Education at a Glance 2012

OECD INDICATORS

OECD
BETTER POLICIES FOR BETTER LIVES

This work is published on the responsibility of the Secretary-General of the OECD. The opinions expressed and arguments employed herein do not necessarily reflect the official views of the Organisation or of the governments of its member countries.

This document and any map included herein are without prejudice to the status of or sovereignty over any territory, to the delimitation of international frontiers and boundaries and to the name of any territory, city or area.

Please cite this publication as:
OECD (2012), *Education at a Glance 2012: OECD Indicators*, OECD Publishing.
http://dx.doi.org/10.1787/eag-2012-en

ISBN 978-92-64-17715-4 (print)
ISBN 978-92-64-17929-5 (PDF)

Revised version, September 2012.
Details of revisions available at: *www.oecd.org/edu/Corrigendum_EAG2012 EN.pdf.*

The statistical data for Israel are supplied by and under the responsibility of the relevant Israeli authorities. The use of such data by the OECD is without prejudice to the status of the Golan Heights, East Jerusalem and Israeli settlements in the West Bank under the terms of international law.

Photo credits:
Stocklib Image Bank © Cathy Yeulet
Fotolia.com © Feng Yu
Getty Images © blue jean images

FOREWORD

Governments are paying increasing attention to international comparisons as they search for effective policies that enhance individuals' social and economic prospects, provide incentives for greater efficiency in schooling, and help to mobilise resources to meet rising demands. As part of its response, the OECD Directorate for Education devotes a major effort to the development and analysis of the quantitative, internationally comparable indicators that it publishes annually in *Education at a Glance*. These indicators enable educational policy makers and practitioners alike to see their education systems in light of other countries' performance and, together with the OECD's country policy reviews, are designed to support and review the efforts that governments are making towards policy reform.

Education at a Glance addresses the needs of a range of users, from governments seeking to learn policy lessons to academics requiring data for further analysis to the general public wanting to monitor how its country's schools are progressing in producing world-class students. The publication examines the quality of learning outcomes, the policy levers and contextual factors that shape these outcomes, and the broader private and social returns that accrue to investments in education.

Education at a Glance is the product of a long-standing, collaborative effort between OECD governments, the experts and institutions working within the framework of the OECD's Indicators of Education Systems (INES) programme and the OECD Secretariat. The publication was prepared by the Innovation and Measuring Progress Division of the OECD Directorate for Education with input from the Centre for Educational Research and Innovation, under the responsibility of Dirk Van Damme and J.D. LaRock, in co-operation with Etienne Albiser, Eric Charbonnier, Ji Eun Chung, Pedro Lenin Garcia de Léon, Bo Hansson, Corinne Heckmann, Estelle Herbaut, Karinne Logez, Koji Miyamoto, Gara Rojas González, Sophie Vayssettes and Jean Yip. Administrative support was provided by Rhodia Diallo and Rebecca Tessier, editing of the report was undertaken by Marilyn Achiron and J.D. LaRock, and additional advice as well as analytical and editorial support were provided by Marika Boiron, Elizabeth Del Bourgo, Joris Ranchin, Giannina Rech, Wida Rogh, JungHyun Ryu, Amy Todd, and Elisabeth Villoutreix. Production of the report was co-ordinated by Elizabeth Del Bourgo and Elisabeth Villoutreix. The development of the publication was steered by member countries through the INES Working Party and facilitated by the INES Networks. The members of the various bodies as well as the individual experts who have contributed to this publication and to OECD INES more generally are listed at the end of the book.

While much progress has been accomplished in recent years, member countries and the OECD continue to strive to strengthen the link between policy needs and the best available internationally comparable data. This presents various challenges and trade-offs. First, the indicators need to respond to educational issues that are high on national policy agendas, and where the international comparative perspective can offer important added value to what can be accomplished through national analysis and evaluation. Second, while the indicators need to be as comparable as possible, they also need to be as country-specific as is necessary to allow for historical, systemic and cultural differences between countries. Third, the indicators need to be presented in as straightforward a manner as possible, while remaining sufficiently complex to reflect multi-faceted educational realities. Fourth, there is a general desire to keep the indicator set as small as possible, but it needs to be large enough to be useful to policy makers across countries that face different educational challenges.

The OECD will continue to address these challenges vigorously and to pursue not just the development of indicators in areas where it is feasible and promising to develop data, but also to advance in areas where a considerable investment still needs to be made in conceptual work. The further development of the OECD Programme for International Student Assessment (PISA) and its extension through the OECD Programme for the International Assessment of Adult Competencies (PIAAC), as well as OECD's Teaching and Learning International Survey (TALIS) are major efforts to this end.

TABLE OF CONTENTS

This book has...

StatLinkS

A service that delivers Excel® files from the printed page!

Look for the *StatLinks* at the bottom left-hand corner of the tables or graphs in this book.
To download the matching Excel® spreadsheet, just type the link into your Internet browser, starting with the *http://dx.doi.org* prefix.
If you're reading the PDF e-book edition, and your PC is connected to the Internet, simply click on the link. You'll find *StatLinks* appearing in more OECD books.

EDITORIAL

Investing in people, skills and education for inclusive growth and jobs

For some time now, the global education and economic landscapes have been in a state of rapid transformation, spurred in significant part by two key changes. The first is the continued ascent of the knowledge economy, which has created powerful new incentives for people to build their skills through education – and for countries to help them do so. The second phenomenon – which is closely related to the first – is the explosive growth of higher education worldwide, which has increased opportunities for millions and is expanding the global talent pool of highly-educated individuals.

This year's *Education at a Glance* examines these landscapes in light of another important change: the full onset of the global recession in 2009 and 2010. As one might expect, our analysis finds that no group or country – no matter how well-educated – is totally immune from the effects of a worldwide economic downturn. At the same time, it also shows the remarkable importance of having a higher level of education for the economy, for the labour market and for the society as a whole.

At the most basic level, it's clear that having more education helped people to keep or change their jobs during the recession. For instance, between the start of the downturn in 2008 and 2010, overall unemployment rates jumped from an already high 8.8% to 12.5% for people without an upper secondary education, and from 4.9% to 7.6% for people with an upper secondary education, on average across OECD countries. By contrast, unemployment rates for people with higher education remained much lower, rising from 3.3% to 4.7% during this same period. While the rate of change between the two groups may be similar, its impact on labour markets is hugely different. For all OECD countries together, the unemployment rate in 2010 was roughly one-third less for men with higher education than for men with upper secondary education; for women with higher education, it was two-fifths less.

The gaps in earnings between people with higher education and those with lower levels of education not only remained substantial during the global recession, but grew even wider. In 2008, a man with higher education could expect to earn 58% more than his counterpart with no more than an upper secondary education, on average across OECD countries. By 2010, this premium increased to 67%. Similarly, in 2008, women with higher education had an average earnings premium of 54% compared to their upper secondary-educated peers. By 2010, this premium grew to 59%. This is no longer just a phenomenon of the industrialised world. Indeed, the country with the greatest earnings premium on higher education is now Brazil, where that advantage is about three times as high as on average across OECD countries. The hunger for education is also mirrored in the educational aspirations of much younger people in the emerging economies. Brazil, Indonesia and the Russian Federation are now among the ten countries with the highest proportion of 15-year-olds aspiring to highly-skilled careers.

These figures suggest that although the downturn certainly had a sweeping impact – especially for people with lower levels of education – the impact of the broader changes occurring on the global education and economic landscapes is even larger. Over the past decade across OECD countries, the percentage of adults who have attained higher education has grown at a rapid clip, from 22% in 2000 to 31% in 2010. Yet despite this burgeoning supply of well-educated individuals – as well as the faltering market conditions from 2008 forward – most people with higher education have continued to reap very good economic benefits. This signals that, overall, the demand for highly-skilled employees to meet the needs of the knowledge economy in OECD countries has continued to grow, even during the crisis.

Consequently, as long as societies continue to need more high-level skills, it's likely that the benefits of having advanced skills will remain solid not only in the short term, but over the long run. For example, this year's *Education at a Glance* estimates that, on average across 28 OECD countries, the long-term personal economic gain of acquiring a tertiary degree instead of an upper secondary degree as part of initial education, minus the associated costs, is over USD 160 000 for men and around USD 110 000 for women.

Importantly, taxpayers are increasingly aware of the economic and social returns on the public funds that are used to help people pursue higher education. On average, OECD countries receive a net return of over USD 100 000 in increased income tax payments and other savings for each man they support in higher education – four times the amount of public investment. For women, the net public return is about 2.5 times the amount of public investment. Of course, the public and private benefits of education go beyond the purely economic. For instance, this edition of *Education at a Glance* finds that higher levels of education are associated with a longer life expectancy, increased voting rates, and more supportive attitudes towards equal rights for ethnic minorities.

Indeed, the fact that investing in education yields strong benefits both for individuals and societies helps to explain one of the most salient findings from this year's *Education at a Glance*: to a notable degree, public and private investments on education rose in many OECD countries during the recession year of 2009. For example, between 2008 and 2009, spending by governments, enterprises and individual students and their families for all levels of education combined, increased in 24 out of 31 OECD countries with available data. This occurred even as national wealth, as measured by GDP, decreased in 26 of these countries. Similarly, expenditure per student by primary, secondary and post-secondary educational institutions increased by 15 percentage points on average across OECD countries between 2005 and 2009. Also here, some of the emerging economies are leading the way. In Brazil and the Russian Federation, for example, spending per student rose by around 60 percentage points over the same period, albeit from comparatively low levels.

Meanwhile, per-student expenditure by tertiary institutions rose an average of 9 percentage points during this same period.

Less surprisingly, while public expenditure on education as a percentage of total public expenditure remained at 13% on average across OECD countries in both 2005 and 2009, it decreased in 19 out of 32 individual countries during this period – an outcome that is almost certainly related to the onset and deepening of the global recession during the latter part of this time frame. Nonetheless, the fact that overall public and private education expenditure rose by any measure during the economic slowdown speaks to the efforts by governments and individuals to preserve what both see as the unique advantages of promoting investments in education.

This is not to say, however, that more spending necessarily equals better results. In recent years, policy makers have continuously emphasised the need for increased investments to be matched by improved outcomes. Moreover, especially in times of fiscal constraint, countries must make smart choices about how to allocate limited resources – a priority that the OECD is helping to address with initiatives like our Skills Strategy. This edition of *Education at a Glance* calls attention to several areas where countries have made noteworthy progress, and identifies others that are likely to require continued attention in the future.

For example – as detailed in our first-ever indicator on early childhood education and care – countries are making admirable strides in expanding schooling for their youngest students, an issue that has become more prominent on countries' education policy agendas in recent years. On average, in OECD countries with data for both years, enrolments in early childhood education programmes rose from 64% of 3-year-olds in 2005 to 69% in 2010, and from 77% of 4-year-olds in 2005 to 81% in 2010. More than three-quarters of 4-year-olds are enrolled in early childhood education across OECD countries as a whole, and in a majority of OECD countries, education now begins for most children well before they are 5 years old. Given that early childhood education is associated with better performance later on in school, these developments bode well for a future in which increasing young people's skills will be more important than ever.

OECD countries are also benefitting from continued gains in women's participation in higher education. For instance, the percentage of women expected to enter a university programme in their lifetime rose from 60%

in 2005 to 69% in 2010, on average across OECD countries, while the proportion for men increased from 48% to 55% during this same period. In addition, women now comprise 59% of all university first degree graduates, on average across OECD countries. While more needs to be done to increase women's participation in fields of study like engineering, manufacturing and computer science – as well as their representation among advanced degree-holders – the progress thus far is nonetheless quite positive.

By contrast, it's clear that increasing educational equity and opportunity for all students, regardless of their background, remains a deep and abiding challenge in all countries. For example, this year's *Education at a Glance* concludes that the reading performance of students from immigrant backgrounds may be particularly negatively affected when they attend schools with large numbers of pupils from families with low levels of education – a finding that suggests the need for effective policy remedies in many OECD countries.

Similarly, policy makers would do well to take note of the increase in the number of 15-29 year-olds who are neither in employment nor in education or training – the so-called "NEET" population – which spiked to nearly 16% across OECD countries in 2010 after several years of decline. This increase reflects the particular hardship that young people have borne as a result of the global recession. Data from the 2012 *OECD Employment Outlook* show that youth unemployment has now reached alarming levels in several OECD countries, underscoring the need for countries to examine measures that can productively engage people in this crucial age group, such as vocational education and training programmes and opportunities for non-formal education and training.

Likewise, in an era when having a higher education degree is increasingly necessary to assure a smooth transition into the labour market, many OECD countries need to do more to increase access to higher education for young people from disadvantaged circumstances. For example, this year's edition finds stark differences in young people's chances of attending higher education, depending on their parents' educational background. On average across OECD countries, young people from families with low levels of education are less than half as likely to be in higher education, compared to the proportion of such families in the population. Meanwhile, a young person with at least one parent who has attained a higher education degree is almost twice as likely to be in higher education, compared to the proportion of these families in the population.

Finally, because changes to the global economy affect both countries and individuals, countries should take care to strike a careful balance between providing appropriate public support for education and requiring students and families to cover some of the costs. As the expenditure data cited earlier suggest, students and families have been bearing an increasing share of the costs of education in many OECD countries. While this general approach is reasonable in that individuals receive many of the benefits of education, it can also lead to scenarios in which individuals face large financial barriers in pursuing more education – a situation that is now the case for people seeking higher education in several OECD countries. In turn, these barriers may impede countries' own goals of increasing educational attainment in their populations.

With the launch of this 20th edition of *Education at a Glance*, the OECD marks its close co-operation with a generation of leaders, policy makers, and researchers in assessing their countries in light of the global education landscape to chart an effective course for the future. As the spectre of another economic downturn is looming large in some countries and is already a reality in others, the findings from this year's edition may be especially relevant. Investing in people, their skills and their education is key for inclusive growth and jobs – it is key for the success of economies, societies and their citizens!

The OECD remains committed to finding new ways to provide accurate, relevant data and policy recommendations on the world's most pressing education issues and to help countries design, promote and implement *better education policies for better lives!*

Angel Gurría
OECD Secretary-General

Introduction:
The Indicators and their Framework

The organising framework

Education at a Glance 2012: OECD Indicators offers a rich, comparable and up-to-date array of indicators that reflects a consensus among professionals on how to measure the current state of education internationally. The indicators provide information on the human and financial resources invested in education, how education and learning systems operate and evolve, and the returns to educational investments. The indicators are organised thematically, and each is accompanied by information on the policy context and the interpretation of the data. The education indicators are presented within an organising framework that:

- distinguishes between the actors in education systems: individual learners and teachers, instructional settings and learning environments, educational service providers, and the education system as a whole;

- groups the indicators according to whether they address learning outcomes for individuals or countries, policy levers or circumstances that shape these outcomes, or to antecedents or constraints that set policy choices into context; and

- identifies the policy issues to which the indicators relate, with three major categories distinguishing between the quality of educational outcomes and educational provision, issues of equity in educational outcomes and educational opportunities, and the adequacy and effectiveness of resource management.

The following matrix describes the first two dimensions:

	1. Education and learning outputs and outcomes	2. Policy levers and contexts shaping educational outcomes	3. Antecedents or constraints that contextualise policy
I. Individual participants in education and learning	**1.I.** The quality and distribution of individual educational outcomes	**2.I.** Individual attitudes, engagement, and behaviour to teaching and learning	**3.I.** Background characteristics of the individual learners and teachers
II. Instructional settings	**1.II.** The quality of instructional delivery	**2.II.** Pedagogy, learning practices and classroom climate	**3.II.** Student learning conditions and teacher working conditions
III. Providers of educational services	**1.III.** The output of educational institutions and institutional performance	**2.III.** School environment and organisation	**3.III.** Characteristics of the service providers and their communities
IV. The education system as a whole	**1.IV.** The overall performance of the education system	**2.IV.** System-wide institutional settings, resource allocations, and policies	**3.IV.** The national educational, social, economic, and demographic contexts

The following sections discuss the matrix dimensions in more detail:

■ Actors in education systems

The OECD Indicators of Education Systems (INES) programme seeks to gauge the performance of national education systems as a whole, rather than to compare individual institutional or other sub-national entities. However, there is increasing recognition that many important features of the development, functioning and impact of education systems can only be assessed through an understanding of learning outcomes and their relationships to inputs and processes at the level of individuals and institutions. To account for this, the indicator framework distinguishes between a macro level, two meso-levels and a micro-level of education systems. These relate to:

- the education system as a whole;
- the educational institutions and providers of educational services;
- the instructional setting and the learning environment within the institutions; and
- the individual participants in education and learning.

To some extent, these levels correspond to the entities from which data are being collected, but their importance mainly centres on the fact that many features of the education system play out quite differently at different levels of the system, which needs to be taken into account when interpreting the indicators. For example, at the level of students within a classroom, the relationship between student achievement and class size may be negative, if students in small classes benefit from improved contact with teachers. At the class or school level, however, students are often intentionally grouped such that weaker or disadvantaged students are placed in smaller classes so that they receive more individual attention. At the school level, therefore, the observed relationship between class size and student achievement is often positive (suggesting that students in larger classes perform better than students in smaller classes). At higher aggregated levels of education systems, the relationship between student achievement and class size is further confounded, e.g. by the socio-economic intake of schools or by factors relating to the learning culture in different countries. Therefore, past analyses that have relied on macro-level data alone have sometimes led to misleading conclusions.

■ Outcomes, policy levers and antecedents

The second dimension in the organising framework further groups the indicators at each of the above levels:

- indicators on observed outputs of education systems, as well as indicators related to the impact of knowledge and skills for individuals, societies and economies, are grouped under the sub-heading *output and outcomes of education and learning;*
- the sub-heading *policy levers and contexts* groups activities seeking information on the policy levers or circumstances which shape the outputs and outcomes at each level; and
- these policy levers and contexts typically have *antecedents* – factors that define or constrain policy. These are represented by the sub-heading *antecedents and constraints*. It should be noted that the antecedents or constraints are usually specific for a given level of the education system and that antecedents at a lower level of the system may well be policy levers at a higher level. For teachers and students in a school, for example, teacher qualifications are a given constraint while, at the level of the education system, professional development of teachers is a key policy lever.

■ Policy issues

Each of the resulting cells in the framework can then be used to address a variety of issues from different policy perspectives. For the purpose of this framework, policy perspectives are grouped into three classes that constitute the third dimension in the organising framework for INES:

- quality of educational outcomes and educational provision;
- equality of educational outcomes and equity in educational opportunities; and
- adequacy, effectiveness and efficiency of resource management.

In addition to the dimensions mentioned above, the time perspective as an additional dimension in the framework allows dynamic aspects in the development of education systems to be modelled as well.

The indicators that are published in *Education at a Glance 2012* fit within this framework, though often they speak to more than one cell.

Most of the indicators in **Chapter A**, *The output of educational institutions and the impact of learning*, relate to the first column of the matrix describing outputs and outcomes of education. Even so, indicators in Chapter A measuring educational attainment for different generations, for instance, not only provide a measure of the output of the education system, but also provide context for current educational policies, helping to shape polices on, for example, lifelong learning.

Chapter B, *Financial and human resources invested in education*, provides indicators that are either policy levers or antecedents to policy, or sometimes both. For example, expenditure per student is a key policy measure that most directly affects the individual learner, as it acts as a constraint on the learning environment in schools and learning conditions in the classroom.

Chapter C, *Access to education, participation and progression*, provides indicators that are a mixture of outcome indicators, policy levers and context indicators. Internationalisation of education and progression rates are, for instance, outcomes measures to the extent that they indicate the results of policies and practices at the classroom, school and system levels. But they can also provide contexts for establishing policy by identifying areas where policy intervention is necessary to, for instance, address issues of inequity.

Chapter D, *The learning environment and organisation of schools*, provides indicators on instruction time, teachers' working time and teachers' salaries that not only represent policy levers which can be manipulated but also provide contexts for the quality of instruction in instructional settings and for the outcomes of individual learners. It also presents data on the profile of teachers, the levels of government at which decisions in education systems are taken, and pathways and gateways to gain access to secondary and tertiary education.

The reader should note that this edition of *Education at a Glance* covers a significant amount of data from non-OECD G20 countries (please refer to the Reader's Guide for details).

READER'S GUIDE

◼ Coverage of the statistics

Although a lack of data still limits the scope of the indicators in many countries, the coverage extends, in principle, to the entire national education system (within the national territory), regardless of who owns or sponsors the institutions concerned and regardless of how education is delivered. With one exception (described below), all types of students and all age groups are included: children (including students with special needs), adults, nationals, foreigners, and students in open-distance learning, in special education programmes or in educational programmes organised by ministries other than the Ministry of Education, provided that the main aim of the programme is to broaden or deepen an individual's knowledge. However, children below the age of three are only included if they participate in programmes that typically cater to children who are at least two years old. Vocational and technical training in the workplace, with the exception of combined school- and work-based programmes that are explicitly deemed to be part of the education system, are not included in the basic education expenditure and enrolment data.

Educational activities classified as "adult" or "non-regular" are covered, provided that the activities involve the same or similar content as "regular" education studies, or that the programmes of which they are a part lead to qualifications similar to those awarded in regular educational programmes. Courses for adults that are primarily for general interest, personal enrichment, leisure or recreation are excluded (except in the indicator on adult learning, C6).

◼ Country coverage

This publication features data on education from the 34 OECD member countries, two non-OECD countries that participate in the OECD Indicators of Education Systems programme (INES), namely Brazil and the Russian Federation, and the other G20 countries that do not participate in INES (Argentina, China, India, Indonesia, Saudi Arabia and South Africa). When data for these latter six countries are available, data sources are specified below the tables and charts.

The statistical data for Israel are supplied by and under the responsibility of the relevant Israeli authorities. The use of such data by the OECD is without prejudice to the status of the Golan Heights, East Jerusalem and Israeli settlements in the West Bank under the terms of international law.

◼ Calculation of international means

For many indicators, an OECD average is presented; for some, an OECD total is shown.

The **OECD average** is calculated as the unweighted mean of the data values of all OECD countries for which data are available or can be estimated. The OECD average therefore refers to an average of data values at the level of the national systems and can be used to answer the question of how an indicator value for a given country compares with the value for a typical or average country. It does not take into account the absolute size of the education system in each country.

The **OECD total** is calculated as a weighted mean of the data values of all OECD countries for which data are available or can be estimated. It reflects the value for a given indicator when the OECD area is considered as a whole. This approach is taken for the purpose of comparing, for example, expenditure charts for individual countries with those of the entire OECD area for which valid data are available, with this area considered as a single entity.

Both the OECD average and the OECD total can be significantly affected by missing data. Given the relatively small number of countries, no statistical methods are used to compensate for this. In cases where a category is not applicable (code "a") in a country or where the data value is negligible (code "n") for the corresponding calculation, the value zero is imputed for the purpose of calculating OECD averages. In cases where both the numerator and the denominator of a ratio are not applicable (code "a") for a certain country, this country is not included in the OECD average.

For financial tables using 1995, 2000 and 2005 data, both the OECD average and OECD total are calculated for countries providing 1995, 2000, 2005 and 2009 data. This allows comparison of the OECD average and OECD total over time with no distortion due to the exclusion of certain countries in the different years.

For many indicators, an EU21 average is also presented. It is calculated as the unweighted mean of the data values of the 21 OECD countries that are members of the European Union for which data are available or can be estimated. These 21 countries are Austria, Belgium, the Czech Republic, Denmark, Estonia, Finland, France, Germany, Greece, Hungary, Ireland, Italy, Luxembourg, the Netherlands, Poland, Portugal, Slovenia, the Slovak Republic, Spain, Sweden and the United Kingdom.

For some indicators, a G20 average is presented. The G20 average is calculated as the unweighted mean of the data values of all G20 countries for which data are available or can be estimated (Argentina, Australia, Brazil, Canada, China, France, Germany, India, Indonesia, Italy, Japan, Korea, Mexico, the Russian Federation, Saudi Arabia, South Africa, Turkey, the United Kingdom and the United States; the European Union is the 20th member of the G20 but is not included in the calculation). The G20 average is not computed if the data for China or India are not available.

Classification of levels of education

The classification of the levels of education is based on the International Standard Classification of Education (ISCED 1997). ISCED 1997 has been recently revised and the new International Standard Classification of Education (ISCED 2011) was formally adopted in November 2011. This new classification should be implemented in data collection in May 2014. ISCED 97 is an instrument for compiling statistics on education internationally and distinguishes among six levels of education.

Term used in this publication	ISCED classification (and subcategories)
Pre-primary education The first stage of organised instruction designed to introduce very young children to the school atmosphere. Minimum entry age of 3.	ISCED 0
Primary education Designed to provide a sound basic education in reading, writing and mathematics and a basic understanding of some other subjects. Entry age: between 5 and 7. Duration: six years.	ISCED 1
Lower secondary education Completes provision of basic education, usually in a more subject-oriented way with more specialist teachers. Entry follows six years of primary education; duration is three years. In some countries, the end of this level marks the end of compulsory education.	ISCED 2 (subcategories: 2A prepares students for continuing academic education, leading to 3A; 2B has stronger vocational focus, leading to 3B; 2C offers preparation of entering workforce)
Upper secondary education Stronger subject specialisation than at lower secondary level, with teachers usually more qualified. Students typically expected to have completed nine years of education or lower secondary schooling before entry and are generally 15 or 16 years old.	ISCED 3 (subcategories: 3A prepares students for university-level education at level 5A; 3B for entry to vocationally oriented tertiary education at level 5B; 3C prepares students for workforce or for post-secondary non-tertiary education at level ISCED 4)

Post-secondary non-tertiary education Internationally, this level straddles the boundary between upper secondary and post-secondary education, even though it might be considered upper secondary or post-secondary in a national context. Programme content may not be significantly more advanced than that in upper secondary, but is not as advanced as that in tertiary programmes. Duration usually the equivalent of between six months and two years of full-time study. Students tend to be older than those enrolled in upper secondary education.	**ISCED 4** (subcategories: 4A may prepare students for entry to tertiary education, both university level and vocationally oriented; 4B typically prepares students to enter the workforce)
Tertiary education	**ISCED 5** (subcategories: 5A and 5B; see below)
Tertiary-type A education Largely theory-based programmes designed to provide sufficient qualifications for entry to advanced research programmes and professions with high skill requirements, such as medicine, dentistry or architecture. Duration at least three years full-time, though usually four or more years. These programmes are not exclusively offered at universities; and not all programmes nationally recognised as university programmes fulfil the criteria to be classified as tertiary-type A. Tertiary-type A programmes include second-degree programmes, such as the American master's degree.	**ISCED 5A**
Tertiary-type B education Programmes are typically shorter than those of tertiary-type A and focus on practical, technical or occupational skills for direct entry into the labour market, although some theoretical foundations may be covered in the respective programmes. They have a minimum duration of two years full-time equivalent at the tertiary level.	**ISCED 5B**
Advanced research programmes Programmes that lead directly to the award of an advanced research qualification, e.g. Ph.D. The theoretical duration of these programmes is three years, full-time, in most countries (for a cumulative total of at least seven years full-time equivalent at the tertiary level), although the actual enrolment time is typically longer. Programmes are devoted to advanced study and original research.	**ISCED 6**

The glossary available at *www.oecd.org/edu/eag2012* also describes these levels of education in detail, and Annex 1 shows the typical age of graduates of the main educational programmes, by ISCED level. Readers should note that the new ISCED 2011 classification will be reflected starting with the 2014 edition of *Education at a Glance*.

Symbols for missing data and abbreviations

These symbols and abbreviations are used in the tables and charts:

a   Data is not applicable because the category does not apply.

c   There are too few observations to provide reliable estimates (e.g. in PISA, there are fewer than 30 students or fewer than five schools with valid data). However, these statistics were included in the calculation of cross-country averages.

m   Data is not available.

n   Magnitude is either negligible or zero.

S.E.   Standard Error.

w   Data has been withdrawn at the request of the country concerned.

x   Data included in another category or column of the table (e.g. x(2) means that data are included in column 2 of the table).

~   Average is not comparable with other levels of education.

■ Further resources

The website *www.oecd.org/edu/eag2012* is a rich source of information on the methods used to calculate the indicators, on the interpretation of the indicators in the respective national contexts, and on the data sources involved. The website also provides access to the data underlying the indicators and to a comprehensive glossary for technical terms used in this publication.

All post-production changes to this publication are listed at *www.oecd.org/edu/eag2012*.

The website *www.pisa.oecd.org* provides information on the OECD Programme for International Student Assessment (PISA), on which many of the indicators in this publication are based.

Education at a Glance uses the OECD's *StatLinks* service. Below each table and chart in *Education at a Glance 2012* is a URL that leads to a corresponding Excel workbook containing the underlying data for the indicator. These URLs are stable and will remain unchanged over time. In addition, readers of the *Education at a Glance* e-book will be able to click directly on these links and the workbook will open in a separate window.

■ Codes used for territorial entities

These codes are used in certain charts. Country or territorial entity names are used in the text. Note that throughout the publication, the Flemish Community of Belgium and the French Community of Belgium may be referred to as "Belgium (Fl.)" and "Belgium (Fr.)", respectively.

ARG	Argentina	LUX	Luxembourg
AUS	Australia	MEX	Mexico
AUT	Austria	NLD	Netherlands
BEL	Belgium	NOR	Norway
BFL	Belgium (Flemish Community)	NZL	New Zealand
BFR	Belgium (French Community)	POL	Poland
BRA	Brazil	PRT	Portugal
CAN	Canada	RUS	Russian Federation
CHE	Switzerland	SAU	Saudi Arabia
CHL	Chile	SCO	Scotland
CHN	China	SVK	Slovak Republic
CZE	Czech Republic	SVN	Slovenia
DEU	Germany	SWE	Sweden
DNK	Denmark	TUR	Turkey
ENG	England	UKM	United Kingdom
ESP	Spain	USA	United States
EST	Estonia	ZAF	South Africa
FIN	Finland		
FRA	France		
GRC	Greece		
HUN	Hungary		
IDN	Indonesia		
IND	India		
IRL	Ireland		
ISL	Iceland		
ISR	Israel		
ITA	Italy		
JPN	Japan		
KOR	Korea		

Chapter

THE OUTPUT OF EDUCATIONAL INSTITUTIONS AND THE IMPACT OF LEARNING

Indicator A1 To what level have adults studied?
StatLink ⬛⬛⬛ http://dx.doi.org/10.1787/888932664100

Indicator A2 How many students are expected to finish secondary education?
StatLink ⬛⬛⬛ http://dx.doi.org/10.1787/888932664328

Indicator A3 How many students are expected to finish tertiary education?
StatLink ⬛⬛⬛ http://dx.doi.org/10.1787/888932664537

Indicator A4 What is the difference between the career aspirations of boys and girls and the fields of study they pursue as young adults?
StatLink ⬛⬛⬛ http://dx.doi.org/10.1787/888932664670

Indicator A5 How well do immigrant students perform in school?
StatLink ⬛⬛⬛ http://dx.doi.org/10.1787/888932664841

Indicator A6 To what extent does parents' education influence access to tertiary education?
StatLink ⬛⬛⬛ http://dx.doi.org/10.1787/888932664936

Indicator A7 How does educational attainment affect participation in the labour market?
StatLink ⬛⬛⬛ http://dx.doi.org/10.1787/888932665031

Indicator A8 What are the earnings premiums from education?
StatLink ⬛⬛⬛ http://dx.doi.org/10.1787/888932665316

Indicator A9 What are the incentives to invest in education?
StatLink ⬛⬛⬛ http://dx.doi.org/10.1787/888932665506

Indicator A10 How does education influence economic growth, labour costs and earning power?
StatLink ⬛⬛⬛ http://dx.doi.org/10.1787/888932665601

Indicator A11 What are the social outcomes of education?
StatLink ⬛⬛⬛ http://dx.doi.org/10.1787/888932665734

TO WHAT LEVEL HAVE ADULTS STUDIED?

- Within most OECD countries, the percentage of 25-34 year-olds with tertiary attainment is moderately to considerably higher than the percentage of 55-64 year-olds with tertiary attainment. Exceptions to this trend include Germany, Israel and the United States.

- The percentage of younger adults (aged 25-34) with an upper secondary education is markedly higher than the percentage of older adults (aged 55-64) with an upper secondary education within most OECD countries. In 2010, 25 OECD countries had upper secondary attainment rates of 80% or more among 25-34 year-olds.

Chart A1.1. **Population that has attained tertiary education (2010)**
Percentage, by age group

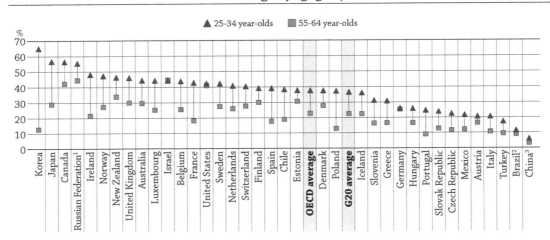

1. Year of reference 2002.
2. Year of reference 2009.
3. Year of reference 2000.
Countries are ranked in descending order of the percentage of 25-34 year-olds who have attained tertiary education.
Source: OECD. Table A1.3a. See Annex 3 for notes (*www.oecd.org/edu/eag2012*).
StatLink ⬛ http://dx.doi.org/10.1787/888932661478

■ Context

Educational attainment is a commonly used proxy for the stock of human capital – that is, the skills available in the population and the labour force. As globalisation and technology continue to re-shape the needs of the global labour market, the demand for individuals who possess a broader knowledge base, more specialised skills, advanced analytical capacities, and complex communication skills continues to rise. As a result, more individuals are pursuing higher levels of education than in previous generations, leading to significant shifts in attainment levels over time within countries.

At the same time, the rise of new economic powers – and sustained efforts by some countries to build and invest in their tertiary education systems – has shifted the global landscape of educational attainment as well. In recent years, countries with strong and long-held leads in attainment have seen their positions erode as individuals in other countries have increased their attainment at an extremely fast pace.

Over the past several years, the global economic crisis has likely affected educational attainment rates in two ways. First, it has provided an additional incentive for people to build their skills and reduce the risk of being unable to secure or retain employment in difficult economic circumstances.

Second, weaker employment prospects have lowered some of the costs of education, such as earnings foregone while studying, providing a different kind of incentive for individuals to pursue more education.

▦ Other findings

▪ If current tertiary attainment rates among 25-34 year-olds are maintained, **the proportion of adults in Ireland, Japan and Korea, among other countries, who have a tertiary education will grow to more than that of other OECD countries,** while the proportion in Austria, Brazil and Germany (among others) will fall further behind other OECD countries.

▪ **Vocational education and training (VET) is a major factor in the educational attainment of people in many countries.** A vocational upper secondary or post-secondary non-tertiary education is the highest level of attainment for more than 50% of 25-64 year-olds in Austria, the Czech Republic, Germany, Hungary, the Slovak Republic and Slovenia.

▪ Despite notable strides, some countries remain far below the OECD average in terms of upper secondary attainment. For example, **in Brazil, China, Mexico, Portugal, and Turkey roughly half of all 25-34 year-olds – or far more – lack an upper secondary education.**

▦ Trends

Efforts to raise people's level of education have led to significant changes in attainment, particularly at the top and bottom ends of the education spectrum. In 1997, on average across OECD countries, 36% of 25-64 year-olds had not completed upper secondary education, 43% had completed upper secondary or post-secondary non-tertiary education, and another 21% had completed tertiary education. By 2010, the proportion of adults who had not attained an upper secondary education had fallen by 10 percentage points, the proportion with a tertiary degree had risen by 10 percentage points, and the proportion with upper secondary or post-secondary non-tertiary education had increased marginally, by one percentage point.

▦ Note

In this publication, different indicators show the level of education among individuals, groups and countries. Indicator A1 shows the level of attainment, i.e. the percentage of a population that has reached a certain level of education. Graduation rates in Indicators A2 and A3 measure the estimated percentage of young adults who are expected to graduate from a particular level of education during their lifetimes. Successful completion of upper secondary programmes in Indicator A2 estimates the proportion of students who enter a programme and complete it successfully within the normal duration of the programme. See Box A2.1 in Indicator A2 for more on this topic.

A1

Analysis

Attainment levels in OECD countries

Tertiary (higher education) attainment

Tertiary attainment levels have increased considerably over the past 30 years. On average across OECD countries, 38% of 25-34 year-olds have a tertiary attainment, compared with 23% of 55-64 year-olds. Canada, Japan, Korea and the Russian Federation lead OECD and G20 countries in the proportion of young adults (25-34 year-olds) with a tertiary attainment, with 55% or more having reached this level of education (Chart A1.1). In France, Ireland, Japan, Korea and Poland, there is a difference of 25 percentage points or more between the proportion of young adults and older adults who have attained this level of education (Table A1.3a).

Chart A1.2. **Population that has attained upper secondary education[1] (2010)**
Percentage, by age group

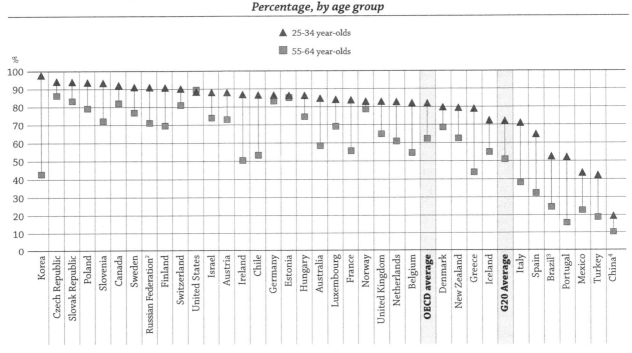

1. Excluding ISCED 3C short programmes.
2. Year of reference 2002.
3. Year of reference 2009.
4. Year of reference 2000.
Countries are ranked in descending order of the percentage of 25-34 year-olds who have attained at least an upper secondary education.
Source: OECD. Table A1.2a. See Annex 3 for notes (*www.oecd.org/edu/eag2012*).
StatLink ᴍᴸᴵꜱ᠊ http://dx.doi.org/10.1787/888932661497

Upper secondary attainment

Across almost all OECD countries, upper secondary attainment is the norm. On average, 74% of 25-64 year-olds have reached this level of attainment, and 82% of 25-34 year-olds have. Only a handful of OECD countries – Greece, Iceland, Italy, Mexico, Portugal, Spain and Turkey – have upper secondary attainment rates below 70% among 25-64 year-olds. At the same time, some of these countries have seen dramatic increases in upper secondary attainment rates from generation to generation. For example, Chile, Greece, Ireland, Italy, Korea, Portugal and Spain have all seen an increase of 30 percentage points or more from the older (55-64 year-old) to the younger (25-34 year-old) age cohorts on this measure (Table A1.2a).

By contrast, this rate has increased only marginally, or even has fallen, in countries with traditionally high levels of upper secondary attainment in previous generations. For instance, in Estonia, Germany and Norway, the upper secondary attainment rate rose by less than 5 percentage points between the 55-64 year-old and 25-34 year-old age cohorts; in the United States, it has decreased slightly (Chart A1.2).

More broadly, differences in upper secondary attainment between age cohorts are less pronounced in OECD countries where the adult population generally has a high level of educational attainment. Among non-OECD G20 countries for which data are available, Brazil, China and the Russian Federation all have made notable progress in increasing upper secondary attainment rates between generations, although 80% of 25-34 year-olds in China still lack an upper secondary education (Table A1.2a).

Evolution of tertiary attainment in the future

Returning to tertiary education, Chart A1.3 compares changes in countries' tertiary attainment figures between generations with tertiary attainment levels among 25-64 year-olds to show how the global landscape of tertiary attainment may evolve over time. For example, the upper-right quadrant of the chart includes countries with already-high levels of tertiary attainment that may increase this advantage in the future.

Chart A1.3. **Proportion of population with tertiary education and potential growth (2010)**

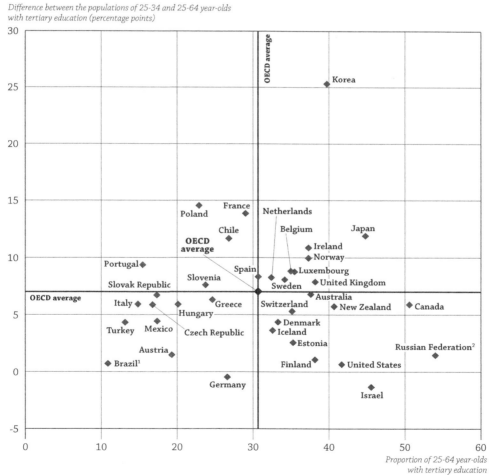

1. Year of reference 2009.
2. Year of reference 2002.
Source: OECD. Table A1.3a. See Annex 3 for notes (*www.oecd.org/edu/eag2012*).
StatLink http://dx.doi.org/10.1787/888932661516

A1

Ireland, Japan and Korea are in this category. The lower-right quadrant includes countries such as Estonia, Finland, Israel, the Russian Federation and the United States that have high levels of attainment, but which may find that an increasing number of countries approach or surpass their levels of tertiary attainment in the coming years.

In the upper-left quadrant, some countries, such as Chile, France and Poland, have tertiary attainment levels that are lower than the OECD average, but given current attainment rates among 25-34 year-olds, these countries' overall tertiary attainment levels could move closer to those of other OECD countries in the future. Countries with lower levels of tertiary attainment that could fall further behind are grouped in the lower-left quadrant of the chart. This disadvantage is particularly marked in Austria, Brazil and Germany. Tertiary graduation rates provide more recent data on the possible evolution of educational attainment (see Indicator A3).

Chart A1.4. **Extent of vocational education and training (2010)**
Percentage of 25-64 year-olds whose highest level of education is upper secondary or post-secondary non-tertiary (ISCED 3/4), by educational orientation

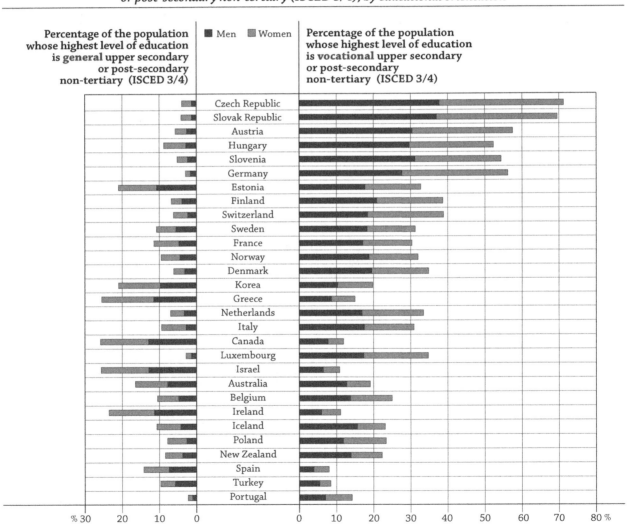

Countries are ranked in descending order of the total (men and women) percentage of 25-64 year-olds whose highest level of education is general or vocational upper secondary or post-secondary non-tertiary level of education (ISCED 3/4).
Source: OECD. Table A1.5. See Annex 3 for notes (*www.oecd.org/edu/eag2012*).
StatLink ᵃˢˡ᷉ http://dx.doi.org/10.1787/888932661535

Vocational education and training (VET) attainment

Obtaining a tertiary education is not the only way for individuals to gain the skills necessary to respond to today's labour-market needs. Vocational education and training (VET) programmes (also known as vocational and technical education or career and technical education), which can include education in advanced manufacturing, a skilled trade, or other specialised areas, offer another approach. Indeed, in light of continued demand for employees with skills that are not typically taught in academically oriented tertiary programmes, some countries, such as the United Kindgom, have introduced policy initiatives in recent years to strengthen this part of the education system.

Vocational education is defined as education that offers participants the opportunity to acquire the practical skills, knowledge, and understanding necessary for employment in a particular occupation or trade or class of occupations or trades. Successful completion of such programmes leads to a labour market-relevant vocational qualification recognised by the competent authorities in the country in which it is obtained (e.g. Ministry of Education, employers' associations, etc.).

Vocational attainment tends to be strongest in countries that have historically emphasised this kind of education or have well-established apprenticeship systems, such as Austria, the Czech Republic, Germany, Hungary, the Slovak Republic and Slovenia. However, vocational education is a significant part of the education systems in many other countries as well. In an additional 10 OECD countries, a vocational upper secondary or post-secondary non-tertiary attainment is the highest educational level for more than 30% of 25-64 year-olds (Table A1.5).

Although vocational education is sometimes thought of as a type of education that is more attractive to male students, it is interesting to note that women represent a substantial proportion of individuals with vocational upper secondary or post-secondary non-tertiary attainments in many countries (Chart A1.4). In fact, in Germany, Luxembourg, Portugal, Spain and Switzerland the percentage of 25-64 year-old women with this attainment level slightly outnumber the percentage of men with this attainment. That said, women tend to outnumber men among 25-64 year-olds with a general upper secondary or post-secondary non-tertiary attainment in many more OECD countries (Table A1.5). In most countries, the difference between the proportion of 24-34 year-olds who have a tertiary education and the proportion of 35-44 year-olds who do is larger among women than among men (Chart A1.5).

Trends in attainment rates in OECD countries

Table A1.4 shows how levels of educational attainment among 25-64 year-olds have evolved from 1997 to 2010. Average annual growth in the proportion of those with a tertiary education has exceeded 5% in Ireland, Korea, Luxembourg, Poland, Portugal and the Slovak Republic. Meanwhile, the proportion of the population that had not attained upper secondary education decreased by 5% or more per year in Canada, the Czech Republic, Ireland, Luxembourg, Poland and the Slovak Republic. No country has seen growth above 5% for upper secondary and post-secondary, non-tertiary attainment. Only Portugal has seen growth rates above 4%.

On average across OECD countries, the proportion of 25-64 year-olds who have not attained an upper secondary education has decreased by 3.2% per year since 1997; the proportion with an upper secondary or post-secondary non-tertiary education has increased by 0.6% per year; and the proportion with tertiary education has increased by 3.7% per year. Most of the changes in educational attainment have occurred at the low and high ends of the skills distribution. One reason could be that older workers with low levels of education are moving out of the labour force. It also could be a result of the expansion of higher education in many countries in recent years.

This expansion generally has been accompanied by an even more rapid shift in the demand for skills in most OECD countries. The relationship between education and demand for skills is explored in labour-market indicators on employment and unemployment (see Indicator A7), earnings (see Indicator A8), incentives to invest in education (see Indicator A9), labour costs and net income (see Indicator A10), and transitions from school to work (see Indicator C5).

A1

Chart A1.5. Difference in the proportion of 25-34 year-olds and 35-44 year-olds with tertiary education, by gender (2010)

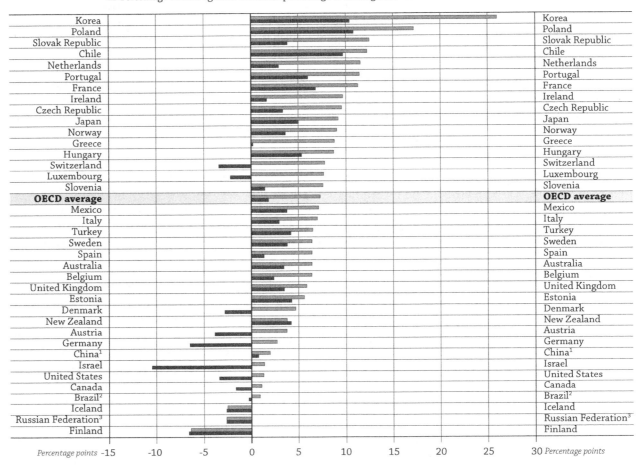

■ Percentage of women aged 25-34 minus percentage of women aged 35-44
■ Percentage of men aged 25-34 minus percentage of men aged 35-44

1. Year of reference 2000.
2. Year of reference 2009.
3. Year of reference 2002.
Countries are ranked in descending order of the difference in the proportion of 25-34 year-old women and 35-44 year-old women with tertiary education.
Source: OECD. Tables A1.3b and A1.3c, available on line. See Annex 3 for notes (*www.oecd.org/edu/eag2012*).
StatLink ᔕᓵᔑ http://dx.doi.org/10.1787/888932661554

Definitions

Levels of education are defined according to the International Standard Classification of Education (ISCED-97). See Annex 3 (*www.oecd.org/edu/eag2012*) for a description of the mapping of ISCED-97 education programmes and attainment levels for each country.

Methodology

Data on population and educational attainment are taken from OECD and Eurostat databases, which are compiled from National Labour Force Surveys. See Annex 3 (*www.oecd.org/edu/eag2012*) for national sources.

Attainment profiles are based on the percentage of the population aged 25 to 64 that has completed a specified level of education.

The statistical data for Israel are supplied by and are under the responsibility of the relevant Israeli authorities. The use of such data by the OECD is without prejudice to the status of the Golan Heights, East Jerusalem and Israeli settlements in the West Bank under the terms of international law.

References

OECD (2004), *OECD Handbook for Internationally Comparative Education Statistics: Concepts, Standards, Definitions and Classifications*, OECD Publishing.

The following additional material relevant to this indicator is available on line:

* *Table A1.1b. Educational attainment: Men (2010)*
  StatLink http://dx.doi.org/10.1787/888932664138

* *Table A1.1c. Educational attainment: Women (2010)*
  StatLink http://dx.doi.org/10.1787/888932664157

* *Table A1.2b. Population of men who have attained at least upper secondary education (2010)*
  StatLink http://dx.doi.org/10.1787/888932664195

* *Table A1.2c. Population of women who have attained at least upper secondary education (2010)*
  StatLink http://dx.doi.org/x10.1787/888932664214

* *Table A1.3b. Population of men who have attained tertiary education (2010)*
  StatLink http://dx.doi.org/10.1787/888932664252

* *Table A1.3c. Population of women who have attained tertiary education (2010)*
  StatLink http://dx.doi.org/10.1787/888932664271

A1

Table A1.1a. Educational attainment: Adult population (2010)

Distribution of 25-64 year-olds, by highest level of education attained

	Pre-primary and primary education	Lower secondary education	ISCED 3C (short programme)	Upper secondary education — ISCED 3C (long programme)/3B	Upper secondary education — ISCED 3A	Post-secondary non-tertiary education	Tertiary education — Type B	Tertiary education — Type A	Tertiary education — Advanced research programmes	All levels of education
	(1)	(2)	(3)	(4)	(5)	(6)	(7)	(8)	(9)	(10)
OECD										
Australia	7	20	a	15	16	4	11	26	1	100
Austria	x(2)	16	1	47	6	10	7	12	x(8)	100
Belgium	13	17	a	10	24	2	18	17	1	100
Canada	3	8	a	x(5)	26	12	24	26	x(8)	100
Chile	15	13	x(5)	x(5)	45	a	10	16	n	100
Czech Republic	n	8	a	40	36	a	x(8)	17	x(8)	100
Denmark	n	23	1	36	6	n	6	27	1	100
Estonia	1	10	a	14	33	7	13	22	n	100
Finland	7	10	a	a	44	1	15	22	1	100
France	11	18	a	30	11	n	12	17	1	100
Germany	3	11	a	49	3	8	10	16	1	100
Greece	24	11	x(5)	6	26	9	7	17	n	100
Hungary	1	17	a	30	29	2	1	19	n	100
Iceland	2	26	6	14	11	9	4	28	1	100
Ireland	11	15	n	x(5)	24	12	16	21	1	100
Israel	11	7	a	9	28	a	15	30	1	100
Italy	12	33	1	7	32	1	n	14	n	100
Japan	x(5)	x(5)	x(5)	x(5)	55	a	19	25	x(8)	100
Korea	9	11	a	20	21	a	12	24	3	100
Luxembourg	10	7	5	18	20	4	15	18	2	100
Mexico	42	22	a	6	13	a	1	16	x(8)	100
Netherlands	8	19	x(4)	15	23	3	3	29	1	100
New Zealand	x(2)	20	7	12	9	11	16	24	x(8)	100
Norway	n	19	a	30	10	3	2	34	1	100
Poland	x(2)	11	a	31	31	4	x(8)	23	x(8)	100
Portugal	49	19	x(5)	x(5)	16	1	x(8)	14	1	100
Slovak Republic	1	8	x(4)	35	39	x(5)	1	16	n	100
Slovenia	2	15	a	26	33	a	11	11	2	100
Spain	19	28	a	8	14	n	9	21	1	100
Sweden	4	9	a	x(5)	46	7	9	25	x(8)	100
Switzerland	3	9	2	40	5	6	11	21	3	100
Turkey	58	11	a	8	10	a	x(8)	13	x(8)	100
United Kingdom	n	11	14	30	7	n	10	27	1	100
United States	4	7	x(5)	x(5)	47	x(5)	10	30	1	100

	Below upper secondary education			Upper secondary level of education			Tertiary level of education			
OECD average	26			44			30			
EU21 average	25			48			28			

Other G20										
Argentina[1]	44	14	a	28	x(5)	a	x(8)	14	x(8)	100
Brazil[2]	45	14	x(5)	x(5)	30	a	x(8)	11	x(8)	100
China[3]	42	40	m	3	10	m	3	1	n	100
India	m	m	m	m	m	m	m	m	m	m
Indonesia[4]	61	15	a	19	x(5)	a	x(8)	5	x(8)	100
Russian Federation[5]	3	8	x(4)	16	18	x(4)	34	20	n	100
Saudi Arabia[6]	54	15	a	15	x(5)	a	x(8)	16	x(8)	100
South Africa[4]	36	36	a	23	x(5)	a	x(8)	5	x(8)	100

	Below upper secondary education			Upper secondary level of education			Tertiary level of education			
G20 average	41			33			26			

Note: Due to discrepancies in the data, averages have not been calculated for each column individually.
1. Year of reference 2003.
2. Year of reference 2009.
3. Year of reference 2000.
4. Year of reference 2007.
5. Year of reference 2002.
6. Year of reference 2004.
Source: OECD. See Annex 3 for notes (*www.oecd.org/edu/eag2012*).
Please refer to the Reader's Guide for information concerning the symbols replacing missing data.
StatLink ⟨ms⟩ http://dx.doi.org/10.1787/888932664119

Table A1.2a. **Population that has attained at least upper secondary education¹ (2010)**
Percentage, by age group

| | Age group | | | | |
	25-64	25-34	35-44	45-54	55-64
	(1)	(2)	(3)	(4)	(5)
OECD					
Australia	73	85	77	69	58
Austria	82	88	86	82	73
Belgium	70	82	78	66	54
Canada	88	92	91	88	82
Chile	71	87	76	67	53
Czech Republic	92	94	95	92	86
Denmark	76	80	81	74	68
Estonia	89	86	91	94	85
Finland	83	91	89	85	70
France	71	84	77	67	56
Germany	86	86	87	86	83
Greece	65	79	72	62	44
Hungary	81	86	83	80	74
Iceland	67	72	72	64	55
Ireland	73	87	80	67	50
Israel	82	88	84	78	74
Italy	55	71	59	51	38
Japan	m	m	m	m	m
Korea	80	98	95	73	43
Luxembourg	78	84	80	75	69
Mexico	36	44	37	33	23
Netherlands	73	83	78	71	61
New Zealand	73	79	77	72	62
Norway	81	83	83	78	79
Poland	89	94	92	89	79
Portugal	32	52	34	22	16
Slovak Republic	91	94	94	91	83
Slovenia	83	93	86	81	72
Spain	53	65	60	48	32
Sweden	87	91	91	87	77
Switzerland	86	90	87	85	81
Turkey	31	42	28	24	19
United Kingdom	75	83	78	74	65
United States	89	88	88	90	90
OECD average	74	82	78	72	62
EU21 average	75	83	80	73	64
Other G20					
Argentina²	42	m	m	m	m
Brazil³	41	53	42	34	25
China⁴	18	20	24	12	10
India	m	m	m	m	m
Indonesia⁵	24	m	m	m	m
Russian Federation⁶	88	91	94	89	71
Saudi Arabia⁷	31	m	m	m	m
South Africa⁵	28	m	m	m	m
G20 Average	56	72	68	61	51

1. Excluding ISCED 3C short programmes.
2. Year of reference 2003.
3. Year of reference 2009.
4. Year of reference 2000.
5. Year of reference 2007.
6. Year of reference 2002.
7. Year of reference 2004.
Source: OECD. See Annex 3 for notes (*www.oecd.org/edu/eag2012*).
Please refer to the Reader's Guide for information concerning the symbols replacing missing data.
StatLink http://dx.doi.org/10.1787/888932664176

A1

Table A1.3a. **Population that has attained tertiary education (2010)**
Percentage by age group
Column 16 refers to absolute numbers in thousands.

	Tertiary-type B education					Tertiary-type A and advanced research programmes					Total tertiary education					25-64 in thousands
	25-64	25-34	35-44	45-54	55-64	25-64	25-34	35-44	45-54	55-64	25-64	25-34	35-44	45-54	55-64	25-64 in thousands
	(1)	(2)	(3)	(4)	(5)	(6)	(7)	(8)	(9)	(10)	(11)	(12)	(13)	(14)	(15)	(16)
Australia	11	10	11	11	10	27	34	28	24	20	38	44	40	35	30	4 299
Austria	7	5	7	8	8	12	15	13	10	8	19	21	21	19	16	890
Belgium	18	20	20	16	14	17	23	19	15	12	35	44	39	31	26	2 051
Canada	24	26	26	24	20	26	31	31	23	22	51	56	57	47	42	9 447
Chile	10	13	13	9	5	17	25	15	12	14	27	38	27	21	19	2 289
Czech Republic	x(11)	x(12)	x(13)	x(14)	x(15)	17	23	16	16	12	17	23	16	16	12	1 023
Denmark	6	6	7	7	5	27	31	30	25	23	33	38	37	31	28	950
Estonia	13	14	12	15	12	22	24	21	23	19	35	38	33	39	31	254
Finland	15	3	18	21	16	23	37	27	18	14	38	39	46	39	30	1 104
France	12	17	14	9	6	18	26	20	13	12	29	43	34	22	18	9 442
Germany	10	7	10	11	10	17	19	18	16	15	27	26	28	27	25	11 825
Greece	7	11	8	6	3	17	20	18	17	13	25	31	27	23	17	1 510
Hungary	1	1	n	n	n	20	25	19	18	16	20	26	19	18	16	1 121
Iceland	4	2	6	4	3	29	34	33	26	19	33	36	39	31	23	53
Ireland	16	18	18	13	10	22	30	24	17	12	37	48	42	30	21	885
Israel	15	12	16	16	17	31	32	33	28	28	46	44	49	44	45	1 614
Italy	n	n	n	1	n	14	20	15	12	10	15	21	16	12	11	4 955
Japan	19	24	24	20	12	25	33	26	26	17	45	57	50	46	29	29 830
Korea	12	26	13	6	2	28	39	34	21	11	40	65	47	27	13	11 397
Luxembourg	15	18	17	12	11	21	26	25	16	15	35	44	41	28	25	95
Mexico	1	1	1	1	1	16	21	15	15	11	17	22	16	16	12	8 615
Netherlands	3	2	3	3	2	30	38	31	27	24	32	41	34	30	26	2 893
New Zealand	16	15	15	18	17	24	31	27	24	17	41	46	42	39	34	870
Norway	2	1	2	3	3	35	46	39	31	25	37	47	41	33	27	929
Poland	x(11)	x(12)	x(13)	x(14)	x(15)	23	37	23	15	13	23	37	23	15	13	4 905
Portugal	x(11)	x(12)	x(13)	x(14)	x(15)	15	25	16	10	9	15	25	16	10	9	919
Slovak Republic	1	1	1	1	1	17	23	15	14	12	17	24	16	15	13	543
Slovenia	11	12	11	10	9	13	19	15	10	8	24	31	27	20	16	280
Spain	9	12	12	7	4	21	27	24	19	14	31	39	35	26	18	8 116
Sweden	9	8	8	9	9	25	34	29	21	18	34	42	37	30	27	1 652
Switzerland	11	10	12	11	9	24	31	26	22	18	35	40	38	33	28	1 524
Turkey	x(11)	x(12)	x(13)	x(14)	x(15)	13	17	12	9	9	13	17	12	9	9	4 290
United Kingdom	10	8	11	12	10	28	38	29	23	20	38	46	41	35	30	12 503
United States	10	10	10	11	9	32	33	33	29	32	42	42	43	40	41	67 207
OECD average	10	11	12	10	8	22	28	24	19	16	31	38	33	28	23	
OECD total (in thousands)																210 281
EU21 average	9	10	11	9	8	20	27	21	17	14	28	35	30	25	20	
Argentina[1]	x(11)	m	m	m	m	x(11)	m	m	m	m	14	m	m	m	m	2 909
Brazil[2]	x(11)	x(12)	x(13)	x(14)	x(15)	11	12	11	11	9	11	12	11	11	9	10 502
China[3]	3	4	3	2	2	1	2	1	1	2	5	6	5	3	3	m
India	m	m	m	m	m	m	m	m	m	m	m	m	m	m	m	m
Indonesia[4]	x(11)	m	m	m	m	x(11)	m	m	m	m	4	m	m	m	m	5 447
Russian Federation[5]	33	34	37	34	26	21	21	21	20	19	54	55	58	54	44	m
Saudi Arabia[6]	x(11)	m	m	m	m	x(11)	m	m	m	m	15	m	m	m	m	1 594
South Africa[4]	x(11)	m	m	m	m	x(11)	m	m	m	m	4	m	m	m	m	1 023
G20 average	13	15	15	12	10	20	25	21	17	15	26	37	33	27	23	m

1. Year of reference 2003. Source: UNESCO/UIS, educational attainment of the population aged 25 and older.
2. Year of reference 2009.
3. Year of reference 2000. Source: 2000 census, Chinese National Bureau of Statistics, education level (college, university and master and above) of 25-64 year-olds.
4. Year of reference 2007. Source: UNESCO/UIS, educational attainment of the population aged 25 and older.
5. Year of reference 2002.
6. Year of reference 2004. Source: UNESCO/UIS, educational attainment of the population aged 25 and older.
Source: OECD. See Annex 3 for notes (www.oecd.org/edu/eag2012).
Please refer to the Reader's Guide for information concerning the symbols replacing missing data.
StatLink ᴍᴤᴸ http://dx.doi.org/10.1787/888932664233

Table A1.4. [1/2] Trends in educational attainment: 25-64 year-olds (1997-2010)

	Percentage, by educational level	1997	1998	1999	2000	2001	2002	2003	2004	2005	2006	2007	2008	2009	2010	2000-10 average annual growth rate
OECD Australia	Below upper secondary	47	44	43	41	41	39	38	36	35	33	32	30	29	27	-4.2
	Upper secondary and post-secondary non-tertiary	29	31	31	31	30	30	31	33	33	34	34	34	34	36	1.3
	Tertiary education	24	25	27	27	29	31	31	31	32	33	34	36	37	38	3.2
Austria	Below upper secondary	26	26	25	24	23	22	21	20	19	20	20	19	18	18	-3.1
	Upper secondary and post-secondary non-tertiary	63	61	61	62	63	64	64	62	63	63	63	63	63	63	0.2
	Tertiary education	11	14	14	14	14	15	15	18	18	18	18	18	19	19	3.3
Belgium	Below upper secondary	45	43	43	41	41	39	38	36	34	33	32	30	29	30	-3.3
	Upper secondary and post-secondary non-tertiary	30	31	31	31	32	33	33	34	35	35	36	37	37	36	1.2
	Tertiary education	25	25	27	27	28	28	29	30	31	32	32	32	33	35	2.6
Canada	Below upper secondary	22	21	20	19	18	17	16	16	15	14	13	13	12	12	-5.0
	Upper secondary and post-secondary non-tertiary	40	40	40	41	40	40	40	40	39	39	38	38	38	38	-0.7
	Tertiary education	37	38	39	40	42	43	44	45	46	47	48	49	50	51	2.4
Chile	Below upper secondary	m	m	m	m	m	m	m	m	m	m	32	32	31	29	
	Upper secondary and post-secondary non-tertiary	m	m	m	m	m	m	m	m	m	m	44	44	45	45	
	Tertiary education	m	m	m	m	m	m	m	m	m	m	24	24	24	27	
Czech Republic	Below upper secondary	15	15	14	14	14	12	14	11	10	10	9	9	9	8	-5.4
	Upper secondary and post-secondary non-tertiary	74	75	75	75	75	76	74	77	77	77	77	76	76	75	0.0
	Tertiary education	11	10	11	11	11	12	12	12	13	14	14	14	16	17	4.3
Denmark	Below upper secondary	m	21	20	21	19	19	19	19	19	18	26	26	25	24	1.3
	Upper secondary and post-secondary non-tertiary	m	53	53	52	52	52	49	48	47	47	43	42	42	42	-2.1
	Tertiary education	m	25	27	26	28	30	32	33	34	35	31	31	32	33	2.4
Estonia	Below upper secondary	m	m	m	m	m	12	12	11	11	12	11	12	11	11	
	Upper secondary and post-secondary non-tertiary	m	m	m	m	m	57	58	57	56	55	56	54	53	54	
	Tertiary education	m	m	m	m	m	30	31	31	33	33	33	34	36	35	
Finland	Below upper secondary	32	31	28	27	26	25	24	22	21	20	19	19	18	17	-4.7
	Upper secondary and post-secondary non-tertiary	39	39	40	41	42	42	43	43	44	44	44	44	45	45	1.0
	Tertiary education	29	30	31	32	32	33	33	34	35	35	36	37	37	38	1.8
France	Below upper secondary	41	39	38	37	36	35	35	34	33	33	32	30	30	29	-2.3
	Upper secondary and post-secondary non-tertiary	39	40	40	41	41	41	41	41	41	41	42	42	42	42	0.2
	Tertiary education	20	21	21	22	23	24	24	24	25	26	27	27	29	29	2.8
Germany	Below upper secondary	17	16	19	18	17	17	17	16	17	17	16	15	15	14	-2.5
	Upper secondary and post-secondary non-tertiary	61	61	58	58	59	60	59	59	59	59	60	60	59	59	0.2
	Tertiary education	23	23	23	23	23	23	24	25	25	24	24	25	26	27	1.3
Greece	Below upper secondary	56	54	52	51	50	48	47	44	43	41	40	39	39	35	-3.7
	Upper secondary and post-secondary non-tertiary	29	29	30	32	32	33	34	35	36	37	37	38	38	41	2.5
	Tertiary education	16	17	17	18	18	19	19	21	21	22	23	23	24	25	3.4
Hungary	Below upper secondary	37	37	33	31	30	29	26	25	24	22	21	20	19	19	-4.9
	Upper secondary and post-secondary non-tertiary	51	50	54	55	56	57	59	59	59	60	61	61	61	61	1.0
	Tertiary education	12	13	14	14	14	14	15	17	17	18	18	19	20	20	3.7
Iceland	Below upper secondary	44	45	44	45	43	41	40	39	37	37	36	36	34	33	-2.8
	Upper secondary and post-secondary non-tertiary	35	34	34	32	32	33	31	32	32	34	34	33	33	34	0.6
	Tertiary education	21	21	22	23	25	26	29	29	31	30	30	31	33	33	3.4
Ireland	Below upper secondary	50	49	45	54	45	40	38	37	35	34	32	31	28	27	-6.9
	Upper secondary and post-secondary non-tertiary	27	30	35	28	32	35	35	35	35	35	36	36	36	36	2.8
	Tertiary education	23	21	20	19	24	25	26	28	29	31	32	34	36	37	7.3
Israel	Below upper secondary	m	m	m	m	m	20	18	21	21	20	20	19	18	18	
	Upper secondary and post-secondary non-tertiary	m	m	m	m	m	38	39	34	33	34	37	37	37	37	
	Tertiary education	m	m	m	m	m	42	43	45	46	46	44	44	45	46	
Italy	Below upper secondary	m	59	58	58	57	56	52	51	50	49	48	47	46	45	-2.5
	Upper secondary and post-secondary non-tertiary	m	32	33	33	33	34	38	37	38	38	39	39	40	40	2.1
	Tertiary education	m	9	9	9	10	10	10	12	12	13	14	14	15	15	4.7
Japan	Below upper secondary	20	20	19	17	17	m	m	m	m	m	m	m	m	m	
	Upper secondary and post-secondary non-tertiary	49	49	49	49	49	63	63	61	60	60	59	57	56	55	1.1
	Tertiary education	31	31	32	34	34	37	37	39	40	40	41	43	44	45	2.9
Korea	Below upper secondary	38	34	33	32	30	29	27	26	24	23	22	21	20	20	-4.7
	Upper secondary and post-secondary non-tertiary	42	44	44	44	45	45	44	44	44	44	43	43	41	41	-0.9
	Tertiary education	20	22	23	24	25	26	29	30	32	33	35	37	39	40	5.2
Luxembourg	Below upper secondary	m	m	44	44	47	38	41	37	34	34	34	32	23	22	-6.5
	Upper secondary and post-secondary non-tertiary	m	m	38	38	35	43	45	40	39	42	39	40	43	42	1.1
	Tertiary education	m	m	18	18	18	19	14	24	27	24	27	28	35	35	6.9

Note: See Annex 3 for breaks in time series.
Source: OECD. See Annex 3 for notes (*www.oecd.org/edu/eag2012*).
Please refer to the Reader's Guide for information concerning the symbols replacing missing data.
StatLink ⟱ http://dx.doi.org/10.1787/888932664290

A1

Table A1.4. [2/2] Trends in educational attainment: 25-64 year-olds (1997-2010)

	Percentage, by educational level	1997	1998	1999	2000	2001	2002	2003	2004	2005	2006	2007	2008	2009	2010	2000-10 average annual growth rate
OECD Mexico	Below upper secondary	72	72	73	71	70	70	70	69	68	68	67	66	65	**64**	-1.0
	Upper secondary and post-secondary non-tertiary	15	15	14	14	15	15	14	15	17	17	17	18	18	**19**	2.7
	Tertiary education	13	13	13	15	15	15	16	17	15	15	16	16	17	**17**	1.7
Netherlands	Below upper secondary	m	36	36	35	35	32	31	29	28	28	27	27	27	**27**	-2.6
	Upper secondary and post-secondary non-tertiary	m	40	40	41	42	43	42	41	42	42	42	41	41	**41**	-0.2
	Tertiary education	m	24	24	23	23	25	28	30	30	30	31	32	33	**32**	3.3
New Zealand	Below upper secondary	40	39	38	37	36	34	33	33	32	31	29	28	28	**27**	-3.1
	Upper secondary and post-secondary non-tertiary	33	34	33	34	35	35	35	32	29	31	30	32	32	**32**	-0.6
	Tertiary education	27	28	29	29	29	31	32	35	39	38	41	40	40	**41**	3.5
Norway	Below upper secondary	17	15	15	15	14	14	13	12	23	21	21	19	19	**19**	2.7
	Upper secondary and post-secondary non-tertiary	57	57	57	57	55	55	56	56	45	46	45	45	44	**43**	-2.7
	Tertiary education	26	27	28	28	30	31	31	32	33	33	34	36	37	**37**	2.8
Poland	Below upper secondary	23	22	22	20	19	19	17	16	15	14	14	13	12	**11**	-5.6
	Upper secondary and post-secondary non-tertiary	67	67	67	69	69	69	68	68	68	68	68	68	67	**66**	-0.4
	Tertiary education	10	11	11	11	12	13	14	16	17	18	19	20	21	**23**	7.2
Portugal	Below upper secondary	m	82	81	81	80	79	77	75	74	72	73	72	70	**68**	-1.7
	Upper secondary and post-secondary non-tertiary	m	10	10	11	11	11	12	13	14	14	14	14	15	**16**	4.6
	Tertiary education	m	8	9	9	9	9	11	13	13	13	13	14	14	**15**	5.7
Slovak Republic	Below upper secondary	21	20	18	16	15	14	13	13	12	11	11	10	9	**9**	-5.7
	Upper secondary and post-secondary non-tertiary	68	70	72	73	74	75	75	74	74	74	75	75	75	**74**	0.0
	Tertiary education	10	10	10	10	11	11	12	13	14	15	14	15	16	**17**	5.3
Slovenia	Below upper secondary	m	m	m	m	m	23	22	20	20	18	18	18	17	**17**	
	Upper secondary and post-secondary non-tertiary	m	m	m	m	m	62	60	61	60	60	60	59	60	**60**	
	Tertiary education	m	m	m	m	m	15	18	19	20	21	22	23	23	**24**	
Spain	Below upper secondary	69	67	65	62	60	59	57	55	51	50	49	49	48	**47**	-2.7
	Upper secondary and post-secondary non-tertiary	13	13	14	16	16	17	18	19	21	21	22	22	22	**22**	3.5
	Tertiary education	19	20	21	23	24	24	25	26	28	28	29	29	30	**31**	3.1
Sweden	Below upper secondary	25	24	24	21	20	19	18	18	17	17	16	16	15	**13**	-4.3
	Upper secondary and post-secondary non-tertiary	54	54	54	54	55	54	54	54	54	54	54	53	53	**52**	-0.4
	Tertiary education	21	22	22	25	26	26	27	28	29	30	30	31	32	**34**	3.3
Switzerland	Below upper secondary	16	16	16	16	15	15	15	15	15	15	14	13	13	**14**	-1.5
	Upper secondary and post-secondary non-tertiary	61	61	60	60	59	60	58	57	56	56	55	53	52	**51**	-1.6
	Tertiary education	22	23	24	24	25	25	27	28	29	30	31	34	35	**35**	3.8
Turkey	Below upper secondary	79	78	78	77	76	75	74	73	72	71	70	70	69	**69**	-1.1
	Upper secondary and post-secondary non-tertiary	13	14	14	15	15	16	17	18	18	18	18	18	18	**18**	1.9
	Tertiary education	8	7	8	8	8	9	10	10	10	11	11	12	13	**13**	4.6
United Kingdom	Below upper secondary	41	40	38	37	37	36	35	34	33	29	28	28	26	**25**	-4.0
	Upper secondary and post-secondary non-tertiary	37	36	37	37	37	37	37	37	37	37	37	36	37	**37**	0.0
	Tertiary education	23	24	25	26	26	27	28	29	30	34	36	35	37	**38**	4.0
United States	Below upper secondary	14	14	13	13	12	13	12	12	12	12	12	11	11	**11**	-1.3
	Upper secondary and post-secondary non-tertiary	52	52	51	51	50	49	49	49	49	48	48	48	47	**47**	-0.7
	Tertiary education	34	35	36	36	37	38	38	39	39	39	40	41	41	**42**	1.3
OECD average	Below upper secondary	36	37	36	36	35	33	32	30	30	29	29	28	27	**26**	-3.2
	Upper secondary and post-secondary non-tertiary	43	42	42	43	43	45	45	44	44	44	44	44	44	**44**	0.6
	Tertiary education	21	21	21	22	22	24	25	26	27	28	28	29	30	**30**	3.7
EU21 average	Below upper secondary	36	38	37	36	35	32	31	30	29	28	27	27	25	**25**	-3.7
	Upper secondary and post-secondary non-tertiary	46	44	44	45	45	47	48	47	48	48	48	48	48	**48**	0.9
	Tertiary education	18	18	19	19	20	21	21	23	24	24	25	26	27	**28**	4.0
Other G20 Argentina		m	m	m	m	m	m	m	m	m	m	m	m	m	**m**	
Brazil	Below upper secondary	m	m	m	m	m	m	m	m	m	m	63	61	59	**m**	
	Upper secondary and post-secondary non-tertiary	m	m	m	m	m	m	m	m	m	m	27	28	30	**m**	
	Tertiary education	m	m	m	m	m	m	m	m	m	m	10	11	11	**m**	
China		m	m	m	m	m	m	m	m	m	m	m	m	m	**m**	
India		m	m	m	m	m	m	m	m	m	m	m	m	m	**m**	
Indonesia		m	m	m	m	m	m	m	m	m	m	m	m	m	**m**	
Russian Federation		m	m	m	m	m	m	m	m	m	m	m	m	m	**m**	
Saudi Arabia		m	m	m	m	m	m	m	m	m	m	m	m	m	**m**	
South Africa		m	m	m	m	m	m	m	m	m	m	m	m	m	**m**	
G20 average		m	m	m	m	m	m	m	m	m	m	m	m	m	**m**	

Note: See Annex 3 for breaks in time series.
Source: OECD. See Annex 3 for notes (www.oecd.org/edu/eag2012).
Please refer to the Reader's Guide for information concerning the symbols replacing missing data.
StatLink ᠁ http://dx.doi.org/10.1787/888932664290

Table A1.5. **Extent of vocational education and training (2010)**
Percentage of 25-64 year-olds whose highest level of education is upper secondary/post-secondary non-tertiary (ISCED 3/4), by educational orientation

A1

	Source[1]	Percentage of the population whose highest level of education is **vocational** upper secondary or post-secondary non-tertiary (ISCED 3/4)			Percentage of the population whose highest level of education is **general** upper secondary or post-secondary non-tertiary (ISCED 3/4)		
		Men	Women	M+W	Men	Women	M+W
		(1)	(2)	(3)	(4)	(5)	(6)
Australia	LFS	12.7	6.4	19.1	7.8	8.7	16.5
Austria	LFS	30.4	27.1	57.5	2.6	3.1	5.7
Belgium	LFS	13.8	11.3	25.0	4.8	5.7	10.5
Canada	LFS	7.7	4.2	11.9	12.9	13.0	25.9
Czech Republic	LFS	37.8	33.5	71.2	1.3	2.6	3.9
Denmark	LFS	19.5	15.4	34.9	3.2	3.0	6.1
Estonia	LFS	17.7	15.1	32.8	10.7	10.3	21.0
Finland	2012_EU_VET	20.9	17.8	38.7	3.9	2.9	6.8
France	LFS	17.1	13.2	30.3	4.8	6.7	11.5
Germany[2]	LFS	27.7	28.5	56.2	1.6	1.3	2.9
Greece	LFS	8.7	6.4	15.0	11.5	14.0	25.5
Hungary	LFS	29.6	22.7	52.4	2.9	5.9	8.8
Iceland	2012_EU_VET	15.6	7.5	23.1	4.3	6.4	10.7
Ireland	2012_EU_VET	6.0	5.1	11.1	11.3	12.2	23.5
Israel	LFS	6.4	4.4	10.8	12.8	12.9	25.7
Italy	LFS	17.6	13.3	30.9	2.8	6.6	9.4
Korea	LFS	10.3	9.4	19.7	9.7	11.2	21.0
Luxembourg	2012_EU_VET	17.3	17.5	34.8	1.4	1.4	2.8
Netherlands	LFS	16.9	16.6	33.5	3.3	3.7	7.0
New Zealand	LFS	13.9	8.4	22.3	3.8	4.6	8.4
Norway	LFS	18.8	13.1	31.9	4.4	5.1	9.5
Poland	LFS	11.8	11.6	23.4	2.6	5.2	7.8
Portugal	2012_EU_VET	7.0	7.2	14.2	1.1	1.2	2.3
Slovak Republic	LFS	37.0	32.5	69.5	1.3	2.8	4.1
Slovenia	2012_EU_VET	31.2	23.2	54.4	2.4	2.8	5.2
Spain	LFS	3.9	4.1	8.0	7.4	6.8	14.2
Sweden	LFS	18.3	12.9	31.2	5.5	5.2	10.7
Switzerland	LFS	18.4	20.5	38.9	2.4	3.9	6.2
Turkey	LFS	5.5	3.0	8.4	5.7	4.0	9.7

1. LFS: Labour Force Survey data provided by countries. EU-VET: European Union LFS provided by Eurostat-Orientation is derived from fields of education.
2. Persons with attainment ISCED 4A in Germany have successfully completed both a general and a vocational programme. In this table they have been allocated to vocational.
Source: OECD. LSO network special data collection on vocational education, Learning and Labour Transitions Working Group. See Annex 3 for notes *(www.oecd.org/edu/eag2012)*.
StatLink ᵐˢᴾ http://dx.doi.org/10.1787/888932664309

HOW MANY STUDENTS ARE EXPECTED TO FINISH SECONDARY EDUCATION?

- Based on current patterns of graduation, it is estimated that an average of 84% of today's young people in OECD countries will complete upper secondary education over their lifetimes; in G20 countries, some 78% of young people will.

- In some countries, it is common for students to graduate from upper secondary programmes after the age of 25. Around 10% of upper secondary graduates in Denmark, Finland and Norway are 25 or older, while 20% in Iceland and more than 40% in Portugal are.

Chart A2.1. Upper secondary graduation rates (2010)

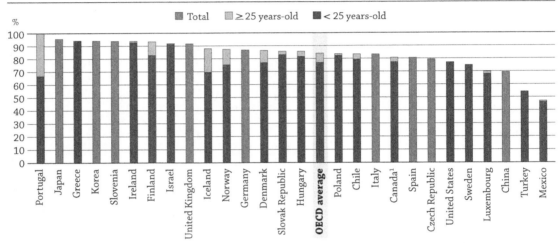

Note: Only first-time graduates in upper secondary programmes are reported in this chart.
1. Year of reference 2009.
Countries are ranked in descending order of the upper secondary graduation rates in 2010.
Source: OECD. China: UNESCO Institute for Statistics (World Education Indicators programme). Table A2.1. See Annex 3 for notes (*www.oecd.org/edu/eag2012*).
StatLink ᓚᕔᔆᑊ http://dx.doi.org/10.1787/888932661573

Context

Upper secondary education provides the basis for advanced learning and training opportunities and prepares some students for direct entry into the labour market. Graduation rates discussed here do not assume that an education system has adequately equipped its graduates with the basic skills and knowledge necessary to enter the labour market, because this indicator does not capture the quality of educational outcomes. However, these rates do give an indication of the extent to which education systems are succeeding in preparing students to meet the labour market's minimum requirements.

Although many countries allow students to leave the education system after completing lower secondary education, students in OECD countries who leave school without an upper secondary qualification tend to face severe difficulties entering – and remaining in – the labour market. Leaving school early is a problem, both for individuals and society. Policy makers are examining ways to reduce the number of early school-leavers, defined as those students who do not complete their upper secondary education. Internationally comparable measures of how many students successfully complete upper secondary programmes – which also imply how many students do not complete those programmes – can assist efforts to that end.

Other findings

- In 23 of 27 countries with available data, **first-time upper secondary graduation rates exceed 75%.** In Finland, Greece, Ireland, Israel, Japan, Korea, Portugal, Slovenia and the United Kingdom, graduation rates equal or exceed 90%.

- **Young women are now more likely than young men to graduate from upper secondary programmes** in almost all OECD countries, a reversal of the historical pattern. Only in Germany are graduation rates for young women slightly lower than those for young men. Young women are also graduating from vocational programmes more often than in the past; consequently, their graduation rates from these programmes are catching up with those of young men.

- In most countries, **upper secondary education is designed to prepare students to enter tertiary-type A (largely theory-based) education.** In Germany, Slovenia, and Switzerland, however, students are more likely to enrol in and graduate from upper secondary programmes that lead to tertiary-type B education, where courses are typically shorter and focus on developing practical, technical or occupational skills.

- **Most boys in vocational programmes at the upper secondary level choose to study engineering, manufacturing and construction,** while girls in such programmes opt for several different fields of study, notably business, law, social sciences, health and welfare, and services.

- This edition marks the second time that comparable data have been published from 25 countries that participated in a special survey on the successful completion of upper secondary programmes. The data show that **70% of students who begin upper secondary education complete the programmes they entered within the theoretical duration of the programme.** However, there are large differences in completion rates, depending on gender and type of programme.

Trends

Since 1995, the upper secondary graduation rate has increased by an average of 8 percentage points among OECD countries with comparable data, which represents an annual growth rate of 0.6%. The greatest increase occurred in Portugal, which showed an annual growth rate of 4.7% between 1995 and 2010.

Note

Graduation rates represent the estimated percentage of people from a certain age cohort that is expected to graduate at some point during their lifetime. This estimate is based on the number of graduates in 2010 and the age distribution of this group. The graduation rates are based on the current pattern of graduation and are thus sensitive to any changes in the education system, such as the introduction of new programmes, and the lengthening or shortening of programme duration. Graduation rates can be very high – even above 100% – during a period when an unexpected category of people goes back to school. For example, this happened in Portugal, when the "New Opportunities" programme was launched to provide a second chance for those individuals who left school early without a secondary diploma.

In this indicator, 25 is regarded as the upper age limit for completing initial education. Among OECD countries, 93% of first-time graduates from upper secondary programmes in 2010 were younger than 25. People who graduate from this level when they are older than 25 are usually enrolled in special programmes.

A2

Analysis

Graduation from upper secondary programmes

Even if completing upper secondary education is considered the norm in most OECD and other G20 countries and economies, the proportion of graduates outside the typical age of graduation varies. First-time graduates are generally between 17 and 20 years old (see Table X1.1a in Annex 1), but some countries also offer second-chance/adult-education programmes. In the Nordic countries, for example, students can leave the education system relatively easily and re-enter it later on. That is why graduation rates for students 25 years or older are relatively high in Denmark, Finland, Iceland and Norway (at least 10% of graduates). Indeed, graduation rates do not imply that all young people have graduated from secondary school by the time they enter the labour market; some students graduate after a period of time spent in work. Policy makers could thus encourage students to complete their upper secondary education before they look for a job, as this is often considered to be the minimum credential for successful entry into the labour market (Chart A2.1). In Portugal, the "New Opportunities" programme, launched in 2005, was introduced to provide a second chance to individuals who left school early or are at risk of doing so, and to assist those in the labour force who want to acquire further qualifications. As a result of the programme, graduation rates in 2010 exceeded 100% and were 41 percentage points higher than in 2008. More than 40% of the students concerned were older than 25.

In most countries, men and women do not have the same level of educational attainment. Women, who often had fewer opportunities and/or incentives to attend higher levels of education, have generally been over-represented among those who had not attained an upper secondary education and were thus under-represented at higher levels of education. But this has changed over the years, and the education gap between men and women has narrowed significantly, and has even been reversed in some cases, among young people (see Indicator A1).

Upper secondary graduation rates for young women exceed those for young men in nearly all countries for which total upper secondary graduation rates can be compared by gender. The gap is greatest in Iceland and Portugal, where graduation rates among young women exceed those of young men by 20 percentage points or more. The exception is Germany, where the graduation rate is slightly higher for young men (Table A2.1).

Most upper secondary programmes are designed primarily to prepare students for tertiary studies, and their orientation may be general, pre-vocational or vocational (see Indicator C1). In 2010, it is estimated that 50% of young people will graduate from general programmes, compared to 46% from pre-vocational or vocational programmes. The rates were 47% and 44%, respectively, in 2005.

For many years now, young women have been more likely to graduate from general programmes than young men. In 2010, the average OECD graduation rate from general programmes was 56% for young women and 44% for young men. In Argentina, Austria, the Czech Republic, Estonia, Italy, Poland, Slovenia and Switzerland, young women outnumber young men as graduates by at least three to two. Only in China, Ireland and Korea is there no, or an extremely narrow, gender gap in graduates from general upper secondary programmes.

On average among countries with available data, there is no clear trend for pre-vocational and vocational upper secondary graduation rates according to gender. Although 47% of boys and 44% of girls in OECD countries graduated from vocational programmes in 2010, graduates who are girls outnumbered graduates who are boys by 10 or more percentage points in Belgium, Finland, Ireland and the Netherlands (Table A2.1).

At this level of education, girls and boys graduate from different fields of education. Differences in young people's choice of field of study can be attributed to traditional perceptions of gender roles and identities as well as the cultural values sometimes associated with particular fields of education. For example, while some fields, especially science, engineering, manufacturing and construction, are often regarded as "masculine" and preferred by men, other (often care-related) fields of study, such as education and health, are sometimes perceived as "feminine" and preferred by women (Eurydice, 2010; see also Indicator A4).

Chart A2.2. Distribution of graduates in upper secondary vocational programmes in OECD countries, by field of education and gender (2010)

A2

⊠ Humanities, arts and education   ▨ Engineering, manufacturing and construction
■ Health and welfare   □ Science
▢ Social sciences, business and law ⫿ Agriculture
▨ Services   ■ Unknown or unspecified

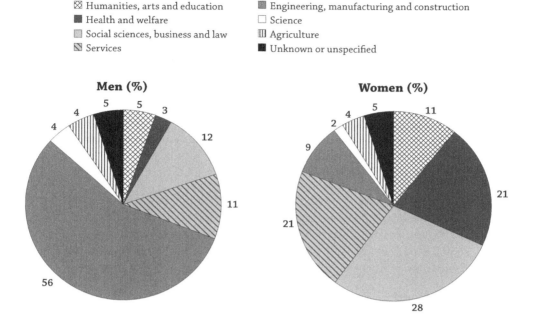

Men (%)

5 5 3
4
4
56
11
12

Women (%)

5 11
2 4
9
21
21
28

Source: OECD. Table A2.4. See Annex 3 for notes (*www.oecd.org/edu/eag2012*).
StatLink ⬛⬛⬛ http://dx.doi.org/10.1787/888932661592

More than one out of two male graduates from upper secondary vocational education programmes studied engineering, manufacturing or construction (Chart A2.2). Futhermore, boys predominated over girls in these fields in almost all countries with available data; in Estonia and Norway, three-quarters of all graduates in these fields were boys (Table A2.4).

For girls, the main field of education varied. In Austria, the Czech Republic, France, Germany, Indonesia, Japan, the Slovak Republic, Slovenia, Spain and Switzerland, girls tended to prefer social sciences, business and law. In Australia, Denmark, Finland, the Netherlands, Norway and Turkey, health and welfare programmes were more popular among girls. Girls in Estonia, Hungary and Poland were more attracted to the service professions, while girls in Iceland, Korea and Sweden tended to pursue studies in education, humanities and the arts. Argentina is the only country where girls preferred engineering, manufacturing and construction (Table A2.4).

Girls and boys might choose different fields of education because of differences in their personal preferences, performance differences in subjects such as reading, mathematics and science, different expectations about labour-market outcomes, or because education policies may lead to gender sorting early in their education. Regardless of social, cultural, or personal differences, girls and boys are equally capable of succeeding in all fields, as indicated by PISA results which show that girls outperform boys in reading in every OECD country, with the average gender gap in reading proficiency equivalent to about a year's worth of schooling. While boys score higher in mathematics, there is no gender gap in science performance (OECD, 2010).

The priority for many countries is to provide young people with the right skills to find a suitable job and to provide adults with an opportunity to update their skills throughout their working lives. As such, governments would be well-advised to link the fields of study at the upper secondary level of education with current or predicted labour-market needs.

A2

The distribution of upper secondary vocational graduates across fields of education sheds light on the prevalence of different fields from country to country. Awareness of this distribution helps policy makers ensure that the demand for qualified vocational trainers who are adequately prepared to teach is met. Policies should also ensure that vocational teachers, trainers and training institutions continue to develop and update their skills and equipment to meet current and future labour-market needs. Efficient and effective delivery of vocational education and training is helpful to raise the status of these programmes, and can also help reduce the proportion of students who drop out from these types of programmes, which is higher than the proportion of general programme dropouts (see section below on successful completion of upper secondary programmes by programme orientation).

Not all countries offer vocational programmes at this level, and thus the level of graduation rates differs quite substantially among countries. Pre-vocational and vocational graduation rates are over 70% in Austria, Finland, the Netherlands, Slovenia and Switzerland; but in Argentina, Brazil, Canada, Estonia, Greece, Hungary, Indonesia, Japan, Korea, Mexico and Turkey, the rates are below 30% (Table A2.1).

Pre-vocational and vocational graduation rates are affected by the proportion of students outside the typical age of graduation, which differs markedly across countries. In Australia, Canada, Denmark, Finland and Iceland, some 40% or more of all graduates are older than 25. In these countries, part-time or evening programmes at this level may be designed especially for older students, i.e. people who drop out during their initial education and who decide to acquire new skills through these types of programmes (Table A2.2).

Graduation from post-secondary non-tertiary programmes

Various kinds of post-secondary non-tertiary programmes are offered in OECD countries. These programmes straddle upper secondary and post-secondary education and may be considered either as upper secondary or post-secondary programmes, depending on the country concerned. Although the content of these programmes may not be significantly more advanced than upper secondary programmes, they broaden the knowledge of individuals who have already attained an upper secondary qualification. Students in these programmes tend to be older than those enrolled in upper secondary schools. These programmes usually offer trade and vocational certificates, and include nursery-teacher training in Austria and vocational training for those who have attained general upper secondary qualifications in the dual system in Germany. Apprenticeships designed for students who have already graduated from an upper secondary programme are also included among these programmes (Table A2.1a available on line).

Transitions following upper secondary education or post-secondary non-tertiary programmes

The vast majority of students who graduate from upper secondary education graduate from programmes designed to provide access to tertiary education (ISCED 3A and 3B). Programmes that facilitate direct entry into tertiary-type A education (ISCED 3A) are preferred by students in all countries except Germany, Slovenia and Switzerland, where the education systems are more strongly oriented towards vocational education and thus, more young people graduate from upper secondary programmes that lead to tertiary-type B programmes. In 2010, graduation rates from long upper secondary programmes (ISCED 3C long) averaged 17% in OECD countries (Table A2.1).

It is interesting to compare the proportion of students who graduate from programmes designed as preparation for entry into tertiary-type A programmes (ISCED 3A and 4A) with the proportion of students who actually enter these programmes under the age of 25. Chart A2.3 shows significant variation in patterns among countries. For instance, in Belgium, Chile, Finland, Ireland and Israel, the difference between these two groups is relatively large, at more than 30 percentage points. This suggests that many students who attain qualifications that would allow them to enter tertiary-type A programmes do not do so, though it should be noted that upper secondary programmes in Belgium and Israel also prepare students for tertiary-type B programmes.

In Israel, the difference may be explained by the wide variation in the age of entry to university, which is partly due to the two to three years of mandatory military service students undertake before entering higher education. In Finland, upper secondary education includes vocational training, and many graduates enter the labour market immediately after completing this level, without any studies at the tertiary level. There is also a *numerus clausus* system in Finnish higher education, which means that the number of entry places is restricted. Therefore, graduates from upper secondary general education may have to take a break of two to three years before obtaining a place in a university or polytechnic institution. In Ireland, the majority of secondary students take the "Leaving Certificate Examination" (ISCED 3A). Although this is designed to allow students to enter tertiary education, not all of the students who take this examination intend to do so. Until the onset of the global economic crisis, school-leavers in Ireland also had strong labour market opportunities, and this also may have had an impact on the difference.

Chart A2.3.   **Access to tertiary-type A education for upper secondary and post-secondary non-tertiary graduates under age 25 (2010)**

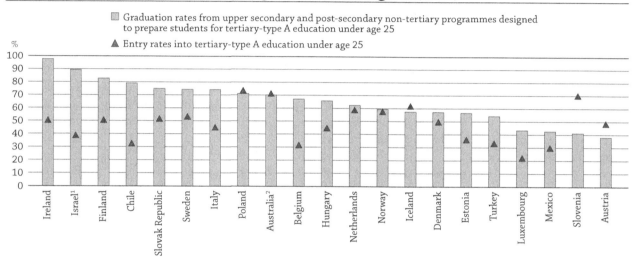

1. Data for post-secondary non-tertiary graduates are missing.
2. Year of reference for graduation rates 2009.
Countries are ranked in descending order of graduation rates from upper secondary programmes designed to prepare students under age 25 for tertiary-type A education in 2010.
Source: OECD. Tables A2.1, A2.1a (available on line) and C3.2. See Annex 3 for notes (*www.oecd.org/edu/eag2012*).
StatLink ⫘ http://dx.doi.org/10.1787/888932661611

In contrast, in Austria and Slovenia, the upper secondary and post-secondary non-tertiary graduation rate is markedly lower – by more than 10 percentage points – than entry rates into tertiary-type A programmes. The large gap for Austria is linked to the high proportion of adults entering tertiary-type A programmes and also to the high proportions of international/foreign students in these programmes (see Indicator C3). Although many students in Slovenia are more likely to graduate from upper secondary programmes leading to tertiary-type B programmes, some may choose to pursue university studies later, and can do so because of the strong pathways between the two types of tertiary programmes in this country.

The availability of pathways between upper secondary/post-secondary non-tertiary and tertiary programmes varies, depending on the country and the relative flexibility of the education system. Switching from vocational to academic programmes, or vice versa, can also occur at the upper secondary level.

Successful completion of upper secondary programmes

This edition of *Education at a Glance* presents, for the second time, an indicator to measure the successful completion of upper secondary programmes and, thus, the pathways between programmes. The indicator sheds light on the time needed to complete these programmes and the proportion of students still in education after the theoretical duration of programmes. It allows for an estimation of the number of students who drop out and a comparison of completion rates by gender and programme orientation.

Box A2.1. Completion and graduation: Two different measures

How is completion measured in *Education at a Glance*? "Successful completion" describes the percentage of students who enter an upper secondary programme for the first time and who graduate from it a given number of years after they entered. It is a measure of how efficiently students flow through upper secondary education. It represents the relationship between the graduates of and the new entrants into the same level of education. The calculation is made using the amount of time normally allocated for completing the programme and also after an additional two years (for students who had to repeat a grade or individual courses, who studied part-time, etc.). This indicator also includes the percentage of students who do not graduate from an upper secondary programme but are still in education. These might include part-time students who need more time to complete their studies and adults who decide to return to school, perhaps while they are working. Only initial education programmes are covered by this indicator.

This measure should not be confused with upper secondary graduation rates. Graduation rates represent the estimated percentage of people from a certain age cohort that is expected to graduate at some point during their lifetime. It measures the production of graduates from upper secondary education, relative to the country's population, and represents the relationship between all the graduates in a given year and a particular population. For each country, for a given year, the number of students who graduate is broken down into age groups. For example, the number of 15-year-old graduates is divided by the total number of 15-year-olds in the country; the number of 16-year-old graduates is divided by the total number of 16-year-olds in the country, etc. The graduation rate is the sum of these age-specific graduation rates.

A third indicator in *Education at a Glance* uses the notion of educational attainment (see Indicator A1). Attainment measures the percentage of a population that has reached a certain level of education, in this case, those who graduated from upper secondary education. It represents the relationship between all graduates (of the given year and previous years) and the total population.

The majority of students who start upper secondary education complete the programmes they entered. It is estimated that 70% of boys and girls who begin an upper secondary programme graduate within the theoretical duration of the programme. However, in some countries, it is relatively common for students and apprentices to take a break from their studies and leave the education system temporarily. Some return quickly to their studies, while others stay away for longer periods of time. In other countries, it is also common for students to repeat a grade or to change programmes; by doing so, their graduation is delayed. Around 85% of students have successfully completed their upper secondary programmes two years after the stipulated time of graduation – 15 percentage points more than the proportion of students who complete their programme within its theoretical duration (Table A2.5).

The proportion of students who complete their education in the stipulated time varies considerably among countries, with Korea having the highest share, at 95%, and Iceland the lowest share, at 44%. Giving two extra years to students to complete the programmes slightly changes the ranking of the countries, with six more countries passing the bar of 80% (Flemish Community of Belgium, Estonia, Finland, France, Spain and the United Kingdom). Iceland remains in last place, at 58%.

In most OECD countries, students may attend regular educational institutions for additional years to complete their upper secondary education whereas in some other countries, older students must attend special programmes designed specifically for them. The difference in the proportion of students who completed their programmes within the stipulated time and that of students who completed after two additional years is 29 percentage points in Luxembourg, where it is common for students to repeat one or more years of school. In contrast, among countries with available data, the difference in New Zealand and in the United States is as low as five and three percentage points, respectively (Chart A2.4). In the United States, it is highly unusual for students over the age of 20 to be enrolled in a regular high school programme.

The large differences in upper secondary completion rates are also linked to the duration of programmes (see section *Successful completion by programme orientation*).

Chart A2.4.   **Successful completion of upper secondary programmes**

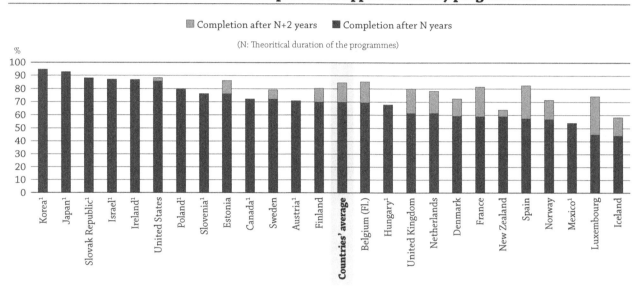

Note: Please refer to Annex 3 for details concerning this indicator, including methods used, programmes included/excluded, year of entry, etc.
1. N+2 information missing.
Countries are ranked in descending order of the successful completion of upper secondary programmes (after N years).
Source: OECD. Table A2.5. See Annex 3 for notes (*www.oecd.org/edu/eag2012*).
StatLink ⟐ http://dx.doi.org/10.1787/888932661630

Successful completion of upper secondary education also depends on how accessible these programmes are. In all of the countries with available data (except Mexico), upper secondary entry rates for students under age 20 are around or over 90%. It is reasonable to expect that a higher percentage of students will graduate from upper secondary education in countries with limited access to this level than in countries that have nearly universal access. In other words, countries where students have to pass an examination to enter upper secondary programmes may have a larger share of higher-achieving students moving on to these programmes, which could produce a higher completion rate (Table A2.4).

Successful completion by gender

In all countries with available data, boys are more likely than girls to drop out of upper secondary school without a diploma. On average, 74% of girls complete their upper secondary education within the stipulated time, compared to 66% of boys. Only in Finland, Japan, Korea, the Slovak Republic and Sweden is the difference in the proportions of boys and girls who leave school early less than five percentage points. In Iceland and Norway, girls outnumbered boys who successfully completed upper secondary education by more than 15 percentage points (Chart A2.5). The gender differences seen in Norway are likely due to the fact that girls tend to have better academic performance than boys in lower secondary school. Controlling for performance in lower secondary school, there is no gender difference, or just a small advantage, for boys (Falch, T., et al., 2010).

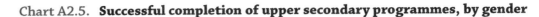

A2

Chart A2.5. **Successful completion of upper secondary programmes, by gender**

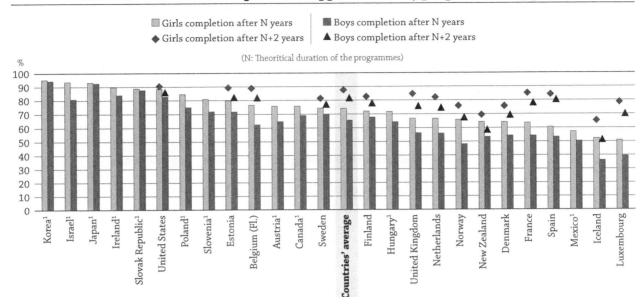

1. N+2 information missing.
Countries are ranked in descending order of the successful completion of girls in upper secondary programmes (after N years).
Source: OECD. Table A2.5. See Annex 3 for notes (*www.oecd.org/edu/eag2012*).
StatLink ⬛ http://dx.doi.org/10.1787/888932661649

The gender gap narrowed slightly, to an average of six percentage points, when completion was delayed by two years because of grade repetition or transfer to a different programme.

The gender gap also varies depending on the programme: 80% of girls complete general programmes, compared to 73% of boys; 64% of girls complete vocational programmes, compared to 59% of boys. In Norway, this gender gap widens to more than 20 percentage points, in favour of girls, in vocational programmes. In Estonia, girls in vocational programmes are not as successful as boys in completing their upper secondary education within the normal duration of the programmes (Table A2.5).

Many studies, including the OECD's PISA analyses, confirm that girls are less likely than boys to leave school early. That said, young women who do leave school early tend to have poorer outcomes than their male counterparts, despite their higher average attainment (see Indicators A1 and C5). The completion rate for upper secondary programmes is also linked to many other issues, such as parental education and immigrant background (Box A2.2).

Successful completion by programme orientation

In several countries, general and vocational programmes are organised separately and students have to opt for one or the other. In other countries, general and vocational programmes are offered in the same programme structure and sometimes in the same school building.

The choice between general and vocational studies is made at different stages in a student's career, depending on the country. In countries with a highly comprehensive system, students follow a common core curriculum until the start of upper secondary education at the age of 16 (e.g. the Nordic countries), while in countries with a highly differentiated system, the choice of a particular programme or type of school can be made during lower secondary education from the age of 10-13 onwards (e.g. Luxembourg).

Students who enter general programmes are more likely to graduate than those who are enrolled in vocational programmes. Among the 20 countries with available data, 77% of students completed their general programme within the theoretical duration of the programme, and that proportion increased by 15 percentage points among students who completed their programme two years after its stipulated duration. In contrast, 61% of students completed their vocational programme within the theoretical duration, and that proportion increased by 16 percentage points two years after the stipulated time. This average difference of 16 percentage points between completion rates for upper secondary general and vocational programmes ranges from around 40 percentage points in Denmark and Estonia, to less than 10 percentage points in France, Japan, Korea and Sweden (Table A2.5).

The large difference in completion rates between upper secondary general and vocational programmes among countries can be explained by the fact that in some countries, low-achieving students may be oriented (or re-oriented) into vocational programmes, while higher-achieving students go into general programmes. Some students may also have difficulty determining which vocational programme is best for them and thus may have to repeat one or more grades at this level of education.

Pathways between these two types of education are well developed in some countries. In Norway, for example, among the 42% of students who entered a vocational programme and graduated within the stipulated time, 47% graduated with a vocational degree, and 53% changed programmes and graduated with a general diploma (Table A2.5).

Some students who begin a vocational programme may leave the education system to enter the labour market directly. Access to employment for people with low educational attainment could also affect successful completion rates and the incidence of dropping out.

Among students who do not complete their programmes within the stipulated time, 59% of those who follow a general programme are still in education, compared to only 45% of those who follow a vocational programme. There is large variation among countries: in Belgium (Flemish Community) and France, 90% or more of students who had not graduated after the theoretical duration of general programmes are still in education, compared to 26% in Israel and only 2% in Korea (Table A2.5).

Chart A2.6. Successful completion of upper secondary programmes, by programme orientation and duration

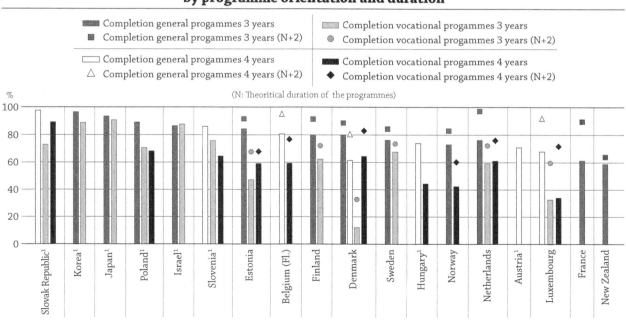

Note: Please refer to Annex 3 for details concerning this indicator, including methods used, programmes included/excluded, year of entry, etc.
1. N+2 information missing.
Countries are ranked in descending order of the successful completion of upper secondary general programmes (after N years).
Source: OECD. Table A2.6. See Annex 3 for notes (*www.oecd.org/edu/eag2012*).
StatLink ⌗⌗⌗ http://dx.doi.org/10.1787/888932661668

A2

The picture is slightly different when it comes to completion of upper secondary programmes (general and vocational) by programme duration. One would assume that completion rates for programmes of longer duration will be lower than those for programmes of shorter duration. Indeed, the completion rate for 4-year general programmes is, on average among countries with available data, 3 percentage points lower than that for 3-year programmes (within the normal duration of the programme, or after 2 more years). But this assumption does not hold for vocational programmes, largely because of differences between the apprenticeship or vocational systems in some countries. For example, in Denmark, completion rates for 3-year vocational programmes are very low (12%), compared to the completion rates for programmes of shorter duration. In some instances, students start the programme, often complete the first school-based part, and then have difficulties finding an employer who will agree to an apprenticeship programme. These students must then wait for an apprenticeship opportunity to arise or give up.

Box A2.2. **Completion by parents' education and immigrant background**

Among the 25 countries that participated in the survey, nine reported completion rates for separate social groups. These rates cannot be directly compared to the overall rates presented above as the cohorts used to calculate them are not the same. A detailed description of the cohort used for each country is presented in Annex 3. The analysis below focuses only on comparing the successful completion of upper secondary programmes as associated with parents' education or an immigrant background.

Successful completion of upper secondary programmes, by parents' education or immigrant background
Ratio of graduates to new entrants based on cohorts

	N = theoretical duration	Successful completion of upper secondary programmes by parental education			Successful completion of upper secondary programmes for immigrant students	
		Below upper secondary education	At upper secondary education	At tertiary education	First generation	Second generation
Denmark	within N	45	56	72	45	47
	2 years after N	56	72	83	55	63
Finland	within N	58	67	75	50	69
	2 years after N	67	77	86	65	74
France	within N	50	59	68	46	49
	2 years after N	70	83	92	68	71
Iceland	within N	m	m	m	26	25
	2 years after N	m	m	m	31	75
Israel	within N	84	91	93	83	m
	2 years after N	m	m	m	m	m
Netherlands	within N	m	m	m	51	53
	2 years after N	m	m	m	65	71
Norway	within N	34	52	70	40	57
	2 years after N	48	68	83	54	70
Sweden	within N	54	70	78	62	65
	2 years after N	61	76	86	70	73
United States	within N	68	83	91	80	84
	2 years after N	74	86	92	85	89

Note: Please refer to Annex 3 for details concerning this Indicator, including methods used, programmes included/excluded, year of entry, etc.
StatLink ⬛🇸 http://dx.doi.org/10.1787/888932664518

Nine countries reported completion rates for immigrant students. Differences in the completion rates of first- and second-generation immigrant students are less than five percentage points in Denmark, France, Iceland, the Netherlands, Sweden and the United States. The exceptions are Finland and Norway, where the completion rates of second-generation immigrant students is more than 17 percentage points higher than the completion rates of first-generation students. Further data will be needed to determine if immigrant students in these two countries are better integrated compared to those in other countries where completion rates are similar between first- and second-generation immigrant students.

...

A2

Seven countries reported completion rates by parents' education level. The difference in upper secondary completion rates between students from families where parents have a tertiary education and those from families where parents have no more than a lower secondary education ranges from 18 percentage points in Finland and France to 36 percentage points in Norway. In Norway, only 34% of students from families with low levels of education complete upper secondary in the stipulated time, compared to 70% of those from highly educated families.

Learning outcomes among students with an immigrant background or from families with low level of education should be an area of focus among education policy makers, particularly in countries where these students show significantly lower completion rates than their peers who do not come from these social groups.

Definitions

First-generation students: both students and parents were born outside the country. **Second-generation students:** students were born in the country, but parents were born outside. More details on the definitions used by countries in Box A2.2 is available in Annex 3.

Graduates in the reference period can be either first-time graduates or repeat graduates. A **first-time graduate** is a student who has graduated for the first time at a given level of education in the reference period. Thus, if a student has graduated multiple times over the years, he or she is counted as a graduate each year, but as a first-time graduate only once.

Net graduation rates represent the estimated percentage of an age group that will complete upper secondary education, based on current patterns of graduation.

Successful completion of upper secondary programmes represents the proportion of new entrants to upper secondary programmes who graduated at the upper secondary level a specific number of years later based on cohorts.

Successful completion of upper secondary general programmes represents the proportion of new entrants to upper secondary general programmes who graduated at the upper secondary level a specific number of years later (based on cohorts).

Successful completion of upper secondary vocational programmes represents the proportion of new entrants to upper secondary general programmes who graduated at the upper secondary level a specific number of years later (based on cohorts).

Methodology

Data refer to the academic year 2009-10 and are based on the UOE data collection on education statistics administered by the OECD in 2011 (for details, see Annex 3 at *www.oecd.org/edu/eag2012*). The fields of education used in the UOE data collection instruments follow the revised ISCED classification by field of education. The same classification is used for all levels of education.

Upper secondary graduation rates (Tables A2.1 to A2.3) are calculated as net graduation rates (i.e. as the sum of age-specific graduation rates) for the years 2005-10. Gross graduation rates are presented for the years 1995 and 2000-04. Gross graduation rates are presented for 2005-10 for countries that are unable to provide such detailed data. In order to calculate gross graduation rates, countries identify the age at which graduation typically occurs. The number of graduates, regardless of their age, is divided by the population at the typical graduation age. The graduation rates take into account students graduating from upper secondary education at the typical graduation ages, as well as older students (e.g. those in "second-chance" programmes) or younger students. Information on the methods used to calculate graduation rates – gross versus net rates – are presented for each level of education in Annex 1.

A2

The count of first-time graduates (Columns 1-3 in Tables A2.1 and Table A2.2) is calculated by netting out students who graduated from another upper secondary programme in a previous year (or another post-secondary non-tertiary programme). As for the others columns of the tables, the net rate is calculated when data are available.

Graduates of ISCED 3A, 3B and 3C (or 4A, 4B, 4C) programmes are not considered as first-time counts. Therefore, gross graduation rates cannot be added, as some individuals graduate from more than one upper secondary programme and would be counted twice. The same applies for graduation rates according to programme orientation, i.e. general or vocational. In addition, the typical graduation ages are not necessarily the same for the different types of programmes (see Annex 1). Pre-vocational and vocational programmes include both school-based programmes and combined school- and work-based programmes that are recognised as part of the education system. Entirely work-based education and training programmes that are not overseen by a formal education authority are not included.

In Table A2.3 (trends in graduation rates at upper secondary level), data for the years 1995, 2000, 2001, 2002, 2003 and 2004 are based on a special survey carried out in January 2007.

In Tables A2.5, A2.6 and Box A2.2, data are based on a special survey carried out in December 2011. Successful completion of upper secondary programmes is calculated as the ratio of the number of students who graduate from an upper secondary programme during the reference year to the number of new entrants in this programme N years before (or N+2), with N being the duration of the programme. The calculation of successful completion is defined from a cohort analysis in three quarters of the countries listed in Table A2.5 (true cohort and longitudinal survey). The estimation for the other countries without a real cohort tracking system assumes constant student flows at the upper secondary level, owing to the need for consistency between the graduate cohort in the reference year and the entrant cohort N years before (Proxy cohort data). This assumption may be an oversimplification. A detailed description of the method used for each country is included in Annex 3 (years of new entrants, years of graduates, programmes taken into account, etc.).

The statistical data for Israel are supplied by and under the responsibility of the relevant Israeli authorities. The use of such data by the OECD is without prejudice to the status of the Golan Heights, East Jerusalem and Israeli settlements in the West Bank under the terms of international law.

References

Education, Audiovisual and Culture Executive Agency (Eurydice) (2010), *Gender Differences in Educational Outcomes: Study on the Measures Taken and the Current Situation in Europe*, Eurydice, Brussels.

Falch, T., et al. (2010), *Completion and Dropout in Upper Secondary Education in Norway: Causes and Consequences*, Centre for Economic Research at Norges Teknisk-Naturvitenskapelige Universitet, Trondheim.

OECD (2010), *PISA 2009 Results: What Students Know and Can Do: Student Performance in Reading, Mathematics and Science* (Volume I), OECD Publishing.

The following additional material relevant to this indicator is available on line:

- *Table A2.1a Post-secondary non-tertiary graduation rates (2010)*
  StatLink ⟨⟨⟨⟩⟩⟩ http://dx.doi.org/10.1787/888932664366

- *Table A2.3a Trends in graduation rates (general and pre-vocational/vocational programmes) at upper secondary level (2005-2010)*
  StatLink ⟨⟨⟨⟩⟩⟩ http://dx.doi.org/10.1787/888932664423

- *Table A2.4a Distribution of upper secondary vocational graduates, by field of education (2010)*
  StatLink ⟨⟨⟨⟩⟩⟩ http://dx.doi.org/10.1787/888932664461

Table A2.1. **Upper secondary graduation rates (2010)**
Sum of age-specific graduation rates, by programme destination, programme orientation and gender

	Total (first-time graduates)			General programmes			Pre-vocational/vocational programmes			ISCED 3A[1]	ISCED 3B[1]	ISCED 3C (long)[1]	ISCED 3C (short)[1]
	M + W	Men	Women	M + W	Men	Women	M + W	Men	Women	M + W	M + W	M + W	M + W
	(1)	(2)	(3)	(4)	(5)	(6)	(7)	(8)	(9)	(10)	(13)	(16)	(19)
OECD													
Australia[2]	m	m	m	70	66	75	49	47	50	70	a	49	a
Austria	m	m	m	18	15	22	76	86	66	18	55	1	21
Belgium	m	m	m	36	31	41	69	63	75	60	a	20	25
Canada[2]	81	77	84	78	74	82	3	4	2	78	a	3	a
Chile	83	80	86	53	50	56	30	30	31	83	a	a	a
Czech Republic	79	76	82	22	17	28	57	59	55	57	n	21	a
Denmark	86	84	89	57	48	66	47	49	44	57	a	46	n
Estonia	m	m	m	58	46	70	20	25	15	58	18	a	2
Finland	93	90	97	46	38	55	94	89	99	93	a	a	a
France	m	m	m	51	45	58	65	65	65	51	14	4	47
Germany	87	87	86	40	35	45	47	52	42	40	46	a	1
Greece	94	92	96	66	59	75	28	34	22	66	a	28	x(16)
Hungary	86	82	89	69	62	77	17	21	13	69	a	17	x(16)
Iceland	88	76	101	69	58	81	54	53	55	65	2	37	18
Ireland	94	93	95	72	73	71	68	53	83	99	a	6	35
Israel	92	88	96	58	52	65	34	35	32	89	a	2	a
Italy	83	81	86	36	25	46	60	67	53	74	1	a	20
Japan	96	95	96	73	70	76	23	25	20	73	1	22	x(16)
Korea	94	93	95	71	70	72	23	23	23	71	a	23	a
Luxembourg	70	67	73	30	27	34	41	42	41	44	7	20	2
Mexico	47	43	51	43	39	47	4	4	4	43	a	4	a
Netherlands	m	m	m	39	36	42	85	76	94	67	a	57	a
New Zealand	m	m	m	m	m	m	m	m	m	m	m	m	m
Norway	87	84	91	60	49	71	36	44	27	60	a	36	m
Poland	84	80	88	52	40	65	38	46	29	75	a	14	a
Portugal[3]	104	92	116	68	60	76	36	32	39	x(1)	x(1)	x(1)	x(1)
Slovak Republic	86	83	88	26	21	31	67	69	64	76	a	15	1
Slovenia	94	92	96	37	29	46	73	80	65	40	44	22	2
Spain	80	76	85	48	41	56	43	43	43	48	19	8	15
Sweden	75	73	77	31	26	36	44	46	41	74	n	n	n
Switzerland	m	m	m	32	25	39	74	78	69	28	71	7	x(16)
Turkey	54	54	54	33	31	35	22	24	19	54	a	a	m
United Kingdom	92	90	94	m	m	m	m	m	m	m	m	74	18
United States	77	73	81	x(1)	x(2)	x(3)	x(1)	x(2)	x(3)	x(1)	x(1)	x(1)	x(1)
OECD average	84	81	87	50	44	56	46	47	44	63	9	17	8
EU21 average	87	84	90	45	39	52	54	55	52	62	11	18	10
Other G20													
Argentina[2]	m	m	m	36	29	44	6	8	5	43	a	a	a
Brazil	m	m	m	63	52	74	10	8	12	63	10	a	a
China	69	69	70	40	39	41	48	47	49	41	x(10)	28	18
India	m	m	m	m	m	m	m	m	m	m	m	m	m
Indonesia	m	m	m	31	29	33	19	22	15	31	19	a	a
Russian Federation	m	m	m	49	x(4)	x(4)	40	x(7)	x(7)	49	18	19	3
Saudi Arabia	m	m	m	m	m	m	m	m	m	m	m	m	m
South Africa	m	m	m	m	m	m	m	m	m	m	m	m	m
G20 average	78	76	80	51	47	56	30	30	28	56	8	13	8

Notes: Columns showing graduation rates for men and women at upper secondary level by programme orientation (i.e. Columns 11-12, 14-15, 17-18, 20-21) are available for consultation on line (see *StatLink* below).

Refer to Annex 1 for information on the method used to calculate graduation rates (gross rates versus net rates) and the corresponding typical ages.

Mismatches between the coverage of the population data and the graduate data mean that the graduation rates for those countries that are net exporters of students may be underestimated (for instance Luxembourg) and those that are net importers may be overestimated.

1. ISCED 3A (designed to prepare for direct entry to tertiary-type A education).
   ISCED 3B (designed to prepare for direct entry to tertiary-type B education).
   ISCED 3C (long) similar to duration of typical 3A or 3B programmes.
   ISCED 3C (short) shorter than duration of typical 3A or 3B programmes.
2. Year of reference 2009.
3. The above 100% first-time graduation rate is an exceptional and temporary situation following the implementation of the "New Opportunities" programme in Portugal. Many individuals went back to school and are now graduated from this programme.
Source: OECD. Argentina, China, Indonesia: UNESCO Institute for Statistics (World Education Indicators programme). See Annex 3 for notes (*www.oecd.org/edu/eag2012*).

Please refer to the Reader's Guide for information concerning the symbols replacing missing data.

StatLink ⬛📉 http://dx.doi.org/10.1787/888932664347

A2

Table A2.2. Upper secondary graduation rates: below 25 years old (2010)

Sum of age-specific graduation rates below age 25, by programme destination, programme orientation and gender

	Total (first-time graduates)				General programmes				Pre-vocational/vocational programmes				ISCED 3A[1]	ISCED 3B[1]	ISCED 3C (long)[1]	ISCED 3C (short)[1]
	M + W	Men	Women	Share of graduates below 25[2]	M + W	Men	Women	Share of graduates below 25[2]	M + W	Men	Women	Share of graduates below 25[2]	M + W	M + W	M + W	M + W
	(1)	(2)	(3)	(4)	(5)	(6)	(7)	(8)	(9)	(10)	(11)	(12)	(13)	(16)	(19)	(22)
OECD																
Australia[3]	m	m	m	m	70	66	75	100	23	25	21	47	70	a	23	a
Austria	m	m	m	m	18	15	22	99	70	79	60	90	18	50	1	20
Belgium	m	m	m	m	36	31	41	100	51	51	52	71	60	a	20	4
Canada[3]	77	74	80	96	76	73	80	98	1	1	1	37	76	a	1	a
Chile	79	77	82	96	49	48	51	94	30	30	30	99	79	a	a	a
Czech Republic	m	m	m	m	m	m	m	m	m	m	m	m	m	n	m	a
Denmark	77	75	78	89	56	47	65	98	28	33	22	58	56	a	28	n
Estonia	m	m	m	m	57	45	69	98	19	24	14	96	57	m	a	1
Finland	83	80	85	89	45	37	54	99	50	53	47	54	83	a	a	a
France	m	m	m	m	51	45	58	100	58	61	55	89	51	14	3	40
Germany	m	m	m	m	m	m	m	m	m	m	m	m	m	m	a	m
Greece	94	92	96	100	66	59	75	100	28	34	22	100	66	a	28	x(16)
Hungary	82	79	84	94	66	59	72	94	17	21	12	96	66	a	17	x(16)
Iceland	70	61	78	80	61	51	71	89	32	32	32	60	57	2	21	13
Ireland	93	92	94	98	70	72	69	97	52	45	60	71	98	a	6	19
Israel	92	88	96	100	58	52	65	100	34	35	32	100	89	a	2	a
Italy	m	m	m	m	36	25	46	100	m	m	m	m	74	m	a	m
Japan	m	m	m	m	m	m	m	m	m	m	m	m	m	m	m	x(16)
Korea	m	m	m	m	m	m	m	m	m	m	m	m	m	a	m	a
Luxembourg	68	65	71	97	30	27	34	100	40	40	39	95	43	7	18	2
Mexico	46	43	50	99	43	39	46	99	4	4	4	94	43	a	4	a
Netherlands	m	m	m	m	39	36	42	100	59	60	58	67	62	a	36	a
New Zealand	m	m	m	m	m	m	m	m	m	m	m	m	m	m	m	m
Norway	75	72	79	86	58	48	69	98	22	30	14	61	58	a	22	m
Poland	82	78	86	98	48	37	60	92	37	46	28	99	71	a	14	a
Portugal	67	59	74	56	40	32	47	50	27	27	27	69	x(1)	x(1)	x(1)	x(1)
Slovak Republic	83	81	85	97	26	21	31	98	63	67	59	94	74	a	15	n
Slovenia	m	m	m	m	37	29	46	100	m	m	m	m	40	m	m	2
Spain	m	m	m	m	m	m	m	m	m	m	m	m	m	m	m	m
Sweden	75	73	77	100	31	26	36	100	44	46	41	100	74	n	n	n
Switzerland	m	m	m	m	m	m	m	m	m	m	m	m	m	m	m	m
Turkey	54	54	54	100	33	31	35	100	22	24	19	100	54	a	a	m
United Kingdom	m	m	m	m	m	m	m	m	m	m	m	m	m	m	m	m
United States	77	73	81	100	x(1)	x(2)	x(3)	m	x(1)	x(2)	x(3)	m	x(1)	x(1)	x(1)	x(1)
OECD average	77	74	80	93	49	44	56	96	35	37	32	79	64	3	11	5
EU21 average	80	78	83	92	44	38	51	96	43	46	40	83	62	5	12	6
Other G20																
Argentina[3]	m	m	m	m	34	27	42	95	6	8	5	100	41	a	a	a
Brazil	m	m	m	m	54	46	61	86	6	5	7	62	54	6	a	a
China	m	m	m	m	m	m	m	m	m	m	m	m	m	m	m	m
India	m	m	m	m	m	m	m	m	m	m	m	m	m	m	m	m
Indonesia	m	m	m	m	31	29	33	100	19	22	15	100	31	19	a	a
Russian Federation	m	m	m	m	m	m	m	m	m	m	m	m	m	m	m	m
Saudi Arabia	m	m	m	m	m	m	m	m	m	m	m	m	m	m	m	m
South Africa	m	m	m	m	m	m	m	m	m	m	m	m	m	m	m	m
G20 average	m	m	m	m	m	m	m	m	m	m	m	m	m	m	m	m

Notes: Columns showing graduation rates for men and women at upper secondary level by programme orientation (i.e. Columns 14-15, 17-18, 20-21, 23-24) are available for consultation on line (see *StatLink* below).

Refer to Annex 1 for information on the method used to calculate graduation rates (gross rates versus net rates) and the corresponding typical ages.

Mismatches between the coverage of the population data and the graduate data mean that the graduation rates for those countries that are net exporters of students may be underestimated (for instance Luxembourg) and those that are net importers may be overestimated.

1. ISCED 3A (designed to prepare for direct entry to tertiary-type A education).
   ISCED 3B (designed to prepare for direct entry to tertiary-type B education).
   ISCED 3C (long) similar to duration of typical 3A or 3B programmes.
   ISCED 3C (short) shorter than duration of typical 3A or 3B programmes.
2. Share of 25-year-old graduates among the total population of graduates.
3. Year of reference 2009.

Source: OECD. Argentina, Indonesia: UNESCO Institute for Statistics (World Education Indicators programme). See Annex 3 for notes (*www.oecd.org/edu/eag2012*).
Please refer to the Reader's Guide for information concerning the symbols replacing missing data.

StatLink ⬛⬛ http://dx.doi.org/10.1787/888932664385

Table A2.3. **Trends in graduation rates (first-time) at upper secondary level (1995-2010)**

	1995	2000	2001	2002	2003	2004	2005	2006	2007	2008	2009	2010	Average annual growth rate 1995-2010[1]
OECD Australia	m	m	m	m	m	m	m	m	m	m	m	**m**	m
Austria	m	m	m	m	m	m	m	m	m	m	m	**m**	m
Belgium	m	m	m	m	m	m	m	m	m	m	m	**m**	m
Canada	m	m	77	79	83	79	80	79	76	79	81	**m**	m
Chile	m	m	m	m	m	79	85	82	82	83	85	**83**	m
Czech Republic	78	m	84	83	88	87	89	90	88	87	84	**79**	0.1%
Denmark	83	95	95	94	88	88	82	84	85	83	85	**86**	0.3%
Estonia	m	m	m	m	m	m	m	m	m	m	m	**m**	m
Finland	91	91	85	84	90	95	94	94	97	93	95	**93**	0.2%
France	m	m	m	m	m	m	m	m	m	m	m	**m**	m
Germany[2]	100	92	92	94	97	99	99	100	100	97	84	**87**	-1.0%
Greece	80	54	76	85	96	93	100	98	96	91	m	**m**	m
Hungary	m	m	83	82	87	86	84	87	84	78	86	**86**	m
Iceland	80	67	70	79	81	87	79	87	86	89	89	**88**	0.7%
Ireland	m	74	77	78	91	92	91	87	90	88	91	**94**	2.3%
Israel	m	m	m	90	89	93	90	90	92	90	89	**92**	m
Italy	m	78	81	78	m	82	85	86	84	86	81	**83**	0.7%
Japan	96	95	93	94	95	96	95	96	96	95	95	**96**	0.0%
Korea	88	96	100	99	92	94	94	93	91	93	89	**94**	0.5%
Luxembourg	m	m	m	69	71	69	75	71	75	73	69	**70**	m
Mexico	m	33	34	35	37	39	40	42	43	44	45	**47**	3.6%
Netherlands	m	m	m	m	m	m	m	m	m	m	m	**m**	m
New Zealand	m	m	m	m	m	m	m	m	m	m	m	**m**	m
Norway	77	99	105	97	92	100	89	88	92	91	91	**87**	0.8%
Poland	m	90	93	91	86	79	85	81	84	83	85	**84**	-0.8%
Portugal[3]	52	52	48	50	60	53	51	54	65	63	96	**104**	4.7%
Slovak Republic	85	87	72	60	56	83	85	86	86	82	82	**86**	0.0%
Slovenia	m	m	m	m	m	m	85	97	91	85	96	**94**	m
Spain	62	60	66	66	67	66	72	72	74	73	74	**80**	1.8%
Sweden	m	75	71	72	76	78	76	75	74	74	74	**75**	0.0%
Switzerland	86	88	91	92	89	87	89	89	89	90	90	**m**	m
Turkey	37	37	37	37	41	55	48	52	58	26	45	**54**	2.6%
United Kingdom	m	m	m	m	m	m	86	88	89	91	92	**92**	m
United States	69	70	71	73	74	75	76	75	75	76	76	**77**	0.7%
OECD average	78	76	77	78	79	81	82	82	83	*81*	83	**84**	m
OECD average for countries with 1995 and 2010 data	78	77										85	0.6%
EU21 average	79	77	79	77	79	78	81	82	84	*84*	85	**86**	m
Other G20 Argentina	m	m	m	m	m	m	m	m	m	m	m	**m**	m
Brazil	m	m	m	m	m	m	m	m	m	m	m	**m**	m
China	m	m	m	m	m	m	m	m	m	m	m	**69**	m
India	m	m	m	m	m	m	m	m	m	m	m	**m**	m
Indonesia	m	m	m	m	m	m	m	m	m	m	m	**m**	m
Russian Federation	m	m	m	m	m	m	m	m	m	m	m	**m**	m
Saudi Arabia	m	m	m	m	m	m	m	m	m	m	m	**m**	m
South Africa	m	m	m	m	m	m	m	m	m	m	m	**m**	m
G20 average	m	m	m	m	m	m	m	m	m	m	m	**m**	m

Notes: Up to 2004, graduation rates at upper secondary level were calculated on a gross basis. From 2005 and for countries with available data, graduation rates are calculated as net graduation rates (i.e. as the sum of age-specific graduation rates).
Refer to Annex 1 for information on the method used to calculate graduation rates (gross rates versus net rates) and the corresponding typical ages.
1. For countries that do not have data for the year 1995, the 2000-10 average annual growth rate is indicated in italics.
2. Break in the series between 2008 and 2009 due to a partial reallocation of vocational programmes into ISCED 2 and ISCED 5B.
3. Year of reference 1997 instead of 1995.
Source: OECD. China: UNESCO Institute for Statistics (World Education Indicators programme). See Annex 3 for notes (*www.oecd.org/edu/eag2012*).
Please refer to the Reader's Guide for information concerning the symbols replacing missing data.
StatLink ᠍᠍ᡅ᠍ http://dx.doi.org/10.1787/888932664404

A2

Table A2.4. Distribution of upper secondary vocational graduates, by field of education and gender (2010)

	Boys									Girls								
	Pre-vocational/ vocational programmes graduation rates	Humanities, arts and education	Health and welfare	Social sciences, business and law	Services	Engineering, manufacturing and construction	Sciences	Agriculture	Unknown or unspecified	Pre-vocational/ vocational programmes graduation rates	Humanities, arts and education	Health and welfare	Social sciences, business and law	Services	Engineering, manufacturing and construction	Sciences	Agriculture	Unknown or unspecified
	(1)	(2)	(5)	(6)	(7)	(8)	(9)	(14)	(15)	(16)	(17)	(20)	(21)	(22)	(23)	(24)	(29)	(30)
Australia[1]	46	2	5	12	12	59	3	4	2	49	6	35	30	17	4	1	2	5
Austria	86	1	2	14	11	59	2	11	n	66	3	10	42	27	7	n	11	n
Belgium	63	17	5	11	8	30	3	2	24	75	22	18	12	19	2	n	1	26
Canada[1]	4	m	m	m	m	m	m	m	m	2	m	m	m	m	m	m	m	m
Chile	30	m	m	m	m	m	m	m	m	31	m	m	m	m	m	m	m	m
Czech Republic	59	3	1	11	13	69	n	3	m	55	6	13	36	29	10	n	5	m
Denmark	49	3	3	15	12	61	n	7	n	44	1	43	36	9	6	n	4	n
Estonia	25	2	n	1	10	76	5	7	n	15	6	n	20	43	22	3	5	n
Finland	89	4	3	9	18	56	4	5	n	99	7	29	21	27	10	1	5	n
France	65	2	3	14	12	63	n	6	n	65	2	30	32	27	6	n	3	n
Germany	52	2	2	27	9	52	3	3	n	42	3	16	53	19	7	1	1	n
Greece	35	m	m	m	m	m	m	m	m	22	m	m	m	m	m	m	m	m
Hungary	21	1	1	6	17	72	n	5	m	13	4	10	30	37	14	n	4	m
Iceland	53	11	1	12	13	59	1	2	n	55	26	19	20	24	6	n	4	n
Ireland	53	7	7	10	7	3	3	5	57	83	6	31	16	5	n	1	2	40
Israel	35	m	m	m	m	m	m	m	m	32	m	m	m	m	m	m	m	m
Italy	67	m	m	m	m	m	m	m	m	53	m	m	m	m	m	m	m	m
Japan	25	n	1	17	2	56	n	11	11	20	n	10	40	13	8	n	11	17
Korea	23	16	n	6	3	62	10	2	n	23	32	1	22	5	26	13	2	n
Luxembourg	42	m	m	m	m	m	m	m	m	41	m	m	m	m	m	m	m	m
Mexico	4	m	m	m	m	m	m	m	m	4	m	m	m	m	m	m	m	m
Netherlands	76	4	8	18	22	37	7	4	n	94	5	58	19	14	2	n	2	n
New Zealand	m	m	m	m	m	m	m	m	m	m	m	m	m	m	m	m	m	m
Norway	44	1	4	2	13	75	3	3	n	27	4	47	11	25	10	n	3	n
Poland	46	1	n	7	14	63	10	5	n	29	3	n	35	46	11	2	4	n
Portugal	32	m	m	m	m	m	m	m	m	39	m	m	m	m	m	m	m	m
Slovak Republic	69	3	2	11	19	61	n	3	n	64	7	11	38	31	9	n	4	n
Slovenia	80	3	4	15	10	57	7	4	n	65	12	21	39	15	7	n	6	n
Spain	43	15	2	10	12	48	8	4	n	43	27	20	30	16	3	2	1	n
Sweden	46	12	5	4	8	64	n	3	4	41	33	21	11	14	10	n	7	4
Switzerland	78	2	2	23	6	57	3	6	n	69	4	24	47	13	9	n	3	n
Turkey	24	1	2	13	4	52	17	n	13	19	5	23	19	8	13	13	n	19
United Kingdom	m	m	m	m	m	m	m	m	m	m	m	m	m	m	m	m	m	m
United States	m	m	m	m	m	m	m	m	m	m	m	m	m	m	m	m	m	m
OECD average	47	5	3	12	11	56	4	4	5	44	11	21	28	21	9	2	4	5
EU21 average	55	4	3	12	13	55	3	5	5	52	8	21	30	24	8	1	4	5
Argentina[1]	8	2	1	9	1	63	6	14	4	5	5	2	27	1	32	13	17	2
Brazil	8	m	m	m	m	m	m	m	m	12	m	m	m	m	m	m	m	m
China	47	m	m	m	m	m	m	m	m	49	m	m	m	m	m	m	m	m
India	m	m	m	m	m	m	m	m	m	m	m	m	m	m	m	m	m	m
Indonesia	22	2	2	49	n	39	n	n	8	15	2	6	49	n	29	n	4	10
Russian Federation	m	m	m	m	m	m	m	m	m	m	m	m	m	m	m	m	m	m
Saudi Arabia	m	m	m	m	m	m	m	m	m	m	m	m	m	m	m	m	m	m
South Africa	m	m	m	m	m	m	m	m	m	m	m	m	m	m	m	m	m	m
G20 average	31	m	m	m	m	m	m	m	m	28	m	m	m	m	m	m	m	m

Note: Columns showing the breakdown of humanities, arts and education (3, 4, 18 and 19) and science (10-13, 25-28) are available for consultation on line (see *StatLink* below).
1. Year of reference 2009.
Source: OECD. Argentina, China, Indonesia: UNESCO Institute for Statistics (World Education Indicators programme). See Annex 3 for notes (*www.oecd.org/edu/eag2012*).
Please refer to the Reader's Guide for information concerning the symbols replacing missing data.
StatLink ᴸ http://dx.doi.org/10.1787/888932664442

Table A2.5. [1/2] Successful completion of upper secondary programmes, by gender and programme orientation

Ratio of graduates to new entrants based on cohorts

A2

	Method	Year used for new entrants / Duration of programme (G: general, V: vocational)	N: theoretical duration	Completion of upper secondary programmes			Completion of general programmes[1]			Proportion of vocational programme graduates[3]	Completion of vocational programmes[2]			Proportion of general programmes graduates[4]
				Total	Men	Women	Total	Men	Women		Total	Men	Women	
Austria	True cohort	2006-07 / 4 years G & V	within N	**71**	65	76	**71**	65	76	3	**m**	m	m	n
			2 years after N	**m**	m	m	**m**	m	m	m	**m**	m	m	m
Belgium (Fl.)	True cohort	2004-05 / 4 years G & V	within N	**69**	62	77	**81**	74	86	13	**59**	54	66	n
			2 years after N	**85**	82	89	**95**	93	97	18	**77**	74	80	n
Canada	Proxy cohort data	2006-07 / 3 years	within N	**72**	69	76	**m**	m	m	m	**m**	m	m	m
			2 years after N	**m**	m	m	**m**	m	m	m	**m**	m	m	m
Denmark	True cohort	2002-03 / 3-4 years G & 2-5 years V	within N	**59**	54	64	**80**	76	82	n	**35**	35	35	3
			2 years after N	**73**	69	76	**88**	87	90	3	**54**	54	54	9
Estonia	True cohort	2004 / 3 years G & 3-4 years V	within N	**76**	72	80	**84**	82	86	n	**48**	52	40	1
			2 years after N	**86**	82	89	**92**	90	93	3	**68**	67	69	3
Finland	True cohort	2004 / 3 years G & V	within N	**70**	68	72	**80**	78	81	1	**62**	61	64	1
			2 years after N	**80**	78	83	**91**	90	93	4	**72**	71	74	1
France	Longitudinal sample survey	1999-2005 / 3 years G & 2 years V	within N	**59**	54	64	**61**	56	66	1	**55**	52	60	n
			2 years after N	**82**	78	85	**90**	88	91	6	**69**	67	73	1
Hungary	Proxy cohort data	2006-07 / 4 years G & V	within N	**68**	64	72	**74**	70	77	m	**44**	45	43	m
			2 years after N	**m**	m	m	**m**	m	m	m	**m**	m	m	m
Iceland	True cohort	2003 / 4 years G & V	within N	**44**	36	52	**44**	35	51	6	**45**	38	55	39
			2 years after N	**58**	51	65	**59**	52	65	15	**57**	50	67	46
Ireland	True cohort	2004 / 2-3 years G & V	within N	**87**	84	90	**m**	m	m	m	**m**	m	m	m
			2 years after N	**m**	m	m	**m**	m	m	m	**m**	m	m	m
Israel	True cohort	2007 / 3 years G & V	within N	**87**	81	94	**87**	78	94	9	**88**	84	92	13
			2 years after N	**m**	m	m	**m**	m	m	m	**m**	m	m	m
Japan	True cohort	2007 / 3 years G & V	within N	**93**	92	93	**93**	93	94	m	**91**	91	91	m
			2 years after N	**m**	m	m	**m**	m	m	m	**m**	m	m	m
Korea	True cohort	2007 / 3 years G & V	within N	**95**	94	95	**97**	96	97	m	**89**	88	89	m
			2 years after N	**m**	m	m	**m**	m	m	m	**m**	m	m	m
Luxembourg	True cohort	2004-05 / 4 years G & 2-5 years V	within N	**45**	39	51	**68**	61	73	1	**35**	31	39	n
			2 years after N	**74**	70	79	**92**	90	93	5	**66**	63	71	n
Mexico	Proxy cohort data	2008 / 3 years G & V	within N	**54**	50	57	**m**	m	m	m	**m**	m	m	m
			2 years after N	**m**	m	m	**m**	m	m	m	**m**	m	m	m
Netherlands	True cohort	2007 / 2-3 years G & 2-4 years V	within N	**61**	56	67	**72**	69	75	2	**55**	50	62	n
			2 years after N	**78**	75	82	**94**	93	95	3	**70**	66	75	1
New Zealand	True cohort	2004 / 3 years G	within N	**59**	53	64	**59**	53	64	m	**m**	m	m	m
			2 years after N	**64**	59	69	**64**	59	69	m	**m**	m	m	m
Norway	True cohort	2004 / 3 years G & 4 years V	within N	**57**	48	66	**73**	68	77	n	**42**	33	54	53
			2 years after N	**72**	68	76	**83**	79	87	1	**62**	59	65	39
Poland	True cohort	2006-07 / 3 years G & 3-4 years V	within N	**80**	75	84	**89**	87	91	m	**69**	67	73	m
			2 years after N	**m**	m	m	**m**	m	m	m	**m**	m	m	m
Slovak Republic	Proxy cohort data	2006 / 4 years G & 2-4 years V	within N	**88**	87	89	**98**	98	97	m	**84**	84	85	m
			2 years after N	**m**	m	m	**m**	m	m	m	**m**	m	m	m
Slovenia	Proxy cohort data	2007 / 4 years G & 3-4 years V	within N	**76**	72	81	**86**	86	86	m	**68**	63	75	m
			2 years after N	**m**	m	m	**m**	m	m	m	**m**	m	m	m
Spain	Proxy cohort data	2006-07 / 2 years G & V	within N	**57**	53	61	**57**	53	61	m	**m**	m	m	m
			2 years after N	**82**	80	84	**82**	80	84	m	**m**	m	m	m
Sweden[6]	True cohort	2006 / 3 years G & V	within N	**72**	70	74	**76**	74	78	1	**68**	66	69	1
			2 years after N	**79**	77	81	**84**	82	86	4	**74**	72	75	3
United Kingdom	True cohort	2006 / 2 years	within N	**61**	56	67	**m**	m	m	m	**m**	m	m	m
			2 years after N	**80**	76	85	**m**	m	m	m	**m**	m	m	m
United States	Longitudinal sample survey	2002 / 3 years G & V	within N	**85**	83	88	**m**	m	m	m	**m**	m	m	m
			2 years after N	**88**	86	90	**m**	m	m	m	**m**	m	m	m
Countries' average[7]			within N	**70**	66	74	**77**	73	80	m	**61**	59	64	m
			2 years after N	**85**	82	87	**92**	90	93	m	**77**	76	80	m

Note: Data presented in this table come from a special survey in which 25 countries participated. Refer to Annex 3 for details concerning this indicator, including methods used, programmes included/excluded, year of entry, etc.
1. ISCED 3 general programme entrants who graduated from either a general or vocational programme.
2. ISCED 3 vocational programme entrants who graduated from either a general or vocational programme.
3. ISCED 3 general programme entrants who graduated from a vocational programme.
4. ISCED 3 vocational programme entrants who graduated from a general programme.
5. Net entry rates at upper secondary level are based on the UOE data collection.
6. Excluding students having continued their studies in the adult education system.
7. Countries' average for N + 2 corresponds to the countries' average for N + the difference (in percentage points) of the average for countries with N and N + 2 data.
Source: OECD. See Annex 3 for notes (*www.oecd.org/edu/eag2012*).
Please refer to the Reader's Guide for information concerning the symbols replacing missing data.
StatLink ⬛ http://dx.doi.org/10.1787/888932664480

A2

Table A2.5. [2/2] Successful completion of upper secondary programmes, by gender and programme orientation

Ratio of graduates to new entrants based on cohorts

	Method	Year used for new entrants / Duration of programme (G: general, V: vocational)	N: theoretical duration	Proportion of students who did not graduate and who are still in education (general programmes)			Proportion of students who did not graduate and who are still in education (vocational programmes)			Net entry rates at upper secondary level for students below 20 years old (2010)[5]
				Total	Men	Women	Total	Men	Women	
Austria	True cohort	2006-07 / 4 years G & V	within N / 2 years after N	76 / m	76 / m	76 / m	m / m	m / m	m / m	m
Belgium (Fl.)	True cohort	2004-05 / 4 years G & V	within N / 2 years after N	90 / 11	90 / 13	89 / 8	70 / 6	71 / 7	69 / 5	89
Canada	Proxy cohort data	2006-07 / 3 years	within N / 2 years after N	m / m	m / m	m / m	m / m	m / m	m / m	m
Denmark	True cohort	2002-03 / 3-4 years G & 2-5 years V	within N / 2 years after N	69 / 34	71 / 35	67 / 33	62 / 34	61 / 33	62 / 36	95
Estonia	True cohort	2004 / 3 years G & 3-4 years V	within N / 2 years after N	54 / 23	51 / 20	57 / 26	51 / 15	44 / 12	63 / 21	100
Finland	True cohort	2004 / 3 years G & V	within N / 2 years after N	81 / 45	78 / 42	83 / 48	46 / 25	44 / 23	48 / 27	m
France	Longitudinal sample survey	1999-2005 / 3 years G & 2 years V	within N / 2 years after N	93 / m	93 / m	94 / m	80 / m	81 / m	79 / m	m
Hungary	Proxy cohort data	2006-07 / 4 years G & V	within N / 2 years after N	m / m	m / m	m / m	m / m	m / m	m / m	98
Iceland	True cohort	2003 / 4 years G & V	within N / 2 years after N	50 / 35	49 / 35	50 / 37	40 / 25	38 / 24	44 / 28	100
Ireland	True cohort	2004 / 2-3 years G & V	within N / 2 years after N	m / m	m / m	m / m	m / m	m / m	m / m	100
Israel	True cohort	2007 / 3 years G & V	within N / 2 years after N	26 / m	25 / m	28 / m	14 / m	12 / m	18 / m	95
Japan	True cohort	2007 / 3 years G & V	within N / 2 years after N	m / m	m / m	m / m	m / m	m / m	m / m	100
Korea	True cohort	2007 / 3 years G & V	within N / 2 years after N	2 / m	1 / m	4 / m	13 / m	8 / m	21 / m	m
Luxembourg	True cohort	2004-05 / 4 years G & 2-5 years V	within N / 2 years after N	90 / 37	91 / 37	89 / 38	73 / 28	72 / 29	74 / 28	91
Mexico	Proxy cohort data	2008 / 3 years G & V	within N / 2 years after N	m / m	m / m	m / m	m / m	m / m	m / m	77
Netherlands	True cohort	2007 / 2-3 years G & 2-4 years V	within N / 2 years after N	73 / 43	71 / 42	75 / 44	25 / 20	26 / 20	25 / 20	m
New Zealand	True cohort	2004 / 3 years G	within N / 2 years after N	34 / 24	34 / 25	35 / 24	m / m	m / m	m / m	99
Norway	True cohort	2004 / 3 years G & 4 years V	within N / 2 years after N	40 / 14	39 / 15	40 / 13	35 / 11	39 / 10	28 / 11	98
Poland	True cohort	2006-07 / 3 years G & 3-4 years V	within N / 2 years after N	m / m	m / m	m / m	m / m	m / m	m / m	89
Slovak Republic	Proxy cohort data	2006 / 4 years G & 2-4 years V	within N / 2 years after N	m / m	m / m	m / m	m / m	m / m	m / m	95
Slovenia	Proxy cohort data	2007 / 4 years G & 3-4 years V	within N / 2 years after N	m / m	m / m	m / m	m / m	m / m	m / m	100
Spain	Proxy cohort data	2006-07 / 2 years G & V	within N / 2 years after N	m / m	m / m	m / m	m / m	m / m	m / m	m
Sweden[6]	True cohort	2006 / 3 years G & V	within N / 2 years after N	50 / 1	49 / 1	51 / 2	35 / 1	35 / 1	35 / 1	98
United Kingdom	True cohort	2006 / 2 years	within N / 2 years after N	m / m	m / m	m / m	m / m	m / m	m / m	m
United States	Longitudinal sample survey	2002 / 3 years G & V	within N / 2 years after N	m / m	m / m	m / m	m / m	m / m	m / m	99
Countries' average[7]			within N / 2 years after N	59 / m	59 / m	60 / m	45 / m	44 / m	47 / m	m

Note: Data presented in this table come from a special survey in which 20 countries participated. Refer to Annex 3 for details concerning this indicator, including methods used, programmes included/excluded, year of entry, etc.
1. ISCED 3 general programme entrants who graduated from either a general or vocational programme.
2. ISCED 3 vocational programme entrants who graduated from either a general or vocational programme.
3. ISCED 3 general programme entrants who graduated from a vocational programme.
4. ISCED 3 vocational programme entrants who graduated from a general programme.
5. Net entry rates at upper secondary level are based on the UOE data collection.
6. Excluding students having continued their studies in the adult education system.
7. Countries' average for N + 2 corresponds to the countries' average for N + the difference (in percentage points) of the average for countries with N and N + 2 data.
Source: OECD. See Annex 3 for notes (*www.oecd.org/edu/eag2012*).
Please refer to the Reader's Guide for information concerning the symbols replacing missing data.

StatLink ⏹⎙⎓⎕ http://dx.doi.org/10.1787/888932664480

Table A2.6. Successful completion of upper secondary programmes, by programme orientation and duration

Ratio of graduates to new entrants based on cohorts

	N: theoretical duration	Completion of general programmes[1]				Completion of vocational programmes[2]				
		Total	2 years	3 years	4 years	Total	2 years	3 years	4 years	5 years
Austria	within N	71	a	a	71	m	n	m	m	a
	2 years after N	m	a	a	m	m	n	m	m	a
Belgium (Fl.)	within N	81	a	a	81	59	a	a	59	a
	2 years after N	95	a	a	95	77	a	a	77	a
Canada	within N	m	m	m	m	m	m	m	m	m
	2 years after N	m	m	m	m	m	m	m	m	m
Denmark	within N	80	m	80	61	35	57	12	64	41
	2 years after N	88	m	89	80	54	72	33	83	59
Estonia	within N	84	a	84	a	48	a	47	59	a
	2 years after N	92	a	92	a	68	a	68	68	a
Finland	within N	80	a	80	n	62	n	62	n	n
	2 years after N	91	a	91	n	72	n	72	n	n
France	within N	61	a	61	a	55	55	m	a	a
	2 years after N	90	a	90	a	69	69	m	a	a
Hungary	within N	74	m	a	74	44	m	a	44	n
	2 years after N	m	m	a	m	m	m	a	m	m
Iceland	within N	44	m	m	m	45	m	m	m	m
	2 years after N	59	m	m	m	57	m	m	m	m
Ireland	within N	m	m	m	m	m	m	m	m	m
	2 years after N	m	m	m	m	m	m	m	m	m
Israel	within N	87	a	87	a	88	a	88	m	a
	2 years after N	m	a	m	m	m	a	m	m	a
Japan	within N	93	a	93	m	91	a	91	m	a
	2 years after N	m	a	m	m	m	a	m	m	a
Korea	within N	97	a	97	a	89	a	89	a	a
	2 years after N	m	a	m	a	m	a	m	a	a
Luxembourg	within N	68	a	a	68	35	52	33	34	36
	2 years after N	92	a	a	92	66	61	60	72	74
Mexico	within N	m	m	m	m	m	m	m	m	m
	2 years after N	m	m	m	m	m	m	m	m	m
Netherlands	within N	72	69	76	m	55	48	59	61	m
	2 years after N	94	91	97	m	70	64	72	76	m
New Zealand	within N	59	m	59	m	m	m	m	m	m
	2 years after N	64	m	64	m	m	m	m	m	m
Norway	within N	73	n	73	n	42	a	m	42	m
	2 years after N	83	n	83	n	62	a	m	62	m
Poland	within N	89	a	89	a	69	a	71	68	a
	2 years after N	m	a	m	a	m	a	m	m	a
Slovak Republic	within N	98	a	a	98	84	73	73	89	a
	2 years after N	m	a	a	m	m	m	m	m	a
Slovenia	within N	86	n	a	86	68	n	76	65	a
	2 years after N	m	n	a	m	m	n	m	m	a
Spain	within N	57	57	a	a	m	m	m	m	m
	2 years after N	82	82	a	a	m	m	m	m	m
Sweden[3]	within N	76	m	76	a	68	m	68	a	a
	2 years after N	84	m	84	a	74	m	74	a	a
United Kingdom	within N	m	m	m	m	m	m	m	m	m
	2 years after N	m	m	m	m	m	m	m	m	m
United States	within N	m	m	m	m	m	m	m	m	m
	2 years after N	m	m	m	m	m	m	m	m	m
Countries' average[4]	within N	77	m	80	77	61	m	64	59	m
	2 years after N	92	m	93	90	77	m	80	78	m

Note: Please refer to Annex 3 for details concerning this indicator, including methods used, programmes included/excluded, year of entry, etc.
1. ISCED 3 general programme entrants who graduated from either a general or vocational programme.
2. ISCED 3 vocational programme entrants who graduated from either a general or vocational programme.
3. Excluding students having continued their studies in the adult education system.
4. Countries' average for N+2 corresponds to the countries' average for N + the difference (in percentage points) of the average for countries with N and N+2 data.
Source: OECD. See Annex 3 for notes (*www.oecd.org/edu/eag2012*).
Please refer to the Reader's Guide for information concerning the symbols replacing missing data.
StatLink ⌐日⌐ http://dx.doi.org/10.1787/888932664499

HOW MANY STUDENTS ARE EXPECTED TO FINISH TERTIARY EDUCATION?

- Based on current patterns of graduation, it is estimated that an average of 39% of today's young adults in OECD countries will complete tertiary-type A (largely theory-based) education over their lifetimes, from 50% or more in Australia, Denmark, Iceland, Poland and the United Kingdom to less than 25% in Mexico, Saudi Arabia and Turkey.

- At the same time, it is expected that only one-third of young adults will complete tertiary-type A education before the age of 30, from a high of more than 40% in Australia, Denmark, Ireland, Poland and the United Kingdom to only 18% in Mexico.

Chart A3.1. **Tertiary-type A graduation rates, by age group (2010)**
Including and excluding international students

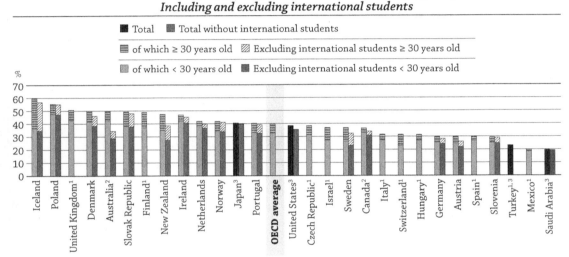

Note: Only first-time graduates in tertiary-type A programmes are reported in this chart.
1. Graduation rates for international students are missing.
2. Year of reference 2009.
3. Graduation rates by age group are missing.
Countries are ranked in descending order of the total graduation rates for tertiary-type A education in 2010.
Source: OECD. Saudi Arabia: Observatory on Higher Education. Table A3.1. See Annex 3 for notes (*www.oecd.org/edu/eag2012*).
StatLink ⟶ http://dx.doi.org/10.1787/888932661687

How to read this chart

This chart shows students' likelihood of graduating from a university-level programme, across OECD and other G20 countries with available data. For example, among a group of 100 young men and women:

- in Iceland, 60 people will graduate from a university-level programme in their lifetimes, but only 36 will do so before the age of 30;

- in Poland, 55 people will graduate from a university-level programme in their lifetimes, and 47 will do so before the age of 30; and

- in Australia, Denmark, and the United Kingdom, about 50 people will graduate from a university-level programme, but just over 40 will do so before the age of 30. If international students are excluded, fewer than 30 Australians will graduate before the age of 30.

■ Context

Tertiary graduation rates indicate a country's capacity to produce workers with advanced, specialised knowledge and skills. In OECD countries, there are strong incentives to obtain a tertiary qualification, including higher salaries and better employment prospects. Tertiary education varies widely in structure and scope among countries, and graduation rates are influenced both by the degree of access to these programmes and the demand for higher skills in the labour market. Expanding participation in tertiary education while maintaining quality is likely to create pressure for countries and tertiary institutions to maintain current levels of spending.

In recent years, the traditional notion of a tertiary student has changed with the influx of older students into tertiary education. In some countries, it is common for tertiary students to have professional experience and be older than 30. Changes in the labour market have provided incentives for adults to study in order to adapt their skills to new labour-market needs. In addition, the global economic crisis has also created incentives for students to enter or remain in tertiary education, instead of risking entry into an unstable labour market.

Other findings

- Based on current patterns of graduation, it is estimated that **an average of 47% of today's young women and 32% of today's young men in OECD countries will complete tertiary-type A education over their lifetimes.** The majority of graduates at all levels of tertiary education are women, except at the doctoral level.

- In spite of rapidly expanding demand for university programmes in recent decades, there is still a place for shorter, vocationally-oriented programmes, or tertiary-type B education. These programmes respond to the need of individuals to pursue shorter programmes of study, as well as the needs of the labour market. **An average of 11% of today's young adults in OECD countries are expected to complete tertiary-type B education over their lifetimes** (12% of young women, compared to 9% of young men).

- **In China, an estimated 14% of today's young people will graduate from a tertiary-type A first-degree programme, and 18% will graduate from a tertiary-type B first-degree programme, during their lifetimes.**

- **International students make a significant contribution to tertiary graduation rates in a number of countries.** For countries with a high proportion of international students, such as Australia, New Zealand and the United Kingdom, graduation rates are artificially inflated.

Trends

Over the past 15 years, tertiary-type A graduation rates have risen by 20 percentage points on average among OECD countries with available data, while rates for tertiary-type B programmes have been stable. While doctorates represent only a small proportion of tertiary programmes, the graduation rate from these types of programmes has doubled over the past 15 years.

Note

Graduation rates represent the estimated percentage of an age cohort that is expected to graduate over their lifetimes. This estimate is based on the number of graduates in 2010 and the age distribution of this group. Therefore, the graduation rates are based on the current pattern of graduation, and thus are sensitive to any changes in the educational system, such as the introduction of new programmes or increases and decreases in programme duration, like those that are occurring with the implementation of the Bologna process.

In this indicator, 30 is regarded as the upper bound for the typical age of first-time graduation from a tertiary-type A or B degree programme. The upper bound for the typical age of graduation from an advanced research programme is 35.

A3

Analysis

Many countries make a clear distinction between first and second university degrees (i.e. undergraduate and graduate programmes). However, in some countries, degrees that are internationally comparable to a master's degree are obtained through a single programme of long duration. In order to make accurate comparisons, data presented in this indicator refer to first-time graduates unless otherwise indicated. The Bologna process aims to harmonise programme duration among European countries (see section on *Structure of tertiary education*).

Based on 2010 patterns of graduation, 39% of young people, on average among the 27 OECD countries with comparable data, will graduate for the first time from tertiary-type A programmes during their lifetimes. The proportion ranges from around 20% in Mexico and Saudi Arabia to 50% or more in Australia, Denmark, Iceland, Poland and the United Kingdom.

These programmes are largely theory-based and are designed to provide qualifications for entry into advanced research programmes and professions with high requirements in knowledge and skills. They are typically delivered by universities, and their duration ranges from three years (e.g. the Honours bachelor's degree in many colleges in Ireland and the United Kingdom, and the *Licence* in France) to five or more years (e.g. the *Diplom* in Germany).

In 2010, graduation rates for tertiary-type B programmes averaged 11% among the 26 OECD countries with comparable data. These programmes are classified at the same academic level as more theory-based programmes, but are often shorter in duration (usually two to three years). They are generally not intended to lead to further university-level degrees, but rather to lead directly to the labour market. In 2010, the graduation rates for women were 12% compared to 9% for men (Table A3.1).

Based on 2010 patterns of graduation, on average among OECD countries, 39% of young people will graduate from tertiary-type A first-degree programmes (often called a bachelor's degree) and 15% from tertiary-type A second degree programmes (often called a master's degree). For first-degree programmes, the graduation rate equals or exceeds 50% in Australia, Iceland, New Zealand, Poland and the Russian Federation but is lower than 20% in Argentina, Belgium, China, Indonesia, Saudi Arabia and South Africa. The low graduation rates in Argentina, Belgium and China are counterbalanced by a higher level of first-degree graduation rates from tertiary-type B programmes. The graduation rate from second-degree programmes equals or exceeds 20% in Belgium, the Czech Republic, Denmark, Finland, Iceland, Ireland, Poland, the Slovak Republic and the United Kingdom (Table A3.3). With the implementation of the Bologna process, programmes at this level of education have developed considerably.

Trend data

In every country for which comparable data are available, tertiary-type A graduation rates increased between 1995 and 2010. The increase was particularly steep between 1995 and 2000, and then levelled off. Over the past three years, tertiary type-A graduation rates have remained relatively stable, at around 39%. The most significant increases since 1995 were in Austria, the Czech Republic, the Slovak Republic, Switzerland and Turkey, where the annual growth rate is over 8% (Table A3.2).

Because of increasing harmonisation among the systems of higher education in European countries and a general shift away from longer programmes in favour of three-year programmes, some countries have seen rapid rises in their graduation rates. Graduation rates rose sharply in the Czech Republic between 2004 and 2007 within the framework of the Bologna process reforms, and also rose in Finland and the Slovak Republic between 2007 and 2008 for the same reason (see section on *Structure of tertiary education*).

Trends in tertiary-type B education between 1995 and 2010 vary, even though the OECD average has been stable. For example, in Spain, the sharp rise in graduation rates from this type of education during this period can be attributed to the development of new advanced-level vocational training programmes. By contrast, in Finland, where tertiary-type B programmes are being phased out, graduation rates from these programmes have fallen sharply in favour of more academically oriented tertiary education (Chart A3.2).

Chart A3.2. **First-time graduation rates in tertiary-type A and B education (1995 and 2010)**

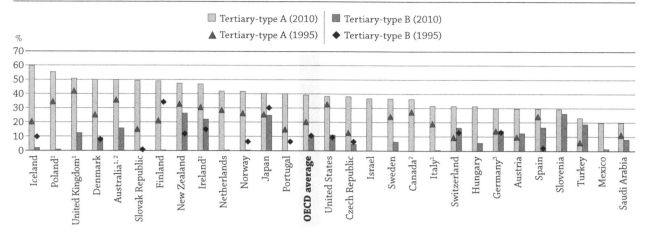

1. Year of reference 2000 instead of 1995.
2. Year of reference 2009 instead of 2010.
3. Break in the series between 2008 and 2009 due to a partial reallocation of vocational programmes into ISCED 2 and ISCED 5B.
Countries are ranked in descending order of first-time graduation rates in tertiary-type A education in 2010.
Source: OECD. Saudi Arabia: Observatory on Higher Education. Table A3.2. See Annex 3 for notes (*www.oecd.org/edu/eag2012*).
StatLink ᴴᴵˢᴾ http://dx.doi.org/10.1787/888932661706

The share of older students as graduates

The proportion of young people who graduate from tertiary education and their ages varies across countries. In some countries, a large proportion of graduates consists of older students. Age differences among graduates may be linked to structural factors, such as the length of tertiary education programmes or the obligation to do military service. Age differences may also be linked to economic factors, such as the existence of policies to encourage those who have already gained experience in the workplace to enrol in tertiary education and raise their skills. In the current global economy, some young people have decided to stay in education instead of risking entry into an unstable labour market (see Indicator C3). The fact that these men and women are entering the labour force later has economic repercussions that policy makers should consider, such as higher expenditure per student and foregone tax revenues as a result of these individuals' shorter working lives.

Among the 24 countries with available data on students' age, students outside the typical age of graduation, i.e. over 30 years old, represent one-quarter of all graduates in Iceland, Israel, New Zealand, Sweden and Switzerland (Chart A3.1).

Of those countries where more than 20% of individuals are first-time graduates from tertiary-type B programmes – namely Canada, Ireland, Japan, New Zealand and Slovenia – New Zealand and Slovenia had the largest proportion of graduates over age 30 (Table A3.1).

The share of international students as graduates

The term "international students" refers to students who have crossed borders expressly with the intention to study. International students have a marked impact on estimated graduation rates, for different reasons. By definition, they are considered first-time graduates, regardless of their previous education in other countries (i.e. an international student who enters and graduates from a second-degree programme will be considered a first-time graduate). Furthermore, as they have crossed borders with the intention to study and not necessarily to work or to stay in the country, they increase the absolute number of graduates among the population. For countries with a high proportion of international students, such as Australia, New Zealand and the United Kingdom, graduation rates are thus artificially inflated. For example, when international students are excluded from consideration, first-time tertiary-type A graduation rates below age 30 for Australia and New Zealand drop by 14 and 8 percentage points, respectively, and first-time tertiary-type B graduation rates below age 30 drop by 5 percentage points in New Zealand (Table A3.1).

The contribution of international students to graduation rates is also significant at the first (i.e. bachelor's-level) stage of tertiary-type A education, although to a lesser extent. In Australia, Austria, New Zealand, Switzerland and the United Kingdom, at least 10% of students graduating with a first degree in tertiary education are international students. Among countries for which data on student mobility are not available, foreign students also represent 10% or more of those earning first degrees in France.

The contribution of international students to graduation rates is also significant in second-degree programmes, such as master's degrees. In Australia and the United Kingdom, graduation rates drop by 11 percentage points in both countries when international graduates are excluded.

Graduation rates for advanced research degrees

Doctoral graduates are those who have obtained the highest level of formal education, and typically include researchers who hold a Ph.D. As such, they are important for creating and diffusing knowledge in society. Based on 2010 patterns of graduation, 1.6% of young people, on average among OECD countries, will graduate from advanced research programmes, compared to 1.0% in 2000. This half percentage-point increase in the past ten years represents an annual growth rate of 5%. At this level of education, the graduation rate for women (1.5%) is lower than that of men (1.7%). (See more on gender equality in access to and graduation from tertiary programmes in Indicator A4).

Some countries promote doctoral education, particularly to international students. In Germany and Switzerland, graduation rates at the doctoral level are high compared to the OECD average, with more than 2.5% of people graduating from this level of education. This is partly due to the high proportion of international students at the doctoral level. In contrast, graduation rates for first and second degrees of tertiary-type A programmes are below the OECD average in these countries.

The international mobility of doctoral students highlights the attractiveness of advanced research programmes in the host countries. International students represent more than 40% of doctoral graduates in Switzerland and the United Kingdom (Table A3.3).

Structure of tertiary education: Main programme blocks

The Bologna process had its origins in the Sorbonne Joint Declaration on Harmonisation of the Architecture of the European Higher Education System, signed in 1998 by France, Germany, Italy and the United Kingdom. Its purpose was to provide a common framework for tertiary education in Europe at the bachelor, master and doctorate levels – often referred to as the BMD structure. Under the new system, the average duration of the bachelor's degree, the master's degree and doctorate have been harmonised in order to improve the comparability of data for European and non-European OECD countries, facilitate student mobility among countries, and recognise equivalence between similar programmes. Less than 15 years later, this process has now spread to 47 countries.

Table A3.4 presents the main programme blocks in tertiary education and the distribution of graduates from the corresponding blocks. The blocks are organised as follows:

- Programmes that last less than three years but are still considered to be part of tertiary education. In 2010, an average of 8% of all graduates graduated from these programmes. The proportion reached between 16% and 40% in Denmark, France, Korea, Ireland, Saudi Arabia, Turkey, the United Kingdom and the United States, while in other countries, less than 6% of all graduates graduated from these programmes.

- Bachelor's programmes or equivalents, which last three to four years. This is the most common programme block across countries. In 2010, an average of 44% of all graduates graduated from this type of programme. In Estonia, Finland, Iceland, the Netherlands, Norway, Portugal and Saudi Arabia more than 60% of all graduates have completed this type of programme.

- Master's programmes or equivalents, which typically last between one and four years and usually prepare students for a second degree/qualification following a bachelor's programme. The cumulative duration of studies at the tertiary level is thus four to eight years, or even longer. In 2010, an average of 19% of all graduates completed this type of programme, although the proportion reaches at least 30% in Belgium, Poland, the Slovak Republic and Sweden.

■ Long programmes and degrees with a single structure and a minimum duration of five years. For the most part, these degrees are equivalent to master's degrees, but in a few cases, the qualification obtained is equivalent to that of a bachelor's programme. These programmes usually concentrate on medical studies, architecture, engineering and theology. In 2010, only 2% of all graduates completed such programmes on average, but the proportion reaches 9% in France and Portugal and more than 16% in Poland. However, a share of graduates at this level is not counted in this category if the programmes still fall outside the Bologna categories.

■ Programmes and degrees at the doctorate/Ph.D. level, which normally corresponds to ISCED 6 and are usually three to four years in duration, depending on the programme and the country. In 2010, an average of 2% of all graduates completed these types of programmes.

Chart A3.3. **Structure of tertiary education: Main programme blocks (2010)**

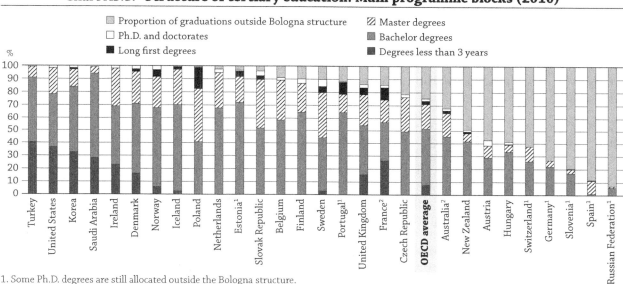

1. Some Ph.D. degrees are still allocated outside the Bologna structure.
2. Year of reference 2009.
Countries are ranked in descending order of the proportion of graduations following the Bologna structure.
Source: OECD. Saudi Arabia: Observatory on Higher Education. Table A3.4. See Annex 3 for notes (*www.oecd.org/edu/eag2012*).
StatLink ᐧᐧᐧᐧ http://dx.doi.org/10.1787/888932661725

One of the beneficial effects of the Bologna process will be better comparability of data. In the short term, however, the process has led to a structural increase in graduation rates in European countries (see trend data and the discussion of Table A3.2). In some countries, certain programmes have not yet shifted to different blocks because of difficulties in classification. In 2010, an average of 25% of all graduates came from such programmes, and more than 50% did so in Austria, Germany, Hungary, Slovenia, Spain and Switzerland. These countries must decide on the appropriate blocks for these programmes if they are to be fully integrated into the Bologna structure, which was scheduled to be operational by 2010.

Definitions

A **first degree** at tertiary-type A level has a minimum cumulative theoretical duration of three years, full-time equivalent, e.g. the bachelor's degrees in many English-speaking countries, the *Diplom* in many German-speaking countries, and the *licence* in many French-speaking countries.

A3

Graduates in the reference period can be either first-time graduates or repeat graduates. A **first-time graduate** is a student who has graduated for the first time at a given level of education – or in the case of ISCED 5, from a type A or type B programme – in the reference period. Therefore, if a student has graduated multiple times over the years, he or she is counted as a graduate each year, but as a first-time graduate only once.

Net graduation rates represent the estimated percentage of people from a specific age cohort who will complete tertiary education over their lifetimes, based on current patterns of graduation.

Second degree and higher theory-based programmes (e.g. master's degree in English-speaking countries and *maîtrise* in French-speaking countries) would be classified in tertiary-type A separately from advanced research qualifications, which would have their own position in ISCED 6.

Tertiary graduates are those who obtain a university degree, vocational qualifications, or advanced research degrees of doctorate standard.

Methodology

Data refer to the academic year 2009-10 and are based on the UOE data collection on education statistics administered by the OECD in 2011 (for details, see Annex 3 at *www.oecd.org/edu/eag2012*).

Data on the impact of international students on tertiary graduation rates are based on a special survey conducted by the OECD in December 2011.

Data on trends in graduation rates at the tertiary level for the years 1995 and 2000 through 2004 are based on a special survey carried out in January 2007.

To allow for comparisons that are independent of differences in national degree structures, university-level degrees are subdivided according to the total theoretical duration of study, in other words, the standard number of years, established by law or regulations, in which a student can complete the programme. Degrees obtained from programmes of less than three years' duration are not considered equivalent to completing this level of education and are not included in this indicator. Second-degree programmes are classified according to the cumulative duration of the first- and second-degree programmes. Individuals who already hold a first degree are not included in the count of first-time graduates.

In Tables A3.1, A3.2 (from 2005 onwards), A3.3, and Tables A3.2a and A3.5 (available on line), graduation rates are calculated as net graduation rates (i.e. as the sum of age-specific graduation rates). Gross graduation rates are presented for countries that are unable to provide such detailed data. In order to calculate gross graduation rates, countries identify the age at which graduation typically occurs (see Annex 1). The number of graduates, regardless of their age, is divided by the population at the typical graduation age. In many countries, defining a typical age of graduation is difficult, however, because graduates are dispersed over a wide range of ages.

The statistical data for Israel are supplied by and under the responsibility of the relevant Israeli authorities. The use of such data by the OECD is without prejudice to the status of the Golan Heights, East Jerusalem and Israeli settlements in the West Bank under the terms of international law.

References

The following additional material relevant to this indicator is available on line:

- *Table A3.2a. Trends in tertiary graduation rates by gender (2005-2010)*
  StatLink ⟨⟨⟩⟩ http://dx.doi.org/10.1787/888932664594

- *Table A3.5. Trends in net graduation rates at advanced research qualification level (1995-2010)*
  StatLink ⟨⟨⟩⟩ http://dx.doi.org/10.1787/888932664651

Table A3.1. Graduation rates at tertiary level (2010)

Sum of age-specific graduation rates, by gender and programme destination

	Rates for tertiary-type B programmes (first-time graduates)							Rates for tertiary-type A programmes (first-time graduates)							Rates for advanced research programmes					
				of which < age 30							of which < age 30							of which < age 35		
	Total	Men	Women	Total	Men	Women	Adjusted (without international students)	Total	Men	Women	Total	Men	Women	Adjusted (without international students)	Total	Men	Women	Total	Men	Women
	(1)	(2)	(3)	(4)	(5)	(6)	(7)	(8)	(9)	(10)	(11)	(12)	(13)	(14)	(15)	(16)	(17)	(18)	(19)	(20)
Australia[1]	16	14	18	11	10	12	8	50	41	59	43	35	50	29	1.9	1.9	1.9	1.0	1.0	1.0
Austria	12	13	11	8	9	7	8	30	25	34	25	20	29	22	2.2	2.5	1.9	1.6	1.8	1.4
Belgium	m	m	m	m	m	m	m	m	m	m	m	m	m	m	1.5	1.7	1.3	1.2	1.3	1.1
Canada[1]	29	23	34	22	19	26	21	36	28	45	33	26	41	31	1.2	1.3	1.0	0.7	0.8	0.7
Chile	m	m	m	m	m	m	m	m	m	m	m	m	m	m	0.2	0.2	0.2	0.1	0.1	0.1
Czech Republic	5	2	7	4	2	6	m	38	28	49	31	23	41	m	1.3	1.4	1.0	0.4	1.1	0.8
Denmark	9	9	9	7	7	8	6	50	38	62	42	31	52	38	2.0	2.2	1.8	1.4	1.7	1.1
Estonia	m	m	m	m	m	m	m	m	m	m	m	m	m	m	0.9	0.9	1.0	0.2	0.2	0.2
Finland	n	n	n	m	n	m	n	49	41	57	37	31	43	m	2.3	2.2	2.5	1.0	1.1	1.0
France[1]	m	m	m	m	m	m	m	m	m	m	m	m	m	m	1.5	1.7	1.3	m	m	m
Germany	14	9	19	m	m	m	m	30	28	32	25	24	27	24	2.6	2.8	2.3	2.1	2.2	1.9
Greece	m	m	m	m	m	m	m	m	m	m	m	m	m	m	1.1	1.2	1.0	m	m	m
Hungary	6	3	8	5	3	7	m	31	23	40	27	20	34	m	0.8	0.8	0.7	0.5	0.5	0.5
Iceland	2	2	2	1	1	1	1	60	41	80	36	27	47	34	0.8	0.9	0.7	0.4	0.5	m
Ireland	22	24	20	16	18	14	15	47	40	53	42	36	48	40	1.6	1.6	1.4	1.1	1.1	1.1
Israel	m	m	m	m	m	m	m	37	31	43	27	21	33	m	1.5	1.4	1.4	0.1	0.1	0.1
Italy	1	1	1	m	m	m	m	32	25	38	27	21	33	m	m	m	m	m	m	m
Japan	25	18	32	m	m	m	m	40	44	36	m	m	m	m	1.1	1.5	0.6	m	m	m
Korea	m	m	m	m	m	m	m	m	m	m	m	m	m	m	1.3	1.8	0.9	0.4	0.5	0.3
Luxembourg	m	m	m	m	m	m	m	m	m	m	m	m	m	m	m	m	m	m	m	m
Mexico	1	2	1	1	2	1	m	20	18	21	18	17	20	m	0.2	0.3	0.2	m	m	m
Netherlands	n	n	1	n	n	n	n	42	37	47	39	33	44	37	1.8	2.1	1.5	m	m	m
New Zealand	26	23	29	16	15	16	11	47	38	57	35	29	41	27	1.7	1.6	1.8	0.9	0.9	0.9
Norway	n	n	1	n	n	n	n	42	30	53	34	26	44	34	1.8	2.1	1.7	0.9	1.0	0.7
Poland	1	n	1	1	n	1	m	55	39	72	47	34	61	47	0.5	0.5	0.5	m	m	m
Portugal	n	n	n	m	n	m	m	40	30	50	33	24	43	32	1.8	1.3	2.2	0.9	0.6	1.2
Slovak Republic	1	1	1	1	n	1	m	49	34	65	38	28	48	38	3.2	3.2	3.2	2.1	2.1	2.1
Slovenia	26	21	31	14	12	18	14	29	15	45	25	13	39	25	1.5	1.5	1.5	0.4	n	n
Spain	16	15	18	15	14	16	m	30	22	37	27	19	34	m	1.1	1.1	1.0	0.7	0.7	0.7
Sweden	6	5	8	4	4	5	4	37	26	47	26	20	33	23	2.8	2.9	2.9	1.6	1.8	1.5
Switzerland	16	20	13	m	m	m	m	31	30	33	23	20	26	m	3.6	4.2	3.0	2.7	3.0	2.4
Turkey	19	20	17	16	m	15	m	23	25	21	m	m	m	m	0.4	0.4	0.4	0.3	0.3	0.3
United Kingdom	12	10	15	7	6	8	m	51	45	57	43	38	47	m	2.3	2.4	2.1	1.6	1.7	1.5
United States	11	8	14	m	m	m	m	38	32	45	m	m	m	m	1.6	1.5	1.8	m	m	m
OECD average	11	9	12	8	6	9	m	39	32	47	33	26	40	m	1.6	1.7	1.5	1.0	1.1	0.9
EU21 average	8	7	9	7	5	8	m	40	31	49	33	26	41	m	1.7	1.8	1.6	1.1	1.2	1.7
Argentina[1]	m	m	m	m	m	m	m	m	m	m	m	m	m	m	0.1	0.1	0.2	m	m	m
Brazil	m	m	m	m	m	m	m	m	m	m	m	m	m	m	0.4	0.4	0.4	0.2	0.2	0.2
China	m	m	m	m	m	m	m	m	m	m	m	m	m	m	2.4	2.6	2.2	m	m	m
India	m	m	m	m	m	m	m	m	m	m	m	m	m	m	m	m	m	m	m	m
Indonesia	m	m	m	m	m	m	m	m	m	m	m	m	m	m	0.1	0.1	n	m	m	m
Russian Federation	m	m	m	m	m	m	m	m	m	m	m	m	m	m	0.4	0.4	0.4	m	m	m
Saudi Arabia	8	11	4	m	m	m	m	20	14	27	m	m	m	m	0.1	0.1	0.1	m	m	m
South Africa[1]	m	m	m	m	m	m	m	m	m	m	m	m	m	m	0.1	0.2	0.1	m	m	m
G20 average	m	m	m	m	m	m	m	m	m	m	m	m	m	m	1.0	1.1	0.9	m	m	m

OECD rows from Australia to United States. Other G20 rows from Argentina to South Africa.

Notes: Refer to Annex 1 for information on the method used to calculate graduation rates (gross rates versus net rates) and the corresponding typical ages. Mismatches between the coverage of the population data and the graduate data mean that the graduation rates for those countries that are net exporters of students may be underestimated, and those that are net importers may be overestimated. The adjusted graduation rates seek to compensate for that.
1. Year of reference 2009.
Source: OECD. Argentina, China, Indonesia: UNESCO Institute for Statistics (World Education Indicators programme). Saudi Arabia: Observatory on Higher Education. South Africa: UNESCO Institute for Statistics. See Annex 3 for notes (*www.oecd.org/edu/eag2012*).
Please refer to the Reader's Guide for information concerning the symbols replacing missing data.
StatLink ᵃˢᶫ http://dx.doi.org/10.1787/888932664556

A3

Table A3.2. Trends in tertiary graduation rates (1995-2010)
Sum of age-specific graduation rates, by programme destination

	Tertiary-type 5A (first-time graduates)						Tertiary-type 5B (first-time graduates)					
	1995	2000	2005	2008	2009	2010	1995	2000	2005	2008	2009	2010
	(1)	(2)	(7)	(10)	(11)	(12)	(13)	(14)	(19)	(22)	(23)	(24)
OECD Australia	m	36	50	49	50	**m**	m	m	m	16	16	**m**
Austria	10	15	20	25	29	**30**	m	m	8	8	10	**12**
Belgium	m	m	m	m	m	**m**	m	m	m	m	m	**m**
Canada	27	27	29	37	36	**m**	m	m	m	29	29	**m**
Chile	m	m	m	m	m	**m**	m	m	m	m	m	**m**
Czech Republic	13	14	23	36	38	**38**	6	5	6	5	4	**5**
Denmark	25	37	46	47	50	**50**	8	10	10	11	11	**9**
Estonia	m	m	m	m	m	**m**	m	m	m	m	m	**m**
Finland	21	40	47	63	44	**49**	34	7	n	n	n	**n**
France	m	m	m	m	m	**m**	m	m	m	m	m	**m**
Germany[1]	14	18	20	25	28	**30**	13	11	11	10	14	**14**
Greece	14	15	25	m	m	**m**	5	6	11	m	m	**m**
Hungary	m	m	33	30	31	**31**	m	m	4	4	5	**6**
Iceland	20	33	56	57	51	**60**	10	5	4	4	2	**2**
Ireland	m	30	38	46	47	**47**	m	15	24	26	26	**22**
Israel	m	m	35	36	37	**37**	m	m	m	m	m	**m**
Italy	m	19	41	33	33	**32**	m	n	1	1	1	**1**
Japan	25	29	37	39	40	**40**	30	30	28	27	26	**25**
Korea	m	m	m	m	m	**m**	m	m	m	m	m	**m**
Luxembourg	m	m	m	m	m	**m**	m	m	m	m	m	**m**
Mexico	m	m	17	18	19	**20**	m	m	1	1	1	**1**
Netherlands	29	35	42	41	42	**42**	m	m	n	n	n	**n**
New Zealand	33	50	51	48	50	**47**	12	17	21	21	24	**26**
Norway	26	37	41	41	41	**42**	6	6	2	1	n	**n**
Poland	m	34	47	50	50	**55**	m	m	n	n	n	**1**
Portugal	15	23	32	45	40	**40**	6	8	9	2	1	**n**
Slovak Republic	15	m	30	58	62	**49**	1	2	2	1	1	**1**
Slovenia	m	m	18	20	27	**29**	m	m	24	26	26	**26**
Spain[2]	24	29	30	27	27	**30**	2	8	15	14	15	**16**
Sweden	24	28	38	40	36	**37**	m	4	5	6	6	**6**
Switzerland	9	12	27	32	31	**31**	13	14	8	19	19	**16**
Turkey	6	9	11	20	21	**23**	2	m	m	13	15	**19**
United Kingdom	m	42	47	48	48	**51**	m	7	11	12	12	**12**
United States	33	34	34	37	38	**38**	9	8	10	10	11	**11**
OECD average	20	28	34	*39*	39	**39**	11	9	*9*	11	11	*10*
OECD average for countries with 1995 and 2010 data	*20*	*27*				**40**	*11*	*10*				*10*
EU21 average	18	27	34	*40*	39	**40**	9	7	*8*	*8*	*8*	*8*
Other G20 Argentina	m	m	m	m	m	**m**	m	m	m	m	m	**m**
Brazil	m	10	m	m	m	**m**	m	m	m	m	m	**m**
China	m	m	m	m	m	**m**	m	m	m	m	m	**m**
India	m	m	m	m	m	**m**	m	m	m	m	m	**m**
Indonesia	m	m	m	m	m	**m**	m	m	m	m	m	**m**
Russian Federation	m	m	m	m	m	**m**	m	m	m	m	m	**m**
Saudi Arabia	11	13	18	21	19	**20**	n	3	5	6	6	**8**
South Africa	m	m	m	m	m	**m**	m	m	m	m	m	**m**
G20 average	m	m	m	m	m	**m**	m	m	m	m	m	**m**

Notes: Years 2001, 2002, 2003, 2004, 2006, 2007 are available for consultation on line (see *StatLink* below).
Up to 2004, graduation rates at the tertiary-type A or B levels were calculated on a gross basis. From 2005 and for countries with available data, graduation rates are calculated as net graduation rates (i.e. as the sum of age-specific graduation rates). Please refer to Annex 1 for information on the method used to calculate graduation rates (gross rates versus net rates) and the corresponding typical ages.
1. Break in time series between 2008 and 2009 due to a partial reallocation of vocational programmes into ISCED 2 and ISCED 5B.
2. Break in time series following methodological change in 2008.
Source: OECD. Saudi Arabia: Observatory on Higher Education. See Annex 3 for notes (*www.oecd.org/edu/eag2012*).
Please refer to the Reader's Guide for information concerning the symbols replacing missing data.
StatLink ms http://dx.doi.org/10.1787/888932664575

Table A3.3. **Graduation rates at different tertiary levels, impact of international/foreign students (2010)**

Sum of age-specific graduation rates, by programme destination

A3

	Tertiary-type B programmes (first-time)		Tertiary-type B programmes (first degree)		Tertiary-type A programmes (first-time)		Tertiary-type A programmes (first degree)		Tertiary-type A programmes (second degree)		Advanced research programmes	
	Graduation rate (all students)	Adjusted graduation rate (without international/ foreign students)	Graduation rate (all students)	Adjusted graduation rate (without international/ foreign students)	Graduation rate (all students)	Adjusted graduation rate (without international/ foreign students)	Graduation rate (all students)	Adjusted graduation rate (without international/ foreign students)	Graduation rate (all students)	Adjusted graduation rate (without international/ foreign students)	Graduation rate (all students)	Adjusted graduation rate (without international/ foreign students)
	(1)	(2)	(3)	(4)	(5)	(6)	(7)	(8)	(9)	(10)	(11)	(12)
OECD												
Australia[1]	**16**	13	22	19	**50**	34	61	44	19	8	1.9	1.3
Austria	**12**	12	12	12	**30**	26	30	26	8	7	2.2	1.7
Belgium	**m**	m	30	30	**m**	m	19	19	24	23	1.5	1.3
Canada[1]	**29**	27	33	32	**36**	34	39	36	9	8	1.2	1.0
Chile[2]	**m**	m	19	19	**m**	m	20	20	6	6	0.2	0.2
Czech Republic[2]	**5**	m	5	m	**38**	m	40	37	21	19	1.3	1.2
Denmark	**9**	8	9	8	**50**	46	49	47	20	18	2.0	1.7
Estonia	**m**	m	19	19	**m**	m	23	23	13	12	0.9	0.9
Finland	**n**	n	n	n	**49**	m	46	45	24	23	2.3	2.2
France[2]	**m**	m	26	25	**m**	m	36	32	14	11	1.5	0.9
Germany	**14**	m	14	m	**30**	28	30	28	3	3	2.6	2.2
Greece	**m**	m	14	m	**m**	m	23	m	7	m	1	m
Hungary[2]	**6**	m	6	6	**31**	m	36	35	8	7	0.8	0.8
Iceland	**2**	2	2	2	**60**	57	63	62	24	22	0.8	0.6
Ireland	**22**	21	22	21	**47**	45	47	45	25	23	1.6	1.3
Israel	**m**	m	m	m	**37**	m	38	38	15	15	1.5	1.4
Italy[2]	**1**	m	1	1	**32**	m	31	30	m	m	m	m
Japan	**25**	24	25	24	**40**	40	40	40	6	5	1.1	0.9
Korea	**m**	m	29	m	**m**	m	46	m	10	m	1.3	m
Luxembourg	**m**	m	m	m	**m**	m	m	m	m	m	m	m
Mexico	**1**	m	1	m	**20**	m	20	m	3	m	0.2	m
Netherlands	**n**	n	n	n	**42**	40	45	43	17	17	1.8	m
New Zealand	**26**	20	31	25	**47**	38	50	43	17	15	1.7	1.2
Norway	**n**	n	n	n	**42**	41	46	45	12	11	1.8	1.6
Poland	**1**	m	1	m	**55**	55	55	55	39	39	0.5	0.5
Portugal	**n**	n	n	n	**40**	39	40	39	15	14	1.8	1.5
Slovak Republic[2]	**1**	m	1	m	**49**	48	49	48	36	35	3.2	3.1
Slovenia	**26**	26	27	27	**29**	29	34	34	5	5	1.5	1.4
Spain	**16**	m	16	m	**30**	m	34	34	6	5	1.1	m
Sweden	**6**	6	6	6	**37**	32	35	34	8	4	2.8	2.2
Switzerland	**16**	m	24	m	**31**	m	29	26	16	13	3.6	2.0
Turkey[2]	**19**	m	19	19	**23**	m	23	m	4	4	0.4	0.4
United Kingdom	**12**	m	16	15	**51**	m	41	36	24	14	2.3	1.3
United States	**11**	11	11	11	**38**	35	38	37	18	16	1.6	1.2
OECD average	**11**	m	14	m	**39**	m	38	m	15	m	1.6	m
EU21 average	**8**	m	11	m	**40**	m	37	m	17	m	1.7	m
Other G20												
Argentina[1]	**m**	m	16	m	**m**	m	12	m	1	m	0.1	m
Brazil[2]	**m**	m	5	m	**m**	m	25	25	1	m	0.4	0.4
China	**m**	m	18	m	**m**	m	14	m	n	m	2.4	m
India	**m**	m	m	m	**m**	m	m	m	m	m	m	m
Indonesia	**m**	m	4	m	**m**	m	14	m	1	m	0.1	m
Russian Federation[2]	**m**	m	28	m	**m**	m	55	54	1	m	0.4	m
Saudi Arabia[2]	**8**	8	8	8	**20**	19	18	18	1	1	0.1	0.1
South Africa[1]	**m**	m	5	m	**m**	m	6	m	3	m	0.1	m
G20 average	**m**	m	16	m	**m**	m	30	m	7	m	1.0	m

Notes: Refer to Annex 1 for information on the method used to calculate graduation rates (gross rates versus net rates) and the corresponding typical ages. Mismatches between the coverage of the population data and the graduate data mean that the graduation rates for those countries that are net exporters of students may be underestimated and those that are net importers may be overestimated. The adjusted graduation rates seek to compensate for that.
1. Year of reference 2009.
2. The graduation rates are calculated for foreign students (defined on the basis of their country of citizenship). These data are not comparable with data on international graduates.
Source: OECD. Argentina, China, Indonesia: UNESCO Institute for Statistics (World Education Indicators programme). Saudi Arabia: Observatory on Higher Education. South Africa: UNESCO Institute for Statistics. See Annex 3 for notes (*www.oecd.org/edu/eag2012*).
Please refer to the Reader's Guide for information concerning the symbols replacing missing data.
StatLink ᵃ᷉ᵈᵊ http://dx.doi.org/10.1787/888932664613

A3

Table A3.4. Structure of tertiary education: Main programme blocks (2010)
Proportion of graduations/graduates following the Bologna structure
(or in programmes that lead to a similar degree in non-European countries)

	Proportion of degrees following the Bologna structure[1] 2010	Of which					Proportion of degrees outside the Bologna structure[1] (ISCED levels 5A, 5B and 6)	Proportion of degrees following the Bologna structure[1] 2009	Proportion of degrees following the Bologna structure[1] 2008
		Degrees less than 3 years but considered to be at tertiary level and part of the Bologna structure[1] (first degree)	Bachelor's degrees 3-4 years of duration (first degree)	Master's degrees 4-8 years of cumulative duration (second degree)	Long first degrees considered to be part of the Bologna structure[1] (duration 5 or more years)	Ph.D. and doctorates			
	(1)	(2)	(3)	(4)	(5)	(6)	(7)	(8)	(9)
OECD									
Australia[2]	68	a	45	19	2	2	32	69	69
Austria	43	n	29	10	n	4	57	38	32
Belgium	91	a	58	31	a	2	9	88	71
Canada	m	m	m	m	m	m	m	m	m
Chile	m	m	m	m	m	m	m	m	m
Czech Republic	79	a	49	27	a	2	21	74	66
Denmark	100	16	55	24	2	3	m	100	100
Estonia[3]	97	a	72	20	4	1	3	97	94
Finland	90	a	65	22	n	3	10	92	56
France[2]	86	26	31	18	9	2	14	86	87
Germany[3]	27	a	22	5	a	a	73	19	14
Greece	m	m	m	m	m	m	m	m	m
Hungary	41	a	33	6	n	2	59	22	3
Iceland	100	3	68	27	2	1	n	100	100
Ireland	100	23	46	29	a	2	a	100	100
Israel	m	m	m	m	m	m	m	m	m
Italy	m	m	m	m	m	m	m	90	85
Japan	m	m	m	m	m	m	m	m	m
Korea	100	32	51	13	1	2	m	100	100
Luxembourg	m	m	m	m	m	m	m	m	m
Mexico	m	m	m	m	m	m	m	m	m
Netherlands	98	a	68	27	a	3	2	98	96
New Zealand	51	n	41	7	1	2	49	52	56
Norway	100	6	62	24	5	3	a	100	100
Poland	99	a	41	42	16	1	1	99	100
Portugal[3]	88	a	65	14	9	1	12	73	57
Slovak Republic	96	a	52	38	3	4	4	96	95
Slovenia[3]	21	a	17	3	n	n	79	13	5
Spain[3]	12	n	1	10	n	n	88	6	4
Sweden	90	3	41	36	5	6	10	91	m
Switzerland[3]	38	n	26	12	n	n	62	33	26
Turkey	100	40	50	8	m	1	a	a	a
United Kingdom	86	16	39	24	5	3	14	86	77
United States	100	37	42	20	a	2	a	100	100
OECD average	75	8	44	19	2	2	25	72	66
EU21 average	69	5	42	18	2	2	31	65	57
Other G20									
Argentina	m	m	m	m	m	m	m	m	m
Brazil	a	a	a	a	a	a	a	a	a
China	m	m	m	m	m	m	m	m	m
India	m	m	m	m	m	m	m	m	m
Indonesia	m	m	m	m	m	m	m	m	m
Russian Federation[3]	7	a	6	1	a	a	93	6	m
Saudi Arabia	100	28	66	5	n	n	n	100	100
South Africa	m	m	m	m	m	m	m	m	m
G20 average	m	m	m	m	m	m	m	m	m

1. Or in programmes that lead to a similar degree in non-European countries.
2. Year of reference 2009.
3. Some countries still allocated Ph.D. graduates in Column (7).
Source: OECD. Saudi Arabia: Observatory on Higher Education. See Annex 3 for notes (*www.oecd.org/edu/eag2012*).
Please refer to the Reader's Guide for information concerning the symbols replacing missing data.
StatLink ⟦⟧ http://dx.doi.org/10.1787/888932664632

WHAT IS THE DIFFERENCE BETWEEN THE CAREER ASPIRATIONS OF BOYS AND GIRLS AND THE FIELDS OF STUDY THEY PURSUE AS YOUNG ADULTS?

- Young women seem to have higher career aspirations than young men, but there is considerable variation in expectations within both genders and among countries.

- On average, girls are 11 percentage points more likely than boys to expect to work as legislators, senior officials, managers and professionals.

- Countries where girls are significantly more ambitious than boys tend to be those where women outnumber men in tertiary-type A programmes.

Chart A4.1. **Percentage of 15-year-old boys and girls who plan to work in ISCO major occupational groups 1 and 2[1], by gender**

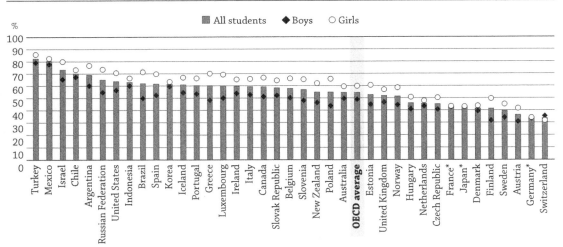

Note: Countries in which gender differences are not statistically significant are shown with an asterisk.
1. Group 1 refers to legislators, senior officials and managers and group 2 refers to professionals in the ISCO classification.
Countries are ranked in descending order of the percentage of 15-year-old students who plan to work in ISCO major occupational groups 1 and 2.
Source: OECD, *PISA 2006 Database*. Table A4.1. See Annex 3 for notes (*www.oecd.org/edu/eag2012*).
StatLink 🔗 http://dx.doi.org/10.1787/888932661744

🔲 Context

Recognising the impact that education has on participation in labour markets, occupational mobility and the quality of life, policy makers and educators emphasise the importance of reducing educational differences between men and women. Significant progress has been achieved in reducing the gender gap in educational attainment, although in certain fields of study, such as mathematics and computer science, gender differences favouring men still exist.

As women have closed the gap and surpassed men in many aspects of education in OECD countries, there is now concern about the underachievement of young men in certain areas, such as reading. Gender differences in student performance, as well as traditional perceptions of some fields, need close attention from policy makers if greater gender equity in educational outcomes is to be achieved. Gender equality is not only a goal in itself (although this is an important intrinsic value), but it is also economically beneficial. Programmes recruiting from almost only one gender are in danger of excluding many potentially able candidates. This is particularly the case with science, engineering, manufacturing and construction, which are often viewed as "masculine" fields and perceived to be more suited for men, and care-related fields, such as education or health, which are sometimes viewed as "feminine" and more appropriate for women.

Furthermore, students' perceptions of what occupations lie ahead for them can affect their academic decisions and performance. Prior studies based on PISA (Marks, 2010; McDaniel, 2010; Sikora and Saha, 2007; Sikora and Saha, 2009) and other surveys of youth going back at least three decades (Croll, 2008; Goyette, 2008; Little, 1978; Reynolds, et al., and Sischo 2006) consistently find that secondary school students tend to be quite ambitious in setting their educational and occupational goals. Strengthening the role that education systems can play in moderating gender differences in performance in various subjects should be an important policy objective.

Other findings

- **Only 5% of 15-year-old girls in OECD countries, on average, expect a career in engineering and computing,** while 18% of boys expect a career in these fields. In every OECD country, more girls than boys expect a career in health and services.

- **Women are also performing strongly in tertiary-type A education:** an estimated 69% of young women in OECD countries are expected to enter these programmes during their lifetimes, compared to 55% of young men.

- **On average in OECD countries, 59% of all graduates of a first tertiary-type A programme are women.** The proportion is below 50% only in China, Japan, Korea and Turkey. However, men are still more likely than women to hold advanced research qualifications, and **73% of all graduates in the fields of engineering, manufacturing and construction are men.**

Trends

Trend data tend to demonstrate that gender gaps still exist both in countries' education systems and in the labour market. However, these gaps have narrowed slightly since 2000. For example, the proportion of women who entered a tertiary-type A programme rose from 60% in 2005 to 69% in 2010, while the proportion of men who entered similar programmes rose from 48% in 2005 to 55% in 2010.

While few girls expect to enter certain science careers, such as engineering and computing, the proportion of women in these fields of education has increased slightly (from 23% to 27%) over the past decade.

Analysis

PISA performance and career expectations of 15-year-olds

Girls outperformed boys on the PISA 2009 reading assessment in every OECD country and by 39 points on average, the equivalent of one year of school. In mathematics, 15-year-old boys tend to perform slightly better than girls in most countries, while in science, patterns of performance related to gender are less pronounced. Moreover, 15-year-old girls are also generally more ambitious than boys in terms of their career expectations. On the 2006 PISA assessment, 15-year-old students were asked what they expect to be doing in early adulthood, around the age of 30. Participants in PISA 2006 expected to pursue highly skilled lines of employment, dominated by professional and managerial positions. Among OECD countries, at least 70% of students in Chile, Israel, Mexico and Turkey expected to work in occupations requiring a tertiary-type A degree at entry. In Argentina, Brazil, Greece, Iceland, Indonesia, Korea, Mexico, Portugal, the Russian Federation, Spain and United States, over 60% of students also hoped to enter highly skilled managerial and professional careers. At the other end of the spectrum, the percentage of high school students planning similar careers in Austria, Germany, and Switzerland, as well as in Sweden, did not exceed 40% (Table A4.1 and Chart A4.1).

The differences in the career ambitions of students across countries can be attributed to a number of factors. These include students' family characteristics and academic performance, but also the specific national labour market conditions and the features of national education systems that provide different options for 15-year-olds (Sikora and Saha, 2010).

In almost all OECD countries, girls have more ambitious aspirations than boys. On average, girls are 11 percentage points more likely than boys to expect to work in high-status careers such as legislators, senior officials, managers and professionals. France, Germany and Japan were the only OECD countries where similar proportions of boys and girls aspired to these careers, while in Switzerland, boys generally had slightly more ambitious aspirations than girls. The gender gap in career expectations was particularly wide in Greece and Poland: in these two countries, the proportion of girls expecting to work as legislators, senior officials, managers and professionals was 20 percentage points higher than the proportion of boys expecting to work in those occupations (Table A4.1).

Not only do boys and girls have different aspirations in general, they also expect to have careers in very different fields. In 25 OECD countries, "a lawyer" is one of the ten careers girls cited most often when asked what they expect to be working as when they are 30. By contrast, it was one of the ten careers boys cited most often in only ten countries. Similarly, in 20 OECD countries, "authors, journalists and other writers" were among the ten careers girls most often expected to pursue, while these careers were among the top ten that boys cited in only four OECD countries (Sikora and Pokropek, 2011).

Countries differ widely in the magnitude of gender differences in various subjects

The fact that the direction of gender differences in reading and mathematics tends to be somewhat consistent among countries suggests that there are underlying features of education systems or societies and cultures that may foster such gender gaps. However, the wide variation among countries in the magnitude of gender differences suggests that current differences may be the result of variations in students' learning experiences, and thus are amenable to changes in policy.

In recent years, girls in many countries have caught up with or even surpassed boys in science proficiency. Better performance in science or mathematics among girls, however, does not necessarily mean that girls want to pursue all types of science-related careers. In fact, careers in "engineering and computing" still attract relatively few girls. On average among OECD countries, fewer than 5% of girls, but 18% of boys, expect to be working in engineering and computing as young adults. This is remarkable, especially because the definition of computing and engineering includes fields like architecture, which is not particularly associated with either gender (Table A4.2 and Chart A4.2).

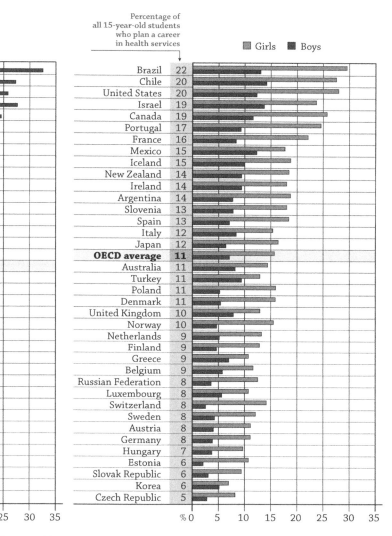

Chart A4.2. Percentage of 15-year-old boys and girls planning a career in engineering or computing

Percentage of all 15-year-old students who plan a career in engineering or computing

Girls ▪ Boys

Country	%
Poland	20
Mexico	17
Chile	16
Slovenia	15
Portugal	15
Spain	14
Turkey	14
Estonia	14
Norway	13
Slovak Republic	13
Italy	13
Czech Republic	13
Greece	13
Russian Federation	12
Belgium	12
Argentina	12
Hungary	12
OECD average	**11**
Brazil	11
Israel	11
Canada	11
Iceland	11
Ireland	11
Luxembourg	10
France	10
Sweden	10
Australia	9
United States	9
Switzerland	9
Austria	9
Japan	9
Germany	9
Denmark	8
New Zealand	8
Korea	8
United Kingdom	7
Finland	6
Netherlands	5

% 0 5 10 15 20 25 30 35

Countries are ranked in descending order of the percentage of all 15-year-old students who plan a career in engineering or computing (including architecture).
Source: OECD, *PISA 2006 Database*. Table A4.2. See Annex 3 for notes (*www.oecd.org/edu/eag2012*).
StatLink ᵐˢᴾ http://dx.doi.org/10.1787/888932661763

Chart A4.3. Percentage of 15-year-old boys and girls planning a career in health services

Percentage of all 15-year-old students who plan a career in health services

Girls ▪ Boys

Country	%
Brazil	22
Chile	20
United States	20
Israel	19
Canada	19
Portugal	17
France	16
Mexico	15
Iceland	15
New Zealand	14
Ireland	14
Argentina	14
Slovenia	13
Spain	13
Italy	12
Japan	12
OECD average	**11**
Australia	11
Turkey	11
Poland	11
Denmark	11
United Kingdom	10
Norway	10
Netherlands	9
Finland	9
Greece	9
Belgium	9
Russian Federation	8
Luxembourg	8
Switzerland	8
Sweden	8
Austria	8
Germany	8
Hungary	7
Estonia	6
Slovak Republic	6
Korea	6
Czech Republic	5

% 0 5 10 15 20 25 30 35

Countries are ranked in descending order of the percentage of all 15-year-old students who plan a career in health services (excluding nurses and midwives).
Source: OECD, *PISA 2006 Database*. Table A4.3. See Annex 3 for notes (*www.oecd.org/edu/eag2012*).
StatLink ᵐˢᴾ http://dx.doi.org/10.1787/888932661782

The number of students expecting a career in engineering and computing varies widely among countries, ranging from relatively high proportions in Chile, Mexico, Poland and Slovenia to very low numbers in Finland and the Netherlands. In no OECD country did the number of girls who expected a career in computing and engineering exceed the number of boys contemplating such a career. Moreover, the ratio of boys to girls who wanted to pursue a career in engineering or computing is large in most OECD countries. On average, there were almost four times as many boys as girls who expected to be employed in these fields. Even among the highest-achieving students, career expectations differed between boys and girls. In fact, their expectations mirrored those of their lower-achieving peers. For example, few top-performing girls expected to enter engineering and computing (Table A4.2 and Chart A4.2).

Although few girls expected to enter certain science careers, such as engineering and computing, in every OECD country more girls than boys reported that they wanted to pursue a career in health services, a science profession with a caring component. This pattern holds even after nurses and midwives (two fields in which girls are over-represented compared to boys) are excluded from the list of health-related careers. On average across OECD countries, 16% of girls expected a career in health services, excluding nursing and midwifery, compared to only 7% of boys. This suggests that although girls who are high achievers in science may not expect to become engineers or computer scientists, they direct their higher ambitions towards achieving the top places in other science-related professions, such as those in the health field. The gender gap in the percentage of students citing future careers in the health sciences was particularly large in Austria, Brazil, Canada, Chile, France, the Netherlands, Norway, Portugal, Switzerland and the United States. By contrast, boys and girls in Greece, Indonesia, Italy, Korea, Mexico and Turkey are closer to their peers of the opposite gender in their intentions to pursue careers in health. Nevertheless, this does not suggest the absence of a gender gap, merely a narrower one (Table A4.3 and Chart A4.3).

Impact of career expectations at age 15 on entry rates into tertiary-type A education

What is the relationship between the career plans of 15-year-olds and access to tertiary-type A education? The link can be measured by analysing the gender differences in the percentage of 15-year-olds who planned to work in certain occupations in 2006 and in the percentage of new entrants into tertiary-type A education several years after, in 2010. Tables A4.1 and A4.4 show a relatively good correlation (R= 0.50) between both measures. Thus, countries where girls have significantly higher career aspirations than boys tend to be those where women are better represented than men in tertiary-type A programmes.

For example, the gender gap in favour of women in access to tertiary-type A education exceeds 20 percentage points in Australia, Denmark, Iceland, New Zealand, Norway, Poland, Portugal, the Slovak Republic, Slovenia and Sweden. Among these countries, only in Australia and Denmark is the gender gap – in favour of girls – in the proportion of students expecting to work as legislators, senior officials, managers and professionals lower than the OECD average of 11 percentage points. In other words, in countries where women are well-represented in tertiary-type A education, girls also tend to have more ambitious career expectations.

Similarly, Tables A4.1 and A4.4 show that in Belgium, Germany, Indonesia, Korea, Mexico, Switzerland and Turkey, where the difference in tertiary-type A entry rates between men and women is lower than 10 percentage points, the proportion of girls expecting to work as legislators, senior officials, managers and professionals is never more than 10 percentage points higher than the proportion of boys expecting to work in those occupations. In other words, in countries where women are not as well represented in tertiary-type A education, girls' career expectations are more similar to boys'.

Gender equality in access to and graduation from tertiary programmes

More generally, the better 15-year-old boys and girls do in school, the more likely they are to continue in education. Between 2005 and 2010, the likelihood that both young men and women would enter a tertiary-type A programme increased dramatically, from 54% to 61%, and by 2010, far more women than men entered these programmes, on average among OECD countries (see Table C3.1). The proportion of women who entered a tertiary-type A programme rose from 60% in 2005 to 69% in 2010, while the proportion of men who entered a similar programme rose from 48% in 2005 to 55% in 2010 (Table A4.4).

Similarly, in most countries, girls leave education with a tertiary qualification in larger numbers than boys. The proportion of women with a first tertiary-type A degree exceed that of men in 35 of the 39 countries for which data are comparable. On average in OECD countries, 59% of all graduates of a first tertiary-type A degree are women. This proportion is below 50% only in China, Japan, Korea and Turkey (Table A4.5 and Chart A4.4).

However, this pattern should not obscure the fact that the higher the level of tertiary education, the lower the proportion of women who graduate. In OECD countries, men are still more likely than women to receive advanced research qualifications (54% on average), such as doctorates. The proportion of advanced research

What is the difference between the career aspirations of boys and girls and the fields of study they pursue as young adults? – INDICATOR A4   CHAPTER A

A4

degrees (e.g. doctorates) awarded to women is lower than for men in all countries except Argentina, Brazil, Estonia, Finland, Israel, Italy, New Zealand, Portugal and the United States. In Japan and Korea, two-thirds or more of advanced research qualifications are awarded to men (Chart A4.4).

Chart A4.4.   **Percentage of tertiary-type A and advanced research qualifications awarded to women (2010)**

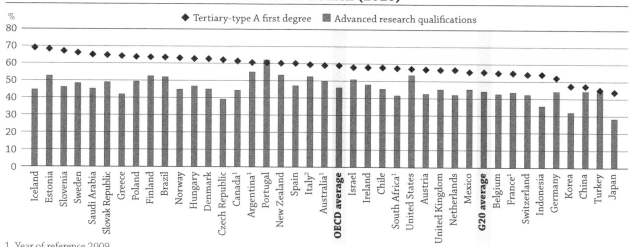

1. Year of reference 2009.
2. Year of reference for advanced research programmes 2008.
Countries are ranked in descending order of the percentage of tertiary-type A (first degree) qualifications awarded to women.
Source: OECD. Argentina, China, Indonesia: UNESCO Institute for Statistics (World Education Indicators programme). Saudi Arabia: Observatory on Higher Education. South Africa: UNESCO Institute for Statistics. Table A4.5. See Annex 3 for notes (*www.oecd.org/edu/eag2012*).
StatLink ⊠⊡⊠ http://dx.doi.org/10.1787/888932661801

Gender differences in fields of education

The distribution of graduates by field of education is driven by the relative popularity of these fields among students, the relative number of students admitted to these fields in universities and equivalent institutions, and the degree structure of the various disciplines in a particular country.

Women predominate among graduates in the field of education: they represent 70% or more of tertiary students (tertiary-type A and advanced research programmes) in this field in all countries except Indonesia (55%), Japan (59%), Saudi Arabia (51%) and Turkey (57%). They also dominate in the fields of health and welfare, accounting for 74% of all degrees awarded in this field, on average (Table A4.6 and Chart A4.5).

In contrast, in all countries except Argentina, Denmark, Estonia, France, Greece, Iceland, Indonesia, Italy, New Zealand, Poland, Portugal, Saudi Arabia, the Slovak Republic, Slovenia and Spain, 30% or fewer of all graduates in the fields of engineering, manufacturing and construction are women.

Moreover, this situation has changed only slightly since 2000, despite many initiatives to promote gender equality in OECD countries and at the EU level. For example, in 2000, the European Union established a goal to increase the number of tertiary-type A graduates in mathematics, science and technology by at least 15% by 2010, and to reduce the gender imbalance in these subjects. So far, however, progress towards this goal has been marginal. The Czech Republic, Germany, the Slovak Republic and Switzerland are the only four countries in which the proportion of women in science grew by at least 10 percentage points between 2000 and 2010. As a result, these countries are now closer to the OECD average in this respect. Among OECD countries, the proportion of women in these fields has grown marginally from 40% in 2000 to 42% in 2010 – even as the proportion of women graduates in all fields grew from 54% to 58% during that period. The proportion of women in engineering, manufacturing and construction is also low and increased slightly (from 23% to 27%) over the past decade (Table A4.6 and Chart A4.5).

A4

Chart A4.5. Percentage of tertiary degrees (tertiary-type A and advanced research programmes) awarded to women, by field of education (2010)

Only those fields in which less than 30% or more than 70% of women graduated in 2010 are shown in the graph

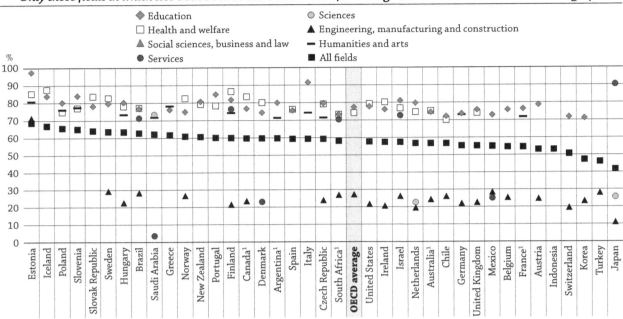

1. Year of reference 2009.

Countries are ranked in descending order of the percentage of tertiary degrees (tertiary-type A and advanced research programmes) awarded to women in 2010.

Source: OECD. Argentina, Indonesia: UNESCO Institute for Statistics (World Education Indicators programme). Saudi Arabia: Observatory on Higher Education. South Africa: UNESCO Institute for Statistics. Table A4.6. See Annex 3 for notes (*www.oecd.org/edu/eag2012*).

StatLink ⟨⟨⟨ http://dx.doi.org/10.1787/888932661820

Box A4.1. Gender equality in employment

Reducing the gender gap in employment is a priority for policy makers in OECD countries. Tertiary education improves job prospects for both men and women, and the gender gap in employment has narrowed at the highest levels of educational attainment. However, the employment rate among women without an upper secondary qualification (49% on average) is particularly low, whereas the rates are 66% and 79%, respectively, for women with an upper secondary and tertiary qualification (see Indicator A7).

The gender gap in employment also decreases with increasing educational attainment. Although there is still a gender gap in employment among those with the highest educational attainment, it is much narrower than among those with lower qualifications, and has decreased compared to 1997. On average among OECD countries, with each additional level of education attained, the difference between the employment ratio of men and women decreases significantly, from 20 percentage points among those with less than upper secondary attainment (26% in 1997), to 15 percentage points among those with an upper secondary education (21% in 1997) and to 9 percentage points among those with tertiary attainment (12% in 1997).

Recent reforms have been implemented by governments to increase equality in employment (see also OECD, 2011). These include:

Extending parental leave to fathers.
Women make more use of flexible working-time arrangements than men, which contributes to persistent gender differences in career profiles. In 2010, on average across OECD countries, 68% of women with a tertiary qualification aged 25-64 worked full-time in the labour market, compared to 83% of men.

...

However, in a number of countries, including the Nordic countries, Germany and Portugal, fathers are granted the exclusive right to part of the parental leave entitlement and/or ample income support during the leave period. This has resulted in more fathers taking more parental leave days; but it is still unclear whether this has led to a better sharing of care responsibilities in the household, and whether these changes are durable.

Instituting quotas to increase the number of women on company boards, empower specialised bodies and take legal action against employers who engage in discriminatory practices.

Wage gaps are often larger at the higher end of the wage distribution, reflecting the so-called "glass ceiling" that blocks women's career progression and consequently leads to loss of talent. Policies can address the reasons for pay gaps and glass ceilings. One approach that is being discussed, especially in Europe, where women hold only 12% of corporate board seats on average, is to introduce quotas on the number of women on company boards. In order to help women break through the glass ceiling, some countries (Iceland, Norway and Spain) have introduced mandatory quotas for women in boardrooms. Depending on the size of the company or the number of board members, firms may be required to have at least 40% of their boardroom seats assigned to women. Similar legislation has been introduced in other OECD countries (Belgium, France, Italy and the Netherlands). Some companies (such as Deutsche Telekom) have introduced voluntary quotas for women in management.

The need to introduce quotas for women in boardrooms or in senior management is being widely debated and merits further analysis to assess its benefits in terms of women's employment outcomes and firm performance.

Moreover, entering the labour force in greater numbers in some fields of education does not guarantee that women will occupy equitable positions in the labour market, despite recent initiatives to reinforce equality in employment (Box A4.1). For example, on average, women represent 67% of all school teachers, but the higher the level of education, the higher the proportion of male teachers. Although women tend to dominate the teaching profession in pre-primary (97% of teachers on average), primary (82% of teachers on average), and lower secondary education, only 56% of the teachers in upper secondary education are women. In addition, in tertiary education, men are in the majority among professors in all countries except Argentina, Finland, New Zealand, the Russian Federation and South Africa (see Indicator D5).

Methodology

The PISA target population is 15-year-old students. Operationally, these are students who were from 15 years and 3 (completed) months to 16 years and 2 (completed) months at the beginning of the testing period, and who were enrolled in an educational institution, regardless of the grade level or type of institution and of whether they participated in school full-time or part-time.

As far as occupational plans are concerned, student preferences tend to centre heavily on occupations that require at least some tertiary study. Table A4.1 is based on categories 1 and 2 of the ISCO88 classification and refer to the 15-year-olds who expect high-status careers. Most occupations grouped in ISCO88 (International Labour Office, 1988) under the label of *i)* Legislators, senior officials and managers or *ii)* Professionals require a minimum of university degree at entry, high levels of numeracy and literacy as well as excellent personal intercommunication skills. These skills are denoted by level 4 in the nomenclature of ISCO88. The occupations listed as *iii)* Technicians and associate professionals require similar skills at a high level and usually require between one to three years of study in a tertiary education institution. Few students see their future in any of the occupations listed in the remaining major groups, i.e. *iv)* Clerks, *v)* Service workers and shop and market sales workers, *vi)* Skilled, agricultural and fishery workers, *vii)* Craft and related workers, *viii)* Plant and machine operators and assemblers and ix) Elementary occupations (see more details on the ISCO classification in the Annex 3).

Data refer to the academic year 2009-10 and are based on the UOE data collection on education statistics administered by the OECD in 2011 (for details, see Annex 3 at *www.oecd.org/edu/eag2012*). The fields of education used in the UOE data collection instruments follow the revised ISCED classification by field of education. The same classification is used for all levels of education.

Data on new entrants and graduates refer to the academic year 2009-10 and are based on the UOE data collection on education statistics administered by the OECD in 2011 (for details, see Annex 3 at *www.oecd.org/edu/eag2012*).

The statistical data for Israel are supplied by and under the responsibility of the relevant Israeli authorities. The use of such data by the OECD is without prejudice to the status of the Golan Heights, East Jerusalem and Israeli settlements in the West Bank under the terms of international law.

References

Croll, P. (2008), "Occupational Choice, Socio-Economic Status and Educational Attainment: A Study of the Occupational Choices and Destinations of Young People in the British Household Panel Survey", *Research Papers in Education,* No. 23, pp.243-268.

Goyette, K. (2008), "College for Some to College for All: Social Background, Occupational Expectations, and Educational Expectations over Time", *Social Science Research,* No. 37, pp. 461-84.

Little, A. (1978), "The Occupational and Educational Expectations of Students in Developed and Less-Developed Countries", Sussex University, Institute of Development Studies, Sussex.

Marks, G.N. (2010), "Meritocracy, modernization and students' occupational expectations: Crossnational evidence", *Research in Social Stratification and Mobility,* No. 28, pp. 275-289

McDaniel, A. (2010), "Cross-National Gender Gaps in Educational Expectations: The Influence of National-Level Gender Ideology and Educational Systems", *Comparative Education Review,* No. 54, pp. 27-50.

OECD (2011), "Report on the Gender Initiative: Gender Equality in Education, Employment and Entrepreneurship", Meeting of the OECD Council at Ministerial Level, 25-26 May 2011, Paris.

Reynolds, J., M. Stewart, R. MacDonald, and L. Sischo (2006), "Have Adolescents Become too Ambitious? High School Seniors' Educational and Occupational Plans 1976 to 2000", *Social Problems,* No. 53, pp. 186-206.

Sikora, J. and L.J. Saha (2007), "Corrosive Inequality? Structural Determinants of Educational and Occupational Expectations in Comparative Perspective", *International Education Journal: Comparative Perspectives,* No. 8, pp. 57-78.

Sikora, J. and L.J. Saha (2009), "Gender and Professional Career Plans of High School Students in Comparative Perspective", *Educational Research and Evaluation,* No. 15, pp. 387-405.

Sikora, J. and L.J. Saha (2010), "New Directions in National Education Policymaking: Student Career Plans in International Achievement Studies", in A.W. Wiseman (ed.), *The Impact of International Achievement Studies on National Education Policymaking,* Vol. 14, International Perspectives on Education and Society Series, Emerald Publishing, Bingley, United Kingdom, pp. 83-115.

Sikora, J. and A. Pokropek (2011), "Gendered Career Expectations of Students: Perspectives from PISA 2006", *OECD Education Working Papers*, No. 57, OECD Publishing.

The following additional material relevant to this indicator is available on line:

- *Table A4.7. Concentration of career plans (percentage of students who expect one of the 10 most popular jobs)*
  StatLink ᵐˢ⁷ http://dx.doi.org/10.1787/888932664803

- *Table A4.8 Science-related graduates among 25-34 year-olds in employment, by gender (2010)*
  StatLink ᵐˢ⁷ http://dx.doi.org/10.1787/888932664822

Table A4.1. Percentage of 15-year-old boys and girls who plan to work in International Standard Classification of Occupations (ISCO) major occupational[1] groups 1 and 2, by gender

A4

	All 15-year-old students		Boys		Girls		Difference (Girls-Boys)	
	%	S.E.	%	S.E.	%	S.E.	%	S.E.
OECD								
Australia	54.5	(0.8)	49.6	(1.1)	59.4	(0.9)	**9.8**	(1.3)
Austria	36.3	(1.5)	30.8	(2.1)	41.5	(2.2)	**10.8**	(3.2)
Belgium	57.7	(1.1)	50.2	(1.6)	65.9	(1.3)	**15.7**	(2.2)
Canada	59.1	(0.6)	51.2	(0.9)	66.6	(0.7)	**15.4**	(1.1)
Chile	70.0	(1.4)	67.2	(2.1)	73.2	(1.3)	**6.0**	(2.2)
Czech Republic	45.1	(1.5)	40.7	(1.8)	50.3	(1.9)	**9.6**	(2.4)
Denmark	41.4	(1.1)	39.3	(1.2)	43.6	(1.5)	**4.3**	(1.7)
Estonia	52.6	(1.0)	44.8	(1.4)	60.5	(1.4)	**15.7**	(1.8)
Finland	41.3	(1.0)	31.6	(1.3)	49.6	(1.3)	**18.0**	(1.7)
France	42.8	(1.5)	42.4	(1.9)	43.2	(1.6)	0.8	(2.0)
Germany	33.6	(1.1)	33.3	(1.5)	33.9	(1.4)	0.7	(1.9)
Greece	60.1	(1.2)	48.3	(1.8)	70.0	(1.2)	**21.7**	(1.9)
Hungary	45.8	(1.5)	40.9	(2.1)	50.7	(2.0)	**9.8**	(2.7)
Iceland	60.9	(0.9)	54.4	(1.4)	66.8	(1.2)	**12.4**	(1.7)
Ireland	59.7	(1.2)	53.8	(1.5)	65.1	(1.4)	**11.3**	(1.8)
Israel	73.2	(1.3)	65.3	(2.4)	79.9	(1.3)	**14.6**	(2.6)
Italy	59.2	(0.8)	52.7	(1.3)	65.6	(1.0)	**12.8**	(1.5)
Japan	42.7	(1.1)	42.5	(1.3)	43.0	(1.7)	0.5	(1.9)
Korea	61.4	(0.9)	59.5	(1.2)	63.3	(1.2)	**3.8**	(1.8)
Luxembourg	59.9	(0.7)	50.0	(0.9)	69.1	(1.1)	**19.1**	(1.5)
Mexico	80.3	(0.6)	77.7	(1.0)	82.5	(0.7)	**4.8**	(1.3)
Netherlands	45.5	(1.1)	43.2	(1.4)	47.8	(1.5)	**4.6**	(1.7)
New Zealand	54.9	(0.8)	46.3	(1.3)	62.0	(1.0)	**15.7**	(1.7)
Norway	51.4	(1.0)	44.4	(1.3)	58.4	(1.4)	**14.0**	(1.7)
Poland	54.8	(1.1)	43.6	(1.3)	65.6	(1.4)	**22.0**	(1.7)
Portugal	60.2	(1.2)	53.5	(1.7)	66.1	(1.2)	**12.6**	(1.8)
Slovak Republic	58.2	(1.5)	52.1	(1.9)	64.3	(1.8)	**12.2**	(2.1)
Slovenia	56.9	(0.8)	47.9	(1.1)	65.1	(1.1)	**17.2**	(1.6)
Spain	61.5	(0.9)	52.3	(1.4)	69.6	(1.1)	**17.3**	(1.7)
Sweden	39.5	(0.9)	34.1	(1.1)	44.9	(1.3)	**10.8**	(1.5)
Switzerland	33.5	(0.8)	35.2	(0.9)	31.6	(1.2)	**-3.6**	(1.3)
Turkey	82.3	(1.0)	79.0	(1.4)	85.8	(1.3)	**6.7**	(1.8)
United Kingdom	51.9	(0.8)	46.5	(1.1)	56.9	(1.1)	**10.4**	(1.4)
United States	63.7	(1.0)	56.4	(1.4)	70.6	(1.3)	**14.2**	(1.9)
OECD average	54.5	(0.2)	48.8	(0.3)	59.8	(0.2)	**10.9**	(0.3)
Other G20								
Argentina	69.1	(1.5)	60.0	(2.1)	76.7	(1.6)	**16.6**	(2.3)
Brazil	61.9	(0.9)	49.9	(1.3)	71.3	(1.0)	**21.4**	(1.5)
China	m	m	m	m	m	m	m	m
India	m	m	m	m	m	m	m	m
Indonesia	63.1	(2.0)	60.0	(2.4)	66.2	(2.0)	**6.2**	(1.7)
Russian Federation	65.0	(1.3)	54.7	(2.0)	73.5	(1.0)	**18.8**	(2.1)
Saudi Arabia	m	m	m	m	m	m	m	m
South Africa	m	m	m	m	m	m	m	m
G20 average	m	m	m	m	m	m	m	m

Note: Values that are statistically significant are indicated in bold.
1. Group 1 refers to legislators, senior officials and managers and group 2 refers to professionals in the ISCO classification.
Source: OECD, *PISA 2006 Database*. See Annex 3 for notes (*www.oecd.org/edu/eag2012*).
Please refer to the Reader's Guide for information concerning the symbols replacing missing data.
StatLink ⌗ http://dx.doi.org/10.1787/888932664689

A4

Table A4.2. Percentage of 15-year-old boys and girls planning a science-related career or a career in engineering and computing at age 30, by gender

	Percentage of 15-year-old boys and girls planning a science-related career				Percentage of 15-year-olds planning a career in engineering and computing ("Including architects" and "Not including architects")							
					Including architects				Not including architects			
	All 15-year-old students	Boys	Girls	Difference (Girls-Boys)	All 15-year-old students	Boys	Girls	Difference (Girls-Boys)	All 15-year-old students	Boys	Girls	Difference (Girls-Boys)
	% S.E.	% S.E.	% S.E.	% S.E.	% S.E.	% S.E.	% S.E.	% S.E.	% S.E.	% S.E.	% S.E.	% S.E.
Australia	33.5 (0.6)	34.2 (0.8)	32.8 (0.9)	-1.4 (1.1)	9.5 (0.4)	16.3 (0.6)	2.8 (0.2)	**-13.5** (0.7)	5.8 (0.3)	10.5 (0.5)	1.2 (0.2)	**-9.3** (0.6)
Austria	29.2 (1.7)	27.3 (2.4)	31.0 (1.8)	3.6 (2.5)	9.1 (1.0)	15.1 (1.6)	3.3 (0.5)	**-11.8** (1.5)	6.3 (0.7)	11.9 (1.3)	0.8 (0.2)	**-11.1** (1.3)
Belgium	31.6 (0.9)	31.4 (1.2)	31.8 (1.0)	0.4 (1.4)	12.2 (0.6)	18.7 (0.9)	5.1 (0.4)	**-13.6** (0.9)	6.6 (0.4)	11.0 (0.7)	1.7 (0.2)	**-9.3** (0.7)
Canada	42.4 (0.7)	39.8 (1.0)	44.9 (0.9)	**5.1** (1.2)	10.7 (0.4)	18.8 (0.7)	3.2 (0.3)	**-15.6** (0.7)	6.2 (0.4)	11.5 (0.7)	1.2 (0.2)	**-10.3** (0.7)
Chile	47.9 (1.4)	49.1 (1.6)	46.6 (1.9)	-2.5 (2.2)	16.4 (0.9)	25.9 (1.4)	5.9 (0.5)	**-20.0** (1.4)	9.6 (0.8)	16.9 (1.2)	1.4 (0.3)	**-15.5** (1.3)
Czech Republic	25.6 (1.2)	26.8 (1.5)	24.3 (1.8)	-2.6 (2.3)	12.9 (1.2)	20.0 (1.6)	4.8 (1.2)	**-15.2** (1.9)	9.6 (1.0)	17.1 (1.6)	0.9 (0.3)	**-16.2** (1.5)
Denmark	28.4 (0.8)	24.3 (1.0)	32.6 (1.1)	**8.3** (1.5)	8.2 (0.4)	13.0 (0.8)	3.3 (0.5)	**-9.7** (1.0)	2.6 (0.3)	4.5 (0.6)	0.7 (0.2)	**-3.7** (0.6)
Estonia	27.7 (0.8)	27.4 (1.1)	28.0 (1.1)	0.6 (1.6)	13.7 (0.6)	18.5 (1.0)	8.8 (0.7)	**-9.7** (1.3)	6.8 (0.5)	12.3 (0.9)	1.3 (0.3)	**-11.0** (1.0)
Finland	23.2 (0.7)	21.3 (1.0)	24.8 (1.1)	**3.5** (1.5)	6.0 (0.4)	10.5 (0.7)	2.1 (0.4)	**-8.3** (0.7)	3.6 (0.3)	7.6 (0.6)	0.2 (0.1)	**-7.4** (0.6)
France	36.2 (1.1)	36.3 (1.6)	36.1 (1.2)	-0.3 (1.8)	10.3 (0.7)	18.3 (1.1)	3.5 (0.5)	**-14.7** (1.2)	5.4 (0.5)	10.1 (0.8)	1.5 (0.3)	**-8.6** (0.9)
Germany	25.8 (0.8)	26.2 (1.2)	25.3 (1.1)	-0.9 (1.6)	8.9 (0.5)	14.2 (1.0)	3.6 (0.4)	**-10.6** (1.1)	5.5 (0.4)	9.9 (0.8)	1.1 (0.2)	**-8.8** (0.8)
Greece	36.3 (0.9)	38.1 (1.4)	34.8 (1.2)	-3.3 (1.9)	12.5 (0.7)	19.2 (1.0)	7.0 (0.7)	**-12.3** (1.1)	9.2 (0.5)	15.9 (0.9)	3.5 (0.4)	**-12.4** (0.9)
Hungary	24.5 (1.4)	26.4 (1.7)	22.6 (1.5)	**-3.8** (1.8)	11.6 (1.0)	19.1 (1.6)	4.1 (0.5)	**-15.0** (1.5)	8.5 (0.9)	14.5 (1.5)	2.4 (0.4)	**-12.1** (1.4)
Iceland	39.8 (0.9)	36.8 (1.3)	42.5 (1.3)	**5.7** (1.9)	10.6 (0.5)	14.1 (0.9)	7.5 (0.7)	**-6.7** (1.2)	3.4 (0.3)	6.7 (0.6)	0.5 (0.2)	**-6.3** (0.6)
Ireland	33.5 (0.9)	34.5 (1.5)	32.6 (1.0)	-1.9 (1.6)	10.5 (0.6)	18.1 (1.0)	3.4 (0.5)	**-14.7** (1.1)	4.5 (0.3)	7.9 (0.6)	1.3 (0.3)	**-6.6** (0.6)
Israel	45.1 (1.4)	43.6 (2.1)	46.3 (1.6)	2.8 (2.5)	10.8 (0.8)	15.6 (1.5)	6.8 (0.8)	**-8.9** (1.7)	9.2 (0.7)	14.9 (1.5)	4.4 (0.6)	**-10.5** (1.7)
Italy	35.6 (1.0)	38.6 (1.3)	32.8 (1.1)	**-5.8** (1.3)	13.1 (0.9)	21.4 (1.3)	4.9 (0.5)	**-16.5** (1.1)	7.6 (0.7)	14.1 (1.1)	1.2 (0.2)	**-12.8** (1.0)
Japan	24.8 (1.5)	23.7 (1.4)	25.9 (2.5)	2.3 (2.6)	9.0 (0.7)	15.1 (1.2)	3.2 (0.4)	**-11.9** (1.2)	9.0 (0.7)	15.1 (1.2)	3.2 (0.4)	**-11.9** (1.2)
Korea	20.7 (0.8)	25.1 (1.1)	16.2 (1.0)	**-8.9** (1.4)	7.5 (0.6)	12.4 (0.8)	2.6 (0.4)	**-9.8** (0.9)	5.2 (0.5)	9.5 (0.7)	0.9 (0.2)	**-8.6** (0.8)
Luxembourg	30.1 (0.8)	31.0 (1.0)	29.3 (1.1)	-1.7 (1.5)	10.4 (0.5)	16.4 (0.9)	4.8 (0.5)	**-11.7** (1.1)	4.5 (0.3)	8.6 (0.6)	0.6 (0.2)	**-7.9** (0.7)
Mexico	45.9 (0.9)	50.9 (1.4)	41.7 (1.1)	**-9.2** (1.7)	16.7 (0.5)	27.3 (0.9)	7.8 (0.5)	**-19.5** (1.0)	8.6 (0.4)	13.7 (0.6)	4.4 (0.3)	**-9.3** (0.6)
Netherlands	27.1 (0.9)	21.6 (0.9)	32.7 (1.3)	**11.1** (1.4)	5.1 (0.4)	7.8 (0.7)	2.4 (0.4)	**-5.5** (0.8)	2.4 (0.3)	4.6 (0.6)	0.2 (0.1)	**-4.4** (0.6)
New Zealand	30.2 (0.9)	27.7 (1.3)	32.3 (1.2)	**4.6** (1.7)	7.6 (0.5)	12.2 (0.9)	3.7 (0.4)	**-8.6** (1.1)	3.9 (0.4)	7.9 (0.8)	0.6 (0.2)	**-7.3** (0.9)
Norway	34.4 (0.8)	30.4 (1.1)	38.3 (1.3)	**7.9** (1.8)	13.4 (0.7)	19.4 (1.1)	7.4 (0.7)	**-12.0** (1.2)	6.0 (0.5)	10.1 (0.8)	2.0 (0.3)	**-8.1** (0.8)
Poland	38.9 (0.8)	43.3 (1.2)	34.7 (1.2)	**-8.6** (1.8)	19.6 (0.7)	32.6 (1.2)	7.2 (0.6)	**-25.3** (1.4)	15.5 (0.7)	28.7 (1.2)	2.8 (0.3)	**-25.8** (1.3)
Portugal	47.5 (1.1)	45.5 (1.5)	49.3 (1.2)	**3.8** (1.7)	14.9 (0.7)	24.6 (1.3)	6.3 (0.6)	**-18.3** (1.4)	11.3 (0.6)	21.0 (1.2)	2.7 (0.4)	**-18.4** (1.3)
Slovak Republic	26.4 (1.4)	30.4 (1.8)	22.5 (1.7)	**-7.9** (2.1)	13.1 (1.1)	23.1 (1.5)	3.1 (0.5)	**-20.0** (1.5)	10.9 (1.1)	20.3 (1.7)	1.5 (0.3)	**-18.8** (1.7)
Slovenia	39.4 (0.8)	43.1 (1.1)	36.0 (1.2)	**-7.1** (1.7)	15.2 (0.5)	27.7 (0.9)	3.6 (0.6)	**-24.1** (1.1)	12.4 (0.5)	24.3 (1.0)	1.3 (0.3)	**-23.0** (1.0)
Spain	38.0 (1.0)	38.1 (1.2)	37.9 (1.1)	-0.2 (1.2)	14.4 (0.6)	23.8 (0.9)	6.1 (0.5)	**-17.7** (0.9)	7.8 (0.4)	14.3 (0.7)	2.0 (0.3)	**-12.3** (0.7)
Sweden	26.9 (0.8)	25.4 (1.2)	28.5 (1.2)	3.1 (1.7)	9.8 (0.6)	15.3 (0.9)	4.4 (0.5)	**-10.9** (0.9)	6.2 (0.5)	11.2 (0.8)	1.1 (0.2)	**-10.2** (0.9)
Switzerland	26.3 (0.5)	25.7 (0.7)	26.9 (0.9)	1.2 (1.1)	9.1 (0.4)	14.8 (0.6)	3.1 (0.4)	**-11.7** (0.7)	5.7 (0.3)	9.8 (0.5)	1.2 (0.2)	**-8.5** (0.6)
Turkey	31.9 (1.6)	33.8 (2.0)	30.0 (1.6)	-3.9 (1.8)	14.1 (0.9)	20.9 (1.4)	7.0 (0.7)	**-13.9** (1.3)	7.1 (0.7)	11.6 (1.1)	2.6 (0.4)	**-9.0** (1.1)
United Kingdom	27.7 (0.7)	27.2 (1.0)	28.1 (0.9)	1.0 (1.2)	7.2 (0.4)	12.6 (0.6)	2.1 (0.2)	**-10.5** (0.7)	4.2 (0.3)	7.6 (0.5)	0.9 (0.2)	**-6.7** (0.5)
United States	44.8 (0.9)	39.9 (1.5)	49.4 (1.1)	**9.5** (1.8)	9.4 (0.5)	16.4 (0.8)	2.7 (0.4)	**-13.7** (0.9)	3.9 (0.3)	6.7 (0.5)	1.3 (0.2)	**-5.4** (0.6)
OECD average	33.2 (0.2)	33.1 (0.2)	33.2 (0.2)	0.1 (0.3)	11.3 (0.1)	18.2 (0.2)	4.6 (0.1)	**-13.6** (0.2)	6.9 (0.1)	12.4 (0.2)	1.6 (0.1)	**-10.8** (0.2)
Argentina	36.2 (1.1)	34.5 (1.4)	37.7 (1.6)	3.2 (1.9)	11.7 (0.9)	18.6 (1.4)	6.0 (0.8)	**-12.6** (1.5)	6.2 (0.6)	10.7 (1.0)	2.4 (0.4)	**-8.3** (1.0)
Brazil	46.1 (0.9)	40.3 (1.3)	50.6 (1.1)	**10.3** (1.5)	11.0 (0.5)	17.3 (0.9)	6.0 (0.6)	**-11.2** (1.0)	9.4 (0.5)	16.2 (0.9)	4.2 (0.4)	**-12.0** (0.9)
China	m m	m m	m m	**m** m	m m	m m	m m	**m** m	m m	m m	m m	**m** m
India	m m	m m	m m	**m** m	m m	m m	m m	**m** m	m m	m m	m m	**m** m
Indonesia	34.2 (2.0)	32.9 (3.6)	35.6 (1.7)	2.6 (3.8)	9.3 (2.4)	11.8 (4.7)	6.6 (1.0)	-5.1 (5.1)	5.9 (0.7)	7.1 (1.8)	4.7 (1.3)	-2.5 (2.8)
Russian Federation	28.7 (1.0)	31.8 (1.8)	26.2 (0.9)	**-5.6** (2.0)	12.4 (1.0)	20.9 (1.6)	5.3 (0.6)	**-15.7** (1.4)	9.6 (0.9)	17.1 (1.5)	3.5 (0.5)	**-13.6** (1.4)
Saudi Arabia	m m	m m	m m	**m** m	m m	m m	m m	**m** m	m m	m m	m m	**m** m
South Africa	m m	m m	m m	**m** m	m m	m m	m m	**m** m	m m	m m	m m	**m** m
G20 average	m m	m m	m m	**m** m	m m	m m	m m	**m** m	m m	m m	m m	**m** m

Note: Values that are statistically significant are indicated in bold.
Source: OECD, *PISA 2006 Database*. See Annex 3 for notes (*www.oecd.org/edu/eag2012*).
Please refer to the Reader's Guide for information concerning the symbols replacing missing data.
StatLink ᔒ http://dx.doi.org/10.1787/888932664708

Table A4.3. Percentage of 15-year-old boys and girls expecting employment in health and services at age 30, by gender

	With nurses and midwives								Without nurses and midwives							
	All 15-year-old students		Boys		Girls		Difference (Girls -Boys)		All 15-year-old students		Boys		Girls		Difference (Girls -Boys)	
	%	S.E.	%	S.E.	%	S.E.	%	S.E.	%	S.E.	%	S.E.	%	S.E.	%	S.E.
OECD																
Australia	13.3	(0.4)	8.3	(0.5)	18.3	(0.6)	**10.0**	(0.7)	11.3	(0.4)	8.2	(0.5)	14.4	(0.5)	**6.2**	(0.7)
Austria	12.7	(0.9)	4.5	(0.7)	20.5	(1.4)	**15.9**	(1.5)	7.7	(0.5)	4.0	(0.6)	11.1	(0.8)	**7.1**	(1.1)
Belgium	11.5	(0.6)	6.2	(0.5)	17.2	(0.7)	**10.9**	(0.8)	8.6	(0.5)	5.7	(0.5)	11.6	(0.7)	**5.9**	(0.8)
Canada	21.2	(0.5)	11.8	(0.6)	30.1	(0.7)	**18.3**	(0.9)	18.9	(0.5)	11.6	(0.6)	25.7	(0.7)	**14.1**	(0.9)
Chile	21.9	(1.0)	14.2	(0.8)	30.6	(1.8)	**16.4**	(1.9)	20.5	(1.0)	14.2	(0.8)	27.5	(1.7)	**13.3**	(1.8)
Czech Republic	6.6	(0.7)	2.8	(0.4)	10.9	(1.3)	**8.1**	(1.2)	5.3	(0.5)	2.8	(0.4)	8.2	(0.9)	**5.4**	(0.8)
Denmark	12.7	(0.6)	5.4	(0.5)	20.2	(1.0)	**14.8**	(1.2)	10.5	(0.5)	5.4	(0.5)	15.8	(1.0)	**10.5**	(1.2)
Estonia	6.5	(0.5)	2.2	(0.3)	10.8	(0.9)	**8.6**	(0.9)	6.4	(0.5)	2.1	(0.3)	10.8	(0.9)	**8.7**	(0.9)
Finland	10.6	(0.6)	4.7	(0.6)	15.6	(0.9)	**10.9**	(1.2)	9.1	(0.6)	4.6	(0.6)	12.8	(0.9)	**8.2**	(1.1)
France	19.2	(0.8)	9.2	(0.8)	27.6	(1.0)	**18.4**	(1.2)	15.8	(0.7)	8.3	(0.7)	22.1	(0.9)	**13.8**	(1.1)
Germany	9.8	(0.6)	4.1	(0.6)	15.4	(1.0)	**11.2**	(1.2)	7.5	(0.4)	3.9	(0.5)	11.1	(0.8)	**7.2**	(1.0)
Greece	10.5	(0.6)	7.3	(0.8)	13.1	(0.8)	**5.8**	(1.1)	9.0	(0.5)	7.0	(0.8)	10.8	(0.7)	**3.8**	(1.0)
Hungary	8.0	(0.7)	3.9	(0.6)	12.1	(1.1)	**8.2**	(1.2)	6.7	(0.5)	3.8	(0.6)	9.7	(0.8)	**5.9**	(1.0)
Iceland	15.8	(0.7)	10.1	(0.8)	20.9	(1.1)	**10.8**	(1.4)	14.6	(0.6)	10.0	(0.9)	18.8	(1.0)	**8.8**	(1.4)
Ireland	16.9	(0.7)	9.5	(0.9)	23.7	(0.8)	**14.2**	(1.2)	13.9	(0.7)	9.4	(0.9)	18.0	(0.8)	**8.6**	(1.2)
Israel	21.0	(1.2)	14.3	(1.4)	26.7	(1.4)	**12.3**	(1.7)	19.1	(1.1)	13.7	(1.3)	23.7	(1.3)	**10.0**	(1.6)
Italy	12.5	(0.7)	8.6	(1.0)	16.4	(0.8)	**7.9**	(1.1)	11.9	(0.7)	8.4	(1.0)	15.3	(0.8)	**7.0**	(1.1)
Japan	11.5	(1.3)	6.4	(0.7)	16.4	(2.0)	**10.0**	(1.9)	11.5	(1.3)	6.4	(0.7)	16.4	(2.0)	**10.0**	(1.9)
Korea	7.4	(0.5)	5.2	(0.4)	9.6	(0.8)	**4.4**	(0.9)	6.0	(0.4)	5.1	(0.4)	6.9	(0.6)	**1.8**	(0.8)
Luxembourg	12.1	(0.6)	6.6	(0.6)	17.4	(1.0)	**10.8**	(1.1)	8.3	(0.5)	5.6	(0.5)	10.8	(0.8)	**5.1**	(1.0)
Mexico	16.8	(0.6)	12.4	(0.8)	20.4	(0.8)	**8.0**	(1.0)	15.2	(0.6)	12.3	(0.8)	17.7	(0.8)	**5.4**	(1.0)
Netherlands	15.6	(0.8)	6.0	(0.6)	25.2	(1.1)	**19.2**	(1.0)	9.2	(0.5)	5.1	(0.6)	13.2	(0.7)	**8.1**	(0.8)
New Zealand	16.1	(0.7)	9.4	(0.8)	21.7	(1.0)	**12.3**	(1.3)	14.3	(0.7)	9.4	(0.8)	18.4	(1.0)	**9.0**	(1.3)
Norway	13.2	(0.6)	4.7	(0.5)	21.8	(1.1)	**17.1**	(1.2)	10.1	(0.5)	4.7	(0.5)	15.5	(0.9)	**10.8**	(1.1)
Poland	11.2	(0.5)	5.7	(0.5)	16.5	(0.8)	**10.8**	(1.0)	10.7	(0.5)	5.2	(0.5)	15.9	(0.8)	**10.7**	(1.0)
Portugal	20.4	(0.8)	10.5	(0.9)	29.0	(1.0)	**18.5**	(1.3)	17.4	(0.7)	9.3	(0.8)	24.6	(1.1)	**15.3**	(1.3)
Slovak Republic	7.6	(0.8)	3.3	(0.5)	11.9	(1.3)	**8.6**	(1.2)	6.3	(0.6)	3.1	(0.5)	9.4	(0.9)	**6.4**	(0.8)
Slovenia	16.0	(0.6)	8.3	(0.7)	23.1	(1.0)	**14.8**	(1.3)	13.1	(0.6)	7.8	(0.7)	18.1	(1.0)	**10.3**	(1.2)
Spain	14.8	(0.6)	7.4	(0.7)	21.4	(0.8)	**14.0**	(1.0)	13.1	(0.5)	7.1	(0.6)	18.4	(0.7)	**11.3**	(0.9)
Sweden	10.2	(0.6)	4.6	(0.6)	15.8	(0.9)	**11.2**	(1.0)	8.2	(0.5)	4.3	(0.5)	12.1	(0.8)	**7.8**	(0.9)
Switzerland	10.2	(0.5)	2.8	(0.3)	18.2	(0.9)	**15.4**	(0.9)	8.2	(0.4)	2.6	(0.3)	14.2	(0.8)	**11.6**	(0.8)
Turkey	12.8	(0.8)	9.5	(0.9)	16.3	(1.4)	**6.8**	(1.5)	11.1	(0.8)	9.4	(0.9)	12.9	(1.1)	**3.5**	(1.2)
United Kingdom	13.0	(0.5)	7.9	(0.6)	17.8	(0.7)	**9.9**	(0.9)	10.5	(0.4)	7.8	(0.6)	12.9	(0.6)	**5.1**	(0.8)
United States	24.3	(0.8)	12.4	(0.8)	35.6	(1.0)	**23.2**	(1.2)	20.3	(0.7)	12.3	(0.8)	27.9	(1.0)	**15.6**	(1.2)
OECD average	13.6	(0.1)	7.4	(0.1)	19.7	(0.2)	**12.3**	(0.3)	11.5	(0.1)	7.1	(0.1)	15.7	(0.2)	**8.6**	(0.2)
Other G20																
Argentina	14.2	(0.8)	7.8	(0.9)	19.5	(1.1)	**11.7**	(1.1)	13.7	(0.8)	7.7	(0.9)	18.7	(1.0)	**11.0**	(1.1)
Brazil	24.1	(0.9)	13.8	(1.0)	32.0	(1.2)	**18.2**	(1.4)	22.3	(0.7)	13.0	(0.8)	29.5	(1.1)	**16.5**	(1.3)
China	m	m	m	m	m	m	m	m	m	m	m	m	m	m	m	m
India	m	m	m	m	m	m	m	m	m	m	m	m	m	m	m	m
Indonesia	18.6	(1.6)	15.1	(1.9)	22.3	(1.5)	**7.3**	(1.9)	16.3	(1.5)	13.5	(1.8)	19.3	(1.5)	**5.8**	(1.7)
Russian Federation	9.5	(0.6)	3.6	(0.4)	14.4	(1.0)	**10.8**	(1.0)	8.5	(0.5)	3.6	(0.4)	12.5	(0.8)	**8.9**	(0.8)
Saudi Arabia	m	m	m	m	m	m	m	m	m	m	m	m	m	m	m	m
South Africa	m	m	m	m	m	m	m	m	m	m	m	m	m	m	m	m
G20 average	m	m	m	m	m	m	m	m	m	m	m	m	m	m	m	m

Note: Values that are statistically significant are indicated in bold.
Source: OECD, *PISA 2006 Database*. See Annex 3 for notes (*www.oecd.org/edu/eag2012*).
Please refer to the Reader's Guide for information concerning the symbols replacing missing data.
StatLink ᴍˢᴾ http://dx.doi.org/10.1787/888932664727

A4

Table A4.4. **Trends in entry rates at tertiary level, by gender (2005-2010)**

	Men								Women							
	Tertiary-type 5A				Tertiary-type 5B				Tertiary-type 5A				Tertiary-type 5B			
	2005	2008	2009	2010	2005	2008	2009	2010	2005	2008	2009	2010	2005	2008	2009	2010
	(1)	(4)	(5)	(6)	(7)	(10)	(11)	(12)	(13)	(16)	(17)	(18)	(19)	(22)	(23)	(24)
OECD																
Australia	74	76	82	**83**	m	m	m	**m**	92	99	107	**110**	m	m	m	**m**
Austria	34	44	48	**56**	7	7	14	**16**	41	56	61	**70**	10	10	16	**19**
Belgium	29	29	29	**32**	29	31	33	**32**	38	32	33	**34**	38	44	46	**45**
Canada	m	m	m	**m**	m	m	m	**m**	m	m	m	**m**	m	m	m	**m**
Chile*	m	m	40	**43**	m	m	60	**58**	m	m	48	**50**	m	m	58	**59**
Czech Republic	39	50	51	**52**	5	6	5	**5**	44	65	68	**70**	12	12	12	**13**
Denmark	45	46	44	**53**	23	21	25	**25**	69	73	67	**78**	23	21	24	**26**
Estonia	55	33	34	**35**	25	22	23	**25**	68	52	50	**50**	44	40	36	**33**
Finland	63	61	60	**61**	a	a	a	**a**	84	79	78	**75**	a	a	a	**a**
France	m	m	m	**m**	m	m	m	**m**	m	m	m	**m**	m	m	m	**m**
Germany[1]	36	36	39	**42**	11	11	12	**13**	36	37	40	**43**	17	17	26	**28**
Greece	39	42	m	**m**	13	27	m	**m**	48	53	m	**m**	13	26	m	**m**
Hungary	57	52	48	**50**	8	7	10	**11**	78	62	57	**58**	13	17	18	**21**
Iceland	53	54	58	**74**	7	5	4	**4**	96	94	97	**113**	7	6	3	**4**
Ireland	39	43	44	**51**	15	19	30	**32**	51	49	58	**61**	13	21	20	**25**
Israel	51	54	53	**53**	24	24	26	**28**	59	66	66	**66**	27	28	28	**29**
Italy	49	43	42	**42**	a	n	n	**n**	64	60	58	**57**	a	n	n	**n**
Japan	47	54	55	**56**	23	22	20	**20**	34	42	43	**45**	38	37	35	**35**
Korea	58	72	72	**71**	50	35	33	**33**	52	70	69	**71**	54	42	40	**40**
Luxembourg	m	25	30	**26**	m	n	1	**10**	m	25	32	**29**	m	n	3	**10**
Mexico	27	30	31	**33**	2	3	3	**3**	27	30	31	**32**	2	2	2	**2**
Netherlands	54	57	58	**61**	a	n	n	**n**	63	67	68	**70**	a	n	n	**n**
New Zealand	64	60	66	**66**	41	41	42	**46**	93	84	93	**93**	54	51	51	**50**
Norway	61	57	64	**64**	1	1	n	**n**	85	86	91	**89**	n	n	n	**n**
Poland	70	76	76	**73**	1	1	n	**n**	83	90	95	**96**	2	2	2	**2**
Portugal	m	71	74	**78**	m	n	n	**n**	m	92	95	**101**	m	n	n	**n**
Slovak Republic	52	59	56	**55**	2	1	1	**1**	67	86	82	**76**	3	1	1	**1**
Slovenia	33	43	48	**64**	46	32	31	**19**	49	69	74	**90**	52	32	32	**19**
Spain	36	36	39	**44**	21	20	22	**24**	51	50	54	**60**	23	23	25	**27**
Sweden	64	53	57	**65**	7	9	10	**12**	89	78	80	**87**	8	10	12	**12**
Switzerland	36	37	40	**43**	19	21	22	**25**	38	39	43	**45**	13	18	20	**21**
Turkey	30	32	42	**40**	22	26	33	**31**	24	28	38	**40**	16	19	27	**24**
United Kingdom	45	50	53	**56**	19	21	22	**19**	58	64	68	**71**	36	39	40	**34**
United States	56	57	62	**67**	x(1)	x(4)	x(5)	**x(6)**	71	72	78	**82**	x(13)	x(16)	x(17)	**x(18)**
OECD average	48	49	52	**55**	16	14	15	**16**	60	63	66	**69**	19	18	19	**19**
EU21 average	47	47	49	**52**	13	12	13	**13**	60	62	64	**67**	17	16	17	**17**
Other G20																
Argentina	m	41	48	**m**	m	26	28	**m**	m	53	63	**m**	m	62	65	**m**
Brazil	m	m	m	**m**	m	m	m	**m**	m	m	m	**m**	m	m	m	**m**
China	m	m	15	**16**	m	m	17	**17**	m	m	18	**18**	m	m	22	**20**
India	m	m	m	**m**	m	m	m	**m**	m	m	m	**m**	m	m	m	**m**
Indonesia	m	m	22	**22**	m	m	4	**4**	m	m	22	**24**	m	m	5	**5**
Russian Federation	m	m	m	**m**	m	m	m	**m**	m	m	m	**m**	m	m	m	**m**
Saudi Arabia	27	35	36	**47**	16	19	23	**16**	47	78	49	**50**	4	5	6	**6**
South Africa	m	m	m	**m**	m	m	m	**m**	m	m	m	**m**	m	m	m	**m**
G20 average	m	m	47	**48**	m	m	17	**16**	m	m	53	**54**	m	m	26	**21**

Notes: Years 2006 and 2007 are available for consultation on line (see *StatLink* below).
Please refer to Annex 1 for information on the method used to calculate entry rates (gross rates versus net rates) and the corresponding age of entry.
1. Break in time series between 2008 and 2009 due to a partial reallocation of vocational programmes into ISCED 2 and ISCED 5B.
* Due to late changes, Chile's data on new entrants are not included in the OECD average calculation.
Source: OECD. Argentina, China, Indonesia: UNESCO Institute for Statistics (World Education Indicators programme). Saudi Arabia: Observatory on Higher Education. See Annex 3 for notes (*www.oecd.org/edu/eag2012*).
Please refer to the Reader's Guide for information concerning the symbols replacing missing data.
StatLink ᵐˢᴾ http://dx.doi.org/10.1787/888932664746

Table A4.5. **Percentage of qualifications awarded to women at different tertiary levels (2010)**

	Tertiary-type B (first degree)	Tertiary-type A (first degree)	Tertiary-type A (second degree)	Advanced research programmes
	(1)	(2)	(3)	(4)
OECD Australia[1]	56	59	50	50
Austria	46	57	43	43
Belgium	64	55	55	43
Canada[1]	60	61	55	44
Chile	53	58	53	45
Czech Republic	72	62	58	39
Denmark	48	63	54	45
Estonia	73	68	71	53
Finland	9	64	55	53
France[1]	56	55	55	44
Germany	68	52	52	44
Greece	56	64	58	42
Hungary	72	63	69	47
Iceland	58	69	62	44
Ireland	46	58	58	48
Israel	m	58	57	51
Italy[2]	48	59	62	52
Japan	63	44	30	28
Korea	58	47	49	32
Luxembourg	m	m	m	m
Mexico	46	55	53	45
Netherlands	55	57	59	42
New Zealand	56	60	63	53
Norway	62	63	55	45
Poland	84	64	69	49
Portugal	58	60	59	62
Slovak Republic	70	65	65	49
Slovenia	57	67	58	46
Spain	54	60	59	47
Sweden	60	66	59	48
Switzerland	47	54	47	42
Turkey	46	45	52	45
United Kingdom	62	57	54	45
United States	63	57	59	53
OECD average	57	59	56	46
EU21 average	58	61	58	47
Other G20 Argentina[1]	70	61	51	55
Brazil	48	63	54	52
China	51	47	46	44
India	m	m	m	m
Indonesia	64	54	42	36
Russian Federation	m	m	m	48
Saudi Arabia	26	65	42	45
South Africa[1]	66	57	60	42
G20 average	56	55	51	45

1. Year of reference 2009.
2. Year of reference 2008 for second degree and advanced research programmes.
Source: OECD. Argentina, China, Indonesia: UNESCO Institute for Statistics (World Education Indicators programme). Saudi Arabia: Observatory on Higher Education. South Africa: UNESCO Institute for Statistics. See Annex 3 for notes (*www.oecd.org/edu/eag2012*).
Please refer to the Reader's Guide for information concerning the symbols replacing missing data.
StatLink ᴍᴺˢᴸ http://dx.doi.org/10.1787/888932664765

A4

Table A4.6. Percentage of qualifications awarded to women in tertiary-type A and advanced research programmes, by field of education (2000, 2010)

	2010									2000								
	All fields	Education	Humanities and arts	Health and welfare	Social sciences, business and law	Services	Engineering, manufacturing and construction	Sciences	Agriculture	All fields	Education	Humanities and arts	Health and welfare	Social sciences, business and law	Services	Engineering, manufacturing and construction	Sciences	Agriculture
	(1)	(2)	(3)	(4)	(5)	(6)	(7)	(8)	(13)	(14)	(15)	(16)	(17)	(18)	(19)	(20)	(21)	(26)
Australia[1]	57	75	64	75	54	55	24	37	55	56	75	67	76	52	55	21	41	44
Austria	53	79	66	66	56	44	25	35	63	46	72	59	59	49	37	18	33	52
Belgium	55	76	65	66	58	39	25	35	54	50	70	62	59	52	44	21	38	40
Canada[1]	60	77	65	83	58	60	24	49	57	58	73	63	74	58	61	23	45	51
Chile	57	72	60	70	52	52	26	33	48	m	m	m	m	m	m	m	m	m
Czech Republic	59	80	71	79	67	43	24	39	60	51	75	64	70	56	27	27	25	38
Denmark	60	74	65	80	52	23	32	37	73	49	59	69	59	44	54	26	42	50
Estonia	69	97	81	85	71	68	38	50	57	m	m	m	m	m	m	m	m	m
Finland	60	82	74	86	66	76	21	46	55	58	82	74	84	64	72	19	46	46
France[1]	55	76	72	60	60	42	30	38	55	56	69	74	60	61	42	24	43	54
Germany	55	74	73	69	53	55	22	44	54	45	71	67	56	42	58	20	32	47
Greece	62	76	78	59	65	n	41	48	48	m	m	m	m	m	m	m	m	m
Hungary	63	80	73	78	68	61	23	39	49	55	72	69	70	54	31	21	31	42
Iceland	67	84	69	88	59	70	40	48	63	67	91	69	82	57	n	25	48	n
Ireland	57	76	62	80	54	52	21	42	53	57	78	67	75	56	66	24	48	41
Israel	57	81	59	77	56	73	26	44	54	60	69	68	56	m	24	43	48
Italy	59	91	74	68	58	50	33	52	33	56	m	m	m	m	m	m	m	m
Japan	42	59	69	56	35	90	11	26	38	36	59	69	50	26	m	9	25	38
Korea	47	71	67	65	43	34	23	39	39	45	73	69	50	40	39	23	47	33
Luxembourg	m	m	m	m	m	m	m	m	m	m	m	m	m	m	m	m	m	m
Mexico	55	73	58	66	59	25	28	48	35	52	66	60	61	55	55	22	46	25
Netherlands	57	80	57	75	53	53	20	23	55	55	76	61	76	49	49	13	28	38
New Zealand	61	81	64	79	57	53	30	44	55	61	84	66	79	53	51	33	45	42
Norway	61	75	59	83	56	46	27	36	58	62	79	62	82	49	36	27	28	46
Poland	66	80	76	75	69	56	33	45	56	64	78	77	68	66	51	24	64	57
Portugal	60	85	61	78	63	46	31	54	58	65	83	67	77	65	57	34	46	58
Slovak Republic	64	78	69	84	69	44	31	43	47	52	75	56	69	56	29	30	30	33
Slovenia	65	84	77	77	69	59	33	50	64	m	m	m	m	m	m	m	m	m
Spain	59	76	65	76	60	56	34	41	49	58	77	64	76	60	60	27	46	46
Sweden	64	80	62	83	61	52	29	47	64	59	79	63	79	58	45	25	47	52
Switzerland	51	72	62	68	47	52	20	34	71	38	63	61	54	34	45	11	24	42
Turkey	46	57	58	61	42	32	28	45	33	41	43	48	53	40	28	24	47	37
United Kingdom	55	76	62	74	54	61	23	38	66	54	73	63	71	55	n	20	44	53
United States	58	78	59	79	54	55	22	44	51	57	76	61	75	54	40	21	44	49
OECD average	58	77	67	74	58	51	27	42	54	54	74	65	68	52	43	23	40	43
EU21 average	60	80	69	75	61	49	28	42	56	55	74	66	69	55	45	23	40	47
Argentina[1]	60	80	71	68	61	47	32	50	38	m	m	m	m	m	m	m	m	m
Brazil	63	77	52	77	57	71	28	38	41	m	m	m	m	m	m	m	m	m
China	47	m	m	m	m	m	m	m	m	m	m	m	m	m	m	m	m	m
India	m	m	m	m	m	m	m	m	m	m	m	m	m	m	m	m	m	m
Indonesia	53	55	52	53	55	n	51	53	52	m	m	m	m	m	m	m	m	m
Russian Federation	m	m	m	m	m	m	m	m	m	m	m	m	m	m	m	m	m	m
Saudi Arabia	62	51	72	58	n	4	50	73	24	m	m	m	m	m	m	m	m	m
South Africa[1]	58	73	63	73	58	70	27	46	46	m	m	m	m	m	m	m	m	m
G20 average	51	m	m	m	m	m	m	m	m	m	m	m	m	m	m	m	m	m

Note: Columns showing the breakdown of science (9-12, 22-25) are available for consultation on line (see StatLink below).
1. Year of reference 2009.
Source: OECD. Argentina, Indonesia: UNESCO Institute for Statistics (World Education Indicators programme). Saudi Arabia: Observatory on Higher Education. South Africa: UNESCO Institute for Statistics. See Annex 3 for notes (www.oecd.org/edu/eag2012).
Please refer to the Reader's Guide for information concerning the symbols replacing missing data.
StatLink 🔗 http://dx.doi.org/10.1787/888932664784

HOW WELL DO IMMIGRANT STUDENTS PERFORM IN SCHOOL?

- Across OECD countries, the higher the proportion of students with low-educated mothers in a school, the lower the reading performance of students in that school.

- The relationship between reading performance and the proportion of students with low-educated mothers in a school is negative, and much stronger than the relationship between reading performance and the proportion of immigrant students who do not speak the primary language of instruction at home, or the relationship between reading performance and the proportion of immigrant students in a school.

- Immigrants – even highly educated ones – tend to be concentrated in socio-economically disadvantaged neighbourhoods, particularly in Europe. Immigrant students from families with low occupational status, but with highly educated mothers, are overrepresented in "disadvantaged schools" (defined as schools with the highest proportion of students whose mothers have low levels of education). In the European Union, these students are more than twice as likely to attend disadvantaged schools than their non-immigrant counterparts.

- For all students – not only immigrant students – the impact on reading scores of being in an advantaged versus a disadvantaged school is larger than the impact of having a low-educated mother in many countries, except Nordic and Eastern European countries, and some countries with a long tradition of attracting immigrants, like Australia, Canada and New Zealand.

Chart A5.1. Correlations between reading performance of immigrant students and various measures of student concentration in schools

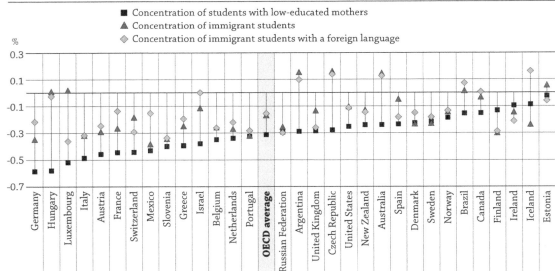

Note: A student with a low-educated mother is one whose mother has not attained an upper secondary education.
Countries are ranked in ascending order of the Pearson correlation between the concentration of students with low-educated mothers and their performance.
Source: OECD, *PISA 2009 Database*, Table A5.1.
StatLink ⟨⟩ http://dx.doi.org/10.1787/888932661839

How to read this chart
For each country, this chart shows three dots, a triangle, a diamond and a square, representing the correlation of three different measures of concentration of students in schools with their performance in reading. These three measures are the concentration in schools of: *i)* immigrant students (triangle); *ii)* immigrant students speaking another language at home (diamond); and *iii)* students (whatever their origin) in a school who have low-educated mothers (square). Countries are ranked in ascending order of the correlation between the concentration of students with low-educated mothers and their performance.

Context

The successful integration of immigrant students in schools is an important policy goal in many OECD countries. A country's success in integrating immigrant students is a key measure of its education system's quality and equity, and also sheds light on the efficacy of its broader social policies (OECD, 2012a).

Designing education policies to address the needs of immigrant students is often difficult and expensive. Policies that work for non-immigrant students may not be sufficient for immigrant students. Successful approaches for immigrant students require a focus on their unique needs, as well as an understanding of the specific factors that can influence their school performance. The diversity of immigrant student populations around the world speaks to the wide variety of challenges these students face. The variance in performance gaps between immigrant and non-immigrant students across countries, even after adjusting for socio-economic background, suggests that policy has an important role to play in eliminating such gaps.

Yet education policy alone is unlikely to address these challenges fully. For example, immigrant children's performance on PISA is more strongly (and negatively) associated with the concentration of educational disadvantage in schools than with the concentration of immigrants per se, or the concentration of students who speak a different language at home than at school. Reducing the concentration of educational disadvantage in schools may imply changes in other areas of social policy – for example, housing policies that promote a more balanced social mix in schools at an early age.

Other findings

- Across OECD countries, **more than one-third of immigrant students attend schools with the highest concentrations of students with low-educated mothers.**

- In many countries, **immigrant students with highly educated mothers are overrepresented in disadvantaged schools.** Across OECD countries, more than a quarter of students with highly educated mothers in disadvantaged schools are immigrant students.

Trends

On average, among OECD countries with comparable data, the percentage of immigrant students increased by two percentage points between 2000 and 2009. The performance difference between immigrant and non-immigrant students remained broadly similar. Non-immigrant students outperformed immigrant students by more than 40 score points on both the 2000 and 2009 PISA assessments.

A5

Analysis

Given that immigrants tend to concentrate in certain neighbourhoods and districts of cities in virtually all countries, the issue of a possible peer effect on outcomes is an especially pertinent one. The school's composition – that is, the characteristics of the student population – can exert a significant influence on the outcomes of students. However, the dimension along which concentration of disadvantages in school occurs and, how they affect outcomes, is not self-evident. Is it the concentration of immigrants per se in certain neighbourhoods which is associated with the less favourable outcomes one observes for the children of immigrants in many countries? Or rather, is it the concentration of students who largely speak another language at home, or the concentration of immigrant students in disadvantaged schools?

These three measures of concentration can be examined and the student sample for each country divided into quartiles on the basis of these three concentration measures. The first quartile is defined to have the lowest value on the measure and the fourth the highest value. The three measures are:

- the percentage of immigrant students in a school;
- the percentage of immigrant students in a school speaking another language at home; and
- the percentage of students (whatever their origin) in a school who have mothers with low levels of education.

The objective is to examine the extent to which concentration measured in these terms affects student outcomes in general, and those of the immigrant students in particular.

Table A5.2 and Chart A5.2 provide summary statistics for these measures. They provide data on the percentage of all immigrant students who are in the high-concentration quartile, according to the measures listed previously, and what share they represent among all students in the quartiles. The figure highlights the relationship between these three measures of concentration across countries.

Note that if the distribution of the immigrant students across quartiles were the same as that for non-immigrants, each quartile would contain 25% of both immigrant and non-immigrant students, and the share of the immigrant students in each quartile would be the same as their share of all students. As is evident from Table A5.2, the observed situation is rather far from this zero hypothesis.

Not surprisingly, the highest concentrations of immigrant students occur for those measures which are themselves based on immigrant characteristics. These characteristics tend to "push" schools with higher percentages of immigrant students into the higher quartiles. For example, in all countries but Luxembourg and Switzerland, more than 50% of the immigrant students are in the high-immigrant concentration quartile. This percentage is higher than 75% in Argentina, the Czech Republic, Estonia, Finland, Iceland and the United Kingdom. In Brazil, 100% of the immigrant students are in the high-immigrant concentration quartile. Immigrant students represent more than 50% of the students in this high-immigrant concentration quartile in Australia, Canada, Luxembourg, New Zealand and the United States.

In the quartile with the highest percentage of students speaking another language at home, around three-quarters of countries have more than 50% of immigrant students included in this quartile. Less than 25% of immigrant students in Brazil and more than 75% of the immigrant students in Finland and the United Kingdom are in this quartile. Immigrant students represent more than 50% of the students in this top quartile in Canada, Luxembourg and the United States.

The same sort of "push effect" is not in principle present when the quartiles are defined on the basis of an external factor, such as the education level of the student's mother. In this case, which does not explicitly include any reference to immigrant characteristics, the fourth quartile also contains significant shares of immigrant students. Across OECD countries, 36% of immigrant students are in the high-concentration quartile of students whose mothers have low levels of education, ranging from around 10% in Portugal to over 55% in the Netherlands.

Chart A5.2. Percentage of all immigrant students and of immigrant students among all students in the top quartile for the three measures of student concentration in schools

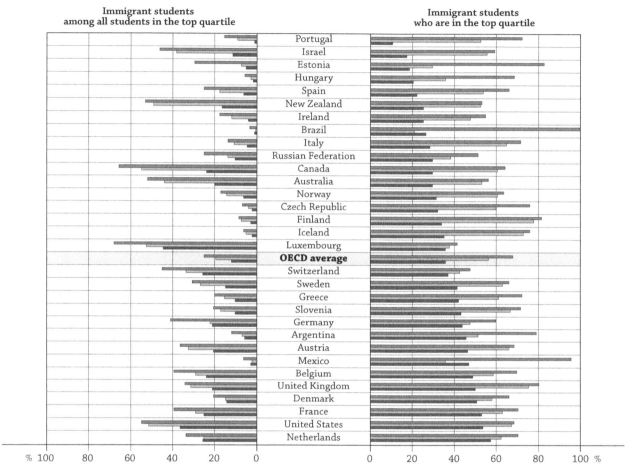

■ Concentration of immigrant students in schools
□ Concentration of immigrant students speaking another language at home
■ Concentration of students with low-educated mothers

Note: A student with a low-educated mother is one whose mother has not attained an upper secondary education.
Countries are ranked in ascending order of the percentage of immigrant students in the top quartile of the measure of school concentration of students with low-educated mothers.
Source: OECD, *PISA 2009 Database*, Table A5.2.
StatLink http://dx.doi.org/10.1787/888932661858

How close is the association between these various concentration measures and reading performance of immigrant students? Contrary to what one might expect, the percentage of students from disadvantaged backgrounds (e.g. with low-educated mothers) in a school is more highly negatively correlated with individual reading performance for the immigrant students in all countries assessed, except Estonia (Chart A5.1) than the two other concentration measures. The percentage of children in a particular school who mostly speak a foreign language at home is next in terms of the strength of the correlation, while the percentage of immigrants is the weakest covariate of the three. In many European countries, the association between immigrant outcomes and school disadvantage is especially high. The exceptions are the Nordic countries, Ireland and Spain, although outcomes for immigrant students in these countries are not always favourable compared to those of non-immigrant students.

Following this initial result, the analysis now turns to examine students in schools that have a high concentration of students whose mothers have low level of education. These schools are referred to as "disadvantaged schools".

A5

In many countries, the educational attainment of immigrants is lower than that of non-immigrants, and the fact that one finds relatively more of their children in disadvantaged schools might simply be a reflection of this. But the story is not so simple. A higher proportion of immigrant students with low-educated mothers than of non-immigrant students with low-educated mothers – 56% and 50%, respectively – are in disadvantaged schools in most countries. The exceptions are Ireland, Israel, Italy, New Zealand, Portugal and Spain.

Chart A5.3. **Percentage of students by mothers' education in disadvantaged schools**

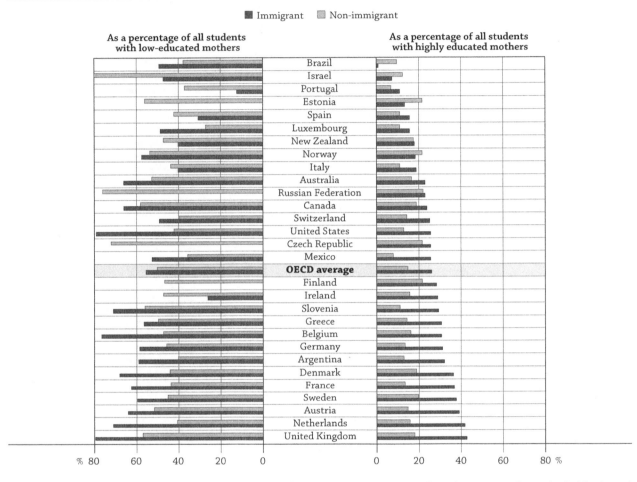

Note: A student with a low-educated mother is one whose mother has not attained an upper secondary education. A student with a highly educated mother is one whose mother has attained a tertiary education.
Countries are ranked in ascending order of the percentage of immigrant students with highly educated mothers in disadvantaged schools.
Source: OECD, *PISA 2009 Database*, Table A5.3.
StatLink 🔗 http://dx.doi.org/10.1787/888932661877

What is even more striking, however, is the even stronger over-representation of immigrant students with highly educated mothers in disadvantaged schools in all countries except Brazil, Estonia, Israel, and Norway (Table A5.3). In Austria, Italy, Luxembourg and the Netherlands, there are in relative terms more than twice as many immigrant students with highly educated mothers, compared to non-immigrant students with highly educated mothers, in disadvantaged schools. Across OECD countries, 26% of students with highly educated mothers are immigrant students in disadvantaged schools, and 14% of students with highly educated mothers are non-immigrant students in disadvantaged schools. Recall that the disadvantage quartiles are characterised not by immigrant characteristics but, rather, by maternal educational disadvantage. The question then is: why the over-representation of immigrant students in disadvantaged schools, at all parental educational levels?

The primary determinant of the socio-economic composition of a neighbourhood is housing costs, and some arriving immigrants may not always have the luxury of choosing their housing freely, either because of more limited funds, lower salaries or because of discrimination in the housing market. The choice of a neighbourhood may initially be motivated as much by the wish to be living near co-nationals or co-ethnics as by the affordability of housing. The two are often linked. The initial choice of housing may not be seen as definitive by the migrant, but may become so because of persistent low income or discrimination in housing, a reluctance to move from what has become a familiar environment, or simply inertia, among other reasons.

OECD research shows, for example, that highly educated immigrants more often tend to be overqualified for the jobs they are doing than is the case for non-immigrants (OECD, 2007). Overqualification is likely to be associated with lower salaries, which would make it more difficult to find housing in less disadvantaged neighbourhoods. It is indeed generally the case that immigrant students in disadvantaged schools, as well as those with highly educated parents, are more often from families with low occupational status than students whose parents are non-immigrants (Chart A5.4).

Chart A5.4. Percentage of students in disadvantaged schools with highly educated mothers from families with low occupational status, by immigrant status

As a percentage of all immigrant and non-immigrant students in disadvantaged schools

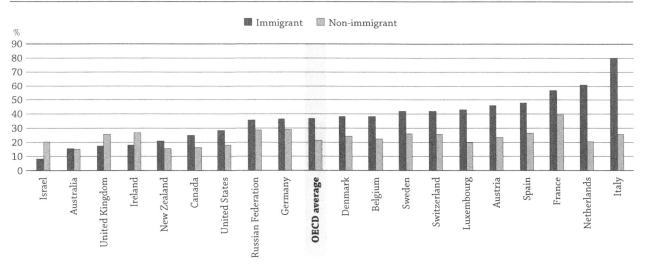

Note: A student with a highly educated mother is one whose mother has attained a tertiary education. Students with low occupational status families are those with a HISEI (Highest International Social and Economic Index) value lower than 40.
Countries are ranked in ascending order of the percentage of immigrant students.
Source: OECD, *PISA 2009 Database*, Table A5.3.
StatLink ᴹˢᴾ http://dx.doi.org/10.1787/888932661896

What is the impact of attending a disadvantaged school on reading performance, and in particular, the impact at different maternal educational attainment levels? The following analysis first shows the association between students attending disadvantaged schools and their reading performance, and then examines the association of their mother's educational attainment and their reading performance.

Chart A5.5 shows reading score differences between students who are in advantaged versus disadvantaged school quartiles and students with highly versus low-educated mothers. The comparison pertains to all students, not only students of immigrant background, to give a general picture of how well national education systems address educational disadvantage in general. For many countries, the picture is not always a positive one.

Indeed, for many students, whether they live in OECD member countries or not, the differences in reading scores associated with attending a disadvantaged school is much larger than those between students with highly versus low-educated mothers. Across OECD countries, the gap between students attending disadvantaged versus advantaged schools is 77 score points, near the equivalent of two school years, and the performance gap between students with low- versus highly educated mothers is 67 score points.

The school disadvantage effect is often substantially stronger than the family background effect. In some OECD countries, including France, Italy, Japan, Luxembourg, Mexico, the Netherlands, Slovenia and Switzerland, and among other G20 countries, such as Argentina, Brazil and Shanghai (China), the school disadvantage effect is even larger than one school year. There are very large differences in scores between schools where there are many students whose mothers have low levels of education and schools where there are very few, except in the Nordic and Eastern European countries included in this analysis (excluding Slovenia), and some countries with a long tradition of attracting immigrants such as Australia, Canada and New Zealand – the effect of parental educational attainment on reading performance is more important than the effect of school disadvantage. In some countries, the school disadvantage effect can be the product of a selection of students into different types of schools based on their academic performance.

Chart A5.5. Difference in scores between students in the top versus bottom school disadvantage quartiles, and those whose mothers have high versus low levels of education

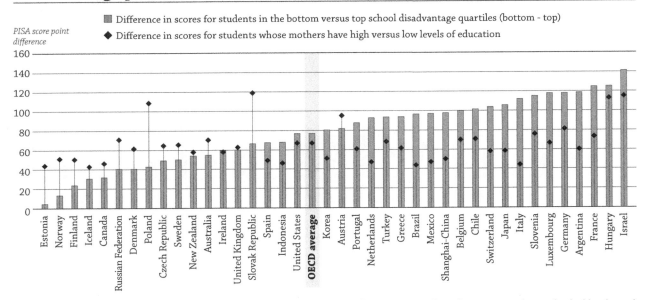

Note: A student with a low-educated mother is one whose mother has not attained an upper secondary education. A student with a highly educated mother is one whose mother has attained a tertiary education.
Countries are ranked in ascending order of the score point difference between top and bottom quartile.
Source: OECD, *PISA 2009 Database*, Table A5.4.
StatLink ᵐᵃˢᵖ http://dx.doi.org/10.1787/888932661915Q

These results highlight the fact that education and social policies interact to limit opportunities for school success among immigrant students. The policy choices available to address the issue of disadvantage are diverse.

One can attempt to overcome the adverse effects of the concentration of disadvantage by investing more in disadvantaged schools. There are a number of ways this could be done, such as attempting to attract better teachers, reducing class sizes, and providing additional remedial or tutoring help. Whether these measures would be effective for 15-year-old immigrant students is a point of empirical research. It is likely that intervention would need to occur much earlier, perhaps even at the pre-primary level. Some attempts to increase funding for disadvantaged schools have not always yielded the expected returns (Bénabou, Kramarz and Prost, 2004).

Other policy options would aim to reduce the concentration of disadvantage itself, for example through a broader dispersal of subsidised low-cost housing or through school choice policies. Such policies are broad in scope and would have implications for other, less disadvantaged neighbourhoods and schools. Again, these would undoubtedly be more effective if implemented early in students' school careers. School choice policies could quickly become controversial if, for example, they involved a departure from neighbourhood schools for young children.

The choices here are not simple ones. Increasing funding for disadvantaged schools may be a more feasible measure politically, but may not be the most effective, and it may be less possible during times of resource constraints. It is clear that attending a disadvantaged school has on average an adverse effect on all students, whatever their origin and whatever the educational attainment of their mothers. If the concentration of disadvantage is not an immigrant-specific phenomenon, immigrant students are still more affected, simply because a higher proportion of them come from disadvantaged families. Addressing the issue of school disadvantage for immigrant students in practice would mean addressing it for all students. This, however, is an objective that goes beyond the immediate goal of successfully integrating immigrant students in school.

Definitions

PISA distinguishes between three types of student immigrant status: *i)* students without an immigrant background, also referred to as **non-immigrant students**, are students who were born in the country where they were assessed by PISA or who had at least one parent born in the country; *ii)* second-generation students are students who were born in the country of assessment but whose parents are foreign-born; and *iii)* first-generation students are foreign-born students whose parents are also foreign-born. In this indicator, **immigrant students** include the students who are first- or second-generation immigrants.

Each sampled school in a country has been placed into a quartile defined according to the estimated (weighted) percentage of students in the school with mothers with less than upper secondary attainment. These students are referred to as students with **low-educated mothers**. The **disadvantaged schools** correspond to the 4th quartile, with the largest proportion of students with low-educated mothers. The advantaged schools are in the 1st quartile, with the smallest proportion of students with low-educated mothers. The students whose mothers have a tertiary education are referred to as students with **highly educated mothers**.

In this indicator, **low-status occupation** is defined as an HISEI (highest international socio-economic index of occupational status) less than 40, which roughly corresponds to service workers (other major groups included are agricultural workers, production and related workers, transport equipment operators and labourers). Occupational data for both the student's father and student's mother were obtained by asking open-ended questions. The response were coded to four-digit ISCO codes (ILO, 1990) and then mapped to the international socio-economic index of occupational status (ISEI) (Ganzeboom, et al., 1992). Three indices were obtained from these scores: father's occupational status (BFMJ); mother's occupational status (BMMJ); and the highest occupational status of parents (HISEI) which corresponds to the higher ISEI score of either parent or to the only available parent's ISEI score. For all three indices, higher ISEI scores indicate higher levels of occupational status. For more information, see: *http://arno.uvt.nl/show.cgi?fid=63721.*

In PISA 2009, **one school year's progress** corresponds to an average of 39 score points on the PISA reading scale. This was determined by calculating the difference in scores among the sizeable number of 15-year-olds in 32 OECD countries who were enrolled in at least two different grade levels.

Methodology

PISA covers students who are between 15 years 3 months and 16 years 2 months of age at the time of assessment, and who have completed at least 6 years of formal schooling, regardless of the type of institution in which they are enrolled and of whether they are in full-time or part-time education, whether they attend general or vocational programmes, and whether they attend public, private or foreign schools within the country (OECD, 2012b).

A5

For further information on the PISA assessment instruments and the methods used in PISA see the PISA website, *www.pisa.oecd.org*.

The statistical data for Israel are supplied by and are under the responsibility of the relevant Israeli authorities. The use of such data by the OECD is without prejudice to the status of the Golan Heights, East Jerusalem and Israeli settlements in the West Bank under the terms of international law.

References

Bénabou, R., F. Kramarz and C. Prost (2004), "Zones d'éducation prioritaire: quels moyens pour quels résultats?", Économie et Statistique, No. 380, INSEE, Paris.

Ganzeboom, H.B.G., P.M. De Graaf and D.J. Treiman (1992), "A Standard International Socio-economic Index of Occupational Status", *Social Science Research*, Vol. 21, No. 1, pp. 1-56.

ILO (International Labour Organization) (1990), "International Standard Classification of Occupations", ISCO-88, Geneva.

OECD (2007), "Matching Educational Background and Employment: A Challenge for Immigrants In Host Countries", in *International Migration Outlook 2007*, OECD Publishing.

OECD (2012a), *Untapped Skills: Realising the Potential of Immigrant Students*, PISA, OECD Publishing.

OECD (2012b), *PISA 2009 Technical Report*, PISA OECD Publishing.

Szulkin, R. and J.O. Jonsson (2007), "Ethnic Segregation and Educational Outcomes in Swedish comprehensive Schools", SULCIS Working Paper, Vol. 2007/2, Stockholm University.

Table A5.1. Correlations between reading performance and various measures of student concentration in schools
Results based on students' self-reports

	Pearson correlation between student performance in reading and concentration measures in schools											
	Immigrant students						Non-immigrant students					
	Percentage of immigrant students in schools		Percentage of immigrant students speaking another language at home		Percentage of students with low-educated mothers[1]		Percentage of immigrant students in schools		Percentage of immigrant students speaking another language at home		Percentage of students with low-educated mothers[1]	
	Corr.	S.E.	Corr.	S.E.	Corr.	S.E.	Corr.	S.E.	Corr.	S.E.	Corr.	S.E.
OECD Australia	0.15	(0.10)	0.13	(0.12)	**-0.24**	(0.05)	**0.11**	(0.03)	**0.09**	(0.04)	**-0.20**	(0.02)
Austria	**-0.29**	(0.08)	**-0.25**	(0.08)	**-0.46**	(0.06)	-0.05	(0.04)	-0.04	(0.05)	**-0.26**	(0.05)
Belgium	**-0.26**	(0.07)	**-0.26**	(0.07)	**-0.35**	(0.05)	**-0.17**	(0.03)	**-0.17**	(0.03)	**-0.34**	(0.03)
Canada	-0.03	(0.04)	0.01	(0.04)	**-0.15**	(0.05)	**0.12**	(0.02)	**0.11**	(0.02)	**-0.12**	(0.02)
Chile	c	c	c	c	c	c	c	c	c	c	**-0.49**	(0.02)
Czech Republic	0.16	(0.08)	**0.14**	(0.07)	**-0.28**	(0.10)	0.07	(0.05)	0.09	(0.05)	**-0.22**	(0.04)
Denmark	**-0.23**	(0.04)	**-0.15**	(0.05)	**-0.23**	(0.04)	-0.03	(0.03)	-0.02	(0.03)	**-0.15**	(0.03)
Estonia	0.06	(0.08)	-0.06	(0.09)	-0.02	(0.06)	**-0.16**	(0.03)	**-0.07**	(0.03)	**-0.06**	(0.03)
Finland	**-0.30**	(0.11)	**-0.29**	(0.10)	-0.13	(0.11)	0.03	(0.03)	0.02	(0.03)	**-0.09**	(0.03)
France	**-0.26**	(0.10)	-0.14	(0.13)	**-0.45**	(0.07)	**-0.21**	(0.05)	**-0.17**	(0.06)	**-0.47**	(0.06)
Germany	**-0.35**	(0.05)	**-0.22**	(0.05)	**-0.58**	(0.05)	**-0.23**	(0.04)	**-0.21**	(0.05)	**-0.52**	(0.04)
Greece	**-0.25**	(0.05)	**-0.19**	(0.04)	**-0.40**	(0.09)	**-0.16**	(0.04)	**-0.17**	(0.03)	**-0.37**	(0.04)
Hungary	0.01	(0.17)	-0.03	(0.09)	**-0.58**	(0.08)	**0.14**	(0.06)	**0.07**	(0.03)	**-0.57**	(0.02)
Iceland	-0.24	(0.14)	0.16	(0.11)	-0.09	(0.10)	-0.01	(0.02)	0.00	(0.02)	**-0.12**	(0.02)
Ireland	-0.14	(0.07)	**-0.21**	(0.07)	-0.10	(0.08)	0.06	(0.04)	0.00	(0.04)	**-0.28**	(0.03)
Israel	-0.11	(0.06)	0.00	(0.06)	**-0.38**	(0.06)	**0.10**	(0.04)	**0.10**	(0.04)	**-0.49**	(0.03)
Italy	**-0.32**	(0.03)	**-0.32**	(0.04)	**-0.49**	(0.03)	**-0.12**	(0.03)	**-0.13**	(0.02)	**-0.47**	(0.02)
Japan	c	c	c	c	c	c	c	c	c	c	**-0.41**	(0.04)
Korea	c	c	c	c	c	c	c	c	c	c	**-0.40**	(0.04)
Luxembourg	0.02	(0.02)	**-0.36**	(0.02)	**-0.52**	(0.01)	**-0.31**	(0.02)	**-0.36**	(0.02)	**-0.40**	(0.02)
Mexico	**-0.38**	(0.10)	**-0.15**	(0.05)	**-0.43**	(0.11)	**-0.24**	(0.03)	-0.06	(0.04)	**-0.45**	(0.02)
Netherlands	**-0.27**	(0.11)	**-0.22**	(0.10)	**-0.34**	(0.09)	**-0.17**	(0.05)	**-0.12**	(0.05)	**-0.35**	(0.05)
New Zealand	**-0.13**	(0.04)	**-0.14**	(0.04)	**-0.24**	(0.05)	0.07	(0.03)	0.04	(0.03)	**-0.23**	(0.04)
Norway	-0.14	(0.08)	-0.13	(0.07)	**-0.19**	(0.06)	0.03	(0.03)	0.02	(0.03)	**-0.06**	(0.03)
Poland	c	c	c	c	c	c	c	c	c	c	**-0.17**	(0.03)
Portugal	**-0.32**	(0.08)	**-0.28**	(0.06)	**-0.33**	(0.07)	-0.01	(0.03)	**-0.10**	(0.04)	**-0.39**	(0.03)
Slovak Republic	c	c	c	c	c	c	c	c	c	c	**-0.33**	(0.04)
Slovenia	**-0.34**	(0.06)	**-0.34**	(0.07)	**-0.40**	(0.05)	**-0.24**	(0.01)	**-0.24**	(0.01)	**-0.51**	(0.01)
Spain	-0.05	(0.05)	**-0.18**	(0.04)	**-0.23**	(0.04)	-0.03	(0.02)	**-0.06**	(0.02)	**-0.31**	(0.03)
Sweden	**-0.23**	(0.07)	**-0.18**	(0.05)	**-0.22**	(0.04)	-0.03	(0.03)	-0.04	(0.03)	**-0.15**	(0.03)
Switzerland	**-0.18**	(0.07)	**-0.29**	(0.03)	**-0.44**	(0.03)	**-0.15**	(0.03)	**-0.18**	(0.04)	**-0.38**	(0.03)
Turkey	c	c	c	c	c	c	c	c	c	c	**-0.47**	(0.03)
United Kingdom	-0.13	(0.09)	**-0.26**	(0.08)	**-0.29**	(0.06)	**-0.07**	(0.03)	**-0.08**	(0.04)	**-0.21**	(0.03)
United States	**-0.10**	(0.04)	**-0.11**	(0.04)	**-0.25**	(0.05)	**-0.08**	(0.03)	**-0.08**	(0.04)	**-0.26**	(0.03)
OECD average	**-0.17**	(0.02)	**-0.15**	(0.01)	**-0.31**	(0.01)	**-0.06**	(0.01)	**-0.06**	(0.01)	**-0.32**	(0.01)
EU21 average	**-0.18**	(0.02)	**-0.20**	(0.02)	**-0.34**	(0.02)	**-0.09**	(0.01)	**-0.09**	(0.01)	**-0.32**	(0.01)
Other G20 Argentina	0.16	(0.17)	0.10	(0.14)	**-0.29**	(0.13)	-0.05	(0.04)	0.01	(0.08)	**-0.47**	(0.03)
Brazil	0.02	(0.15)	0.07	(0.19)	-0.15	(0.22)	**-0.15**	(0.03)	0.01	(0.05)	**-0.43**	(0.02)
Indonesia	c	c	c	c	c	c	c	c	c	c	**-0.40**	(0.05)
Russian Federation	-0.25	(0.13)	**-0.30**	(0.10)	**-0.29**	(0.09)	-0.08	(0.05)	**-0.13**	(0.05)	**-0.16**	(0.03)
Shanghai-China	c	c	c	c	c	c	c	c	c	c	**-0.46**	(0.04)
G20 average	**-0.14**	(0.03)	**-0.11**	(0.03)	**-0.33**	(0.03)	**-0.09**	(0.01)	**-0.06**	(0.01)	**-0.37**	(0.01)

Note: Values that are statistically significant are indicated in bold.
1. Low-educated mothers are those with an educational attainment level lower than upper secondary education.
Source: OECD, *PISA 2009 Database.*
Please refer to the Reader's Guide for information concerning the symbols replacing missing data.
StatLink ᴹˢᴾ http://dx.doi.org/10.1787/888932664860

A5

Table A5.2. **Concentration of immigrant students in schools according to various characteristics**
Results based on students' self-reports

	Percentage of all immigrant students who are in the top quartile						Immigrant students as a percentage of all students in the top quartile					
	Concentration quartiles defined by:						Concentration quartiles defined by:					
	Percentage of immigrant students in schools		Percentage of immigrant students speaking another language at home		Percentage of students with low-educated mothers[1]		Percentage of immigrant students in schools		Percentage of immigrant students speaking another language at home		Percentage of students with low-educated mothers[1]	
	%	S.E.	%	S.E.	%	S.E.	%	S.E.	%	S.E.	%	S.E.
OECD												
Australia	55.9	(3.7)	53.4	(4.3)	30.0	(4.2)	51.6	(2.0)	44.0	(3.5)	20.1	(3.7)
Austria	68.3	(4.4)	65.8	(5.3)	46.5	(5.9)	36.1	(2.3)	32.2	(3.0)	20.5	(3.4)
Belgium	69.6	(3.4)	58.4	(5.1)	48.6	(4.4)	39.0	(2.6)	29.0	(3.2)	23.7	(3.2)
Canada	64.0	(4.1)	60.4	(4.5)	29.8	(4.4)	65.4	(2.0)	54.4	(4.1)	23.7	(3.9)
Chile	c	c	c	c	c	c	1.7	(0.3)	0.5	(0.2)	0.2	(0.1)
Czech Republic	76.0	(5.8)	59.8	(7.4)	32.1	(8.8)	6.5	(0.5)	3.9	(0.7)	2.3	(0.8)
Denmark	66.3	(3.5)	58.0	(4.8)	51.0	(4.0)	20.6	(1.7)	14.9	(1.9)	13.9	(1.9)
Estonia	82.4	(2.6)	29.7	(7.1)	18.5	(6.1)	29.5	(2.3)	7.3	(2.3)	4.9	(2.0)
Finland	81.2	(4.2)	78.0	(5.4)	34.3	(8.4)	8.5	(0.7)	7.5	(0.9)	2.9	(1.0)
France	70.3	(4.8)	63.3	(5.8)	53.0	(6.7)	39.0	(3.0)	29.2	(4.0)	24.7	(4.8)
Germany	59.7	(4.7)	47.7	(5.4)	43.9	(4.9)	40.9	(2.9)	21.8	(2.8)	21.1	(3.2)
Greece	72.0	(4.0)	61.3	(5.7)	42.1	(5.8)	19.9	(1.7)	15.0	(2.2)	10.3	(2.0)
Hungary	68.3	(6.5)	35.7	(6.6)	20.8	(4.9)	5.5	(0.5)	2.7	(0.6)	1.4	(0.5)
Iceland	76.2	(5.7)	73.1	(6.0)	35.1	(6.1)	6.3	(0.9)	5.3	(0.9)	2.4	(0.6)
Ireland	55.0	(5.9)	47.8	(5.7)	25.6	(5.0)	17.3	(1.0)	12.1	(1.8)	3.7	(1.3)
Israel	59.4	(4.7)	55.4	(5.2)	17.5	(4.2)	45.9	(2.6)	37.9	(4.2)	11.2	(3.5)
Italy	71.9	(2.3)	64.8	(2.7)	28.4	(3.2)	13.3	(0.5)	10.9	(0.7)	4.3	(0.7)
Japan	c	c	c	c	c	c	1.1	(0.2)	0.4	(0.1)	0.4	(0.2)
Korea	c	c	c	c	c	c	0.1	(0.1)	0.1	(0.1)	0.0	(0.0)
Luxembourg	41.7	(0.8)	37.5	(0.8)	35.9	(0.8)	67.6	(1.2)	52.4	(1.1)	44.2	(1.1)
Mexico	95.8	(1.2)	36.0	(3.6)	47.1	(5.5)	6.0	(0.4)	2.0	(0.3)	2.7	(0.4)
Netherlands	70.2	(4.8)	62.4	(6.8)	57.5	(6.6)	33.7	(4.2)	25.2	(5.2)	25.6	(4.9)
New Zealand	53.3	(3.3)	52.6	(3.3)	25.2	(3.5)	52.7	(1.4)	48.9	(2.0)	16.5	(2.9)
Norway	63.8	(5.1)	60.5	(5.1)	31.4	(5.5)	17.2	(1.6)	14.3	(2.0)	5.9	(1.8)
Poland	c	c	c	c	c	c	0.1	(0.1)	0.0	(0.0)	0.0	(0.0)
Portugal	72.3	(3.4)	52.3	(6.8)	10.5	(2.7)	15.3	(1.0)	8.8	(1.7)	1.0	(0.5)
Slovak Republic	c	c	c	c	c	c	2.0	(0.4)	0.9	(0.3)	0.9	(0.4)
Slovenia	71.9	(2.5)	66.6	(3.1)	43.2	(2.7)	20.1	(1.2)	17.0	(1.2)	10.4	(0.9)
Spain	66.2	(3.3)	54.1	(4.4)	22.3	(3.7)	25.2	(1.1)	17.4	(1.7)	6.2	(1.3)
Sweden	66.0	(5.0)	62.9	(4.8)	41.6	(6.6)	30.6	(2.8)	26.7	(2.9)	14.8	(3.5)
Switzerland	47.5	(4.0)	42.9	(4.0)	37.0	(3.8)	44.7	(1.5)	33.4	(3.7)	25.3	(3.1)
Turkey	c	c	c	c	c	c	2.1	(0.5)	0.6	(0.2)	0.2	(0.1)
United Kingdom	80.0	(2.7)	75.0	(4.2)	50.1	(6.7)	34.3	(2.8)	31.2	(3.4)	20.9	(3.8)
United States	68.7	(4.2)	67.5	(4.8)	53.5	(6.4)	54.8	(2.2)	51.2	(3.5)	36.4	(4.8)
OECD average	67.6	(0.8)	56.5	(1.0)	36.2	(1.0)	25.1	(0.3)	19.4	(0.4)	11.8	(0.4)
EU21 average	68.9	(1.0)	56.9	(1.2)	37.1	(1.3)	24.0	(0.4)	17.4	(0.5)	12.3	(0.5)
Other G20												
Argentina	79.0	(5.0)	51.5	(9.7)	45.5	(9.3)	11.8	(1.5)	6.7	(2.0)	5.4	(1.5)
Brazil	100.0	(0.0)	21.2	(8.5)	26.4	(9.8)	3.0	(0.4)	0.6	(0.3)	0.8	(0.3)
Indonesia	c	c	c	c	c	c	1.2	(0.4)	1.1	(0.4)	0.3	(0.2)
Russian Federation	51.3	(6.6)	38.3	(7.7)	29.7	(8.2)	25.0	(2.9)	13.7	(4.1)	10.0	(4.6)
Shanghai-China	c	c	c	c	c	c	2.1	(0.3)	0.8	(0.2)	1.1	(0.3)
G20 average	72.4	(1.2)	52.6	(1.8)	39.8	(2.0)	22.0	(0.4)	16.8	(0.6)	10.7	(0.7)

1. Low-educated mothers are those with an educational attainment level lower than upper secondary education.
Source: OECD, *PISA 2009 Database.*
Please refer to the Reader's Guide for information concerning the symbols replacing missing data.
StatLink ⤳ http://dx.doi.org/10.1787/888932664879

Table A5.3. Percentage of students in disadvantaged schools, by educational level of their mother, and from low occupational status families

Results based on students' self-reports

A5

	Students with low-educated mothers in disadvantaged schools, as a percentage of all students with low-educated mothers[1]				Students with highly educated mothers in disadvantaged schools, as a percentage of all students with highly educated mothers[2]				Students in disadvantaged schools with highly educated mothers from families with low occupational status[3]			
	Immigrant students		Non-immigrant students		Immigrant students		Non-immigrant students		Immigrant students		Non-immigrant students	
	%	S.E.	%	S.E.	%	S.E.	%	S.E.	%	S.E.	%	S.E.
OECD												
Australia	66.0	(6.3)	52.6	(4.3)	22.7	(4.0)	16.6	(2.3)	15.5	(2.7)	15.1	(1.6)
Austria	64.2	(5.7)	51.7	(6.4)	39.1	(7.3)	14.5	(2.8)	46.2	(7.9)	23.6	(4.3)
Belgium	76.5	(3.7)	47.0	(4.3)	30.6	(4.5)	16.0	(2.2)	38.2	(5.5)	22.7	(2.2)
Canada	66.4	(6.3)	58.3	(4.4)	23.8	(3.9)	18.6	(2.0)	25.1	(2.6)	16.4	(1.6)
Chile	c	c	46.7	(5.2)	c	c	7.3	(1.4)	m	m	29.9	(4.3)
Czech Republic	c	c	72.2	(4.7)	25.5	(9.5)	21.6	(3.5)	c	c	16.6	(3.5)
Denmark	68.3	(5.0)	44.4	(5.1)	36.4	(4.6)	18.6	(3.0)	38.2	(5.7)	24.4	(2.8)
Estonia	c	c	56.1	(5.0)	13.4	(5.4)	21.5	(2.8)	c	c	17.9	(2.3)
Finland	c	c	46.6	(5.2)	28.6	(8.0)	21.7	(3.3)	c	c	21.8	(1.9)
France	62.8	(6.4)	43.8	(5.3)	36.5	(7.4)	13.1	(2.4)	56.9	(8.2)	39.4	(4.9)
Germany	58.5	(6.4)	45.8	(4.9)	31.3	(5.3)	13.0	(2.5)	36.6	(6.8)	29.1	(5.6)
Greece	56.8	(10.7)	49.6	(4.6)	30.6	(4.3)	14.1	(2.7)	c	c	15.5	(4.6)
Hungary	c	c	60.8	(4.6)	c	c	9.1	(1.3)	c	c	25.0	(3.9)
Iceland	c	c	43.2	(1.9)	c	c	17.6	(0.8)	c	c	6.4	(1.6)
Ireland	26.2	(8.8)	47.2	(5.6)	28.6	(6.0)	15.6	(3.2)	18.1	(8.2)	26.9	(3.1)
Israel	47.2	(7.1)	80.6	(2.7)	7.3	(3.0)	12.3	(1.6)	8.3	(4.1)	20.5	(3.6)
Italy	40.1	(5.4)	43.7	(2.1)	18.7	(4.2)	11.0	(1.0)	80.4	(6.5)	26.0	(2.6)
Japan	c	c	66.0	(4.4)	c	c	14.9	(1.6)	c	c	28.7	(2.6)
Korea	m	m	54.7	(5.0)	c	c	14.7	(2.8)	m	m	16.1	(3.8)
Luxembourg	48.7	(1.8)	27.4	(2.2)	15.7	(1.8)	11.1	(0.9)	43.0	(6.6)	19.9	(4.2)
Mexico	52.5	(5.9)	35.7	(2.2)	25.8	(7.3)	7.5	(0.7)	c	c	34.2	(2.6)
Netherlands	71.4	(6.0)	40.6	(5.2)	41.7	(9.1)	15.3	(2.7)	61.2	(8.4)	20.8	(2.9)
New Zealand	40.1	(6.0)	47.3	(4.7)	18.0	(3.0)	17.3	(2.7)	20.9	(4.9)	15.6	(3.1)
Norway	57.8	(8.0)	53.6	(5.6)	18.1	(4.8)	21.4	(3.0)	c	c	10.4	(1.4)
Poland	c	c	55.3	(5.3)	m	m	14.9	(3.1)	m	m	5.1	(2.1)
Portugal	12.4	(3.8)	37.0	(4.2)	10.8	(3.3)	6.7	(1.2)	c	c	24.1	(4.6)
Slovak Republic	c	c	83.1	(3.7)	c	c	18.4	(3.0)	m	m	22.5	(2.6)
Slovenia	71.1	(4.5)	56.0	(2.6)	29.4	(6.6)	11.0	(0.8)	c	c	11.6	(2.4)
Spain	30.8	(5.0)	42.3	(4.1)	15.3	(3.6)	10.7	(1.5)	48.1	(9.9)	26.4	(3.9)
Sweden	59.7	(8.1)	45.0	(5.1)	37.5	(6.7)	19.6	(2.8)	42.1	(4.9)	26.3	(2.3)
Switzerland	49.3	(4.3)	39.7	(4.5)	25.1	(3.9)	14.2	(2.2)	42.2	(5.9)	25.7	(4.5)
Turkey	c	c	30.0	(3.8)	c	c	2.7	(0.9)	m	m	c	c
United Kingdom	79.8	(8.1)	57.1	(4.6)	42.5	(7.0)	17.7	(2.3)	17.5	(3.5)	25.7	(2.6)
United States	79.0	(4.2)	42.3	(6.4)	25.4	(5.7)	12.8	(2.5)	28.5	(4.9)	18.0	(2.2)
OECD average	55.9	(1.3)	50.1	(0.8)	26.1	(1.1)	14.5	(0.4)	37.0	(1.5)	21.5	(0.6)
EU21 average	55.2	(1.6)	50.1	(1.0)	28.4	(1.4)	15.0	(0.5)	43.9	(2.0)	22.4	(0.8)
Other G20												
Argentina	59.1	(10.1)	40.2	(5.3)	32.2	(9.8)	12.7	(2.1)	c	c	45.0	(3.9)
Brazil	49.1	(15.1)	37.6	(3.5)	0.9	(1.0)	9.6	(1.4)	c	c	41.5	(3.6)
Indonesia	c	c	35.5	(4.6)	c	c	4.6	(1.4)	m	m	c	c
Russian Federation	c	c	75.9	(6.1)	23.0	(5.6)	21.9	(3.6)	35.9	(7.2)	28.9	(2.3)
Shanghai-China	c	c	44.7	(4.8)	c	c	8.6	(1.6)	c	c	27.0	(4.1)
G20 average	60.8	(2.7)	47.4	(1.2)	26.0	(1.9)	12.2	(0.5)	40.1	(2.3)	28.9	(1.0)

Note: Disadvantaged schools are those in the country-specific fourth quartile of the concentration measure of students with low-educated mothers at the school level (these are the 25% of school with the highest proportion of students with low-educated mothers).

1. Students with low-educated mothers are those whose mother has not attained an upper secondary education.

2. Students with highly educated mothers are those whose mother has attained a tertiary education.

3. Students from families with low occupational status are those with a HISEI lower than 40. HISEI is the highest international social and economic index.

Source: OECD, *PISA 2009 Database.*

Please refer to the Reader's Guide for information concerning the symbols replacing missing data.

StatLink ᵐˢᴸ http://dx.doi.org/10.1787/888932664898

A5

Table A5.4. Performance among students in the school disadvantage quartiles and those whose mothers have high or low levels of education

Results based on students' self-reports

	Mean performance on the reading scale of students...												Difference in scores between...			
	In the bottom quartile of school disadvantage		In the second quartile of school disadvantage		In the third quartile of school disadvantage		In the top quartile of school disadvantage		With low-educated mothers		With highly educated mothers		Students in the bottom and top school disadvantage quartiles		Students whose mothers have high or low levels of education	
	Mean score	S.E.	Mean score	S.E.	Mean score	S.E.	Mean score	S.E.	Mean score	S.E.	Mean score	S.E.	Score dif.	S.E.	Score dif.	S.E.
Australia	544	(5.3)	523	(4.5)	506	(4.8)	489	(6.0)	471	(4.3)	541	(2.8)	**55**	(7.9)	**70**	(4.3)
Austria	520	(7.3)	493	(9.5)	499	(8.8)	438	(10.3)	404	(6.6)	499	(4.0)	**82**	(13.6)	**95**	(7.1)
Belgium	563	(7.9)	534	(6.1)	499	(6.3)	463	(6.4)	465	(3.9)	535	(2.5)	**100**	(10.8)	**70**	(4.5)
Canada	544	(3.5)	530	(3.0)	527	(4.5)	512	(3.7)	491	(4.7)	537	(1.7)	**31**	(5.0)	**46**	(4.8)
Chile	511	(5.5)	462	(5.7)	432	(5.1)	409	(5.6)	416	(3.4)	487	(3.6)	**102**	(7.6)	**71**	(4.4)
Czech Republic	503	(6.4)	502	(5.7)	491	(8.7)	454	(7.3)	432	(7.4)	496	(4.9)	**49**	(9.7)	**65**	(7.9)
Denmark	525	(5.1)	496	(6.0)	487	(4.8)	484	(4.5)	451	(3.7)	512	(2.5)	**40**	(6.7)	**62**	(4.1)
Estonia	506	(5.1)	510	(7.1)	507	(5.4)	502	(3.9)	467	(6.6)	511	(3.4)	4	(6.7)	**44**	(7.0)
Finland	546	(4.2)	537	(4.5)	536	(4.5)	523	(4.3)	496	(4.7)	547	(2.4)	**23**	(5.9)	**50**	(4.5)
France	565	(11.7)	539	(8.1)	477	(9.2)	441	(11.0)	456	(4.6)	529	(4.4)	**125**	(17.7)	**73**	(6.4)
Germany	571	(5.6)	543	(5.6)	518	(7.4)	453	(7.8)	448	(4.2)	529	(4.2)	**118**	(10.0)	**81**	(5.7)
Greece	527	(4.4)	503	(7.4)	494	(6.5)	433	(11.7)	444	(6.2)	506	(3.9)	**94**	(12.4)	**62**	(5.5)
Hungary	566	(5.2)	533	(6.2)	501	(6.1)	440	(6.6)	421	(6.0)	534	(4.6)	**125**	(8.3)	**113**	(7.4)
Iceland	518	(3.0)	504	(2.9)	492	(3.3)	488	(3.2)	477	(3.2)	520	(2.2)	**30**	(4.4)	**43**	(4.1)
Ireland	533	(5.5)	506	(6.1)	488	(8.5)	474	(6.8)	461	(4.0)	519	(3.3)	**60**	(8.7)	**58**	(4.2)
Israel	536	(5.7)	514	(5.3)	474	(8.1)	395	(7.1)	401	(6.3)	516	(3.8)	**141**	(9.1)	**115**	(6.7)
Italy	544	(3.3)	514	(3.7)	478	(4.5)	432	(4.5)	459	(2.6)	503	(2.4)	**112**	(5.6)	**44**	(3.2)
Japan	561	(7.6)	553	(5.6)	519	(6.4)	456	(8.4)	483	(7.3)	542	(3.6)	**106**	(11.2)	**59**	(7.6)
Korea	572	(5.0)	559	(4.7)	540	(6.4)	492	(7.7)	504	(7.2)	555	(4.9)	**80**	(9.3)	**51**	(7.2)
Luxembourg	539	(2.0)	503	(2.1)	425	(2.7)	421	(2.3)	436	(2.6)	503	(2.7)	**118**	(3.1)	**67**	(3.6)
Mexico	485	(3.6)	440	(3.9)	418	(3.1)	388	(4.3)	408	(1.9)	455	(2.4)	**97**	(5.5)	**47**	(2.3)
Netherlands	551	(7.8)	535	(17.1)	498	(10.3)	458	(7.4)	479	(5.8)	526	(5.5)	**93**	(11.1)	**47**	(5.3)
New Zealand	553	(5.5)	542	(6.7)	529	(4.7)	499	(6.9)	493	(4.0)	551	(3.2)	**54**	(9.1)	**58**	(4.5)
Norway	508	(5.0)	511	(5.3)	502	(5.4)	495	(3.9)	465	(6.0)	516	(2.8)	**13**	(6.3)	**51**	(5.7)
Poland	519	(5.4)	503	(6.1)	501	(4.7)	476	(4.2)	444	(5.1)	553	(3.9)	**43**	(7.1)	**109**	(6.4)
Portugal	538	(5.7)	499	(3.7)	478	(6.7)	450	(6.1)	470	(3.2)	531	(4.5)	**88**	(8.7)	**61**	(4.8)
Slovak Republic	514	(5.7)	510	(4.7)	474	(7.8)	447	(8.4)	384	(11.3)	503	(4.2)	**66**	(10.5)	**119**	(11.9)
Slovenia	548	(1.9)	532	(2.5)	464	(1.9)	433	(2.0)	440	(3.8)	516	(2.7)	**115**	(2.8)	**76**	(3.4)
Spain	518	(3.9)	490	(3.4)	471	(4.0)	450	(4.2)	460	(2.5)	509	(2.8)	**68**	(5.6)	**49**	(3.4)
Sweden	526	(6.0)	497	(5.8)	486	(5.4)	476	(5.6)	447	(6.1)	513	(3.2)	**50**	(8.5)	**66**	(6.5)
Switzerland	555	(8.0)	525	(7.5)	483	(4.8)	451	(3.8)	463	(3.9)	522	(3.5)	**104**	(9.2)	**58**	(4.7)
Turkey	527	(7.3)	471	(8.1)	447	(5.7)	434	(4.7)	454	(3.2)	523	(7.5)	**94**	(8.5)	**68**	(7.3)
United Kingdom	531	(5.5)	511	(4.4)	490	(6.4)	471	(6.5)	454	(5.4)	516	(2.7)	**60**	(9.2)	**63**	(6.3)
United States	538	(8.5)	514	(5.4)	483	(7.0)	461	(4.7)	458	(4.3)	525	(4.8)	**77**	(9.7)	**67**	(5.8)
OECD average	535	(1.0)	513	(1.1)	489	(1.1)	458	(1.1)	453	(0.9)	520	(0.6)	**77**	(1.5)	**67**	(1.0)
EU21 average	536	(1.3)	514	(1.5)	489	(1.4)	458	(1.5)	448	(1.2)	518	(0.8)	**78**	(2.0)	**70**	(1.3)
Argentina	481	(8.4)	415	(10.5)	386	(7.7)	362	(9.6)	369	(4.8)	429	(5.6)	**119**	(12.3)	**60**	(6.4)
Brazil	486	(5.7)	412	(8.3)	402	(4.9)	389	(3.8)	393	(2.6)	437	(4.9)	**97**	(6.8)	**44**	(4.9)
Indonesia	442	(8.5)	408	(7.4)	389	(6.2)	374	(5.6)	390	(3.2)	437	(8.3)	**68**	(9.9)	**46**	(8.1)
Russian Federation	472	(5.4)	470	(4.7)	472	(5.9)	432	(7.1)	397	(12.3)	468	(3.2)	**40**	(7.7)	**71**	(12.0)
Shanghai-China	608	(4.9)	568	(5.2)	541	(6.5)	510	(7.2)	532	(3.5)	582	(3.2)	**98**	(9.0)	**50**	(4.8)
G20 average	529	(1.6)	498	(1.5)	475	(1.5)	443	(1.7)	448	(1.3)	507	(1.1)	**86**	(2.4)	**59**	(1.6)

Notes: Disadvantage quartiles are defined at the country level, ranking schools according to the proportion of students with low-educated mothers. The highest disadvantage quartile, the top quartile, is the one with the 25% of schools where the proportion of students with low-educated mothers is highest. The opposite is true for the lowest disadvantaged quartile, the bottom quartile. Low-educated mothers are those with an educational attainment level lower than upper secondary education. Highly educated mothers are those with a tertiary level of education. Values that are statistically significant are indicated in bold.

Source: OECD, *PISA 2009 Database.*

Please refer to the Reader's Guide for information concerning the symbols replacing missing data.

StatLink ᓍᓕᓐᓚ http://dx.doi.org/10.1787/888932664917

TO WHAT EXTENT DOES PARENTS' EDUCATION INFLUENCE ACCESS TO TERTIARY EDUCATION?

- The odds that a 20-34 year-old will attend higher education are low if his or her parents have not completed upper secondary education. On average across OECD countries, young people from families with low levels of education are less than one-half (odds of 0.44) as likely to be in higher education, compared to the proportion of such families in the population.

- On average across OECD countries, a young person with at least one parent who has attained a tertiary degree is almost twice as likely (odds of 1.9) to be in higher education, compared to the proportion of such families in the population. Only in Denmark, Estonia, Finland, Iceland, Luxembourg, Norway and Sweden is this over-representation of students from high educational backgrounds below 50% (odds below 1.5).

- Inequalities in early schooling due to different socio-economic backgrounds are strongly linked to inequalities at the tertiary level of education. In addition, the impact of socio-economic background on student performance at age 15 (PISA 2000) explains 37% of the between-country variance in the intake of students to higher education from low educational backgrounds in 2009.

- Young people (25-34 year-old non-students) from families with low levels of education enjoy the greatest educational opportunities in Australia, Canada, Denmark, Finland, France, Iceland, Ireland, the Netherlands, Spain and Sweden, where at least 25% of this cohort have attained a tertiary degree, and less than 30% have not completed at least an upper secondary education.

Chart A6.1. Participation in higher education of students whose parents have low levels of education (2009)

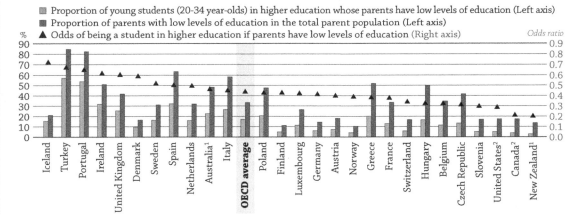

■ Proportion of young students (20-34 year-olds) in higher education whose parents have low levels of education (Left axis)
■ Proportion of parents with low levels of education in the total parent population (Left axis)
▲ Odds of being a student in higher education if parents have low levels of education (Right axis)

Note: The number of students attending higher education are under-reported for Australia, Canada, New Zealand and the United States compared to the other countries as they only include students who attained ISCED 5A, while the other countries include students who attained ISCED 5A and/or 5B. Therefore, the omission of data on 5B qualifications may understate intergenerational mobility in these countries.
1. Data source from Adult Literacy and Lifeskills Survey (ALL) of 2006.
2. Data source from Adult Literacy and Lifeskills Survey (ALL) of 2003.
Countries are ranked in descending order of the odds of attending higher education.
Source: OECD. Table A6.1. See Annex 3 for notes (*www.oecd.org/edu/eag2012*).
StatLink ⟶ http://dx.doi.org/10.1787/888932661934

How to read this chart
The chart shows the odds of someone from a low educational background attending higher education. The odds ratio is calculated by comparing the proportion of parents with low levels of education in the total parent population to the proportion of students in higher education whose parents have low levels of education. Taking the results for the United Kingdom as an example: 25% of all students in tertiary education have parents with low levels of education (light blue bar), while 42% of the parent population have a low levels of education (dark blue bar). This results in an odds ratio of 0.61 (dark triangle). If young people from a low educational background in the United Kingdom were as likely to attend higher education as those from more educated families, 42% of the student population would come from low educational backgrounds, giving an odds ratio equal to 1.

Context

Because of its strong links to earnings, employment, overall wealth and the well-being of individuals, education is a key element in combating inequalities in societies. Giving all young people a fair chance to obtain a quality education is a fundamental part of the social contract. Addressing inequalities in education is critically important for maintaining social mobility and broadening the pool of candidates for higher education and high-skilled jobs.

It is crucial for countries to have an educated and skilled workforce if they want to compete in the knowledge-based global marketplace and promote future growth. The transfer of low-skilled jobs to countries with substantially lower cost structures further suggests that having a large population of low-skilled workers will lead to an increasing social burden and deepening inequalities that are both difficult and costly to address once people have left initial education.

It is important, then, to level the playing field for young people from weak educational backgrounds. Various policy options, such as maintaining reasonable costs for higher education and robust student support systems, can help these students. Ensuring access to and success in higher education for all is important, but so is addressing inequalities at the earliest stages of schooling. Little can be done to remedy poor outcomes at the last stage of the education ladder without also compromising the quality of higher education.

Other findings

- On average across OECD countries, 66% of students with at least one parent who had attained a tertiary degree also attained a tertiary degree, while just 37% of students whose parents attained an upper secondary or post-secondary non-tertiary level of education (ISCED 3/4) completed a tertiary education. **Only one in five (20%) individuals who come from families with low levels of education attains a tertiary degree**.

- **In Italy, Portugal, Turkey and the United States, young people from families with low levels of education have the least chance of attaining a higher level of education than their parents.** In these countries, more than 40% of these young people have not completed upper secondary education, and fewer than 20% have made it to tertiary education.

- **Young women have a clear advantage over young men in attaining a higher level of education than their parents.** The differences in this upward mobility are particularly stark in Greece, Iceland, Norway, Portugal, Slovenia and Spain, where young women are at least 10 percentage points more likely than young men to belong to this group.

- **At the upper secondary or post-secondary non-tertiary level, 21% of young people attain the same educational level as their parents and go no further.** In Austria, the Czech Republic, Germany, the Slovak Republic, Slovenia and Switzerland, this figure exceeds 30%, which largely reflects the importance of this level of education – particularly, the importance of vocational education – in these countries.

Trends

The expansion of education systems in many OECD countries, both at the upper secondary or post-secondary non-tertiary and the tertiary levels of education, has given young people an opportunity to attain a higher level of education than their parents. On average, 37% of young people have achieved a higher level of education than their parents, while only 13% have not been able to reach their parents' educational level. In all countries except Estonia, Germany and Iceland, upward mobility in education is more common than downward mobility, reflecting the expansion of education systems in most OECD countries. The expansion of education has been particularly pronounced in Australia, the Czech Republic, Greece, Hungary, Ireland, Italy and Poland, where the difference between upward and downward educational mobility is 40 percentage points or more.

A6

Analysis

Inequalities in access to higher education across OECD countries

Some caution is needed in interpreting the results in Table A6.1, as the Adult Literacy and Lifeskills (ALL) survey, used as a source for Australia, Canada, New Zealand and the United States, does not include data on the ISCED 5B level of higher education. This can distort the comparability with remaining countries sourced from the 2009 Transition Ad Hoc Module, which includes ISCED 5B data (see *Definitions* section at the end of this indicator for further information). The omission of data on type 5B qualifications may understate mobility, in that those whose parents have low levels of education and who earn qualifications at ISCED 5B level will be excluded from the counts of those with tertiary education.

Assessing inequalities in access to higher education is achieved by comparing the proportion of students from a certain educational background who attend higher education to the proportion of parents with this level of education in the total parent population. The odds of someone coming from a family with low levels of education, for instance, is calculated as the proportion of students in higher education students whose parents have low levels of education compared with the proportion of parents with low levels of education in the total parent population. Odds below 1 indicate a small likelihood of enrolling in higher education; odds close to 1 indicate an equal opportunity; and odds exceeding 1 indicate a greater likelihood of enrolling in higher education.

As shown in the introductory chart (Chart A6.1), the chance that a young person whose parents have not attained an upper secondary education will attend higher education is limited. The odds – calculated as the proportion of students in higher education whose parents have low levels of education, compared to the proportion of parents with low levels of education in the total parent population – are substantially below one (e.g. even odds) in all countries.

The chance that these young people will enrol in higher education exceeds 50% in only nine countries: Denmark, Iceland, Ireland, the Netherlands, Portugal, Spain, Sweden, Turkey and the United Kingdom. In Canada, New Zealand and the United States, the likelihood that a 20-34 year-old whose parents have low levels of education will enrol in higher education is less than 30% (Table A6.1).

Considering that one-third of all parents in OECD countries have not completed upper secondary education, the scope of this issue is significant in many countries. However, in Finland, Germany, Norway and New Zealand, 15% or fewer of parents have not completed upper secondary education, which means that fewer young people have to overcome this particular barrier to higher education (Chart A6.1).

Chart A6.2 shows the other side of this situation. It provides information on the likelihood that young people with one or two highly educated parents will enrol in tertiary education as well.

On average across OECD countries, almost half (48%) of the student population comes from highly educated families where at least one of the parents has attained tertiary education. In Canada, Denmark, Estonia, Finland, New Zealand and the United States, over 60% of students in higher education have at least one parent who has attained a higher education. However, at least 40% of parents in these countries have attained a tertiary education, among the highest levels of attainment in the OECD area. As such, the odds are generally lower than in other countries, except New Zealand (Chart A6.2).

In general, students whose parents have higher levels of education are more likely to enter tertiary education. On average, a 20-34 year-old from a highly educated family is almost twice (1.9) as likely to be in higher education, as compared with the proportion of such families in the population. The greatest likelihood that those from highly educated families will continue into higher education is found in Portugal and Turkey, where this ratio exceeds three. In Austria, the Czech Republic, Greece, Hungary, Italy, the Slovak Republic and Spain, young people are more than twice as likely to be in higher education if their parents hold a tertiary degree, as compared to the percentage of such families in the population (Table A6.1).

Chart A6.2. **Participation in higher education of students whose parents have high levels of education (2009)**

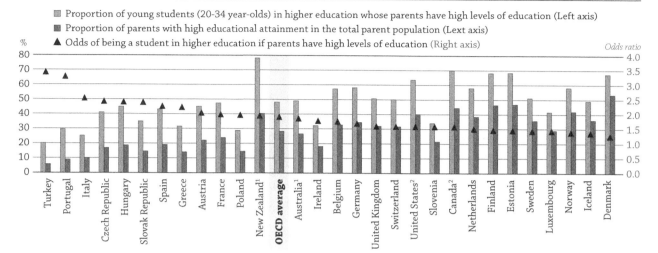

Note: The number of students attending higher education are under-reported for Australia, Canada, New Zealand and the United States compared to the other countries as they only include students who attained ISCED 5A, while the other countries include students who attained ISCED 5A and/or 5B. Therefore, the omission of data on 5B qualifications may understate intergenerational mobility in these countries.
1. Data source from Adult Literacy and Lifeskills Survey (ALL) of 2006.
2. Data source from Adult Literacy and Lifeskills Survey (ALL) of 2003.
Countries are ranked in descending order of the odds of attending higher education.
Source: OECD. Table A6.1. See Annex 3 for notes (*www.oecd.org/edu/eag2012*).
StatLink http://dx.doi.org/10.1787/888932661953

The advantage of having highly educated parents is smaller in countries where overall tertiary attainment is high, as well as in countries where the private costs of education are relatively low. The Nordic countries – Denmark, Finland, Iceland, Norway and Sweden – as well as Estonia and Luxembourg stand out in this respect. In these countries, a student's odds of being in higher education if he or she comes from a highly educated family are below 1.5 (Chart A6.2).

The entry into higher education of young people with at least one parent who has attained an upper secondary or post-secondary non-tertiary education (ISCED 3/4) is proportional to their share of the general parent population, on average. Young women and men in Italy, Portugal and Turkey have a clear advantage if their parents have an upper secondary education (the odds exceed 1.5 in all of these countries). However, for young men in Canada, New Zealand and the United States, the odds ratio of participating in higher education when a parent has only an upper secondary education is less than 50% (Table A6.1).

Inequalities in higher education and at earlier stages of schooling

Countries that have expanded tertiary education in recent years will generally have a higher intake of students from less-advantaged backgrounds. However, increasing tertiary attainment levels, as shown in the difference in attainment between 25-34 year-olds and 45-54 year-olds, explains less than 5% of the variation between countries in the odds of attending higher education if the parents have low levels of education (see Indicator A1, Table A1.3a).

Previous schooling has a substantially greater impact on preparing students from less-educated families to enter higher education. Results from the PISA 2000 assessment provide an opportunity to address this issue. Both PISA and the data used in this indicator provide a representative picture of the quality and inequalities in education at age 15 and in higher education across OECD countries. The data on access to higher education is from 2009 – when most of the PISA 2000 cohort were 24 years old, the prime age for being in tertiary education in many countries. A caveat is the broad age span used in assessing access to higher education (20-34 year-olds), which is likely to weaken the potential association between the two measures.

A6

Chart A6.3 plots countries by the influence of socio-economic background on students' performance in PISA 2000, and the odds of someone whose parents have low levels of education attending higher education. There is a strong link between inequalities in early schooling and students from families with low levels of education enrolling in higher education (this factor explains 37% of the variance). Countries that succeed in providing high-quality compulsory schooling to all students, regardless of their background, are also those that show better odds for students from low educational backgrounds to be enrolled in higher education (Chart A6.3).

The results of breaking down the impact of the *PISA index of economic, social, and cultural status* (ESCS) on student reading performance into within-school and between-school association make intuitive sense (Table A6.1 and Table A6.4, available on line). There is a positive link between the odds for someone with low-educated parents of attending higher education and a low school-level impact of ESCS on the reading performance of students (this explains approximately 20-25% of the between-country variance, depending on the model used). This suggests that countries that succeed in providing high-quality education in less advantaged schools are also those countries that will see more students from families with low educational backgrounds attend higher education.

Chart A6.3. **The influence of socio-economic background on students' performance in PISA 2000, and the odds of someone whose parents have low levels of education of attending higher education (2009)**

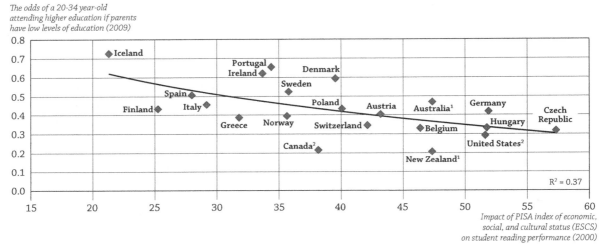

Note: The number of students attending higher education are under-reported for Australia, Canada, New Zealand and the United States compared to the other countries as they only include students who attained ISCED 5A, while the other countries include students who attained ISCED 5A and/or 5B. Therefore, the omission of data on 5B qualifications may understate intergenerational mobility in these countries.
1. Data source from Adult Literacy and Lifeskills Survey (ALL) of 2006.
2. Data source from Adult Literacy and Lifeskills Survey (ALL) of 2003.
Source: OECD. Table A6.1 and Table A6.4, available on line. See Annex 3 for notes (*www.oecd.org/edu/eag2012*).
StatLink ᴍᴤᴸ http://dx.doi.org/10.1787/888932661972

The within-school association between student performance and socio-economic background, on the other hand, is strongly related to lower odds of entering tertiary education for those coming from a high educational background (this explains approximately 27% of the between-country variance). Similarly, the odds of attending higher education among those with highly educated parents is substantially reduced in countries where the overall quality of compulsory education is high. The association between the mean reading performance in PISA 2000 and the odds of 20-34 year-olds from high educational backgrounds attending higher education explains one-third of the between-country variance. (Using PISA 2003 mean scores explains close to half, R^2; 0.44, of the between-country variation.)

Overall, high-quality schooling, as demonstrated by a high average PISA score, and keeping schools mixed in terms of social backgrounds, as demonstrated by larger within-school association of ESCS, appears to be important in enabling students from low educational backgrounds to attain the advantage that many from high educational backgrounds have. These results suggest that peer-learning effects are important, and that having good parental support is less important in countries with high-quality teaching in schools. Making sure that no schools are allowed to fail, manifested by a low school-level impact of ESCS, is an important factor to increase the entry of students from low educational backgrounds into higher education.

Attaining a higher education – Where do those from a weak educational background succeed?

Completing a tertiary education brings substantial benefits to individuals and society. Ensuring that those pursuing a higher education also complete their studies thus makes strong economic sense, particularly for those coming from disadvantaged backgrounds. Table A6.2 shows educational attainment among 25-34 year-old non-students by their parents' level of educational attainment.

On average across OECD countries, 66% of individuals with at least one highly educated parent succeeded in attaining a tertiary degree, while 37% of individuals whose parents attained upper secondary or post-secondary non-tertiary education (ISCED 3/4) completed a tertiary education. Only 20% of individuals whose parents have low levels of education have a tertiary degree.

The chances of obtaining a tertiary degree are substantially lower for young men than for young women. On average, the difference amounts to seven percentage points if the parents have low levels of education, nine percentage points if the parents have attained secondary or post-secondary non-tertiary education (ISCED 3/4), and ten percentage points if the parents have completed a tertiary degree.

Chart A6.4. **Where do individuals from low educational backgrounds succeed? (2009)**
Educational achievement among 25-34 year-old non-students with parents who have not attained an upper secondary education

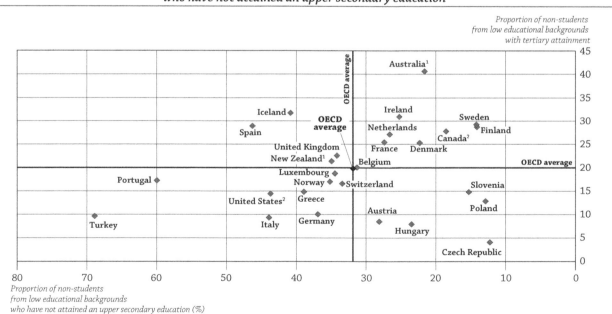

Note: The number of students attending higher education are under-reported for Australia, Canada, New Zealand and the United States compared to the other countries as they only include students who attained ISCED 5A, while the other countries include students who attained ISCED 5A and/or 5B. Therefore, the omission of data on 5B qualifications may understate intergenerational mobility in these countries.
1. Data source from Adult Literacy and Lifeskills Survey (ALL) of 2006.
2. Data source from Adult Literacy and Lifeskills Survey (ALL) of 2003.
Source: OECD. Table A6.2. See Annex 3 for notes (*www.oecd.org/edu/eag2012*).
StatLink ⛶ http://dx.doi.org/10.1787/888932661991

A6

Chart A6.4 takes a closer look at upward educational mobility for those whose parents have low levels of education by examining the proportion of non-students from such backgrounds who have not attained an upper secondary education and the proportion who have attained a tertiary education (the intermediate between those two attainment levels is upper secondary or post-secondary non-tertiary attainment).

Young people from low educational backgrounds have the greatest chances of upward educational mobility in the countries clustered in the upper right quadrant of the chart. The chances of completing a tertiary education exceeds 25% in Canada, Denmark, Finland, France, the Netherlands and Sweden, and is greater than 30% in Australia and Ireland. In all countries, fewer than 30% of these young people have not completed at least an upper secondary education (Chart A6.4).

In Austria, the Czech Republic, Hungary, Poland and Slovenia (lower right quadrant), fewer young people have attained tertiary education, but few have not completed upper secondary education. In Iceland, New Zealand, Spain and the United Kingdom, a relatively large proportion have acquired a tertiary degree, but a substantial portion of 24-35 year-old non-students remain at their parents' low educational level (upper left quadrant).

In Italy, Portugal, Turkey and the United States (lower left quadrant), more than 40% of young people from low educational backgrounds have not completed upper secondary education, and less than 20% of those young people have enrolled in tertiary education.

Intergenerational mobility in education

Overall, educational mobility is strongly associated with the expansion of education, both at the upper secondary (ISCED 3/4) and tertiary levels. In countries where the upper levels of education have not expanded to the same extent, educational mobility is linked to the strength of the relationship between young people's education and their parents' education.

On average across OECD countries, approximately half of 25-34 year-old non-students have achieved the same level of education as their parents: 13% have a low level of education (ISCED 0/1/2), 22% have a medium level of education (ISCED 3/4), and a further 15% have attained tertiary education (ISCED 5/6). More than one-third (37%) of all young people have surpassed their parents' educational level, while 13% have not reached their parents' level of education (Table A6.3).

There is no gender difference in the proportion of 25-34 year-old non-students who have achieved the same educational level as their parents (status quo). However, young women are five percentage points more likely than young men to be upwardly mobile in educational attainment (40% compared with 35%), and young men are more likely than young women to be downwardly mobile in educational attainment (15% compared with 11%). The differences in upward mobility are particularly stark in Greece, Iceland, Norway, Portugal, Slovenia and Spain, where young women are at least 10 percentage points more likely than young men to belong to this group.

Chart A6.5 shows intergenerational mobility in education in OECD countries by analysing the percentage of 25-34 year-old non-students whose educational attainment is higher than that of their parents (upward mobility), lower than that of their parents (downward mobility) or the same (status quo) according to their parents' level of education (low, medium, high).

In Hungary, Poland and Ireland, over half of all 25-34 year-olds have attained a higher educational level than their parents, and few have not achieved at least the same level as their parents. In Australia, the Czech Republic, France, Greece, Italy, Spain and Sweden, at least 45% of young people have surpassed their parents' level of education. However, in France and Sweden, at least 10% of young people have not achieved as high a level of education as their parents.

In Estonia, Germany, Norway, the Slovak Republic and the United States, 25% or less of young people have attained a higher level of education than their parents. In all these countries except the Slovak Republic, downward educational mobility is nearly equal to upward educational mobility. In Estonia, Germany and Iceland, downward educational mobility is more common than an upward mobility, reflecting a contraction of the education systems.

Chart A6.5. Intergenerational mobility in education (2009)
Percentage of 25-34 year-old non-students having an educational attainment higher than their parents,
(upward mobility), a lower one (downward mobility) or the same (status quo)
and status quo by parents' education level (low, medium, high)

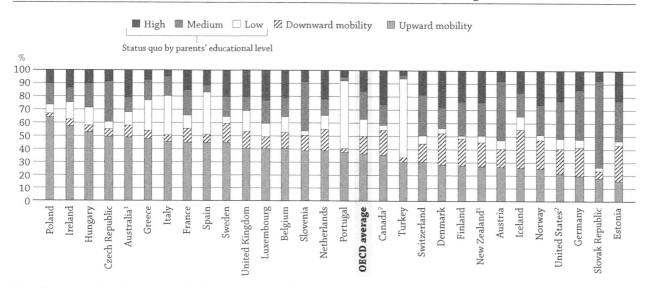

Note: The number of students attending higher education are under-reported for Australia, Canada, New Zealand and the United States compared to the other countries as they only include students who attained ISCED 5A, while the other countries include students who attained ISCED 5A and/or 5B. Therefore, the omission of data on 5B qualifications may understate intergenerational mobility in these countries.
1. Data source from Adult Literacy and Lifeskills Survey (ALL) of 2006.
2. Data source from Adult Literacy and Lifeskills Survey (ALL) of 2003.
Countries are ranked in descending order of upward mobility.
Source: OECD. Table A6.3. See Annex 3 for notes (*www.oecd.org/edu/eag2012*).
StatLink ▒▒▒ http://dx.doi.org/10.1787/888932662010

Despite an expansion of the education system, more than 20% of young people in Greece, Italy, Portugal, Spain and Turkey remain at the same low levels of education as their parents. More than 30% of young people in Austria, the Czech Republic, Estonia, Germany, the Slovak Republic, Slovenia and Switzerland end their educational careers at the same upper secondary or post-secondary non-tertiary level as their parents, largely reflecting the significance of this level of education and the importance of vocational education in these countries (see Indicator A1).

Definitions

Three broad educational categories are used in this comparison of parents' and young people's educational attainment for most countries: low levels of education (ISCED levels 0-2 completed, the person has not completed upper secondary education); mid-levels of education (ISCED levels 3-4 completed, the person has completed upper secondary or post-secondary non-tertiary education); and high levels of education (ISCED levels 5-6 completed, the person has completed tertiary education).

For student attendance data, the four countries (Australia, Canada, New Zealand and the United States) sourced from ALL have slightly different categories than the rest of the countries. The low level of education category groups people who are attending upper secondary or less than high school (ISCED 0-3) education; the mid level category, those who are attending post-secondary non-tertiary education or tertiary but not university (ISCED 4 and 5B); and the high level category, those attending university courses (ISCED 5A and 6). This disparity between ALL and the 2009 Transition Ad Hoc Module categories might distort comparability to some extent, as young people from lower socio-economic backgrounds are more likely to enter ISCED 5B as opposed to ISCED 5A-types of education.

A6

Methodology

The 2009 Transition Ad Hoc Module, a supplement to the 2009 EU Labour Force Surveys, was used for most of the countries in this analysis. The Adult Literacy and Lifeskills Survey (ALL) was used as a data source for Australia, Canada, New Zealand and the United States. The first wave, which took place in 2003, includes Canada and the United States. The second wave, which took place in 2006, includes New Zealand and Australia.

Only respondents between the ages of 25 and 34 were included in the analysis of the educational attainment data. In the analysis of the school-attendance data, only respondents between the ages of 20 and 34 were included. Respondents were excluded from the analysis if the education level of at least one of their parents was not available.

There may be some differences in the information collected from the countries, as well as differences between the two data sources. These differences could affect the results.

Assessing inequalities in access to higher education is achieved by comparing the proportion of students from a certain educational background who attend higher education to the proportion of parents with this level of education in the total parent population. The odds of someone coming from a family with low levels of education, for instance, is calculated as the proportion of students in higher education whose parents have low levels of education compared with the proportion of parents with low levels of education in the total parent population. Odds below 1 indicate a small likelihood of enrolling in higher education; odds close to 1 indicate an equal opportunity; and odds exceeding 1 indicate a great likelihood of enrolling in higher education.

Inequalities in educational attainment (completed education) are examined by comparing the educational attainment of 25-34 year-old non-students to that of their parents.

Because the data on students in higher education pertains to students aged 20, there may be under-reporting of participation, as some students begin higher education before the age of 20. Upward and downward mobility trends are therefore affected.

The statistical data for Israel are supplied by and under the responsibility of the relevant Israeli authorities. The use of such data by the OECD is without prejudice to the status of the Golan Heights, East Jerusalem and Israeli settlements in the West Bank under the terms of international law.

References

The following additional material relevant to this indicator is available on line:

• *Table A6.4. Mean reading performance in PISA 2000, 2003 and relationship between reading performance and the PISA index of economic, social, and cultural status (ESCS) in PISA 2000*
  StatLink http://dx.doi.org/10.1787/888932665012

Table A6.1. [1/2] Participation in higher education, by parents' educational attainment (2009)

Proportion of 20-34 year-olds in higher education by parents' educational background, the distribution (proportion) of parents' educational attainment among 20-34 year-olds, and the corresponding odds of being in higher education by educational background

Reading the columns for those with parents whose level of education is low: 23% of all students in tertiary education (M+W) in Australia have parents with low levels of education (Column 1) while 48% of parents attained low level of education (Column 5) and the corresponding odds of being in higher education for someone whose parents have low educational attainment is 0.47 in Australia (Column 9).

		Proportion of 20-34 year-old students in higher education by parents' educational attainment				Parents' educational attainment in the total parent population (students and non-students)				Odds (ratio) to access higher education by parents' educational background		
		Low (0/1/2)	Medium (3/4)	High (5/6)	Total	Low (0/1/2)	Medium (3/4)	High (5/6)	Total	Low (0/1/2)	Medium (3/4)	High (5/6)
		(1)	(2)	(3)	(4)	(5)	(6)	(7)	(8)	(9)	(10)	(11)
Australia[1]	Men	22	29	49	100	48	25	27	100	0.46	1.17	1.79
	Women	23	28	49	100	48	26	26	100	0.47	1.08	1.91
	M+W	23	28	49	100	48	25	27	100	0.47	1.12	1.85
Austria	Men	6	50	44	100	18	59	23	100	0.34	0.84	1.91
	Women	9	46	46	100	18	61	21	100	0.47	0.75	2.17
	M+W	7	48	45	100	18	60	22	100	0.40	0.80	2.04
Belgium	Men	11	30	58	100	34	32	34	100	0.33	0.95	1.73
	Women	11	32	56	100	35	34	32	100	0.33	0.95	1.78
	M+W	11	31	57	100	35	33	33	100	0.33	0.96	1.75
Canada[2]	Men	6	17	77	100	15	40	45	100	0.39	0.42	1.71
	Women	2	33	65	100	20	37	44	100	0.12	0.91	1.48
	M+W	4	26	70	100	17	38	44	100	0.22	0.69	1.57
Chile	Men	m	m	m	m	m	m	m	m	m	m	m
	Women	m	m	m	m	m	m	m	m	m	m	m
	M+W	m	m	m	m	m	m	m	m	m	m	m
Czech Republic	Men	12	46	42	100	42	41	17	100	0.28	1.12	2.53
	Women	14	46	40	100	41	42	17	100	0.35	1.09	2.34
	M+W	13	46	41	100	42	42	17	100	0.32	1.11	2.43
Denmark	Men	11	23	66	100	17	32	51	100	0.65	0.71	1.29
	Women	9	23	68	100	16	28	56	100	0.56	0.82	1.22
	M+W	10	23	67	100	16	30	53	100	0.59	0.76	1.26
Estonia	Men	c	28	69	100	6	50	43	100	c	0.55	1.58
	Women	c	30	68	100	6	44	50	100	c	0.69	1.35
	M+W	c	29	68	100	6	47	47	100	c	0.62	1.46
Finland	Men	4	27	69	100	12	42	46	100	0.36	0.63	1.51
	Women	5	28	67	100	10	43	47	100	0.51	0.65	1.43
	M+W	5	27	68	100	11	42	46	100	0.43	0.64	1.47
France	Men	13	37	50	100	33	43	24	100	0.39	0.85	2.12
	Women	13	42	45	100	34	42	24	100	0.37	1.01	1.87
	M+W	13	40	47	100	33	43	24	100	0.38	0.93	1.99
Germany	Men	5	36	59	100	14	50	35	100	0.33	0.73	1.66
	Women	7	35	57	100	14	52	34	100	0.52	0.68	1.71
	M+W	6	36	58	100	14	51	34	100	0.42	0.70	1.69
Greece	Men	17	48	35	100	53	33	14	100	0.33	1.44	2.47
	Women	23	49	28	100	51	35	14	100	0.45	1.41	1.98
	M+W	20	49	31	100	52	34	14	100	0.39	1.43	2.23
Hungary	Men	14	36	50	100	50	31	19	100	0.29	1.16	2.59
	Women	18	41	41	100	50	31	18	100	0.36	1.29	2.27
	M+W	17	39	45	100	50	31	19	100	0.33	1.23	2.41
Iceland	Men	21	35	44	100	21	47	32	100	0.98	0.74	1.39
	Women	12	36	52	100	21	39	41	100	0.57	0.94	1.28
	M+W	15	36	49	100	21	43	36	100	0.73	0.83	1.36
Ireland	Men	31	35	34	100	51	30	18	100	0.60	1.18	1.82
	Women	32	37	31	100	51	31	18	100	0.64	1.17	1.73
	M+W	32	36	32	100	51	31	18	100	0.62	1.17	1.77
Israel	Men	m	m	m	m	m	m	m	m	m	m	m
	Women	m	m	m	m	m	m	m	m	m	m	m
	M+W	m	m	m	m	m	m	m	m	m	m	m
Italy	Men	23	49	28	100	59	32	9	100	0.40	1.53	2.98
	Women	29	48	23	100	58	32	11	100	0.50	1.52	2.20
	M+W	27	48	25	100	58	32	10	100	0.46	1.52	2.54
Japan	Men	m	m	m	m	m	m	m	m	m	m	m
	Women	m	m	m	m	m	m	m	m	m	m	m
	M+W	m	m	m	m	m	m	m	m	m	m	m

Notes: The number of students attending higher education are under-reported for Australia, Canada, New Zealand and the United States compared to the other countries as they only include students who attained ISCED 5A, while the other countries include students who attained ISCED 5A and/or 5B. Therefore, the omission of data on 5B qualifications may understate intergenerational mobility in these countries.

The odds (ratio) of accessing higher education by parents' educational background is the proportion of students in higher education and their parents' educational attainment over parents' educational attainment in the total population (students and non-students).

1. Data source from Adult Literacy and Lifeskills Survey (ALL) of 2006.
2. Data source from Adult Literacy and Lifeskills Survey (ALL) of 2003.

Source: OECD. Transition Ad Hoc Module, EU Labour Force Survey 2009 and Adult Literacy and Lifeskills Survey (ALL). See Annex 3 for notes (*www.oecd.org/edu/eag2012*).

Please refer to the Reader's Guide for information concerning the symbols replacing missing data.

StatLink http://dx.doi.org/10.1787/888932664955

A6

Table A6.1. [2/2] Participation in higher education, by parents' educational attainment (2009)

Proportion of 20-34 year-olds in higher education by parents' educational background, the distribution (proportion) of parents' educational attainment among 20-34 year-olds, and the corresponding odds of being in higher education by educational background

Reading the columns for those with parents whose level of education is low: 23% of all students in tertiary education (M+W) in Australia have parents with low levels of education (Column 1) while 48% of parents attained low level of education (Column 5) and the corresponding odds of being in higher education for someone whose parents have low educational attainment is 0.47 in Australia (Column 9).

| | | Proportion of 20-34 year-old students in higher education by parents' educational attainment | | | | Parents' educational attainment in the total parent population (students and non-students) | | | | Odds (ratio) to access higher education by parents' educational background | | |
| | | Low (0/1/2) | Medium (3/4) | High (5/6) | Total | Low (0/1/2) | Medium (3/4) | High (5/6) | Total | Low (0/1/2) | Medium (3/4) | High (5/6) |
		(1)	(2)	(3)	(4)	(5)	(6)	(7)	(8)	(9)	(10)	(11)
Korea	Men	m	m	m	m	m	m	m	m	m	m	m
	Women	m	m	m	m	m	m	m	m	m	m	m
	M+W	m	m	m	m	m	m	m	m	m	m	m
Luxembourg	Men	10	47	42	100	25	44	31	100	0.42	1.08	1.36
	Women	12	47	41	100	28	45	27	100	0.43	1.04	1.53
	M+W	11	47	42	100	27	44	29	100	0.43	1.06	1.43
Mexico	Men	m	m	m	m	m	m	m	m	m	m	m
	Women	m	m	m	m	m	m	m	m	m	m	m
	M+W	m	m	m	m	m	m	m	m	m	m	m
Netherlands	Men	14	25	60	100	30	31	39	100	0.47	0.83	1.55
	Women	18	27	55	100	33	29	38	100	0.53	0.93	1.47
	M+W	16	26	58	100	32	30	38	100	0.50	0.88	1.51
New Zealand[1]	Men	c	13	84	100	13	45	42	100	c	0.30	2.00
	Women	c	26	71	100	14	47	39	100	c	0.56	1.83
	M+W	3	19	78	100	14	46	40	100	0.21	0.41	1.94
Norway	Men	3	34	63	100	10	48	41	100	0.26	0.70	1.53
	Women	5	41	54	100	11	47	42	100	0.50	0.87	1.27
	M+W	4	38	58	100	10	48	42	100	0.39	0.79	1.39
Poland	Men	16	48	36	100	48	38	15	100	0.33	1.29	2.42
	Women	24	52	23	100	48	38	14	100	0.51	1.38	1.62
	M+W	21	51	29	100	48	38	15	100	0.43	1.34	1.97
Portugal	Men	48	16	36	100	81	9	10	100	0.59	1.85	3.53
	Women	60	17	23	100	84	8	8	100	0.72	2.01	2.94
	M+W	54	17	30	100	82	9	9	100	0.65	1.92	3.28
Slovak Republic	Men	c	61	38	100	7	78	15	100	c	0.78	2.63
	Women	c	67	32	100	7	79	15	100	c	0.85	2.23
	M+W	c	65	35	100	7	78	15	100	c	0.82	2.40
Slovenia	Men	5	59	37	100	17	61	22	100	0.27	0.96	1.67
	Women	6	63	31	100	17	62	21	100	0.33	1.01	1.51
	M+W	5	61	34	100	17	62	21	100	0.30	0.99	1.58
Spain	Men	31	22	47	100	63	17	19	100	0.49	1.27	2.42
	Women	33	27	40	100	63	18	19	100	0.52	1.52	2.13
	M+W	32	25	43	100	63	18	19	100	0.51	1.41	2.26
Sweden	Men	15	31	55	100	30	33	37	100	0.49	0.92	1.50
	Women	18	34	48	100	32	34	35	100	0.55	1.02	1.39
	M+W	16	33	51	100	31	33	36	100	0.52	0.98	1.43
Switzerland	Men	6	46	48	100	16	52	33	100	0.36	0.89	1.48
	Women	6	42	52	100	18	52	31	100	0.33	0.81	1.71
	M+W	6	44	50	100	17	52	32	100	0.34	0.85	1.59
Turkey	Men	58	23	19	100	85	10	6	100	0.68	2.43	3.23
	Women	56	22	22	100	85	9	6	100	0.67	2.30	3.67
	M+W	57	23	20	100	85	10	6	100	0.68	2.38	3.42
United Kingdom	Men	24	23	53	100	41	26	32	100	0.57	0.88	1.65
	Women	27	25	48	100	42	27	31	100	0.65	0.93	1.54
	M+W	25	24	51	100	42	26	32	100	0.61	0.91	1.59
United States[2]	Men	c	19	77	100	20	41	39	100	c	0.48	1.97
	Women	c	44	50	100	14	45	41	100	c	0.99	1.21
	M+W	5	31	64	100	17	43	40	100	0.29	0.74	1.58
OECD average	Men	17	34	51	100	33	39	28	100	0.44	0.99	2.00
	Women	19	38	46	100	33	38	28	100	0.48	1.07	1.82
	M+W	17	36	48	100	33	39	28	100	0.44	1.03	1.90
EU21 average	Men	16	37	48	100	35	39	26	100	0.42	1.03	2.04
	Women	19	39	43	100	35	39	26	100	0.49	1.08	1.83
	M+W	18	38	46	100	35	39	26	100	0.45	1.06	1.93

Notes: The number of students attending higher education are under-reported for Australia, Canada, New Zealand and the United States compared to the other countries as they only include students who attained ISCED 5A, while the other countries include students who attained ISCED 5A and/or 5B. Therefore, the omission of data on 5B qualifications may understate intergenerational mobility in these countries.

The odds (ratio) of accessing higher education by parents' educational background is the proportion of students in higher education and their parents' educational attainment over parents' educational attainment in the total population (students and non-students).

1. Data source from Adult Literacy and Lifeskills Survey (ALL) of 2006.

2. Data source from Adult Literacy and Lifeskills Survey (ALL) of 2003.

Source: OECD. Transition Ad Hoc Module, EU Labour Force Survey 2009 and Adult Literacy and Lifeskills Survey (ALL). See Annex 3 for notes (www.oecd.org/edu/eag2012).

Please refer to the Reader's Guide for information concerning the symbols replacing missing data.

StatLink ᴍᴤ𝕃 http://dx.doi.org/10.1787/888932664955

Table A6.2. [1/3] **Educational attainment level of 25-34 year-old non-student population, by educational attainment level of their parents (2009)**

	25-34 year-olds' attainment (%)	25-34 year-olds				25-34 year-old men				25-34 year-old women			
		Parents' attainment (%)				Parents' attainment (%)				Parents' attainment (%)			
		Low	Medium	High	Total	Low	Medium	High	Total	Low	Medium	High	Total
		(1)	(2)	(3)	(4)	(5)	(6)	(7)	(8)	(9)	(10)	(11)	(12)
Australia[1]	Low	22	12	3	14	19	10	c	14	20	7	c	14
	Medium	38	41	19	34	41	31	13	34	35	42	21	34
	High	41	47	78	52	39	60	86	52	45	51	76	52
	Total	46	27	27	100	60	22	18	100	60	21	19	100
Austria	Low	28	8	6	12	22	6	c	10	34	9	7	15
	Medium	63	75	49	68	70	79	51	72	57	72	48	65
	High	8	17	44	20	8	15	44	18	9	18	45	21
	Total	23	60	18	100	22	59	18	100	23	60	17	100
Belgium	Low	31	11	5	17	33	15	7	19	30	7	3	15
	Medium	49	45	25	40	52	52	30	45	46	39	19	36
	High	20	44	70	43	16	33	64	36	25	53	78	49
	Total	38	32	30	100	38	30	32	100	38	34	28	100
Canada[2]	Low	19	10	5	10	20	12	6	11	17	8	5	9
	Medium	54	42	31	40	57	38	37	41	51	46	26	39
	High	28	48	63	50	23	50	57	48	31	46	70	52
	Total	21	37	41	100	18	42	41	100	25	33	42	100
Chile	Low	m	m	m	m	m	m	m	m	m	m	m	m
	Medium	m	m	m	m	m	m	m	m	m	m	m	m
	High	m	m	m	m	m	m	m	m	m	m	m	m
	Total	m	m	m	m	m	m	m	m	m	m	m	m
Czech republic	Low	12	2	1	6	10	2	1	5	15	1	1	7
	Medium	84	77	36	75	86	79	42	77	81	75	29	71
	High	4	21	64	19	4	19	57	17	4	24	71	21
	Total	46	40	13	100	47	39	13	100	45	41	14	100
Denmark	Low	22	10	14	14	23	11	18	16	21	10	10	12
	Medium	52	47	29	39	59	54	34	46	45	39	24	32
	High	25	43	58	47	18	36	48	38	34	52	67	56
	Total	18	34	49	100	19	36	45	100	17	31	52	100
Estonia	Low	45	17	7	15	50	20	9	18	c	13	c	12
	Medium	48	60	38	50	46	60	48	54	51	60	29	45
	High	c	23	55	35	c	20	43	28	c	27	66	44
	Total	8	50	42	100	8	54	38	100	8	46	46	100
Finland	Low	14	12	6	10	17	15	8	13	11	8	4	7
	Medium	57	56	34	47	64	63	42	55	48	48	26	39
	High	29	32	60	43	19	22	50	32	42	43	71	54
	Total	15	46	40	100	16	46	39	100	14	46	40	100
France	Low	27	11	6	16	28	13	c	17	27	10	c	15
	Medium	47	46	22	41	50	50	23	45	44	41	20	38
	High	25	43	73	43	22	37	70	38	29	49	76	47
	Total	38	41	21	100	37	43	21	100	39	40	22	100
Germany	Low	38	10	6	14	35	10	7	14	41	10	6	14
	Medium	52	72	46	60	56	73	46	61	47	71	46	60
	High	10	18	48	26	9	17	48	25	11	19	48	27
	Total	17	52	31	100	18	51	32	100	16	54	31	100
Greece	Low	39	10	3	26	46	15	4	32	32	6	c	20
	Medium	46	51	26	46	43	52	32	44	50	50	21	47
	High	15	39	70	28	11	34	64	23	19	44	76	33
	Total	59	30	11	100	60	29	10	100	57	32	11	100
Hungary	Low	23	3	c	14	23	4	c	14	24	2	c	14
	Medium	69	63	29	61	72	70	36	66	65	57	21	56
	High	8	34	70	25	5	26	63	20	11	42	78	30
	Total	56	30	15	100	55	30	15	100	56	29	14	100

Note: The number of students attending higher education are under-reported for Australia, Canada, New Zealand and the United States compared to the other countries as they only include students who attained ISCED 5A, while the other countries include students who attained ISCED 5A and/or 5B. Therefore, the omission of data on 5B qualifications may understate intergenerational mobility in these countries.
1. Data source from Adult Literacy and Lifeskills Survey (ALL) of 2006.
2. Data source from Adult Literacy and Lifeskills Survey (ALL) of 2003.
Source: OECD. Transition Ad Hoc Module, EU Labour Force Survey 2009 and Adult Literacy and Lifeskills Survey (ALL). See Annex 3 for notes (*www.oecd.org/edu/eag2012*).
Please refer to the Reader's Guide for information concerning the symbols replacing missing data.
StatLink http://dx.doi.org/10.1787/888932664974

A6

Table A6.2. [2/3] Educational attainment level of 25-34 year-old non-student population, by educational attainment level of their parents (2009)

	25-34 year-olds' attainment (%)	25-34 year-olds				25-34 year-old men				25-34 year-old women			
		Parents' attainment (%)				Parents' attainment (%)				Parents' attainment (%)			
		Low	Medium	High	Total	Low	Medium	High	Total	Low	Medium	High	Total
		(1)	(2)	(3)	(4)	(5)	(6)	(7)	(8)	(9)	(10)	(11)	(12)
Iceland	Low	41	33	26	33	50	41	32	40	30	21	20	23
	Medium	27	41	20	31	18	40	19	29	37	44	21	34
	High	32	25	54	36	31	19	49	30	32	36	59	43
	Total	24	44	31	100	22	50	28	100	27	37	36	100
Ireland	Low	25	5	3	15	29	7	3	18	22	4	3	13
	Medium	44	36	17	37	46	42	20	40	42	31	15	34
	High	31	59	80	48	25	51	77	42	36	65	82	53
	Total	52	31	17	100	53	30	18	100	52	31	17	100
Israel	Low	m	m	m	m	m	m	m	m	m	m	m	m
	Medium	m	m	m	m	m	m	m	m	m	m	m	m
	High	m	m	m	m	m	m	m	m	m	m	m	m
	Total	m	m	m	m	m	m	m	m	m	m	m	m
Italy	Low	44	12	5	33	48	15	7	37	39	9	4	28
	Medium	47	58	30	49	45	62	35	49	48	55	25	48
	High	9	30	65	19	6	23	58	14	12	36	71	23
	Total	67	26	7	100	68	26	6	100	66	26	8	100
Japan	Low	m	m	m	m	m	m	m	m	m	m	m	m
	Medium	m	m	m	m	m	m	m	m	m	m	m	m
	High	m	m	m	m	m	m	m	m	m	m	m	m
	Total	m	m	m	m	m	m	m	m	m	m	m	m
Korea	Low	m	m	m	m	m	m	m	m	m	m	m	m
	Medium	m	m	m	m	m	m	m	m	m	m	m	m
	High	m	m	m	m	m	m	m	m	m	m	m	m
	Total	m	m	m	m	m	m	m	m	m	m	m	m
Luxembourg	Low	34	8	c	14	36	9	c	15	33	7	c	14
	Medium	47	42	16	36	50	44	19	38	44	39	11	33
	High	19	51	81	50	14	47	78	47	23	54	86	53
	Total	30	42	29	100	29	41	31	100	31	43	26	100
Mexico	Low	m	m	m	m	m	m	m	m	m	m	m	m
	Medium	m	m	m	m	m	m	m	m	m	m	m	m
	High	m	m	m	m	m	m	m	m	m	m	m	m
	Total	m	m	m	m	m	m	m	m	m	m	m	m
Netherlands	Low	27	14	6	16	31	16	7	19	23	12	4	14
	Medium	46	47	31	41	45	47	34	41	48	48	28	41
	High	27	39	63	43	24	37	58	40	29	41	67	45
	Total	39	27	35	100	37	27	36	100	40	26	34	100
New Zealand[1]	Low	35	14	4	13	41	15	3	14	31	12	4	12
	Medium	44	51	29	42	42	51	36	45	45	51	22	40
	High	21	35	67	45	17	34	60	41	24	37	74	48
	Total	14	49	36	100	13	51	37	100	16	48	36	100
Norway	Low	35	17	7	15	34	20	9	17	37	15	5	14
	Medium	48	47	27	39	54	55	35	47	41	38	19	31
	High	17	36	66	45	12	25	56	35	22	47	76	56
	Total	11	50	39	100	11	51	38	100	12	48	40	100
Poland	Low	13	3	1	8	14	3	c	9	11	2	c	7
	Medium	74	46	17	57	77	55	21	63	71	37	13	52
	High	13	51	83	35	9	42	77	28	17	61	87	42
	Total	53	35	12	100	53	35	11	100	52	35	13	100
Portugal	Low	60	16	8	53	67	17	c	59	53	15	c	47
	Medium	23	42	19	24	22	46	23	24	24	38	c	24
	High	17	43	73	23	11	38	67	18	23	48	80	28
	Total	85	8	7	100	85	8	7	100	86	8	6	100

Note: The number of students attending higher education are under-reported for Australia, Canada, New Zealand and the United States compared to the other countries as they only include students who attained ISCED 5A, while the other countries include students who attained ISCED 5A and/or 5B. Therefore, the omission of data on 5B qualifications may understate intergenerational mobility in these countries.
1. Data source from Adult Literacy and Lifeskills Survey (ALL) of 2006.
2. Data source from Adult Literacy and Lifeskills Survey (ALL) of 2003.
Source: OECD. Transition Ad Hoc Module, EU Labour Force Survey 2009 and Adult Literacy and Lifeskills Survey (ALL). See Annex 3 for notes (www.oecd.org/edu/eag2012).
Please refer to the Reader's Guide for information concerning the symbols replacing missing data.
StatLink ⬛⬛⬛ http://dx.doi.org/10.1787/888932664974

Table A6.2. [3/3] Educational attainment level of 25-34 year-old non-student population, by educational attainment level of their parents (2009)

A6

	25-34 year-olds' attainment (%)	25-34 year-olds				25-34 year-old men				25-34 year-old women			
		Parents' attainment (%)				Parents' attainment (%)				Parents' attainment (%)			
		Low	Medium	High	Total	Low	Medium	High	Total	Low	Medium	High	Total
		(1)	(2)	(3)	(4)	(5)	(6)	(7)	(8)	(9)	(10)	(11)	(12)
Slovak Republic	Low	33	3	c	5	27	3	c	5	39	2	c	5
	Medium	65	83	31	75	70	85	33	78	58	80	29	73
	High	c	15	68	20	c	12	66	17	c	18	71	22
	Total	9	80	11	100	9	79	12	100	9	81	11	100
Slovenia	Low	15	6	2	8	17	7	c	8	13	5	c	7
	Medium	70	62	46	61	75	72	56	70	64	51	34	51
	High	15	32	52	32	8	22	41	22	22	44	64	42
	Total	23	60	17	100	23	60	17	100	23	61	17	100
Spain	Low	46	16	8	36	52	20	10	41	40	11	6	30
	Medium	25	35	17	25	24	37	18	25	26	34	15	25
	High	29	49	75	39	24	44	72	34	34	55	79	44
	Total	69	16	15	100	69	15	16	100	69	16	15	100
Sweden	Low	14	7	6	9	16	9	7	11	13	5	4	7
	Medium	57	48	33	46	62	52	38	50	53	43	26	41
	High	29	45	61	45	23	39	55	39	35	52	69	51
	Total	35	32	33	100	34	32	34	100	36	31	32	100
Switzerland	Low	33	6	3	10	29	4	3	8	37	8	3	13
	Medium	50	60	33	50	54	58	31	49	47	61	35	51
	High	17	34	64	40	17	38	66	43	16	31	62	37
	Total	19	51	29	100	18	51	31	100	21	51	28	100
Turkey	Low	69	20	7	62	61	16	5	55	76	24	9	69
	Medium	21	36	21	23	28	38	22	28	15	34	20	17
	High	10	44	73	15	11	46	74	17	8	42	72	14
	Total	87	8	5	100	88	8	5	100	87	8	5	100
United Kingdom	Low	34	14	6	21	35	16	8	22	33	13	4	19
	Medium	43	43	25	38	44	44	28	39	42	42	23	36
	High	23	43	69	41	20	40	65	38	25	46	73	44
	Total	45	25	29	100	46	25	30	100	45	26	29	100
United States[2]	Low	44	10	5	14	41	12	6	17	47	8	4	12
	Medium	42	65	34	49	42	67	38	51	42	64	31	47
	High	14	25	61	37	17	22	56	32	10	28	66	40
	Total	19	44	37	100	23	42	35	100	15	45	40	100
OECD average	Low	32	11	6	18	33	12	8	20	30	9	5	17
	Medium	49	52	29	46	52	55	32	49	47	49	25	43
	High	20	37	66	36	16	33	61	32	23	42	71	40
	Total	37	38	25	100	37	38	25	100	37	38	25	100
EU21 average	Low	30	9	5	17	31	11	7	19	28	8	5	15
	Medium	53	54	29	48	55	58	34	52	50	50	25	45
	High	19	37	66	34	14	31	60	29	23	42	72	40
	Total	39	38	23	100	39	38	23	100	39	38	23	100

Note: The number of students attending higher education are under-reported for Australia, Canada, New Zealand and the United States compared to the other countries as they only include students who attained ISCED 5A, while the other countries include students who attained ISCED 5A and/or 5B. Therefore, the omission of data on 5B qualifications may understate intergenerational mobility in these countries.

1. Data source from Adult Literacy and Lifeskills Survey (ALL) of 2006.
2. Data source from Adult Literacy and Lifeskills Survey (ALL) of 2003.

Source: OECD. Transition Ad Hoc Module, EU Labour Force Survey 2009 and Adult Literacy and Lifeskills Survey (ALL). See Annex 3 for notes (*www.oecd.org/edu/eag2012*).

Please refer to the Reader's Guide for information concerning the symbols replacing missing data.

StatLink ᵐˢᵖ http://dx.doi.org/10.1787/888932664974

A6

Table A6.3. Educational mobility of 25-34 year-old non-students by parent's level of education (2009)

	Men and Women (%)						Men (%)						Women (%)					
	Downward mobility	Upward mobility	Status quo				Downward mobility	Upward mobility	Status quo				Downward mobility	Upward mobility	Status quo			
			Low	Medium	High	Total			Low	Medium	High	Total			Low	Medium	High	Total
	(1)	(2)	(3)	(4)	(5)	(6)	(7)	(8)	(9)	(10)	(11)	(12)	(13)	(14)	(15)	(16)	(17)	(18)
Australia[1]	9	49	10	12	21	42	4	61	12	7	16	34	6	59	11	9	14	35
Austria	14	26	6	45	8	59	14	26	5	47	8	60	15	26	8	44	8	59
Belgium	12	40	12	14	21	47	16	36	12	16	20	48	9	45	11	13	22	47
Canada[2]	19	36	4	16	26	46	22	35	4	16	23	42	15	36	4	15	29	49
Chile	m	m	m	m	m	m	m	m	m	m	m	m	m	m	m	m	m	m
Czech Republic	6	49	6	31	9	45	6	50	5	31	8	43	5	48	7	31	10	47
Denmark	24	28	4	16	28	48	27	27	4	19	22	45	20	29	4	12	35	50
Estonia	27	16	3	30	23	57	33	15	4	32	17	53	22	17	c	28	30	61
Finland	21	27	2	26	24	51	26	23	3	29	19	51	16	32	1	22	29	52
France	10	45	10	19	15	45	12	42	10	21	14	46	9	48	10	16	16	43
Germany	22	20	6	37	15	59	22	20	6	37	15	58	21	20	7	38	15	59
Greece	6	48	23	15	8	46	8	43	27	15	7	49	5	53	18	16	9	42
Hungary	5	53	13	19	10	42	7	50	13	21	9	43	4	55	14	17	11	41
Iceland	29	26	10	18	17	45	34	21	11	20	14	45	22	32	8	16	21	46
Ireland	5	57	13	11	14	38	6	53	15	13	13	41	4	61	12	10	14	35
Israel	m	m	m	m	m	m	m	m	m	m	m	m	m	m	m	m	m	m
Italy	6	45	29	15	5	49	7	41	33	16	4	53	5	50	26	14	6	46
Japan	m	m	m	m	m	m	m	m	m	m	m	m	m	m	m	m	m	m
Korea	m	m	m	m	m	m	m	m	m	m	m	m	m	m	m	m	m	m
Luxembourg	9	41	10	17	23	51	10	38	10	18	24	52	7	44	10	17	22	50
Mexico	m	m	m	m	m	m	m	m	m	m	m	m	m	m	m	m	m	m
Netherlands	17	39	10	13	22	45	19	36	12	13	21	45	14	41	9	13	23	45
New Zealand[1]	18	27	5	25	24	55	22	24	5	26	22	53	15	29	5	25	26	56
Norway	22	25	4	23	26	53	27	20	4	28	21	53	17	30	4	18	31	53
Poland	3	64	7	16	10	33	4	60	8	19	9	36	2	67	6	13	12	30
Portugal	3	38	51	3	5	59	4	31	57	4	5	65	2	44	46	3	5	54
Slovak Republic	6	18	3	66	8	77	6	16	2	68	8	78	5	20	3	64	8	75
Slovenia	12	39	3	37	9	49	14	32	4	43	7	54	9	46	3	31	11	45
Spain	6	45	32	5	12	49	7	40	36	6	11	53	5	50	28	5	12	45
Sweden	15	45	5	15	20	40	18	41	5	16	19	40	11	48	5	14	22	40
Switzerland	14	31	6	31	19	56	13	32	5	30	20	55	15	29	8	31	17	56
Turkey	3	31	60	3	4	66	3	37	54	3	3	60	3	24	66	3	4	73
United Kingdom	13	41	15	11	20	47	14	39	16	11	19	46	11	42	15	11	21	47
United States[2]	19	22	8	29	23	60	20	23	10	28	19	57	17	20	7	29	26	62
OECD average	13	37	13	21	16	50	15	35	13	22	14	50	11	40	13	20	17	50
EU21 average	12	39	13	22	15	49	13	36	14	24	13	50	10	42	12	21	16	48

Note: The number of students attending higher education are under-reported for Australia, Canada, New Zealand and the United States compared to the other countries as they only include students who attained ISCED 5A, while the other countries include students who attained ISCED 5A and/or 5B. Therefore, the omission of data on 5B qualifications may understate intergenerational mobility in these countries.

1. Data source from Adult Literacy and Lifeskills Survey (ALL) of 2006.
2. Data source from Adult Literacy and Lifeskills Survey (ALL) of 2003.

Source: OECD. Transition Ad Hoc Module, EU Labour Force Survey 2009 and Adult Literacy and Lifeskills Survey (ALL). See Annex 3 for notes (www.oecd.org/edu/eag2012).

Please refer to the Reader's Guide for information concerning the symbols replacing missing data.

StatLink ⟐ᴍˢᴸ http://dx.doi.org/10.1787/888932664993

HOW DOES EDUCATIONAL ATTAINMENT AFFECT PARTICIPATION IN THE LABOUR MARKET?

- Across OECD countries, individuals with at least an upper secondary education have a greater chance of being employed than people without an upper secondary education. On average, employment rates are 18 percentage points higher for those with an upper secondary education and 28 percentage points higher for those with a tertiary education, compared to individuals who have not completed an upper secondary education. In Iceland, Norway, Sweden and Switzerland, for example, the average employment rate of tertiary-educated individuals is over 88%.

- During the recent economic crisis, the increase in the average unemployment rate for individuals without an upper secondary education was 1.1 percentage points higher than for those with at least an upper secondary degree and 2.4 percentage points higher than for those with a tertiary education.

- Despite the fact that women have higher tertiary attainment rates on average across OECD countries, their employment rates are much lower than those for men. The difference is greater than 25 percentage points in favour of men in some countries.

Chart A7.1. **Percentage of 25-64 year-olds in employment, by educational attainment level (2010)**

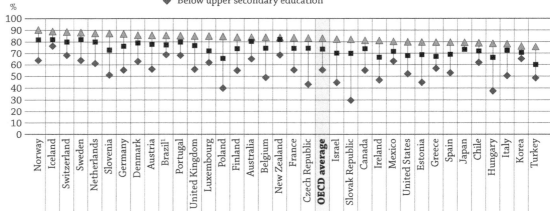

1. Year of reference 2009.
Countries are ranked in descending order of the employment rate of tertiary-educated individuals.
Source: OECD. Table A7.3a. See Annex 3 for notes (*www.oecd.org/edu/eag2012*).
StatLink ᵐᵍᶫ http://dx.doi.org/10.1787/888932662029

How to read this chart
The chart shows a positive relationship between education and employment. The likelihood of being in employment increases with higher levels of education. Individuals with tertiary education have the highest employment rate, compared to those with upper secondary education and below upper secondary education. However, the magnitude of this employment advantage varies across countries.

■ Context

Unemployment rates increased substantially in most OECD countries in 2009 and have remained higher ever since. There is considerable variation among countries, with some more severely affected than others. The impact of economic conditions on the likelihood that an individual will be employed varies significantly by both educational attainment and gender. Data on the relationship between educational attainment and both employment and unemployment provide valuable information to policy makers seeking to understand and respond to challenging economic circumstances.

Rapid technological progress has also been transforming the needs of the global labour market. People with higher or specific skills are in strong demand, while low-skilled workers face a greater likelihood that their jobs will be automated. Therefore, when designing education policies, it is critical to understand the changing needs of employers and identify current and potential skills gaps and mismatches. It is particularly important for policy makers to distinguish between the impact of the economic crisis and the long-term structural changes occurring in OECD economies.

Other findings

- In most OECD countries, **individuals without an upper secondary education are more likely to be unemployed.** On average among OECD countries, men without an upper secondary education are almost twice as likely to be unemployed as men with an upper secondary education, and almost three times as likely to be unemployed as men with a tertiary education.

- Although the gap in the employment rate between men and women narrows among tertiary-educated individuals, **the employment rate of women is far below that of men at all levels of education**. Policies boosting the labour market participation of women can help utilise the skills of women in the workforce more effectively.

- **The probability of working full time generally increases with higher levels of education for both men and women, but most full-time earners are men.** The proportion of individuals working full time is 10 percentage points higher among those with a tertiary education than among those without an upper secondary education. However, among tertiary-educated earners, only 69% of women work full time, while 84% of men are full-time earners, on average across OECD countries.

- **Individuals with a vocational upper secondary education have higher employment rates compared to people with a general upper secondary education**. On average, the employment rate of people who attained a vocational upper secondary education (ISCED level 3/4) as their highest qualification is 4.8 percentage points higher than the rate for those with a general upper secondary education (ISCED 3/4). In addition, the rate of inactivity in the labour force is about five percentage points lower among 25-64 year-olds with a vocational education, compared to those with a general education.

Trends

Education is generally good insurance against unemployment, even in difficult economic times. Over the past 13 years, employment rates for tertiary-educated men and women across OECD countries have consistently been higher than the rates for people without a tertiary degree. On average across OECD countries, unemployment rates for people with tertiary education have remained below 5% while they have remained below 8% for those with an upper secondary education, and have exceeded 10% several times between 1998 and 2010 for those who have not attained an upper secondary education.

A7

Analysis

Labour market outcomes by education attainment and age group

Higher levels of education generally lead to better prospects for employment across OECD countries. The average employment rate for individuals with a lower secondary qualification was 69.1% for men and 48.7% for women, while the average employment rate for individuals with a tertiary-type A (largely theory-based) qualification was 88.3% for men and 79.3% for women in 2010 (Table A7.1a).

On average, the employment rate is 18.2 percentage points higher for people with an upper secondary education, compared to the rate for people without an upper secondary education. The difference is exceptionally large in Belgium, the Czech Republic, Hungary, Poland and the Slovak Republic. In the Slovak Republic, for example, the average employment rate of people with an upper secondary education is 70%, but falls to 30% for those without an upper secondary degree, meaning that only 3 out of 10 people at this educational level are employed. This suggests that holding at least an upper secondary degree is especially important for employability in these countries (Table A7.1b, available on line).

Tertiary education increases the likelihood of being employed even further. Tertiary-educated individuals are employed at a higher rate than people with an upper secondary or post-secondary non-tertiary education. On average, 83% of 25-64 year-olds with a tertiary education were employed in 2010, compared to 74% of those with an upper secondary education. In Ireland, Poland and Turkey, for instance, the employment rate for individuals with a tertiary education is notably higher than the rate for individuals with an upper secondary education, by 15, 19 and 16 percentage points, respectively (Table A7.3a and Chart A7.1).

Unemployment rates vary considerably, depending on the age group. Overall, unemployment rates among 55-64 year-olds are much lower than those for the younger age cohort (25-34 year-olds). On average across OECD countries, among individuals without an upper secondary education aged 25 to 34, the unemployment rate in 2010 was 19.1%, whereas among 55-64 year-olds the rate was 8.8% – less than half that of the younger cohort. At the same time, tertiary-educated individuals had the lowest unemployment rates for both age groups. For 55-64 year-olds with a tertiary education, the unemployment rate was 4%, while it was 6.5% for 25-34 year-olds (Tables A7.4d and A7.4e, available on line).

The effect of the global economic crisis on labour market outcomes

An individual's employment prospects depend largely on whether his or her skills meet the requirements of the labour market. Unemployment rates are therefore a good indication of whether education systems are producing the supply of skills the labour market demands. High unemployment rates among people with different levels of educational attainment suggest that there are mismatches between the supply of and the demand for skills in the labour market. In the increasingly knowledge-based global economy, people with high skills are in greater demand in the labour market, while those with less education are more likely to be at risk of being unemployed, especially during periods of economic downturn.

Since the onset of the global recession in 2008, individuals without an upper secondary education have been hardest hit by unemployment. Unemployment rates among 25-64 year-olds without an upper secondary education rose by 3.8 percentage points between 2008 and 2010, whereas for individuals with an upper secondary education, the unemployment rate increased by 2.7 percentage points. Among tertiary-educated individuals, the rate rose by 1.4 percentage points between 2008 and 2010 (Table A7.4a and Chart A7.2).

The increase in the unemployment rate was particularly evident among men without an upper secondary education compared to women with the same level of education: it increased by 4.3 percentage points compared to 2.3 percentage points for women (Tables A7.4b and A7.4c, available on line).

The younger age cohort (25-34 year-olds) without an upper secondary education was also hit harder by the crisis than 55-64 year-olds without an upper secondary education. On average across OECD countries, the increase in the unemployment rate among 25-34 year-olds without an upper secondary education was 5.6 percentage points, while among 55-64 year-olds with the same educational attainment, the unemployment rate increased by 2.6 percentage points (Tables A7.4d and A7.4e, available on line). This may be due to the greater prevalence of young men in private sector fields such as the construction industry, which was hit harder by the crisis (Veric, 2009).

Estonia, Iceland, Ireland, Spain and the United States reported the most significant increase in unemployment rates among people without an upper secondary education between 2008 and 2009. This continued in 2010 for Estonia, Ireland and Spain, although the increase was smaller than in 2009 (Table A7.4a and Chart A7.2).

Chart A7.2. **Unemployment rates of 25-64 year-olds, by educational attainment level (2008, 2009 and 2010)**

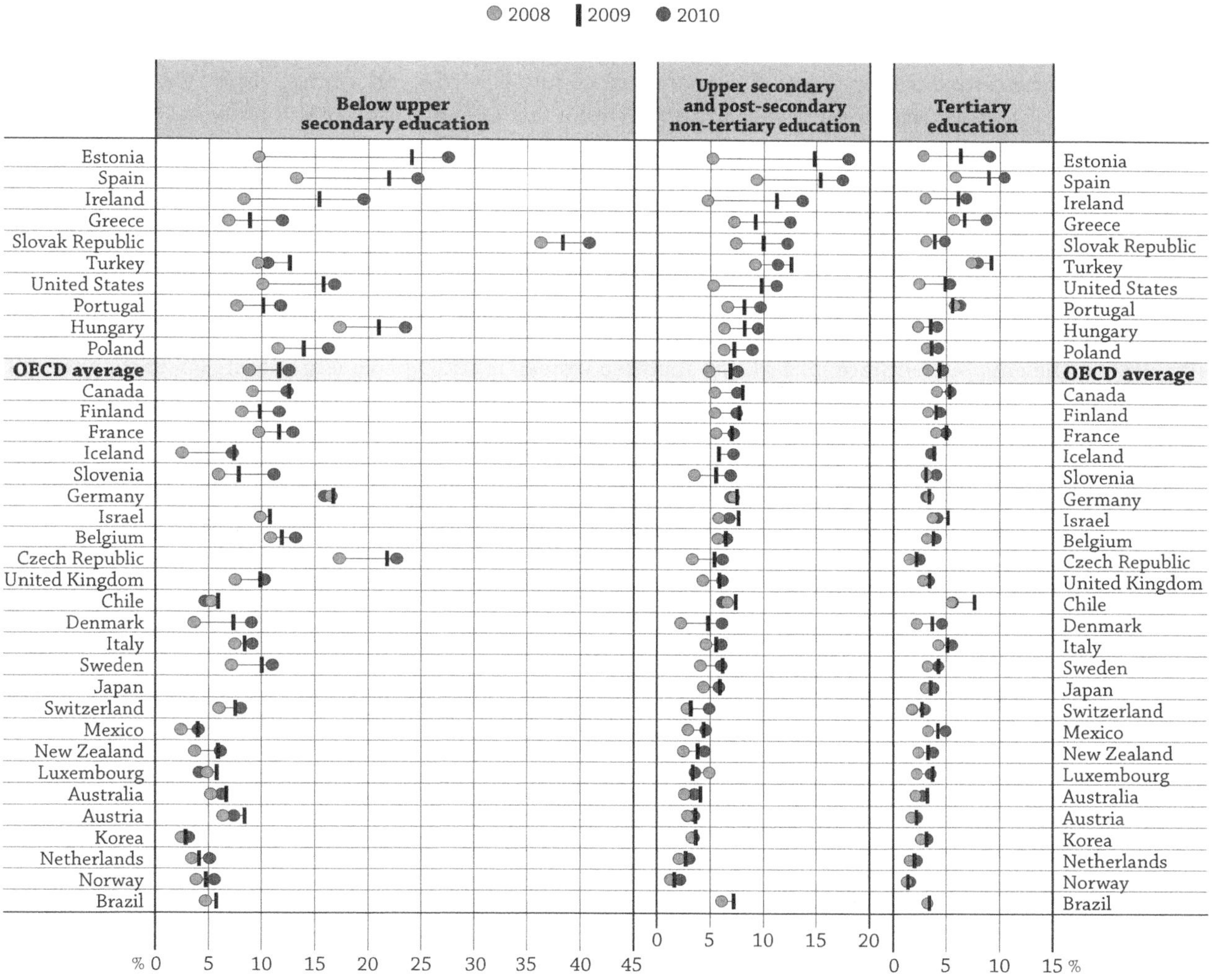

● 2008 | 2009 ● 2010

Countries are ranked in descending order of 2010 unemployment rate for individuals with upper secondary and post-secondary non-tertiary education.
Source: OECD. Table A7.4a. See Annex 3 for notes (*www.oecd.org/edu/eag2012*).
StatLink ⟶ http://dx.doi.org/10.1787/888932662048

The economic crisis also affected individuals with upper secondary education and tertiary education, but to a lesser degree. On average across OECD countries, the unemployment rate among 25-64 year-olds with an upper secondary or post-secondary non-tertiary education increased 2.7 percentage points between 2008 and 2010, which is 1.1 percentage points less than the increase among individuals who have not attained that level of education (Table A7.4a and Chart A7.2).

Tertiary-educated people also fared better than their less-educated counterparts during the same period. Overall, unemployment rates among 25-64 year-olds with a tertiary education rose 1.4 percentage points between 2008 and 2010, from 3.3% to 4.7%. Even in countries where the crisis hit hardest, individuals with a tertiary education managed to retain high employment rates and low unemployment rates compared to individuals with lower levels of education. In general, those with a tertiary education tend to be less likely to lose their jobs during an economic crisis and also tend to have a higher likelihood of re-entering the labour market. This holds for both men and women, and for younger and older age cohorts (Table A7.4a and Chart A7.2). Studies show a positive correlation between re-employment rates and educational attainment among unemployed job-seekers, and a negative correlation with the probability of job loss (Riddell and Song, 2011).

Labour-market participation of women

Fully using the skills available in the labour market is vital for spurring long-term economic growth, especially in ageing societies and during periods of economic recession. However, on average across OECD countries, the employment rate among 25-64 year-old women with a tertiary education is still remarkably low at 79%, compared to 88% for men (Tables A7.3b and A7.3c, available on line).

On average in OECD countries in 2010, 32% of 25-64 year-old women had a tertiary education, compared to 29% of men. In 24 of 34 OECD countries, an equal or greater proportion of women attained a university-level qualification compared to men (see Indicator A1, Tables A1.3b and A1.3c, available on line). However, the employment rates of women are lower than those of men, without exception across OECD countries. Although the gap between men's and women's employment rates narrows considerably with higher educational attainment, the employment rate for tertiary-educated women is still 9 percentage points lower than that of men, on average across OECD countries. The difference in employment rates between tertiary-educated men and women is particularly large in Chile, the Czech Republic, Japan, Korea, Mexico and Turkey, where it is as high as 29 percentage points. By contrast, the countries with the highest overall employment rates for 25-64 year-olds – Iceland, Norway, Sweden and Switzerland – also have some of the highest employment rates among women (Tables A7.1a, Chart A7.3 and Table A7.3c, available on line).

In Canada, Japan, New Zealand and the United States, where there are large proportions of tertiary-educated women compared to the OECD average, the employment rate among women is still below the OECD average, and far behind the rate for men. Consequently, efforts to remove barriers that hinder highly-educated women from participating in the labour market could benefit overall growth. Examples of policy measures to increase women's participation include providing childcare subsidies with employment; increasing the availability of affordable, flexible, high-quality childcare services, especially for single mothers; providing maternity and paternity leave; and offering flexible working hours. In the Nordic countries, where the proportion of women in the workforce is highest, childcare services were expanded specifically to make it easier for women to work. In Sweden, the expansion of childcare services during the 1970s is thought to have helped increase women's employment rates from 60% to over 80% (Kamerman and Moss, 2009).

Women are also over- and under-represented in some fields of education, contributing to gender gaps in occupations. In 2010, in every OECD country except Japan and Turkey, more than 70% of tertiary-type A and advanced research qualifications in the field of education were awarded to women. On average across OECD countries, 74% of the degrees awarded in the field of health and welfare also went to women. By contrast, on average across OECD countries, fewer than 30% of all graduates in the fields of engineering, manufacturing and construction were women (Table A4.6 and Chart A4.5). Perhaps not surprisingly, women are thus under-represented in high-technology industries (see Indicator A4).

Analysing data on the proportion of full-time earners is another way of examining the use of labour resources in different countries. Chart A7.4 provides a breakdown of the proportion of full-time earners (among all earners) with a tertiary education, by gender. The proportion of full-time earners varies considerably among countries, among different educational groups and, more significantly, between men and women.

Chart A7.3. **Percentage of 25-64 year-olds with tertiary education, and their employment rate, by gender (2010)**

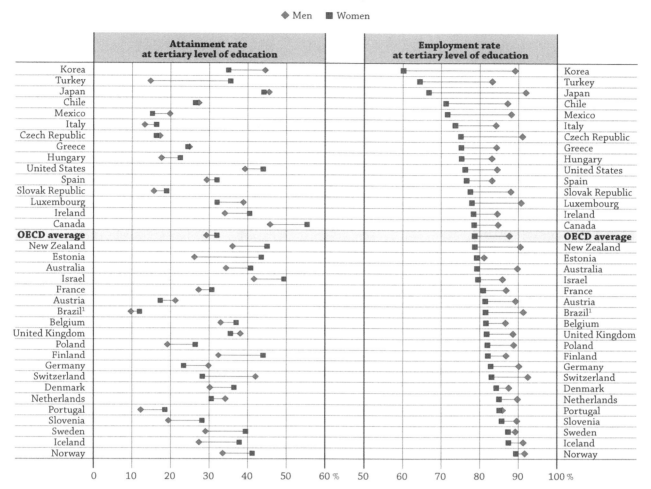

◆ Men   ■ Women

1. Year of reference 2009.
Countries are ranked in ascending order of 2010 employment rate for women with tertiary education.
Source: OECD. Tables A1.3b, A1.3c, A7.3b and Table A7.3c, available on line. See Annex 3 for notes (*www.oecd.org/edu/eag2012*).
StatLink ᴍᴤᴾ http://dx.doi.org/10.1787/888932662067

Full-time earners among tertiary-educated individuals

Full-time work generally increases with higher levels of education. Among wage-earners across OECD countries, 67% of people who have not attained an upper secondary education work full time, 73% of those with an upper secondary education do, and 76% of those with a tertiary education do. Much of the increase in the proportion of full-time workers is the result of the greater proportion of highly educated women now in the labour force (Table A7.5).

The largest difference in the proportion of full-time workers is between men and women. In all OECD countries except Hungary, smaller proportions of women are working full time compared to men (Table A7.5). Despite the fact that the proportion of women working full time increases with higher level of education, on average across OECD countries and among all wage earners, only 69% of tertiary-educated women work full time, while 84% of tertiary-educated men do. In the Netherlands, the proportion of tertiary-educated women working full time is particularly low, at 27.2%. At the same time, the overall employment rate among women in the Netherlands is significantly higher than the OECD average, suggesting that a large proportion of women with a tertiary education are participating in the labour market on a part-time basis (Chart A7.4).

A7

In Canada, Ireland, Luxembourg and the Slovak Republic employment rates of tertiary-educated women are lower than the OECD average, and the percentage of women working full time is also lower than the OECD average. In countries such as Finland and Portugal, employment rates among women are substantially higher than the OECD average, and most tertiary-educated women work full time (Charts A7.3 and A7.4).

Chart A7.4. **Proportion of full-time earners among 25-64 year-old tertiary-educated individuals with earnings from employment, by gender (2010)**

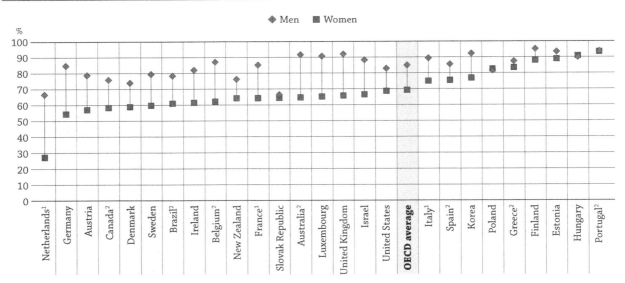

1. Year of reference 2008.
2. Year of reference 2009.
Countries are ranked in ascending order of proportion of full time women earners with tertiary education.
Source: OECD. Table A7.5. See Annex 3 for notes (*www.oecd.org/edu/eag2012*).
StatLink ᐧᔑ𝘴ᔑ http://dx.doi.org/10.1787/888932662086

Labour-force status by vocational and general orientation of education

Matching the supply of and demand for skills not only concerns the level of education that individuals attain, but also the specificity of skills they acquire in the educational system. The International Standard Classification of Education (ISCED-97) defines vocational education and training (VET) as "education which is mainly designed to lead participants to acquire the practical skills, know-how and understanding necessary for employment in a particular occupation or trade or class of occupations or trades. Successful completion of such programmes leads to a labour-market relevant vocational qualification recognised by the competent authorities in the country in which it is obtained."

In other words, VET is generally geared towards giving students with upper secondary and/or post-secondary non-tertiary education relevant labour-market skills for a particular occupation or industry, even if reforms have made direct access to tertiary education easier in some countries. This type of specialisation may also include apprenticeship or work-study programmes, which can help to ensure a closer match between employers' needs for specific skills and the skills workers make available to the labour market (OECD, 2010). VET and programmes that contain work-based elements are often developed in close co-operation with employers, reducing the need for extensive initial on-the-job training and increasing the immediate and long-term productivity of new hires. Research has shown that VET can yield good economic returns on public investment, and countries with strong VET systems, like Germany, have been relatively successful in tackling youth unemployment (CEDEFOP, 2011). A potential drawback is that the versatility of skills that individuals acquire through VET might be limited in times of changing demand.

VET systems vary widely among countries. Therefore, cross-country comparability is somewhat more limited than in other areas of the ISCED classification, and this needs to be kept in mind when comparing VET participation and outcomes across different OECD countries. For example, about 70% of the adult population in the Czech Republic and the Slovak Republic attained an upper secondary VET qualification as their highest level of education, whereas in Spain and Turkey, less than 10% of the adult population attained an upper secondary VET qualification (Table A1.5). Enrolment rates also show a similar tendency. In Austria, Belgium, the Czech Republic, Italy, the Slovak Republic and Slovenia, more than 40% of 15-19 year-olds participate in pre-vocational or vocational programmes at the upper secondary level on a full-time basis. However, in Argentina, Australia, Brazil, Japan, Korea, Mexico, New Zealand, the Russian Federation and Spain, less than 14% of 15-19 year-old students were enrolled in pre-vocational or vocational programmes at that level on a full-time basis in 2010 (see Indicator C1, Table C1.3).

Table A7.6 provides a breakdown of labour-market outcomes by vocational and general education attainment at the upper secondary and/or post-secondary non-tertiary (ISCED 3/4) levels of education. The average employment rate among individuals with a vocational upper secondary (ISCED 3/4) qualification is 75.5%, which is 4.8 percentage points higher than the rate among individuals with a general upper secondary (ISCED 3/4) education as their highest qualification (Table A7.6 and Chart A7.5).

Chart A7.5. **Employment rates of individuals with vocational and general education attainment at ISCED 3/4 level (2010)**

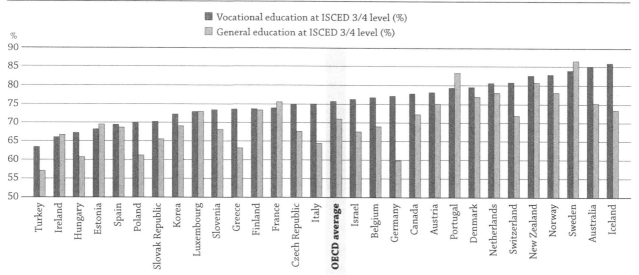

Countries are ranked in ascending order of the employment rate of 25-64 year-olds with vocational education at ISCED 3/4 level.
Source: OECD. Table A7.6. See Annex 3 for notes (*www.oecd.org/edu/eag2012*).
StatLink http://dx.doi.org/10.1787/888932662105

While unemployment rates among people with vocational education and among those with general education are similar, the inactivity rate of individuals with vocational upper secondary education is, on average across countries with comparable data, about 5 percentage points lower than that for individuals with general upper secondary education (Table A7.6 and Chart A7.5).

The stronger labour-market outcomes among individuals with a vocational upper secondary education as their highest degree compared to individuals with a general upper secondary education may be due to the fact that the former group learns specific skills that are immediately needed in the labour market. In addition, they appear to use previous work experience to land their first job (CEDEFOP, 2012). By contrast, skills learned in general education at an upper secondary level tend to have fewer obvious links to the labour market and are

A7

designed to prepare individuals to choose more specific fields of education at the tertiary level. Therefore, it might be more difficult for those with a general upper secondary degree than those with a vocational qualification to find a job.

Further refinement of the cross-country comparability of this aspect of the ISCED classification will improve the precision of estimates and allow for more explicit analysis.

Definitions

Under the auspices of the International Labour Organization (ILO) and their conferences of labour statisticians, concepts and definitions for measuring labour-force participation were established and are now used as a common reference (ILO, 1982).

Employed individuals are those who, during the survey reference week: *i)* work for pay (employees) or profit (self-employed and unpaid family workers) for at least one hour; or *ii)* have a job but are temporarily not at work (through injury, illness, holiday, strike or lock-out, educational or training leave, maternity or parental leave, etc.).

The **employment rate** refers to the number of persons in employment as a percentage of the working-age population.

Full-time basis refers to people who have worked all year long and at least 30 hours per week. The length of the reference period varies from one week to one year. Self-employed people are excluded in some countries.

Unemployed individuals are those who are, during the survey reference week, without work, actively seeking employment and currently available to start work.

The **unemployment rate** refers to unemployed persons as a percentage of the civil labour force.

The statistical data for Israel are supplied by and under the responsibility of the relevant Israeli authorities. The use of such data by the OECD is without prejudice to the status of the Golan Heights, East Jerusalem and Israeli settlements in the West Bank under the terms of international law.

References

CEDEFOP (2011), *The Benefits of Vocational Education and Training*, Publications Office, Luxembourg.

CEDEFOP (2012), *From Education to Working Life: The Labour-Market Outcomes of Vocational Education and Training*, Publications Office, Luxembourg.

ILO (International Labour Organization) (1982), "Resolution concerning statistics of the economically active population, employment, unemployment and underemployment", adopted by the Thirteenth International Conference of Labour Statisticians, October 1982, Geneva.

Kamerman, S.B. and P. Moss (2009), *The Politics of Parental Leave Policy*, Policy Press, Bristol.

OECD (2006), *Employment Outlook 2006: Boosting Jobs and Incomes*, OECD Publishing.

OECD (2010), *Learning For Jobs*, OECD Reviews of Vocational Education and Training, OECD Publishing.

Riddell, C.W. and X. Song (2011), "Impact of Education on Unemployment Incidence and Re-employment Success: Evidence from the U.S. Labour Market", IZA Discussion Paper, No. 5572.

Veric, S. (2009), "Who Is Hit Hardest during a Financial Crisis? The Vulnerability of Young Men and Women to Unemployment in an Economic Downturn", *IZA Discussion Paper*, No. 4359.

The following additional material relevant to this indicator is available on line:

• *Table A7.1b. Employment rates, by educational attainment (2010)*
    StatLink ᔖ http://dx.doi.org/10.1787/888932665069

- *Table A7.2b. Unemployment rates, by educational attainment (2010)*
  StatLink http://dx.doi.org/10.1787/888932665107

- *Table A7.3b. Trends in employment rates of 25-64 year-old men, by educational attainment (1997-2010)*
  StatLink http://dx.doi.org/10.1787/888932665145

- *Table A7.3c. Trends in employment rates of 25-64 year-old women, by educational attainment (1997-2010)*
  StatLink http://dx.doi.org/10.1787/888932665164

- *Table A7.4b. Trends in unemployment rates of 25-64 year-old men, by educational attainment (1997-2010)*
  StatLink http://dx.doi.org/10.1787/888932665202

- *Table A7.4c. Trends in unemployment rates of 25-64 year-old women, by educational attainment (1997-2010)*
  StatLink http://dx.doi.org/10.1787/888932665221

- *Table A7.4d. Trends in unemployment rates of 55-64 year-olds, by educational attainment (1997-2010)*
  StatLink http://dx.doi.org/10.1787/888932665240

- *Table A7.4e. Trends in unemployment rates of 25-34 year-olds, by educational attainment (1997-2010)*
  StatLink http://dx.doi.org/10.1787/888932665259

A7

Table A7.1a. [1/2] Employment rates, by educational attainment and gender (2010)

Number of 25-64 year-olds in employment as a percentage of the population aged 25-64

		Pre-primary and primary education	Lower secondary education	Upper secondary education ISCED 3C Short	Upper secondary education ISCED 3C Long/3B	Upper secondary education ISCED 3A	Post-secondary non-tertiary education	Tertiary education Type B	Tertiary education Type A and advanced research programmes	All levels of education
		(1)	(2)	(3)	(4)	(5)	(6)	(7)	(8)	(9)
Australia	Men	67.0	81.1	a	88.8	85.3	91.7	88.3	90.3	85.9
	Women	37.3	60.1	a	74.1	66.3	80.7	75.4	80.9	69.6
Austria	Men	x(2)	63.8	79.3	81.2	77.2	87.9	86.8	90.9	81.2
	Women	x(2)	50.3	64.5	71.4	73.5	82.4	79.7	82.3	70.0
Belgium	Men	46.2	67.5	a	81.7	81.1	86.7	85.4	87.6	76.5
	Women	27.6	47.1	a	64.3	66.8	77.8	80.2	83.5	64.0
Canada	Men	53.4	66.7	a	x(5)	77.1	80.9	84.3	85.1	79.4
	Women	31.8	51.4	a	x(5)	67.4	72.3	77.8	79.2	71.7
Chile	Men	78.6	87.0	x(5)	88.4	88.2	a	88.4	86.5	86.3
	Women	39.0	46.3	x(5)	57.6	56.3	a	69.1	72.7	56.2
Czech Republic	Men	c	54.4	a	80.8	87.1	x(5)	x(8)	91.0	83.0
	Women	c	39.0	a	59.6	69.2	x(5)	x(8)	75.0	63.7
Denmark	Men	73.2	69.5	75.4	81.2	79.3	c	86.7	87.8	80.2
	Women	41.3	55.7	67.6	77.4	74.7	c	80.1	84.9	74.5
Estonia	Men	c	49.7	a	69.8	73.3	70.2	74.2	84.4	70.7
	Women	c	45.8	a	62.4	66.6	61.9	77.1	80.6	69.4
Finland	Men	47.2	68.3	a	a	75.9	90.4	82.0	89.3	76.3
	Women	41.3	55.6	a	a	71.3	92.5	81.5	82.5	73.0
France	Men	47.4	71.0	a	78.0	80.8	c	88.0	86.2	76.3
	Women	36.6	57.9	a	68.6	72.0	c	82.2	79.9	66.9
Germany	Men	56.8	68.6	a	81.3	63.4	86.3	88.9	90.9	81.8
	Women	35.8	51.8	a	71.3	55.4	80.3	83.7	82.3	70.5
Greece	Men	70.6	79.5	82.0	83.3	79.2	83.3	81.2	85.8	79.3
	Women	36.8	46.8	63.3	54.5	50.0	62.5	72.3	76.2	53.9
Hungary	Men	20.0	46.6	a	68.6	75.6	77.4	82.2	83.1	69.4
	Women	12.4	34.3	a	57.1	61.9	65.3	81.2	75.1	57.6
Iceland	Men	78.1	80.5	84.6	89.0	76.4	87.5	91.0	91.3	85.8
	Women	c	71.0	83.6	80.4	71.6	81.7	91.6	86.7	79.1
Ireland	Men	45.9	63.5	66.2	a	74.9	69.9	81.9	86.1	72.0
	Women	25.8	42.3	54.3	a	59.3	60.6	74.3	81.6	61.5
Israel	Men	53.8	65.8	a	80.1	73.7	a	83.7	87.0	76.8
	Women	20.3	43.3	a	66.9	63.5	a	73.9	82.2	65.7
Italy	Men	48.4	73.2	77.2	82.0	81.7	84.6	80.8	84.3	75.8
	Women	15.4	39.6	55.1	59.3	63.8	68.7	70.7	73.7	51.4
Japan	Men	x(5)	x(5)	x(5)	x(5)	85.7	a	91.6	92.0	88.5
	Women	x(5)	x(5)	x(5)	x(5)	61.2	a	65.8	68.4	63.7
Korea	Men	73.1	80.2	a	86.1	83.2	a	89.3	89.0	85.5
	Women	55.8	58.3	a	57.0	56.7	a	59.4	60.5	58.0
Luxembourg	Men	70.3	78.5	78.9	79.5	83.7	76.8	89.5	91.5	83.6
	Women	54.2	48.5	53.0	56.2	67.2	72.6	78.1	77.8	65.1
Mexico	Men	86.0	90.7	a	89.3	90.3	a	86.4	88.2	88.2
	Women	39.9	47.7	a	57.3	55.5	a	70.3	71.7	49.6
Netherlands	Men	64.8	78.3	x(4)	81.0	87.8	83.3	84.9	90.2	84.0
	Women	37.4	54.0	x(4)	69.6	78.4	76.0	76.9	85.7	70.7
New Zealand	Men	x(2)	73.3	86.5	86.4	88.4	90.2	88.7	91.6	86.2
	Women	x(2)	57.7	72.1	70.9	74.4	76.9	76.7	80.1	72.4
Norway	Men	c	68.4	a	85.3	80.8	85.7	90.3	91.8	83.8
	Women	c	60.3	a	78.8	75.8	82.6	94.6	89.2	79.1

Source: OECD. See Annex 3 for a description of ISCED-97 levels, ISCED-97 country mappings and national data sources (*www.oecd.org/edu/eag2012*).
Please refer to the Reader's Guide for information concerning the symbols replacing missing data.
StatLink ᖂᓭ᛫ http://dx.doi.org/10.1787/888932665050

Table A7.1a. [2/2] Employment rates, by educational attainment and gender (2010)
Number of 25-64 year-olds in employment as a percentage of the population aged 25-64

		Pre-primary and primary education	Lower secondary education	Upper secondary education			Post-secondary non-tertiary education	Tertiary education		All levels of education
				ISCED 3C Short	ISCED 3C Long/3B	ISCED 3A		Type B	Type A and advanced research programmes	
		(1)	(2)	(3)	(4)	(5)	(6)	(7)	(8)	(9)
OECD										
Poland	Men	x(2)	49.6	a	70.9	78.2	79.5	x(8)	88.8	74.3
	Women	x(2)	30.9	a	50.7	58.7	65.7	x(8)	82.0	60.1
Portugal	Men	72.4	82.8	x(5)	x(5)	83.5	86.9	x(8)	85.9	78.1
	Women	56.8	70.2	x(5)	x(5)	76.5	70.7	x(8)	85.1	67.7
Slovak Republic	Men	c	39.9	x(4)	73.0	82.3	x(5)	78.4	88.3	76.0
	Women	c	26.1	x(4)	53.3	67.8	x(5)	66.5	78.1	61.0
Slovenia	Men	34.8	64.3	a	73.7	78.4	a	84.7	93.5	76.4
	Women	23.0	45.0	a	65.3	71.0	a	82.1	88.6	68.8
Spain	Men	52.8	70.1	a	77.8	74.4	c	80.8	84.4	71.9
	Women	31.9	49.3	a	61.3	62.3	c	70.4	78.6	57.3
Sweden	Men	61.8	78.5	a	x(5)	85.2	87.4	86.4	90.1	84.8
	Women	35.5	59.9	a	x(5)	78.1	76.9	83.1	88.9	78.4
Switzerland	Men	68.9	78.3	87.0	87.2	78.1	87.5	95.3	91.0	87.9
	Women	57.4	62.3	74.3	74.5	67.7	80.6	88.8	81.1	74.9
Turkey	Men	71.9	76.4	a	81.0	77.9	a	x(8)	83.2	75.7
	Women	24.4	21.2	a	30.9	27.0	a	x(8)	64.4	29.3
United Kingdom	Men	c	53.7	75.7	82.4	83.9	c	87.2	88.7	81.2
	Women	c	34.2	59.2	73.0	72.6	c	78.3	80.9	68.8
United States	Men	63.6	59.8	x(5)	x(5)	72.2	x(5)	78.6	86.1	75.7
	Women	39.5	42.8	x(5)	x(5)	63.5	x(5)	74.3	76.8	66.9
OECD average	Men	60.3	69.1	79.3	81.0	80.1	83.7	85.5	88.3	80.0
	Women	35.7	48.7	64.7	63.8	65.4	74.4	77.2	79.3	65.0
EU21 average	Men	54.2	65.3	76.4	78.0	79.4	82.2	83.9	88.0	77.8
	Women	34.1	46.9	59.6	63.3	67.5	72.4	77.7	81.1	65.4
Other G20										
Argentina		m	m	m	m	m	m	m	m	m
Brazil[1]	Men	83.4	87.4	x(5)	x(5)	88.8	a	x(8)	91.3	86.3
	Women	51.8	58.9	x(5)	x(5)	67.7	a	x(8)	81.5	61.2
China		m	m	m	m	m	m	m	m	m
India		m	m	m	m	m	m	m	m	m
Indonesia		m	m	m	m	m	m	m	m	m
Russian Federation		m	m	m	m	m	m	m	m	m
Saudi Arabia		m	m	m	m	m	m	m	m	m
South Africa		m	m	m	m	m	m	m	m	m
G20 average		m	m	m	m	m	m	m	m	m

1. Year of reference 2009.
Source: OECD. See Annex 3 for a description of ISCED-97 levels, ISCED-97 country mappings and national data sources (*www.oecd.org/edu/eag2012*).
Please refer to the Reader's Guide for information concerning the symbols replacing missing data.
StatLink ᵐˢᴸ http://dx.doi.org/10.1787/888932665050

A7

Table A7.2a. [1/2]   Unemployment rates, by educational attainment and gender (2010)
Number of 25-64 year-olds in unemployment as a percentage of the labour force aged 25-64

| | | Pre-primary and primary education | Lower secondary education | Upper secondary education | | | Post-secondary non-tertiary education | Tertiary education | | All levels of education |
| | | | | ISCED 3C Short | ISCED 3C Long/3B | ISCED 3A | | Type B | Type A and advanced research programmes | |
		(1)	(2)	(3)	(4)	(5)	(6)	(7)	(8)	(9)
Australia	Men	9.0	5.8	a	2.9	3.7	c	2.9	2.7	3.8
	Women	6.9	5.6	a	4.3	4.5	3.8	2.8	2.8	4.0
Austria	Men	x(2)	10.2	c	3.5	4.9	3.6	c	2.6	4.0
	Women	x(2)	5.9	c	3.5	4.0	2.5	c	3.1	3.5
Belgium	Men	18.3	10.0	a	6.5	5.3	c	3.7	4.2	6.8
	Women	17.9	11.9	a	9.7	7.1	c	3.6	4.7	7.2
Canada	Men	14.1	12.1	a	x(5)	8.3	7.5	6.1	5.2	7.3
	Women	14.7	11.3	a	x(5)	6.9	7.0	5.5	5.0	6.3
Chile	Men	3.8	3.7	x(5)	6.8	5.4	a	5.3	5.0	4.9
	Women	5.0	7.4	x(5)	8.2	7.3	a	6.5	6.1	6.7
Czech Republic	Men	c	24.1	a	6.1	3.7	x(8)	x(8)	2.5	5.4
	Women	c	21.8	a	10.8	5.3	x(8)	x(8)	2.5	7.8
Denmark	Men	c	10.0	c	6.6	7.6	c	4.7	5.3	6.9
	Women	c	8.3	c	5.0	6.9	c	5.4	3.9	5.3
Estonia	Men	c	30.4	a	19.8	16.4	20.6	16.5	10.2	17.8
	Women	c	18.6	a	23.8	14.9	23.2	8.0	6.7	13.1
Finland	Men	10.7	12.1	a	a	8.0	c	5.5	4.2	7.3
	Women	9.4	12.9	a	a	6.9	c	3.9	4.5	6.1
France	Men	13.6	12.4	a	6.3	7.0	c	4.8	4.7	7.5
	Women	13.0	13.3	a	8.5	7.4	c	4.4	5.6	8.2
Germany	Men	23.1	16.9	a	7.8	8.6	5.2	2.8	3.1	7.2
	Women	19.1	12.1	a	6.6	7.9	4.0	2.9	3.5	6.3
Greece	Men	9.7	11.5	7.2	9.5	8.7	10.2	8.3	5.9	8.9
	Women	13.0	17.7	c	24.9	15.5	18.4	15.0	9.5	14.5
Hungary	Men	36.3	24.4	a	11.1	7.1	9.1	c	4.3	10.3
	Women	47.8	21.1	a	11.7	8.0	12.6	c	3.8	9.7
Iceland	Men	c	9.3	c	c	c	c	c	c	6.6
	Women	c	6.3	c	c	c	c	c	c	5.2
Ireland	Men	23.1	23.3	c	a	14.7	20.9	10.4	6.3	15.2
	Women	10.9	11.4	c	a	8.7	10.6	6.9	5.2	7.9
Israel	Men	11.9	8.8	a	6.5	6.5	a	4.3	4.0	6.0
	Women	10.5	6.9	a	9.0	6.7	a	5.3	3.8	5.6
Italy	Men	11.0	7.5	9.3	4.9	5.0	8.8	6.3	4.4	6.2
	Women	12.7	10.8	14.4	7.1	7.3	11.9	6.0	6.6	8.3
Japan	Men	x(5)	x(5)	x(5)	x(5)	6.4	a	4.9	3.4	5.2
	Women	x(5)	x(5)	x(5)	x(5)	5.0	a	4.2	3.2	4.5
Korea	Men	3.9	4.2	a	3.8	4.1	a	4.3	2.9	3.7
	Women	2.1	2.3	a	3.0	2.6	a	3.7	2.9	2.8
Luxembourg	Men	c	c	c	2.6	3.3	c	3.3	2.7	2.9
	Women	c	c	c	5.3	4.7	c	4.1	4.8	4.7
Mexico	Men	4.1	4.3	a	3.5	4.8	a	3.2	5.1	4.4
	Women	3.2	4.8	a	4.0	5.3	a	1.9	5.2	4.2
Netherlands	Men	6.8	4.9	x(4)	3.9	3.2	2.4	2.7	2.6	3.4
	Women	2.8	5.2	x(4)	3.7	2.9	2.1	4.0	2.3	3.0
New Zealand	Men	x(2)	7.4	3.6	5.6	3.3	2.9	4.4	2.8	4.2
	Women	x(2)	6.4	4.3	7.5	4.0	3.5	5.0	3.5	4.9
Norway	Men	c	7.2	a	2.1	c	c	c	1.5	3.0
	Women	c	3.8	a	c	c	c	c	1.7	1.9

Source: OECD. See Annex 3 for a description of ISCED-97 levels, ISCED-97 country mappings and national data sources (*www.oecd.org/edu/eag2012*). *Please refer to the Reader's Guide for information concerning the symbols replacing missing data.*
StatLink ᜎᜒᎦᒪ http://dx.doi.org/10.1787/888932665088

A7

Table A7.2a. [2/2] Unemployment rates, by educational attainment and gender (2010)

Number of 25-64 year-olds in unemployment as a percentage of the labour force aged 25-64

			Pre-primary and primary education	Lower secondary education	Upper secondary education: ISCED 3C Short	Upper secondary education: ISCED 3C Long/3B	Upper secondary education: ISCED 3A	Post-secondary non-tertiary education	Tertiary education: Type B	Tertiary education: Type A and advanced research programmes	All levels of education
			(1)	(2)	(3)	(4)	(5)	(6)	(7)	(8)	(9)
OECD	Poland	Men	x(2)	15.8	a	9.3	6.8	8.1	x(8)	4.0	7.9
		Women	x(2)	16.9	a	11.9	9.2	7.2	x(8)	4.4	8.5
	Portugal	Men	11.3	9.1	x(5)	x(5)	7.5	c	x(8)	5.5	9.4
		Women	12.0	15.7	x(5)	x(5)	11.7	c	x(8)	6.8	11.6
	Slovak Republic	Men	90.0	40.8	x(4)	13.9	8.5	a	c	5.1	12.0
		Women	c	38.9	x(4)	20.3	9.4	a	c	4.3	13.1
	Slovenia	Men	21.6	11.4	a	6.6	6.7	a	5.7	2.6	6.7
		Women	c	9.6	a	8.0	7.0	a	4.3	4.0	6.6
	Spain	Men	28.1	21.5	a	15.3	16.3	c	12.2	8.1	17.6
		Women	27.7	25.1	a	19.1	19.3	c	15.7	9.8	18.6
	Sweden	Men	14.0	8.0	a	x(5)	6.1	4.7	6.2	4.2	6.0
		Women	22.0	10.4	a	x(5)	6.2	7.5	4.6	3.8	5.9
	Switzerland	Men	10.4	9.2	c	5.4	c	c	1.8	3.7	4.7
		Women	11.1	6.8	c	4.5	6.9	c	c	3.3	4.5
	Turkey	Men	11.0	10.7	a	8.2	9.8	x(8)	x(8)	6.1	9.8
		Women	8.2	19.5	a	19.8	20.9	x(8)	x(8)	11.3	11.6
	United Kingdom	Men	c	14.9	8.9	6.4	5.3	c	4.6	3.6	6.2
		Women	c	12.0	6.7	5.7	4.3	c	3.7	3.0	5.1
	United States	Men	15.0	19.5	x(5)	x(5)	12.8	x(5)	8.9	5.1	10.5
		Women	15.6	14.7	x(5)	x(5)	9.3	x(5)	6.1	4.3	7.5
	OECD average	Men	17.4	13.2	7.3	7.1	7.3	8.7	5.8	4.4	7.3
		Women	13.6	12.4	8.5	9.8	7.9	8.8	5.6	4.7	7.2
	EU21 average	Men	22.7	16.0	8.5	8.3	7.7	9.4	6.5	4.6	8.4
		Women	17.4	15.0	10.6	10.9	8.3	10.0	6.2	4.9	8.3
Other G20	Argentina		m	m	m	m	m	m	m	m	m
	Brazil[1]	Men	3.6	4.8	x(5)	x(5)	5.0	a	X(8)	2.8	4.1
		Women	7.6	10.2	x(5)	x(5)	9.7	a	X(8)	4.0	8.1
	China		m	m	m	m	m	m	m	m	m
	India		m	m	m	m	m	m	m	m	m
	Indonesia		m	m	m	m	m	m	m	m	m
	Russian Federation		m	m	m	m	m	m	m	m	m
	Saudi Arabia		m	m	m	m	m	m	m	m	m
	South Africa		m	m	m	m	m	m	m	m	m
	G20 average		m	m	m	m	m	m	m	m	m

1. Year of reference 2009.

Source: OECD. See Annex 3 for a description of ISCED-97 levels, ISCED-97 country mappings and national data sources *(www.oecd.org/edu/eag2012)*.

Please refer to the Reader's Guide for information concerning the symbols replacing missing data.

StatLink http://dx.doi.org/10.1787/888932665088

A7

Table A7.3a. [1/2] Trends in employment rates of 25-64 year-olds, by educational attainment (1998-2010)

Number of 25-64 year-olds in employment as a percentage of the population aged 25-64

		1998	1999	2000	2001	2002	2003	2004	2005	2006	2007	2008	2009	2010
Australia	Below upper secondary	59.5	59.1	60.8	59.9	60.0	61.0	60.6	62.9	63.5	63.9	61.5	66.1	65.1
	Upper secondary and post-secondary non-tertiary	75.9	76.2	76.7	78.0	77.8	78.7	78.8	79.8	80.4	80.5	80.9	80.2	80.5
	Tertiary education	83.8	82.0	82.9	83.1	83.5	83.2	83.3	84.4	84.4	84.8	83.1	84.3	84.0
Austria	Below upper secondary	52.6	53.3	53.7	53.5	54.4	55.0	52.2	53.3	55.7	57.9	57.0	55.6	56.1
	Upper secondary and post-secondary non-tertiary	75.0	75.6	74.8	74.8	75.3	75.6	73.9	74.3	75.8	76.9	78.1	77.6	77.9
	Tertiary education	85.8	86.2	87.5	86.6	86.0	85.0	82.5	84.5	85.9	86.8	86.4	86.7	85.7
Belgium	Below upper secondary	47.5	49.1	50.5	49.0	48.8	48.9	48.8	49.0	49.0	49.8	49.4	48.0	48.9
	Upper secondary and post-secondary non-tertiary	72.0	74.5	75.1	73.9	73.8	72.8	73.1	74.0	73.2	74.2	74.7	74.0	74.5
	Tertiary education	84.3	85.4	85.3	84.5	83.7	83.6	83.9	84.2	83.6	84.9	84.7	84.2	84.0
Canada	Below upper secondary	53.5	54.4	54.7	54.4	55.0	56.4	57.1	56.4	56.8	57.2	57.7	55.0	55.1
	Upper secondary and post-secondary non-tertiary	74.4	75.3	76.0	75.4	75.8	76.3	76.7	76.3	76.0	76.5	76.5	73.7	74.0
	Tertiary education	82.4	82.4	82.7	81.9	82.0	82.1	82.2	82.1	82.5	82.8	82.6	81.7	81.3
Chile	Below upper secondary	m	m	m	m	m	m	m	m	m	59.4	58.9	58.3	61.8
	Upper secondary and post-secondary non-tertiary	m	m	m	m	m	m	m	m	m	69.3	70.1	69.2	71.8
	Tertiary education	m	m	m	m	m	m	m	m	m	77.9	79.5	78.0	79.1
Czech Republic	Below upper secondary	49.5	46.9	46.9	46.7	45.3	46.0	42.3	41.2	43.9	45.7	46.5	43.9	43.2
	Upper secondary and post-secondary non-tertiary	78.2	76.4	75.5	75.7	76.2	75.8	74.8	75.5	75.6	76.1	76.6	75.1	74.5
	Tertiary education	88.7	87.4	86.8	87.8	87.1	86.5	86.4	85.8	85.1	85.2	85.1	84.3	83.3
Denmark	Below upper secondary	60.9	61.7	62.2	61.5	61.2	62.6	61.7	61.5	62.8	67.5	68.4	65.2	62.9
	Upper secondary and post-secondary non-tertiary	79.1	80.7	81.0	81.0	80.3	79.8	79.9	79.9	81.3	82.3	82.7	80.0	79.1
	Tertiary education	87.5	87.9	88.6	87.2	86.0	85.2	85.5	86.4	87.4	87.2	88.5	86.8	85.7
Estonia	Below upper secondary	m	m	m	m	44.1	49.0	50.9	50.0	56.5	56.7	58.3	47.4	44.8
	Upper secondary and post-secondary non-tertiary	m	m	m	m	71.9	72.9	72.6	73.6	78.1	79.4	79.7	71.6	68.6
	Tertiary education	m	m	m	m	81.6	80.3	82.4	84.5	87.7	87.4	85.8	82.8	79.9
Finland	Below upper secondary	56.2	58.6	57.3	58.2	57.7	57.9	57.1	57.9	58.4	58.6	59.3	56.8	55.0
	Upper secondary and post-secondary non-tertiary	73.1	74.3	74.9	75.5	74.4	74.4	74.4	75.2	75.6	76.2	77.3	74.8	74.1
	Tertiary education	83.2	84.7	84.4	85.1	85.1	85.0	84.2	84.1	85.0	85.2	85.6	84.4	84.1
France	Below upper secondary	56.3	56.4	57.0	57.7	57.8	58.9	59.1	58.6	58.2	57.8	57.4	56.2	55.4
	Upper secondary and post-secondary non-tertiary	75.0	75.1	75.8	76.5	76.7	76.3	75.7	75.7	75.6	75.7	75.8	74.8	74.4
	Tertiary education	81.6	81.8	83.1	83.7	83.3	83.3	82.9	83.0	83.0	83.4	84.6	83.5	83.6
Germany	Below upper secondary	46.1	48.7	50.6	51.8	50.9	50.2	48.6	51.6	53.8	54.6	55.3	54.9	55.3
	Upper secondary and post-secondary non-tertiary	67.9	69.9	70.4	70.5	70.3	69.7	69.5	70.6	72.5	74.4	75.3	75.5	76.3
	Tertiary education	82.2	83.0	83.4	83.4	83.6	83.0	82.7	82.9	84.3	85.5	85.8	86.4	86.9
Greece	Below upper secondary	57.1	57.0	57.5	57.2	58.3	59.7	59.7	59.1	59.5	59.9	60.3	59.7	56.7
	Upper secondary and post-secondary non-tertiary	64.8	64.6	64.6	65.0	65.3	66.8	68.1	68.7	69.7	69.4	69.8	68.4	67.1
	Tertiary education	80.5	80.7	80.9	80.3	81.2	81.5	81.4	81.8	83.1	82.6	82.6	82.2	79.8
Hungary	Below upper secondary	36.2	35.8	35.8	36.6	36.7	37.4	36.9	38.1	38.2	38.5	38.7	37.4	37.6
	Upper secondary and post-secondary non-tertiary	70.9	72.1	72.1	71.9	71.7	71.4	70.9	70.4	70.4	70.2	68.7	67.0	66.2
	Tertiary education	81.0	82.1	82.4	82.6	82.0	82.7	82.9	83.0	81.8	80.4	79.9	78.8	78.6
Iceland	Below upper secondary	85.6	87.2	87.3	87.2	86.4	83.7	81.6	83.0	83.6	84.1	83.1	77.1	76.5
	Upper secondary and post-secondary non-tertiary	88.6	90.5	89.0	89.7	89.4	88.7	87.8	88.2	88.6	88.6	86.3	82.6	82.0
	Tertiary education	94.7	95.1	95.0	94.7	95.4	92.7	92.0	92.0	92.0	92.2	91.0	88.3	89.1
Ireland	Below upper secondary	53.4	54.4	60.7	58.4	56.7	56.6	56.5	58.4	58.7	58.7	56.8	50.0	46.8
	Upper secondary and post-secondary non-tertiary	71.7	74.8	77.0	77.3	76.6	75.6	75.9	76.7	77.3	77.1	75.5	69.1	66.4
	Tertiary education	85.2	87.2	87.2	87.0	86.3	86.1	86.2	86.8	86.5	86.7	85.2	82.0	81.1
Israel	Below upper secondary	m	m	m	m	43.5	42.7	40.4	41.2	41.8	42.7	44.8	44.3	44.7
	Upper secondary and post-secondary non-tertiary	m	m	m	m	66.6	65.9	66.4	66.6	67.5	69.2	70.0	69.0	70.1
	Tertiary education	m	m	m	m	79.1	79.3	79.2	80.3	81.2	83.0	82.8	82.4	82.4
Italy	Below upper secondary	47.8	48.0	48.6	49.4	50.5	50.7	51.7	51.7	52.5	52.8	52.5	51.2	50.4
	Upper secondary and post-secondary non-tertiary	70.1	70.3	71.2	72.1	72.3	72.4	73.5	73.5	74.4	74.5	74.3	73.1	72.6
	Tertiary education	80.8	80.7	81.4	81.6	82.2	82.0	81.2	80.4	80.6	80.2	80.7	79.2	78.3
Japan	Below upper secondary	68.8	68.2	67.1	67.6	m	m	m	m	m	m	m	m	m
	Upper secondary and post-secondary non-tertiary	75.8	74.2	73.8	74.3	71.8	71.8	72.0	72.3	73.2	74.4	74.4	73.1	73.3
	Tertiary education	79.5	79.2	79.0	79.9	78.9	79.2	79.3	79.4	79.8	80.1	79.7	79.7	79.5
Korea	Below upper secondary	66.1	66.9	68.0	67.8	68.4	66.5	66.4	65.9	66.2	66.0	66.1	65.3	65.0
	Upper secondary and post-secondary non-tertiary	66.5	66.4	68.7	69.3	70.5	69.6	70.1	70.1	70.3	70.7	70.7	69.7	70.6
	Tertiary education	76.1	74.6	75.4	75.7	76.1	76.4	76.7	76.8	77.2	77.2	77.1	76.3	76.3
Luxembourg	Below upper secondary	m	56.5	58.3	60.0	59.3	60.3	59.1	61.8	60.8	62.3	61.1	61.6	61.9
	Upper secondary and post-secondary non-tertiary	m	73.9	74.6	74.8	73.6	73.3	72.6	71.7	73.4	73.9	70.7	70.2	72.1
	Tertiary education	m	85.0	84.3	85.5	85.2	82.3	84.1	84.0	85.2	84.5	84.7	85.1	85.0

Source: OECD. See Annex 3 for notes (*www.oecd.org/edu/eag2012*).
Please refer to the Reader's Guide for information concerning the symbols replacing missing data.
StatLink ⫘ http://dx.doi.org/10.1787/888932665126

Table A7.3a. [2/2] Trends in employment rates of 25-64 year-olds, by educational attainment (1998-2010)

Number of 25-64 year-olds in employment as a percentage of the population aged 25-64

A7

		1998	1999	2000	2001	2002	2003	2004	2005	2006	2007	2008	2009	2010
OECD Mexico	Below upper secondary	61.3	61.4	60.7	60.5	61.3	60.9	62.2	61.8	62.8	63.0	63.6	61.7	63.0
	Upper secondary and post-secondary non-tertiary	69.1	69.1	70.7	69.8	69.7	69.5	70.3	71.2	73.1	73.5	72.9	71.5	71.6
	Tertiary education	83.2	82.0	82.5	80.9	80.9	81.2	81.4	82.0	83.3	83.0	82.8	81.5	80.4
Netherlands	Below upper secondary	55.3	60.7	57.6	58.8	60.7	59.4	59.4	59.5	60.6	61.9	63.7	63.6	61.1
	Upper secondary and post-secondary non-tertiary	76.8	79.5	79.4	80.0	79.8	78.8	77.9	77.9	79.1	80.3	81.5	81.7	80.0
	Tertiary education	85.4	87.2	86.3	86.3	86.4	85.9	85.3	85.6	86.4	87.7	88.3	88.1	87.5
New Zealand	Below upper secondary	62.4	63.6	64.8	66.0	67.1	67.4	68.9	70.0	70.4	71.0	70.5	69.0	68.4
	Upper secondary and post-secondary non-tertiary	79.1	79.7	80.0	80.2	81.2	81.4	82.7	84.2	84.2	84.6	83.3	82.4	82.0
	Tertiary education	81.5	81.9	82.2	83.6	83.0	82.7	83.4	84.1	84.5	83.7	84.5	84.0	83.8
Norway	Below upper secondary	67.7	67.1	65.3	63.3	64.2	64.1	62.1	64.3	64.7	66.3	66.0	65.4	63.9
	Upper secondary and post-secondary non-tertiary	83.9	82.9	82.7	82.7	81.5	79.6	78.8	82.4	83.1	84.0	84.4	83.1	81.8
	Tertiary education	90.2	90.2	89.9	89.6	89.5	88.8	89.3	88.8	89.2	90.4	90.6	90.2	90.4
Poland	Below upper secondary	49.1	46.6	42.8	41.5	39.1	38.2	37.5	37.7	38.6	41.0	43.0	41.6	39.9
	Upper secondary and post-secondary non-tertiary	71.1	69.7	66.6	64.8	62.5	61.6	61.3	61.7	62.9	65.2	67.0	66.3	65.6
	Tertiary education	87.2	86.6	84.5	84.1	83.1	82.6	82.3	82.7	83.5	84.5	85.1	85.3	84.8
Portugal	Below upper secondary	71.6	71.8	72.8	73.1	73.0	72.4	71.9	71.5	71.7	71.6	71.7	69.0	68.2
	Upper secondary and post-secondary non-tertiary	80.1	81.9	83.3	82.7	82.2	81.5	80.3	79.3	80.2	79.8	80.6	80.1	79.9
	Tertiary education	89.4	90.0	90.6	90.8	88.6	87.5	88.0	87.3	86.4	85.9	86.7	86.7	85.4
Slovak Republic	Below upper secondary	37.4	33.2	30.9	30.5	28.2	28.5	26.6	26.3	28.9	29.1	32.3	30.3	29.7
	Upper secondary and post-secondary non-tertiary	75.1	72.5	70.6	70.2	70.5	71.2	70.3	70.8	71.9	73.2	74.8	72.0	69.9
	Tertiary education	88.6	87.0	85.6	86.7	86.6	87.1	83.6	84.0	84.9	84.2	85.5	83.2	82.2
Slovenia	Below upper secondary	m	m	m	m	55.6	54.2	55.9	56.1	55.9	56.2	55.0	53.7	51.1
	Upper secondary and post-secondary non-tertiary	m	m	m	m	74.0	72.7	74.4	74.6	74.1	75.1	76.4	74.6	73.0
	Tertiary education	m	m	m	m	86.1	86.1	86.8	87.0	88.2	87.7	87.9	88.4	87.3
Spain	Below upper secondary	49.5	51.0	53.8	55.1	55.7	56.6	57.6	58.6	59.8	60.5	59.1	54.0	52.9
	Upper secondary and post-secondary non-tertiary	67.5	69.6	72.1	71.8	71.6	72.4	73.2	74.7	75.9	76.3	75.2	70.6	68.9
	Tertiary education	76.3	77.6	79.7	80.7	80.8	81.6	81.9	82.4	83.4	84.4	83.6	81.1	79.7
Sweden	Below upper secondary	66.4	66.5	68.0	68.8	68.2	67.5	67.0	66.1	66.9	66.6	66.2	64.2	63.8
	Upper secondary and post-secondary non-tertiary	79.3	79.6	81.7	81.9	81.8	81.3	80.7	81.3	81.9	83.1	83.3	81.3	82.0
	Tertiary education	85.5	85.6	86.7	86.9	86.5	85.8	85.4	87.3	87.3	88.6	89.2	88.1	88.1
Switzerland	Below upper secondary	68.8	68.3	64.5	69.6	68.2	66.3	65.4	65.3	64.5	66.0	67.6	67.5	68.3
	Upper secondary and post-secondary non-tertiary	80.8	80.9	81.4	81.3	81.1	80.5	79.9	80.0	80.2	81.1	82.0	81.7	80.0
	Tertiary education	90.3	90.7	90.4	91.3	90.6	89.7	89.7	90.0	90.2	90.0	90.5	89.6	88.7
Turkey	Below upper secondary	57.4	55.8	53.1	51.9	50.5	49.1	47.7	47.2	47.3	46.9	46.7	46.3	48.5
	Upper secondary and post-secondary non-tertiary	66.0	63.9	64.0	62.4	61.8	61.1	60.3	61.8	61.5	60.9	60.8	58.3	60.0
	Tertiary education	81.3	79.0	78.5	78.3	76.3	74.9	74.5	75.2	74.5	74.6	74.5	73.6	75.7
United Kingdom	Below upper secondary	64.5	65.0	65.3	65.5	65.3	66.0	65.4	65.5	63.1	63.3	59.3	56.9	56.0
	Upper secondary and post-secondary non-tertiary	80.1	80.5	81.1	80.9	81.1	81.5	81.2	81.6	81.6	82.3	80.1	78.3	76.8
	Tertiary education	87.1	87.7	87.8	88.1	87.6	87.8	87.7	88.0	87.5	87.4	85.0	84.5	85.1
United States	Below upper secondary	57.6	57.8	57.8	58.4	57.0	57.8	56.5	57.2	58.0	58.3	56.2	52.5	52.1
	Upper secondary and post-secondary non-tertiary	75.8	76.2	76.7	76.2	74.0	73.3	72.8	72.8	73.3	73.6	72.8	68.9	67.9
	Tertiary education	85.3	84.6	85.0	84.4	83.2	82.2	82.0	82.5	82.7	83.3	83.1	80.8	80.0
OECD average	Below upper secondary	57.4	57.7	57.8	58.0	56.5	56.6	56.1	56.5	57.3	58.1	58.0	56.1	55.5
	Upper secondary and post-secondary non-tertiary	74.6	75.0	75.4	75.4	74.6	74.4	74.3	74.8	75.5	76.0	76.0	74.1	73.7
	Tertiary education	84.4	84.5	84.7	84.7	84.2	83.7	83.6	84.0	84.5	84.5	84.5	83.6	83.1
EU21 average	Below upper secondary	53.2	53.7	54.2	54.4	53.7	54.1	53.6	54.0	54.9	55.8	55.8	53.4	52.3
	Upper secondary and post-secondary non-tertiary	73.8	74.5	74.8	74.8	74.4	74.2	74.0	74.4	75.3	76.0	76.1	74.1	73.3
	Tertiary education	84.5	84.9	85.1	85.2	84.7	84.3	84.2	84.6	85.1	85.2	85.3	84.4	83.6
Other G20 Argentina		m	m	m	m	m	m	m	m	m	m	m	m	m
Brazil	Below upper secondary	m	m	m	m	m	m	m	m	m	68.8	69.4	68.7	m
	Upper secondary and post-secondary non-tertiary	m	m	m	m	m	m	m	m	m	76.9	77.7	77.4	m
	Tertiary education	m	m	m	m	m	m	m	m	m	85.8	86.0	85.6	m
China		m	m	m	m	m	m	m	m	m	m	m	m	m
India		m	m	m	m	m	m	m	m	m	m	m	m	m
Indonesia		m	m	m	m	m	m	m	m	m	m	m	m	m
Russian Federation		m	m	m	m	m	m	m	m	m	m	m	m	m
Saudi Arabia		m	m	m	m	m	m	m	m	m	m	m	m	m
South Africa		m	m	m	m	m	m	m	m	m	m	m	m	m
G20 average		m	m	m	m	m	m	m	m	m	m	m	m	m

Source: OECD. See Annex 3 for notes (*www.oecd.org/edu/eag2012*).
Please refer to the Reader's Guide for information concerning the symbols replacing missing data.
StatLink ᎕᎒᎓ http://dx.doi.org/10.1787/888932665126

A7

Table A7.4a. [1/2] **Trends in unemployment rates of 25-64 year-olds, by educational attainment (1998-2010)**

Number of 25-64 year-olds unemployed as a percentage of the labour force aged 25-64

		1998	1999	2000	2001	2002	2003	2004	2005	2006	2007	2008	2009	2010
Australia	Below upper secondary	9.0	8.4	7.5	7.6	7.5	7.0	6.2	6.3	5.6	5.1	5.2	6.6	6.2
	Upper secondary and post-secondary non-tertiary	5.8	5.1	4.5	4.7	4.3	4.3	3.9	3.4	3.8	3.0	2.6	4.1	3.6
	Tertiary education	3.3	3.4	3.6	3.1	3.3	3.0	2.8	2.5	2.3	2.2	2.1	3.3	2.8
Austria	Below upper secondary	6.8	5.9	6.2	6.2	6.7	7.8	7.8	8.6	7.9	7.4	6.3	8.4	7.3
	Upper secondary and post-secondary non-tertiary	3.7	3.2	2.9	3.0	3.4	3.4	3.8	3.9	3.7	3.3	2.9	3.6	3.5
	Tertiary education	1.9	1.8	1.5	1.5	1.8	2.0	2.9	2.6	2.5	2.4	1.7	2.2	2.3
Belgium	Below upper secondary	13.1	12.0	9.8	8.5	10.3	10.7	11.7	12.4	12.3	11.3	10.8	11.9	13.2
	Upper secondary and post-secondary non-tertiary	7.4	6.6	5.3	5.5	6.0	6.7	6.9	6.9	6.7	6.2	5.7	6.5	6.6
	Tertiary education	3.2	3.1	2.7	2.7	3.5	3.5	3.9	3.7	3.7	3.3	3.2	3.8	4.0
Canada	Below upper secondary	11.9	10.8	10.2	10.5	11.0	10.8	10.1	9.7	9.3	9.5	9.1	12.6	12.4
	Upper secondary and post-secondary non-tertiary	7.5	6.7	5.9	6.3	6.7	6.5	6.1	5.9	5.6	5.5	5.4	8.1	7.5
	Tertiary education	4.7	4.5	4.1	4.7	5.1	5.2	4.8	4.6	4.1	3.9	4.1	5.3	5.4
Chile	Below upper secondary	m	m	m	m	m	m	m	m	m	4.6	5.2	5.9	4.6
	Upper secondary and post-secondary non-tertiary	m	m	m	m	m	m	m	m	m	6.0	6.6	7.4	6.2
	Tertiary education	m	m	m	m	m	m	m	m	m	6.0	5.5	7.7	5.6
Czech Republic	Below upper secondary	14.5	18.8	19.3	19.2	18.8	18.3	23.0	24.4	22.3	19.1	17.3	21.8	22.7
	Upper secondary and post-secondary non-tertiary	4.6	6.5	6.7	6.2	5.6	6.0	6.4	6.2	5.5	4.3	3.3	5.4	6.2
	Tertiary education	1.9	2.6	2.5	2.0	1.8	2.0	2.0	2.0	2.2	1.5	1.5	2.2	2.5
Denmark	Below upper secondary	7.0	7.0	6.9	6.2	6.4	6.7	8.2	6.5	5.5	4.3	3.6	7.3	9.0
	Upper secondary and post-secondary non-tertiary	4.6	4.1	3.9	3.7	3.7	4.4	4.8	4.0	2.7	2.6	2.3	4.8	6.1
	Tertiary education	3.3	3.0	3.0	3.6	3.9	4.7	4.4	3.7	3.2	3.0	2.2	3.7	4.6
Estonia	Below upper secondary	m	m	m	m	19.0	14.8	15.4	13.0	11.7	8.6	9.7	24.1	27.5
	Upper secondary and post-secondary non-tertiary	m	m	m	m	10.5	9.5	9.5	8.4	5.7	4.6	5.2	14.8	18.0
	Tertiary education	m	m	m	m	5.8	6.5	5.0	3.8	3.8	3.2	2.4	2.8	6.3	9.1
Finland	Below upper secondary	13.8	13.1	12.1	11.4	12.2	11.2	11.3	10.7	10.1	8.9	8.1	9.8	11.6
	Upper secondary and post-secondary non-tertiary	10.6	9.5	8.9	8.5	8.8	8.3	7.9	7.4	7.0	6.1	5.4	7.7	7.5
	Tertiary education	5.8	4.7	4.7	4.4	4.5	4.1	4.5	4.4	3.7	3.6	3.3	4.0	4.4
France	Below upper secondary	14.9	15.3	13.9	11.9	11.8	10.4	10.7	11.1	11.0	10.2	9.7	11.6	12.9
	Upper secondary and post-secondary non-tertiary	9.6	9.2	7.9	6.9	6.8	6.6	6.7	6.6	6.6	5.9	5.5	7.0	7.2
	Tertiary education	6.6	6.1	5.1	4.8	5.2	5.3	5.7	5.4	5.1	4.7	4.0	5.0	4.9
Germany	Below upper secondary	16.5	15.6	13.7	13.5	15.3	18.0	20.4	20.2	19.9	18.0	16.5	16.7	15.9
	Upper secondary and post-secondary non-tertiary	10.3	8.6	7.8	8.2	9.0	10.2	11.2	11.0	9.9	8.3	7.2	7.5	6.9
	Tertiary education	5.5	4.9	4.0	4.2	4.5	5.2	5.6	5.5	4.8	3.8	3.3	3.4	3.1
Greece	Below upper secondary	7.7	8.8	8.2	8.2	7.8	7.2	8.7	8.3	7.2	7.0	6.8	8.8	11.9
	Upper secondary and post-secondary non-tertiary	10.7	11.5	11.2	10.4	10.5	10.1	10.0	9.6	8.9	8.2	7.2	9.2	12.5
	Tertiary education	6.8	8.0	7.5	7.2	6.8	6.5	7.4	7.1	6.3	6.1	5.7	6.7	8.7
Hungary	Below upper secondary	11.4	11.1	9.9	10.0	10.5	10.6	10.8	12.4	14.8	16.0	17.3	21.0	23.5
	Upper secondary and post-secondary non-tertiary	6.2	5.8	5.3	4.6	4.4	4.8	5.0	6.0	6.1	5.9	6.3	8.2	9.5
	Tertiary education	1.7	1.4	1.3	1.2	1.5	1.4	1.9	2.3	2.2	2.6	2.3	3.5	4.1
Iceland	Below upper secondary	3.2	2.0	2.6	2.6	3.2	3.3	2.5	2.3	c	c	2.5	7.4	7.2
	Upper secondary and post-secondary non-tertiary	c	c	c	c	c	c	c	c	c	c	c	5.8	7.2
	Tertiary education	c	c	c	c	c	c	c	c	c	c	c	3.9	3.5
Ireland	Below upper secondary	11.6	9.2	5.6	5.2	5.9	6.3	6.1	6.0	5.7	6.1	8.2	15.4	19.5
	Upper secondary and post-secondary non-tertiary	4.5	3.5	2.3	2.4	2.8	2.9	3.0	3.1	3.2	3.5	4.8	11.3	13.7
	Tertiary education	3.0	1.7	1.6	1.8	2.2	2.6	2.2	2.0	2.2	2.3	3.0	6.1	6.8
Israel	Below upper secondary	m	m	m	m	14.0	15.2	15.6	14.0	12.8	12.4	9.8	10.8	9.8
	Upper secondary and post-secondary non-tertiary	m	m	m	m	9.8	10.3	10.6	9.5	8.7	7.2	5.8	7.7	6.8
	Tertiary education	m	m	m	m	6.4	6.4	6.1	5.1	4.5	3.8	3.7	5.2	4.2
Italy	Below upper secondary	10.8	10.6	10.0	9.2	9.0	8.8	8.2	7.8	6.9	6.3	7.4	8.4	9.1
	Upper secondary and post-secondary non-tertiary	8.1	7.9	7.2	6.6	6.4	6.1	5.4	5.2	4.6	4.1	4.6	5.6	6.1
	Tertiary education	6.9	6.9	5.9	5.3	5.3	5.3	5.3	5.7	4.8	4.2	4.3	5.1	5.6
Japan	Below upper secondary	4.3	5.6	6.0	5.9	m	m	m	m	m	m	m	m	m
	Upper secondary and post-secondary non-tertiary	3.3	4.4	4.7	4.8	5.6	5.7	5.1	4.9	4.5	4.1	4.4	5.9	5.8
	Tertiary education	2.6	3.3	3.5	3.1	3.8	3.7	3.3	3.1	3.0	2.9	3.1	3.6	3.8
Korea	Below upper secondary	6.0	5.4	3.7	3.1	2.2	2.2	2.6	2.9	2.6	2.4	2.5	2.9	3.1
	Upper secondary and post-secondary non-tertiary	6.8	6.4	4.1	3.6	3.0	3.3	3.5	3.8	3.5	3.3	3.3	3.7	3.5
	Tertiary education	4.9	4.7	3.6	3.5	3.2	3.1	2.9	2.9	2.9	2.9	2.6	3.2	3.3
Luxembourg	Below upper secondary	m	3.4	3.1	1.7	3.8	3.3	5.7	5.1	4.9	4.1	4.8	5.8	4.1
	Upper secondary and post-secondary non-tertiary	m	1.1	1.4	1.0	1.2	2.6	3.7	3.2	3.8	2.8	4.9	3.4	3.6
	Tertiary education	m	c	c	c	1.8	4.0	3.2	3.2	2.9	3.0	2.2	3.7	3.6

Source: OECD. See Annex 3 for notes (*www.oecd.org/edu/eag2012*).
Please refer to the Reader's Guide for information concerning the symbols replacing missing data.
StatLink ⬛⬛⬛ http://dx.doi.org/10.1787/888932665183

Table A7.4a. [2/2] Trends in unemployment rates of 25-64 year-olds, by educational attainment (1998-2010)
Number of 25-64 year-olds unemployed as a percentage of the labour force aged 25-64

		1998	1999	2000	2001	2002	2003	2004	2005	2006	2007	2008	2009	2010
Mexico	Below upper secondary	2.3	1.5	1.5	1.6	1.7	1.8	2.2	2.3	2.2	2.2	2.4	4.0	4.0
	Upper secondary and post-secondary non-tertiary	3.3	2.5	2.2	2.3	2.3	2.2	3.0	3.1	2.6	2.8	2.9	4.4	4.6
	Tertiary education	3.1	3.5	2.4	2.5	3.0	3.0	3.7	3.7	2.9	3.6	3.3	4.2	5.0
Netherlands	Below upper secondary	0.9	4.3	3.9	2.9	3.0	4.5	5.5	5.8	4.8	4.0	3.4	4.1	5.1
	Upper secondary and post-secondary non-tertiary	1.7	2.3	2.3	1.6	2.0	2.8	3.8	4.1	3.5	2.7	2.1	2.7	3.1
	Tertiary education	m	1.7	1.9	1.2	2.1	2.5	2.8	2.8	2.3	1.8	1.6	2.0	2.3
New Zealand	Below upper secondary	8.9	7.8	6.6	5.8	5.0	4.3	3.7	3.4	3.2	3.1	3.7	5.9	6.1
	Upper secondary and post-secondary non-tertiary	5.1	5.0	3.9	3.7	3.6	3.4	2.3	2.3	2.1	2.0	2.5	3.9	4.5
	Tertiary education	4.0	3.7	3.3	2.8	3.1	3.0	2.7	2.3	2.4	2.2	2.4	3.3	3.8
Norway	Below upper secondary	2.9	2.5	2.2	3.4	3.4	3.9	4.0	7.3	4.7	3.3	3.8	4.7	5.5
	Upper secondary and post-secondary non-tertiary	2.4	2.5	2.6	2.7	2.9	3.6	3.8	2.6	2.1	1.3	1.3	1.7	2.2
	Tertiary education	1.5	1.4	1.9	1.7	2.1	2.5	2.4	2.1	1.8	1.4	1.3	1.4	1.6
Poland	Below upper secondary	13.9	16.4	20.6	22.6	25.2	25.9	27.8	27.1	21.5	15.5	11.5	13.9	16.2
	Upper secondary and post-secondary non-tertiary	9.1	10.7	13.9	15.9	17.8	17.8	17.4	16.6	12.7	8.7	6.3	7.2	8.9
	Tertiary education	2.5	3.1	4.3	5.0	6.3	6.6	6.2	6.2	5.0	3.8	3.1	3.6	4.2
Portugal	Below upper secondary	4.4	4.0	3.6	3.6	4.4	5.7	6.4	7.5	7.6	8.0	7.6	10.1	11.8
	Upper secondary and post-secondary non-tertiary	5.1	4.5	3.5	3.3	4.4	5.3	5.6	6.7	7.1	6.8	6.6	8.2	9.7
	Tertiary education	2.8	3.1	2.7	2.8	3.9	4.9	4.4	5.4	5.4	6.6	5.8	5.6	6.3
Slovak Republic	Below upper secondary	24.3	30.3	36.3	38.7	42.3	44.9	47.7	49.2	44.0	41.3	36.3	38.3	40.8
	Upper secondary and post-secondary non-tertiary	8.8	11.9	14.3	14.8	14.2	13.5	14.6	12.7	10.0	8.5	7.4	10.0	12.3
	Tertiary education	3.3	4.0	4.6	4.2	3.6	3.7	4.8	4.4	2.6	3.3	3.1	3.9	4.8
Slovenia	Below upper secondary	m	m	m	m	8.4	8.7	8.4	8.7	7.0	6.5	5.9	7.8	11.2
	Upper secondary and post-secondary non-tertiary	m	m	m	m	5.2	5.5	5.3	5.7	5.6	4.3	3.5	5.6	6.9
	Tertiary education	m	m	m	m	2.3	3.0	2.8	3.0	3.0	3.2	3.1	3.1	4.1
Spain	Below upper secondary	17.0	14.7	13.7	10.2	11.2	11.3	11.0	9.3	9.0	9.0	13.2	21.9	24.7
	Upper secondary and post-secondary non-tertiary	15.3	12.9	10.9	8.4	9.4	9.5	9.4	7.3	6.9	6.8	9.3	15.4	17.4
	Tertiary education	13.1	11.1	9.5	6.9	7.7	7.7	7.3	6.1	5.5	4.8	5.8	9.0	10.4
Sweden	Below upper secondary	10.4	9.0	8.0	5.9	5.8	6.1	6.5	8.5	7.3	7.0	7.1	10.0	11.0
	Upper secondary and post-secondary non-tertiary	7.8	6.5	5.3	4.6	4.6	5.2	5.8	6.0	5.1	4.2	4.1	6.2	6.1
	Tertiary education	4.4	3.9	3.0	2.6	3.0	3.9	4.3	4.5	4.2	3.4	3.3	4.3	4.3
Switzerland	Below upper secondary	5.7	4.7	4.8	3.4	4.3	5.9	7.1	7.2	7.5	6.7	6.0	7.5	8.0
	Upper secondary and post-secondary non-tertiary	2.9	2.5	2.2	2.1	2.4	3.2	3.7	3.7	3.3	3.0	2.9	3.2	4.9
	Tertiary education	2.8	1.7	1.4	1.3	2.2	2.9	2.8	2.7	2.2	2.1	1.8	2.7	3.0
Turkey	Below upper secondary	4.4	5.3	4.6	6.7	8.5	8.8	8.7	9.1	8.8	8.5	9.6	12.6	10.6
	Upper secondary and post-secondary non-tertiary	6.6	8.2	5.5	7.4	8.7	7.8	10.1	9.1	9.0	9.0	9.2	12.6	11.3
	Tertiary education	4.8	5.1	3.9	4.7	7.5	6.9	7.9	6.9	6.9	6.8	7.3	9.2	7.9
United Kingdom	Below upper secondary	7.5	7.1	6.6	6.1	6.0	5.2	5.3	5.1	6.6	6.3	7.5	9.9	10.3
	Upper secondary and post-secondary non-tertiary	4.4	4.4	4.0	3.5	3.6	3.5	3.3	3.1	3.7	3.3	4.3	5.9	6.2
	Tertiary education	2.6	2.6	2.1	2.0	2.4	2.3	2.2	2.1	2.4	2.2	2.8	3.4	3.4
United States	Below upper secondary	8.5	7.7	7.9	8.1	10.2	9.9	10.5	9.0	8.3	8.5	10.1	15.8	16.8
	Upper secondary and post-secondary non-tertiary	4.5	3.7	3.6	3.8	5.7	6.1	5.6	5.1	4.6	4.5	5.3	9.8	11.2
	Tertiary education	2.1	2.1	1.8	2.1	3.0	3.4	3.3	2.6	2.5	2.1	2.4	4.9	5.3
OECD average	Below upper secondary	9.4	9.3	9.0	8.7	9.8	10.0	10.6	10.7	10.1	9.1	8.8	11.6	12.5
	Upper secondary and post-secondary non-tertiary	6.5	6.1	5.7	5.5	6.1	6.3	6.5	6.2	5.6	4.9	4.9	6.9	7.6
	Tertiary education	4.0	3.8	3.5	3.3	3.8	4.1	4.1	3.9	3.5	3.4	3.3	4.4	4.7
EU21 average	Below upper secondary	11.5	11.4	11.1	10.6	11.6	11.7	12.7	12.8	11.8	10.7	10.4	13.7	15.2
	Upper secondary and post-secondary non-tertiary	7.4	6.9	6.6	6.3	6.7	6.9	7.1	6.8	6.1	5.3	5.2	7.4	8.5
	Tertiary education	4.4	4.1	3.8	3.5	3.8	4.2	4.2	4.1	3.7	3.4	3.2	4.3	4.9
Argentina		m	m	m	m	m	m	m	m	m	m	m	m	m
Brazil	Below upper secondary	m	m	m	m	m	m	m	m	m	5.6	4.7	5.7	m
	Upper secondary and post-secondary non-tertiary	m	m	m	m	m	m	m	m	m	7.0	6.1	7.2	m
	Tertiary education	m	m	m	m	m	m	m	m	m	3.3	3.3	3.5	m
China		m	m	m	m	m	m	m	m	m	m	m	m	m
India		m	m	m	m	m	m	m	m	m	m	m	m	m
Indonesia		m	m	m	m	m	m	m	m	m	m	m	m	m
Russian Federation		m	m	m	m	m	m	m	m	m	m	m	m	m
Saudi Arabia		m	m	m	m	m	m	m	m	m	m	m	m	m
South Africa		m	m	m	m	m	m	m	m	m	m	m	m	m
G20 average		m	m	m	m	m	m	m	m	m	m	m	m	m

Source: OECD. See Annex 3 for notes (*www.oecd.org/edu/eag2012*).
Please refer to the Reader's Guide for information concerning the symbols replacing missing data.
StatLink ᕤᓯᒧ http://dx.doi.org/10.1787/888932665183

A7

Table A7.5. [1/2] Proportion of wage earners who worked full-time among all earners, by educational attainment and age group[1] (2010)

			Below upper secondary education			Upper secondary and post-secondary non-tertiary education			Tertiary education			All levels of education		
			25-64	35-44	55-64	25-64	35-44	55-64	25-64	35-44	55-64	25-64	35-44	55-64
			(1)	(2)	(3)	(4)	(5)	(6)	(7)	(8)	(9)	(10)	(11)	(12)
Australia	2009	Men	89	94	79	91	93	85	92	95	83	91	94	83
		Women	47	43	42	53	51	52	65	56	60	57	52	51
		M+W	69	69	61	77	77	74	77	75	72	75	75	69
Austria	2010	Men	61	58	67	76	78	81	79	84	82	75	78	79
		Women	39	38	42	42	38	46	57	48	76	45	40	51
		M+W	48	46	52	60	59	68	69	67	80	60	59	68
Belgium	2009	Men	79	82	73	86	91	64	87	90	73	84	89	69
		Women	37	40	35	43	38	38	62	59	51	51	48	42
		M+W	62	65	56	68	67	54	74	75	64	69	70	59
Canada	2009	Men	66	73	64	70	76	65	76	81	71	72	78	67
		Women	49	54	44	54	58	51	58	60	49	56	59	49
		M+W	59	65	55	63	68	59	67	70	61	65	69	59
Chile			m	m	m	m	m	m	m	m	m	m	m	m
Czech Republic			m	m	m	m	m	m	m	m	m	m	m	m
Denmark	2010	Men	49	49	48	57	61	53	74	80	68	60	65	56
		Women	44	42	43	51	54	46	59	61	57	53	55	49
		M+W	46	46	45	55	57	50	65	70	62	56	60	53
Estonia	2010	Men	94	95	81	96	96	90	93	98	84	95	96	88
		Women	86	90	86	87	86	89	89	91	83	88	88	86
		M+W	91	93	83	92	91	89	90	93	83	91	92	87
Finland	2010	Men	92	94	89	93	95	90	95	97	89	94	96	90
		Women	79	80	77	82	83	80	88	86	85	85	85	81
		M+W	86	89	82	88	90	84	91	90	87	89	90	85
France	2008	Men	75	84	53	83	89	57	85	89	76	82	88	60
		Women	46	44	40	57	56	50	64	62	58	57	56	47
		M+W	61	65	46	71	74	54	74	75	68	70	73	54
Germany	2010	Men	88	88	95	79	83	79	85	88	81	82	85	81
		Women	36	29	26	44	38	39	54	49	57	47	41	42
		M+W	61	58	54	62	61	60	71	71	71	65	64	63
Greece	2009	Men	80	85	73	88	90	92	87	88	89	85	88	82
		Women	65	65	63	73	76	73	83	86	80	75	77	70
		M+W	75	77	70	82	85	86	85	87	86	81	83	78
Hungary	2010	Men	78	81	75	85	86	82	90	92	86	85	87	81
		Women	77	79	72	84	85	82	91	91	89	85	86	81
		M+W	78	80	73	85	86	82	90	91	88	85	86	81
Iceland			m	m	m	m	m	m	m	m	m	m	m	m
Ireland	2010	Men	63	69	56	69	74	56	82	87	71	72	77	60
		Women	25	21	16	46	49	47	61	57	66	50	48	45
		M+W	49	51	45	58	61	51	71	73	69	62	64	54
Israel	2010	Men	87	91	82	91	95	86	88	93	87	89	93	86
		Women	48	54	39	67	69	59	66	71	56	66	70	56
		M+W	77	85	67	82	84	75	77	82	73	79	83	73
Italy	2008	Men	85	87	77	89	91	89	89	93	88	87	90	83
		Women	60	53	60	77	73	84	75	68	91	71	66	74
		M+W	76	75	71	84	82	87	82	79	89	81	79	80
Japan			m	m	m	m	m	m	m	m	m	m	m	m
Korea	2010	Men	83	84	83	92	93	90	92	93	85	91	93	86
		Women	76	76	74	80	79	70	77	72	65	78	76	72
		M+W	80	81	78	87	86	85	87	87	81	86	86	80
Luxembourg	2010	Men	88	91	80	91	93	75	91	98	82	90	94	79
	2010	Women	43	50	27	53	46	41	65	55	63	54	51	40
	2010	M+W	67	71	54	76	75	64	78	76	76	74	74	64

Note: The length of the reference period varies from one week to one year. Self-employed individuals are excluded in some countries. See Annex 3 for details.
1. Full-time basis refers to people who have worked all year long and at least 30 hours per week.
Source: OECD, LSO Network special data collection on full-time, full-year earnings, Economic Working Group. See Annex 3 for notes (*www.oecd.org/edu/eag2012*). *Please refer to the Reader's Guide for information concerning the symbols replacing missing data.*
StatLink ⌘Ⅶ51■ http://dx.doi.org/10.1787/888932665278

Table A7.5. [2/2] Proportion of wage earners who worked full-time among all earners, by educational attainment and age group[1] (2010)

			Below upper secondary education			Upper secondary and post-secondary non-tertiary education			Tertiary education			All levels of education		
			25-64	35-44	55-64	25-64	35-44	55-64	25-64	35-44	55-64	25-64	35-44	55-64
			(1)	(2)	(3)	(4)	(5)	(6)	(7)	(8)	(9)	(10)	(11)	(12)
OECD Mexico			m	m	m	m	m	m	m	m	m	m	m	m
Netherlands	2008	Men	63	65	61	66	68	65	67	68	62	65	67	63
		Women	14	13	11	18	15	18	27	22	23	20	17	16
		M+W	41	43	39	43	42	47	48	47	49	45	44	45
New Zealand	2010	Men	72	74	63	72	76	60	76	79	64	73	77	62
		Women	58	56	58	59	56	57	64	58	58	62	57	58
		M+W	65	64	60	67	68	59	70	68	61	68	67	60
Norway			m	m	m	m	m	m	m	m	m	m	m	m
Poland	2010	Men	85	87	86	88	90	86	82	83	85	86	88	86
		Women	79	78	77	85	86	84	82	85	84	84	85	83
		M+W	82	83	83	87	88	85	82	85	84	85	86	85
Portugal	2009	Men	99	99	99	97	98	97	94	95	89	98	98	98
		Women	91	92	86	95	96	94	93	94	89	92	93	87
		M+W	95	96	94	96	97	96	94	95	89	95	96	93
Slovak Republic	2010	Men	53	52	57	63	65	64	66	67	70	62	64	64
		Women	47	43	48	59	60	61	64	68	67	59	60	59
		M+W	49	47	52	61	62	63	65	67	69	61	62	62
Slovenia			m	m	m	m	m	m	m	m	m	m	m	m
Spain	2009	Men	76	76	80	82	86	84	86	90	87	81	83	83
		Women	51	49	55	63	58	85	75	75	85	64	63	69
		M+W	66	66	71	74	73	85	80	82	86	73	74	78
Sweden	2010	Men	74	77	69	79	84	63	79	86	71	78	84	67
		Women	37	46	30	48	49	43	60	58	59	52	53	47
		M+W	60	65	55	65	69	53	68	70	64	66	69	57
Switzerland			m	m	m	m	m	m	m	m	m	m	m	m
Turkey			m	m	m	m	m	m	m	m	m	m	m	m
United Kingdom	2010	Men	86	83	84	93	96	86	92	95	78	92	94	84
		Women	43	42	41	53	50	47	66	59	55	58	54	49
		M+W	67	67	63	75	74	69	79	78	68	76	76	68
United States	2010	Men	62	62	66	74	76	73	83	87	78	77	79	75
		Women	53	53	59	64	65	64	69	68	66	66	66	65
		M+W	59	59	63	70	71	68	76	77	73	71	73	70
OECD average		Men	77	79	74	82	85	77	84	88	79	82	85	77
		Women	53	53	50	62	61	60	69	66	67	63	62	59
		M+W	67	68	63	73	74	70	76	77	74	73	74	69
Other G20 Argentina			m	m	m	m	m	m	m	m	m	m	m	m
Brazil	2009	Men	74	76	74	79	82	79	78	79	76	76	78	75
		Women	46	48	41	62	63	57	61	61	55	54	55	45
		M+W	63	65	61	71	73	70	69	69	67	66	68	63
China			m	m	m	m	m	m	m	m	m	m	m	m
India			m	m	m	m	m	m	m	m	m	m	m	m
Indonesia			m	m	m	m	m	m	m	m	m	m	m	m
Russian Federation			m	m	m	m	m	m	m	m	m	m	m	m
Saudi Arabia			m	m	m	m	m	m	m	m	m	m	m	m
South Africa			m	m	m	m	m	m	m	m	m	m	m	m
G20 average			m	m	m	m	m	m	m	m	m	m	m	m

Note: The length of the reference period varies from one week to one year. Self-employed individuals are excluded in some countries. See Annex 3 for details.
1. Full-time basis refers to people who have worked all year long and at least 30 hours per week.
Source: OECD, LSO Network special data collection on full-time, full-year earnings, Economic Working Group. See Annex 3 for notes (*www.oecd.org/edu/eag2012*).
Please refer to the Reader's Guide for information concerning the symbols replacing missing data.
StatLink ᵐˢ🔗 http://dx.doi.org/10.1787/888932665278

A7

Table A7.6. Labour market outcomes of 25-64 year-olds, by programme orientation at ISCED 3/4 level (2010)

Labour status of 25-64 year-olds whose highest level of education is upper secondary and post-secondary non-tertiary education (ISCED 3/4), by educational orientation

	Employment rate (%)						Unemployment rate (%)						Inactivity rate (%)					
	ISCED 3/4 Vocational			ISCED 3/4 General			ISCED 3/4 Vocational			ISCED 3/4 General			ISCED 3/4 Vocational			ISCED 3/4 General		
	Men	Women	M+W	Men	Women	M+W	Men	Women	M+W	Men	Women	M+W	Men	Women	M+W	Men	Women	M+W
Australia	89.3	76.3	84.9	85.3	66.3	75.3	2.7	4.1	3.1	3.7	4.5	4.1	8.2	20.4	12.3	11.3	30.6	21.5
Austria	82.2	73.7	78.2	77.2	73.5	75.2	3.6	3.3	3.4	4.9	4.0	4.5	14.8	23.8	19.0	18.8	23.5	21.3
Belgium	83.2	69.0	76.8	76.9	62.2	68.9	5.0	7.5	6.0	7.6	8.4	8.0	12.4	25.4	18.2	16.8	32.1	25.1
Canada	80.9	72.3	77.9	77.1	67.4	72.2	7.5	7.0	7.3	8.3	6.9	7.7	12.6	22.3	16.0	15.9	27.6	21.8
Chile	m	m	m	m	m	m	m	m	m	m	m	m	m	m	m	m	m	m
Czech Republic	83.5	65.2	74.9	77.6	62.5	67.6	5.1	7.7	6.2	5.7	7.0	6.5	12.1	29.4	20.2	17.7	32.8	27.7
Denmark	81.2	77.4	79.5	79.3	74.7	77.1	6.6	5.0	5.9	7.6	6.9	7.3	13.1	18.5	15.5	14.2	19.8	16.9
Estonia	71.7	64.0	68.1	72.4	66.4	69.5	18.1	20.0	18.9	17.3	15.5	16.5	12.5	20.1	16.0	12.4	21.4	16.8
Finland	76.0	71.0	73.7	75.9	69.9	73.4	8.3	7.1	7.8	8.0	5.3	6.9	17.1	23.6	20.1	17.4	26.2	21.2
France	78.0	68.6	73.9	80.6	72.0	75.6	6.3	8.5	7.2	7.0	7.4	7.2	16.7	25.0	20.3	13.3	22.2	18.5
Germany[1]	81.9	72.6	77.2	63.4	55.4	59.8	7.4	6.2	6.9	8.6	7.9	8.3	11.5	22.6	17.1	30.7	39.9	34.8
Greece	83.3	60.5	73.6	79.2	50.0	63.2	9.8	20.0	13.6	8.7	15.5	11.8	7.7	24.4	14.8	13.3	40.8	28.4
Hungary	71.7	61.2	67.1	69.5	56.5	60.7	9.7	9.6	9.7	7.0	9.0	8.2	20.6	32.3	25.7	25.3	38.0	33.8
Iceland	88.4	80.7	85.9	76.3	71.6	73.5	5.9	7.0	6.2	12.6	7.0	9.4	6.1	13.2	8.4	12.7	23.0	18.9
Ireland	70.0	61.3	66.0	74.9	59.1	66.7	20.9	10.3	16.7	14.7	8.8	12.1	11.5	31.7	20.8	12.2	35.2	24.1
Israel	81.2	69.3	76.4	72.7	62.4	67.5	6.3	8.2	7.0	6.6	6.8	6.7	13.4	24.5	17.9	22.2	33.0	27.6
Italy	82.9	64.7	75.1	75.0	60.0	64.4	4.8	7.6	5.8	6.7	6.9	6.8	12.9	30.0	20.3	19.6	35.5	30.9
Japan	m	m	m	m	m	m	m	m	m	m	m	m	m	m	m	m	m	m
Korea	86.1	57.0	72.2	83.2	56.7	69.0	3.8	3.0	3.5	4.1	2.6	3.4	10.5	41.3	25.2	13.2	41.8	28.5
Luxembourg	81.9	64.0	72.9	84.9	61.6	73.0	2.4	4.4	3.3	1.7	3.3	2.4	16.1	33.0	24.6	13.6	36.3	25.2
Netherlands	85.5	75.5	80.6	83.6	73.1	78.0	2.9	2.9	2.9	1.6	2.4	2.0	12.0	22.2	17.0	15.0	25.1	20.4
New Zealand	88.9	72.2	82.6	88.4	74.4	80.7	3.9	6.6	4.8	3.3	4.0	3.7	7.6	22.7	13.3	8.6	22.5	16.2
Norway	85.4	79.1	82.8	80.8	75.8	78.1	2.2	1.3	1.9	4.9	1.8	3.3	12.7	19.8	15.6	15.1	22.9	19.2
Poland	78.9	60.8	70.0	75.1	54.0	61.2	6.3	8.6	7.3	9.2	10.9	10.2	15.8	33.5	24.5	17.2	39.4	31.8
Portugal	83.1	75.7	79.4	87.0	80.0	83.3	7.8	12.0	9.9	6.2	10.8	8.6	9.9	14.0	11.9	7.3	10.3	8.9
Slovak Republic	77.3	62.2	70.2	74.9	61.1	65.5	11.5	13.6	12.4	10.3	10.5	10.4	12.7	28.1	19.9	16.5	31.8	26.9
Slovenia	76.4	69.4	73.4	71.8	65.0	68.1	6.2	7.1	6.6	12.5	9.4	10.9	18.6	25.3	21.4	17.9	28.3	23.6
Spain	77.8	61.3	69.4	74.4	62.3	68.6	13.5	19.1	17.1	16.3	19.3	17.6	8.1	24.3	16.4	11.0	22.8	16.7
Sweden	86.9	79.5	83.9	88.5	84.4	86.5	5.3	5.3	5.3	4.2	3.9	4.0	8.2	16.0	11.5	7.7	12.2	9.9
Switzerland	87.2	75.0	80.7	79.9	67.0	71.9	5.4	4.3	4.9	4.6	7.4	6.2	7.8	21.7	15.1	16.2	27.7	23.3
Turkey	81.0	30.9	63.4	77.9	27.0	57.0	8.2	19.8	10.5	9.8	20.9	12.2	11.7	61.5	29.2	13.6	65.9	35.1
United Kingdom	m	m	m	m	m	m	m	m	m	m	m	m	m	m	m	m	m	m
United States	m	m	m	m	m	m	m	m	m	m	m	m	m	m	m	m	m	m
OECD average	81.4	67.9	75.5	78.1	64.6	70.7	7.2	8.5	7.7	7.7	8.1	7.8	12.2	25.9	18.2	15.4	29.9	23.3
Argentina	m	m	m	m	m	m	m	m	m	m	m	m	m	m	m	m	m	m
Brazil	m	m	m	m	m	m	m	m	m	m	m	m	m	m	m	m	m	m
China	m	m	m	m	m	m	m	m	m	m	m	m	m	m	m	m	m	m
India	m	m	m	m	m	m	m	m	m	m	m	m	m	m	m	m	m	m
Indonesia	m	m	m	m	m	m	m	m	m	m	m	m	m	m	m	m	m	m
Russian Federation	m	m	m	m	m	m	m	m	m	m	m	m	m	m	m	m	m	m
Saudi Arabia	m	m	m	m	m	m	m	m	m	m	m	m	m	m	m	m	m	m
South Africa	m	m	m	m	m	m	m	m	m	m	m	m	m	m	m	m	m	m
G20 average	m	m	m	m	m	m	m	m	m	m	m	m	m	m	m	m	m	m

1. Individuals with attainment ISCED 4A in Germany have successfully completed both a general and a vocational programme. In this table they have been allocated to vocational.

Source: OECD, LSO network special data collection on vocational education, Learnings and Labour Transitions Working Group. See Annex 3 for notes (*www.oecd.org/edu/eag2012*).

Please refer to the Reader's Guide for information concerning the symbols replacing missing data.

StatLink http://dx.doi.org/10.1787/888932665297

WHAT ARE THE EARNINGS PREMIUMS FROM EDUCATION?

- People with tertiary (higher) education reap a substantial earnings premium in the labour market. On average across OECD countries, a person with a tertiary degree can expect to earn 55% more than a person with an upper secondary or post-secondary non-tertiary education.

- Similarly, people who lack an upper secondary education face a severe earnings penalty in the labour market. A person without an upper secondary degree can expect to earn 23% less than a person who has completed this level of education, on average across OECD countries.

- The earnings premium for tertiary-educated individuals also increases with age. A 25-34 year-old with this level of education can expect to earn 37% more than a similarly-aged person who has completed an upper secondary education, while a 55-64 year-old with a tertiary education can expect to earn 69% more than a similarly-aged counterpart with an upper secondary education.

Chart A8.1. Relative earnings from employment among 25-64 year-olds, by level of educational attainment (2010 or latest available year)

Upper secondary and post-secondary non-tertiary education = 100

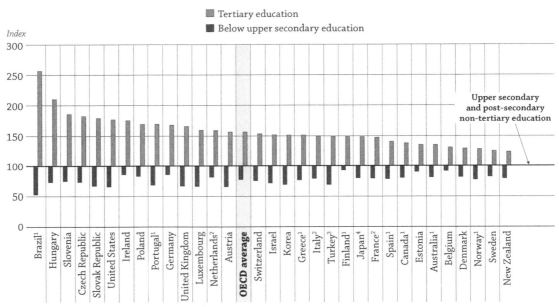

Note: Belgium, Korea and Turkey report earnings net of income tax.
1. Year of reference 2009.
2. Year of reference 2008.
3. Year of reference 2005.
4. Year of reference 2007.
Countries are ranked in descending order of the relative earnings of 25-64 year-olds with tertiary education.
Source: OECD. Table A8.1. See Annex 3 for notes (*www.oecd.org/edu/eag2012*).
StatLink ᴍᴤᴸ http://dx.doi.org/10.1787/888932662124

▉ Context

The potential for greater earnings provides a powerful incentive for individuals to pursue education and develop their skills. In addition to increasing a person's chances of employment and decreasing his or her chances of unemployment (see Indicator A7), having a higher level of education is generally a good way to secure a better income – and to increase it over time. As of 2010, this continued to be the case across most OECD and G20 countries, even in the face of the global economic crisis.

At the same time, the prospect of better earnings is not the only factor individuals consider when deciding to pursue more education. The cost of education – particularly at the tertiary level – is an increasingly important consideration in some countries, especially as shrinking public budgets have led to increases in tuition fees and reductions to tertiary student aid (see Indicator B5). The field of education individuals choose when deciding to pursue more education is another important consideration, as not all fields generate the same economic rewards (Carnevale, 2012).

From a broader perspective, the earnings premiums seen among people with higher levels of education relate to the skills and competences that are most in demand in the global labour market, especially as national economies continue to become more knowledge-based. High and rising earnings premiums can indicate that highly educated individuals are in short supply, while lower and falling premiums can indicate the opposite. Relative earnings, and trend data on the earnings premium in particular, are thus important indicators of the match between the skills national education systems are helping individuals to develop, and the demand for those skills in the labour market.

Other findings

- **Earnings increase with each level of education.** Those who have attained upper secondary, post-secondary non-tertiary education or tertiary education enjoy substantial earnings advantages compared with individuals of the same gender who have not completed upper secondary education. The earnings premium for tertiary education is substantial in most countries, and exceeds 50% in 17 of 32 countries.

- In Brazil, the Czech Republic, France, Germany, Greece, Hungary, Ireland, Israel, Poland, the Slovak Republic and the United States, **men holding a degree from a university or an advanced research programme earn at least 80% more than men who have an upper secondary or post-secondary non-tertiary education**. In Brazil, Canada, Greece, Hungary, Ireland, Japan, the United Kingdom and the United States, women have a similar advantage.

- **An individual with a tertiary-type B degree** (a degree from a shorter programme, designed to lead directly to the labour market) **can expect an earnings premium of 24%,** compared to his or her counterpart with an upper secondary education. However, this earnings premium is less likely to increase over time, compared to the premium for a person with a tertiary-type A (university) degree.

- Relative earnings for individuals with a tertiary education are higher for people in older age groups in all countries except Ireland and Turkey. **For those who have not attained an upper secondary education, the earnings disadvantage generally increases with age**.

Trends

The trend data on relative earnings suggest that the demand for tertiary-educated individuals has kept up with the increasing supply from higher educational institutions in most OECD countries. Despite an increase in the proportion of 25-64 year-olds with tertiary attainment from 21% in 2000 to 30% in 2010 (see Indicator A1), the earnings premium for those with a tertiary education held firm over the same period.

A8

Analysis

Earnings differentials and educational attainment

Variations in relative earnings (before taxes) among countries reflect a number of factors, including the demand for skills in the labour market, minimum wage laws, the strength of labour unions, the coverage of collective-bargaining agreements, the supply of workers at various levels of educational attainment, and the relative incidence of part-time and seasonal work.

Still, earnings differentials are among the more straightforward indications of whether the supply of educated individuals meets demand, particularly in light of changes over time. Chart A8.2 shows a strong positive relationship between educational attainment and average earnings. In all countries, people with tertiary education earn more overall than those with upper secondary and post-secondary non-tertiary education.

Chart A8.2.   Relative earnings from employment among 25-64 year-olds, by level of educational attainment and gender (2010 or latest available year)

Upper secondary and post-secondary non-tertiary education = 100

■ Tertiary-type A and advanced research programmes
□ Tertiary-type B education
■ Below upper secondary education

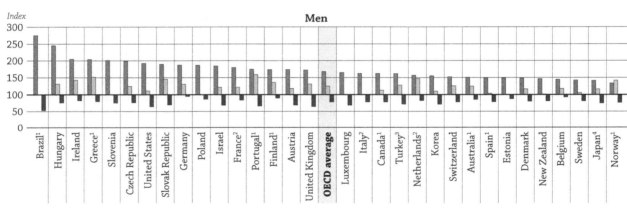

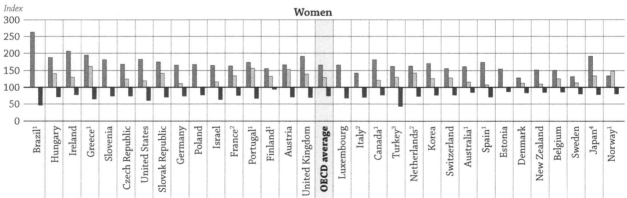

Note: Belgium, Korea and Turkey report earnings net of income tax.
1. Year of reference 2009.
2. Year of reference 2008.
3. Year of reference 2005.
4. Year of reference 2007.
Countries are ranked in descending order of the relative earnings of 25-64 year-old men with tertiary-type A education (including advanced research programmes).
Source: OECD. Table A8.1. See Annex 3 for notes (*www.oecd.org/edu/eag2012*).
StatLink ᴍ⑤ᴸ http://dx.doi.org/10.1787/888932662143

Earnings differentials between those with tertiary education – especially tertiary-type A (largely theory-based) education and advanced research programmes – and those with upper secondary education are generally more pronounced than the differentials between upper secondary and lower secondary or below. This suggests that in many countries, upper secondary education is the level beyond which additional education implies a particularly high earnings premium. Since private investment costs beyond upper secondary education rise considerably in most countries, a high earnings premium helps to ensure that there will be an adequate supply of individuals willing to invest time and money in further education (Table A8.1).

The earnings premium for men with a degree from a university or advanced research programme exceeds 100% in Brazil, Greece, Hungary and Ireland, and nearly does so in the Czech Republic and the United States. Meanwhile, women with these degrees earn 80% or more than women with an upper secondary or post-secondary non-tertiary education in Brazil, Canada, Greece, Hungary, Ireland, Japan, the United Kingdom and the United States (Table A8.1).

Women who have not attained an upper secondary education are particularly disadvantaged in Brazil, Greece, Israel, Italy, Luxembourg, Portugal, Turkey, the United Kingdom and the United States, where their earnings represent less than 70% those of women with an upper secondary education. In Austria, Brazil, Israel, Luxembourg, Portugal, the Slovak Republic, the United Kingdom and the United States, men who have not attained an upper secondary education are in a similar situation (Table A8.1).

The relative earnings premium for those with a tertiary education has held steady in most countries over the past ten years, indicating that the demand for more educated individuals still exceeds supply in most countries. On average among OECD countries with available data, the tertiary earnings premium increased by 10 percentage points between 2000 and 2010 (Table A8.2a). In Germany and Hungary, the earnings premium has increased by over 10 percentage points; however, tertiary attainment levels are low in these countries compared to the OECD average (see Indicator A1). In Ireland, the earnings premium has increased by 22 points between 2000 and 2010. Nevertheless, in some cases the earnings premium could reflect lower earnings for less-educated workers, rather than wage increases for more highly educated workers. This relationship could be driven by the migration of high-paying factory jobs, formerly held by less-educated workers, to developing countries.

Canada, Finland, France, Norway, Portugal, Slovenia, Sweden and Switzerland have seen a slight decrease in earnings premiums for those with a tertiary education in the years since 2000, although the premium still exceeds the 2010 OECD average in Portugal and Slovenia. It is unclear whether this indicates weakening demand, an excess supply of tertiary-educated workers, or whether these figures reflect the fact that younger tertiary-educated individuals have entered the labour market making relatively low starting salaries. In all countries but Turkey and Norway, the trends in relative earnings are different for men and women (Tables A8.2b and A8.2c).

Education, earnings and age

Table A8.1 shows how relative earnings vary with age. The earnings premium for tertiary-educated 55-64 year-olds is generally larger than that for 25-64 year-olds: on average, the earnings differential increases by 15 percentage points. Both employment opportunities and earnings advantages for older people with a tertiary education improve in most countries (see Indicator A7). Earnings are relatively higher for older individuals with tertiary education in all countries except Germany, Greece, Ireland, Turkey and the United Kingdom.

For those who have not attained an upper secondary education, the earnings disadvantage increases for older workers (55-64 year-olds) in all countries except Australia, Denmark, Finland, Ireland, Norway, the Slovak Republic, Sweden, the United Kingdom and the United States. The increase in this disadvantage is not as marked as the increase in the earnings advantage for those with a tertiary education – an indication that tertiary education is the key to higher earnings at an older age. In most countries, then, tertiary education not only improves the prospect of being employed at an older age, but is also associated with greater earnings and productivity differentials throughout a person's working life.

A8

Chart A8.3. **Difference in relative earnings among 55-64 year-olds and 25-64 year-olds (2010 or latest available year)**

Earnings relative to upper secondary and post-secondary non-tertiary education

■ Below upper secondary education   ▓ Tertiary education

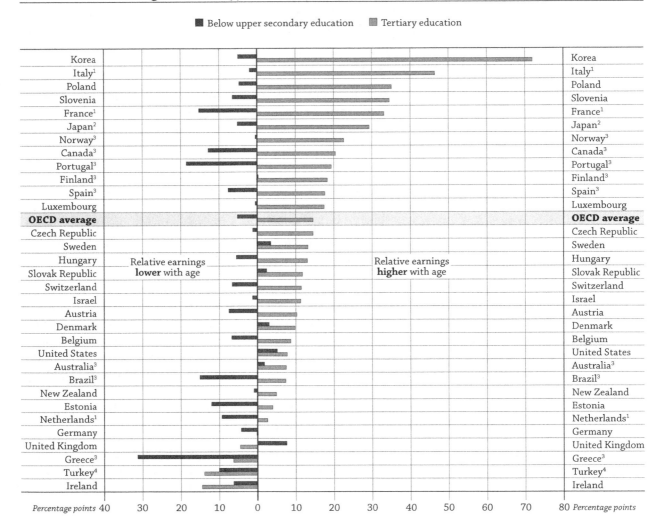

Relative earnings **lower** with age

Relative earnings **higher** with age

Percentage points 40   30   20   10   0   10   20   30   40   50   60   70   80 Percentage points

Notes: Belgium, Korea and Turkey report earnings net of income tax.
1. Year of reference 2008.
2. Year of reference 2007.
3. Year of reference 2009.
4. Year of reference 2005.
Countries are ranked in descending order of the difference in relative earnings among 55-64 year-olds and the total population (25-64 year-olds) at the tertiary level of education.
Source: OECD, Table A8.1. See Annex 3 for notes (*www.oecd.org/edu/eag2012*).
StatLink ⟐⟐⟐ http://dx.doi.org/10.1787/888932662162

Education and gender disparities in earnings

More education does little to narrow the gender gap in earnings. Across OECD countries, the difference in full-time earnings between 25-64 year-old men and women is the smallest among those with an upper secondary and post-secondary non-tertiary education and largest among those with a tertiary education. Only in five countries – Finland, New Zealand, Slovenia, Spain, and the United Kingdom – do the earnings of tertiary-educated women amount to 75% or more of men's earnings. In Brazil, Estonia, Italy and Korea, women who have obtained a tertiary degree earn 65% or less of what tertiary-educated men earn (Table A8.3a).

The gender gap in earnings does not narrow over the working life of women with a tertiary education. In fact, on average across OECD countries, a 55-64 year-old woman with a tertiary degree can expect to earn 71% of a man's wages – a percentage point less than the gender differential in earnings that exists among the total tertiary-educated population (Table A8.3a). The gender gap in earnings is partly due to differences in occupations, differences in the fields men and women tend to study during education (see Indicator A4), and the amount of time spent in the labour force (see Indicator C5). However, low earnings, particularly for women who have completed tertiary education, could adversely affect the labour supply and the full use of skills developed in the education system. This, in turn, could hamper economic growth.

Chart A8.4. **Differences in earnings distribution, by educational attainment (2010 or latest available year)**

Proportion of 25-64 year-olds at or below half the median and the proportion of the population earning more than twice the median, for below upper secondary education and tertiary-type A and advanced research programmes

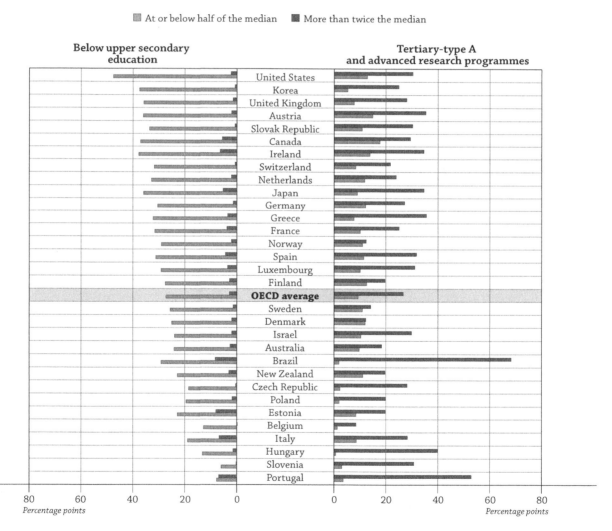

Notes: Estonia and Slovenia refer to all tertiary education. Year of reference for Australia, Brazil, Canada, Finland, Greece, Norway, Portugal and Spain is 2009; for France, Italy and the Netherlands is 2008 and for Japan is 2007.

Countries are ranked in descending order of the difference in proportion of 25-64 year-olds at or below half the median and the proportion of the population earning more than twice the median for below upper secondary education.

Source: OECD. Table A8.4a, available on line. See Annex 3 for notes (*www.oecd.org/edu/eag2012*).

StatLink http://dx.doi.org/10.1787/888932662181

A8

Distribution of earnings within levels of educational attainment

Since this indicator includes earnings from all employed individuals (except in Table A8.3a), the supply of labour in terms of hours worked influences earnings differences, in general, and the distribution in earnings, in particular. Nevertheless, data on the distribution of earnings among different educational groups can show how tightly earnings centre around the country median. In addition to providing information on equity in earnings, these data indicate the risks associated with investing in education (as risk is typically measured by the variation in outcomes).

Tables A8.4a, A8.4b and A8.4c (available on line) show the distribution of earnings among 25-64 year-olds according to their level of educational attainment. Distributions are provided for the entire adult population and are also broken down for women and men. For people with wages from work, the five earnings categories reported range from "At or below half of the median" to "More than twice the median", while the proportion of people without earnings from work is reported in a separate column.

Chart A8.4 contrasts the results for those who do not have an upper secondary education with those who have completed a tertiary-type A or an advanced research programme by comparing the proportion of wage-earners at or below one-half of the median to those at more than twice the median. As expected, there is a large difference between these two educational categories. On average, tertiary-educated individuals are substantially more likely to earn twice as much as the median worker and are substantially less likely to be in the low-earnings category than those who have not completed an upper secondary education.

There are, however, some notable differences in how well tertiary-educated individuals fare in different countries. In Brazil, Hungary and Portugal, 40% or more of those who have completed a university or an advanced research programme earn twice as much as the median worker; in Canada, nearly 18% of those with such a degree are found in the lowest-earnings category (at or below half of the median); and in Denmark and Norway, an individual with such a degree is roughly as likely to fall into the lowest as the highest earnings category. This signals the risk in investing in education (Table A8.4a, available on line).

Box A8.1. High education and low income: disentangling the paradox in Canada

Ever since 2005, when the distribution of earnings by level of educational attainment was published for the first time in *Education at a Glance*, international data have shown that compared to other OECD countries, Canada has had the highest percentage of tertiary-educated workers who earned less than half of the national median employment income. For instance, recent data show that 17.6% of ISCED 5A/6-educated adults and 23.1% of ISCED 5B-educated adults aged 25 to 64 in Canada earned less than half the national median employment income in 2009. This meant that these workers' annual earnings were less than CAD 37 766 before taxes and transfers.

Given the importance of post-secondary education in Canada, such findings raise pertinent questions. Does this ranking suggest, for example, that structural factors in Canada could lead to such a result? Is Canada producing too many ISCED 5B and ISCED 5A/6 graduates for the labour market to absorb? Or is Canada not producing the right mix of post-secondary graduates?

In order to answer these questions, it is important to know who these tertiary-educated workers in low-earnings situations are. Based on data for 2006, Statistics Canada researchers examined the characteristics of these workers in order to identify demographic and employment characteristics that could suggest reasons for their low employment-earnings situation (McMullen, 2009; Zeman et al., 2010). The definition on which the indicator of low earnings was based includes all workers who reported non-zero earnings from employment in 2006. However, working may not have been their main activity for the year.

...

Overall, for the ISCED 5A/6-educated population, 43% of low earners reported an activity other than working as their main activity for the year, though they did report having some employment earnings during the year. Another 24% were self-employed, and 5% were both self-employed and reported an activity other than working as their main activity. When only ISCED 5A/6 graduates who reported working for an employer are considered, only 5% of ISCED 5A/6 graduates were in the lowest earnings category in 2006.

Among ISCED 5B graduates, one-third of low earners reported an activity other than working as their main activity for the year; 27% were self-employed and 4% were both self-employed and reported an activity other than working as their main activity. Again, when only those who reported working for an employer are considered, just 8% of ISCED 5B graduates were in the lowest earnings category in 2006.

Work schedule played an important role as well. Just 11% of both ISCED 5B and 5A/6 graduates who were working full-time, full-year fell into the lowest earnings category, compared to 49% of ISCED 5B graduates and 42% of ISCED 5A/6 graduates who worked part time.

With this, it is already clear that being in a situation of low earnings is largely a function of the nature of an individual's participation in the labour market. Yet while it is understandable that low attachment to the labour market leads to low earnings, the high proportion of highly-educated individuals for whom labour market participation is not the main activity poses questions about a possible under-utilisation of skills that are rather costly – both privately and publicly – to produce.

After taking employment characteristics into account, the analysis found that certain other characteristics were associated with higher probabilities of falling into the lowest earnings category. One of these characteristics was gender, with ISCED 5B- and 5A/6-educated women being more likely than their male counterparts to be in the lowest earnings category. Age was another factor, with older workers (age 55 to 64) being more likely to fall into low earnings categories. Individuals' province of residence had an effect as well, with workers in Newfoundland and Labrador, Nova Scotia and New Brunswick – three provinces in the eastern part of Canada – being more likely to fall into low earnings compared to workers in the other provinces.

Differences were found by field of study: workers who had studied arts and communications technologies, parks, recreation and fitness or the humanities were more likely than individuals in other fields of study to be in a low-earnings situation. Conversely, workers in certain occupations such as those in management, business administration, science and technical professions, health and occupations in social science were less likely than those in other occupations to have low earnings. This was also the case for those employed in primary industries and public administration.

Finally, immigrant status also had a strong effect, after controlling for other factors. Notably, the effect of immigration status became particularly strong after controlling for education, suggesting that a recent (less than ten years in Canada) immigrant aged 25 to 64 with the same education as a Canadian-born worker was almost twice as likely to fall into the lowest earnings category. Immigrants who had been in Canada between 10 and 29 years were also more likely than Canadian-born workers to fall into low earnings. This effect was particularly strong after controlling for their main activity during the year. In other words, after controlling for whether or not a person was working as the main activity during the year, immigrant workers aged 25 to 64 were more likely to fall into low earnings.

The fact that Canada ranks high compared to other OECD countries in terms of the proportion of ISCED 5B and 5A/6 graduates earning less than half the median earnings therefore raises the question: Are Canadians more likely than workers in other countries to report an activity other than working as their main activity for the year? A useful avenue for future research would be to undertake an international comparison of the characteristics of highly-educated low earners in order to determine the extent to which differences in labour market attachment behaviours contribute to this finding.

A8

Low earnings differentials and the supply of labour can help explain why some highly educated individuals can fall into a low-income group. For instance, in Denmark and Norway, the earnings premiums for someone with a university or an advanced research degree are 32% and 27%, respectively (Table A8.1). The relatively low economic reward for higher education is likely influencing the supply of labour, in terms of hours worked, and as such low earnings premiums can be detrimental to the overall supply and use of skills in those economies.

Not completing upper secondary education is associated with large earnings disadvantages in all countries. On average across OECD countries, only 2.9% of those who have not attained an upper secondary education earn twice the national median. In Brazil, Canada, Estonia, Ireland, Italy, Japan and Portugal, this proportion is above 5%, but in no country does it exceed 10%. On average, more than 27% of those who have not completed an upper secondary education earn less than half of the national median (Table A8.4, available on line).

Definitions

For the definition of **full-time earnings**, countries were asked whether they had applied a self-designated full-time status or a threshold value of typical number of hours worked per week. Ireland, Italy, Luxembourg, Portugal, Spain, Sweden and the United Kingdom reported self-designated full-time status; the other countries defined the full-time status by the number of working hours per week. The threshold was 36 hours per week in Austria, Hungary and the Slovak Republic, 35 hours in Australia, Brazil, Canada, Estonia, Germany and the United States, and 30 hours in the Czech Republic, Greece and New Zealand. Other participating countries did not report a minimum normal number of working hours for full-time work.

For some countries, data on **full-time, full-year earnings** are based on the European Survey on Income and Living Conditions (EU-SILC), which uses a self-designated approach in establishing full-time status.

The **length of the reference period for earnings** also differed. Australia, New Zealand and the United Kingdom reported data on weekly earnings, while Belgium, Estonia, Finland, Hungary, Korea and Portugal reported monthly data. In Austria, the Czech Republic, Denmark, Germany, Greece, Ireland, Israel, Italy, Luxembourg, the Netherlands, Norway, the Slovak Republic, Slovenia, Spain, Sweden and the United States, the reference period for the earnings data was 12 months. For France, the length of the reference period, up to and including 2007, was one month; the new reference period for France from 2008 onwards is 12 months.

Methodology

The indicator is based on two different data collections. One is the regular data collection that takes account of earnings from work for all individuals during the reference period, even if the individual has worked part-time or part-year. The second collects data on the earnings of those working full-time and full-year. This data collection supplies the data for Table A8.3a (gender differences in full-time earnings). The regular data collection is used for all other tables.

Earnings data in Tables A8.1, A8.2 and A8.4 (regular earnings data collection) are based on an annual reference period in Austria, Brazil, Canada, the Czech Republic, Denmark, Ireland, Italy, Korea, Luxembourg, the Netherlands, Norway, Slovenia, Spain, Sweden, Turkey and the United States. Earnings are reported weekly in Australia, New Zealand and the United Kingdom, and monthly in Belgium, Estonia, Finland, France, Hungary, Portugal and Switzerland. Data on earnings are before income tax, except for Belgium, Korea and Turkey, where earnings reported are net of income tax. Data on earnings for individuals in part-time work are also excluded in the regular data collection for the Czech Republic, Hungary, Portugal, Slovenia, and data on part-year earnings are excluded for the Czech Republic, Hungary and Portugal.

Since earnings data differ across countries in a number of ways, the results should be interpreted with caution. For example, in countries reporting annual earnings, differences in the incidence of seasonal work among individuals with different levels of educational attainment will have an effect on relative earnings that is not similarly reflected in the data for countries reporting weekly or monthly earnings.

The statistical data for Israel are supplied by and are under the responsibility of the relevant Israeli authorities. The use of such data by the OECD is without prejudice to the status of the Golan Heights, East Jerusalem and Israeli settlements in the West Bank under the terms of international law.

References

Carnevale, A. (2012), *Hard Times: College Majors, Unemployment and Earnings: Not All College Degrees Are Created Equal,* Center on Education and the Workforce, Washington, D.C.

McMullen, K. (2009), "College and university graduates with low earnings in Canada: Demographic and labour market characteristics", *Education Matters*, Vol. 6 No. 2, Statistics Canada, Ottawa.

Zeman, K., K. McMullen, and P. de Broucker (2010), "The High Education/Low Income Paradox: College and University Graduates with Low Earnings", Ontario, 2006, *Culture, Tourism and the Centre for Education Statistics Research Papers,* No. 81, Statistics Canada, Ottawa.

The following additional material relevant to this indicator is available on line:

- *Table A8.4a Distribution of 25-64 year-olds, by level of earnings and educational attainment (2010 or latest available year)*
  StatLink ⟐ http://dx.doi.org/10.1787/888932665449

- *Table A8.4b Distribution of 25-64 year-old men, by level of earnings and educational attainment (2010 or latest available year)*
  StatLink ⟐ http://dx.doi.org/10.1787/888932665468

- *Table A8.4c Distribution of 25-64 year-old women, by level of earnings and educational attainment (2010 or latest available year)*
  StatLink ⟐ http://dx.doi.org/10.1787/888932665487

A8

Table A8.1. [1/2] Relative earnings of the population with income from employment
(2010 or latest available year)
By level of educational attainment, gender and age groups
(upper secondary and post-secondary non-tertiary education = 100)

			Below upper secondary education			Post-secondary non-tertiary education			Tertiary-type B education			Tertiary-type A and advanced research programmes			All tertiary education		
			25-64	25-34	55-64	25-64	25-34	55-64	25-64	25-34	55-64	25-64	25-34	55-64	25-64	25-34	55-64
			(1)	(2)	(3)	(4)	(5)	(6)	(7)	(8)	(9)	(10)	(11)	(12)	(13)	(14)	(15)
Australia	2009	Men	85	78	88	103	110	100	125	100	131	151	122	163	144	117	155
		Women	85	75	88	95	107	94	116	105	118	162	151	169	148	141	150
		M+W	81	77	82	93	103	95	111	96	113	145	126	157	135	119	143
Austria	2010	Men	69	70	66	135	120	189	118	118	110	174	139	191	153	133	160
		Women	71	64	63	124	120	148	153	115	163	167	166	212	162	155	187
		M+W	66	68	58	124	114	168	130	118	123	171	144	200	156	137	167
Belgium	2010	Men	92	93	86	96	96	90	117	110	118	145	129	153	133	120	139
		Women	86	90	80	98	99	107	125	122	128	151	144	159	136	132	139
		M+W	91	93	85	95	95	95	117	112	119	147	133	161	131	122	140
Canada	2009	Men	78	80	67	109	113	107	113	115	123	162	131	200	139	123	169
		Women	77	91	65	98	102	90	121	129	111	181	182	177	150	159	140
		M+W	80	87	67	109	111	105	110	113	114	165	140	199	138	128	158
Chile			m	m	m	m	m	m	m	m	m	m	m	m	m	m	m
Czech Republic	2010	Men	76	77	78	m	m	m	124	123	172	199	166	207	195	162	206
		Women	74	76	70	m	m	m	125	120	129	168	155	178	163	148	175
		M+W	73	76	72	m	m	m	120	115	144	187	159	199	182	153	197
Denmark	2010	Men	80	76	86	70	49	103	117	120	114	148	116	164	141	117	153
		Women	83	76	86	39	42	81	112	120	107	128	123	134	126	123	130
		M+W	81	78	84	63	47	111	116	119	111	132	114	145	129	114	139
Estonia	2010	Men	88	91	75	m	m	m	m	m	m	m	m	m	149	118	162
		Women	87	98	76	m	m	m	m	m	m	m	m	m	154	161	146
		M+W	90	95	78	m	m	m	m	m	m	m	m	m	136	120	139
Finland	2009	Men	90	89	92	m	m	m	136	132	135	174	138	211	162	137	179
		Women	94	89	93	m	m	m	133	128	126	155	142	191	146	141	154
		M+W	93	92	93	m	m	m	128	120	128	161	130	206	149	129	167
France	2008	Men	84	81	68	m	m	m	121	119	108	180	142	252	153	133	199
		Women	75	76	65	m	m	m	134	133	109	163	151	181	151	144	157
		M+W	79	80	64	m	m	m	123	121	107	165	140	221	147	132	180
Germany	2010	Men	95	90	100	120	123	105	131	131	118	187	159	177	171	154	160
		Women	74	73	70	119	117	115	111	127	79	166	149	183	153	144	163
		M+W	85	83	81	115	117	104	130	121	119	181	150	183	168	144	167
Greece	2009	Men	80	85	50	106	101	97	151	133	130	204	139	251	153	133	137
		Women	65	79	35	114	104	211	162	140	165	195	182	m	163	141	165
		M+W	76	88	45	106	99	136	149	128	139	204	152	276	151	128	145
Hungary	2010	Men	76	76	74	125	116	131	131	120	126	245	206	253	244	205	252
		Women	71	77	63	116	111	118	140	143	154	188	179	195	187	178	195
		M+W	73	77	67	120	114	124	134	130	145	211	188	224	210	188	223
Iceland			m	m	m	m	m	m	m	m	m	m	m	m	m	m	m
Ireland	2010	Men	82	77	70	86	99	76	143	119	152	205	208	162	180	177	158
		Women	78	77	68	99	90	102	130	162	141	206	252	165	178	223	155
		M+W	85	74	79	90	95	86	135	125	147	200	205	169	175	179	161
Israel	2010	Men	68	76	69	109	115	122	122	122	121	184	159	198	164	149	172
		Women	63	79	61	116	110	155	116	100	116	165	139	180	150	130	156
		M+W	71	79	70	108	114	125	115	109	115	169	143	189	152	134	163
Italy	2008	Men	78	83	76	m	m	m	m	m	m	162	110	212	162	110	212
		Women	70	74	76	m	m	m	m	m	m	142	119	168	142	119	168
		M+W	79	85	77	m	m	m	m	m	m	150	109	196	150	109	196
Japan	2007	Men	74	88	71	m	m	m	116	111	126	141	126	157	139	125	154
		Women	78	73	77	m	m	m	134	134	146	191	171	225	161	155	178
		M+W	80	90	74	m	m	m	90	96	106	168	139	197	148	129	178
Korea	2010	Men	71	82	70	m	m	m	110	115	141	155	136	222	143	128	213
		Women	77	66	81	m	m	m	126	115	128	171	141	243	155	130	221
		M+W	69	80	64	m	m	m	115	112	137	167	136	236	151	126	223
Luxembourg	2010	Men	68	68	83	105	99	74	m	m	m	165	143	188	165	143	188
		Women	68	61	49	113	61	91	m	m	m	166	167	150	166	167	150
		M+W	66	67	66	119	109	80	m	m	m	159	151	177	159	151	177
Mexico			m	m	m	m	m	m	m	m	m	m	m	m	m	m	m

Note: Belgium, Korea and Turkey report earnings net of income tax.
Source: OECD. See Annex 3 for notes (*www.oecd.org/edu/eag2012*).
Please refer to the Reader's Guide for information concerning the symbols replacing missing data.
StatLink ᴹ⁵ᴾ http://dx.doi.org/10.1787/888932665335

A8

Table A8.1. [2/2] Relative earnings of the population with income from employment
(2010 or latest available year)
By level of educational attainment, gender and age groups
(upper secondary and post-secondary non-tertiary education = 100)

			Below upper secondary education			Post-secondary non-tertiary education			Tertiary-type B education			Tertiary-type A and advanced research programmes			All tertiary education		
			25-64	25-34	55-64	25-64	25-34	55-64	25-64	25-34	55-64	25-64	25-34	55-64	25-64	25-34	55-64
			(1)	(2)	(3)	(4)	(5)	(6)	(7)	(8)	(9)	(10)	(11)	(12)	(13)	(14)	(15)
OECD Netherlands	2008	Men	82	87	79	114	120	110	147	145	130	157	139	160	156	139	158
		Women	73	75	67	117	115	112	143	137	143	163	150	161	162	149	160
		M+W	81	87	72	115	119	107	149	141	142	160	140	163	159	140	162
New Zealand	2010	Men	81	87	84	100	103	100	101	93	101	147	117	167	130	109	140
		Women	85	83	81	90	86	92	110	104	109	152	136	152	135	128	128
		M+W	79	86	78	109	106	108	97	94	97	140	119	158	124	112	129
Norway	2009	Men	76	73	76	120	117	127	142	130	145	134	106	154	134	107	152
		Women	80	77	77	117	110	127	148	145	150	134	128	148	135	128	148
		M+W	77	74	77	125	123	133	150	129	165	127	107	149	128	108	151
Poland	2010	Men	86	85	84	110	106	113	m	m	m	186	160	223	186	160	223
		Women	77	87	66	118	110	118	m	m	m	168	155	182	168	155	182
		M+W	83	87	78	109	102	114	m	m	m	169	148	204	169	148	204
Portugal	2009	Men	66	77	51	84	91	81	159	145	151	175	160	187	172	158	180
		Women	67	76	48	103	107	118	156	148	156	173	168	209	171	166	196
		M+W	68	79	50	92	98	92	157	146	154	171	161	198	169	159	188
Slovak Republic	2010	Men	70	59	78	m	m	m	145	145	143	189	157	200	188	157	198
		Women	71	70	67	m	m	m	141	135	137	175	156	184	172	155	180
		M+W	67	62	69	m	m	m	132	131	132	182	151	194	179	151	191
Slovenia	2010	Men	75	75	72	m	m	m	m	m	m	m	m	m	201	164	232
		Women	74	79	59	m	m	m	m	m	m	m	m	m	181	156	204
		M+W	75	79	68	m	m	m	m	m	m	m	m	m	186	151	220
Spain	2009	Men	79	89	76	161	112	160	103	113	114	149	137	164	133	127	153
		Women	71	80	57	120	131	83	108	107	106	174	166	181	159	152	170
		M+W	78	88	70	135	119	141	107	113	114	155	146	169	141	135	158
Sweden	2010	Men	81	79	83	122	79	127	105	96	111	142	118	159	133	113	147
		Women	80	75	84	108	85	125	114	95	121	132	130	148	127	124	138
		M+W	82	78	85	120	80	133	105	94	111	133	118	152	125	113	139
Switzerland	2010	Men	78	87	78	104	104	101	126	122	121	152	131	167	143	128	150
		Women	77	62	67	111	100	113	128	112	126	156	123	163	148	120	150
		M+W	75	76	69	107	102	107	138	121	135	161	127	182	153	126	165
Turkey	2005	Men	72	77	60	m	m	m	128	154	121	162	178	133	153	171	129
		Women	43	37	49	m	m	m	131	93	m	162	150	307	154	133	307
		M+W	69	70	59	m	m	m	125	131	128	157	166	138	149	156	135
United Kingdom	2010	Men	64	62	73	m	m	m	131	128	138	172	159	159	162	153	153
		Women	69	75	80	m	m	m	140	120	159	191	191	191	177	178	180
		M+W	67	67	74	m	m	m	131	120	142	178	166	170	165	158	161
United States	2010	Men	64	65	68	m	m	m	111	110	102	192	165	199	184	159	191
		Women	61	61	70	m	m	m	119	132	114	182	186	176	175	181	168
		M+W	66	67	71	m	m	m	111	115	105	184	167	193	177	161	184
OECD average		Men	78	79	75	110	104	111	126	122	127	170	145	187	160	140	173
		Women	74	75	69	106	100	116	130	124	130	166	157	183	157	149	169
		M+W	77	80	72	108	104	114	124	118	127	165	144	186	155	137	169
Other G20 Argentina			m	m	m	m	m	m	m	m	m	m	m	m	m	m	m
Brazil	2009	Men	53	58	38	m	m	m	m	m	m	275	279	265	275	279	265
		Women	47	52	34	m	m	m	m	m	m	263	262	273	263	262	273
		M+W	53	59	38	m	m	m	m	m	m	256	256	264	256	256	264
China			m	m	m	m	m	m	m	m	m	m	m	m	m	m	m
India			m	m	m	m	m	m	m	m	m	m	m	m	m	m	m
Indonesia			m	m	m	m	m	m	m	m	m	m	m	m	m	m	m
Russian Federation			m	m	m	m	m	m	m	m	m	m	m	m	m	m	m
Saudi Arabia			m	m	m	m	m	m	m	m	m	m	m	m	m	m	m
South Africa			m	m	m	m	m	m	m	m	m	m	m	m	m	m	m
G20 average			m	m	m	m	m	m	m	m	m	m	m	m	m	m	m

Note: Belgium, Korea and Turkey report earnings net of income tax.
Source: OECD. See Annex 3 for notes (*www.oecd.org/edu/eag2012*).
Please refer to the Reader's Guide for information concerning the symbols replacing missing data.
StatLink http://dx.doi.org/10.1787/888932665335

A8

Table A8.2a. [1/2] Trends in relative earnings: Total population (2000-10)
By educational attainment, for 25-64 year-olds (upper secondary and post-secondary non-tertiary education = 100)

		2000	2001	2002	2003	2004	2005	2006	2007	2008	2009	2010
Australia	Below upper secondary	m	77	m	m	m	82	m	m	m	81	m
	Tertiary	m	133	m	m	m	134	m	m	m	135	m
Austria	Below upper secondary	m	m	m	m	m	71	66	67	68	65	66
	Tertiary	m	m	m	m	m	152	157	155	160	155	156
Belgium	Below upper secondary	92	m	91	89	90	89	m	m	m	91	91
	Tertiary	128	m	132	130	134	133	m	m	m	131	131
Canada	Below upper secondary	82	79	79	81	81	78	77	83	82	80	m
	Tertiary	142	141	135	138	137	135	136	140	138	138	m
Czech Republic	Below upper secondary	m	m	m	m	73	72	74	73	72	71	73
	Tertiary	m	m	m	m	182	181	183	183	183	188	182
Denmark	Below upper secondary	m	87	88	82	82	82	83	82	83	81	81
	Tertiary	m	124	124	127	126	125	126	125	125	127	129
Estonia	Below upper secondary	m	m	m	m	m	m	m	m	91	91	90
	Tertiary	m	m	m	m	m	m	m	m	129	137	136
Finland	Below upper secondary	95	95	95	94	94	94	94	94	93	93	m
	Tertiary	153	150	150	148	149	149	149	148	147	149	m
France	Below upper secondary	m	m	84	84	85	86	85	84	79	m	m
	Tertiary	m	m	150	146	147	144	149	150	147	m	m
Germany	Below upper secondary	75	m	77	87	88	88	90	91	90	87	85
	Tertiary	143	m	143	153	153	156	164	162	167	157	168
Greece	Below upper secondary	m	m	m	m	m	m	m	m	m	76	m
	Tertiary	m	m	m	m	m	m	m	m	m	151	m
Hungary	Below upper secondary	71	71	74	74	73	73	73	72	73	71	73
	Tertiary	194	194	205	219	217	215	219	211	210	211	210
Ireland	Below upper secondary	89	m	76	m	79	78	83	77	74	83	85
	Tertiary	153	m	144	m	174	177	157	161	153	164	175
Israel	Below upper secondary	m	m	m	m	m	79	78	83	75	80	71
	Tertiary	m	m	m	m	m	151	151	153	152	154	152
Italy	Below upper secondary	78	m	78	m	79	m	76	m	79	m	m
	Tertiary	138	m	153	m	165	m	155	m	150	m	m
Japan	Below upper secondary	m	m	m	m	m	m	m	80	m	m	m
	Tertiary	m	m	m	m	m	m	m	148	m	m	m
Korea	Below upper secondary	m	69	71	68	69	68	69	70	69	69	69
	Tertiary	m	144	143	145	144	149	147	150	150	172	151
Luxembourg	Below upper secondary	m	m	78	m	m	m	74	m	m	66	66
	Tertiary	m	m	145	m	m	m	153	m	m	162	159
Netherlands	Below upper secondary	m	m	84	m	m	85	m	81	m	m	m
	Tertiary	m	m	148	m	m	154	m	159	m	m	m
New Zealand	Below upper secondary	79	78	81	77	75	77	82	76	82	79	79
	Tertiary	123	120	123	123	116	120	115	117	118	118	124
Norway	Below upper secondary	79	79	79	78	78	78	78	79	78	77	m
	Tertiary	129	131	130	131	130	129	129	128	127	128	m
Poland	Below upper secondary	m	81	81	m	82	m	84	m	83	m	83
	Tertiary	m	166	172	m	179	m	173	m	167	m	169
Portugal	Below upper secondary	m	m	m	m	67	67	68	m	m	68	m
	Tertiary	m	m	m	m	178	177	177	m	m	169	m
Slovak Republic	Below upper secondary	m	m	m	m	m	m	m	m	69	66	67
	Tertiary	m	m	m	m	m	m	m	m	181	184	179
Slovenia	Below upper secondary	m	m	m	81	73	m	74	74	m	73	75
	Tertiary	m	m	m	m	198	m	193	192	m	191	186
Spain	Below upper secondary	m	78	m	79	82	80	m	81	78	78	m
	Tertiary	m	129	m	128	135	137	m	138	141	141	m

Note: Belgium, Korea and Turkey report earnings net of income tax.
Source: OECD. See Annex 3 for notes (www.oecd.org/edu/eag2012).
Please refer to the Reader's Guide for information concerning the symbols replacing missing data.
StatLink ⬛📊 http://dx.doi.org/10.1787/888932665354

Table A8.2a. [2/2] Trends in relative earnings: Total population (2000-10)

By educational attainment, for 25-64 year-olds (upper secondary and post-secondary non-tertiary education = 100)

			2000	2001	2002	2003	2004	2005	2006	2007	2008	2009	2010
OECD	Sweden	Below upper secondary	m	86	87	87	87	86	85	84	83	83	**82**
		Tertiary	m	131	130	128	127	126	126	126	126	126	**125**
	Switzerland	Below upper secondary	m	76	75	74	74	75	74	74	74	76	**75**
		Tertiary	m	156	155	157	157	155	156	160	155	154	**153**
	Turkey	Below upper secondary	m	m	m	m	65	69	m	m	m	m	**m**
		Tertiary	m	m	m	m	141	149	m	m	m	m	**m**
	United Kingdom	Below upper secondary	69	70	68	69	69	71	71	70	71	70	**67**
		Tertiary	160	160	157	162	157	158	160	157	154	159	**165**
	United States	Below upper secondary	68	m	66	66	65	67	66	65	66	64	**66**
		Tertiary	176	m	172	172	172	175	176	172	177	179	**177**
	OECD average	Below upper secondary	80	79	79	79	78	78	78	78	78	77	**76**
		Tertiary	149	145	148	147	155	151	157	154	153	155	**159**
Other G20	Argentina		m	m	m	m	m	m	m	m	m	m	**m**
	Brazil	Below upper secondary	m	m	m	m	m	m	m	51	52	53	**m**
		Tertiary	m	m	m	m	m	m	m	268	254	256	**m**
	China		m	m	m	m	m	m	m	m	m	m	**m**
	India		m	m	m	m	m	m	m	m	m	m	**m**
	Indonesia		m	m	m	m	m	m	m	m	m	m	**m**
	Russian Federation		m	m	m	m	m	m	m	m	m	m	**m**
	Saudi Arabia		m	m	m	m	m	m	m	m	m	m	**m**
	South Africa		m	m	m	m	m	m	m	m	m	m	**m**
	G20 average		m	m	m	m	m	m	m	m	m	m	**m**

Note: Belgium, Korea and Turkey report earnings net of income tax.

Source: OECD. See Annex 3 for notes *(www.oecd.org/edu/eag2012)*.

Please refer to the Reader's Guide for information concerning the symbols replacing missing data.

StatLink http://dx.doi.org/10.1787/888932665354

A8

Table A8.2b. [1/2] Trends in relative earnings: Men (2000-10)

By educational attainment, for 25-64 year-olds (upper secondary and post-secondary non-tertiary education = 100)

		2000	2001	2002	2003	2004	2005	2006	2007	2008	2009	2010
Australia	Below upper secondary	m	84	m	m	m	88	m	m	m	85	m
	Tertiary	m	142	m	m	m	140	m	m	m	144	m
Austria	Below upper secondary	m	m	m	m	m	76	72	72	71	68	69
	Tertiary	m	m	m	m	m	149	155	151	159	153	153
Belgium	Below upper secondary	93	m	91	90	91	91	m	m	m	93	92
	Tertiary	128	m	132	132	137	137	m	m	m	134	133
Canada	Below upper secondary	83	79	81	81	81	78	78	85	82	78	m
	Tertiary	148	145	141	141	139	136	137	143	139	139	m
Czech Republic	Below upper secondary	m	m	m	m	79	79	81	78	76	75	76
	Tertiary	m	m	m	m	193	190	194	192	193	201	195
Denmark	Below upper secondary	m	87	87	82	82	82	82	81	82	80	80
	Tertiary	m	132	131	134	133	133	133	133	133	136	141
Estonia	Below upper secondary	m	m	m	m	m	m	m	m	91	88	88
	Tertiary	m	m	m	m	m	m	m	m	135	142	149
Finland	Below upper secondary	92	92	92	92	91	91	91	90	90	90	m
	Tertiary	169	163	163	160	161	162	162	161	159	162	m
France	Below upper secondary	m	m	88	88	89	90	89	87	84	m	m
	Tertiary	m	m	159	151	154	152	157	158	153	m	m
Germany	Below upper secondary	80	m	84	90	91	93	92	90	97	91	95
	Tertiary	141	m	140	150	149	151	163	158	163	154	171
Greece	Below upper secondary	m	m	m	m	m	m	m	m	m	80	m
	Tertiary	m	m	m	m	m	m	m	m	m	153	m
Hungary	Below upper secondary	75	75	78	77	76	76	75	74	77	75	76
	Tertiary	232	232	245	255	253	253	259	247	248	247	244
Ireland	Below upper secondary	84	m	71	m	78	78	82	71	71	80	82
	Tertiary	138	m	141	m	170	176	149	151	156	162	180
Israel	Below upper secondary	m	m	m	m	74	76	80	72	77	68
	Tertiary	m	m	m	m	m	159	166	165	164	162	164
Italy	Below upper secondary	71	m	74	m	78	m	73	m	78	m	m
	Tertiary	143	m	162	m	188	m	178	m	162	m	m
Japan	Below upper secondary	m	m	m	m	m	m	m	74	m	m	m
	Tertiary	m	m	m	m	m	m	m	139	m	m	m
Korea	Below upper secondary	m	76	78	74	74	73	73	73	72	68	71
	Tertiary	m	135	135	136	134	139	140	141	142	168	143
Luxembourg	Below upper secondary	m	m	79	m	m	m	74	m	m	69	68
	Tertiary	m	m	149	m	m	m	158	m	m	171	165
Netherlands	Below upper secondary	m	m	84	m	m	m	87	m	82	m	m
	Tertiary	m	m	143	m	m	m	151	m	156	m	m
New Zealand	Below upper secondary	82	81	84	80	77	83	85	78	87	82	81
	Tertiary	133	124	131	135	126	129	123	128	126	127	130
Norway	Below upper secondary	80	80	80	79	79	78	79	79	78	76	m
	Tertiary	133	134	133	134	134	134	134	134	133	134	m
Poland	Below upper secondary	m	85	84	m	86	m	86	m	87	m	86
	Tertiary	m	185	194	m	204	m	194	m	188	m	186
Portugal	Below upper secondary	m	m	m	m	64	64	66	m	m	66	m
	Tertiary	m	m	m	m	183	183	183	m	m	172	m
Slovak Republic	Below upper secondary	m	m	m	81	m	m	m	m	72	70	70
	Tertiary	m	m	m	m	m	m	m	m	187	192	188
Slovenia	Below upper secondary	m	m	m	m	74	m	75	75	m	73	75
	Tertiary	m	m	m	m	217	m	210	208	m	208	201
Spain	Below upper secondary	m	79	m	81	84	80	m	83	80	79	m
	Tertiary	m	138	m	125	132	133	m	133	135	133	m

Note: Belgium, Korea and Turkey report earnings net of income tax.
Source: OECD. See Annex 3 for notes (www.oecd.org/edu/eag2012).
Please refer to the Reader's Guide for information concerning the symbols replacing missing data.
StatLink http://dx.doi.org/10.1787/888932665373

Table A8.2b. [2/2] Trends in relative earnings: Men (2000-10)

By educational attainment, for 25-64 year-olds (upper secondary and post-secondary non-tertiary education = 100)

		2000	2001	2002	2003	2004	2005	2006	2007	2008	2009	2010
OECD													
Sweden	Below upper secondary	m	84	85	85	85	84	83	83	82	82	**81**
	Tertiary	m	141	139	137	135	135	135	135	134	134	**133**
Switzerland	Below upper secondary	m	84	79	77	77	80	78	77	78	80	**78**
	Tertiary	m	141	138	140	140	141	139	145	139	141	**143**
Turkey	Below upper secondary	m	m	m	m	67	72	m	m	m	m	**m**
	Tertiary	m	m	m	m	139	153	m	m	m	m	**m**
United Kingdom	Below upper secondary	74	73	72	71	70	72	73	69	68	69	**64**
	Tertiary	152	147	147	152	146	146	148	145	145	151	**162**
United States	Below upper secondary	65	m	63	63	62	64	63	63	65	62	**64**
	Tertiary	181	m	178	177	179	183	183	180	188	190	**184**
OECD average	Below upper secondary	80	81	81	81	79	79	79	78	79	77	**77**
	Tertiary	154	151	153	151	161	155	163	157	158	160	**167**
Other G20													
Argentina		m	m	m	m	m	m	m	m	m	m	**m**
Brazil	Below upper secondary	m	m	m	m	m	m	m	51	52	53	**m**
	Tertiary	m	m	m	m	m	m	m	284	263	275	**m**
China		m	m	m	m	m	m	m	m	m	m	**m**
India		m	m	m	m	m	m	m	m	m	m	**m**
Indonesia		m	m	m	m	m	m	m	m	m	m	**m**
Russian Federation		m	m	m	m	m	m	m	m	m	m	**m**
Saudi Arabia		m	m	m	m	m	m	m	m	m	m	**m**
South Africa		m	m	m	m	m	m	m	m	m	m	**m**
G20 average		m	m	m	m	m	m	m	m	m	m	**m**

Note: Belgium, Korea and Turkey report earnings net of income tax.
Source: OECD. See Annex 3 for notes (*www.oecd.org/edu/eag2012*).
Please refer to the Reader's Guide for information concerning the symbols replacing missing data.
StatLink ⬛⬛⬛ http://dx.doi.org/10.1787/888932665373

A8

Table A8.2c. [1/2] Trends in relative earnings: Women (2000-10)
By educational attainment, for 25-64 year-olds (upper secondary and post-secondary non-tertiary education = 100)

		2000	2001	2002	2003	2004	2005	2006	2007	2008	2009	2010
Australia	Below upper secondary	m	84	m	m	m	88	m	m	m	85	m
	Tertiary	m	146	m	m	m	147	m	m	m	148	m
Austria	Below upper secondary	m	m	m	m	m	74	71	73	74	70	71
	Tertiary	m	m	m	m	m	156	158	160	159	158	162
Belgium	Below upper secondary	82	m	83	81	82	81	m	m	m	84	86
	Tertiary	132	m	139	132	137	134	m	m	m	135	136
Canada	Below upper secondary	72	70	67	73	70	70	68	72	73	77	m
	Tertiary	140	146	134	144	140	140	141	144	146	150	m
Czech Republic	Below upper secondary	m	m	m	m	73	72	73	74	73	72	74
	Tertiary	m	m	m	m	160	161	163	165	164	166	163
Denmark	Below upper secondary	m	90	90	85	85	84	84	83	84	83	83
	Tertiary	m	124	123	127	126	126	125	124	123	125	126
Estonia	Below upper secondary	m	m	m	m	m	m	m	m	82	86	87
	Tertiary	m	m	m	m	m	m	m	m	146	162	154
Finland	Below upper secondary	99	98	98	97	97	98	97	96	95	94	m
	Tertiary	146	146	146	146	146	145	146	146	145	146	m
France	Below upper secondary	m	m	81	81	82	81	82	82	75	m	m
	Tertiary	m	m	146	146	145	142	146	147	151	m	m
Germany	Below upper secondary	72	m	73	81	81	77	83	84	80	79	74
	Tertiary	137	m	137	145	148	151	153	159	158	154	153
Greece	Below upper secondary	m	m	m	m	m	m	m	m	m	65	m
	Tertiary	m	m	m	m	m	m	m	m	m	163	m
Hungary	Below upper secondary	71	71	71	72	71	72	72	71	71	68	71
	Tertiary	164	164	176	192	190	188	189	185	183	185	187
Ireland	Below upper secondary	65	m	60	m	63	61	63	67	65	73	78
	Tertiary	163	m	153	m	171	172	180	185	162	171	178
Israel	Below upper secondary	m	m	m	m	m	72	67	67	67	70	63
	Tertiary	m	m	m	m	m	157	150	155	153	159	150
Italy	Below upper secondary	84	m	78	m	73	m	74	m	70	m	m
	Tertiary	137	m	147	m	138	m	143	m	142	m	m
Japan	Below upper secondary	m	m	m	m	m	m	m	78	m	m	m
	Tertiary	m	m	m	m	m	m	m	161	m	m	m
Korea	Below upper secondary	m	76	76	75	77	76	76	75	75	72	77
	Tertiary	m	158	151	157	158	160	156	155	154	176	155
Luxembourg	Below upper secondary	m	m	74	m	m	m	73	m	m	65	68
	Tertiary	m	m	131	m	m	m	134	m	m	160	166
Netherlands	Below upper secondary	m	m	72	m	m	m	75	m	73	m	m
	Tertiary	m	m	155	m	m	m	159	m	162	m	m
New Zealand	Below upper secondary	86	82	86	84	83	79	89	85	83	82	85
	Tertiary	126	130	131	127	123	123	122	126	125	123	135
Norway	Below upper secondary	81	81	81	81	81	81	81	81	80	80	m
	Tertiary	132	135	135	137	136	135	134	134	133	135	m
Poland	Below upper secondary	m	74	73	m	74	m	76	m	75	m	77
	Tertiary	m	155	159	m	166	m	165	m	161	m	168
Portugal	Below upper secondary	m	m	m	m	66	66	67	m	m	67	m
	Tertiary	m	m	m	m	173	173	173	m	m	171	m
Slovak Republic	Below upper secondary	m	m	m	m	m	m	m	m	72	70	71
	Tertiary	m	m	m	m	m	m	m	m	176	177	172
Slovenia	Below upper secondary	m	m	m	m	71	m	72	72	m	72	74
	Tertiary	m	m	m	m	190	m	188	187	m	185	181
Spain	Below upper secondary	m	64	m	69	71	73	m	70	69	71	m
	Tertiary	m	125	m	143	150	155	m	149	156	159	m

Note: Belgium, Korea and Turkey report earnings net of income tax.
Source: OECD. See Annex 3 for notes *(www.oecd.org/edu/eag2012)*.
Please refer to the Reader's Guide for information concerning the symbols replacing missing data.
StatLink ⟿ http://dx.doi.org/10.1787/888932665392

Table A8.2c. [2/2] Trends in relative earnings: Women (2000-10)

By educational attainment, for 25-64 year-olds (upper secondary and post-secondary non-tertiary education = 100)

		2000	2001	2002	2003	2004	2005	2006	2007	2008	2009	2010
OECD Sweden	Below upper secondary	m	87	87	88	87	86	85	84	82	81	**80**
	Tertiary	m	129	129	128	127	126	126	127	126	127	**127**
Switzerland	Below upper secondary	m	73	74	76	77	76	76	76	76	78	**77**
	Tertiary	m	148	148	152	153	149	160	157	157	152	**148**
Turkey	Below upper secondary	m	m	m	m	46	43	m	m	m	m	**m**
	Tertiary	m	m	m	m	164	154	m	m	m	m	**m**
United Kingdom	Below upper secondary	69	73	69	69	72	71	70	70	73	68	**69**
	Tertiary	176	187	177	182	180	181	182	181	177	176	**177**
United States	Below upper secondary	66	m	63	66	62	63	63	61	60	63	**61**
	Tertiary	169	m	165	167	166	167	170	167	171	173	**175**
OECD average	Below upper secondary	77	79	77	78	75	75	76	76	75	75	**75**
	Tertiary	148	145	146	148	154	152	155	156	154	158	**159**
Other G20 Argentina		m	m	m	m	m	m	m	m	m	m	**m**
Brazil	Below upper secondary	m	m	m	m	m	m	m	51	52	53	**m**
	Tertiary	m	m	m	m	m	m	m	284	263	275	**m**
China		m	m	m	m	m	m	m	m	m	m	**m**
India		m	m	m	m	m	m	m	m	m	m	**m**
Indonesia		m	m	m	m	m	m	m	m	m	m	**m**
Russian Federation		m	m	m	m	m	m	m	m	m	m	**m**
Saudi Arabia		m	m	m	m	m	m	m	m	m	m	**m**
South Africa		m	m	m	m	m	m	m	m	m	m	**m**
G20 average		m	m	m	m	m	m	m	m	m	m	**m**

Note: Belgium, Korea and Turkey report earnings net of income tax.
Source: OECD. See Annex 3 for notes (*www.oecd.org/edu/eag2012*).
Please refer to the Reader's Guide for information concerning the symbols replacing missing data.
StatLink ⬛🔢 http://dx.doi.org/10.1787/888932665392

A8

Table A8.3a. Differences in earnings between women and men (2010 or latest available year)

*Average annual full-time, full-year earnings of women as a percentage of men's earnings,
by level of educational attainment and age groups*

		Below upper secondary education			Upper secondary and post-secondary non-tertiary education			Tertiary education			All levels of education		
		25-64	35-44	55-64	25-64	35-44	55-64	25-64	35-44	55-64	25-64	35-44	55-64
		(1)	(2)	(3)	(4)	(5)	(6)	(7)	(8)	(9)	(10)	(11)	(12)
OECD Australia	2009	76	76	83	73	68	75	72	70	73	77	74	80
Austria	2010	72	73	72	76	76	79	73	77	69	75	75	74
Belgium	2009	48	58	42	61	60	52	68	68	53	64	65	47
Canada	2009	70	73	67	70	67	74	74	72	63	75	73	67
Chile		m	m	m	m	m	m	m	m	m	m	m	m
Czech Republic	2010	79	77	80	81	74	87	70	67	84	75	67	78
Denmark	2010	82	80	82	80	77	82	74	74	73	79	78	79
Estonia	2010	62	62	69	62	62	73	63	54	67	69	66	79
Finland	2010	79	76	79	78	76	79	75	74	74	80	78	77
France	2008	74	63	79	78	75	76	74	77	66	79	79	70
Germany	2010	76	85	83	82	84	82	68	75	70	75	80	77
Greece	2009	60	65	51	75	73	90	74	78	92	78	80	76
Hungary	2010	81	79	81	88	83	96	67	58	73	83	77	83
Iceland		m	m	m	m	m	m	m	m	m	m	m	m
Ireland	2010	87	82	87	79	87	78	73	75	58	84	82	78
Israel	2010	76	71	65	74	68	67	66	68	61	73	73	65
Italy	2008	73	76	77	75	75	73	65	91	52	77	84	71
Japan		m	m	m	m	m	m	m	m	m	m	m	m
Korea	2010	67	68	65	64	61	59	65	68	54	61	59	48
Luxembourg	2010	80	78	56	74	81	80	73	81	64	80	84	69
Mexico		m	m	m	m	m	m	m	m	m	m	m	m
Netherlands	2008	80	83	78	78	83	77	72	78	70	80	85	76
New Zealand	2010	83	86	84	76	75	76	78	76	71	80	78	75
Norway		m	m	m	m	m	m	m	m	m	m	m	m
Poland	2010	71	66	73	80	73	94	71	66	76	84	80	90
Portugal	2009	74	74	73	71	71	71	69	73	69	79	79	69
Slovak Republic	2010	74	72	74	76	72	84	67	58	75	74	67	79
Slovenia	2010	85	84	83	87	84	102	79	79	89	93	91	107
Spain	2009	74	77	69	79	79	79	89	91	90	89	92	86
Sweden	2010	84	90	86	83	85	79	74	68	77	82	80	86
Switzerland		m	m	m	m	m	m	m	m	m	m	m	m
Turkey		m	m	m	m	m	m	m	m	m	m	m	m
United Kingdom	2010	92	74	98	84	80	83	82	80	90	88	84	92
United States	2010	70	70	70	72	72	70	68	70	62	72	73	64
OECD average		75	75	74	76	75	78	72	73	71	78	77	76
Other G20 Argentina		m	m	m	m	m	m	m	m	m	m	m	m
Brazil	2009	64	63	63	62	60	56	61	64	61	76	75	71
China		m	m	m	m	m	m	m	m	m	m	m	m
India		m	m	m	m	m	m	m	m	m	m	m	m
Indonesia		m	m	m	m	m	m	m	m	m	m	m	m
Russian Federation		m	m	m	m	m	m	m	m	m	m	m	m
Saudi Arabia		m	m	m	m	m	m	m	m	m	m	m	m
South Africa		m	m	m	m	m	m	m	m	m	m	m	m
G20 average		m	m	m	m	m	m	m	m	m	m	m	m

Note: Belgium and Korea report earnings net of income tax.
Source: OECD. LSO Network special data collection on full-time, full-year earnings, Economic Working Group. See Annex 3 for notes (*www.oecd.org/edu/eag2012*).
Please refer to the Reader's Guide for information concerning the symbols replacing missing data.
StatLink ⬛ᴍ⬛ http://dx.doi.org/10.1787/888932665411

Table A8.3b. [1/2] Trends in differences in earnings between women and men (2000-10)
Average annual earnings of women as a percentage of men's earnings, by level of educational attainment of 25-64 year-olds

		2000	2001	2002	2003	2004	2005	2006	2007	2008	2009	2010
Australia	Below upper secondary	m	62	m	m	m	61	m	m	m	59	m
	Upper secondary and post-secondary non-tertiary	m	62	m	m	m	61	m	m	m	59	m
	Tertiary	m	63	m	m	m	64	m	m	m	61	m
Austria	Below upper secondary	m	m	m	m	m	57	58	60	61	62	61
	Upper secondary and post-secondary non-tertiary	m	m	m	m	m	60	59	58	59	61	60
	Tertiary	m	m	m	m	m	62	60	62	59	63	63
Belgium	Below upper secondary	64	m	65	66	66	67	m	m	m	70	72
	Upper secondary and post-secondary non-tertiary	72	m	72	74	74	75	m	m	m	77	77
	Tertiary	74	m	76	74	74	73	m	m	m	78	79
Canada	Below upper secondary	53	52	52	53	53	55	54	53	54	61	m
	Upper secondary and post-secondary non-tertiary	61	59	63	59	61	61	61	63	60	62	m
	Tertiary	57	60	60	60	61	62	63	63	64	67	m
Chile		m	m	m	m	m	m	m	m	m	m	m
Czech Republic	Below upper secondary	m	m	m	m	74	74	73	75	75	77	79
	Upper secondary and post-secondary non-tertiary	m	m	m	m	80	80	80	79	78	80	82
	Tertiary	m	m	m	m	67	68	67	68	67	66	68
Denmark	Below upper secondary	m	74	75	73	74	73	72	73	74	80	80
	Upper secondary and post-secondary non-tertiary	m	71	73	71	71	71	71	72	72	77	76
	Tertiary	m	67	68	67	67	67	67	67	67	71	68
Estonia	Below upper secondary	m	m	m	m	m	m	m	m	54	57	59
	Upper secondary and post-secondary non-tertiary	m	m	m	m	m	m	m	m	59	58	60
	Tertiary	m	m	m	m	m	m	m	m	64	67	62
Finland	Below upper secondary	76	76	76	76	76	78	77	76	76	78	m
	Upper secondary and post-secondary non-tertiary	71	71	72	72	72	73	72	71	72	75	m
	Tertiary	61	63	64	66	65	65	64	65	66	68	m
France	Below upper secondary	m	m	70	68	68	68	68	70	62	m	m
	Upper secondary and post-secondary non-tertiary	m	m	77	75	74	75	74	75	69	m	m
	Tertiary	m	m	70	72	70	70	69	70	67	m	m
Germany	Below upper secondary	56	m	53	54	54	52	56	55	49	51	49
	Upper secondary and post-secondary non-tertiary	63	m	61	60	60	62	62	59	60	59	62
	Tertiary	61	m	60	58	60	62	58	59	58	59	56
Greece	Below upper secondary	m	m	m	m	m	m	m	m	m	55	m
	Upper secondary and post-secondary non-tertiary	m	m	m	m	m	m	m	m	m	67	m
	Tertiary	m	m	m	m	m	m	m	m	m	71	m
Hungary	Below upper secondary	83	83	85	89	89	88	93	87	85	84	83
	Upper secondary and post-secondary non-tertiary	88	88	93	95	96	93	96	91	93	91	89
	Tertiary	62	62	67	71	72	69	70	68	69	68	68
Iceland		m	m	m	m	m	m	m	m	m	m	m
Ireland	Below upper secondary	46	m	48	m	48	49	42	46	51	58	60
	Upper secondary and post-secondary non-tertiary	60	m	57	m	59	63	54	49	56	63	64
	Tertiary	71	m	62	m	59	62	66	60	58	67	63
Israel	Below upper secondary	m	m	m	m	m	57	56	52	57	58	60
	Upper secondary and post-secondary non-tertiary	m	m	m	m	m	59	64	63	62	64	65
	Tertiary	m	m	m	m	m	58	57	59	58	62	60
Italy	Below upper secondary	76	m	70	m	67	m	67	m	63	m	m
	Upper secondary and post-secondary non-tertiary	65	m	66	m	71	m	66	m	71	m	m
	Tertiary	62	m	60	m	52	m	53	m	62	m	m
Japan	Below upper secondary	m	m	m	m	m	m	m	43	m	m	m
	Upper secondary and post-secondary non-tertiary	m	m	m	m	m	m	m	41	m	m	m
	Tertiary	m	m	m	m	m	m	m	47	m	m	m
Korea	Below upper secondary	m	60	60	59	60	61	62	60	63	63	64
	Upper secondary and post-secondary non-tertiary	m	60	60	58	58	59	59	59	60	61	59
	Tertiary	m	70	67	67	68	67	66	65	65	60	64
Luxembourg	Below upper secondary	m	m	80	m	m	m	87	m	m	61	63
	Upper secondary and post-secondary non-tertiary	m	m	86	m	m	m	88	m	m	65	64
	Tertiary	m	m	75	m	m	m	75	m	m	61	64
Mexico		m	m	m	m	m	m	m	m	m	m	m

Note: Belgium, Korea and Turkey report earnings net of income tax.
Source: OECD. See Annex 3 for notes (*www.oecd.org/edu/eag2012*).
Please refer to the Reader's Guide for information concerning the symbols replacing missing data.
StatLink ⏷ http://dx.doi.org/10.1787/888932665430

A8

Table A8.3b. [2/2] Trends in differences in earnings between women and men (2000-10)

Average annual earnings of women as a percentage of men's earnings, by level of educational attainment of 25-64 year-olds

		2000	2001	2002	2003	2004	2005	2006	2007	2008	2009	2010
Netherlands	Below upper secondary	m	m	49	m	m	m	48	m	49	m	**m**
	Upper secondary and post-secondary non-tertiary	m	m	58	m	m	m	55	m	55	m	**m**
	Tertiary	m	m	62	m	m	m	58	m	57	m	**m**
New Zealand	Below upper secondary	67	63	67	67	68	61	68	68	61	67	**69**
	Upper secondary and post-secondary non-tertiary	64	63	65	64	63	64	64	62	64	67	**65**
	Tertiary	61	65	65	60	62	61	64	61	64	65	**68**
Norway	Below upper secondary	63	63	64	66	66	65	65	65	66	68	**m**
	Upper secondary and post-secondary non-tertiary	62	62	63	64	64	63	63	63	64	65	**m**
	Tertiary	62	63	64	65	65	63	63	63	64	65	**m**
Poland	Below upper secondary	m	72	73	m	73	m	71	m	69	m	**72**
	Upper secondary and post-secondary non-tertiary	m	83	84	m	84	m	81	m	80	m	**81**
	Tertiary	m	69	68	m	68	m	69	m	68	m	**72**
Portugal	Below upper secondary	m	m	m	m	73	73	73	m	m	72	**m**
	Upper secondary and post-secondary non-tertiary	m	m	m	m	70	71	71	m	m	71	**m**
	Tertiary	m	m	m	m	67	67	67	m	m	71	**m**
Slovak Republic	Below upper secondary	m	m	m	m	m	m	m	m	72	73	**73**
	Upper secondary and post-secondary non-tertiary	m	m	m	m	m	m	m	m	72	72	**73**
	Tertiary	m	m	m	m	m	m	m	m	68	67	**67**
Slovenia	Below upper secondary	m	m	m	m	84	m	82	81	m	86	**85**
	Upper secondary and post-secondary non-tertiary	m	m	m	m	88	m	86	84	m	88	**87**
	Tertiary	m	m	m	m	77	m	77	76	m	78	**79**
Spain	Below upper secondary	m	58	m	m	63	m	m	58	60	62	**m**
	Upper secondary and post-secondary non-tertiary	m	71	m	m	68	m	m	68	69	69	**m**
	Tertiary	m	64	m	m	73	m	m	77	80	83	**m**
Sweden	Below upper secondary	m	74	74	75	75	74	74	73	73	74	**73**
	Upper secondary and post-secondary non-tertiary	m	71	72	73	73	73	73	72	73	74	**74**
	Tertiary	m	65	67	68	69	68	68	68	69	70	**71**
Switzerland	Below upper secondary	m	51	53	55	55	54	55	56	53	56	**58**
	Upper secondary and post-secondary non-tertiary	m	58	56	56	56	57	56	57	55	57	**59**
	Tertiary	m	61	60	61	61	60	65	61	62	62	**61**
Turkey	Below upper secondary	m	m	m	m	52	47	m	m	m	m	**m**
	Upper secondary and post-secondary non-tertiary	m	m	m	m	75	78	m	m	m	m	**m**
	Tertiary	m	m	m	m	89	78	m	m	m	m	**m**
United Kingdom	Below upper secondary	50	52	53	53	55	55	53	56	59	57	**70**
	Upper secondary and post-secondary non-tertiary	54	52	55	55	54	56	56	55	55	58	**65**
	Tertiary	63	66	67	66	66	69	69	69	68	68	**71**
United States	Below upper secondary	60	m	63	67	63	63	65	64	60	69	**63**
	Upper secondary and post-secondary non-tertiary	60	m	63	64	63	65	65	66	65	68	**66**
	Tertiary	56	m	58	61	59	59	60	61	59	62	**63**
OECD average	Below upper secondary	63	65	65	66	66	63	66	64	63	66	**68**
	Upper secondary and post-secondary non-tertiary	65	67	68	67	70	67	69	65	66	68	**70**
	Tertiary	63	65	65	65	67	66	65	64	64	67	**67**
Argentina		m	m	m	m	m	m	m	m	m	m	**m**
Brazil	Below upper secondary	m	m	m	m	m	m	m	49	49	50	**m**
	Upper secondary and post-secondary non-tertiary	m	m	m	m	m	m	m	58	56	57	**m**
	Tertiary	m	m	m	m	m	m	m	55	57	55	**m**
China		m	m	m	m	m	m	m	m	m	m	**m**
India		m	m	m	m	m	m	m	m	m	m	**m**
Indonesia		m	m	m	m	m	m	m	m	m	m	**m**
Russian Federation		m	m	m	m	m	m	m	m	m	m	**m**
Saudi Arabia		m	m	m	m	m	m	m	m	m	m	**m**
South Africa		m	m	m	m	m	m	m	m	m	m	**m**
G20 average		m	m	m	m	m	m	m	m	m	m	**m**

Note: Belgium, Korea and Turkey report earnings net of income tax.
Source: OECD. See Annex 3 for notes (*www.oecd.org/edu/eag2012*).
Please refer to the Reader's Guide for information concerning the symbols replacing missing data.
StatLink ⟐⟐⟐⟐ http://dx.doi.org/10.1787/888932665430

WHAT ARE THE INCENTIVES TO INVEST IN EDUCATION?

- On average across 28 OECD countries, the total return (net present value), both private and public, to a man who successfully completes upper secondary or post-secondary non-tertiary and tertiary education is USD 388 300. The equivalent return for a woman is USD 250 700.

- The net public return on an investment in tertiary education is over USD 100 000 for men, on average – almost three times the amount of public investment. For women, the net public return is almost twice the amount of public investment.

- On average, the gross earnings premium for an individual with a tertiary degree exceeds USD 340 000 for men and USD 235 000 for women across OECD countries.

Chart A9.1. Distribution of public/private costs/benefits for a woman obtaining tertiary education as part of initial education, ISCED 5/6 (2008 or latest available year)

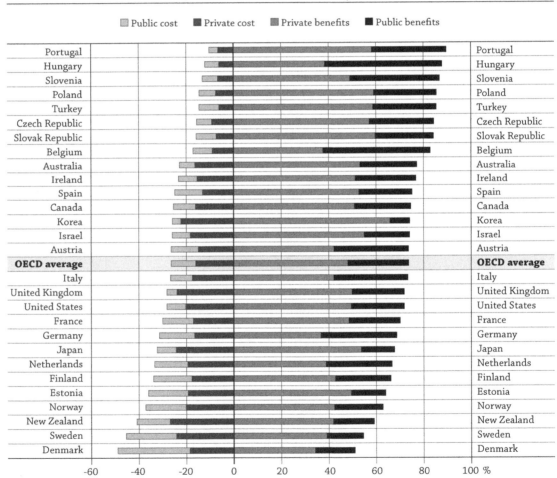

Notes: Australia, Belgium and Turkey refer to 2005; Portugal refers to 2006. Japan and Slovenia refer to 2007. All other countries refer to 2008.

Cashflows are discounted at a 3% interest rate.

Countries are ranked in descending order of the benefits (public + private) as a proportion of total (public + private) values for women immediately after acquiring tertiary education, ISCED 5/6.

Source: OECD. Tables A9.3 and A9.4. See Annex 3 for notes (www.oecd.org/edu/eag2012).

StatLink ᵃˢᵖ http://dx.doi.org/10.1787/888932662200

Context

The financial benefits of completing higher levels of education motivate individuals to postpone consumption and earnings today for future rewards. From a policy perspective, awareness of economic incentives is crucial to understanding how individuals move through the education system. Large upward shifts in the demand for education can drive up earnings and returns considerably before supply catches up. This provides a strong signal, both to individuals and to education systems, of the need for additional investment in education.

In some countries, however, the labour market may not effectively signal demand because of rigid labour laws and structures that tend to compress wages across different educational groups. Apart from these labour-related issues, major components of the return to education are directly linked to policy: access to education, taxes and the costs of education for the individual. The economic benefits of education flow not only to individuals but also to society through lower social transfers and in the additional revenue earned through taxes individuals pay once they enter the labour market. Building an educated populace can help reduce public expenditure on social welfare programmes and assist employers looking for personnel with specialised skills if the supply of those skills is insufficient to meet demand. In shaping policies, it is important to consider the balance between private and public returns.

Other findings

- In Austria, Ireland, Norway, Portugal, the United Kingdom and the United States, a man with an upper secondary or post-secondary non-tertiary education **can expect a gross earnings premium of more than USD 200 000** over his working life, compared with a man who has not attained that level of education.

- **The value of the gross earnings premium for men and women with a tertiary education is substantial.** For example, over the course of their working lives, tertiary-educated men in Austria, the Czech Republic, Hungary, Ireland, Italy, the Netherlands, Portugal and Slovenia can expect to earn at least USD 400 000 more than those with an upper secondary or post-secondary non-tertiary education. In the United States, this figure is almost USD 675 000.

- On average across OECD countries with comparable data, people who invest in tertiary education can expect a substantial **net gain of just over USD 160 000 for a man and almost USD 110 000 for a woman.** In Ireland, Portugal, Slovenia and the United States, the investment generates a net present value over USD 150 000 for a woman – a strong incentive to complete this level of education.

- **An individual invests an average of about USD 55 000 to acquire a tertiary qualification, when direct and indirect costs are taken into account.** In Japan, the Netherlands, the United Kingdom and the United States, this investment exceeds USD 100 000 in the case of a man who obtains a tertiary education.

A9

Analysis

Financial returns on investment in education

The overall economic benefits of education can be assessed by estimating the economic value of the investment in education, which essentially measures the degree to which the costs of attaining higher levels of education translate into higher levels of earnings.

To understand how costs and benefits are shared between the private and public side, one must understand each calculation. The calculation of benefits includes earnings, taxes, social contributions and social transfers as well as differences in the probability of finding work by educational level. The cost components include public and private direct costs, as well as foregone earnings while in school, adjusted for the probability of finding work and for foregone taxes, social contributions and social transfers. This indicator relies on 2008 data or the most recent available year.

In practice, raising levels of education will give rise to a complex set of fiscal effects beyond those taken into account here. As earnings generally increase with educational attainment, individuals with higher levels of education typically consume more goods and services, and thus pay additional taxes on their consumption. Public returns are thus underestimated in this indicator.

Individuals with higher earnings typically also pay more into their pensions and, after leaving the labour force, will have a further income advantage that is not taken into account in the calculations here. Similarly, many governments have programmes that provide loans to students at interest rates below those used in this indicator. These subsidies can often make a substantial difference in the returns to education for the individual. Given these factors, the returns on education in different countries should be assessed with caution.

Both costs and benefits are discounted back in time at a real discount rate of 3%, reflecting the fact that the calculations are made in constant prices (see the *Methodology* section for further discussion of the discount rate). The economic benefits of tertiary education are compared to those of upper secondary or post-secondary non-tertiary education; for upper secondary or post-secondary non-tertiary education, below upper secondary education is used as a point of reference. In the calculations, women are benchmarked against women, and men against men.

Incentives for individuals to invest in education

Upper secondary or post-secondary non-tertiary education

Table A9.1 shows the value of each component and the net present value of the overall investment for a man and a woman attaining an upper secondary or a post-secondary non-tertiary education.

The direct costs of education for a man investing in an upper secondary or post-secondary non-tertiary education are usually negligible; the main investment cost is foregone earnings (Chart A9.2). Depending on the length of education, salary levels and the possibility of finding a job, foregone earnings vary substantially among countries. In Estonia, Hungary, the Slovak Republic, Spain and Turkey, foregone earnings are less than USD 15 000, while in Austria, Denmark, Germany, Italy and Norway, they exceed USD 35 000. Good labour-market prospects for young individuals who have not attained an upper secondary or post-secondary non-tertiary education increase the costs of further investment in education.

Gross earnings and reduced risk of unemployment over an individual's working life make up the benefit side. In most countries, men with an upper secondary or post-secondary non-tertiary education enjoy a significant earnings premium over those who have not attained that level of education. The value of reduced chances of unemployment can also be large. In the Czech Republic, Germany and the Slovak Republic, the better employment prospects for men with this level of education are valued at USD 75 000 or more (Table A9.1).

Additional education produces large returns from both the individual's and the public's perspective. A man who invests in upper secondary or post-secondary non-tertiary education can expect a net gain of more than USD 90 000 during his working life over a man who has not attained that level of education. However, the amount varies significantly among countries: in Ireland, Korea, the Slovak Republic and the United States, this level of education generates over USD 150 000; but in Estonia, Finland, Germany, Poland and Turkey, the net benefits are less than USD 40 000 (Table A9.1).

Chart A9.2. **Components of the private net present value for a man obtaining an upper secondary or post-secondary non-tertiary education, ISCED 3/4 (2008 or latest available year)**

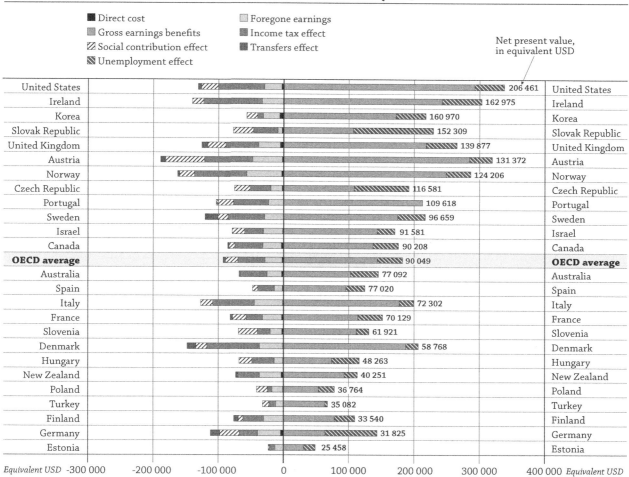

- ■ Direct cost
- □ Foregone earnings
- ▨ Gross earnings benefits
- ▨ Income tax effect
- ▧ Social contribution effect
- ■ Transfers effect
- ▨ Unemployment effect

Net present value, in equivalent USD

Country	Net present value (Equivalent USD)
United States	206 461
Ireland	162 975
Korea	160 970
Slovak Republic	152 309
United Kingdom	139 877
Austria	131 372
Norway	124 206
Czech Republic	116 581
Portugal	109 618
Sweden	96 659
Israel	91 581
Canada	90 208
OECD average	**90 049**
Australia	77 092
Spain	77 020
Italy	72 302
France	70 129
Slovenia	61 921
Denmark	58 768
Hungary	48 263
New Zealand	40 251
Poland	36 764
Turkey	35 082
Finland	33 540
Germany	31 825
Estonia	25 458

Equivalent USD -300 000   -200 000   -100 000   0   100 000   200 000   300 000   400 000 *Equivalent USD*

Notes: Japan is not included in the chart because the data at lower and upper secondary level of education are not broken down. Belgium and the Netherlands are not included in the chart because upper secondary education is compulsory. Australia and Turkey refer to 2005. Portugal refers to 2006. Slovenia refers to 2007. All other countries refer to 2008.
Cashflows are discounted at a 3% interest rate.
Countries are ranked in descending order of the net present value.
Source: OECD, Table A9.1. See Annex 3 for notes (*www.oecd.org/edu/eag2012*).
StatLink ⟨⟩ http://dx.doi.org/10.1787/888932662219

Men generally enjoy better financial returns on their upper secondary or post-secondary non-tertiary education than women, except in Estonia, Hungary, Italy, Poland and Spain. On average across OECD countries, a woman can expect a net gain of USD 67 000 over her working life. Some countries' social safety nets may work against women investing in further education and upper secondary education, in particular. In these countries, low wages for women who do not have an upper secondary or post-secondary non-tertiary education may be supplemented by social benefit systems, removing some of the income advantage in completing an upper secondary education (Table A9.1).

Tertiary education

The net returns to individuals (both men and women) with a tertiary education are, on average, more than 60% larger than the returns for those with an upper secondary or post-secondary non-tertiary education, reflecting the fact that an upper secondary or post-secondary non-tertiary education has become the norm in OECD countries. In some countries, individuals need to obtain tertiary education to reap the full financial rewards of education beyond compulsory schooling (Tables A9.1 and A9.3).

The returns for investing in tertiary education are typically higher for men, except in Australia, where average returns are nearly identical between men and women, and in Spain and Turkey, where the returns are higher for women (Table A9.3). On average across OECD countries, a woman investing in tertiary education can expect a net gain of USD 110 000, while a man can expect a net gain of USD 162 000.

Chart A9.3.   Components of the private net present value for a man obtaining tertiary education, ISCED 5/6 (2008 or latest available year)

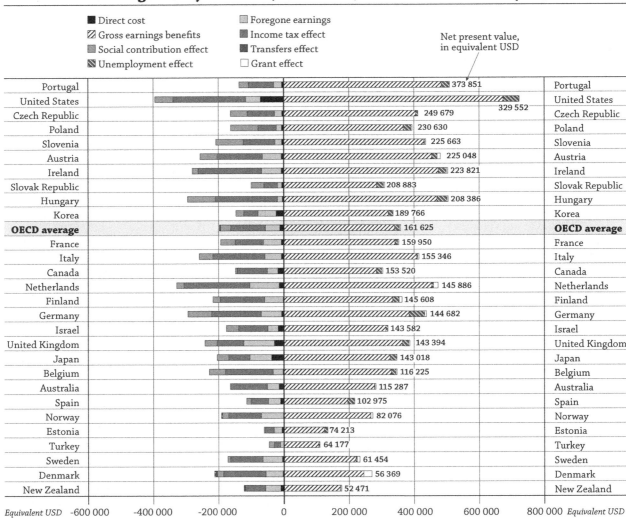

Notes: Australia, Belgium and Turkey refer to 2005. Portugal refers to 2006. Japan and Slovenia refer to 2007. All other countries refer to 2008. Cashflows are discounted at a 3% interest rate.
Countries are ranked in descending order of the net present value.
Source: OECD. Table A9.3. See Annex 3 for notes (*www.oecd.org/edu/eag2012*).
StatLink ᵇᵐˢᵖ http://dx.doi.org/10.1787/888932662238

A9

The value of the gross earnings premium for men and women with tertiary education is substantial. Men in Austria, the Czech Republic, Hungary, Ireland, Italy, the Netherlands, Portugal, Slovenia and the United States can expect to earn at least an additional USD 400 000 over their working lives compared to an individual with an upper secondary or post-secondary non-tertiary education. Women in Austria, Ireland, the Netherlands, Portugal, Slovenia, the United Kingdom and the United States can expect to earn at least an additional USD 300 000 over their working lives compared to a woman with an upper secondary or post-secondary non-tertiary education.

Chart A9.3 shows the components of the returns on tertiary education for men in different countries. Compared with upper secondary or post-secondary non-tertiary education, the impact of unemployment benefits is less pronounced than the earnings differential; and taxes and the direct costs of education are more substantial.

Box A9.1. **Estimating returns to education**

There are two main approaches to estimating the financial returns to education: one founded on financed-based investment theory, the other on labour economics-based econometric specification.

The basis for an investment approach is the discount rate (the time-value of money), which makes it possible to compare costs or payments (cash flows) over time. The discount rate can be estimated either by raising it to the level at which financial benefits equal costs, which is then the internal rate of return, or by setting the discount rate at a rate that takes into consideration the risk involved in the investment, which is then a net present value calculation, with the gains expressed in monetary units.

The econometric approach taken in labour economics originates from Mincer (1974). In this approach, returns to education are estimated in a regression relating earnings to years of education, labour market experience and tenure. This basic model has been extended in subsequent work to include educational levels, employment effects and additional control variables such as gender and work characteristics (part-time, firm size, contracting arrangements, utilisation of skills, etc.). The drawback of a regression approach is typically the scarcity of information beyond gross earnings to determine public and private returns, which makes it difficult to assess the actual incentives for individuals to invest in education.

Apart from availability of data, the main difference between the two approaches is that the investment approach is forward-looking (although historical data are typically used), whereas an econometric approach tries to establish the actual contribution of education to gross earnings by controlling for other factors that can influence earnings and returns. This distinction has implications for the assumptions and for the interpretation of returns to education. As the investment approach focuses on the incentives at the time of the investment decision, it is prudent not to remove the effects of (controlling for) other factors such as work characteristics, as these are not known ex-ante and could be seen as part of the average returns that an individual can expect to receive when deciding to invest in education.

Depending on the impact of the control variables and how steep the earnings curves are, the results of the two approaches can diverge quite substantially. Returns may differ within discounting models, too, depending on other underlying assumptions, the size of cash flows and how these are distributed over the life span. It is therefore generally not advisable to compare rates of return from different approaches or studies.

Tertiary education brings substantial net returns for men in Portugal and the United States, where an investment generates over USD 300 000 and thus provides a strong incentive to complete this level of education. This is the case for women in Portugal as well, where an investment generates over USD 200 000. The returns on tertiary education are lower in Denmark, Estonia, New Zealand, Sweden and Turkey, where a man with a tertiary education can expect a net gain of between USD 52 000 and USD 74 000 over his working life. For women, the returns are lower in Denmark, Estonia, New Zealand and Sweden, where the net gain ranges from USD 32 000 to USD 47 000. Much of the difference between countries is driven by earnings differentials. Factors such as supply and demand for highly educated individuals are important in some countries, while the overall reward structure in the labour market (overall wage compression) plays an important role in other countries.

One way to mitigate weak labour market returns is to provide higher education at lower costs for the individual. Apart from subsidising the direct costs of education, a number of countries also provide students with loans and grants to improve incentives and access to education. Grants are particularly important in Austria, Finland, and the Netherlands, where they account for between 14% and 15% of the total private investment cost (direct costs and foregone earnings) for both men and women (Table A9.3). In Denmark, about 45% of the total private investment is covered by government grants.

Many countries also have favourable and substantial student loans that further lower investment costs and make investing more attractive. Both grants and loans are particularly important tools for recruiting students from less affluent backgrounds. There is, of course, a danger in focusing only on the supply side of the investment. As younger generations become more mobile, a reward structure that does not adequately compensate more highly educated individuals could eventually lead to a loss of these individuals to countries with higher earnings potentials.

There are some trade-offs between taxes and the direct costs of education (tuition fees) that are linked to government support for higher education. In countries with low or no tuition fees, individuals typically pay back public subsidies later in life through progressive tax systems. In countries in which a larger portion of the investment falls on the individual, in the form of tuition fees, earnings differentials tend to be larger, and a larger portion of them accrues to the individual. In general there is a positive link, albeit a weak one, between the private direct costs of education and the overall net present value of the education.

Public rate of return on investments in education

Tables A9.2 and A9.4 show the public returns to individuals who obtain upper secondary or post-secondary non-tertiary and tertiary education as part of initial education. Chart A9.4 shows the public and private costs for men who obtain tertiary education. On average across OECD countries, over USD 92 000 is invested in a man's tertiary education, taking into account public and private spending, as well as indirect costs in the form of public and private foregone earnings and taxes. In the Netherlands, the United Kingdom and the United States, the value of the investment exceeds USD 150 000 (Chart A9.4).

Direct costs for education are generally borne by the public sector, except in Australia, Japan, Korea, the United Kingdom and the United States, where private direct costs such as tuition fees constitute over half of the overall direct investment costs. Together with foregone public earnings in the form of taxes and social contributions, direct and indirect public investment costs for a man with a tertiary education exceed USD 50 000 in Denmark, Finland, Germany, the Netherlands, Norway and Sweden. In Korea and Turkey, the total public investment cost does not exceed USD 15 000. On average among OECD countries, the total value of the public costs for a man who obtains a tertiary qualification is around USD 36 000 (Table A9.4).

Although public investments in tertiary education are large in many countries, private investment costs are larger in most countries. In the Netherlands, the United Kingdom and the United States, both men and women invest over USD 100 000, on average, to acquire a tertiary qualification, when direct and indirect costs are taken into account. On average across OECD countries, direct costs, such as tuition fees, constitute about one-fifth of the total investment made by a tertiary graduate. In the United States, direct costs represent more than 60% of the investment and in Canada, Israel and Japan, between 35% and 43%, depending on the gender of the individual (Table A9.3).

The decision to continue education at the tertiary level is a difficult one to take, since much is at stake, particularly for young individuals from less affluent backgrounds. To alleviate the financial burden, most countries provide grants to students. These are particularly large in Denmark (USD 25 200) and the Netherlands (USD 14 400).

Chart A9.4. **Public versus private investment for a man obtaining tertiary education, ISCED 5/6 (2008 or latest available year)**

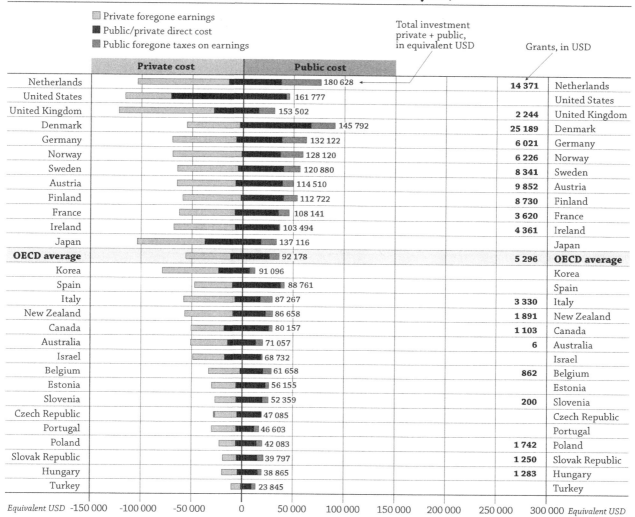

Notes: Australia, Belgium and Turkey refer to 2005. Portugal refers to 2006. Japan and Slovenia refer to 2007. All other countries refer to 2008. Cashflows are discounted at a 3% interest rate.
Countries are ranked in descending order of the total public + private cost.
Source: OECD. Tables A9.3 and A9.4. See Annex 3 for notes (*www.oecd.org/edu/eag2012*).
StatLink ⬛ᵐˢ᪭ http://dx.doi.org/10.1787/888932662257

Note that these grants are not included in the private and public costs shown in Chart A9.4 but are displayed to illustrate the magnitude of these transfers between the private and public side. With the substantial private and public gains from tertiary investments, financial support in the form of grants and loans are important to ensure that financial constrains do not prevent people from making these investments.

For an individual, foregone earnings make up a substantial part of overall investment costs. In countries with lengthy tertiary education, such as Finland, Germany, the Netherlands and Sweden, foregone earnings are large (see Indicator B1). Earnings foregone also depend on expected wage levels and the probability of finding a job. As the labour market for young adults worsens (see Indicator C5), investment costs will fall. As higher-educated people typically fare better in the labour market in times of economic hardship (see Indicator A7), larger earnings differentials further improve the benefit side. The incentives to invest in education from both the private and public side are likely to be greater in most OECD countries as the analysis in this indicator moves beyond 2008 and considers subsequent years of the global economic crisis.

A9

Investments in education also generate public returns from higher income levels in the form of income taxes, increased social insurance payments and lower social transfers. Chart A9.5 compares the public costs and economic benefits when a man invests in upper secondary or post-secondary non-tertiary education and in tertiary education.

The public returns for a man investing in upper secondary or post-secondary non-tertiary education are positive in all countries except Estonia. On average across OECD countries, this level of education generates a net return of USD 36 000. In Austria, Ireland and the United Kingdom, it generates a net return of more than USD 70 000. The public returns to a woman investing in this level of education are USD 14 000 less than for a man, on average across OECD countries (Table A9.2). Nonetheless, the public benefits are about twice as large, on average, as the overall public costs for upper secondary or post-secondary non-tertiary education, for both men and women. In a few countries, students need to continue beyond upper secondary or post-secondary non-tertiary education for the public sector to reap the full benefits.

Chart A9.5. **Public cost and benefits for a man obtaining upper secondary or post-secondary non-tertiary education and tertiary education (2008 or latest available year)**

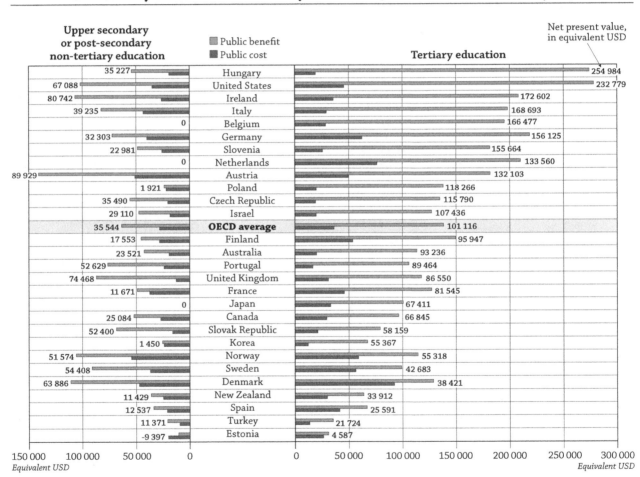

Notes: Japan is not included in the left-hand side of the chart because the data at lower and upper secondary levels of education are not broken down. Belgium and the Netherlands are not included in the left-hand side of the chart because upper secondary education is compulsory.
Australia and Turkey refer to 2005; Portugal refers to 2006. Japan and Slovenia refer to 2007. All other countries refer to 2008.
Cashflows are discounted at a 3% interest rate.
Countries are ranked in descending order of the net present value at tertiary level of education.
Source: OECD, Tables A9.2 and A9.4. See Annex 3 for notes (*www.oecd.org/edu/eag2012*).
StatLink http://dx.doi.org/10.1787/888932669040

The public returns to tertiary education are substantially larger than the public returns to upper secondary or post-secondary non-tertiary education, in part because a larger share of the investment costs are borne by the individuals themselves. The main contributing factors are, however, the higher taxes and social contributions that flow from the higher income levels of those with tertiary qualifications. In Hungary and the United States, these benefits exceed USD 260 000 over an individual's working life (Table A9.4 and Chart A9.5).

On average across OECD countries, the net public return on an investment in tertiary education is over USD 100 000 for a man and over USD 52 000 for a woman at this level of education. Even after taking into account student grants, the public benefits outweigh the costs by a factor of three for men and a factor of two for women, on average. In Hungary, the benefits are 14 times larger than the public sector's initial investment in a man's tertiary education.

Returns on investments, taxation and labour market rewards

Overall wage dispersion drives much of the returns for both the individual and the public sector. A compressed wage structure will typically generate lower returns to higher education. This is particularly true in the Nordic countries, Denmark, Norway and Sweden, and in New Zealand. The Nordic countries have generally offset the effects of this weak reward structure by providing a higher education system almost free of charge and by having a generous student-grant system (see Indicator B5); New Zealand has shared some of the direct costs with the individual and has kept income taxes low.

A number of countries have substantially larger overall income inequality, which is also reflected in the gross earnings benefits for those with tertiary education. In some countries with overall lower cost structures, supply and demand appears to drive earnings differentials.

Although overall costs and income levels are low in the Czech Republic, Hungary, Poland, Portugal and Slovenia, higher education generates a substantially larger gross earnings premium over an individual's working life than in the previous group of countries. Tertiary attainment levels in the working-age population are considerably below the OECD average (see Indicator A1), and the earnings premiums for tertiary-educated individuals are above the OECD average (see Indicator A8). This suggests a short supply of higher-educated individuals, which has driven up wages and overall wage inequality over the years. As a result, individuals in these countries have strong incentives to make further investments in education, a premise that is supported by the increasingly high entry rates into tertiary education in these countries (see Indicator C3). Given the likelihood that the demand for more highly educated workers will continue to grow in these countries, it will take some time before a balance is reached.

Because earnings premiums and gross earnings benefits vary substantially among OECD countries, tax payments and benefits to the public sector also vary in ways that are somewhat contradictory to common perception. Due to low earnings premiums in the Nordic countries, average tertiary earnings are typically below the income bracket where high marginal taxes are levied. Instead, the largest public gains in tax and social security benefits from higher education typically occur in countries where earnings differentials are large, or where average earnings levels reach high income-tax brackets.

The additional taxes and social contributions paid by those with a tertiary education are large in Germany, Hungary, the Netherlands and the United States, for example, stressing the importance for public policy to take a broad approach to strategic decisions on educational investments. Taxation and social policies also play an important role in promoting the supply of labour and are thus key to reaping the full benefits of the investments made in education.

It is important to note, however, that a number of countries have tax policies that effectively lower the actual tax paid by individuals, particularly by those in high income brackets. Tax relief for interest payments on mortgage debt has been introduced in many OECD countries to encourage homeownership. These benefits essentially favour those with higher education and high marginal taxes. The tax incentives for housing are particularly large in the Czech Republic, Denmark, Finland, Greece, the Netherlands, Norway, Sweden and the United States. For further information, see Andrews, et al. (2011).

Methodology

In calculating the returns to education, the approach taken here is the **net present value (NPV)** of the investment. In this framework, lifetime costs and benefits are transferred back to the start of the investment. This is done by discounting all cash flows back to the beginning of the investment with a set rate of interest (discount rate). The choice of interest rate is difficult, as it should reflect not only the overall time horizon of the investment, but also the cost of borrowing or the perceived risk of the investment. To keep things simple, and to make the interpretation of results easier, the same discount rate is applied across all OECD countries.

To arrive at a reasonable discount rate, long-term government bonds have been used as a benchmark. The average long-term interest rate across OECD countries was approximately 4.9% in 2008. Assuming that countries' central banks have succeeded in anchoring inflation expectations at or below 2% per year, a long-term nominal interest rate of 4.9% implies a real interest rate of 2.5% to 3%. The 3% real discount rate used in this indicator reflects the fact that calculations are made in constant prices. The change in the discount rate since the 2009 edition of *Education at a Glance* has a substantial impact on the net present value of education, and that must be taken into account if returns are compared across different editions of the publication.

Discounting the costs and benefits to the present value with this interest rate makes the financial returns on the overall investment and values of the different components comparable across time and countries. Using the same unit of analysis also has the advantage of making it possible to add or subtract components across different educational levels or between the private and public sectors to understand how different factors interact.

NPV calculations are based on the same method as **internal rate of return (IRR)** calculations. The main difference between the two methods lies in how the interest rate is set. For calculations developed within the IRR framework, the interest rate is raised to the level at which the economic benefits equal the cost of the investment and it pinpoints the discount rate at which the investment breaks even.

In calculating the NPV, private investment costs include after-tax foregone earnings adjusted for the probability of finding a job (unemployment rate) and direct private expenditures on education. Both of these investment streams take into account the duration of studies. On the benefit side, age-earnings profiles are used to calculate the earnings differential between different educational groups (below upper secondary education; upper secondary or post-secondary non-tertiary education; and tertiary education).

These gross earnings differentials are adjusted for differences in income taxes, social contributions and social transfers, including housing benefits and social assistance related to earnings level, to arrive at net earnings differentials. The cash flows are further adjusted for probability of finding a job (unemployment rates). The calculations are done separately for men and women to account for differences in earnings differentials and unemployment rates.

In calculating public NPV, public costs include lost tax receipts during the years of schooling (income tax and social contributions) and public expenditures, taking into account the duration of studies. Lost tax receipts are low in some countries because young individuals have low earnings levels. Public expenditures on education include direct expenditures, such as payment of teachers' salaries or spending for the construction of school buildings, purchase of textbooks, etc., and public-private transfers, such as public subsidies to households for scholarships and other grants and to other private entities for providing training at the workplace, etc. The benefits for the public sector are additional tax and social contribution receipts associated with higher earnings and savings on transfers, i.e. housing benefits and social assistance that the public sector does not have to pay because of higher levels of earnings.

It is important to consider some of the broad **conceptual limitations** on the estimates of financial returns discussed here:

- The data reported are accounting-based values only. The results no doubt differ from econometric estimates that would use the same data on the micro level rather than a lifetime stream of earnings derived from average earnings.

▪ The approach used here estimates future earnings for individuals with different levels of educational attainment, based on knowledge of how average present gross earnings vary by level of attainment and age. However, the relationship between different levels of educational attainment and earnings may differ in the future. Technological, economic and social changes may all alter how wage levels relate to levels of educational attainment.

▪ Differences in returns across countries partly reflect different institutional and non-market conditions that bear on earnings, such as institutional conditions that limit flexibility in relative earnings.

▪ In estimating benefits, the effect of education on the likelihood of finding employment when wanting to work is taken into account. However, this also makes the estimate sensitive to the stage in the economic cycle at which the data are collected. As more highly educated individuals typically have a stronger attachment to the labour market, the value of education generally increases in times of poor economic growth.

The calculations also involve a number of restrictive assumptions needed for international comparability. For calculating the investments in education, foregone earnings have been standardised at the level of the legal minimum wage or the equivalent in countries in which earnings data include part-time work. When no national minimum wage was available, the wage was selected from wages set in collective agreements. This assumption aims to counterbalance the very low earnings recorded for 15-24 year-olds that led to excessively high estimates in earlier editions of *Education at a Glance*. In the Czech Republic, Hungary, Japan, the Netherlands, Portugal and the United Kingdom, actual earnings are used in calculating foregone earnings, as part-time work is excluded in these earnings data collections.

For the methods employed for calculating the rates of return, please see Annex 3 at *www.oecd.org/edu/eag2012*

Cost and benefits for upper secondary or post-secondary non-tertiary education cannot be computed for Belgium and the Netherlands because upper secondary education is compulsory in both countries. The fact that upper secondary education is compulsory in these countries prevents a consistent application of the methodology for this indicator, because it uses an investment approach. The investment approach assumes that individuals make a choice to invest in a given level of education in order to obtain the benefits. In countries where a particular level of education is compulsory, individuals do not face this choice, thereby making the methodology inapplicable in such instances.

The statistical data for Israel are supplied by and under the responsibility of the relevant Israeli authorities. The use of such data by the OECD is without prejudice to the status of the Golan Heights, East Jerusalem and Israeli settlements in the West Bank under the terms of international law.

References

Andrews, D., A. Caldera Sánches and A. Johansson (2011), "Housing Markets and Structural Policies in OECD Countries", *OECD Economics Department Working Papers*, No. 836, OECD Publishing.

Mincer, J. (1974), *Schooling, Experience, and Earnings*, National Bureau of Economic Research, New York.

OECD (2011), "A User's Guide to Indicator A9 – Incentives to Invest in Education" (available at *www.oecd.org/edu/eag2011*).

A9

Table A9.1. [1/2] Private net present value and internal rate of return for an individual obtaining upper secondary or post-secondary non-tertiary education as part of initial education (2008 or latest available year)

In equivalent USD converted using PPPs for GDP

	Year	Direct cost	Foregone earnings	Total costs	Gross earnings benefits	Income tax effect	Social contribution effect	Transfers effect	Unemployment effect	Total benefits	Net present value	Internal rate of return
							Per man					
Australia	2005	-2 891	-22 748	**-25 639**	103 116	-41 661	0	-886	42 163	**102 731**	77 092	14.2%
Austria	2008	-1 801	-45 844	**-47 645**	284 884	-73 822	-59 487	-7 587	35 029	**179 017**	131 372	12.4%
Belgium[1]												
Canada	2008	-3 142	-28 731	**-31 873**	136 984	-42 770	-10 510	-385	38 762	**122 081**	90 208	13.6%
Chile		m	m	**m**	m	m	m	m	m	**m**	m	m
Czech Republic	2008	-2 142	-17 517	**-19 659**	108 257	-31 801	-23 905	0	83 688	**136 240**	116 581	21.2%
Denmark	2008	-746	-36 225	**-36 971**	187 370	-80 160	-17 256	-13 571	19 357	**95 739**	58 768	11.2%
Estonia	2008	-190	-12 503	**-12 693**	31 071	-9 246	-1 260	0	17 586	**38 151**	25 458	9.1%
Finland	2008	-210	-30 193	**-30 403**	77 946	-31 681	-6 879	-6 961	31 518	**63 943**	33 540	8.4%
France	2008	-2 632	-29 772	**-32 404**	114 056	-24 881	-20 862	-3 284	37 503	**102 532**	70 129	10.7%
Germany	2008	-3 877	-35 678	**-39 555**	63 972	-27 911	-29 948	-14 223	79 490	**71 380**	31 825	6.7%
Greece		m	m	**m**	m	m	m	m	m	**m**	m	m
Hungary	2008	-880	-13 073	**-13 953**	73 813	-34 401	-19 706	0	42 510	**62 216**	48 263	15.2%
Iceland		m	m	**m**	m	m	m	m	m	**m**	m	m
Ireland	2008	-620	-32 896	**-33 515**	243 036	-89 225	-17 630	0	60 310	**196 490**	162 975	14.7%
Israel	2008	-1 266	-30 056	**-31 322**	143 387	-28 405	-18 920	0	26 841	**122 903**	91 581	9.7%
Italy	2008	-986	-43 886	**-44 872**	177 073	-63 514	-18 903	0	22 519	**117 174**	72 302	8.1%
Japan[2]												
Korea	2008	-6 069	-25 378	**-31 447**	171 945	-8 892	-16 444	0	45 808	**192 417**	160 970	16.5%
Luxembourg		m	m	**m**	m	m	m	m	m	**m**	m	m
Mexico		m	m	**m**	m	m	m	m	m	**m**	m	m
Netherlands[1]												
New Zealand	2008	-3 244	-33 866	**-37 111**	93 186	-33 648	-1 463	-971	20 258	**77 362**	40 251	7.3%
Norway	2008	-2 859	-53 840	**-56 699**	248 839	-80 412	-22 351	-3 187	38 016	**180 905**	124 206	11.9%
Poland	2008	-916	-16 602	**-17 518**	53 311	-6 965	-16 753	0	24 689	**54 282**	36 764	10.3%
Portugal	2006	-12	-23 445	**-23 456**	212 846	-53 287	-23 133	0	-3 353	**133 074**	109 618	11.5%
Slovak Republic	2008	-2 358	-6 324	**-8 682**	106 965	-37 696	-30 699	0	122 421	**160 991**	152 309	40.8%
Slovenia	2007	-2 176	-18 284	**-20 460**	111 618	-19 595	-28 948	0	19 307	**82 381**	61 921	12.1%
Spain	2008	-1 464	-12 551	**-14 015**	95 667	-25 708	-7 912	0	28 987	**91 035**	77 020	11.4%
Sweden	2008	-21	-29 425	**-29 446**	174 618	-55 711	-15 255	-20 046	42 499	**126 105**	96 659	14.9%
Switzerland		m	m	**m**	m	m	m	m	m	**m**	m	m
Turkey	2005	-336	-11 218	**-11 554**	63 318	-10 584	-10 115	0	4 017	**46 637**	35 082	9.5%
United Kingdom	2008	-4 880	-33 603	**-38 483**	218 579	-50 129	-27 713	-9 149	46 772	**178 360**	139 877	12.5%
United States	2008	-2 888	-26 755	**-29 643**	292 656	-70 774	-25 846	-5 325	45 392	**236 104**	206 461	20.2%
OECD average		-1 944	-26 817	**-28 761**	143 540	-41 315	-18 876	-3 423	38 884	**118 810**	90 049	13.4%
EU21 average		-1 524	-25 754	**-27 278**	137 358	-42 102	-21 544	-4 401	41 814	**111 124**	83 846	13.6%

Note: Values are based on the difference between people who attained an upper secondary or post-secondary non tertiary education compared with those who have not attained that level of education.
1. Belgium and the Netherlands are not included in the table because upper secondary education is compulsory.
2. Japan is not included in the table because the data at the lower and upper secondary levels of education are not broken down.
Source: OECD. See Annex 3 for notes (*www.oecd.org/edu/eag2012*).
Please refer to the Reader's Guide for information concerning the symbols replacing missing data.
StatLink ᐧᒥᔅᐧ http://dx.doi.org/10.1787/888932665525

A9

Table A9.1. [2/2] Private net present value and internal rate of return for an individual obtaining upper secondary or post-secondary non-tertiary education as part of initial education (2008 or latest available year)

In equivalent USD converted using PPPs for GDP

	Year	Direct cost	Foregone earnings	Total costs	Gross earnings benefits	Income tax effect	Social contribution effect	Transfers effect	Unemployment effect	Total benefits	Net present value	Internal rate of return
					Per woman							
Australia	2005	-2 891	-23 470	**-26 361**	88 809	-28 020	0	-17 611	23 261	**66 440**	40 079	11.3%
Austria	2008	-1 801	-44 864	**-46 665**	188 626	-29 485	-43 040	-22 993	29 567	**122 675**	76 010	9.3%
Belgium[1]												
Canada	2008	-3 142	-29 730	**-32 871**	109 365	-23 190	-11 278	-2 192	19 739	**92 443**	59 572	8.8%
Chile		m	m	**m**	m	m	m	m	m	**m**	m	m
Czech Republic	2008	-2 142	-15 950	**-18 092**	97 445	-26 652	-20 933	0	69 776	**119 635**	101 543	21.8%
Denmark	2008	-746	-35 265	**-36 011**	137 856	-50 090	-12 363	0	10 066	**85 469**	49 458	9.6%
Estonia	2008	-180	-10 993	**-11 173**	46 597	-11 311	-1 535	0	12 466	**46 217**	35 044	20.9%
Finland	2008	-210	-30 803	**-31 013**	54 469	-17 246	-5 083	-15 568	26 412	**42 985**	11 972	4.9%
France	2008	-2 632	-28 347	**-30 980**	108 028	-19 605	-19 025	-10 229	31 096	**90 265**	59 285	9.4%
Germany	2008	-3 877	-35 784	**-39 662**	122 989	-31 876	-34 864	-36 714	43 778	**63 313**	23 651	5.8%
Greece		m	m	**m**	m	m	m	m	m	**m**	m	m
Hungary	2008	-880	-12 304	**-13 184**	85 252	-32 820	-21 045	0	38 518	**69 905**	56 721	16.3%
Iceland		m	m	**m**	m	m	m	m	m	**m**	m	m
Ireland	2008	-620	-36 155	**-36 775**	218 100	-23 313	-16 064	0	19 774	**198 498**	161 723	23.5%
Israel	2008	-1 266	-29 067	**-30 333**	107 391	-6 276	-6 332	-82	16 175	**110 876**	80 544	9.7%
Italy	2008	-986	-38 624	**-39 610**	152 167	-51 238	-17 293	0	29 983	**113 620**	74 010	8.4%
Japan[2]												
Korea	2008	-6 069	-25 021	**-31 090**	71 331	-1 971	-9 207	0	50 039	**110 192**	79 101	12.5%
Luxembourg		m	m	**m**	m	m	m	m	m	**m**	m	m
Mexico		m	m	**m**	m	m	m	m	m	**m**	m	m
Netherlands[1]												
New Zealand	2008	-3 244	-33 447	**-36 691**	81 687	-19 232	-1 205	-10 028	11 252	**62 474**	25 783	6.1%
Norway	2008	-2 859	-54 055	**-56 914**	149 381	-41 441	-13 140	-13 729	20 335	**101 406**	44 492	6.3%
Poland	2008	-916	-14 879	**-15 794**	74 416	-8 271	-19 448	0	16 433	**63 130**	47 335	10.5%
Portugal	2006	-12	-20 631	**-20 642**	150 215	-31 104	-17 731	0	10 416	**111 796**	91 153	11.7%
Slovak Republic	2008	-2 358	-4 464	**-6 822**	81 611	-27 655	-22 522	0	87 101	**118 534**	111 712	42.8%
Slovenia	2007	-2 176	-18 557	**-20 733**	118 292	-16 877	-28 104	-708	9 009	**81 612**	60 879	11.3%
Spain	2008	-1 464	-11 638	**-13 102**	127 362	-23 551	-9 849	0	28 607	**122 569**	109 467	20.4%
Sweden	2008	-21	-29 252	**-29 273**	132 070	-42 495	-12 280	-28 046	43 892	**93 141**	63 868	10.6%
Switzerland		m	m	**m**	m	m	m	m	m	**m**	m	m
Turkey	2005	-336	-12 058	**-12 394**	75 879	-8 395	-9 432	0	-12 434	**45 618**	33 223	9.2%
United Kingdom	2008	-4 880	-34 465	**-39 345**	110 415	-27 011	-15 010	-35 051	39 416	**72 759**	33 414	6.6%
United States	2008	-2 888	-27 307	**-30 195**	229 708	-43 137	-19 464	-10 332	24 981	**181 756**	151 561	17.8%
OECD average		-1 944	-26 285	**-28 229**	116 778	-25 690	-15 450	-8 131	27 986	**95 493**	67 264	13.0%
EU21 average		-1 944	-26 285	**-28 229**	116 778	-25 690	-15 450	-8 131	27 986	**95 493**	67 264	13.0%

Note: Values are based on the difference between people who attained an upper secondary or post-secondary non tertiary education compared with those who have not attained that level of education.

1. Belgium and the Netherlands are not included in the table because upper secondary education is compulsory.
2. Japan is not included in the table because the data at the lower and upper secondary levels of education are not broken down.

Source: OECD. See Annex 3 for notes (*www.oecd.org/edu/eag2012*).

Please refer to the Reader's Guide for information concerning the symbols replacing missing data.

StatLink ᵐˢᴾ http://dx.doi.org/10.1787/888932665525

A9

Table A9.2. [1/2] Public net present value and internal rate of return for an individual obtaining upper secondary or post-secondary non-tertiary education as part of initial education (2008 or latest available year)

In equivalent USD converted using PPPs for GDP

	Year	Direct cost	Foregone taxes on earnings	Total costs	Income tax effect	Social contribution effect	Transfers effect	Unemployment effect	Total benefits	Net present value	Internal rate of return
						Per man						
Australia	2005	-14 757	-4 270	**-19 027**	32 427	0	886	9 234	**42 548**	23 521	8.0%
Austria	2008	-42 641	-8 326	**-50 967**	69 564	53 202	7 587	10 543	**140 896**	89 929	9.4%
Belgium[1]											
Canada	2008	-23 735	-3 282	**-27 018**	35 892	7 681	374	8 155	**52 101**	25 084	6.5%
Chile		m	m	**m**	m	m	m	m	**m**	m	m
Czech Republic	2008	-20 272	56	**-20 215**	21 869	13 500	0	20 336	**55 705**	35 490	9.9%
Denmark	2008	-30 821	-16 280	**-47 102**	74 608	15 050	13 571	7 758	**110 987**	63 886	8.4%
Estonia	2008	-18 086	-1 817	**-19 902**	6 334	805	0	3 367	**10 506**	-9 397	0.3%
Finland	2008	-20 895	-7 073	**-27 968**	25 458	4 927	6 961	8 175	**45 521**	17 553	6.7%
France	2008	-31 556	-5 799	**-37 355**	20 634	15 760	3 284	9 349	**49 027**	11 671	4.4%
Germany	2008	-26 098	-13 681	**-39 779**	15 256	13 631	14 223	28 972	**72 082**	32 303	8.4%
Greece		m	m	**m**	m	m	m	m	**m**	m	m
Hungary	2008	-15 738	-3 142	**-18 880**	27 606	12 527	0	13 974	**54 107**	35 227	9.3%
Iceland		m	m	**m**	m	m	m	m	**m**	m	m
Ireland	2008	-25 948	-164	**-26 113**	82 207	14 857	0	9 790	**106 855**	80 742	9.3%
Israel	2008	-16 918	-1 298	**-18 216**	26 378	17 092	0	3 855	**47 325**	29 110	6.9%
Italy	2008	-32 919	-10 264	**-43 183**	59 003	16 776	0	6 638	**82 418**	39 235	6.0%
Japan[2]											
Korea	2008	-21 272	-2 614	**-23 887**	8 106	12 993	0	4 237	**25 337**	1 450	3.3%
Luxembourg		m	m	**m**	m	m	m	m	**m**	m	m
Mexico		m	m	**m**	m	m	m	m	**m**	m	m
Netherlands[1]											
New Zealand	2008	-19 455	-5 198	**-24 653**	29 331	1 201	971	4 578	**36 082**	11 429	4.9%
Norway	2008	-36 851	-17 525	**-54 376**	72 824	19 403	3 187	10 537	**105 950**	51 574	7.2%
Poland	2008	-16 232	-5 565	**-21 797**	5 188	11 477	0	7 053	**23 718**	1 921	3.4%
Portugal	2006	-19 937	-3 854	**-23 791**	53 798	23 500	0	-879	**76 420**	52 629	7.7%
Slovak Republic	2008	-13 158	-2 837	**-15 995**	17 648	14 372	0	36 375	**68 395**	52 400	15.0%
Slovenia	2007	-20 398	-5 164	**-25 562**	17 749	24 705	0	6 089	**48 543**	22 981	6.2%
Spain	2008	-19 800	-1 282	**-21 083**	23 319	6 085	0	4 216	**33 620**	12 537	4.7%
Sweden	2008	-28 557	-8 046	**-36 603**	46 631	12 302	20 046	12 033	**91 012**	54 408	13.5%
Switzerland		m	m	**m**	m	m	m	m	**m**	m	m
Turkey	2005	-4 776	-4 551	**-9 327**	9 997	9 514	0	1 188	**20 699**	11 371	6.4%
United Kingdom	2008	-17 187	4 665	**-12 522**	43 564	23 960	9 149	10 317	**86 990**	74 468	20.6%
United States	2008	-33 006	-1 851	**-34 857**	64 903	22 394	5 325	9 323	**101 944**	67 088	9.6%
OECD average		-22 841	-5 166	**-28 007**	35 612	14 709	3 422	9 809	**63 551**	35 544	7.8%
EU21 average		-23 544	-5 210	**-28 754**	35 908	16 320	4 401	11 418	**68 047**	39 293	8.4%

Note: Values are based on the difference between people who attained an upper secondary or post-secondary non tertiary education compared with those who have not attained that level of education.
1. Belgium and the Netherlands are not included in the table because upper secondary education is compulsory.
2. Japan is not included in the table because the data at the lower and upper secondary level of education are not broken down.
Source: OECD. See Annex 3 for notes (*www.oecd.org/edu/eag2012*).
Please refer to the Reader's Guide for information concerning the symbols replacing missing data.
StatLink ⟨⟨⟩⟩ http://dx.doi.org/10.1787/888932665544

Table A9.2. [2/2] Public net present value and internal rate of return for an individual obtaining upper secondary or post-secondary non-tertiary education as part of initial education (2008 or latest available year)

In equivalent USD converted using PPPs for GDP

	Year	Direct cost	Foregone taxes on earnings	Total costs	Income tax effect	Social contribution effect	Transfers effect	Unemployment effect	Total benefits	Net present value	Internal rate of return
						Per woman					
Australia	2005	-14 757	-4 405	**-19 163**	23 936	0	17 611	4 084	**45 630**	26 468	17.1%
Austria	2008	-42 641	-8 148	**-50 789**	28 780	37 860	22 993	5 886	**95 519**	44 729	7.2%
Belgium[1]											
Canada	2008	-24 447	-3 498	**-27 946**	21 740	9 998	2 192	2 731	**36 661**	8 715	4.2%
Chile		m	m	**m**	m	m	m	m	**m**	m	m
Czech Republic	2008	-20 272	51	**-20 221**	19 849	12 252	0	15 484	**47 586**	27 365	8.7%
Denmark	2008	-30 821	-15 849	**-46 670**	47 639	11 027	0	3 787	**62 453**	15 783	4.9%
Estonia	2008	-17 047	-1 597	**-18 645**	9 543	1 213	0	2 090	**12 846**	-5 799	0.7%
Finland	2008	-20 895	-7 216	**-28 111**	12 908	3 450	15 568	5 971	**37 896**	9 786	5.8%
France	2008	-31 556	-5 522	**-37 078**	16 827	14 808	10 229	6 994	**48 859**	11 781	4.4%
Germany	2008	-26 098	-13 722	**-39 820**	28 195	25 933	36 714	12 612	**103 454**	63 634	10.6%
Greece		m	m	**m**	m	m	m	m	**m**	m	m
Hungary	2008	-15 738	-2 957	**-18 696**	27 536	14 539	0	11 789	**53 865**	35 169	8.9%
Iceland		m	m	**m**	m	m	m	m	**m**	m	m
Ireland	2008	-25 948	-181	**-26 129**	22 747	15 644	0	985	**39 377**	13 247	4.9%
Israel	2008	-16 918	-1 255	**-18 173**	6 031	5 694	82	883	**12 690**	-5 483	1.8%
Italy	2008	-32 919	-9 033	**-41 952**	47 153	14 467	0	6 910	**68 530**	26 578	5.2%
Japan[2]											
Korea	2008	-21 272	-2 513	**-23 785**	1 607	5 442	0	4 129	**11 178**	-12 606	-0.5%
Luxembourg		m	m	**m**	m	m	m	m	**m**	m	m
Mexico		m	m	**m**	m	m	m	m	**m**	m	m
Netherlands[1]											
New Zealand	2008	-19 455	-5 133	**-24 589**	17 143	1 060	10 028	2 235	**30 465**	5 877	4.1%
Norway	2008	-36 851	-17 595	**-54 446**	38 484	11 570	13 729	4 528	**68 310**	13 865	4.5%
Poland	2008	-16 232	-4 987	**-21 219**	7 206	15 942	0	4 571	**27 719**	6 500	4.2%
Portugal	2006	-19 937	-2 842	**-22 779**	30 147	16 590	0	2 098	**48 835**	26 056	6.1%
Slovak Republic	2008	-13 158	-2 003	**-15 160**	13 424	10 932	0	25 821	**50 177**	35 017	12.6%
Slovenia	2007	-20 398	-5 241	**-25 639**	16 274	26 130	708	2 577	**45 690**	20 050	5.8%
Spain	2008	-19 800	-1 189	**-20 989**	22 400	8 051	0	2 950	**33 400**	12 411	4.7%
Sweden	2008	-28 557	-7 999	**-36 556**	33 919	9 236	28 046	11 620	**82 821**	46 265	12.7%
Switzerland		m	m	**m**	m	m	m	m	**m**	m	m
Turkey	2005	-4 776	-4 892	**-9 668**	10 025	11 264	0	-3 463	**17 827**	8 159	5.8%
United Kingdom	2008	-17 187	2 255	**-14 932**	22 136	12 175	35 051	7 710	**77 072**	62 140	13.2%
United States	2008	-33 006	-1 889	**-34 895**	41 060	17 570	10 332	3 971	**72 932**	38 037	7.6%
OECD average		-22 828	-5 094	**-27 922**	22 668	12 514	8 131	5 958	**49 272**	21 350	6.6%
EU21 average		-23 483	-5 069	**-28 552**	23 923	14 721	8 783	7 639	**55 065**	26 512	7.1%

Note: Values are based on the difference between people who attained an upper secondary or post-secondary non tertiary education compared with those who have not attained that level of education.

1. Belgium and the Netherlands are not included in the table because upper secondary education is compulsory.

2. Japan is not included in the table because the data at the lower and upper secondary level of education are not broken down.

Source: OECD. See Annex 3 for notes (*www.oecd.org/edu/eag2012*).

Please refer to the Reader's Guide for information concerning the symbols replacing missing data.

StatLink ᴍ〿ᶩ〿 http://dx.doi.org/10.1787/888932665544

A9

Table A9.3. [1/2] Private net present value and internal rate of return for an individual obtaining tertiary education as part of initial education (2008 or latest available year)

In equivalent USD converted using PPPs for GDP

	Year	Direct cost	Foregone earnings	Total costs	Gross earnings benefits	Income tax effect	Social contribution effect	Transfers effect	Unemploy-ment effect	Grants effect	Total benefits	Net present value	Internal rate of return
							Per man						
Australia	2005	-14 426	-36 560	**-50 986**	278 519	-113 313	0	0	1 061	6	**166 273**	115 287	9.8%
Austria	2008	-7 082	-57 842	**-64 924**	455 326	-139 387	-52 154	0	16 336	9 852	**289 972**	225 048	10.6%
Belgium	2005	-2 133	-30 842	**-32 975**	330 066	-145 966	-50 056	0	14 294	862	**149 200**	116 225	12.0%
Canada	2008	-18 094	-32 494	**-50 588**	284 705	-92 145	-5 371	0	15 816	1 103	**204 108**	153 520	10.8%
Chile		m	m	**m**	m	m	m	m	m	m	**m**	m	m
Czech Republic	2008	-5 062	-22 919	**-27 981**	405 482	-83 316	-51 577	0	7 072		**277 660**	249 679	19.7%
Denmark	2008	-3 124	-52 320	**-55 444**	244 798	-130 076	-19 062	-4 821	-4 215	25 189	**111 813**	56 369	7.9%
Estonia	2008	-6 117	-23 805	**-29 922**	124 705	-27 313	-3 507	0	10 250		**104 135**	74 213	0
Finland	2008	-1 925	-57 211	**-59 136**	334 537	-135 987	-22 276	0	19 740	8 730	**204 744**	145 608	10.9%
France	2008	-7 868	-54 588	**-62 456**	341 205	-86 399	-44 451	0	8 431	3 620	**222 406**	159 950	9.9%
Germany	2008	-6 542	-63 113	**-69 654**	384 499	-151 331	-73 282	0	48 429	6 021	**214 336**	144 682	9.6%
Greece		m	m	**m**	m	m	m	m	m	m	**m**	m	m
Hungary	2008	-4 426	-15 223	**-19 649**	470 934	-190 103	-85 379	0	31 301	1 283	**228 035**	208 386	24.8%
Iceland		m	m	**m**	m	m	m	m	m	m	**m**	m	m
Ireland	2008	-7 482	-60 313	**-67 795**	475 563	-194 735	-17 926	0	24 353	4 361	**291 616**	223 821	12.8%
Israel	2008	-17 469	-31 486	**-48 955**	313 487	-89 214	-37 998	0	6 263		**192 538**	143 582	10.3%
Italy	2008	-7 285	-50 608	**-57 893**	408 011	-159 562	-41 835	0	3 295	3 330	**213 239**	155 346	8.1%
Japan	2007	-37 215	-66 750	**-103 965**	326 614	-64 523	-36 039	0	20 931		**246 983**	143 018	7.4%
Korea	2008	-23 592	-55 397	**-78 989**	321 520	-43 198	-24 275	0	14 708		**268 754**	189 766	9.3%
Luxembourg		m	m	**m**	m	m	m	m	m	m	**m**	m	m
Mexico		m	m	**m**	m	m	m	m	m	m	**m**	m	m
Netherlands	2008	-14 113	-90 118	**-104 231**	455 296	-202 175	-22 153	0	4 778	14 371	**250 117**	145 886	7.9%
New Zealand	2008	-9 476	-47 386	**-56 861**	172 607	-63 341	-2 254	-6	434	1 891	**109 332**	52 471	6.1%
Norway	2008	-1 180	-68 022	**-69 202**	267 137	-99 740	-20 722	0	-1 623	6 226	**151 278**	82 076	6.1%
Poland	2008	-6 291	-15 995	**-22 287**	367 019	-55 868	-83 937	0	23 960	1 742	**252 917**	230 630	23.4%
Portugal	2006	-5 903	-24 146	**-30 050**	484 640	-77 432	-28 586	0	25 278		**403 901**	373 851	18.5%
Slovak Republic	2008	-5 543	-13 269	**-18 812**	285 337	-41 848	-38 547	0	21 503	1 250	**227 695**	208 883	24.2%
Slovenia	2007	-5 895	-20 705	**-26 600**	430 880	-97 103	-84 520	0	2 805	200	**252 262**	225 663	19.1%
Spain	2008	-10 051	-37 385	**-47 436**	195 793	-53 120	-13 796	0	21 534		**150 411**	102 975	9.3%
Sweden	2008	-4 913	-59 657	**-64 570**	221 486	-99 336	-7 997	0	3 530	8 341	**126 024**	61 454	6.4%
Switzerland		m	m	**m**	m	m	m	m	m	m	**m**	m	m
Turkey	2005	-1 061	-9 402	**-10 463**	106 985	-18 682	-16 424	0	2 761		**74 640**	64 177	19.3%
United Kingdom	2008	-28 704	-93 851	**-122 555**	364 136	-82 074	-37 666	0	19 310	2 244	**265 949**	143 394	7.4%
United States	2008	-71 053	-45 170	**-116 223**	674 277	-223 008	-55 326	0	49 832		**445 775**	329 552	11.5%
OECD average		-11 929	-44 163	**-56 093**	340 199	-105 725	-34 897	-172	14 720	5 296	**217 718**	161 625	12.4%
EU21 average		-7 307	-42 527	**-49 833**	352 609	-106 176	-41 559	-284	16 642	5 859	**225 713**	175 879	13.9%

Notes: Estonia estimate assumes duration of tertiary education is 5.5 years.

Values are based on the difference between people who attained a tertiary education compared with those who have attained an upper secondary or post-secondary non-tertiary education.

Source: OECD. See Annex 3 for notes *(www.oecd.org/edu/eag2012)*.

Please refer to the Reader's Guide for information concerning the symbols replacing missing data.

StatLink ⊞ℨℙ￭ http://dx.doi.org/10.1787/888932665563

Table A9.3. [2/2] Private net present value and internal rate of return for an individual obtaining tertiary education as part of initial education (2008 or latest available year)

In equivalent USD converted using PPPs for GDP

	Year	Direct cost	Foregone earnings	Total costs	Gross earnings benefits	Income tax effect	Social contribution effect	Transfers effect	Unemploy-ment effect	Grants effect	Total benefits	Net present value	Internal rate of return
					Per woman								
Australia	2005	-14 426	-36 510	**-50 936**	225 540	-74 614	0	0	15 136	6	**166 068**	115 132	11.8%
Austria	2008	-7 082	-57 719	**-64 801**	309 444	-88 580	-57 804	0	10 068	9 852	**182 980**	118 179	8.6%
Belgium	2005	-2 133	-29 666	**-31 799**	255 953	-103 549	-57 031	0	36 371	862	**132 606**	100 806	14.4%
Canada	2008	-18 094	-33 461	**-51 555**	229 354	-59 998	-17 327	0	9 909	1 103	**163 042**	111 487	11.0%
Chile		m	m	**m**	m	m	m	m	m	m	**m**	m	m
Czech Republic	2008	-4 915	-22 214	**-27 129**	229 623	-49 088	-30 987	0	18 444		**167 992**	140 864	16.3%
Denmark	2008	-3 124	-51 865	**-54 989**	146 733	-55 606	-12 209	-7 081	4 395	25 189	**101 420**	46 432	8.7%
Estonia	2008	-6 117	-23 843	**-29 961**	91 458	-20 035	-2 591	0	8 254		**77 086**	47 125	9.6%
Finland	2008	-1 925	-57 436	**-59 361**	203 311	-71 668	-13 866	-1 661	18 032	8 730	**142 879**	83 518	9.0%
France	2008	-7 868	-52 263	**-60 131**	227 629	-45 923	-33 756	-84	19 076	3 620	**170 561**	110 430	9.4%
Germany	2008	-6 542	-63 643	**-70 185**	266 912	-80 528	-60 157	-926	24 178	6 021	**155 499**	85 314	8.2%
Greece		m	m	**m**	m	m	m	m	m	m	**m**	m	m
Hungary	2008	-4 426	-14 717	**-19 143**	253 441	-110 971	-47 460	0	25 593	1 283	**121 885**	102 742	18.1%
Iceland		m	m	**m**	m	m	m	m	m	m	**m**	m	m
Ireland	2008	-7 482	-63 062	**-70 544**	341 156	-92 253	-29 519	0	10 885	4 361	**234 630**	164 087	11.5%
Israel	2008	-17 469	-30 773	**-48 242**	177 689	-29 269	-20 793	0	16 951		**144 578**	96 336	9.9%
Italy	2008	-7 285	-47 826	**-55 111**	223 811	-79 954	-21 986	0	7 563	3 330	**132 764**	77 652	6.9%
Japan	2007	-37 215	-49 265	**-86 481**	231 306	-20 848	-29 117	0	9 951		**191 293**	104 812	7.8%
Korea	2008	-23 592	-47 607	**-71 199**	205 230	-8 892	-18 027	0	31 992		**210 303**	139 104	9.7%
Luxembourg		m	m	**m**	m	m	m	m	m	m	**m**	m	m
Mexico		m	m	**m**	m	m	m	m	m	m	**m**	m	m
Netherlands	2008	-14 113	-87 458	**-101 571**	339 338	-129 641	-30 381	0	9 467	14 371	**203 152**	101 581	7.0%
New Zealand	2008	-9 476	-47 867	**-57 343**	123 296	-34 553	-1 645	-2 591	2 863	1 891	**89 261**	31 918	5.8%
Norway	2008	-1 180	-68 812	**-69 992**	214 414	-60 617	-16 984	0	3 998	6 226	**147 038**	77 046	7.3%
Poland	2008	-6 291	-15 058	**-21 350**	215 086	-24 687	-52 035	0	27 164	1 742	**167 270**	145 920	19.9%
Portugal	2006	-5 903	-20 483	**-26 386**	355 880	-92 120	-36 253	0	9 848		**237 354**	210 968	18.4%
Slovak Republic	2008	-5 543	-12 580	**-18 123**	183 917	-34 359	-27 821	0	24 459	1 250	**147 446**	129 323	20.8%
Slovenia	2007	-5 895	-20 090	**-25 984**	319 493	-74 631	-74 593	0	22 535	200	**193 005**	167 020	17.7%
Spain	2008	-10 051	-35 821	**-45 872**	235 494	-61 742	-16 761	0	28 175		**185 166**	139 293	11.3%
Sweden	2008	-4 913	-59 179	**-64 092**	134 336	-39 174	-10 088	0	10 293	8 341	**103 709**	39 616	5.7%
Switzerland		m	m	**m**	m	m	m	m	m	m	**m**	m	m
Turkey	2005	-1 061	-8 185	**-9 246**	116 530	-21 267	-19 627	0	14 075		**89 711**	80 466	19.2%
United Kingdom	2008	-28 704	-93 777	**-122 481**	352 964	-72 696	-40 014	-2 242	14 270	2 244	**254 525**	132 044	7.3%
United States	2008	-71 053	-46 090	**-117 143**	389 714	-98 287	-31 645	0	25 624		**285 407**	168 264	8.8%
OECD average		-11 924	-42 760	**-54 684**	235 680	-61 984	-28 946	-521	16 413	5 296	**164 237**	109 553	11.4%
EU21 average		-7 298	-41 857	**-49 155**	240 629	-64 354	-33 406	-706	16 661	5 859	**163 304**	102 892	10.8%

Notes: Estonia estimate assumes duration of tertiary education is 5.5 years.

Values are based on the difference between people who attained a tertiary education compared with those who have attained an upper secondary or post-secondary non-tertiary education.

Source: OECD. See Annex 3 for notes (*www.oecd.org/edu/eag2012*).

Please refer to the Reader's Guide for information concerning the symbols replacing missing data.

StatLink ⫘ http://dx.doi.org/10.1787/888932665563

A9

Table A9.4. [1/2] Public net present value and internal rate of return for an individual obtaining tertiary education as part of initial education (2008 or latest available year)

In equivalent USD converted using PPPs for GDP

	Year	Direct cost	Foregone taxes on earnings	Total costs	Income tax effect	Social contribution effect	Transfers effect	Unemploy-ment effect	Grants effect	Total benefits	Net present value	Internal rate of return
						Per man						
Australia	2005	-13 209	-6 863	**-20 071**	112 914	0	0	400	-6	**113 307**	93 236	13.0%
Austria	2008	-39 081	-10 505	**-49 586**	136 010	49 715	0	5 816	-9 852	**181 689**	132 103	8.8%
Belgium	2005	-20 552	-8 132	**-28 684**	141 569	48 060	0	6 394	-862	**195 160**	166 477	14.8%
Canada	2008	-25 745	-3 823	**-29 569**	89 048	4 483	0	3 985	-1 103	**96 413**	66 845	8.9%
Chile		m	m	**m**	m	m	m	m	m	**m**	m	m
Czech Republic	2008	-19 177	74	**-19 104**	82 126	50 695	0	2 073		**134 894**	115 790	16.2%
Denmark	2008	-66 835	-23 514	**-90 349**	131 307	19 544	4 821	-1 713	-25 189	**128 770**	38 421	4.3%
Estonia	2008	-22 774	-3 459	**-26 233**	25 505	3 242	0	2 073		**30 820**	4 587	4.0%
Finland	2008	-40 184	-13 402	**-53 586**	130 540	21 044	0	6 680	-8 730	**149 533**	95 947	7.8%
France	2008	-35 052	-10 633	**-45 686**	85 338	43 297	0	2 216	-3 620	**127 231**	81 545	7.5%
Germany	2008	-38 267	-24 201	**-62 467**	139 891	63 980	0	20 742	-6 021	**218 592**	156 125	9.4%
Greece		m	m	**m**	m	m	m	m	m	**m**	m	m
Hungary	2008	-15 556	-3 659	**-19 215**	180 835	80 072	0	14 575	-1 283	**274 199**	254 984	27.2%
Iceland		m	m	**m**	m	m	m	m	m	**m**	m	m
Ireland	2008	-35 397	-302	**-35 699**	189 708	16 765	0	6 188	-4 361	**208 300**	172 602	13.3%
Israel	2008	-18 417	-1 360	**-19 776**	88 357	37 478	0	1 377		**127 213**	107 436	12.7%
Italy	2008	-17 538	-11 836	**-29 374**	157 696	41 484	0	2 217	-3 330	**198 067**	168 693	10.1%
Japan	2007	-17 897	-15 254	**-33 151**	62 285	33 612	0	4 665		**100 562**	67 411	8.4%
Korea	2008	-6 770	-5 337	**-12 107**	42 363	23 177	0	1 934		**67 474**	55 367	11.6%
Luxembourg		m	m	**m**	m	m	m	m	m	**m**	m	m
Mexico		m	m	**m**	m	m	m	m	m	**m**	m	m
Netherlands	2008	-37 382	-39 015	**-76 397**	201 244	21 220	0	1 863	-14 371	**209 957**	133 560	7.4%
New Zealand	2008	-22 524	-7 273	**-29 797**	63 170	2 248	6	177	-1 891	**63 709**	33 912	6.3%
Norway	2008	-36 777	-22 141	**-58 918**	99 985	20 848	0	-372	-6 226	**114 236**	55 318	5.4%
Poland	2008	-14 435	-5 361	**-19 796**	53 177	78 804	0	7 824	-1 742	**138 062**	118 266	15.0%
Portugal	2006	-11 848	-4 706	**-16 553**	73 993	27 167	0	4 858		**106 018**	89 464	18.1%
Slovak Republic	2008	-15 033	-5 953	**-20 985**	38 685	35 766	0	5 943	-1 250	**79 145**	58 159	11.3%
Slovenia	2007	-19 911	-5 848	**-25 759**	96 667	83 921	0	1 035	-200	**181 423**	155 664	16.3%
Spain	2008	-37 506	-3 819	**-41 325**	49 879	12 434	0	4 603		**66 916**	25 591	5.3%
Sweden	2008	-39 997	-16 313	**-56 310**	98 282	7 794	0	1 257	-8 341	**98 992**	42 683	5.1%
Switzerland		m	m	**m**	m	m	m	m	m	**m**	m	m
Turkey	2005	-9 567	-3 814	**-13 381**	18 209	16 010	0	886		**35 106**	21 724	9.3%
United Kingdom	2008	-15 151	-15 796	**-30 947**	78 788	35 928	0	5 025	-2 244	**117 497**	86 550	11.0%
United States	2008	-42 430	-3 124	**-45 554**	212 253	51 525	0	14 556		**278 334**	232 779	14.5%
OECD average		-26 250	-9 835	**-36 085**	102 851	33 225	172	4 546	-5 296	**137 201**	101 116	10.8%
EU21 average		-28 455	-9 367	**-37 822**	102 849	39 509	284	5 377	-5 859	**143 538**	105 716	11.2%

Notes: Estonia estimate assumes duration of tertiary education is 5.5 years.

Values are based on the difference between people who attained a tertiary education compared with those who have attained an upper secondary or post-secondary non-tertiary education.

Source: OECD. See Annex 3 for notes (*www.oecd.org/edu/eag2012*).

Please refer to the Reader's Guide for information concerning the symbols replacing missing data.

StatLink ⫍⫎ http://dx.doi.org/10.1787/888932665582

Table A9.4. [2/2] Public net present value and internal rate of return for an individual obtaining tertiary education as part of initial education (2008 or latest available year)

In equivalent USD converted using PPPs for GDP

	Year	Direct cost	Foregone taxes on earnings	Total costs	Income tax effect	Social contribution effect	Transfers effect	Unemploy-ment effect	Grants effect	Total benefits	Net present value	Internal rate of return
						Per woman						
Australia	2005	-13 209	-6 853	**-20 062**	71 195	0	0	3 419	-6	**74 608**	54 546	13.1%
Austria	2008	-39 081	-10 483	**-49 564**	87 056	55 999	0	3 328	-9 852	**136 531**	86 968	7.2%
Belgium	2005	-20 552	-7 822	**-28 374**	94 858	52 075	0	13 646	-862	**159 718**	131 345	17.5%
Canada	2008	-25 745	-3 937	**-29 682**	58 596	16 632	0	2 097	-1 103	**76 222**	46 539	8.5%
Chile		m	m	**m**	m	m	m	m	m	**m**	m	m
Czech Republic	2008	-18 619	71	**-18 547**	46 477	28 689	0	4 909		**80 074**	61 527	12.7%
Denmark	2008	-66 835	-23 309	**-90 144**	54 341	11 718	7 081	1 757	-25 189	**49 707**	-40 437	1.0%
Estonia	2008	-22 774	-3 465	**-26 239**	18 703	2 377	0	1 545		**22 626**	-3 612	2.2%
Finland	2008	-40 184	-13 454	**-53 639**	67 724	12 745	1 661	5 065	-8 730	**78 465**	24 826	4.7%
France	2008	-35 052	-10 181	**-45 233**	43 527	31 158	84	4 994	-3 620	**76 144**	30 911	5.6%
Germany	2008	-38 267	-24 404	**-62 671**	76 514	55 196	926	8 974	-6 021	**135 590**	72 920	7.4%
Greece		m	m	**m**	m	m	m	m	m	**m**	m	m
Hungary	2008	-15 556	-3 537	**-19 094**	104 090	43 123	0	11 218	-1 283	**157 149**	138 055	20.9%
Iceland		m	m	**m**	m	m	m	m	m	**m**	m	m
Ireland	2008	-35 397	-315	**-35 712**	90 864	28 943	0	1 964	-4 361	**117 411**	81 699	9.6%
Israel	2008	-18 417	-1 329	**-19 745**	28 170	19 701	0	2 191		**50 063**	30 317	7.8%
Italy	2008	-17 538	-11 185	**-28 723**	77 919	21 270	0	2 750	-3 330	**98 610**	69 886	8.0%
Japan	2007	-17 897	-10 654	**-28 551**	20 218	27 924	0	1 822		**49 965**	21 414	6.2%
Korea	2008	-6 770	-4 588	**-11 358**	8 331	15 613	0	2 976		**26 919**	15 561	8.0%
Luxembourg		m	m	**m**	m	m	m	m	m	**m**	m	m
Mexico		m	m	**m**	m	m	m	m	m	**m**	m	m
Netherlands	2008	-37 382	-35 640	**-73 022**	128 001	28 440	0	3 582	-14 371	**145 652**	72 630	6.2%
New Zealand	2008	-22 524	-7 347	**-29 871**	33 955	1 608	2 591	634	-1 891	**36 897**	7 026	4.2%
Norway	2008	-36 777	-22 398	**-59 175**	59 828	16 674	0	1 098	-6 226	**71 374**	12 199	3.8%
Poland	2008	-14 435	-5 047	**-19 482**	22 460	46 221	0	8 041	-1 742	**74 980**	55 498	10.9%
Portugal	2006	-11 848	-3 689	**-15 537**	89 669	35 321	0	3 385		**128 374**	112 837	17.6%
Slovak Republic	2008	-15 033	-5 644	**-20 676**	30 346	24 560	0	7 273	-1 250	**60 929**	40 253	9%
Slovenia	2007	-19 911	-5 674	**-25 585**	70 951	69 680	0	8 594	-200	**149 024**	123 439	13.4%
Spain	2008	-37 506	-3 659	**-41 165**	58 077	14 980	0	5 445		**78 503**	37 338	6.3%
Sweden	2008	-39 997	-16 182	**-56 179**	36 903	9 372	0	2 986	-8 341	**40 920**	-15 259	1.8%
Switzerland		m	m	**m**	m	m	m	m	m	**m**	m	m
Turkey	2005	-9 567	-3 320	**-12 887**	19 194	17 528	0	4 171		**40 894**	28 006	9.1%
United Kingdom	2008	-15 151	-6 193	**-21 344**	70 462	38 754	2 242	3 494	-2 244	**112 709**	91 365	14.8%
United States	2008	-42 430	-3 188	**-45 618**	94 347	29 697	0	5 887		**129 931**	84 313	9.7%
OECD average		-26 230	-9 051	**-35 281**	59 385	27 000	521	4 545	-5 296	**87 857**	52 575	8.8%
EU21 average		-28 423	-8 609	**-37 031**	61 534	31 183	706	5 043	-5 859	**93 985**	56 954	9.0%

Notes: Estonia estimate assumes duration of tertiary education is 5.5 years.

Values are based on the difference between people who attained a tertiary education compared with those who have attained an upper secondary or post-secondary non-tertiary education.

Source: OECD. See Annex 3 for notes (*www.oecd.org/edu/eag2012*).

Please refer to the Reader's Guide for information concerning the symbols replacing missing data.

StatLink ᵐˢ⁴ http://dx.doi.org/10.1787/888932665582

HOW DOES EDUCATION INFLUENCE ECONOMIC GROWTH, LABOUR COSTS AND EARNING POWER?

- Over the past decade, more than half of the GDP growth in OECD countries is related to labour income growth among tertiary-educated individuals.

- For workers in their prime years (45-54 year-olds), employers pay almost twice as much for a tertiary-educated worker, on average, than for someone without an upper secondary education.

- On average across OECD countries, an individual without an upper secondary education can expect to keep 62% of labour costs in net income, while a tertiary-educated worker can expect to keep 56% of those costs.

- The most attractive wages for tertiary-educated individuals are found in Australia, Austria, Ireland, Luxembourg, the Netherlands, the United Kingdom and the United States, where average spending power exceeds USD 40 000 per year.

Chart A10.1. **Average GDP growth (real percentage change from the previous year) and labour income growth in GDP, by educational categories (2000-10)**
*Countries with at least five years of growth estimates by educational categories;
GDP growth estimates are matched with years of education growth estimates*

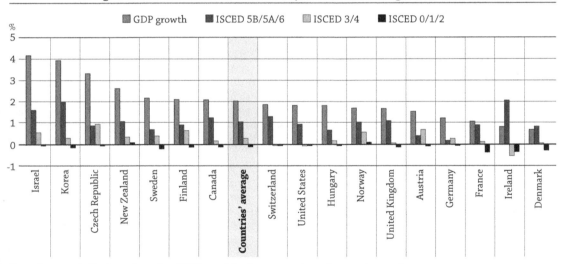

Countries are ranked in descending order of GDP growth (real percentage change from previous year).
Source: OECD. Table A10.1. See Annex 3 for notes (*www.oecd.org/edu/eag2012*).
StatLink ⬛⬛⬛ http://dx.doi.org/10.1787/888932662276

■ Context

The skills available in the labour force, and the price of those skills, determine how countries fare in the global market. OECD countries face increasing competition in the lower and, more recently, the mid-range skills segments. But even at these levels, many countries maintain a competitive advantage through technological advances, innovation and capital investments that boost productivity levels.

As services and production systems become more complex, they require workers with higher levels of education. A highly qualified workforce is thus important, not only for jobs in the high-end skills sector, but also for maintaining an overall cost advantage in the lower skills segments.

As the mobility of the global workforce increases, it is more important to strike the right balance between fostering overall equity in societies and offering strong economic incentives to attract and retain skilled workers. As such, Purchasing Power Parity (USD) – adjusted earnings provide a good gauge of the potential living standards that people with different educational levels can expect to gain in different countries.

The shift in the demand for skills and the shift in the composition of the workforce generate a substantial impact on the overall economy as well. Rising attainment levels in the population, better employment prospects and the increasing earnings that come with higher educational attainment can all contribute to growth and prosperity in OECD countries. In this context, labour income growth in GDP by educational categories provides a simple measure to illustrate this move towards higher skills segments and the impact it has on economic growth.

Other findings

- **Labour income growth among tertiary graduates has contributed over one percentage point in annual GDP growth over the past decade.** Even during the recent economic downturn, labour income growth among this group generated a positive impact on GDP of more than a half percentage point per year (between 2008 and 2010). While GDP shrank by almost 4% across OECD countries in 2009, labour income growth among tertiary graduates still made a positive contribution to GDP of 0.4%.

- **Labour income growth at the upper secondary or post-secondary non-tertiary levels of education has, on average, also made a positive contribution to growth over the past decade by adding 0.3% to GDP per year.** In Austria, the Czech Republic and Germany, these levels of education are more important to GDP growth than tertiary-level education, due to the significance of vocational education in these countries (over 55% of 25-64 year-olds hold a vocational qualification; see Indicator A1).

- **Annual labour costs increase substantially with educational attainment.** On average across OECD countries, a person without an upper secondary (ISCED 3/4) education costs USD 38 000 to employ, an individual with an upper secondary education costs USD 46 000, and a tertiary-educated person costs USD 68 000 per year.

- In Austria, Denmark, Ireland, Italy, Luxembourg, the Netherlands, Norway and the United States, over the course of a year, employers pay at least USD 20 000 more than the OECD average to employ individuals with tertiary degrees. **Earnings differentials for those with a tertiary education are typically large in many countries with overall low cost structures** (see Indicator A8); **yet in an OECD country comparison, the relative cost advantage is still for those with tertiary attainment.**

- On average across OECD countries, an employer can expect to pay an additional USD 25 000 per year for an experienced tertiary graduate (45-54 years old), compared to a recent graduate (25-34 years old). However, that cost climbs to almost USD 40 000 for an experienced tertiary graduate over someone with similar experience who has not completed an upper secondary education. **This skills premium increases markedly if there is a short supply of highly-educated workers.**

A10

Analysis

Long-term GDP growth and contribution of educational categories

With high labour costs and advanced industry structures, OECD countries need a steady supply of skills to move their economies forward. Education plays a key role in providing the labour market with those skills. The supply of highly-educated workers has increased rapidly in most OECD countries over the past several decades (see Indicator A1). Other indicators in *Education at a Glance* suggest that there is little evidence that this expansion has led to an excess supply; on the contrary, most indicators suggest that the expansion of higher education has not kept pace with the demand for those skills. As a result, there is a widening gap in employment prospects among individuals with different levels of education (see Indicator A7) and increasing earnings differentials in most countries (see Indicator A8).

Indicator A10 takes a closer look at how this evolution has influenced the economic growth of countries over the past decade by examining overall earnings growth for three broad educational categories in relation to GDP. Annual changes in total earnings for those without an upper secondary education (ISCED 0/1/2), for those with an upper secondary or post-secondary non-tertiary level of education (ISCED 3/4), and for those with a tertiary education (ISCED 5/6) are related to GDP growth and are compared over time. (See the *Methodology* section for the approach taken in this indicator.)

Chart A10.1 provides a breakdown of the contribution of these three educational categories to GDP growth over the past decade. The chart includes the results for countries with at least five years of growth estimates for the educational categories. GDP growth estimates are matched with the years of education growth estimates to gauge the impact of education on GDP growth. As such, comparing GDP growth across countries is not straightforward, since not all countries have data over the same or whole period.

On average for the 17 countries with a sufficient number of observations, about half of the GDP growth is related to labour income growth at the tertiary level of education. In France, Norway, Switzerland and the United Kingdom, 60% or more of growth is generated by those who have attained a tertiary education. In Denmark and Ireland, the labour income growth of those with tertiary education exceeds GDP growth, largely as a consequence of a strong shift towards higher skills and the impact of the global economic crisis on overall economic activity in these countries (Table A10.1).

In all these 17 countries except Austria, the Czech Republic and Germany, labour income growth among those with tertiary education make up the main source of income growth in GDP. Labour income growth at the upper secondary or post-secondary non-tertiary level of education (ISCED 3/4) has, on average, made a positive contribution to growth over the past decade by adding 0.3% to GDP per year. Labour income growth among those without an upper secondary education has been negative, with an annual impact on GDP of -0.1% over the period.

Shifting demand for skills during the height of the recession

In times of economic recession, large changes in demand for labour typically occur due to structural and transitory adjustments of the production of goods and services. In 2009, the economies of OECD countries shrank by almost 4% (3.8%) on average, and most countries faced economic hardship. Changes in total labour income for different educational categories provide a good yardstick of changing skill demand, as they comprise changes in part-time jobs, employment and earnings. Chart A10.2 examines the change in annual labour income growth related to GDP for the three educational categories during this year.

Despite the severe recession, labour income growth among tertiary graduates increased in 14 out of 20 countries in 2009, and on average added close to 0.4% to GDP during this difficult year. Economic activity in Denmark, Germany, Slovak Republic and the United Kingdom contracted by over 4.5% in 2009, yet at the same time, labour income growth among those with a tertiary education generated a positive impact on GDP. Similarly, in Norway and Switzerland, labour income growth among tertiary graduates added over 1.5% to GDP, in spite of the overall contraction of economic activity.

Chart A10.2. Change in annual labour-income growth in GDP, by educational categories (2009)
2009 GDP growth shown next to country names (%)

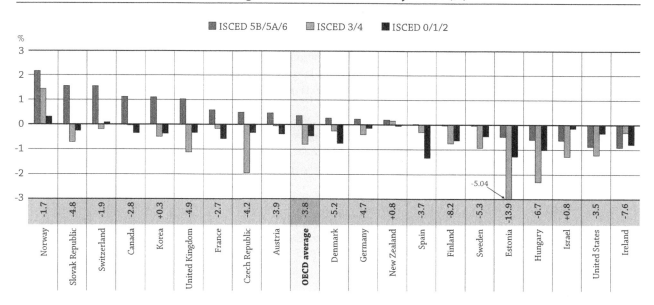

Countries are ranked in descending order of income growth in GDP among those with tertiary education (real percentage change from previous year).
Source: OECD. Table A10.1. See Annex 3 for notes (*www.oecd.org/edu/eag2012*).
StatLink http://dx.doi.org/10.1787/888932662295

Those with mid-range jobs and skills felt the most severe impact of the 2009 drop in GDP. On average across OECD countries, labour income growth for those with an upper secondary or post-secondary non-tertiary level of education had a negative impact on GDP of - 0.8% in 2009. The largest shift in the demand for high and mid-range skills appeared in the Czech Republic, Estonia, Slovak Republic and the United Kingdom, where the difference between the labour income growth of tertiary graduates and those with upper secondary or post-secondary non-tertiary education exceeded two percentage points of GDP. Only in New Zealand and Norway did the labour income growth of those with an upper secondary or post-secondary non-tertiary level of education contribute positively to GDP growth.

In 2009, labour income among those without an upper secondary education had, on average, a negative impact on GDP of -0.5%. In Estonia, Hungary and Spain, the contraction of labour income for this group generated a negative impact on GDP growth exceeding -1%.

The shift in the demand for skills has been accentuated by the recent economic downturn, which also revealed the vulnerability of those holding mid-level education and jobs. On average, labour income among those with an upper secondary or post-secondary non-tertiary education generated a negative annual impact on GDP growth of -0.2% between 2008 and 2010, the same as for those without an upper secondary education (Table A10.1).

Notwithstanding the severity of the recession, higher-educated individuals have succeeded in finding and keeping jobs as well as maintaining their bargaining position and earnings throughout the economic downturn and generated, through their labour income growth, a positive impact on GDP of over a half percentage point (0.55%) per year between 2008 and 2010.

Labour costs by skill (educational) levels across OECD countries

Table A10.2 presents annual labour costs, gross earnings and net earnings based on a direct exchange-rate comparison and Purchasing Power Parity (PPP)-adjusted comparison for three broad educational levels. Average labour costs have attracted considerable attention in cross-country comparisons in recent years.

However, average labour costs say little about the price that employers need to pay for different skills levels, which is a focus of this indicator.

Among 25-64 year-olds, annual labour costs increase sharply for both men and women with higher levels of education. On average across OECD countries, labour costs for those without an upper secondary education are USD 41 000 for men and USD 31 000 for women. Labour costs increase at the upper secondary level to USD 51 000 for men and USD 38 000 for women. The largest increase in labour costs is for highly-skilled workers: employers pay USD 77 000, on average, for a tertiary-educated man and USD 55 000 for a tertiary-educated woman.

Chart A10.3 shows how the price of labour varies among countries by educational attainment. On average, annual labour costs for men and women without an upper secondary education are USD 38 000; for those with an upper secondary education, USD 46 000; and for those with a tertiary education, USD 68 000 (Table A10.2).

Chart A10.3.   **Deviation from the OECD mean in annual labour costs, by educational attainment (2009 or latest available year)**

In equivalent USD, for 25-64 year-olds

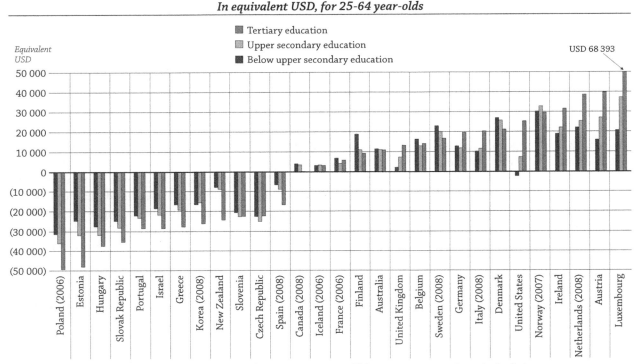

Countries are ranked in ascending order of the deviation from the OECD mean in annual labour costs of tertiary-educated individuals.
Source: OECD. Table A10.2. See Annex 3 for notes (*www.oecd.org/edu/eag2012*).
StatLink ⟲ http://dx.doi.org/10.1787/888932662314

The overall cost structure in Estonia, Hungary, Poland, Portugal and the Slovak Republic is considerably lower than in other OECD countries, and annual labour costs are at least USD 20 000 below the OECD average across all educational levels. Even though these countries have among the largest earnings differentials for tertiary-educated individuals (see Indicator A8), their relative cost advantage is still in the high-end skills segment. This suggests that earnings differentials will stay well above those in other OECD countries until a balance is reached between supply and demand (Table A10.2).

There is a substantial cost advantage in the high-end skills market in Greece, Israel, Korea, New Zealand and Spain, where those with higher education are relatively inexpensive compared to their less-educated peers.

A10

In the Czech Republic and Slovenia, the cost advantage is similar across all educational groups. Canada, France and Iceland deviate little from the OECD average in all segments. A few countries with overall higher cost levels show decreasing labour costs as educational levels rise. Among OECD countries, in Belgium, Denmark, Finland and Sweden, individuals with tertiary education are less expensive to employ than their counterparts with less education. A compressed wage structure and strong labour unions may explain these results to some extent (Chart A10.3).

Average labour costs for individuals with tertiary education increase substantially in other countries. In Austria, Ireland, Italy, Luxembourg, the Netherlands, Norway and the United States, annual labour costs are higher than the OECD average by some USD 20 000 or more, largely as a result of an overall higher cost structure and higher productivity differentials between educational categories.

Labour costs in the high-end skills segment

Given their high overall cost structure, OECD countries typically face stronger competition in the lower skills segments, where products and services are easier to replicate in other contexts, and where production can be shifted to low-cost countries. Their pricing power is still in the high-end skills market, even if labour costs are higher.

Employers pay an additional premium not only for education, but also for labour-market experience. A comparison between tertiary labour costs for 25-34 year-old men who recently graduated and those of 45-54 year-old men with 20-30 years of experience in the labour market indicates that costs vary substantially among countries. On average across OECD countries, an employer can expect to pay an additional USD 29 000 (approximately 50% more) per year for an experienced tertiary graduate. In Italy and Portugal, employers pay 120% or more for an experienced tertiary worker, while in Estonia, new graduates are paid more than their experienced peers (Tables A10.3 and A10.5).

Chart A10.4. **Labour cost ratio and attainment levels (2009 or latest available year)**
*Labour cost ratio of tertiary-educated individuals (5/6) to below upper secondary-educated individuals (0/1/2)
and attainment levels of 45-54 year-olds*

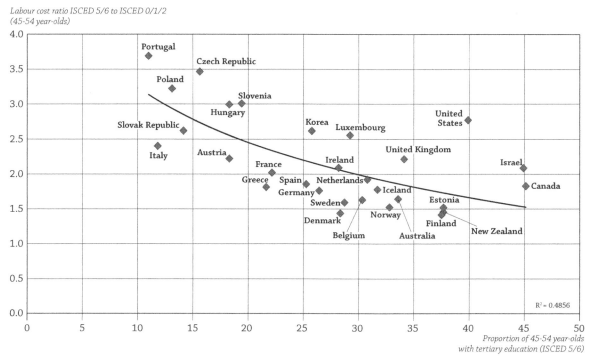

A10

However, the main difference in labour costs is linked to skill levels. Chart A10.4 compares the skills premium among 45-54 year-olds (labour costs for tertiary-educated individuals compared to individuals without an upper secondary education) and tertiary attainment levels for the same age group.

For a tertiary graduate, labour costs vary from over 3.5 times as much as those for an individual without an upper secondary education in Portugal, to less than 1.5 times as much in Denmark, Finland and New Zealand. The skills premium falls as the level of tertiary attainment rises. The skills premium for experienced workers is particularly high in countries with low educational attainment (Chart A10.4).

In the Czech Republic, Poland, Portugal and Slovenia, labour costs are three times as high for tertiary workers as for those without an upper secondary education, and fewer than 20% of individuals attain a tertiary education. This suggests that having too few highly-educated individuals leads to upward pressure on labour costs as employers compete for a small pool of skilled workers. The labour costs for tertiary graduates in the United States are more than 2.5 times those for individuals without an upper secondary education, even though tertiary attainment levels are high (40%). This is likely a reflection that demand still outstrips even a relatively large supply of tertiary graduates, or that productivity differentials between these two educational categories are particularly large (Chart A10.4).

Attractiveness of labour markets in OECD countries

There are substantial differences in labour-related tax policies among OECD countries. After accounting for employer non-tax compulsory payments, social contributions and income taxes, an individual between the ages of 45 and 54 without an upper secondary education can, on average across OECD countries, expect to keep 62% of labour costs in net income, while a tertiary-educated worker can expect to keep 56% of those costs (Chart A10.5).

An individual with a tertiary education can expect to receive 70% or more of the total labour costs in Israel, Korea and New Zealand, while such an individual receives less than 50% of total labour costs in Austria, Belgium, France, Germany, Hungary, Italy, the Netherlands and Sweden. However, the difference in average taxes and social contributions paid on labour costs between workers with high and low levels of education is largely driven by earnings differentials and to a lesser extent, by progressive tax rates. The difference is 10 percentage points or more in Hungary, Ireland, Israel, Luxembourg and Portugal, while in the Nordic countries it is typically below 5% (Table A10.5).

Chart A10.5. **Net income as a percentage of labour costs (2009 or latest available year)**
45-54 year-olds with below upper secondary education and tertiary education

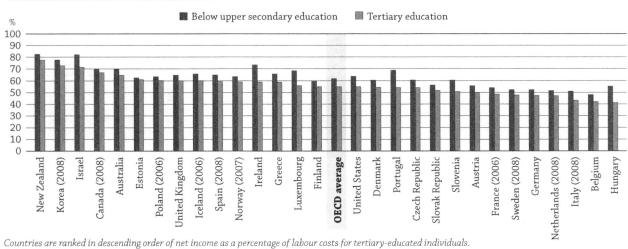

Countries are ranked in descending order of net income as a percentage of labour costs for tertiary-educated individuals.
Source: OECD. Table A10.5. See Annex 3 for notes (*www.oecd.org/edu/eag2012*).
StatLink ⎯⎯ http://dx.doi.org/10.1787/888932662352

The reward structure and overall tax rates have an impact on individuals' net income. The overall cost structure in different countries further determines the purchasing power of net earnings. Tables A10.2 through A10.6 provide information on net earnings by ISCED levels in Purchasing Power Parity (PPP)-adjusted USD to weigh the attractiveness of labour markets from the individual's perspective.

Chart A10.6 shows the PPP-adjusted net income differences by ISCED levels as a measure of the living standards that people with different educational levels can expect across OECD countries. The most attractive wages for tertiary-educated individuals are found in Australia, Austria, Ireland, Luxembourg, the Netherlands, the United Kingdom and the United States, where average net spending power exceeds USD 40 000 per year.

Chart A10.6. Net income differences by ISCED levels in PPP-adjusted USD (2009 or latest available year)
25-64 year-olds

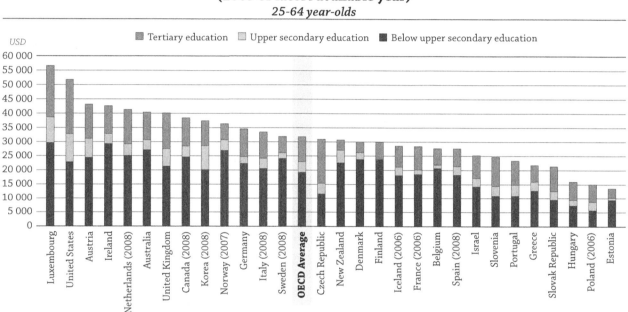

Countries are ranked in descending order of net income for all education levels.
Source: OECD. Table A10.2. See Annex 3 for notes (*www.oecd.org/edu/eag2012*).
StatLink ᵃ°ⁱˢᴸ http://dx.doi.org/10.1787/888932662371

The largest absolute gains in living standards are enjoyed by those with a tertiary education in Austria, the Czech Republic, Luxembourg, the Netherlands, the United Kingdom and the United States, where a person with a tertiary education can expect to have between USD 12 000 and USD 20 000 more in annual spending power compared to someone with an upper secondary education. On average across OECD countries, a tertiary education generates close to USD 9 000 and an upper secondary education close to USD 4 000 in additional net purchasing power every year (Chart A10.6).

The after-tax gains in purchasing power between those without an upper secondary education and those with a tertiary education is smallest in Belgium, Denmark, Estonia, Finland and Sweden, where the difference is less than USD 8 000 per year. The highest net earnings among those with low levels of education are found in Australia, Ireland, Luxembourg, the Netherlands and Norway, where an individual without an upper secondary education can expect to earn (PPP) at least USD 25 000 per year (Table A10.2).

Definitions

The data used for calculating **labour income growth in GDP by educational categories** (Table A10.1) uses earnings data for all employed individuals and includes part-time and part-year workers.

A10

Labour costs, gross and net income (Tables A10.2 through A10.6) are based on the earnings of individuals who work full-time, full-year, supplemented by employer cost data and employee income-tax data (see Annex 3 for deviations between countries in full-time definition and status). A three-year average USD exchange rate is used to determine the comparative advantages and assess average tax rates for different educational groups across OECD countries. To further explore the attractiveness of labour markets across OECD countries, net income differences are also given in Purchasing Power Parities (see Table X2.1 for exchange rates).

Purchasing Power Parities (PPP) are currency conversion rates that equalise the purchasing power in different countries by eliminating differences in price levels between countries.

Methodology

There are three methods to measure the level of activity in the economy: the expenditures (Gross Domestic Product or GDP), the income (Gross Domestic Income or GDI), and the value added approach. Gross Domestic Income (GDI) is analytically equivalent to Gross Domestic Product (GDP). Due to measurement errors, slight differences can sometimes occur among the measures.

A simple and relatively straightforward way of measuring the contribution of education to GDP growth is to relate changes in total labour income to the overall changes of GDP between years. To link education and growth, changes in total labour income by different educational categories are related to GDP and provide an indication of the economic benefits that different educational groups generate to the economy. The approach is analogous to the GDP growth (percentage change from previous year) equation $((GDP(t)-GDP(t-1))/GDP(t-1)$ and measures the share of labour compensation in GDP growth for different educational groups. All factors at market prices are deflated by constant prices (GDP deflator). Data on GDP and labour income was extracted from the OECD National Account statistics database on 14 September 2011 for the purpose of calculating this indicator.

Even if there is no doubt about the relationship between the educational attainment levels of a population and its productivity, there is no consensus on whether this relationship can be appropriately demonstrated by showing the development of income levels by educational attainment levels. Using the income approach to measure GDP may say more about the distribution than the production of GDP. Thus, data in Indicator A10 may primarily indicate the success of different social groups, defined by their educational attainment, in securing additional income generated through economic growth. Whether or not the increase in income of one group really reflects its contribution to economic growth is an assumption that requires further testing.

GDP measured by the income side includes compensation of employees, gross operating surplus, gross mixed income, and adjustments for taxes and subsidies on production and imports. Broken down, compensation of employees constitutes the total remuneration for work and includes wages and salaries, as well as employer contributions towards social security and similar programmes.

Employer contributions are not included in the INES LSO earnings data collection, which is generally based on labour force and household surveys. As such, the total earnings by different educational categories are scaled to fit the total labour income measure in National Accounts (NA). Differences in employment measures in national accounts and labour force surveys have been explored in earlier work (OECD, 1998).

The underlying assumption for this adjustment is that labour force (household) survey earnings accurately reflect the overall distribution of earnings across different educational levels, and that employer contributions are not too progressive/regressive across different earnings levels. A sensitivity analysis of progressive/regressive employer contribution has been made, and within a reasonable difference between educational groups in the employer rate of contributions (+/-15%), the impact on the growth estimates is on the second decimal (and marginally so).

Examining wages to compute the contribution of different labour/educational categories to economic growth combines two concepts – increases in employment and increases in total factor productivity (TFP) – into one single measure. However, this examination misses a key aspect of education that relates to the additional positive effects over and above those of earnings (spill-over and other positive externalities). The shifts in the contribution of educational categories to growth documented in this indicator should thus be considered as a lower bound for the overall effect that education has on economic activity. For discussions on whether education has a permanent or transitory effect, see also Arnold, et al. (2007).

For Tables A10.2 to A10.6, the full-time and full-year earnings are supplemented with information on employers' social contributions and non-tax compulsory payments from the OECD's *Taxing Wages Database*. Employer's social contributions (which are generally paid directly to government) and non-tax compulsory payments (which are stipulated by law but are typically paid into private insurance schemes) make up the additional compensation paid by employers on top of gross earnings. In some countries, social contributions are borne almost exclusively by the individual and paid out of the salary received. In this case, social contributions are included in gross earnings. Some countries apply a flat rate that is independent of the level of earnings, while others have a progressive rate, or floors or caps on social contributions, which change the level of contributions depending on the level of earnings.

The OECD calculates taxes based on the Taxing Wages model. The annual *Taxing Wages* publication provides details of taxes paid on wages in all 34 OECD countries. The information contained in the report covers the personal income tax and social security contributions paid by employees and their employers, and cash benefits received by families. The results allow quantitative cross-country comparisons of labour-cost levels and the overall tax-and-benefit position of single persons and families. The 2010 edition of the *Taxing Wages* report (OECD, 2010) offers accurate estimates of the tax/benefit position of employees in 2009. It also shows definitive data on the tax/benefit position of employees for the year 2008 and tax burdens for the period 2000-09.

The statistical data for Israel are supplied by and under the responsibility of the relevant Israeli authorities. The use of such data by the OECD is without prejudice to the status of the Golan Heights, East Jerusalem and Israeli settlements in the West Bank under the terms of international law.

References

Arnold, J., A. Bassanini and S. Scarpetta (2007), "Solow or Lucas?: Testing Growth Models Using Panel Data from OECD Countries", *OECD Economics Department Working Papers*, No. 592, OECD Publishing.

OECD (1998), "Employment Measures in the OECD National Accounts: Comparison between National Accounts and Labour Force Statistics", OECD Meeting of National Accounts Experts, OECD Publishing.

OECD (2010), *Taxing Wages 2009*, OECD Publishing.

The following additional material relevant to this indicator is available on line:

- *Table A10.4. Annual labour costs, full-time gross and net earnings by ISCED levels in equivalent USD, 35-44 year-olds (2009 or latest available year)*
  StatLink 🔗 http://dx.doi.org/10.1787/888932665677

- *Table A10.6. Annual labour costs, full-time gross and net earnings by ISCED levels in equivalent USD, 55-64 year-olds (2009 or latest available year)*
  StatLink 🔗 http://dx.doi.org/10.1787/888932665715

A10

Table A10.1. [1/3] GDP growth (real percentage change from previous year) and labour income growth, by educational category (2000-10) (%)

	ISCED/growth	2000	2001	2002	2003	2004	2005	2006	2007	2008	2009	2010	Average	Average 2
Australia	0/1/2	m	m	m	m	m	m	m	m	m	m	m	m	m
	3/4	m	m	m	m	m	m	m	m	m	m	m	m	m
	5B/5A/6	m	m	m	m	m	m	m	m	m	m	m	m	m
	Total labour income growth	0.83	0.93	1.44	1.59	1.81	1.46	2.32	1.89	-0.36	1.00	m	1.29	m
	GDP growth	2.07	3.90	3.27	4.16	2.96	3.08	3.56	3.83	1.45	2.28	2.58	3.01	m
Austria	0/1/2	m	m	m	m	m	-0.23	0.44	-0.19	-0.38	-0.04	-0.08	-0.08
	3/4	m	m	m	m	m	m	1.21	0.85	1.10	-0.06	0.26	0.67	0.67
	5B/5A/6	m	m	m	m	m	m	0.41	0.17	0.72	0.46	0.20	0.39	0.39
	Total labour income growth	1.16	0.01	0.20	0.46	0.15	0.73	1.38	1.46	1.63	0.02	0.42	0.69	0.98
	GDP growth	3.65	0.52	1.65	0.80	2.54	2.46	3.60	3.73	2.18	-3.89	1.96	1.75	1.52
Belgium	0/1/2	m	m	m	m	m	-0.52	m	m	m	m	0.19	-0.17	-0.17
	3/4	m	m	m	m	m	0.76	m	m	m	m	-0.83	-0.03	-0.03
	5B/5A/6	m	m	m	m	m	0.26	m	m	m	m	0.60	0.43	0.43
	Total labour income growth	1.36	1.76	0.94	-0.07	0.29	0.50	1.17	1.42	1.75	0.09	-0.04	0.83	0.23
	GDP growth	3.68	0.79	1.37	0.79	3.23	1.71	2.69	2.92	1.00	-2.75	2.18	1.60	1.95
Canada	0/1/2	-0.21	-0.17	0.20	-0.18	-0.20	0.03	-0.16	0.03	-0.12	-0.35	m	-0.11	-0.11
	3/4	0.30	0.48	0.45	-0.38	-0.07	0.68	0.25	-0.13	0.03	-0.01	m	0.16	0.16
	5B/5A/6	2.03	1.41	0.87	1.25	1.58	0.49	2.02	1.29	0.17	1.12	m	1.22	1.22
	Total labour income growth	2.12	1.72	1.52	0.69	1.31	1.21	2.11	1.19	0.09	0.76	0.69	1.22	1.27
	GDP growth	5.23	1.78	2.92	1.88	3.12	3.02	2.82	2.20	0.69	-2.77	3.21	2.19	2.09
Chile		m	m	m	m	m	m	m	m	m	m	m	m	m
Czech Republic	0/1/2	m	m	m	m	m	0.01	0.04	0.07	0.10	-0.33	0.03	-0.01	-0.01
	3/4	m	m	m	m	m	1.74	2.02	1.69	1.41	-1.95	0.66	0.93	0.93
	5B/5A/6	m	m	m	m	m	1.32	0.83	0.74	0.99	0.49	0.73	0.85	0.85
	Total labour income growth	1.72	1.39	1.72	2.20	0.82	3.06	2.89	2.50	2.49	-1.79	1.42	1.67	1.76
	GDP growth	3.65	2.46	1.90	3.60	4.48	6.32	6.81	6.13	2.46	-4.15	2.35	3.27	3.32
Denmark	0/1/2	m	m	-0.16	-0.63	-0.29	-0.05	0.17	0.26	-0.13	-0.76	-0.90	-0.28	-0.28
	3/4	m	m	0.18	-0.01	-0.11	0.32	0.28	0.91	0.22	-0.26	-1.06	0.05	0.05
	5B/5A/6	m	m	0.66	1.18	0.76	0.76	1.46	1.12	0.88	0.26	0.29	0.82	0.82
	Total labour income growth	0.68	1.48	0.68	0.53	0.37	1.03	1.91	2.29	0.97	-0.75	-1.66	0.68	0.60
	GDP growth	3.53	0.70	0.47	0.38	2.30	2.45	3.39	1.58	-1.12	-5.21	1.75	0.93	0.66
Estonia	0/1/2	m	m	m	m	m	m	m	m	m	-1.27	-0.59	-0.93	-0.93
	3/4	m	m	m	m	m	m	m	m	m	-5.04	-1.43	-3.23	-3.23
	5B/5A/6	m	m	m	m	m	m	m	m	m	-0.49	-1.34	-0.91	-0.91
	Total labour income growth	3.44	2.68	3.17	3.40	3.24	4.03	4.85	5.44	2.06	-6.80	-3.36	2.01	-5.08
	GDP growth	9.97	7.52	7.94	7.56	7.23	9.43	10.56	6.92	-5.06	-13.90	3.11	4.66	-5.40
Finland	0/1/2	-0.11	0.00	-0.24	-0.06	-0.10	-0.07	-0.05	-0.03	0.07	-0.64	m	-0.12	-0.12
	3/4	0.78	0.88	0.33	0.85	0.73	1.01	0.84	0.72	0.89	-0.75	m	0.63	0.63
	5B/5A/6	1.02	0.72	0.72	0.93	1.10	1.35	1.00	0.72	1.30	0.00	m	0.89	0.89
	Total labour income growth	1.69	1.61	0.81	1.72	1.73	2.29	1.79	1.41	2.26	-1.39	0.92	1.35	1.39
	GDP growth	5.32	2.28	1.83	2.01	4.12	2.92	4.41	5.34	0.98	-8.23	3.64	2.24	2.10
France	0/1/2	m	m	m	m	-0.49	0.07	-0.61	-0.55	-0.02	-0.58	m	-0.36	-0.36
	3/4	m	m	m	m	0.26	0.40	-0.28	0.51	-0.03	-0.17	m	0.12	0.12
	5B/5A/6	m	m	m	m	1.17	0.42	2.00	0.77	0.33	0.58	m	0.88	0.88
	Total labour income growth	2.00	1.28	0.98	0.47	0.94	0.89	1.11	0.73	0.28	-0.16	0.68	0.84	0.63
	GDP growth	3.68	1.84	0.93	0.90	2.54	1.83	2.47	2.29	-0.08	-2.73	1.48	1.38	1.05
Germany	0/1/2	-0.75	m	m	1.18	-0.20	0.10	-0.25	-0.18	0.06	-0.14	-0.10	-0.03	-0.03
	3/4	1.00	m	m	-0.28	0.05	-0.75	0.86	0.48	1.72	-0.40	-0.32	0.26	0.26
	5B/5A/6	2.23	m	m	-1.27	-0.24	0.01	-0.15	-0.13	-0.47	0.23	1.37	0.18	0.18
	Total labour income growth	2.48	0.26	-0.47	-0.37	-0.39	-0.65	0.46	0.17	1.31	-0.32	0.95	0.31	0.41
	GDP growth	3.21	1.24	0.00	-0.22	1.21	0.75	3.37	2.66	0.99	-4.72	3.63	1.10	1.21
Greece	0/1/2	m	m	m	m	m	m	m	m	m	m	m	m	m
	3/4	m	m	m	m	m	m	m	m	m	m	m	m	m
	5B/5A/6	m	m	m	m	m	m	m	m	m	m	m	m	m
	Total labour income growth	1.12	0.82	3.88	1.50	1.74	1.01	1.54	1.98	1.40	0.49	-3.04	1.13	m
	GDP growth	4.48	4.20	3.44	5.94	4.37	2.28	5.17	4.28	1.02	-2.04	-4.47	2.61	m
Hungary	0/1/2	0.54	m	m	0.03	0.01	-0.10	-0.10	0.17	0.19	-1.01	0.06	-0.02	-0.02
	3/4	1.62	m	m	0.58	0.84	1.59	-0.36	0.54	-0.11	-2.31	-0.87	0.17	0.17
	5B/5A/6	1.08	m	m	2.06	0.77	1.04	1.56	-0.22	0.42	-0.61	-0.32	0.64	0.64
	Total labour income growth	3.24	2.44	2.45	2.68	1.63	2.52	1.10	0.49	0.50	-3.93	-1.12	1.09	0.79
	GDP growth	4.90	3.77	4.14	3.98	4.52	3.17	3.63	0.77	0.83	-6.69	1.17	2.20	1.81

Note: In the column listing Average 2, GDP is matched to years with labour income growth estimates for educational categories to provide comparable GDP figures to the years of income growth by educational level.
Source: OECD. LSO Network special data collection on full-time, full-year earnings, Economic Working Group.
Please refer to the Reader's Guide for information concerning the symbols replacing missing data.
StatLink ⟦≡⟧ http://dx.doi.org/10.1787/888932665620

Table A10.1. [2/3] GDP growth (real percentage change from previous year) and labour income growth, by educational category (2000-10) (%)

A10

	ISCED/growth	2000	2001	2002	2003	2004	2005	2006	2007	2008	2009	2010	Average	Average 2
Iceland		m	m	m	m	m	m	m	m	m	m	m	m	m
Ireland	0/1/2	m	m	m	m	m	0.58	0.11	-0.06	-0.57	-0.80	-1.34	-0.35	-0.35
	3/4	m	m	m	m	m	1.48	-3.48	0.47	0.57	-0.31	-1.87	-0.53	-0.53
	5B/5A/6	m	m	m	m	m	1.72	5.86	2.52	1.24	-0.91	1.99	2.07	2.07
	Total labour income growth	3.01	2.22	0.96	2.07	2.54	3.77	2.49	2.93	1.25	-2.02	-1.23	1.64	1.20
	GDP growth	9.71	5.70	6.55	4.41	4.60	6.02	5.32	5.63	-3.55	-7.58	-1.04	3.25	0.80
Israel	0/1/2	m	m	m	m	m	m	0.14	0.11	-0.02	-0.15	-0.18	-0.02	-0.02
	3/4	m	m	m	m	m	m	1.11	1.24	0.50	-1.28	1.11	0.54	0.54
	5B/5A/6	m	m	m	m	m	m	2.17	2.07	2.24	-0.63	2.09	1.59	1.59
	Total labour income growth	4.56	1.60	-1.60	-0.56	1.47	2.46	3.42	3.42	2.72	-2.05	3.02	1.68	2.10
	GDP growth	9.25	-0.22	-0.58	1.51	4.84	4.94	5.59	5.50	4.03	0.84	4.85	3.69	4.16
Italy	0/1/2	m	m	m	m	m	m	m	m	m	m	m	m	m
	3/4	m	m	m	m	m	m	m	m	m	m	m	m	m
	5B/5A/6	m	m	m	m	m	m	m	m	m	m	m	m	m
	Total labour income growth	0.91	0.98	0.51	0.31	0.37	1.06	1.11	0.53	0.45	-1.42	0.09	0.45	m
	GDP growth	3.69	1.82	0.45	-0.02	1.53	0.66	2.04	1.48	-1.32	-5.22	1.30	0.58	m
Japan	0/1/2	m	m	m	m	m	m	m	m	m	m	m	m	m
	3/4	m	m	m	m	m	m	m	m	m	m	m	m	m
	5B/5A/6	m	m	m	m	m	m	m	m	m	m	m	m	m
	Total labour income growth	1.23	0.28	-0.50	0.05	0.11	1.07	1.50	0.07	0.61	-2.03	m	0.24	m
	GDP growth	2.86	0.18	0.26	1.41	2.74	1.93	2.04	2.36	-1.17	-6.29	3.94	0.94	m
Korea	0/1/2	m	m	0.25	-0.65	-0.01	-0.07	0.05	-0.11	-0.24	-0.37	m	-0.14	-0.14
	3/4	m	m	0.85	-0.18	0.75	0.71	0.71	0.13	-0.17	-0.50	m	0.29	0.29
	5B/5A/6	m	m	1.76	3.12	1.53	2.33	2.04	2.17	1.69	1.10	m	1.97	1.97
	Total labour income growth	3.73	2.44	2.87	2.29	2.27	2.97	2.80	2.19	1.28	0.23	m	2.31	2.11
	GDP growth	8.80	3.97	7.15	2.80	4.62	3.96	5.18	5.11	2.30	0.32	6.16	4.58	3.93
Luxembourg	0/1/2	m	m	m	m	m	m	m	m	m	m	0.14	m	m
	3/4	m	m	m	m	m	m	m	m	m	m	0.02	m	m
	5B/5A/6	m	m	m	m	m	m	m	m	m	m	-1.21	m	m
	Total labour income growth	4.28	4.40	2.13	-1.38	1.85	1.43	-0.07	2.09	1.19	1.40	-1.05	1.48	m
	GDP growth	8.44	2.52	4.11	1.55	4.40	5.43	4.97	6.64	1.44	-3.64	3.52	3.58	m
Mexico		m	m	m	m	m	m	m	m	m	m	m	m	m
Netherlands	0/1/2	m	m	m	m	m	m	m	m	m	m	m	m	m
	3/4	m	m	m	m	m	m	m	m	m	m	m	m	m
	5B/5A/6	m	m	m	m	m	m	m	m	m	m	m	m	m
	Total labour income growth	1.57	1.09	0.59	0.36	0.72	-0.51	1.12	1.91	1.33	0.65	-0.57	0.75	m
	GDP growth	3.94	1.93	0.08	0.34	2.24	2.05	3.39	3.92	1.88	-3.92	1.77	1.60	m
New Zealand	0/1/2	-0.13	-0.22	0.57	-0.12	0.36	0.12	0.92	-0.85	0.29	-0.05	m	0.09	0.09
	3/4	0.24	1.16	0.39	1.03	-0.32	-1.14	1.16	-0.99	1.71	0.16	m	0.34	0.34
	5B/5A/6	0.65	0.46	1.64	1.00	1.99	3.25	-0.78	2.97	-0.82	0.20	m	1.05	1.05
	Total labour income growth	0.76	1.39	2.60	1.91	2.02	2.23	1.30	1.14	1.18	0.31	m	1.48	1.48
	GDP growth	2.45	3.47	4.89	3.88	3.57	3.25	2.23	2.86	-1.07	0.79	2.50	2.62	2.63
Norway	0/1/2	m	0.83	0.29	-0.33	-0.26	-0.36	0.04	0.55	-0.18	0.31	m	0.10	0.10
	3/4	m	2.51	1.24	-0.30	-0.24	-0.66	-0.09	1.30	-0.19	1.43	m	0.56	0.56
	5B/5A/6	m	2.49	1.38	0.45	0.32	0.01	0.36	1.61	0.36	2.17	m	1.02	1.02
	Total labour income growth	-4.18	1.88	2.92	-0.19	-0.18	-1.02	0.31	3.46	-0.01	3.91	-1.28	0.51	1.23
	GDP growth	3.25	1.99	1.50	1.01	3.86	2.74	2.28	2.73	0.73	-1.71	0.35	1.70	1.68
Poland	0/1/2	m	m	-0.46	m	m	m	m	m	m	m	m	m	m
	3/4	m	m	-1.34	m	m	m	m	m	m	m	m	m	m
	5B/5A/6	m	m	0.49	m	m	m	m	m	m	m	m	m	m
	Total labour income growth	0.44	1.29	-1.31	0.52	-0.09	0.93	1.92	2.43	3.70	0.18	2.63	1.15	m
	GDP growth	4.26	1.21	1.44	3.87	5.34	3.62	6.23	6.79	5.13	1.61	3.80	3.93	m
Portugal	0/1/2	m	m	m	m	m	-0.29	-0.74	m	m	m	m	-0.51	-0.51
	3/4	m	m	m	m	m	0.32	0.40	m	m	m	m	0.36	0.36
	5B/5A/6	m	m	m	m	m	1.18	0.43	m	m	m	m	0.81	0.81
	Total labour income growth	2.52	0.95	0.57	-0.17	0.46	1.22	0.08	0.42	0.88	0.48	0.10	0.68	0.65
	GDP growth	3.93	1.97	0.71	-0.93	1.56	0.76	1.44	2.39	-0.01	-2.51	1.33	0.97	1.10
Slovak Republic	0/1/2	m	m	m	m	m	m	m	m	m	-0.26	-0.04	-0.15	-0.15
	3/4	m	m	m	m	m	m	m	m	m	-0.71	0.00	-0.36	-0.36
	5B/5A/6	m	m	m	m	m	m	m	m	m	1.55	0.31	0.93	0.93
	Total labour income growth	0.48	0.36	1.75	1.03	-0.10	2.85	2.61	3.37	2.27	0.58	0.27	1.41	0.43
	GDP growth	1.37	3.48	4.58	4.77	5.06	6.66	8.50	10.52	5.83	-4.78	4.02	4.55	-0.38

Note: In the column listing Average 2, GDP is matched to years with labour income growth estimates for educational categories to provide comparable GDP figures to the years of income growth by educational level.
Source: OECD. LSO Network special data collection on full-time, full-year earnings, Economic Working Group.
Please refer to the Reader's Guide for information concerning the symbols replacing missing data.
StatLink ⇒ http://dx.doi.org/10.1787/888932665620

A10

Table A10.1. [3/3] GDP growth (real percentage change from previous year) and labour income growth, by educational category (2000-10) (%)

	ISCED/growth	2000	2001	2002	2003	2004	2005	2006	2007	2008	2009	2010	Average	Average 2
OECD Slovenia	0/1/2	m	m	m	m	m	m	m	0.13	m	m	-0.13	0.00	0.00
	3/4	m	m	m	m	m	m	m	1.35	m	m	0.07	0.71	0.71
	5B/5A/6	m	m	m	m	m	m	m	1.32	m	m	1.20	1.26	1.26
	Total labour income growth	3.60	1.97	1.08	1.18	2.45	2.07	2.47	2.81	2.87	-1.89	1.14	1.80	1.97
	GDP growth	4.27	2.94	3.83	2.93	4.40	4.01	5.85	6.87	3.59	-8.01	1.38	2.91	4.12
Spain	0/1/2	m	m	m	m	m	m	m	m	-0.31	-1.34	m	-0.82	-0.82
	3/4	m	m	m	m	m	m	m	m	0.13	-0.30	m	-0.09	-0.09
	5B/5A/6	m	m	m	m	m	m	m	m	1.76	0.03	m	0.89	0.89
	Total labour income growth	2.47	1.44	0.86	1.13	0.90	1.43	1.69	2.17	1.58	-1.62	-1.21	0.99	0.99
	GDP growth	5.05	3.65	2.70	3.10	3.27	3.61	4.02	3.57	0.86	-3.72	-0.14	2.36	-1.43
Sweden	0/1/2	m	m	-0.18	-0.18	-0.12	-0.17	-0.22	0.00	-0.32	-0.47	-0.13	-0.20	-0.20
	3/4	m	m	0.41	0.31	0.75	0.62	0.46	1.30	-0.15	-0.93	0.65	0.38	0.38
	5B/5A/6	m	m	0.66	0.55	0.91	0.91	0.72	1.22	0.28	-0.03	0.84	0.67	0.67
	Total labour income growth	4.54	2.42	0.90	0.68	1.53	1.36	0.97	2.52	-0.19	-1.43	1.36	1.33	0.86
	GDP growth	4.45	1.26	2.48	2.34	4.23	3.16	4.30	3.31	-0.61	-5.33	5.69	2.30	2.17
Switzerland	0/1/2	-0.33	0.16	-0.08	-0.13	-0.13	0.10	-0.03	-0.15	-0.08	0.08	0.57	0.00	0.00
	3/4	0.93	0.62	1.05	-1.53	-1.11	0.53	0.08	-0.09	-0.11	-0.19	-0.14	0.00	0.00
	5B/5A/6	1.31	2.25	0.42	1.09	0.95	1.59	1.27	1.93	1.74	1.55	-0.02	1.28	1.28
	Total labour income growth	1.90	3.02	1.40	-0.57	-0.28	2.21	1.32	1.69	1.55	1.44	0.41	1.28	1.28
	GDP growth	3.58	1.15	0.44	-0.20	2.53	2.64	3.63	3.64	2.10	-1.88	2.71	1.85	1.85
Turkey		m	m	m	m	m	m	m	m	m	m	m	m	m
United Kingdom	0/1/2	0.00	0.09	-0.28	-0.15	0.06	-0.22	-0.13	0.05	-0.16	-0.33	-0.26	-0.12	-0.12
	3/4	1.46	1.03	0.19	-0.39	0.10	0.91	-0.51	-0.11	0.00	-1.12	-0.88	0.06	0.06
	5B/5A/6	1.78	0.96	0.64	1.58	1.03	0.77	1.79	1.36	-0.21	1.02	1.18	1.08	1.08
	Total labour income growth	3.25	2.08	0.54	1.03	1.19	1.47	1.15	1.31	-0.37	-0.43	0.03	1.02	1.02
	GDP growth	3.92	2.46	2.10	2.81	2.95	2.17	2.79	2.68	-0.07	-4.87	1.35	1.66	1.66
United States	0/1/2	0.08	0.21	-0.17	-0.06	0.05	0.04	0.03	-0.23	0.00	-0.34	-0.06	-0.04	-0.04
	3/4	0.52	-0.25	-0.20	0.15	0.36	0.11	-0.03	0.52	-0.37	-1.22	-0.26	-0.06	-0.06
	5B/5A/6	2.75	0.63	0.71	1.24	0.75	1.07	1.42	0.90	0.67	-0.87	0.85	0.92	0.92
	Total labour income growth	3.35	0.59	0.33	1.32	1.16	1.23	1.42	1.19	0.30	-2.43	0.54	0.82	0.82
	GDP growth	4.17	1.09	1.83	2.55	3.48	3.08	2.66	1.91	-0.36	-3.53	3.02	1.81	1.81
OECD average	0/1/2	-0.11	0.13	-0.02	-0.11	-0.10	-0.05	-0.06	-0.02	-0.09	-0.46	-0.17	-0.19	-0.19
	3/4	0.86	0.92	0.32	-0.01	0.15	0.51	0.26	0.59	0.40	-0.80	-0.31	0.08	0.08
	5B/5A/6	1.61	1.27	0.90	1.10	0.97	1.09	1.36	1.25	0.74	0.36	0.55	0.91	0.91
	Total labour income growth	2.01	1.56	1.13	0.86	1.07	1.54	1.67	1.89	1.23	-0.63	0.00	1.14	0.79
	GDP growth	4.69	2.39	2.48	2.33	3.60	3.34	4.16	4.02	0.84	-3.81	2.30	2.39	1.50
EU21 average	0/1/2	-0.08	0.05	-0.26	0.03	-0.16	-0.06	-0.18	0.03	-0.12	-0.64	-0.24	-0.26	-0.26
	3/4	1.21	0.95	-0.04	0.18	0.38	0.76	0.13	0.79	0.52	-1.10	-0.43	0.01	0.01
	5B/5A/6	1.53	0.84	0.63	0.84	0.79	0.89	1.45	0.87	0.66	0.20	0.45	0.74	0.74
	Total labour income growth	2.19	1.57	1.09	0.92	1.06	1.55	1.61	1.92	1.41	-0.96	-0.16	1.11	0.49
	GDP growth	4.72	2.58	2.51	2.42	3.63	3.40	4.52	4.31	0.78	-4.87	1.89	2.35	1.02
Other G20 Argentina		m	m	m	m	m	m	m	m	m	m	m	m	m
Brazil		m	m	m	m	m	m	m	m	m	m	m	m	m
China		m	m	m	m	m	m	m	m	m	m	m	m	m
India		m	m	m	m	m	m	m	m	m	m	m	m	m
Indonesia		m	m	m	m	m	m	m	m	m	m	m	m	m
Russian Federation		m	m	m	m	m	m	m	m	m	m	m	m	m
Saudi Arabia		m	m	m	m	m	m	m	m	m	m	m	m	m
South Africa		m	m	m	m	m	m	m	m	m	m	m	m	m
G20 average		m	m	m	m	m	m	m	m	m	m	m	m	m

Note: In the column listing Average 2, GDP is matched to years with labour income growth estimates for educational categories to provide comparable GDP figures to the years of income growth by educational level.
Source: OECD. LSO Network special data collection on full-time, full-year earnings, Economic Working Group.
Please refer to the Reader's Guide for information concerning the symbols replacing missing data.
StatLink ᨏᨏᨏ http://dx.doi.org/10.1787/888932665620

Table A10.2. [1/2] Annual labour costs, full-time gross earnings and annual net income, by ISCED levels in equivalent USD, 25-64 year-olds (2009 or latest available year)

A10

	Year	Source	Gender	Annual labour costs — Three-year average exchange rate			Gross annual full-time earnings — Three-year average exchange rate			Annual net income — Three-year average exchange rate			Annual net income — PPP-adjusted exchange rate		
				0/1/2 (1)	3/4 (2)	5B/5A/6 (3)	0/1/2 (4)	3/4 (5)	5B/5A/6 (6)	0/1/2 (7)	3/4 (8)	5B/5A/6 (9)	0/1/2 (10)	3/4 (11)	5B/5A/6 (12)
Australia	2009	National	Men	53 552	61 793	89 543	46 404	53 545	77 591	36 798	41 584	56 837	28 985	32 754	44 769
			Women	40 934	44 910	64 474	35 471	38 915	55 869	29 746	31 968	43 175	23 430	25 180	34 008
			M+W	49 269	57 321	78 520	42 693	49 670	68 040	34 404	38 929	51 249	27 099	30 663	40 368
Austria	2009	National	Men	61 766	78 976	117 697	47 833	61 160	93 561	33 247	40 341	58 734	27 198	33 001	48 047
			Women	45 068	61 308	88 336	34 902	47 479	68 409	25 957	33 047	44 096	21 234	27 034	36 073
			M+W	53 804	73 291	107 502	41 667	56 758	84 077	29 771	38 061	52 762	24 354	31 136	43 162
Belgium	2009	National	Men	56 736	61 589	90 186	44 043	47 666	69 090	27 340	28 974	38 234	21 229	22 497	29 688
			Women	46 288	52 525	69 782	36 242	40 899	53 784	24 122	26 021	31 732	18 730	20 204	24 639
			M+W	54 166	59 178	81 671	42 124	45 867	62 661	26 573	28 162	35 627	20 633	21 867	27 663
Canada	2008	National	Men	46 627	55 506	77 717	41 841	50 306	71 623	32 054	37 727	51 953	26 870	31 626	43 552
			Women	30 365	39 840	55 392	27 252	35 712	50 197	22 325	28 056	37 652	18 715	23 519	31 563
			M+W	41 953	49 846	67 880	37 598	44 896	62 132	29 313	34 003	45 849	24 573	28 504	38 434
Chile				m	m	m	m	m	m	m	m	m	m	m	m
Czech Republic	2009	National	Men	17 285	22 938	50 361	12 899	17 118	37 583	10 208	13 115	27 215	12 841	16 498	34 234
			Women	13 341	18 289	34 055	9 956	13 648	25 414	8 180	10 724	18 831	10 290	13 490	23 688
			M+W	15 278	21 271	45 300	11 401	15 874	33 806	9 176	12 258	24 613	11 543	15 419	30 961
Denmark	2009	National	Men	69 973	78 538	100 461	69 566	78 131	100 054	42 057	45 599	53 749	25 572	27 725	32 681
			Women	57 858	63 125	77 094	57 451	62 718	76 686	35 171	38 188	45 062	21 385	23 219	27 398
			M+W	64 825	71 997	88 720	64 417	71 589	88 312	39 148	43 167	49 384	23 803	26 246	30 026
Estonia	2009	National	Men	15 725	17 631	24 925	11 746	13 170	18 618	9 627	10 731	14 960	11 064	12 334	17 194
			Women	9 091	10 612	16 901	6 791	7 927	12 624	5 780	6 662	10 308	6 643	7 656	11 847
			M+W	13 147	14 346	19 480	9 820	10 716	14 551	8 132	8 827	11 804	9 346	10 144	13 566
Finland	2009	National	Men	62 416	63 764	90 035	50 745	51 841	73 199	36 384	37 007	48 384	25 531	25 968	33 952
			Women	49 065	49 862	67 126	39 890	40 538	54 574	30 129	30 505	38 510	21 142	21 406	27 024
			M+W	56 688	57 290	76 893	46 088	46 577	62 515	33 724	34 008	42 720	23 665	23 864	29 977
France	2006	National	Men	51 569	54 324	83 916	36 240	38 175	58 911	26 596	27 918	41 131	20 498	21 516	31 700
			Women	32 828	40 988	61 474	26 068	30 464	43 200	20 488	22 652	31 349	15 790	17 458	24 161
			M+W	44 687	50 525	73 450	32 457	35 602	51 598	24 013	26 160	36 911	18 506	20 162	28 447
Germany	2009	National	Men	55 204	62 916	93 756	46 206	52 660	79 674	28 585	31 585	44 336	23 774	26 269	36 874
			Women	40 259	48 450	73 011	33 696	40 553	61 110	22 393	25 849	35 311	18 624	21 498	29 369
			M+W	50 688	58 084	87 175	42 425	48 616	73 764	26 767	29 721	41 556	22 262	24 719	34 562
Greece	2009	National	Men	24 316	29 506	45 779	18 988	23 041	35 748	15 950	18 735	26 740	14 547	17 086	24 388
			Women	14 596	22 253	33 648	11 397	17 377	26 275	9 574	14 597	20 772	8 732	13 313	18 945
			M+W	21 216	27 012	39 987	16 567	21 094	31 225	13 916	17 508	23 891	12 692	15 968	21 789
Hungary	2009	National	Men	11 384	15 136	37 177	8 594	11 416	27 926	6 149	7 513	14 964	7 861	9 605	19 130
			Women	9 414	13 772	24 978	7 090	10 394	18 789	5 307	7 125	10 669	6 784	9 108	13 640
			M+W	10 361	14 531	30 169	7 813	10 963	22 677	5 711	7 341	12 497	7 302	9 385	15 976
Iceland	2006	SILC	Men	45 790	54 477	87 223	40 107	47 715	76 397	29 610	34 197	51 489	19 788	22 854	34 410
			Women	34 140	38 578	54 998	29 903	33 790	48 172	23 458	25 801	34 472	15 677	17 243	23 038
			M+W	41 062	49 768	70 780	35 966	43 591	61 995	27 113	31 711	42 806	18 120	21 192	28 607
Ireland	2009	National	Men	57 668	74 764	112 853	52 070	67 507	101 899	42 309	50 029	67 490	29 546	34 937	47 130
			Women	52 343	57 739	81 435	47 262	52 135	73 530	39 080	42 342	53 042	27 290	29 568	37 040
			M+W	56 709	68 332	99 201	51 205	61 699	89 572	41 877	47 125	61 064	29 244	32 908	42 643
Israel	2009	National	Men	20 350	27 006	45 174	18 955	25 090	42 323	16 857	21 243	32 150	14 777	18 622	28 184
			Women	14 535	19 600	31 409	13 590	18 266	29 267	12 889	16 365	23 971	11 299	14 346	21 014
			M+W	19 276	24 553	39 216	17 968	22 819	36 671	16 153	19 614	28 784	14 160	17 194	25 233
Italy	2008	National	Men	51 725	64 474	105 150	37 082	46 222	75 383	26 183	31 507	46 394	21 854	26 298	38 724
			Women	37 925	48 119	68 502	27 189	34 497	49 110	20 105	24 586	32 990	16 781	20 522	27 536
			M+W	48 071	57 902	87 867	34 463	41 510	62 993	24 566	28 927	40 100	20 504	24 145	33 470
Japan				m	m	m	m	m	m	m	m	m	m	m	m
Korea	2008	National	Men	25 585	36 323	46 605	21 689	30 792	39 522	19 748	27 238	34 055	24 114	33 261	41 584
			Women	15 830	20 723	29 775	13 420	17 568	25 241	12 326	16 060	22 814	15 051	19 611	27 858
			M+W	21 263	30 679	41 506	18 025	26 007	35 186	16 470	23 434	30 668	20 111	28 615	37 449

Note: Labour costs include non-tax compulsory payments (NTCP) and employer social contributions based on the OECD Taxing Wages Database (Centre for Tax Policy and Administration), except for the United States, for which Bureau of Labor Statistics information is used, and the United Kingdom, for which EU Labour Cost Survey data is used. SILC: Statistics on Income and Living Conditions (Eurostat). USD based on three-year moving average of currency exchange rates (OECD annual exchange rates) and last three columns on net income in USD (PPP) Purchasing Power Parity-adjusted for private consumption (see Table X2.1 for exchange rates).
Source: OECD. LSO Network special data collection on full-time, full-year earnings, Economic Working Group.
Please refer to the Reader's Guide for information concerning the symbols replacing missing data.
StatLink ⬛ http://dx.doi.org/10.1787/888932665639

A10

Table A10.2. [2/2] Annual labour costs, full-time gross earnings and annual net income, by ISCED levels in equivalent USD, 25-64 year-olds (2009 or latest available year)

	Year	Source	Gender	Annual labour costs — Three-year average exchange rate			Gross annual full-time earnings — Three-year average exchange rate			Annual net income — Three-year average exchange rate			Annual net income — PPP-adjusted exchange rate		
				0/1/2	3/4	5B/5A/6	0/1/2	3/4	5B/5A/6	0/1/2	3/4	5B/5A/6	0/1/2	3/4	5B/5A/6
				(1)	(2)	(3)	(4)	(5)	(6)	(7)	(8)	(9)	(10)	(11)	(12)
OECD															
Luxembourg	2009	National	Men	63 254	88 508	153 423	55 987	78 340	135 797	43 349	55 538	85 960	31 512	40 373	62 487
			Women	47 152	69 404	106 298	41 734	61 431	94 085	34 242	46 493	63 862	24 892	33 798	46 423
			M+W	58 537	83 572	136 036	51 811	73 970	120 407	40 809	53 215	77 812	29 665	38 684	56 564
Mexico				m	m	m	m	m	m	m	m	m	m	m	m
Netherlands	2008	National	Men	61 702	74 983	114 078	48 675	59 012	91 441	31 870	37 643	54 272	25 732	30 394	43 820
			Women	48 634	58 241	83 567	38 899	46 008	65 693	26 891	30 391	41 360	21 712	24 538	33 395
			M+W	59 900	71 642	106 273	47 273	56 411	84 771	31 085	36 199	51 183	25 099	29 228	41 326
New Zealand	2009	National	Men	33 188	40 417	48 869	33 188	40 417	48 869	26 993	31 836	37 451	24 557	28 964	34 072
			Women	25 610	31 081	37 439	25 610	31 081	37 439	21 402	25 599	29 840	19 471	23 289	27 148
			M+W	29 953	37 380	43 323	29 953	37 380	43 323	24 833	29 801	33 783	22 593	27 112	30 735
Norway	2007	National	Men	74 405	87 410	115 327	65 025	76 353	100 670	46 994	54 088	67 511	29 098	33 490	41 802
			Women	56 450	63 239	78 219	49 384	55 298	68 347	36 953	40 750	49 127	22 880	25 231	30 418
			M+W	68 068	79 101	97 211	59 504	69 115	84 890	43 450	49 620	58 801	26 903	30 723	36 408
Poland	2006	SILC	Men	7 531	11 437	21 445	6 359	9 658	18 108	4 719	7 017	12 905	6 450	9 592	17 641
			Women	4 946	8 484	15 709	4 176	7 164	13 265	3 198	5 279	9 531	4 371	7 217	13 028
			M+W	6 559	10 298	18 233	5 538	8 695	15 395	4 147	6 347	11 015	5 668	8 675	15 057
Portugal	2009	National	Men	17 504	26 730	47 152	14 145	21 600	38 103	11 976	17 010	27 027	11 887	16 883	26 825
			Women	12 978	19 028	32 434	10 487	15 376	26 209	9 333	12 912	20 029	9 264	12 816	19 880
			M+W	15 697	22 953	39 210	12 684	18 548	31 685	10 866	15 011	23 497	10 785	14 899	23 322
Slovak Republic	2009	National	Men	15 601	20 446	37 840	10 729	14 062	26 132	8 547	10 884	19 352	10 949	13 944	24 791
			Women	11 342	15 401	25 942	7 801	10 592	17 855	6 492	8 450	13 558	8 317	10 826	17 369
			M+W	13 073	18 194	32 185	8 991	12 513	22 198	7 327	9 798	16 653	9 387	12 552	21 335
Slovenia	2009	National	Men	18 242	24 871	51 681	15 712	21 422	44 515	10 968	14 487	26 283	11 441	15 113	27 418
			Women	15 618	21 822	40 442	13 453	18 796	34 834	9 721	12 986	21 834	10 141	13 546	22 776
			M+W	17 179	23 602	45 089	14 797	20 329	38 836	10 369	13 866	23 673	10 817	14 464	24 695
Spain	2008	National	Men	33 502	40 846	54 198	25 790	31 444	41 723	21 552	25 544	32 475	19 400	22 993	29 232
			Women	25 366	31 874	46 609	19 528	24 537	35 881	17 125	20 660	28 535	15 415	18 597	25 686
			M+W	31 288	37 376	50 777	24 086	28 773	39 090	20 340	23 675	30 699	18 308	21 311	27 633
Sweden	2008	National	Men	62 867	70 040	101 110	43 231	48 164	69 530	32 772	36 147	47 740	24 835	27 393	36 178
			Women	52 304	58 646	67 238	35 968	40 329	46 237	27 654	30 731	34 828	20 957	23 288	26 393
			M+W	60 746	66 451	84 297	41 773	45 696	57 968	31 750	34 457	42 131	24 061	26 112	31 928
Switzerland				m	m	m	m	m	m	m	m	m	m	m	m
Turkey				m	m	m	m	m	m	m	m	m	m	m	m
United Kingdom	2009	National	Men	43 079	59 194	89 513	35 138	48 282	73 012	27 670	36 739	53 803	22 693	30 131	44 125
			Women	33 070	43 408	68 908	26 974	35 406	56 205	22 036	27 855	42 206	18 073	22 844	34 615
			M+W	40 049	53 601	80 843	32 666	43 720	65 940	25 964	33 591	48 923	21 294	27 549	40 124
United States	2009	National	Men	39 405	60 563	109 383	31 274	48 066	86 812	24 869	36 252	59 506	24 869	36 252	59 506
			Women	28 652	44 306	73 568	22 739	35 163	58 387	18 842	27 616	42 509	18 842	27 616	42 509
			M+W	35 701	53 659	92 863	28 334	42 586	73 701	22 793	32 859	51 793	22 793	32 859	51 793
OECD average			Men	41 309	50 521	77 330	34 147	41 806	63 925	25 241	29 939	42 521	20 671	24 771	35 660
			Women	31 241	38 470	55 475	26 011	31 864	45 748	20 032	23 802	32 137	16 274	19 586	26 844
			M+W	37 904	46 336	67 643	31 383	38 331	55 861	23 468	27 841	38 009	19 148	22 976	31 836
EU21 average			Men	40 907	49 600	77 273	32 942	40 004	62 381	23 717	27 813	40 102	19 353	22 883	33 631
			Women	31 404	38 731	56 357	25 569	31 346	45 418	19 190	22 765	30 877	15 551	18 664	25 758
			M+W	37 746	45 783	68 112	30 479	36 930	54 954	22 192	26 068	36 120	18 045	21 402	30 201
Other G20															
Argentina				m	m	m	m	m	m	m	m	m	m	m	m
Brazil	2009	National	Men	m	m	m	5 391	9 890	25 762	m	m	m	m	m	m
			Women	m	m	m	3 476	6 125	15 602	m	m	m	m	m	m
			M+W	m	m	m	4 840	8 354	20 706	m	m	m	m	m	m
China				m	m	m	m	m	m	m	m	m	m	m	m
India				m	m	m	m	m	m	m	m	m	m	m	m
Indonesia				m	m	m	m	m	m	m	m	m	m	m	m
Russian Federation				m	m	m	m	m	m	m	m	m	m	m	m
Saudi Arabia				m	m	m	m	m	m	m	m	m	m	m	m
South Africa				m	m	m	m	m	m	m	m	m	m	m	m
G20 average				m	m	m	m	m	m	m	m	m	m	m	m

Note: Labour costs include non-tax compulsory payments (NTCP) and employer social contributions based on the OECD Taxing Wages Database (Centre for Tax Policy and Administration), except for the United States, for which Bureau of Labor Statistics information is used, and the United Kingdom, for which EU Labour Cost Survey data is used. SILC: Statistics on Income and Living Conditions (Eurostat). USD based on three-year moving average of currency exchange rates (OECD annual exchange rates) and last three columns on net income in USD (PPP) Purchasing Power Parity-adjusted for private consumption (see Table X2.1 for exchange rates).

Source: OECD. LSO Network special data collection on full-time, full-year earnings, Economic Working Group.

Please refer to the Reader's Guide for information concerning the symbols replacing missing data.

StatLink ⫴ http://dx.doi.org/10.1787/888932665639

Table A10.3. [1/2] Annual labour costs, full-time gross earnings and annual net income, by ISCED levels in equivalent USD, 25-34 year-olds (2009 or latest available year)

A10

	Year	Source	Gender	Annual labour costs — Three year-average exchange rate 0/1/2 (1)	3/4 (2)	5B/5A/6 (3)	Gross annual full-time earnings — Three year-average exchange rate 0/1/2 (4)	3/4 (5)	5B/5A/6 (6)	Annual net income — Three year-average exchange rate 0/1/2 (7)	3/4 (8)	5B/5A/6 (9)	Annual net income — PPP-adjusted exchange rate 0/1/2 (10)	3/4 (11)	5B/5A/6 (12)
Australia	2009	National	Men	45 598	58 205	68 989	39 512	50 436	59 781	32 353	39 454	45 855	25 483	31 077	36 119
			Women	40 451	45 953	59 245	35 051	39 819	51 337	29 476	32 551	40 071	23 217	25 639	31 563
			M+W	44 355	54 730	64 308	38 435	47 425	55 725	31 658	37 457	43 077	24 936	29 504	33 930
Austria	2009	National	Men	53 833	62 820	92 673	41 690	48 649	71 768	29 784	33 707	45 836	24 365	27 574	37 496
			Women	41 121	50 277	69 267	31 845	38 935	53 642	24 234	28 231	36 447	19 825	23 095	29 815
			M+W	49 330	58 653	82 160	38 203	45 422	63 626	27 818	31 888	41 619	22 757	26 086	34 046
Belgium	2009	National	Men	51 406	54 826	74 146	40 063	42 617	57 043	25 644	26 796	33 201	19 912	20 806	25 779
			Women	38 849	44 510	59 633	30 940	34 914	46 206	22 253	23 713	28 315	17 279	18 412	21 986
			M+W	48 036	52 381	66 640	37 547	40 792	51 438	24 552	25 973	30 674	19 064	20 167	23 817
Canada	2008	National	Men	38 370	48 603	56 129	34 400	43 708	50 901	27 242	33 322	38 137	22 837	27 933	31 970
			Women	31 765	32 044	46 064	28 502	28 751	41 328	23 246	23 430	31 720	19 487	19 641	26 591
			M+W	36 634	43 351	51 355	32 850	38 851	46 338	26 292	30 112	34 996	22 040	25 243	29 336
Chile				m	m	m	m	m	m	m	m	m	m	m	m
Czech Republic	2009	National	Men	17 254	22 686	37 834	12 876	16 930	28 234	10 192	12 985	20 774	12 821	16 334	26 132
			Women	14 267	18 679	28 803	10 647	13 939	21 495	8 656	10 925	16 130	10 889	13 742	20 291
			M+W	16 279	21 450	34 422	12 149	16 007	25 688	9 691	12 350	19 020	12 190	15 535	23 925
Denmark	2009	National	Men	62 628	69 495	80 829	62 220	69 087	80 421	37 907	41 787	46 450	23 048	25 407	28 243
			Women	51 013	56 307	67 415	50 605	55 899	67 007	31 205	34 272	40 612	18 974	20 838	24 693
			M+W	58 847	64 127	73 747	58 440	63 719	73 340	35 743	38 754	43 817	21 733	23 563	26 642
Estonia	2009	National	Men	19 149	19 298	26 755	14 303	14 415	19 985	11 611	11 698	16 021	13 345	13 445	18 413
			Women	9 337	11 013	18 141	6 974	8 226	13 551	5 923	6 895	11 027	6 807	7 924	12 674
			M+W	15 649	16 237	21 773	11 689	12 129	16 264	9 582	9 923	13 133	11 013	11 405	15 094
Finland	2009	National	Men	57 799	58 963	73 738	46 991	47 937	59 949	34 248	34 789	41 360	24 033	24 412	29 023
			Women	46 321	46 943	59 419	37 660	38 165	48 308	28 835	29 129	35 000	20 234	20 440	24 560
			M+W	54 619	54 582	65 659	44 406	44 375	53 381	32 748	32 731	37 878	22 980	22 968	26 580
France	2006	National	Men	38 801	43 477	65 717	29 286	31 805	46 182	22 015	23 567	33 386	16 967	18 163	25 730
			Women	22 767	31 061	51 458	19 576	25 117	36 162	16 564	20 036	26 543	12 766	15 442	20 456
			M+W	33 928	39 903	58 779	26 661	29 879	41 307	20 769	22 298	30 056	16 007	17 185	23 164
Germany	2009	National	Men	42 248	53 050	70 673	35 362	44 403	59 153	23 246	27 724	34 469	19 334	23 058	28 668
			Women	35 678	44 868	62 123	29 863	37 554	51 997	20 395	24 356	31 282	16 962	20 257	26 018
			M+W	40 097	49 634	66 540	33 561	41 543	55 694	22 323	26 335	32 949	18 566	21 903	27 403
Greece	2009	National	Men	20 565	24 005	34 406	16 059	18 745	26 867	13 489	15 746	21 145	12 302	14 360	19 285
			Women	15 663	18 943	25 455	12 231	14 792	19 877	10 274	12 425	16 697	9 370	11 332	15 228
			M+W	19 677	22 263	28 970	15 365	17 384	22 622	12 907	14 603	18 471	11 771	13 318	16 846
Hungary	2009	National	Men	10 762	14 356	29 766	8 119	10 832	22 375	5 883	7 291	12 355	7 521	9 321	15 795
			Women	9 510	13 312	22 465	7 163	10 050	16 906	5 348	6 964	9 784	6 837	8 904	12 509
			M+W	10 295	13 945	25 764	7 763	10 524	19 377	5 683	7 174	10 946	7 266	9 171	13 993
Iceland	2006	SILC	Men	44 217	49 822	71 507	38 729	43 658	62 632	28 779	31 739	43 190	19 233	21 211	28 864
			Women	26 264	34 238	43 995	23 004	29 989	38 534	19 299	23 510	28 662	12 898	15 712	19 155
			M+W	39 032	44 667	55 371	34 187	39 123	48 499	26 041	29 017	34 669	17 403	19 392	23 169
Ireland	2009	National	Men	55 153	52 521	80 299	49 800	47 423	72 505	40 882	39 194	52 529	28 549	27 370	36 682
			Women	40 413	46 288	73 236	36 491	41 795	66 127	32 646	35 197	49 339	22 798	24 579	34 455
			M+W	51 712	50 030	76 485	46 693	45 174	69 061	38 675	37 597	50 806	27 008	26 255	35 479
Israel	2009	National	Men	18 259	22 103	32 990	17 032	20 566	30 767	15 485	18 007	24 946	13 575	15 785	21 869
			Women	12 844	16 157	24 542	12 008	15 100	22 809	11 389	14 107	19 606	9 984	12 366	17 188
			M+W	17 727	20 228	29 047	16 543	18 827	27 027	15 136	16 776	22 515	13 269	14 707	19 738
Italy	2008	National	Men	45 073	53 694	60 333	32 314	38 494	43 253	23 248	27 059	29 980	19 404	22 585	25 024
			Women	31 364	37 952	44 342	22 485	27 208	31 789	17 219	20 117	22 926	14 372	16 791	19 136
			M+W	41 795	47 325	52 266	29 963	33 928	37 470	21 806	24 238	26 431	18 201	20 231	22 062
Japan				m	m	m	m	m	m	m	m	m	m	m	m
Korea	2008	National	Men	23 029	25 393	32 201	19 523	21 526	27 298	17 821	19 600	24 502	21 761	23 933	29 919
			Women	22 703	20 428	25 002	19 246	17 318	21 195	17 573	15 836	19 305	21 458	19 337	23 574
			M+W	22 987	23 565	29 101	19 487	19 977	24 670	17 788	18 225	22 346	21 721	22 255	27 287

Note: Labour costs include non-tax compulsory payments (NTCP) and employer social contributions based on the OECD Taxing Wages Database (Centre for Tax Policy and Administration), except for the United States, for which Bureau of Labor Statistics information is used, and the United Kingdom, for which EU Labour Cost Survey data is used. SILC: Statistics on Income and Living Conditions (Eurostat). USD based on three-year moving average of currency exchange rates (OECD annual exchange rates) and last three columns on net income in USD (PPP) Purchasing Power Parity-adjusted for private consumption (see Table X2.1 for exchange rates).

Source: OECD. LSO Network special data collection on full-time, full-year earnings, Economic Working Group.

Please refer to the Reader's Guide for information concerning the symbols replacing missing data.

StatLink ᵐˢ᷈ http://dx.doi.org/10.1787/888932665658

A10

Table A10.3. [2/2] Annual labour costs, full-time gross earnings and annual net income, by ISCED levels in equivalent USD, 25-34 year-olds (2009 or latest available year)

	Year	Source	Gender	Annual labour costs — Three year-average exchange rate			Gross annual full-time earnings — Three year-average exchange rate			Annual net income — Three year-average exchange rate			Annual net income — PPP-adjusted exchange rate		
				0/1/2	3/4	5B/5A/6	0/1/2	3/4	5B/5A/6	0/1/2	3/4	5B/5A/6	0/1/2	3/4	5B/5A/6
				(1)	(2)	(3)	(4)	(5)	(6)	(7)	(8)	(9)	(10)	(11)	(12)
Luxembourg	2009	National	Men	47 828	62 499	118 314	42 333	55 319	104 721	34 655	42 936	69 514	25 192	31 212	50 532
			Women	37 869	53 501	86 741	33 519	47 354	76 776	28 438	37 981	54 715	20 672	27 609	39 774
			M+W	45 166	59 206	102 318	39 977	52 404	90 563	33 044	41 167	62 007	24 021	29 926	45 075
Mexico				m	m	m	m	m	m	m	m	m	m	m	m
Netherlands	2008	National	Men	51 710	59 763	80 449	41 175	47 165	63 266	27 983	31 025	40 002	22 594	25 050	32 298
			Women	43 345	50 838	69 208	34 985	40 529	54 517	25 012	27 674	35 139	20 195	22 344	28 372
			M+W	50 309	57 174	75 804	40 138	45 218	59 651	27 486	29 972	37 993	22 193	24 199	30 676
New Zealand	2009	National	Men	30 422	35 132	39 235	30 422	35 132	39 235	25 163	28 295	31 044	22 893	25 742	28 243
			Women	24 283	30 955	35 996	24 283	30 955	35 996	20 354	25 515	28 873	18 517	23 213	26 268
			M+W	28 563	33 699	37 650	28 563	33 699	37 650	23 735	27 335	29 982	21 593	24 869	27 277
Norway	2007	National	Men	65 965	79 337	88 403	57 672	69 321	77 218	42 274	49 752	54 565	26 175	30 805	33 786
			Women	49 151	56 144	67 039	43 026	49 117	58 608	32 871	36 782	42 875	20 353	22 774	26 547
			M+W	60 867	72 060	76 705	53 232	62 981	67 028	39 423	45 682	48 280	24 410	28 286	29 894
Poland	2006	SILC	Men	8 438	9 801	16 004	7 125	8 276	13 514	5 253	6 055	9 704	7 180	8 276	13 264
			Women	5 761	6 841	12 370	4 864	5 777	10 445	3 677	4 313	7 566	5 026	5 895	10 342
			M+W	7 881	8 811	13 989	6 654	7 440	11 812	4 925	5 472	8 518	6 732	7 480	11 644
Portugal	2009	National	Men	15 186	19 940	31 982	12 271	16 113	25 844	10 552	13 316	19 790	10 474	13 316	19 643
			Women	11 968	15 641	26 016	9 671	12 639	21 023	8 607	10 832	16 633	8 543	10 751	16 509
			M+W	13 968	17 756	28 421	11 287	14 349	22 966	9 783	12 131	17 905	9 710	12 041	17 772
Slovak Republic	2009	National	Men	15 282	20 719	32 100	10 511	14 249	22 139	8 393	11 016	16 612	10 753	14 112	21 281
			Women	12 547	15 793	24 213	8 629	10 862	16 653	7 074	8 639	12 702	9 062	11 068	16 272
			M+W	14 230	18 939	28 627	9 787	13 026	19 639	7 886	10 157	14 830	10 102	13 013	18 998
Slovenia	2009	National	Men	16 308	22 618	38 581	14 046	19 482	33 230	9 878	13 384	21 097	10 304	13 961	22 007
			Women	13 509	17 847	28 636	11 635	15 372	24 665	8 764	10 746	16 331	9 143	11 210	17 036
			M+W	15 694	20 785	32 421	13 518	17 902	27 925	9 764	12 401	18 185	10 185	12 936	18 970
Spain	2008	National	Men	32 083	35 226	43 894	24 699	27 118	33 790	20 775	22 497	27 126	18 701	20 251	24 417
			Women	25 054	26 577	39 371	19 287	20 460	30 309	16 973	17 758	24 768	15 278	15 985	22 295
			M+W	30 294	31 704	41 646	23 321	24 407	32 060	19 795	20 568	25 959	17 818	18 514	23 367
Sweden	2008	National	Men	60 168	62 307	78 106	41 375	42 846	53 711	31 471	32 508	39 947	23 849	24 635	30 272
			Women	56 400	48 339	54 424	38 784	33 241	37 426	29 641	25 731	28 683	22 462	19 499	21 736
			M+W	59 985	58 656	66 130	41 250	40 336	45 475	31 383	30 738	34 309	23 782	23 294	26 000
Switzerland				m	m	m	m	m	m	m	m	m	m	m	m
Turkey				m	m	m	m	m	m	m	m	m	m	m	m
United Kingdom	2009	National	Men	37 563	50 267	72 369	30 639	41 001	59 028	24 565	31 715	44 154	20 147	26 011	36 212
			Women	30 734	40 982	61 802	25 068	33 427	50 410	20 722	26 489	38 207	16 994	21 725	31 335
			M+W	35 878	47 240	67 374	29 264	38 532	54 954	23 617	30 012	41 343	19 369	24 613	33 907
United States	2009	National	Men	33 613	50 978	81 641	26 677	40 458	64 794	21 622	31 356	46 394	21 622	31 356	46 394
			Women	26 284	37 516	61 386	20 861	29 775	48 719	17 515	23 810	36 648	17 515	23 810	36 648
			M+W	31 416	45 947	71 415	24 933	36 466	56 678	20 391	28 536	41 473	20 391	28 536	41 473
OECD average			Men	36 507	42 824	58 968	30 249	35 438	48 607	22 842	26 152	33 934	18 772	21 638	28 392
			Women	28 525	33 446	46 476	23 755	27 830	38 407	18 765	21 309	27 814	15 445	17 598	23 208
			M+W	34 319	39 622	52 578	28 478	32 823	43 377	21 739	24 470	30 834	17 870	20 227	25 778
EU21 average			Men	36 154	41 540	58 998	29 203	33 472	47 475	21 508	24 138	32 164	17 657	19 984	26 962
			Women	28 261	33 167	46 883	22 996	26 965	37 871	17 736	20 115	26 612	14 499	16 564	22 166
			M+W	33 984	38 610	52 848	27 506	31 166	42 586	20 475	22 690	29 374	16 784	18 752	24 546
Argentina				m	m	m	m	m	m	m	m	m	m	m	m
Brazil	2009	National	Men	m	m	m	4 479	7 509	19 003	m	m	m	m	m	m
			Women	m	m	m	3 248	5 132	12 779	m	m	m	m	m	m
			M+W	m	m	m	4 158	6 517	15 668	m	m	m	m	m	m
China				m	m	m	m	m	m	m	m	m	m	m	m
India				m	m	m	m	m	m	m	m	m	m	m	m
Indonesia				m	m	m	m	m	m	m	m	m	m	m	m
Russian Federation				m	m	m	m	m	m	m	m	m	m	m	m
Saudi Arabia				m	m	m	m	m	m	m	m	m	m	m	m
South Africa				m	m	m	m	m	m	m	m	m	m	m	m
G20 average				m	m	m	m	m	m	m	m	m	m	m	m

Note: Labour costs include non-tax compulsory payments (NTCP) and employer social contributions based on the OECD Taxing Wages Database (Centre for Tax Policy and Administration), except for the United States, for which Bureau of Labor Statistics information is used, and the United Kingdom, for which EU Labour Cost Survey data is used. SILC: Statistics on Income and Living Conditions (Eurostat). USD based on three-year moving average of currency exchange rates (OECD annual exchange rates) and last three columns on net income in USD (PPP) Purchasing Power Parity-adjusted for private consumption (see Table X2.1 for exchange rates).
Source: OECD. LSO Network special data collection on full-time, full-year earnings, Economic Working Group.
Please refer to the Reader's Guide for information concerning the symbols replacing missing data.
StatLink ⏱ http://dx.doi.org/10.1787/888932665658

A10

Table A10.5. [1/2] Annual labour costs, full-time gross earnings and annual net income, by ISCED levels in equivalent USD, 45-54 year-olds (2009 or latest available year)

	Year	Source	Gender	Annual labour costs — Three-year average exchange rate			Gross annual full-time earnings — Three-year average exchange rate			Annual net income — Three-year average exchange rate			Annual net income — PPP-adjusted exchange rate		
				0/1/2	3/4	5B/5A/6	0/1/2	3/4	5B/5A/6	0/1/2	3/4	5B/5A/6	0/1/2	3/4	5B/5A/6
				(1)	(2)	(3)	(4)	(5)	(6)	(7)	(8)	(9)	(10)	(11)	(12)
Australia	2009	National	Men	56 719	64 114	96 536	49 148	55 556	83 650	38 572	42 961	60 381	30 382	33 840	47 561
			Women	38 969	44 491	63 641	33 768	38 552	55 146	28 648	31 734	42 681	22 565	24 996	33 619
			M+W	49 496	58 728	81 329	42 890	50 890	70 474	34 531	39 765	52 673	27 200	31 322	41 489
Austria	2009	National	Men	63 250	87 951	129 756	48 982	68 111	104 778	33 895	43 942	65 797	27 728	35 947	53 825
			Women	44 508	67 942	98 839	34 468	52 615	76 543	25 713	35 915	48 309	21 034	29 381	39 519
			M+W	52 957	80 957	117 733	41 011	62 695	93 594	29 401	41 136	58 755	24 052	33 652	48 064
Belgium	2009	National	Men	60 454	63 292	101 143	46 819	48 938	77 655	28 592	29 547	41 707	22 201	22 942	32 385
			Women	46 587	57 918	81 443	36 465	44 925	62 491	24 191	27 738	35 558	18 784	21 538	27 610
			M+W	57 549	61 714	93 841	44 650	47 760	71 947	27 614	29 016	39 393	21 441	22 530	30 587
Canada	2008	National	Men	44 973	62 367	84 692	40 331	56 864	78 464	31 073	42 242	55 936	26 048	35 411	46 890
			Women	33 867	44 886	67 041	30 379	40 253	61 330	24 595	31 022	45 311	20 617	26 006	37 984
			M+W	41 929	55 373	76 699	37 577	50 179	70 625	29 299	37 640	51 324	24 561	31 553	43 024
Chile				m	m	m	m	m	m	m	m	m	m	m	m
Czech Republic	2009	National	Men	17 017	22 307	56 461	12 699	16 647	42 135	10 070	12 790	30 352	12 668	16 089	38 180
			Women	13 089	18 051	37 090	9 768	13 471	27 679	8 051	10 602	20 391	10 127	13 337	25 651
			M+W	14 557	20 572	50 455	10 863	15 352	37 653	8 806	11 898	27 263	11 077	14 967	34 295
Denmark	2009	National	Men	72 604	82 202	111 303	72 197	82 521	110 896	43 392	47 231	57 780	26 384	28 717	35 132
			Women	59 767	66 095	81 520	59 359	65 687	81 113	36 276	39 866	46 707	22 057	24 239	28 399
			M+W	66 640	75 526	95 771	66 233	75 119	95 363	40 174	44 479	52 005	24 427	27 044	31 620
Estonia	2009	National	Men	13 281	18 124	22 131	9 921	13 538	16 531	8 210	11 017	13 341	9 435	12 662	15 332
			Women	7 971	10 592	15 362	5 954	7 912	11 475	5 131	6 650	9 416	5 897	7 643	10 822
			M+W	11 220	14 271	17 059	8 381	10 660	12 742	7 015	8 783	10 400	8 062	10 095	11 952
Finland	2009	National	Men	63 088	65 945	96 917	51 291	53 614	78 794	36 694	38 001	51 350	25 749	26 666	36 034
			Women	49 851	50 816	70 066	40 530	41 314	56 965	30 500	30 955	39 778	21 403	21 722	27 913
			M+W	57 130	58 161	80 800	46 447	47 285	65 691	33 933	34 419	44 404	23 811	24 152	31 159
France	2006	National	Men	52 007	60 919	100 542	36 547	42 810	70 530	26 806	31 083	47 836	20 659	23 956	36 867
			Women	32 744	46 006	73 817	26 023	33 167	51 854	20 466	24 498	37 059	15 773	18 880	28 561
			M+W	44 127	55 900	89 129	32 155	39 283	62 554	23 807	28 674	43 233	18 348	22 099	33 320
Germany	2009	National	Men	59 453	63 451	99 342	49 762	53 108	84 690	30 255	31 788	46 639	25 163	26 438	38 790
			Women	40 702	47 813	80 656	34 067	40 019	67 909	22 584	25 586	38 691	18 783	21 280	32 179
			M+W	53 401	58 200	94 189	44 696	48 713	80 063	27 864	29 767	44 515	23 175	24 757	37 023
Greece	2009	National	Men	28 665	32 717	48 279	22 384	25 549	37 700	18 321	20 315	27 970	16 709	18 527	25 509
			Women	16 127	23 943	37 851	12 594	18 697	29 557	10 579	15 705	22 840	9 648	14 323	20 831
			M+W	24 188	29 639	43 885	18 888	23 143	34 269	15 866	18 799	25 809	14 470	17 145	23 538
Hungary	2009	National	Men	11 866	15 431	40 098	8 962	11 638	30 115	6 355	7 597	15 992	8 124	9 712	20 445
			Women	9 338	13 861	25 894	7 032	10 461	19 475	5 274	7 150	10 992	6 743	9 141	14 052
			M+W	10 336	14 670	30 943	7 794	11 067	23 257	5 701	7 380	12 769	7 288	9 435	16 324
Iceland	2006	SILC	Men	46 545	55 553	88 694	40 768	48 658	77 686	30 008	34 765	52 265	20 055	23 234	34 929
			Women	36 713	43 613	61 691	32 157	38 200	54 034	24 817	28 460	38 006	16 585	19 020	25 400
			M+W	42 180	51 870	75 045	36 945	45 432	65 731	27 704	32 821	45 058	18 514	21 934	30 112
Ireland	2009	National	Men	59 879	104 896	134 737	54 067	94 714	121 659	43 308	63 636	77 781	30 243	44 438	54 317
			Women	50 388	65 726	97 912	45 497	59 346	88 408	37 826	45 948	60 482	26 415	32 087	42 236
			M+W	58 023	89 446	121 353	52 391	80 764	109 573	42 470	56 659	71 529	29 658	39 567	49 951
Israel	2009	National	Men	23 042	30 350	52 029	21 430	28 262	48 824	18 622	23 318	35 921	16 325	20 442	31 490
			Women	15 424	22 109	35 316	14 421	20 972	32 972	13 596	18 011	26 380	11 919	15 789	23 126
			M+W	21 408	27 304	44 677	19 927	25 373	41 851	17 551	21 440	31 876	15 386	18 795	27 944
Italy	2008	National	Men	53 969	74 492	146 289	38 691	53 404	104 876	27 180	35 196	61 436	22 686	29 377	51 279
			Women	37 032	58 018	83 495	26 549	41 594	59 858	19 712	28 978	38 507	16 453	24 187	32 141
			M+W	49 329	67 853	118 553	35 364	48 644	84 992	25 118	32 751	51 275	20 966	27 336	42 798
Japan				m	m	m	m	m	m	m	m	m	m	m	m
Korea	2008	National	Men	26 747	43 192	61 355	22 675	36 615	52 522	20 616	31 771	44 549	25 174	38 796	54 399
			Women	16 833	22 225	37 279	14 270	18 841	31 603	13 094	17 207	27 858	15 988	21 011	34 017
			M+W	21 773	36 217	57 020	18 458	30 702	48 701	16 861	27 159	41 473	20 589	33 163	50 642

Note: Labour costs include non-tax compulsory payments (NTCP) and employer social contributions based on the OECD Taxing Wages Database (Centre for Tax Policy and Administration), except for the United States, for which Bureau of Labor Statistics information is used, and the United Kingdom, for which EU Labour Cost Survey data is used. SILC: Statistics on Income and Living Conditions (Eurostat). USD based on three-year moving average of currency exchange rates (OECD annual exchange rates) and last three columns on net income in USD (PPP) Purchasing Power Parity-adjusted for private consumption (see Table X2.1 for exchange rates).
Source: OECD. LSO Network special data collection on full-time, full-year earnings, Economic Working Group.
Please refer to the Reader's Guide for information concerning the symbols replacing missing data.
StatLink ▨▨▨ http://dx.doi.org/10.1787/888932665696

A10

Table A10.5. [2/2] Annual labour costs, full-time gross earnings and annual net income, by ISCED levels in equivalent USD, 45-54 year-olds (2009 or latest available year)

	Year	Source	Gender	Annual labour costs — Three-year average exchange rate			Gross annual full-time earnings — Three-year average exchange rate			Annual net income — Three-year average exchange rate			Annual net income — PPP-adjusted exchange rate		
				0/1/2	3/4	5B/5A/6	0/1/2	3/4	5B/5A/6	0/1/2	3/4	5B/5A/6	0/1/2	3/4	5B/5A/6
				(1)	(2)	(3)	(4)	(5)	(6)	(7)	(8)	(9)	(10)	(11)	(12)
OECD Luxembourg	2009	National	Men	67 423	99 120	167 109	59 677	87 732	148 753	45 496	60 511	93 326	33 072	43 988	67 842
			Women	56 536	79 465	157 450	50 041	70 335	139 361	39 698	51 289	87 852	28 858	37 284	63 862
			M+W	64 296	95 664	164 389	56 909	84 674	146 033	43 885	58 899	91 685	31 901	42 816	66 649
Mexico				m	m	m	m	m	m	m	m	m	m	m	m
Netherlands	2008	National	Men	65 368	82 507	127 016	51 528	64 868	102 497	33 467	40 898	59 393	27 021	33 022	47 955
			Women	49 975	62 678	97 527	39 891	49 434	77 297	27 367	32 295	47 722	22 097	26 075	38 531
			M+W	63 095	79 195	121 311	49 759	62 290	97 622	32 477	39 456	57 135	26 222	31 857	46 131
New Zealand	2009	National	Men	35 855	43 364	52 929	35 855	43 364	52 929	28 779	33 810	39 967	26 182	30 760	36 361
			Women	25 676	30 880	38 338	25 676	30 880	38 338	21 454	25 466	30 443	19 519	23 168	27 696
			M+W	31 032	39 003	45 149	31 032	39 003	45 149	25 566	30 888	35 007	23 259	28 101	31 848
Norway	2007	National	Men	80 224	93 152	131 865	70 093	81 355	115 077	50 248	56 849	75 464	31 113	35 200	46 725
			Women	59 866	66 567	85 953	52 360	58 197	75 083	38 863	42 610	53 387	24 063	26 383	33 056
			M+W	72 054	83 809	109 894	62 977	73 216	95 938	45 679	52 253	64 899	28 284	32 354	40 184
Poland	2006	SILC	Men	7 363	12 066	23 039	6 217	10 189	19 454	4 620	7 387	13 843	6 315	10 098	18 922
			Women	5 069	9 291	18 667	4 280	7 845	15 762	3 270	5 754	11 271	4 470	7 865	15 406
			M+W	6 337	10 830	20 427	5 351	9 145	17 248	4 016	6 660	12 306	5 490	9 104	16 822
Portugal	2009	National	Men	19 089	36 306	70 426	15 426	29 338	56 910	12 950	22 079	37 640	12 853	21 914	37 360
			Women	13 564	24 762	50 139	10 961	20 010	40 516	9 755	15 969	28 354	9 683	15 850	28 143
			M+W	16 805	31 034	62 003	13 579	25 078	50 104	11 546	19 289	33 642	11 460	19 145	33 391
Slovak Republic	2009	National	Men	15 869	19 971	40 648	10 914	13 735	28 085	8 676	10 655	20 662	11 115	13 650	26 470
			Women	11 298	15 232	26 975	7 770	10 476	18 573	6 471	8 369	14 070	8 290	10 721	18 025
			M+W	12 721	17 566	33 340	8 749	12 081	23 001	7 158	9 495	17 226	9 170	12 164	22 069
Slovenia	2009	National	Men	19 033	25 742	58 044	16 393	22 173	49 995	11 414	14 914	28 802	11 906	15 558	30 045
			Women	16 037	24 154	48 953	13 814	20 804	42 165	9 958	14 136	25 203	10 387	14 746	26 291
			M+W	17 532	25 007	52 735	15 101	21 539	45 422	10 568	14 554	26 700	11 024	15 182	27 853
Spain	2008	National	Men	34 250	46 743	62 240	26 366	35 984	47 914	21 962	28 605	36 649	19 769	25 748	32 989
			Women	25 613	35 770	54 724	19 718	27 536	42 127	17 245	22 795	32 747	15 523	20 519	29 477
			M+W	31 697	42 489	58 847	24 401	32 709	45 302	20 564	26 397	34 888	18 510	23 761	31 404
Sweden	2008	National	Men	63 619	74 925	119 984	43 748	51 523	82 509	33 127	38 448	53 753	25 104	29 137	40 735
			Women	53 436	63 116	79 692	36 746	43 402	54 801	28 205	32 889	40 598	21 374	24 924	30 766
			M+W	61 212	70 881	97 566	42 094	48 743	67 092	31 974	36 545	46 554	24 230	27 695	35 279
Switzerland				m	m	m	m	m	m	m	m	m	m	m	m
Turkey				m	m	m	m	m	m	m	m	m	m	m	m
United Kingdom	2009	National	Men	45 226	63 970	102 188	36 889	52 177	83 351	28 878	39 427	60 408	23 684	32 335	49 542
			Women	32 979	43 821	74 094	26 900	35 743	60 436	21 986	28 087	45 125	18 031	23 035	37 009
			M+W	40 661	55 863	90 076	33 165	45 565	73 471	26 309	34 865	54 120	21 576	28 594	44 385
United States	2009	National	Men	42 523	65 994	123 879	33 748	52 377	98 317	26 617	38 865	66 115	26 617	38 865	66 115
			Women	28 421	46 556	80 081	22 556	36 949	63 556	18 712	28 877	45 643	18 712	28 877	45 643
			M+W	37 348	57 404	103 501	29 641	45 559	82 144	23 716	34 732	56 769	23 716	34 732	56 769
OECD average			Men	43 083	55 582	87 920	35 639	46 047	72 665	26 145	32 402	47 347	21 396	26 809	39 808
			Women	32 013	41 600	64 190	26 690	34 388	52 980	20 484	25 330	36 255	16 614	20 829	30 275
			M+W	39 001	50 522	77 507	32 325	41 816	64 055	24 040	29 883	42 575	19 582	24 657	35 764
EU21 average			Men	42 513	54 943	88 462	34 261	44 396	71 420	24 460	30 241	44 879	19 933	24 806	37 617
			Women	32 029	42 146	66 294	26 116	34 038	53 541	19 536	24 342	35 318	15 801	19 942	29 401
			M+W	38 753	50 259	78 781	31 333	40 586	63 666	22 679	28 091	40 743	18 398	23 004	34 029
Other G20 Argentina				m	m	m	m	m	m	m	m	m	m	m	m
Brazil	2009	National	Men	m	m	m	5 987	12 762	31 720	m	m	m	m	m	m
			Women	m	m	m	3 614	7 765	18 667	m	m	m	m	m	m
			M+W	m	m	m	5 253	10 772	25 518	m	m	m	m	m	m
China				m	m	m	m	m	m	m	m	m	m	m	m
India				m	m	m	m	m	m	m	m	m	m	m	m
Indonesia				m	m	m	m	m	m	m	m	m	m	m	m
Russian Federation				m	m	m	m	m	m	m	m	m	m	m	m
Saudi Arabia				m	m	m	m	m	m	m	m	m	m	m	m
South Africa				m	m	m	m	m	m	m	m	m	m	m	m
G20 average				m	m	m	m	m	m	m	m	m	m	m	m

Note: Labour costs include non-tax compulsory payments (NTCP) and employer social contributions based on the OECD Taxing Wages Database (Centre for Tax Policy and Administration), except for the United States, for which Bureau of Labor Statistics information is used, and the United Kingdom, for which EU Labour Cost Survey data is used. SILC: Statistics on Income and Living Conditions (Eurostat). USD based on three-year moving average of currency exchange rates (OECD annual exchange rates) and last three columns on net income in USD (PPP) Purchasing Power Parity-adjusted for private consumption (see Table X2.1 for exchange rates).
Source: OECD. LSO Network special data collection on full-time, full-year earnings, Economic Working Group.
Please refer to the Reader's Guide for information concerning the symbols replacing missing data.
StatLink ⬛⬛⬛ http://dx.doi.org/10.1787/888932665696

WHAT ARE THE SOCIAL OUTCOMES OF EDUCATION?

- Education is an important predictor of life expectancy. On average, among 15 OECD countries, a 30-year-old male tertiary graduate can expect to live another 51 years, while a 30-year-old man who has not completed upper secondary education can expect to live an additional 43 years. Differences in life expectancy by education are particularly large among men in Central European countries. On average, a 30-year-old male tertiary graduate in the Czech Republic can expect to live 17 years longer than a 30-year-old man who has not completed upper secondary education.

- There are substantial gender differences in life expectancy. Moreover, the gender differences exist in the relationship between education and life expectancy. Differences in life expectancy by education are generally much smaller among women in 15 OECD countries. On average, male tertiary graduates can expect to live 8 years longer than those who have not attained upper secondary education, while a tertiary-educated woman can expect to live 4 years longer than a woman without an upper secondary education. In Portugal, the latter figure is 1 year.

- Although all OECD countries encourage electoral participation, voting rates vary across age groups and there are significant differences in voting behaviour associated with educational attainment in most countries. On average, the gap in the voting rate between adults with high and low levels of education (25-64 year-olds) is 14.8 percentage points. This gap widens considerably to 26.8 percentage points among younger adults (25-34 year-olds). For younger adults in Germany, the corresponding figure is 49.6 percentage points.

Chart A11.1. **Difference in life expectancy by educational attainment at age 30 (2010)**
Differences between those with "tertiary eduation"
and "below upper secondary education" at age 30, by gender

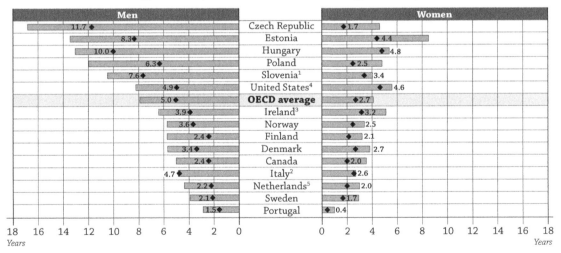

Note: The figures describe the differences in the expected years of life remaining at age 30 across education levels.
1. Year of reference 2009.
2. Year of reference 2008.
3. Year of reference 2006.
4. Year of reference 2005.
5. Year of reference 2007-10.
Countries are ranked in descending order of the difference in life expectancy among men at age 30.
Source: OECD. Table A11.1. See Annex 3 for notes (*www.oecd.org/edu/eag2012*).
StatLink ᔏᓵᔑ http://dx.doi.org/10.1787/888932662390

Context

The idea that education produces social benefits is not new. Early philosophers such as Aristotle and Plato pointed out that education is central to the well-being of society. Most if not all policy makers, school administrators, teachers and parents are aware of the wider benefits of learning. Over the last several decades, social science research has consistently pointed out the correlation between higher levels of education among individuals and better health conditions, lower incidence of criminal activity, and higher levels of societal engagement. More recently, researchers have started to present evidence suggesting the causal effects of education on diverse social outcomes (OECD, 2010).

National policy initiatives are also recognising the links between education and positive social outcomes to a greater degree. For example, dropout-prevention programmes, after-school programmes, and other educational interventions have been adopted as an element of anti-crime policies in some countries. More recently, health policies have started to emphasise school-based efforts, such as programmes that encourage young people to lead healthy lifestyles. Generally, more policy makers appear to be embracing the idea that preventive, education-based efforts may be a resource-efficient way to address broader social challenges – especially in the current economic climate.

In addition, well-being and social progress, in and of themselves, are emerging more prominently in national policy. For example, some heads of state (e.g. in France and the United Kingdom) and prominent economists (e.g. Joseph Stiglitz and Amartya Sen) have underscored the importance of looking beyond economic indicators such as GDP and national income in benchmarking national goals. There has since been strong policy interest in addressing well-being and social progress based on a whole-of-government approach in which the education sector can play a key role.

Other findings

- **Education predicts a variety of social outcomes.** Adults with higher levels of educational attainment are generally more likely than those with lower levels of attainment to engage in social activities, exhibit greater satisfaction with life and vote. An individual's social engagement and life satisfaction vary across different levels of educational attainment, even after accounting for differences in age, gender and income. This suggests that education may have an impact on these outcomes by raising skills and abilities, although other factors related to the choice of education or the effect of credentials may also be at play.

- **Students' competencies on civic matters help to explain their social values and attitudes.** In all the OECD countries surveyed by the International Civic and Citizenship Education Study (ICCS) 2009, lower secondary school students (grade 8) with higher measured levels of civic competencies (i.e. knowing and understanding elements and concepts of citizenship) showed higher levels of supportive attitudes towards equal rights for ethnic minorities.

A11

Analysis

Educational attainment is positively associated with diverse measures of social outcomes, including life expectancy, life satisfaction, electoral participation and social engagement (Charts A11.1 and A11.2, Tables A11.1, A11.2, A11.3 and A11.4). The strengths of these associations are sometimes substantial. For instance, the difference in life expectancy between those with high (i.e. tertiary attainment) and low (i.e. below upper secondary attainment) education among 30-year-old Hungarian men is 13.1 years. Similarly, the difference in voting rates between those with high and low levels of education in the United States is 45.6 percentage points. Finally, the difference in social engagement between those with high and low levels of education in Estonia is 33 percentage points. In many countries, some of these associations are statistically significant, even after accounting for individual differences in age, gender and income (Tables A11.3 and A11.5, available on line).

There is evidence suggesting that such associations are likely to reflect causal effects. For instance, Lleras-Muney (2005), Glied and Lleras-Muney (2008) and Cipollone and Rosolia (2011) show that a one-year increase in schooling reduces mortality in the United States and Italy. Lleras-Muney (2005) calculated that an additional year of education increased life expectancy at age 35 by as much as 1.7 years. Moreover, Miligan, et al. (2004) find that an extra year of schooling also raised voter turnout in the United States.

Chart A11.2. **Voting gaps between adults with high and low levels of education (2008, 2010)**
Differences in voting rates between those with "tertiary education" and "below upper secondary education" among younger adults (25-34 year-olds) and older adults (55-64 year-olds)

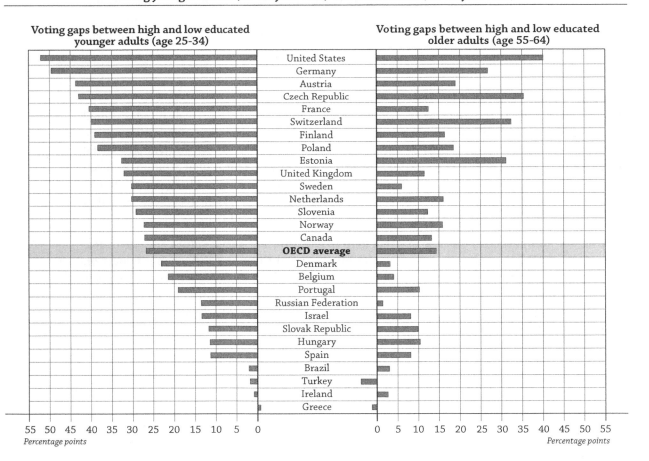

Countries are ranked in descending order of the proportion of adults aged 25-34 reporting electoral participation.
Source: OECD. Table A11.2. See Annex 3 for notes (*www.oecd.org/edu/eag2012*).
StatLink ⧉ http://dx.doi.org/10.1787/888932662409

The associations between education and social outcomes can be quite different across population groups. For instance, while the association between education and life expectancy is substantial for men, this relationship appears to be rather limited among women (Chart A11.1 and Table A11.1). Moreover, while the association between education and voting is small among older adults (age 55-64), this relationship is very pronounced among younger adults (age 25-34) (Chart A11.2 and Table A11.2).

Education can enhance social outcomes by helping individuals make informed and competent decisions. Education imparts knowledge and information, improves cognitive skills and strengthens socio-emotional capabilities, such as conscientiousness, self-efficacy and social skills. As such, education can help individuals pursue healthier lifestyles and increase their engagement in civil society. Educational institutions can also offer a positive environment for children to develop healthy habits and participatory attitudes and norms conducive to social cohesion. For instance, an open classroom climate, practical involvement in civic matters and school climates that promote active citizenship can foster civic participation.

Chart A11.3. **Students' attitudes towards equal rights for ethnic minorities (2009)**
Mean ICCS scale of "support for equal rights for ethnic minorities" among grade 8 students, by level of civic knowledge

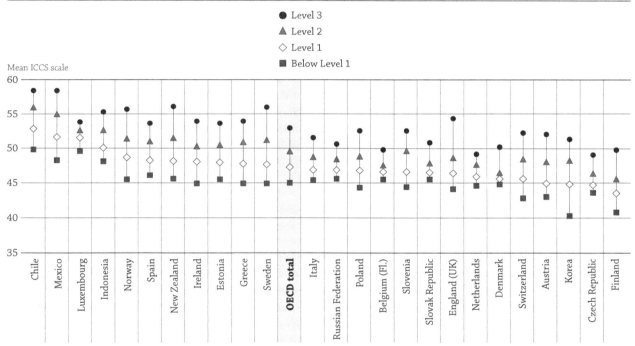

Note: Countries are ranked in descending order of the mean scales of Grade 8 students' attitudes towards equal rights for ethnic minorities, among those who have achieved Level 1 in civic knowledge. Mean ICCS scales are based on Rasch Partial Credit Model and the resulting weighted likelihood estimates (WLEs) were transformed into a metric with a mean of 50 and a standard deviation of 10. The *Definitions* section at the end of this indicator provides details on the ICCS scale.
Source: OECD. Table A11.4. See Annex 3 for notes (*www.oecd.org/edu/eag2012*).
StatLink http://dx.doi.org/10.1787/888932662428

In all OECD countries surveyed by ICCS, students in grade 8 (approximately 14 years old) with higher levels of civic competencies show supportive attitudes towards equal rights for ethnic minorities (Chart A11.3 and Table A11.4), as well as higher levels of expected adult electoral participation and supportive attitudes towards gender equality (Chart A11.3 and Table A11.2 in *Education at a Glance 2011*). In New Zealand, for example, those who are at the lowest level on a civic competency scale score only an average of 45.6 points on the ICCS scale of "support for equal rights for ethnic minorities", whereas those who are at the highest level on the scale score 56.1 points (Table A11.4, see *Definitions* section at the end of this indicator for details on the scales).

A11

Definitions

This section describes the education variables (i.e. educational attainment and civic competency) and social outcome variables. See Annex 3 (*www.oecd.org/edu/eag2012*) for detailed descriptions of the variables, including the actual questions used in each survey.

Civic knowledge means knowing about and understanding elements and concepts of citizenship, as well as those of traditional civics (Schultz, et al., 2010). The ICCS assessment is based on a 79-item test administered to lower-secondary students (8th grade) and covers issues related to civic society and systems, civic principles, civic participation and civic identities. Three-quarters of the test items involve reasoning and analysis associated with civics and citizenship, while the rest focuses on knowledge about civics and citizenship. Civic knowledge is measured on a scale with an international average of 500 points and a standard deviation of 100. There is significant variation across and within countries in civic knowledge: half of the total variance in civic knowledge was found to be at the student level, a quarter at the school level, and a quarter across countries. See Schulz, et al. (2010) for more details on how civic knowledge is conceptualised.

Educational attainment variables in each data source are converted to three categories of educational attainment (below upper secondary education, upper secondary education and tertiary education) based on the ISCED-97 classification system. Those in the "upper secondary education" category include those who have attained post-secondary non-tertiary education (ISCED 4).

Electoral participation (voting) is captured by the percentage of adults who reported voting during the previous national election. European Social Survey (ESS) 2008 and 2010, General Social Survey (GSS) 2008 for Canada, the Current Population Survey (CPS) 2008 for the United States and Estudo Eleitoral Brasileiro (ESEB) 2010 for Brazil provide this information. The analysis in this chapter is limited to adults who are eligible to vote. Countries with compulsory voting are included in the data (i.e. Belgium, Greece and Turkey). For countries with a voting-registration requirement that is not enforced or automated (e.g. Ireland, the United Kingdom and the United States), the analysis includes those who are potentially eligible (e.g. are citizens of the country) but have not registered for voting.

Engagement in social activities is based on a question asking students how often they take part in social activities compared to other people of the same age. Social activities relate to events and encounters by choice and for enjoyment rather than for reasons of work or duty.

Life expectancy is calculated using a well established statistical method and information from life tables. Note that there are certain discrepancies across countries depending on the available data source (i.e. registered or survey data) and how death has been identified. As with other indicators, it is important to emphasise that the indicators are meant to be compared across gender and education groups within each country. Note also that life expectancy is calculated based on various factors that individuals have experienced in the past, which will not necessarily be those constituting the environment of similar individuals in the present or in the future. This indicator can be considered a robust measure assuming that the socio-economic, cultural and environmental conditions that drive life expectancy are relatively stable over time within a country.

Life satisfaction is captured by the percentage of adults who reported being satisfied with life. ESS 2010, GSS 2008 for Canada and New Zealand and Lifelong Education Survey 2010 for Korea provide this information.

Students' attitudes towards equal rights for ethnic minorities are captured by the mean ICCS scale of students' responses to a series of questions related to attitudes towards minorities' rights. The questions ask if students express support for equal rights for all ethnic groups. These scales are set to have an international mean of 50 scale points and a standard deviation of 10 points. See Lauglo (2011) for more details on how this scale is developed.

Methodology

Given the potentially significant cross-country differences in norms (e.g. social desirability of expressing one's satisfaction with life) and institutional contexts (e.g. eligibility and compulsory nature of voting), indicators related to social outcomes should be interpreted with caution. The main focus should be on *within-country* differences in social outcomes across levels of educational attainment and civic competencies, rather than *cross-country* comparisons.

The indicators presented in this chapter are based on developmental work jointly conducted by the INES Network on Labour Market, Economic and Social Outcomes of Learning (LSO) and the OECD Centre for Educational Research and Innovation (CERI). The life expectancy indicators are based on past research by Eurostat. The conceptual framework for the indicators was developed by CERI's Social Outcomes of Learning project (OECD, 2007; OECD, 2010), and the empirical strategies were developed by the INES LSO Network. See Annex 3 at *www.oecd.org/edu/eag2012* for details on the calculation of the indicators.

In this year's edition of *Education at a Glance*, we present four new indicators (Tables A11.1, A11.2, A11.3 and A11.4), as well as updates of indicators presented in *Education at a Glance 2011* (Table A11.5) that can be found on line. Updated indicators are included since the primary data source, ESS, released revised measures of educational attainment in 2010 that are more comparable across countries. The new indicators were calculated using micro-data from the ESS 2008 and 2010, EUROSTAT's Statistical Database, STATCAN's CANSIM Database for Canada , CDC/NCHS, National Longitudinal Mortality Study, National Vital Statistics System, and the U.S. Census Bureau for the United States. Updates of indicators presented in *Education at a Glance 2011* were calculated using the ESS 2010. Surveys were selected on the basis of the following factors:

Age restriction: For indicators using surveys that cover only adults (i.e. Tables A11.2, A11.3 and A11.5), data on adults aged 25 to 64 were used. For surveys that cover students (i.e. Tables A11.4), data on children enrolled in grade 8 (approximately 14 years old) were used.

Comparability of educational attainment variables: The general principle is to use micro-data for which the distribution of educational attainment was within 10 percentage points of figures published for comparable years in *Education at a Glance*. A number of exceptions, however, were made on the recommendation of the country representatives of INES Working Party and/or INES LSO Network (i.e. Denmark [ESS], France [ESS], Norway [ESS] and Poland [ESS]). For some countries, the discrepancy in the educational attainment distributions may be driven by the possibility that ESS's educational attainment category "Lower secondary or second stage of basic" level includes those who have attained ISCED 3C (long), which is classified as upper secondary education in A11.

Comparability of social outcomes variables: Surveys are selected on the basis of the comparability of social outcomes variables.

Country coverage: An important objective is to select surveys that represent a large number of OECD countries. This was the motivation to select the European Social Survey, which covers a large number of European Union (EU) member countries and other countries for the adult population. For the ICCS, a large number of EU and other countries were included, including Austria, Belgium (Flanders), Chile, the Czech Republic, Denmark, Estonia, Finland, Greece, Indonesia, Ireland, Italy, Korea, Luxembourg, Mexico, the Netherlands, New Zealand, Norway, Poland, the Russian Federation, the Slovak Republic, Slovenia, Spain, Sweden, Switzerland and the United Kingdom (England).

Sample size: Surveys with a minimum sample of approximately 1 000 observations per country were used.

To calculate incremental percentage-point differences, country-specific regression models were estimated to predict each dichotomous outcome variable (e.g. high versus low level of interest in politics) from individuals' educational attainment level, with and without control variables for age, gender and family income. In preliminary analyses, both probit and ordinary least squares (OLS) regressions were used, and were found to produce very similar estimates of incremental differences. Because OLS regression provides more readily interpretable coefficients, OLS was used for the final analysis to generate incremental differences (Tables A11.3 and A11.5).

References

Cipollone, P. and A. Rosolia (2011) "Schooling and Youth Mortality: Learning from a Mass Military Exemption," *CEPR Discussion Papers*, No. 8431.

Eurostat (2012), Statistical Database, *http://epp.eurostat.ec.europa.eu/portal/page/portal/population/data/database.*

Glied, S. and A. Lleras-Muney (2008), "Health, Inequality, Education and Medical Innovation", *Demography*, Vol. 45, pp.741-761.

Lauglo, J. (2011), *Statistics of Possible Interest to OECD Based on Data from the IEA International Civic and Citizenship Education Study 2009*, unpublished mimeo, Norwegian Social Research (NOVA), Oslo.

Lleras-Muney, A. (2005), "The Relationship between Education and Adult Mortality in the United States", *Review of Economic Studies*, Vol. 72, pp. 189-221.

Miligan, K., E. Moretti and P. Oreopoulos (2004), "Does Education Improve Citizenship?" Evidence from the United States and the United Kingdom", *Journal of Public Economics*, Vol. 88, pp. 1667-1695.

OECD (2007), *Understanding the Social Outcomes of Learning*, OECD Publishing.

OECD (2010), *Improving Health and Social Cohesion through Education*, OECD Publishing.

Schulz, et al., (2010), *ICCS 2009 International Report: Civic Knowledge, Attitudes, and Engagement Among Lower-Secondary School Students in 38 countries*, IEA, Amsterdam.

The following additional material relevant to this indicator is available on line:

* *Table A11.5. Incremental percentage point differences in adult voting and life satisfaction associated with an increase in the level of educational attainment (2010) (with and without adjustments for age, gender and income)*
  StatLink ᗰᏚᏞᎦ http://dx.doi.org/10.1787/888932665829

Table A11.1. Additional years of life expectancy at age 30, by level of educational attainment and gender (2010)

	Men			Women			Total		
	Below upper secondary education	Upper secondary education	Tertiary education	Below upper secondary education	Upper secondary education	Tertiary education	Below upper secondary education	Upper secondary education	Tertiary education
Australia	m	m	m	m	m	m	m	m	m
Austria	m	m	m	m	m	m	m	m	m
Belgium	m	m	m	m	m	m	m	m	m
Canada	45.9	48.3	50.9	51.6	53.6	55.2	48.8	51.0	53.1
Chile	m	m	m	m	m	m	m	m	m
Czech Republic	34.1	45.8	50.9	49.7	51.4	54.3	43.8	48.6	52.6
Denmark	44.9	48.3	50.6	49.8	52.5	53.6	47.4	50.2	52.2
Estonia	34.2	42.6	47.7	46.1	50.5	54.6	39.1	46.7	52.1
Finland	45.3	47.7	51.0	52.1	54.2	55.3	48.4	51.0	53.3
France	m	m	m	m	m	m	m	m	m
Germany	m	m	m	m	m	m	m	m	m
Greece	m	m	m	m	m	m	m	m	m
Hungary	34.3	44.3	47.4	46.1	50.9	51.5	40.8	47.5	49.5
Iceland	m	m	m	m	m	m	m	m	m
Ireland	45.3	49.2	51.7	50.2	53.4	55.3	47.2	51.2	53.4
Israel	m	m	m	m	m	m	m	m	m
Italy	48.3	53.0	53.2	54.2	56.7	56.9	51.3	55.0	55.1
Japan	m	m	m	m	m	m	m	m	m
Korea	m	m	m	m	m	m	m	m	m
Luxembourg	m	m	m	m	m	m	m	m	m
Mexico	m	m	m	m	m	m	m	m	m
Netherlands	47.9	50.1	52.3	50.0	55.3	56.3	50.6	52.6	54.5
New Zealand	m	m	m	m	m	m	m	m	m
Norway	46.6	50.2	52.4	52.0	54.4	55.3	49.4	52.3	53.9
Poland	37.3	43.6	49.3	49.0	51.4	53.8	43.0	47.4	51.7
Portugal	47.1	48.7	50.0	53.3	53.7	54.3	50.2	51.1	52.3
Slovak Republic	m	m	m	m	m	m	m	m	m
Slovenia	40.4	48.0	50.9	50.9	54.3	55.0	46.3	51.0	53.0
Spain	m	m	m	m	m	m	m	m	m
Sweden	48.4	50.5	52.3	52.5	54.1	55.4	50.3	52.3	54.0
Switzerland	m	m	m	m	m	m	m	m	m
Turkey	m	m	m	m	m	m	m	m	m
United Kingdom	m	m	m	m	m	m	m	m	m
United States	47.2	52.1	55.4	47.8	52.4	53.4	47.4	52.3	54.4
OECD average	43.1	48.2	51.1	50.3	53.3	54.7	46.9	50.7	53.0
EU21 average	42.3	47.6	50.6	50.3	53.2	54.7	46.5	50.4	52.8
Argentina	m	m	m	m	m	m	m	m	m
Brazil	m	m	m	m	m	m	m	m	m
China	m	m	m	m	m	m	m	m	m
India	m	m	m	m	m	m	m	m	m
Indonesia	m	m	m	m	m	m	m	m	m
Russian Federation	m	m	m	m	m	m	m	m	m
Saudi Arabia	m	m	m	m	m	m	m	m	m
South Africa	m	m	m	m	m	m	m	m	m
G20 average	m	m	m	m	m	m	m	m	m

Note: Figures for Canada are based on the average between 1991 and 2006. Weighted average of "Level 3 (short of a university bachelor's degree)" and "Level 4: University degree (bachelor's or higher)" are used to calculate the figures for Tertiary education. Figures for Ireland are calculated based on the weighted average of figures for ages 20 and 35. Census (2006) is used to calculate the total figure. Figures for Italy are based on 2008. Figures for the Netherlands are based on the average between 2007-10. Figures for Slovenia are based on 2009. Figures for the United States are based on 2005 using adjusted, revised state with 2003 degree-based education items presented in tables 8 and 9 of *http://www.cdc.gov/nchs/data/series/sr_02/sr02_151.pdf.*

Sources: EUROSTAT (2010): *http://epp.eurostat.ec.europa.eu/portal/page/portal/population/data/database;* Statistics Canada (2012): *http://www5.statcan.gc.ca/cansim/home-accueil?lang=eng&p2=50;* FitzGerald, Byre and Znuderl (2011) for Ireland; CDC (2010): *http://www.cdc.gov/nchs/data/series/sr_02/sr02_151.pdf* for the United States. See Annex 3 for notes (*www.oecd.org/edu/eag2012*).

Please refer to the Reader's Guide for information concerning the symbols replacing missing data.

StatLink 🔗 http://dx.doi.org/10.1787/888932665753

A11

Table A11.2. Proportions of adults voting, by level of educational attainment and age group (2008, 2010)

	Younger (25-34 years old)			Older (55-64 years old)			Total (25-64 years old)		
	Below upper secondary education	Upper secondary education	Tertiary education	Below upper secondary education	Upper secondary education	Tertiary education	Below upper secondary education	Upper secondary education	Tertiary education
Australia	m	m	m	m	m	m	m	m	m
Austria	36.6	63.7	80.4	72.7	81.8	91.7	67.9	77.6	88.5
Belgium	71.6	90.7	93.2	89.5	92.8	93.5	87.5	92.3	93.4
Canada	41.1	55.1	68.2	77.2	87.1	90.3	63.4	72.4	78.4
Chile	m	m	m	m	m	m	m	m	m
Czech Republic	34.2	46.9	77.3	47.0	63.5	82.4	44.8	59.6	81.0
Denmark	71.0	88.2	94.2	92.9	94.6	96.1	90.8	93.6	95.7
Estonia	43.7	56.1	76.3	53.6	66.5	84.7	50.8	64.3	82.6
Finland	47.1	61.7	86.1	73.7	80.7	90.1	71.7	76.1	89.0
France	28.0	53.4	68.5	72.3	77.9	84.8	69.0	73.8	80.4
Germany	44.7	74.2	94.3	67.4	81.7	94.2	62.0	80.3	94.2
Greece	83.6	86.5	83.0	91.0	90.5	89.7	90.2	89.5	87.5
Hungary	70.2	69.9	81.7	79.4	79.1	89.8	77.6	76.8	87.1
Iceland	m	m	m	m	m	m	m	m	m
Ireland	58.3	69.5	59.3	83.8	87.8	86.3	81.3	84.6	77.9
Israel	65.5	65.2	78.9	79.8	82.1	87.9	78.1	77.2	85.4
Italy	m	m	m	m	m	m	m	m	m
Japan	m	m	m	m	m	m	m	m	m
Korea	m	m	m	m	m	m	m	m	m
Luxembourg	m	m	m	m	m	m	m	m	m
Mexico	m	m	m	m	m	m	m	m	m
Netherlands	64.6	80.5	94.9	78.3	89.6	94.3	76.9	87.8	94.4
New Zealand	m	m	m	m	m	m	m	m	m
Norway	59.4	67.4	86.8	78.1	88.2	93.9	75.9	84.2	92.0
Poland	40.6	63.3	79.1	69.6	77.6	88.1	65.1	73.8	84.2
Portugal	58.6	66.9	77.7	75.1	81.1	85.3	72.8	76.2	82.7
Slovak Republic	68.3	72.5	80.2	74.4	82.2	84.2	74.1	80.2	82.9
Slovenia	47.4	56.8	76.6	73.7	74.6	86.0	72.0	69.7	83.1
Spain	70.8	80.4	82.2	82.4	87.0	90.3	80.5	85.0	87.5
Sweden	65.4	85.8	95.7	90.9	93.5	96.9	89.4	91.3	96.6
Switzerland	19.0	38.9	59.0	46.5	64.9	78.9	42.8	59.5	75.0
Turkey	84.4	84.1	86.2	94.6	95.0	90.7	91.6	89.7	87.8
United Kingdom	35.0	54.2	67.1	68.9	74.0	80.3	63.6	69.2	77.3
United States	29.9	58.0	82.0	51.3	79.2	91.5	41.8	69.5	87.4
OECD average	53.6	67.6	80.4	74.6	82.1	88.9	71.3	78.2	86.1
EU21 average	55.2	68.0	81.7	74.9	81.6	88.8	72.3	78.2	86.5
Argentina	m	m	m	m	m	m	m	m	m
Brazil	91.1	86.8	93.1	97.1	100.0	100.0	92.5	89.1	93.1
China	m	m	m	m	m	m	m	m	m
India	m	m	m	m	m	m	m	m	m
Indonesia	m	m	m	m	m	m	m	m	m
Russian Federation	46.1	56.5	59.7	73.9	72.1	75.3	67.1	68.5	71.2
Saudi Arabia	m	m	m	m	m	m	m	m	m
South Africa	m	m	m	m	m	m	m	m	m
G20 average	m	m	m	m	m	m	m	m	m

Notes: Figures presented in the column "Below upper secondary education" describe the proportion of adults who have attained below upper secondary education reporting electoral participation. Likewise, figures presented in columns "Upper secondary education" and "Tertiary education" describe the proportion of adults who have attained upper secondary and tertiary education reporting electoral participation. The analysis is limited to adults who are eligible to vote. Countries with compulsory voting are included in the data, i.e. Belgium, Greece and Turkey. For countries with a voting registration requirement which is not enforced or automated (e.g. Ireland, the United Kingdom and the United States), the analysis includes those who are potentially eligible (e.g. are citizens of the country) but have not registered for voting. Data for Brazil for older age groups is likely to be affected by small cell size.

Source: European Social Survey (ESS) 2008 and 2010; General Social Survey (GSS) 2008 for Canada; Estudo Eleitoral Brasileiro (ESEB) 2010 – CESOP-UNICAMP. See Annex 3 for notes (www.oecd.org/edu/eag2012).

Please refer to the Reader's Guide for information concerning the symbols replacing missing data.

StatLink ⟡⟐ http://dx.doi.org/10.1787/888932665772

Table A11.3. Incremental percentage point differences in "engagement in social activities" associated with an increase in the level of educational attainment (2010) (with and without adjustments for age, gender and income)

Percentage of 25-64 years-old, by level of educational attainment

	Proportion of adults engaged in social activities among those who have attained upper secondary education	Difference in outcome from below upper secondary to upper secondary			Difference in outcome from upper secondary to tertiary		
		No adjustments	Adjustments age, gender	Adjustments age, gender, income	No adjustments	Adjustments age, gender	Adjustments age, gender, income
OECD							
Australia	m	m	m	m	m	m	m
Austria	69.2	17.2	17.5	16.6	2.6	2.8	2.3
Belgium	55.4	10.1	8.5	7.8	14.2	13.1	13.0
Canada	m	m	m	m	m	m	m
Chile	m	m	m	m	m	m	m
Czech Republic	58.2	19.0	19.5	15.7	9.3	8.4	5.6
Denmark	67.2	3.7	3.9	3.0	8.8	7.7	5.5
Estonia	44.4	18.1	17.2	15.8	14.9	15.3	12.5
Finland	51.3	4.7	6.4	5.1	12.7	13.0	10.2
France	83.9	14.1	15.1	10.3	-4.1	-3.5	-8.5
Germany	58.2	-0.5	0.3	-1.8	6.0	6.6	3.8
Greece	m	m	m	m	m	m	m
Hungary	47.7	21.6	19.0	15.8	9.6	9.4	6.5
Iceland	m	m	m	m	m	m	m
Ireland	m	m	m	m	m	m	m
Israel	59.4	1.6	0.4	0.1	6.0	5.7	5.2
Italy	m	m	m	m	m	m	m
Japan	m	m	m	m	m	m	m
Korea	m	m	m	m	m	m	m
Luxembourg	m	m	m	m	m	m	m
Mexico	m	m	m	m	m	m	m
Netherlands	67.3	10.1	10.3	9.7	5.6	5.8	4.5
New Zealand	m	m	m	m	m	m	m
Norway	77.3	13.7	14.5	12.9	0.6	0.2	-2.1
Poland	60.1	6.0	5.8	4.5	1.7	1.3	-0.1
Portugal	76.8	17.2	15.0	15.0	5.2	5.5	5.5
Slovak Republic	m	m	m	m	m	m	m
Slovenia	59.1	m	m	m	m	m	m
Spain	71.5	13.8	12.2	10.0	6.5	6.4	4.0
Sweden	65.8	9.3	9.5	6.9	6.5	7.2	3.8
Switzerland	56.9	1.2	1.3	0.5	6.0	6.2	5.7
Turkey	m	m	m	m	m	m	m
United Kingdom	56.8	-1.1	-0.7	-2.6	6.9	6.9	3.2
United States	m	m	m	m	m	m	m
OECD average	62.4	10.0	9.8	8.1	6.6	6.6	4.5
EU21 average	62.1	10.9	10.6	8.8	7.1	7.1	4.8
Other G20							
Argentina	m	m	m	m	m	m	m
Brazil	m	m	m	m	m	m	m
China	m	m	m	m	m	m	m
India	m	m	m	m	m	m	m
Indonesia	m	m	m	m	m	m	m
Russian Federation	61.5	7.0	7.6	6.7	0.0	0.4	-2.0
Saudi Arabia	m	m	m	m	m	m	m
South Africa	m	m	m	m	m	m	m
G20 average	m	m	m	m	m	m	m

Notes: This indicator is based on a question "Compared to other people of your age, how often would you say you take part in social activities?". Social activities relate to events/encounters with other people, by choice and for enjoyment rather than for reasons of work or duty. Those responded that they take part in activities "about the same" or more are considered engaged. Except for the first column, calculations are based on ordinary least squares regressions among adults aged 25-64. Cells highlighted in grey are statistically significant and different from zero at the 5% level. Non-linear models (probit models) produce similar results.

Source: European Social Survey (ESS) 2010. See Annex 3 for notes (*www.oecd.org/edu/eag2012*).

Please refer to the Reader's Guide for information concerning the symbols replacing missing data.

StatLink ᘉᕟᔮ http://dx.doi.org/10.1787/888932665791

A11

Table A11.4. Mean scores of "students' attitudes towards equal rights for ethnic minorities", by their proficiency level of civic knowledge (2009)

| | Proficiency levels of civic knowledge | | | | | | | |
| | Below Level 1 | | Level 1 | | Level 2 | | Level 3 | |
	Mean scores	Standard error	Mean scores	Standard error	Mean scores	Standard error	Mean scores	Standard error
OECD Australia	m	m	m	m	m	m	m	m
Austria	43.0	(0.6)	44.9	(0.5)	48.1	(0.4)	52.0	(0.4)
Belgium (Fl.)	45.5	(0.8)	46.6	(0.5)	47.6	(0.4)	49.8	(0.5)
Canada	m	m	m	m	m	m	m	m
Chile	49.8	(0.5)	52.8	(0.4)	56.0	(0.3)	58.4	(0.3)
Czech Republic	43.6	(0.5)	44.7	(0.3)	46.4	(0.3)	49.1	(0.4)
Denmark	44.8	(1.6)	45.6	(0.6)	46.5	(0.5)	50.2	(0.4)
Estonia	45.5	(0.8)	48.0	(0.4)	50.5	(0.3)	53.6	(0.3)
Finland	40.8	(1.8)	43.5	(0.7)	45.6	(0.4)	49.8	(0.3)
France	m	m	m	m	m	m	m	m
Germany	m	m	m	m	m	m	m	m
Greece	44.9	(0.6)	47.8	(0.5)	50.9	(0.4)	53.9	(0.4)
Hungary	m	m	m	m	m	m	m	m
Iceland	m	m	m	m	m	m	m	m
Ireland	44.9	(0.8)	48.1	(0.6)	50.3	(0.5)	53.9	(0.4)
Israel	m	m	m	m	m	m	m	m
Italy	45.4	(0.5)	46.9	(0.4)	48.8	(0.4)	51.5	(0.3)
Japan	m	m	m	m	m	m	m	m
Korea	40.3	(1.2)	44.8	(0.5)	48.3	(0.3)	51.3	(0.2)
Luxembourg	49.6	(0.5)	51.5	(0.3)	52.6	(0.3)	53.8	(0.3)
Mexico	48.3	(0.4)	51.6	(0.3)	55.0	(0.2)	58.4	(0.3)
Netherlands	44.6	(1.2)	45.9	(0.8)	47.7	(0.8)	49.2	(0.9)
New Zealand	45.6	(0.9)	48.2	(0.6)	51.5	(0.5)	56.1	(0.4)
Norway	45.5	(0.8)	48.7	(0.5)	51.4	(0.4)	55.7	(0.4)
Poland	44.3	(0.7)	46.8	(0.4)	48.9	(0.3)	52.5	(0.4)
Portugal	m	m	m	m	m	m	m	m
Slovak Republic	45.5	(0.8)	46.5	(0.4)	47.9	(0.4)	50.8	(0.4)
Slovenia	44.4	(0.7)	46.6	(0.4)	49.7	(0.3)	52.5	(0.4)
Spain	46.1	(0.7)	48.3	(0.4)	51.0	(0.4)	53.6	(0.4)
Sweden	44.9	(1.0)	47.7	(0.5)	51.2	(0.5)	56.0	(0.4)
Switzerland	42.8	(1.2)	45.6	(0.7)	48.5	(0.5)	52.2	(0.3)
Turkey	m	m	m	m	m	m	m	m
United Kingdom (England)	44.1	(0.6)	46.4	(0.6)	48.7	(0.6)	54.3	(0.5)
United States	m	m	m	m	m	m	m	m
OECD total	45.0	(0.2)	47.3	(0.1)	49.6	(0.1)	52.9	(0.1)
EU21 average	44.8	m	46.8	m	49.0	m	52.1	m
Other G20 Argentina	m	m	m	m	m	m	m	m
Brazil	m	m	m	m	m	m	m	m
China	m	m	m	m	m	m	m	m
India	m	m	m	m	m	m	m	m
Indonesia	48.2	(0.3)	50.1	(0.3)	52.6	(0.3)	55.3	(0.5)
Russian Federation	45.6	(0.5)	46.9	(0.3)	48.5	(0.3)	50.6	(0.4)
Saudi Arabia	m	m	m	m	m	m	m	m
South Africa	m	m	m	m	m	m	m	m
G20 average	m	m	m	m	m	m	m	m

Notes: Figures presented in the column "Below Level 1" describe the mean scales of Grade 8 students' civic engagement (i.e. express support for equal rights for all ethnic groups) among those who have scored "Below Level 1" in civic knowledge. Likewise, figures presented in the columns "Level 1", "Level 2" and "Level 3" describe the mean scales of students' civic engagement among those who have scored at "Level 1", "Level 2" and "Level 3" in civic knowledge. EU21 average represents weighted average of EU member countries that are also OECD countries. They include Austria, Belgium (Flanders), the Czech Republic, Denmark, Estonia, Finland, Greece, Ireland, Italy, Luxembourg, the Netherlands, Poland, the Slovak Republic, Slovenia, Spain, Sweden and the United Kingdom (England). Mean ICCS scales are based on Rasch Partical Credit Model, and the resulting weighted likelihood estimates (WLEs) were transformed into a metric with a mean of 50 and a standard deviation of 10. The *Definitions* section provides more details on the ICCS scale.
Source: International Civic and Citizenship Education Study (ICCS), 2009. See Annex 3 for notes (*www.oecd.org/edu/eag2012*).
Please refer to the Reader's Guide for information concerning the symbols replacing missing data.
StatLink ᵐˢᴾ http://dx.doi.org/10.1787/888932665810

Chapter

FINANCIAL AND HUMAN RESOURCES INVESTED IN EDUCATION

Classification of educational expenditure

Educational expenditure in this chapter is classified through three dimensions:

- The first dimension – represented by the horizontal axis in the diagram below – relates to the location where spending occurs. Spending on schools and universities, education ministries and other agencies directly involved in providing and supporting education is one component of this dimension. Spending on education outside these institutions is another.

- The second dimension – represented by the vertical axis in the diagram below – classifies the goods and services that are purchased. Not all expenditure on educational institutions can be classified as direct educational or instructional expenditure. Educational institutions in many OECD countries offer various ancillary services – such as meals, transport, housing, etc. – in addition to teaching services to support students and their families. At the tertiary level, spending on research and development can be significant. Not all spending on educational goods and services occurs within educational institutions. For example, families may purchase textbooks and materials themselves or seek private tutoring for their children.

- The third dimension – represented by the colours in the diagram below – distinguishes among the sources from which funding originates. These include the public sector and international agencies (indicated by light blue), and households and other private entities (indicated by medium-blue). Where private expenditure on education is subsidised by public funds, this is indicated by cells in the grey colour.

| | Public sources of funds | Private sources of funds | Private funds publicly subsidised |

	Spending on educational institutions (e.g. schools, universities, educational administration and student welfare services)	Spending on education outside educational institutions (e.g. private purchases of educational goods and services, including private tutoring)
Spending on core educational services	e.g. public spending on instructional services in educational institutions	e.g. subsidised private spending on books
	e.g. subsidised private spending on instructional services in educational institutions	e.g. private spending on books and other school materials or private tutoring
	e.g. private spending on tuition fees	
Spending on research and development	e.g. public spending on university research	
	e.g. funds from private industry for research and development in educational institutions	
Spending on educational services other than instruction	e.g. public spending on ancillary services such as meals, transport to schools, or housing on the campus	e.g. subsidised private spending on student living costs or reduced prices for transport
	e.g. private spending on fees for ancillary services	e.g. private spending on student living costs or transport

Coverage diagrams

For Indicators **B1, B2, B3 and B6**

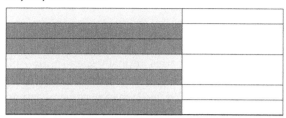

For Indicators **B4 and B5**

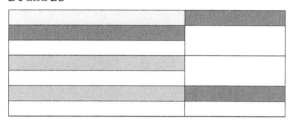

HOW MUCH IS SPENT PER STUDENT?

- On average, OECD countries spend USD 9 252 annually per student from primary through tertiary education: USD 7 719 per primary student, USD 9 312 per secondary student and USD 13 728 per tertiary student.

- Excluding activities peripheral to instruction (research and development and ancillary services such as welfare services to students), OECD countries annually spend USD 7 620 from primary through tertiary education, on average. This lower figure results mainly from the much lower expenditure per student at the tertiary level (USD 8 944) when peripheral activities are excluded.

- At the primary and secondary levels, 94% of total expenditure per student is devoted to core educational services (i.e. excluding activities peripheral to education). Greater differences are seen at the tertiary level, partly because expenditure on R&D represents an average of 31% of total expenditure per student, and can account for more than 40% in Norway, Portugal, Sweden and Switzerland.

- As of 2009, the economic crisis had not yet affected the investment on education in the majority of OECD countries. From 2005 to 2009, expenditure per student by primary, secondary and post-secondary non-tertiary educational institutions increased by 15 percentage points on average in OECD countries, following a previous significant increase between 2000 and 2005. A similar pattern is observed at the tertiary level, with increases of 5 percentage points over the 2000-05 period and 9 percentage points over the 2005-09 period.

Chart B1.1. Annual expenditure per student by educational institutions in primary through tertiary education, by type of service (2009)

In equivalent USD converted using PPPs, for primary to tertiary education, based on full-time equivalents

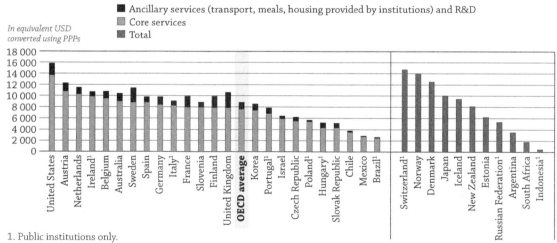

1. Public institutions only.
Countries are ranked in descending order of expenditure per student by educational institutions for core services.
Source: OECD. Argentina, Indonesia: UNESCO Institute for Statistics (World Education Indicators programme). South Africa: UNESCO Institute for Statistics. Table B1.2. See Annex 3 for notes (*www.oecd.org/edu/eag2012*).
StatLink ⬛⬛ http://dx.doi.org/10.1787/888932662447

How to read this chart
The amount of expenditure per student by educational institutions provides a measure of the unit costs of formal education. This chart shows annual expenditure (from public and private sources) per student by educational institutions in equivalent USD converted using purchasing power parities (PPPs), based on the number of full-time equivalent students. It distinguishes expenditure by type of services: core educational services, ancillary services, and research and development. Expenditure on core educational services includes all expenditure that is directly related to instruction in educational institutions. This covers all expenditure on teachers, school buildings, teaching materials, books, and the administration of schools.

■ Context

The demand for high-quality education, which can translate into higher costs per student, must be balanced against other demands on public expenditure and the overall burden of taxation. Policy makers must also balance the importance of improving the quality of educational services with the desirability of expanding access to educational opportunities, notably at the tertiary level. A comparative review of trends in expenditure per student by educational institutions shows that in many OECD countries, expenditure has not kept up with expanding enrolments. In addition, some OECD countries emphasise broad access to higher education, while others invest in near-universal education for children as young as three or four. Both investment in education and the number of students enrolled in education can be affected by financial crises. Consequently, the recent global economic crisis is likely to have resulted in changes in the level of expenditure per student. However, because the crisis began in late 2008, available data cannot show yet the full extent of this impact.

Expenditure per student by educational institutions is largely influenced by teachers' salaries (see Indicators B6 and D3), pension systems, instructional and teaching hours (see Indicator B7), the cost of teaching materials and facilities, the programme provided (e.g. general or vocational), and the number of students enrolled in the education system (see Indicator C1). Policies to attract new teachers or to reduce average class size or change staffing patterns (see Indicator D2) have also contributed to changes in expenditure per student by educational institutions over time. Ancillary and R&D services can also influence the level of expenditure per student.

■ Other findings

- Among the ten countries with the largest expenditure per student by educational institutions in secondary education, **high teachers' salaries and low student-teacher ratios are often the main factors explaining the level of expenditure.**

- At the primary and secondary levels, there is a strong positive relationship between spending per student by educational institutions and GDP per capita. The relationship is weaker at the tertiary level, mainly because financing mechanisms and enrolment patterns differ more at this level.

- On average, **OECD countries spend nearly twice as much per student at the tertiary level than at the primary level**. However, R&D activities or ancillary services can account for a significant proportion of expenditure at the tertiary level. When these are excluded, expenditure per student on core educational services at the tertiary level is still, on average, 10% higher than at the primary, secondary and post-secondary non-tertiary levels.

- **The orientation of programmes provided to students at the secondary level influences the level of expenditure per student** in most countries. Among the 17 OECD countries with separate data on expenditure for general and vocational programmes at the upper secondary level, an average of USD 1 124 more per student was spent on vocational programmes than on general programmes.

■ Trends

Expenditure per primary, secondary and post-secondary non-tertiary student by educational institutions increased in every country with available data, and by an average of more than 36% between 2000 and 2009, a period of relatively stable student enrolment in most countries.

During the same period, **spending per tertiary student fell in 6 of the 27 countries** with available data, as expenditure did not keep up with expanding enrolments at this level. Iceland, Israel and the United States, which saw significant increases in student enrolment between 2000 and 2009, did not increase spending at the same pace as enrolment growth. As a result, expenditure per student decreased in these countries. This is also the case in Brazil, Hungary and Switzerland, where public expenditure per student (data on private expenditure are not available) decreased during this period.

B1

Analysis

Expenditure per student by educational institutions in equivalent USD

Spending per student from primary through tertiary education in 2009 ranged from USD 4 000 per student or less in Argentina, Brazil, Chile, Indonesia, Mexico and South Africa, to more than USD 10 000 per student in Australia, Austria, Belgium, Denmark, Ireland, Japan, the Netherlands, Norway, Sweden, Switzerland and the United Kingdom, and up over USD 15 000 in the United States. In 14 of 35 countries with available data, it ranged from USD 8 000 to less than USD 11 000 per student from primary through tertiary education (Chart B1.1 and Table B1.1a).

Countries have different priorities for allocating their resources (see Indicator B7). For example, among the ten countries with the largest expenditure per student by educational institutions at the secondary level, Belgium, Denmark, Ireland, Luxembourg, the Netherlands, Switzerland and the United States are among the ten countries with the highest teachers' salaries at the secondary level (see Indicator D3), while Austria, Belgium, Denmark and Norway are among the countries with the lowest student-to-teacher ratios at the secondary level (see Indicator D2).

Even if spending per student from primary through tertiary education is similar in some OECD countries, the ways in which resources are allocated among the different levels of education vary widely. Spending per student by educational institutions in a typical OECD country (as represented by the simple mean across all OECD countries) amounts to USD 7 719 at the primary level, USD 9 312 at the secondary level and USD 13 728 at the tertiary level (Table B1.1a and Chart B1.2). At the tertiary level, this amount is affected by high expenditure in a few OECD countries – most notably Canada, Switzerland and the United States.

These averages mask a broad range of expenditure per student by educational institutions across countries. At the primary and secondary levels, expenditure per student by educational institutions varies by a factor of 8 and 9, respectively. At the primary level, expenditures range from USD 2 185 or less per student in Indonesia, Mexico and South Africa to USD 16 494 in Luxembourg. At the secondary level, expenditure ranges from USD 2 235 or less per student in Brazil, Indonesia and South Africa to USD 19 324 in Luxembourg. Expenditure per tertiary student by educational institutions ranges from USD 7 000 or less in Argentina, Chile, Estonia, Indonesia, the Slovak Republic and South Africa to more than USD 19 000 in Canada, Norway, Sweden, Switzerland and the United States (Table B1.1a and Chart B1.2).

These comparisons are based on purchasing power parities (PPPs) for GDP, not on market exchange rates. Therefore, they reflect the amount of a national currency required to produce the same basket of goods and services in a given country as produced by the United States in USD.

Expenditure per student on core educational services

On average across OECD countries, expenditure on core educational services represents 82% of total expenditure per student from primary through tertiary education, and exceeds 95% in Brazil, Mexico and Poland. In 6 of the 24 countries for which data are available – Finland, France, Hungary, the Slovak Republic, Sweden and the United Kingdom – core educational services account for less than 85% of total expenditure per student. Annual expenditure on R&D and ancillary services influence the ranking of countries for all services combined. However, this overall picture masks large variations among the levels of education (Table B1.2).

At the primary and secondary levels, expenditure is dominated by spending on core educational services. On average, OECD countries for which data are available spend 94% of the total expenditure per student by educational institutions on core educational services at the primary, secondary and post-secondary non-tertiary levels. This corresponds to USD 8 103 at these levels. In 9 of the 23 countries for which data are available, ancillary services provided by these institutions account for less than 5% of the total expenditure per student. The proportion exceeds 10% of total expenditure per student in Finland, France, Hungary, Korea, the Slovak Republic, Sweden and the United Kingdom (Table B1.2).

Chart B1.2. **Annual expenditure per student by educational institutions for all services, by level of education (2009)**

In equivalent USD converted using PPPs, based on full-time equivalents

B1

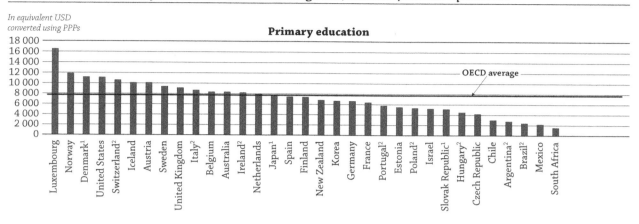

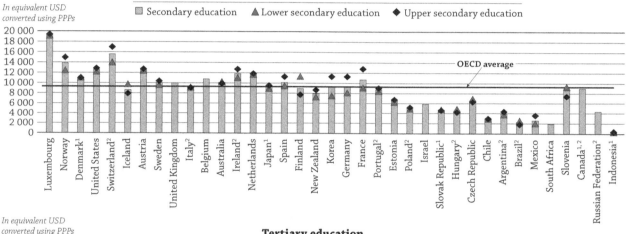

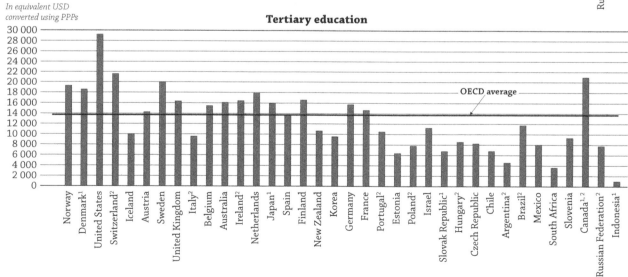

1. Some levels of education are included with others. Refer to "x"code in Table B1.1a for details.

2. Public institutions only (for Canada, in tertiary education only; for Italy, except in tertiary education).

Countries are ranked in descending order of expenditure on educational institutions per student in primary education.

Source: OECD. Argentina, Indonesia: UNESCO Institute for Statistics (World Education Indicators programme). South Africa: UNESCO Institute for Statistics. Table B1.1a. See Annex 3 for notes (*www.oecd.org/edu/eag2012*).

StatLink 🔗 http://dx.doi.org/10.1787/888932662466

B1

Greater differences are seen at the tertiary level, partly because R&D expenditure can account for a significant proportion of educational spending. The OECD countries in which most R&D is performed in tertiary educational institutions (e.g. Portugal, Sweden and Switzerland) tend to report higher expenditure per student than those in which a large proportion of R&D is performed in other public institutions or in industry (e.g. the United States).

Excluding R&D activities and ancillary services (peripheral services such as student welfare services), expenditure on core educational services in tertiary institutions is, on average, USD 8 944 per student. It ranges from USD 5 000 or less in Estonia and the Slovak Republic to more than USD 10 000 in Brazil, Canada, Finland, Ireland, the Netherlands and Norway, and more than USD 23 000 in the United States (Table B1.2).

On average in OECD countries, expenditure on R&D and ancillary services at the tertiary level represents 31% and 4%, respectively, of all expenditure per student by tertiary institutions. In 8 of the 29 OECD countries for which data on R&D and ancillary services are available separately from total expenditure – Australia, Germany, Italy, Norway, Portugal, Sweden, Switzerland and the United Kingdom – expenditure on R&D and ancillary services represents at least 40 % of total tertiary expenditure per student by educational institutions. This can translate into significant amounts: in Australia, Canada, Norway, Sweden, Switzerland and the United Kingdom, expenditure for R&D and ancillary services amounts to more than USD 6 500 per student (Table B1.2).

Expenditure per student by educational institutions at different levels of education

Expenditure per student by educational institutions rises with the level of education in almost all countries, but the size of the differentials varies markedly (Table B1.1a and Chart B1.3). At the secondary level, the expenditure is, on average, 1.2 times greater than at the primary level. This ratio exceeds 1.5 in the Czech Republic, France and Portugal. In these countries, this is mainly due to a simultaneous increase in the number of instructional hours for students and a significant decrease in the number of teachers' teaching hours between primary and secondary education, as compared to the OECD average (see Indicators B7, D1 and D4).

Chart B1.3. **Expenditure per student by educational institutions at various levels of education, for all services, relative to primary education (2009)**
Primary education = 100

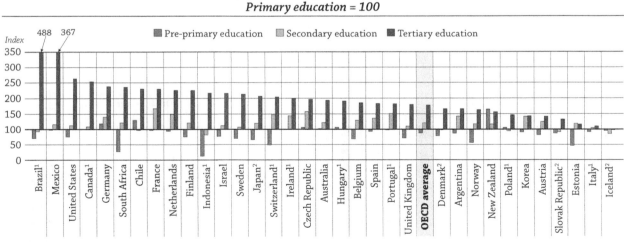

Notes: A ratio of 300 for tertiary education means that expenditure per tertiary student by educational institutions is three times the expenditure per primary student by educational institutions.

A ratio of 50 for pre-primary education means that exenditure per pre-primary student by educational institutions is half the expenditure per primary student by educational institutions.

1. Public institutions only.

2. Some levels of education are included with others. Refer to "x" code in Table B1.1a for details.

Countries are ranked in descending order of expenditure per student by educational institutions in tertiary education relative to primary education.

Source: OECD. Argentina, Indonesia: UNESCO Institute for Statistics (World Education Indicators programme). South Africa: UNESCO Institute for Statistics. Table B1.1a. See Annex 3 for notes (*www.oecd.org/edu/eag2012*).

StatLink ⟲ http://dx.doi.org/10.1787/888932662485

Educational institutions in OECD countries spend, on average, 1.8 times more per tertiary student than per primary student, but spending patterns vary widely, mainly because education policies vary more at the tertiary level (see Indicator B5). For example, Austria, Estonia, Iceland, Italy, Korea, Poland and the Slovak Republic spend less than 1.5 times more on a tertiary student than on a primary student, but Brazil and Mexico spend about three times as much or even more (Table B1.1a and Chart B1.3).

Differences in educational expenditure per student between general and vocational programmes

In the 17 OECD countries for which data are available, expenditure per student in upper secondary vocational programmes represents, on average, USD 1 124 more than expenditure per student in general programmes. The countries with large enrolments in dual-system apprenticeship programmes at the upper secondary level (e.g. Austria, France, Germany, Hungary, Luxembourg, the Netherlands and Switzerland) tend to be those with the largest differences, compared to the OECD average, between expenditure per student enrolled in general and vocational programmes. Finland, Germany, Luxembourg, the Netherlands, and Switzerland spend, respectively, USD 1 289, USD 3 857, USD 1 521, USD 3 094 and USD 7 712 more per student in vocational programmes than they spend per student in general programmes. Meanwhile, the Czech Republic, France and the Slovak Republic spend, respectively, USD 1 067, USD 930, and USD 1 104 more per student in vocational programmes than they spend per student in general programmes. Exceptions to this pattern are Austria, which has approximately the same level of expenditure per student in the two types of programmes, and Hungary, where expenditure per student enrolled in a general programme is slightly higher than expenditure per student in an apprenticeship programme. The underestimation of the expenditure made by private enterprises on dual vocational programmes can partly explain the small differences in Austria, France and Hungary (Box B3.1 in *Education at a Glance 2011*, Table B1.6, Table C1.3).

Expenditure per student by educational institutions over the average duration of tertiary studies

Given that the duration and intensity of tertiary education vary from country to country, differences in annual expenditure on educational services per student (Chart B1.2) do not necessarily reflect differences in the total cost of educating the typical tertiary student. For example, if the typical duration of tertiary studies is long, comparatively low annual expenditure per student by educational institutions can result in comparatively high overall costs for tertiary education. Chart B1.4 shows the average expenditure per student throughout the course of tertiary studies. The figures account for all students for whom expenditure is incurred, including those who do not finish their studies. Although the calculations are based on a number of simplified assumptions, and therefore should be treated with caution (see Annex 3 at *www.oecd.org/edu/eag2012*), there are some notable differences between annual and aggregate expenditure in the ranking of countries.

For example, annual spending per tertiary student in Japan is about the same as in Belgium, at USD 15 957 and USD 15 443, respectively (Table B1.1a). However, the average duration of tertiary studies is more than one year longer in Japan than in Belgium (4.2 and 3.0 years, respectively). As a consequence, the cumulative expenditure for each tertiary student is nearly USD 20 000 less in Belgium (USD 46 175) than in Japan (USD 66 856) (Chart B1.4 and Table B1.3a).

The total cost of tertiary-type A education in Switzerland (USD 126 021) is more than twice the amount reported by other countries, with the exception of Austria, Finland, France, Germany, Japan, the Netherlands, Spain and Sweden (Table B1.3a). These figures must be interpreted bearing in mind differences in national degree structures and possible differences in the qualifications students obtain after completing their studies. Tertiary-type B (shorter and vocationally oriented) programmes tend to be less expensive than tertiary-type A programmes, largely because of their shorter duration.

Expenditure per student by educational institutions relative to GDP per capita

Since access to education is universal (and usually compulsory) at the lower levels of schooling in most OECD countries, spending per student by educational institutions at those levels relative to GDP per capita can be interpreted as the resources spent on the school-age population relative to a country's ability to pay.

At higher levels of education, this measure is more difficult to interpret because student enrolment levels vary sharply among countries. At the tertiary level, for example, OECD countries may rank relatively high on this measure if a large proportion of their wealth is spent on educating a relatively small number of students.

Chart B1.4. Cumulative expenditure per student by educational institutions over the average duration of tertiary studies (2009)

Annual expenditure per student by educational institutions multiplied by the average duration of studies, in equivalent USD converted using PPPs

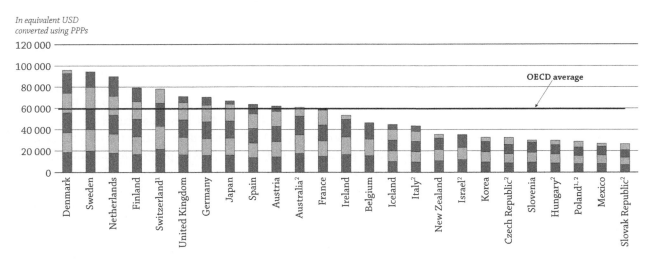

Note: Each segment of the bar represents the annual expenditure by educational institutions per student. The number of segments represents the average number of years a student remains in tertiary education.
1. Public institutions only.
2. Tertiary-type A and advanced research programmes only.
Countries are ranked in descending order of the total expenditure per student by educational institutions over the average duration of tertiary studies.
Source: OECD. Table B1.3a. See Annex 3 for notes (*www.oecd.org/edu/eag2012*).
StatLink ᴍˢᴸ http://dx.doi.org/10.1787/888932662504

In OECD countries, expenditure per student by educational institutions averages 23% of GDP per capita at the primary level, 27% at the secondary level and 42% at the tertiary level. Overall, from the primary to tertiary levels of education, expenditure per student averages 29% of the GDP per capita in OECD countries (Table B1.4). Countries with low levels of expenditure may nonetheless show distributions of investment relative to GDP per capita that are similar to those of countries with a high level of spending per student. For example, Korea and Portugal – countries with below-OECD-average expenditure per student by educational institutions at the secondary level of education and below-OECD-average GDP per capita – spend more per student relative to GDP per capita than the OECD average.

The relationship between GDP per capita and expenditure per student by educational institutions is difficult to interpret. However, as one would expect, there is a clear positive relationship between the two at both the primary and secondary levels of education – in other words, poorer countries tend to spend less per student than richer ones. Although the relationship is generally positive at these levels, there are variations, even among countries with similar levels of GDP per capita, and especially those in which GDP per capita exceeds USD 30 000. Australia and Austria, for example, have similar levels of GDP per capita (see Table X2.1 in Annex 2) but spend very different proportions of it at the primary and secondary levels. In Australia, the proportions are 21% at the primary level and 25% at the secondary level (below the OECD averages of 23% and 27%, respectively), while in Austria, the proportions are among the highest, at 26% and 32%, respectively (Table B1.4 and Chart B1.5).

Chart B1.5. **Annual expenditure per student by educational institutions relative to GDP per capita (2009)**

In equivalent USD converted using PPPs, by level of education

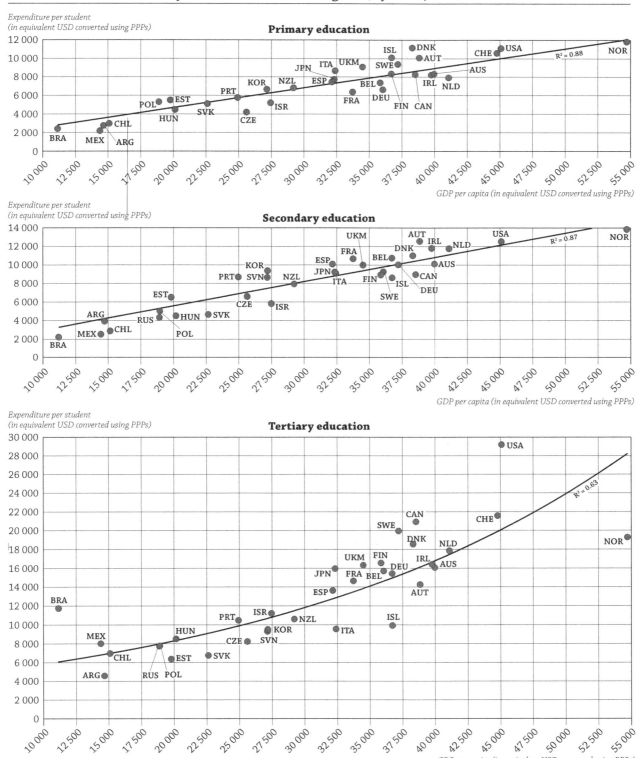

Note: Please refer to the Reader's Guide for the list of country codes used in this chart.
Source: OECD. Argentina: UNESCO Institute for Statistics (World Education Indicators programme). Tables B1.1a, B1.4 and Annex 2. See Annex 3 for notes (*www.oecd.org/edu/eag2012*).

StatLink ⬛ᵐˢ⬛ http://dx.doi.org/10.1787/888932662523

B1

There is more variation in spending levels at the tertiary level, and the relationship between countries' relative wealth and their expenditure levels varies as well. Italy and Spain, for example, have similar levels of GDP per capita (USD 32 397 and USD 32 146, respectively) but very different levels of spending on tertiary education (USD 9 562 and USD 13 614, respectively), even when taking into account core expenditure only (USD 5 688 and USD 9 186). Canada, Mexico, Sweden and the United States spend more than 50% of GDP per capita on each tertiary student – among the highest proportions after Brazil and Saudi Arabia (Table B1.4 and Chart B1.5). Brazil spends the equivalent of 105% of GDP per capita on each tertiary student; however, it is important to bear in mind that tertiary students represent only 3% of students enrolled in all levels of education combined (Table B1.7, available on line).

Change in expenditure per student by educational institutions between 1995 and 2009

Changes in expenditure by educational institutions largely reflect changes in the size of the school-age population and in teachers' salaries. These tend to rise over time in real terms, as teachers' salaries, the main component of costs, have increased in the majority of countries during the past decade (see Indicator D3).

Chart B1.6. Changes in the number of students and changes in expenditure per student by educational institutions, by level of education (2000, 2009)

Index of change between 2000 and 2009 (2000 = 100, 2009 constant prices)

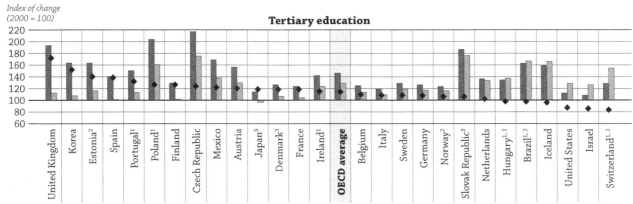

1. Public institutions only.
2. Public expenditure only.
3. Some levels of education are included with others. Refer to "x" code in Table B1.1a for details.
Countries are ranked in descending order of change in expenditure per student by educational institutions.
Source: OECD. Tables B1.5a and B1.5b. See Annex 3 for notes (*www.oecd.org/edu/eag2012*).
StatLink 🔗 http://dx.doi.org/10.1787/888932662542

The size of the school-age population influences both enrolment levels and the amount of resources and organisational effort a country must invest in its education system. The larger this population, the greater the potential demand for educational services.

Expenditure per primary, secondary and post-secondary non-tertiary student by educational institutions increased in every country by an average of 56% between 1995 and 2009, a time during which student enrolment at these levels was relatively stable. The increase was relatively similar over the periods 2000-05 and 2005-09, showing that the global economic crisis had not yet affected the investment in education in the majority of countries. Only Hungary and Mexico showed a decrease between 2005 and 2009 in expenditure per primary, secondary and post-secondary non-tertiary student (Table B1.5a).

Between 2000 and 2009, in 24 of the 29 countries for which data are available, expenditure per primary, secondary and post-secondary non-tertiary student by educational institutions increased by at least 16%. The increase exceeded 50% in Brazil, the Czech Republic, Estonia, Hungary, Ireland, Korea, Poland, the Slovak Republic and the United Kingdom. By contrast, in France, Israel and Italy, this expenditure increased by only 10% or less between 2000 and 2009 (Chart B1.6).

In most countries, changes in enrolments do not seem to have been the main factor behind changes in expenditure at these levels. In fact, in the Czech Republic, Estonia, Hungary, Poland, the Slovak Republic and the United Kingdom, a decrease in enrolment of more than 5% coincided with significant increases (over 5%) in spending per student by educational institutions between 2000 and 2009. In Germany, Japan and Portugal, a similar decline in enrolment at the primary, secondary and post-secondary non-tertiary levels coincided with a slight increase only in expenditure at those levels (Chart B1.6).

The pattern is different at the tertiary level. In some cases, spending per student fell between 1995 and 2009, as expenditure did not keep up with expanding enrolments. On average among OECD countries, expenditure per tertiary student by educational institutions remained stable from 1995 to 2000 but then increased from 2000-05 and 2005-09. Between 2000 and 2009, Estonia, Korea, Portugal, Spain and the United Kingdom increased expenditure per student by 30% or more.

By contrast, between 2000 and 2009, of the 27 countries for which data are available, Iceland, Israel and the United States recorded a decrease in expenditure per student in tertiary education. This is also the case in Brazil, Hungary and Switzerland, where public expenditure per student (data on private expenditure are not available) decreased during the period. In all of these countries, the decline was mainly the result of a rapid increase of 25% or more in the number of tertiary students (Table B1.5 and Chart B1.6).

Definitions

Ancillary services are defined as services provided by educational institutions that are peripheral to the main educational mission. The main component of ancillary services is student welfare services. In primary, secondary and post-secondary non-tertiary education, student welfare services include things such as meals, school health services, and transportation to and from school. At the tertiary level, they include residence halls (dormitories), dining halls, and health care.

Core educational services include all expenditure that is directly related to instruction in educational institutions. This covers all expenditure on teachers, school buildings, teaching materials, books, and administration of schools.

Research and development (R&D) includes all expenditure on research performed at universities and other tertiary educational institutions, regardless of whether the research is financed from general institutional funds or through separate grants or contracts from public or private sponsors. The classification of expenditure is based on data collected from the institutions carrying out R&D, rather than on the sources of funds.

Methodology

Reference year: Data refer to the financial year 2009 and are based on the UOE data collection on education statistics administered by the OECD in 2011 (for details see Annex 3 at *www.oecd.org/edu/eag2012*).

Table B1.5 shows the changes in expenditure per student by educational institutions between the financial years 1995, 2000, 2005 and 2009. OECD countries were asked to collect 1995, 2000 and 2005 data according to the definitions and coverage of UOE 2011 data collection. All expenditure data and GDP information for 1995, 2000 and 2005 are adjusted to 2009 prices using the GDP price deflator.

Data coverage: The indicator shows direct public and private expenditure by educational institutions in relation to the number of full-time equivalent students enrolled. Public subsidies for students' living expenses outside educational institutions have been excluded to ensure international comparability.

Core educational services are estimated as the residual of all expenditure, that is, total expenditure on educational institutions net of expenditure on R&D and ancillary services.

Expenditure per student by educational institutions at a particular level of education is calculated by dividing the total expenditure by educational institutions at that level by the corresponding full-time equivalent enrolment. Only educational institutions and programmes for which both enrolment and expenditure data are available are taken into account. Expenditure in national currency is converted into equivalent USD by dividing the national currency figure by the purchasing power parity (PPP) index for GDP. The PPP exchange rate is used because the market exchange rate is affected by many factors (interest rates, trade policies, expectations of economic growth, etc.) that have little to do with current relative domestic purchasing power in different OECD countries (see Annex 2 for further details).

Expenditure data for students in private educational institutions are not available for certain countries, and some other countries provide incomplete data on independent private institutions. Where this is the case, only expenditure on public and government dependent private institutions has been taken into account.

Expenditure per student by educational institutions relative to GDP per capita is calculated by expressing expenditure per student by educational institutions in units of national currency as a percentage of GDP per capita, also in national currency. In cases where the educational expenditure data and the GDP data pertain to different reference periods, the expenditure data are adjusted to the same reference period as the GDP data, using inflation rates for the OECD country in question (see Annex 2).

Cumulative expenditure over the average duration of tertiary studies (Table B1.3a) is calculated by multiplying current annual expenditure by the typical duration of tertiary studies. The methodology used to estimate the typical duration of tertiary studies is described in Annex 3 (*www.oecd.org/edu/eag2012*). For estimates of the duration of tertiary education, data are based on a survey carried out in OECD countries in 2011.

Full-time equivalent student: The ranking of OECD countries by annual expenditure on educational services per student is affected by differences in how countries define full-time, part-time and full-time equivalent enrolment. Some OECD countries count every participant at the tertiary level as a full-time student, while others determine a student's intensity of participation by the credits that he/she obtains for successful completion of specific course units during a specified reference period. OECD countries that can accurately account for part-time enrolment have higher apparent expenditure per full-time equivalent student by educational institutions than OECD countries that cannot differentiate among the different types of student attendance.

OECD total: The OECD total reflects the value of the indicator if the OECD region is considered as a whole (see the Reader's Guide for details).

The statistical data for Israel are supplied by and are under the responsibility of the relevant Israeli authorities. The use of such data by the OECD is without prejudice to the status of the Golan Heights, East Jerusalem and Israeli settlements in the West Bank under the terms of international law.

References

The following additional material relevant to this indicator is available on line:

- *Chart 1.7. Cumulative expenditure per student by educational institutions over the theoretical duration of primary and secondary studies (2009)*
  StatLink 🔗 http://dx.doi.org/10.1787/888932662561

- *Table B1.1b. Annual expenditure per student by educational institutions for core services (2009)*
  StatLink 🔗 http://dx.doi.org/10.1787/888932665886

- *Table B1.3b. Cumulative expenditure per student by educational institutions for all services over the theoretical duration of primary and secondary studies (2009)*
  StatLink 🔗 http://dx.doi.org/10.1787/888932665943

- *Table B1.7. Distribution of expenditure (as a percentage) by educational institutions compared to the number of students enrolled at each level of education (2009)*
  StatLink 🔗 http://dx.doi.org/10.1787/888932666038

B1

Table B1.1a. Annual expenditure per student by educational institutions, for all services (2009)
In equivalent USD converted using PPPs for GDP, by level of education, based on full-time equivalents

| | Pre-primary education (for children aged 3 and older) | Primary education | Secondary education | | | Post-secondary non-tertiary education | Tertiary education (including R&D activities) | | | All tertiary education excluding R&D activities | Primary to tertiary education |
			Lower secondary education	Upper secondary education	All secondary education		Tertiary-type B education	Tertiary-type A & advanced research programmes	All tertiary education		
	(1)	(2)	(3)	(4)	(5)	(6)	(7)	(8)	(9)	(10)	(11)
Australia	8 493	8 328	10 273	9 916	10 137	7 445	9 158	17 460	16 074	9 867	**10 407**
Austria	8 202	10 080	12 442	12 737	12 589	x(4)	14 210	14 258	14 257	9 811	**12 285**
Belgium	5 696	8 341	x(5)	x(5)	10 775	x(5)	x(9)	x(9)	15 443	10 001	**10 758**
Canada[1,2]	x(2)	8 262	x(2)	10 340	8 997	m	13 605	25 341	20 932	15 126	**m**
Chile[3]	3 885	2 981	2 893	2 892	2 892	a	4 132	8 935	6 863	6 390	**3 860**
Czech Republic	4 452	4 196	6 973	6 293	6 602	1 915	3 407	8 615	8 237	6 672	**6 216**
Denmark	8 785	11 166	11 078	10 996	11 036	x(4,9)	x(9)	x(9)	18 556	m	**12 523**
Estonia	2 551	5 493	6 225	6 756	6 519	7 604	5 186	6 981	6 373	3 968	**6 210**
Finland	5 553	7 368	11 338	7 739	8 947	x(5)	n	16 569	16 569	10 085	**9 910**
France	6 185	6 373	9 111	12 809	10 696	m	12 102	15 494	14 642	10 042	**9 913**
Germany	7 862	6 619	8 130	11 287	9 285	8 843	8 192	17 306	15 711	9 594	**9 779**
Greece	x(2)	m	x(5)	x(5)	m	m	m	m	m	m	**m**
Hungary[2]	4 745	4 467	4 874	4 181	4 514	4 701	5 402	8 725	8 518	6 645	**5 227**
Iceland	9 636	10 099	9 778	7 934	8 644	x(5)	x(9)	x(9)	9 939	m	**9 429**
Ireland[2]	m	8 219	11 069	12 731	11 831	9 047	x(9)	x(9)	16 420	11 256	**10 713**
Israel	3 998	5 202	x(5)	x(5)	5 842	4 871	9 393	11 621	11 214	m	**6 410**
Italy[2]	7 948	8 669	9 165	9 076	9 112	m	9 565	9 562	9 562	5 980	**9 055**
Japan	5 103	7 729	8 985	9 527	9 256	x(4,9)	10 125	17 511	15 957	m	**10 035**
Korea	6 047	6 658	7 536	11 300	9 399	a	6 313	10 499	9 513	8 096	**8 542**
Luxembourg	16 247	16 494	19 202	19 443	19 324	m	m	m	m	m	**m**
Mexico	2 158	2 185	2 014	3 534	2 536	a	x(9)	x(9)	8 020	6 756	**2 875**
Netherlands	7 437	7 917	11 708	11 880	11 793	11 642	10 056	17 854	17 849	11 479	**11 493**
New Zealand	11 202	6 812	7 304	8 670	7 960	9 421	8 521	11 185	10 619	8 939	**8 117**
Norway	6 696	11 833	12 505	14 983	13 883	x(5)	x(9)	x(9)	19 269	11 290	**14 020**
Poland[2]	5 610	5 302	4 871	5 159	5 026	7 865	5 691	7 800	7 776	6 502	**5 666**
Portugal[2]	5 661	5 762	8 448	9 015	8 709	m	x(9)	x(9)	10 481	5 504	**7 829**
Slovak Republic	4 433	5 099	4 747	4 578	4 658	x(4)	x(4)	6 758	6 758	5 919	**5 134**
Slovenia	7 979	x(3)	9 386	7 409	8 476	x(4)	x(9)	x(9)	9 311	7 510	**8 826**
Spain	6 946	7 446	9 484	11 265	10 111	m	10 990	14 191	13 614	9 656	**9 800**
Sweden	6 549	9 382	9 642	10 375	10 050	5 974	6 658	21 144	19 961	9 464	**11 400**
Switzerland[2]	5 147	10 597	14 068	17 013	15 645	x(4)	5 502	23 111	21 577	9 465	**14 716**
Turkey	m	m	a	m	m	a	m	m	m	m	**m**
United Kingdom	6 493	9 088	10 124	9 929	10 013	x(4)	x(9)	x(9)	16 338	9 889	**10 587**
United States	8 396	11 109	12 247	12 873	12 550	m	x(9)	x(9)	29 201	26 313	**15 812**
OECD average	6 670	7 719	8 854	9 755	9 312	4 958	~	~	13 728	9 341	**9 252**
OECD total	6 208	7 550	~	~	9 264	~	~	~	18 572	15 399	**10 380**
EU21 average	6 807	7 762	9 369	9 666	9 513	6 399	~	~	12 967	8 332	**9 122**
Argentina[2]	2 398	2 757	3 727	4 307	3 932	a	3 034	5 284	4 579	m	**3 512**
Brazil[2]	1 696	2 405	2 523	1 763	2 235	a	x(9)	x(9)	11 741	11 107	**2 647**
China	m	m	m	m	m	m	m	m	m	m	**m**
India	m	m	m	m	m	m	m	m	m	m	**m**
Indonesia[3]	57	449	366	374	369	a	1 509	818	972	592	**467**
Russian Federation[2]	m	x(5)	x(5)	x(5)	4 325	x(5)	4 539	8 627	7 749	7 368	**5 354**
Saudi Arabia[2,3]	m	m	m	m	m	m	x(9)	x(9)	16 297	m	**m**
South Africa[2]	420	1 536	x(5)	x(5)	1 872	4 183	x(9)	x(9)	3 616	m	**1 824**
G20 average	m	m	m	m	m	m	m	m	m	m	**m**

1. Year of reference 2008.
2. Public institutions only (for Canada, in tertiary education only; for Italy, except in tertiary education).
3. Year of reference 2010.
Source: OECD. Argentina, Indonesia: UNESCO Institute for Statistics (World Education Indicators programme). Saudi Arabia: Observatory on Higher Education. South Africa: UNESCO Institute for Statistics. See Annex 3 for notes (www.oecd.org/edu/eag2012).
Please refer to the Reader's Guide for information concerning the symbols replacing missing data.
StatLink http://dx.doi.org/10.1787/888932665867

Table B1.2. **Annual expenditure per student by educational institutions on core services, ancillary services and R&D (2009)**

In equivalent USD converted using PPPs for GDP, by level of education and type of service, based on full-time equivalents

	Primary, secondary and post-secondary non-tertiary education			Tertiary education				Primary to tertiary education		
	Educational core services	Ancillary services (transport, meals, housing provided by institutions)	Total	Educational core services	Ancillary services (transport, meals, housing provided by institutions)	R&D	Total	Educational core services	Ancillary services (transport, meals, housing provided by institutions) and R&D	Total
	(1)	(2)	(3)	(4)	(5)	(6)	(7)	(8)	(9)	(10)
Australia	8 937	202	**9 139**	9 267	600	6 208	**16 074**	8 997	1 410	**10 407**
Austria	11 146	535	**11 681**	9 689	123	4 446	**14 257**	10 804	1 480	**12 285**
Belgium	9 501	283	**9 783**	9 474	527	5 442	**15 443**	9 496	1 262	**10 758**
Canada[1, 2, 3]	8 515	481	**8 997**	14 014	1 113	5 806	**20 932**	m	m	**m**
Chile[4]	2 708	227	**2 935**	6 390	x(4)	472	**6 863**	3 575	285	**3 860**
Czech Republic	5 178	437	**5 615**	6 586	86	1 565	**8 237**	5 501	715	**6 216**
Denmark[1]	11 094	a	**11 094**	x(7)	a	x(7)	**18 556**	x(10)	x(10)	**12 523**
Estonia	x(3)	x(3)	**6 149**	3 968	x(4)	2 405	**6 373**	x(10)	x(10)	**6 210**
Finland	7 402	912	**8 314**	10 085	n	6 484	**16 569**	7 898	2 011	**9 910**
France	7 694	1 166	**8 861**	9 284	758	4 600	**14 642**	7 984	1 930	**9 913**
Germany	8 303	232	**8 534**	8 885	709	6 117	**15 711**	8 403	1 375	**9 779**
Greece	m	m	**m**	m	m	m	**m**	m	m	**m**
Hungary[3]	3 949	557	**4 506**	6 168	477	1 873	**8 518**	4 348	880	**5 227**
Iceland	x(3)	x(3)	**9 309**	x(7)	x(7)	x(7)	**9 939**	x(10)	x(10)	**9 429**
Ireland[3]	9 615	m	**9 615**	11 256	m	5 164	**16 420**	9 880	833	**10 713**
Israel	5 172	292	**5 464**	9 857	1 357	n	**11 214**	5 927	483	**6 410**
Italy[3, 5]	8 632	311	**8 943**	5 688	293	3 581	**9 562**	8 260	795	**9 055**
Japan[1]	x(3)	x(3)	**8 502**	x(7)	x(7)	x(7)	**15 957**	x(10)	x(10)	**10 035**
Korea	7 155	967	**8 122**	8 030	65	1 418	**9 513**	7 420	1 123	**8 542**
Luxembourg	17 190	828	**18 018**	m	m	m	**m**	m	m	**m**
Mexico	x(3)	x(3)	**2 339**	6 756	m	1 264	**8 020**	2 756	119	**2 875**
Netherlands	10 030	n	**10 030**	11 479	n	6 370	**17 849**	10 301	1 191	**11 493**
New Zealand	x(3)	x(3)	**7 556**	8 939	x(4)	1 680	**10 619**	x(10)	x(10)	**8 117**
Norway	x(3)	x(3)	**12 971**	11 105	185	7 979	**19 269**	x(10)	x(10)	**14 020**
Poland[3]	5 148	19	**5 167**	6 502	n	1 274	**7 776**	5 407	259	**5 666**
Portugal[3]	7 121	167	**7 288**	5 504	x(4)	4 977	**10 481**	6 860	969	**7 829**
Slovak Republic[1]	4 254	526	**4 781**	4 674	1 246	839	**6 758**	4 329	805	**5 134**
Slovenia	8 108	562	**8 670**	7 480	30	1 802	**9 311**	7 955	871	**8 826**
Spain	8 366	452	**8 818**	9 186	470	3 957	**13 614**	8 799	1 001	**9 800**
Sweden	8 697	1 012	**9 709**	9 464	n	10 497	**19 961**	8 823	2 576	**11 400**
Switzerland[3]	x(3)	x(3)	**13 411**	9 465	x(4)	12 113	**21 577**	x(10)	x(10)	**14 716**
Turkey	m	m	**m**	m	m	m	**m**	m	m	**m**
United Kingdom	7 767	1 835	**9 602**	8 368	1 521	6 449	**16 338**	7 855	2 732	**10 587**
United States	10 902	928	**11 831**	23 079	3 234	2 888	**29 201**	13 693	2 119	**15 812**
OECD average	8 103	539	**8 617**	8 944	582	4 202	**13 728**	7 621	1 184	**9 252**
EU21 average	8 379	546	**8 759**	7 986	390	4 325	**12 967**	7 818	1 276	**9 122**
Argentina[3]	x(3)	x(3)	**3 296**	x(7)	x(7)	x(7)	**4 579**	x(10)	x(10)	**3 512**
Brazil[3]	x(3)	x(3)	**2 304**	11 107	x(4)	634	**11 741**	2 624	23	**2 647**
China	m	m	**m**	m	m	m	**m**	m	m	**m**
India	m	m	**m**	m	m	m	**m**	m	m	**m**
Indonesia[4]	x(3)	x(3)	**418**	x(7)	x(7)	x(7)	**972**	x(10)	x(10)	**467**
Russian Federation[3]	x(3)	x(3)	**4 325**	x(7)	x(7)	380	**7 749**	x(10)	x(10)	**5 354**
Saudi Arabia[3, 4]	m	m	**m**	x(7)	x(7)	x(7)	**16 297**	m	m	**m**
South Africa[2]	x(3)	x(3)	**1 697**	x(7)	x(7)	x(7)	**3 616**	x(10)	x(10)	**1 824**
G20 average	m	m	**m**	m	m	m	**m**	m	m	**m**

1. Some levels of education are included with others. Refer to "x" code in Table B1.1a for details.
2. Year of reference 2008.
3. Public institutions only (for Canada, in tertiary education only; for Italy, except in tertiary education).
4. Year of reference 2010.
5. Exclude post-secondary non-tertiary education.

Source: OECD. Argentina, Indonesia: UNESCO Institute for Statistics (World Education Indicators programme). Saudi Arabia: Observatory on Higher Education. South Africa: UNESCO Institute for Statistics. See Annex 3 for notes (*www.oecd.org/edu/eag2012*).
Please refer to the Reader's Guide for information concerning the symbols replacing missing data.

StatLink ⏢⏢ http://dx.doi.org/10.1787/888932665905

B1

Table B1.3a. Cumulative expenditure per student by educational institutions for all services over the average duration of tertiary studies (2009)

In equivalent USD converted using PPPs for GDP, by type of programme

	Method[1]	Average duration of tertiary studies in 2008 (in years)			Cumulative expenditure per student over the average duration of tertiary studies (in USD)		
		Tertiary-type B education	Tertiary-type A and advanced research programmes	All tertiary education	Tertiary-type B education	Tertiary-type A and advanced research programmes	All tertiary education
		(1)	(2)	(3)	(4)	(5)	(6)
OECD Australia	CM	m	3.48	**m**	m	60 762	**m**
Austria	AF	1.89	4.80	**4.34**	26 900	68 418	**61 920**
Belgium	CM	2.41	3.67	**2.99**	x(6)	x(6)	**46 175**
Canada		m	m	**m**	m	m	**m**
Chile		m	m	**m**	m	m	**m**
Czech Republic[2]	CM	m	3.76	**m**	m	32 381	**m**
Denmark	AF	2.51	5.97	**5.19**	x(6)	x(6)	**96 230**
Estonia		m	m	**m**	m	m	**m**
Finland	CM	a	4.78	**4.78**	a	79 199	**79 199**
France[2]	CM	3.00	4.74	**4.02**	36 305	73 442	**58 860**
Germany	CM	2.50	5.16	**4.48**	20 500	89 317	**70 353**
Greece		m	m	**m**	m	m	**m**
Hungary[3]	AF	1.84	3.74	**3.48**	9 916	32 632	**29 681**
Iceland	CM	x(3)	x(3)	**4.49**	x(6)	x(6)	**44 624**
Ireland[3]	CM	2.21	4.02	**3.24**	x(6)	x(6)	**53 201**
Israel	CM	m	3.03	**m**	m	35 211	**m**
Italy	AF	m	4.52	**m**	m	43 218	**m**
Japan	CM	2.09	4.57	**4.19**	21 193	80 021	**66 856**
Korea	CM	2.07	4.22	**3.43**	13 068	44 308	**32 630**
Luxembourg		m	m	**m**	m	m	**m**
Mexico	AF	1.72	3.49	**3.35**	x(6)	x(6)	**26 868**
Netherlands	CM	m	5.02	**5.02**	m	89 626	**89 604**
New Zealand	CM	2.22	3.90	**3.32**	18 951	43 647	**35 287**
Norway		m	m	**m**	m	m	**m**
Poland[3]	CM	m	3.68	**m**	m	28 705	**m**
Portugal		m	m	**m**	m	m	**m**
Slovak Republic	AF	2.47	3.90	**3.82**	m	26 356	**m**
Slovenia	AF	2.63	3.64	**3.21**	x(6)	x(6)	**29 873**
Spain	CM	2.15	5.54	**4.66**	23 629	78 616	**63 440**
Sweden	CM	2.20	4.89	**4.73**	14 648	103 341	**94 375**
Switzerland[3]	CM	2.19	5.45	**3.62**	12 032	126 021	**78 201**
Turkey	CM	2.73	2.37	**2.65**	m	m	**m**
United Kingdom[2]	CM	3.52	5.86	**4.34**	x(6)	x(6)	**70 951**
United States		m	m	**m**	m	m	**m**
OECD total		2.23	4.33	**3.97**	~	~	**59 386**
EU21 average		2.26	4.57	**4.16**	~	~	**64 913**
Other G20 Argentina		m	m	**m**	m	m	**m**
Brazil		m	m	**m**	m	m	**m**
China		m	m	**m**	m	m	**m**
India		m	m	**m**	m	m	**m**
Indonesia		m	m	**m**	m	m	**m**
Russian Federation		m	m	**m**	m	m	**m**
Saudi Arabia		m	m	**m**	m	m	**m**
South Africa		m	m	**m**	m	m	**m**

1. Either the Chain Method (CM) or an Approximation Formula (AF) was used to estimate the duration of tertiary studies.
2. Average duration of tertiary studies is estimated based on national data.
3. Public institutions only.
Source: OECD. See Annex 3 for notes (*www.oecd.org/edu/eag2012*).
Please refer to the Reader's Guide for information concerning the symbols replacing missing data.
StatLink ⟨ᵃⁱˢ⟩ http://dx.doi.org/10.1787/888932665924

Table B1.4. **Annual expenditure per student by educational institutions for all services relative to GDP per capita (2009)**
By level of education, based on full-time equivalents

B1

| | Pre-primary education (for children 3 years and older) | Primary education | Secondary education | | | Post-secondary non-tertiary education | Tertiary education (including R&D activities) | | | All tertiary education excluding R&D activities | Primary to tertiary education |
| | | | Lower secondary education | Upper secondary education | All secondary education | | Tertiary-type B education | Tertiary-type A and advanced research programmes | All tertiary education | | |
	(1)	(2)	(3)	(4)	(5)	(6)	(7)	(8)	(9)	(10)	(11)
Australia	21	21	26	25	25	19	23	44	40	25	**26**
Austria	21	26	32	33	32	m	37	37	37	25	**32**
Belgium	16	23	x(5)	x(5)	29	x(5)	x(9)	x(9)	42	27	**29**
Canada[1, 2]	x(2)	21	x(2)	27	23	m	35	66	54	39	**m**
Chile[3]	26	20	19	19	19	a	27	59	45	42	**26**
Czech Republic	17	16	27	25	26	7	13	34	32	26	**24**
Denmark	23	29	29	29	29	x(4,9)	x(9)	x(9)	48	m	**33**
Estonia	13	28	31	34	33	38	26	35	32	20	**31**
Finland	15	21	32	22	25	x(5)	n	46	46	28	**28**
France	18	19	27	38	32	m	36	46	43	30	**29**
Germany	22	18	23	31	26	25	23	48	44	27	**27**
Greece	x(2)	m	x(5)	x(5)	m	m	m	m	m	m	**m**
Hungary[2]	24	22	24	21	22	23	27	43	42	33	**26**
Iceland	26	28	27	22	24	x(5)	x(9)	x(9)	27	m	**26**
Ireland[2]	m	21	28	32	30	23	x(9)	x(9)	41	28	**27**
Israel	15	19	x(5)	x(5)	21	18	34	42	41	m	**23**
Italy[2]	25	27	28	28	28	m	30	30	30	18	**28**
Japan	16	24	28	29	29	x(4,9)	31	54	49	m	**31**
Korea	22	25	28	42	35	a	23	39	35	30	**31**
Luxembourg	20	20	23	23	23	m	m	m	m	m	**m**
Mexico	15	15	14	25	18	a	x(9)	x(9)	56	47	**20**
Netherlands	18	19	28	29	29	28	24	43	43	28	**28**
New Zealand	38	23	25	30	27	32	29	38	36	31	**28**
Norway	12	22	23	27	25	x(5)	x(9)	x(9)	35	21	**26**
Poland[2]	30	28	26	27	27	42	30	41	41	34	**30**
Portugal[2]	23	23	34	36	35	m	x(9)	x(9)	42	22	**31**
Slovak Republic	20	23	21	20	21	x(4)	x(4)	30	30	26	**23**
Slovenia	29	x(3)	35	27	32	x(4)	x(9)	x(9)	34	28	**33**
Spain	22	23	30	35	31	a	34	44	42	30	**30**
Sweden	18	25	26	28	27	16	18	57	54	25	**31**
Switzerland[2]	11	24	31	38	35	x(4)	12	52	48	21	**33**
Turkey	m	m	a	m	m	a	m	m	m	m	**m**
United Kingdom	19	26	29	29	29	x(4)	x(9)	x(9)	47	29	**31**
United States	19	25	27	29	28	m	x(9)	x(9)	65	58	**35**
OECD average	20	23	26	29	27	17	26	44	42	30	**29**
EU21 average	21	22	25	29	27	13	26	42	39	29	**28**
Argentina[2]	16	19	25	29	27	a	21	36	31	m	**24**
Brazil[2]	15	22	23	16	20	a	x(9)	x(9)	105	100	**24**
China	m	m	m	m	m	m	m	m	m	m	**m**
India	m	m	m	m	m	m	m	m	m	m	**m**
Indonesia[3]	1	10	8	9	8	a	34	19	22	13	**11**
Russian Federation[1]	m	x(5)	x(5)	x(5)	23	a	24	46	41	39	**28**
Saudi Arabia[2, 3]	m	m	m	m	m	m	x(9)	x(9)	69	m	**m**
South Africa[2]	4	15	x(5)	x(5)	18	41	x(9)	x(9)	35	m	**18**
G20 average	m	m	m	m	m	m	m	m	m	m	**m**

1. Year of reference 2008.
2. Public institutions only (for Canada, in tertiary education only. For Italy, except in tertiary education).
3. Year of reference 2010.
Source: OECD. Argentina, Indonesia: UNESCO Institute for Statistics (World Education Indicators programme). Saudi Arabia: Observatory on Higher Education. South Africa: UNESCO Institute for Statistics. See Annex 3 for notes (*www.oecd.org/edu/eag2012*).
Please refer to the Reader's Guide for information concerning the symbols replacing missing data.
StatLink http://dx.doi.org/10.1787/888932665962

B1

Table B1.5a. Change in expenditure per student by educational institutions for all services relative to different factors, at the primary, secondary and post-secondary non-tertiary levels (1995, 2000, 2005, 2009)

Index of change between 1995, 2000, 2005 and 2009 (GDP deflator 2005 = 100, constant prices)

	Primary, secondary and post-secondary non-tertiary education								
	Change in expenditure (2005 = 100)			Change in the number of students (2005 = 100)			Change in expenditure per student (2005 = 100)		
	1995	2000	2009	1995	2000	2009	1995	2000	2009
Australia	65	84	127	87	93	100	74	91	127
Austria	90	97	109	m	101	97	m	95	112
Belgium	m	94	113	m	91	96	m	103	118
Canada[1, 2]	91	86	113	m	99	99	m	87	115
Chile[3]	m	m	118	m	m	94	m	m	124
Czech Republic	86	76	111	115	107	91	75	71	123
Denmark[1]	72	86	105	91	95	101	79	91	104
Estonia[4]	62	80	117	119	122	86	53	66	137
Finland	72	81	108	88	95	100	81	85	108
France	90	100	103	m	102	100	m	98	104
Germany	94	100	105	99	102	94	95	97	112
Greece[1]	50	78	m	107	101	m	46	77	m
Hungary[4, 5]	69	69	88	113	108	91	61	64	97
Iceland	m	72	101	93	94	102	m	77	100
Ireland[5]	57	68	138	102	97	107	56	70	130
Israel	79	95	116	84	94	106	95	101	110
Italy[5, 6]	97	96	100	101	99	100	96	97	101
Japan[1]	97	99	101	124	109	96	78	91	105
Korea	m	69	130	110	102	96	m	68	136
Luxembourg[4, 5, 7]	m	m	108	m	m	105	m	m	103
Mexico	65	80	104	88	95	104	74	85	99
Netherlands	68	83	114	94	97	102	73	86	112
New Zealand[4]	65	92	120	m	m	101	m	m	120
Norway[4]	85	89	114	84	95	102	101	95	112
Poland[5]	63	89	118	121	110	85	52	81	139
Portugal[5]	74	98	109	113	109	103	66	90	106
Slovak Republic[1]	71	73	129	114	108	87	62	68	148
Slovenia	m	m	104	m	m	91	m	m	113
Spain	92	93	120	127	107	104	73	87	116
Sweden	71	88	103	85	98	94	84	90	109
Switzerland[5]	75	87	108	93	98	99	81	89	109
Turkey	m	m	m	m	m	m	m	m	m
United Kingdom	58	70	105	98	113	100	59	62	105
United States	74	92	116	93	98	100	79	95	116
OECD average	75	85	112	102	101	98	74	85	115
EU21 average	74	85	110	105	103	97	69	83	115
Argentina	m	m	m	m	m	m	m	m	m
Brazil[4, 5]	58	66	156	84	98	94	69	67	166
China	m	m	m	m	m	m	m	m	m
India	m	m	m	m	m	m	m	m	m
Indonesia	m	m	m	m	m	m	m	m	m
Russian Federation[4]	m	66	139	m	m	88	m	m	158
Saudi Arabia	m	m	m	m	m	m	m	m	m
South Africa	m	m	m	m	m	m	m	m	m
G20 average	m	m	m	m	m	m	m	m	m

1. Some levels of education are included with others. Refer to "x" code in Table B1.1a for details.
2. Year of reference 2008 instead of 2009.
3. Year of reference 2010 instead of 2009.
4. Public expenditure only.
5. Public institutions only.
6. Excluding post-secondary non-tertiary education.
7. Including pre-primary education.
Source: OECD. See Annex 3 for notes (*www.oecd.org/edu/eag2012*).
Please refer to the Reader's Guide for information concerning the symbols replacing missing data.
StatLink ⟐ﬁﬆ⟐ http://dx.doi.org/10.1787/888932665981

Table B1.5b. Change in expenditure per student by educational institutions for all services relative to different factors, at the tertiary level (1995, 2000, 2005, 2009)

Index of change between 1995, 2000, 2005 and 2009 (GDP deflator 2005 = 100, constant prices)

B1

	Tertiary education								
	Change in expenditure (2005 = 100)			Change in the number of students (2005 = 100)			Change in expenditure per student (2005 = 100)		
	1995	2000	2009	1995	2000	2009	1995	2000	2009
OECD Australia	74	83	124	73	m	117	**102**	**m**	**106**
Austria	72	75	117	93	103	133	**77**	**73**	**87**
Belgium	m	98	123	m	94	107	**m**	**104**	**114**
Canada[1, 2, 3]	64	86	109	m	m	m	**m**	**m**	**m**
Chile[4]	m	m	156	m	m	149	**m**	**m**	**104**
Czech Republic	64	65	141	46	72	127	**139**	**90**	**111**
Denmark[1]	78	86	109	94	98	104	**83**	**88**	**104**
Estonia[5]	64	92	150	51	85	99	**124**	**108**	**151**
Finland	77	86	112	85	95	97	**91**	**91**	**115**
France	85	93	116	m	95	99	**m**	**98**	**116**
Germany	89	94	119	96	93	109	**92**	**101**	**109**
Greece[1]	28	42	m	46	68	m	**61**	**63**	**m**
Hungary[3, 5]	64	81	109	38	66	91	**167**	**122**	**119**
Iceland	m	69	110	53	68	112	**m**	**103**	**98**
Ireland[3]	58	100	143	72	85	105	**80**	**118**	**136**
Israel	64	90	97	59	82	104	**107**	**110**	**94**
Italy	73	93	110	90	89	98	**82**	**104**	**113**
Japan[1]	82	94	108	98	99	95	**84**	**95**	**113**
Korea	m	79	129	63	93	101	**m**	**84**	**128**
Luxembourg	m	m	m	m	m	m	**m**	**m**	**m**
Mexico	57	73	123	64	83	114	**89**	**88**	**108**
Netherlands	82	86	117	82	85	114	**100**	**101**	**103**
New Zealand[5]	87	84	133	m	m	130	**m**	**m**	**102**
Norway[5]	92	86	106	88	88	102	**104**	**98**	**104**
Poland[3]	34	57	117	35	60	96	**97**	**96**	**122**
Portugal[3]	51	70	105	69	90	103	**74**	**78**	**103**
Slovak Republic[1]	54	67	125	51	71	125	**106**	**94**	**99**
Slovenia	m	m	110	m	m	107	**m**	**m**	**102**
Spain	63	88	123	108	107	109	**59**	**82**	**113**
Sweden	70	86	112	68	82	98	**102**	**105**	**114**
Switzerland[3, 5]	69	77	99	75	79	122	**92**	**97**	**81**
Turkey	m	m	m	m	m	m	**m**	**m**	**m**
United Kingdom	61	65	127	83	93	105	**74**	**70**	**120**
United States	60	85	95	81	89	114	**74**	**96**	**83**
OECD average	67	81	118	72	86	110	**94**	**95**	**109**
EU21 average	65	80	120	71	86	107	**95**	**94**	**113**
Other G20 Argentina	m	m	m	m	m	m	**m**	**m**	**m**
Brazil[3, 5]	66	79	128	56	70	117	**118**	**112**	**109**
China	m	m	m	m	m	m	**m**	**m**	**m**
India	m	m	m	m	m	m	**m**	**m**	**m**
Indonesia	m	m	m	m	m	m	**m**	**m**	**m**
Russian Federation[5]	m	44	168	m	m	175	**m**	**m**	**96**
Saudi Arabia	m	m	m	m	m	m	**m**	**m**	**m**
South Africa	m	m	m	m	m	m	**m**	**m**	**m**
G20 average	m	m	m	m	m	m	**m**	**m**	**m**

1. Some levels of education are included with others. Refer to "x" code in Table B1.1a for details.
2. Year of reference 2008 instead of 2009.
3. Public institutions only.
4. Year of reference 2010 instead of 2009.
5. Public expenditure only.
Source: OECD. See Annex 3 for notes (*www.oecd.org/edu/eag2012*).
Please refer to the Reader's Guide for information concerning the symbols replacing missing data.
StatLink ▆▆ॿ▊ http://dx.doi.org/10.1787/888932666000

B1

Table B1.6. Annual expenditure per student by educational institutions for all services, by type of programme, at the secondary level (2009)

In equivalent US dollars converted using PPPs for GDP, by level of education, based on full-time equivalents

	Secondary education								
	Lower secondary education			Upper secondary education			All secondary education		
	All programmes	General programmes	Vocational/ Pre-vocational programmes	All programmes	General programmes	Vocational/ Pre-vocational programmes	All programmes	General programmes	Vocational/ Pre-vocational programmes
	(1)	(2)	(3)	(4)	(5)	(6)	(7)	(8)	(9)
OECD									
Australia	**10 273**	10 618	6 146	**9 916**	11 299	6 657	**10 137**	10 835	6 506
Austria	**12 442**	12 442	a	**12 737**	12 387	12 852	**12 589**	12 432	12 852
Belgium[1]	**x(7)**	x(7)	x(7)	**x(7)**	x(7)	x(7)	**10 775**	x(7)	x(7)
Canada[1, 2]	**x(7)**	x(7)	x(7)	**10 340**	x(4)	x(4)	**8 997**	x(7)	x(7)
Chile[3]	**2 893**	2 893	a	**2 892**	2 842	2 992	**2 892**	2 863	2 992
Czech Republic	**6 973**	6 951	x(1)	**6 293**	5 512	6 579	**6 602**	6 599	6 606
Denmark	**11 078**	11 078	a	**10 996**	x(4)	x(4)	**11 036**	x(7)	x(7)
Estonia	**6 225**	x(1)	x(1)	**6 756**	6 922	6 433	**6 519**	x(7)	x(7)
Finland[1]	**11 338**	11 338	a	**7 739**	6 823	8 112	**8 947**	9 693	8 112
France	**9 111**	9 111	a	**12 809**	12 443	13 373	**10 696**	10 153	13 373
Germany	**8 130**	8 130	a	**11 287**	9 171	13 028	**9 285**	8 345	13 028
Greece	**m**	m	m	**m**	m	m	**m**	m	m
Hungary[4]	**4 874**	4 876	4 637	**4 181**	4 251	3 988	**4 514**	4 599	4 007
Iceland[1]	**9 778**	9 778	a	**7 934**	x(4)	x(4)	**8 644**	x(7)	x(7)
Ireland[4]	**11 069**	x(1)	x(1)	**12 731**	x(4)	x(4)	**11 831**	x(7)	x(7)
Israel	**x(7)**	x(7)	x(7)	**x(7)**	x(7)	x(7)	**5 842**	4 453	11 394
Italy[4]	**9 165**	x(1)	x(1)	**9 076**	x(4)	x(4)	**9 112**	x(7)	x(7)
Japan[1]	**8 985**	8 985	a	**9 527**	x(4)	x(4)	**9 256**	x(7)	x(7)
Korea	**7 536**	7 536	a	**11 300**	x(4)	x(4)	**9 399**	x(7)	x(7)
Luxembourg	**19 202**	19 202	a	**19 443**	18 536	20 057	**19 324**	19 007	20 057
Mexico	**2 014**	2 376	459	**3 534**	3 486	4 004	**2 536**	2 786	1 186
Netherlands	**11 708**	10 392	15 045	**11 880**	9 765	12 860	**11 793**	10 202	13 508
New Zealand	**7 304**	7 304	a	**8 670**	7 940	10 764	**7 960**	7 563	10 764
Norway[1]	**12 505**	12 505	a	**14 983**	x(4)	x(4)	**13 883**	x(7)	x(7)
Poland[4]	**4 871**	x(1)	x(1)	**5 159**	4 974	5 327	**5 026**	x(7)	x(7)
Portugal[4]	**8 448**	x(1)	x(1)	**9 015**	x(4)	x(4)	**8 709**	x(7)	x(7)
Slovak Republic[1]	**4 747**	4 747	x(6)	**4 578**	3 833	4 937	**4 658**	4 502	4 937
Slovenia[1]	**9 386**	9 386	a	**7 409**	x(4)	x(4)	**8 670**	x(7)	x(7)
Spain	**9 484**	x(1)	x(1)	**11 265**	x(4)	x(4)	**10 111**	x(7)	x(7)
Sweden	**9 642**	9 739	a	**10 375**	10 599	10 221	**10 050**	10 033	10 085
Switzerland[1, 4]	**14 068**	14 068	a	**17 013**	12 188	19 900	**15 645**	13 501	19 900
Turkey	**a**	a	a	**m**	m	m	**m**	m	m
United Kingdom[1]	**x(7)**	x(7)	x(7)	**x(7)**	x(7)	x(7)	**10 013**	x(7)	x(7)
United States	**12 247**	12 247	a	**12 873**	12 873	a	**12 550**	12 550	a
OECD average	**8 854**	~	~	**9 755**	8 410	9 534	**9 312**	8 598	9 957
EU21 average	**9 327**	~	~	**9 652**	8 768	9 814	**9 513**	9 556	10 657
Other G20									
Argentina[4]	**3 727**	3 727	a	**4 307**	x(4)	x(4)	**3 932**	x(7)	x(7)
Brazil[4]	**2 523**	2 523	a	**1 763**	x(4)	x(4)	**2 235**	x(7)	x(7)
China	**m**	m	m	**m**	m	m	**m**	m	m
India	**m**	m	m	**m**	m	m	**m**	m	m
Indonesia[3]	**366**	366	a	**374**	472	232	**369**	397	232
Russian Federation[1]	**m**	m	m	**m**	m	m	**m**	m	m
Saudi Arabia	**m**	m	m	**m**	m	m	**m**	m	m
South Africa[4]	**x(7)**	x(7)	x(7)	**x(7)**	x(7)	x(7)	**1 872**	x(7)	x(7)
G20 average	**m**	m	m	**m**	m	m	**m**	m	m

1. Some levels of education are included with others. Refer to "x" code in Table B1.1a for details.
2. Year of reference 2008.
3. Year of reference 2010.
4. Public institutions only.

Source: OECD. Argentina, Indonesia: UNESCO Institute for Statistics (World Education Indicators programme). South Africa: UNESCO Institute for Statistics. See Annex 3 for notes (*www.oecd.org/edu/eag2012*).

Please refer to the Reader's Guide for information concerning the symbols replacing missing data.

StatLink ᵐˢ🔗 http://dx.doi.org/10.1787/888932666019

WHAT PROPORTION OF NATIONAL WEALTH IS SPENT ON EDUCATION?

■ In 2009, OECD countries spent on average 6.2% of their GDP on educational institutions. This proportion exceeded 7% in Denmark, Iceland, Israel, Korea, New Zealand and the United States. Only 7 of the 37 countries for which data are available spent less than 5%, namely the Czech Republic, Hungary, India, Indonesia, Italy, the Slovak Republic and South Africa.

■ Between 2000 and 2009, expenditure for all levels of education combined increased at a faster rate than GDP growth during this period in almost all countries for which data are available. During this period, the increase exceeded one percentage point in Brazil, Denmark, Ireland, Korea, Mexico, the Netherlands, Norway, the Russian Federation and the United Kingdom.

■ Based on the proportion of GDP devoted to the sector, education was not an early casualty of the economic crisis. Between 2008 and 2009, expenditure for all levels of education combined increased in 24 out of the 31 countries with available data, while GDP in 26 of these 31 countries decreased.

Chart B2.1. Expenditure on educational institutions as a percentage of GDP for all levels of education (2000 and 2009) and index of change between 2000 and 2009 (2000=100, constant prices)

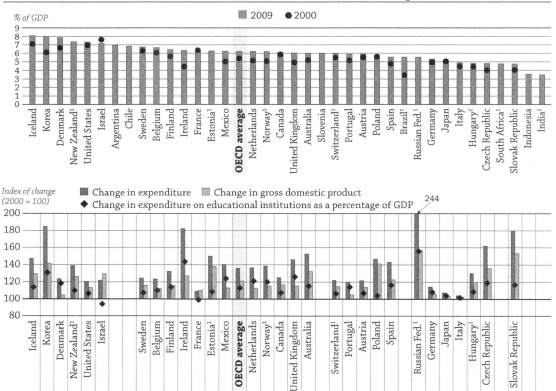

1. Public expenditure only (for Switzerland, in tertiary education only; for Norway, in primary, secondary and post-secondary non-tertiary education only; for Estonia, New Zealand and the Russian Federation, for 2000 only).
Countries are ranked in descending order of expenditure from both public and private sources on educational institutions in 2009.
Source: OECD. Argentina, India, Indonesia: UNESCO Institute for Statistics (World Education Indicators programme). South Africa: UNESCO Institute for Statistics. Table B2.1 and Table B2.5, available on line. See Annex 3 for notes (*www.oecd.org/edu/eag2012*).
StatLink ⧉ http://dx.doi.org/10.1787/888932662580

How to read this chart
The chart shows investment in education as a proportion of the national income that countries devoted to spending on educational institutions in 2000 and 2009, and changes in overall spending on educational institutions between 2000 and 2009. It includes direct and indirect expenditure on educational institutions, from both public and private sources of funds.

Context

This indicator presents a measure of expenditure on educational institutions relative to a nation's wealth. The national wealth is estimated based on the GDP, and expenditure on education includes spending by governments, enterprises and individual students and their families.

Countries invest in educational institutions to help foster economic growth, enhance productivity, contribute to personal and social development, and reduce social inequality, among other reasons. The proportion of education expenditure relative to GDP depends on the different preferences of various public and private actors. Nevertheless, expenditure on education largely comes from public budgets and is closely scrutinised by governments. During times of financial crisis, even core sectors like education can be subject to budget cuts.

The level of expenditure on educational institutions is affected by the size of a country's school-age population, enrolment rates, level of teachers' salaries and the organisation and delivery of instruction. At the primary and lower secondary levels of education (corresponding broadly to the 5-14 year-old population), enrolment rates are close to 100% in OECD countries and changes in the number of students are closely related to demographic changes. This is not as much the case for upper secondary and tertiary education, because part of the concerned population has left the education system (see Indicator C1).

Other findings

■ **Expenditure on pre-primary education accounts for 9% of expenditure on educational institutions**, or 0.5% of the GDP, on average in OECD countries. There are large differences among countries. For instance, expenditure on pre-primary education is less than 0.2% of GDP in Australia, India, Indonesia, Ireland and South Africa, but about 0.9% or more in Denmark, Iceland, Israel, Spain and the Russian Federation.

■ **Primary, secondary and post-secondary non-tertiary education accounts for 64% of expenditure on educational institutions**, or 4.0% of the GDP, on average in OECD countries. Iceland and New Zealand spend more than 5% of their GDP at these levels, while the Czech Republic, Hungary, India, Indonesia, Japan and the Russian Federation spend 3% or less.

■ **Tertiary education accounts for nearly one-quarter of expenditure on educational institutions**, or 1.6% of the GDP, on average in OECD countries. Canada, Chile, Korea and the United States spend between 2.4% and 2.6% of their GDP on tertiary institutions.

■ **Private expenditure on educational institutions as a percentage of GDP is highest in tertiary education.** This share is between 1.6% and 1.9% in Chile, Korea and the United States.

Trends

For all levels of education combined, public and private investment in education increased by an average of 36% in OECD countries between 2000 and 2009.

Investment in education increased in all countries between 2000 and 2009, but the increase was smaller than the rate of GDP growth in France and Israel. However, between 1995 and 2000, there was a decrease in expenditure on educational institutions in 18 out of 28 countries with comparable data for both years.

B2

Analysis

Overall investment relative to GDP

The share of national wealth devoted to educational institutions is substantial in all OECD and G20 countries with available data. In 2009, OECD countries spent on average 6.2% of their GDP on educational institutions; and OECD countries as a whole spent 6.4% of their combined GDP on educational institutions, taking into account both public and private sources of funds.

Expenditure on educational institutions (all levels combined) relative to GDP was above 6% in nearly half of the OECD and G20 countries, and even above 7% in six of them: Denmark (7.9%), Iceland (8.1%), Israel (7.2%), Korea (8.0%), New Zealand (7.4%) and the United States (7.3%). At the other end of the spectrum, seven countries spent less than 5% of their GDP on education, namely the Czech Republic (4.8%), Hungary (4.8%), India (3.5%), Indonesia (3.6%), Italy (4.9%), the Slovak Republic (4.7%) and South Africa (4.8%).

Expenditure on educational institutions by level of education

More than 64% of the expenditure on education in all OECD countries goes on average to primary, secondary and post-secondary non-tertiary education, while 25% is devoted to tertiary education, and more than 9% to pre-primary education. Primary and lower secondary education receive on average nearly 42% of the educational expenditure of all OECD countries. Expenditure on educational institutions depends on the age of the population. In most cases, countries with above-average expenditure on educational institutions relative to GDP are usually those with an above-average proportion of people whose age corresponds to primary and lower secondary education (Table B2.2).

In all OECD and G20 countries with available data, the level of national resources devoted to primary, secondary and post-secondary non-tertiary education combined is the largest share of the total expenditure on educational institutions (compared with the share devoted to pre-primary and tertiary education). This share exceeds 60% in most countries, with only six exceptions: Chile (53%), Israel (56%), Japan (57%), Korea (58%), the Russian Federation (43%) and the United States (58%). For primary, secondary and post-secondary non-tertiary education, expenditure as a percentage of GDP ranges from 3% or below in the Czech Republic (2.9%), Hungary (3.0%), India (2.2%), Indonesia (2.5%), Japan (3.0%) and the Russian Federation (2.4%) to above 5% in Iceland (5.2%) and New Zealand (5.2%).

Expenditure on primary and lower secondary education amounts to more than 1.3% of GDP in all countries, and more than 3% in Argentina (3.8%), Australia (3.3%), Brazil (3.6%), Denmark (3.4%), Iceland (3.7%), Ireland (3.4%), Korea (3.1%), Mexico (3.1%), New Zealand (3.3%) and the United States (3.2%).

Every country except Denmark and Iceland spends less than 1% of GDP on pre-primary education. Nevertheless, data on pre-primary education should be analysed with care because there are large differences among countries in enrolment rates, the age at which pre-primary education begins, and the extent to which privately funded early childhood education is accounted for (see Indicator C1).

Expenditure on tertiary education amounts to more than 1.5% of GDP in nearly half of all countries, and exceeds 2.5% in Korea (2.6%) and the United States (2.6%). Four countries devote less than 1% of GDP to tertiary education, namely Brazil (0.8%), Indonesia (0.7%), the Slovak Republic (0.9%) and South Africa (0.6%) (Table B2.2 and Chart B2.2).

Changes in overall spending on educational institutions between 2000 and 2009

The expansion in the number of students enrolled in upper secondary and tertiary education between 2000 and 2009 was accompanied in most countries by an increase in the financial investment at these levels.

Over the period 2000-09, expenditure on education in France and Israel increased by 9% and 22%, respectively, but GDP increased more rapidly (by 10% and 29%, respectively), leading to a decrease in expenditure as a proportion of GDP (Chart B2.1 and Table B2.5, available on line). In all other countries with comparable data, expenditure on educational institutions (all levels of education combined) as a percentage of GDP increased during this period, as expenditure grew more than GDP (Chart B2.1). The increase was above one percentage point in Brazil (from 3.5% to 5.5%), Denmark (from 6.6% to 7.9%), Ireland (from 4.4% to 6.3%), Korea (from 6.1% to 8.0%), Mexico (from 5.0% to 6.2%), the Netherlands (from 5.1% to 6.2%), Norway (from 5.1% to 6.2%), the Russian Federation (from 2.9% to 5.5%) and the United Kingdom (from 4.9% to 6.0%) (Table B2.1).

There were similar changes in expenditure for primary, secondary and post-secondary non-tertiary education combined, as well as for tertiary education.

Chart B2.2.   **Expenditure on educational institutions as a percentage of GDP (2009)**
From public and private sources, by level of education and source of funds

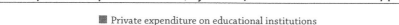

■ Private expenditure on educational institutions
▨ Public expenditure on educational institutions

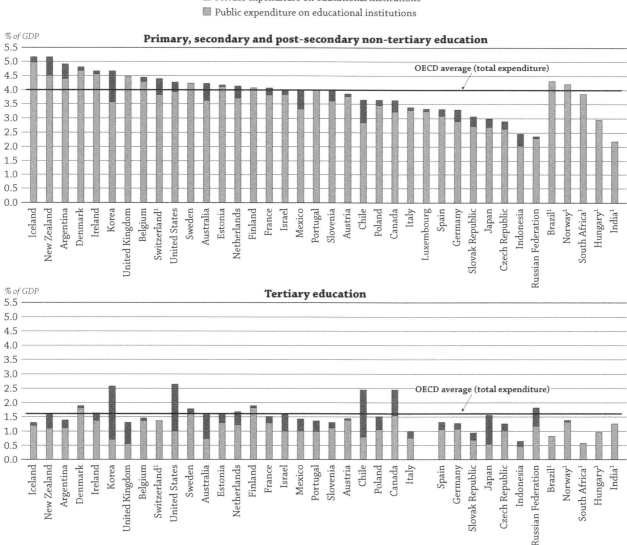

1. Public expenditure only (for Switzerland, in tertiary education only; for Norway, in primary, secondary and post-secondary non-tertiary education only).
Countries are ranked in descending order of expenditure from both public and private sources on educational institutions in primary, secondary and post-secondary non-tertiary education.
Source: OECD. Argentina, India, Indonesia: UNESCO Institute for Statistics (World Education Indicators programme). South Africa: UNESCO Institute for Statistics. Table B2.3. See Annex 3 for notes (*www.oecd.org/edu/eag2012*).
StatLink ᓂᔅᒷ http://dx.doi.org/10.1787/888932662599

Expenditure on instruction, research and development, and ancillary services

On average among OECD countries, some 91% of all expenditure on primary, secondary and post-secondary non-tertiary education combined is devoted to core services. This share is significantly smaller at the tertiary level (an OECD average of 70%), because other services, particularly those related to research and development (R&D), can represent a large proportion of total spending on education.

At the tertiary level, the share of R&D expenditure as a percentage of GDP ranges from below 0.2% in Brazil (0.04%), Chile (0.17%) and the Slovak Republic (0.12%) to above 0.6% in Australia (0.62%), Canada (0.61%), Finland (0.74%), Sweden (0.94%) and Switzerland (0.72%). These differences among countries help to explain differences in overall expenditure per tertiary-level student by country (Table B2.4 and Chart B2.3). For example, the high levels of R&D spending in the above-mentioned countries imply that spending on educational institutions per student in these countries would be considerably lower if the R&D component was excluded (Table B1.2 on Indicator B1).

Chart B2.3.   Expenditure on education core services, R&D and ancillary services in tertiary educational institutions as a percentage of GDP (2009)

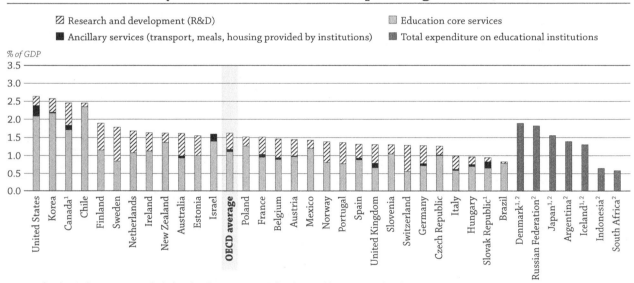

1. Some levels of education are included with others. Refer to "x" code in Table B1.1a for details.
2. Total expenditure at the tertiary level including expenditure on research and development (R&D).
Countries are ranked in descending order of total expenditure on educational institutions in tertiary institutions.
Source: OECD. Argentina, Indonesia: UNESCO Institute for Statistics (World Education Indicators programme). South Africa: UNESCO Institute for Statistics. Table B2.4. See Annex 3 for notes (*www.oecd.org/edu/eag2012*).
StatLink ⟋⟍⟋ http://dx.doi.org/10.1787/888932662618

In many OECD countries, schools and universities provide student welfare services, and in some cases, services for the general public. This expenditure on ancillary services is defrayed by the public sector and by fees paid by students and their families. The share of ancillary services at the primary, secondary and post-secondary non-tertiary levels of education combined as a percentage of GDP is 0.26%, on average across OECD countries. It is above 0.40% in Finland (0.45%), France (0.53%), Korea (0.55%), Sweden (0.44%) and the United Kingdom (0.86%).

Ancillary services are financed by private users more often at the tertiary level than at any other level. At the tertiary level, expenditure on ancillary services accounts for 0.06% of GDP, on average in OECD countries. This proportion is above 0.1% in Canada (0.13%), Israel (0.20%), the Slovak Republic (0.17%), the United Kingdom (0.12%) and the United States (0.29%).

Expenditure on educational institutions by source of funding

Education is funded from both public and private sources. Increased expenditure on educational institutions in response to enrolment growth and other factors implies a heavier financial burden for society as a whole. However, this burden does not fall entirely on public funding. On average, of the 6.4% of the combined GDP in the OECD area devoted to education, three-quarters come from public sources for all levels of education combined (Table B2.3). Public funds are the major funding source for education in all countries and account for at least 61% (Korea) up to nearly 98% (Finland) of total expenditure. However, differences among countries in the breakdown of educational expenditure by source of funding and by level of education are great (see Indicator B3).

Box B2.1. **The financial crisis and expenditure on educational institutions (2008-09)**

In most countries, more than 75% of education expenditure comes from public sources. Since public budgets in most countries are approved many months before the funds are actually spent, there are certain built-in rigidities to the funding of education. Moreover, most governments try to protect education from dramatic reductions in public investment.

The global economic crisis that began in 2008 had (and is still having) a major negative impact on the different sectors of the economy. It is too early to assess, with only 2009 data, the full impact of the crisis on the funding of the educational institutions, but its impact on the broader economy can already be observed. Between 2008 and 2009, GDP (expressed in constant prices) increased in only 5 out of the 31 countries with available data: Australia, Israel, Korea, New Zealand and Poland.

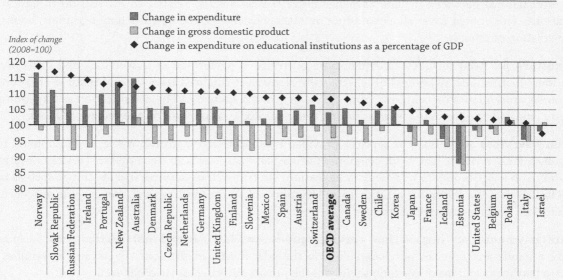

Index of change between 2008 and 2009 in expenditure on educational institutions as a percentage of GDP, for all levels of education (2008=100, constant prices)

Countries are ranked in descending order of the change in expenditure on educational institutions as a percentage of GDP.
Source: OECD. See Annex 3 for notes (*www.oecd.org/edu/eag2012*).
StatLink ᐅᔐᔓ http://dx.doi.org/10.1787/888932669306

How to read this chart
The chart shows investment in education as the proportion of national income that countries devoted to spending on educational institutions in 2008 and 2009, and changes in overall spending on educational institutions between 2008 and 2009. It includes direct and indirect expenditure on educational institutions from both public and private sources of funds.

...

B2

Although the initial impact of the crisis hit at different times and in different degrees, depending on the country, 2009 data also sheds light on the first measures some countries took to respond to the crisis). For example, was spending on education cut as a result of the crisis? Our findings show that the education sector was spared from early budget cuts.

Among the 31 countries with available data for these two years, only Israel shows a decrease in expenditure on educational institutions as a percentage of GDP. In Israel, GDP grew only slightly between 2008 and 2009, and expenditure on education shrank during the period.

The picture is different in other countries. Even though the crisis had already begun, between 2008 and 2009, expenditure on educational institutions started to fall only in Belgium, Estonia, Iceland, Italy, Japan and the United States, but the reductions seen in these six countries were smaller than the drop in GDP and not necessary linked to the crisis. As a result, the share of GDP devoted to education continued to rise.

In all of the 24 remaining countries with available data, education expenditure increased by an average of 4%. This increase was larger than 10% in Australia (14.7%), New Zealand (13.5%), Norway (16.4%) and the Slovak Republic (11.0%). The significant increase seen in Australia's 2009 education expenditure is mostly due to the Building the Education Revolution spending programme (BER). In 2009, the government announced a AUD 16.2 billion BER spending programme over four years to build or upgrade large scale infrastructure, such as libraries and halls in primary and secondary schools throughout Australia. These higher than normal spending patterns should continue for a few years (see more in Annex 3 at *www.oecd.org/edu/eag2012*).

In more than half of these 24 countries, the increase in expenditure on education as a percentage of GDP was higher than 10% because of decreases or small increases in GDP between 2008 and 2009.

Definitions

Core educational services include all expenditure that is directly related to instruction in educational institutions. This should cover all expenditure on teachers, school buildings, teaching materials, books, and administration of schools.

Expenditure on R&D includes all expenditure on research performed at universities and other tertiary educational institutions, regardless of whether the research is financed from general institutional funds or through separate grants or contracts from public or private sponsors. The classification of expenditure is based on data collected from the institutions carrying out R&D, rather than on the sources of funds.

Ancillary services are defined as services provided by educational institutions that are peripheral to the main educational mission. The main component of ancillary services is student welfare services. In primary, secondary and post-secondary non-tertiary education, student welfare services include things such as meals, school health services, and transportation to and from school. At the tertiary level, they include residence halls (dormitories), dining halls and health care.

Private payments on instruction services/goods outside educational institutions include the education goods and services purchased outside the educational institutions. For example, families may purchase textbooks and materials themselves or seek private tutoring for their children.

Methodology

Reference year: Data refer to the financial year 2009 and are based on the UOE data collection on education statistics administered by the OECD in 2011 (for details see Annex 3 at *www.oecd.org/edu/eag2012*).

OECD total: The OECD total reflects the value of the indicator if the OECD region is considered as a whole (see the Reader's Guide at the beginning of this book for details).

The statistical data for Israel are supplied by and under the responsibility of the relevant Israeli authorities. The use of such data by the OECD is without prejudice to the status of the Golan Heights, East Jerusalem and Israeli settlements in the West Bank under the terms of international law.

References

OECD (2011), *Education at a Glance 2011: OECD Indicators*, OECD Publishing.

The following additional material relevant to this indicator is available on line:

• *Table B2.5. Change in expenditure on educational institutions and in GDP (1995, 2000, 2005, 2009)*
  StatLink ⌗⌗ http://dx.doi.org/10.1787/888932666152

B2

Table B2.1. Expenditure on educational institutions as a percentage of GDP, by level of education (1995, 2000, 2009)

From public and private sources, by year

	Primary, secondary and post-secondary non-tertiary education				Tertiary education				Total for all levels of education			
	1995	2000	2005	2009	1995	2000	2005	2009	1995	2000	2005	2009
	(1)	(2)	(3)	(4)	(5)	(6)	(7)	(8)	(9)	(10)	(11)	(12)
Australia	3.4	3.6	3.6	4.2	1.6	1.4	1.5	1.6	5.0	5.2	5.3	6.0
Austria	4.2	3.9	3.7	3.9	1.2	1.1	1.3	1.4	6.1	5.5	5.5	5.9
Belgium	m	4.1	4.1	4.4	m	1.3	1.2	1.5	m	6.1	6.0	6.7
Canada[1,2]	4.3	3.3	3.7	3.6	2.1	2.3	2.7	2.5	6.7	5.9	6.5	6.1
Chile[3]	m	m	3.4	3.6	m	m	1.8	2.5	m	m	5.7	6.8
Czech Republic	3.3	2.7	2.9	2.9	0.9	0.8	1.0	1.3	4.8	4.0	4.5	4.8
Denmark[2]	4.0	4.1	4.5	4.8	1.6	1.6	1.7	1.9	6.2	6.6	7.4	7.9
Estonia[4]	4.9	4.5	4.0	4.2	1.1	1.2	1.3	1.6	6.7	6.2	5.8	6.3
Finland	4.0	3.6	3.9	4.1	1.9	1.7	1.7	1.9	6.3	5.6	6.0	6.4
France	4.5	4.3	4.0	4.1	1.4	1.3	1.3	1.5	6.6	6.4	6.0	6.3
Germany	3.4	3.3	3.2	3.3	1.1	1.1	1.1	1.3	5.1	4.9	5.0	5.3
Greece[2]	2.0	2.7	2.8	m	0.6	0.8	1.5	m	2.7	3.6	4.3	m
Hungary[4]	3.2	2.8	3.3	3.0	0.8	0.9	0.9	1.0	4.8	4.4	5.1	4.8
Iceland	m	4.8	5.4	5.2	m	1.1	1.2	1.3	m	7.1	8.0	8.1
Ireland	3.8	2.9	3.4	4.7	1.3	1.5	1.1	1.6	5.2	4.4	4.5	6.3
Israel	4.6	4.3	4.0	4.0	1.7	1.9	1.9	1.6	7.8	7.6	7.5	7.2
Italy	3.5	3.1	3.1	3.4	0.7	0.9	0.9	1.0	4.6	4.5	4.4	4.9
Japan[2]	3.1	3.0	2.9	3.0	1.3	1.4	1.4	1.6	5.0	5.0	4.9	5.2
Korea	m	3.5	4.1	4.7	m	2.2	2.3	2.6	m	6.1	6.7	8.0
Luxembourg	m	m	3.7	3.3	m	m	m	m	m	m	m	m
Mexico	3.7	3.5	4.0	4.0	1.0	1.0	1.2	1.4	5.1	5.0	5.9	6.2
Netherlands	3.4	3.4	3.8	4.1	1.6	1.4	1.5	1.7	5.4	5.1	5.8	6.2
New Zealand[4]	m	m	4.6	5.2	m	m	1.5	1.6	m	m	6.5	7.4
Norway[4]	4.3	3.8	3.8	4.2	1.6	1.2	1.3	1.4	5.9	5.1	5.6	6.2
Poland	3.6	3.9	3.7	3.6	0.8	1.1	1.6	1.5	5.2	5.6	5.9	5.8
Portugal	3.5	3.7	3.7	4.0	0.9	1.0	1.3	1.4	4.9	5.2	5.5	5.9
Slovak Republic[2]	3.1	2.7	2.9	3.1	0.7	0.8	0.9	0.9	4.6	4.1	4.4	4.7
Slovenia	m	m	4.1	4.0	m	m	1.3	1.3	m	m	6.0	6.0
Spain	3.8	3.2	2.9	3.3	1.0	1.1	1.1	1.3	5.3	4.8	4.6	5.6
Sweden	4.1	4.2	4.2	4.2	1.5	1.6	1.6	1.8	6.0	6.3	6.4	6.7
Switzerland[4]	3.9	4.1	4.4	4.4	1.1	1.1	1.4	1.3	5.3	5.5	6.1	6.0
Turkey[4]	1.2	1.8	m	m	0.5	0.8	m	m	1.7	2.5	m	m
United Kingdom	3.6	3.5	4.4	4.5	1.1	1.0	1.3	1.3	5.2	4.9	6.0	6.0
United States	3.8	3.9	3.7	4.3	2.3	2.7	2.8	2.6	6.6	6.9	6.9	7.3
OECD average	3.6	3.5	3.8	4.0	1.2	1.3	1.5	1.6	5.4	5.3	5.8	6.2
OECD total	3.7	3.6	3.6	3.9	1.6	1.8	1.9	1.9	5.8	5.9	6.0	6.4
EU21 average	3.7	3.5	3.6	3.8	1.1	1.1	1.3	1.4	5.3	5.2	5.5	5.9
OECD mean for countries with 1995, 2000, 2005 and 2009 data (25 countries)	3.8	3.6	3.7	3.9	1.3	1.3	1.5	1.6	5.6	5.4	5.7	6.0
Argentina	m	m	m	4.9	m	m	m	1.4	m	m	m	7.0
Brazil[4]	2.6	2.4	3.2	4.3	0.7	0.7	0.8	0.8	3.7	3.5	4.4	5.5
China	m	m	m	m	m	m	m	m	m	m	m	m
India[4]	m	m	m	2.2	m	m	m	1.3	m	m	m	3.5
Indonesia[3]	m	m	m	2.5	m	m	m	0.7	m	m	m	3.6
Russian Federation[4]	m	1.7	1.5	2.4	m	0.5	0.6	1.8	m	2.9	2.9	5.5
Saudi Arabia[3,4]	m	m	m	m	m	m	m	2.3	m	m	m	m
South Africa[4]	m	m	m	3.9	m	m	m	0.6	m	m	m	4.8
G20 average	m	m	m	3.7	m	m	m	1.5	m	m	m	5.7

1. Year of reference 2008 instead of 2009.
2. Some levels of education are included with others. Refer to "x" code in Table B1.1a for details.
3. Year of reference 2010 instead of 2009.
4. Public expenditure only (for Switzerland, in tertiary education only; for Norway, in primary, secondary and post-secondary non-tertiary education only; for Estonia, New Zealand and the Russian Federation, for 1995 and 2000 only).
Source: OECD. Argentina, India, Indonesia: UNESCO Institute for Statistics (World Education Indicators programme). Saudi Arabia: Observatory on Higher Education. South Africa: UNESCO Institute for Statistics. See Annex 3 for notes (www.oecd.org/edu/eag2012).
Please refer to the Reader's Guide for information concerning the symbols replacing missing data.
StatLink 🔗 http://dx.doi.org/10.1787/888932666076

Table B2.2. **Expenditure on educational institutions as a percentage of GDP, by level of education (2009)**
From public and private sources of funds[1]

B2

	Pre-primary education (for children aged 3 and older)	Primary, secondary and post-secondary non-tertiary education				Tertiary education			All levels of education combined (including undistributed programmes)
		All primary, secondary and post-secondary non-tertiary education	Primary and lower secondary education	Upper secondary education	Post-secondary non-tertiary education	All tertiary education	Tertiary-type B education	Tertiary-type A education and advanced research programmes	
	(1)	(2)	(3)	(4)	(5)	(6)	(7)	(8)	(9)
OECD Australia	0.1	4.2	3.3	0.8	0.1	1.6	0.2	1.4	**6.0**
Austria	0.6	3.9	2.4	1.4	n	1.4	n	1.4	**5.9**
Belgium[2]	0.6	4.4	1.5	2.9	x(4)	1.5	x(6)	x(6)	**6.7**
Canada[3]	x(3)	3.6	2.2	1.5	x(7)	2.5	1.0	1.5	**6.1**
Chile[4]	0.7	3.6	2.4	1.2	a	2.5	0.7	1.8	**6.8**
Czech Republic	0.5	2.9	1.7	1.1	n	1.3	n	1.2	**4.8**
Denmark	1.0	4.8	3.4	1.3	x(4, 6)	1.9	x(6)	x(6)	**7.9**
Estonia	0.5	4.2	2.6	1.4	0.2	1.6	0.4	1.2	**6.3**
Finland	0.4	4.1	2.5	1.6	x(4)	1.9	n	1.9	**6.4**
France	0.7	4.1	2.6	1.4	n	1.5	0.3	1.2	**6.3**
Germany	0.6	3.3	2.1	1.1	0.2	1.3	0.1	1.2	**5.3**
Greece	m	m	m	m	m	m	m	m	**m**
Hungary[5]	0.7	3.0	1.8	1.0	0.1	1.0	n	0.9	**4.8**
Iceland	1.0	5.2	3.7	1.5	x(4)	1.3	x(6)	x(6)	**8.1**
Ireland	0.1	4.7	3.4	0.9	0.3	1.6	x(6)	x(6)	**6.3**
Israel	0.9	4.0	2.3	1.7	n	1.6	0.2	1.4	**7.2**
Italy	0.5	3.4	2.0	1.2	0.1	1.0	n	1.0	**4.9**
Japan	0.2	3.0	2.1	0.9	x(4, 6)	1.6	0.2	1.3	**5.2**
Korea	0.3	4.7	3.1	1.6	a	2.6	0.4	2.2	**8.0**
Luxembourg	0.6	3.3	2.4	1.0	m	m	m	m	**m**
Mexico	0.6	4.0	3.1	0.9	a	1.4	x(6)	x(6)	**6.2**
Netherlands	0.4	4.1	2.8	1.3	n	1.7	n	1.7	**6.2**
New Zealand	0.6	5.2	3.3	1.6	0.3	1.6	0.3	1.3	**7.4**
Norway[5]	0.4	4.2	2.8	1.4	x(4)	1.4	x(6)	x(6)	**6.2**
Poland	0.6	3.6	2.5	1.1	n	1.5	n	1.5	**5.8**
Portugal	0.4	4.0	2.7	1.2	m	1.4	x(6)	x(6)	**5.9**
Slovak Republic	0.5	3.1	1.9	1.1	x(4)	0.9	x(4)	0.9	**4.7**
Slovenia	0.7	4.0	2.7	1.2	x(4)	1.3	x(6)	x(6)	**6.0**
Spain	0.9	3.3	2.6	0.8	a	1.3	0.2	1.1	**5.6**
Sweden	0.7	4.2	2.8	1.4	n	1.8	x(6)	x(6)	**6.7**
Switzerland[5]	0.2	4.4	2.7	1.7	x(4)	1.3	n	1.2	**6.0**
Turkey	m	m	m	m	a	m	m	m	**m**
United Kingdom	0.3	4.5	3.0	1.5	n	1.3	x(6)	x(6)	**6.0**
United States	0.4	4.3	3.2	1.1	m	2.6	x(6)	x(6)	**7.3**
OECD average	0.5	4.0	2.6	1.3	n	1.6	0.2	1.4	**6.2**
OECD total	0.5	3.9	2.7	1.2	n	1.9	0.2	1.3	**6.4**
EU21 average	0.6	3.8	2.5	1.3	n	1.4	0.1	1.3	**5.9**
Other G20 Argentina	0.7	4.9	3.8	1.1	a	1.4	0.4	0.9	**7.0**
Brazil[5]	0.4	4.3	3.6	0.7	a	0.8	x(6)	x(6)	**5.5**
China	m	m	m	m	m	m	m	m	**m**
India[5]	n	2.2	1.3	0.9	n	m	m	1.3	**3.5**
Indonesia[4]	n	2.5	2.0	0.5	a	0.7	x(6)	x(6)	**3.6**
Russian Federation[5]	0.9	2.4	x(2)	x(2)	x(2)	1.8	0.2	1.6	**5.5**
Saudi Arabia[4, 5]	m	m	m	m	m	2.3	x(6)	x(6)	**m**
South Africa[5]	n	3.9	x(2)	x(2)	0.1	0.6	x(6)	x(6)	**4.8**
G20 average	0.4	3.2	2.1	1.1	n	m	m	1.1	**4.9**

1. Including international sources.
2. Column 3 only refers to primary education and Column 4 refers to all secondary education.
3. Year of reference 2008.
4. Year of reference 2010.
5. Public expenditure only (for Switzerland, in tertiary education only; for Norway, in primary, secondary and post-secondary non-tertiary education only).
Source: OECD. Argentina, India, Indonesia: UNESCO Institute for Statistics (World Education Indicators programme). Saudi Arabia: Observatory on Higher Education. South Africa: UNESCO Institute for Statistics. See Annex 3 for notes (*www.oecd.org/edu/eag2012*).
Please refer to the Reader's Guide for information concerning the symbols replacing missing data.
StatLink ⟡⟡⟡ http://dx.doi.org/10.1787/888932666095

B2

Table B2.3. Expenditure on educational institutions as a percentage of GDP, by source of fund and level of education (2009)

From public and private sources of funds

	Pre-primary education			Primary, secondary and post-secondary non-tertiary education			Tertiary education			Total all levels of education		
	Public[1]	Private[2]	Total	Public[1]	Private[2]	Total	Public[1]	Private[2]	Total	Public[1]	Private[2]	Total
	(1)	(2)	(3)	(4)	(5)	(6)	(7)	(8)	(9)	(10)	(11)	(12)
Australia	0.06	0.05	**0.11**	3.6	0.6	**4.2**	0.7	0.9	**1.6**	4.5	1.5	**6.0**
Austria	0.55	0.04	**0.59**	3.8	0.1	**3.9**	1.4	0.1	**1.4**	5.7	0.2	**5.9**
Belgium	0.60	0.02	**0.62**	4.3	0.2	**4.4**	1.4	0.1	**1.5**	6.4	0.3	**6.7**
Canada[3, 4]	x(4)	x(5)	**x(6)**	3.2	0.4	**3.6**	1.5	0.9	**2.5**	4.8	1.3	**6.1**
Chile[5]	0.60	0.14	**0.74**	2.9	0.8	**3.6**	0.8	1.6	**2.5**	4.3	2.6	**6.8**
Czech Republic	0.47	0.04	**0.51**	2.6	0.3	**2.9**	1.0	0.2	**1.3**	4.2	0.6	**4.8**
Denmark[4]	0.91	0.13	**1.04**	4.7	0.1	**4.8**	1.8	0.1	**1.9**	7.5	0.3	**7.9**
Estonia	0.48	0.01	**0.49**	4.1	0.1	**4.2**	1.3	0.3	**1.6**	5.9	0.4	**6.3**
Finland	0.40	0.04	**0.45**	4.1	n	**4.1**	1.8	0.1	**1.9**	6.3	0.1	**6.4**
France	0.68	0.04	**0.72**	3.8	0.2	**4.1**	1.3	0.2	**1.5**	5.8	0.5	**6.3**
Germany	0.44	0.19	**0.63**	2.9	0.4	**3.3**	1.1	0.2	**1.3**	4.5	0.8	**5.3**
Greece	m	m	**m**	m	m	**m**	m	m	**m**	m	m	**m**
Hungary	0.72	m	**m**	3.0	m	**m**	1.0	m	**m**	4.8	m	**m**
Iceland	0.79	0.23	**1.02**	5.0	0.2	**5.2**	1.2	0.1	**1.3**	7.3	0.7	**8.1**
Ireland	n	n	**n**	4.6	0.1	**4.7**	1.4	0.3	**1.6**	6.0	0.4	**6.3**
Israel	0.68	0.18	**0.87**	3.8	0.2	**4.0**	1.0	0.6	**1.6**	5.8	1.3	**7.2**
Italy	0.46	0.04	**0.51**	3.3	0.1	**3.4**	0.8	0.2	**1.0**	4.5	0.4	**4.9**
Japan[4]	0.10	0.12	**0.22**	2.7	0.3	**3.0**	0.5	1.0	**1.6**	3.6	1.7	**5.2**
Korea	0.11	0.15	**0.26**	3.6	1.1	**4.7**	0.7	1.9	**2.6**	4.9	3.1	**8.0**
Luxembourg	0.59	0.01	**0.60**	3.2	0.1	**3.3**	m	m	**m**	m	m	**m**
Mexico	0.53	0.12	**0.65**	3.3	0.7	**4.0**	1.0	0.4	**1.4**	5.0	1.2	**6.2**
Netherlands	0.41	n	**0.41**	3.7	0.4	**4.1**	1.2	0.5	**1.7**	5.3	0.9	**6.2**
New Zealand	0.48	0.10	**0.58**	4.5	0.7	**5.2**	1.1	0.5	**1.6**	6.1	1.3	**7.4**
Norway	0.35	0.06	**0.41**	4.2	m	**m**	1.3	0.1	**1.4**	6.1	m	**m**
Poland	0.52	0.12	**0.64**	3.5	0.2	**3.6**	1.1	0.5	**1.5**	5.0	0.8	**5.8**
Portugal	0.40	n	**0.40**	4.0	n	**4.0**	1.0	0.4	**1.4**	5.5	0.4	**5.9**
Slovak Republic[4]	0.42	0.08	**0.50**	2.7	0.3	**3.1**	0.7	0.3	**0.9**	4.1	0.6	**4.7**
Slovenia	0.56	0.15	**0.71**	3.6	0.3	**4.0**	1.1	0.2	**1.3**	5.3	0.7	**6.0**
Spain	0.71	0.21	**0.92**	3.1	0.2	**3.3**	1.1	0.3	**1.3**	4.9	0.7	**5.6**
Sweden	0.73	n	**0.73**	4.2	n	**4.2**	1.6	0.2	**1.8**	6.6	0.2	**6.7**
Switzerland	0.21	m	**m**	3.8	0.6	**4.4**	1.4	m	**m**	5.5	m	**m**
Turkey	m	m	**m**	m	m	**m**	m	m	**m**	m	m	**m**
United Kingdom	0.26	n	**0.26**	4.5	n	**4.5**	0.6	0.7	**1.3**	5.3	0.7	**6.0**
United States	0.34	0.08	**0.43**	3.9	0.3	**4.3**	1.0	1.6	**2.6**	5.3	2.1	**7.3**
OECD average	0.47	0.08	**0.55**	3.7	0.3	**4.0**	1.1	0.5	**1.6**	5.4	0.9	**6.3**
OECD total	0.37	0.09	**0.47**	3.6	0.3	**3.9**	1.0	1.0	**1.9**	5.0	1.4	**6.4**
EU21 average	0.52	0.06	**0.56**	3.7	0.2	**3.9**	1.2	0.3	**1.5**	5.5	0.5	**6.0**
Argentina	0.46	0.21	**0.66**	4.4	0.5	**4.9**	1.1	0.3	**1.4**	6.0	1.0	**7.0**
Brazil	0.40	m	**m**	4.3	m	**m**	0.8	m	**m**	5.5	m	**m**
China	m	m	**m**	m	m	**m**	m	m	**m**	m	m	**m**
India	0.04	m	**m**	2.2	m	**m**	1.3	m	**m**	3.5	m	**m**
Indonesia[5]	0.02	0.02	**0.04**	2.0	0.4	**2.5**	0.5	0.2	**0.7**	3.0	0.6	**3.6**
Russian Federation	0.74	0.13	**0.87**	2.3	0.1	**2.4**	1.2	0.6	**1.8**	4.7	0.8	**5.5**
Saudi Arabia[5]	m	m	**m**	m	m	**m**	2.3	m	**m**	m	m	**m**
South Africa	0.05	m	**m**	3.9	m	**m**	0.6	m	**m**	4.8	m	**m**
G20 average	0.35	m	**m**	3.0	m	**m**	0.9	m	**m**	4.4	m	**m**

1. Including public subsidies to households attributable for educational institutions, and direct expenditure on educational institutions from international sources.
2. Net of public subsidies attributable for educational institutions.
3. Year of reference 2008.
4. Some levels of education are included with others. Refer to "x" code in Table B1.1a for details.
5. Year of reference 2010.

Source: OECD. Argentina, India, Indonesia: UNESCO Institute for Statistics (World Education Indicators programme). Saudi Arabia: Observatory on Higher Education. South Africa: UNESCO Institute for Statistics. See Annex 3 for notes (*www.oecd.org/edu/eag2012*).
Please refer to the Reader's Guide for information concerning the symbols replacing missing data.
StatLink ⟨⟨s⟩⟩ http://dx.doi.org/10.1787/888932666114

Table B2.4. **Expenditure on educational institutions, by service category as a percentage of GDP (2009)**
Expenditure on instruction, R&D and ancillary services in educational institutions and private expenditure on educational goods purchased outside educational institutions

	Primary, secondary and post-secondary non-tertiary education				Tertiary education				
	Expenditure on educational institutions			Private payments on instructional services/ goods outside educational institutions	Expenditure on educational institutions				Private payments on instruction services/ goods outside educational institutions
	Core education services	Ancillary services (transport, meals, housing provided by institutions)	Total		Core education services	Ancillary services (transport, meals, housing provided by institutions)	Research & development at tertiary institutions	Total	
	(1)	(2)	(3)	(4)	(5)	(6)	(7)	(8)	(9)
OECD									
Australia	4.13	0.09	**4.22**	0.08	0.93	0.06	0.62	**1.62**	0.11
Austria	3.69	0.18	**3.86**	m	0.98	0.01	0.45	**1.44**	m
Belgium	4.31	0.13	**4.44**	0.12	0.89	0.05	0.51	**1.46**	0.19
Canada[1, 2, 3]	3.44	0.20	**3.63**	m	1.71	0.13	0.61	**2.45**	0.12
Chile[4]	3.37	0.28	**3.65**	m	2.28	x(5)	0.17	**2.45**	n
Czech Republic	2.67	0.23	**2.90**	0.05	1.01	0.01	0.24	**1.26**	0.03
Denmark[2]	x(3)	x(3)	**4.77**	m	x(8)	a	x(8)	**1.89**	m
Estonia	x(3)	x(3)	**4.17**	m	0.99	x(5)	0.60	**1.59**	m
Finland	3.65	0.45	**4.10**	m	1.15	a	0.74	**1.89**	m
France	3.53	0.53	**4.07**	0.17	0.96	0.08	0.47	**1.51**	0.07
Germany	3.22	0.09	**3.31**	0.15	0.72	0.06	0.50	**1.28**	0.08
Greece	m	m	**m**	m	m	m	m	**m**	m
Hungary[3]	2.59	0.37	**2.95**	m	0.70	0.05	0.21	**0.97**	m
Iceland	x(3)	x(3)	**5.16**	m	x(8)	x(8)	x(8)	**1.30**	m
Ireland[3]	4.66	m	**4.66**	0.05	1.12	m	0.51	**1.63**	m
Israel	3.82	0.22	**4.03**	0.26	1.40	0.20	m	**1.59**	n
Italy[3]	3.27	0.11	**3.39**	0.41	0.59	0.03	0.37	**0.99**	0.14
Japan[2]	x(3)	x(3)	**2.99**	0.80	x(8)	x(8)	x(8)	**1.56**	0.04
Korea	4.12	0.55	**4.66**	m	2.18	0.02	0.38	**2.58**	m
Luxembourg	3.18	0.15	**3.33**	0.05	m	m	m	**m**	m
Mexico	3.99	m	**3.99**	0.20	1.20	m	0.22	**1.43**	0.05
Netherlands	4.14	n	**4.14**	0.13	1.08	n	0.60	**1.68**	0.07
New Zealand	x(3)	x(3)	**5.16**	0.03	1.37	x(8)	0.26	**1.62**	m
Norway	x(3)	x(3)	**4.16**	m	0.81	n	0.57	**1.38**	m
Poland[3]	3.63	0.01	**3.64**	0.24	1.27	n	0.25	**1.51**	0.05
Portugal[3]	3.90	0.08	**3.98**	0.18	0.78	x(8)	0.58	**1.36**	m
Slovak Republic[2]	2.73	0.34	**3.07**	0.30	0.65	0.17	0.12	**0.95**	0.05
Slovenia	3.71	0.26	**3.96**	m	1.05	n	0.25	**1.30**	m
Spain	3.15	0.17	**3.32**	m	0.88	0.05	0.38	**1.31**	m
Sweden	3.79	0.44	**4.24**	m	0.85	n	0.94	**1.78**	m
Switzerland[3]	x(3)	x(3)	**4.39**	m	0.56	x(8)	0.72	**1.28**	m
Turkey	m	m	**m**	m	m	m	m	**m**	m
United Kingdom	3.62	0.86	**4.48**	m	0.67	0.12	0.51	**1.30**	0.10
United States	3.94	0.34	**4.27**	m	2.09	0.29	0.26	**2.64**	a
OECD average	3.61	0.26	**3.97**	0.20	1.10	0.06	0.45	**1.58**	0.07
EU21 average	3.52	0.26	**3.84**	0.17	0.90	0.04	0.46	**1.43**	0.09
Other G20									
Argentina	x(3)	x(3)	**4.91**	m	x(8)	x(8)	x(8)	**1.39**	m
Brazil[3]	x(3)	x(3)	**4.32**	m	0.79	x(5)	0.04	**0.83**	m
China	m	m	**m**	m	m	m	m	**m**	m
India	x(3)	x(3)	**2.19**	m	x(8)	x(8)	x(8)	**1.26**	m
Indonesia[4]	x(3)	x(3)	**2.46**	m	x(8)	x(8)	x(8)	**0.65**	m
Russian Federation[3]	x(3)	x(3)	**2.37**	m	x(8)	x(8)	x(8)	**1.82**	m
Saudi Arabia[3, 4]	m	m	**m**	m	x(8)	x(8)	x(8)	**2.28**	m
South Africa[3]	x(3)	x(3)	**3.86**	m	x(8)	x(8)	x(8)	**0.58**	m
G20 average	m	m	**3.22**	m	m	m	m	**1.17**	m

1. Year of reference 2008.
2. Some levels of education are included with others. Refer to "x" code in Table B1.1a for details.
3. Public institutions only (for Canada, in tertiary education only; for Italy, except in tertiary education).
4. Year of reference 2010.
Source: OECD. Argentina, India, Indonesia: UNESCO Institute for Statistics (World Education Indicators programme). Saudi Arabia: Observatory on Higher Education. South Africa: UNESCO Institute for Statistics. See Annex 3 for notes (*www.oecd.org/edu/eag2012*).
Please refer to the Reader's Guide for information concerning the symbols replacing missing data.
StatLink ᒪᓯᒪ http://dx.doi.org/10.1787/888932666133

HOW MUCH PUBLIC AND PRIVATE INVESTMENT IN EDUCATION IS THERE?

- Public funding accounts for 84% of all funds for educational institutions, on average in OECD countries.

- At the primary, secondary and post-secondary non-tertiary levels of education, 91% of the funds for educational institutions come from public sources, on average in OECD countries; only in Chile, Korea and the United Kingdom is this share less than 80%.

- Tertiary institutions and, to a lesser extent, pre-primary institutions obtain the largest proportions of funds from private sources, at 30% and 18%, respectively. However, these proportions vary more widely among countries than those for primary, secondary and post-secondary non-tertiary education.

- Public funding on educational institutions, for all levels combined, increased between 2000 and 2009 in all countries for which comparable data are available. However, more pressure has been put on households to share the cost of education, and private funding increased at an even greater rate in more than three-quarters of countries. As a result, on average among OECD countries, the share of private funding for educational institutions increased between 2000 and 2009.

Chart B3.1. **Share of private expenditure on educational institutions (2009)**

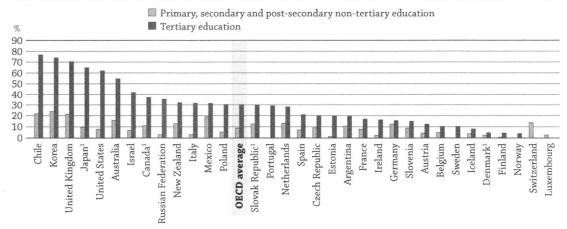

1. Some levels of education are included with others. Refer to "x" code in Table B1.1a for details.
Countries are ranked in descending order of the share of private expenditure on educational institutions for tertiary education.
Source: OECD. Argentina: UNESCO Institute for Statistics (World Education Indicators programme). Tables B3.2a and B3.2b. See Annex 3 for notes (*www.oecd.org/edu/eag2012*).
StatLink ⬛⬛⬛ http://dx.doi.org/10.1787/888932662637

> **How to read this chart**
> The chart shows private spending on educational institutions as a percentage of total spending on educational institutions. This includes all money transferred to educational institutions from private sources, including public funding via subsidies to households, private fees for educational services, or other private spending (e.g. on room and board) that goes through the educational institution.

■ Context

Today, more people are participating in a wider range of educational programmes offered by increasing numbers of providers. As a result, the question of who should support people's efforts to acquire more education – governments or individuals themselves – is becoming increasingly important. In the current economic environment, many governments are finding it difficult to provide the necessary resources to support the increased demand for education in their countries through public funds alone. In addition, some policy makers assert that those who benefit the most from education – the individuals who receive it – should bear at least some of the costs. While public funding still represents a very large part of countries' investment in education, the role of private sources of funding is becoming increasingly prominent.

The balance between public and private financing of education is an important policy issue in many OECD countries, especially at the pre-primary and tertiary levels of education, for which full or nearly full public funding is less common. At these levels, private funding comes mainly from households, raising concerns about equity of access to education. The debate is particularly intense with respect to funding for tertiary education. Some stakeholders are concerned that the balance between public and private funding should not become so tilted as to discourage potential students from entering tertiary education. Others believe that countries should significantly increase public support to students, while others support efforts to increase the amount of funding to tertiary education provided by private enterprises. By contrast, primary, secondary and post-secondary non-tertiary education, which is mainly compulsory, is usually conceived as a public good and is thus mainly financed by public funds.

Other findings

- Public funds are mainly allocated to public institutions, but also to private institutions to varying degrees. **For all levels of education combined, public expenditure on public institutions, per student, is nearly twice the level of public expenditure on private institutions, on average in OECD countries.** However, the ratio varies from less than twice (1.8) for primary, secondary and post-secondary non-tertiary education, to nearly two-and-a-half times (2.4) at the pre-primary level, and to nearly three times (2.9) at the tertiary level.

- **At the tertiary level, the countries with the lowest amounts of public expenditure per student in public and private institutions are also those with the fewest students enrolled in public tertiary institutions,** except for Poland and Argentina.

- **In most countries for which data are available, individual households account for most of the private expenditure on tertiary education.** Exceptions are Austria, the Czech Republic, the Slovak Republic and Sweden, where private expenditure from entities other than households (e.g. private businesses and non-profit organisations) is more significant than private expenditure from households, mainly because tuition fees charged by tertiary institutions are low or negligible in these countries.

Trends

Between 1995 and 2009, the share of public funding for tertiary institutions decreased from 78% in 1995, to 77% in 2000, to 73% in 2005 and then stabilised at 73% in 2009 (on average among the OECD countries for which trend data are available for all years). This trend is mainly influenced by non-European countries, where tuition fees are generally higher and enterprises participate more actively in providing grants to finance tertiary institutions.

Between 2000 and 2009, the share of private funding for tertiary education increased in more than two-thirds of the countries for which comparable data are available (18 out of 25 countries). The share increased by five percentage points, on average, and by more than ten percentage points in Mexico, Portugal, the Slovak Republic and the United Kingdom. The share of private funding also rose at the primary, secondary, post-secondary non-tertiary levels and at all levels of education combined, on average between OECD countries, and most significantly in the Slovak Republic and the United Kingdom.

B3

Analysis

Public and private expenditure on educational institutions

Educational institutions in OECD countries are mainly publicly funded, although there is a substantial and growing level of private funding at the tertiary level. On average in OECD countries, 84% of all funds for educational institutions come directly from public sources, and 16% come from private sources (Table B3.1).

However, the share of public and private funding varies widely among countries. Comparing expenditure on all levels of education, the share of private funds exceeds 20% in Canada, Israel and Mexico, 25% in Australia, Japan, the United Kingdom and the United States, and 40% in Chile and Korea (Table B3.1).

Private spending on education for all levels of education combined increased from 2000 to 2009; and in most countries, private expenditure as a percentage of total expenditure on educational institutions also increased. As a result, the share of public funding for educational institutions decreased by at least 5 percentage points in Mexico and Portugal and by 12 percentage points in the Slovak Republic and the United Kingdom. These decreases are mainly due to significant increases in the level of private expenditure during this same period. For example, in Portugal and the United Kingdom, the tuition fees charged by tertiary educational institutions increased substantially (Table B3.1).

However, decreases in the public share of total expenditure on educational institutions (and consequent increases in the share of private expenditure) have not generally gone hand-in-hand with cuts (in real terms) in public expenditure on educational institutions (Table B3.1). In fact, many of the OECD countries with the greatest growth in private spending have also had the largest increases in public funding. This indicates that an increase in private spending tends to complement public investment, rather than replace it. However, the share of private expenditure on educational institutions varies across countries and by level of education.

Public and private expenditure on pre-primary, primary, secondary and post-secondary non-tertiary educational institutions

Investment in early childhood education is essential for building a strong foundation for lifelong learning and for ensuring equitable access to learning opportunities later in school. In pre-primary education, the share of total payments to educational institutions from private sources averages more than 18% in OECD countries – a higher rate than for all levels of education combined. However, this proportion varies widely among countries, ranging from 5% or less in Belgium, Estonia, Luxembourg, the Netherlands and Sweden, to 25% or more in Argentina, Austria and Germany, and 48% or more in Australia, Japan and Korea (Table B3.2a). The proportions of public and private funds may be related to the availability of public institutions at this level (see below and Indicators C1 and C2).

Public funding dominates primary, secondary and post-secondary non-tertiary education in all countries. Less than 10% of funding for these levels of education comes from private sources, except in Argentina, Australia, Canada, Chile, Germany, Korea, Mexico, the Netherlands, New Zealand, the Slovak Republic, Switzerland and the United Kingdom (Table B3.2a and Chart B3.2). In most countries, the largest share of private expenditure at these levels comes from households and goes mainly towards tuition. In Germany, the Netherlands and Switzerland, however, most private expenditure takes the form of contributions from the business sector to the dual system of apprenticeship in upper secondary and post-secondary non-tertiary education (see Box B3.1 in *Education at a Glance 2011*).

Between 2000 and 2009, more than half the countries for which comparable data are available (15 out of 25 countries) showed a decrease in the share of public funding for primary, secondary and post-secondary non-tertiary education. However, among these countries, the corresponding increase in the private share is three percentage points or more only in Canada (from 7.6% to 10.9%), Korea (from 19.2% to 23.8%), Mexico (from 13.9% to 19.0%), the Slovak Republic (from 2.4% to 12.5%) and the United Kingdom (from 11.3% to 21.3%). In the other countries, shifts in the opposite direction, i.e. towards public funding, do not exceed 2 percentage points (Table B3.2a).

Chart B3.2. Distribution of public and private expenditure on educational institutions (2009)
By level of education

■ All private sources, including subsidies for payments
   to educational institutions received from public sources
■ Expenditure of other private entities
□ Household expenditure
▨ Public expenditure on educational institutions

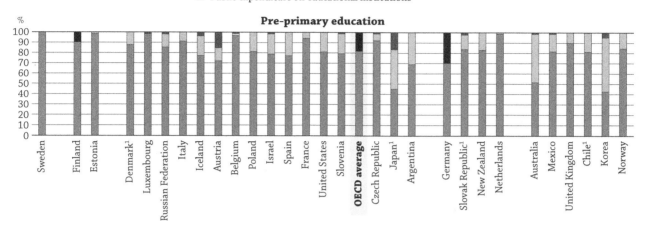

Pre-primary education

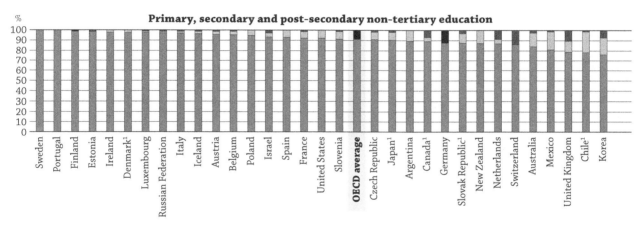

Primary, secondary and post-secondary non-tertiary education

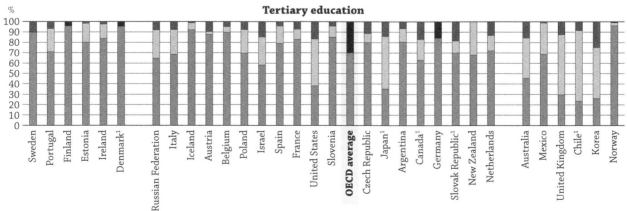

Tertiary education

1. Some levels of education are included with others. Refer to "x" code in Table B1.1a for details.
Countries are ranked in descending order of the proportion of public expenditure on educational institutions in primary, secondary and post-secondary non-tertiary education.
Source: OECD. Argentina: UNESCO Institute for Statistics (World Education Indicators programme). Tables B3.2a and B3.2b. See Annex 3 for notes (*www.oecd.org/edu/eag2012*).
StatLink ⧉ http://dx.doi.org/10.1787/888932662656

B3

In spite of these differences, between 2000 and 2009 the amount of public expenditure on educational institutions at these levels of education increased in all countries with comparable data. In contrast with general trends, increases in the amount of public expenditure for these levels of education have been accompanied by decreases in the amount of private expenditure on education in Japan, Portugal and Sweden. However, in Portugal and Sweden, less than 1% of expenditure on educational institutions was provided by private sources in 2009 (Table B3.2a).

Public and private expenditure on tertiary educational institutions

At the tertiary level, high private returns (see Indicator A9) suggest that a greater contribution to the costs of education by individuals and other private entities may be justified, as long as there are ways to ensure that funding is available to students regardless of their economic backgrounds (see Indicator B5). In all countries, the proportion of private expenditure on education is far higher for tertiary education – an average of 30% of total expenditure at this level – than it is for primary, secondary and post-secondary non-tertiary education (Tables B3.2a and B3.2b).

The proportion of expenditure on tertiary institutions covered by individuals, businesses and other private sources, including subsidised private payments, ranges from less than 5% in Denmark, Finland and Norway (tuition fees charged by tertiary institutions are low or negligible in these countries), to more than 40% in Australia, Israel, Japan and the United States, and to over 70% in Chile, Korea and the United Kingdom (Chart B3.2 and Table B3.2b). Of these countries, in Korea and the United Kingdom, most students are enrolled in private institutions (around 80% in private universities in Korea; 100% in government-dependent private institutions in the United Kingdom), and most of the budget of educational institutions comes from tuition fees (more than 70% in Korea, and more than 50% in the United Kingdom).

The contribution from private entities other than households to financing educational institutions is higher for tertiary education than for other levels of education, on average across OECD countries. In Australia, Canada, the Czech Republic, Israel, Japan, Korea, the Netherlands, the Slovak Republic, Sweden, the United Kingdom and the United States, 10% or more of expenditure on tertiary institutions is covered by private entities other than households. In Sweden, these contributions are largely directed to sponsoring research and development.

In many OECD countries, greater participation in tertiary education (see Indicator C1) reflects strong individual and social demand. The increases in enrolment have been accompanied by increases in the level of investment of countries, from both public and private sources, and resulted in changes in the proportions of public and private expenditure. On average among the OECD countries for which trend data are available for all reference years, the share of public funding for tertiary institutions decreased slightly from 78% in 1995, to 77% in 2000, to 73% in 2005 and then stabilised at 73% in 2009. This trend is apparent primarily in non-European countries, where tuition fees are generally higher and enterprises participate more actively, largely through grants to tertiary institutions (Table B3.3, Chart B3.3 and Indicator B5).

In 18 of the 25 countries for which comparable data are available for 2000 and 2009 showed an increase in the share of private funding for tertiary education. Similarly, in 11 of the 22 countries with comparable data for 1995 and 2009, the private share of expenditure on tertiary education increased by at least three percentage points during this period. This increase exceeded 10 percentage points in Australia, Italy, Portugal, the Slovak Republic, and exceeded 50 percentage points in the United Kingdom. In Australia, this increase was largely due to changes to the Higher Education Contribution Scheme/Higher Education Loan Programme implemented in 1997. In the United Kingdom, the huge increase is the result of successive increases in tuition fees during the past decade (for more details, see Indicator B5 and Annex 3).

Only the Czech Republic and Ireland – and, to a lesser extent, Canada, Norway and Spain – show a significant decrease in the share of private expenditure on tertiary educational institutions between 1995 and 2009 (Table B3.3 and Chart B3.3). In Ireland, tuition fees for tertiary first-degree programmes were gradually eliminated over the past decade, leading to a reduction in the share of private spending at this level.

Private expenditure on educational institutions generally increased faster than public expenditure between 2000 and 2009. Nevertheless, public investment in tertiary education also increased in all countries for which 2000 and 2009 data are available, regardless of the changes in private spending (Table B3.2b). Three of the nine countries with the largest increases in private expenditure during this period (the Czech Republic, Mexico and Poland) are also among the ten countries with the largest increases in public expenditure. In these countries, tertiary educational institutions charge low or no tuition fees and tertiary attainment is relatively low (see Indicators A1 and B5). In the other six countries among the nine with the largest increases in public expenditure over the period (Estonia, Iceland, Ireland, Korea, New Zealand and Spain), private expenditure increased less than public expenditure. Among these six countries, Korea is the only one where tertiary institutions rely heavily on private funding. In Estonia, Iceland, Ireland, New Zealand and Spain, private funding represents 8% to 32% of expenditure on educational institutions (Table B3.2b).

Chart B3.3.   **Share of private expenditure on tertiary educational institutions (2000, 2005 and 2009) and change, in percentage points, in the share of private expenditure between 2000 and 2009**

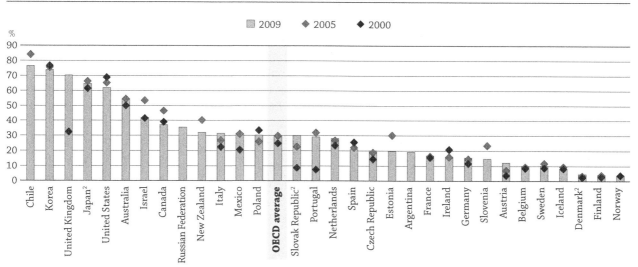

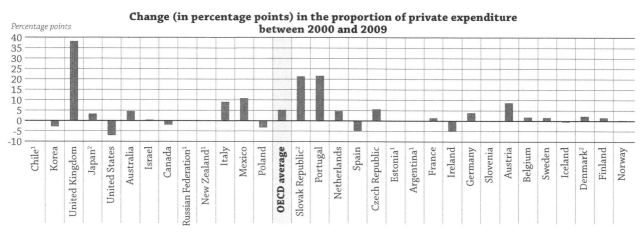

1. The change between between 2000 and 2009 is not available as the value for 2000 is missing
2. Some levels of education are included with others. Refer to "x" code in Table B1.1a for details.
Countries are ranked in descending order of the share of private expenditure on educational institutions in 2009.
Source: OECD. Argentina: UNESCO Institute for Statistics (World Education Indicators programme). Table B3.3. See Annex 3 for notes (*www.oecd.org/edu/eag2012*).

StatLink ᕯᕟᎦ http://dx.doi.org/10.1787/888932662675

B3

Public expenditure on educational institutions per student, by type of institution

The level of public expenditure partly shows the degree to which governments value education (see Indicators B2 and B4). Naturally, public funds go to public institutions; but in some cases a significant part of the public budget may be devoted to private educational institutions.

Table B3.4 shows public investment in educational institutions relative to the size of the education system, focusing on public expenditure, per student, on public and private educational institutions (private funds are excluded from Table B3.4, although in some countries they represent a significant share of the resources of educational institutions, especially at the tertiary level). This can be considered a measure that complements public expenditure relative to national income (see Indicator B2).

On average among OECD countries, at all levels of education combined, public expenditure, per student, on public institutions is nearly twice the public expenditure, per student, on private institutions (USD 8 329 and USD 4 301, respectively). However, the difference varies according to the level of education. Public expenditure, per student, on public institutions is more than twice that on private institutions at the pre-primary level (USD 6 426 and USD 2 701, respectively), somewhat under twice (1.8) that for primary, secondary and post-secondary non-tertiary education (USD 8 511 and USD 4 810, respectively), and nearly three times (2.9) that at the tertiary level (USD 10 906 and USD 3 812, respectively).

At the pre-primary level, public expenditure per student for both public and private institutions averages USD 5 379 in OECD countries but varies from USD 1 839 or less in Argentina and Mexico to more than USD 15 500 in Luxembourg. Public expenditure per student is usually higher for public institutions than for private institutions, but private institutions generally enrol fewer pupils than public institutions. For example, in Mexico and the Netherlands, public expenditure per student for private institutions is negligible, and a relatively small proportion of pupils is enrolled in private institutions. In contrast, private institutions enrol nearly all pupils in New Zealand and public expenditure per student in private institutions is higher-than-average (USD 9 415) (Tables B3.4 and C2.2).

At the primary, secondary and post-secondary non-tertiary level of education (the level with the largest proportion of public funds, Table B3.2a), public expenditure per student for both public and private institutions averages USD 7 745 in OECD countries, but varies from USD 1 893 in Mexico to approximately USD 17 000 in Luxembourg. At this level, most students are enrolled in public institutions, and public expenditure per student is usually higher for public than for private institutions, except in Finland, Israel and Sweden. In these three OECD countries, between 7% and 25% of pupils are enrolled in private institutions. In Mexico and the Netherlands, the amount of public expenditure, per student, on private institutions is small or negligible, as the private sector is marginal and receives little or no public funds (Table C1.4).

At the tertiary level, public expenditure per student for both public and private institutions averages USD 8 810 in OECD countries, but varies from about USD 1 500 in Chile to more than USD 17 000 in Denmark, Norway and Sweden, three countries in which the level of private expenditure is small or negligible. In all countries with available data, public expenditure per student is higher for public than for private institutions (Table B3.4 and Chart B3.4).

At this level, patterns in the allocation of public funds to public and private institutions differ. In Denmark and the Netherlands, at least 90% of students are enrolled in public institutions, and most public expenditure goes to these institutions. Public expenditure, per student, on public institutions is higher than the OECD average, and public expenditure per student on private institutions is negligible. In these countries, private funds complement public funds to varying degrees: private expenditure is less than 5% of expenditure for public and private educational institutions in Denmark and above 28% in the Netherlands.

In Belgium, Estonia, Finland, Hungary, Iceland and Sweden, public expenditure goes to both public and private institutions, and public expenditure, per student, on private institutions represents at least 59% – and up to nearly 100% – of the level of public expenditure, per tertiary student, on public institutions (Table B3.4).

Chart B3.4. Annual public expenditure on educational institutions per student in tertiary education, by type of institution (2009)

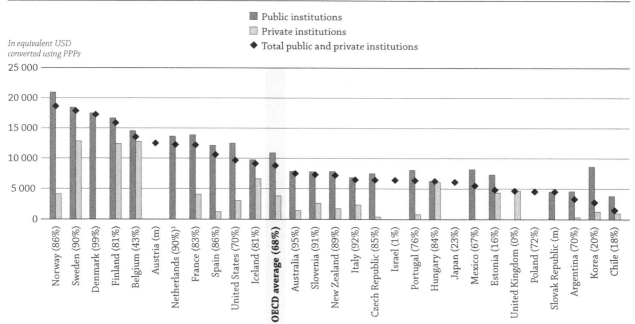

Note: The figures into brackets represent the percentage of students enrolled in public institutions in tertiary education, based on full-time equivalents.
1. Government-dependent private institutions are included with public institutions.
Countries are ranked in descending order of public expenditure on public and private educational institutions per student.
Source: OECD. Argentina: UNESCO Institute for Statistics (World Education Indicators programme). Table B3.4. See Annex 3 for notes (*www.oecd.org/edu/eag2012*).
StatLink ⬛ᵢₛ▟ http://dx.doi.org/10.1787/888932662694

However, these countries show different participation patterns. In Finland, Hungary, Iceland and Sweden, at least 80% of students are enrolled in public institutions, whereas in Belgium and Estonia, tertiary students are mainly enrolled in private institutions. In all these countries, private expenditure on tertiary institutions is below the OECD average.

In the remaining countries, public expenditure goes mainly to public institutions: public expenditure, per student, on private institutions is less than 35% of public expenditure, per student, on public institutions (Chart B3.1 and Table B3.2b).

Definitions

Other private entities include private businesses and non-profit organisations, e.g. religious organisations, charitable organisations and business and labour associations.

Private spending includes all direct expenditure on educational institutions, whether partially covered by public subsidies or not. Expenditure by private companies on the work-based element of school- and work-based training of apprentices and students is also taken into account. Public subsidies attributable to households, included in private spending, are shown separately.

Public expenditure is related to all students at public and private institutions, whether these institutions receive public funding or not.

The **public and private proportions of expenditure on educational institutions** are the percentages of total spending originating in, or generated by, the public and private sectors.

Methodology

Reference year: Data refer to the financial year 2009 and are based on the UOE data collection on education statistics administered by the OECD in 2011 (for details see Annex 3 at *www.oecd.org/edu/eag2012*).

Data coverage: Not all spending on instructional goods and services occurs within educational institutions. For example, families may purchase commercial textbooks and materials or seek private tutoring for their children outside educational institutions. At the tertiary level, students' living expenses and foregone earnings can also account for a significant proportion of the costs of education. All expenditure outside educational institutions, even if publicly subsidised, is excluded from this indicator. Public subsidies for educational expenditure outside institutions are discussed in Indicators B4 and B5.

A portion of the budgets of educational institutions is related to ancillary services offered to students, including student welfare services (student meals, housing and transport). Part of the cost of these services is covered by fees collected from students and is included in the indicator.

The data on expenditure for 1995 and 2000 were obtained by a survey updated in 2011, in which expenditure for 1995 and 2000 were adjusted to the methods and definitions used in the current UOE data collection.

OECD total: The OECD total reflects the value of the indicator if the OECD region is considered as a whole (see the Reader's Guide at the beginning of this book for details).

The statistical data for Israel are supplied by and under the responsibility of the relevant Israeli authorities. The use of such data by the OECD is without prejudice to the status of the Golan Heights, East Jerusalem and Israeli settlements in the West Bank under the terms of international law.

Table B3.1. **Relative proportions of public and private expenditure on educational institutions, for all levels of education (2000, 2009)**

Distribution of public and private sources of funds for educational institutions after transfers from public sources, by year

	2009					2000		Index of change between 2000 and 2009 in expenditure on educational institutions	
		Private sources							
	Public sources	Household expenditure	Expenditure of other private entities	All private sources[1]	Private: of which, subsidised	Public sources	All private sources[1]	Public sources	All private sources[1]
	(1)	(2)	(3)	(4)	(5)	(6)	(7)	(8)	(9)
OECD Australia	**73.2**	20.8	6.0	**26.8**	1.3	74.1	25.9	151	158
Austria	**91.4**	3.9	4.7	**8.6**	5.5	94.0	6.0	118	175
Belgium	**94.3**	4.6	1.1	**5.7**	1.8	94.3	5.7	123	122
Canada[2]	**78.6**	10.5	10.9	**21.4**	m	79.9	20.1	123	133
Chile[3]	**58.9**	37.9	3.2	**41.1**	3.3	m	m	m	m
Czech Republic	**88.0**	7.8	4.3	**12.0**	m	89.9	10.1	158	194
Denmark	**95.8**	4.2	m	**4.2**	m	96.0	4.0	123	130
Estonia	**94.2**	5.3	0.5	**5.8**	n	m	m	150	m
Finland	**97.6**	x(4)	x(4)	**2.4**	n	98.0	2.0	132	157
France	**90.2**	7.0	2.7	**9.8**	m	91.2	8.8	108	121
Germany	**85.0**	x(4)	x(4)	**15.0**	m	86.1	13.9	113	123
Greece	**m**	m	m	**m**	m	93.8	6.2	m	m
Hungary	**m**	m	m	**m**	m	m	m	130	m
Iceland	**90.8**	7.9	1.3	**9.2**	m	90.0	10.0	148	135
Ireland	**94.2**	5.2	0.6	**5.8**	n	90.5	9.5	191	112
Israel	**79.2**	14.6	6.2	**20.8**	2.3	79.8	20.2	121	125
Italy	**90.7**	7.7	1.6	**9.3**	1.7	94.3	5.7	104	177
Japan	**68.1**	21.6	10.3	**31.9**	m	71.0	29.0	103	118
Korea	**60.0**	27.3	12.8	**40.0**	1.0	59.2	40.8	187	182
Luxembourg	**m**	m	m	**m**	m	m	m	m	m
Mexico	**78.8**	21.1	0.2	**21.2**	1.9	85.3	14.7	130	203
Netherlands	**83.7**	7.0	9.3	**16.3**	2.1	84.1	15.9	135	140
New Zealand	**82.6**	17.4	x(2)	**17.4**	m	m	m	139	m
Norway	**m**	m	m	**m**	m	95.0	5.0	138	51
Poland	**86.7**	x(4)	x(4)	**13.3**	m	89.0	11.0	142	177
Portugal	**93.5**	5.0	1.5	**6.5**	m	98.6	1.4	112	534
Slovak Republic	**83.9**	10.1	6.0	**16.1**	2.3	96.4	3.6	147	751
Slovenia	**88.5**	10.2	1.3	**11.5**	n	m	m	m	m
Spain	**87.1**	12.0	1.0	**12.9**	0.4	87.4	12.6	142	147
Sweden	**97.4**	n	2.6	**2.6**	a	97.0	3.0	124	108
Switzerland	**m**	m	m	**m**	m	91.8	8.2	122	154
Turkey	**m**	m	m	**m**	m	98.6	1.4	m	m
United Kingdom	**68.9**	20.7	10.4	**31.1**	19.2	85.2	14.8	117	303
United States	**72.0**	22.0	6.0	**28.0**	m	67.3	32.7	129	103
OECD average	**84.0**	~	~	**16.0**	2.5	87.8	12.2	133	186
EU21 average	**89.5**	~	~	**10.5**	2.7	92.1	7.9	132	217
Other G20 Argentina	**85.7**	13.0	1.3	**14.3**	0.1	m	m	m	m
Brazil	**m**	m	m	**m**	m	m	m	215	m
China	**m**	m	m	**m**	m	m	m	m	m
India	**m**	m	m	**m**	m	m	m	m	m
Indonesia	**m**	m	m	**m**	m	m	m	m	m
Russian Federation	**84.8**	11.6	3.5	**15.2**	m	m	m	244	m
Saudi Arabia	**m**	m	m	**m**	m	m	m	m	m
South Africa	**m**	m	m	**m**	m	m	m	m	m
G20 average	**m**	m	m	**m**	m	m	m	m	m

1. Including subsidies attributable to payments to educational institutions received from public sources.
2. Year of reference 2008 instead of 2009.
3. Year of reference 2010 instead of 2009.
Source: OECD. Argentina: UNESCO Institute for Statistics (World Education Indicators programme). See Annex 3 for notes (*www.oecd.org/edu/eag2012*).
Please refer to the Reader's Guide for information concerning the symbols replacing missing data.
StatLink ▨▨ http://dx.doi.org/10.1787/888932666190

B3

Table B3.2a. Relative proportions of public and private expenditure on educational institutions, as a percentage, by level of education (2000, 2009)

Distribution of public and private sources of funds for educational institutions after transfers from public sources, by year

	Pre-primary education (for children 3 years and older)					Primary, secondary and post-secondary non-tertiary education								
	2009					2009					2000		Index of change between 2000 and 2009 in expenditure on educational institutions	
		Private sources			Private: of which, subsidised		Private sources			Private: of which, subsidised				
	Public sources	Household expenditure	Expenditure of other private entities	All private sources[1]		Public sources	Household expenditure	Expenditure of other private entities	All private sources[1]		Public sources	All private sources[1]	Public sources	All private sources[1]
	(1)	(2)	(3)	(4)	(5)	(6)	(7)	(8)	(9)	(10)	(11)	(12)	(13)	(14)
Australia	**51.4**	48.2	0.3	**48.6**	1.8	**84.1**	13.3	2.6	**15.9**	1.6	83.7	16.3	155	150
Austria	**72.0**	12.8	15.2	**28.0**	21.5	**95.7**	2.9	1.4	**4.3**	1.8	95.8	4.2	112	115
Belgium	**96.5**	3.3	0.1	**3.5**	0.8	**95.3**	4.6	0.1	**4.7**	1.3	94.7	5.3	121	108
Canada[2,3]	**x(6)**	x(7)	x(8)	**x(9)**	x(6)	**89.1**	3.9	6.9	**10.9**	x(6)	92.4	7.6	128	188
Chile[4]	**81.1**	18.6	m	**18.9**	n	**78.2**	21.5	0.3	**21.8**	a	m	m	m	m
Czech Republic	**92.0**	6.6	1.4	**8.0**	m	**91.0**	7.2	1.9	**9.0**	n	91.7	8.3	145	159
Denmark[3]	**87.6**	12.4	n	**12.4**	m	**97.5**	2.5	n	**2.5**	m	97.8	2.2	121	139
Estonia	**98.6**	1.4	n	**1.4**	n	**98.7**	1.2	0.1	**1.3**	m	m	m	147	m
Finland	**90.3**	x(4)	x(4)	**9.7**	n	**99.2**	x(9)	x(9)	**0.8**	n	99.3	0.7	133	160
France	**94.1**	5.9	n	**5.9**	m	**92.2**	6.2	1.6	**7.8**	m	92.6	7.4	103	110
Germany	**70.2**	x(4)	x(4)	**29.8**	n	**87.6**	x(9)	x(9)	**12.4**	m	87.1	12.9	106	102
Greece	**m**	m	m	**m**	m	**m**	m	n	**m**	m	91.7	8.3	m	m
Hungary	**m**	m	m	**m**	m	**m**	m	m	**m**	n	92.7	7.3	128	m
Iceland	**77.1**	19.1	3.7	**22.9**	a	**96.3**	3.4	0.2	**3.7**	a	96.4	3.6	139	142
Ireland	**m**	m	m	**m**	m	**97.7**	2.3	m	**2.3**	m	96.0	4.0	208	116
Israel	**78.7**	19.7	1.6	**21.3**	n	**93.2**	3.9	2.9	**6.8**	1.8	94.1	5.9	122	142
Italy	**91.2**	8.8	n	**8.8**	n	**97.0**	2.8	0.1	**3.0**	n	97.8	2.2	108	146
Japan[3]	**45.0**	38.3	16.7	**55.0**	m	**90.4**	7.7	2.0	**9.6**	m	89.8	10.2	103	96
Korea	**42.6**	52.7	4.7	**57.4**	0.5	**76.2**	16.6	7.3	**23.8**	0.3	80.8	19.2	178	234
Luxembourg	**98.6**	1.2	0.2	**1.4**	m	**97.4**	1.9	0.7	**2.6**	m	m	m	m	m
Mexico	**81.4**	18.5	0.1	**18.6**	0.2	**81.0**	18.9	0.1	**19.0**	2.2	86.1	13.9	122	178
Netherlands	**98.7**	1.3	a	**1.3**	1.1	**86.8**	4.4	8.8	**13.2**	2.9	85.7	14.3	139	126
New Zealand	**82.9**	17.1	x(2)	**17.1**	m	**87.2**	12.8	x(7)	**12.8**	m	m	m	131	m
Norway	**84.4**	15.6	n	**15.6**	n	**m**	m	m	**m**	m	99.0	1.0	127	m
Poland	**81.1**	18.9	m	**18.9**	n	**94.7**	5.3	m	**5.3**	m	95.4	4.6	131	154
Portugal	**m**	m	m	**m**	m	**100.0**	n	m	**n**	m	99.9	0.1	112	85
Slovak Republic[3]	**83.6**	14.3	2.2	**16.4**	0.4	**87.5**	9.4	3.1	**12.5**	1.0	97.6	2.4	150	882
Slovenia	**79.3**	20.6	0.1	**20.7**	n	**91.2**	8.2	0.5	**8.8**	n	m	m	m	m
Spain	**77.1**	22.9	m	**22.9**	n	**92.9**	7.1	m	**7.1**	a	93.0	7.0	128	129
Sweden	**100.0**	n	n	**n**	n	**100.0**	n	a	**n**	n	99.9	0.1	116	51
Switzerland	**m**	m	m	**m**	m	**86.3**	n	13.7	**13.7**	0.8	88.9	11.1	121	154
Turkey	**m**	m	m	**m**	m	**m**	m	m	**m**	m	m	m	m	m
United Kingdom	**89.9**	10.1	n	**10.1**	26.0	**78.7**	10.8	10.5	**21.3**	21.1	88.7	11.3	133	283
United States	**80.9**	19.1	a	**19.1**	a	**92.1**	7.9	m	**7.9**	m	91.6	8.4	126	118
OECD average	**81.7**	~	~	**18.3**	2.5	**91.2**	~	~	**8.8**	1.7	92.9	7.1	131	171
EU21 average	**88.3**	~	~	**11.7**	1.6	**93.7**	~	~	**6.3**	0.7	94.3	5.7	131	192
Argentina	**69.0**	31.0	n	**31.0**	m	**89.4**	10.6	a	**10.6**	m	m	m	m	m
Brazil	**m**	m	m	**m**	m	**m**	m	m	**m**	m	m	m	237	m
China	**m**	m	m	**m**	m	**m**	m	m	**m**	m	m	m	m	m
India	**m**	m	m	**m**	m	**m**	m	m	**m**	m	m	m	m	m
Indonesia	**m**	m	m	**m**	m	**m**	m	m	**m**	m	m	m	m	m
Russian Federation	**85.2**	12.9	1.9	**14.8**	m	**97.2**	1.4	1.5	**2.8**	m	m	m	212	m
Saudi Arabia	**m**	m	m	**m**	m	**m**	m	m	**m**	m	m	m	m	m
South Africa	**m**	m	m	**m**	m	**m**	m	m	**m**	m	m	m	m	m
G20 average	**m**	m	m	**m**	m	**m**	m	m	**m**	m	m	m	m	m

1. Including subsidies attributable to payments to educational institutions received from public sources.
To calculate private funds net of subsidies, subtract public subsidies (Columns 5, 10) from private funds (Columns 4, 9).
To calculate total public funds, including public subsidies, add public subsidies (Columns 5, 10) to direct public funds (Columns 1, 6).
2. Year of reference 2008 instead of 2009.
3. Some levels of education are included with others. Refer to "x" code in Table B1.1a for details.
4. Year of reference 2010 instead of 2009.
Source: OECD. Argentina: UNESCO Institute for Statistics (World Education Indicators programme). See Annex 3 for notes (*www.oecd.org/edu/eag2012*).
Please refer to the Reader's Guide for information concerning the symbols replacing missing data.
StatLink ⏷ http://dx.doi.org/10.1787/888932666209

Table B3.2b. Relative proportions of public and private expenditure on educational institutions, as a percentage, for tertiary education (2000, 2009)

Distribution of public and private sources of funds for educational institutions after transfers from public sources, by year

	Tertiary education								
	2009					2000		Index of change between 2000 and 2009 in expenditure on educational institutions	
		Private sources							
	Public sources	Household expenditure	Expenditure of other private entities	All private sources[1]	Private: of which, subsidised	Public sources	All private sources[1]	Public sources	All private sources[1]
	(1)	(2)	(3)	(4)	(5)	(6)	(7)	(8)	(9)
Australia	45.4	39.1	15.4	54.6	0.5	49.9	50.1	135	161
Austria	87.7	2.9	9.4	12.3	8.8	96.3	3.7	142	518
Belgium	89.7	5.5	4.8	10.3	3.9	91.5	8.5	123	151
Canada[2,3]	62.9	20.2	16.9	37.1	m	61.0	39.0	130	121
Chile[4]	23.4	68.1	8.5	76.6	9.3	m	m	m	m
Czech Republic	79.9	8.8	11.3	20.1	m	85.4	14.6	202	298
Denmark[3]	95.4	x(4)	x(4)	4.6	m	97.6	2.4	121	236
Estonia	80.2	18.2	1.6	19.8	n	m	m	163	m
Finland	95.8	x(4)	x(4)	4.2	n	97.2	2.8	127	198
France	83.1	9.7	7.3	16.9	m	84.4	15.6	122	134
Germany	84.4	x(4)	x(4)	15.6	m	88.2	11.8	120	166
Greece	m	m	m	m	m	99.7	0.3	m	m
Hungary	m	m	m	m	m	76.7	23.3	135	m
Iceland	92.0	7.4	0.6	8.0	a	91.8	8.2	159	154
Ireland	83.8	13.8	2.4	16.2	m	79.2	20.8	152	111
Israel	58.2	27.3	14.6	41.8	5.0	58.5	41.5	108	109
Italy	68.6	23.8	7.6	31.4	8.5	77.5	22.5	104	164
Japan[3]	35.3	50.7	14.1	64.7	m	38.5	61.5	105	120
Korea	26.1	49.2	24.8	73.9	1.4	23.3	76.7	183	157
Luxembourg	m	m	m	m	m	m	m	m	m
Mexico	68.7	30.9	0.4	31.3	1.8	79.4	20.6	146	256
Netherlands	72.0	14.9	13.1	28.0	0.4	76.5	23.5	127	161
New Zealand	67.9	32.1	m	32.1	m	m	m	157	m
Norway	96.1	3.0	m	3.9	m	96.3	3.7	124	131
Poland	69.7	22.8	7.5	30.3	m	66.6	33.4	211	183
Portugal	70.9	22.3	6.8	29.1	m	92.5	7.5	109	548
Slovak Republic[3]	70.0	11.7	18.3	30.0	2.0	91.2	8.8	139	620
Slovenia	85.1	10.8	4.2	14.9	n	m	m	m	m
Spain	79.1	16.8	4.1	20.9	1.7	74.4	25.6	149	115
Sweden	89.8	n	10.2	10.2	n	91.3	8.7	125	150
Switzerland	m	m	m	m	m	m	m	129	m
Turkey	m	m	m	m	m	95.4	4.6	m	m
United Kingdom	29.6	58.1	12.3	70.4	10.8	67.7	32.3	117	334
United States	38.1	45.3	16.6	61.9	m	31.1	68.9	138	101
OECD average	70.0	~	~	30.0	3.2	77.1	22.9	138	216
EU21 average	78.6	~	~	21.4	2.5	85.2	14.8	138	255
Argentina	80.6	12.9	6.5	19.4	m	m	m	m	m
Brazil	m	m	m	m	m	m	m	162	m
China	m	m	m	m	m	m	m	m	m
India	m	m	m	m	m	m	m	m	m
Indonesia	m	m	m	m	m	m	m	m	m
Russian Federation	64.6	27.4	8.0	35.4	m	m	m	379	m
Saudi Arabia	m	m	m	m	m	m	m	m	m
South Africa	m	m	m	m	m	m	m	m	m
G20 average	m	m	m	m	m	m	m	m	m

1. Including subsidies attributable to payments to educational institutions received from public sources.
To calculate private funds net of subsidies, subtract public subsidies (Column 5) from private funds (Column 4).
To calculate total public funds, including public subsidies, add public subsidies (Column 5) to direct public funds (Column 1).
2. Year of reference 2008 instead of 2009.
3. Some levels of education are included with others. Refer to "x" code in Table B1.1a for details.
4. Year of reference 2010 instead of 2009.
Source: OECD. Argentina: UNESCO Institute for Statistics (World Education Indicators programme). See Annex 3 for notes *(www.oecd.org/edu/eag2012)*.
Please refer to the Reader's Guide for information concerning the symbols replacing missing data.
StatLink http://dx.doi.org/10.1787/888932666228

B3

Table B3.3. Trends in relative proportions of public expenditure[1] on educational institutions and index of change between 1995 and 2009 (2000 = 100), for tertiary education (1995, 2000, 2005 and 2009)

	Share of public expenditure on tertiary educational institutions (%)				Index of change between 1995 and 2009 in public expenditure on tertiary educational institutions (2000 = 100, constant prices)			
	1995	2000	2005	2009	1995	2000	2005	2009
	(1)	(2)	(3)	(4)	(5)	(6)	(7)	(8)
Australia	64.6	49.9	45.4	45.4	116	100	109	135
Austria	96.1	96.3	92.9	87.7	96	100	129	142
Belgium	m	91.5	90.6	89.7	m	100	101	123
Canada[2, 3]	56.6	61.0	53.4	62.9	69	100	108	130
Chile[4]	m	m	15.9	23.4	m	m	m	m
Czech Republic	71.5	85.4	81.2	79.9	84	100	148	202
Denmark[2]	99.4	97.6	96.7	95.4	93	100	115	121
Estonia	m	m	69.9	80.2	69	100	109	163
Finland	97.8	97.2	96.1	95.8	90	100	115	127
France	85.3	84.4	83.6	83.1	93	100	106	122
Germany	89	88.2	85.3	84.4	96	100	102	120
Greece[2]	m	99.7	96.7	m	63	100	229	m
Hungary	80.3	76.7	78.5	m	80	100	124	135
Iceland[2]	m	91.8	90.5	92.0	m	100	142	159
Ireland	69.7	79.2	84.0	83.8	50	100	106	152
Israel	62.5	58.5	46.5	58.2	75	100	88	108
Italy	82.9	77.5	73.2	68.6	85	100	101	104
Japan[2]	35.1	38.5	33.7	35.3	80	100	93	105
Korea	m	23.3	24.3	26.1	m	100	132	183
Luxembourg	m	m	m	m	m	m	m	m
Mexico	77.4	79.4	69.0	68.7	75	100	119	146
Netherlands	79.4	76.5	73.3	72.0	99	100	111	127
New Zealand	m	m	59.7	67.9	103	100	119	157
Norway	93.7	96.3	m	96.1	107	100	116	124
Poland	m	66.6	74.0	69.7	89	100	193	211
Portugal	96.5	92.5	68.1	70.9	77	100	102	109
Slovak Republic[2]	95	91.2	77.3	70.0	86	100	127	139
Slovenia	m	m	76.5	85.1	m	m	m	m
Spain	74.4	74.4	77.9	79.1	72	100	119	149
Sweden	93.6	91.3	88.2	89.8	84	100	111	125
Switzerland	m	m	m	m	90	100	130	129
Turkey	96.3	95.4	m	m	55	100	m	m
United Kingdom	80.0	67.7	m	29.6	111	100	m	117
United States	37.4	31.1	34.7	38.1	85	100	132	138
OECD average	78.9	77.1	70.2	70.0	85	100	122	138
OECD average for countries with data available for all reference years	77.9	77.3	73.0	72.8	85	100	114	133
EU21 average	87.0	87.1	82.9	81.6	85	100	115	134
Argentina	m	m	m	m	m	m	m	m
Brazil	m	m	m	m	84	100	127	162
China	m	m	m	m	m	m	m	m
India	m	m	m	m	m	m	m	m
Indonesia	m	m	m	m	m	m	m	m
Russian Federation	m	m	m	64.6	m	100	226	379
Saudi Arabia	m	m	m	m	m	m	m	m
South Africa	m	m	m	m	m	m	m	m
G20 average	m	m	m	m	m	m	m	m

1. Excluding international funds in public and total expenditure on educational institutions.
2. Some levels of education are included with others. Refer to "x" code in Table B1.1a for details.
3. Year of reference 2008 instead of 2009.
4. Year of reference 2010 instead of 2009.
Source: OECD. See Annex 3 for notes (*www.oecd.org/edu/eag2012*).
Please refer to the Reader's Guide for information concerning the symbols replacing missing data.
StatLink ᴍᴸᴸ http://dx.doi.org/10.1787/888932666247

Table B3.4. Annual public expenditure on educational institutions per student, by type of institution (2009)

In equivalent USD converted using PPPs for GDP, by level of education and type of institution

	Pre-primary education			Primary, secondary and post-secondary non-tertiary education			Tertiary education				Total all levels of education		
	Public institutions	Private institutions	Total public and private	Public institutions	Private institutions	Total public and private	Public institutions	Private institutions	Total public and private	of which: R&D activities	Public institutions	Private institutions	Total public and private
	(1)	(2)	(3)	(4)	(5)	(6)	(7)	(8)	(9)	(10)	(11)	(12)	(13)
OECD Australia	x(3)	x(3)	**4 368**	8 744	6 825	**8 124**	7 836	1 418	**7 496**	5 565	x(13)	x(13)	**8 001**
Austria	x(3)	x(3)	**5 906**	x(6)	x(6)	**11 184**	x(9)	x(9)	**12 500**	4 446	x(13)	x(13)	**10 697**
Belgium	5 997	5 050	**5 499**	10 343	8 616	**9 318**	14 529	12 765	**13 524**	4 367	10 626	8 733	**9 530**
Canada[1]	x(4)	m	**m**	8 389	m	**m**	13 468	m	**m**	m	9 561	m	**m**
Chile[2]	4 755	2 441	**3 151**	3 174	1 652	**2 296**	3 795	995	**1 501**	219	3 381	1 564	**2 218**
Czech Republic	4 113	3 024	**4 096**	5 271	3 023	**5 107**	7 517	422	**6 455**	1 485	5 649	2 078	**5 365**
Denmark	8 568	1 510	**7 698**	11 480	6 543	**10 820**	17 473	a	**17 252**	x(9)	12 281	5 425	**11 508**
Estonia	2 538	1 760	**2 514**	6 123	4 594	**6 063**	7 339	4 331	**4 818**	1 951	5 452	4 298	**5 202**
Finland	5 112	3 979	**5 015**	8 214	9 214	**8 291**	16 664	12 423	**15 868**	5 270	9 113	9 710	**9 170**
France	6 221	3 013	**5 822**	8 903	5 361	**8 202**	13 863	4 063	**12 189**	4 373	9 165	4 898	**8 392**
Germany	m	m	**m**	m	m	**m**	m	m	**m**	m	m	m	**m**
Greece	m	m	**m**	m	m	**m**	m	m	**m**	m	m	m	**m**
Hungary	x(3)	x(3)	**4 433**	x(6)	x(6)	**4 302**	6 289	6 061	**6 253**	1 202	4 760	5 161	**4 810**
Iceland	7 872	3 942	**7 431**	9 095	5 725	**8 970**	9 748	6 647	**9 144**	x(9)	9 561	5 765	**9 284**
Ireland	m	m	**3 410**	9 098	m	**m**	13 902	m	**m**	4 410	9 873	m	**m**
Israel	4 101	1 645	**3 336**	5 108	5 259	**5 145**	x(9)	x(9)	**6 431**	m	5 327	4 849	**5 150**
Italy[3]	7 552	575	**5 410**	8 718	1 464	**8 193**	6 837	2 366	**6 483**	3 335	8 234	1 208	**7 470**
Japan	x(3)	x(3)	**2 565**	x(6)	x(6)	**7 779**	x(9)	x(9)	**6 102**	x(9)	x(13)	x(13)	**7 405**
Korea	7 995	1 144	**2 746**	6 564	5 021	**6 291**	8 625	1 287	**2 751**	954	7 629	2 453	**5 639**
Luxembourg	16 751	3 341	**15 693**	18 629	6 856	**17 040**	m	m	**m**	m	m	m	**m**
Mexico	2 052	10	**1 757**	2 118	6	**1 893**	8 200	a	**5 509**	1 264	2 586	6	**2 252**
Netherlands[4]	7 211	n	**7 186**	8 773	n	**8 557**	13 638	n	**12 252**	5 025	9 376	n	**9 043**
New Zealand	2 535	9 415	**9 285**	6 957	2 213	**6 593**	7 852	1 771	**7 212**	1 680	7 111	5 228	**6 857**
Norway	6 382	4 762	**5 654**	12 923	11 645	**12 862**	20 958	4 106	**18 623**	7 160	13 806	9 621	**13 359**
Poland	x(3)	x(3)	**3 987**	x(6)	x(6)	**4 588**	x(9)	x(9)	**4 535**	776	x(13)	x(13)	**4 506**
Portugal	5 661	1 848	**3 819**	7 253	3 627	**6 723**	8 110	852	**6 372**	3 567	7 504	2 549	**6 494**
Slovak Republic	3 662	2 590	**3 626**	3 991	3 911	**3 984**	4 490	m	**4 500**	748	4 188	3 849	**4 166**
Slovenia	6 527	1 341	**6 341**	7 905	5 627	**7 876**	7 803	2 626	**7 312**	1 430	7 715	3 192	**7 567**
Spain	7 830	2 384	**5 876**	10 105	3 735	**8 122**	12 141	1 227	**10 616**	2 937	10 094	3 206	**8 076**
Sweden	6 649	6 008	**6 549**	9 687	9 880	**9 709**	18 408	12 830	**17 848**	8 343	10 387	9 332	**10 260**
Switzerland	5 147	m	**m**	11 388	m	**m**	21 577	m	**m**	m	12 431	m	**m**
Turkey	m	m	**m**	m	m	**m**	m	m	**m**	m	m	m	**m**
United Kingdom	7 655	845	**5 840**	8 562	3 611	**7 555**	a	4 644	**4 644**	4 590	8 496	3 896	**7 041**
United States	11 348	1 486	**6 992**	12 272	1 038	**11 264**	12 481	3 044	**9 679**	x(9)	12 248	1 891	**10 517**
OECD average	6 426	2 701	**5 379**	8 511	4 810	**7 745**	10 906	3 812	**8 810**	3 265	8 329	4 301	**7 407**
EU21 average	6 803	2 485	**5 722**	8 941	5 071	**8 091**	10 563	4 615	**9 613**	3 427	8 307	4 502	**7 606**
Other G20 Argentina	2 398	671	**1 839**	3 296	1 454	**2 845**	4 579	359	**3 309**	m	3 393	1 142	**2 801**
Brazil	1 696	m	**m**	2 304	m	**m**	11 741	m	**m**	634	2 545	m	**m**
China	m	m	**m**	m	m	**m**	m	m	**m**	m	m	m	**m**
India	m	m	**m**	m	m	**m**	m	m	**m**	m	m	m	**m**
Indonesia	m	m	**m**	m	m	**m**	m	m	**m**	m	m	m	**m**
Russian Federation	m	m	**m**	4 203	m	**m**	4 988	m	**m**	m	5 994	m	**m**
Saudi Arabia[2]	m	m	**m**	m	m	**m**	16 297	m	**m**	m	m	m	**m**
South Africa	420	m	**m**	1 697	m	**m**	3 616	m	**m**	m	1 863	m	**m**
G20 average	m	m	**m**	m	m	**m**	m	m	**m**	m	m	m	**m**

1. Year of reference 2008.
2. Year of reference 2010.
3. Exclude post-secondary non-tertiary education.
4. Government-dependent private institutions are included with public institutions.
Source: OECD. Argentina: UNESCO Institute for Statistics (World Education Indicators programme). Saudi Arabia: Observatory on Higher Education. South Africa: UNESCO Institute for Statistics. See Annex 3 for notes (*www.oecd.org/edu/eag2012*).
Please refer to the Reader's Guide for information concerning the symbols replacing missing data.
StatLink http://dx.doi.org/10.1787/888932666266

WHAT IS THE TOTAL PUBLIC SPENDING ON EDUCATION?

- Education accounts for 13% of total public spending, on average in OECD countries, ranging from less than 10% in the Czech Republic, Italy, Japan and the Slovak Republic, to more than 19% in Chile, Mexico and New Zealand.

- The proportion of public expenditure devoted to education increased slightly between 1995 and 2009 in most countries with available data for all years. Among these countries, it increased by 0.5 percentage point on average during this period.

- However, during the period 2005-09, the proportion of public expenditure devoted to education decreased for most countries. The beginning of the economic crisis in 2008, which put more pressure on public budgets, may be related to decreases in the later years.

Chart B4.1. Total public expenditure on education as a percentage of total public expenditure (2000, 2005, 2009)

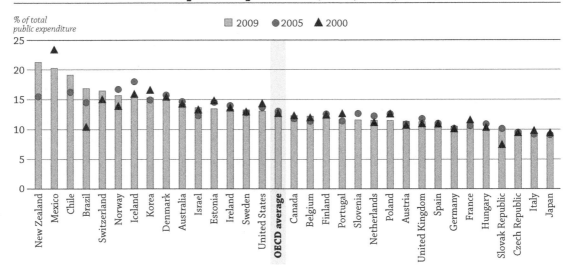

Countries are ranked in descending order of total public expenditure on education at all levels as a percentage of total public expenditure in 2009.
Source: OECD. Table B4.3. See Annex 3 for notes (*www.oecd.org/edu/eag2012*).
StatLink ⬛⬛⬛ http://dx.doi.org/10.1787/888932662713

How to read this chart
This chart shows direct public expenditure on educational institutions, plus public support to households (which includes subsidies for living costs, such as scholarships and grants to students/households and student loans) and to other private entities, as a percentage of total public expenditure, by year.

▣ Context

This indicator presents total public spending on education, both relative to the country's total public spending and to its gross domestic product, to account for the relative sizes of the public budgets. In addition, this indicator includes data on the different sources of the public funding invested in education (central, regional and local government) and on the transfers of funds between these levels of government.

Countries' decisions concerning budget allocations to various sectors, including education, health care, social security or defence, depend not only on their priorities but also on whether markets, alone, can provide those services adequately. Markets may fail to do so if the public benefits are greater than the private benefits. For example, government funding can help increase access to education for members of society. However, the economic crisis has put pressure on public budgets to the extent that fewer public resources may be allocated to education. This, in turn, may affect access to or the outcomes of education. On the other hand, the demand for education and training from people who are not in work may increase, requiring more spending on education.

■ Other findings

■ Most OECD countries **spend more than twice as much on primary, secondary and post-secondary non-tertiary education than on tertiary education**.

■ **Public funding is more decentralised at the primary, secondary and post-secondary non-tertiary level than at the tertiary level**. On average, more than 50% of the initial public funds for these levels of education comes from the central government in OECD countries.

■ **Some 85% of public funding for tertiary education comes from the central government**, before transfers of public funds from central to regional and local levels of government are taken into account.

■ **At the primary, secondary and post-secondary non-tertiary level of education, only one country had an entirely centralised public funding system** (New Zealand), while six countries (Chile, Iceland, the Netherlands, New Zealand, Norway and the United Kingdom) have an entirely centralised funding system for tertiary education.

■ Trends

Over the past 15 years (1995-2009), the percentage of total public expenditure devoted to education (all levels of education combined) increased slightly in two-thirds of countries with available data, with an increase of 0.5 percentage point, on average. Nevertheless, the evolution is different when looking at data from 2005 to 2009. During this period, public expenditure on education as a percentage of total public expenditure decreased in just under two-thirds of countries with available data. The decrease was especially substantial in Estonia, Iceland, Mexico, Norway, Poland and Slovenia (1 percentage point or more).

Similar changes occurred for public expenditure on education as a percentage of GDP over the 1995-2009 period. However, between 2005 and 2009, the variations are different. Whereas the share of public expenditure devoted to education decreased in most countries between 2005 and 2009, expenditure on education as a percentage of GDP increased in almost all countries during this period. On average in OECD countries with available data on both years, it increased by nearly 0.4 percentage point.

B4

Analysis

Overall level of public resources invested in education

In 2009, total public expenditure on education as a percentage of total public expenditure averaged 13.0% in OECD countries and ranged from below 10% in the Czech Republic (9.8%), Italy (9.0%), Japan (8.9%) and the Slovak Republic (9.8%) to above 19% in Chile (19.1%), Mexico (20.3%) and New Zealand (21.2%) (Chart B4.1 and Table B4.1).

In most countries, about two-thirds of total public expenditure on education is devoted to primary, secondary and post-secondary non-tertiary education, both as a percentage of total public expenditure and as a percentage of GDP. This is primarily explained by the near-universal enrolment rates at these levels of education (see Indicator C2) and the demographic structure of the population.

Pre-primary education accounts for 8% of public expenditure on education, on average in OECD countries. The percentage of public expenditure devoted to the pre-primary level differs greatly among countries. It ranges from below 5% in Australia (1.1%), Ireland (0.8%), Japan (2.7%), Korea (2.2%), Norway (4.8%) and Switzerland (3.7%) to over 13% in Chile (13.4%), Hungary (14.0%) and Spain (14.4%). This diversity is mainly explained by the differences among countries in enrolment rates (see Indicator C2).

Public expenditure devoted to the tertiary level amounts to 23.5% of total public expenditure on education, on average in OECD countries. In OECD and G20 countries, the percentages range from below 15% in the United Kingdom (14.4%) to over 30% in Canada (38.0%), Finland (31.7%) and Norway (30.4%).

When public expenditure on education is considered as a proportion of total public spending, the relative sizes of public budgets must be taken into account. Indeed, the picture is different when looking at total public expenditure on education as a percentage of gross domestic product for all levels of education combined, compared with the picture described above on the total public expenditure on education as a percentage of total public expenditure. While OECD countries like the Czech Republic, Italy, Japan and the Slovak Republic are still among those with the lowest rates of public expenditure on education related to GDP in 2009 (4.4%, 4.7%, 3.8% and 4.1%, respectively), other countries are also below 5%, namely Chile (4.5%), India (3.5%), Indonesia (3.0%), the Russian Federation (4.7%) and South Africa (4.8%). At the other end of the spectrum, only Denmark spends more than 8% of its GDP on education (8.7%). This rate is well above the OECD average of 5.8%.

Despite what one might think, the countries with the highest total public expenditure on education as a percentage of total public expenditure – namely Brazil, Chile, Mexico, New Zealand and Switzerland (Chart B4.1) – are at the bottom end in terms of total public expenditure on all services as a percentage of GDP (Chart B4.2).

When looking at total public expenditure on all services (e.g. health, social security, environment), and not simply public expenditure on education, as a proportion of GDP, rates differ greatly among countries. In 2009, around one-third of the countries reported this proportion of total public expenditure on all services in relation to GDP as greater than 50%, and in four of them the percentage was above 55% (58.0% in Denmark, 55.6% in Finland and 56.7% in France and 55.1% in Sweden). At the other extreme, this proportion represents less than 30% of GDP in Chile (23.4%) and Mexico (26.2%) (Chart B4.2). Despite what one might think, countries with larger total public expenditure on all services are not the ones with the higher rates of total public expenditure on education as a percentage of total public expenditure. Only Denmark and Iceland are simultaneously among the top ten countries for public spending on public services overall and among the top ten countries in terms of public spending on education (Charts B4.1 and B4.2).

Changes in public expenditure in education between 1995 and 2009

Over the past 15 years (1995-2009), public expenditure on education (all levels combined) as a percentage of total public expenditure has increased slightly in two-thirds of countries with available data for both 1995 and 2009 (on average, by 0.5 percentage point in these countries). Nevertheless, spending patterns differ among countries. In Brazil, Denmark, the Netherlands, New Zealand, Sweden and Switzerland, there have been increases of more than two percentage points, while in others, there have been large decreases (for instance, 1.9 percentage point in Mexico) (Table B4.3).

In addition, spending patterns changed considerably between 2005 to 2009. During this five-year period, public expenditure on education as a percentage of total public expenditure decreased in less than two-thirds of countries with available data (19 out of 32 countries). The largest changes were seen in Mexico (a decrease of 3.1 percentage points) and New Zealand (an increase of 5.8 percentage points). These variations observed between 2005 and 2009 are likely linked to the first effects of the global economic crisis, which began in 2008. The crisis put more pressure on overall public budgets, requiring governments to prioritise allocations among education and other key public sectors, such as health and social security.

Between 1995 and 2009, the evolution of public expenditure on education as a percentage of GDP is similar to the evolution of public expenditure on education as a percentage of total public expenditure. Relative to GDP, public expenditure on education increased by more than one percentage point in Brazil, Denmark, Ireland, Mexico and New Zealand, and decreased by more than one percentage point in Canada.

Comparing 2009 with 2005, public expenditure on education as a percentage of GDP increased in all countries except Hungary, Poland, Slovenia and Switzerland. On average in OECD countries with available data for all years, the increase was 0.4 percentage point. Nevertheless, these figures should be interpreted with caution as the GDP in this five-year period was stable or even decreased in some countries. This means that expenditure on education relative to GDP might have increased not only because of an increase in the expenditure on education, but also because of a decrease in GDP in many countries (see Box B2.1 in Indicator B2).

Many countries reported great changes in the level of total public expenditure on all services as a percentage of GDP between 2000 and 2009. This share increased in most countries, except three where it decreased: Israel (by 4.2 percentage points), the Slovak Republic (by 10.7 percentage points), and Switzerland (by 0.7 percentage points) (Chart B4.2). Increases in the other countries ranged from 1 percentage point or below in Austria, Brazil, Canada and Sweden to 17 percentage points in Ireland.

Chart B4.2. **Total public expenditure on all services as a percentage of GDP (2000, 2009)**

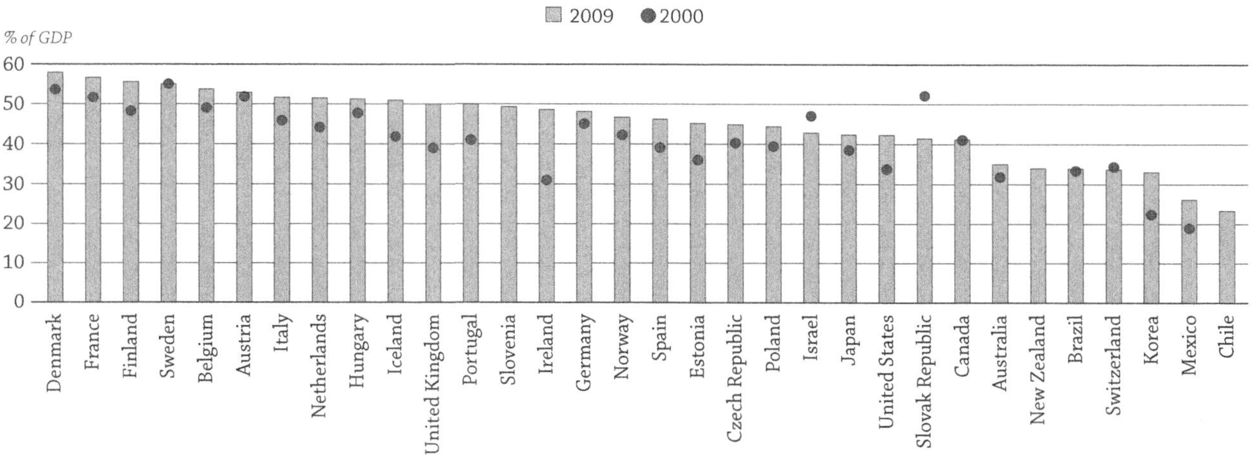

Note: This chart represents public expenditure on all services and not simply public expenditure on education.
Countries are ranked in descending order of total public expenditure as a percentage of GDP in 2009.
Source: OECD. Annex 2. See Annex 3 for notes (*www.oecd.org/edu/eag2012*).
StatLink ⬛🇸🇱🔳 http://dx.doi.org/10.1787/888932662732

Sources of public funding invested in education

All government sources (apart from international sources) for expenditure on education are classified in three different levels of government: central, regional and local. In some countries the funding of education is centralised while in others, the funding can become very decentralised after transfers between the different levels of government.

In recent years, many schools have become more autonomous and decentralised organisations and have become more accountable to students, parents and the public at large for their outcomes. PISA results suggest that when autonomy and accountability are intelligently combined, they tend to be associated with better student performance.

Chart B4.3. Distribution (in percentage) of initial sources of public funds for education, by level of government in primary, secondary and post-secondary non-tertiary education (2009)

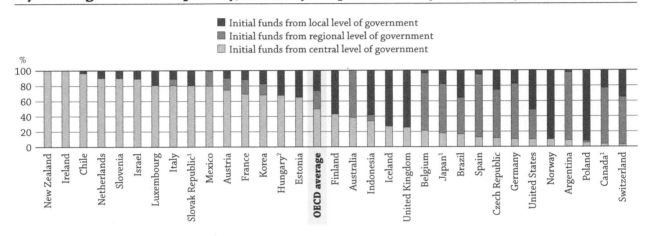

Change (in percentage points) in the proportion of educational funds received from the different levels of governement between initial and final purchasers of educational resources, at primary, secondary and post-secondary non-tertiary level (2009)

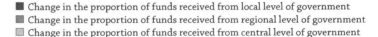

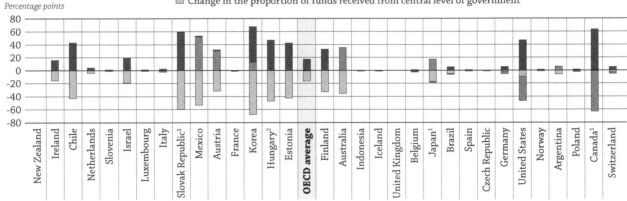

1. Some levels of education are included with others. Refer to "x" code in Table B1.1a for details.
2. Funds from local level includes funds from regional level of governement.
Countries are ranked in descending order of the share of initial sources of funds from the central level of government.
Source: OECD. Argentina, Indonesia: UNESCO Institute for Statistics (World Education Indicators programme). Table B4.2. See Annex 3 for notes (*www.oecd.org/edu/eag2012*).

StatLink http://dx.doi.org/10.1787/888932662751

Public funding is more centralised at the tertiary level than at lower levels of education. In 2009, 50.7% of public funds for primary, secondary and post-secondary non-tertiary education combined before transfers came from the central government, on average in OECD countries, compared with 84.5% for tertiary education (Tables B4.2 and B4.4, available on line).

For primary, secondary and post-secondary non-tertiary education combined, the share of initial public funds from the central government differed greatly among countries. Five countries reported a share below 10%, namely Argentina (8.7%), Canada (3.5%), Norway (9.7%), Poland (5.4%) and Switzerland (2.9%). At the other extreme, more than 90% of initial public funds came from the central government in Chile and the Netherlands (96.4% and 90.1%, respectively), and public funds come nearly exclusively from the central government in Ireland and New Zealand. Nevertheless, this picture changes dramatically when transfers between levels of government are taken into account. After these transfers, less than 5% of public funds came from central sources in Argentina (2.7%), Canada (2.8%), Poland (4.2%) and Switzerland (0.2%), but this was also the case in four other countries: Australia (3.3%), Japan (0.7%), Korea (0.7%) and the United States (0.4%). Only New Zealand still has an entirely centralised funding system (Chart B4.3 and Table B4.2).

The transfers of funds from central to regional and local levels of government at the primary, secondary and post-secondary non-tertiary levels combined are larger than at the tertiary level, on average in OECD countries, extending the scope of decentralisation at these levels of education. At the primary, secondary and post-secondary non-tertiary levels combined, on average in OECD countries, nearly 44% of public funds came from local sources after transfers, compared with 27% before transfers. At the tertiary level, public funds from local sources represented less than 3% of the funds before and after transfers, on average in OECD countries (Table B4.4, available on line).

At the primary, secondary and post-secondary non-tertiary levels combined, the extent of transfers from central to lower sources of public funds vary largely between countries, but represent more than 40 percentage points in Chile, Estonia, Hungary, Korea, Mexico and the Slovak Republic. Transfers from regional to local sources of public funds exceed 35 percentage points in Canada and the United States.

At the tertiary level of education, the proportions of public funds coming from the central government are relatively high, both before and after transfers between levels of government. Shares of public funds from central government are the lowest in Belgium (26.0% and 24.7%, before and after transfers, respectively), Germany (24.1% and 19.2%) and Spain (15.8% and 15.5%). At the other extreme, in nine countries these shares reach nearly 100% both before and after transfers: Chile, Estonia (99.7% after transfers), Iceland, the Netherlands, New Zealand, Norway, Portugal, the Slovak Republic and the United Kingdom (Table B4.4, available on line).

Definitions

Public expenditure on education covers expenditure on educational institutions and support for students' living costs and for other private expenditure outside institutions. It includes expenditure by all public entities, including ministries other than ministries of education, local and regional governments, and other public agencies. OECD countries differ in the ways in which they use public money for education. Public funds may flow directly to institutions or may be channelled to institutions via government programmes or via households. They may also be restricted to the purchase of educational services or be used to support student living costs.

All government sources (apart from international sources) for expenditure on education can be classified into three levels: central (national) government, regional government (province, state, *Land,* etc.), local government (municipality, district, commune, etc.). The terms "regional" and "local" apply to governments whose responsibilities are exercised within certain geographical subdivisions of a country. They do not apply to government bodies whose roles are not geographically circumscribed but are defined in terms of responsibility for particular services, functions, or categories of students.

B4

Total public expenditure, also referred to as total public spending, corresponds to the non-repayable current and capital expenditure of all levels of government: central, regional and local. It includes direct public expenditure on educational institutions as well as public support to households (e.g. scholarships and loans to students for tuition fees and student living costs) and to other private entities for education (e.g. subsidies to companies or labour organisations that operate apprenticeship programmes).

Methodology

Reference year: Data refer to the financial year 2009 and are based on the UOE data collection on education statistics administered by the OECD in 2011 (for details see Annex 3 at *www.oecd.org/edu/eag2012*).

Data coverage: Figures for total public expenditure have been taken from the OECD National Accounts Database (see Annex 2) and use the System of National Accounts 1993.

Educational expenditure is expressed as a percentage of a country's total public sector expenditure and as a percentage of GDP.

Though expenditure on debt servicing (e.g. interest payments) is included in total public expenditure, it is excluded from public expenditure on education. The reason is that some countries cannot separate interest payments for education from those for other services. This means that public expenditure on education as a percentage of total public expenditure may be underestimated in countries in which interest payments represent a large proportion of total public expenditure on all services.

OECD total: The OECD total reflects the value of the indicator if the OECD region is considered as a whole (see the Reader's Guide at the beginning of this book for details).

The statistical data for Israel are supplied by and under the responsibility of the relevant Israeli authorities. The use of such data by the OECD is without prejudice to the status of the Golan Heights, East Jerusalem and Israeli settlements in the West Bank under the terms of international law.

References

The following additional material relevant to this indicator is available on line:

- *Table B4.4. Sources of public educational funds, before and after transfers, by level of government, for tertiary education (2009)*
  StatLink ⬛🔢⬛ http://dx.doi.org/10.1787/888932666361

- *Table B4.5. Distribution of total public expenditure on education (2009)*
  StatLink ⬛🔢⬛ http://dx.doi.org/10.1787/888932666380

Table B4.1. **Total public expenditure on education (2009)**

Direct public expenditure on educational institutions plus public subsidies to households[1] and other private entities,
as a percentage of total public expenditure and as a percentage of GDP, by level of education

	Public expenditure[1] on education as a percentage of total public expenditure				Public expenditure[1] on education as a percentage of GDP			
	Pre-primary education	Primary, secondary and post-secondary non-tertiary education	Tertiary education	All levels of education combined	Pre-primary education	Primary, secondary and post-secondary non-tertiary education	Tertiary education	All levels of education combined
	(1)	(2)	(3)	(4)	(5)	(6)	(7)	(8)
Australia	0.2	10.8	3.1	**14.2**	0.1	3.8	1.1	**5.0**
Austria	1.0	7.3	3.0	**11.4**	0.6	3.9	1.6	**6.0**
Belgium	1.1	8.1	2.7	**12.2**	0.6	4.3	1.5	**6.6**
Canada[2, 3]	x(2)	8.3	4.7	**12.3**	x(6)	3.2	1.8	**5.1**
Chile[4]	2.6	12.3	4.3	**19.1**	0.6	2.9	1.0	**4.5**
Czech Republic	1.1	6.2	2.3	**9.8**	0.5	2.8	1.0	**4.4**
Denmark[3]	1.7	8.7	4.2	**15.1**	1.0	5.1	2.4	**8.7**
Estonia	1.1	9.4	3.0	**13.5**	0.5	4.2	1.3	**6.1**
Finland	0.7	7.6	3.9	**12.2**	0.4	4.2	2.2	**6.8**
France	1.2	6.8	2.4	**10.4**	0.7	3.9	1.3	**5.9**
Germany	0.9	6.6	2.8	**10.5**	0.4	3.2	1.3	**5.1**
Greece	m	m	m	**m**	m	m	m	**m**
Hungary	1.4	6.0	2.2	**10.0**	0.7	3.1	1.1	**5.1**
Iceland	1.5	9.9	3.1	**15.3**	0.8	5.0	1.6	**7.8**
Ireland	0.1	10.1	3.2	**13.4**	0.1	4.9	1.5	**6.5**
Israel	1.6	8.9	2.4	**13.6**	0.7	3.8	1.0	**5.8**
Italy	0.9	6.5	1.7	**9.0**	0.5	3.3	0.9	**4.7**
Japan[3]	0.2	6.4	1.8	**8.9**	0.1	2.7	0.8	**3.8**
Korea	0.3	10.8	2.6	**15.3**	0.1	3.6	0.9	**5.0**
Luxembourg	1.4	7.5	m	**m**	0.6	3.2	m	**m**
Mexico	2.0	13.5	4.1	**20.3**	0.5	3.5	1.1	**5.3**
Netherlands	0.8	7.6	3.2	**11.5**	0.4	3.9	1.6	**5.9**
New Zealand	1.4	14.1	5.7	**21.2**	0.5	4.8	1.9	**7.2**
Norway	0.7	9.6	4.8	**15.7**	0.3	4.5	2.2	**7.3**
Poland	1.2	7.9	2.4	**11.5**	0.5	3.5	1.1	**5.1**
Portugal	0.8	8.3	2.2	**11.6**	0.4	4.2	1.1	**5.8**
Slovak Republic[3]	1.0	6.4	1.9	**9.8**	0.4	2.7	0.8	**4.1**
Slovenia	1.1	7.6	2.8	**11.6**	0.6	3.8	1.4	**5.7**
Spain	1.6	6.8	2.5	**10.8**	0.7	3.1	1.1	**5.0**
Sweden	1.3	8.2	3.7	**13.2**	0.7	4.5	2.0	**7.3**
Switzerland	0.6	11.4	4.1	**16.4**	0.2	3.8	1.4	**5.5**
Turkey	m	m	m	**m**	m	m	m	**m**
United Kingdom	0.6	9.0	1.6	**11.3**	0.3	4.5	0.8	**5.6**
United States	0.8	9.3	3.0	**13.1**	0.3	3.9	1.3	**5.5**
OECD average	1.1	8.7	3.1	**13.0**	0.6	3.8	1.4	**5.8**
EU21 average	1.1	7.6	2.7	**11.5**	0.6	3.8	1.4	**5.8**
Argentina	m	m	m	**m**	0.5	4.4	1.1	**6.0**
Brazil	1.2	13.0	2.7	**16.8**	0.4	4.4	0.9	**5.7**
China	m	m	m	**m**	m	m	m	**m**
India	m	m	m	**m**	n	2.2	1.3	**3.5**
Indonesia[4]	m	m	m	**m**	n	2.1	0.5	**3.0**
Russian Federation	m	m	m	**m**	0.7	2.3	1.2	**4.7**
Saudi Arabia[4]	m	m	m	**m**	m	m	2.3	**m**
South Africa	m	m	m	**m**	n	3.9	0.7	**4.8**
G20 average	m	m	m	**m**	0.6	3.4	1.5	**5.0**

1. Public expenditure presented in this table includes public subsidies to households for living costs (scholarships and grants to students/households and students loans), which are not spent on educational institutions. Thus the figures presented here exceed those on public spending on institutions found in Table B2.4.
2. Year of reference 2008 instead of 2009.
3. Some levels of education are included with others. Refer to "x" code in Table B1.1a for details.
4. Year of reference 2010 instead of 2009.
Source: OECD. Argentina, India, Indonesia: UNESCO Institute for Statistics (World Education Indicators programme). Saudi Arabia: Observatory on Higher Education. South Africa: UNESCO Institute for Statistics. See Annex 3 for notes *(www.oecd.org/edu/eag2012).*
Please refer to the Reader's Guide for information concerning the symbols replacing missing data.
StatLink ▓▓▒ http://dx.doi.org/10.1787/888932666304

B4

Table B4.2. Sources of public educational funds, before and after transfers, by level of government for primary, secondary and post-secondary non-tertiary education (2009)

	Initial funds (before transfers between levels of government)				Final funds (after transfers between levels of government)			
	Central	Regional	Local	Total	Central	Regional	Local	Total
	(1)	(2)	(3)	(4)	(5)	(6)	(7)	(8)
OECD Australia	38.7	61.3	m	100.0	3.3	96.7	m	100.0
Austria	74.5	15.4	10.2	100.0	42.7	46.7	10.5	100.0
Belgium	21.4	74.6	4.0	100.0	22.6	73.4	4.0	100.0
Canada[1,2]	3.5	73.7	22.8	100.0	2.8	11.1	86.1	100.0
Chile[3]	96.4	a	3.6	100.0	53.7	a	46.3	100.0
Czech Republic	11.4	63.2	25.3	100.0	11.4	63.3	25.3	100.0
Denmark[2]	m	m	m	100.0	39.7	n	60.3	100.0
Estonia	65.1	a	34.9	100.0	22.8	a	77.2	100.0
Finland	43.0	a	57.0	100.0	10.2	a	89.8	100.0
France	69.2	19.0	11.9	100.0	69.0	19.0	12.0	100.0
Germany	10.3	72.2	17.5	100.0	8.5	68.5	23.0	100.0
Greece	m	m	m	m	m	m	m	m
Hungary	67.6	x(3)	32.4	100.0	20.8	x(7)	79.2	100.0
Iceland	27.0	a	73.0	100.0	26.8	a	73.2	100.0
Ireland	100.0	a	n	100.0	84.3	a	15.7	100.0
Israel	89.2	a	10.8	100.0	70.0	a	30.0	100.0
Italy	80.5	8.5	11.0	100.0	79.9	6.7	13.4	100.0
Japan[2]	18.0	64.2	17.8	100.0	0.7	81.5	17.8	100.0
Korea	68.2	14.2	17.6	100.0	0.7	26.9	72.4	100.0
Luxembourg	80.6	a	19.4	100.0	79.3	a	20.7	100.0
Mexico	79.7	20.1	0.2	100.0	26.4	73.4	0.2	100.0
Netherlands	90.1	n	9.9	100.0	86.1	n	13.9	100.0
New Zealand	100.0	n	n	100.0	100.0	n	n	100.0
Norway	9.7	n	90.3	100.0	8.5	n	91.5	100.0
Poland	5.4	2.4	92.2	100.0	4.2	2.2	93.5	100.0
Portugal	m	m	m	m	m	m	m	m
Slovak Republic[2]	80.4	a	19.6	100.0	20.7	a	79.3	100.0
Slovenia	89.9	a	10.1	100.0	88.6	a	11.4	100.0
Spain	12.7	81.6	5.7	100.0	11.8	82.5	5.7	100.0
Sweden	m	m	m	m	m	m	m	m
Switzerland	2.9	62.1	35.0	100.0	0.2	59.5	40.3	100.0
Turkey	m	m	m	m	m	m	m	m
United Kingdom	25.4	a	74.6	100.0	25.4	a	74.6	100.0
United States	10.0	38.7	51.3	100.0	0.4	1.6	98.0	100.0
OECD average	50.7	24.0	27.1	100.0	34.1	24.6	43.6	100.0
EU21 average	54.6	21.1	25.6	100.0	40.4	21.3	39.4	100.0
Other G20 Argentina	8.7	88.4	3.0	100.0	2.7	94.3	3.0	100.0
Brazil	16.8	47.7	35.5	100.0	11.8	47.5	40.7	100.0
China	m	m	m	m	m	m	m	m
India	m	m	m	m	m	m	m	m
Indonesia[3]	34.1	7.8	58.2	100.0	34.1	7.8	58.2	100.0
Russian Federation	m	m	m	m	3.3	30.9	65.9	100.0
Saudi Arabia	m	m	m	m	m	m	m	m
South Africa	m	m	m	m	m	m	m	m
G20 average	m	m	m	m	m	m	m	m

1. Year of reference 2008.
2. Some levels of education are included with others. Refer to "x" code in Table B1.1a for details.
3. Year of reference 2010.
Source: OECD. Argentina, Indonesia: UNESCO Institute for Statistics (World Education Indicators programme). See Annex 3 for notes (*www.oecd.org/edu/eag2012*). *Please refer to the Reader's Guide for information concerning the symbols replacing missing data.*
StatLink 🔗 http://dx.doi.org/10.1787/888932666323

B4

Table B4.3. Total public expenditure on education (1995, 2000, 2005, 2009)

Direct public expenditure on educational institutions plus public subsidies to households[1] and other private entities,
as a percentage of total public expenditure and as a percentage of GDP, for all levels of education combined by year

	Public expenditure[1] on education as a percentage of total public expenditure				Public expenditure[1] on education as a percentage of GDP			
	1995	2000	2005	2009	1995	2000	2005	2009
	(1)	(2)	(3)	(4)	(5)	(6)	(7)	(8)
OECD								
Australia	13.8	14.3	14.6	14.2	4.8	4.6	4.5	5.0
Austria	10.8	10.7	10.9	11.4	6.1	5.6	5.4	6.0
Belgium	m	12.0	11.4	12.2	m	5.9	5.9	6.6
Canada[2, 3]	12.7	12.4	11.8	12.3	6.2	5.1	5.1	5.1
Chile[4]	m	m	16.2	19.1	m	m	3.2	4.5
Czech Republic	8.7	9.5	9.5	9.8	4.5	3.8	4.1	4.4
Denmark[3]	12.3	15.4	15.7	15.1	7.3	8.3	8.3	8.7
Estonia	13.9	14.8	14.5	13.5	5.8	5.4	4.9	6.1
Finland	11.1	12.5	12.6	12.2	6.8	6.0	6.3	6.8
France	11.5	11.6	10.6	10.4	6.3	6.0	5.7	5.9
Germany	8.6	10.1	9.8	10.5	4.7	4.6	4.6	5.1
Greece	5.6	7.3	m	m	2.6	3.4	4.1	m
Hungary	9.4	10.4	10.9	10.0	5.3	5.0	5.5	5.1
Iceland	m	15.9	18.0	15.3	m	6.7	7.6	7.8
Ireland	12.2	13.7	14.0	13.4	5.0	4.2	4.7	6.5
Israel	12.7	13.4	12.3	13.6	6.6	6.3	5.6	5.8
Italy	9.0	9.8	9.2	9.0	4.7	4.5	4.4	4.7
Japan[3]	9.7	9.5	9.1	8.9	3.6	3.6	3.5	3.8
Korea	m	16.6	14.9	15.3	m	3.7	4.0	5.0
Luxembourg	m	m	m	m	m	m	m	m
Mexico	22.2	23.4	23.4	20.3	4.2	4.4	5.0	5.3
Netherlands	9.1	11.2	12.2	11.5	5.1	5.0	5.5	5.9
New Zealand	16.5	m	15.5	21.2	5.6	6.7	6.0	7.2
Norway	15.6	14.0	16.7	15.7	7.9	5.9	7.0	7.3
Poland	11.9	12.7	12.6	11.5	5.2	5.0	5.5	5.1
Portugal	11.9	12.7	11.4	11.6	4.9	5.2	5.2	5.8
Slovak Republic[3]	9.4	7.5	10.1	9.8	4.6	3.9	3.8	4.1
Slovenia	m	m	12.7	11.6	m	m	5.7	5.7
Spain	10.3	10.9	11.0	10.8	4.6	4.3	4.2	5.0
Sweden	10.9	13.0	12.8	13.2	7.1	7.2	6.9	7.3
Switzerland	13.0	15.1	12.7	16.4	5.5	5.2	5.7	5.5
Turkey	m	m	m	m	m	m	m	m
United Kingdom	11.4	11.0	11.8	11.3	5.0	4.3	5.2	5.6
United States	12.5	14.4	13.6	13.1	4.7	4.9	5.0	5.5
OECD average	11.7	12.6	13.0	13.0	5.3	5.2	5.3	5.8
EU21 average	10.4	11.4	11.8	11.5	5.3	5.1	5.3	5.8
OECD average (countries with available data for all years)	11.5	12.2	12.1	12.0	5.6	5.2	5.3	5.7
Other G20								
Argentina	m	m	m	m	m	m	m	6.0
Brazil	11.2	10.5	14.5	16.8	3.9	3.5	4.5	5.7
China	m	m	m	m	m	m	m	m
India	m	m	m	m	m	m	m	3.5
Indonesia[4]	m	m	m	m	m	m	m	3.0
Russian Federation	m	10.6	11.0	m	m	m	m	4.7
Saudi Arabia	m	m	m	m	m	m	m	m
South Africa	m	m	m	m	m	m	m	4.8
G20 average	m	m	m	m	m	m	m	4.5

1. Public expenditure presented in this table includes public subsidies to households for living costs (scholarships and grants to students/households and students loans), which are not spent on educational institutions. Thus the figures presented here exceed those on public spending on institutions found in Table B2.4.
2. Year of reference 2008 instead of 2009.
3. Some levels of education are included with others. Refer to "x" code in Table B1.1a for details.
4. Year of reference 2010 instead of 2009.
Source: OECD. Argentina, India, Indonesia: UNESCO Institute for Statistics (World Education Indicators programme). South Africa: UNESCO Institute for Statistics. See Annex 3 for notes (*www.oecd.org/edu/eag2012*).
Please refer to the Reader's Guide for information concerning the symbols replacing missing data.
StatLink ⌐🔢 http://dx.doi.org/10.1787/888932666342

HOW MUCH DO TERTIARY STUDENTS PAY AND WHAT PUBLIC SUPPORT DO THEY RECEIVE?

- OECD and G20 countries differ significantly in the amount of tuition fees charged by their tertiary institutions. In eight OECD countries, public institutions charge no tuition fees, but in one-third of OECD countries with available data, public institutions charge annual tuition fees in excess of USD 1 500 for national students.

- Countries with high levels of tuition fees tend to be those where private entities (e.g. enterprises) also contribute the most to funding tertiary institutions.

- An increasing number of OECD countries are charging higher tuition fees for international students than for national students, and many also differentiate tuition fees by field of education, largely because of the difference in the public cost of studies.

- An average of 21% of public spending on tertiary education is devoted to supporting students, households and other private entities. In Australia, Chile, the Netherlands, New Zealand, Norway and the United Kingdom, grants/scholarships and loans are particularly developed, and public support to households account for at least 27% of public tertiary education budgets.

Chart B5.1. Relationship between average tuition fees charged by public institutions and proportion of students who benefit from public loans and/or scholarships/grants in tertiary-type A education (academic year 2008-09)

For full-time national students, in USD converted using PPPs

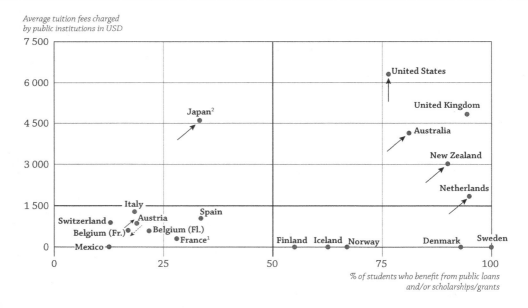

1. Average tuition fees from USD 190 to 1 309 for university programmes dependent on the Ministry of Education.
2. Tuition fees refer to public institutions but more than two-thirds of students are enrolled in private institutions.
Source: OECD. Tables B5.1 and B5.2. See Annex 3 for notes (*www.oecd.org/edu/eag2012*).
StatLink ⧉ http://dx.doi.org/10.1787/888932662770

How to read this chart
This graph shows the relationship, at the tertiary-type A level of education, between annual tuition fees charged by educational institutions and public support to households for students' living costs. Arrows show how the average tuition fees and the proportion of students who benefit from public support have changed since 1995 following reforms (solid arrow) and how they may change due to policy changes that have been planned since 2008-09 (dashed arrow).

Context

Many countries have similar goals for tertiary education, such as strengthening the knowledge economy, increasing access for students, encouraging high completion rates, and ensuring the financial stability of their higher education systems. Yet OECD countries differ dramatically in the way the cost of higher education is shared between governments, students and their families and other private entities – and in the financial support they provide to students.

Policy decisions relating to tuition fees affect both the cost of tertiary education to students and the resources available to tertiary institutions. Public support to students and their families also enables governments to encourage participation in education – particularly among low-income students – by covering part of the cost of education and related expenses. In this way, governments can address issues of access and equality of opportunity. The impact of such support must therefore be judged, at least partly, by examining tertiary education participation, retention and completion.

Public support to students also indirectly funds tertiary institutions. Channelling funding to institutions through students may also help increase competition among institutions. Since aid for students' living costs can serve as a substitute for income from work, public subsidies may enhance educational attainment by enabling students to work less.

Public support for students comes in many forms: as means-based subsidies, family allowances for students, tax allowances for students or their parents, or other household transfers. Based on a given amount of subsidies, public support such as tax reductions or family allowances may provide less support for low-income students than means-tested subsidies, as the former are not targeted specifically to support low-income students. However, they may still help to reduce financial disparities among households with and without children in education.

Other findings

- Among the European countries for which data are available, only **public tertiary institutions in Italy, the Netherlands, Portugal and the United Kingdom (government-dependent private institutions) charge annual tuition fees of more than USD 1 200 per full-time national student.**

- **The high entry rates into tertiary education in some countries that charge no tuition fees likely result in part from their highly-developed student financial support systems** to cover living expenses, not just the absence of tuition fees.

- OECD countries in which **students are required to pay tuition fees but can benefit from sizeable financial support do not have below-average levels of access to tertiary-type A education.**

- **Student financial support systems that offer loans with income-contingent repayment to all students combined with means-tested grants can be an effective way to promote access and equity** while sharing the costs of higher education between the state and students.

Trends

Since 1995, **14 out of the 25 countries with available information implemented reforms to tuition fees.** Most of these reforms led to an increase in the average level of tuition fees charged by tertiary educational institutions. In all of these 14 countries except Iceland and the Slovak Republic, the reforms were combined with a change in the level of public support available to students (Box B5.1 and Chart B5.1).

Since 2009, further changes have been made to tuition fees and public support systems in various countries. For example, in the United Kingdom, tuition fees are scheduled to double or nearly triple in some universities in 2012, as part of a government plan to stabilise university finances. Similarly, in 2011, Korea implemented reforms to increase the level of public support available to students for higher education, with the goal of strengthening access and equity in tertiary-type A education.

B5

Analysis

Annual tuition fees charged by tertiary-type A institutions for national students

The cost of higher education and the best way to support students in paying for it are among the most hotly debated public policy topics in education today. The level of tuition fees charged by tertiary institutions – as well as the level and type of financial assistance countries provide through their student support systems – can have dramatic repercussions on access and equity in tertiary education.

Striking the right balance between providing sufficient support to institutions through tuition fees and maintaining access and equity is not easy. On the one hand, higher tuition fees increase the resources available to educational institutions, support their efforts to maintain quality academic programmes and develop new ones, and can help institutions accommodate increases in student enrolment. However, they may also restrict access to higher education for students – particularly those from low-income backgrounds – in the absence of a strong system of public support to help them pay or reimburse the cost of their studies. In addition, high tuition fees may prevent some students from pursuing fields that require extended periods of study if labour market opportunities are not sufficient.

Chart B5.2. Average annual tuition fees charged by tertiary-type A public institutions for full-time national students, in USD converted using PPPs (academic year 2008-09)

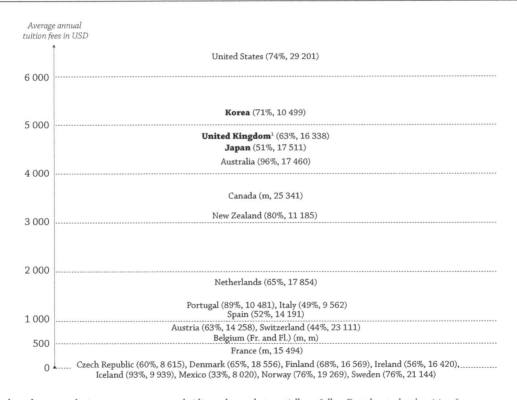

Note: This chart does not take into account grants, subsidies or loans that partially or fully offset the student's tuition fees.

1. Public institutions do not exist at this level of education and almost all students are enrolled in government-dependent private institutions.

Source: OECD. Tables B1.1a, B5.1 and Indicator C3. See Annex 3 for notes (www.oecd.org/edu/eag2012).

Please refer to the Reader's Guide for information concerning the symbols replacing the missing data.

StatLink ⟐⟐ http://dx.doi.org/10.1787/888932662789

How to read this chart
This chart shows the annual tuition fees charged in equivalent USD, converted using PPPs. Countries in bold denote cases in which more than two-thirds of students are enrolled in private institutions, but where the tuition fee levels still refer to public institutions. The net entry rate (2010) and expenditure per student (in USD, 2009) in tertiary-type A programmes are added next to country names.

On the other hand, lower tuition fees can help promote student access and equity in higher education, particularly among disadvantaged populations. However, they may also constrain the ability of tertiary institutions to maintain an appropriate quality of education, especially in light of the massive expansion of tertiary education in all OECD countries in recent years. Moreover, budgetary pressures stemming from the global economic crisis may make it more difficult for countries that have lower tuition fees to sustain this model in the future.

There are large differences among countries in the average tuition fees charged by tertiary-type A institutions for national students. In the five Nordic countries with more progressive tax structures (Denmark, Finland, Iceland, Norway and Sweden), and in the Czech Republic and Mexico, public institutions do not charge tuition fees. Ireland could also be included in this category, as the tuition fees charged by public institutions (for full-time undergraduate students from the European Union) are paid directly by the government. By contrast, tuition fees are higher than USD 1 500 in one-third of the countries with available data, and they reach more than USD 5 000 in Korea and the United States. Meanwhile, in Austria, Belgium, France, Ireland, Italy, Portugal, Switzerland and Spain, students pay small tuition fees for tertiary-type A education. Among the EU21 countries for which data are available, only the Netherlands and the United Kingdom have annual tuition fees that exceed USD 1 500 per full-time national student (Table B5.1 and Chart B5.2).

Differentiation of tuition fees by citizenship and field of education

National policies regarding tuition fees and financial aid to students generally cover all students studying in the country's educational institutions. Countries' policies also take international students into account. Differences between national and international students in terms of the fees they are charged or the financial help they may receive from the country in which they study, can, along with other factors, have an impact on the flows of international students. These differences can attract students to study in some countries or discourage students from studying in others (see Indicator C4), especially in a context where an increasing number of OECD countries are charging higher tuition fees for international students.

In nearly half of the countries with available data, the tuition fees charged by public educational institutions may differ between national and international students enrolled in the same programme. In Austria, for example, the average tuition fees charged by public institutions for students who are not citizens of EU or European Economic Area (EEA) countries are twice the fees charged for citizens of these countries. Similar policies are found in Canada, Denmark (as of 2006-07), Ireland, the Netherlands, New Zealand (except for foreign doctoral students), Poland, the Slovak Republic, Slovenia, Sweden (as of 2011), Switzerland, the United Kingdom and the United States. In these countries, the level of tuition fees varies based on citizenship or on an individual's residence (see Indicator C4 and Box C4.3). In Australia, international students are not eligible for the same supports available to national students and it is estimated that around 10% of national students at the tertiary level pay full fees.

Tuition fees are also differentiated by field of education in more than half of the countries with available data. The exceptions are Austria, Belgium (Flemish Community and French Community), Japan (in national universities), Mexico, the Netherlands, Slovenia, Sweden and Switzerland. The main rationale for differentiating fees is the public cost of the field of study – for example, Ireland, Italy, New Zealand, Poland and the Slovak Republic use this basis for differentiating tuition fees. In these countries, the higher the cost of the field of study, the higher the level of tuition fees charged by educational institutions.

However, in a few countries, the basis for differentiating tuition fees by field of education is the priority given by the country to specific fields. In Australia for example, tuition fee differentiation is linked to skills shortages in the labour market and the level of salaries that graduates in certain disciplines can expect to receive. In Iceland and the United Kingdom, tuition fees vary by fields of education because of differences in both the cost of studies and in labour-market opportunities (Box B5.1).

OECD countries use different mixes of grants and loans to subsidise students' education costs

A key question in many OECD countries is whether financial support for households should be provided primarily in the form of grants or loans. Governments subsidise students' living or educational costs through different combinations of these two types of support. Advocates of student loans argue that loans allow available resources to be spread further: if the amount spent on grants were used to guarantee or subsidise loans instead, aid would be available to more students, and overall access to higher education would increase. Loans also shift some of the cost of education to those who benefit most from higher education – namely, the individual students. Opponents of loans argue that student loans are less effective than grants in encouraging low-income students to pursue their education. They also argue that loans may be less efficient than anticipated because of the various types of support provided to borrowers or lenders and the costs of administration and servicing.

OECD countries spend an average of about 21% of their public budgets for tertiary education on support to households and other private entities (Chart B5.3). In Australia, Chile, Denmark, Japan, the Netherlands, New Zealand, Norway and the United Kingdom, public support accounts for more than 25% of public spending on tertiary education. Only Argentina, the Czech Republic, Indonesia and Poland spend less than 5% of total public spending on tertiary education on support. However, in the two European countries, subsidies for student grants are directly sent to institutions, which are responsible for distributing them among students (Table B5.3).

OECD research suggests that the existence of a robust financial support system is important to assure good outcomes for higher education students, and that the type of aid is also critical. Chart B5.3 presents the proportion of public tertiary education expenditure dedicated to loans, grants and scholarships, and other types of support given to households.

More than one-third of the 32 countries for which data are available rely exclusively on scholarships/grants and transfers/payments to other private entities. Iceland provides only student loans, while other countries make a combination of grants and loans available. Both types of support are used extensively in Australia, Chile, the Netherlands, New Zealand, Norway, Sweden, the United Kingdom and the United States.

Chart B5.3.   **Public support for education in tertiary education (2009)**
Public support for education to households and other private entities as a percentage of total public expenditure on education, by type of subsidy

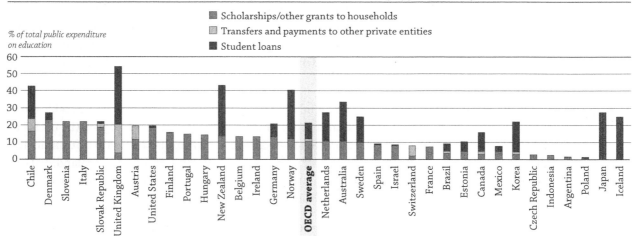

Countries are ranked in descending order of the share of scholarships/other grants to households and transfers and payments to other private entities in total public expenditure on education.

Source: OECD. Argentina, Indonesia: UNESCO Institute for Statistics (World Education Indicators programme). Table B5.3. See Annex 3 for notes (*www.oecd.org/edu/eag2012*).

StatLink ⟶ http://dx.doi.org/10.1787/888932662808

B5

In general, the largest support to students is provided by countries that offer student loans; in most cases, these countries also spend an above-average proportion of their tertiary education budgets on grants and scholarships (Chart B5.3 and Table B5.3).

Country approaches to funding tertiary education

As noted above, the cost of higher education, and the level of support available to students, varies markedly across OECD countries. This section provides a taxonomy of approaches to funding tertiary education in countries with available data, and analyses the impact of these models on access to tertiary education. Countries are grouped in four models, according to two factors: the level of tuition fees and the level of financial support available through the country's student financial aid system for tertiary education.

There is no single model for financing tertiary-type A education. Some countries in which tertiary-type A institutions charge similar tuition fees may have differences in the proportion of students benefiting from public support and/or differences in the average amount of these subsidies (Tables B5.1, B5.2 and B5.3, Table B5.4 available on line, and Chart B5.1). Moreover, arrangements regarding the tuition fees charged by tertiary educational institutions have been the subject of reforms in many OECD countries since 1995, and some countries have moved from one model to another over this period (Box B5.1 and Chart B5.1).

Box B5.1. Changes in tuition-fees policies and public support to students since 1995

Since 1995, more than half of the 25 countries with available information have undertaken reforms of their tuition fee systems using different approaches. Tuition fees have been introduced in some German federal states or have been increased since 1995 in Australia, Austria, Japan, the Netherlands, New Zealand, Portugal, the United Kingdom and the United States. Similarly, Denmark, Ireland and the Slovak Republic increased tuition fees charged for international students (only international students are charged tuition fees in these countries).

However, some countries simultaneously implemented policies to limit the variation in the level of tuition fees charged in tertiary-type A institutions for each field of education. These approaches were sometimes implemented at the state/regional level, as tuition fee rates can vary within the country (**Canada**). Approaches include linking the level of tuition fees to labour-market opportunities, so that fields with skills shortages have lower tuition fees than others, in order to attract more students (**Australia**); setting an upper limit on tuition fees to ensure that students from socio-economically disadvantaged backgrounds have access to tertiary education (**Italy**); and temporarily freezing the level of fees in return for a higher government subsidy (**New Zealand**).

A few countries even reduced tuition fees: in **Austria**, tuition fees introduced in the 2001-02 academic year were eliminated for the majority of students as of the summer term of 2009; while in **Ireland**, tuition fees for most full-time undergraduate students have been paid by the state since 1995-96 through a transfer to public institutions. In **Hungary** (not included in the table below) a general tuition fee system was introduced in 1996, but this system was abolished in 1998. Since then, there has been a special dual system in operation, in which some tertiary students can study free of charge, while others must pay a fee. The status of students is determined mainly during the application and admission procedure.

Increases in tuition fees are usually combined with increases in student support. Changes in support for students usually aim to give students from disadvantaged backgrounds greater access to tertiary studies or to reduce the liquidity constraints on all students, through grants/scholarships or loans, or by introducing different levels of tuition fees. These kinds of systems have been developed in **Australia**, **Austria** and **Canada**. A specific loan for tuition fees has been introduced in the **Netherlands**. In the **United States**, where tuition fees are among the highest in the world, recent reforms have increased funding for means-tested grants, lowered interest rates on student loans, instituted an income-based repayment system for government loans, and expanded loan forgiveness for students who go on to work in public sector and public service professions.

...

B5

	Reforms have been implemented since 1995	Reforms have been combined with a change in the level of public subsidies available to students	Tertiary educational institutions differentiate tuition fees between national and international students	Tertiary educational institutions differentiate tuition fees by field of education
Australia	Yes	Yes	Yes	Yes
Austria	Yes	Yes	No	No
Belgium (Fl.)	Yes	No	Yes	No
Belgium (Fr.)	Yes	No	Yes	No
Canada	Yes	Yes	Yes	Yes
Denmark	Yes	Yes	Yes	No
Finland	No	No	No	No
France	No	No	No	Yes
Iceland	Yes	No	No	Yes
Ireland	Yes	Yes	Yes	Yes
Italy	Yes	Yes	No	Yes
Japan	Yes	Yes	No	No
Korea	Yes	Yes	No	Yes
Mexico	No	No	No	No
Netherlands	Yes	Yes	Yes	No
New Zealand	Yes	Yes	Yes	Yes
Norway	No	No	No	No
Poland	Yes	Yes	Yes	Yes
Slovak Republic	Yes	No	Yes	Yes
Slovenia	No	No	Yes	No
Spain	No	No	No	Yes
Sweden	No	No	No	No
Switzerland	No	No	Yes	No
United Kingdom	Yes	Yes	Yes	Yes
United States[1]	Yes	Yes	Yes	Yes

1. In the United States, public institutions offer lower fees to in-state students than out-of-state students. International students generally pay the same fees as out-of-state students.

Other countries have devoted more public funds to support tertiary institutions, either directly or indirectly. This is the case in **New Zealand**, where the government required institutions to freeze their fees between 2001 and 2003, in return for proportional increases in subsidies to individuals. This limited the cost of study for students, while offering indirect funding to institutions as a way of meeting the costs of foregoing increases in fees.

Only a few countries (the **Flemish Community of Belgium** and the **Slovak Republic**) did not change student support systems further while also changing their systems of tuition fees. In **Belgium (Flemish Community)**, reforms aimed to make tuition fees more flexible since 2007, based on the number of credits in which students are enrolled in the programme. In the **Slovak Republic**, reforms allowed tertiary institutions to charge tuition fees for part-time students and for students who stay longer in a programme than theoretically expected.

Model 1: Countries with no or low tuition fees but generous student support systems

This group is composed of the Nordic countries (Denmark, Finland, Iceland, Norway and Sweden). These countries have more progressive tax structures, and students pay no tuition fees and benefit from generous public support for higher education. However, individuals face high income tax rates. At 76%, the average entry rate into tertiary-type A education for this group is significantly above the OECD average of 61% (see Indicator C3). These high entry rates may also be due to these countries' highly-developed student financial support systems, not just the absence of tuition fees. For instance, in these countries, more than 55% of students benefit from public grants, public loans, or a combination of both (Tables B5.1, B5.2 and Chart B5.1).

B5

The approach to funding tertiary education in this model reflects these countries' deeply rooted social values, such as equality of opportunity and social equity. The notion that government should provide its citizens with tertiary education at no charge to the individual is a salient feature of the educational culture in these countries: the funding of both institutions and students is based on the principle that access to tertiary education is a right, rather than a privilege. However, during the past decade, Denmark and Sweden (as of 2011) decided to introduce tuition fees for international students to increase the resources available for their tertiary institutions. This approach has also been considered in Iceland (Box B5.1).

Model 2: Countries with high levels of tuition fees and well-developed student-support systems

The second group includes Australia, Canada, the Netherlands, New Zealand, the United Kingdom and the United States. These countries have potentially high financial barriers to entry into tertiary-type A education, but also large public support to students. The average entry rate to tertiary-type A education for this group of countries is, at 76%, significantly above the OECD average and higher than most countries with low tuition fees (except the Nordic countries). The Netherlands and, to a lesser extent, the United Kingdom, have moved from Model 4 (countries with lower tuition fees and less-developed student support systems) to Model 2 since 1995 (Chart B5.1). Countries in Model 2 tend to be those where private entities (e.g. private businesses and non-profit organisations) contribute the most to the financing of tertiary institutions; in other words, in Model 2 countries, the cost of education is shared between government, households and private companies (Chart B3.2 and Table B3.2b).

Tuition fees charged by public tertiary-type A institutions exceed USD 1 500 in all these countries, but more than 75% of tertiary-type A students receive public support (in Australia, the Netherlands, New Zealand, the United Kingdom and the United States, the five countries for which data are available; Tables B5.1 and B5.2). Student support systems are well-developed and mostly accommodate the needs of the entire student population. As a result, the share of public expenditure on tertiary education that is devoted to public support in these countries is higher than the OECD average (21%) in four out of the six countries: Australia (33%), the Netherlands (27%), New Zealand (43%) and the United Kingdom (54%), and nearly at the average for Canada (16%) and the United States (20%) (Table B5.3).

In this group of countries, access to tertiary-type A education is not lower than in other groups. For example, Australia and New Zealand have among the highest entry rates into tertiary-type A education (96% and 80%, respectively), although these rates also reflect the high proportion of international students enrolled in tertiary-type A education. Entry rates into tertiary-type A education were also above the OECD average (61%) in the Netherlands (65%), the United Kingdom (63%) and the United States (74%) in 2010. These countries spend more on core services per tertiary student than the OECD average and have a relatively high level of revenue from income tax as a percentage of GDP, compared to the OECD average. The Netherlands is an outlier, as its level of income taxation is below the OECD average (Table B1.1b and Table C3.1).

OECD research (OECD, 2008) suggests that in general, this model can be an effective way for countries to increase access to higher education. However, during periods of economic crisis, high levels of tuition fees can put a considerable financial burden on students and their families and can discourage some of them to enter tertiary education, even when relatively high levels of student support are available. This topic is highly debated in Canada, the United Kingdom and the United States.

Model 3: Countries with high levels of tuition fees but less-developed student support systems

In Japan and Korea, most students are charged high tuition fees (on average, more than USD 4 500 in tertiary-type A institutions), but student support systems are somewhat less developed than those in Models 1 and 2. This has the potential to place a large financial burden on students and their families. With entry rates into tertiary-type A institutions at 51% and 71%, respectively, Japan is below and Korea is significantly above the OECD average. In Japan and Korea, some students who excel academically but have difficulty financing their studies can benefit from reduced tuition and/or admission fees or receive total exemptions. The below-average access to tertiary-type A education in Japan is counterbalanced by an above-average entry rate into tertiary-type B (shorter and more practically oriented) programmes (see Indicator C3).

B5

Japan and Korea are among the countries with the lowest levels of public expenditure allocated to tertiary education as a percentage of GDP (Table B4.1). This partially explains the small proportion of students who benefit from public loans. It should be noted, however, that both countries have recently implemented reforms to improve their student-support systems. As a result, these countries are moving closer to Model 2.

Model 4: Countries with low levels of tuition fees and less-developed student-support systems

The fourth group includes all other European countries for which data are available (Austria, Belgium, the Czech Republic, France, Ireland, Italy, Poland, Portugal, Switzerland and Spain), as well as Mexico. All of these countries charge moderate tuition fees compared to those in Models 2 and 3, although since 1995, reforms have been implemented in some of these countries – particularly Austria and Italy – to increase tuition fees in public institutions (Chart B5.1 and Box B5.1). Model 4 countries share relatively low financial barriers to entry into tertiary education (or no tuition-fee barriers, as in the Czech Republic, Ireland and Mexico), combined with relatively low support for students, which are mainly targeted to specific groups. Tuition fees charged by public institutions in this group never exceed USD 1 300, and in countries for which data are available, the proportion of students who benefit from public support is below 40% (Tables B5.1 and B5.2).

In Model 4 countries, tertiary institutions usually depend heavily on the state for funding, and participation levels in tertiary education are typically below the OECD average. The average tertiary-type A entry rate in this group of countries is relatively low at 56%; in Belgium, this low rate is counterbalanced by high entry rates into tertiary-type B education. Similarly, expenditure per student for tertiary-type A education is also comparatively low (see Indicator B1 and Chart B5.2). While high tuition fees can raise potential barriers to student participation, Model 4 suggests that lower tuition fees, which are assumed to ease access to education, do not necessarily ensure high levels of access to and the quality of tertiary-type A education.

In these countries, students and their families can benefit from support provided by sources other than the ministry of education (e.g. housing allowances, tax reductions and/or tax credits for education); but these are not covered in this analysis. In France, for example, housing allowances represent about 90% of scholarships/ grants, and about one-third of students benefit from them. Poland is notable in that most students enrolled in public institutions have their studies fully subsidised by the state, while students enrolled in part-time studies pay the full costs of tuition.

In Model 4 countries, loan systems, such as public loans or loans guaranteed by the state, are not available or are only available to a small proportion of students in these countries (Table B5.2). At the same time, the level of public spending and the tax revenue from income as a percentage of GDP vary significantly more among this group of countries than in the other groups. Policies on tuition fees and public support are not necessarily the main factors that influence students' decisions to enter tertiary-type A education.

Definitions

Average tuition fees charged in public and private tertiary-type A institutions does not distinguish tuition fees by type of programme. This indicator gives an overview of tuition fees at this level by type of institution and shows the proportions of students who do or do not receive scholarships/grants that fully or partially cover tuition fees. Levels of tuition fees and associated proportions of students should be interpreted with caution as they are derived from the weighted average of the main tertiary-type A programmes and do not cover all educational institutions.

Public spending transferred to students, families and other private entities includes funds that may go indirectly to educational institutions, such as the supports that are used to cover tuition fees, and funds that do not go, even indirectly, to educational institutions, such as subsidies for students' living costs.

Public subsidies to households include: *i)* grants/scholarships (non-repayable subsidies); *ii)* public student loans, which must be repaid; *iii)* family or child allowances contingent on student status; *iv)* public support in cash or in kind, specifically for housing, transport, medical expenses, books and supplies, social, recreational and other purposes; and *v)* interest-related support for private loans.

B5

However, public support does not distinguish among different types of grants or loans, such as scholarships, family allowances and in-kind subsidies. Governments can also support students and their families by providing housing allowances, tax reductions and/or tax credits for education. These subsidies are not covered here. Financial aid to students in some countries may therefore be substantially underestimated.

It is also common for governments to guarantee the repayment of loans to students made by private lenders. In some OECD countries, this indirect form of support is as significant as, or even more significant than, direct financial aid to students. However, for reasons of comparability, the indicator only takes into account the amounts relating to public transfers for private loans that are made to private entities, not the total value of loans generated. Some qualitative information is nevertheless presented in some of the tables to give some insight on this type of support.

Student loans refer to the full volume of student loans in order to provide information on the level of support received by current students. The gross amount of loans provides an appropriate measure of the financial aid to current participants in education. Interest payments and repayments of principal by borrowers should be taken into account in order to assess the net cost of student loans to public and private lenders. However, such payments are usually made by former students rather than by current students and are not covered in this indicator. In most countries, moreover, loan repayments do not flow to the education authorities, and the money is not available to them to cover other educational expenditures. OECD indicators take the full amount of scholarships and loans (gross) into account when discussing financial aid to current students. Some OECD countries also have difficulty quantifying the amount of loans to students. Therefore, data on student loans should be treated with some caution.

Methodology

Data refer to the financial year 2009 and are based on the UOE data collection on education statistics administered by the OECD in 2011 (for details see Annex 3 at *www.oecd.org/edu/eag2012*).

Data on tuition fees charged by educational institutions, financial aid to students and on reforms implemented since 1995 were collected through a special survey undertaken in 2010 and refer to the academic year 2008-09. Amounts of tuition fees and amounts of loans in national currency are converted into equivalent USD by dividing the national currency by the purchasing power parity (PPP) index for GDP. Amounts of tuition fees and associated proportions of students should be interpreted with caution as they represent the weighted average of the main tertiary-type A programmes and do not cover all the educational institutions.

Public costs related to private loans guaranteed by governments are included as subsidies to other private entities. Unlike public loans, only the net cost of these loans is included.

The value of tax reductions or credits to households and students is not included.

The statistical data for Israel are supplied by and under the responsibility of the relevant Israeli authorities. The use of such data by the OECD is without prejudice to the status of the Golan Heights, East Jerusalem and Israeli settlements in the West Bank under the terms of international law.

References

OECD (2011), *OECD Tax Statistics: Volume 2011, Issue I: Revenue Statistics*, OECD Publishing.

OECD (2008), *OECD Reviews of Tertiary Education: Tertiary Education for the Knowledge Society*, OECD Publishing.

The following additional material relevant to this indicator is available on line:

- *Table B5.4. Public subsidies for households and other private entities as a percentage of total public expenditure on education and GDP, for primary, secondary and post-secondary non-tertiary education (2009)*
  StatLink 🔗 http://dx.doi.org/10.1787/888932666475

B5

Table B5.1. [1/2] Estimated annual average tuition fees charged by tertiary-type A educational institutions[1] for national students (academic year 2008-09)

In equivalent USD converted using PPPs, by type of institutions, based on full-time students

Tuition fees and associated proportions of students should be interpreted with caution as they result from the weighted average of the main tertiary-type A programmes and do not cover all educational institutions. However, the figures reported can be considered as good proxies and show the difference among countries in tuition fees charged by main educational institutions and for the majority of students.

	Percentage of tertiary full-time students enrolled in tertiary-type A programmes	Percentage of tertiary-type A full-time students enrolled in:			Annual average tuition fees in USD charged by institutions (for full-time students)			Comment
		Public institutions	Government-dependent private institutions	Independent private institutions	Public institutions	Government-dependent private institutions	Independent private institutions	
		(1)	(2)	(3)	(4)	(5)	(6)	(7)
Australia	84	97	a	3	4 222	a	9 112	93% of national students in public institutions are in subsidised places and pay an average USD 3 817 tuition fee, including HECS/HELP subsidies. There was a significant increase (~50%) in scholarships for domestic students from 2007 to 2009 as a result of government reforms aimed at doubling the number of Commonwealth Scholarships by 2012. The new scholarships were mostly targeted towards students studying national priority subjects, students who needed to relocate to study specialist subjects, and Indigenous students.
Austria[2]	87	87	13	m	859	859	235 to 11 735	As of summer term 2009, tuition fees have to be paid by national students and students from EU/EEA countries when they exceed the theoretical duration of the study programme by two semesters and by students from non-EU/EEA countries (except students from least-developed countries).
Belgium (Fl.)	69	51	49	m	x(5)	545 to 618	m	Tuition fees refer to the minimum and maximum amount that institutions may charge according to the decree (indexed figures). They refer to those for students enrolled in first (Bachelor) and second (Master) degree programmes. The information does not refer to further degree programmes (for example Master after Master). This information refers to students without a scholarship (student with a scholarship benefit from lower tuition fees, see more details in Annex 3).
Belgium (Fr.)	91	33	67	m	608	694	m	Tuition fees charged for programmes are the same in public as in private institutions but the distribution of students differs between public and private institutions, so the weighted average is not the same.
Canada	66	100	m	m	3 774	x(4)	x(4)	
Chile	60	m	m	m	m	m	m	
Czech Republic	86	87	a	13	No tuition fees	a	m	The average fee in public institutions is negligible because fees are paid only by student studying too long (larger than the standard length of the programme plus 1 year): about 4% of students.
Denmark[3]	88	m	m	m	No tuition fees	m	a	
Estonia	62	m	m	m	a	m	m	
Finland	100	82	18	a	No tuition fees	No tuition fees	a	Excluding membership fees to student unions.
France	72	87	5	8	190 to 1 309	1 127 to 8 339	1 128 to 8 339	Tuition fees in public insitutions refer to University programmes dependent from the Ministry of Education.
Germany	83	96	4	x(2)	m	m	m	There is no national nor subnational average levels of tuition fees. Since 2005 the 16 German *Länder* have been free to decide on the imposition of tuition fees. A few *Länder* have tuitions fees, but the level of fees differs between *Länder*. In some *Länder*, the higher education institutions themselves are free to decide on the imposition of study fees and the amount thereof. Most of the 16 *Länder* did not impose tuition fees for initial education. Some German *Bundesländer*, which had introduced tuition fees meanwhile, did abolish these fees.
Greece	60	m	m	m	m	m	m	
Hungary	90	m	m	m	m	m	m	There is no general tuition fee imposed. However, there is a special dual system in operation, in which one part of tertiary students can study free of charge by state subsidy while the other part of students can study by paying a "training contribution" (the term "tuition fee" is not in use). The status of students is determined mainly during the application and admission procedure (with the principle that the state finances studies for the first degree by levels within a quota determined annually by the government). In 2008-09 the proportion of State-financed full-time students was 75% (19% for part-time students) – while the proportion of contribution-paying full-time student was 25% (81% for part-time students). The amount of training contributions is defined by the higher education institutions but according to the current regulation it should be at least as high as the State-provided subsidy to the HEIs for the training of a student in the particular field of study.

1. Scholarships/grants that the student may receive are not taken into account.
2. Including students in advanced research programmes.
3. Tuition fees in total tertiary education.
Source: OECD. See Annex 3 for notes (*www.oecd.org/edu/eag2012*).
Please refer to the Reader's Guide for information concerning the symbols replacing missing data.
StatLink ᴍᴤᴸ http://dx.doi.org/10.1787/888932666418

Table B5.1. [2/2] Estimated annual average tuition fees charged by tertiary-type A educational institutions[1] for national students (academic year 2008-09)

In equivalent USD converted using PPPs, by type of institutions, based on full-time students

Tuition fees and associated proportions of students should be interpreted with caution as they result from the weighted average of the main tertiary-type A programmes and do not cover all educational institutions. However, the figures reported can be considered as good proxies and show the difference among countries in tuition fees charged by main educational institutions and for the majority of students.

	Percentage of tertiary full-time students enrolled in tertiary-type A programmes	Percentage of tertiary-type A full-time students enrolled in:			Annual average tuition fees in USD charged by institutions (for full-time students)			Comment
		Public institutions	Government-dependent private institutions	Independent private institutions	Public institutions	Government-dependent private institutions	Independent private institutions	
		(1)	(2)	(3)	(4)	(5)	(6)	(7)
OECD								
Iceland	97	79	21	n	No tuition fees	2 311 to 6 831	8 433 to 12 650	Subsidised student loans that cover tution fees are available for all students. Almost no scholarships/ grants exist.
Ireland	74	97	a	3	from 2 800 to 10 000	a	m	The tuition fees charged by public institutions are paid directly by the government in respect of full-time, undergraduate students from the European Union, only. About one half of all tuition fee income is derived from households (mainly for part-time or postgraduate or non-EU students).
Israel	76	m	m	m	a	m	m	
Italy	98	92	a	8	1 289	a	4 741	The annual average tuition fees do not take into account the scholarships/grants that fully cover tuition fees but partial reductions of fees cannot be excluded.
Japan	75	25	a	75	4 602	a	7 247	Excludes admission fee charged by the school for the first year (USD 2 398 on average).
Korea	74	24	a	76	5 193	a	9 366	Tuition fees in first degree programmes only. Excludes admission fees to university, but includes supporting fees.
Luxembourg	m	m	m	m	m	m	m	
Mexico	96	66	a	34	No tuition fees	a	5 218	
Netherlands	100	m	a	m	1 861	a	m	
New Zealand	77	97	2	1	3 031	4 177	m	
Norway	95	86	14	x(2)	No tuition fees	n	5 503	Student fees are representative of the dominant private ISCED 5 institution in Norway.
Poland	96	87	a	13	n	a	1 889 to 2 537	
Portugal[3]	96	m	m	m	1 259	5 094	m	
Slovak Republic	96	96	a	4	Maximum 2 707	a	m	Generally, full-time students do not pay the tuition fees, but students who are simultaneously enrolled in one academic year in two or more study programmes offered by a public university in the same level, are required to pay annual tuition fees for the second and the other study programmes in the academic year. In addition, students studying longer than the standard duration of study are required to pay annual tuition for each additional year of study.
Slovenia	72	96	4	n	m	m	m	In public and government-dependent private institutions: First and second level full-time students do not pay tuition fees. But second cycle students who already obtained a qualification/degree equivalent to the second cycle pay tuition fees.
Spain	81	87	a	13	1 052	a	m	
Sweden	86	92	8	n	No tuition fees	No tuition fees	m	Excluding mandatory membership fees to student unions.
Switzerland	83	99	m	1	889	m	7 342	
Turkey	69	m	m	m	m	a	m	
United Kingdom	87	a	100	n	a	4 731	m	English students from low-income households can access non-repayable grants and bursaries. Loans for tuition fees and living costs are available to all eligible students.
United States	80	68	a	32	6 312	a	22 852	Including non national students.
Other G20								
Brazil	90	m	m	m	m	a	m	
Russian Federation	75	m	m	m	m	a	m	

1. Scholarships/grants that the student may receive are not taken into account.
2. Including students in advanced research programmes.
3. Tuition fees in total tertiary education.
Source: OECD. See Annex 3 for notes (*www.oecd.org/edu/eag2012*).
Please refer to the Reader's Guide for information concerning the symbols replacing missing data.
StatLink ⟨⟩ http://dx.doi.org/10.1787/888932666418

B5

Table B5.2. Distribution of financial aid to students compared to amount of tuition fees charged in tertiary-type A education (academic year 2008-09)

Based on full-time students

	Distribution of financial aid to students Percentage of students who:				Distribution of scholarships/grants in support of tuition fees Percentage of students who:			
	benefit from public loans only	benefit from scholarships/ grants only	benefit from public loans AND scholarships/ grants	DO NOT benefit from public loans OR scholarships/ grants	receive scholarships/ grants that are higher than the tuition fees	receive scholarships/ grants whose amount is equivalent to the tuition fees	receive scholarships/ grants that partially cover the tuition fees	DO NOT receive scholarships/ grants in support of tuition fees
	(1)	(2)	(3)	(4)	(5)	(6)	(7)	(8)
Australia[1]	74	1	7	19	n	n	7.3	92.7
Austria	a	19	a	81	16.8	n	1.5	81.7
Belgium (Fl.)[2]	a	22	a	78	21.7	x(5)	x(5)	78.3
Belgium (Fr.)	n	17	n	83	16.9	x(5)	x(5)	83.1
Canada	m	m	m	m	m	m	m	m
Chile	m	m	m	m	m	m	m	m
Czech Republic	m	m	a	m	m	m	m	m
Denmark[2]	m	93	m	m	m	m	m	m
Estonia	m	m	m	m	m	m	m	m
Finland	a	55	a	45	a	a	a	a
France[2]	a	28	a	72	24.0	4.0	a	72.0
Germany	m	m	m	m	m	m	m	m
Greece	m	m	m	m	m	m	m	m
Hungary	21	35	m	m	a	a	a	100.0
Iceland	63	m	m	37	a	a	a	100.0
Ireland[3]	a	39	a	m	x(6)	85.5	m	14.5
Israel	m	m	m	m	m	m	m	m
Italy	n	18	n	82	8.2	3.1	7.0	81.7
Japan	33	1	n	67	a	a	a	100.0
Korea	m	m	m	m	a	1.8	38.8	59.5
Luxembourg	m	m	m	m	m	m	m	m
Mexico[2]	1	12	m	87	m	m	m	m
Netherlands[3]	11	63	21	5	67.8	n	12.2	20.0
New Zealand	51	4	35	10	m	m	m	m
Norway[4]	12	4	52	33	m	m	m	m
Poland	m	m	m	m	m	m	m	m
Portugal	m	m	m	m	m	m	m	m
Slovak Republic	m	m	m	m	m	m	m	m
Slovenia[5]	a	21	n	m	m	m	m	m
Spain	n	34	n	66	23.5	3.5	10.4	62.6
Sweden	n	19	50	32	a	a	a	a
Switzerland	2	11	m	87	m	m	m	m
Turkey	m	m	m	m	m	m	m	m
United Kingdom	37	8	50	6	m	m	m	42.7
United States[2]	12	27	38	24	m	m	m	m
Brazil	m	m	m	m	m	m	m	m
Russian Federation	m	m	m	m	m	m	m	m

1. Excludes foreign students.
2. Distribution of students in total tertiary education (only Public University, including tertiary-type B in France).
3. Public institutions only.
4. Data refer to academic year 2007-08.
5. Column 2 only includes scholarships.
Source: OECD. See Annex 3 for notes (*www.oecd.org/edu/eag2012*).
Please refer to the Reader's Guide for information concerning the symbols replacing missing data.
StatLink ⧉ http://dx.doi.org/10.1787/888932666437

Table B5.3. Public support for households and other private entities as a percentage of total public expenditure on education and GDP, for tertiary education (2009)

Direct public expenditure on educational institutions and subsidies for households and other private entities

	Direct public expenditure for institutions	Public subsidies for education to private entities						Subsidies for education to private entities as a percentage of GDP
		Financial aid to students			Scholarships/ other grants to households attributable for educational institutions	Transfers and payments to other private entities	Total	
		Scholarships/ other grants to households	Student loans	Total				
	(1)	(2)	(3)	(4)	(5)	(6)	(7)	(8)
Australia	**66.5**	10.7	22.8	33.5	0.7	n	**33.5**	0.37
Austria	**80.4**	11.5	a	11.5	m	8.1	**19.6**	0.31
Belgium	**86.6**	13.4	n	13.4	3.8	n	**13.4**	0.20
Canada[1]	**84.2**	3.0	11.1	14.1	m	1.7	**15.8**	m
Chile[2]	**57.5**	16.4	18.8	35.3	15.6	7.3	**42.5**	0.42
Czech Republic	**97.2**	2.8	a	2.8	m	n	**2.8**	0.03
Denmark[3]	**72.9**	23.0	4.2	27.1	n	n	**27.1**	0.65
Estonia	**89.7**	4.7	5.6	10.3	m	n	**10.3**	0.14
Finland	**84.2**	15.4	n	15.4	n	0.3	**15.8**	0.34
France	**92.6**	7.4	m	7.4	m	n	**7.4**	0.10
Germany	**79.3**	13.1	7.6	20.7	m	n	**20.7**	0.28
Greece	**m**	m	m	m	m	m	**m**	m
Hungary	**85.7**	14.3	n	14.3	n	n	**14.3**	0.16
Iceland	**75.1**	a	24.9	24.9	a	n	**24.9**	0.40
Ireland	**86.8**	13.2	n	13.2	m	n	**13.2**	0.20
Israel	**91.4**	8.2	0.4	8.6	7.9	n	**8.6**	0.09
Italy	**78.0**	22.0	n	22.0	9.7	n	**22.0**	0.19
Japan[3]	**72.5**	0.7	26.8	27.5	m	n	**27.5**	0.21
Korea	**78.0**	3.0	17.7	20.7	2.9	1.3	**22.0**	0.19
Luxembourg	**m**	m	m	m	m	m	**m**	m
Mexico	**92.3**	4.7	3.0	7.7	2.4	a	**7.7**	0.08
Netherlands	**72.6**	10.6	16.4	27.0	n	0.4	**27.4**	0.45
New Zealand	**56.9**	13.6	29.6	43.1	m	n	**43.1**	0.84
Norway	**59.7**	12.1	28.2	40.3	m	n	**40.3**	0.90
Poland	**98.6**	0.7	0.7	1.4	m	n	**1.4**	0.01
Portugal	**85.2**	14.8	m	14.8	m	m	**14.8**	0.16
Slovak Republic[3]	**77.9**	18.7	1	19.9	m	2.2	**22.1**	0.18
Slovenia	**77.9**	22.1	n	22.1	m	n	**22.1**	0.31
Spain	**90.8**	8.6	0.6	9.2	2.0	n	**9.2**	0.11
Sweden	**75.1**	10.0	15.0	24.9	n	m	**24.9**	0.51
Switzerland	**92.0**	2.1	n	2.1	m	5.9	**8.0**	0.11
Turkey	**m**	m	m	m	m	m	**m**	m
United Kingdom	**45.8**	3.7	33.8	37.5	x(4)	16.6	**54.2**	0.44
United States	**80.4**	18.5	1.1	19.6	m	m	**19.6**	0.24
OECD average	**79.5**	10.4	9.3	19.1	3.2	1.6	**20.5**	0.29
Argentina	**98.4**	1.5	n	1.5	m	0.1	**1.6**	0.02
Brazil	**90.8**	3.5	4.4	7.9	x(2)	1.3	**9.2**	0.08
China	**m**	m	m	m	m	m	**m**	m
India	**m**	m	m	m	m	m	**m**	m
Indonesia[2]	**97.4**	2.6	m	2.6	m	m	**2.6**	0.01
Russian Federation	**m**	m	a	m	m	m	**m**	m
Saudi Arabia	**m**	m	m	m	m	m	**m**	m
South Africa	**89.1**	x(4)	x(4)	10.9	x(4)	n	**10.9**	0.07
G20 average	**m**	m	m	m	m	m	**m**	m

1. Year of reference 2008.
2. Year of reference 2010.
3. Some levels of education are included with others. Refer to "x" code in Table B1.1a for details.
Source: OECD. Argentina, Indonesia : UNESCO Institute for Statistics (World Education Indicators programme). South Africa: UNESCO Institute for Statistics. See Annex 3 for notes (*www.oecd.org/edu/eag2012*).
Please refer to the Reader's Guide for information concerning the symbols replacing missing data.
StatLink ⟡⟡⟡ http://dx.doi.org/10.1787/888932666456

ON WHAT RESOURCES AND SERVICES IS EDUCATION FUNDING SPENT?

- More than 90% of total expenditure on education is devoted to current expenditure on average in OECD countries and for most OECD and other G20 countries, both at the primary, secondary, post-secondary non-tertiary levels of education combined and at the tertiary level.

- At the tertiary level of education, the share of total expenditure devoted to capital expenditure is higher than that for primary, secondary and post-secondary non-tertiary education combined in 18 out of the 31 countries with available data. This may be linked to the expansion of tertiary education in recent years, and a consequent need for new buildings to be constructed.

- In OECD and other G20 countries with available data, most current expenditure goes to compensating education staff (teachers and others).

- Current expenditure devoted to purposes other than the compensation of staff is largest at the tertiary level, where it reaches 32% of all current expenditure, on average in OECD countries. This could be explained by the higher costs of facilities and equipment in tertiary education, compared to other levels of education.

Chart B6.1. **Distribution of current expenditure by educational institutions for primary, secondary and post-secondary non-tertiary education (2009)**

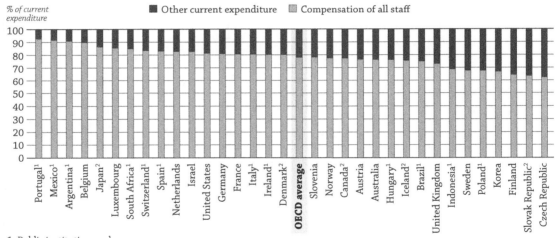

1. Public institutions only.
2. Some levels of education are included with others. Refer to "x" code in Table B1.1a for details.
Countries are ranked in descending order of the share of compensation of all staff in primary, secondary and post-secondary non-tertiary education.
Source: OECD. Argentina, Indonesia: UNESCO Institute for Statistics (World Education Indicators programme). South Africa: UNESCO Institute for Statistics. Table B6.2. See Annex 3 for notes (*www.oecd.org/edu/eag2012*).
StatLink ▒▒▒ http://dx.doi.org/10.1787/888932662827

Context

Decisions about how resources are allocated affect the material conditions under which instruction takes place and can also influence the nature of instruction.

While savings can be made by cutting capital expenditure (such as not building new schools) and some current expenditure (not purchasing certain teaching materials), when pressures on education budgets increase, changes in spending on staff have the greatest impact on overall spending. Saving money by reducing salaries and benefits or cutting the number of teachers and other staff is unpopular politically and possibly counterproductive, in that it discourages good teachers from wanting to enter or remain in the profession. Therefore, in addition to managing material resources more efficiently, it is essential to improve the management of human resources to raise the quality of education systems.

This indicator describes the resources and services on which money for education is spent. It shows the difference between current and capital expenditure. Capital expenditure can be affected by expanding enrolments, which often require the construction of new buildings. This indicator also presents details on where current expenditure is spent, either on compensation of education staff or elsewhere. Current expenditure is mainly affected by teachers' salaries (see Indicator D3), but also by pension systems, the age distribution of teachers, and the size of the non-teaching staff employed in education. In addition, educational institutions offer not only instruction but other services, such as meals, transport, housing services and/or research activities. All these expenditures are addressed in this indicator.

Other findings

- At the **primary, secondary and post-secondary non-tertiary levels of education, OECD countries spend an average of 22% of current expenditure for purposes other than compensating education personnel**. There is little difference between primary and secondary education in terms of the proportion of current expenditure used for purposes other than compensation. In fact, the difference exceeds 6 percentage points only in Iceland, Korea, South Africa and the United Kingdom, and reaches 13 percentage points in Ireland.

- In all countries except the Czech Republic and Indonesia, **most current expenditure at the tertiary level of education is related to compensation of staff**. Over 80% of current expenditure is devoted to compensation of staff in Argentina, Brazil, Denmark and Israel (88%, 80%, 83% and 80%, respectively).

- The share of **current expenditure devoted to purposes other than compensation of staff is larger at the tertiary level than at the primary, secondary and post-secondary non-tertiary levels combined in almost all countries** except Brazil, Denmark, Iceland, Poland and the United Kingdom.

Analysis

Current and capital expenditure by educational institutions

Education expenditure includes both current and capital expenditure. Current expenditure by educational institutions takes account of the spending on school resources used each year to operate schools. It includes, for instance, the compensation of teachers and other staff, maintenance of school buildings, students' meals or the rental of school buildings and other facilities. Capital expenditure by educational institutions refers to spending on assets that last longer than one year. It includes, for instance, spending on the construction, renovation and major repair of school buildings.

The largest share of expenditure is current expenditure, given the labour-intensive nature of instruction. In 2009, more than 90% of total expenditure was devoted to current expenditure at the primary, secondary and post-secondary non-tertiary levels of education combined (91.3%) and at the tertiary level (91.0%), on average in OECD countries. Current expenditure amounts to more than 79% of total expenditure at each level of education in every country, except for tertiary education in Indonesia and Saudi Arabia. The share varies from 80% (Australia) to 98% (Portugal) in primary education; from 85% (Norway) to 98% (Austria) in secondary education; and from 70% (Saudi Arabia) to almost 100% (Iceland) in tertiary education. The OECD average presents similar values for each level of education, accounting for a difference of only 0.3 percentage points (91.3% in primary, secondary and post-secondary non-tertiary education combined against 91.0% in tertiary education) (Tables B6.1 and B6.2 and Chart B6.2).

Chart B6.2.   **Distribution of current and capital expenditure on educational institutions (2009)**
By resource category and level of education

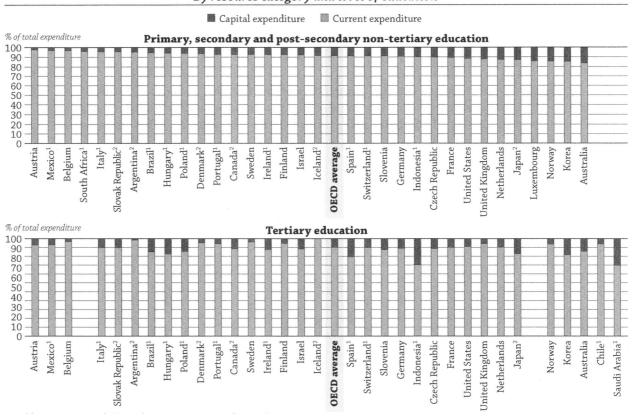

1. Public institutions only (for Italy, except in tertiary education).
2. Some levels of education are included with others. Refer to "x" code in Table B1.1a for details.
Countries are ranked in descending order of the share of current expenditure on primary, secondary and post-secondary non-tertiary education.
Source: OECD. Argentina, Indonesia: UNESCO Institute for Statistics (World Education Indicators programme). Saudi Arabia: Observatory on Higher Education. South Africa: UNESCO Institute for Statistics. Table B6.2. See Annex 3 for notes (*www.oecd.org/edu/eag2012*).
StatLink ⌹ http://dx.doi.org/10.1787/888932662846

Nevertheless, differences between current expenditure in primary, secondary and post-secondary non-tertiary education combined and tertiary education can be relatively large. In most countries, the share of current expenditure in the former levels of education is larger than in the latter level. The three main exceptions are Iceland, Norway and the United Kingdom, where the share of current expenditure in tertiary education exceeds the share in primary, secondary and post-secondary non-tertiary education combined by seven to nine percentage points. In contrast, the share of current expenditure at primary, secondary and post-secondary non-tertiary education combined exceeds the share in the tertiary level by ten percentage points or more in Hungary, Indonesia and Spain.

The differences between countries are likely to reflect how the different levels of education are organised in each country, as well as the degree to which the expansion in enrolments requires the construction of new buildings, especially at the tertiary level. Capital expenditure in tertiary education exceeds 15% in Hungary (15.9%), Indonesia (27.1%), Japan (15.5%), Korea (16.5%), Saudi Arabia (30.2%) and Spain (18.8%). The ways countries report expenditure related to university buildings may also explain differences in the share of current and capital expenditure at the tertiary level (Box B6.1).

Box B6.1. **Expenditure on university buildings**

The real estate and facility management of institutions of tertiary education is heterogeneous in OECD countries. This is because the buildings and lands used for education can be either owned, used free of charge or rented by the institutions. Energy costs can also be recognised in different ways. The amount of current and capital expenditure partly depends on the type of real estate management used in the country. For example, in some countries, current expenditure by educational institutions includes rents. Rents (considered as current expenditure) can be seen as equivalents for capital costs and depreciations. To illustrate the differences between countries, a short survey was initiated in 2012.

Twenty-seven out of the 36 countries that were contacted (all OECD countries, Brazil and the Russian Federation) returned the questionnaire. The responses show that there is a wide variety of real estate management practices.

Ten countries reported that rents for institutions of tertiary education are included in the data they report for current expenditure; seven of them report concrete figures. The percentage of rents reported as "current expenditure other than compensation of personnel" varies significantly. The Slovak Republic spends 0.8% for rents of buildings used for education, the Netherlands spends 5.2%, Germany 9.5%, Switzerland 12.4%, Norway 31.6% and Sweden 38.2%. The high rental cost in Sweden is attributed to the fact that tertiary institutions normally do not own their buildings and thus have to pay rent for them.

Different real estate management practices not only affect current expenditure; there can also be capital expenditure on buildings rented by educational institutions. This is relevant in some countries. For instance, Switzerland reports this kind of expenditure as the main component of total capital expenditure on public educational institutions (97.1%).

Distribution of current expenditure

Current expenditure by educational institutions can be subdivided further into three broad functional categories: compensation of teachers, compensation of other staff, and other current expenditures. Other current expenditures include, for instance, teaching materials and supplies, maintenance of school buildings, students' meals and rental of school facilities. The amount allocated to each of these categories depends partly on current and projected changes in enrolments, on salaries of educational personnel, and on the costs of maintenance and construction of educational facilities. Despite the fact that the shares of these categories do not undergo large changes every year, countries' decisions might affect not only the amounts but also these shares.

B6

At the primary, secondary and post-secondary non-tertiary levels, over 62% of current expenditure is devoted to compensating teachers, 16% to compensating other staff, and 22% to expenditure other than compensation, on average in OECD countries. For tertiary education, 42% of current expenditure is devoted to the compensation of teachers, on average across OECD countries, as larger shares are devoted to compensating other staff (26%) and other current expenditure (32%).

There are relatively large differences in how current expenditure is allocated between the primary, secondary, and post-secondary non-tertiary levels combined and tertiary education. For instance, in all countries, the share devoted to compensation of teachers is larger at the combined primary, secondary and post-secondary non-tertiary level of education than at the tertiary level. The only exception is Denmark, where the share at the tertiary level exceeds the share at the combined lower levels by one percentage point. The share for other current expenditure is more than 30% in primary, secondary and post-secondary non-tertiary education combined in only seven countries, namely the Czech Republic (37.6%), Finland (35.6%), Indonesia (31.1%), Korea (33.1%), Poland (32.4%), the Slovak Republic (36.4%) and Sweden (32.2%). In contrast, at the tertiary level, this share is more than 30% in over half of OECD countries and below 20% in only four countries, Argentina (12.2%), Brazil (19.7%), Denmark (16.7%) and Israel (19.7%).

The variation in current expenditure not devoted to compensation of staff between levels of education illustrates the difference in the size of administrative systems (for instance, the number of employees or the equipment available to administrative staff) across these levels. The cost of facilities and equipment is expected to be higher in tertiary education than in other levels of education. Meanwhile, the differences among countries in compensation of other staff likely reflect the degree to which education personnel, such as principals, guidance counsellors, bus drivers, school nurses, janitors and maintenance workers, are included in the category "non-teaching staff" (see indicator D2). Compensation of staff involved in research and development at the tertiary level may also explain part of the differences, between countries and between levels of education, in the share of current expenditure devoted to compensation of other staff.

Definitions

Capital expenditure refers to spending on assets that last longer than one year, including construction, renovation or major repair of buildings and new or replacement equipment. The capital expenditure reported here represents the value of educational capital acquired or created during the year in question – that is, the amount of capital formation – regardless of whether the capital expenditure was financed from current revenue or through borrowing. Neither current nor capital expenditure includes debt servicing.

Current expenditure refers to spending on goods and services consumed within the current year and requiring recurrent production in order to sustain educational services. Current expenditure by educational institutions other than on compensation of personnel includes expenditure on sub-contracted services such as support services (e.g. maintenance of school buildings), ancillary services (e.g. preparation of meals for students) and rental of school buildings and other facilities. These services are obtained from outside providers, unlike the services provided by the education authorities or by the educational institutions using their own personnel.

Methodology

Data refer to the financial year 2009 and are based on the UOE data collection on education statistics administered by the OECD in 2011 (for details see Annex 3 at *www.oecd.org/edu/eag2012*).

Calculations cover expenditure by public institutions or, where available, by both public and private institutions.

The statistical data for Israel are supplied by and under the responsibility of the relevant Israeli authorities. The use of such data by the OECD is without prejudice to the status of the Golan Heights, East Jerusalem and Israeli settlements in the West Bank under the terms of international law.

Table B6.1. Expenditure by educational institutions, by resource category in primary and secondary education (2009)

Distribution of total and current expenditure by educational institutions from public and private sources

	Primary education						Secondary education					
	Percentage of total expenditure		Percentage of current expenditure				Percentage of total expenditure		Percentage of current expenditure			
	Current	Capital	Compensation of teachers	Compensation of other staff	Compensation of all staff	Other current expenditure	Current	Capital	Compensation of teachers	Compensation of other staff	Compensation of all staff	Other current expenditure
	(1)	(2)	(3)	(4)	(5)	(6)	(7)	(8)	(9)	(10)	(11)	(12)
OECD												
Australia	79.7	20.3	62.8	14.4	77.2	22.8	86.8	13.2	59.9	16.1	76.0	24.0
Austria	97.2	2.8	61.2	13.4	74.6	25.4	98.0	2.0	67.8	9.8	77.6	22.4
Belgium[1]	96.0	4.0	71.2	18.8	90.0	10.0	97.3	2.7	73.6	16.3	89.9	10.1
Canada[1, 2]	92.8	7.2	62.4	15.1	77.4	22.6	92.8	7.2	62.4	15.1	77.4	22.6
Chile	m	m	m	m	m	m	m	m	m	m	m	m
Czech Republic	88.1	11.9	46.3	19.5	65.8	34.2	90.5	9.5	47.3	13.9	61.2	38.8
Denmark[1]	90.8	9.2	50.3	29.9	80.2	19.8	94.3	5.7	52.0	29.8	81.8	18.2
Estonia	m	m	m	m	m	m	m	m	m	m	m	m
Finland[1]	93.1	6.9	56.7	9.0	65.7	34.3	92.3	7.7	51.7	12.2	63.9	36.1
France	91.7	8.3	57.1	20.3	77.4	22.6	88.7	11.3	59.5	22.7	82.2	17.8
Germany	91.7	8.3	x(5)	x(5)	82.8	17.2	90.3	9.7	x(11)	x(11)	80.9	19.1
Greece	m	m	m	m	m	m	m	m	m	m	m	m
Hungary[3]	94.4	5.6	x(5)	x(5)	76.3	23.7	94.1	5.9	x(11)	x(11)	76.2	23.8
Iceland[1]	89.7	10.3	x(5)	x(5)	78.7	21.3	93.3	6.7	x(11)	x(11)	72.6	27.4
Ireland[3]	90.5	9.5	76.1	12.7	88.7	11.3	95.2	4.8	69.2	6.3	75.5	24.5
Israel	91.0	9.0	x(5)	x(5)	82.0	18.0	93.6	6.4	x(11)	x(11)	83.6	16.4
Italy[3]	95.3	4.7	63.8	16.9	80.6	19.4	96.6	3.4	64.6	18.8	83.5	16.5
Japan[1]	86.6	13.4	x(5)	x(5)	86.3	13.7	87.7	12.3	x(11)	x(11)	86.4	13.6
Korea	83.3	16.7	58.7	12.1	70.9	29.1	86.7	13.3	56.0	8.6	64.6	35.4
Luxembourg	85.4	14.6	78.8	5.0	83.7	16.3	86.2	13.8	74.7	12.1	86.7	13.3
Mexico[3]	97.4	2.6	83.2	9.5	92.7	7.3	96.4	3.6	76.5	14.1	90.6	9.4
Netherlands	87.2	12.8	x(5)	x(5)	84.5	15.5	87.7	12.3	x(11)	x(11)	81.8	18.2
New Zealand	m	m	m	m	m	m	m	m	m	m	m	m
Norway[1]	85.9	14.1	x(5)	x(5)	78.0	22.0	85.4	14.6	x(11)	x(11)	77.2	22.8
Poland[3]	92.8	7.2	x(5)	x(5)	69.7	30.3	94.9	5.1	x(11)	x(11)	66.1	33.9
Portugal[3]	98.1	1.9	80.7	14.0	94.6	5.4	89.4	10.6	79.7	11.5	91.2	8.8
Slovak Republic[1]	95.7	4.3	47.7	14.0	61.7	38.3	95.6	4.4	50.4	14.1	64.4	35.6
Slovenia[1]	x(7)	x(8)	x(9)	x(10)	x(11)	x(12)	91.1	8.9	x(11)	x(11)	78.3	21.7
Spain[3]	91.9	8.1	71.4	10.4	81.8	18.2	90.6	9.4	75.3	8.6	83.9	16.1
Sweden	93.1	6.9	52.5	17.9	70.4	29.6	92.6	7.4	49.7	16.2	66.0	34.0
Switzerland[1, 3]	90.1	9.9	66.2	15.6	81.9	18.1	91.8	8.2	72.6	12.1	84.6	15.4
Turkey	m	m	m	m	m	m	m	m	m	m	m	m
United Kingdom[1]	87.1	12.9	46.8	30.1	76.9	23.1	88.4	11.6	57.1	13.3	70.4	29.6
United States	88.6	11.4	55.3	26.1	81.4	18.6	88.6	11.4	55.3	26.1	81.4	18.6
OECD average	90.9	9.1	62.5	16.2	79.0	21.0	91.6	8.4	62.8	14.9	77.8	22.2
EU21 average	92.2	7.8	61.5	16.6	78.1	21.9	92.3	7.7	62.3	14.7	76.9	23.1
Other G20												
Argentina[3]	95.3	4.7	68.8	22.0	90.8	9.2	95.2	4.8	67.4	23.6	91.0	9.0
Brazil[2]	94.6	5.4	x(5)	x(5)	73.2	26.8	94.6	5.4	x(11)	x(11)	76.3	23.7
China	m	m	m	m	m	m	m	m	m	m	m	m
India	m	m	m	m	m	m	m	m	m	m	m	m
Indonesia[3, 4]	89.2	10.8	x(5)	x(5)	70.0	30.0	92.3	7.7	x(11)	x(11)	66.8	33.2
Russian Federation	m	m	m	m	m	m	m	m	m	m	m	m
Saudi Arabia	m	m	m	m	m	m	m	m	m	m	m	m
South Africa[3]	94.7	5.3	78.6	4.8	83.4	16.6	97.6	2.4	84.8	4.8	89.6	10.4
G20 average	m	m	m	m	m	m	m	m	m	m	m	m

1. Some levels of education are included with others. Refer to "x" code in Table B1.1a for details.
2. Year of reference 2008.
3. Public institutions only.
4. Year of reference 2010.
Source: OECD. Argentina, Indonesia: UNESCO Institute for Statistics (World Education Indicators programme). South Africa: UNESCO Institute for Statistics. See Annex 3 for notes (*www.oecd.org/edu/eag2012*).
Please refer to the Reader's Guide for information concerning the symbols replacing missing data.
StatLink ⬛ http://dx.doi.org/10.1787/888932666513

B6

Table B6.2. **Expenditure by educational institutions, by resource category and level of education (2009)**
Distribution of total and current expenditure by educational institutions from public and private sources

	Primary, secondary and post-secondary non-tertiary education						Tertiary education					
	Percentage of total expenditure		Percentage of current expenditure				Percentage of total expenditure		Percentage of current expenditure			
	Current	Capital	Compensation of teachers	Compensation of other staff	Compensation of all staff	Other current expenditure	Current	Capital	Compensation of teachers	Compensation of other staff	Compensation of all staff	Other current expenditure
	(1)	(2)	(3)	(4)	(5)	(6)	(7)	(8)	(9)	(10)	(11)	(12)
OECD												
Australia	83.6	16.4	60.8	15.6	76.4	23.6	86.9	13.1	33.1	28.7	61.7	38.3
Austria	97.8	2.2	65.7	10.8	76.5	23.5	93.5	6.5	53.6	8.7	62.3	37.7
Belgium	96.8	3.2	72.8	17.2	89.9	10.1	96.9	3.1	49.6	27.5	77.1	22.9
Canada[1,2]	92.8	7.2	62.4	15.1	77.4	22.6	89.5	10.5	36.2	27.0	63.1	36.9
Chile[3,4]	m	m	m	m	m	m	94.7	5.3	x(11)	x(11)	62.6	37.4
Czech Republic	89.9	10.1	47.1	15.3	62.4	37.6	89.8	10.2	31.3	17.8	49.1	50.9
Denmark[2]	93.5	6.5	47.9	32.3	80.2	19.8	95.7	4.3	48.9	34.4	83.3	16.7
Estonia	m	m	m	m	m	m	m	m	m	m	m	m
Finland	92.5	7.5	53.3	11.1	64.4	35.6	95.2	4.8	33.7	27.9	61.6	38.4
France	89.6	10.4	58.7	21.9	80.7	19.3	91.0	9.0	46.3	29.5	75.8	24.2
Germany	90.6	9.4	x(5)	x(5)	81.0	19.0	90.2	9.8	x(11)	x(11)	65.8	34.2
Greece	m	m	m	m	m	m	m	m	m	m	m	m
Hungary[3]	94.2	5.8	x(5)	x(5)	76.2	23.8	84.1	15.9	x(11)	x(11)	61.8	38.2
Iceland[2]	91.5	8.5	x(5)	x(5)	75.6	24.4	100.0	n	x(11)	x(11)	77.7	22.3
Ireland[3]	92.7	7.3	71.1	9.2	80.3	19.7	88.8	11.2	38.8	26.2	65.0	35.0
Israel	92.2	7.8	x(5)	x(5)	82.7	17.3	89.5	10.5	x(11)	x(11)	80.3	19.7
Italy[3]	95.7	4.3	62.5	18.1	80.5	19.5	90.8	9.2	35.9	30.0	65.9	34.1
Japan[2]	87.2	12.8	x(5)	x(5)	86.3	13.7	84.5	15.5	x(11)	x(11)	60.0	40.0
Korea	85.4	14.6	57.0	9.9	66.9	33.1	83.5	16.5	34.9	18.5	53.4	46.6
Luxembourg	85.9	14.1	76.4	9.1	85.5	14.5	m	m	m	m	m	m
Mexico[3]	96.9	3.1	80.1	11.6	91.7	8.3	93.6	6.4	61.5	14.6	76.1	23.9
Netherlands	87.5	12.5	x(5)	x(5)	82.8	17.2	91.2	8.8	x(11)	x(11)	69.1	30.9
New Zealand	m	m	m	m	m	m	m	m	m	m	m	m
Norway	85.6	14.4	x(5)	x(5)	77.5	22.5	94.4	5.6	x(11)	x(11)	68.0	32.0
Poland[3]	93.9	6.1	x(5)	x(5)	67.6	32.4	86.9	13.1	x(11)	x(11)	77.2	22.8
Portugal[3]	92.8	7.2	80.1	12.5	92.6	7.4	94.8	5.2	x(11)	x(11)	74.1	25.9
Slovak Republic[2]	95.6	4.4	49.6	14.0	63.6	36.4	90.7	9.3	32.4	23.4	55.8	44.2
Slovenia	91.1	8.9	x(5)	x(5)	78.3	21.7	88.6	11.4	x(11)	x(11)	66.5	33.5
Spain[3]	91.1	8.9	73.7	9.3	83.0	17.0	81.2	18.8	56.1	21.3	77.3	22.7
Sweden	92.8	7.2	50.9	16.9	67.8	32.2	96.5	3.5	x(11)	x(11)	62.9	37.1
Switzerland[3]	91.1	8.9	70.0	13.5	83.5	16.5	90.9	9.1	46.6	27.9	74.5	25.5
Turkey	m	m	m	m	m	m	m	m	m	m	m	m
United Kingdom	87.9	12.1	52.9	20.1	73.1	26.9	94.9	5.1	43.1	36.8	79.9	20.1
United States	88.6	11.4	55.3	26.1	81.4	18.6	91.9	8.1	25.8	36.5	62.3	37.7
OECD average	**91.3**	**8.7**	62.4	15.5	78.1	21.9	**91.0**	**9.0**	41.6	25.7	67.9	32.1
EU21 average	**92.2**	**7.8**	61.6	15.6	77.2	22.8	**91.2**	**8.8**	42.7	25.8	68.4	31.6
Other G20												
Argentina[3]	95.2	4.8	68.0	22.9	90.9	9.1	98.6	1.4	54.6	33.3	87.8	12.2
Brazil[3]	94.6	5.4	x(5)	x(5)	75.0	25.0	86.4	13.6	x(11)	x(11)	80.3	19.7
China	m	m	m	m	m	m	m	m	m	m	m	m
India	m	m	m	m	m	m	m	m	m	m	m	m
Indonesia[3,4]	90.3	9.7	x(5)	x(5)	68.9	31.1	72.9	27.1	x(11)	x(11)	40.2	59.8
Russian Federation	m	m	m	m	m	m	m	m	m	m	m	m
Saudi Arabia[3,4]	m	m	m	m	m	m	69.8	30.2	x(11)	x(11)	51.8	48.2
South Africa[3]	96.0	4.0	80.0	4.9	84.9	15.1	m	m	m	m	m	m
G20 average	**m**	**m**	m	m	m	m	**m**	**m**	m	m	m	m

1. Year of reference 2008.
2. Some levels of education are included with others. Refer to "X" code in Table B1.1a for details.
3. Public institutions only (For Italy, except in tertiary education).
4. Year of reference 2010.
Source: OECD. Argentina, Indonesia: UNESCO Institute for Statistics (World Education Indicators programme). Saudi Arabia: Observatory on Higher Education. South Africa: UNESCO Institute for Statistics. See Annex 3 for notes (*www.oecd.org/edu/eag2012*).
Please refer to the Reader's Guide for information concerning the symbols replacing missing data.
StatLink ⟲ http://dx.doi.org/10.1787/888932666532

WHICH FACTORS INFLUENCE THE LEVEL OF EXPENDITURE?

- Four factors influence expenditures on education related to the per student salary cost of teachers: instruction time of students, teaching time of teachers, teachers' salaries and estimated class size. Consequently, a given level of teachers' salary cost per student may result from different combinations of these four factors.

- There are large differences in the salary cost of teachers per student between countries. In 2010, the salary cost of teachers per student varied by a ratio of 1 to 14 or 15 at the primary, lower secondary and upper secondary levels of education.

- The salary cost of teachers per student increased substantially between 2000 and 2010 at the primary and lower secondary levels of education in most countries. On average, it increased by one-third and one-quarter, respectively, among countries with available data in both years: from USD 1 733 to USD 2 307 at the primary level, and from USD 2 273 to USD 2 856 at the lower secondary level.

- France and Italy are the only countries where the salary cost of teachers per student decreased (slightly) between 2000 and 2010.

Chart B7.1. **Change (in USD) in the salary cost of teacher per student at the primary level of education (2000, 2010)**

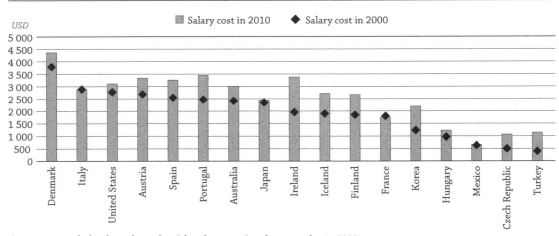

Countries are ranked in descending order of the salary cost of teacher per student in 2000.
Source: OECD. Table B7.2. See Annex 3 for notes (*www.oecd.org/edu/eag2012*).
StatLink http://dx.doi.org/10.1787/888932662865

Context

The relationship between the resources devoted to education and the outcomes achieved has been a significant area of focus among governments as they seek to provide more and better education for their populations. At the same time, given the increasing pressure on public budgets, there is intense interest in ensuring that public funding is directed so as to achieve the desired outcomes as efficiently as possible.

Teachers' compensation is usually the largest part of expenditure on education and thus of expenditure per student. It is a function of the instruction time of students, the teaching time of teachers, teachers' salaries and the number of teachers needed to teach students, which depends on estimated class size (Box B7.1). Differences among countries in these four factors may explain differences in the level of expenditure per student. Similarly, a given level of expenditure may result from a different combination of these factors. This indicator examines the choices countries make when investing their resources in primary and secondary education and explores how changing policy choices between 2000 and 2010 relating to these four factors affected the level of salary cost of teachers.

Other findings

- **Similar levels of expenditure among countries can mask a variety of contrasting policy choices.** This helps to explain why there is no simple relationship between overall spending on education and the level of student performance. For example, at the upper secondary level of education, Germany and Spain have similar levels of salary costs of teachers per student, both higher than the average. However, this mainly results from higher-than-average salaries of teachers in Germany, whereas in Spain, it results from the combination of below-average estimated class size, above-average instruction time and above-average salaries of teachers.

- **Teachers' salaries are most often the main driver** of the difference from the average salary cost of teachers per student at each level of education. **Estimated class size is the second main driver** of the difference at each level.

- Comparing salary cost to GDP per capita is a way to account for differences in country wealth. **Teachers' salaries (as a percentage of GDP per capita) are less often the main driver of the difference from the average salary cost of teachers per student when that cost is compared to GDP per capita.**

- **The increase in the salary cost of teachers per student as the level of education increases is mainly influenced by decreases in the numbers of hours teachers are required to teach, followed by increases in the number of hours of instruction that students receive.** Increases in teachers' salaries between different levels of education play a minor role compared to these other two factors. Increasing class sizes as the level of education increases counterbalances the effect of the three other factors on the salary cost of teachers per student.

Trends

The increase in the salary cost of teachers per student between 2000 and 2010 has mostly been influenced by the changes in two factors: teachers' salaries and estimated class size. Between 2000 and 2010, among countries with available data in both years, teachers' salaries increased on average by about 16% at the primary level and 14% at lower secondary level, while estimated class sizes decreased on average by 14% at the primary level and by 7% at the lower secondary level.

At the primary level, most countries simultaneously increased teachers' salaries and decreased the estimated class size between 2000 and 2010. The impact of the change in teachers' salaries on the salary cost is usually larger than the impact of the change in estimated class size, even if it varies between countries. At the lower secondary level, most countries also increased teachers' salaries and decreased the estimated class size between 2000 and 2010, and the effect of these changes on the per student teacher salary cost is usually of a similar magnitude.

Some countries introduced reforms between 2000 and 2010 that affected the salary cost of teachers per student. For instance, Austria's decision to slightly decrease the instruction time of students at the secondary level (from school year 2003-04) resulted in a decrease of the public funds devoted to the salaries of teachers. In Hungary, teaching time was increased at the secondary level in 2006. This increased the number of teachers necessary for teaching students at this level, which increased expenditure on teachers' salaries. Reforms on class size were also taken in Italy to increase slightly the number of students per classroom. This resulted in a decrease in the salary cost of teachers per student.

Analysis

The salary cost of teachers per student

Per-student expenditure reflects the structural and institutional factors that relate to the organisation of schools and curricula. Expenditure can be broken down into the compensation of teachers and other expenditure (defined as expenditure for all purposes other than teacher compensation). Teacher compensation usually constitutes the largest part of expenditure on education. As a result, the level of teacher compensation divided by the number of students (referred to here as "salary cost of teachers per student") is the main proportion of expenditure per student.

Box B7.1. Relationship between salary cost of teachers per student and instruction time of students, teaching time of teachers, teachers' salaries and class size

One way to analyse the factors that have an impact on expenditure per student and to measure the extent of their effects is to compare the differences between national figures and the OECD average. This analysis computes the differences in expenditure per student among countries and the OECD average, and then calculates the contribution of these different factors to the variation from the OECD average.

This exercise is based on a mathematical relationship between the different factors and follows the method presented in the Canadian publication *Education Statistics Bulletin* (2005) (see explanations in Annex 3). Educational expenditure is mathematically linked to factors related to a country's school context (number of hours of instruction time for students, number of teaching hours for teachers, estimated class size) and one factor relating to teachers (statutory salary).

Expenditure is broken down into compensation of teachers and other expenditure (defined as all expenditure other than compensation of teachers). Compensation of teachers divided by the number of students, or "the salary cost per student" (CCS), is estimated through the following calculation:

$$CCS = SAL \times instT \times \frac{1}{teachT} \times \frac{1}{ClassSize} = \frac{SAL}{Ratiostud/teacher}$$

SAL: teachers' salaries (estimated by statutory salary after 15 years of experience)
instT: instruction time of students (estimated as the annual intended instruction time, in hours, for students)
teachT: teaching time of teachers (estimated as the annual number of teaching hours for teachers)
ClassSize: a proxy for class size
Ratiostud/teacher: the ratio of students to teaching staff

With the exception of class size (which is not computed at the upper secondary level, as class size is difficult to define and compare because students at this level may attend several classes depending on the subject area), values for the different variables can be obtained from the indicators published in *Education at a Glance* (Chapter D). However, for the purpose of the analysis, an "estimated" class size or proxy class size is computed based on the ratio of students to teaching staff and the number of teaching hours and instruction hours (Box D2.1). As a proxy, this estimated class size should be interpreted with caution.

Using this mathematical relationship and comparing a country's values for the four factors to the OECD averages makes it possible to measure both the direct and indirect contribution of each of these four factors to the variation in salary cost per student between that country and the OECD average (for more details, see Annex 3). For example, in the case where only two factors interact, if a worker receives a 10% increase in the hourly wage and increases the number of hours of work by 20%, his/her earnings will increase by 32% as a result of the direct contribution of each of these variations (0.1 + 0.2) and the indirect contribution of these variations due to the combination of the two factors (0.1 * 0.2).

To account for differences in countries' level of wealth when comparing salary costs per student, salary cost per student, as well as teachers' salaries, can be divided by GDP per capita (on the assumption that GDP per capita is an estimate of countries' level of wealth). This makes it possible to compare countries' "relative" salary cost per student (see *Education at a Glance 2012* tables, available on line).

The compensation of teachers is a function of the instruction time of students, the teaching time of teachers, teachers' salaries and the number of teachers needed to teach students, which depends on estimated class size (Box B7.1). As a consequence, differences among countries in these four factors may explain differences in the level of expenditure. In the same way, a given level of expenditure may result from a different combination of these factors.

Differences in the salary cost of teachers per student result from differences in the combination of factors

There are large differences in the salary cost of teachers per student between countries. In 2010, the salary cost of teachers per student varied by a ratio of 1 to 14 at the primary level (USD 662 in Mexico to USD 9 404 in Luxembourg), 1 to 15 at the lower secondary level (USD 729 in Mexico to USD 11 145 in Luxembourg) and 1 to 15 at the upper secondary level (USD 758 in Estonia to USD 11 145 in Luxembourg).

This results from the fact that the four factors vary largely between countries. At the primary, lower secondary and upper secondary levels, the salary of teachers is the factor that varies the most between countries, and instruction time is the factor that varies the least between countries (Tables B7.1a, B7.1b and B7.1c). At the upper secondary level of education, the salary cost of teachers per student varies from less than 1 000 USD in Chile, Estonia and the Slovak Republic to more than USD 11 000 in Luxembourg. These large variations are explained by significant differences in the four factors between countries. For instance, the annual teachers' salary varies by a ratio of 1 to 8 (from USD 12 576 in Estonia to USD 101 775 in Luxembourg), instruction time by a ratio of less than 1 to 2 between countries (from 741 hours in Sweden to 1 197 hours in Chile), teaching time varies by a ratio of 1 to 3 between countries (from less than 380 teaching hours in Denmark to 1 087 hours in Chile); and estimated class size varies by a ratio of more than 1 to 3 (from 8.8 students in Portugal to 28.7 in Chile).

Chart B7.2a. Contribution (in USD) of various factors to salary cost of teachers per student, at the upper secondary level of education (2010)

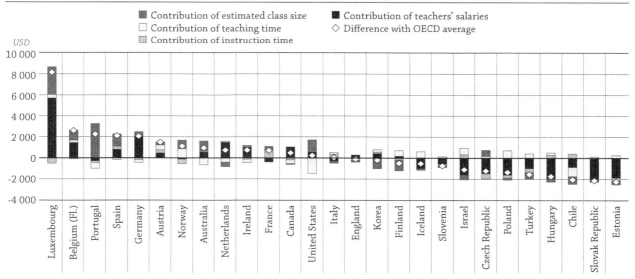

Countries are ranked in descending order of the difference between the salary cost of teacher per student and the OECD average.
Source: OECD. Table B7.4. See Annex 3 for notes (*www.oecd.org/edu/eag2012*).
StatLink ⌗ http://dx.doi.org/10.1787/888932662884

How to read this chart
This chart shows the contribution (in USD) of the factors to the difference in salary cost of teachers per student between the country and the OECD average. For example, in Spain, the salary cost of teachers per student is USD 2 105 higher than the OECD average. This is because Spain has higher teachers' salaries (+ USD 783) than the OECD average, annual instruction time for students close to the OECD average (+ USD 320) and above-average teaching time for teachers (- USD 150), compared to the OECD average. However, these effects are sharply diminished by significantly smaller class sizes (+ USD 1 153) than the OECD average.

The variety of combinations of the four factors that can result in a given level of salary cost of teachers makes it difficult to find correlations between the level of expenditure and educational outcomes. At the upper secondary level of education, Germany and Spain have similar levels of salary cost of teachers per student – both higher than the average. However, this mainly results from higher-than-average teachers' salaries in Germany, whereas it results from a combination of below-average estimated class size, above-average instruction time and above-average salaries of teachers in Spain (Chart B7.2a and Table B7.4).

However, the level of teachers' salaries and, as a consequence, the level of the salary cost of teachers per student, depend on a country's relative wealth. To control for these differences in wealth level between countries, the analysis has also been made using levels of teachers' salaries (and salary cost per student) relative to GDP per capita. Comparing the relative salary cost of teachers per student under this analysis provides a different picture. There are still large variations between countries: at the upper secondary level, the relative salary cost of teachers per student represents 9.4% of the GDP per capita, on average among countries with available data in 2010, and varies from 4.2% (Slovak Republic) to 23.3% (Portugal) of the GDP per capita. However, compared to the analysis in USD, the position of a minority of countries changes significantly. This is for example the case for Luxembourg, which has the highest salary cost of teachers per student in USD (mainly as a consequence of the high level of salaries in USD), but not in proportion of the GDP per capita, as salaries as a proportion of GDP in Luxembourg are at the OECD average. As a consequence, salaries of teachers (as a percentage of the GDP per capita) do not increase the salary cost of teachers per student (as a percentage of GDP per capita). In the United States, while the salary cost of teachers per student is above the OECD average, computed in USD, it is below the OECD average as a proportion of GDP per capita (Table B7.4 continued and Chart B7.2b, available on line).

Main drivers of the level of salary cost of teachers per student

Differences in the salary cost of teachers per student between countries may result from different factors. One factor may have a larger impact than the others on the salary cost of teachers per student. Comparing the salary costs of countries to the OECD average rate shows the impact of each of the factors.

Teachers' salaries are most often the main driver of the difference to the average at each level of education in the salary cost of teachers per student. Among countries with available data in 2010, they are the main driver in 18 out of 31 countries at the primary level, 15 out of 30 countries at the lower secondary level, and 17 out of 27 countries at the upper secondary level. This is true both in countries with the highest and lowest levels of salary cost of teachers per student. For example, at the upper secondary level, the above-average salaries of teachers are the main driver of the difference in the country with the highest level of salary cost (Luxembourg), as well as in nine of the ten countries with the lowest levels of salary cost of teachers per student (the Czech Republic, Estonia, Hungary, Iceland, Israel, Poland, the Slovak Republic, Slovenia and Turkey) (Chart B7.2a).

Estimated class size is the second most influential driver of the difference at each level of education. This is the case for 9 countries at the primary level, 13 countries at the lower secondary level, and 5 countries at the upper secondary level. At the upper secondary level, below-average estimated class size is the main driver of the difference with the average salary cost of teachers per student in two out of the four countries with the highest salary cost of teachers per student, Portugal and Spain (Box B7.2).

When differences in countries wealth are accounted for, comparing the relative salary cost of teachers per student offers a similar picture. Salaries of teachers (as a percentage of GDP per capita) and estimated class sizes are the main drivers of the difference to the average in the salary cost of teachers per student, at each level of education. However, each of these two factors is the main driver in approximately the same number of countries. Teachers' salaries (as a percentage of GDP per capita) are the main driver of the difference to the average in 12 out of 31 countries at the primary level, 12 out of 30 countries at the lower secondary level, and 14 out of 27 countries at the upper secondary level. Class size is the main driver in 11 countries at primary level, 14 countries at the lower secondary level and 6 countries at the upper secondary level. Instruction time and teaching time are more often the main drivers of the difference with the OECD average than in the analysis computed in USD.

Box B7.2. **Main driver of salary cost of teachers per student, by level of education (2010)**

	Primary education	Lower secondary education	Upper secondary education
Salary	**18 countries** AUS (+), BFR (+), CAN (+), CHL (-), CZE (-), DNK (+), EST (-), DEU (+), HUN (-), ISL (-), IRL (+), ISR (-), KOR (+), LUX (-), MEX (-), NLD (+), POL (-), SVK (-)	**15 countries** CAN (+), CHL (-), CZE (-), DNK (+), EST (-), DEU (+), HUN (-), ISL (-), IRL (+), ISR (-), LUX (+), NLD (+), POL (-), SVK (-), ESP (+)	**17 countries** AUT (+), BFL (+), CAN (+), CZE (-), ENG (+), EST (-), DEU (+), HUN (-), ISL (-), IRL (+), ISR (-), LUX (+), NLD (+), POL (-), SVK (-), SVN (-), TUR (-)
Instruction time	**2 countries** FIN (-), SVN (-)	**0 countries**	**2 countries** FRA (+), ITA (+)
Teaching time	**2 countries** FRA (-), USA (-)	**2 countries** ITA (+), USA (-)	**3 countries** CHL (-), NOR (+), USA (-)
Estimated class size	**9 countries** AUT (+), BFL (+), ENG (-), ITA (+), JPN (-), NOR (+), PRT (+), ESP (+), TUR (-)	**13 countries** AUS (+), AUT (+), BFL (+), BFR (+), ENG (-), FIN (+), FRA (-), JPN (-), KOR (-), MEX (-), NOR (+), PRT (+), SVN (+)	**5 countries** AUS (+), FIN (-), KOR (-), PRT (+), ESP (+)

Note: The positive or negative signs show whether the factor increases or decreases the salary cost of teachers per student.
Source: OECD. See Annex 3 for notes *(www.oecd.org/edu/eag2012)*.
Please refer to the Reader's Guide for the list of country codes used in this table.
StatLink ⟨⟨⟨ http://dx.doi.org/10.1787/888932669325

In fact, teachers' salaries are no more the main driver of the difference with the OECD average in countries that have both high levels of teachers' salaries and GDP per capita compared to other countries (for example, Luxembourg) and also in countries that have both low levels of teachers' salaries and GDP per capita compared to other countries (for example, Chile and Turkey). As a result, teachers' salaries as a percentage of GDP per capita are less often the driver of the diference in salary cost of teachers per student with the average (Box B7.2 continued, available on line).

Change in the salary cost of teachers per student between primary and secondary levels

The level of salary cost of teachers per student increases as the level of education increases. This is consistent with increases in teachers' salaries and in the instruction time of students at higher educational levels, but also with the fact that estimated class size and teaching time generally decrease as the level of education increases (Tables B7.1a, B7.1b and B7.1c).

Which factors most influence the increases in the salary cost of teachers per student at successive levels of schooling? The increase is mainly influenced by teaching time, followed by instruction time. Increases in teachers' salaries between the different levels of education play a minor role compared to the other two factors. This may be linked to the fact that the qualifications required to be teachers at the primary and secondary levels of education are similar in some countries and thus, teachers' salaries are similar as well (Chart B7.3 and Table B7.5). In sum, then, education expenditure increases at successive levels of education (from the primary to the secondary level) mainly because teachers spend less time teaching, and pupils have more instruction hours – and to a lesser degree, because teachers have slightly better salaries at higher levels of education. However, as shown in Chart B7.3, increased class sizes at higher schooling levels counterbalances the increase in expenditure.

Change in the salary cost of teachers per student between 2000 and 2010

Changes in the salary cost of teachers per student are only analysed at the primary and lower secondary levels of education because trend data are not available at the upper secondary level, on countries with data on both 2000 and 2010 reference years (17 countries at the primary level and 16 countries at the lower secondary level).

B7

Chart B7.3. Contributions (in USD) of four factors to the average change in salary cost of teachers per student between primary, lower secondary and upper secondary levels of education (2010)

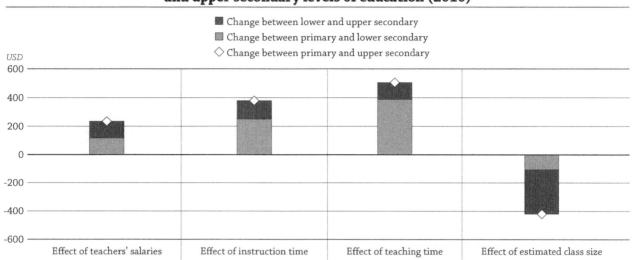

Source: OECD. Table B7.6, available on line. See Annex 3 for notes (*www.oecd.org/edu/eag2012*).
StatLink ⟪≡⟫ http://dx.doi.org/10.1787/888932662922

General pattern of change in salary cost of teachers per student

The salary cost of teachers per student varied largely between 2000 and 2010. At the primary and lower secondary levels of education, the salary cost of teachers per student increased in nearly all countries. It increased by a third and one-quarter, respectively, on average among countries with available data in both years: from USD 1 733 to USD 2 307 at the primary level (among the 17 countries with available data for both years) and from USD 2 273 to USD 2 856 at the lower secondary level (among the 16 countries with available data for both years).

There are two exceptions to this general pattern. In France and Italy, the salary cost of teachers per student decreased at both the primary and lower secondary levels between 2000 and 2010, but the decrease was marginal at the primary level. At the lower secondary level, the decrease of the salary cost of teachers per student in France resulted mainly from a decrease in teachers' salaries (by nearly 8%) during this period, as other factors did not vary by more than 4%. In Italy, the decrease in the salary cost of teachers resulted from an increase in the estimated class size (by 9%), whereas the effect of the increase of teaching time (by 3.6%) was balanced by the effect of the increase of teachers salaries (by 4.6%).

Changes in the four factors explain the overall change in the level of salary cost of teachers per student between 2000 and 2010. At both the primary and lower secondary levels of education, the increase was mostly influenced by the changes in two of the four factors: teachers' salaries and estimated class size. Between 2000 and 2010, among countries with available data in both years, teachers' salaries increased on average by 16% at the primary level and by 14% at lower secondary level, whereas estimated class sizes decreased on average by about 14% at the primary level and by 7% at the lower secondary level. These results are not surprising, because many countries implemented reforms between 2000 and 2010 to decrease class size and/or increase teachers' salaries.

In more than three-quarters of the countries with comparable data for 2000 and 2010, estimated class size tended to become smaller in primary education, most notably in countries that had a relatively large estimated class size in 2000 (for example, the Czech Republic, Ireland, Japan, Korea and Turkey). Similarly, teachers' salaries increased in real terms in most countries over the same period, with the largest increases – well over 50% – seen in the Czech Republic, Estonia and Turkey (Table B7.1a).

There was little or no change with respect to the two other factors (instruction time and teaching time) on average between 2000 and 2010. However, in a small number of countries, instruction time and/or teaching time changed significantly. At the primary level, teaching time increased most significantly in the Czech Republic, with 200 hours of teaching time added between 2000 and 2010 (the salary of teachers also doubled in the Czech Republic during this time). During this period, instruction time increased the most in Iceland (by nearly 200 hours).

At the lower secondary level, significant changes in teaching and/or instruction time occurred between 2000 and 2010 in three countries. In Greece, instruction time decreased by one-quarter or more (by 268 hours). In Portugal, teaching time increased by more than a quarter (166 hours) and in Spain, both instruction time and teaching time increased by about one-quarter (205 more instruction hours and 149 more teaching hours).

Pattern of change at the primary level

In monetary terms, all of these changes in the features of education systems are reflected in the salary cost of teachers per student. Thus, the majority of countries simultaneously increased teacher's salaries and decreased the estimated class size between 2000 and 2010, which resulted in an increase of the salary cost of teachers per student. On average in countries with available data, the impact of the changes in teachers' salaries on the salary cost of teachers per student is usually larger than the impact of the change in estimated class size (USD 316 and about USD 267, respectively).

However, the impact of each of these two factors on the salary cost varies largely between countries. These two factors combined increased the salary cost by USD 500 or more in Australia, Austria, Denmark, Finland, Hungary, Portugal, Spain and Turkey, by more than USD 1 000 in the Czech Republic and Korea, and by more than USD 1 500 in Ireland. These large increases in the salary cost of teachers per student occurred in countries with either a high salary cost of teachers per student in 2000 (Denmark) or low levels of salary cost of teachers per student in 2000 (the Czech Republic or Korea, for example). Similarly, the decrease in estimated class size had a large impact on the salary cost in both countries with below-average estimated class size in 2000 (Finland) or above-average estimated class size in 2000 (the Czech Republic, Ireland and Korea). Increases in teachers' salaries had also a large impact on the salary cost in countries with below-average salaries in 2000 (in the Czech Republic, Hungary and Turkey, for example) and in countries with above-average salaries in 2000 (Denmark) (Chart B7.4 and Table B7.2).

Chart B7.4.   Contribution (in USD) of various factors to the change in salary cost of teachers per student, at primary level of education (2000, 2010)

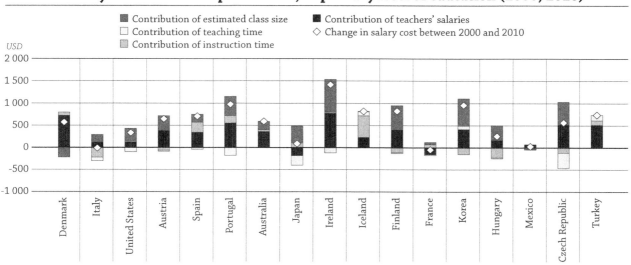

Countries are ranked in descending order of the salary cost of teachers per student in 2000.
Source: OECD. Table B7.2. See Annex 3 for notes (*www.oecd.org/edu/eag2012*).
StatLink http://dx.doi.org/10.1787/888932662941

These changes in teachers' salaries and in estimated class size explain most of the increase in the salary cost of teachers per student. However, changes in teaching and instruction times balanced or significantly complemented (by USD 200 or more) the increase in salary cost. The salary cost of teachers per student also increased by more than USD 200 as a result of a a combined decrease in instruction time and an increase of teaching time in Iceland and Turkey. By contrast, the salary cost of teachers per student decreased by more than USD 200 as a result of the combined increase in both instruction time and teaching time in the Czech Republic, Hungary and Italy.

Pattern of change at the lower secondary level

As with the primary level, at the lower secondary level of education, most countries simultaneously increased teachers' salaries and decreased estimated class size between 2000 and 2010. These two changes increased the salary cost by USD 355 and USD 412 per student respectively, on average among countries with available data. Nevertheless, there are large variations between countries in the impact of changes in teachers' salaries and estimated class size, and the extent of the impact of these two factors varies within countries (Table B7.3 and Chart B7.5).

Chart B7.5.   **Change (in USD) in the salary cost of teachers per student at the lower secondary level of education (2000, 2010)**

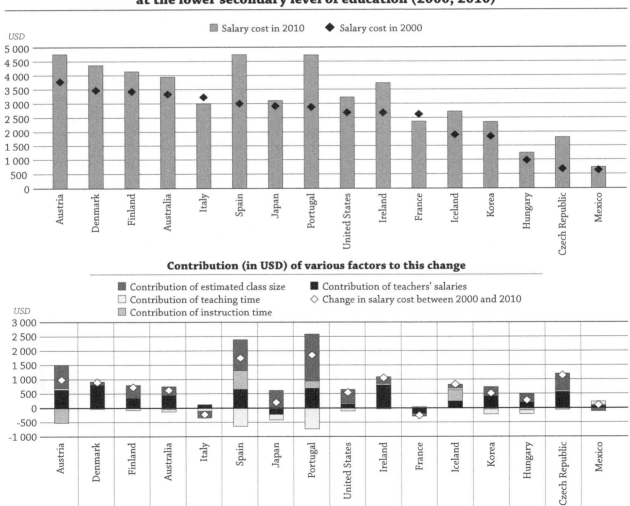

Countries are ranked in descending order of the salary cost of teachers per student in 2000.
Source: OECD. Table B7.3. See Annex 3 for notes (*www.oecd.org/edu/eag2012*).
StatLink ⬛⬛⬛ http://dx.doi.org/10.1787/888932662960

The combined impact of the increase in teachers' salaries and of the decrease in estimated class size is particularly large in Portugal and Spain (+ USD 2 317 and + USD 1 730 respectively), as teachers' salaries increased by 25% and 16% respectively, and estimated class size decreased by 34% and 28% respectively (from 14.8 to 9.8 students in Portugal, and from 20.6 to 14.9 students in Spain). However, the total change in the salary cost of teachers per student between 2000 and 2010 is a bit smaller in Portugal (+ USD 1 849), as the changes in teaching and instruction times did not completely cancel each other out. In Spain, changes in teaching and instruction times did balance, so that the salary cost of teachers per student increased between 2000 and 2010 by USD 1 746 (USD 16 more than the combined effect of the changes in estimated class size and teachers' salaries). The impact of the increase in teachers' salaries and of the decrease in estimated class size is also large in Austria, the Czech Republic and Ireland, where their combined effects increased the salary cost by more than USD 1 000.

Changes in teaching time and instruction time balanced or complemented the increase in salary cost, but their effect was most significant in Austria, Iceland and Portugal. Mexico is the only country where changes in teaching time increased the salary cost by more than USD 100 per student because the number of teaching hours decreased by more than 100 hours between 2000 and 2010 (from 1 182 hours in 2000 to 1 047 hours in 2010).

As the preceding discussion shows, changes in the four factors certainly impact countries' expenditures on education. At the same time, the choices countries make among these four factors can also affect the outcomes of education. Results from the PISA assessment suggest that at the secondary level, high-performing education systems are generally prioritising the quality of teachers over the size of classes. In the challenging economic climate that countries face today, the efficiency of their choices regarding educational expenditures are likely to be scrutinised more than ever.

Methodology

Reference year: Data referring to the 2010 school year are based on the UOE data collection on education statistics, as well as on the Survey on Teachers and the Curriculum Survey, which were both administered by the OECD in 2011. Data referring to the 2000 school year are based on the UOE data collection on education statistics, and on the Survey on Teachers and the Curriculum Survey, which were both administered by the OECD and published in the 2012 editions (for trend data on teaching time and salary of teachers) and 2002 (ratio of student to teaching staff and instruction time) of *Education at a Glance*. The consistency of 2000 and 2010 data has been validated (for details see Annex 3 at *www.oecd.org/edu/eag2012*).

Salary cost of teachers per student is calculated based on teachers' salaries, the number of hours of instruction for students, the number of hours of teaching for teachers and the estimated class size (a proxy of the class size; see Box D2.1). In most cases, the values for these variables are derived from *Education at a Glance 2012*, and refer to the school year 2009-10 and 1999-2000. Data for school year 1999-2000 are derived from *Education at a Glance 2002* when they are not available in the current edition. The data for 2000 have been checked to ensure the consistency with 2010 data. Teachers' salaries in national currencies are converted into equivalent USD by dividing the national currency figure by the purchasing power parity (PPP) index for private consumption, following the methodology used in Indicator D3 on teachers' salaries, which results in the salary cost per student expressed in equivalent USD. Further details on the analysis of these factors are available in Annex 3 at *www.oecd.org/edu/eag2012*.

The statistical data for Israel are supplied by and under the responsibility of the relevant Israeli authorities. The use of such data by the OECD is without prejudice to the status of the Golan Heights, East Jerusalem and Israeli settlements in the West Bank under the terms of international law.

References

The following additional material relevant to this indicator is available on line at:

- *Box B7.2. (continued) Main driver of salary cost of teacher per student as a percentage of GDP per capita, by level of education (2010)*
   StatLink ᔧᔧᔧ http://dx.doi.org/10.1787/888932671776

B7

- *Chart B7.2b. Contribution (in percentage points of GDP per capita) of various factors to salary cost of teacher per student, at the upper secondary level of education (2010)*
  StatLink ⫶⫶⫶ http://dx.doi.org/10.1787/888932662903

- *Table B7.2a. (continued) Contribution, in percentage points of GDP per capita, of various factors to salary cost of teacher per student at primary level of education (2000, 2010)*
  StatLink ⫶⫶⫶ http://dx.doi.org/10.1787/888932666646

- *Table B7.3. (continued) Contribution, in percentage points of GDP per capita, of various factors to salary cost of teacher per student at lower secondary level of education (2000, 2010)*
  StatLink ⫶⫶⫶ http://dx.doi.org/10.1787/888932666684

- *Table B7.4. (continued) Contribution, in percentage points of GDP per capita, of various factors to salary cost of teacher per student at upper secondary level of education (2010)*
  StatLink ⫶⫶⫶ http://dx.doi.org/10.1787/888932666722

- *Table B7.6. Contribution, in USD, of various factors to salary cost of teacher per student at primary, lower secondary and upper secondary levels of education (2010)*
  StatLink ⫶⫶⫶ http://dx.doi.org/10.1787/888932666760

Table B7.1a. Factors used to compute the salary cost of teachers per student, at the primary level of education (2000, 2010)

	Teachers' salary (annual, in USD, 2010 constant prices)			Instruction time (for students, hours per year)			Teaching time (for teachers, hours per year)			Ratio of students to teaching staff (number of students per teacher)			Estimated class size (number of students per classroom)		
	2010	2000	Variation 2000-2010 (%)	2010	2000	Variation 2000-2010 (%)	2010	2000	Variation 2000-2010 (%)	2010	2000	Variation 2000-2010 (%)	2010	2000	Variation 2000-2010 (%)
	(1)	(2)	(3)	(4)	(5)	(6)	(7)	(8)	(9)	(10)	(11)	(12)	(13) = (10) x (4) / (7)	(14) = (11) x (5) / (8)	(15)
Australia[1]	47 445	41 925	13.2	984	987	-0.3	868	882	-1.6	15.7	17.3	-9.1	17.8	19.3	-7.8
Austria[1]	40 818	35 479	15.0	811	833	-2.6	779	779	0.0	12.2	13.2	-7.3	12.7	14.1	-9.7
Belgium (Fl.)	44 076	39 784	10.8	835	m	m	761	767	-0.8	12.4	m	m	13.6	m	m
Belgium (Fr.)	42 792	38 518	11.1	930	930	0.0	732	804	-9.0	12.4	m	m	15.7	m	m
Canada	54 978	m	m	921	m	m	799	m	m	17.9	18.1	-1.1	20.7	m	m
Chile	23 411	m	m	1 083	1 060	2.2	1 087	m	m	24.6	m	m	24.6	m	m
Czech Republic[1,2]	19 949	9 859	102.3	706	752	-6.2	862	650	32.7	18.7	19.7	-5.2	15.3	22.8	-32.9
Denmark[1]	50 253	39 486	27.3	813	790	2.8	650	640	1.6	11.5	10.4	10.6	14.4	12.9	12.0
England	44 145	40 510	9.0	899	890	1.0	684	m	m	19.8	21.2	-6.6	26.1	m	m
Estonia	12 576	7 530	67.0	683	m	m	630	630	0.0	16.2	m	m	17.5	m	m
Finland[1]	37 455	31 095	20.5	683	694	-1.5	680	656	3.8	14.0	16.9	-16.8	14.1	17.8	-21.0
France[1]	32 733	35 692	-8.3	847	814	4.1	918	907	1.2	18.7	19.8	-5.7	17.3	17.8	-3.0
Germany	55 771	m	m	793	796	-0.4	805	783	2.8	16.7	19.8	-15.7	16.5	20.1	-18.3
Greece	32 387	27 825	16.4	812	928	-12.5	589	609	-3.2	m	13.4	m	m	20.4	m
Hungary[1]	13 228	10 609	24.7	724	834	-13.2	604	583	3.6	10.8	10.9	-1.6	12.9	15.7	-17.6
Iceland[1]	27 930	24 112	15.8	889	692	28.4	624	629	-0.8	10.3	12.7	-19.1	14.6	14.0	4.7
Ireland[1]	53 677	42 010	27.8	915	941	-2.7	915	915	0.0	15.9	21.5	-25.9	15.9	22.1	-27.9
Israel	25 181	19 193	31.2	990	m	m	820	731	12.1	20.6	m	m	24.8	m	m
Italy[1]	32 658	31 050	5.2	924	1 020	-9.4	770	744	3.5	11.3	10.7	5.6	13.6	14.7	-7.6
Japan[1]	44 788	49 033	-8.7	800	761	5.1	707	635	11.3	18.4	20.9	-11.9	20.8	25.0	-16.8
Korea[1]	46 338	39 720	16.7	703	737	-4.6	807	865	-6.7	21.1	32.1	-34.3	18.4	27.4	-32.8
Luxembourg	95 043	m	m	924	m	m	739	m	m	10.1	15.9	-36.6	12.6	m	m
Mexico[1]	18 621	17 201	8.3	800	800	0.0	800	800	0.0	28.1	27.2	3.6	28.1	27.2	3.6
Netherlands	50 621	m	22.8	940	1 000	-6.0	930	930	0.0	15.7	16.8	-6.3	15.9	18.1	-11.9
New Zealand	41 009	38 066	7.7	m	985	m	930	985	-5.6	16.2	20.6	-21.4	m	20.6	m
Norway	35 991	m	m	773	703	9.9	741	713	4.0	10.5	12.4	-15.7	10.9	12.2	-10.9
Poland	15 186	m	m	763	m	m	502	m	m	10.0	12.7	-21.4	15.1	m	m
Portugal[1]	37 542	29 981	25.2	888	833	6.6	865	815	6.1	10.9	12.1	-10.2	11.2	12.4	-9.9
Scotland	48 188	39 724	21.3	a	950	m	855	950	-10.0	19.8	21.2	-6.6	m	21.2	m
Slovak Republic	12 688	m	m	794	m	m	841	m	m	17.1	18.3	-6.9	16.1	m	m
Slovenia	32 436	m	m	721	m	m	690	m	m	16.2	m	m	17.0	m	m
Spain[1]	42 846	38 080	12.5	875	795	10.1	880	880	0.0	13.2	14.9	-11.9	13.1	13.5	-3.0
Sweden	33 374	30 898	8.0	741	741	0.0	a	a	m	11.7	12.8	-8.7	m	m	m
Switzerland	m	m	m	m	m	m	m	884	m	14.9	m	m	m	m	m
Turkey[1]	24 761	12 276	101.7	864	796	8.5	621	639	-2.8	21.7	30.5	-29.0	30.1	38.0	-20.7
United States[1]	45 226	43 867	3.1	980	980	0.0	1 097	1 080	1.6	14.5	15.8	-8.0	13.0	14.3	-9.4
OECD average	37 603	31 289	22.5	843	853	0.8	782	782	1.6	15.7	17.6	-11.5	17.1	19.2	-12.1
Average for 17 countries with all data available	36 251	31 263	16.0	836	827	1.1	791	771	2.7	15.7	18.0	-12.9	16.6	19.4	-14.3

Note: Data in this table come either from Chapter D (for 2010 data and 2000 data relating to salaries of teachers and teaching time) or from *Education at a Glance 2002* (for 2000 data on ratio of student to teaching staff and instruction time). Some 2000 data have been revised to ensure consistency with 2010 data.

1. Countries with all data available for both 2000 and 2010.

2. Current instruction time for 2000, minimum instruction time for 2010.

Source: OECD. See Annex 3 for notes (*www.oecd.org/edu/eag2012*).

Please refer to the Reader's Guide for information concerning the symbols replacing missing data.

StatLink ⟡⟡ http://dx.doi.org/10.1787/888932666570

B7

Table B7.1b. Factors used to compute the salary cost of teachers per student, at the lower secondary level of education (2000, 2010)

	Teachers' salary (annual, in USD, 2010 constant prices)			Instruction time (for students, hours per year)			Teaching time (for teachers, hours per year)			Ratio of students to teaching staff (number of students per teacher)			Estimated class size (number of students per classroom)		
	2010	2000	Variation 2000-2010 (%)	2010	2000	Variation 2000-2010 (%)	2010	2000	Variation 2000-2010 (%)	2010	2000	Variation 2000-2010 (%)	2010	2000	Variation 2000-2010 (%)
	(1)	(2)	(3)	(4)	(5)	(6)	(7)	(8)	(9)	(10)	(11)	(12)	(13) = (10) x (4) / (7)	(14) = (11) x (5) / (8)	(15)
Australia[1]	47 445	41 942	13.1	997	1 019	-2.2	819	811	1.1	12.0	12.6	-4.6	14.6	15.8	-7.7
Austria[1]	44 179	36 976	19.5	959	1 148	-16.5	607	607	0.0	9.3	9.8	-5.2	14.7	18.5	-20.9
Belgium (Fl.)	44 076	41 952	5.1	960	m	m	675	682	-1.0	8.1	m	m	11.5	m	m
Belgium (Fr.)	42 792	40 999	4.4	1 020	1 075	-5.1	671	728	-7.8	8.1	m	m	12.3	m	m
Canada	54 978	m	m	922	m	m	740	m	m	17.9	18.1	-1.1	22.3	m	m
Chile	23 411	m	m	1 083	1 080	0.3	1 087	m	m	25.1	m	m	25.0	m	m
Czech Republic[1,2]	20 217	9 859	105.1	862	867	-0.5	647	650	-0.5	11.2	14.7	-23.7	14.9	19.6	-23.7
Denmark[1]	50 253	39 486	27.3	900	890	1.1	650	640	1.6	11.5	11.4	1.2	15.9	15.8	0.8
England	44 145	40 510	9.0	925	940	-1.6	703	m	m	17.1	17.6	-2.7	22.5	m	m
Estonia	12 576	7 530	67.0	802	m	m	630	630	0.0	14.9	m	m	19.0	m	m
Finland[1]	40 451	36 501	10.8	829	808	2.6	595	570	4.4	9.8	10.7	-8.4	13.6	15.1	-9.9
France[1]	35 583	38 528	-7.6	1 065	1 042	2.2	646	639	1.1	15.0	14.7	2.3	24.8	24.0	3.4
Germany	61 784	m	m	887	903	-1.8	756	732	3.2	14.9	15.7	-5.2	17.4	19.3	-9.8
Greece	32 387	27 825	16.4	796	1 064	-25.2	415	426	-2.6	m	10.8	m	m	26.9	m
Hungary[1]	13 228	10 609	24.7	885	925	-4.3	604	555	8.8	10.7	10.9	-2.1	15.7	18.2	-13.8
Iceland[1]	27 930	24 112	15.8	969	809	19.8	624	629	-0.8	10.3	12.7	-19.1	16.0	16.3	-2.3
Ireland[1]	53 677	42 462	26.4	929	907	2.3	735	735	0.0	14.4	15.9	-9.2	18.2	19.6	-7.1
Israel	23 047	21 333	8.0	981	m	m	598	579	3.3	12.8	m	m	20.9	m	m
Italy[1]	35 583	34 010	4.6	1 023	1 020	0.3	630	608	3.6	11.9	10.6	12.6	19.3	17.7	9.0
Japan[1]	44 788	49 033	-8.7	877	875	0.2	602	557	8.0	14.4	16.8	-14.4	21.0	26.5	-20.6
Korea[1]	46 232	39 577	16.8	859	867	-1.0	627	570	10.0	19.7	21.5	-8.6	27.0	32.8	-17.7
Luxembourg	101 775	m	m	908	m	m	634	m	m	9.1	m	m	13.1	m	m
Mexico[1]	23 854	21 768	9.6	1 167	1 167	0.0	1 047	1 182	-11.4	32.7	34.8	-6.0	36.5	34.3	6.2
Netherlands	61 704	m	39.8	1 000	1 067	-6.3	750	867	-13.5	16.5	17.1	-3.5	22.0	21.0	4.6
New Zealand	42 062	38 066	10.5	m	948	m	845	968	-12.7	16.3	19.9	-18.1	m	19.5	m
Norway	35 991	m	m	836	827	1.1	654	633	3.2	9.9	9.9	0.2	12.7	12.9	-1.9
Poland	17 300	m	m	820	m	m	497	m	m	12.7	11.5	10.7	20.9	m	m
Portugal[1]	37 542	29 981	25.2	934	842	10.9	761	595	27.9	7.9	10.4	-23.8	9.8	14.8	-33.9
Scotland	48 188	39 724	21.3	a	a	m	855	893	-4.3	17.1	17.6	-2.7	m	m	m
Slovak Republic	12 688	m	m	851	m	m	652	m	m	13.6	13.5	0.4	17.7	m	m
Slovenia	32 436	m	m	817	m	m	690	m	m	8.0	m	m	9.5	m	m
Spain[1]	47 816	41 144	16.2	1 050	845	24.3	713	564	26.3	10.1	13.7	-26.6	14.9	20.6	-27.8
Sweden	34 481	30 898	11.6	741	741	0.0	a	a	a	11.4	12.8	-11.2	m	m	m
Switzerland	m	m	m	m	m	m	m	859	m	11.8	m	m	m	m	m
Turkey	a	m	m	864	796	8.5	a	a	a	a	a	a	m	m	m
United States[1]	45 049	43 697	3.1	980	980	0.0	1 068	1 080	-1.1	14.0	16.3	-14.2	12.8	14.8	-13.2
OECD average	39 401	33 141	18.2	924	940	0.4	704	703	1.8	14	15	-7.0	17.9	20	-9.8
Average for 16 countries with all data available	38 364	33 730	13.7	955	938	1.8	711	687	3.5	13	15	-9.5	18.0	19.4	-6.8

Note: Data in this table come either from Chapter D (for 2010 data and 2000 data relating to salaries of teachers and teaching time) or from *Education at a Glance 2002* (for 2000 data on ratio of student to teaching staff and instruction time). Some 2000 data have been revised to ensure consistency with 2010 data.

1. Countries with all data available for both 2000 and 2010.

2. Current instruction time for 2000, minimum instruction time for 2010.

Source: OECD. See Annex 3 for notes (www.oecd.org/edu/eag2012).

Please refer to the Reader's Guide for information concerning the symbols replacing missing data.

StatLink ⬛≣🖵 http://dx.doi.org/10.1787/888932666589

Table B7.1c. Factors used to compute the salary cost of teachers per student, at upper secondary level of education (2010)

	Teachers' salary (annual, in USD)	Instruction time (for students, hours per year)	Teaching time (for teachers, hours per year)	Ratio of students to teaching staff (number of students per teacher)	Estimated class size (number of students per classroom)
	(1)	(2)	(3)	(4)	(5) = (4) x (2) / (3)
Australia[1]	47 445	982	803	12.0	14.7
Austria[1]	45 425	1 050	589	10.1	18.1
Belgium (Fl.)[1]	56 638	960	630	10.1	15.4
Belgium (Fr.)	55 157	m	610	10.1	m
Canada[1]	55 191	919	744	15.9	19.6
Chile[1]	24 820	1 197	1 087	26.1	28.7
Czech Republic[1]	21 449	794	617	12.1	15.5
Denmark	58 256	930	377	m	m
England[1]	44 145	950	703	15.2	20.6
Estonia	12 576	840	578	16.6	24.1
Finland[1]	42 809	913	553	17.1	28.2
France[1]	35 819	1 147	632	9.7	17.6
Germany[1]	66 895	933	713	13.2	17.3
Greece	32 387	773	415	m	m
Hungary[1]	15 616	1 106	604	12.5	22.8
Iceland[1]	28 103	987	544	11.3	20.6
Ireland[1]	53 677	935	735	14.4	18.3
Israel[1]	21 009	1 101	521	11.0	23.3
Italy[1]	36 582	1 089	630	12.1	20.9
Japan	44 788	m	500	12.2	m
Korea[1]	46 232	1 020	616	16.5	27.4
Luxembourg[1]	101 775	900	634	9.1	13.0
Mexico	m	799	843	26.9	25.5
Netherlands[1]	61 704	1 000	750	16.5	22.0
New Zealand	43 116	m	760	14.4	m
Norway[1]	38 817	858	523	9.4	15.5
Poland[1]	19 791	865	494	12.1	21.1
Portugal[1]	37 542	934	761	7.2	8.8
Scotland	48 188	a	855	15.2	m
Slovak Republic[1]	12 698	936	624	14.6	21.9
Slovenia[1]	32 436	908	633	14.3	20.5
Spain[1]	48 818	1 050	693	9.6	14.5
Sweden	36 429	741	a	13.1	m
Switzerland	m	m	m	10.3	m
Turkey[1]	25 411	810	551	17.6	25.8
United States[1]	48 446	980	1 051	15.0	14.0
OECD average	41 182	949	658	13.6	19.9
Average for 26 countries with all data available	40 069	969	667	13.4	19.4

Note: Data in this table come from Chapter D.
1. Countries with all data available for 2010.
Source: OECD. See Annex 3 for notes *(www.oecd.org/edu/eag2012)*.
Please refer to the Reader's Guide for information concerning the symbols replacing missing data.
StatLink 🔗 http://dx.doi.org/10.1787/888932666608

B7

Table B7.2. Contribution, in USD, of various factors to salary cost of teachers per student at the primary level of education (2000, 2010)

In equivalent USD, converted using PPPs for private consumption

	Salary cost of teacher per student		Difference (in USD) from the 2000 OECD average of USD 1 733			Effect (in USD) of teachers' salary below/above the 2000 OECD average of USD 31 263			Effect (in USD) of instruction time (for students) below/above the 2000 OECD average of 827 hours			Effect (in USD) of teaching time (for teachers) below/above the 2000 OECD average of 771 hours			Effect (in USD) of estimated class size below/above the 2000 OECD average of 19.4 students per class		
	2010	2000	2010	2000	variation 2000-2010	2010	2000	variation 2000-2010	2010	2000	variation 2000-2010	2010	2000	variation 2000-2010	2010	2000	variation 2000-2010
	(1)	(2)	(3)	(4)	(5)	(6)	(7)	(8)	(9)	(10)	(11)	(12)	(13)	(14)	(15)	(16)	(17)
Australia	3 015	2 423	1 283	690	**593**	965	606	**359**	407	366	**41**	- 283	- 283	**0**	194	1	**192**
Austria	3 335	2 688	1 602	955	**647**	657	277	**380**	- 49	16	**- 65**	- 29	- 25	**- 3**	1 023	687	**336**
Belgium (Fl.)	3 556	m	m	m	**m**	m	m	**m**	m	m	**m**	m	m	**m**	m	m	**m**
Belgium (Fr.)	3 452	m	m	m	**m**	m	m	**m**	m	m	**m**	m	m	**m**	m	m	**m**
Canada	3 067	m	m	m	**m**	m	m	**m**	m	m	**m**	m	m	**m**	m	m	**m**
Chile	950	m	m	m	**m**	m	m	**m**	m	m	**m**	m	m	**m**	m	m	**m**
Czech Republic	1 068	500	- 665	-1 232	**567**	- 621	-1 142	**521**	- 222	- 104	**- 118**	- 158	191	**- 349**	336	- 178	**514**
Denmark	4 364	3 791	2 631	2 059	**573**	1 341	618	**724**	- 51	- 123	**71**	492	493	**- 1**	849	1 071	**- 222**
England	2 226	m	m	m	**m**	m	m	**m**	m	m	**m**	m	m	**m**	m	m	**m**
Estonia	776	m	m	m	**m**	m	m	**m**	m	m	**m**	m	m	**m**	m	m	**m**
Finland	2 670	1 844	937	112	**825**	395	- 10	**405**	- 423	- 316	**- 107**	273	290	**- 18**	692	147	**545**
France	1 751	1 800	19	68	**- 49**	80	235	**- 155**	43	- 29	**71**	- 306	- 289	**- 16**	202	151	**51**
Germany	3 338	m	m	m	**m**	m	m	**m**	m	m	**m**	m	m	**m**	m	m	**m**
Greece	m	m	m	m	**m**	m	m	**m**	m	m	**m**	m	m	**m**	m	m	**m**
Hungary	1 228	969	- 505	- 764	**259**	-1 335	-1 500	**166**	- 212	12	**- 224**	390	412	**- 22**	652	312	**339**
Iceland	2 718	1 899	986	166	**820**	- 251	- 482	**231**	160	- 330	**489**	464	375	**89**	613	602	**11**
Ireland	3 373	1 956	1 640	224	**1 416**	1 332	550	**783**	256	240	**16**	- 440	- 321	**- 119**	492	- 245	**737**
Israel	1 224	m	m	m	**m**	m	m	**m**	m	m	**m**	m	m	**m**	m	m	**m**
Italy	2 881	2 891	1 148	1 159	**- 11**	100	- 16	**115**	252	475	**- 223**	2	80	**- 78**	794	619	**176**
Japan	2 437	2 350	704	617	**88**	744	925	**- 181**	- 68	- 172	**104**	180	400	**- 220**	- 151	- 536	**385**
Korea	2 194	1 236	461	- 497	**958**	775	360	**415**	- 324	- 172	**- 152**	- 93	- 172	**80**	103	- 512	**616**
Luxembourg	9 404	m	m	m	**m**	m	m	**m**	m	m	**m**	m	m	**m**	m	m	**m**
Mexico	662	633	-1 071	-1 099	**28**	- 572	- 646	**74**	- 38	- 37	**- 1**	- 43	- 42	**- 1**	- 418	- 374	**- 44**
Netherlands	3 215	m	m	m	**m**	m	m	**m**	m	m	**m**	m	m	**m**	m	m	**m**
New Zealand	m	m	m	m	**m**	m	m	**m**	m	m	**m**	m	m	**m**	m	m	**m**
Norway	3 442	m	m	m	**m**	m	m	**m**	m	m	**m**	m	m	**m**	m	m	**m**
Poland	1 524	m	m	m	**m**	m	m	**m**	m	m	**m**	m	m	**m**	m	m	**m**
Portugal	3 447	2 471	1 715	738	**976**	465	- 89	**553**	182	16	**167**	- 299	- 119	**- 180**	1 366	930	**436**
Scotland	m	m	m	m	**m**	m	m	**m**	m	m	**m**	m	m	**m**	m	m	**m**
Slovak Republic	744	m	m	m	**m**	m	m	**m**	m	m	**m**	m	m	**m**	m	m	**m**
Slovenia	1 998	m	m	m	**m**	m	m	**m**	m	m	**m**	m	m	**m**	m	m	**m**
Spain	3 257	2 549	1 524	817	**707**	766	421	**345**	139	- 86	**225**	- 330	- 287	**- 44**	949	768	**181**
Sweden	m	m	m	m	**m**	m	m	**m**	m	m	**m**	m	m	**m**	m	m	**m**
Switzerland	m	m	m	m	**m**	m	m	**m**	m	m	**m**	m	m	**m**	m	m	**m**
Turkey	1 142	402	- 590	-1 331	**740**	- 336	- 852	**516**	64	- 38	**102**	315	194	**122**	- 633	- 634	**0**
United States	3 110	2 776	1 378	1 043	**334**	887	762	**125**	412	385	**27**	- 878	- 779	**- 98**	957	676	**280**
Average for countries with available data in both 2000 and 2010	2 307	1 733	776	219	**557**			**316**			**25**			**- 51**			**267**

Source: OECD. See Annex 3 for notes (*www.oecd.org/edu/eag2012*).
Please refer to the Reader's Guide for information concerning the symbols replacing missing data.
StatLink ᔛᔑ http://dx.doi.org/10.1787/888932666627

Table B7.3. Contribution, in USD, of various factors to salary cost of teachers per student at the lower secondary level of education (2000, 2010)

In equivalent USD, converted using PPPs for private consumption

	Salary cost of teacher per student		Difference (in USD) from the 2000 OECD average of USD 2 273			Effect (in USD) of teachers' salary below/above the 2000 OECD average of USD 33 730			Effect (in USD) of instruction time (for students) below/above the 2000 OECD average of 938 hours			Effect (in USD) of teaching time (for teachers) below/above the 2000 OECD average of 687 hours			Effect (in USD) of estimated class size below/above the 2000 OECD average of 20.3 students per class		
	2010	2000	2010	2000	variation 2000-2010	2010	2000	variation 2000-2010	2010	2000	variation 2000-2010	2010	2000	variation 2000-2010	2010	2000	variation 2000-2010
	(1)	(2)	(3)	(4)	(5)	(6)	(7)	(8)	(9)	(10)	(11)	(12)	(13)	(14)	(15)	(16)	(17)
Australia	3 946	3 329	1 673	1 056	**617**	1 041	606	**435**	187	232	**- 45**	- 550	- 466	**- 84**	995	684	**311**
Austria	4 756	3 773	2 483	1 500	**983**	907	273	**634**	73	596	**- 523**	422	368	**53**	1 081	264	**818**
Belgium (Fl.)	5 440	m	m	m	**m**	m	m	**m**	m	m	**m**	m	m	**m**	m	m	**m**
Belgium (Fr.)	5 281	m	m	m	**m**	m	m	**m**	m	m	**m**	m	m	**m**	m	m	**m**
Canada	3 067	m	m	m	**m**	m	m	**m**	m	m	**m**	m	m	**m**	m	m	**m**
Chile	933	m	m	m	**m**	m	m	**m**	m	m	**m**	m	m	**m**	m	m	**m**
Czech Republic	1 803	671	- 469	-1 602	**1 133**	-1 060	-1 618	**557**	- 176	- 116	**- 59**	126	82	**44**	641	50	**590**
Denmark	4 364	3 471	2 091	1 199	**893**	1 274	447	**827**	- 136	- 151	**15**	180	201	**- 21**	773	701	**73**
England	2 577	m	m	m	**m**	m	m	**m**	m	m	**m**	m	m	**m**	m	m	**m**
Estonia	844	m	m	m	**m**	m	m	**m**	m	m	**m**	m	m	**m**	m	m	**m**
Finland	4 143	3 426	1 871	1 154	**717**	572	224	**348**	- 396	- 429	**33**	451	528	**- 77**	1 244	831	**413**
France	2 368	2 623	95	350	**- 255**	125	326	**- 201**	296	258	**38**	143	178	**- 34**	- 469	- 411	**- 58**
Germany	4 154	m	m	m	**m**	m	m	**m**	m	m	**m**	m	m	**m**	m	m	**m**
Greece	m	2 579	m	m	**m**	m	m	**m**	m	m	**m**	m	m	**m**	m	m	**m**
Hungary	1 236	971	-1 037	-1 302	**265**	-1 646	-1 831	**186**	- 106	- 24	**- 82**	239	370	**- 131**	477	184	**293**
Iceland	2 718	1 899	446	- 373	**819**	- 475	- 706	**231**	81	- 313	**394**	241	187	**55**	599	459	**140**
Ireland	3 728	2 678	1 455	406	**1 049**	1 366	570	**797**	- 31	- 83	**52**	- 202	- 167	**- 35**	322	86	**236**
Israel	1 807	m	m	m	**m**	m	m	**m**	m	m	**m**	m	m	**m**	m	m	**m**
Italy	2 994	3 222	722	950	**- 228**	140	23	**117**	226	228	**- 1**	226	332	**- 106**	129	368	**- 239**
Japan	3 107	2 911	834	639	**195**	757	978	**- 221**	- 182	- 184	**2**	356	550	**- 194**	- 98	- 706	**608**
Korea	2 348	1 837	75	- 435	**510**	740	336	**403**	- 208	- 165	**- 43**	214	393	**- 178**	- 671	- 999	**329**
Luxembourg	11 145	m	m	m	**m**	m	m	**m**	m	m	**m**	m	m	**m**	m	m	**m**
Mexico	729	626	-1 543	-1 647	**104**	- 482	- 571	**89**	319	304	**16**	- 582	- 699	**118**	- 799	- 680	**- 118**
Netherlands	3 740	m	m	m	**m**	m	m	**m**	m	m	**m**	m	m	**m**	m	m	**m**
New Zealand	m	1 914	m	m	**m**	m	m	**m**	m	m	**m**	m	m	**m**	m	m	**m**
Norway	3 630	m	m	m	**m**	m	m	**m**	m	m	**m**	m	m	**m**	m	m	**m**
Poland	1 364	m	m	m	**m**	m	m	**m**	m	m	**m**	m	m	**m**	m	m	**m**
Portugal	4 723	2 873	2 450	601	**1 849**	373	- 306	**679**	- 15	- 280	**266**	- 362	372	**- 734**	2 454	816	**1 638**
Scotland	m	m	m	m	**m**	m	m	**m**	m	m	**m**	m	m	**m**	m	m	**m**
Slovak Republic	933	m	m	m	**m**	m	m	**m**	m	m	**m**	m	m	**m**	m	m	**m**
Slovenia	4 060	m	m	m	**m**	m	m	**m**	m	m	**m**	m	m	**m**	m	m	**m**
Spain	4 743	2 997	2 470	724	**1 746**	1 169	522	**648**	383	- 276	**659**	- 127	516	**- 643**	1 045	- 37	**1 082**
Sweden	m	m	m	m	**m**	m	m	**m**	m	m	**m**	m	m	**m**	m	m	**m**
Switzerland	m	m	m	m	**m**	m	m	**m**	m	m	**m**	m	m	**m**	m	m	**m**
Turkey	m	m	m	m	**m**	m	m	**m**	m	m	**m**	m	m	**m**	m	m	**m**
United States	3 223	2 683	950	410	**540**	813	658	**155**	123	111	**12**	-1 265	-1 161	**- 104**	1 278	802	**477**
Average for countries with available data in both 2000 and 2010	2 856	2 273	910	227	**684**			**355**			**46**			**- 129**			**412**

Source: OECD. See Annex 3 for notes (*www.oecd.org/edu/eag2012*).
Please refer to the Reader's Guide for information concerning the symbols replacing missing data.
StatLink http://dx.doi.org/10.1787/888932666665

B7

Table B7.4. Contribution, in USD, of various factors to salary cost of teachers per student at the upper secondary level of education (2010)

In equivalent USD, converted using PPPs for private consumption

| | Salary cost of teacher per student | Difference (in USD) from the 2000 OECD average of **USD 29 94** | Contribution of the underlying factors to the difference from the OECD average | | | |
			Effect (in USD) of teachers' salary below/above the 2000 OECD average of **USD 40 069**	Effect (in USD) of instruction time (for students) below/above the 2000 OECD average of **969 hours**	Effect (in USD) of teaching time (for teachers) below/above the 2000 OECD average of **667 hours**	Effect (in USD) of estimated class size below/above the 2000 OECD average of **19.4 students per class**
	(1)	(2) = (3)+(4)+(5)+(6)	(3)	(4)	(5)	(6)
Australia	3 946	952	587	46	-651	969
Austria	4 480	1 486	462	296	461	266
Belgium (Fl.)	5 588	2 594	1 434	-40	241	959
Belgium (Fr.)	m	m	m	m	m	m
Canada	3 475	481	1 040	-172	-357	-30
Chile	951	-2 043	-862	405	-877	-709
Czech Republic	1 775	-1 219	-1 477	-480	189	549
Denmark	m	m	m	m	m	m
England	2 901	-94	286	-59	-155	-166
Estonia	758	-2 236	-1 862	-256	266	-384
Finland	2 509	-485	184	-165	524	-1 029
France	3 705	711	-377	565	182	341
Germany	5 052	2 058	2 018	-153	-270	462
Greece	m	m	m	m	m	m
Hungary	1 252	-1 742	-1 902	288	216	-344
Iceland	2 477	-518	-976	50	566	-158
Ireland	3 728	733	982	-120	-327	198
Israel	1 903	-1 091	-1 585	323	626	-455
Italy	3 029	34	-275	352	173	-216
Japan	m	m	m	m	m	m
Korea	2 798	-196	420	150	234	-1 000
Luxembourg	11 145	8 150	5 696	-501	345	2 610
Mexico	m	m	m	m	m	m
Netherlands	3 740	745	1 462	107	-401	-423
New Zealand	m	m	m	m	m	m
Norway	4 115	1 121	-113	-435	865	804
Poland	1 642	-1 352	-1 612	-268	720	-193
Portugal	5 246	2 252	-277	-155	-562	3 246
Scotland	m	m	m	m	m	m
Slovak Republic	870	-2 124	-1 963	-67	129	-224
Slovenia	2 267	-727	-552	-172	139	-142
Spain	5 100	2 105	783	320	-150	1 153
Sweden	m	m	m	m	m	m
Switzerland	m	m	m	m	m	m
Turkey	1 444	-1 550	-970	-388	422	-613
United States	3 233	239	608	36	-1 461	1 057

Source: OECD. See Annex 3 for notes (*www.oecd.org/edu/eag2012*).

Please refer to the Reader's Guide for information concerning the symbols replacing missing data.

StatLink ⟡⟡⟡ http://dx.doi.org/10.1787/888932666703

B7

Table B7.5. [1/5] Main reforms implemented between 1995 and 2009 on the four factors used to calculate the salary cost of teachers per student

	Salary of teachers (statutory salaries)	Annual amount of instruction time for students	Annual teaching time for teachers (in public institutions)	Class size or ratio of students to teaching staff
Australia	There have been no substantial policy reforms on teachers' salaries at the national level over the previous ten years that can be identified as affecting this Indicator directly. However, under the recent Teacher Quality National Partnership Agreement, the Commonwealth government is working with state and territory governments on a range of reforms to improve the quality of teaching and school leadership in schools. These reforms will include improvements to teacher pay to reward quality teaching and improve reward structures for teachers and leaders who work in disadvantaged indigenous, rural/remote and hard-to-staff schools. These reforms are still in the early stages and it is not yet possible to determine how they will affect teachers' salaries.	There was no reform in this area.	There was no reform in this area.	There have been no substantial policy reforms directly concerning class sizes at the national level over the previous ten years that can be identified as affecting this Indicator directly. However, several states/territories have made resourcing commitments to help improve class sizes within their state/territory.
Austria	There was no reform in this area.	Decrease in instruction time for students. Beginning with the school year 2003-04, the number of teaching periods was reduced by 2 periods per class (ISCED 3) and 1.5 periods per class (on average, ISCED 2). The number of teaching periods is stipulated in the various curricula which are federal ordinances enacted by the Ministry of Education. As a consequence, public expenditure on teacher salaries decreased.	There was no reform in this area.	Beginning with the school year 2007-08, the maximum number of pupils per class was reduced by five in schools at ISCED 1 and 2. At ISCED 1 (primary schools) and ISCED 2 (*Hauptschulen:* general secondary schools), the regional provinces were responsible for amending the respective regional School Organisation Acts. In respect of ISCED 2 (*Allgemein bildenden höhere Schulen:* academic secondary schools) the Federal School Organisation Act was amended. At ISCED 3 the maximum number of pupils per class was left unchanged. However, possibilities for splitting classes into small groups were enlarged for certain subjects. As a result, expenditure on teacher salaries will rise considerably up to 2010-11.
Belgium (Flemish Community)	Identical teacher's salaries in primary and lower secondary education. Before September 2000, the statutory salary was different for teachers in ISCED 1 and ISCED 2. Since 1 September 2000, the statutory salary of these two types of teachers gradually became the same. The implementation ended on 1 September 2004.	There was no reform in this area.	Since September 1997, the weekly teaching time for teachers in primary education has been a maximum of 27 hours of 50 minutes (previously 28 hours of 50 minutes). Similar reforms were introduced in 1989 in secondary education.	As of 1 September 2002, there is an integrated support provision for children from deprived backgrounds for equal opportunities in education. Extra support for additional needs in schools has been made available. The support is aimed at schools that have a rather large number of pupils with certain socio-economic indicators. This extra support consists of additional teaching periods. Compared to 2002, about 1.7% additional teaching hours have been awarded on this basis to schools in regular secondary education.

Source: OECD. See Annex 3 for notes (*www.oecd.org/edu/eag2012*).
StatLink ⟨⟩ http://dx.doi.org/10.1787/888932666741

B7

Table B7.5. [2/5] **Main reforms implemented between 1995 and 2009 on the four factors used to calculate the salary cost of teachers per student**

	Salary of teachers (statutory salaries)	Annual amount of instruction time for students	Annual teaching time for teachers (in public institutions)	Class size or ratio of students to teaching staff
Czech Republic	Statutory rule 469/2002 Sb., subsequently amended: The salary scales have 16 categories (according to the complexity of work) and 12 steps (according to the length of service). The tariffs in the scale valid for the remuneration of teachers overrides those in the basic scale, but are lower than in the scale for some other groups of employees, e.g. in health services. All teachers who are fully qualified are entitled to salary advancement within the salary scale, irrespective of the type of contract or the form of the employment relationship. Educational staff are placed in the range between 8th and 13th categories, with the 14th category being used for educational staff only in exceptional circumstances. Statutory rule 74/2009 Sb.: Non-pedagogical staff has been included in salary scales of pedagogical staff (salaries of non-pedagogical staff increased).	The reform of curricula (transfer to Framework Educational Programme [FEP]) which started in 2005 will be implemented from 2007-08 to 2011-12 in primary and secondary education. Substantial changes were done in the timetable of FEP, e.g. more hours are flexible. The FEP sets key competences, outputs of educational areas composed of educational fields, which are compulsory, and recommended content of education. It also sets the cross-curricular topics. The school educational programmes set the individual subjects – the subjects can be the same as the educational fields and cross-curricular topics, they can integrate the fields/topics or the fields can be divided into more subjects. The form of modules or courses can also be used. The outputs must be fulfilled and the time allocated to individual educational areas/fields must be observed. All schools must teach according to their school educational programme.	Since 2005: Headmasters can increase the number of teaching time for teachers of 3 hours per week (within a limit of 24 hours per week).	There was no reform in this area.
Finland	A new salary system has been implemented for education staff since 2007. Earlier salaries were based on the number of teaching hours and years of service. In the new system, the salaries are based on the tasks and their requirements and the results of the work, the professionalism of the staff and work experience. In addition, a bonus can be paid based on the results of the institution. There is also room for local flexibility in the salary system. The Trade Union of Education hopes that employers (that is, local authorities) will make more frequent use of this opportunity to pay their employees more than the minimum salaries determined in national agreements. It is too early to determine the quantitative impact of the new salary system.	Since 1 August 2001, all programmes leading to upper secondary vocational qualifications take three years to complete and comprise 120 credits (one credit is equal to 40 hours of students' average workload). Before that, the completion of an initial vocational qualification took 2-3 years. In 1999, slightly less than one-third of students started in study programmes lasting 2 or 2.5 years. The distribution of lesson hours in general upper secondary education was also reformed by a Government Decree in 2002, which did not change the minimum total number of students' courses.	The conditions of service for teachers, including teaching time, are agreed in a collective bargaining process and in the relevant legislation (length of school year, etc.). Most teachers' working hours are based on teaching duties. In some fields of vocational upper secondary education and training, teachers have overall teaching/working hours. This was introduced in different years in different fields.	There was no reform in this area.
France	There was no reform in this area.	At the start of the 2008 school year, a new organisation of the school week was introduced in primary schools. Saturday morning classes were removed. The school week is now composed of 24 hours of teaching over four days (Monday, Tuesday, Thursday and Friday), or nine half-days including Wednesday mornings. The maximum duration of a school day is still six hours. When the need arises, pupils may receive two hours of tutoring per week by a teacher (in the school), on top of the 24 hours of regular classes. The school year now has 864 hours of instruction instead of 962 hours previously.	There was no reform in this area.	There was no reform in this area.
Hungary	There was no reform in this area.	In 2004-05, a modified National Core Curriculum was introduced at grade 1. From 2003-04 new (also recommended) frame curricula with fewer lessons were introduced in grades 5, 9 and 10. In 2005-06 this curriculum was extended to grades 3 and 7. Altogether, the changes resulted in an 8-10% decrease in the amount of compulsory instruction time.	Since 2006: Increase in the number of compulsory hours of teaching from 20 to 22 at ISCED 2 and 3. The change resulted in a 10% increase in teachers' compulsory teaching time.	There was no reform in this area.

Source: OECD. See Annex 3 for notes (www.oecd.org/edu/eag2012).
StatLink ⫘⫘⫘ http://dx.doi.org/10.1787/888932666741

Table B7.5. [3/5] Main reforms implemented between 1995 and 2009 on the four factors used to calculate the salary cost of teachers per student

	Salary of teachers (statutory salaries)	Annual amount of instruction time for students	Annual teaching time for teachers (in public institutions)	Class size or ratio of students to teaching staff
Italy	More autonomy for schools to set teacher's salaries. The salary is made up of basic and additional compensation. The increase for both parts is defined on the basis of the price index. Owing to the law on autonomy, from 2000 the additional salary is assigned according to criteria defined at the level of the school.	Establishment of the minimum and maximum number of instruction hours in 2005 and 2009.	There was no reform in this area.	In 2006: Increase of 0.40 in the average number of students per class in primary and secondary education. Since 2009, no fewer than 15 and at most 25 in primary education, no fewer than 18 and at most 25 in lower secondary, and no fewer than 27 in upper secondary education.
Mexico	There was no reform in this area.	There was no reform in this area.	There was no reform in this area.	There was no reform in this area.
Netherlands	Reduction of career line: In 2000 with 2 steps (years), in 2001 with three steps, in 2002 with two steps. At that moment (in 2002) the career line had 18 steps. This reduction cost about EUR 100 million and EUR 60 million in primary and secondary education, respectively. Teachers with the maximum salary will get an extra allowance of EUR 1 850 and EUR 1 000 in primary and secondary education, respectively.	Reduction of instruction time from 1 067 to 1 040 and finally to 1 000 hours in 2009 in lower secondary education.	Reduction of teaching time from 867 hours in 2001 to a maximum of 750 hours in 2009. School boards for secondary education have a large degree of autonomy on decision making, including on teaching time. Since 2004 the collective labour agreement no longer contains formal regulations on teaching time for teachers in secondary education. In the past there was a maximum of 750 (or 867) clock hours a year. In the new collective labour agreement 2008-10 teacher unions and the employers organisation for secondary education have noted that the maximum teaching time will be 750 clock hours again, with commencing date 1 August 2009. From that date, the individual (full time) teacher yearly has the right to exchange 24 hours of teaching time for other school activities or payment. In addition to this, an analysis on the integral workforce count of teachers in secondary education (IPTO-VO) has shown that, converted to the average of a full time teacher, teaching time is 690 clock hours, assuming that the number of weeks a teacher teaches per annum is 38.5.	Investments in reduction of class size. Reduction of pupil to teacher ratio from 18.6 in 2000 to 16.2 in 2008 (special education excluded). Growth in the number of teacher aides from 5 000 FTE in 2002 to 8 000 FTE in 2007.
Norway	The first deal between the government and teacher unions was signed in May 2000 (*skolepakke 1*) and the second in October 2001 (*skolepakke 2*). Teachers were awarded two pay grades from 1 August 2000 in the first deal, and three pay grades in the second deal (one pay grade from 1 January 2002 and two pay grades from August 2002). The total increase of five pay grades was equivalent to approximately an 8% increase in salaries.	Increase of 3 hours a week (85.5 hours a year) in reading, writing and literature at grades 1-4 in 2002, increase of 3 hours a week (85.5 hours a year) in reading, writing and literature and 2 hours a week (57 hours a year) in mathematics at grades 1-4 in 2004, increase of 1 hour a week (28.5 hours a year) in mathematics, science, social studies and modern foreign languages at grades 1-4 in 2005, increase of 76 hours a year in mathematics and reading, writing and literature, and 38 hours in modern foreign languages at grades 1-4 in 2008, increase of 76 hours a year in physical education at grades 5-7 in 2009 and increase of 38 hours a year at any subject or grade according to school owners' assessment in 2010.	1 hour increase in teaching hours per week in primary school was included in the second deal (*skolepakke 2*). 1 % increase from 1 January 2002, and 3 % increase from 1 August 2002 (4% = 1 hour).	Norway used to have a fairly rigid system, with permanent classes and a maximum number of students per class, depending on the age of the students (28 per class in primary school – grades 1-7, 30 in lower secondary – grades 8-10, and in upper secondary, 15 in professionally oriented upper secondary). In 2003, this system was abandoned. The system of classes and maximum numbers was replaced by a more liberal system which conferred a large degree of discretionary power on the municipalities. The key words are "justifiable", "pedagogy", and "security". A condition of the introduction of this system was that the municipalities might not use it to save money.

Source: OECD. See Annex 3 for notes (*www.oecd.org/edu/eag2012*).
StatLink ⟦ᵐⁱˢ⟧ http://dx.doi.org/10.1787/888932666741

B7

**Table B7.5. [4/5] Main reforms implemented between 1995 and 2009 on the four factors used
to calculate the salary cost of teachers per student**

	Salary of teachers (statutory salaries)	Annual amount of instruction time for students	Annual teaching time for teachers (in public institutions)	Class size or ratio of students to teaching staff
Portugal	1999, 2007 and 2009: Revision of the salaries and years to go from minimum to maximum salary.	Reorganisation of (upper) secondary education. The total compulsory flexible curriculum increased from 2 disciplines (6 sessions per week) to 3 disciplines (9 sessions per week) and 205.2 sessions (307.8 hours) to 307.8 sessions (461.7 hours) per year, respectively. Consequently, the total intended curriculum increased from 581.4 sessions (872.1 hours) to 615.6 sessions (923.4 hours).	Changes to the Teacher's Career Statute. The Decree-Law nr. 15/2007 increased the number of teaching hours per week in upper secondary education from 20 hours per week to 22 hours per week (respectively, an increase in the number of hours a teacher teaches per year from 684 hours per year to 752.4 hours per year).	There was no reform in this area.
Spain	New Education Act passed 3 May 2006, implemented from 2007-08 to 2010-11. The reforms established by this Act do not affect the subjects included in this survey. These subjects remain the same as those in the Teachers and Curriculum Survey 2009.			
Sweden	There have been no reforms/changes since 2000 in Swedish education policy with consequences for the factors used in the analysis for this Indicator.			
Switzerland	According to this important feature of federally organised Switzerland, teachers' salaries, the annual hours of instruction time for students and the annual hours of teaching time for teachers are determined by each *canton* individually. In the context of the questions on metadata for this Indicator, this means that there are no reforms that are valid on the national level. There have been relevant reforms in the last ten years in single *cantons*, but their impact affects only some Swiss teachers and/or students. In the *canton* of St. Gall, for example, the total instruction time in primary school (6 years) increased from 5 100 to 5 460 hours between 1998 and 2008. But primary school students in St. Gall represent only about 7 % of total Swiss primary school students (and 8% of teachers).			
United Kingdom	Between 1999 and April 2002 starting pay for teachers in England and Wales was based on a nine-point scale. They were then able to progress to a post-threshold higher five-point scale. From September 2002 the pay scales were revised (shortened) to the current main (six-point) and upper (three-point) scales. A review in November 2003 led to the introduction of new (higher) pay scales for those working in outer London and the Fringe (around London). Management allowances were also reformed. Scotland: A new pay structure was introduced in 2002 following a review in 2000.	The school year in England consists of 380 half-day sessions; one in the morning between around 9 am and 12 noon, the other in the afternoon usually between 1 pm and 3:30 pm. There is no fixed number of lessons per week. Recommended minimum weekly lesson times (excluding breaks) are: 21 hours for 5-7 year-olds; 23.5 hours for 7-11 year-olds; 24 hours for 11-14 year-olds; and 25 hours for 14-16 year-olds.	Teachers are contracted to work 1 265 hours per year. There is no statutory amount of teaching time within this. From 1 September 2005, all teachers at a school (including head teachers) with timetabled teaching commitments, have a contractual entitlement to guaranteed planning, preparation and assessment time for a minimum of at least 10% of their timetabled teaching time. Scotland: An annual working week of 35 hours was introduced from August 2001, with class contact time reduced in stages, ultimately to 22.5 hours per week in 2006.	The (English) government pledged in its 1997 election manifesto to limit the size of classes for 5, 6 and 7 year-olds to no more than 30 pupils. The School Standards and Framework Act placed a duty on schools to limit the size of classes for 5, 6 and 7 year-olds taught by one qualified teacher to 30 or fewer pupils. The limit became a statutory duty from September 2001, the start of the 2001-02 school year. Scotland: A 1999 regulation limited class sizes in the first three years of primary school (P1, P2 and P3) to a maximum of 30 from August 1999, August 2000 and August 2001, respectively. The P1 limit was reduced to 25 in 2007-08 (Government Circular 1/2007). (Other primary classes have a limit of 33.) In secondary education, maths and English classes were reduced to a maximum of 20 pupils by Government Circular 1/2007.
United States	Teachers' salaries in the United States are determined by individual states and districts.	State requirements for the number of instructional days and hours per year vary. While there is no national standard, the general trend since 1980 has been to increase instructional time (ECS, Zaleski and Colasanti, June 2008, *www.ecs.org/html/educationIssues/ECSStateNotes.asp?nIssueID=102v*). National average is 180 school days per year.	State and district requirements on the number of teaching hours within public institutions vary. Additionally, hours per school day vary among states.	There are no nationally set guidelines on student to teacher ratios. NCLB-Title II Teacher Quality Block Grants may be used to reduce class size, but do not legislate what is required (*www.ed.gov/offices/OESE/ClassSize/index.html*). Some districts, such as New York City, have negotiated caps with the local teachers unions.

Source: OECD. See Annex 3 for notes (*www.oecd.org/edu/eag2012*).
StatLink ᴍˢᴾ http://dx.doi.org/10.1787/888932666741

Table B7.5. [5/5] **Main reforms implemented between 1995 and 2009 on the four factors used to calculate the salary cost of teachers per student**

		Salary of teachers (statutory salaries)	Annual amount of instruction time for students	Annual teaching time for teachers (in public institutions)	Class size or ratio of students to teaching staff
Other G20	Brazil	In 2007, a law created the Fund for Development of Basic Education and Teaching Valuation (Fundeb). This fund's resources were destined to state and municipal teaching nets based on the number of students enrolled in ISCED 0, 1, 2 and 3. At least 60% of the total annual resources of this fund, in each state and in the Federal District, must be destined for the payment of professionals who are acting in ISCED 0, 1, 2 and 3. A law of 2008 establishes a minimum national salary to teachers of ISCED 0, 1, 2 and 3.	There was no reform in this area.	There was no reform in this area.	There was no reform in this area.

Source: OECD. See Annex 3 for notes (*www.oecd.org/edu/eag2012*).

StatLink ⌨📊 http://dx.doi.org/10.1787/888932666741

Chapter

ACCESS TO EDUCATION, PARTICIPATION AND PROGRESSION

Indicator C1 Who participates in education?
StatLink ⬛ᴵˢ⬛ http://dx.doi.org/10.1787/888932666779

Indicator C2 How do early childhood education systems differ around the world?
StatLink ⬛ᴵˢ⬛ http://dx.doi.org/10.1787/888932667007

Indicator C3 How many students are expected to enter tertiary education?
StatLink ⬛ᴵˢ⬛ http://dx.doi.org/10.1787/888932667083

Indicator C4 Who studies abroad and where?
StatLink ⬛ᴵˢ⬛ http://dx.doi.org/10.1787/888932667216

Indicator C5 Transition from school to work: where are the 15-29 year-olds?
StatLink ⬛ᴵˢ⬛ http://dx.doi.org/10.1787/888932667368

Indicator C6 How many adults participate in education and learning?
StatLink ⬛ᴵˢ⬛ http://dx.doi.org/10.1787/888932667577

WHO PARTICIPATES IN EDUCATION?

- Access to education is universal between the ages of 5 and 14 among all OECD and other G20 countries with available data.

- In 25 of 33 OECD countries, 80% or more of 15-19 year-olds participate in education. This is true for more than 90% of this age group in Belgium, the Czech Republic, Hungary, Ireland, the Netherlands, Poland and Slovenia.

- From 1995 to 2010, enrolment rates among 20-29 year-olds increased by 10.1 percentage points in OECD countries with available data.

- After years of relatively stable level enrolment rates among 20-29 year-olds across OECD countries, the proportion of this age group participating in education increased by more than one percentage point in 13 out of 31 countries between 2009 and 2010. In Iceland, Ireland, Spain, Sweden and Turkey, the increase in enrolment rates was more than two percentage points higher than the annual average growth rate for the entire decade.

- In 2015, if current enrolment rates remain constant, the number of 20-29 year-olds in education is likely to increase by more than 30% in Austria and Greece, and by more than 70% in Turkey, compared to 2005 levels. Hungary, Japan, Poland and Portugal will likely see a decrease in the number of students this age of more than 13%.

Chart C1.1. Enrolment rates of 20-29 year-olds (1995, 2000 and 2010)
Full-time and part-time students in public and private institutions

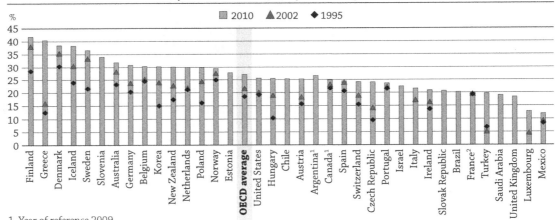

1. Year of reference 2009.
2. Excludes overseas departments for 1995.
Countries are ranked in descending order of the enrolment rates of 20-29 year-olds in 2010.
Source: OECD. Argentina: UNESCO Institute for Statistics (World Education Indicators programme). Saudi Arabia: UNESCO Institute for Statistics. Table C1.2. See Annex 3 for notes (*www.oecd.org/edu/eag2012*).
StatLink ᴍꜱ᠍᠍᠍᠍ http://dx.doi.org/10.1787/888932662979

■ Context

In past decades, education systems in all OECD and other G20 countries have managed to provide universal access to basic education. Participation in education is now expanding to upper and lower levels of education. Access to upper secondary education is becoming almost universal in most countries, as is pre-primary education (see Indicator C2). The expansion of upper secondary education has been driven by increasing demand and policy changes ranging from a more flexible curriculum, a reshaping of vocational studies, and efforts to expand access to education to the entire population. The same applies to tertiary education, although participation rates at this level of education are significantly lower.

Upper secondary education has become a minimum qualification to transition successfully into the labour market and to lower the risk of unemployment (see Indicator A7). Successful completion of upper secondary programmes is vital for addressing equity issues in countries (OECD, 2010a; OECD, 2011a), but completion rates vary widely among OECD countries (see Indicator A2). Efforts to expand this level of education further and to help ensure good returns for individuals will require education systems to provide the skills students need to make them employable in the short term, as well as generic skills and knowledge to enable them to pursue increasingly flexible pathways through lifelong learning and their working lives (OECD, 2010b).

Demographic pressures, such as smaller school-age populations, are likely to influence education policies in the future. While countries with fewer students will have opportunities to increase per-student resources (see Indicator B1) and reduce student-teacher ratios (see Indicator D2), reallocating human resources to other levels of education may require changes in teacher training and recruitment that need long-term planning. Countries facing historically large populations of students have the opportunity to shape their future labour force and skills profile through education reforms. On the other hand, the pressures on these countries' education budgets, particularly in light of the present economic situation, are likely to intensify. The potentially greater prevalence of skilled workers could lead to skill mismatches and lower private and public returns on education (see Indicator A9). However, the deep structural changes in the global labour market over the past decades suggest that individuals in increasingly better-educated populations will continue to find solid positions in the labour market, as long as economies keep evolving to become more knowledge-based.

Other findings

- **Under present enrolment conditions, a 5-year-old in an OECD country can expect to participate in more than 17 years of full-time and part-time education before reaching the age of 40.** Expected years in education range from more than 19 years in Finland, Iceland and Sweden to around 15 years in Luxembourg (where student mobility is high), Mexico and Turkey, to 14 years in Indonesia.

- **Virtually all people in OECD countries have access to at least 13 years of formal education.** In Belgium, Norway and Sweden, at least 90% of the population are enrolled in education for 15 years or more. By contrast, in Chile, Indonesia, Saudi Arabia and Turkey, at least 90% of the population are enrolled for between 8 and 10 years.

Trends

Countries with stronger correlations between the evolution of unemployment and enrolment rates for 20-29 year-olds between 2005 and 2010 also saw the largest increases in enrolment among this age group between 2009 and 2010, revealing a return to education among unemployed people in Estonia, Greece, Iceland, Ireland, Spain and Turkey.

Because of demographic changes in the 5-14 year-old cohort, demand for education at all levels is likely to decrease over the next five to ten years. In 2015, that drop could exceed 20% in Eastern European countries, such as Poland and the Slovak Republic, and in Korea, compared to 2005 levels. At the same time, enrolment is expected to increase by 21% in Israel and by 16% in Ireland.

C1

Analysis

In half of OECD countries, full enrolment in education (defined here as enrolment rates exceeding 90%) begins between the ages of 3 and 4; in the other half of countries, full enrolment starts between ages 5 and 7. In almost two-thirds of OECD countries, at least 75% of 3-4 year-olds are enrolled in either pre-primary or primary programmes; participation is higher in European countries than in other OECD countries (78% and 72%, respectively) (Table C1.1a and see Indicator C2). In Belgium, Denmark, France, Iceland, Norway and Spain, enrolment of 3-4 year-olds reached 95% or more in 2010.

Box C1.1. **Expected years in education**

Under present enrolment patterns, children entering education can expect to spend an additional year in education for each age in which there is full enrolment in a country. Unlike graduation rates, which measure the expected percentage of the population just beginning education to graduate from a specific level, expected years in education takes account of all participation in education, including discontinuous and incomplete participation in education programmes.

Some countries, such as the Nordic countries, Australia, Belgium and New Zealand, have significant shares of the adult population in education – even beyond the age of 40. This is explained by higher part-time enrolment and by lifelong learning. For instance, credit-based systems in Sweden allow adults to participate in formal education as a way to increase their skills. Expected years in education is only an estimate of the potential number of years an individual may expect to be in education. This measure does not correspond to present educational attainment, and may also differ from projections of future attainment, because the time spent in a programme may differ within the population.

On average, a 5-year-old child in an OECD country is expected to remain in education more than 17.5 years before reaching age 40. This same child is expected to be enrolled in full-time studies for 16.5 years: 9.5 years in primary and lower secondary education, 3.3 years in upper secondary education, and 2.6 years in tertiary education. She or he can also expect to participate in an additional 1.2 years of part-time studies, mainly at the tertiary level of education.

Among countries with available data, education expectancy ranges from 12.4 years in China (full-time only) and 14.2 years in Indonesia to 19 years or more in Iceland and Sweden to almost 20 years in Finland. (Table C1.7a).

Participation in compulsory education

Compulsory education includes primary and lower secondary programmes in all OECD countries, as well as upper secondary education in most countries. Between the ages of 5 and 14, enrolment rates are above 90% in all OECD and other G20 countries except India. In all countries except India, Poland, the Russian Federation and Turkey, the rates in 2010 were higher than 95% (Table C1.1a).

Using demographic projections and assuming that present near-full enrolment will stay constant, it is anticipated that in 26 out of 37 countries with available data, the population of students between ages 5 and 14 is likely to decrease or stay constant in 2015, compared to 2005 levels. The notable exceptions to this are Ireland, Israel and Spain, which are likely to see increases of more than 10% in this cohort. Mainly Eastern European countries, Germany and Korea are likely to see students in this age group decrease, ranging from -25% in Korea to -10% in Estonia (Table C1.6 and Chart C1.3). Since most education expenditure is allocated to basic education, this change could have a sizeable budgetary impact in some countries (see Indicator B4).

Participation in upper secondary education

In recent decades, countries have increased the diversity of upper secondary programmes. This diversification has been driven by the increasing demand for upper secondary education and an evolution of the curriculum from general knowledge taught in general programmes and practical skills reserved to vocational studies, to more comprehensive programmes leading to more flexible pathways.

Enrolment rates for 15-19 year-olds indicate the number of individuals participating in upper secondary education, which is part of compulsory education in most OECD countries (Table C1.1b, available on line), or in transition to upper levels of education. In Argentina, Austria, Brazil, Chile, China, Indonesia, Israel, Luxembourg, Mexico, New Zealand, Turkey and the United Kingdom, more than 20% of 15-19 year-olds are not enrolled in education (Table C1.1a and Chart C1.2).

In all countries with available data (except Argentina for 16-year-olds, China, Indonesia, Mexico and Turkey), at least 85% of 15-16 year-olds are enrolled in upper secondary education. In most OECD and other G20 countries, the sharpest decline in enrolment rates occurs at the end of upper secondary education.

Different age patterns of enrolment reflect different requirements in terms of level completion or enrolment in upper secondary within an age limit. Some countries like Belgium, Germany and Portugal allow older students to complete upper secondary education on a part-time basis. In the Netherlands, upper secondary vocational programmes have a duration that goes beyond 20 years old. This factor – combined with longer programmes, repetition of grades, late entry into the labour market or participation in education while employed – has led to larger numbers of older students in upper secondary education. In some OECD countries, one-quarter or more of 20-year-olds are still enrolled in upper secondary education. This is the case in Denmark (31%), Germany (26%), Iceland (38%), Luxembourg (27%) and the Netherlands (27%), (Table C1.1b, available on line).

Enrolment rates among 15-19 year-olds in OECD countries increased on average by 10.4 percentage points between 1995 and 2010. This is mostly due to a convergence of enrolment rates in OECD countries in the past 15 years. While the rates increased by more than 20 percentage points during this period in the Czech Republic, Greece, Hungary and Turkey (despite having the largest increase in cohort size among OECD countries), and by nearly 15 points or more in Ireland, Mexico, Poland and Portugal, they have remained virtually unchanged in Belgium, Canada (until 2009), Germany, Israel and the Netherlands. In all of these countries except Israel, more than 85% of 15-19 year-olds are enrolled in education. In France, the enrolment rate among this age group decreased from 89% to 84% during this period (Table C1.2 and Chart C1.2).

Chart C1.2. **Enrolment rates of 15-19 year-olds (1995, 2000 and 2010)**
Full-time and part-time students in public and private institutions

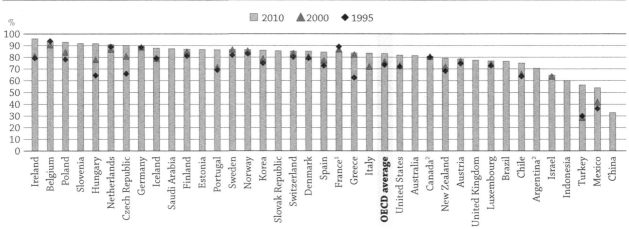

1. Excludes overseas departments for 1995.
2. Year of reference 2009.
Countries are ranked in descending order of the enrolment rates of 15-19 year-olds in 2010.
Source: OECD. Argentina, China, India and Indonesia: UNESCO Institute for Statistics (World Education Indicators programme). Saudi Arabia: UNESCO Institute for Statistics. Table C1.2. See Annex 3 for notes (*www.oecd.org/edu/eag2012*).
StatLink ⌐┓╕┗ http://dx.doi.org/10.1787/888932662998

C1

Chart C1.3. **Evolution in the number of students from 2005 (2010 and 2015)**

Evolution in the number of students, projections to 2015 are made assuming 2010 enrolment rates stay constant.
Full-time and part-time students in public and private institutions, 2005 = 0

■ 2010   ▢ Projection to 2015

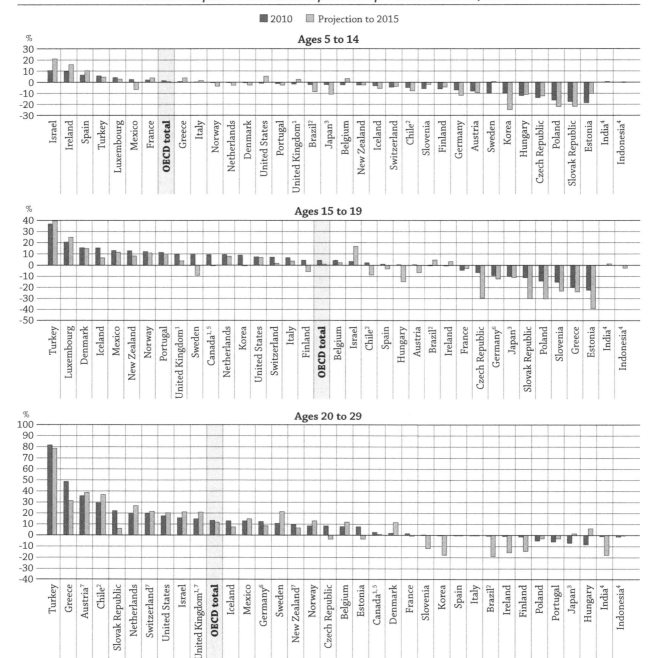

1. Change compared to 2006.
2. Change compared to 2007.
3. Excluding tertiary levels of education.
4. Change compared to 2010.
5. Reference year 2009 instead of 2010.
6. Excludes advanced research programmes.
7. A high proportion of students between the ages of 20 and 29 are international students, changes in migration patterns may affect projections.
Countries are ranked in descending order of the change in the number of students between 2005 and 2010.
Source: OECD Education Database, OECD (2011), "Labour Force Statistics: Population projections", OECD Employment and Labour Market Statistics (database). Argentina, China, India and Indonesia: UNESCO Institute for Statistics (World Education Indicators programme). Table C1.6. See Annex 3 for notes (*www.oecd.org/edu/eag2012*).

StatLink ⟐⟐⟐ http://dx.doi.org/10.1787/888932663017

C1

Enrolment rates for 15-19 year-olds increased steadily in nearly all OECD countries between 1995 and 2005. The enrolment rate for 15-19 year-olds increased from an average of 73% in 1995 to 81% in 2005. The pace slowed between 2005 and 2009, with rates rising to 82% in 2009 and about one-half of countries showing variations around or below one percentage point. In Estonia, rates decreased by nearly 3 percentage points during this period, only to recover again in 2010. In Greece, rates decreased by nearly 14 percentage points between 2005 and 2010.

In around one-third of countries, the largest increase in enrolment among 15-19 year-olds since 2005 occurred between 2009 and 2010. In Iceland, Ireland, Spain, Turkey and the United Kingdom, enrolment rates increased by around 3% or more. All of these countries have also experienced significant increases in youth unemployment between 2008 and 2009.

Many countries have reached near universal access to education for 15-19 year-olds. In Belgium, Hungary, Ireland, the Netherlands, Poland and Slovenia, enrolment rates reached more than 90% in 2010 (in Belgium, they had already reached this level in 1995) (Table C1.2). A decline in the population of 15-19 year-olds since 2005 may have helped to augment enrolment rates even further in Eastern European countries within the existing system capacity (Table C1.6).

Even though the size of the 15-19 year-old cohort across all OECD countries has been stable in recent years and is likely to remain so in the near future, there are stark differences between countries. While some countries like Turkey (37%), Luxembourg (20%) and Denmark and Iceland (15%) experienced large increases in this cohort between 2005 and 2010, Eastern European countries show decreases in this cohort ranging from 7% in the Czech Republic to 22% in Estonia (Table C1.6 and Chart C1.3).

Looking at the demographic evolution in different countries, this scenario is likely to intensify in the coming years. Since enrolment rates for 15-19 year-olds are still increasing in most countries, the projection using demographic evolution gives a lower bound to the expected number of students. If present enrolment rates remain constant, Estonia will have 39% fewer students in this cohort in 2015 compared to 2005, and 35% fewer in 2020. This is likely due to Estonia's negative immigration balance and a drastic decline in its birth rate in the 1990s. The Czech Republic, Greece, Poland, the Slovak Republic and Slovenia are expected to see cohort decreases of more than 20% (Table C1.6 and Chart C1.3). On the other hand, countries such as Denmark and Norway are likely to see this cohort increase by around 10% or more in 2015 compared to a decade earlier. This is also the case in Israel, Luxembourg, Mexico, Portugal and Turkey.

Vocational and apprenticeship programmes

The structure of vocational education and training (VET) programmes varies between countries. In many countries, the current structure of vocational education was established as far back as the Industrial Revolution (CEDEFOP, 2004), but these systems are likely to evolve given the increased demand for acquired skills in the labour market, as well as the increasing flexibility and diversification of education systems. Recent policies have placed a new emphasis on vocational education, as countries with well-established vocational and apprenticeship programmes have been more effective in holding the line on youth unemployment by smoothing the transition from education to work (see Indicator C5). For example, the European Union has launched the Copenhagen Process, which aims to promote reforms to national qualification frameworks (CEDEFOP, 2010) and an outcomes-based approach for VET. An apprenticeship pilot programme has been developed in Sweden as part of this process. At the same time, some consider vocational education a less-attractive option than more academic education, and some research suggests that participation in vocational education increases the risk of unemployment at later ages (Hanushek, et al., 2011).

Detailed classifications of vocational programmes can be hard to determine between and sometimes even within countries. Nonetheless, three main models exist:

- In some countries, like Sweden, academic and vocational upper secondary programmes have a common core curriculum. In the United States, vocational programmes are prevalent in some states but not in others; apprenticeship programmes also exist, but they generally are not part of the formal education system.

C1

■ Other countries provide distinctive vocational and general education with parallel work-based and school-based programmes. This model is prevalent in Germanic countries and the former Austro-Hungarian region, and has led to significant participation in vocational education.

■ A third set of countries provides vocational training independently from general programmes, and both systems have evolved independently. This is the case in France, Italy and Norway.

Definitions of the scope of general, pre-vocational, vocational, and school- and work-based programmes are provided below.

Vocational programmes in OECD countries offer different combinations of vocational or pre-vocational studies along with apprenticeship programmes. Upper secondary students in many education systems can enrol in vocational programmes, but some OECD countries delay vocational training until students graduate from upper secondary education. While vocational programmes are offered as advanced upper secondary education in Austria, Hungary and Spain, similar programmes are offered as post-secondary education in Canada.

Among countries for which data are available, in 14 out of 38 countries, the majority of upper secondary students pursues pre-vocational or vocational programmes. However, in 16 out of 38 countries, at least 60% of upper secondary students are enrolled in general programmes, even though pre-vocational and/or vocational programmes are offered (Table C1.3). In Brazil, Canada, Japan, Korea and Mexico more than three-quarters of students are in general programmes.

In many OECD countries, upper secondary vocational education is school-based. However, in Austria and the Czech Republic, at least 30% of students in vocational education participate in programmes that combine school- and work-based elements. In Denmark, Germany and Switzerland, at least 45% of students in vocational education are enrolled in those kinds of programmes.

Table C1.3 includes enrolments in apprenticeship programmes that are a recognised part of countries' education systems. In most countries except Argentina, Brazil, Chile, China, Greece, Indonesia, Italy, Japan, Korea, Mexico, New Zealand and Portugal, some form of apprenticeship system exists. The majority of countries has combined school- and work-based apprenticeship programmes.

In most countries, a student who successfully completes an apprenticeship programme is usually awarded an upper secondary or post-secondary qualification. In some countries, higher qualifications are possible (such as an Advanced Diploma in Australia).

The importance of VET programmes can also be seen in enrolment rates by age groups. More than 40% of 15-19 year-olds participate in pre-vocational or vocational programmes at the upper secondary level in Austria, Belgium, the Czech Republic, Italy, the Slovak Republic and Slovenia.

Across OECD countries, there is no clear correlation between higher VET participation levels and lower unemployment rates among 15-29 year-olds in 2010 (see Indicator C5 and Table C1.3). However, participation in VET programmes may be a factor in lowering youth inactivity levels. Among the 13 OECD countries with above-average participation of 15-19 year-olds in upper secondary VET programmes, only the Slovak Republic and Italy have higher-than-average levels of 15-29 year-olds who are inactive and not in education (NEETs). The inverse is also true: 13 out of 15 countries with above-average NEET levels also have lower-than-average participation in VET programmes (see Table C5.2a in Indicator C5).

Participation of young adults in education

On average in OECD countries, 27% of 20-29 year-olds were enrolled in education – mostly tertiary education – in 2010. In Australia, Belgium, Denmark, Finland, Germany, Greece, Iceland, Korea, the Netherlands, New Zealand, Slovenia and Sweden, 30% or more of people in this age group were enrolled in education (Table C1.1a and Chart C1.1).

C1

Policies to expand education have led to greater access to tertiary education in many OECD and other G20 countries in the last 15 years. So far, this has more than compensated for the declines in cohort sizes that had led to predictions of stable or declining demand for education in some OECD countries. On average, in all OECD countries with comparable data, participation rates for 20-29 year-olds grew by 10.1 percentage points from 1995 to 2010. Almost all OECD and other G20 countries saw some increase in participation rates among 20-29 year-olds in this period. Growth of at least 12 percentage points was seen in the Czech Republic, Finland, Greece, Hungary, Iceland, Korea, New Zealand, Poland, Sweden and Turkey. This growth was particularly significant in the Czech Republic and Hungary, which previously ranked low among OECD countries on this measure, but have recently moved to the middle (Table C1.2).

As with 15-19 year-olds, the increase in enrolment rates for 20-29 year-olds slowed before 2009. Almost one-third of countries showed less than one percentage point of variation between 2005 and 2009 (Table C1.2 and Chart C1.1).

Trends changed significantly from 2009 to 2010. In 18 out of 32 OECD countries, the largest increase in enrolment rates among 20-29 year-olds between 2005 and 2010 occurred between 2009 and 2010. The same is true for the whole decade, on average, in OECD countries and more specifically in Austria, France, Spain, Sweden, Switzerland and Turkey. These increases may reveal the general awareness of the benefits of participating in education in a restricted labour market.

Returning to or continuing studies is an option for adults to increase and diversify their skills and make them more adaptable to the changing demands of the labour market. In the current context of higher unemployment and changing skills needs in the labour market, some countries, such as Chile, have established specific policies to encourage adults to follow tertiary-type B studies.

Chart C1.4 shows the relationship between changes in the proportion of the unemployed population and changes in enrolment rates among 20-29 year-olds after 2005. The vertical axis displays the correlation between changes in enrolment rates and changes in the proportion of the unemployed population between 2005 and 2010. This is compared to the change in enrolment rates between 2009 and 2010, on the horizontal axis.

Countries with stronger correlations between the evolution of unemployment and enrolment rates in the 2005-2010 period for those aged 20 and 29 saw the highest increases in enrolment between 2009 and 2010. This revealed a return to education among unemployed individuals in Estonia, Iceland, Ireland, Spain, Sweden, Turkey and especially in Greece, which saw an increase in enrolment of nearly 12 percentage points between 2008 and 2010. These countries, except Iceland, Sweden and Turkey, were the countries with the four highest percentages of unemployed 20-29 year-olds (according to figures from OECD, 2011b). On the other hand, some countries with high youth unemployment, such as Italy, Poland, Portugal, the Slovak Republic and Luxembourg (where student mobility is high) showed an inverse correlation between unemployment and enrolment in the last five years. In these countries, enrolment rates remained virtually constant or decreased slightly between 2009 and 2010, except for Luxembourg, where data is available only for 2008 and 2010 (Table C1.2, Table C1.8, available on line, and Chart C1.4).

In 17 out of 32 OECD countries, the correlation between unemployment and enrolment is higher than 0.6, indicating a high level of synchronisation between participation in education and labour market variations for 20-29 year-olds.

After an average cohort expansion of 13% between 2005 and 2010 in OECD countries, the enrolment rates of 20-29 year-olds will likely continue to expand through 2015. Assuming that present enrolment rates stay constant, in 15 out of 23 OECD countries, the increase in the number of 20-29 year-old students seen between 2005 and 2010 is likely to continue and lead to an increase of more than 10% in 2015 over 2005 levels, putting further pressure on educational systems. The number of students in this age group is likely to increase more than 11% on average compared with 2005 levels, more than 30% in Austria and Greece, and more than 70% in Turkey. On the other hand, Hungary, Japan, Poland and Portugal are expected to see a decrease of more than 13% in the number of students in this age group, compared with 2005 levels (Table C1.6).

Chart C1.4. **Unemployment and enrolment among 20-29 year-olds (2005 to 2010)**

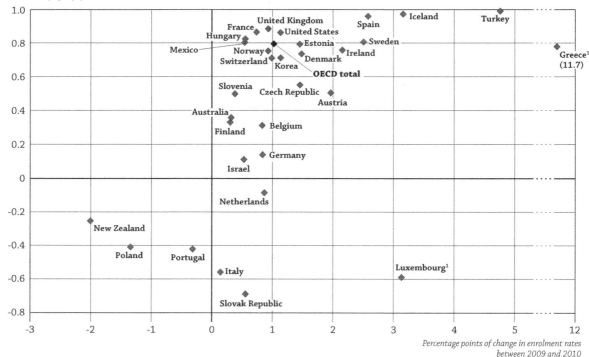

Correlation between changes in the proportion
of the population enrolled and changes
in the unemployed population between 2005 and 2010

Percentage points of change in enrolment rates
between 2009 and 2010

Note: Correlation is calculated by comparing the change in enrolment in a specific year and the change in the proportion of unemployed persons in the previous year.
1. Change in enrolment rates between 2008 and 2010.
Source: OECD. Table C1.2 and Table C1.8 available on line. See Annex 3 for notes (*www.oecd.org/edu/eag2012*).
StatLink ⎙⎙⎙⎙ http://dx.doi.org/10.1787/888932663036

Gender differences

As is the case for entry and graduation rates, the enrolment rate for 15-19 year-olds is higher for girls than for boys in nearly all countries (84% for girls compared to 82% for boys, on average across OECD countries). The difference in favour of girls is especially large in Argentina, at more than 10 percentage points. The reverse gender gap is larger than one percentage point in Switzerland and Turkey. This gap is especially large in Saudi Arabia, where boys' enrolment rates are 49 percentage points higher than girls'.

In some countries, higher enrolment levels for young women are linked to improved access to education, but they can also imply a later entry into the labour market than for men. On the other hand, less access to child care and cultural barriers may lead to lower levels of participation among women.

On average across OECD countries, more 20-29 year-old women than men participate in education. The difference among 20-29 year-olds is higher than ten percentage points in Slovenia and Sweden. However, the gender gap favours men by more than one percentage point in Germany, Indonesia, Ireland, Korea, Saudi Arabia and Turkey. In Korea, there is a 17 percentage-point gender gap, which is mainly due to delayed graduation among men pursuing their mandatory military service. In all of these countries, gender differences are smaller among 30-39 year-olds. In Ireland and Mexico, more 30-39 year-old women than men are enrolled in education. This may be because women enter education later for family reasons. In the countries in which more 15-19 year-old boys than girls are enrolled, such as Indonesia, Saudi Arabia, Switzerland and Turkey, the trend continues among 20-29 year-olds (Table C1.1a).

C1

Part-time studies

Students in tertiary education are more likely to study full time rather than part time, whether they are enrolled in tertiary-type A (academically-oriented) or B (shorter vocationally oriented) programmes. Students may opt for part-time studies because they may also participate in the labour market at the same time, because of family constraints (particularly for women), because of preferences for different fields of education, or other reasons. On average, there is little gender difference among part-time tertiary students, although slightly more women than men choose this mode of study.

The picture is more diverse at the country level. In tertiary-type B programmes, which are designed for direct entry into the labour market, the proportion of women in part-time enrolment is more than 10 percentage points higher than the proportion of men in Ireland, the Netherlands, Norway and the Slovak Republic. The opposite is true in Germany, Iceland, Luxembourg and Switzerland, where a higher proportion of men is enrolled in part-time studies. It should be noted that in some countries such as Iceland, the Netherlands, Norway and the Slovak Republic, tertiary-type B studies represent a small part of total tertiary enrolment. Gender differences are weaker in tertiary-type A programmes and advanced research programmes. However, in Hungary, Iceland, Norway, the Russian Federation and the Slovak Republic, the proportion of women in part-time studies is more than five percentage points greater than that for men. The reverse is true in Estonia and Finland (Table C1.5).

The relative size of the public and the private sectors

In OECD and other G20 countries, primary and secondary education is mostly provided by public institutions. On average, 90% of primary education students in OECD countries are enrolled in public schools. The proportion is slightly smaller in secondary education, with 86% of lower secondary students and 81% of upper secondary students taught in public schools. Public and government-dependent institutions combined enrol 97% of students at the lower secondary level and 95% of students at the upper secondary level. On the other hand, Indonesia has a significant share (36%) of students at the lower secondary level enrolled in independent private schools. Indonesia, Japan, Mexico and Portugal are the exceptions at the upper secondary level, as independent private providers (those that receive less than 50% of their funds from government sources) take in 50%, 31%, 18% and 19% of students, respectively (Table C1.4 and Indicator D5).

At the tertiary level, the pattern is quite different: private providers generally play a more significant role. For example, 41% of students enrolled in tertiary-type B programmes attend programmes that are totally or partially funded privately, and 32% of students enrolled in tertiary-type A education and advanced research programmes attend independent private or government-dependent private institutions. In the United Kingdom, virtually all tertiary education is provided through government-dependent private institutions. In Israel, 64% of students enrolled in tertiary-type B programmes and 76% of students enrolled in tertiary-type A and advanced research programmes attend these types of institutions. In Estonia, 92% of students enrolled in tertiary-type A and advanced research programmes attend government-dependent private institutions. Independent private institutions are more prominent at the tertiary level than at the pre-tertiary levels (an average of more than 15% of tertiary students attend such institutions), particularly in Brazil, Chile, Japan and Korea, where more than 85% of students enrolled in tertiary-type B programmes attend independent private institutions. More than half of students in these countries and in Indonesia attend tertiary-type A and advanced research programmes in independent private institutions (Table C1.5).

Definitions

Programmes at the secondary level can be subdivided into three categories, based on the degree to which they are oriented towards a specific class of occupations or trades and lead to a qualification that is relevant to the labour market:

In **combined school- and work-based programmes**, less than 75% of the curriculum is presented in the school environment or through distance education. These programmes can be organised in conjunction with educational authorities or institutions and include apprenticeship programmes that involve concurrent

C1

school-based and work-based training, and programmes that involve alternating periods of attendance at educational institutions and participation in work-based training (sometimes referred to as "sandwich" programmes).

General education programmes are not explicitly designed to prepare participants for specific occupations or trades, or for entry into further vocational or technical education programmes (less than 25% of programme content is vocational or technical).

Pre-vocational or pre-technical education programmes are mainly designed to introduce participants to the world of work and to prepare them for entry into further vocational or technical education programmes. Successful completion of such programmes does not lead to a vocational or technical qualification that is directly relevant to the labour market (at least 25% of programme content is vocational or technical).

The degree to which a programme has a vocational or general orientation does not necessarily determine whether participants have access to tertiary education. In several OECD countries, vocationally oriented programmes are designed to prepare students for further study at the tertiary level, and in some countries general programmes do not always provide direct access to further education.

In **school-based programmes**, instruction takes place (either partially or exclusively) in educational institutions. These include special training centres run by public or private authorities or enterprise-based special training centres if these qualify as educational institutions. These programmes can have an on-the-job training component involving some practical experience at the workplace. Programmes are classified as school-based if at least 75% of the programme curriculum is presented in the school environment. This may include distance education.

Vocational or technical education programmes prepare participants for direct entry into specific occupations without further training. Successful completion of such programmes leads to a vocational or technical qualification that is relevant to the labour market.

Vocational and pre-vocational programmes are further divided into two categories (school-based and combined school- and work-based programmes) based on the amount of training provided in school as opposed to the workplace.

Methodology

Data on enrolments are for the school year 2009-10 and are based on the UOE data collection on educational systems administered annually by the OECD.

Except where otherwise noted, figures are based on head counts; that is, they do not distinguish between full-time and part-time study because the concept of part-time study is not recognised by some countries. In some OECD countries, part-time education is only partially covered in the reported data.

Net enrolment rates, expressed as percentages in Tables C1.1a and C1.2, are calculated by dividing the number of students of a particular age group enrolled in all levels of education by the size of the population of that age group. In Table C1.1b, available on line, the net enrolment rate is calculated for students at a particular level of education.

In Table C1.2, data on trends in enrolment rates for the years 1995, 2000, 2001, 2002, 2003 and 2004 are based on a special survey carried out in January 2007 among OECD countries and four of six partner countries at the time (Brazil, Chile, Israel and the Russian Federation).

Expected years in education are calculated as the proportion of the population enrolled at specific ages summed over an age range. The main assumption is that every year of full enrolment would correspond to a full year of expected education for an individual below that age.

Enrolment projections are done using OECD demographic projections available on line (OECD, 2011c). All enrolment rates have been assumed to remain constant as they were in 2010.

The statistical data for Israel are supplied by and under the responsibility of the relevant Israeli authorities. The use of such data by the OECD is without prejudice to the status of the Golan Heights, East Jerusalem and Israeli settlements in the West Bank under the terms of international law.

References

CEDEFOP (2004), *Towards a history of vocational education and training (VET) in Europe in a comparative perspective*, European Centre for the Development of Vocational Training, Publications Office of the European Union, Luxembourg.

CEDEFOP (2010), *The Bruges Communiqué on enhanced European Cooperation in Vocational Education and Training*, European Centre for the Development of Vocational Training, Publications Office of the European Union, Luxembourg.

Hanushek, E., L. Woessmann and L. Zhang, (2011), "General Education, Vocational Education, and Labor-Market Outcomes over the Life-Cycle", *Forschungsinstitut zur Zukunft der Arbeit*, Discussion Paper No. 6083, October 2011.

OECD (2010a), *PISA 2009 Results: Overcoming Social Background: Equity in Learning Opportunities and Outcomes*, OECD Publishing.

OECD (2010b), *Learning for Jobs*, OECD Publishing.

OECD (2011a), *Equity and Quality in Education: Supporting disadvantaged students and schools*, OECD Publishing.

OECD (2011b), *Key Short-Term Economic Indicators, http://stats.oecd.org/Index.aspx?DataSetCode=KEI,* accessed 20 June 2011.

OECD (2011c), "Labour Force Statistics: Population projections", OECD Employment and Labour Market Statistics Database.

The following additional material relevant to this indicator is available on line:

- *Table C1.1b. Transition characteristics from age 15 to 20, by level of education (2010)*
  StatLink ▦⬛ http://dx.doi.org/10.1787/888932666817

- *Table C1.7b. Education expectancy (2010)*
  StatLink ▦⬛ http://dx.doi.org/10.1787/888932666950

- *Table C1.7c. Expected years in tertiary education (2010)*
  StatLink ▦⬛ http://dx.doi.org/10.1787/888932666969

- *Table C1.8 Unemployment and variations in enrolment rates among the population aged 20-29 (2004 to 2010)*
  StatLink ▦⬛ http://dx.doi.org/10.1787/888932666988

C1

Table C1.1a. Enrolment rates, by age (2010)

Full-time and part-time students in public and private institutions

	Starting age of compulsory education	Ending age of compulsory education	Number of years during which over 90% of the population are enrolled	Age range at which over 90% of the population are enrolled	Students as a percentage of the population of a specific age group						
					Age 2 and under[1]	Ages 3 and 4	Ages 5-14	Ages 15-19 Men + Women	Ages 20-29 Men + Women	Ages 30-39 Men + Women	Ages 40 and over
	(1)	(2)	(3)	(4)	(5)	(6)	(7)	(8)	(11)	(14)	(17)
Australia	6	17	12	5 - 16	a	30.9	99.2	81.4	31.9	12.0	4.7
Austria	6	15	11	5 - 15	3.6	75.1	98.4	78.4	25.2	5.4	0.8
Belgium	6	18	15	3 - 17	16.9	98.9	98.6	93.3	30.3	8.9	3.7
Canada[2]	6	16-18	12	6 - 17	a	24.1	98.7	80.8	24.9	5.7	1.2
Chile	6	18	10	6 - 15	0.4	56.5	95.1	74.8	25.2	4.3	0.7
Czech Republic	6	15	13	5 - 17	5.8	72.5	98.1	90.2	24.0	3.9	0.5
Denmark	6	16	13	4 - 16	a	92.3	99.1	85.0	38.4	8.1	1.5
Estonia	7	16	14	4 - 17	n	89.2	96.4	86.5	27.7	6.4	0.8
Finland	7	16	13	6 - 18	a	51.7	95.5	86.8	41.7	15.4	3.6
France	6	16	14	3 - 16	5.1	*100.0*	99.6	84.2	19.9	2.7	x(14)
Germany	6	18	14	4 - 17	7.8	92.4	99.4	89.5	30.8	3.0	0.2
Greece	5	14-15	13	5 - 17	n	25.9	*100.0*	83.4	40.3	1.0	m
Hungary	5	18	14	4 - 17	a	82.2	98.5	91.7	25.4	4.4	0.6
Iceland	6	16	14	3 - 16	a	95.8	98.5	87.8	38.2	13.6	3.7
Ireland	6	16	14	5 - 18	n	66.9	*100.0*	95.7	20.9	4.9	1.1
Israel	6	17	12	5 - 16	n	82.6	97.8	64.6	22.4	5.8	1.0
Italy	6	16	14	3 - 16	4.9	94.8	99.5	83.3	21.5	3.2	0.1
Japan	6	15	14	4 - 17	0.1	86.1	*100.0*	m	m	m	m
Korea	6	14	12	6 - 17	31.6	80.2	99.7	85.9	30.2	2.0	0.5
Luxembourg[3]	4	15	12	4 - 15	1.4	84.5	95.8	76.7	12.8	1.5	0.2
Mexico	4	15	11	4 - 14	n	69.4	*100.0*	53.8	11.9	4.0	0.8
Netherlands	5	18	14	4 - 17	n	50.1	99.5	90.7	30.0	3.0	0.8
New Zealand	5	16	13	4 - 16	n	90.5	*100.0*	79.1	30.1	11.8	4.7
Norway	6	16	15	3 - 17	a	95.7	99.5	86.3	29.4	7.0	1.7
Poland	5	16	13	6 - 18	1.3	52.5	94.9	92.7	29.9	5.0	x(14)
Portugal	6	15	13	5 - 17	n	79.5	*100.0*	86.4	23.5	9.1	2.8
Slovak Republic	6	16	11	6 - 16	2.8	66.5	95.8	85.3	20.6	4.3	0.7
Slovenia	6	15	13	6 - 18	n	83.7	97.1	91.8	34.0	5.0	0.7
Spain	6	16	14	3 - 16	26.5	99.0	99.5	84.3	24.4	4.7	1.1
Sweden	7	16	16	3 - 18	a	92.0	98.5	86.4	36.5	13.7	2.8
Switzerland	5-7	15	13	5 - 17	a	22.4	*100.0*	85.1	24.1	4.3	0.5
Turkey	6	14	8	6 - 13	m	10.3	94.1	56.2	19.6	3.2	0.4
United Kingdom	4-5	16	13	4 - 16	3.1	90.0	*100.0*	77.4	18.2	5.9	1.6
United States	4-6	17	11	6 - 16	n	59.9	96.8	81.7	25.5	6.6	1.5
OECD average	6	16	13	4 - 16	3.3	71.9	95.9	82.9	27.0	6.1	1.5
EU21 average	6	16	13	4 - 16	3.8	78.1	98.7	86.7	27.4	5.7	1.3
Argentina[2]	5	17	11	5 - 15	n	55.3	*100.0*	70.4	26.6	7.8	1.4
Brazil	6	17	11	6 - 16	7.7	43.9	96.2	76.4	20.2	8.4	2.6
China	m	m	m	m	m	m	m	32.8	m	m	m
India	m	m	m	m	m	m	77.7	m	m	m	m
Indonesia	m	15	8	6 - 14	n	13.3	*100.0*	60.0	10.3	n	n
Russian Federation	7	17	m	7 - 14	17.3	71.1	93.1	m	m	m	m
Saudi Arabia	6	11	7	11 - 17	m	m	m	87.1	19.2	1.4	0.1
South Africa[2]	7	15	m	m	m	m	m	m	m	m	m
G20 average	m	m	m	m	m	m	92.1	73.4	m	m	m

(OECD countries grouped under label "OECD"; Argentina through South Africa grouped under "Other G20")

Note: Ending age of compulsory education is the age at which compulsory schooling ends. For example, an ending age of 18 indicates that all students under 18 are legally obliged to participate in education. Mismatches between the coverage of the population data and the enrolment data mean that the participation rates may be underestimated for countries such as Luxembourg that are net exporters of students, and may be overestimated for those that are net importers. Rates above 100% in the calculation are shown in italics. Enrolment rates by gender for the 15-19, 20-29 and 30-39 year-old age groups are available for consultation on line (see StatLink below).

1. Includes only institution-based pre-primary programmes. These are not the only form of early childhood education available below the age of 3, therefore inferences about access to and quality of pre-primary education and care should be made with caution. In countries where an integrated system of pre-primary and care exists enrolment rate is noted as not applicable for children aged 2 and under.
2. Year of reference 2009.
3. Underestimated because many resident students go to school in the neighbouring countries.
Source: OECD. Argentina, China, India and Indonesia: UNESCO Institute for Statistics (World Education Indicators programme). Saudi Arabia and South Africa: UNESCO Institute for Statistics. See Annex 3 for notes (*www.oecd.org/edu/eag2012*).
Please refer to the Reader's Guide for information concerning the symbols replacing missing data.
StatLink ⫯⫯⫯ http://dx.doi.org/10.1787/888932666798

Table C1.2. **Trends in enrolment rates (1995-2010)**
Full-time and part-time students in public and private institutions

C1

		15-19 year-olds						20-29 year-olds					
		Students as a percentage of the population of this age group						Index of change in the number of students (1995 = 100)	Students as a percentage of the population of this age group					Index of change in the number of students (1995 = 100)
		1995	2000	2005	2008	2009	2010		1995	2000	2005	2008	2009	2010	
OECD	Australia	m	m	m	m	80	81	**m**	23	28	33	33	32	32	**162**
	Austria	75	77	80	79	79	78	**115**	16	18	19	22	23	25	**139**
	Belgium	94	91	94	92	93	93	**106**	24	25	29	29	30	30	**116**
	Canada	80	81	80	81	81	m	**119**	22	23	26	25	25	m	**129**
	Chile	64	66	74	74	73	75	**150**	m	m	m	21	23	25	**1016**
	Czech Republic	66	81	90	90	89	90	**95**	10	14	20	21	23	24	**243**
	Denmark	79	80	85	84	84	85	**115**	30	35	38	37	37	38	**103**
	Estonia	m	m	87	84	85	87	**m**	m	m	27	26	26	28	**m**
	Finland	81	85	87	87	87	87	**109**	28	38	43	43	41	42	**148**
	France	89	87	85	84	84	84	**101**	19	19	20	19	19	20	**100**
	Germany	88	88	89	89	88	89	**103**	20	24	28	28	30	31	**126**
	Greece	62	82	97	83	m	83	**99**	13	16	24	29	m	40	**283**
	Hungary	64	78	87	89	90	92	**101**	10	19	24	25	25	25	**230**
	Iceland	79	79	85	84	85	88	**127**	24	31	37	35	35	38	**181**
	Ireland	79	81	89	90	92	96	**99**	14	16	21	18	19	21	**192**
	Israel[1]	m	64	65	64	64	65	**112**	m	m	20	21	22	22	**125**
	Italy[1]	m	72	80	82	82	83	**112**	m	17	20	21	21	21	**102**
	Japan	m	m	m	m	m	m	**m**	m	m	m	m	m	m	**m**
	Korea	75	79	86	89	87	86	**100**	15	24	27	28	29	30	**159**
	Luxembourg[1]	73	74	72	75	m	77	**130**	m	5	6	10	m	13	**m**
	Mexico	36	42	48	52	52	54	**155**	8	9	11	11	11	12	**155**
	Netherlands	89	87	86	90	90	91	**112**	21	22	26	29	29	30	**117**
	New Zealand	68	72	74	74	81	79	**139**	17	23	30	29	32	30	**185**
	Norway	83	86	86	87	86	86	**124**	25	28	29	29	29	29	**108**
	Poland	78	84	92	93	93	93	**94**	16	24	31	30	31	30	**223**
	Portugal	69	71	73	81	85	86	**89**	22	22	22	23	24	24	**94**
	Slovak Republic[2]	m	m	85	85	85	85	**95**	m	m	16	19	20	21	**165**
	Slovenia	m	m	91	91	91	92	**m**	m	m	32	33	34	34	**m**
	Spain	73	77	81	81	81	84	**81**	21	24	22	21	22	24	**109**
	Sweden	82	86	87	86	87	86	**132**	22	33	36	33	34	36	**163**
	Switzerland	80	83	83	85	85	85	**122**	15	19	22	23	23	24	**149**
	Turkey	30	28	41	46	53	56	**179**	7	5	10	13	15	20	**331**
	United Kingdom	m	m	m	73	74	77	**m**	m	m	m	17	17	18	**m**
	United States	72	73	79	81	81	82	**136**	19	20	23	23	24	26	**151**
	OECD average	73	76	81	81	82	83	**116**	18	22	25	25	26	27	**190**
	OECD average for countries with data available for all reference years	73	77	81	82	83	83		18	22	26	26	27	28	
	EU21 average	78	81	86	85	86	87	**105**	19	22	25	25	27	27	**156**
Other G20	Argentina	m	m	m	71	70	m	**m**	m	m	m	25	27	m	**m**
	Brazil[1]	m	m	m	76	75	76	**m**	m	m	m	21	21	20	**m**
	China	m	m	m	m	m	33	**m**	m	m	m	m	m	m	**m**
	India	m	m	m	m	m	m	**m**	m	m	m	m	m	m	**m**
	Indonesia	m	m	m	m	62	60	**m**	m	m	m	m	m	m	**m**
	Russian Federation	m	71	74	77	m	m	**m**	m	m	19	20	m	m	**m**
	Saudi Arabia	m	m	m	m	m	87	**m**	m	m	m	m	m	19	**m**
	South Africa	m	m	m	m	m	m	**m**	m	m	m	m	m	m	**m**
	G20 average	m	m	m	m	m	m	**m**	m	m	m	m	m	m	**m**

Note: Columns showing years 2001 and 2003, 2004, 2006 and 2007 are available for consultation on line (see *StatLink* below).
1. 1997=100.
2. 1998=100.
Source: OECD. Argentina, China, India and Indonesia: UNESCO Institute for Statistics (World Education Indicators programme). Saudi Arabia: UNESCO Institute for Statistics. See Annex 3 for notes (*www.oecd.org/edu/eag2012*).
Please refer to the Reader's Guide for information concerning the symbols replacing missing data.
StatLink ᐧᐧᐧ http://dx.doi.org/10.1787/888932666836

C1

Table C1.3. Upper secondary and post-secondary non-tertiary enrolment patterns (2010)

Enrolment in upper secondary programmes in public and private institutions, by programme orientation, and enrolment rates by age group, including students in public and private institutions

	Upper secondary education							Post-secondary non-tertiary education						
	Share of students by orientation			Vocational combined school- and work-based	Enrolment rates among 15-19 year-olds			Share of students by orientation			Combined school- and work-based	Enrolment rates among 15-24 year-olds		
					Prevocational and vocational							Prevocational and vocational		
	General	Pre-vocational	Vocational		Full-time + part-time	Part-time	Combined work- and school-based	General	Pre-vocational	Vocational		Full-time + part-time	Part-time	Combined work- and school-based
	(1)	(2)	(3)	(4)	(5)	(6)	(7)	(11)	(12)	(13)	(14)	(15)	(16)	(17)
Australia	52.5	a	47.5	m	8.1	6.9	m	a	a	100.0	m	1.9	1.2	m
Austria	23.2	5.7	71.0	34.6	47.3	m	21.3	n	n	100.0	19.6	5.6	m	m
Belgium	27.0	a	73.0	3.1	41.2	2.5	1.8	0.7	a	99.3	19.9	1.8	n	0.4
Canada[1]	94.4	x(3)	5.6	a	m	m	m	m	m	m	m	m	m	m
Chile	66.8	a	33.2	a	20.7	n	a	a	a	a	a	a	a	a
Czech Republic	26.9	n	73.1	31.9	52.4	n	22.9	36.5	n	63.5	8.9	1.9	n	0.3
Denmark	53.5	a	46.5	45.3	15.6	n	15.2	100.0	a	a	a	a	a	a
Estonia	65.8	a	34.2	0.3	18.9	n	0.1	a	a	100.0	4.4	3.1	n	0.1
Finland	30.3	a	69.7	13.4	30.2	n	5.8	a	a	100.0	68.8	0.1	n	0.1
France	55.7	a	44.3	12.2	25.1	m	6.9	38.4	n	61.6	1.5	0.3	m	n
Germany	48.5	a	51.5	45.5	18.7	n	m	26.0	a	74.0	m	4.0	n	m
Greece	69.3	a	30.7	a	15.3	0.6	a	a	a	100.0	a	1.4	n	m
Hungary	74.2	10.4	15.4	15.4	19.6	0.1	11.7	a	a	100.0	a	4.4	0.5	a
Iceland	65.7	1.9	32.3	14.6	m	m	6.6	n	n	100.0	13.7	0.4	0.1	n
Ireland	62.5	32.5	5.0	5.0	17.0	n	2.3	a	a	100.0	27.1	8.0	0.5	2.2
Israel	61.8	a	38.2	3.9	21.5	n	2.2	88.8	11.2	a	a	0.1	n	a
Italy	40.0	a	60.0	a	44.2	n	a	a	a	100.0	a	0.2	n	a
Japan	76.5	0.9	22.6	a	13.3	0.3	a	a	a	a	a	m	a	a
Korea	76.3	a	23.7	a	13.6	n	a	a	a	a	a	a	a	a
Luxembourg	38.5	a	61.5	14.5	36.0	n	8.5	a	a	100.0	n	0.6	n	n
Mexico	90.8	a	9.2	a	3.0	n	a	a	a	a	a	a	a	a
Netherlands	33.0	a	67.0	20.9	28.8	n	9.0	a	a	100.0	83.8	0.1	n	0.1
New Zealand	69.9	4.0	26.1	a	6.2	4.0	a	14.7	0.8	84.5	a	3.2	2.1	a
Norway	46.1	a	53.9	15.3	30.9	0.7	8.8	12.0	a	88.0	n	0.9	0.1	a
Poland	51.8	a	48.2	6.6	31.7	0.6	4.4	a	a	100.0	a	3.5	2.9	a
Portugal	61.2	3.9	34.9	a	21.7	n	a	a	a	100.0	a	0.4	n	a
Slovak Republic	28.7	a	71.3	28.9	49.5	0.1	20.1	a	a	100.0	a	0.2	n	a
Slovenia	35.4	a	64.6	n	45.7	1.3	0.2	61.2	a	38.8	n	0.2	0.1	n
Spain	55.4	a	44.6	2.2	13.1	1.5	0.7	a	a	a	a	a	a	a
Sweden	43.9	1.1	55.0	1.5	36.3	0.2	n	15.7	n	84.3	n	0.6	0.1	n
Switzerland	33.8	a	66.2	60.6	36.2	n	33.2	61.6	a	38.4	n	0.4	0.1	n
Turkey[2]	57.1	a	42.9	n	m	m	m	a	a	a	a	a	a	a
United Kingdom[3]	67.9	x(7)	32.1	m	18.6	1.3	m	m	m	m	m	m	m	m
United States	m	m	m	m	m	m	m	a	a	100.0	m	m	m	m
OECD average	54	2.0	44.0	12.1	26.0	0.7	9.5	41.4	6.0	88.8	27.5	1.8	0.4	0.3
EU21 average	47	2.7	50.1	14.0	29.8	0.4	6.9	13.9	n	81.1	12.3	1.8	0.2	0.2
Argentina[1]	75	a	25.3	a	9.2	n	a	a	a	a	a	a	a	a
Brazil	87	a	12.7	a	3.3	x(5)	a	a	a	a	a	a	a	a
China	48	x(3)	51.8	a	m	m	a	75.2	x(12)	24.8	a	m	a	a
India	m	m	m	m	m	m	m	m	m	m	m	m	m	m
Indonesia	59	a	40.6	a	14.8	n	a	a	a	a	a	a	a	a
Russian Federation	51	22.5	26.1	n	8.0	n	m	a	a	100.0	m	m	m	m
Saudi Arabia	m	m	m	m	m	m	m	m	m	m	m	m	m	m
South Africa	m	m	m	m	m	m	m	m	m	m	m	m	m	m
G20 average	65.4	m	33.1	m	m	m	m	46.5	m	80.1	m	m	m	m

Note: Different duration of upper secondary programmes between countries must be taken into account when comparing enrolment rates at this level of education. Columns showing enrolment rates in upper secondary vocational programmes for 20-24 year-olds and in post-secondary non-tertiary vocational programmes for 25-29 year-olds are available for consultation on line (see *StatLink* below).

1. Year of reference 2009.

2. Excludes ISCED 3C.

3. Includes post-secondary non-tertiary education.

Source: OECD. Argentina, China, India and Indonesia: UNESCO Institute for Statistics (World Education Indicators programme). See Annex 3 for notes (*www.oecd.org/edu/eag2012*).

Please refer to the Reader's Guide for information concerning the symbols replacing missing data.

StatLink 🔗 http://dx.doi.org/10.1787/888932666855

Table C1.4. Students in primary and secondary education, by type of institution or mode of enrolment (2010)

Distribution of students, by mode of enrolment and type of institution

		Type of institution									Mode of enrolment	
		Primary			Lower secondary			Upper secondary			Primary and secondary	
		Public	Government-dependent private	Independent private	Public	Government-dependent private	Independent private	Public	Government-dependent private	Independent private	Full-time	Part-time
		(1)	(2)	(3)	(4)	(5)	(6)	(7)	(8)	(9)	(10)	(11)
OECD	Australia[1]	**69.1**	30.9	a	**65.5**	34.5	m	**68.3**	31.5	0.2	**83.6**	16.4
	Austria	**94.3**	5.7	x(2)	**91.0**	9.0	x(5)	**89.3**	10.7	x(8)	**m**	m
	Belgium[1]	**46.2**	53.8	m	**40.2**	59.8	m	**43.3**	56.7	m	**79.5**	20.5
	Canada[2]	**94.0**	6.0	x(2)	**91.4**	8.6	x(5)	**94.2**	5.8	x(8)	**100.0**	a
	Chile	**42.1**	51.0	6.9	**47.1**	46.2	6.7	**40.2**	52.8	7.0	**100.0**	a
	Czech Republic	**98.5**	1.5	a	**97.3**	2.7	a	**85.6**	14.4	a	**99.9**	0.1
	Denmark	**86.3**	13.5	0.2	**74.1**	25.2	0.7	**98.0**	1.9	0.1	**97.0**	3.0
	Estonia	**95.9**	a	4.1	**96.8**	a	3.2	**96.6**	a	3.4	**95.2**	4.2
	Finland	**98.5**	1.5	a	**95.5**	4.5	a	**83.9**	16.1	a	**100.0**	a
	France	**85.2**	14.3	0.5	**78.2**	21.5	0.3	**68.4**	30.6	0.9	**m**	m
	Germany	**95.9**	4.1	x(2)	**90.8**	9.2	x(5)	**92.7**	7.3	x(8)	**99.6**	0.4
	Greece	**92.8**	a	7.2	**94.9**	a	5.1	**95.5**	a	4.5	**97.6**	2.4
	Hungary	**91.3**	8.7	a	**90.5**	9.5	a	**79.3**	20.7	a	**95.7**	4.3
	Iceland	**98.0**	2.0	n	**99.2**	0.8	n	**79.1**	20.2	0.7	**89.5**	10.5
	Ireland	**99.3**	a	0.7	**100.0**	a	a	**98.5**	a	1.5	**99.9**	0.1
	Israel	**m**	m	a	**m**	m	a	**m**	m	a	**100.0**	a
	Italy	**93.2**	a	6.8	**95.9**	a	4.1	**89.0**	5.9	5.1	**99.0**	1.0
	Japan	**98.9**	a	1.1	**92.8**	a	7.2	**69.0**	a	31.0	**98.7**	1.3
	Korea	**98.6**	a	1.4	**81.8**	18.2	a	**54.8**	45.2	a	**100.0**	a
	Luxembourg	**91.4**	0.4	8.2	**81.2**	10.6	8.2	**84.2**	6.5	9.3	**99.9**	0.1
	Mexico	**91.8**	a	8.2	**88.5**	a	11.5	**82.3**	a	17.7	**100.0**	a
	Netherlands	**m**	a	m	**m**	a	m	**m**	a	m	**99.0**	1.0
	New Zealand	**97.9**	n	2.1	**95.1**	n	4.9	**86.0**	9.1	4.9	**90.6**	9.4
	Norway	**97.7**	2.3	x(2)	**96.8**	3.2	x(5)	**88.4**	11.6	x(8)	**98.5**	1.5
	Poland	**97.2**	0.8	2.1	**95.8**	1.2	3.0	**86.3**	1.2	12.5	**94.9**	5.1
	Portugal	**87.8**	3.9	8.4	**81.3**	6.1	12.7	**76.4**	4.9	18.6	**100.0**	a
	Slovak Republic	**94.0**	6.0	n	**93.6**	6.4	n	**85.9**	14.1	n	**98.8**	1.2
	Slovenia	**99.6**	0.4	n	**99.9**	0.1	n	**96.6**	2.1	1.4	**94.3**	5.7
	Spain	**68.2**	28.0	3.8	**69.0**	27.9	3.2	**78.0**	12.2	9.7	**91.8**	8.2
	Sweden	**91.9**	8.1	n	**88.5**	11.5	n	**84.3**	15.7	n	**84.6**	15.4
	Switzerland	**95.4**	1.5	3.1	**92.0**	3.0	5.0	**93.2**	2.9	3.9	**99.8**	0.2
	Turkey	**97.7**	a	2.3	**a**	a	a	**97.2**	a	2.8	**m**	m
	United Kingdom	**95.0**	0.2	4.9	**78.5**	15.6	5.8	**54.0**	40.2	5.8	**96.8**	3.2
	United States	**91.1**	a	8.9	**91.6**	a	8.4	**91.6**	a	8.4	**100.0**	a
	OECD average	**89.7**	7.4	2.9	**86.1**	10.5	3.4	**81.4**	13.3	5.3	**96.3**	3.7
	EU21 average	**90.1**	7.2	2.8	**86.8**	10.5	2.7	**83.3**	12.4	4.3	**96.0**	4.0
Other G20	Argentina[2]	**76.4**	18.1	5.6	**77.4**	17.0	5.7	**70.1**	21.4	8.6	**100.0**	a
	Brazil	**86.7**	a	13.3	**89.3**	a	10.7	**85.0**	a	15.0	**m**	m
	China	**95.1**	4.9	x(2)	**92.1**	7.9	x(5)	**89.1**	10.9	x(8)	**97.9**	2.1
	India	**m**	m	m	**m**	m	m	**m**	m	m	**m**	m
	Indonesia	**83.2**	a	16.8	**63.7**	a	36.3	**50.2**	a	49.8	**100.0**	a
	Russian Federation	**99.4**	a	0.6	**99.5**	a	0.5	**98.0**	a	2.0	**99.9**	0.1
	Saudi Arabia	**m**	m	m	**m**	m	m	**m**	m	m	**100.0**	a
	South Africa	**m**	m	m	**m**	m	m	**m**	m	m	**m**	m
	G20 average	**90.7**	11.2	m	**85.1**	16.6	m	**78.4**	22.1	m	**98.3**	3.5

1. Excludes independent private institutions.
2. Year of reference 2009.

Source: OECD. Argentina, China, India and Indonesia: UNESCO Institute for Statistics (World Education Indicators programme). Saudi Arabia: UNESCO Institute for Statistics. See Annex 3 for notes *(www.oecd.org/edu/eag2012)*.

Please refer to the Reader's Guide for information concerning the symbols replacing missing data.

StatLink http://dx.doi.org/10.1787/888932666874

C1

Table C1.5. Students in tertiary education, by type of institution or mode of enrolment (2010)
Distribution of students, by mode of enrolment, type of institution and programme destination

	Type of institution						Mode of study							
	Tertiary-type B education			Tertiary-type A and advanced research programmes			Tertiary-type B education				Tertiary-type A and advanced research programmes			
							Full-time Men + Women	Part-time			Full-time Men + Women	Part-time		
	Public	Government-dependent private	Independent private	Public	Government-dependent private	Independent private		M + W	Men	Women		M + W	Men	Women
	(1)	(2)	(3)	(4)	(5)	(6)	(7)	(8)	(9)	(10)	(11)	(12)	(13)	(14)
Australia	76.1	13.1	10.9	95.9	a	4.1	47.3	52.7	51.8	53.5	70.8	29.2	27.8	30.2
Austria	70.2	29.8	x(2)	85.3	14.7	x(5)	m	m	m	m	m	m	m	m
Belgium[1]	43.0	57.0	m	44.0	56.0	m	63.1	36.9	39.6	35.0	84.1	15.9	17.6	14.3
Canada[2]	m	m	m	m	m	m	76.0	24.0	20.2	27.0	82.1	17.9	17.2	18.5
Chile	5.6	2.7	91.7	27.5	21.5	50.9	m	m	m	m	m	m	m	m
Czech Republic	69.6	28.4	2.1	86.0	a	14.0	90.5	9.5	11.6	8.6	97.4	2.6	1.8	3.3
Denmark	98.7	0.7	0.6	98.2	1.8	n	70.2	29.8	27.8	31.9	90.2	9.8	8.6	10.7
Estonia	48.9	18.2	33.0	0.3	92.0	7.7	89.7	10.3	12.7	8.7	86.8	13.2	16.5	11.1
Finland	100.0	n	a	81.2	18.8	a	100.0	a	a	a	55.7	44.3	49.8	39.7
France	69.7	9.9	20.4	83.9	0.8	15.3	m	m	m	m	m	m	m	m
Germany[3]	57.2	42.8	x(2)	94.2	5.8	x(5)	87.4	12.6	23.5	7.4	94.8	5.2	5.6	4.7
Greece	100.0	a	a	100.0	a	a	100.0	a	a	a	100.0	a	a	a
Hungary	52.1	47.9	a	86.7	13.3	a	73.6	26.4	20.2	29.6	64.8	35.2	30.8	38.8
Iceland	31.6	68.4	n	81.2	18.8	n	45.1	54.9	66.3	41.2	71.1	28.9	25.3	30.9
Ireland	97.0	a	3.0	95.1	a	4.9	71.3	28.7	23.4	35.5	87.3	12.7	12.5	12.9
Israel	36.5	63.5	a	9.7	76.2	14.1	100.0	a	a	a	82.1	17.9	17.1	18.5
Italy	85.4	a	14.6	91.5	a	8.5	100.0	a	a	a	100.0	a	a	a
Japan	8.0	a	92.0	24.6	a	75.4	97.0	3.0	2.1	3.6	90.8	9.2	7.2	12.1
Korea	2.8	a	97.2	24.4	a	75.6	m	m	m	m	m	m	m	m
Luxembourg	n	100.0	n	n	100.0	m	41.3	58.7	67.5	50.2	95.0	5.0	m	m
Mexico	95.3	a	4.7	66.7	a	33.3	100.0	a	a	a	100.0	a	a	a
Netherlands	m	a	m	m	a	m	50.0	50.0	40.0	57.5	85.9	14.1	13.0	15.0
New Zealand	62.7	35.0	2.3	96.7	3.0	0.3	36.0	64.0	62.8	65.1	59.9	40.1	37.5	42.0
Norway	42.4	28.7	28.9	86.0	4.5	9.5	46.0	54.0	40.3	61.1	71.3	28.7	25.0	31.0
Poland	75.9	a	24.1	67.1	a	32.9	67.8	32.2	33.9	31.8	45.2	54.8	52.1	56.6
Portugal	79.6	a	20.4	76.6	a	23.4	m	m	m	m	m	m	m	m
Slovak Republic	81.0	19.0	n	83.6	n	16.4	78.0	22.0	13.7	26.1	64.4	35.6	30.7	38.9
Slovenia	78.2	5.0	16.8	89.2	6.4	4.5	53.9	46.1	45.5	46.7	75.0	25.0	25.4	24.7
Spain	79.9	14.2	5.9	86.1	n	13.9	94.9	5.1	3.4	6.7	75.8	24.2	26.1	22.7
Sweden	57.9	42.1	n	93.4	6.6	n	90.0	10.0	11.8	8.2	48.2	51.8	49.5	53.4
Switzerland	34.5	33.5	32.0	95.3	3.1	1.6	25.7	74.3	78.8	68.8	88.5	11.5	13.6	9.5
Turkey	96.7	a	3.3	94.1	a	5.9	100.0	n	n	n	100.0	n	n	n
United Kingdom	a	100.0	n	a	100.0	n	26.4	73.6	72.5	74.2	75.5	24.5	22.4	26.2
United States	78.2	a	21.8	70.9	a	29.1	48.2	51.8	51.0	52.3	66.3	33.7	31.3	35.6
OECD average	59.3	22.8	17.9	68.2	16.2	15.5	71.4	28.6	28.3	28.6	79.6	20.4	20.1	21.5
EU21 average	67.2	24.5	8.3	71.6	19.7	8.8	74.9	25.1	24.8	25.4	79.2	20.8	21.3	21.9
Argentina[2]	59.1	16.9	24.0	79.1	a	20.9	94.0	6.0	7.8	5.0	53.2	46.8	45.9	47.4
Brazil	14.8	a	85.2	29.0	a	71.0	m	m	m	m	m	m	m	m
China	m	m	m	m	m	m	70.1	29.9	31.7	28.1	76.4	23.6	23.8	23.4
India	m	m	m	m	m	m	m	m	m	m	m	m	m	m
Indonesia	50.4	a	49.6	39.4	a	60.6	100.0	a	0.0	0.0	100.0	a	0.0	0.0
Russian Federation[3]	97.2	a	2.8	83.1	a	16.9	67.7	32.3	34.4	30.5	48.9	51.1	46.6	54.6
Saudi Arabia	99.3	0.0	0.7	95.6	0.0	4.4	100.0	0.0	0.0	0.0	81.4	18.6	22.4	15.7
South Africa[2]	100.0	n	n	100.0	n	n	m	m	m	m	m	m	m	m
G20 average	m	m	m	m	m	m	78.0	22.0	22.7	21.7	81.4	18.6	17.5	19.4

1. Excludes independent private institutions.
2. Year of reference 2009.
3. Excludes advanced research programmes.
Source: OECD. Argentina, China, India and Indonesia: UNESCO Institute for Statistics (World Education Indicators programme). Saudi Arabia: Observatory on Higher Education. South Africa: UNESCO Institute for Statistics. See Annex 3 for notes (www.oecd.org/edu/eag2012).
Please refer to the Reader's Guide for information concerning the symbols replacing missing data.
StatLink ᵀᵐˢᴸ http://dx.doi.org/10.1787/888932666893

Table C1.6. **Projections of the number of students (2010, 2015 and 2020)**
Assuming enrolment rates in 2010 stay constant
Full-time and part-time students in public and private institutions, by age group, in thousands

	Number of students in 2010						Projections of the number of students in 2015						Individuals in the following age ranges as a percentage of the total population		
	Ages 5-14		Ages 15-19		Ages 20-29		Ages 5-14		Ages 15-19		Ages 20-29		Ages 5-14	Ages 15-19	Ages 20-29
	No. of students	2005=100	No. of students	2005=100	No. of students	2005=100	No. of students	2005=100	No. of students	2005=100	No. of students	2005=100	2010	2010	2010
	(1)	(2)	(3)	(4)	(5)	(6)	(7)	(8)	(9)	(10)	(11)	(12)	(19)	(21)	(23)
Australia[1]	2 747	m	1 221	m	1 056	m	2 874	m	1 210	m	1 060	m	12.4	6.7	14.8
Austria	838	92	393	100	272	136	826	91	365	93	278	139	10.2	6.0	12.9
Belgium	1 187	98	607	104	410	108	1 255	103	595	102	426	112	11.1	6.0	12.5
Canada[2,3]	3 774	m	1 838	109	1 147	102	3 692	m	1 678	100	1 128	101	11.5	6.8	13.8
Chile[4]	2 442	95	1 114	102	702	129	2 365	92	994	91	744	137	15.0	8.7	16.3
Czech Republic	912	86	556	93	350	108	928	88	420	71	311	96	8.8	5.9	13.9
Denmark	669	100	298	115	245	102	653	97	297	115	268	112	12.2	6.3	11.5
Estonia	122	81	73	78	58	108	134	90	57	61	52	96	9.4	6.3	15.5
Finland	564	94	291	104	279	98	573	96	262	94	282	100	11.0	6.3	12.5
France	7 933	102	3 358	96	1 622	101	8 072	104	3 416	97	1 584	99	12.3	6.2	12.6
Germany[5]	7 566	93	3 862	91	3 056	112	7 174	88	3 730	88	2 948	108	9.3	5.3	12.1
Greece	1 061	101	477	80	567	149	1 095	104	452	76	500	131	9.3	5.1	12.4
Hungary	973	88	553	101	343	91	985	89	469	85	321	86	9.9	6.0	13.5
Iceland	43	97	21	115	18	113	42	94	19	107	17	107	13.6	7.5	14.8
Ireland	615	110	263	100	142	99	649	116	272	103	118	82	13.5	6.1	15.2
Israel	1 317	110	385	103	257	116	1 442	121	435	117	269	121	17.9	7.9	15.3
Italy	5 605	100	2 471	107	1 422	99	5 672	102	2 403	104	1 366	96	9.3	4.9	11.0
Japan[6]	11 811	98	3 530	90	40	93	10 770	89	3 483	89	37	85	9.1	4.8	11.3
Korea	5 689	90	2 922	109	2 064	100	4 738	75	2 676	100	2 006	97	11.7	7.0	14.0
Luxembourg	58	104	23	120	m	m	57	103	24	125	m	m	12.0	5.9	12.8
Mexico	22 628	103	5 634	113	2 237	113	20 630	94	5 565	112	2 276	115	19.8	9.7	17.4
Netherlands	1 979	100	921	109	603	120	1 923	97	908	108	637	127	12.0	6.1	12.1
New Zealand	588	97	255	113	182	110	588	98	245	108	176	106	13.3	7.4	13.8
Norway	611	100	278	112	180	108	588	96	275	111	188	113	12.6	6.6	12.6
Poland	3 636	84	2 345	86	1 865	95	3 380	78	1 906	70	1 594	81	10.0	6.6	16.3
Portugal	1 123	99	490	111	320	94	1 107	97	483	110	287	84	10.3	5.3	12.8
Slovak Republic	528	83	314	89	180	122	500	78	248	70	156	106	10.2	6.8	16.1
Slovenia	179	94	97	85	96	100	187	98	88	77	84	88	9.0	5.2	13.8
Spain	4 388	106	1 888	101	1 464	99	4 552	110	1 809	97	1 164	79	9.6	4.9	13.0
Sweden	987	90	552	110	430	111	1 098	101	456	91	471	121	10.7	6.8	12.6
Switzerland	800	96	387	107	235	120	805	96	368	102	239	122	10.3	5.8	12.6
Turkey	11 956	106	3 506	137	2 506	182	11 828	105	3 577	140	2 465	179	17.5	8.6	17.6
United Kingdom[3]	7 234	98	3 048	110	1 548	115	7 544	102	2 879	104	1 632	121	11.3	6.3	13.7
United States	39 339	99	17 555	107	11 059	118	41 879	105	17 446	107	11 317	120	13.2	7.0	14.1
OECD Total	151 902	101	61 525	104	36 955	113	150 605	101	59 507	101	36 401	112	12.5	6.6	13.9
EU21 Total	48 157		22 880		15 271		48 364		21 538		14 480				
Argentina[2]	7 226	m	2 430	m	1 743	m	m	m	m	m	m	m	16.8	8.6	16.3
Brazil[4]	30 920	98	12 986	100	6 927	99	28 932	92	13 572	105	6 637	95	16.8	8.9	18.0
China[7]	m	m	m	m	m	m	m	m	m	m	m	m	m	m	m
India[7]	191 511	100	m	100	m	100	193 609	101	m	101	m	106	20.1	9.8	17.9
Indonesia[7]	40 640	100	13 086	100	4 326	100	40 754	100	12 758	97	4 262	99	18.0	9.0	18.0
Russian Federation	12 523	102	m	m	m	m	14 096	115	m	m	m	m	9.5	6.0	17.3
Saudi Arabia	1 910	m	1 923	m	846	m	m	m	m	m	m	m	9.4	5.7	17.4
South Africa[2]	m	m	m	m	m	m	m	m	m	m	m	m	20.1	10.0	19.5
G20 total	m		m		m		m		m		m		m	m	m

Note: The predicted values shown in this table are calculated assuming that the percentage of the population enrolled at each age will remain constant in the future; thus they may deviate from the values calculated by national authorities under different assumptions. Predictions for ages concerning compulsory education are more likely to follow the evolution of the population given near-full enrolment rates in most countries. These predictions can be considered as a lower bound for later ages given that participation is still increasing in most countries. Columns showing projections for 2020 are available for consultation on line (see *StatLink* below).

1. A high proportion of students between the ages of 20 to 29 are international students, changes in migration patterns may affect projections.
2. Reference year 2009 instead of 2010.
3. 2006=100.
4. 2007=100.
5. Excludes advanced research programmes.
6. Excluding tertiary levels of education.
7. 2010=100.

Source: OECD. Argentina, China, India and Indonesia: UNESCO Institute for Statistics (World Education Indicators programme). Saudi Arabia: UNESCO Institute for Statistics. South Africa: UNESCO Institute for Statistics. See Annex 3 for notes (*www.oecd.org/edu/eag2012*).
Please refer to the Reader's Guide for information concerning the symbols replacing missing data.

StatLink ⧉ http://dx.doi.org/10.1787/888932666912

C1

Table C1.7a. Expected years in education from age 5 through age 39 (2010)

Expected years of education under countries' current education system (excluding education for children under the age of 5 and individuals over 40), by gender and mode of study

	Full-time							Part-time[1]							Full-time + Part-time[1]
	All levels of education combined			Primary and lower secondary education	Upper secondary education	Post-secondary non-tertiary	Tertiary education	All levels of education combined			Primary and lower secondary education	Upper secondary education	Post-secondary non-tertiary	Tertiary education	All levels of education combined
	M+W	Men	Women	M+W				M+W	Men	Women	M+W				M+W
	(1)	(2)	(3)	(4)	(5)	(6)	(7)	(8)	(9)	(10)	(11)	(12)	(13)	(14)	(15)
Australia	15.3	14.9	15.6	10.9	1.8	0.1	2.5	3.2	3.4	3.1	0.6	1.1	0.3	1.0	18.5
Austria	m	m	m	m	m	m	m	m	m	m	m	m	m	m	16.9
Belgium	16.3	16.0	16.5	8.4	4.1	0.3	2.4	2.5	2.2	2.8	0.3	1.3	0.1	0.8	18.7
Canada[2]	m	m	m	12.4	x(4)	m	2.4	m	m	m	x(4)	x(4)	m	0.5	17.0
Chile[3]	16.2	16.2	16.2	8.1	3.8	a	3.4	x(1)	x(2)	x(3)	x(4)	x(5)	a	x(7)	16.2
Czech Republic	17.3	16.9	17.7	9.0	3.8	0.3	2.8	0.5	0.4	0.6	n	n	0.3	0.1	17.8
Denmark	18.1	17.6	18.5	9.5	3.6	n	3.0	0.7	0.7	0.8	n	0.3	n	0.2	18.8
Estonia	16.6	16.0	17.3	9.0	2.8	0.4	2.8	0.8	0.8	0.9	0.1	0.3	n	0.4	17.4
Finland	18.0	17.5	18.5	9.0	4.8	0.2	2.4	1.6	1.7	1.6	n	n	n	1.6	19.6
France[3]	16.4	16.1	16.7	9.3	3.3	0.1	2.7	x(1)	x(2)	x(3)	x(4)	x(5)	x(6)	x(7)	16.4
Germany[4]	17.7	17.8	17.6	10.3	3.0	0.6	2.4	0.2	0.2	0.2	n	n	n	0.1	17.9
Greece	18.1	17.9	18.4	9.3	3.0	0.2	4.6	0.4	0.5	0.2	0.1	0.2	n	n	18.5
Hungary	16.3	16.2	16.3	8.1	4.1	0.4	2.0	1.2	1.0	1.5	n	0.4	0.1	0.8	17.5
Iceland	17.3	16.7	17.8	9.9	3.9	0.1	2.5	2.2	1.8	2.5	n	1.3	0.1	0.8	19.4
Ireland	17.5	17.5	17.5	11.0	2.8	1.3	3.9	0.4	0.4	0.4	n	n	0.1	0.3	17.9
Israel	15.4	15.1	15.7	8.8	2.8	0.1	2.5	0.4	0.3	0.5	n	n	n	0.4	15.8
Italy	17.0	16.5	17.4	8.2	m	n	3.0	0.1	0.1	0.1	0.1	m	n	n	17.1
Japan[3]	15.8	m	m	9.2	m	n	m	0.4	m	m	m	m	n	m	16.2
Korea[3]	17.7	18.5	16.8	9.0	2.9	a	4.8	x(1)	x(2)	x(3)	x(4)	x(5)	a	x(7)	17.7
Luxembourg[5]	14.8	14.7	14.9	9.3	3.8	0.1	0.7	0.1	0.1	0.1	n	n	n	0.1	14.9
Mexico[3]	14.9	14.7	15.0	10.5	2.0	a	1.4	x(1)	x(2)	x(3)	x(4)	x(5)	a	x(7)	14.9
Netherlands	17.4	17.4	17.4	10.3	3.4	n	2.7	0.4	0.4	0.5	n	0.1	n	0.3	17.8
New Zealand	15.3	15.0	15.6	10.2	2.8	0.2	2.1	2.9	2.7	3.0	n	0.9	0.5	1.5	18.2
Norway	16.9	16.7	17.2	10.0	3.6	0.1	2.3	1.0	0.8	1.2	n	0.2	n	0.7	17.9
Poland	15.3	15.1	15.6	8.9	3.0	0.1	1.7	2.9	2.5	3.4	n	0.5	0.4	2.0	18.2
Portugal[3]	18.0	17.7	18.2	10.6	3.6	0.1	2.7	x(1)	x(2)	x(3)	x(4)	x(5)	x(6)	x(7)	18.0
Slovak Republic	15.5	15.3	15.8	8.8	3.7	n	1.8	0.9	0.6	1.2	n	0.1	n	0.8	16.4
Slovenia	16.8	16.2	17.5	8.7	3.9	0.1	3.1	1.5	1.4	1.7	0.1	0.4	n	1.0	18.4
Spain	16.1	15.7	16.4	10.4	2.1	a	2.6	1.2	1.2	1.3	0.4	0.3	a	0.6	17.3
Sweden	16.2	15.9	16.5	9.1	3.2	0.1	1.8	3.0	2.4	3.7	0.7	0.9	n	1.4	19.2
Switzerland	16.6	16.6	16.5	9.6	3.4	0.1	1.8	0.6	0.7	0.5	n	n	0.1	0.5	17.2
Turkey[3]	15.2	15.7	14.7	8.5	3.4	a	2.8	x(1)	x(2)	x(3)	x(4)	x(5)	a	x(7)	15.2
United Kingdom	15.7	15.4	15.9	9.5	4.2	n	1.9	1.0	0.8	1.1	0.1	0.2	n	0.6	16.6
United States	15.4	15.0	15.8	9.1	2.8	0.1	2.8	1.7	1.5	2.0	n	n	n	1.5	17.1
OECD average	16.5	16.3	16.7	9.5	3.3	0.2	2.6	1.2	1.1	1.4	0.1	0.4	0.1	0.7	17.4
EU21 average	16.7	16.5	17.0	9.3	3.5	0.2	2.5	1.1	1.0	1.2	0.1	0.3	0.1	0.6	17.7
Argentina[2]	16.5	15.6	17.4	11.0	2.3	a	m	16.5	15.6	17.4	11.0	2.3	a	m	17.8
Brazil[3]	16.3	16.0	16.5	10.1	3.1	a	1.8	16.3	16.0	16.5	10.1	3.1	a	1.8	16.3
China	12.4	12.3	12.6	8.1	m	m	1.0	12.4	12.3	12.6	8.1	m	m	1.0	m
India	m	m	m	m	m	m	m	m	m	m	m	m	m	m	m
Indonesia	14.2	14.2	14.2	10.5	1.9	a	1.2	14.2	14.2	14.2	10.5	1.9	a	1.2	14.2
Russian Federation	m	m	m	8.7	m	m	m	m	m	m	8.7	m	m	m	m
Saudi Arabia	m	m	m	8.3	m	a	1.7	m	m	m	8.3	m	a	1.7	m
South Africa	m	m	m	m	m	m	m	m	m	m	m	m	m	m	m
G20 average	15.7	15.6	15.9	9.6	m	m	2.3	6.6	7.1	7.5	4.8	m	m	0.9	m

1. Expected years in part-time education must be interpreted with caution since they may reflect variations due to different intensities of participation among countries, levels and individuals of different ages.
2. Year of reference 2009.
3. Full time + Part time.
4. Excludes advanced research programmes.
5. High levels of enrolment abroad and immigration may affect expected years in education.
Source: OECD. Argentina, China, Indonesia: UNESCO Institute for Statistics (World Education Indicators programme). Saudi Arabia: UNESCO Institute for Statistics. See Annex 3 for notes (*www.oecd.org/edu/eag2012*).
Please refer to the Reader's Guide for information concerning the symbols replacing missing data.
StatLink 🔗 http://dx.doi.org/10.1787/888932666931

HOW DO EARLY CHILDHOOD EDUCATION SYSTEMS DIFFER AROUND THE WORLD?

- Early childhood education is associated with better performance later on in school. Fifteen-year-old pupils who attended pre-primary education perform better on PISA than those who did not, even after accounting for their socio-economic backgrounds.

- In a majority of OECD countries, education now begins for most children well before they are 5 years old. Belgium, France, Iceland, Italy, Norway, Spain and Sweden have the highest enrolment rates of 3-year-olds in early childhood education, where more than 90% are enrolled.

- More than three-quarters of 4-year-olds (79%) are enrolled in early childhood education across OECD countries as a whole. This rises to 83%, on average, among OECD countries that are part of the European Union.

Chart C2.1. **Enrolment rates in early childhood and primary education at age 4 (2005 and 2010)**

Full-time and part-time pupils in public and private institutions

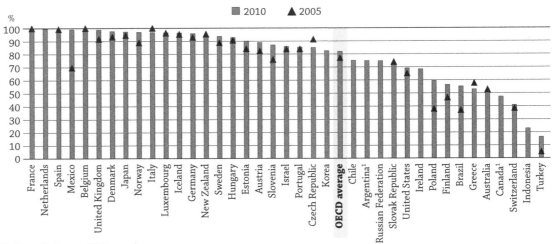

1. Year of reference 2009.
Countries are ranked in descending order of the enrolment rates of 4-year-olds in 2010.
Source: OECD. Argentina and Indonesia: UNESCO Institute for Statistics (World Education Indicators programme). Table C2.1. See Annex 3 for notes (*www.oecd.org/edu/eag2012*).
StatLink ᴍⁱˢᴸ http://dx.doi.org/10.1787/888932663055

▨ Context

A growing body of research recognises that early childhood (pre-primary) education improves children's cognitive abilities, helps to create a foundation for lifelong learning, makes learning outcomes more equitable, reduces poverty, and improves social mobility from generation to generation.

Enrolling pupils in early childhood education can also mitigate social inequalities and promote better student outcomes overall. Many of the inequalities that exist within school systems are already present when pupils enter formal schooling and persist as pupils progress through the school system (Entwisle, et al., 1997; Downey, et al., 2004). Because inequalities tend to grow when school is not compulsory, earlier entrance into the school system may reduce educational inequalities. In addition, schooling experiences in pre-primary education helps pupils become better prepared to enter and succeed in formal schooling (Hart and Risely, 1995; Heckman, 2000).

As countries continue to expand their early childhood education programmes, it will be important to consider parents' needs and expectations regarding accessibility, cost, programme quality and accountability. When parents' needs with respect to program quality and accountability are not met, some may be more inclined to send their children to private pre-primary institutions, child care, or extra-curricular activities. This can result in heavy financial burdens for parents, even when government subsidies are provided (Shin, et al., 2009).

Other findings

- **Publicly-funded pre-primary education tends to be more strongly developed in the European than in the non-European countries of the OECD.** Private funding varies widely between countries, ranging from 5% or less in Belgium, Estonia, Luxembourg, the Netherlands and Sweden, to 25% or more in Argentina, Austria and Germany, and to over 48% in Australia, Japan and Korea.

- **As a percentage of GDP, expenditure on pre-primary education accounts for 9% of OECD expenditure on educational institutions, or on average 0.5% of GDP.** Differences between countries are significant. For example, while 0.1% or less of GDP is spent on pre-primary education in Australia, India, Indonesia, Ireland and South Africa, 0.8% or more is spent in Denmark, Iceland, Israel, the Russian Federation and Spain.

- The ratio of pupils to teaching staff is also an important indicator of the resources devoted to pre-primary education. **The pupil-teacher ratio excluding non-professional staff (e.g. teachers' aides) ranges from more than 20 pupils per teacher in China, France, Israel, Mexico and Turkey, to fewer than 10 in Chile, Iceland, New Zealand, Slovenia and Sweden.**

- **Some countries make extensive use of teachers' aides at the pre-primary level.** Fifteen countries reported smaller ratios of pupils to contact staff than of pupils to teaching staff. As a result, the ratios of pupils to contact staff are substantially lower than the ratios of pupils to teaching staff (at least two fewer pupils) in Austria, Brazil, China, France, Germany, Ireland, Israel and the United States.

Trends

Over the past decade, many countries have expanded pre-primary education programmes. This increased focus on early childhood education has resulted in the extension of compulsory education to lower ages in some countries, free early childhood education, and the creation of programmes that integrate care with formal pre-primary education.

On average for OECD countries with 2005 and 2010 data, enrolments in early childhood education programmes have risen from 64% of 3-year-olds in 2005 to 69% in 2010, and similarly from 77% of 4-year-olds in 2005 to 81% in 2010. The enrolment rates of 4-year-olds in early childhood education programmes increased more than 20 percentage points in Mexico and Poland between 2005 and 2010.

C2

Analysis

Early childhood education is the initial stage of organised instruction for many children and can play a significant role in their development. While primary and lower secondary enrolment patterns are fairly similar throughout the OECD, there is significant variation in early childhood education programmes among OECD and other G20 countries. This includes the overall level of participation in programmes, the typical starting age for children, and programme length.

This indicator shows enrolment rates in ISCED 0 (pre-primary) programmes by individual year of age, as well as the transition into primary education. Expenditure by public and private sources, pupil/staff ratios and information on starting ages and program length are also presented to enable further comparisons of early childhood education systems throughout OECD countries.

Enrolment in early childhood education

In a majority of OECD countries, education now begins for most children well before they are 5 years old. More than three-quarters (79%) of 4-year-olds are enrolled in in early childhood education programmes across OECD countries as a whole, and this rises to 83%, on average, in the OECD countries that are part of the European Union. Enrolment rates for early childhood education at this age vary from over 95% in Belgium, France, Germany, Iceland, Italy, Japan, Luxembourg, Mexico, the Netherlands, New Zealand, Norway, Spain and the United Kingdom, at one end of the spectrum, to less than 60% in Australia, Brazil, Canada, Finland, Greece, Indonesia, Poland, Switzerland and Turkey (Table C2.1 and Chart C2.1).

Results from the OECD's PISA assessment support these figures. On average across OECD countries, 72% of the 15-year-old pupils assessed by PISA reported that they had attended more than one year of pre-primary education. According to pupils' responses, enrolment in more than one year of pre-primary education was nearly universal about ten years ago in Belgium, France, Hungary, Iceland, Japan and the Netherlands, where over 90% of 15-year-olds reported that they had attended pre-primary education for more than one year. More than 90% of pupils in 27 OECD countries had attended pre-primary education for at least some time, and more than 98% of pupils in France, Hungary, Japan and the United States reported having done so. Pre-primary education is rare in Turkey, where less than 30% of 15-year-olds attended pre-primary education for any period of time. More than one year of pre-primary education is uncommon in Canada, Chile, Ireland and Poland, where less than 50% of pupils had attended pre-primary education for that length of time (see OECD, 2010, Table II.5.5, and Table C2.2 at the end of this indicator).

Notably, PISA analyses also find that in most countries, pupils who have attended pre-primary education programmes tend to perform better than those who have not, even after accounting for pupils' socio-economic background. PISA research also shows that the relationship between pre-primary attendance and performance tends to be greater in school systems with a longer duration of pre-primary education, smaller pupil-to-teacher ratios in pre-primary education and higher public expenditure per child at the pre-primary level (OECD [2010], Table II.5.6).

At the same time, the availability of early childhood education programmes for even younger children is still a work in progress. In some countries, demand for early childhood education for children aged 3 and under far outstrips supply. The highest enrolment rates of 3-year-olds in early childhood education are found in Belgium, France, Iceland, Italy, Norway and Spain. OECD research has found that the demand for services for young children is significantly higher than the places available in many countries, even in those with provisions for long parental leave. In countries where public funding for parental leave is limited, many working parents must either seek solutions in the private market, where parents' ability to pay significantly influences access to quality services, or else rely on informal arrangements with family, friends and neighbours (OECD, 2011).

Early childhood education helps to build a strong foundation for lifelong learning and ensure equity in education later on. Some countries have recognised this by making access to pre-primary education almost universal for children by the time they are three. Early childhood education is growing quickly in the majority of countries.

On average for OECD countries with 2005 and 2010 data, enrolments rose from 64% of 3-year-olds in 2005 to 69% in 2010, and from 77% of 4-year-olds in 2005 to 81% in 2010. In Mexico and Poland, the enrolment rates of 4-year-olds increased more than 20 percentage points during this period (Table C2.1).

Financing early childhood education

Sustained public funding is critical to supporting the growth and quality of early childhood education programmes. Appropriate funding helps to ensure the recruitment of professional staff who are qualified to support children's cognitive, social and emotional development. Investment in early childhood facilities and materials also helps support the development of child-centred environments for learning. In the absence of direct public funding or parental subsidies, there is greater risk that early childhood education programmes will vary in quality, or that access will be restricted to more affluent families (OECD, 2006).

Public expenditure on education is mainly used to support public pre-primary institutions, but also funds private institutions in some countries to varying degrees. On average among OECD countries, the level of public expenditure on public pre-primary institutions, per pupil, is more than twice the level of public expenditure on private pre-primary institutions (USD 6 426 and USD 2 701, respectively) (see Table B3.4). At the pre-primary level, annual expenditure per pupil for both public and private institutions averages USD 6 670 in OECD countries. However, expenditure varies from USD 2 500 or less in Argentina, Brazil, Indonesia, Mexico and South Africa to more than USD 10 000 in Luxembourg and New Zealand (Table C2.2, and see Table B3.4 in Indicator B3).

**Chart C2.2. Expenditure on early childhood educational institutions
as a percentage of GDP (2009)**
By funding source

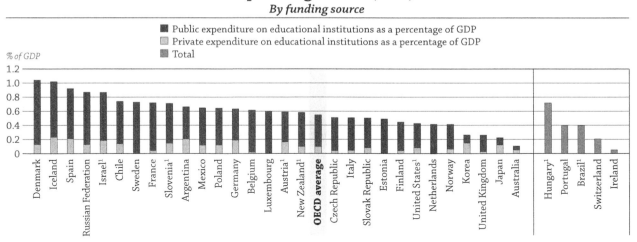

1. Includes some expenditure on child care.
Countries are ranked in descending order of public and private expenditure on educational institutions.
Source: OECD. Argentina: UNESCO Institute for Statistics (World Education Indicators programme). Table C2.2. See Annex 3 for notes (*www.oecd.org/edu/eag2012*).
StatLink ⧉ http://dx.doi.org/10.1787/888932663074

Expenditure on pre-primary education accounts for 9% of OECD expenditure on educational institutions, or 0.5% of the collective GDP. Differences between countries are significant. For example, while 0.1% or less of GDP is spent on pre-primary education in Australia, India, Indonesia, Ireland and South Africa, 0.8% or more is spent in Denmark, Iceland, Israel, the Russian Federation and Spain (Table C2.2, and see Table B2.1 in Indicator B2).

These differences can largely be explained by enrolment rates and the differing starting age for primary education in some countries, but are also influenced by the extent to which this indicator covers private early childhood education. In Ireland, for example, most early childhood education is delivered by private institutions that were not captured by the Irish data for the year 2009. In Australia, the Netherlands and Switzerland, the absence of data on integrated programmes is also likely to understate the true level of expenditure and enrolments in early childhood education programmes, and may affect the comparability of the data to other countries. Inferences on access to and quality of early childhood education and care should therefore be made with caution. Countries with integrated early childhood programmes may vary in the extent of expenditure that is devoted to the "care" component of the programme (ideally only education expenditures should be included) (Table C2.2, Chart C2.2 and Indicator B2).

Publicly-funded pre-primary education tends to be more strongly developed in the European than the non-European countries of the OECD. In Europe, the concept of universal access to education for 3- to 6-year-olds is generally accepted. Most countries in this region provide all children with at least two years of free, publicly-funded pre-primary education before they begin primary education. With the exception of Ireland and the Netherlands, such access is generally a statutory right from the age of 3 and in some countries, even before that and for at least two years. Early education programmes in Europe are often free and located in schools. Compared to primary, secondary and post-secondary non-tertiary education, pre-primary institutions obtain the largest proportion of funds from private sources, at 18%. However, this proportion varies widely between countries, ranging from 5% or less in Belgium, Estonia, Luxembourg, the Netherlands and Sweden, and 25% or more in Argentina, Austria and Germany, to over 48% in Australia, Japan and Korea (Table C2.2 and OECD, 2011).

Ratio of pupils to teaching staff

The ratio of pupils to teaching staff is obtained by dividing the number of full-time equivalent pupils at a given level of education by the number of full-time equivalent teachers at that level and in similar types of institutions. However, this ratio does not take into account instruction time compared to the length of a teacher's working day, nor how much time teachers spend teaching. Therefore, it cannot be interpreted in terms of class size. The number of pupils per class summarises different factors, but distinguishing between them would allow an understanding of the differences between countries in terms of the quality of the educational system (see Indicator D2).

Chart C2.3. **Ratio of pupils to teaching staff in early childhood education (2010)**
Public and private institutions

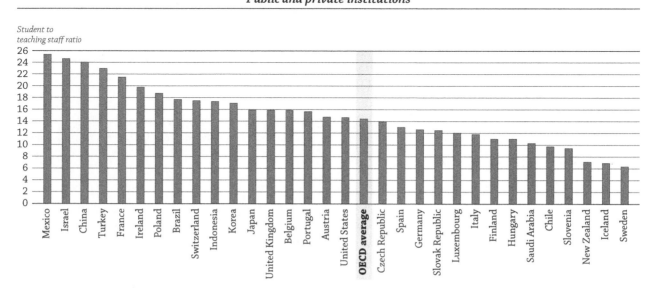

Countries are ranked in descending order of students to teaching staff ratios in early childhood education.
Source: OECD. China and Indonesia: UNESCO Institute for Statistics (World Education Indicators programme). Saudi Arabia: UNESCO Institute for Statistics. Table C2.2. See Annex 3 for notes (*www.oecd.org/edu/eag2012*).
StatLink ⬛️⬛️⬛️ http://dx.doi.org/10.1787/888932663093

C2

The ratio of pupils to teaching staff is also an important indicator of the resources devoted to education. Table C2.2 shows, for the pre-primary level, the ratio of student to teaching staff and also the ratio of pupils to contact staff (e.g. teachers and non-professional staff [teacher aides]) in early childhood education. Some countries make extensive use of teachers' aides at the pre-primary level. Fifteen countries reported smaller ratios of pupils to contact staff (Column 4 of Table C2.2) than of pupils to teaching staff. As a result, the ratios of pupils to contact staff are substantially lower in Austria, Brazil, China, France, Germany, Ireland, Israel and the United States. The difference is particularly large in Ireland and Israel, where there are at least ten fewer pupils per contact staff than per teaching staff. Globally, at the pre-primary level, there are 14 pupils for every teacher, on average in OECD countries. The student-teacher ratio (excluding teacher aides) ranges from more than 20 pupils per teacher in China, France, Israel, Mexico and Turkey, to fewer than 10 in Chile, Iceland, New Zealand, Slovenia and Sweden (Table C2.2 and Chart C2.3).

Definitions and methodologies

How is early childhood education defined?

Early childhood education or pre-primary education (ISCED 0) is defined as the initial stage of *organised instruction*, designed primarily to introduce very young children to a school-type environment.

The distinction between programmes that are classified as ISCED 0 and programmes that are outside of the scope of ISCED 0 is based primarily on the *educational properties* of the programme. As the educational properties of these programmes are difficult to assess directly, several proxy measures are used. ISCED 0 programmes:

- Include early childhood programmes that:
  - are in a centre or are school-based;
  - are designed to meet the educational and developmental needs of children;
  - are typically designed for children at least 3 years old and not older than 6; and
  - have staff that are adequately trained (i.e. qualified) to provide an educational programme for the children.

- Exclude early childhood programmes that fail to meet these criteria.

How are early childhood education programmes classified as full-time or part-time, and what effect does this have?

There are two methods used to classify pupils as full-time/part-time in *Education at a Glance*:

1. Based on national definitions for early childhood education programmes.
2. A proxy method, derived from the duration of the first grade in primary education (ISCED 1).

Though the classification method used by countries differs, the issue does not affect enrolment rates (Table C2.1), as these are based on the total number of enrolments as a proportion of the population, regardless of whether pupils are full-time or part-time. The differences in classification methods may have some effect on expenditure per student and the teacher/student ratio, as these data are based on full-time equivalent student figures.

What are the differences between *education only* and *integrated* programmes?

In some countries, institutions providing early childhood education also provide extended day or evening child care. For the purposes of reporting in *Education at a Glance*, these programmes are referred to as *integrated programmes* (i.e. they integrate education and care in the same programme). *Education only* programmes are those that do not include extended day or evening child care services (i.e. they only provide educational programmes).

Is child care expenditure on integrated programmes reported in *Education at a Glance*?

The focus of ISCED 0 is on the educational properties of the programme. Therefore, the child care component of integrated programmes is excluded from expenditure reporting in *Education at a Glance*. Countries that are not able to remove child care expenditure from data reported in *Education at a Glance* have been footnoted in Table C2.2. The amount of child care expenditure included is likely to vary between countries and care should be taken when interpreting these results.

How are variations at the national level represented?

Some variations at the national level are not able to be presented and information on the "characteristics of programmes" has been simplified in some cases. For example, in some countries the starting age of early childhood education programmes differs among jurisdictions or regions. In these instances, the information that is the most common or typical is reported.

The statistical data for Israel are supplied by and under the responsibility of the relevant Israeli authorities. The use of such data by the OECD is without prejudice to the status of the Golan Heights, East Jerusalem and Israeli settlements in the West Bank under the terms of international law.

References

Downey, D.B., P.T. von Hippel and B.A. Broh, "Are Schools the Great Equalizer? Cognitive Inequality during the Summer Months and the School Year", *American Sociological Review*, Vol. 69, No. 5, pp. 613-635.

Entwisle, D.R., K. Alexander and L.S. Olson (1997), *Children, Schools and Inequality*, Westview, Boulder.

Hart, B. and I. Risley (1995), *Meaningful Differences in the Everyday Experience of Young American Children*, Paul H. Brookes Publishing, Baltimore.

Heckman, J.J. (2000), *The Case for Investing in Disadvantaged Young Children*, CESifo DICE Report, Ifo Institute for Economic Research at the University of Munich, Vol. 6, No. 2, pages 3-8, 07.

OECD (2006), *Starting Strong II: Early Childhood Education and Care*, OECD Publishing.

OECD (2010), *PISA 2009 Results: Overcoming Social Background: Equity in Learning Opportunities and Outcomes* (Volume II), PISA, OECD Publishing.

OECD (2011), *Starting Strong III: A Quality Toolbox for Early Childhood Education and Care*, OECD Publishing.

Shin, E., M. Jung and E. Park, E. (2009), "A Survey on the Development of the Pre-school Free Service Model", Research Report of the Korean Educational Development Institute, Seoul.

Table C2.1. Enrolment rates in early childhood and primary education, by age (2005, 2010)

Full-time and part-time students in public and private institutions

	Enrolment rates (2010)										Enrolment rates (2005)									
	Age 3	Age 4			Age 5			Age 6			Age 3	Age 4			Age 5			Age 6		
	ISCED 0	ISCED 0	ISCED 1	Total	ISCED 0	ISCED 1	Total	ISCED 0	ISCED 1	Total	ISCED 0	ISCED 0	ISCED 1	Total	ISCED 0	ISCED 1	TOTAL	ISCED 0	ISCED 1	Total
	(1)	(2)	(3)	(4)	(5)	(6)	(7)	(8)	(9)	(10)	(11)	(12)	(13)	(14)	(15)	(16)	(17)	(18)	(19)	(20)
OECD Australia	10	**51**	1	52	17	82	99	n	*100*	100	17	**51**	2	53	18	72	91	n	*100*	100
Austria	61	**89**	n	89	95	n	95	41	59	100	47	**82**	n	82	93	n	93	39	57	96
Belgium	99	**99**	n	99	98	1	99	5	94	99	*100*	**100**	n	*100*	99	1	100	6	94	100
Canada[1]	1	**47**	n	47	94	n	94	n	m	99	m	**m**	m	m	m	m	m	m	m	m
Chile	38	**m**	m	75	m	m	87	m	m	92	m	**m**	m	m	m	m	m	m	m	m
Czech Republic	60	**85**	n	85	92	1	93	46	51	97	65	**91**	n	91	97	n	97	49	51	*100*
Denmark	87	**98**	n	98	98	n	98	97	2	99	91	**93**	n	93	84	n	84	95	3	98
Estonia	88	**90**	n	90	91	n	91	77	14	91	81	**84**	n	84	88	n	88	*100*	12	*100*
Finland	47	**56**	n	56	64	n	64	99	n	99	38	**47**	n	47	56	n	56	98	1	99
France	*100*	**100**	n	*100*	*100*	1	*100*	2	99	100	*100*	**100**	n	*100*	99	1	*100*	2	94	96
Germany[2]	89	**96**	n	96	96	n	97	35	64	99	82	**93**	n	93	93	n	93	38	58	96
Greece	a	**53**	a	53	94	a	94	2	98	100	a	**58**	a	58	83	2	84	n	*100*	100
Hungary	72	**93**	n	93	96	n	96	73	22	95	73	**91**	n	91	97	n	97	74	25	99
Iceland	95	**96**	n	96	95	n	95	n	98	98	94	**95**	n	95	96	n	96	n	98	98
Ireland	65	**27**	41	68	n	*100*	100	n	*100*	100	m	**m**	m	m	m	m	m	m	m	m
Israel	79	**86**	n	86	96	n	96	14	83	97	67	**84**	n	84	93	n	94	13	81	95
Italy	93	**97**	a	97	89	8	98	1	98	99	97	**100**	a	*100*	94	7	*100*	1	*100*	100
Japan	75	**97**	a	97	99	a	99	a	*100*	100	69	**95**	a	95	99	a	99	a	*100*	100
Korea	78	**82**	n	82	88	1	89	4	98	100	m	**m**	m	m	m	m	m	m	m	m
Luxembourg	73	**97**	n	97	88	5	93	3	95	98	62	**96**	n	96	92	3	95	3	97	100
Mexico	40	**99**	n	99	99	29	*100*	1	*100*	100	23	**70**	a	70	88	10	98	1	100	100
Netherlands	m	**100**	a	100	99	a	99	a	99	99	m	**m**	m	m	m	m	m	m	m	m
New Zealand	86	**95**	n	95	2	98	*100*	n	*100*	100	85	**96**	n	96	3	100	*100*	n	*100*	100
Norway	95	**97**	n	97	97	n	97	1	*100*	100	83	**89**	n	89	91	n	91	1	99	100
Poland	46	**59**	a	59	75	x(9)	75	91	4	95	28	**38**	a	38	48	m	48	98	1	99
Portugal	73	**85**	n	85	93	1	93	3	97	100	61	**84**	n	84	87	3	90	3	*100*	100
Slovak Republic	60	**73**	n	73	82	n	82	41	51	92	61	**74**	n	74	85	n	85	40	54	94
Slovenia	81	**87**	n	87	90	x(9)	90	5	94	99	67	**76**	n	76	84	n	84	4	96	*100*
Spain	99	**99**	n	99	99	n	*100*	1	97	98	95	**99**	2	99	*100*	n	*100*	1	99	100
Sweden	90	**94**	n	94	95	n	95	96	1	97	84	**89**	n	89	90	n	90	96	3	99
Switzerland	3	**40**	n	41	94	1	95	56	43	100	8	**38**	n	39	90	1	91	60	40	100
Turkey	4	**17**	m	17	61	n	61	m	96	96	2	**5**	n	5	23	8	32	n	83	83
United Kingdom	83	**65**	31	97	1	99	100	n	99	99	78	**60**	32	92	n	*100*	100	n	*100*	100
United States	51	**69**	n	69	74	6	80	16	80	96	35	**65**	n	65	72	6	78	15	80	95
OECD average	66	**79**	3	81	78	15	93	26	72	99	64	**77**	1	79	77	12	88	30	69	100
OECD average for countries with 2005 and 2010 data	69	**81**	1	83	80	13	93	29	70	99	64	**77**	1	79	76	12	88	31	69	100
EU21 average	73	**83**	3	86	82	11	93	34	64	98	69	**82**	2	84	82	7	89	40	61	100
Other G20 Argentina[1]	36	**75**	n	75	*100*	1	*100*	1	*100*	100	m	**m**	m	m	m	m	m	m	m	m
Brazil	32	**55**	n	55	77	1	78	47	45	92	21	**37**	n	37	62	1	63	63	21	83
China	m	**m**	n	m	m	n	m	n	m	m	m	**m**	m	m	m	m	m	m	m	m
India	m	**m**	5	m	m	44	m	m	99	m	m	**m**	m	m	m	m	m	m	m	m
Indonesia	4	**23**	n	23	43	5	48	23	75	98	m	**m**	m	m	m	m	m	m	m	m
Russian Federation	68	**75**	a	75	76	1	77	70	14	84	*100*	**m**	a	m	m	1	1	m	23	23
Saudi Arabia	m	**m**	m	m	m	m	m	m	m	m	m	**m**	m	m	m	m	m	m	m	m
South Africa	m	**m**	m	m	m	m	m	m	m	m	m	**m**	m	m	m	m	m	m	m	m
G20 average	m	**m**	3	m	m	17	m	m	86	m	m	**m**	m	m	m	m	m	m	m	m

Note: Enrolment rates at young ages should be interpreted with care; mismatches between the date of reference of ages and the date of data collection may lead to overestimations. Underestimation in enrolment rates may be due to uncounted late entrants. Rates above 100% are shown in italics.
1. Year of reference 2009 instead of 2010.
2. Year of reference 2006 instead of 2005.
Source: OECD. Argentina, India and Indonesia: UNESCO Institute for Statistics (World Education Indicators programme). See Annex 3 for notes (www.oecd.org/edu/eag2012).
Please refer to the Reader's Guide for information concerning the symbols replacing missing data.
StatLink http://dx.doi.org/10.1787/888932667026

Table C2.2. **Characteristics of early childhood education programmes (2010)**

	Distribution of pupils in ISCED 0, by type of institution (2010)			Ratio of pupils to teaching staff (2010)		Expenditure on educational institutions (2009)				Characteristics of early childhood education programmes						
	Public	Government-dependent private	Independent private	Pupils to contact staff (teachers and teachers' aides)	Pupils to teaching staff	Total expenditure (from public and private sources) as a % of GDP	Proportion of total expenditure from public sources	Proportion of total expenditure from private sources	Annual expenditure per pupil (in USD)	Earliest starting age	Usual starting age	Usual duration (in years)	Usual starting age in ISCED 1	Entry age for compulsory programmes (if applicable)	Length of compulsory programmes (if applicable)(in years)	Full-time (FT)/ Part-time (PT)
	ISCED 0	ISCED 0	ISCED 0	ISCED 0	ISCED 0	ISCED 0	ISCED 0	ISCED 0	ISCED 0	ISCED 0	ISCED 0	ISCED 0	ISCED 1	ISCED 0	ISCED 0	ISCED 0
	(1)	(2)	(3)	(4)	(5)	(6)	(7)	(8)	(9)	(10)	(11)	(12)	(13)	(14)	(15)	(16)
OECD																
Australia	25.0	75.0	n	m	m	0.1	51.4	48.6	8 493	3	4	1	5	a	a	PT
Austria[1]	71.9	28.1	x(2)	10.3	14.7	0.6	72.0	28.0	8 202	3	3	3	6	5	1	FT
Belgium	47.2	52.8	m	15.9	15.9	0.6	96.5	3.5	5 696	3	2.5	3 to 4	6	a	a	FT
Canada[2]	93.0	7.0	x(2)	m	m	m	m	m	m	2.5 to 5	4.5 to 5	1	6	a	a	FT/PT
Chile	34.1	59.3	6.7	9.4	9.7	0.7	81.1	18.9	3 885	0	4	2	m	a	a	FT/PT
Czech Republic	98.4	1.6	a	13.6	13.9	0.5	92.0	8.0	4 452	3	3	3	6	a	a	FT
Denmark	79.1	20.9	n	m	m	1.0	87.6	12.4	8 785	0	1	6	7	m	m	FT
Estonia	97.4	a	2.6	m	6.0	0.5	98.6	1.4	2 551	0	3	4	7	m	m	FT
Finland	91.2	8.8	a	m	11.0	0.4	90.3	9.7	5 553	0	a	a	7	a	a	FT
France	87.1	12.5	0.4	14.2	21.5	0.7	94.1	5.9	6 185	2	2 to 3	3	6	a	a	FT
Germany	35.2	64.8	x(2)	9.9	12.6	0.6	70.2	29.8	7 862	3	3	3	6	a	a	FT
Greece	92.6	a	7.4	m	m	m	m	m	m	4	4	1 to 2	6	m	m	FT
Hungary[1]	93.9	6.1	a	m	11.0	0.7	m	m	4 745	3	3	3	7	5	1	FT
Iceland	88.0	12.0	n	6.9	6.9	1.0	77.1	22.9	9 636	0	2	4	6	a	a	FT/PT
Ireland	2.5	a	97.5	9.0	19.8	0.1	m	m	m	3	3	1	4 to 5	a	a	FT/PT
Israel[1, 3]	95.6	a	4.4	12.5	24.6	0.9	78.7	21.3	3 998	3	3	3	6	3	3	FT
Italy	68.6	a	31.4	11.8	11.8	0.5	91.2	8.8	7 948	m	m	m	m	a	a	FT
Japan	30.4	a	69.6	15.1	15.9	0.2	45.0	55.0	5 103	3	3	3	6	a	a	FT
Korea	17.2	3.7	79.1	17.1	17.1	0.3	42.6	57.4	6 047	m	m	m	m	m	m	FT
Luxembourg	91.6	n	8.4	m	12.0	0.6	98.6	1.4	16 247	3	3	3	6	4	2	FT
Mexico	85.9	a	14.1	25.4	25.4	0.6	81.4	18.6	2 158	3	3 to 4	3	6	4	2	FT
Netherlands	100.0	a	m	m	m	0.4	98.7	1.3	7 437	4	4	2	6	5	1	FT
New Zealand[1]	1.7	98.3	n	7.1	7.1	0.6	82.9	17.1	11 202	m	3	2	5	a	a	FT/PT
Norway	55.1	44.9	a	m	m	0.4	84.4	15.6	6 696	0	1	5	6	a	a	FT/PT
Poland	86.7	1.2	12.1	m	18.7	0.6	81.1	18.9	5 610	3	3	4	7	6	1	FT
Portugal	51.4	31.3	17.3	m	15.7	0.4	m	m	5 661	m	m	m	m	m	m	FT
Slovak Republic	96.4	3.6	n	12.4	12.5	0.5	83.6	16.4	4 433	2	3	3	6	a	a	FT
Slovenia[1]	96.4	3.1	0.5	9.4	9.4	0.7	79.3	20.7	7 979	3	3	3	6	a	a	FT
Spain	64.2	24.7	11.0	m	13.0	0.9	77.1	22.9	6 946	0	2 to 3	3 to 4	6	a	a	FT
Sweden	83.8	16.2	n	6.3	6.3	0.7	100.0	n	6 549	3	-	4	7	a	a	FT
Switzerland[4]	96.1	0.3	3.5	m	17.5	0.2	m	m	5 147	4	5	2	6	5	1	FT
Turkey	91.0	a	9.0	m	23.0	m	m	m	m	3	5	1 to 3	6	a	a	m
United Kingdom	79.0	0.2	20.8	15.0	15.9	0.3	89.9	10.1	6 493	3	3	1.5	5	a	a	FT/PT
United States[1, 5]	55.5	a	44.5	11.4	14.6	0.4	80.9	19.1	8 396	3	4	1	6	a	a	FT/PT
OECD average	62.7	21.5	15.8	12.3	14.4	0.5	81.7	18.3	6 670							
OECD total						0.5	-	-	6 208							
EU21 average	75.1	12.8	12.0	11.6	13.4	0.6	88.3	11.7	6 807							
Other G20																
Argentina	m	m	m	m	m	0.7	69.0	31.0	2 398	m	m	m	m	m	m	FT
Brazil[1]	72.7	a	27.3	13.0	17.7	0.4	m	m	1 696	0	m	5	6	4	2	FT
China	m	m	m	21.6	24.0	m	m	m	m	m	m	m	m	m	m	FT
India	m	m	m	m	m	n	m	m	m	m	m	m	m	m	m	m
Indonesia	2.5	a	97.5	16.1	17.4	n	m	m	57	m	m	m	m	m	m	FT
Russian Federation	98.9	a	1.1	m	m	0.9	85.2	14.8	m	m	m	m	m	m	m	m
Saudi Arabia	m	m	m	m	10.3	m	m	m	m	m	m	m	m	m	m	m
South Africa	m	m	m	m	m	n	m	m	420	m	m	m	m	m	m	m
G20 average	60.1	m	m	15.5	17.5	0.4	m	m	m	m	m	m	m	m	m	m

1. Includes some expenditure on child care.

2. ISCED 0 programmes are compulsory for all pupils in two of the 13 jurisdictions. Earliest stating age, typical starting age and duration of ISCED 0 programmes vary by jurisdiction.

3. By recently enacted law, ISCED 0 programmes have been made compulsory and free nationwide. Implementation will commence gradually from 2013.

4. In jurisdictions where ISCED 0 programmes are compulsory, it is compulsory for two years in some jurisdictions and only one year in others.

5. ISCED 0 programmes are compulsory in about one-third of U.S. states.

Source: OECD. Argentina, China and Indonesia: UNESCO Institute for Statistics (World Education Indicators programme). Saudi Arabia and South Africa: UNESCO Institute for Statistics. See Annex 3 for notes (*www.oecd.org/edu/eag2012*).

Please refer to the Reader's Guide for information concerning the symbols replacing missing data.

StatLink ⬛⬛⬛ http://dx.doi.org/10.1787/888932667045

Table C2.3. **Characteristics of education-only and integrated early childhood education programmes (2010)**

	Education-only programmes			Integrated programmes (includes education and child care services)			Relative proportion of enrolments reported in *Education at a Glance* (%)		
	Exist nationally	Delivered by qualified teacher	Have a formal curriculum	Exist nationally	Delivered by qualified teacher	Have a formal curriculum	Education-only programmes	Integrated programmes	Total
	(1)	(2)	(3)	(4)	(5)	(6)	(7)	(8)	(9)
OECD Australia	Yes	Yes	Yes	Yes	Yes	Yes	100	m	100
Austria	Yes	Yes	Yes	Yes	a	No	3	97	100
Belgium	Yes	Yes	Yes	No	a	a	100	a	100
Canada	Yes	Yes1	Yes	Yes	Yes	Yes	100	m	100
Chile	Yes	Yes	Yes	Yes	Yes	Yes	x(9)	x(9)	100
Czech Republic	Yes	Yes	Yes	No	a	a	100	a	100
Denmark	m	m	m	m	m	m	m	m	m
Estonia	No	a	a	Yes	Yes	Yes	a	100	100
Finland	Yes	Yes	Yes	Yes	Yes	Yes	37	63	100
France	Yes	Yes	Yes	No	a	a	100	a	100
Germany	Yes	Yes	Yes	No	a	a	100	a	100
Greece	Yes	Yes	Yes	No	a	a	100	a	100
Hungary	No	a	a	Yes	Yes	Yes	a	100	100
Iceland	Yes	Yes	Yes	Yes	Yes	Yes	1	99	100
Ireland	Yes	Yes	Yes	No	a	a	100	a	100
Israel	Yes	Yes	Yes	Yes	Yes	Yes	98	2	100
Italy	m	m	m	m	m	m	m	m	m
Japan	Yes	Yes	Yes	Yes	Varies	Varies	x(9)	x(9)	100
Korea	Yes	Yes	Yes	Yes	Yes	Yes	x(9)	x(9)	100
Luxembourg	Yes	Yes	Yes	No	a	a	100	a	100
Mexico	Yes	Yes	Yes	Yes	Yes	Yes	99	1	100
Netherlands[2]	Yes	Yes	Yes	Yes	No	Varies	100	m	100
New Zealand	No	a	a	Yes	Yes	Yes	a	100	100
Norway	No	a	a	Yes	Yes	Yes	a	100	100
Poland	Yes	Yes	Yes	No	a	a	100	a	100
Portugal	m	m	m	m	m	m	m	m	m
Slovak Republic	Yes	Yes	Yes	No	a	a	100	a	100
Slovenia	No	a	a	Yes	Yes	Yes	a	100	100
Spain	Yes	Yes	Yes	No	a	a	100	a	100
Sweden	Yes	Yes	Yes	Yes	Yes	Yes	30	70	100
Switzerland	Yes	Yes	Yes	Yes	Yes	m	100	m	100
Turkey	Yes	Yes	Yes	No	a	a	100	a	100
United Kingdom	Yes	Yes	Yes	Yes	Varies	Yes	x(9)	x(9)	100
United States	Yes	Varies	Varies	Yes	Varies	Yes	x(9)	x(9)	100
Other G20 Argentina	m	m	m	m	m	m	m	m	m
Brazil	Yes	Yes	No	Yes	Yes	No	x(9)	x(9)	100
China	m	m	m	m	m	m	m	m	m
India	m	m	m	m	m	m	m	m	m
Indonesia	m	m	m	m	m	m	m	m	m
Russian Federation	m	m	m	m	m	m	m	m	m
Saudi Arabia	m	m	m	m	m	m	m	m	m
South Africa	m	m	m	m	m	m	m	m	m

1. For most jurisdictions.
2. The teachers in integrated programmes are qualified nursery personnel with additional training for early childhood education. These integrated programmes are only offered to the 3-year-old children in ISCED 0 (who are missing in table C2.1).
Source: OECD, INES Working Party special data collection on early childhood education programmes.
Please refer to the Reader's Guide for information concerning the symbols replacing missing data.
StatLink ▆▆ᔕ▙ http://dx.doi.org/10.1787/888932667064

HOW MANY STUDENTS ARE EXPECTED TO ENTER TERTIARY EDUCATION?

- Based on current patterns of entry, it is estimated that an average of 62% of today's young adults in OECD countries will enter tertiary-type A (largely theory-based) programmes over their lifetimes, and 49% before the age of 25.

- In 2010, one in five students who entered a tertiary-type A programmes for the first time was older than 25, on average among OECD countries with available data. This varied from more than one student in three in Iceland, Israel and Portugal to less than one in ten in Belgium, Italy and Mexico.

- Poland and Slovenia are the two countries with the largest proportion of young adults who are expected to enter tertiary-type A education under the age of 25 when international students – students who left their country of origin and moved to another country for the purpose of study – are not counted.

Chart C3.1. Entry rates into tertiary-type A education, by age group (2010)
Including and excluding international students

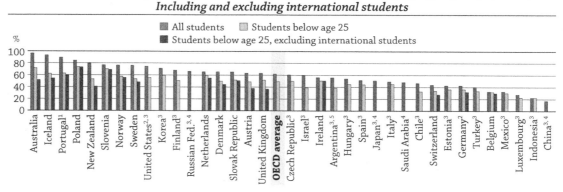

1. Entry rates may be overestimated as they include all students who entered the first year of a programme, not just those students who entered a tertiary-type A or B programme for the first time.
2. The entry rates for tertiary-type A programmes include the entry rates for tertiary-type B programmes.
3. New entrants data for international students are missing.
4. New entrants data by age are missing.
5. Year of reference 2009.
Countries are ranked in descending order of entry rates for tertiary-type A education in 2010.
Source: OECD. Argentina, China, Indonesia: UNESCO Institute for Statistics (World Education Indicators programme). Saudi Arabia: Observatory on Higher Education. Tables C3.1 and C3.2. See Annex 3 for notes (*www.oecd.org/edu/eag2012*).
StatLink ⟲ http://dx.doi.org/10.1787/888932663112

How to read this chart
This chart shows the likelihood of people entering a tertiary-type A programme across OECD countries. For example, among a group of 100 young men and women:

- in Australia, more than 95 people are expected to enter a university-level programme in their lifetimes, but only 71 will do so before the age of 25;

- in Poland, 84 people are expected to enter a university-level programme in their lifetimes, and 74 will do so before the age of 25; and

- if international students are excluded from consideration, only 51 people in Australia will enter such a programme before the age of 25, compared to 73 students in Poland.

■ Context

Entry rates estimate the proportion of people who are expected to enter a specific type of tertiary education programme during their lifetimes. They also indicate the accessibility of tertiary education and the perceived value of attending tertiary programmes, and provide some indication of the degree to which a population is acquiring the high-level skills and knowledge valued by today's labour market. High entry and enrolment rates in tertiary education imply that a highly educated labour force is being developed and maintained.

In OECD countries, the belief that skills acquired through higher education are valued more than those held by people with lower educational attainment stems from the depreciation, both real and feared, of "routine" jobs that could be performed instead in low-wage countries or mechanised, as well as from the growing understanding that knowledge and innovation are key to sustaining economic growth in countries. Tertiary institutions will be challenged not only to meet growing demand by expanding the number of places offered, but also to adapt programmes and teaching methods to match the diverse needs of a new generation of students.

Other findings

- Based on current patterns of entry, it is estimated that **an average of 17% of today's young adults will enter tertiary-type B (shorter and largely vocational) programmes over their lifetimes:** 19% of women and 16% of men. In 2010, more than 40% of students entered this type of programme for the first time after the age of 25, on average among OECD countries with available data.

- **In 2010, the expected rate of entry into tertiary-type A programmes was 25% higher for women than for men.**

- In the 24 OECD countries with available data, **an estimated 2.8% of today's young adults will enter advanced research programmes.**

- In all countries except Finland, Korea and Saudi Arabia, **the most popular fields of education chosen by new entrants into tertiary programmes are social sciences, business and law.**

Trends

Between 1995 and 2010, entry rates for tertiary-type A programmes increased by nearly 25 percentage points, on average across OECD countries, while entry rates for tertiary-type B programmes remained stable. This increase is due to the increased accessibility of tertiary education in many countries, but also because of structural changes in the educational systems of some countries, such as the creation of new programmes (in relation to labour market needs) or shorter programmes (with the implementation of the Bologna process). Entry rates for tertiary programmes have also risen due to the expansion of access to such programmes to a wider population, including international students (see Indicator C4) and older students. In addition, the increases in entry rates may be overstated, as part of the increase can be attributed to better data coverage. In the past decade, many countries have improved their data collection systems, and the 2010 data better reflect access to tertiary education.

Note

Entry rates represent the estimated percentage of an age cohort that is expected to enter a tertiary programme over a lifetime. This estimate is based on the number of new entrants in 2010 and the age distribution of this group. Therefore, the entry rates are based on a "synthetic cohort" assumption, according to which the current pattern of entry constitutes the best estimate of the lifecycle behaviour of today's young adults. These entry rates are thus sensitive to any changes in the education system, such as the introduction of new programmes or the variation in the number of international students. Entry rates can be very high, and even greater than 100% (thus clearly indicating that the synthetic cohort assumption is implausible), during a period when an unexpected category of people decides to enter tertiary education. For example, this is the case in Australia, where in 2010 a large proportion of students came from other countries (the entry rate decreases from 96% to 67% when international students are excluded from consideration) or in Iceland, where a large number of women went to university to pursue their studies (entry rates for women decrease from 113% to 74% when students above the age of 25 are excluded from consideration).

Analysis

Overall access to tertiary education

It is estimated that 62% of young adults in OECD countries will enter tertiary-type A programmes during their lifetimes if current patterns of entry continue. In several countries, at least 70% of young adults are expected to enter these programmes, while in Belgium, China, Indonesia, Luxembourg and Mexico, not more than 35% are expected to do so (Chart C3.1).

The proportion of students entering tertiary-type B programmes is generally smaller, mainly because these programmes are less developed in most OECD countries. In OECD countries for which data are available, an average of 17% of young adults will enter these types of programmes. Proportions range from 3% or less in Italy, Mexico, the Netherlands, Norway, Poland, Portugal and the Slovak Republic, to 30% or more in Argentina, Belgium, Korea and New Zealand, to more than 50% in Chile. Although the Netherlands offers relatively few of these programmes, this is expected to change with the introduction of new associate degrees. Finland and Norway have, respectively, no or only one tertiary-type B programme in their education systems (Table C3.1).

Belgium, Chile and China are the three countries where the expected proportion of students who will enter tertiary-type B programmes is higher than those expected to enter tertiary-type A programmes. In Belgium and Chile, broad access to tertiary-type B programmes counterbalances comparatively low entry rates into academic tertiary programmes. Other countries, most notably Israel and the United Kingdom, have entry rates around the OECD average for academic (type A) programmes, and comparatively high entry rates for vocational (type B) programmes. New Zealand's entry rates for both types of programmes are among the highest in OECD countries. However, these entry rates are inflated by a greater population of older and international students (Table C3.1).

Chart C3.2. **Entry rates into tertiary-type A and B education (2000 and 2010)**

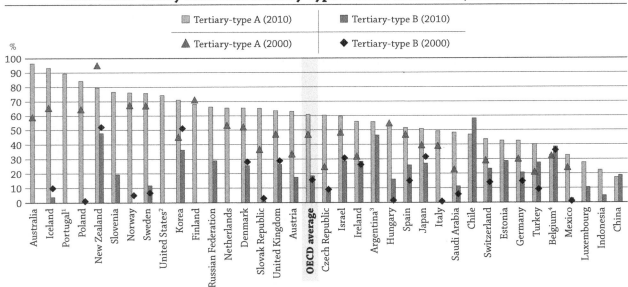

1. Entry rates may be overestimated as they include all students who entered the first year of a programme, not just those students who entered a tertiary-type A or B programme for the first time.
2. In 2010, the entry rates for tertiary-type A programmes include the entry rates for tertiary-type B programmes.
3. Year of reference 2009 instead of 2010.
4. Year of reference 2001 instead of 2000.
Countries are ranked in descending order of entry rates for tertiary-type A education in 2010.
Source: OECD. Argentina, China, Indonesia: UNESCO Institute for Statistics (World Education Indicators programme). Saudi Arabia: Observatory on Higher Education. Table C3.3. See Annex 3 for notes (*www.oecd.org/edu/eag2012*).
StatLink ⟨ms⟩ http://dx.doi.org/10.1787/888932663131

C3

On average, across all OECD countries with comparable data, the proportion of young adults expected to enter tertiary-type A programmes increased by 15 percentage points between 2000 and 2010, and by nearly 25 percentage points between 1995 and 2010 (Table C3.3). Entry rates into these programmes increased by more than 20 percentage points between 2000 and 2010 in Australia, Austria, the Czech Republic, Iceland, Ireland, Korea, Saudi Arabia and the Slovak Republic. In Korea, the increase is mainly due to a reclassification of tertiary-type B programmes into tertiary-type A programmes. Finland, Hungary and New Zealand are the only OECD countries that show a decline in entry rates into these programmes. However, in Hungary, the decrease is counterbalanced by a significant increase in entry rates into tertiary-type B programmes during the same period. In New Zealand, the rise and fall of entry rates between 2000 and 2010 mirrored the rise and fall of the number of international students over the same period (Chart C3.2).

Among OECD countries, overall net entry rates into tertiary-type B programmes between 2000 and 2010 have remained relatively stable except in Hungary, Spain and Turkey, where they have increased by more than 10 percentage points, and in Korea, where they have decreased by 15 percentage points (Chart C3.2).

It is expected that 2.8% of today's young adults in the 24 OECD countries with comparable data will enter advanced research programmes during their lifetimes. Among all countries with available data, the proportions range from less than 1% in Argentina, Chile, Indonesia, Mexico, Saudi Arabia and Turkey to at least 4% in Austria, the Slovak Republic, Slovenia and Switzerland (Table C3.1).

Age of new entrants into tertiary education

On average among OECD countries, 80% of all first-time entrants into tertiary-type A programmes and 58% of first-time entrants into tertiary-type B programmes are under 25 years old. Some 55% of students who enter an advanced research programme are younger than 30 (Table C3.2).

The age of new entrants into tertiary education varies among OECD countries because of differences in the typical graduation ages from upper secondary education (see Tables X1.1a and X1.1b), the intake capacity of institutions (admissions with *numerus clausus,* one of many methods used to limit the number of students who may study at a tertiary institution) and the opportunities to enter the labour market before enrolling in tertiary education.

Traditionally, students enter academic programmes immediately after having completed upper secondary education, and this remains true in many countries. For example, in Belgium, Indonesia, Italy and Mexico, 90% of all first-time entrants into tertiary-type A or B programmes are under 25. In other OECD countries, the transition from upper secondary to tertiary education may occur at a later age because of time spent in the labour force or the military. In such cases, first-time entrants into tertiary-type A or B programmes typically represent a much wider age range. In Iceland, Israel and Portugal, only two-thirds of all first-time entrants into tertiary-type A programmes are under 25 (Table C3.2).

The proportion of older first-time entrants into these programmes (tertiary-type A and B) may reflect the flexibility of the programmes and their suitability to students outside the typical age group. It may also reflect the value placed on work experience before entering higher education, which is characteristic of the Nordic countries and is also common in Australia, Hungary, New Zealand and Switzerland, where a sizeable proportion of new entrants is much older than the typical age of entry. It may also reflect some countries' mandatory military service, which postpones entry into tertiary education. For example, Israel – where more than half of students entering tertiary-type A education for the first time are 24 or older – has mandatory military service for 18-21 year-old men and 18-20 year-old women. Nevertheless, entering tertiary education at a later stage also has some consequences for the economy, such as foregone tax revenue. Some governments are encouraging students to make the most of their capacities by moving more rapidly into and through tertiary education, and are providing universities with more incentives to promote on-time completion.

During the recent economic crisis, some young people have postponed entry into the labour market and remained in education. Some governments have also developed second-chance programmes, aimed at people who have left school early, to raise the skills level of the workforce and increase opportunities for people to

C3

acquire practical education and skills. In some countries, high entry rates may reflect a temporary phenomenon, such as university reforms, the economic crisis, or a surge in international students.

Impact of international students on entry rates into tertiary-type A programmes

By definition, all international students enrolling for the first time in a country are counted as new entrants, regardless of their previous education in other countries. To highlight the impact of international students on entry rates into tertiary-type A programmes, both unadjusted and adjusted entry rates (i.e. the entry rate when international students are excluded from consideration) are presented in Tables C3.1 and C3.2.

In Australia, the difference between the unadjusted and adjusted entry rates is 29 percentage points – the largest among all countries with comparable data. In Austria, Iceland, New Zealand, Sweden, Switzerland and the United Kingdom, the presence of international students also affects entry rates greatly, with differences from 11 to 22 percentage points (Table C3.1).

Unsurprisingly, the greatest impact of international students on entry and graduation rate indicators (see Indicator A3) is seen among countries with the largest proportions of international students, e.g. Australia, New Zealand and the United Kingdom. To improve the comparability of these indicators, international students should be presented separately whenever possible.

The expected percentage of new entrants into tertiary-type A education changes dramatically when older and international students are not considered. These two groups are important components of the student population in countries, but they can artificially inflate the expected proportion of today's young adults that will enter a tertiary programme. When international and older students are not counted, Poland and Slovenia become the two countries with the largest proportion of people who are expected to enter tertiary-type A education under the age of 25. The results in Poland follow the 1999 education reforms in that country, which aimed to increase the quality of its secondary and higher education systems and increase equal educational opportunities. Poland and Slovenia are also two of the six countries with the highest percentage of the population that has attained at least an upper secondary education.

When international as well as older students are excluded, Australia, with its large proportion of older and international students, slips from first to seventh place in terms of entry rates; Iceland from second to sixth place; and New Zealand from fifth to twelfth place (Chart C3.1).

Pathways between academic and vocational programmes

In some countries, tertiary-type A and B programmes are provided by different types of institutions, but this is changing. It is increasingly common for universities or other institutions to offer both types of programmes. The two types of programmes are also gradually becoming more similar in terms of curriculum, orientation and learning outcomes.

Graduates from tertiary-type B programmes can often gain entry into tertiary-type A programmes, usually in the second or third year, or even into a master's programme. Adding entry rates into these two types of programmes together to obtain overall tertiary-level entry rates would thus result in overcounting. Entry is often subject to certain conditions, such as passing a special examination, past personal or professional achievements, and/or completion of a "bridging" programme, depending on the country or programme. In some cases, students who leave an academic programme before graduating can be successfully re-oriented towards vocational programmes.

Countries with high rates of entry into tertiary education may also be those that offer pathways between the two types of programmes.

Entry rate into tertiary programmes, by field of education (Tertiary-type A and B)

In almost all countries, a large proportion of students pursues tertiary programmes in the fields of social sciences, business and law. In 2010, these fields received the highest share of new entrants in all countries except Finland, Korea and Saudi Arabia. In Finland, the proportion of new entrants was highest in engineering, manufacturing and construction, while in Korea and Saudi Arabia the proportion was highest in humanities, arts and education (Chart C3.3).

Science-related fields, which include science and engineering, manufacturing and construction, are less popular. On average, only one quarter of all students enter these fields (Table C3.4). This low level of participation is partly due to the under-representation of women: on average in 2010, only 13% of new entrants into tertiary education who were women chose these fields, compared with 38% of new entrants who were men. Among the new entrant population, the proportion of women who chose science-related fields ranged from 5% in Belgium to 20% in Mexico, while among the male population, the proportion in these fields ranged from 26% in the Netherlands to 58% in Finland (Table C3.4a, available on line). The demand for science graduates in the labour market and the under-representation of women are explored further in Indicator A4.

Chart C3.3. Distribution of new entrants into tertiary programmes, by field of education (2010)
*Only those fields in which more than 20% of students entered a tertiary programme in 2010
are shown in the graph below*

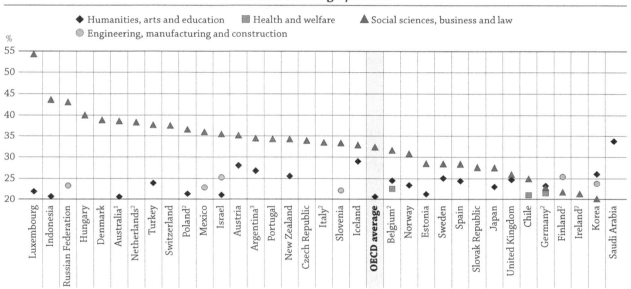

1. Excludes tertiary-type B programmes.
2. Excludes advanced research programmes.
3. Year of reference 2009.
Countries are ranked in descending order of new entrants in social sciences, business and law programmes in 2010.
Source: OECD. Argentina, China, Indonesia: UNESCO Institute for Statistics (World Education Indicators programme). Saudi Arabia: Observatory on Higher Education. Table C3.4. See Annex 3 for notes (*www.oecd.org/edu/eag2012*).
StatLink ⟨ᴍᴵˢ⟩ http://dx.doi.org/10.1787/888932663150

The distribution of entrants into advanced research programmes by field of education is very different from that of tertiary education as a whole. In 2010, 22% of new doctoral entrants undertook studies in science, compared to 10% of all new tertiary entrants who chose this field. In Israel and Luxembourg, more than 30% of advanced research students chose science (Table C3.4b, available on line).

Definitions

Advanced research programmes (ISCED 6) are at the doctorate level.

Students are classified as **international students** if they left their country of origin and moved to another country for the purpose of study. International students enrolling for the first time in a postgraduate programme are considered first-time entrants.

New (first-time) entrants are students who enrol at the relevant level of education for the first time.

The **tertiary-level entry rate** is an estimated probability, based on current entry patterns, that a young adult will enter tertiary education during his or her lifetime.

Tertiary-type A programmes (ISCED 5A) are largely theory-based and designed to provide qualifications for entry into advanced research programmes and highly skilled professions.

Tertiary-type B programmes (ISCED 5B) are classified at the same level of competence as tertiary-type A programmes, but are more occupationally oriented and provide direct access to the labour market. They tend to be of shorter duration than academic programmes (typically two to three years) and are generally not designed to lead to university degrees.

Methodology

Data refer to the academic year 2009-10 and are based on the UOE data collection on education statistics administered by the OECD in 2011 (for details, see Annex 3 at *www.oecd.org/edu/eag2012*). The fields of education used in the UOE data collection instruments follow the revised ISCED classification by field of education. The same classification is used for all levels of education.

Data on trends in entry rates (Table C3.3) for the years 1995, 2000, 2001, 2002, 2003 and 2004 are based on a special survey carried out in OECD countries in January 2007.

Data on the impact of international students on tertiary entry rates are based on a special survey carried out by the OECD in December 2011.

Tables C3.1, C3.2 and C3.3 show the sum of net entry rates for all ages. The net entry rate for a specific age is obtained by dividing the number of first-time entrants of that age for each type of tertiary education by the total population in the corresponding age group. The sum of net entry rates is calculated by adding the rates for each year of age. The result represents an estimate of the probability that a young person will enter tertiary education in his/her lifetime if current age-specific entry rates continue. Table C3.1 also shows the 20th, 50th and 80th percentiles of the age distribution of first-time entrants, i.e. the age below which 20%, 50% and 80% of first-time entrants are found.

Not all countries can distinguish between students entering a tertiary programme for the first time and those transferring between different levels of tertiary education or repeating or re-entering a level after an absence. Thus, first-time entry rates for tertiary-type A or tertiary-type B cannot be added to form a total tertiary-level entrance rate because it would result in counting entrants twice.

The statistical data for Israel are supplied by and under the responsibility of the relevant Israeli authorities. The use of such data by the OECD is without prejudice to the status of the Golan Heights, East Jerusalem and Israeli settlements in the West Bank under the terms of international law.

References

The following additional material relevant to this indicator is available on line:

- *Table C3.4a. Distribution of tertiary new entrants, by field of education and gender (2010)*
  StatLink ▄▄▄ http://dx.doi.org/10.1787/888932667178

- *Table C3.4b. Distribution of new entrants into advanced research programmes, by field of education (2010)*
  StatLink ▄▄▄ http://dx.doi.org/10.1787/888932667197

Table C3.1. **Entry rates into tertiary education and age distribution of new entrants (2010)**
Sum of age-specific entry rates, by gender and programme destination

	Tertiary-type B				Tertiary-type A							Advanced research programmes			
	Net entry rates				Net entry rates				Age at:			Net entry rates			
	M+W	Men	Women	Adjusted from international students[1]	M+W	Men	Women	Adjusted from international students[1]	20th percentile[2]	50th percentile[2]	80th percentile[2]	M+W	Men	Women	Adjusted from international students[1]
	(1)	(2)	(3)	(4)	(5)	(6)	(7)	(8)	(9)	(10)	(11)	(12)	(13)	(14)	(15)
OECD Australia	m	m	m	m	96	83	110	67	19	21	27	3.3	3.4	3.2	2.1
Austria	17	16	19	17	63	56	70	49	20	21	26	5.5	5.5	5.5	4.0
Belgium	38	32	45	36	33	32	34	30	18	19	20	m	m	m	m
Canada	m	m	m	m	m	m	m	m	m	m	m	m	m	m	m
Chile*	58	58	59	m	47	43	50	m	19	20	29	n	n	n	n
Czech Republic	9	5	13	m	60	52	70	m	20	20	25	3.8	4.1	3.4	m
Denmark	25	25	26	23	65	53	78	57	21	22	26	3.8	3.9	3.6	2.8
Estonia	29	25	33	m	43	35	50	m	19	20	23	2.7	2.4	3.0	m
Finland	a	a	a	a	68	61	75	m	20	21	27	m	m	m	m
France	m	m	m	m	m	m	m	m	m	m	m	m	m	m	m
Germany	21	13	28	m	42	42	43	36	20	21	24	m	m	m	m
Greece	m	m	m	m	m	m	m	m	m	m	m	m	m	m	m
Hungary	16	11	21	m	54	50	58	m	19	20	25	1.6	1.6	1.6	m
Iceland	4	4	4	m	93	74	113	80	21	22	29	2.3	2.0	2.6	1.8
Ireland	28	32	25	25	56	51	61	56	18	19	21	m	m	m	m
Israel	29	28	29	m	60	53	66	m	22	24	27	2.0	1.9	2.1	m
Italy	n	n	n	n	49	42	57	m	19	20	21	2.3	2.1	2.4	m
Japan	27	20	35	m	51	56	45	m	18	19	19	1.0	1.3	0.6	m
Korea	36	33	40	m	71	71	71	m	18	19	24	2.7	3.2	2.2	m
Luxembourg	10	10	10	m	28	26	29	m	21	22	25	1.0	1.1	0.9	m
Mexico	3	3	2	m	33	33	32	m	18	19	21	n	n	n	m
Netherlands	n	n	n	n	65	61	70	61	18	20	22	m	m	m	m
New Zealand	48	46	50	39	80	66	93	63	19	21	32	2.9	2.9	2.8	1.5
Norway	n	n	n	n	76	64	89	73	20	21	27	2.9	3.0	2.8	2.8
Poland	1	n	2	m	84	73	96	83	19	20	23	m	m	m	m
Portugal[3]	n	n	n	m	89	78	101	84	19	22	32	3.3	3.3	3.4	2.8
Slovak Republic	1	1	1	m	65	55	76	63	20	21	26	4.0	4.2	3.8	3.7
Slovenia	19	19	19	m	77	64	90	75	19	20	22	5.5	4.7	6.3	5.0
Spain	26	24	27	m	52	44	60	m	18	19	25	1.8	1.7	1.9	m
Sweden	12	12	12	12	76	65	87	65	20	22	28	2.9	3.0	2.9	2.0
Switzerland	23	25	21	m	44	43	45	33	20	22	27	5.0	5.5	4.5	2.4
Turkey	28	31	24	m	40	40	40	m	19	20	24	0.9	1.0	0.7	m
United Kingdom	26	19	34	24	63	56	71	41	18	20	25	2.8	3.0	2.7	1.6
United States	x(5)	x(6)	x(7)	m	74	67	82	m	18	20	27	m	m	m	m
OECD average	17	16	19	m	62	55	69	m	19	21	25	2.8	2.8	2.8	m
EU21 average	15	13	17	m	60	52	67	m	19	21	25	3.1	3.1	3.2	m
Other G20 Argentina[4]	46	28	65	m	56	48	63	m	19	21	28	0.4	0.4	0.5	m
Brazil	m	m	m	m	m	m	m	m	m	m	m	m	m	m	m
China	19	17	20	m	17	16	18	m	m	m	m	2.7	m	m	m
India	m	m	m	m	m	m	m	m	m	m	m	m	m	m	m
Indonesia	5	4	5	m	22	22	23	m	18	19	19	0.2	0.2	0.1	m
Russian Federation	29	x(1)	x(1)	m	66	x(5)	x(5)	m	m	m	m	2.4	x(12)	x(12)	m
Saudi Arabia	11	16	6	11	48	47	50	47	m	m	m	n	n	n	m
South Africa	m	m	m	m	m	m	m	m	m	m	m	m	m	m	m
G20 average	21	17	24	m	52	48	54	m	m	m	m	1.6	1.5	1.3	m

Note: Mismatches between the coverage of the population data and the new-entrants data mean that the entry rates for those countries that are net exporters of students may be underestimated and those that are net importers may be overestimated. The adjusted entry rates seek to compensate for that. Please refer to Annex 1 for information on the method used to calculate entry rates (gross rates versus net rates) and the corresponding age of entry.

1. Adjusted entry rates correspond to the entry rate when international students are excluded.
2. Respectively 20%, 50% and 80% of new entrants are below this age.
3. Entry rates may be overestimated as they include all students who entered the first year of a programme, not just those students who entered a tertiary-type A or B programme for the first time.
4. Year of reference 2009.
* Due to late changes, Chile's data on new entrants are not included in the OECD average calculation.
Source: OECD. Argentina, China, Indonesia: UNESCO Institute for Statistics (World Education Indicators programme). Saudi Arabia: Observatory on Higher Education. See Annex 3 for notes *(www.oecd.org/edu/eag2012)*.
Please refer to the Reader's Guide for information concerning the symbols replacing missing data.

StatLink http://dx.doi.org/10.1787/888932667102

C3

Table C3.2. Entry rates into tertiary education below the typical age of entry (2010)

Sum of age-specific entry rates up to age 25 for tertiary-type A or B, and up to age 30 for advanced researh programmes, by gender and programme destination

	Tertiary-type B (below 25)					Tertiary-type A (below 25)					Advanced research programmes (below 30)				
	M+W	Men	Women	Adjusted from international students[1]	Share of below 25-year-old new entrants[2]	M+W	Men	Women	Adjusted from international students[1]	Share of below 25-year-old new entrants[2]	M+W	Men	Women	Adjusted from international students[1]	Share of below 30-year-old new entrants[2]
	(1)	(2)	(3)	(4)	(5)	(6)	(7)	(8)	(9)	(10)	(11)	(12)	(13)	(14)	(15)
OECD															
Australia	m	m	m	m	m	71	61	82	51	73	1.5	1.6	1.5	0.9	48
Austria	8	8	9	8	46	49	40	57	38	75	3.7	3.6	3.8	2.8	66
Belgium	37	31	43	35	95	32	30	33	30	97	m	m	m	m	m
Canada	m	m	m	m	m	m	m	m	m	m	m	m	m	m	m
Chile*	39	38	39	m	70	33	29	36	m	74	n	n	n	m	47
Czech Republic	7	4	11	m	81	50	44	56	m	80	3.0	3.2	2.8	m	77
Denmark	13	13	13	11	49	50	39	61	44	76	2.4	2.7	2.1	1.7	61
Estonia	21	20	23	m	76	36	30	42	m	86	1.7	1.6	1.9	m	66
Finland	a	a	a	a	a	51	46	55	m	74	m	m	m	m	m
France	m	m	m	m	m	m	m	m	m	m	m	m	m	m	m
Germany	16	8	24	m	75	36	35	38	32	85	m	m	m	m	m
Greece	m	m	m	m	m	m	m	m	m	m	m	m	m	m	m
Hungary	13	9	18	m	83	45	41	48	m	81	1.2	1.1	1.2	m	70
Iceland	1	1	n	m	17	62	51	74	54	67	0.6	0.7	0.6	n	29
Ireland	23	26	20	21	75	50	45	56	50	88	m	m	m	m	m
Israel	20	16	25	m	72	39	29	49	m	66	0.7	0.6	0.8	m	35
Italy	m	m	m	m	m	45	38	53	m	91	m	m	m	m	m
Japan	m	m	m	m	m	m	m	m	m	m	m	m	m	m	m
Korea	31	29	34	m	84	60	58	61	m	82	1.0	1.1	0.9	m	35
Luxembourg	2	2	3	m	18	22	21	24	m	77	0.6	0.6	0.5	m	55
Mexico	3	3	2	m	94	30	30	30	m	93	n	n	n	m	43
Netherlands	n	n	n	n	25	59	55	63	55	90	m	m	m	m	m
New Zealand	22	22	21	16	48	53	45	61	41	69	1.4	1.5	1.4	0.6	50
Norway	n	n	n	n	49	58	48	68	55	75	1.6	1.8	1.4	1.5	51
Poland	1	n	1	m	79	74	65	83	73	86	m	m	m	m	m
Portugal[3]	n	n	n	n	16	62	54	72	59	64	1.3	1.2	1.4	1.1	35
Slovak Republic	1	1	1	m	80	52	45	59	51	77	3.0	3.0	2.9	2.9	74
Slovenia	12	13	11	m	58	70	59	82	69	89	3.6	3.1	4.1	3.3	65
Spain	20	19	21	m	71	44	37	52	m	79	1.1	0.9	1.2	m	54
Sweden	6	6	6	6	53	53	46	61	48	72	1.7	1.9	1.6	1.0	58
Switzerland	10	10	10	m	41	34	32	36	27	75	3.7	4.1	3.4	1.8	73
Turkey	22	25	19	m	80	33	32	35	m	83	n	n	n	m	58
United Kingdom	8	7	10	7	31	51	47	56	37	81	1.7	1.8	1.6	0.9	62
United States	x(6)	x(7)	x(8)	m	m	56	52	59	m	76	m	m	m	m	m
OECD average	11	10	12	m	58	49	43	55	m	80	1.7	1.7	1.7	m	55
EU21 average	10	9	12	m	56	49	43	55	m	81	2.1	2.1	2.1	m	62
Other G20															
Argentina[4]	28	20	37	m	62	38	34	43	m	72	m	m	m	m	m
Brazil	m	m	m	m	m	m	m	m	m	m	m	m	m	m	m
China	m	m	m	m	m	m	m	m	m	m	m	m	m	m	m
India	m	m	m	m	m	m	m	m	m	m	m	m	m	m	m
Indonesia	5	4	5	m	100	22	22	23	m	100	0.1	0.2	0.1	m	92
Russian Federation	m	m	m	m	m	m	m	m	m	m	m	m	m	m	m
Saudi Arabia	m	m	m	m	m	m	m	m	m	m	m	m	m	m	m
South Africa	m	m	m	m	m	m	m	m	m	m	m	m	m	m	m
G20 average	m	m	m	m	m	m	m	m	m	m	m	m	m	m	m

Note: Mismatches between the coverage of the population data and the new entrants data mean that the entry rates for those countries that are net exporters of students may be underestimated and those that are net importers may be overestimated. The adjusted entry rates seek to compensate for that. Please refer to Annex 1 for information on the method used to calculate entry rates (gross rates versus net rates) and the corresponding age of entry.

1. Adjusted entry rates correspond to the entry rate when international students are excluded.

2. Share of 25-year-old new entrants among the total population of new entrants.

3. Entry rates may be overestimated as they include students who enrolled in the first year of a programme, instead of for the first time in tertiary-type A or B programmes.

4. Year of reference 2009.

* Due to late changes, Chile's data on new entrants are not included in the OECD average calculation.

Source: OECD. Argentina, Indonesia: UNESCO Institute for Statistics (World Education Indicators programme). See Annex 3 for notes (www.oecd.org/edu/eag2012). *Please refer to the Reader's Guide for information concerning the symbols replacing missing data.*

StatLink http://dx.doi.org/10.1787/888932667121

Table C3.3. Trends in entry rates at the tertiary level (1995-2010)

		Tertiary-type 5A[1]						Tertiary-type 5B					
		1995	2000	2005	2008	2009	2010	1995	2000	2005	2008	2009	2010
		(1)	(2)	(7)	(10)	(11)	(12)	(13)	(14)	(19)	(22)	(23)	(24)
OECD	Australia	m	59	82	87	94	**96**	m	m	m	m	m	**m**
	Austria	27	34	37	50	54	**63**	m	m	8	9	15	**17**
	Belgium	m	m	33	31	31	**33**	m	m	34	37	39	**38**
	Canada	m	m	m	m	m	**m**	m	m	m	m	m	**m**
	Chile*	m	m	m	m	44	**47**	m	m	m	m	59	**58**
	Czech Republic	m	25	41	57	59	**60**	m	9	8	9	8	**9**
	Denmark	40	52	57	59	55	**65**	33	28	23	21	25	**25**
	Estonia	m	m	55	42	42	**43**	m	m	34	31	30	**29**
	Finland	39	71	73	70	69	**68**	32	a	a	a	a	**a**
	France	m	m	m	m	m	**m**	m	m	m	m	m	**m**
	Germany[2]	26	30	36	36	40	**42**	15	15	14	14	19	**21**
	Greece	15	30	43	42	m	**m**	5	21	13	26	m	**m**
	Hungary	m	55	68	57	53	**54**	m	1	11	12	14	**16**
	Iceland	38	66	74	73	77	**93**	12	10	7	6	4	**4**
	Ireland	m	32	45	46	51	**56**	m	26	14	20	25	**28**
	Israel	m	48	55	60	60	**60**	m	31	25	26	27	**29**
	Italy	m	39	56	51	50	**49**	m	1	n	n	n	**n**
	Japan	31	40	42	48	49	**51**	33	32	31	29	27	**27**
	Korea	41	45	51	71	71	**71**	27	51	48	38	36	**36**
	Luxembourg	m	m	m	25	31	**28**	m	m	m	n	2	**10**
	Mexico	m	24	27	30	31	**33**	m	1	2	2	2	**3**
	Netherlands	44	53	59	62	63	**65**	a	a	a	n	n	**n**
	New Zealand	83	95	79	72	80	**80**	44	52	48	46	47	**48**
	Norway	59	67	73	71	77	**76**	5	5	0	n	n	**n**
	Poland	36	65	76	83	85	**84**	1	1	1	1	1	**1**
	Portugal[3]	m	m	m	81	84	**89**	m	m	m	n	n	**n**
	Slovak Republic	28	37	59	72	69	**65**	1	3	2	1	1	**1**
	Slovenia	m	m	40	56	61	**77**	m	m	49	32	32	**19**
	Spain	m	47	43	43	46	**52**	3	15	22	22	23	**26**
	Sweden	57	67	76	65	68	**76**	m	7	7	10	11	**12**
	Switzerland	17	29	37	38	41	**44**	29	14	16	19	21	**23**
	Turkey	18	21	27	30	40	**40**	9	9	19	23	30	**28**
	United Kingdom	m	47	51	57	61	**63**	m	29	28	30	31	**26**
	United States	m	42	64	64	70	**74**	m	13	x(7)	x(10)	x(11)	**x(12)**
	OECD average	37	47	54	56	59	**62**	17	16	17	16	17	**17**
	OECD average for countries with data available from 2000 to 2010		48				**63**		17				**20**
	EU21 average	35	46	53	54	56	**60**	11	11	15	14	15	**15**
Other G20	Argentina	m	m	m	47	56	**m**	m	m	m	44	46	**m**
	Brazil	m	m	m	m	m	**m**	m	m	m	m	m	**m**
	China	m	m	m	m	17	**17**	m	m	m	m	19	**19**
	India	m	m	m	m	m	**m**	m	m	m	m	m	**m**
	Indonesia	m	m	m	m	22	**22**	m	m	m	m	5	**5**
	Russian Federation	m	m	67	68	69	**66**	m	m	33	30	27	**29**
	Saudi Arabia	24	23	37	42	43	**48**	4	6	10	12	15	**11**
	South Africa	m	m	m	m	m	**m**	m	m	m	m	m	**m**
	G20 average	m	m	m	m	51	**52**	m	m	m	m	22	**19**

Note: Columns showing entry rates for the years 2001-04, 06, 07 (i.e. Columns 3-6, 8-9, 15-18, 20-21) are available for consultation on line (see *StatLink* below). Please refer to Annex 1 for information on the method used to calculate entry rates (gross rates versus net rates) and the corresponding age of entry.

1. The entry rates for tertiary-type A programmes include advanced research programmes for 1995, 2000-03 (except for Belgium and Germany).
2. Break in time series between 2008 and 2009 due to a partial reallocation of vocational programmes into ISCED 2 and ISCED 5B.
3. Entry rates may be overestimated as they include all students who entered the first year of a programme, not just those students who entered a tertiary-type A or B programme for the first time.

* Due to late changes, Chile's data on new entrants are not included in the OECD average calculation.

Source: OECD. Argentina, China, Indonesia: UNESCO Institute for Statistics (World Education Indicators programme). Saudi Arabia: Observatory on Higher Education. See Annex 3 for notes *(www.oecd.org/edu/eag2012)*.

Please refer to the Reader's Guide for information concerning the symbols replacing missing data.

StatLink http://dx.doi.org/10.1787/888932667140

Table C3.4. **Distribution of tertiary new entrants, by field of education (2010)**

	Humanities, arts and education	Health and welfare	Social sciences, business and law	Services	Engineering, manufacturing and construction	Sciences	Agriculture	Unknown or unspecified
	(1)	(4)	(5)	(6)	(7)	(8)	(13)	(14)
Australia[1]	21	16	39	4	9	11	1	n
Austria	28	7	35	3	17	10	1	n
Belgium[2]	25	23	32	2	11	5	3	n
Canada	m	m	m	m	m	m	m	m
Chile*	17	21	25	10	17	7	2	n
Czech Republic	17	12	34	6	15	12	4	n
Denmark	16	20	39	2	12	9	2	n
Estonia	21	11	29	9	15	13	3	n
Finland[2]	15	20	22	7	25	9	2	n
France	m	m	m	m	m	m	m	m
Germany[2]	23	21	23	3	16	12	1	1
Greece	m	m	m	m	m	m	m	m
Hungary	13	9	40	14	14	8	2	n
Iceland	29	12	33	2	11	12	1	n
Ireland[2]	14	12	21	4	11	14	2	22
Israel	21	6	36	n	25	8	n	3
Italy[2]	19	13	33	3	15	9	2	4
Japan	23	15	28	9	15	2	2	7
Korea	26	14	20	8	24	8	1	n
Luxembourg	22	5	54	n	8	11	n	n
Mexico	14	9	36	4	23	11	3	2
Netherlands[2]	19	18	38	8	9	6	1	1
New Zealand	26	11	34	6	6	16	1	n
Norway	23	17	31	7	8	9	1	4
Poland[2]	21	8	37	9	15	9	2	n
Portugal	18	14	34	7	18	8	1	n
Slovak Republic	20	17	28	7	17	9	2	n
Slovenia	13	9	33	11	22	8	4	n
Spain[2]	24	13	28	8	17	8	1	n
Sweden	25	13	28	4	19	10	1	n
Switzerland	17	12	38	8	15	9	1	1
Turkey	24	8	38	4	14	8	4	n
United Kingdom	25	18	26	1	8	14	1	7
United States	m	m	m	m	m	m	m	m
OECD average	21	13	32	6	15	10	2	2
EU21 average	20	14	32	6	15	10	2	2
Argentina[3]	27	13	34	4	8	10	3	1
Brazil	m	m	m	m	m	m	m	m
China	m	m	m	m	m	m	m	m
India	m	m	m	m	m	m	m	m
Indonesia	21	5	44	n	16	10	5	1
Russian Federation	11	5	43	5	23	7	2	2
Saudi Arabia	34	7	15	n	13	12	n	20
South Africa	m	m	m	m	m	m	m	m
G20 average	m	m	m	m	m	m	m	m

Note: Columns showing the breakdown of humanities, arts and education (2 and 3) and science (9-12) are available for consultation on line (see *StatLink* below).
1. Excludes tertiary-type B programmes.
2. Excludes advanced research programmes.
3. Year of reference 2009.
* Due to late changes, Chile's data on new entrants are not included in the OECD average calculation.
Source: OECD. Argentina, Indonesia: UNESCO Institute for Statistics (World Education Indicators programme). Saudi Arabia: Observatory on Higher Education. See Annex 3 for notes *(www.oecd.org/edu/eag2012)*.
Please refer to the Reader's Guide for information concerning the symbols replacing missing data.
StatLink ᴹˢᴾ http://dx.doi.org/10.1787/888932667159

WHO STUDIES ABROAD AND WHERE?

In reading this indicator, a distinction should be made between students who have moved from their country of origin with the purpose of studying (international students) and those who are not citizens of the country where they are enrolled (foreign students) but may, in some cases, be long-term residents or, indeed, have been born in the country (see *Definitions* section). International students are thus a subset of foreign students.

- In 2010, more than 4.1 million tertiary students were enrolled outside their country of citizenship.

- Luxembourg (where mobility is high due to strong integration with neighbouring countries), Australia, the United Kingdom, Austria, Switzerland and New Zealand have, in descending order, the highest percentages of international students among their tertiary enrolments.

- In absolute terms, the largest numbers of foreign students are from China, India and Korea. Asian students represent 52% of foreign students enrolled worldwide.

- The number of foreign students enrolled in OECD countries was almost three times the number of citizens from an OECD country studying abroad in 2010. In the 21 European countries that are members of the OECD, there were 2.7 foreign students per each European citizen enrolled abroad.

- Some 83% of all foreign students are enrolled in G20 countries, while 77% of all foreign students are enrolled in OECD countries. These proportions have remained stable during the past decade.

Chart C4.1. **Evolution in the number of students enrolled outside their country of citizenship, by region of destination (2000 to 2010)**

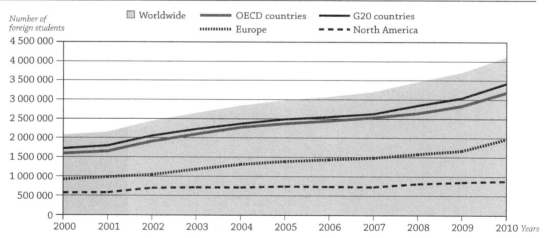

Source: OECD and UNESCO Institute for Statistics for most data on non-OECD countries. Table C4.6. See Annex 3 for notes (*www.oecd.org/edu/eag2012*).
StatLink ᘻ᠊ᣙ http://dx.doi.org/10.1787/888932663169

■ Context

As national economies become more interconnected and participation in education expands, governments and individuals are looking to higher education to broaden students' horizons and help them to better understand the world's languages, cultures and business methods. One way for students to expand their knowledge of other societies and languages, and thus improve their prospects in globalised sectors of the labour market, such as multinational corporations or research, is to study in tertiary institutions in countries other than their own.

The factors driving the general increase in student mobility range from the exploding demand for higher education worldwide and the perceived value of studying at prestigious post-secondary institutions abroad to specific policies aiming to foster student mobility within a geographic region (as is the case in Europe), to efforts by governments to support students in studying specific fields that are growing rapidly in the country of origin. In addition, some countries and institutions undertake major marketing efforts to attract students from outside their boundaries.

A significant portion of students coming from G20 non-OECD countries includes the better performing students, natural candidates for public or private support, or have a relatively high socio-economic background. This implies that student mobility can not only bring stature to tertiary institutions' academic programmes, but also economic benefits to the host education systems.

In the current economic context, shrinking support for scholarships and grants to support student mobility – as well as tightening budgets among individuals – may diminish the pace of student mobility. On the other hand, limited labour market opportunities in students' countries of origin may lower the opportunity costs of studying abroad, and help increase student mobility.

The increase in student mobility in tertiary education can also provide an opportunity for smaller and/or less-developed host education systems to improve the cost efficiency of their education systems. For example, it can help countries focus limited resources on educational programmes with potential economies of scale, or expand participation in tertiary education without having to expand the tertiary system within the country itself. For host countries, enrolling international students can not only help raise revenues from higher education, but also can be part of a broader strategy to recruit highly skilled immigrants.

International students tend to choose different programmes of study than local students (see Indicator A4, in *Education at a Glance 2011*), indicating either a degree of specialisation of countries in the programmes offered, a lack of programmes in the countries of origin, and/or better employment opportunities associated with specific fields of education.

Other findings

- Australia, France, Germany, the United Kingdom and the United States each receive more than 6% of all foreign students worldwide.

- International students from OECD countries mainly come from Canada, France, Germany, Japan, Korea, Turkey and the United States.

- International students make up 10% or more of the enrolments in tertiary education in Australia, Austria, Luxembourg, New Zealand, Switzerland and the United Kingdom. They also account for more than 20% of enrolments in advanced research programmes in Australia, Austria, Canada, Denmark, Ireland, Luxembourg, New Zealand, Sweden, Switzerland, the United Kingdom and the United States.

Trends

Since 2000 and up to 2010, the number of foreign tertiary students enrolled worldwide has increased by 99%, for an average annual growth rate of 7.1%. The number of foreign tertiary students enrolled in OECD countries doubled since 2000, for an average annual increase growth rate of 7.2%.

Europe is the preferred destination for students studying outside their country, with 41% of all international students. North America has 21% of all international students. Nevertheless, the fastest growing regions of destination are Latin America and the Caribbean, Oceania and Asia, mirroring the internationalisation of universities in an increasing set of countries (Chart C4.1).

Analysis

Trends

OECD and UNESCO Institute for Statistics data make it possible to examine longer-term trends in tertiary student mobility. These data illustrate the dramatic growth in foreign enrolments (Box C4.1). Over the past three decades, the number of students enrolled outside their country of citizenship has risen dramatically, from 0.8 million worldwide in 1975 to 4.1 million in 2010, more than a fivefold increase. Growth in the internationalisation of tertiary education has accelerated during the past several decades, reflecting the globalisation of economies and societies, and also the expansion of tertiary systems and institutions throughout the world.

The rise in the number of students enrolled abroad since 1975 stems from various factors, from an interest in promoting academic, cultural, social and political ties between countries (especially as the European Union was taking shape), to a substantial increase in global access to tertiary education, to reduced transportation costs. The internationalisation of labour markets for highly skilled individuals has also given people an incentive to gain international experience as part of their studies.

The increase in the number of foreign students can be compared with the increase in tertiary enrolment worldwide. According to UNESCO data, 177 million students participated in formal tertiary education around the world in 2010, an increase of 77 million students since 2000, or 77% (UNESCO Institute for Statistics, 2011). During this same period, the number of foreign students increased from 2.1 to 4.1 million students, an increase of 99%. Consequently, the share of tertiary students who are foreign students grew by more than 10% between 2000 and 2010 (Chart C4.1).

Most of the new foreign tertiary students come from countries outside the OECD area, and are likely to gradually increase the proportion of foreign students in advanced research programmes in OECD and other G20 countries in the coming years.

The internationalisation of tertiary education is particularly pronounced among OECD countries. In absolute terms, the number of foreign students enrolled in tertiary education has more than doubled since 2005 in Brazil, Chile, Estonia, Iceland, Indonesia, Ireland, Korea, Luxembourg, Saudi Arabia, the Slovak Republic and Spain. In contrast, the number of foreign students enrolled in France, Germany, Mexico and New Zealand grew by less than 10% (Table C4.1).

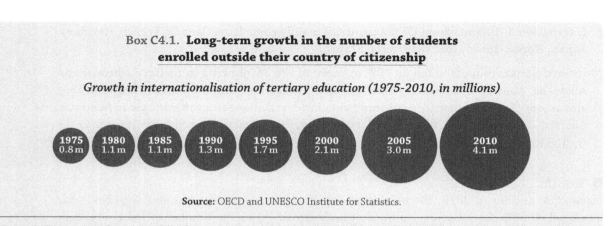

Box C4.1. Long-term growth in the number of students enrolled outside their country of citizenship

Growth in internationalisation of tertiary education (1975-2010, in millions)

1975	1980	1985	1990	1995	2000	2005	2010
0.8 m	1.1 m	1.1 m	1.3 m	1.7 m	2.1 m	3.0 m	4.1 m

Source: OECD and UNESCO Institute for Statistics.

Data on foreign enrolment worldwide comes from both the OECD and the UNESCO Institute for Statistics (UIS). UIS provided the data on all countries for 1975-95 and most of the non-OECD countries for 2000, 2005 and 2010. The OECD provided the data on OECD countries and the other non-OECD economies in 2000 and 2010. Both sources use similar definitions, thus making their combination possible. Missing data were imputed with the closest data reports to ensure that breaks in data coverage do not result in breaks in time series.

StatLink 🔗 http://dx.doi.org/10.1787/888932663283

In relative terms, the percentage of international students in tertiary enrolment has also increased since 2005 in all 18 OECD countries with available data, except New Zealand, Norway and the United States.

Global student mobility mirrors inter- and intra-regional migration patterns to a great extent. The growth in the internationalisation of tertiary enrolment in OECD countries, as well as the high proportion of intra-regional student mobility, show the growing importance of regional mobility over global mobility. Furthermore, student flows in European countries and in Eastern Asia and Oceania tend to reflect the evolution of geopolitical areas, such as closer ties between Asia-Pacific countries and further co-operation between European countries beyond the European Union (UNESCO, 2009).

Major destinations of foreign students

G20 countries attract 83% of foreign students worldwide. Some 77% of foreign students are enrolled in an OECD country. Within the OECD area, EU21 countries host the highest number of foreign students, with 40% of total foreign students worldwide. These 21 countries also host 98% of foreign students in the European Union. EU mobility policies become evident when analysing the composition of this population. Within the share of foreign students enrolled in EU21 countries, 76% of students come from another EU21 country (Tables C4.4 and C4.6).

North America is the second most attractive region for foreign students, with 21% of all foreign students. The profile of international students in North America is more diverse than in the European Union: in the United States, only 4.1% of international students come from Canada, and in Canada only 7.4% of international students come from the United States (Tables C4.3 and C4.4).

In 2010, almost one out of two foreign students went to one of the five countries that host higher shares of students enrolled outside of their country of citizenship. The United States received the most (in absolute terms), with 17% of all foreign students worldwide, followed by the United Kingdom (13%), Australia (7%), Germany (6%) and France (6%). Although these destinations account for half of all tertiary students pursuing their studies abroad, some new players have emerged on the international education market in the past few years (Chart C4.2 and Table C4.7, available on line). Besides the five major destinations, significant numbers of foreign students were enrolled in Canada (5%), Japan (3%), the Russian Federation (4%) and Spain (2%) in 2010. The figures for Australia and the United States refer to international students (Table C4.4).

New players in the international education market

Over a ten-year period, the share of international students who chose the United States as their destination dropped from 23% to 17%, and the share of international students who chose Germany fell by more than two percentage points. In contrast, the shares of international students who chose Australia and New Zealand as their destination grew by more than one percentage point, while the share of students who chose the United Kingdom and the Russian Federation grew by around two percentage points (Chart C4.3). Some of these changes reflect the differences in countries' internationalisation approaches, ranging from proactive marketing in the Asia-Pacific region to a more local and university-driven approach in the traditionally dominant United States.

Underlying factors in students' choice of a country of study

Language of instruction

The language spoken and used in instruction sometimes determines in which country a student chooses to study. Countries whose language of instruction is widely spoken and read, such as English-, French-, German-, Russian- and Spanish-speaking countries, are therefore leading destinations of foreign students, both in absolute and relative terms. Japan is a notable exception: despite a language of instruction that is not widespread, it enrols large numbers of foreign students, 93% of whom are from Asia (Table C4.3 and Chart C4.2).

C4

Chart C4.2. **Distribution of foreign students in tertiary education, by country of destination (2010)**
Percentage of foreign tertiary students reported to the OECD who are enrolled in each country of destination

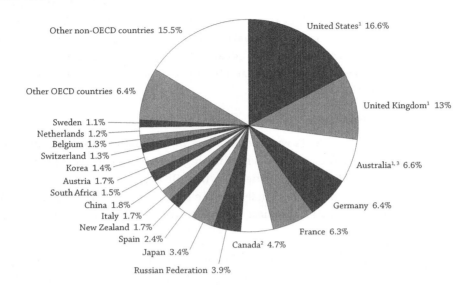

1. Data relate to international students defined on the basis of their country of residence.
2. Year of reference 2009.
3. Student stocks are derived from different sources; therefore, results should be interpreted with some caution.
Source: OECD and UNESCO Institute for Statistics for most data on non-OECD destinations. Tables C4.4 and C4.7, available on line. See Annex 3 for notes (*www.oecd.org/edu/eag2012*).
StatLink 🔗 http://dx.doi.org/10.1787/888932663188

Chart C4.3. **Trends in international education market shares (2000, 2010)**
Percentage of all foreign tertiary students enrolled, by destination

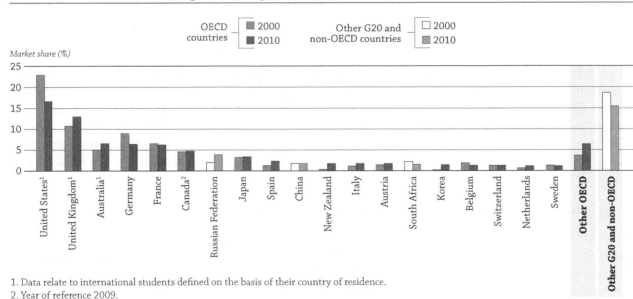

1. Data relate to international students defined on the basis of their country of residence.
2. Year of reference 2009.
Countries are ranked in descending order of 2010 market shares.
Source: OECD and UNESCO Institute for Statistics for most data on non-OECD countries. Table C4.7, available on line. See Annex 3 for notes (*www.oecd.org/edu/eag2012*).
StatLink 🔗 http://dx.doi.org/10.1787/888932663207

The dominance (in absolute numbers) of English-speaking destinations (Australia, Canada, New Zealand, the United Kingdom and the United States) reflects the progressive adoption of English as a global language. It may also reflect the fact that students intending to study abroad are likely to have learned English in their home country or wish to improve their English language skills through immersion in a native English-speaking context. The rapid increase in foreign enrolments in Australia (index change of 153), Canada (132), Ireland (227) and the United Kingdom (168) between 2005 and 2010 can be partly attributed to linguistic considerations (Table C4.1). The high number of countries using English either as an official language or as *lingua franca* reinforces this pattern. All English-speaking OECD countries have between one-fifth and one-third of foreign students coming from other English-speaking countries. In the whole OECD area, around one out of four foreign students comes from a country with the same official or widely-spoken language as the country of destination (Table C4.5).

Given this pattern, an increasing number of institutions in non-English-speaking countries now offer courses in English to overcome their linguistic disadvantage in attracting foreign students. This trend is especially noticeable in countries in which the use of English is widespread, such as the Nordic countries (Box C4.2).

Box C4.2. **Countries offering tertiary programmes in English (2010)**

Use of English in instruction	
All or nearly all programmes offered in English	Australia, Canada,[1] Ireland, New Zealand, the United Kingdom, the United States
Many programmes offered in English	Denmark, Finland, the Netherlands, Sweden
Some programmes offered in English	Belgium (Fl.),[2] the Czech Republic, France, Germany, Hungary, Iceland, Japan, Korea, Norway, Poland, Portugal, the Slovak Republic, Switzerland,[3] Turkey
No or nearly no programmes offered in English	Austria, Belgium (Fr.), Brazil, Chile, Greece, Israel, Italy, Luxembourg, Mexico,[3] the Russian Federation, Spain

Note: The extent to which a country offers a few or many programmes in English takes into account the size of the population in the country. Hence, France and Germany are classified among countries with comparatively few English programmes, although they have more English programmes than Sweden, in absolute terms.

1. In Canada, tertiary institutions are either French- (mostly Quebec) or English-speaking.

2. Master's programmes.

3. At the discretion of tertiary education institutions.

Source: OECD, compiled from brochures for prospective international students by OAD (Austria), CHES and NARIC (Czech Republic), Cirius (Denmark), CIMO (Finland), EduFrance (France), DAAD (Germany), Campus Hungary (Hungary), University of Iceland (Iceland), JPSS (Japan), NIIED (Korea), NUFFIC (Netherlands), SIU (Norway), CRASP (Poland), Swedish Institute (Sweden) and Middle-East Technical University (Turkey).

Quality of programmes

International students increasingly select their study destination based on the quality of education offered, as perceived from a wide array of information on and rankings of higher education programmes now available, both in print and on line. For instance, the high proportion of top-ranked higher education institutions in the principal destination countries and the emergence in rankings of institutions based in fast-growing student destinations draws attention to the increasing importance of the perception of quality, even if a correlation between patterns of student mobility and quality judgments on individual institutions is hard to establish.

Tuition fees

Among most EU countries, including Austria, Belgium (Flemish Community), the Czech Republic, Denmark, Estonia, Finland, France, Germany, Ireland, Italy, the Netherlands, the Slovak Republic, Spain, Sweden and the United Kingdom, international students from other EU countries are treated as domestic students with respect to tuition fee charges. This is also true in Ireland, but only if the EU student has lived in Ireland for three out of the five previous years. If this condition is satisfied, the EU student is eligible for free tuition in a given academic year. In Finland, Germany and Italy, this applies to non-EU international students as well.

While there are no tuition fees in Finland and Sweden, in Germany, tuition fees are collected at all government-dependent private institutions and, in some *Bundesländer*, tuition fees have been introduced at public tertiary institutions as well. In Denmark, students from some Nordic countries (Norway and Iceland) and EU countries are treated like domestic students and pay no tuition fees, as their education is fully subsidised. Most international students from non-EU or non-European Economic Area (EEA) countries, however, must pay the full amount of tuition fees, although a limited number of talented students from non-EU/EEA countries can obtain scholarships covering all or part of their tuition fees (Box C4.3).

Box C4.3. **Structure of tuition fees**

Tuition fee structure	OECD and other G20 countries
Higher tuition fees for international students than for domestic students	Australia[1], Austria,[2] Belgium,[2, 3] Canada, the Czech Republic,[2, 4] Denmark,[2, 4] Estonia,[2] Ireland,[4] the Netherlands,[2] New Zealand,[5] the Russian Federation, Turkey, the United Kingdom,[2] the United States[6]
Same tuition fees for international and domestic students	France, Germany, Italy, Japan, Korea, Mexico,[7] Spain
No tuition fees for either international or domestic students	Finland, Iceland, Norway, Sweden

1. International students are not eligible for government subsidised places in Australia and therefore are full-fee paying. While this typically results in international students having higher tuition fees than domestic students (who usually attend subsidised places), it should be noted that some domestic students in public universities and all students in independent-private universities are full-fee paying and pay the same tuition fees as international students.

2. For non-European Union or non-European Economic Area students.

3. In Belgium (Fl.), different tuition allowed only if institutions reach 2% of students from outside the EEA area.

4. No tuition fees for full-time domestic students in public institutions.

5. Except students in advanced research programmes, or students from Australia.

6. In public institutions, international students pay the same fees as domestic out-of-state students. However since most domestic students are enrolled in-state, international students pay higher tuition fees than most domestic students, in practice. In private universities, the fees are the same for national and international students.

7. Some institutions charge higher tuition fees for international students.

Source: OECD. Indicator B5. See Annex 3 for notes (*www.oecd.org/edu/eag2012*).

Among some non-EU countries, including Iceland, Japan, Korea, Norway and the United States, the same treatment applies to all domestic and international students. In Norway, tuition fees are the same for both domestic and international students: no fees in public institutions, but fees in some private institutions. In Iceland, all students have to pay registration fees, and students in private institutions have to pay tuition fees as well. In Japan, domestic and international students are generally charged the same tuition fees, although international students with Japanese government scholarships do not have to pay tuition fees, and many scholarships are available for privately financed international students.

In Korea, tuition fees and subsidies for international students vary, depending on the contract between their school of origin and the school they attend in Korea. In general, most international students in Korea pay tuition fees that are somewhat lower than those paid by domestic students. In New Zealand, international students, except those in advanced research programmes, generally pay higher tuition fees; however, international students from Australia receive the same subsidies as domestic students. In Australia (with the exceptions noted in Box C4.3) and in Canada, all international students pay higher tuition fees than domestic students. This is also true in the Russian Federation, unless students are subsidised by the Russian government.

The fact that Finland, Iceland and Norway do not have tuition fees for international students, combined with the availability of programmes taught in English, probably explains part of the robust growth in the number of foreign students enrolled in some of these countries between 2005 and 2010 (Table C4.1). However, given the absence of fees, the high unit costs of tertiary education mean that international students place a heavy

C4

financial burden on their countries of destination (see Table B1.1a). For this reason, Denmark, which previously had no tuition fees, adopted tuition fees for non-EU and non-EEA international students as of 2006-07. Similar options are being discussed in Finland and were adopted in Sweden, where foreign enrolments grew by 14% and 57%, respectively, between 2005 and 2010 (see Indicator B5). Sweden introduced tuition fees, compensated by scholarships, for students from outside the EU/EEA starting from the academic year 2011-12, which is not covered by figures in *Education at a Glance 2012*.

Countries that charge international students the full cost of education reap significant economic benefits. Several countries in the Asia-Pacific region have actually made international education an explicit part of their socio-economic development strategy and have initiated policies to attract international students on a revenue-generating or at least a cost-recovery basis. Australia and New Zealand have successfully adopted differentiated tuition fees for international students, and this has not hampered some of the strongest growth in foreign students in the past years (Table C4.1). This shows that tuition costs do not necessarily discourage prospective international students, as long as the quality of education provided is high and its likely returns make the investment worthwhile.

However, in choosing between similar educational opportunities, cost considerations may play a role, especially for students from developing countries. In this respect, the deterioration of the United States' market share, may be attributed to the comparatively high tuition fees charged to international students in a context of fierce competition from other, primarily English-speaking, destinations offering similar educational opportunities at lower cost (Chart C4.3). Advanced research programmes in New Zealand, for example, have become more attractive since 2005, when tuition fees for international students were reduced to the same level as those paid by domestic students (Box C4.3).

Public funding that is "portable" across borders, or student support for tertiary education, can ease the cost of studying abroad, as is evident in Chile, Finland, Iceland, the Netherlands, Norway and Sweden.

Immigration policy

In recent years, several OECD countries have eased their immigration policies to encourage the temporary or permanent immigration of international students (OECD, 2008). This makes these countries more attractive to students and strengthens the country's labour force. As a result, immigration considerations as well as tuition fees may also affect some students' decisions on where to study abroad (OECD, 2011).

Other factors

Students also make decisions on where to study based on the academic reputation of particular institutions or programmes; the flexibility of programmes in counting time spent abroad towards degree requirements; recognition of foreign degrees; the limitations of tertiary education in the home country; restrictive university admission policies at home; geographical, trade or historical links between countries; future job opportunities; cultural aspirations; and/or government policies to facilitate transfer of credits between home and host institutions.

Extent of student mobility in tertiary education

The preceding analysis has focused on trends in absolute numbers of foreign students and their distribution by countries of destination, since time series or global aggregates on student mobility do not exist. It is also possible to measure the extent of student mobility in each country of destination by examining the proportion of international students in total tertiary enrolments. Doing so takes into account the size of different tertiary education systems and highlights those that are highly internationalised, regardless of their size and the importance of their market share.

Among countries for which data on student mobility are available, Australia, Austria, Luxembourg, New Zealand, Switzerland and the United Kingdom show the highest levels of incoming student mobility, measured as the proportion of international students in their total tertiary enrolment. In Australia, 21.2% of tertiary students have come to the country in order to pursue their studies. Similarly, international students represent 15.4%

C4

of total tertiary enrolments in Austria, 41.4% in Luxembourg (mainly due to a high level of integration with neighbour countries), 14.2% in New Zealand, 15.4% in Switzerland and 16.0% in the United Kingdom. In contrast, incoming student mobility accounts for less than 2% of total tertiary enrolments in Chile, Estonia, Norway, Poland and Slovenia (Table C4.1 and Chart C4.4).

Among countries for which data based on the preferred definition of international students are not available, foreign enrolments constitute a large group of tertiary students in France (11.6%). On the other hand, foreign enrolments represent 1% or less of total tertiary enrolments in Brazil, China, Indonesia and Turkey (Table C4.1).

Chart C4.4. **Student mobility in tertiary education (2010)**
Percentage of international and foreign students in tertiary enrolments

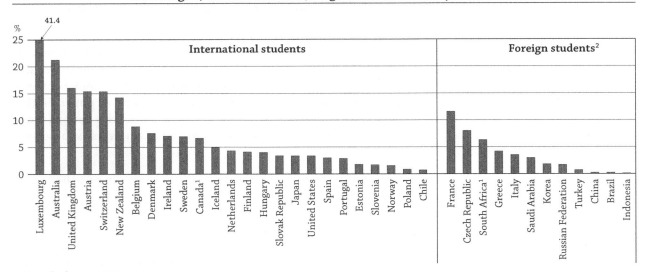

1. Year of reference 2009.
2. Foreign students are defined on the basis of their country of citizenship. These data are not comparable with data on international students and are therefore presented separately in the chart.
Countries are ranked in descending order of the percentage of international students in tertiary education.
Source: OECD. Table C4.1. See Annex 3 for notes (*www.oecd.org/edu/eag2012*).
StatLink ⫘⫘⫘ http://dx.doi.org/10.1787/888932663226

Proportion of international students at different levels and types of tertiary education

The proportion of international students in different types of tertiary education in each country of destination also sheds light on patterns of student mobility. With the exception of Japan, Luxembourg, New Zealand, Norway and Spain, tertiary-type B (shorter and vocationally-oriented) programmes are less internationalised than tertiary-type A (largely theory-based) programmes. With the exception of Greece and Italy, this observation also holds true for countries for which data using the preferred definition of international students are not available (Table C4.1).

All reporting countries show higher incoming student mobility relative to total enrolments in advanced research programmes, compared to tertiary-type A programmes. The proportion is more than 15 percentage points higher in advanced research programmes in Ireland, Luxembourg, New Zealand, Sweden, Switzerland, the United Kingdom and the United States, as well as in France, which reports foreign students and for which data using the preferred definition of international student are not available. This may be due to the attractiveness of advanced research programmes in these countries, or to a preference for recruiting international students at higher levels of education because of their potential contribution to domestic research and development, or in anticipation of recruiting these students as highly qualified immigrants (Table C4.1).

Examining the proportion of international and foreign students by level and type of tertiary education reveals what kinds of programmes countries offer. In some countries, a comparatively large proportion of international students are enrolled in tertiary-type B programmes. This is the case in Belgium (26%), Chile (34%), Japan (24%), Luxembourg (27%), New Zealand (30%) and Spain (31%). The same pattern is true in Greece (36%) and in Saudi Arabia (95%) (Table C4.1).

In other countries, a large proportion of international students enrol in advanced research programmes. This is particularly true in Switzerland (25%). This concentration can also be observed to a lesser extent in Ireland (17%), Spain (15%), Sweden (15%) and the United States (19%). Among countries for which data using the preferred definition of international students are not available, 21% of foreign students in China and 12% of foreign students in France are enrolled in advanced research programmes (Table C4.1). All of these countries are likely to benefit from the contribution of these high-level international students to domestic research and development. In countries that charge full tuition to foreign students, these students are also a source of revenue (Box C4.3).

Profile of international student intake in different destinations

Global balance of student mobility in OECD countries

OECD countries receive more foreign students than they send to study abroad for tertiary education. In 2010, OECD countries hosted 2.9 foreign students per each student studying outside his or her country of origin. In absolute terms, this represents for 3.2 million foreign students in OECD countries, compared to more than one million students outside of their OECD country of citizenship. As 93% of OECD citizens study in another OECD country, more than two-thirds of foreign students in the OECD area come from a non-OECD country (Tables C4.4 and C4.5).

At the country level, the balance varies greatly. While in Australia there are 21 foreign students for each Australian student studying abroad, the ratio is 12 to 1 in New Zealand, and the balance is negative in Argentina, Brazil, Chile, Estonia, Greece, Iceland, Indonesia, Israel, Korea, Luxembourg, Mexico, Norway, Poland, Portugal, Saudi Arabia, the Slovak Republic, Slovenia and Turkey. The United Kingdom and the United States also show high ratios of foreign to national students, with more than 12 foreign students for each citizen studying abroad (Table C4.5).

Main regions of origin

Asian students form the largest group of international students enrolled in countries reporting data to the OECD or the UNESCO Institute for Statistics: 52% of the total in all reporting destinations (51% of the total in OECD countries, and 55% of the total in non-OECD countries).

The predominance of international or foreign Asian students in OECD countries is greatest in Australia (80%), Japan (93%) and Korea (95%). In OECD countries, the Asian group is followed by Europeans (24%), particularly EU21 citizens (17%). Students from Africa account for 9.6% of all international students in OECD countries, while those from North America account for only 3.3%. Students from Latin America and the Caribbean represent 6% of the total. Altogether, 30% of international students enrolled in the OECD area originate from another OECD country (Table C4.3).

Main countries of origin

The predominance of students from Asia and Europe is also clear when looking at individual countries of origin within the OECD area. Students from France (2.0%), Germany (3.8%), and Korea (4.6%) represent the largest groups of international OECD students enrolled in OECD countries, followed by students from Canada (1.6%), Japan (1.5%) and the United States (1.6%) (Table C4.3).

Among international students originating from non-member countries, students from China represent by far the largest group, with 19% of all international students enrolled in the OECD area (not including an additional 1.2% from Hong Kong, China) (Table C4.3). Some 20% of all Chinese students studying abroad head for the United States, while 13.8% choose Australia and 13.6% choose Japan. In OECD countries, students from China are followed by those from India (7.0%), Malaysia (1.8%), Morocco (1.5%), Vietnam (1.6%) and the Russian Federation (1.3%). A significant number of Asian students studying abroad also come from Indonesia, Iran, Nepal, Pakistan, Singapore and Thailand (Table C4.4).

Chart C4.5. **Distribution of foreign students in tertiary education, by region of origin (2010)**
Percentage of foreign tertiary students enrolled worldwide

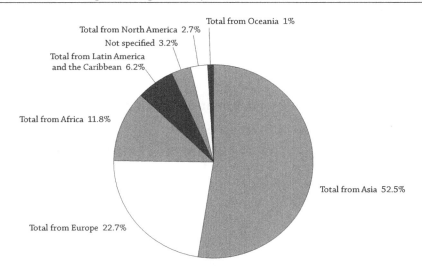

Source: OECD and UNESCO Institute for Statistics for most data on non-OECD destinations. Table C4.3.
See Annex 3 for notes (*www.oecd.org/edu/eag2012*).
StatLink ⟨⟩ http://dx.doi.org/10.1787/888932663264

A large proportion of foreign students in OECD countries comes from neighbouring countries. In all OECD countries, around 21% of all foreign students come from countries that share land or maritime borders with the host country. Higher levels of mobility from neighbouring countries is not only the consequence of a particular central geographic situation, as in the Czech Republic, but may also reveal cost, quality and enrolment advantages that are more apparent to students in neighbouring countries. On the other hand, higher percentages of foreign students from countries beyond the immediate borders are seen in countries that have the largest market shares in international education and in countries like Portugal and Spain that have close historic and cultural ties with other countries further afield (Table C4.5 and Table C4.7, available on line).

Among OECD countries, the highest percentages of mobility from neighbouring countries are found in Korea (79%), Greece (79%), Estonia, where 77% of foreign students come from Finland, Latvia, the Russian Federation or Sweden; and in the Czech Republic, where 66% of foreign students come from Austria, Germany, Poland or the Slovak Republic. Foreign students from neighbouring countries are also strongly represented in Austria, Belgium, the Netherlands, Poland, the Russian Federation, the Slovak Republic, Slovenia and Switzerland. On the other hand, in Australia, only 5% of students come from Indonesia, New Zealand or Papua New Guinea, and only 1.8% come from other countries in Oceania. In Canada, just 5% of foreign students come from the United States; in Portugal, only 4% of foreign students come from Spain or Morocco; and in the United States, 7% of students come from the Bahamas, Canada, Mexico or the Russian Federation (Table 4.5 and Table 4.7, available on line). Linguistic criteria are responsible for student mobility in Portugal, where 69% of foreign students come from Angola, Brazil, Cape Verde, Guinea-Bissau, Sao Tomé and Principe or Timor-Leste, all countries where Portuguese is an official language (Table 4.5 and Table 4.7, available on line).

Destinations of citizens enrolled abroad

OECD students usually enrol in another OECD country if they are looking to pursue tertiary studies outside their country of citizenship. On average, 93% of foreign students from OECD countries are enrolled in other OECD countries. The proportion of foreign students from the other G20 countries enrolled in OECD countries is also high, with 83% of foreign students from Argentina, Brazil, China, India, Indonesia, the Russian Federation, Saudi Arabia and South Africa enrolled in an OECD country. Notably, students from Belgium (1.9%), the Czech Republic (1.4%), Iceland (0.6%), Ireland (0.7%), Luxembourg (0.4%), the Netherlands (1.5%), Poland (1.2%) and the Slovak Republic (0.4%) show an extremely low propensity to study outside of the OECD area (Table C4.4).

Language and cultural considerations, geographic proximity and similarity of education systems are all factors that students weigh when determining where they will study. Geographic considerations and differences in entry requirements (as *numerus clausus* or stronger selectivity for some programmes) are the most likely explanations of the concentration of students from Germany in Austria, from Belgium in France and the Netherlands, from France in Belgium, from Canada in the United States, from New Zealand in Australia, etc. Language and academic traditions also explain the propensity for English-speaking students to concentrate in other countries of the British Commonwealth or in the United States, even those that are distant geographically. This is also true for other historic geopolitical areas, such as the former Soviet Union, the *Francophonie* and Latin America. Migration networks also play a role, as illustrated by the concentration of students with Portuguese citizenship in France, students from Turkey in Germany or those from Mexico in the United States.

The destinations of international students also highlight the attractiveness of specific education systems, whether because of their academic reputation or because of subsequent immigration opportunities. It is noteworthy, for example, that students from China are mostly in Australia, Canada, France, Germany, Japan, Korea, New Zealand, the United Kingdom and the United States, most of which have policies to facilitate the immigration of international students. Similarly, students from India favour Australia, the United Kingdom and the United States. In fact, these three destinations attract 76 % of Indian citizens enrolled abroad (Table C4.4).

Definitions

The **country of prior education** is defined as the country in which students obtained the qualification required to enrol in their current level of education, i.e. the country in which students obtained their upper secondary or post-secondary, vocationally oriented education for international students enrolled in academically or vocationally oriented tertiary programmes, and the country in which they obtained their academically oriented tertiary education for international students enrolled in advanced research programmes. Country-specific operational definitions of international students are indicated in the tables as well as in Annex 3 (*www.oecd.org/edu/eag2012*).

Students are classified as **foreign students** if they are not citizens of the country in which the data are collected. While pragmatic and operational, this classification is inappropriate for capturing student mobility because of differing national policies regarding the naturalisation of immigrants. For instance, Australia has a greater propensity to grant permanent residence to its immigrant populations than Switzerland. This implies that even when the proportion of foreign students in tertiary enrolment is similar for both countries, the proportion of international student in tertiary enrolment is lower in Switzerland than in Australia. Therefore, for student mobility and bilateral comparisons, interpretations of data based on the concept of foreign students should be made with caution.

Students are classified as **international students** if they left their country of origin and moved to another country for the purpose of study. Depending on country-specific immigration legislation, mobility arrangements, such as the free mobility of individuals within the EU and the EEA, and data availability, international students may be defined as students who are not permanent or usual residents of their country of study or alternatively as students who obtained their prior education in a different country, including another EU country.

Permanent or usual residence in the reporting country is defined according to national legislation. In practice, this means holding a student visa or permit, or electing a foreign country of domicile in the year prior to entering the education system of the country reporting data.

Methodology

Data refer to the academic year 2009-10 and are based on the UOE data collection on education statistics administered by the OECD in 2011 (for details, see Annex 3 at *www.oecd.org/edu/eag2012*). The fields of education used in the UOE data collection instruments follow the revised ISCED classification by field of education. The same classification is used for all levels of education.

Data on international and foreign students refer to the academic year 2009-10 and are based on the UOE data collection on education statistics administered by the OECD in 2011 (for details see Annex 3 at *www.oecd.org/edu/eag2012*). Additional data from the UNESCO Institute for Statistics are also included.

Data on international and foreign students are obtained from enrolments in their countries of destination. The method used for obtaining data on international and foreign students is therefore the same as that used for collecting data on total enrolments, i.e. records of regularly enrolled students in an educational programme. Domestic and international students are usually counted on a specific day or period of the year. This procedure makes it possible to measure the proportion of international enrolments in an education system, but the actual number of individuals involved may be much higher since many students study abroad for less than a full academic year, or participate in exchange programmes that do not require enrolment, such as interuniversity exchanges or short-term advanced research programmes.

Moreover, the international student body includes some distance-learning students who are not, strictly speaking, international students. This pattern of distance enrolments is fairly common in the tertiary institutions of Australia, the United Kingdom and the United States (OECD, 2004).

Since data on international and foreign students are obtained from tertiary enrolments in their country of destination, the data relate to incoming students rather than to students going abroad. Countries of destination covered by this indicator include all OECD and other G20 countries except Chile, Luxembourg, Mexico, the Russian Federation and Slovenia, as well as countries reporting similar data to the UNESCO Institute for Statistics. These data are used to derive global figures and to examine the destinations of students and trends in market shares.

Data on students enrolled abroad as well as trend analyses are not based on the numbers of international students, but on the number of foreign citizens on whom data consistent across countries and over time are readily available. The data do not include students enrolled in countries that did not report foreign students to the OECD or to the UNESCO Institute for Statistics. All statements on students enrolled abroad may therefore underestimate the real number of citizens studying abroad (Table C4.3), especially in cases where many citizens study in countries that do not report their foreign students to the OECD or UNESCO Institute for Statistics, such as China and India.

The statistical data for Israel are supplied by and under the responsibility of the relevant Israeli authorities. The use of such data by the OECD is without prejudice to the status of the Golan Heights, East Jerusalem and Israeli settlements in the West Bank under the terms of international law.

References

The relative importance of international students in the education system affects tertiary entry and graduation rates, and may artificially increase them in some fields or levels of education (see Indicators A2 and A3). It may also affect the mix recorded between public and private expenditure (see Indicator B3).

In countries in which different tuition fees are applied to international students, student mobility may boost the financial resources of tertiary education institutions and help to finance the education system.

International students may represent a heavy financial burden for countries in which tertiary tuition fees are low or non-existent, given the high level of unit costs in tertiary education (see Indicator B5).

International students enrolled in a country different from their own are only one aspect of the internationalisation of tertiary education. New forms of cross-border education have emerged in the past decade, including the mobility of educational programmes and institutions across borders. Yet, cross-border tertiary education has developed quite differently and in response to different rationales in different world regions. For a detailed analysis of these issues, as well as the trade and policy implications of the internationalisation of tertiary education, see OECD (2004).

Kelo, M., U. Teichler and B. Wächter (eds.) (2005), *EURODATA: Student Mobility in European Higher Education*, Verlags and Mediengesellschaft, Bonn.

OECD (2004), *Internationalisation and Trade in Higher Education: Opportunities and Challenges*, OECD Publishing.

OECD (2008), *OECD Review of Tertiary Education: Tertiary Education for the Knowledge Society,* OECD Publishing.

OECD (2011), *International Migration Outlook 2011*, OECD Publishing.

UNESCO (2009), *Global Education Digest 2009*, UNESCO Institute for Statistics, Montreal.

UNESCO Institute for Statistics (2011), *Education Database, www.uis.unesco.org,* accessed 1 July 2011.

Varghese, N.V. (2009), *Globalization, economic crisis and national strategies for higher education development*, IIEP UNESCO, Paris.

The following additional material relevant to this indicator is available on line:

* *Table C4.7. Number of foreign students in tertiary education, by country of origin and destination (2010) and market shares in international education (2000, 2010)*
  StatLink ᴍᴤ╝ http://dx.doi.org/10.1787/888932667349

Table C4.1. Student mobility and foreign students in tertiary education (2005, 2010)

International and foreign students enrolled as a percentage of all students (international plus domestic) and distribution of international mobility by level and type of tertiary education

Reading the first column: 21.2% of all students in tertiary education in Australia are international students and 15.4% of all students in tertiary education in Switzerland are international students. The data presented in this table on student mobility represent the best available proxy of student mobility for each country. Reading the first column on the second part of the table: 11.6% of all students in tertiary education in France are not French citizens, and 3.5% of all students in tertiary education in Italy are not Italian citizens.

	International students as a percentage of all tertiary enrolment						Distribution of international or foreign students		
	Total tertiary	Tertiary-type B programmes	Tertiary-type A programmes	Advanced research programmes	Index of change in the **percentage** of international/ foreign students, total tertiary (2005=100)	Index of change in the **number** of foreign students, total tertiary (2005=100)	Tertiary-type B programmes	Tertiary-type A programmes	Advanced research programmes
	(1)	(2)	(3)	(4)	(5)	(6)	(7)	(8)	(9)
OECD Australia	**21.2**	17.3	21.8	28.7	123	153	14.3	80.7	5.0
Austria	**15.4**	1.8	16.5	22.3	139	199	1.2	87.7	11.1
Belgium	**8.8**	5.4	10.6	18.5	135	122	26.4	62.9	10.7
Canada[1,2]	**6.6**	4.3	7.1	20.5	m	132	19.6	71.2	9.2
Chile	**0.7**	0.6	0.7	13.3	m	489	33.5	58.8	7.6
Denmark	**7.5**	12.3	6.4	20.8	171	150	19.4	71.6	9.0
Estonia	**1.8**	0.2	2.3	5.8	137	289	4.4	83.2	12.4
Finland	**4.1**	n	3.8	8.0	114	167	0.0	86.8	13.2
Germany[4]	**m**	m	8.7	m	m	102	m	m	m
Hungary	**4.0**	0.3	4.4	5.7	147	133	0.8	96.7	2.5
Iceland	**4.9**	0.6	4.8	17.3	m	223	0.2	93.7	6.1
Ireland	**7.0**	3.7	6.9	27.1	102	227	12.0	71.1	16.9
Israel	**m**	m	m	m	m	m	m	m	m
Japan	**3.4**	4.0	2.9	17.3	118	112	23.7	66.4	9.9
Luxembourg	**41.4**	60.0	33.4	80.2	m	437	26.5	60.6	12.9
Mexico	**m**	m	m	m	m	100	m	m	m
Netherlands[5]	**4.3**	0.3	4.4	m	m	m	0.0	100.0	0.0
New Zealand	**14.2**	16.6	12.4	37.2	84	102	29.7	62.7	7.6
Norway	**1.5**	1.7	1.4	4.7	83	117	0.5	89.3	10.2
Poland	**0.9**	0.1	0.8	2.3	m	180	0.1	95.4	4.5
Portugal	**2.9**	n	2.6	7.8	m	113	0.0	88.0	12.0
Slovak Republic	**3.4**	0.7	3.2	7.1	382	503	0.2	90.1	9.7
Slovenia	**1.7**	0.7	1.8	7.3	174	178	9.3	77.9	12.8
Spain	**3.0**	6.2	2.0	12.2	305	216	31.0	53.7	15.3
Sweden	**6.9**	0.2	6.5	24.2	157	114	0.2	84.5	15.3
Switzerland[6]	**15.4**	m	16.1	48.3	116	146	m	74.6	25.4
United Kingdom[7]	**16.0**	5.4	17.6	41.7	115	168	6.6	84.5	8.9
United States[7]	**3.4**	1.0	3.3	27.8	98	116	6.8	73.7	19.4
OECD average	**8.0**	6.0	7.8	21.1	150	192	12.1	78.6	11.2
Other G20 Argentina	**m**	m	m	m	m	m	m	m	m
India	**m**	m	m	m	m	m	m	m	m
Foreign students[8]									
OECD Czech Republic	**8.0**	1.2	8.4	10.8	145	189	1.1	90.9	8.0
France	**11.6**	4.2	12.8	42.0	107	110	9.0	79.4	11.5
Greece[3,4]	**4.2**	4.4	4.3	m	172	171	35.8	64.2	0.0
Italy	**3.5**	5.8	3.4	9.3	158	156	0.4	94.5	5.1
Korea	**1.8**	0.4	2.1	7.1	375	382	5.5	88.1	6.4
Turkey	**0.7**	0.1	1.0	2.5	85	142	5.3	90.3	4.4
Other G20 Brazil	**0.2**	0.2	0.2	1.9	369	1319	9.3	82.4	8.2
China	**0.2**	0.0	0.4	0.8	m	m	1.4	77.7	20.9
Indonesia	**0.1**	n	0.2	n	m	200	m	m	m
Russian Federation[3,5,6]	**1.7**	0.6	2.0	m	142	178	5.5	94.5	0.0
Saudi Arabia	**3.0**	0.8	3.3	17.2	m	244	94.5	1.6	3.8
South Africa[1]	**6.3**	x(1)	x(1)	x(1)	m	125	m	m	m

1. Year of reference 2009.
2. Index of change based on year 2004=100 instead of 2005 and year of reference 2009.
3. Excludes private institutions.
4. Excludes advanced research programmes.
5. Percentage in total tertiary underestimated because of the exclusion of certain programmes.
6. Excludes tertiary-type B programmes.
7. International students in Column 6.
8. Foreign students are defined on the basis of their country of citizenship, these data are not comparable with data on international students and are therefore presented separately in the table.
Source: OECD. China, Indonesia, and Mexico for Column 6: **UNESCO Institute for** Statistics (World Education Indicators programme). Saudi Arabia: Observatory on Higher Education. South Africa: UNESCO Institute for Statistics. See Annex 3 for notes (*www.oecd.org/edu/eag2012*).
Please refer to the Reader's Guide for information concerning the symbols replacing missing data.

StatLink 🔗 http://dx.doi.org/10.1787/888932667235

Table C4.2. Distribution of international and foreign students enrolled in tertiary programmes, by field of education (2010)

C4

	Humanities, arts and education	Health and welfare	Social sciences, business and law	Services	Engineering, manufacturing and construction	Sciences	Agriculture	Not known or unspecified	Total all fields of education
	(1)	(4)	(5)	(6)	(7)	(8)	(13)	(14)	(15)
International students									
Australia	8.7	10.0	55.6	2.0	11.1	11.6	0.9	0.1	100.0
Austria[1]	23.1	8.1	39.5	1.4	13.6	11.8	2.0	0.3	100.0
Belgium	15.4	29.6	11.2	1.3	10.7	5.7	4.9	21.2	100.0
Canada[2]	9.6	6.0	40.5	1.5	15.7	15.4	1.0	10.3	100.0
Chile	12.8	14.2	37.2	7.1	14.0	11.1	3.6	n	100.0
Denmark	13.0	12.6	39.5	0.8	19.3	10.3	4.5	n	100.0
Estonia	22.4	9.8	45.2	1.7	3.4	6.5	11.0	n	100.0
Finland[1]	12.1	8.7	28.6	6.1	31.7	11.2	1.6	n	100.0
Germany[1,3]	24.9	6.4	27.1	1.7	21.6	16.3	1.5	0.5	100.0
Greece	m	m	m	m	m	m	m	m	m
Hungary	12.2	42.0	20.0	3.0	9.3	4.5	9.0	n	100.0
Iceland	44.2	3.5	23.6	0.6	8.9	18.8	0.4	n	100.0
Ireland	n	m	m	m	m	m	m	m	100.0
Israel	n	m	m	m	m	m	m	m	m
Japan	27.5	2.1	38.4	2.2	15.0	1.2	2.1	11.5	100.0
Korea	n	m	m	m	m	m	m	m	m
Luxembourg	15.0	3.4	61.6	n	5.1	15.0	n	n	100.0
Mexico	n	m	m	m	m	m	m	m	m
Netherlands[3]	14.8	17.2	49.2	9.3	3.9	3.4	1.2	1.0	100.0
New Zealand	14.5	6.6	39.5	6.8	7.0	19.1	1.3	5.2	100.0
Norway	32.0	11.5	28.5	4.4	4.7	12.0	2.3	4.7	100.0
Portugal	14.9	8.5	45.0	6.5	16.3	7.2	1.6	n	100.0
Slovenia	21.1	8.8	37.2	4.6	15.9	10.3	2.1	n	100.0
Spain[1,3]	16.4	26.0	32.6	5.1	9.5	7.2	1.2	1.9	100.0
Sweden	13.4	9.0	23.8	1.3	34.5	17.2	0.7	0.1	100.0
Switzerland[1]	21.2	7.4	33.6	2.5	15.9	17.0	0.7	1.7	100.0
United Kingdom	15.9	8.9	43.2	2.1	14.9	13.7	0.8	0.6	100.0
United States	15.3	6.6	32.7	2.1	18.4	17.5	0.8	6.6	100.0
Argentina	m	m	m	m	m	m	m	m	m
Brazil	m	m	m	m	m	m	m	m	m
China	m	m	m	m	m	m	m	m	m
India	m	m	m	m	m	m	m	m	m
Indonesia	m	m	m	m	m	m	m	m	m
Russian Federation	m	m	m	m	m	m	m	m	m
Saudi Arabia	m	m	m	m	m	m	m	m	m
South Africa	m	m	m	m	m	m	m	m	m
Foreign students[4]									
Czech Republic	13.8	15.4	40.0	3.1	10.5	14.8	2.2	0.2	100.0
France	19.2	8.0	40.3	1.7	13.0	17.4	0.3	n	100.0
Italy[1,3]	18.1	16.3	30.2	1.6	17.0	4.8	1.2	10.9	100.0
Poland	17.0	30.2	36.7	4.7	5.1	5.3	0.9	0.1	100.0
Slovak Republic	20.0	45.0	18.7	2.7	8.7	2.3	2.7	n	100.0
Turkey	22.3	14.4	35.5	2.7	14.5	8.1	2.5	n	100.0

Note: Columns showing the breakdown of humanities, arts and education (2 and 3) and science (9-12) are available for consultation on line (see *StatLink* below).

1. Excludes tertiary-type B programmes.

2. Year of reference 2009.

3. Excludes advanced research programmes.

4. Foreign students are defined on the basis of their country of citizenship; these data are not comparable with data on international students and are therefore presented separately in the table.

Source: OECD. See Annex 3 for notes (*www.oecd.org/edu/eag2012*).

Please refer to the Reader's Guide for information concerning the symbols replacing missing data.

StatLink 🔗 http://dx.doi.org/10.1787/888932667254

Table C4.3. [1/2] Distribution of international and foreign students in tertiary education, by country of origin (2010)

Number of international and foreign students enrolled in tertiary education from a given country of origin as a percentage of all international or foreign students in the country of destination, based on head counts

The table shows for each country the proportion of international students in tertiary education who are residents of or had their prior education in a given country of origin. When data on student mobility are not available, the table shows the proportion of foreign students in tertiary education that have citizenship of a given country of origin.
Reading the second column: 15.3% of international tertiary students in Belgium come from France, 8.6% of international tertiary students in Belgium come from the Netherlands, etc.
Reading the sixth column: 48.0% of international tertiary students in Estonia come from Finland, 1.6% of international tertiary students in Estonia come from Italy, etc.
Reading the 22nd column: 36.7% of foreign tertiary students in Austria are German citizens, 2.5% of foreign tertiary students in Austria are Hungarian citizens, etc.

C4

	Australia	Belgium	Canada[1,2]	Chile	Denmark	Estonia	Germany[3,4]	Hungary	Iceland	Ireland	Luxembourg	Netherlands[2,4]	New Zealand	Portugal	Slovak Republic	Slovenia	Spain[3]	Sweden[5]	Switzerland[3]	United Kingdom	United States
Countries of origin	(1)	(2)	(3)	(4)	(5)	(6)	(7)	(8)	(9)	(10)	(11)	(12)	(13)	(14)	(15)	(16)	(17)	(18)	(19)	(20)	(21)
Australia	a	0.1	0.3	n	0.3	n	0.2	0.1	0.8	0.5	0.1	0.1	7.8	0.1	n	0.2	0.1	0.2	0.3	0.4	0.5
Austria	0.1	0.1	0.1	n	0.3	0.2	3.4	0.7	n	0.3	0.8	0.5	0.1	0.3	1.0	1.7	0.2	0.3	2.5	0.4	0.1
Belgium	n	a	0.2	n	0.4	0.3	0.5	0.1	0.6	0.5	14.0	4.1	n	1.1	n	0.2	0.5	0.1	0.7	0.7	0.1
Canada	1.6	0.2	a	0.1	0.3	0.2	0.3	1.1	3.0	4.4	0.2	0.1	1.1	0.3	0.1	0.3	0.2	0.8	1.0	1.4	4.1
Chile	0.2	0.1	0.2	a	0.1	0.1	0.4	n	0.2	n	n	0.1	0.3	0.2	n	n	3.4	0.1	0.3	0.1	0.3
Czech Republic	n	0.1	n	n	0.7	0.2	0.8	0.4	2.6	0.3	0.4	0.2	0.1	0.3	58.2	0.4	0.2	0.1	0.3	0.3	0.1
Denmark	0.1	n	0.1	n	a	0.7	0.2	0.1	3.6	0.2	0.3	0.2	0.3	n	0.1	0.4	0.1	0.7	0.2	0.4	0.1
Estonia	n	0.1	n	n	1.0	a	0.3	0.1	0.4	0.1	0.1	0.1	n	0.1	n	n	0.1	0.3	0.1	0.2	n
Finland	0.1	0.1	0.1	n	0.9	48.0	0.4	0.3	4.7	0.3	0.2	0.5	0.1	0.1	0.2	0.1	4.4	0.2	0.4	0.1	0.1
France	0.5	15.3	6.1	1.1	1.2	0.7	3.0	0.9	5.2	3.4	33.1	1.5	0.8	3.0	0.2	0.3	3.3	1.4	15.7	3.4	1.1
Germany	0.8	1.3	0.7	0.9	8.5	1.9	a	12.1	15.0	4.2	16.0	61.0	2.7	1.8	4.8	0.8	2.6	3.6	28.3	3.8	1.4
Greece	n	0.5	0.1	n	0.7	0.2	1.2	1.2	0.3	0.4	1.0	0.5	n	0.2	9.7	0.4	0.4	0.7	1.0	2.9	0.3
Hungary	n	0.2	0.1	n	1.4	0.4	1.0	a	0.7	0.4	0.6	0.6	0.1	0.1	0.9	0.6	0.1	0.1	0.5	0.3	0.1
Iceland	n	n	n	n	6.4	0.2	n	0.5	a	n	n	0.1	n	n	0.1	n	n	0.6	n	0.1	0.1
Ireland	0.1	0.1	0.1	n	0.2	n	0.2	0.2	0.3	a	0.1	0.2	0.1	n	0.4	n	0.1	0.1	0.1	4.1	0.2
Israel	0.1	n	0.3	0.1	0.1	0.5	0.8	5.2	n	0.1	n	0.2	n	n	1.2	n	0.1	0.1	0.3	0.1	0.4
Italy	0.2	1.0	0.3	0.2	1.7	1.6	2.1	0.4	3.6	2.2	2.3	0.9	0.1	2.4	0.1	8.2	5.6	0.9	7.9	1.6	0.6
Japan	0.9	0.2	1.9	n	0.1	n	1.0	1.0	1.8	0.3	0.2	0.2	1.8	0.1	0.1	n	0.2	0.5	0.6	0.8	3.6
Korea	2.7	n	4.5	0.5	n	n	2.2	0.7	0.4	0.2	n	0.4	4.5	n	0.1	n	0.2	0.3	0.4	1.1	10.4
Luxembourg	n	1.2	n	n	n	0.1	1.5	n	n	0.1	a	0.2	n	0.3	n	n	n	n	1.0	0.2	n
Mexico	0.2	0.2	1.3	2.9	0.3	0.4	0.8	0.1	0.3	0.2	0.3	0.1	0.3	0.1	0.1	0.1	5.2	0.6	0.6	0.3	1.9
Netherlands	0.1	8.6	0.2	0.1	0.9	0.4	0.4	0.2	1.1	0.6	0.5	a	0.2	0.6	0.1	0.1	0.5	0.4	0.6	0.8	0.3
New Zealand	0.9	n	0.1	n	0.1	n	0.1	n	0.4	0.2	n	n	a	n	n	n	0.1	0.1	0.1	0.2	0.2
Norway	0.5	0.1	0.2	0.1	13.2	0.6	0.2	4.7	2.8	0.3	n	0.6	0.5	0.1	3.6	0.1	0.1	1.4	0.2	0.8	0.2
Poland	0.1	0.8	0.2	n	4.4	0.2	4.5	0.3	6.7	2.7	1.7	1.7	n	1.8	1.4	0.7	0.8	0.7	1.2	2.1	0.3
Portugal	n	0.3	0.1	n	0.4	0.2	0.2	0.4	0.4	0.4	1.5	0.3	0.1	a	0.2	0.3	4.6	0.3	0.4	0.7	0.1
Slovak Republic	n	0.1	n	n	0.5	0.1	0.5	14.0	0.8	0.3	0.3	0.3	n	0.1	a	0.4	0.2	0.1	0.3	0.3	0.1
Slovenia	n	n	n	n	0.2	n	0.1	0.1	0.1	0.1	0.1	0.1	n	0.1	1.9	a	n	0.1	0.1	n	n
Spain	0.1	0.4	0.1	0.9	1.3	0.4	2.2	1.0	6.0	1.8	1.3	0.8	0.1	7.7	0.1	0.4	a	0.8	1.4	1.4	0.6
Sweden	0.3	0.1	0.1	0.1	10.8	1.5	0.3	2.7	4.3	0.4	0.2	0.4	0.3	0.1	0.8	0.2	0.2	a	0.5	0.8	0.5
Switzerland	0.1	0.1	0.3	0.1	0.3	0.2	1.0	0.1	0.9	0.2	0.3	0.2	0.1	0.5	0.2	0.1	0.8	0.2	a	0.6	0.2
Turkey	0.2	0.5	0.6	n	0.6	1.4	3.4	1.9	n	0.3	0.5	0.7	0.1	0.4	0.2	0.2	0.3	1.7	1.6	0.8	1.8
United Kingdom	0.6	0.3	0.8	0.1	1.0	0.6	0.7	1.0	3.5	13.2	0.7	0.8	1.3	1.9	0.8	0.1	0.9	0.5	0.9	a	1.3
United States	1.1	0.5	7.4	1.2	1.2	1.8	1.9	1.8	6.4	7.5	1.2	0.5	6.7	1.5	0.1	0.4	1.0	1.6	1.9	3.5	a
OECD total	11.6	32.7	26.6	8.7	59.4	62.8	35.7	54.5	77.4	46.1	78.4	78.2	29.8	25.7	84.6	16.3	32.1	24.0	71.2	35.3	31.1
Argentina	n	n	0.1	5.9	0.1	n	0.2	n	0.1	n	0.2	n	0.1	0.3	n	0.2	5.4	0.1	0.4	0.1	0.3
Brazil	0.3	0.3	0.6	3.1	0.3	0.3	1.2	0.1	0.2	0.3	0.3	0.3	0.4	25.4	n	0.2	3.5	0.4	1.2	0.3	1.3
China	32.3	2.3	24.7	0.6	7.3	5.1	11.5	1.5	2.5	8.2	1.7	7.0	23.9	0.5	0.4	0.9	1.3	11.8	2.1	14.0	18.5
India	7.5	1.1	4.8	n	1.6	0.2	2.1	0.3	1.0	10.2	0.7	0.2	17.6	0.3	0.1	0.8	0.3	5.1	1.4	9.6	15.2
Indonesia	3.7	0.2	0.8	n	n	0.3	0.9	n	0.4	0.1	0.1	1.2	0.8	0.1	n	n	0.3	0.1	0.3	1.0	
Russian Federation	0.3	0.5	0.5	0.1	0.5	10.3	5.2	0.8	1.3	0.2	1.1	0.7	0.8	0.5	0.4	1.2	1.1	1.5	1.9	0.8	0.7
Saudi Arabia	2.0	n	1.7	n	n	n	0.1	1.0	n	0.7	n	n	1.7	n	1.1	n	n	0.1	n	2.0	2.3
South Africa	0.3	0.1	0.2	n	0.1	n	0.1	n	n	0.6	0.1	0.1	0.3	0.5	n	n	n	0.1	0.2	0.4	0.2
G20 total	46.5	4.6	33.4	9.8	10.0	16.3	21.2	3.8	5.6	20.4	4.2	9.6	45.7	27.6	2.0	3.3	11.7	19.2	7.4	27.4	39.5
Main geographic regions																					
Africa	2.8	5.9	11.5	0.1	2.5	1.5	9.0	3.1	1.6	7.3	9.2	2.0	1.0	40.1	1.4	0.9	9.8	5.7	5.5	9.3	5.4
Asia	79.8	7.7	54.6	1.5	15.4	11.9	33.1	21.1	8.7	35.1	5.3	12.2	64.7	3.8	8.2	2.8	3.8	45.3	10.4	50.5	70.0
Europe	4.3	36.4	11.4	4.1	72.4	83.1	42.7	72.6	76.5	40.5	82.6	81.4	8.2	26.0	89.8	92.7	30.4	23.3	73.4	31.0	10.3
of which, EU21 countries	3.1	30.6	9.5	3.6	36.4	57.6	23.3	37.3	60.0	32.0	75.4	74.8	6.6	22.3	79.0	15.0	20.6	15.8	63.9	25.1	7.4
North America	2.7	0.7	7.8	1.3	1.5	2.0	2.2	2.9	9.4	12.0	1.4	0.7	7.8	1.8	0.2	0.6	1.2	2.4	2.9	5.0	4.1
Oceania	1.7	0.1	0.5	0.1	0.4	n	0.3	0.1	1.2	0.7	0.4	0.1	17.0	0.2	n	0.2	0.1	0.3	0.4	0.6	0.7
Latin America and the Caribbean	1.4	1.6	7.2	75.9	1.3	1.6	4.6	0.2	2.4	1.1	1.0	2.4	1.3	28.0	0.4	0.8	54.3	2.3	5.1	2.0	9.5
Not specified	7.3	47.5	6.9	16.9	6.5	n	8.1	n	0.2	3.3	n	1.2	n	n	n	2.0	0.4	20.6	2.3	1.6	n
Total all countries	100.0	100.0	100.0	100.0	100.0	100.0	100.0	100.0	100.0	100.0	100.0	100.0	100.0	100.0	100.0	100.0	100.0	100.0	100.0	100.0	100.0

OECD destination countries — International students

1. Year of reference 2009.
2. Excludes private institutions.
3. Excludes tertiary-type B programmes.
4. Excludes advanced research programmes.
5. Students with origin not specified come mainly from other nordic countries.
6. Foreign students are defined on the basis of their country of citizenship; these data are not comparable with data on international students and are therefore presented separately in the table.
Source: OECD. See Annex 3 for notes (*www.oecd.org/edu/eag2012*).
Please refer to the Reader's Guide for information concerning the symbols replacing missing data.
StatLink ▒▒▒ http://dx.doi.org/10.1787/888932667273

Table C4.3. [2/2] Distribution of international and foreign students in tertiary education, by country of origin (2010)

Number of international and foreign students enrolled in tertiary education from a given country of origin as a percentage of all international or foreign students in the country of destination, based on head counts

The table shows for each country the proportion of international students in tertiary education who are residents of or had their prior education in a given country of origin. When data on student mobility are not available, the table shows the proportion of foreign students in tertiary education that have citizenship of a given country of origin.
Reading the second column: 15.3% of international tertiary students in Belgium come from France, 8.6% of international tertiary students in Belgium come from the Netherlands, etc.
Reading the sixth column: 48.0% of international tertiary students in Estonia come from Finland, 1.6% of international tertiary students in Estonia come from Italy, etc.
Reading the 22nd column: 36.7% of foreign tertiary students in Austria are German citizens, 2.5% of foreign tertiary students in Austria are Hungarian citizens, etc.

	Countries of destination															
	OECD												Other G20			
	Foreign students												Foreign students			
Countries of origin	Austria[3,6]	Czech Republic[6]	Greece[6]	Finland[6]	France[6]	Italy[6]	Japan[6]	Korea[6]	Norway[6]	Poland[6]	Turkey[6]	Total OECD destinations	Brazil[6]	Russian Federation[2,4,6]	Total non-OECD destinations	Total all reporting destinations
	(22)	(23)	(24)	(25)	(26)	(27)	(28)	(29)	(30)	(31)	(32)	(33)	(34)	(35)	(36)	(37)
OECD																
Australia	0.1	n	0.1	0.3	0.1	0.1	0.2	0.1	0.3	0.1	0.2	**0.4**	0.1	n	**0.1**	**0.3**
Austria	a	0.2	0.2	0.3	0.2	0.2	n	0.1	0.3	0.3	0.2	**0.4**	0.2	n	**0.1**	**0.4**
Belgium	0.2	n	0.2	0.2	1.2	0.2	n	n	0.3	0.1	0.2	**0.4**	0.4	n	**n**	**0.3**
Canada	0.2	0.1	0.1	0.8	0.6	0.1	0.3	0.5	0.6	2.5	0.1	**1.6**	0.3	n	**0.2**	**1.3**
Chile	n	n	n	0.1	0.3	0.2	n	n	0.5	n	n	**0.3**	3.0	n	**0.3**	**0.3**
Czech Republic	1.1	a	0.1	0.4	0.3	0.3	n	n	0.4	2.0	n	**0.4**	n	n	**n**	**0.3**
Denmark	0.1	n	n	0.3	0.1	0.1	n	n	5.1	0.2	0.1	**0.2**	0.1	n	**n**	**0.2**
Estonia	0.1	n	n	5.0	n	0.1	n	n	0.4	0.1	n	**0.1**	n	0.3	**0.1**	**0.1**
Finland	0.3	n	0.1	a	0.1	0.1	0.1	n	2.0	0.1	n	**0.3**	0.1	n	**0.2**	**0.2**
France	0.9	0.4	0.2	1.1	a	1.2	0.4	0.2	1.0	0.8	0.3	**2.0**	2.3	0.1	**0.2**	**1.6**
Germany	36.7	1.1	1.1	3.4	2.7	1.8	0.3	0.2	5.2	3.4	3.1	**3.8**	1.9	0.1	**0.3**	**3.0**
Greece	0.6	0.9	a	0.5	0.7	5.0	n	n	0.2	0.2	3.7	**0.9**	0.1	0.1	**0.5**	**0.9**
Hungary	2.5	0.4	0.1	0.9	0.2	0.3	0.1	n	0.3	0.4	0.1	**0.3**	n	n	**n**	**0.2**
Iceland	n	n	n	0.1	n	n	n	n	1.9	n	n	**0.1**	n	n	**n**	**0.1**
Ireland	0.1	0.1	n	0.3	0.2	n	n	n	0.1	0.2	n	**0.7**	n	n	**n**	**0.6**
Israel	0.2	0.4	0.2	0.1	0.1	2.2	n	n	0.1	0.2	0.1	**0.3**	0.1	0.4	**0.9**	**0.4**
Italy	11.1	0.1	0.3	1.3	2.3	a	0.1	n	0.4	0.4	0.1	**1.4**	1.6	0.1	**0.2**	**1.1**
Japan	0.6	0.1	0.1	0.9	0.7	0.4	a	1.9	0.3	0.2	0.1	**1.5**	1.2	0.1	**0.2**	**1.2**
Korea	0.7	0.1	0.1	0.3	0.9	0.6	18.1	a	0.2	0.2	0.1	**4.6**	1.6	0.4	**0.6**	**3.7**
Luxembourg	1.0	n	n	n	0.5	n	n	n	n	n	n	**0.3**	n	n	**n**	**0.2**
Mexico	0.2	0.1	n	0.7	0.8	0.3	0.1	0.1	0.3	0.2	n	**0.9**	0.6	n	**0.2**	**0.8**
Netherlands	0.4	n	0.1	0.6	0.3	0.1	0.1	n	1.5	0.2	0.3	**0.5**	0.1	n	**n**	**0.4**
New Zealand	n	n	n	0.1	n	n	0.1	0.1	0.1	n	n	**0.2**	n	n	**n**	**0.1**
Norway	0.1	0.8	n	0.5	0.1	0.1	0.1	n	a	7.1	n	**0.5**	0.1	n	**0.1**	**0.4**
Poland	2.7	0.9	0.5	1.6	1.1	1.8	0.1	n	1.9	a	0.1	**1.1**	0.1	n	**0.1**	**0.9**
Portugal	0.2	1.3	0.1	0.3	1.2	0.1	n	n	0.3	0.1	n	**0.4**	5.6	n	**0.2**	**0.4**
Slovak Republic	2.4	64.1	n	0.2	0.2	0.3	n	n	0.2	1.0	n	**1.1**	n	n	**n**	**0.9**
Slovenia	1.2	0.1	n	0.1	n	0.4	n	n	n	0.1	n	**0.1**	n	n	**n**	**0.1**
Spain	0.9	0.1	0.2	1.1	1.6	0.6	0.1	n	0.6	0.9	0.1	**0.8**	1.4	n	**0.1**	**0.7**
Sweden	0.3	0.4	0.1	3.8	0.2	0.2	0.1	n	8.8	5.1	0.1	**0.6**	0.1	n	**0.1**	**0.5**
Switzerland	1.3	n	0.2	0.3	0.7	1.2	n	n	0.3	0.1	0.1	**0.4**	0.4	n	**0.1**	**0.3**
Turkey	4.3	0.2	0.6	1.0	0.9	0.8	0.1	0.1	0.7	0.9	a	**1.2**	0.1	0.3	**2.1**	**1.4**
United Kingdom	0.5	1.2	0.5	1.3	1.0	0.3	0.3	0.1	2.1	0.6	0.4	**0.8**	2.2	n	**0.2**	**0.7**
United States	0.9	0.5	0.6	1.7	1.3	0.4	1.6	1.7	2.2	5.4	0.5	**1.6**	2.9	0.1	**0.7**	**1.4**
OECD total	72.1	73.7	6.0	29.8	20.6	19.5	22.6	5.3	39.2	33.1	9.9	**30.3**	26.7	2.1	**7.8**	**25.2**
Other G20																
Argentina	n	n	n	0.1	0.3	0.4	n	0.1	0.2	n	n	**0.3**	5.1	n	**0.3**	**0.3**
Brazil	0.3	n	0.1	0.5	1.4	1.2	0.4	0.1	0.6	0.2	n	**0.9**	a	0.1	**0.4**	**0.8**
China	2.0	0.4	n	14.9	9.5	6.7	61.1	77.3	4.8	2.2	0.8	**18.7**	2.4	5.8	**10.9**	**17.0**
India	0.6	0.3	n	2.8	0.6	0.6	0.4	0.8	1.5	1.9	n	**7.0**	0.1	2.4	**2.3**	**5.9**
Indonesia	0.1	n	n	0.2	0.1	0.1	1.4	0.7	0.5	0.1	0.4	**0.9**	0.1	n	**1.6**	**1.1**
Russian Federation	1.3	6.6	1.4	11.3	1.5	1.6	0.2	0.6	5.7	3.0	1.9	**1.3**	0.2	a	**2.5**	**1.6**
Saudi Arabia	n	n	n	n	0.2	n	0.1	0.1	n	0.8	0.1	**1.2**	n	n	**1.4**	**1.3**
South Africa	0.1	0.1	0.2	0.1	n	n	n	n	0.2	0.1	n	**0.2**	1.2	n	**0.2**	**0.2**
G20 total	4.4	7.6	1.8	30.0	13.6	10.8	63.8	79.7	13.5	8.2	3.2	**30.6**	9.1	8.3	**19.6**	**28.1**
Main geographic regions																
Africa	1.5	1.4	3.4	18.6	42.8	11.0	0.8	1.0	10.0	4.2	2.8	**9.6**	28.3	4.1	**19.1**	**11.8**
Asia	12.3	9.8	55.8	36.7	21.8	18.0	93.2	94.5	19.6	19.0	57.4	**51.7**	7.2	58.6	**54.9**	**52.5**
Europe	83.8	86.5	37.0	39.1	21.3	50.5	2.6	1.5	47.7	68.0	23.3	**24.5**	17.7	32.6	**16.8**	**22.7**
of which, EU21 countries	63.5	71.3	3.9	22.7	14.1	13.1	1.9	0.8	31.6	16.3	8.8	**16.7**	16.3	0.9	**2.5**	**13.5**
North America	1.1	0.7	0.7	2.5	1.9	0.5	1.8	2.2	2.8	7.9	0.6	**3.3**	3.2	0.1	**0.8**	**2.7**
Oceania	0.1	n	0.1	0.4	0.2	0.1	0.4	0.2	0.4	0.1	0.2	**0.8**	0.7	n	**1.5**	**1.0**
Latin America and the Caribbean	1.1	0.6	0.3	2.5	5.5	7.5	1.1	0.5	2.7	0.8	0.1	**6.0**	29.6	0.6	**6.9**	**6.2**
Not specified	n	0.9	2.7	0.2	6.5	12.4	n	n	16.8	0.1	15.6	**4.1**	13.3	4.0	**m**	**3.2**
Total from all countries	100.0	100.0	100.0	100.0	100.0	100.0	100.0	100.0	100.0	100.0	100.0	**100.0**	100.0	100.0	**100.0**	**100.0**

1. Year of reference 2009.
2. Excludes private institutions.
3. Excludes tertiary-type B programmes.
4. Excludes advanced research programmes.
5. Students with origin not specified come mainly from other nordic countries.
6. Foreign students are defined on the basis of their country of citizenship; these data are not comparable with data on international students and are therefore presented separately in the table.
Source: OECD. See Annex 3 for notes (*www.oecd.org/edu/eag2012*).
Please refer to the Reader's Guide for information concerning the symbols replacing missing data.
StatLink ⫍⫎ http://dx.doi.org/10.1787/888932667273

C4

Table C4.4. [1/2] Citizens studying abroad in tertiary education, by country of destination (2010)

Number of foreign students enrolled in tertiary education in a given country of destination as a percentage of all students enrolled abroad, based on head counts

The table shows for each country the proportion of students studying abroad in tertiary education in a given country of destination.
Reading the second column: 5.7% of Czech citizens enrolled in tertiary education abroad study in Austria, 12.9% of Italian citizens enrolled in tertiary education abroad study in Austria, etc.
Reading the first row: 2.7% of Australian citizens enrolled in tertiary education abroad study in France, 23.1% of Australian citizens enrolled in tertiary education abroad study in New Zealand, etc.

Country of origin	Australia (1)	Austria[1] (2)	Belgium (3)	Canada[2,3] (4)	Chile (5)	Czech Republic (6)	Denmark (7)	Estonia (8)	Finland (9)	France (10)	Germany[4] (11)	Greece[5] (12)	Hungary (13)	Iceland (14)	Ireland[6] (15)	Israel (16)	Italy (17)	Japan (18)	Korea (19)	Luxembourg[5] (20)
OECD																				
Australia	a	0.6	0.3	3.9	n	n	0.5	n	0.3	2.7	3.3	0.2	0.1	0.1	1.0	0.1	0.3	2.4	0.5	n
Austria	1.8	a	0.6	1.0	n	0.3	0.5	n	0.3	3.0	51.0	0.3	0.8	0.1	0.2	0.1	1.0	0.4	0.2	0.1
Belgium	0.7	1.2	a	3.1	n	0.1	0.6	n	0.3	25.4	8.4	0.5	0.2	n	0.6	0.4	1.2	0.4	n	2.2
Canada	9.1	0.3	0.3	a	n	0.1	0.2	n	0.2	3.0	1.3	0.1	0.4	0.1	1.1	0.2	0.2	0.8	0.7	n
Chile	4.0	0.3	1.0	3.5	a	0.1	0.3	n	0.2	6.9	6.2	0.1	n	n	0.1	n	1.4	0.4	0.1	n
Czech Republic	0.7	5.7	0.6	0.7	n	a	1.0	n	0.4	5.9	13.5	0.1	0.5	0.2	0.7	n	1.5	0.3	0.1	0.1
Denmark	2.8	1.3	0.7	1.5	n	0.1	a	0.1	0.6	2.7	6.5	0.2	0.1	1.0	0.4	0.1	0.8	0.4	0.2	0.1
Estonia	0.5	1.8	0.7	0.4	n	0.1	4.7	a	13.2	2.1	11.7	0.2	0.4	0.1	1.5	n	1.0	0.4	n	n
Finland	1.4	2.0	0.5	0.9	n	0.1	2.2	4.6	a	2.9	7.3	0.2	0.4	0.4	0.6	0.1	0.6	0.8	0.1	0.1
France	1.9	0.8	22.9	10.4	0.1	0.2	0.4	n	0.2	a	8.6	0.1	0.2	0.1	0.6	0.2	1.1	0.8	0.1	1.1
Germany	1.7	20.4	0.8	1.0	0.1	0.3	1.9	n	0.4	5.8	a	0.2	1.6	0.1	0.8	0.1	1.0	0.4	0.1	0.3
Greece	0.2	1.1	1.5	0.3	n	0.8	0.4	n	0.2	5.0	15.8	a	0.5	n	0.2	n	9.2	n	n	0.1
Hungary	0.5	16.7	1.3	1.0	n	1.4	2.8	n	1.2	5.9	21.0	0.2	a	0.1	1.0	0.1	1.8	0.9	0.1	0.1
Iceland	0.8	0.8	0.2	1.0	n	n	41.4	0.1	0.3	0.8	2.5	n	1.8	a	1.5	n	0.2	0.5	n	0.1
Ireland	0.9	0.3	0.3	0.9	n	0.2	0.2	n	0.1	1.5	1.4	n	0.7	n	a	n	0.1	0.1	n	n
Israel	0.9	0.7	0.2	6.0	n	0.8	0.2	n	0.1	1.4	8.9	0.4	4.5	n	0.1	a	8.5	0.2	n	n
Italy	0.7	12.9	4.3	0.6	n	0.1	0.7	n	0.3	9.9	15.0	0.1	0.1	0.1	0.9	0.1	a	0.3	n	0.2
Japan	5.6	1.0	0.3	4.9	n	0.1	0.1	n	0.3	4.0	4.9	0.1	0.4	n	0.1	n	0.7	a	2.7	n
Korea	5.4	0.3	n	6.2	n	n	n	n	n	1.6	3.9	n	0.1	n	n	n	0.3	18.8	a	n
Luxembourg	0.3	8.3	22.7	0.1	n	n	n	n	n	17.5	36.9	0.1	0.1	n	0.1	n	0.3	0.1	n	a
Mexico	1.9	0.4	0.4	5.6	0.7	0.1	0.2	n	0.3	6.6	5.4	n	n	n	0.1	n	0.7	0.6	0.1	n
Netherlands	1.6	1.4	27.6	2.0	0.1	0.1	1.4	n	0.4	3.6	8.0	0.2	0.2	0.1	1.0	0.1	0.5	0.6	0.1	n
New Zealand	43.6	0.2	0.3	2.7	n	0.1	0.2	n	0.2	1.2	1.6	n	0.1	0.1	0.8	n	1.4	0.9	n	n
Norway	9.2	0.5	0.2	1.3	n	1.7	18.3	n	0.5	2.0	2.7	n	4.6	0.2	0.2	0.1	0.4	0.5	n	0.2
Poland	0.3	3.9	1.6	1.3	n	0.7	2.3	n	0.5	5.8	25.4	0.3	0.2	0.2	2.8	n	2.6	0.2	n	0.6
Portugal	0.5	0.6	4.7	1.3	n	2.0	0.5	n	0.2	13.8	8.1	0.1	0.3	n	0.6	n	0.4	0.1	n	0.1
Slovak Republic	0.2	4.9	0.3	0.4	n	67.3	0.3	n	0.1	1.2	3.8	n	7.5	n	0.4	n	0.6	0.1	n	n
Slovenia	0.8	27.4	1.0	0.5	n	0.8	1.4	0.1	0.6	2.1	17.1	0.1	0.8	0.1	0.4	0.1	9.8	0.4	n	0.1
Spain	0.5	2.0	3.9	0.7	0.2	0.1	1.0	n	0.5	13.4	17.0	0.2	0.5	0.2	1.5	n	1.3	0.4	0.1	0.2
Sweden	4.3	1.2	0.3	1.0	0.1	0.7	13.0	n	2.8	2.3	3.6	0.2	2.3	0.2	0.6	0.1	0.6	0.9	0.1	n
Switzerland	2.8	7.3	1.3	3.4	0.1	0.1	0.7	n	0.3	14.8	21.4	0.4	0.2	0.1	0.4	0.1	6.9	0.5	0.1	0.1
Turkey	0.6	3.7	0.5	1.2	n	0.1	0.7	n	0.2	2.9	37.8	0.2	0.4	n	0.1	n	0.7	0.2	0.1	n
United Kingdom	4.7	0.9	1.0	5.7	n	1.2	1.6	n	0.5	7.7	5.6	0.4	0.4	0.1	11.0	0.1	0.5	1.4	0.1	0.1
United States	5.3	1.1	0.5	15.9	0.1	0.3	0.6	n	0.4	6.0	6.9	0.3	0.5	0.1	2.2	1.4	0.5	3.9	1.7	n
OECD total	2.9	4.5	3.2	3.6	0.1	2.4	1.4	0.1	0.4	4.9	10.5	0.1	0.8	0.1	1.0	0.1	1.2	2.9	0.3	0.2
EU21 total	1.4	7.0	5.4	2.4	n	4.0	1.5	0.1	0.5	5.9	10.5	0.2	1.0	0.1	1.4	0.1	1.5	0.4	0.1	0.4
Other G20																				
Argentina	0.7	0.2	0.3	3.8	3.6	n	0.2	n	0.1	5.8	3.2	0.1	n	n	0.1	0.1	2.0	0.5	0.3	n
Brazil	2.2	0.5	0.7	3.4	0.7	n	0.4	n	0.2	10.3	7.5	0.1	0.1	n	0.3	0.1	2.5	1.8	0.1	n
China	13.8	0.2	0.2	5.6	n	n	0.3	n	0.3	3.9	3.8	n	n	n	0.4	n	0.7	13.6	7.2	n
India	9.0	0.2	0.2	4.4	n	n	0.2	n	0.2	0.6	1.9	n	n	n	0.8	n	0.2	0.3	0.2	n
Indonesia	24.0	0.2	0.3	2.5	n	0.1	n	n	0.1	0.9	6.1	n	n	n	n	n	0.2	4.7	1.0	n
Russian Federation	1.3	1.3	0.9	2.5	n	3.4	0.6	n	2.4	5.7	20.2	0.6	0.3	n	0.3	n	1.7	0.5	0.5	0.1
Saudi Arabia	11.7	0.1	n	3.6	n	n	n	n	n	1.0	0.4	n	0.3	n	0.1	n	n	0.4	0.1	n
South Africa	6.9	0.6	0.5	3.5	n	0.4	0.3	n	0.1	0.9	1.4	0.4	n	n	2.0	0.2	0.1	0.2	0.1	n
Other G20 total	11.7	0.3	0.3	4.8	0.1	0.2	0.2	0.1	0.4	3.3	4.5	0.0	0.1	0.0	0.4	0.0	0.7	8.4	4.4	0.0
Total all countries	6.6	1.7	1.3	4.7	0.2	0.8	0.6	0.1	0.3	6.3	6.4	0.7	0.4	n	0.7	0.1	1.7	3.4	1.4	0.1

Note: The proportion of students abroad is based only on the total of students enrolled in countries reporting data to the OECD and UNESCO Institute for Statistics.
1. Excludes tertiary-type B programmes.
2. Year of reference 2009.
3. Excludes private institutions.
4. Excludes advanced research programmes.
5. Total based on the estimation by the UNESCO Institute for Statistics.
6. Excludes part-time students.
Source: OECD. See Annex 3 for notes (*www.oecd.org/edu/eag2012*).
Please refer to the Reader's Guide for information concerning the symbols replacing missing data.
StatLink ᘛ᙭ᘰᕟ http://dx.doi.org/10.1787/888932667292

Table C4.4. [2/2] Citizens studying abroad in tertiary education, by country of destination (2010)

Number of foreign students enrolled in tertiary education in a given country of destination as a percentage of all students enrolled abroad, based on head counts

The table shows for each country the proportion of students studying abroad in tertiary education in a given country of destination.
Reading the second column: 5.7% of Czech citizens enrolled in tertiary education abroad study in Austria, 12.9% of Italian citizens enrolled in tertiary education abroad study in Austria, etc.
Reading the first row: 2.7% of Australian citizens enrolled in tertiary education abroad study in France, 23.1% of Australian citizens enrolled in tertiary education abroad study in New Zealand, etc.

C4

Country of origin	Mexico[5]	Netherlands[3,4]	New Zealand	Norway	Poland	Portugal	Slovak Republic	Slovenia	Spain	Sweden	Switzerland	Turkey	United Kingdom	United States	Total OECD destinations	Total EU21 destinations	Brazil	Russian Federation[3,4]	Total non-OECD destinations	Total all reporting destinations
	(21)	(22)	(23)	(24)	(25)	(26)	(27)	(28)	(29)	(30)	(31)	(32)	(33)	(34)	(35)	(36)	(37)	(38)	(39)	(40)
OECD																				
Australia	m	0.5	23.1	0.4	0.1	0.2	n	n	0.4	0.8	0.7	0.3	28.5	24.8	96.1	39.7	0.1	n	3.9	100.0
Austria	m	1.7	0.6	0.3	0.3	0.2	0.5	0.2	1.4	1.0	8.3	0.3	12.8	6.1	95.3	76.1	0.2	0.1	4.7	100.0
Belgium	m	17.7	0.4	0.4	0.1	1.1	n	n	4.5	0.5	3.3	0.4	17.9	6.6	98.1	82.4	0.4	0.1	1.9	100.0
Canada	m	0.4	1.5	0.2	1.0	0.3	n	n	0.4	0.5	0.7	n	14.8	58.8	96.6	24.5	0.1	n	3.4	100.0
Chile	m	0.4	1.5	0.6	n	0.3	n	n	25.1	1.4	0.9	n	4.9	17.5	77.2	48.7	3.8	n	22.8	100.0
Czech Republic	m	1.2	0.4	0.5	2.7	0.4	36.1	0.1	1.3	0.5	1.2	n	15.9	6.0	98.6	88.4	n	0.2	1.4	100.0
Denmark	m	2.2	2.1	11.0	0.6	0.1	0.1	0.1	1.2	10.9	1.4	0.2	34.3	13.3	97.2	63.0	0.2	n	2.8	100.0
Estonia	m	1.3	0.1	1.2	0.2	0.2	n	n	1.6	4.4	0.7	n	25.9	4.1	78.7	71.2	0.1	10.5	21.3	100.0
Finland	m	2.1	0.4	2.8	0.2	0.2	n	n	1.1	25.9	1.2	0.1	22.0	5.8	87.0	72.9	0.1	0.6	13.0	100.0
France	m	1.2	0.5	0.2	0.2	0.7	n	n	4.4	0.6	7.4	0.1	22.6	9.8	97.4	65.8	0.4	0.1	2.6	100.0
Germany	m	17.9	1.3	0.7	0.5	0.3	0.3	n	2.4	1.4	11.2	0.6	16.4	7.7	97.6	72.7	0.2	0.2	2.4	100.0
Greece	m	2.2	n	0.1	0.1	0.1	2.0	n	1.0	0.9	1.2	2.6	36.1	4.8	86.5	77.3	n	0.5	13.5	100.0
Hungary	m	3.3	0.6	0.4	0.7	0.2	0.8	0.1	1.3	1.1	2.2	0.2	22.4	6.3	95.6	83.3	0.1	0.4	4.4	100.0
Iceland	m	2.3	0.1	7.2	0.1	n	0.1	n	0.5	10.4	0.5	n	16.7	9.6	99.4	79.7	n	0.1	0.6	100.0
Ireland	m	0.6	0.9	0.1	0.1	n	0.1	n	0.5	0.3	0.2	n	85.2	15.3	99.3	91.8	n	n	0.7	100.0
Israel	m	0.8	0.3	0.1	0.2	n	0.5	n	0.7	0.2	0.5	0.1	4.0	15.3	55.6	32.1	0.1	3.5	44.4	100.0
Italy	m	1.4	0.1	0.2	0.1	0.8	0.1	0.2	10.3	0.7	10.1	n	19.3	6.8	96.6	77.5	0.4	0.1	3.4	100.0
Japan	m	0.4	2.3	0.1	0.1	n	n	n	0.4	0.5	0.6	n	8.9	57.1	95.8	22.5	0.4	0.3	4.2	100.0
Korea	m	0.2	2.1	n	n	n	n	n	0.3	0.1	0.2	n	3.8	52.4	95.9	10.8	0.2	0.5	4.1	100.0
Luxembourg	m	1.0	0.1	n	n	0.4	n	n	0.6	0.1	4.7	n	5.6	0.7	99.6	93.7	n	n	0.4	100.0
Mexico	a	0.7	0.4	0.2	0.1	0.1	n	n	15.5	0.6	0.8	n	5.2	45.1	92.4	36.8	0.3	0.1	7.6	100.0
Netherlands	m	a	2.5	1.2	0.2	0.5	n	n	2.4	1.6	2.3	0.4	29.7	9.1	98.5	78.6	0.1	n	1.5	100.0
New Zealand	m	0.3	a	0.2	0.1	n	n	n	0.1	0.4	0.6	n	24.2	19.1	98.1	29.7	n	n	1.9	100.0
Norway	m	2.2	1.2	a	8.2	0.1	1.8	n	0.7	7.7	0.6	n	23.3	9.1	97.8	75.5	0.1	0.1	2.2	100.0
Poland	m	1.9	0.1	0.6	a	0.5	0.3	n	2.4	1.4	1.1	n	37.1	4.6	98.8	90.2	n	0.1	1.2	100.0
Portugal	m	1.7	0.1	0.2	0.1	a	0.1	n	16.5	0.6	5.8	n	29.9	4.5	92.9	80.2	3.7	n	7.1	100.0
Slovak Republic	m	0.5	0.1	0.1	0.6	0.1	a	n	0.6	0.1	0.6	n	8.3	1.4	99.6	96.8	n	0.1	0.4	100.0
Slovenia	m	3.0	0.1	0.1	0.4	0.8	0.2	a	1.6	0.8	2.0	0.2	12.8	6.3	91.6	81.2	n	0.1	8.4	100.0
Spain	m	2.6	0.2	0.3	0.6	3.5	n	n	a	1.2	5.1	0.1	27.3	12.8	97.5	76.9	0.6	0.1	2.5	100.0
Sweden	m	1.3	0.8	7.4	5.0	0.1	0.3	n	1.3	a	1.4	0.1	26.7	16.4	95.1	62.3	0.1	0.1	4.9	100.0
Switzerland	m	1.4	0.8	0.4	0.1	1.0	0.1	n	6.1	0.7	a	0.2	12.5	10.7	95.1	75.8	0.5	0.1	4.9	100.0
Turkey	m	1.3	n	0.1	0.2	0.1	n	n	0.3	0.6	1.3	a	5.6	15.6	74.7	55.5	n	0.6	25.3	100.0
United Kingdom	m	2.4	16.3	1.0	0.3	0.4	0.2	n	3.2	1.7	1.3	0.3	a	24.9	94.9	39.0	0.9	0.1	5.1	100.0
United States	m	0.9	5.7	0.6	1.7	0.3	n	n	1.9	1.1	1.2	0.2	27.5	a	89.1	52.8	0.7	0.1	10.9	100.0
OECD total	m	3.2	1.9	0.6	0.6	0.4	0.6	n	2.9	1.2	3.4	0.2	18.1	19.4	93.4	57.8	0.4	0.3	6.6	100.0
EU21 total	m	5.1	1.5	0.8	0.5	0.5	1.1	n	3.4	1.5	5.4	0.4	23.9	8.2	96.3	75.5	0.4	0.2	3.7	100.0
Other G20																				
Argentina	m	0.2	0.5	0.2	n	0.2	n	n	38.7	0.3	0.9	n	2.4	15.8	80.2	53.8	5.6	n	19.8	100.0
Brazil	m	0.5	0.9	0.3	0.1	12.8	n	n	9.9	0.5	1.5	n	7.0	25.2	89.6	53.3	a	0.4	10.4	100.0
China	m	0.6	2.3	0.1	0.1	n	n	n	0.3	0.6	0.2	n	9.8	19.9	83.9	21.3	0.1	1.5	16.1	100.0
India	m	0.2	3.7	0.1	0.2	n	n	n	0.1	0.6	0.3	n	21.0	46.0	90.5	26.4	n	1.7	9.5	100.0
Indonesia	m	2.3	1.2	0.2	n	n	n	n	0.1	0.2	0.2	0.2	3.0	16.3	63.7	13.4	n	0.1	36.3	100.0
Russian Federation	m	0.7	0.8	1.3	0.8	0.3	0.1	0.1	1.9	1.0	1.4	0.7	6.8	7.1	65.7	49.9	n	a	34.3	100.0
Saudi Arabia	m	n	1.4	n	0.3	n	0.2	n	0.1	n	n	n	17.7	33.9	71.6	20.3	n	n	28.4	100.0
South Africa	m	0.7	18.1	0.2	0.1	0.7	n	n	0.2	0.3	0.4	n	35.9	13.4	87.7	44.6	1.4	n	12.3	100.0
Other G20 total	m	0.5	2.5	0.2	0.1	0.5	0.0	0.0	1.1	0.5	0.3	0.1	12.1	25.1	83.0	25.5	0.1	1.2	17.0	100.0
Total all countries	n	1.2	1.7	0.4	0.4	0.5	0.2	0.1	2.4	1.1	1.3	0.6	13.0	16.6	77.3	40.0	0.4	3.9	22.7	100.0

Note: The proportion of students abroad is based only on the total of students enrolled in countries reporting data to the OECD and UNESCO Institute for Statistics.
1. Excludes tertiary-type B programmes.
2. Year of reference 2009.
3. Excludes private institutions.
4. Excludes advanced research programmes.
5. Total based on the estimation by the UNESCO Institute for Statistics.
6. Excludes part-time students.
Source: OECD. See Annex 3 for notes (www.oecd.org/edu/eag2012).
Please refer to the Reader's Guide for information concerning the symbols replacing missing data.
StatLink http://dx.doi.org/10.1787/888932667292

Table C4.5. Mobility patterns of foreign and international students (2010)

Regional and cross-border mobility, balance on mobility and use of the official language of the host country in countries of origin

	Percentage of national tertiary students enrolled abroad	Number of foreign students per national student abroad	Percentage of foreign students coming from neighbouring countries[1]	Percentage of students from countries with the same official language
	(1)	(2)	(3)	(4)
OECD Australia	1.3	20.6	33.6	20.3
Austria	5.2	4.2	56.6	50.5
Belgium	3.0	4.3	48.0	65.5
Canada[2]	3.4	4.1	4.6	31.3
Chile	1.2	0.8	31.4	57.4
Czech Republic[3]	3.3	2.6	66.3	n
Denmark	3.2	3.6	36.9	n
Estonia	7.2	0.5	76.9	n
Finland	3.7	1.3	20.6	3.8
France[3]	3.8	3.3	14.5	28.4
Germany	4.9	2.1	15.3	9.0
Greece[3]	5.8	0.7	78.7	49.1
Hungary	2.7	1.7	47.8	0.1
Iceland	19.6	0.3	9.4	n
Ireland	13.0	1.1	13.2	36.5
Israel[3]	4.8	0.2	0.3	n
Italy[3]	3.0	1.2	30.6	5.0
Japan	1.2	3.3	18.8	n
Korea[3]	4.1	0.4	79.2	n
Luxembourg	71.6	0.4	m	30.0
Mexico	1.0	0.1	m	m
Netherlands	3.1	2.5	51.6	6.2
New Zealand	2.4	12.4	11.4	42.6
Norway	6.7	1.0	25.7	n
Poland	2.2	0.4	53.9	n
Portugal	5.6	0.9	5.7	68.5
Slovak Republic	12.8	0.3	62.9	n
Slovenia	2.6	0.7	42.7	7.4
Spain	1.7	3.2	21.4	43.3
Sweden	4.3	2.4	19.5	6.5
Switzerland	5.4	4.5	51.0	55.4
Turkey[3]	2.2	0.3	30.0	8.4
United Kingdom	1.7	15.1	14.0	35.8
United States	0.3	12.0	7.0	28.6
OECD total	2.0	2.9	20.7	26.1
EU21 total	3.6	2.7	23.4	27.3
Other G20 Argentina	0.6	0.2	m	73.5
Brazil[3]	0.5	0.4	23.0	30.0
China[3]	2.0	m	m	m
India	m	m	m	m
Indonesia[3]	0.8	0.1	88.1	41.5
Russian Federation[3]	0.8	2.4	60.6	37.5
Saudi Arabia[3]	5.0	0.7	9.9	12.5
South Africa[3]	1.3	5.1	55.4	60.6

1. Neighbour countries are those that have land or maritime borders with the host country.
2. Year of reference 2009.
3. National tertiary students are calculated as total enrolment minus foreign students instead of total enrolment minus international students.
Source: OECD. CIA World Factbook 2012 for worldwide official languages. See Annex 3 for notes (*www.oecd.org/edu/eag2012*).
Please refer to the Reader's Guide for information concerning the symbols replacing missing data.
StatLink ⟪ms⟫ http://dx.doi.org/10.1787/888932667311

Table C4.6. Trends in the number of foreign students enrolled outside their country of origin, by destination region and origin (2000 to 2010)

Number of foreign students enrolled in tertiary education outside their country of origin, head counts

Foreign students enrolled in the following destinations	Number of foreign students					Index of change (2010)				Foreign students enrolled in OECD countries from the following regions of origin (2010)
	2010	2009	2008	2005	2000	2009 = 100	2008 = 100	2005 = 100	2000 = 100	
Africa	155 293	147 338	142 811	107 851	99 117	105	109	144	157	344 072
Asia	486 076	446 055	398 817	322 449	214 744	109	122	151	226	1 523 272
Europe	1 968 418	1 665 829	1 580 212	1 388 027	920 140	118	125	142	214	867 514
North America	880 427	850 966	809 943	738 401	569 640	103	109	119	155	98 214
Latin America & the Caribbean	77 735	77 546	60 889	39 227	31 058	100	128	198	250	200 463
Oceania	350 013	335 305	298 176	251 904	118 646	104	117	139	295	25 927
Worldwide	**4 119 002**	**3 707 756**	**3 459 354**	**2 982 588**	**2 071 963**	**111**	**119**	**138**	**199**	**3 181 939**
OECD	3 181 939	2 838 027	2 646 999	2 373 011	1 588 862	112	120	134	200	1 021 625
EU countries	1 686 306	1 413 462	1 322 936	1 201 503	806 286	119	127	140	209	704 310
of which in EU21 countries	1 647 730	1 378 961	1 287 768	1 174 107	776 672	119	128	140	212	598 087
G20 countries	3 418 367	3 040 151	2 849 469	2 488 585	1 718 429	112	120	137	199	1 550 532

Note: Figures are based on the number of foreign students enrolled in OECD and non-OECD countries reporting data to the OECD and to the UNESCO Institute for Statistics, in order to provide a global picture of foreign students worldwide. The coverage of these reporting countries has evolved over time, therefore missing data have been imputed when necessary to ensure the comparability of time series over time. Given the inclusion of UNESCO data for non-OECD countries and the imputation of missing data, the estimates of the number of foreign students may differ from those published in previous editions of *Education at a Glance*. Totals refering to years 2006 to 2008 and 2001 to 2004 are available for consultation on line (see *StatLink* below).

Source: OECD and UNESCO Institute for Statistics for most data on non-OECD countries. See Annex 3 for notes *(www.oecd.org/edu/eag2012)*.

Please refer to the Reader's Guide for information concerning the symbols replacing missing data.

StatLink ᴍᴤᴸ http://dx.doi.org/10.1787/888932667330

TRANSITION FROM SCHOOL TO WORK: WHERE ARE THE 15-29 YEAR-OLDS?

INDICATOR C5

- On average across OECD countries in 2010, 16% of individuals between the ages of 15 and 29 were neither employed, nor in education or training (the "NEET" population).

- Overall, the proportion of NEETs in 2010 was 4 percentage points higher among 15-29 year-old women than among 15-29 year-old men, but situations vary widely from one country to another.

- On average across OECD countries, the proportion of NEETs between the ages of 15 and 29 increased substantially in 2009 (above 1999 levels) and in 2010.

- The lack of an upper secondary qualification is a serious impediment to finding a job, while holding a tertiary degree increases the likelihood of being employed, particularly during difficult economic times.

Chart C5.1. **Percentage of 15-29 year-olds neither in education nor employed (2010)**

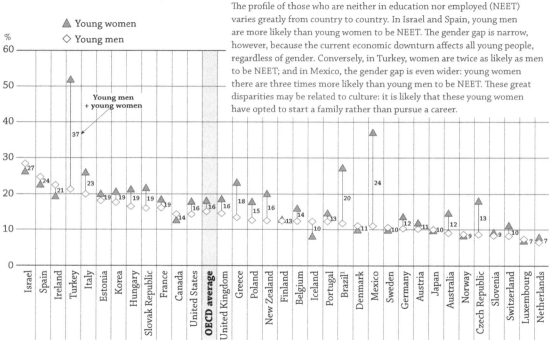

The profile of those who are neither in education nor employed (NEET) varies greatly from country to country. In Israel and Spain, young men are more likely than young women to be NEET. The gender gap is narrow, however, because the current economic downturn affects all young people, regardless of gender. Conversely, in Turkey, women are twice as likely as men to be NEET; and in Mexico, the gender gap is even wider: young women there are three times more likely than young men to be NEET. These great disparities may be related to culture: it is likely that these young women have opted to start a family rather than pursue a career.

1. Year of reference 2009.
Countries are ranked in descending order of the percentage of young men who are neither in education nor employed.
Source: OECD. Tables C5.4a, C5.4b and C5.4c (available on line). See Annex 3 for notes (*www.oecd.org/edu/eag2012*).
StatLink ᴍꜱᴘ http://dx.doi.org/10.1787/888932663302

▮ Context

The transition from education to work is a complex process that is affected by the length and quality of schooling that individuals receive, labour market conditions, the economic environment and demography.

National traditions also play an important role. For example, in some countries, young people traditionally complete schooling before they look for work; in others, education and employment are concurrent. In some cultures, young women and men transition from school to work in similar proportions, while in others, significant proportions of young women raise families full-time after leaving the education system.

The ageing of the population and the declining size of the population of 15-19 year-olds in OECD countries should favour employment among young adults. However, during recessionary periods, high general unemployment rates make the transition from school to work substantially more difficult for the younger population, as those with more work experience are favoured over new entrants into the labour market. In addition, when labour market conditions are unfavourable, younger people often tend to stay in education longer, because high unemployment rates drive down the opportunity costs of education. In these circumstances, public investment in education can be a sensible way to counterbalance inactivity and invest in future economic growth by building needed skills.

To improve the transition of young people from school to work in any economic climate, education systems should work to ensure that individuals have skills that match the requirements of the labour market, and to minimise the proportion of young adults who are neither in school nor in work.

INDICATOR C5

Other findings

- On average across OECD countries, **a 15-year-old in 2010 could expect to spend about 7.0 additional years in formal education** (compared to 6.8 years in 2008). In addition, he/she can expect to hold a job for 5.5 of the subsequent 15 years, to be unemployed for a total of 0.8 years and to be out of the labour force – that is, neither in education nor seeking work – for 1.3 years (Table C5.1a and Table C5.1b, available on line).

- In 2010, **a 15-year-old girl in an OECD country could expect to spend an average of 7.2 additional years in formal education,** or 0.3 years more than a 15-year-old boy. As a woman, she can expect to hold a job for 5.0 years (0.9 years less than a man), and be unemployed (0.8 years) for less time than a man (1.2 years). However, women are twice as likely as men to be inactive. Women can expect to be completely out of the labour force for 1.8 years, compared to 0.9 years for men (Table C5.1a).

- **The amount of time a 15-29 year-old can expect to be in education changes over time and varies greatly from country to country.** In Spain, expected years in education decreased from 6.8 in 1998 to 6.0 in 2010. Between 1998 and 2010 in Hungary, Luxembourg and Turkey, expected years in education increased by more than one year and a half, and in the Czech Republic and the Slovak Republic, expected years in education increased by more than two years (Table C5.1b).

- **On average in 2010, completion of upper secondary education reduced unemployment among 20-24 year-olds who are not in school by 8 percentage points, and among 25-29 year-olds by 6.7 percentage points.** On average, completion of tertiary education reduces unemployment among 25-29 year-olds by 2.3 percentage points, compared to individuals who completed upper secondary education (Table C5.3, available on line). It also reduces long-term unemployment among 15-29 year-olds (Table C5.2d).

Trends

Efforts by governments to raise people's level of education have led to significant changes in educational participation. In 1998, on average across OECD countries, 41.1% of 15-29 year-olds were in education. By 2010, the proportion of young adults (15-29 year-olds) in education reached 47.1%.

During the same period, the proportion of 15-29 year-olds not in education but employed fell from 42.8% to 37.1%. While the percentage of individuals in education increased steadily between 1998 and 2010, youth employment trends have been marked by two periods of large decrease, between 2000 and 2003 (-3.3 percentage points) and between 2008-10 (-3.5 percentage points). Interestingly, these decreases in youth employment occurred at the same time as the burst of the so-called "Internet bubble" (2000-03) and the burst of the real estate bubble in 2008.

The proportion of 15-29 year-olds not in education and not employed (NEET) decreased from 16.0% in 1998 to 15.8% in 2010. During this 13-year period, however, the NEET population decreased substantially on two occasions – consecutively between 1998 and 2001 (-1.3 percentage points) and between 2002 and 2008 (-1.6 percentage points). It then increased substantially by 2.1 percentage points between 2008 and 2010, during the emergence of the global economic crisis.

C5

Analysis

Young adults represent the principal source of labour with new skills. On average across OECD countries in 2010, a 15-year-old could expect to spend the next 15 years of his or her life as follows: 7.0 years in education, 5.5 years in a job, unemployed for a total of 1 year, and out of the labour force entirely (neither in education nor seeking work) for 1.3 years (Table C5.1a). Looking at the population of 15-29 year-olds as a whole, 47.1% are in education, 37.1% hold a job, 6.7% are unemployed, and 9.1% are outside of the labour force (Table C5.2a).

Youth in education

On average across OECD countries in 2010, 47% of 15-29 year-olds were in education (Table C5.4a). This proportion varies across countries. In Denmark, Finland, Germany, Iceland, Luxembourg, Netherlands, Slovenia and Sweden, more than 50% of 15-29 year-olds were in education. In Denmark, Finland, Germany, Iceland, the Netherlands and Sweden, the average duration of tertiary studies is also above the OECD average (see Table B1.3a). Conversely, less than 35% of 15-29 year-olds were in education in Mexico and Turkey, and the average duration of tertiary studies for individuals in these countries tends to be shorter. While individuals in Slovenia do not have a particularly long duration in tertiary education, Project Learning for Young Adults (PLYA) – an initiative begun in 1999 to assist 15-25 year-olds – has boosted education participation among the 20-29 year-old age group due to a rising number of student workers who are not in regular employment (OECD, 2009, page 106).

The proportion of individuals in education decreases with age in all OECD countries. On average across OECD countries in 2010, 86% of 15-19 year-olds were in education (Table C5.4a). In most OECD countries, education policy seeks to encourage youth to complete at least upper secondary education. The effect of these efforts is seen in young people's strong participation in education beyond compulsory schooling (Table C5.4a).

In Belgium, the Czech Republic, Estonia, Finland, Germany, Hungary, Luxembourg, Poland, the Slovak Republic and Slovenia, more than 90% of 15-19 year-olds were in education in 2010. In Mexico and Turkey, less than 61% of 15-19 year-olds were in education.

In 2010, 44% of 20-24 year-olds were in education, on average across OECD countries. Figures range from more than 60% in Luxembourg and Slovenia to around 25% in Mexico and Turkey (Table C5.4a).

Some 16% of 25-29 year-olds were in education in 2010, on average across OECD countries, with more than 30% in Iceland and Slovenia to less than 10% in Belgium, France, Greece, Hungary, Korea, Mexico, the Slovak Republic and Turkey (Table C5.4a).

Between 1998 and 2010, the proportion of 15-19 year-olds in education increased on average by 6 percentage points (an increase of 8%). The proportion of 20-24 year-olds in education increased on average by 10 percentage points (an increase of 28%), while the proportion of 25-29 year-olds in education increased on average by 3 percentage points (an increase of 26%) (Table C5.4a).

The average number of years expected in formal education after compulsory schooling has changed considerably over the past decade. In the Czech Republic, Hungary, Luxembourg, the Slovak Republic and Turkey, the average number of years in education increased by at least 1.5 years between 1998 and 2010, while in Estonia (between 2003 and 2010) and Spain, it decreased by at least 5 months (Table C5.1b, available on line).

In 2010, for all countries except Germany, Japan, Korea, Mexico, the Netherlands, Switzerland and Turkey, young women spend more time in education than young men. In Iceland, Norway and Sweden, young women are likely to spend one full year more in education than their male counterparts. Mexico and Turkey are the countries with the lowest average number of years in education for women between the ages of 15 and 29 – 5.0 and 4.3 years, respectively. In these two countries, women also have the highest average number of years expected outside the labour force – 5.1 and 7.0 years, respectively. These figures likely reflect the high numbers of women in Mexico and Turkey who start families following education, rather than entering the workforce (Table C5.1a).

Chart C5.2. **Education and employment among young people (2010)**
Distribution of the population by education and work status

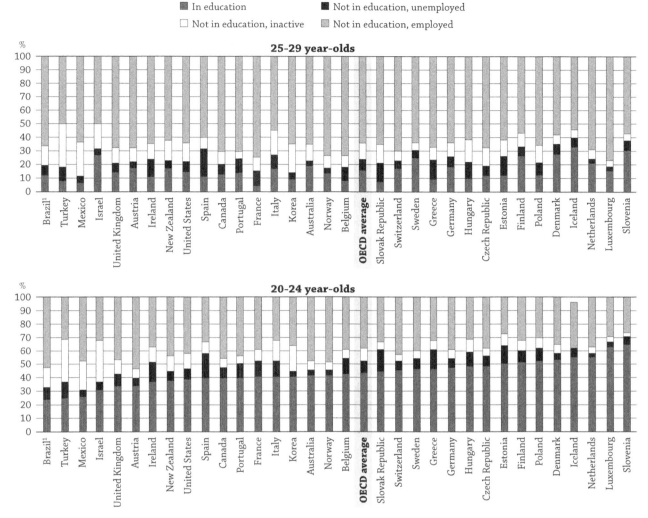

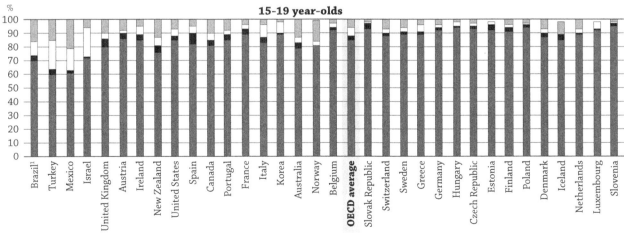

Note: Missing bars refer to cells below reliability thresholds.

1. Year of reference 2009.

Countries are ranked in ascending order of the percentage of 20-24 year-olds in education.

Source: OECD. Table C5.2a. See Annex 3 for notes (*www.oecd.org/edu/eag2012*).

StatLink ⌐ℴ⌐ http://dx.doi.org/10.1787/888932663321

C5

The Anglo-Saxon and Nordic countries, which have long traditions of working students, now have the highest percentage of unemployment among students, with more than 4% of 15-29 year-olds not working in Denmark, Finland, New Zealand and Sweden. In Australia, Canada, Denmark, Finland, Iceland, the Netherlands, New Zealand, Sweden, the United Kingdom and the United States, unemployment among 15-29 year-olds who are still in school ranges from 2% to 6.5% (Table C5.2a).

Youth in employment (excluding work-study programmes)

In Australia, Canada, Denmark, Iceland, the Netherlands and Norway, more than 60% of 15-29 year-olds were employed in 2010, while in Hungary, Israel, Italy, the Slovak Republic and Turkey, less than 40% of 15-29 year-olds were employed. On average across OECD countries in 2010, 48% of 15-29 year-olds were in employment (Table C5.2a).

Almost one quarter of these individuals were still in education. On average across OECD countries in 2010, 11% of 15-29 year-olds had a job and were in education. In some countries, being a student and holding a job is driven by national traditions, and may also reflect the condition of the labour market and the structure of the education system (e.g. the presence of vocational education and training programmes). In Denmark and the Netherlands, more than 30% of 15-29 year-olds held a job while they also participated in education. As a result, the employment rate among the student population in this cohort surpassed 50% in these countries, and this was true even among the youngest cohorts.

In Denmark and the Netherlands, the proportion of 15-19 year-olds in education and employment is the highest among OECD countries, at 43% and 46%, respectively. Among 20-24 year-olds, the proportion of those in education and employment is also highest in these two countries, at 32% and 36%, respectively. On average across OECD countries, 60% of students in the 25-29 year-old cohort held a job in 2010, and in the Netherlands, the proportion reached more than 75%. Conversely, in Belgium, the Czech Republic, Greece, Hungary, Italy, Luxembourg, Portugal, the Slovak Republic and Spain, less than 5% of 15-29 year-olds held a job while in education, representing less than 12% of students (Table C5.2a).

In 2010, on average across OECD countries, 12% of 15-29 year-old women held a job and participated in education, compared to 10.2% of young men. Men aged 15-29 year-old are more likely to have a job and participate in education than young women only in France, Greece, Luxembourg, Mexico and Turkey (Tables C5.2b and C5.2c, available on line).

Most individuals currently in temporary employment but not working one year earlier were either unemployed or pursuing full-time studies at that time. Temporary jobs are particularly important points of entry into the labour market for the unemployed in Spain, while over one-quarter of temporary workers in Denmark were full-time students (OECD, 2002). In periods of economic crisis, when the number of unemployed people increases, it may be more difficult for students to obtain a temporary position. On average across OECD countries, the proportion of 15-29 year-olds who held a job and were in education decreased from 11.7% in 2009 (see Table C4.2a in OECD, 2011) to 11.1% in 2010 (Table C5.2a), suggesting that individuals with more work experience may have been favoured over students.

Individuals who are neither employed, nor in education and training (NEET)

The transition from education to work is closely related to general economic activity. On average across OECD countries in 2010, 37.1% of 15-29 year-olds had a job and were no longer in education (Table C5.2a). In 2000, the proportion of young adults in employment (not in education) represented 43.6% of 15-29 year-olds; by 2003, this proportion had fallen 3.3 percentage points, to 40.3%. The proportion of young adults in employment (not in education) then stabilised (decreasing to 39.9% by 2005 and increasing slightly to 40.7% by 2008), before decreasing to 38.4% in 2009 and 37.1% in 2010 (Table C5.4a). Although the reasons for this progression are unclear, it is interesting to note that decreases correspond with the burst of the Internet bubble between 2000 and 2003, and the burst of the real estate bubble between 2008 and 2010.

The worsening conditions in the labour market between 2008 and 2010 had more severe effects for younger workers than older workers. Among 15-19 year-olds, the proportion of those employed fell from 8.5% in 2008 to 6.6% in 2010, representing a 22% decrease, while among 25-29 year-olds, employment rates fell from 68.3% to 64.3% during the same period, representing a 6% decrease. Similarly, between 2000 and 2003, among 15-19 year-olds, the proportion of those employed fell from 11.4% in 2000 to 8.7% in 2003, representing a 24% decrease, while among 25-29 year-olds employment rates fell from 68.7% to 66.6% during the same period, representing a 3% decrease (Table C5.4a).

In 2010, the majority of 15-19 year-olds were still in education (85.6% compared to 84.4% in 2009). Those who were not (14.4%) were, in many instances, unemployed (3.0% compared to 3.1% in 2009), out of the labour force (5.3% compared to 5.5% in 2009) or employed (6.6% compared to 7.4% in 2009). These numbers for those not in education who are unemployed or not in the labour force range from 3.2% in Slovenia (2.2% unemployed and 1.0%, not in the labour force), to 25.6% in Turkey (4.7% unemployed and 20.9% not in the labour force) (see Table C5.2a and Table C4.2a in OECD, 2011).

Chart C5.3.   **Percentage of 15-19 year-olds not in education and unemployed or not in the labour force (2010)**

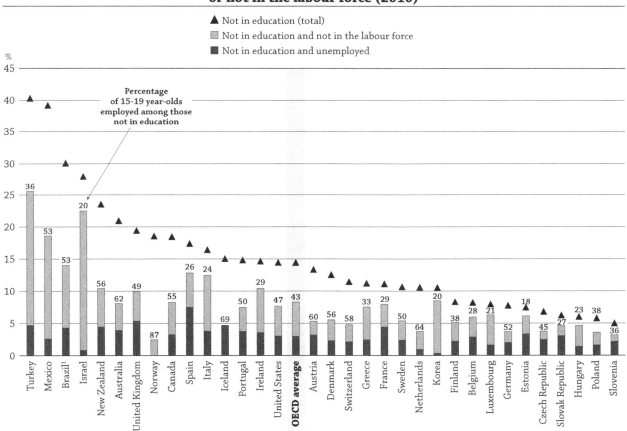

Note: Missing bars refer to cells below reliability thresholds.
1. Year of reference 2009.
Countries are ranked in descending order of the percentage of 15-19 year-olds not in education.
Source: OECD. Table C5.2a. See Annex 3 for notes (*www.oecd.org/edu/eag2012*).
StatLink http://dx.doi.org/10.1787/888932663340

Young adults leaving school and entering a difficult labour market may be unemployed or may exit the labour force entirely. Unemployment and employment rates are useful indicators of the performance of youth in the labour market, but young people are particularly likely to drop out of the labour force and become inactive.

Chart C5.4.   Change in the percentage of 15-29 year-olds neither in education nor employed between 2005 and 2010

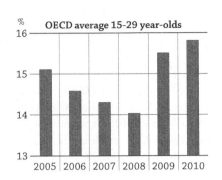

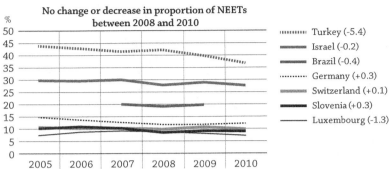

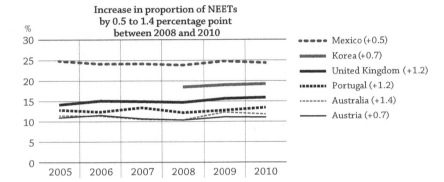

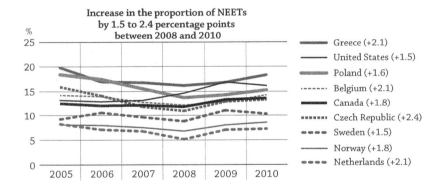

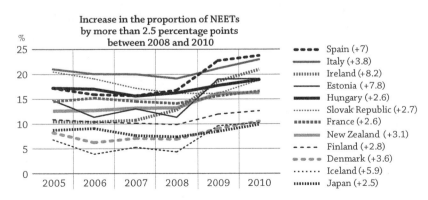

Countries are ranked in ascending order of the percentage of 15-29 year-olds who are neither in education nor employed (NEETs) in 2010.
Source: OECD. Table C5.4a. See Annex 3 for notes (*www.oecd.org/edu/eag2012*).
StatLink ᵐˢᵖ http://dx.doi.org/10.1787/888932663359

While a growing share of young people tend to stay in education beyond the age of compulsory schooling and are counted as inactive individuals too, it would be inappropriate to consider these young people as a high-risk group. Consequently, the proportion of young people not in employment, education or training is a better measure of young adults' difficulty in finding a job.

The size of the NEET population often reflects declining economic situations and increasing uncertainty regarding the future. More seriously, it can also reflect the disenfranchisement of people from the traditional pathway from school to work or family life. In some countries, the NEET population is a source of concern for authorities, because people who are not in education or the labour force may be more likely to be involved in the "informal" (e.g. underground) economy and criminal activity. Individuals in the NEET population are also less likely to be reintegrated in the labour market and more likely to experience long-term effects in terms of their future employment and earnings prospects, which also results in a loss of human capital and foregone tax revenues for national economies. Many studies have confirmed the association between unemployment and poor mental health, including depression, which may also result in extra social costs for society (OECD, 2008).

At the same time, the size of the NEET population can also be influenced by other factors. In some countries such as Mexico, the high percentage of NEETs may reflect the large population of women who are not in education or employment because they are raising families. In Korea, data on the category ISCED 4 are not available, and the NEET population include some people who are not classified as being in formal education, but who are training (in education) for employment or for tertiary entrance examinations.

In Ireland, Israel, Italy, Mexico, Spain and Turkey, more than 20% of 15-29 year-olds were not in education or employment. In Luxembourg, the Netherlands, Norway, Slovenia and Switzerland, less than 10% of 15-29 year-olds were not in education or employment. On average across OECD countries in 2010, 16% of 15-29 year-olds were not in education or employment (Table C5.4a).

In 2010, on average among OECD countries, young men between the ages of 15 and 29 are likely to work 5.9 years after leaving the education system, 0.9 years longer than young women. When not in education, young women are less likely than men to work and more likely than men to be outside of the labour market. Young men can expect to spend 2.1 years not in education and not employed (1.2 years unemployed and 0.9 year inactive), while young women can expect to spend 2.6 years not in education and not employed (0.8 years unemployed and 1.8 year inactive). In Brazil, Israel, Mexico and Turkey, there is a much stronger tendency for young women to spend time out of the education system and not working, either because they are unemployed or are not in the labour force. In Finland, Japan, Luxembourg, Norway and Sweden, young men and women differ by less than 0.1 year on this measure (Table C5.1a).

In most countries, when not working and not in school, young men are more likely to be unemployed (e.g. willing to work and actively looking for a job), while young women are more likely to be inactive (not looking for employment). In all countries but Israel, the proportion of 15-29 year-olds not in education and inactive is higher for young women than for young men. In all countries but Brazil and Greece, the proportion of 15-29 year-olds not in education and unemployed is higher for young men than for young women (Tables C5.2b and C5.2c, available on line). Overall, between 1998 and 2010, the NEET population among women has been rather stable compared to men. The NEET population among 15-29 year-old women steadily decreased from 21.6% in 1998, to 20.0% in 2000, and 17.1% in 2008 and then slightly increased to 17.9% in 2009 (+ 0.8 percentage points, representing a 5% increase). In 2010, the percentage remained stable at 17.9% (Table C5.4c, available on line). Over the same period, the evolution of the NEET population among 15-29 year-old men held steady at 10.9% in 1998, 10.6% in 2000, and 10.6% in 2008 but then jumped to 13.0% in 2009 (+ 2.4 percentage points, representing a 23% increase). In 2010, the percentage reached 13.7% (Table C5.4b, available on line). This suggests that the population of young men has been more severely affected by the global economic crisis.

Variation in unemployment among individuals not in school

In Estonia, Ireland, the Slovak Republic and Spain, more than 13% of young men (15-29 year-olds) are unemployed. In all of these countries except Ireland, more than 59% of this unemployed population have been

C5

looking for a job for more than 6 months. In Ireland, long-term unemployment is less prevalent but increasing: the proportion of 15-29 year-olds unemployed for more than 6 months doubled between 2009 and 2010, from 0.5% of 15-29 year-olds in 2009 (Table C4.2a in OECD, 2011) to 1.1% in 2010 (Table C5.2a).

On average across OECD countries, the proportion of individuals unemployed for more than 6 months increased from 2.4% of 15-29 year-olds in 2009 (Table C4.2a in OECD, 2011), representing 16% of the NEET population, to 3.1% of 15-29 year-olds in 2010 (Table C5.2a), representing 20% of the NEET population. Younger people in this age cohort have been less affected: 1.3% of 15-19 year-olds were unemployed for more than 6 months in 2010, the same rate as in 2009. Conversely, 25-29 year-olds have been the most affected: 4.2% of 25-29 year-olds were unemployed for more than 6 months in 2010, an increase of 1.2 percentage points from 2009.

Because of the expansion of upper secondary education over the years, fewer 15-19 year-olds are outside the education system. Those not engaged in employment, education or training are at particular risk, as they receive little or no support from welfare systems in most countries. Compared with older age groups, they are twice as likely to give up looking for work and lose contact with the labour market (Quintini, et al., 2007). Inactive individuals – those out of the labour force – represent 37% of 15-19 year-olds who are not in school, 18% of 20-24 year-olds who are not in school, and 14% of 25-29 year-olds who are not in school (Table C5.2a).

When the labour market deteriorates, young people making the transition from school to work are often the first to encounter difficulties. In these circumstances, it is often very difficult for young people to gain a foothold in the labour market, as employers tend to prefer more experienced workers for the few jobs on offer. Some countries are more able than others to provide employment for young adults (15-19 year-olds) with relatively low levels of educational attainment (indicated by the difference between the bars and the triangles in Chart C5.3). In Austria, Australia, Iceland, the Netherlands and Norway, 60% or more of young adults with relatively low levels of educational attainment who are not in education find employment.

In the past, the transition between education and work has typically been smoother in countries with work-study programmes at the upper secondary and post-secondary non-tertiary levels of education. In the crisis period, the relative advantage of countries with work-study programmes weakened on average. Australia, Austria, Belgium , the Czech Republic, Germany, Italy, the Slovak Republic, Switzerland and the United Kingdom offer work-study programmes at these levels of education, although participation in Belgium and Italy is somewhat lower. In 2010, average youth unemployment in these countries was almost the same as the OECD average (6.6% compared to 6.7% on average across the OECD) though it ranged from a low of 3.9% in Australia to 11.3% in the Slovak Republic. On average across countries with work study-programmes, 3.8% of 15-29 year-olds were unemployed for more than 6 months, compared to the OECD average of 3.1% (Table C5.2a). The situation was better in Australia, Austria and Switzerland, where youth unemployment was below 2%, than in the Slovak Republic, where youth unemployment was above 8%.

On average, completing upper secondary education reduces the unemployment rate among 20-24 year-olds who are not in school by 8 percentage points (10.2 percentage points for young men and 5.2 percentage points for young women; Table C5.3, available on line). Since it has become the norm in most OECD countries to complete upper secondary education (see Indicator A2), those who do not are potentially more likely to have difficulty finding employment when they enter the labour market. In Estonia, France, Ireland, the Slovak Republic and Spain, at least 25% of 20-24 year-olds who have not attained an upper secondary education are not in school and unemployed. By contrast, in Denmark, Korea, Mexico and the Netherlands, that proportion is between 4.9% and 6.8%. Notably, in Brazil, the proportion of unemployed 20-24 year-olds who are not in school, but who have attained an upper secondary or post-secondary non-tertiary education, is greater than that of the same age group who have not attained an upper secondary education (10.5% and 8.9%; Table C5.3).

Completing tertiary education reduces the unemployment rate among 25-29 year-olds who are not in school by an average of 2.3 percentage points, compared to those who completed upper secondary education. In Australia, Austria and the Netherlands, the unemployment rate among 25-29 year-olds who are not in school and who have completed tertiary education is 3% or less. In Greece, Italy, Spain and Turkey, this rate is between 10.4% and 15.6%. In Canada, Hungary, Ireland and the Slovak Republic, completing tertiary education reduces the unemployment rate among 25-29 year-olds who are not in school by five percentage points or more. Some countries are an exception to this pattern: in Denmark, Greece, Italy, Korea, Mexico, Slovenia and Turkey, unemployment rates among 25-29 year-old upper secondary and post-secondary non-tertiary graduates who are not in education are lower than the rate for those with tertiary qualifications in this age cohort (Table C5.3).

Chart C5.5.   **Percentage of 25-29 year-olds not in education and unemployed, by educational attainment level (2010)**

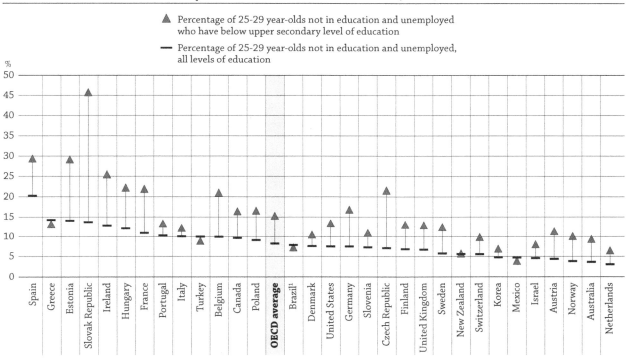

1. Year of reference 2009.
Countries are ranked in descending order of the percentage of 25-29 year-olds not in education and unemployed, all levels of education.
Source: OECD. Table C5.3, available on line. See Annex 3 for notes (*www.oecd.org/edu/eag2012*).
StatLink ⌘⬛ http://dx.doi.org/10.1787/888932663378

Individuals with a tertiary education are also less likely to become inactive. In 2010, 16.0% of young people who had not attained an upper secondary education were not in school and were either unemployed (6.0%) or inactive (10.0%). For those with tertiary education, the distribution was more balanced, with 6.5% unemployed and 6.7% inactive (Table C5.2d).

The incidence of long-term unemployment decreases as the level of educational attainment rises. On average across OECD countries, the proportion of 15-29 year-olds who have completed upper secondary education, are not in school, and who have been unemployed for more than 6 months is 0.6 percentage point higher than the proportion of 15-29 year-olds who have completed tertiary education (3.5% and 2.9%, respectively). The proportion of 15-29 year-olds who have completed upper secondary education, are not in school, and who have been unemployed for less than 6 months is 0.2 percentage points lower than the proportion of 15-29 year-olds who have completed tertiary education (4.1% and 3.9%, respectively).

Further education improves young people's economic opportunities, but the economic downturn over the past several years has created difficulties for young people to find long-term, stable employment.

Definitions

The labour-force status categories shown in this indicator are defined according to the International Labour Organization (ILO) guidelines, with one exception. For the purposes of this indicator, the term being in education and employed is used to describe persons in work-study programmes (see Annex 3), without reference to their ILO labour-force status during the survey reference week. This is because they may not necessarily be in the work component of their programmes during the survey reference week and may therefore not count as being employed at that point. The category "other employed" includes individuals employed according to the ILO definition, but excludes those attending work-study programmes who are already counted as employed. The category "not in the labour force" includes individuals who are not working and who are not unemployed, i.e. individuals who are not looking for a job.

Methodology

Data for this indicator are collected as part of the annual OECD Labour Force Survey (for certain European countries the data are from the annual European Labour Force Survey; see Annex 3) and usually refer to the first quarter, or the average of the first three months of the calendar year, thereby excluding summer employment.

The unemployment and employment rates are examined by considering their proportion in the total population, not only the labour force.

The statistical data for Israel are supplied by and under the responsibility of the relevant Israeli authorities. The use of such data by the OECD is without prejudice to the status of the Golan Heights, East Jerusalem and Israeli settlements in the West Bank under the terms of international law.

References

OECD (2002), *OECD Employment Outlook,* Chapter 3: Taking the measure of temporary employment, (*www.oecd.org/dataoecd/36/8/17652675.pdf*).

OECD (2008), *Mental Health in OECD Countries*, OECD policy brief, November 2008.

OECD (2009), Economic Surveys: Slovenia (*http://publications.oecd.org/acrobatebook/1009071e.pdf*).

OECD (2011), *Education at a Glance 2011: OECD Indicators,* OECD Publishing.

Quintini, G., Martin, J. and Martin, S. (2007): *The Changing Nature of the School-to-Work, Transition Process in OECD Countries*, IZA Discussion Paper No. 2582, January 2007.

The following additional material relevant to this indicator is available on line:

- *Table C5.1b. Trends in expected years in education and not in education for 15-29 year-olds, by gender (1998-2010)*
  StatLink http://dx.doi.org/10.1787/888932667406

- *Table C5.2b. Percentage of 15-29 year-old young men in education and not in education, by age group (2010)*
  StatLink http://dx.doi.org/10.1787/888932667444

- *Table C5.2c. Percentage of 15-29 year-old young women in education and not in education, by age group (2010)*
  StatLink http://dx.doi.org/10.1787/888932667463

- *Table C5.3. Percentage of the cohort population not in education and unemployed (2010)*
  StatLink http://dx.doi.org/10.1787/888932667501

- *Table C5.4b. Trends in the percentage of young men in education and not in education (1997-2010)*
  StatLink http://dx.doi.org/10.1787/888932667539

- *Table C5.4c. Trends in the percentage of young women in education and not in education (1997-2010)*
  StatLink http://dx.doi.org/10.1787/888932667558

**Table C5.1a. [1/2] Expected years in education and not in education
for 15-29 year-olds (2010)**
By gender and work status

		Expected years in education			Expected years not in education			
		Not employed	Employed (including work-study programmes)	Sub-total	Employed	Unemployed	Not in the labour force	Sub-total
		(1)	(2)	(3)	(4)	(5)	(6)	(7)
Australia	Young men	3.2	3.6	6.7	6.9	0.7	0.6	8.3
	Young women	3.1	3.8	6.9	5.8	0.5	1.7	8.1
	M+W	3.2	3.7	6.8	6.4	0.6	1.2	8.2
Austria	Young men	3.8	2.9	6.7	6.8	0.8	0.8	8.3
	Young women	4.4	2.4	6.8	6.4	0.5	1.2	8.2
	M+W	4.1	2.6	6.7	6.6	0.7	1.0	8.3
Belgium	Young men	6.4	0.6	7.0	6.2	1.3	0.6	8.0
	Young women	6.5	0.6	7.1	5.5	1.2	1.3	7.9
	M+W	6.4	0.6	7.0	5.9	1.2	0.9	8.0
Canada	Young men	4.1	2.2	6.3	6.6	1.2	0.9	8.7
	Young women	3.8	3.1	6.9	6.2	0.6	1.3	8.1
	M+W	3.9	2.7	6.6	6.4	0.9	1.1	8.4
Chile		m	m	m	m	m	m	m
Czech Republic	Young men	5.1	1.8	6.8	6.9	1.0	0.3	8.2
	Young women	6.4	1.3	7.6	4.6	0.8	2.0	7.4
	M+W	5.7	1.5	7.2	5.8	0.9	1.1	7.8
Denmark	Young men	3.9	4.2	8.2	5.2	0.9	0.8	6.8
	Young women	4.0	5.1	9.0	4.5	0.6	0.9	6.0
	M+W	4.0	4.6	8.6	4.8	0.7	0.8	6.4
Estonia	Young men	5.7	1.2	6.9	5.4	2.0	0.7	8.1
	Young women	6.3	1.5	7.7	4.2	1.2	1.8	7.3
	M+W	6.0	1.3	7.3	4.8	1.6	1.2	7.7
Finland	Young men	6.0	2.0	8.1	5.1	1.1	0.7	6.9
	Young women	6.1	2.7	8.7	4.3	0.6	1.3	6.3
	M+W	6.1	2.3	8.4	4.7	0.9	1.0	6.6
France	Young men	5.4	1.0	6.4	6.3	1.6	0.7	8.6
	Young women	5.9	0.8	6.7	5.6	1.2	1.5	8.3
	M+W	5.6	0.9	6.6	5.9	1.4	1.1	8.4
Germany	Young men	4.9	2.9	7.8	5.6	1.1	0.5	7.2
	Young women	4.9	2.6	7.6	5.4	0.6	1.4	7.4
	M+W	4.9	2.8	7.7	5.5	0.8	0.9	7.3
Greece	Young men	6.0	0.5	6.5	6.5	1.4	0.6	8.5
	Young women	6.3	0.4	6.7	4.8	1.9	1.6	8.3
	M+W	6.2	0.4	6.6	5.7	1.6	1.1	8.4
Hungary	Young men	6.8	0.3	7.1	5.4	1.6	0.9	7.9
	Young women	7.1	0.3	7.4	4.4	0.9	2.3	7.6
	M+W	6.9	0.3	7.2	4.9	1.3	1.6	7.8
Iceland	Young men	4.1	3.6	7.7	5.5	1.5	c	7.0
	Young women	4.2	4.9	9.1	4.7	c	0.9	5.6
	M+W	4.1	4.3	8.4	5.1	1.0	0.6	6.6
Ireland	Young men	4.9	1.0	5.9	5.7	2.3	1.1	9.1
	Young women	4.8	1.3	6.1	6.0	1.0	2.0	8.9
	M+W	4.8	1.2	6.0	5.9	1.6	1.5	9.0
Israel	Young men	5.2	1.4	6.5	4.2	0.6	3.7	8.5
	Young women	4.9	1.8	6.7	4.4	0.5	3.4	8.3
	M+W	5.0	1.6	6.6	4.3	0.5	3.6	8.4
Italy	Young men	6.0	0.4	6.3	5.7	1.4	1.6	8.7
	Young women	6.8	0.5	7.3	3.8	1.2	2.7	7.7
	M+W	6.4	0.4	6.8	4.8	1.3	2.2	8.2
Japan[1]	Young men	5.6	0.8	6.3	2.7	0.5	0.5	3.7
	Young women	5.2	0.8	6.0	3.0	0.3	0.7	4.0
	M+W	5.4	0.8	6.2	2.8	0.4	0.6	3.8
Korea	Young men	6.6	0.7	7.3	5.1	0.5	2.1	7.7
	Young women	5.6	0.8	6.4	5.5	0.4	2.7	8.6
	M+W	6.1	0.8	6.8	5.3	0.4	2.4	8.2
Luxembourg	Young men	7.0	0.9	7.9	6.0	0.6	0.5	7.1
	Young women	8.0	0.6	8.5	5.4	0.3	0.6	6.5
	M+W	7.5	0.7	8.2	5.7	0.4	0.6	6.8
Mexico	Young men	3.9	1.4	5.2	8.1	0.8	0.9	9.8
	Young women	4.1	0.9	5.0	4.4	0.4	5.1	10.0
	M+W	4.0	1.1	5.1	6.2	0.6	3.1	9.9

1. Data refer to 15-24 year-olds.
2. Year of reference 2009.
Source: OECD. See Annex 3 for notes (*www.oecd.org/edu/eag2012*).
Please refer to the Reader's Guide for information concerning the symbols replacing missing data.
StatLink http://dx.doi.org/10.1787/888932667387

C5

Table C5.1a. [2/2] Expected years in education and not in education for 15-29 year-olds (2010)

By gender and work status

		Expected years in education			Expected years not in education			
		Not employed	Employed (including work-study programmes)	Sub-total	Employed	Unemployed	Not in the labour force	Sub-total
		(1)	(2)	(3)	(4)	(5)	(6)	(7)
Netherlands	Young men	3.4	4.9	8.4	5.7	0.4	0.6	6.6
	Young women	3.3	4.9	8.3	5.5	0.3	0.9	6.7
	M+W	3.4	4.9	8.3	5.6	0.3	0.7	6.7
New Zealand	Young men	4.2	2.5	6.7	6.4	0.9	0.9	8.3
	Young women	4.1	2.7	6.8	5.2	0.7	2.3	8.2
	M+W	4.2	2.6	6.8	5.8	0.8	1.6	8.2
Norway	Young men	4.6	1.8	6.4	7.3	0.6	0.7	8.6
	Young women	4.6	2.9	7.5	6.3	0.3	1.0	7.5
	M+W	4.6	2.3	6.9	6.8	0.4	0.8	8.1
Poland	Young men	5.7	1.3	7.0	6.1	1.2	0.7	8.0
	Young women	6.4	1.4	7.8	4.5	0.9	1.8	7.2
	M+W	6.1	1.4	7.4	5.3	1.1	1.2	7.6
Portugal	Young men	5.8	0.6	6.4	6.8	1.3	0.5	8.6
	Young women	5.9	0.7	6.5	6.3	1.3	0.9	8.5
	M+W	5.8	0.6	6.5	6.5	1.3	0.7	8.5
Slovak Republic	Young men	5.7	0.9	6.5	6.1	2.1	0.3	8.5
	Young women	6.4	0.8	7.3	4.5	1.3	2.0	7.7
	M+W	6.0	0.9	6.9	5.3	1.7	1.1	8.1
Slovenia	Young men	5.9	2.7	8.6	5.1	0.9	0.4	6.4
	Young women	6.5	3.0	9.6	4.0	0.7	0.7	5.4
	M+W	6.2	2.9	9.1	4.6	0.8	0.5	5.9
Spain	Young men	5.2	0.6	5.8	5.5	2.8	0.9	9.2
	Young women	5.5	0.8	6.3	5.3	2.1	1.3	8.7
	M+W	5.3	0.7	6.0	5.4	2.5	1.1	9.0
Sweden	Young men	6.4	1.3	7.7	5.7	1.0	0.6	7.3
	Young women	6.7	2.0	8.7	4.8	0.6	0.9	6.3
	M+W	6.6	1.6	8.2	5.3	0.8	0.7	6.8
Switzerland	Young men	3.3	4.3	7.6	6.1	0.7	0.5	7.4
	Young women	3.3	3.9	7.1	6.2	0.7	1.0	7.9
	M+W	3.3	4.1	7.4	6.2	0.7	0.7	7.6
Turkey	Young men	4.2	0.9	5.2	6.6	1.7	1.5	9.8
	Young women	3.7	0.6	4.3	2.9	0.8	7.0	10.7
	M+W	4.0	0.8	4.7	4.8	1.3	4.2	10.3
United Kingdom	Young men	4.3	2.0	6.3	6.7	1.3	0.7	8.7
	Young women	4.0	2.3	6.3	5.9	0.7	2.0	8.7
	M+W	4.2	2.2	6.3	6.3	1.0	1.4	8.7
United States	Young men	4.8	2.0	6.7	6.2	1.1	1.1	8.3
	Young women	4.7	2.4	7.1	5.2	0.8	1.9	7.9
	M+W	4.7	2.2	6.9	5.7	0.9	1.5	8.1
OECD average excluding Japan	Young men	5.1	1.8	6.9	5.9	1.2	0.9	8.0
	Young women	5.3	2.0	7.2	5.0	0.8	1.8	7.7
	M+W	5.2	1.9	7.0	5.5	1.0	1.3	7.8
EU21 average	Young men	5.4	1.6	7.1	5.9	1.3	0.7	7.9
	Young women	5.8	1.7	7.5	5.0	0.9	1.5	7.5
	M+W	5.6	1.7	7.3	5.5	1.1	1.1	7.7
Argentina		m	m	m	m	m	m	m
Brazil[2]	Young men	2.8	2.4	5.2	8.1	0.9	0.9	9.8
	Young women	3.5	1.9	5.5	5.4	1.2	2.9	9.5
	M+W	3.2	2.2	5.3	6.7	1.0	1.9	9.7
China		m	m	m	m	m	m	m
India		m	m	m	m	m	m	m
Indonesia		m	m	m	m	m	m	m
Russian Fed.		m	m	m	m	m	m	m
Saudi Arabia		m	m	m	m	m	m	m
South Africa		m	m	m	m	m	m	m
G20 average		m	m	m	m	m	m	m

1. Data refer to 15-24 year-olds.
2. Year of reference 2009.
Source: OECD. See Annex 3 for notes *(www.oecd.org/edu/eag2012)*.
Please refer to the Reader's Guide for information concerning the symbols replacing missing data.
StatLink ⬛⬛⬛ http://dx.doi.org/10.1787/888932667387

C5

Table C5.2a. [1/3] Percentage of 15-29 year-olds in education and not in education, by 5-year age group and work status (2010)

	Age group	In education							Not in education						Total in education and not in education
				Unemployed						Unemployed					
		Students in work-study programmes[1]	Other employed	For any length	Less than 6 months	More than 6 months	Not in the labour force	Sub-total	Employed	For any length	Less than 6 months	More than 6 months	Not in the labour force	Sub-total	
		(1)	(2)	(3)	(4)	(5)	(6)	(7)	(8)	(9)	(10)	(11)	(12)	(13)	(14)
Australia	15-19	5.8	28.0	5.3	4.3	1.0	39.9	**79.0**	12.9	3.9	2.9	1.1	4.1	**21.0**	100
	20-24	4.3	22.6	1.1	0.9	0.2	13.4	**41.5**	47.3	4.2	3.1	1.2	7.0	**58.5**	100
	25-29	1.0	12.5	0.4	0.4	c	5.0	**18.9**	65.2	3.7	2.6	1.1	12.2	**81.1**	100
	15-29	3.6	20.9	2.2	1.8	0.4	18.9	**45.6**	42.6	3.9	2.8	1.1	7.9	**54.4**	100
Austria	15-19	23.8	5.5	1.0	0.9	0.1	56.3	**86.6**	8.1	3.2	1.7	1.5	2.1	**13.4**	100
	20-24	2.5	10.5	1.4	0.8	0.5	20.0	**34.4**	53.0	5.4	3.7	1.7	7.2	**65.6**	100
	25-29	0.3	11.2	0.8	0.7	0.1	5.2	**17.5**	67.8	4.4	2.9	1.5	10.3	**82.5**	100
	15-29	8.4	9.2	1.1	0.8	0.2	26.1	**44.8**	44.1	4.3	2.8	1.6	6.7	**55.2**	100
Belgium	15-19	1.5	2.1	c	c	c	87.9	**91.8**	2.3	2.9	1.4	1.5	3.1	**8.2**	100
	20-24	1.4	3.0	0.9	c	c	37.8	**43.0**	38.9	11.3	4.2	7.2	6.7	**57.0**	100
	25-29	c	3.0	0.8	c	c	3.6	**8.1**	73.6	10.0	3.3	6.6	8.3	**91.9**	100
	15-29	1.2	2.7	0.7	0.4	0.3	42.2	**46.8**	39.0	8.1	3.0	5.1	6.1	**53.2**	100
Canada	15-19	a	27.3	6.6	5.9	0.5	47.6	**81.5**	10.2	3.3	3.0	0.2	5.0	**18.5**	100
	20-24	a	19.4	1.6	1.4	0.1	18.5	**39.5**	45.1	7.6	6.6	0.8	7.7	**60.5**	100
	25-29	a	7.1	0.6	0.5	0.1	5.2	**12.9**	70.4	7.2	5.9	1.2	9.5	**87.1**	100
	15-29	a	17.8	2.9	2.5	0.2	23.3	**43.9**	42.5	6.1	5.2	0.7	7.5	**56.1**	100
Chile		m	m	m	m	m	m	**m**	m	m	m	m	m	**m**	m
Czech Republic	15-19	20.4	0.9	c	c	c	71.7	**93.2**	3.0	2.5	1.3	1.2	1.3	**6.8**	100
	20-24	1.2	5.2	0.6	0.4	c	41.4	**48.4**	38.1	7.6	2.9	4.7	6.0	**51.6**	100
	25-29	c	4.9	0.5	c	c	6.7	**12.0**	67.6	7.1	2.8	4.3	13.4	**88.0**	100
	15-29	6.4	3.8	0.4	0.3	c	37.5	**48.1**	38.7	5.9	2.4	3.5	7.3	**51.9**	100
Denmark	15-19	a	42.7	7.4	6.1	1.3	37.3	**87.4**	7.0	2.3	1.8	c	3.2	**12.6**	100
	20-24	a	32.5	3.8	3.4	c	17.0	**53.4**	34.5	5.3	3.7	1.5	6.9	**46.6**	100
	25-29	a	15.9	1.2	1.0	c	10.5	**27.6**	58.1	7.6	4.3	3.2	6.8	**72.4**	100
	15-29	a	30.9	4.3	3.6	0.7	22.1	**57.2**	32.3	5.0	3.2	1.7	5.6	**42.8**	100
Estonia	15-19	a	c	c	c	c	88.2	**92.5**	c	3.4	c	c	2.8	**7.5**	100
	20-24	a	14.5	4.1	c	2.4	31.6	**50.2**	27.3	13.6	4.5	9.1	8.8	**49.8**	100
	25-29	a	8.2	c	c	c	2.9	**12.1**	61.9	14.1	5.0	9.1	12.0	**87.9**	100
	15-29	a	8.8	2.4	1.3	1.2	37.4	**48.7**	32.2	10.9	3.9	7.0	8.2	**51.3**	100
Finland	15-19	a	11.7	6.3	5.8	c	73.7	**91.7**	3.2	2.2	1.6	c	2.9	**8.3**	100
	20-24	a	19.2	4.8	4.5	c	28.0	**52.0**	32.2	8.4	5.5	2.7	7.4	**48.0**	100
	25-29	a	16.0	2.1	1.9	c	8.2	**26.3**	56.9	6.8	4.1	2.4	10.0	**73.7**	100
	15-29	a	15.6	4.4	4.0	0.3	36.1	**56.0**	31.3	5.8	3.7	1.9	6.8	**44.0**	100
France	15-19	a	7.4	0.5	0.4	0.1	81.0	**88.9**	3.2	4.4	1.9	2.4	3.5	**11.1**	100
	20-24	a	9.1	0.7	0.3	0.2	30.7	**40.4**	39.0	12.4	5.9	6.3	8.3	**59.6**	100
	25-29	a	2.1	0.1	0.0	0.1	2.1	**4.3**	74.7	11.0	4.9	6.0	10.1	**95.7**	100
	15-29	a	6.2	0.4	0.3	0.1	37.2	**43.8**	39.5	9.3	4.3	4.9	7.3	**56.2**	100
Germany	15-19	16.5	6.7	1.2	0.7	0.5	67.9	**92.3**	4.1	2.0	0.8	1.2	1.7	**7.7**	100
	20-24	15.1	8.2	0.9	0.7	0.2	23.3	**47.5**	38.8	7.1	3.2	3.8	6.6	**52.5**	100
	25-29	2.4	7.3	0.5	0.3	0.1	8.1	**18.3**	63.9	7.5	3.3	4.1	10.2	**81.7**	100
	15-29	11.1	7.4	0.9	0.5	0.3	31.9	**51.3**	36.7	5.7	2.5	3.1	6.3	**48.7**	100
Greece	15-19	a	1.5	c	c	c	87.1	**88.8**	3.7	2.5	c	c	5.1	**11.2**	100
	20-24	a	4.6	c	c	c	40.9	**46.6**	31.8	14.8	6.6	8.2	6.7	**53.4**	100
	25-29	a	2.6	c	c	c	5.8	**9.2**	67.2	14.3	5.1	9.2	9.4	**90.8**	100
	15-29	a	2.9	0.7	c	c	40.3	**43.9**	37.8	11.0	4.4	6.6	7.3	**56.1**	100
Hungary	15-19	a	c	c	c	c	93.5	**94.0**	1.4	1.4	c	0.9	3.3	**6.0**	100
	20-24	a	2.6	c	c	c	44.9	**48.1**	30.4	10.9	3.6	7.3	10.6	**51.9**	100
	25-29	a	3.1	c	c	c	6.4	**9.8**	61.5	12.1	3.9	8.2	16.5	**90.2**	100
	15-29	a	2.0	0.4	c	0.3	45.9	**48.3**	32.8	8.4	2.7	5.7	10.5	**51.7**	100

1. Students in work-study programmes are considered to be both in education and employed, irrespective of their labour market status according to the ILO definition.
2. Year of reference 2009.
Source: OECD. See Annex 3 for notes (*www.oecd.org/edu/eag2012*).
Please refer to the Reader's Guide for information concerning the symbols replacing missing data.
StatLink ▬▬ http://dx.doi.org/10.1787/888932667425

C5

Table C5.2a. [2/3] Percentage of 15-29 year-olds in education and not in education, by 5-year age group and work status (2010)

	Age group	In education							Not in education						Total in education and not in education
		Students in work-study programmes[1]	Other employed	Unemployed			Not in the labour force	Sub-total	Employed	Unemployed			Not in the labour force	Sub-total	
				For any length	Less than 6 months	More than 6 months				For any length	Less than 6 months	More than 6 months			
		(1)	(2)	(3)	(4)	(5)	(6)	(7)	(8)	(9)	(10)	(11)	(12)	(13)	(14)
OECD															
Iceland	15-19	a	38.7	6.5	c	c	39.8	**85.0**	8.2	4.7	c	c	c	**15.0**	100
	20-24	a	29.2	c	c	c	22.7	**55.3**	34.1	7.3	5.0	c	c	**44.7**	100
	25-29	a	19.5	c	c	m	13.0	**32.9**	54.3	6.9	c	c	5.9	**67.1**	100
	15-29	a	28.4	3.2	2.6	c	24.2	**55.8**	33.9	6.4	4.2	2.1	3.9	**44.2**	100
Ireland	15-19	a	6.5	1.0	1.0	m	77.9	**85.3**	4.2	3.6	3.4	c	6.9	**14.7**	100
	20-24	a	12.3	1.1	1.1	c	23.2	**36.6**	36.9	15.2	13.2	1.7	11.3	**63.4**	100
	25-29	a	5.3	0.6	0.6	m	5.0	**10.9**	64.7	12.8	11.4	1.4	11.5	**89.1**	100
	15-29	a	7.7	0.9	0.9	c	31.4	**40.0**	39.0	10.9	9.6	1.1	10.1	**60.0**	100
Israel	15-19	a	3.8	0.8	0.7	0.1	67.4	**72.0**	5.5	0.8	0.3	0.4	21.6	**28.0**	100
	20-24	a	12.1	1.4	1.2	m	17.4	**30.9**	32.1	5.5	3.7	1.5	31.5	**69.1**	100
	25-29	a	16.3	1.0	0.7	0.2	9.7	**27.0**	50.1	4.6	3.0	1.4	18.3	**73.0**	100
	15-29	a	10.5	1.1	0.9	0.1	32.4	**44.0**	28.6	3.6	2.3	1.1	23.8	**56.0**	100
Italy	15-19	c	0.6	0.3	0.2	c	82.5	**83.6**	4.0	3.8	1.5	2.3	8.7	**16.4**	100
	20-24	0.3	3.6	1.0	0.4	0.6	35.9	**40.8**	32.1	11.4	3.9	7.5	15.7	**59.2**	100
	25-29	0.1	3.7	1.2	0.7	0.6	11.8	**16.9**	54.9	10.1	3.6	6.4	18.1	**83.1**	100
	15-29	0.2	2.7	0.9	0.4	0.5	41.5	**45.3**	31.7	8.6	3.0	5.5	14.4	**54.7**	100
Japan	15-24	a	7.8	0.2	m	m	53.6	**61.7**	28.4	3.9	m	m	6.0	**38.3**	100
Korea	15-19	a	4.0	0.5	0.3	m	84.9	**89.4**	2.1	0.3	0.3	0.0	8.1	**10.6**	100
	20-24	a	8.7	0.9	0.5	0.0	31.3	**40.9**	35.5	3.7	3.1	0.2	19.8	**59.1**	100
	25-29	a	3.3	0.3	0.2	m	5.6	**9.2**	64.9	4.8	4.0	0.4	21.1	**90.8**	100
	15-29	a	5.0	0.5	0.3	0.0	39.9	**45.4**	35.3	3.0	2.5	0.2	16.3	**54.6**	100
Luxembourg	15-19	a	5.4	0.0	m	m	86.7	**92.1**	c	1.6	c	c	4.7	**7.9**	100
	20-24	a	2.5	c	c	c	59.0	**63.1**	29.4	3.9	c	1.8	3.6	**36.9**	100
	25-29	a	6.4	c	c	c	7.8	**15.5**	76.9	3.0	1.9	c	4.6	**84.5**	100
	15-29	a	4.8	1.0	0.6	c	48.9	**54.7**	38.1	2.8	1.5	1.1	4.3	**45.3**	100
Mexico	15-19	a	9.7	0.7	0.6	0.0	50.3	**60.8**	20.6	2.6	2.4	0.1	16.0	**39.2**	100
	20-24	a	7.8	0.9	0.8	0.1	17.4	**26.1**	47.3	4.9	4.4	0.3	21.7	**73.9**	100
	25-29	a	3.4	0.3	0.3	0.1	3.0	**6.7**	63.5	4.8	4.2	0.4	25.1	**93.3**	100
	15-29	a	7.3	0.6	0.6	0.0	26.1	**34.1**	41.5	4.0	3.5	0.2	20.4	**65.9**	100
Netherlands	15-19	a	46.3	5.8	3.8	1.7	37.3	**89.4**	6.8	1.0	0.6	0.3	2.8	**10.6**	100
	20-24	a	36.1	2.5	1.7	0.5	16.9	**55.4**	36.8	2.8	1.6	1.0	5.0	**44.6**	100
	25-29	a	16.0	0.8	0.5	0.2	4.3	**21.1**	68.9	3.1	1.8	1.1	7.0	**78.9**	100
	15-29	a	32.9	3.0	2.0	0.8	19.6	**55.5**	37.3	2.3	1.3	0.8	4.9	**44.5**	100
New Zealand	15-19	a	22.8	7.3	5.1	1.8	46.3	**76.5**	13.1	4.4	3.0	1.1	6.0	**23.5**	100
	20-24	a	18.3	3.3	2.7	0.5	16.6	**38.2**	43.4	6.5	4.7	1.2	11.9	**61.8**	100
	25-29	a	9.9	1.5	1.0	0.4	5.9	**17.2**	62.2	5.6	3.9	1.3	14.9	**82.8**	100
	15-29	a	17.3	4.1	3.0	0.9	23.7	**45.1**	38.6	5.5	3.8	1.2	10.8	**54.9**	100
Norway	15-19	a	22.1	4.0	3.7	c	55.3	**81.4**	15.1	c	c	c	2.5	**18.6**	100
	20-24	a	18.7	1.7	1.6	c	21.8	**42.2**	48.8	3.7	2.4	c	5.4	**57.8**	100
	25-29	a	5.6	c	c	c	7.4	**13.5**	73.5	3.9	2.7	c	9.1	**86.5**	100
	15-29	a	15.6	2.0	1.9	c	28.5	**46.2**	45.3	3.0	2.0	0.8	5.5	**53.8**	100
Poland	15-19	a	3.5	0.9	0.6	0.2	89.9	**94.2**	2.2	1.6	1.0	0.6	2.0	**5.8**	100
	20-24	a	15.1	3.7	2.2	1.4	34.0	**52.8**	29.6	9.6	4.9	4.6	8.1	**47.2**	100
	25-29	a	8.0	1.0	0.5	0.4	3.4	**12.3**	65.7	9.1	4.2	4.9	12.9	**87.7**	100
	15-29	a	9.0	1.8	1.1	0.7	38.5	**49.3**	35.4	7.1	3.5	3.6	8.2	**50.7**	100
Portugal	15-19	a	0.9	c	c	c	83.7	**85.2**	7.4	3.8	2.3	1.4	3.7	**14.8**	100
	20-24	a	4.8	1.2	c	c	33.5	**39.6**	44.1	11.2	4.7	6.5	5.2	**60.4**	100
	25-29	a	6.3	1.6	c	1.1	5.9	**13.8**	70.5	10.3	4.5	5.8	5.4	**86.2**	100
	15-29	a	4.2	1.2	0.5	0.7	37.7	**43.1**	43.5	8.6	3.9	4.7	4.8	**56.9**	100

1. Students in work-study programmes are considered to be both in education and employed, irrespective of their labour market status according to the ILO definition.
2. Year of reference 2009.
Source: OECD. See Annex 3 for notes (*www.oecd.org/edu/eag2012*).
Please refer to the Reader's Guide for information concerning the symbols replacing missing data.
StatLink ⟨⟩ http://dx.doi.org/10.1787/888932667425

C5

Table C5.2a. [3/3] Percentage of 15-29 year-olds in education and not in education, by 5-year age group and work status (2010)

	Age group	In education: Students in work-study programmes[1]	In education: Other employed	In education: Unemployed: For any length	In education: Unemployed: Less than 6 months	In education: Unemployed: More than 6 months	In education: Not in the labour force	In education: Sub-total	Not in education: Employed	Not in education: Unemployed: For any length	Not in education: Unemployed: Less than 6 months	Not in education: Unemployed: More than 6 months	Not in education: Not in the labour force	Not in education: Sub-total	Total in education and not in education
		(1)	(2)	(3)	(4)	(5)	(6)	(7)	(8)	(9)	(10)	(11)	(12)	(13)	(14)
OECD															
Slovak Republic	15-19	10.5	c	c	c	m	82.9	**93.8**	1.7	3.1	0.9	2.1	1.5	**6.2**	100
	20-24	c	3.6	0.6	c	c	40.4	**44.8**	33.0	16.1	3.4	12.7	6.0	**55.2**	100
	25-29	c	3.1	0.1	m	c	3.9	**7.3**	65.1	13.7	3.1	10.6	13.8	**92.7**	100
	15-29	3.3	2.4	0.3	c	c	40.0	**45.9**	35.2	11.3	2.5	8.8	7.5	**54.1**	100
Slovenia	15-19	a	10.0	0.3	m	c	84.7	**95.0**	1.8	2.2	1.2	1.0	1.0	**5.0**	100
	20-24	a	24.4	2.6	1.2	1.3	38.3	**65.3**	25.5	5.6	2.6	3.1	3.6	**34.7**	100
	25-29	a	20.7	2.4	0.4	2.1	7.3	**30.4**	57.2	7.3	3.2	4.1	5.1	**69.6**	100
	15-29	a	19.1	1.9	0.6	1.3	39.5	**60.6**	30.7	5.3	2.4	2.9	3.5	**39.4**	100
Spain	15-19	a	2.0	2.4	1.3	1.0	78.2	**82.6**	4.6	7.5	3.2	4.0	5.4	**17.4**	100
	20-24	a	7.1	3.8	1.5	2.1	28.4	**39.3**	33.3	19.4	7.5	11.1	8.0	**60.7**	100
	25-29	a	4.8	1.9	0.8	1.0	4.5	**11.3**	60.1	20.3	8.0	11.5	8.3	**88.7**	100
	15-29	a	4.7	2.6	1.2	1.4	32.9	**40.3**	35.9	16.4	6.5	9.2	7.4	**59.7**	100
Sweden	15-19	a	10.5	8.4	7.0	c	70.4	**89.3**	5.3	2.4	1.8	c	3.0	**10.7**	100
	20-24	a	12.2	7.5	5.2	1.9	26.6	**46.3**	39.4	8.6	5.8	2.4	5.7	**53.7**	100
	25-29	a	9.9	3.3	2.4	c	11.6	**24.8**	63.9	5.7	3.8	1.8	5.6	**75.2**	100
	15-29	a	10.9	6.5	4.9	1.1	37.2	**54.6**	35.2	5.5	3.7	1.5	4.7	**45.4**	100
Switzerland	15-19	37.2	6.8	2.4	0.6	1.5	42.1	**88.5**	6.7	2.1	1.1	1.0	2.6	**11.5**	100
	20-24	11.1	17.2	1.6	0.6	0.5	16.0	**45.8**	43.1	6.3	4.3	2.0	4.8	**54.2**	100
	25-29	1.0	10.6	0.7	0.4	0.2	5.0	**17.2**	70.0	5.6	3.2	2.4	7.2	**82.8**	100
	15-29	15.8	11.6	1.5	0.5	0.7	20.4	**49.3**	41.1	4.7	2.9	1.8	5.0	**50.7**	100
Turkey	15-19	a	4.4	0.9	0.5	0.4	54.4	**59.7**	14.7	4.7	2.9	1.8	20.9	**40.3**	100
	20-24	a	6.6	2.8	1.5	1.3	15.8	**25.2**	31.1	11.4	5.7	5.7	32.3	**74.8**	100
	25-29	a	4.3	1.1	0.4	0.7	2.6	**8.1**	50.1	10.0	5.2	4.8	31.9	**91.9**	100
	15-29	a	5.0	1.5	0.8	0.8	24.8	**31.4**	32.0	8.5	4.5	4.0	28.1	**68.6**	100
United Kingdom	15-19	4.3	14.8	5.3	2.9	2.5	56.1	**80.6**	9.4	5.3	2.8	2.5	4.7	**19.4**	100
	20-24	2.5	12.4	1.9	1.2	0.7	16.9	**33.7**	46.9	8.6	4.5	4.1	10.7	**66.3**	100
	25-29	1.2	8.3	0.6	0.5	c	4.2	**14.3**	67.6	6.7	3.5	3.1	11.4	**85.7**	100
	15-29	2.6	11.8	2.6	1.5	1.1	25.1	**42.1**	42.0	6.9	3.6	3.3	9.0	**57.9**	100
United States	15-19	a	15.8	4.8	3.6	1.2	64.9	**85.5**	6.8	3.0	2.3	0.8	4.6	**14.5**	100
	20-24	a	18.8	2.3	1.6	0.7	17.6	**38.6**	42.0	8.3	4.8	3.4	11.2	**61.4**	100
	25-29	a	9.0	1.0	0.5	0.4	4.7	**14.6**	64.2	7.5	4.3	3.2	13.7	**85.4**	100
	15-29	a	14.5	2.7	1.9	0.8	28.9	**46.0**	37.8	6.3	3.8	2.5	9.8	**54.0**	100
OECD average	15-19		12.5	3.2	2.5	0.9	67.8	**85.6**	6.6	3.0	1.8	1.3	5.3	**14.4**	100
	20-24		13.2	2.2	1.6	0.8	27.4	**43.9**	37.5	8.7	4.6	4.2	10.0	**56.1**	100
	25-29		8.4	1.0	0.7	0.5	6.1	**15.7**	64.3	8.2	4.1	4.2	11.9	**84.3**	100
	15-29		11.1	1.9	1.4	0.6	32.5	**47.1**	37.1	6.7	3.5	3.1	9.1	**52.9**	100
EU21 average	15-19		9.9	2.9	2.5	0.9	75.0	**89.4**	4.4	3.0	1.7	1.6	3.5	**10.6**	100
	20-24		11.6	2.4	1.8	1.1	31.8	**46.8**	35.8	10.0	4.8	5.2	7.5	**53.2**	100
	25-29		7.9	1.2	0.8	0.6	6.2	**15.4**	65.2	9.4	4.2	5.3	10.0	**84.6**	100
	15-29		9.5	1.8	1.4	0.7	35.7	**48.6**	36.6	7.6	3.6	4.0	7.2	**51.4**	100
Other G20															
Argentina		m	m	m	m	m	m	**m**	m	m	m	m	m	**m**	m
Brazil[2]	15-19	a	20.4	6.6	m	m	42.9	**69.9**	16.1	4.3	m	m	9.7	**30.1**	100
	20-24	a	14.1	2.8	m	m	7.0	**23.9**	52.8	8.8	m	m	14.5	**76.1**	100
	25-29	a	8.9	1.1	m	m	2.1	**12.0**	66.4	7.3	m	m	14.3	**88.0**	100
	15-29	a	14.5	3.5	m	m	17.5	**35.6**	44.9	6.8	m	m	12.8	**64.4**	100
China		m	m	m	m	m	m	**m**	m	m	m	m	m	**m**	m
India		m	m	m	m	m	m	**m**	m	m	m	m	m	**m**	m
Indonesia		m	m	m	m	m	m	**m**	m	m	m	m	m	**m**	m
Russian Federation		m	m	m	m	m	m	**m**	m	m	m	m	m	**m**	m
Saudi Arabia		m	m	m	m	m	m	**m**	m	m	m	m	m	**m**	m
South Africa		m	m	m	m	m	m	**m**	m	m	m	m	m	**m**	m
G20 average		m	m	m	m	m	m	**m**	m	m	m	m	m	**m**	m

1. Students in work-study programmes are considered to be both in education and employed, irrespective of their labour market status according to the ILO definition.
2. Year of reference 2009.

Source: OECD. See Annex 3 for notes *(www.oecd.org/edu/eag2012)*.

Please refer to the Reader's Guide for information concerning the symbols replacing missing data.

StatLink http://dx.doi.org/10.1787/888932667425

C5

Table C5.2d. [1/3]   Percentage of 15-29 year-olds in education and not in education, by educational attainment and work status (2010)

	Educational attainment	In education							Not in education						Total in education and not in education
		Students in work-study programmes[1]	Other employed	Unemployed			Not in the labour force	Sub-total	Employed	Unemployed			Not in the labour force	Sub-total	
				For any length	Less than 6 months	More than 6 months				For any length	Less than 6 months	More than 6 months			
		(1)	(2)	(3)	(4)	(5)	(6)	(7)	(8)	(9)	(10)	(11)	(12)	(13)	(14)
Australia	0/1/2	5.4	18.9	3.9	3.0	0.9	34.8	**63.0**	21.7	5.3	3.4	1.9	10.0	**37.0**	100
	3/4	4.2	23.2	1.9	1.7	0.2	13.8	**43.1**	45.4	3.9	3.0	0.9	7.6	**56.9**	100
	5/6	0.3	19.0	0.4	0.4	m	7.6	**27.3**	64.8	2.2	1.8	0.4	5.6	**72.7**	100
	Total	3.6	20.9	2.2	1.8	0.4	18.9	**45.6**	42.6	3.9	2.8	1.1	7.9	**54.4**	100
Austria	0/1/2	20.9	3.9	1.2	1.0	0.2	47.5	**73.5**	13.6	4.7	2.4	2.3	8.3	**26.5**	100
	3/4	1.6	10.4	0.9	0.7	0.2	14.6	**27.5**	62.2	4.3	3.0	1.3	6.0	**72.5**	100
	5/6	0.1	24.5	1.3	0.7	0.5	10.2	**36.0**	56.5	3.1	2.4	0.7	4.3	**64.0**	100
	Total	8.4	9.2	1.1	0.8	0.2	26.1	**44.8**	44.1	4.3	2.8	1.6	6.7	**55.2**	100
Belgium	0/1/2	1.3	1.8	c	c	c	64.3	**67.8**	15.1	8.5	2.5	5.9	8.6	**32.2**	100
	3/4	1.4	2.6	0.8	c	c	37.1	**42.0**	44.0	9.2	3.5	5.7	4.8	**58.0**	100
	5/6	c	4.5	c	c	c	13.5	**19.2**	71.1	5.5	2.8	2.6	4.2	**80.8**	100
	Total	1.2	2.7	0.7	0.4	0.3	42.2	**46.8**	39.0	8.1	3.0	5.1	6.1	**53.2**	100
Canada	0/1/2	a	20.8	6.0	5.5	0.4	43.8	**70.7**	15.1	5.4	4.6	0.7	8.9	**29.3**	100
	3/4	a	18.3	2.2	1.9	0.2	19.1	**39.6**	45.0	7.4	6.4	0.7	8.0	**60.4**	100
	5/6	a	14.2	0.9	0.8	0.0	10.9	**26.0**	63.8	4.9	4.0	0.8	5.3	**74.0**	100
	Total	a	17.8	2.9	2.5	0.2	23.3	**43.9**	42.5	6.1	5.2	0.7	7.5	**56.1**	100
Chile		m	m	m	m	m	m	**m**	m	m	m	m	m	**m**	m
Czech Republic	0/1/2	19.7	0.7	c	c	c	63.5	**84.0**	5.9	4.2	1.0	3.2	5.8	**16.0**	100
	3/4	0.7	4.0	0.4	0.3	c	27.2	**32.3**	52.1	7.2	3.1	4.1	8.3	**67.7**	100
	5/6	a	10.6	c	c	c	21.5	**33.1**	56.7	4.0	2.2	1.7	6.2	**66.9**	100
	Total	6.4	3.8	0.4	0.3	c	37.5	**48.1**	38.7	5.9	2.4	3.5	7.3	**51.9**	100
Denmark	0/1/2	a	36.4	5.8	4.8	1.0	30.6	**72.8**	16.7	4.0	2.3	1.7	6.4	**27.2**	100
	3/4	a	26.6	3.1	2.8	c	14.7	**44.4**	45.9	5.5	4.0	1.5	4.3	**55.6**	100
	5/6	a	24.5	2.0	c	c	9.4	**35.8**	53.5	7.0	4.8	2.1	3.7	**64.2**	100
	Total	a	30.9	4.3	3.6	0.7	22.1	**57.2**	32.3	5.0	3.2	1.7	5.6	**42.8**	100
Estonia	0/1/2	a	2.7	c	c	c	65.8	**70.3**	11.9	9.5	2.6	7.0	8.2	**29.7**	100
	3/4	a	12.4	3.5	1.5	2.0	26.7	**42.6**	35.9	14.3	5.3	9.0	7.1	**57.4**	100
	5/6	a	11.9	c	c	c	9.0	**21.7**	62.3	4.8	c	c	11.2	**78.3**	100
	Total	a	8.8	2.4	1.3	1.2	37.4	**48.7**	32.2	10.9	3.9	7.0	8.2	**51.3**	100
Finland	0/1/2	a	11.0	5.3	4.8	c	64.6	**80.9**	8.7	3.4	1.8	1.3	7.0	**19.1**	100
	3/4	a	18.6	4.4	4.1	c	22.3	**45.4**	39.8	7.7	5.2	2.4	7.1	**54.6**	100
	5/6	a	17.8	1.9	1.6	c	5.9	**25.6**	63.3	5.9	3.8	1.9	5.3	**74.4**	100
	Total	a	15.6	4.4	4.0	0.3	36.1	**56.0**	31.3	5.8	3.7	1.9	6.8	**44.0**	100
France	0/1/2	a	4.7	0.2	0.2	0.0	58.9	**63.8**	16.5	10.0	3.9	6.1	9.7	**36.2**	100
	3/4	a	7.2	0.7	0.4	0.2	30.7	**38.5**	44.2	10.0	4.8	5.2	7.3	**61.5**	100
	5/6	a	6.4	0.3	0.1	0.1	17.7	**24.4**	64.3	7.2	4.1	2.9	4.1	**75.6**	100
	Total	a	6.2	0.4	0.3	0.1	37.2	**43.8**	39.5	9.3	4.3	4.9	7.3	**56.2**	100
Germany	0/1/2	18.1	5.6	1.0	0.5	0.5	51.2	**75.9**	11.3	5.7	1.8	3.7	7.1	**24.1**	100
	3/4	6.7	8.8	0.8	0.6	0.2	19.6	**35.9**	52.1	6.0	3.1	2.9	6.0	**64.1**	100
	5/6	1.3	9.0	0.7	0.6	c	6.6	**17.6**	74.6	3.4	2.5	0.9	4.3	**82.4**	100
	Total	11.1	7.4	0.9	0.5	0.3	31.9	**51.3**	36.7	5.7	2.5	3.1	6.3	**48.7**	100
Greece	0/1/2	a	c	c	c	c	57.1	**58.2**	25.9	7.0	2.9	4.0	8.9	**41.8**	100
	3/4	a	4.4	1.1	c	c	39.1	**44.6**	37.2	11.3	4.5	6.8	7.0	**55.4**	100
	5/6	a	3.1	c	c	c	5.9	**9.7**	66.6	19.2	7.5	11.7	4.6	**90.3**	100
	Total	a	2.9	0.7	c	c	40.3	**43.9**	37.8	11.0	4.4	6.6	7.3	**56.1**	100
Hungary	0/1/2	a	c	c	c	c	72.6	**73.1**	8.2	6.3	1.9	4.4	12.3	**26.9**	100
	3/4	a	2.8	c	c	c	35.3	**38.5**	41.7	10.1	3.4	6.6	9.7	**61.5**	100
	5/6	a	4.5	0.6	m	c	7.5	**12.5**	71.3	7.8	2.4	5.4	8.3	**87.5**	100
	Total	a	2.0	0.4	c	0.3	45.9	**48.3**	32.8	8.4	2.7	5.7	10.5	**51.7**	100

1.Students in work-study programmes are considered to be both in education and employed, irrespective of their labour market status according to the ILO definition.
2. Data refer to 15-24 year-olds.
3. Year of reference 2009.
Source: OECD. See Annex 3 for notes (*www.oecd.org/edu/eag2012*).
Please refer to the Reader's Guide for information concerning the symbols replacing missing data.
StatLink ⟧ http://dx.doi.org/10.1787/888932667482

Table C5.2d. [2/3]　Percentage of 15-29 year-olds in education and not in education, by educational attainment and work status (2010)

	Educational attainment	In education							Not in education						Total in education and not in education
		Students in work-study programmes[1]	Other employed	Unemployed			Not in the labour force	Sub-total	Employed	Unemployed			Not in the labour force	Sub-total	
				For any length	Less than 6 months	More than 6 months				For any length	Less than 6 months	More than 6 months			
		(1)	(2)	(3)	(4)	(5)	(6)	(7)	(8)	(9)	(10)	(11)	(12)	(13)	(14)
Iceland	0/1/2	a	28.9	4.5	3.5	c	26.2	**59.7**	28.5	6.7	4.1	c	5.2	**40.3**	100
	3/4	a	30.4	c	c	c	25.5	**58.2**	32.4	7.3	5.1	c	c	**41.8**	100
	5/6	a	20.3	0.0	m	m	c	**28.6**	64.8	3.0	c	m	c	**71.4**	100
	Total	a	28.4	3.2	2.6	c	24.2	**55.8**	33.9	6.4	4.2	2.1	3.9	**44.2**	100
Ireland	0/1/2	a	3.1	0.6	0.6	m	63.1	**66.8**	9.8	8.8	7.2	1.6	14.6	**33.2**	100
	3/4	a	10.7	1.2	1.2	c	23.9	**35.8**	41.4	13.7	12.3	1.3	9.1	**64.2**	100
	5/6	a	9.0	0.7	0.6	m	9.0	**18.7**	67.1	8.9	8.4	c	5.2	**81.3**	100
	Total	a	7.7	0.9	0.9	c	31.4	**40.0**	39.0	10.9	9.6	1.1	10.1	**60.0**	100
Israel	0/1/2	a	3.4	0.8	0.7	0.0	67.7	**71.9**	10.4	2.6	1.3	1.1	15.1	**28.1**	100
	3/4	a	13.3	1.2	1.0	0.1	19.4	**33.9**	30.7	3.9	2.6	1.1	31.5	**66.1**	100
	5/6	a	15.2	1.0	0.7	0.2	6.5	**22.8**	58.9	4.3	3.0	1.1	14.1	**77.2**	100
	Total	a	10.5	1.1	0.9	0.1	32.4	**44.0**	28.6	3.6	2.3	1.1	23.8	**56.0**	100
Italy	0/1/2	c	0.6	0.3	0.2	c	54.3	**55.2**	20.8	6.9	2.1	4.8	17.0	**44.8**	100
	3/4	0,2	3.8	1.2	0.4	0.7	32.0	**37.2**	40.4	10.0	3.7	6.3	12.3	**62.8**	100
	5/6	0,5	7.1	2.2	1.4	0.8	27.7	**37.5**	41.0	9.1	4.0	5.1	12.4	**62.5**	100
	Total	0,2	2.7	0.9	0.4	0.5	41.5	**45.3**	31.7	8.6	3.0	5.5	14.4	**54.7**	100
Japan[2]	1/2/3	a	13.4	0.5	m	m	37.6	**51.5**	33.9	5.5	m	m	9.2	**48.5**	100
	5/6	a	a	0.0	m	m	a	**0.0**	81.5	8.2	m	m	10.3	**100.0**	100
	Total	a	7.8	0.2	m	m	53.6	**61.7**	28.4	3.9	m	m	6.0	**38.3**	100
Korea	0/1/2	a	1.3	0.2	0.2	m	90.5	**92.0**	2.6	0.3	0.3	0.0	5.1	**8.0**	100
	3/4	a	8.5	0.9	0.9	0.0	27.1	**36.5**	35.6	3.1	2.9	0.2	24.8	**63.5**	100
	5/6	a	1.5	0.1	0.1	m	1.7	**3.3**	71.4	5.6	5.1	0.5	19.7	**96.7**	100
	Total	a	5.0	0.5	0.3	0.0	39.9	**45.4**	35.3	3.0	2.5	0.2	16.3	**54.6**	100
Luxembourg	0/1/2	a	4.1	0.0	m	m	70.0	**74.1**	16.0	3.7	1.8	1.6	6.2	**25.9**	100
	3/4	a	4.1	c	c	m	44.2	**49.6**	45.1	2.6	c	c	2.7	**50.4**	100
	5/6	a	6.3	2.4	m	c	9.5	**18.1**	77.1	1.7	c	m	c	**81.9**	100
	Total	a	4.8	1.0	0.6	c	48.9	**54.7**	38.1	2.8	1.5	1.1	4.3	**45.3**	100
Mexico	0/1/2	a	5.8	0.4	0.4	0.0	26.3	**32.6**	40.1	3.5	3.2	0.2	23.8	**67.4**	100
	3/4	a	11.7	1.1	1.0	0.0	30.5	**43.3**	38.5	3.8	3.4	0.2	14.4	**56.7**	100
	5/6	a	7.6	1.0	0.9	0.1	11.9	**20.5**	62.2	8.5	7.2	0.7	8.8	**79.5**	100
	Total	a	7.3	0.6	0.6	0.0	26.1	**34.1**	41.5	4.0	3.5	0.2	20.4	**65.9**	100
Netherlands	0/1/2	a	36.8	4.7	3.0	1.4	30.2	**71.7**	19.2	2.5	1.2	1.2	6.6	**28.3**	100
	3/4	a	34.3	2.3	1.6	0.5	15.1	**51.6**	42.1	2.1	1.3	0.6	4.2	**48.4**	100
	5/6	a	23.4	1.2	0.9	c	7.9	**32.6**	63.3	1.9	1.4	0.3	2.2	**67.4**	100
	Total	a	32.9	3.0	2.0	0.8	19.6	**55.5**	37.3	2.3	1.3	0.8	4.9	**44.5**	100
New Zealand	0/1/2	a	11.4	4.9	3.1	1.5	36.1	**52.4**	26.3	6.0	3.7	1.7	15.3	**47.6**	100
	3/4	a	24.1	4.0	3.1	0.8	22.3	**50.4**	36.8	4.7	3.7	0.9	8.1	**49.6**	100
	5/6	a	14.6	3.1	2.4	0.2	6.9	**24.6**	61.9	6.0	4.5	1.0	7.5	**75.4**	100
	Total	a	17.3	4.1	3.0	0.9	23.7	**45.1**	38.6	5.5	3.8	1.2	10.8	**54.9**	100
Norway	0/1/2	a	15.2	3.1	2.7	c	38.8	**57.1**	30.7	4.3	2.7	1.4	7.9	**42.9**	100
	3/4	a	16.8	c	c	c	18.6	**36.9**	56.7	2.2	1.6	c	4.2	**63.1**	100
	5/6	a	17.7	c	c	c	18.5	**37.3**	59.1	c	c	c	c	**62.7**	100
	Total	a	15.6	2.0	1.9	c	28.5	**46.2**	45.3	3.0	2.0	0.8	5.5	**53.8**	100
Poland	0/1/2	a	3.6	0.6	0.3	0.3	75.7	**79.8**	8.0	4.2	1.7	2.5	7.9	**20.2**	100
	3/4	a	10.7	2.5	1.5	1.0	24.5	**37.7**	42.8	9.3	4.6	4.7	10.2	**62.3**	100
	5/6	a	14.2	2.0	1.3	0.7	9.2	**25.4**	61.9	7.2	4.0	3.2	5.6	**74.6**	100
	Total	a	9.0	1.8	1.1	0.7	38.5	**49.3**	35.4	7.1	3.5	3.6	8.2	**50.7**	100
Portugal	0/1/2	a	2.9	1.0	0.5	0.5	42.1	**46.0**	38.7	9.0	3.6	5.4	6.3	**54.0**	100
	3/4	a	5.1	1.2	c	c	40.5	**46.8**	42.4	7.8	4.0	3.9	3.0	**53.2**	100
	5/6	a	7.7	2.0	c	c	12.2	**22.0**	66.2	9.1	5.5	3.7	2.7	**78.0**	100
	Total	a	4.2	1.2	0.5	0.7	37.7	**43.1**	43.5	8.6	3.9	4.7	4.8	**56.9**	100

1. Students in work-study programmes are considered to be both in education and employed, irrespective of their labour market status according to the ILO definition.
2. Data refer to 15-24 year-olds.
3. Year of reference 2009.
Source: OECD. See Annex 3 for notes (*www.oecd.org/edu/eag2012*).
Please refer to the Reader's Guide for information concerning the symbols replacing missing data.
StatLink ᴀ⃫ˢ⃥ http://dx.doi.org/10.1787/888932667482

C5

Table C5.2d. [3/3] Percentage of 15-29 year-olds in education and not in education, by educational attainment and work status (2010)

	Educational attainment	In education		Unemployed					Not in education		Unemployed					Total in education and not in education
		Students in work-study programmes[1]	Other employed	For any length	Less than 6 months	More than 6 months	Not in the labour force	Sub-total	Employed	For any length	Less than 6 months	More than 6 months	Not in the labour force	Sub-total	
		(1)	(2)	(3)	(4)	(5)	(6)	(7)	(8)	(9)	(10)	(11)	(12)	(13)	(14)
Slovak Republic	0/1/2	9.9	c	c	c	m	74.2	**84.5**	2.2	7.1	1.3	5.8	6.1	**15.5**	100
	3/4	c	2.4	c	c	c	24.9	**27.8**	49.1	14.6	3.4	11.3	8.5	**72.2**	100
	5/6	a	8.2	c	c	c	18.1	**26.9**	59.4	7.2	2.1	5.1	6.4	**73.1**	100
	Total	3.3	2.4	0.3	c	c	40.0	**45.9**	35.2	11.3	2.5	8.8	7.5	**54.1**	100
Slovenia	0/1/2	a	10.6	1.1	c	0.9	72.6	**84.3**	8.5	3.5	1.0	2.5	3.7	**15.7**	100
	3/4	a	23.1	2.5	0.7	1.7	31.0	**56.6**	34.7	5.4	2.6	2.8	3.3	**43.4**	100
	5/6	a	19.8	1.1	c	c	4.6	**25.5**	62.2	8.7	4.7	4.1	3.5	**74.5**	100
	Total	a	19.1	1.9	0.6	1.3	39.5	**60.6**	30.7	5.3	2.4	2.9	3.5	**39.4**	100
Spain	0/1/2	a	1.9	1.9	0.8	1.1	39.1	**43.0**	27.9	19.8	7.4	11.7	9.3	**57.0**	100
	3/4	a	6.5	3.6	1.6	1.7	36.5	**46.6**	35.6	12.6	5.4	6.8	5.3	**53.4**	100
	5/6	a	9.2	3.1	1.5	1.5	13.5	**25.8**	55.5	13.1	5.8	6.5	5.7	**74.2**	100
	Total	a	4.7	2.6	1.2	1.4	32.9	**40.3**	35.9	16.4	6.5	9.2	7.4	**59.7**	100
Sweden	0/1/2	a	11.2	9.4	7.2	1.3	61.0	**81.7**	9.3	4.3	2.8	1.2	4.8	**18.3**	100
	3/4	a	10.0	5.8	4.1	1.3	20.5	**36.2**	50.1	8.0	5.4	2.2	5.7	**63.8**	100
	5/6	a	16.1	4.8	4.0	c	18.3	**39.2**	54.5	3.5	2.6	c	2.7	**60.8**	100
	Total	a	10.9	6.5	4.9	1.1	37.2	**54.6**	35.2	5.5	3.7	1.5	4.7	**45.4**	100
Switzerland	0/1/2	37.4	5.6	2.1	0.4	1.1	34.4	**79.5**	11.3	3.9	2.2	1.7	5.4	**20.5**	100
	3/4	3.7	15.5	1.4	0.8	0.6	13.7	**34.3**	55.3	5.5	3.7	1.8	4.9	**65.7**	100
	5/6	0.8	14.3	0.5	0.1	0.2	7.4	**23.0**	68.6	4.5	2.2	2.2	3.9	**77.0**	100
	Total	15.8	11.6	1.5	0.5	0.7	20.4	**49.3**	41.1	4.7	2.9	1.8	5.0	**50.7**	100
Turkey	0/1/2	a	3.1	0.8	0.4	0.4	28.7	**32.5**	28.3	7.2	4.4	2.8	31.9	**67.5**	100
	3/4	a	7.6	2.7	1.4	1.3	23.0	**33.3**	31.9	9.7	4.6	5.2	25.1	**66.7**	100
	5/6	a	10.2	3.4	1.6	1.8	5.7	**19.3**	55.2	13.5	5.0	8.5	12.0	**80.7**	100
	Total	a	5.0	1.5	0.8	0.8	24.8	**31.4**	32.0	8.5	4.5	4.0	28.1	**68.6**	100
United Kingdom	0/1/2	3.5	2.3	1.7	0.8	0.9	48.5	**56.1**	18.2	9.2	3.5	5.6	16.5	**43.9**	100
	3/4	3.2	15.5	3.6	2.0	1.6	24.1	**46.5**	39.4	6.6	3.7	2.9	7.6	**53.5**	100
	5/6	0.8	12.2	0.8	0.6	c	8.8	**22.6**	68.4	5.2	3.3	1.8	3.9	**77.4**	100
	Total	2.6	11.8	2.6	1.5	1.1	25.1	**42.1**	42.0	6.9	3.6	3.3	9.0	**57.9**	100
United States	0/1/2	a	9.1	3.7	2.8	1.0	59.8	**72.6**	13.7	4.5	2.6	1.9	9.2	**27.4**	100
	3/4	a	18.1	2.9	2.0	0.9	19.0	**40.0**	40.5	7.9	4.7	3.1	11.6	**60.0**	100
	5/6	a	13.6	0.8	0.5	0.2	8.7	**23.1**	65.1	5.1	3.3	1.7	6.7	**76.9**	100
	Total	a	14.5	2.7	1.9	0.8	28.9	**46.0**	37.8	6.3	3.8	2.5	9.8	**54.0**	100
OECD average	0/1/2		9.2	2.5	2.0	0.7	52.9	**67.1**	16.9	6.0	2.8	3.1	10.0	**32.9**	100
	3/4		12.8	2.2	1.6	0.8	25.5	**41.0**	42.7	7.4	4.1	3.5	9.0	**59.0**	100
	5/6		12.5	1.4	1.1	0.5	10.7	**23.8**	63.5	6.5	3.9	2.9	6.7	**76.2**	100
	Total		11.0	1.8	1.4	0.6	33.1	**47.5**	36.9	6.6	3.5	3.1	9.0	**52.5**	100
EU21 average	0/1/2		8.0	2.3	1.9	0.7	57.5	**69.7**	14.9	6.8	2.7	4.0	8.6	**30.3**	100
	3/4		10.7	2.2	1.6	1.0	27.8	**41.1**	43.7	8.5	4.3	4.4	6.6	**58.9**	100
	5/6		11.9	1.7	1.2	0.7	11.7	**25.2**	62.7	6.8	3.9	3.5	5.3	**74.8**	100
	Total		9.5	1.8	1.4	0.7	35.7	**48.6**	36.6	7.6	3.6	4.0	7.2	**51.4**	100
Argentina		m	m	m	m	m	m	**m**	m	m	m	m	m	**m**	m
Brazil[3]	0/1/2	a	14.9	4.5	m	m	26.2	**45.6**	34.9	5.2	m	m	14.3	**54.4**	100
	3/4	a	14.7	2.3	m	m	6.4	**23.4**	55.7	9.3	m	m	11.6	**76.6**	100
	5/6	a	9.6	0.9	m	m	4.0	**14.5**	74.2	5.8	m	m	5.5	**85.5**	100
	Total	a	14.5	3.5	m	m	17.5	**35.6**	44.9	6.8	m	m	12.8	**64.4**	100
China		m	m	m	m	m	m	**m**	m	m	m	m	m	**m**	m
India		m	m	m	m	m	m	**m**	m	m	m	m	m	**m**	m
Indonesia		m	m	m	m	m	m	**m**	m	m	m	m	m	**m**	m
Russian Federation		m	m	m	m	m	m	**m**	m	m	m	m	m	**m**	m
Saudi Arabia		m	m	m	m	m	m	**m**	m	m	m	m	m	**m**	m
South Africa		m	m	m	m	m	m	**m**	m	m	m	m	m	**m**	m
G20 average		m	m	m	m	m	m	**m**	m	m	m	m	m	**m**	m

OECD

Other G20

1. Students in work-study programmes are considered to be both in education and employed, irrespective of their labour market status according to the ILO definition.
2. Data refer to 15-24 year-olds.
3. Year of reference 2009.
Source: OECD. See Annex 3 for notes (www.oecd.org/edu/eag2012).
Please refer to the Reader's Guide for information concerning the symbols replacing missing data.
StatLink ᏋᏍᏝ http://dx.doi.org/10.1787/888932667482

C5

Table C5.4a. [1/6] **Trends in the percentage of the youth population in education and not in education (1997[1]-2010)**

By 5-year age group and work status

	Age group	1998			1999			2000			2001			2002			2003			2004		
		In education	Not in education		In education	Not in education		In education	Not in education		In education	Not in education		In education	Not in education		In education	Not in education		In education	Not in education	
		Total	Employed	Not employed	Total	Employed	Not employed	Total	Employed	Not employed	Total	Employed	Not employed	Total	Employed	Not employed	Total	Employed	Not employed	Total	Employed	Not employed
		(4)	(5)	(6)	(7)	(8)	(9)	(10)	(11)	(12)	(13)	(14)	(15)	(16)	(17)	(18)	(19)	(20)	(21)	(22)	(23)	(24)
OECD Australia	15-19	77.3	13.8	8.8	78.2	14.4	7.4	79.5	13.7	6.8	79.5	13.0	7.6	79.7	13.3	7.0	79.6	13.6	6.8	78.4	14.1	7.5
	20-24	32.7	51.3	16.0	34.9	50.6	14.5	35.9	50.9	13.3	36.5	49.6	13.9	38.7	48.1	13.2	39.7	47.0	13.3	39.0	48.7	12.3
	25-29	13.7	67.1	19.2	15.0	66.5	18.5	15.5	65.5	19.0	15.8	67.0	17.2	16.5	65.7	17.8	17.7	64.7	17.6	17.7	65.0	17.3
	15-29	40.0	45.1	14.9	41.9	44.5	13.6	42.8	44.0	13.2	43.4	43.6	13.0	44.5	42.7	12.7	45.4	42.0	12.6	45.4	42.3	12.3
Austria	15-19	m	m	m	m	m	m	m	m	m	m	m	m	81.5	12.1	6.3	83.6	10.7	5.6	83.3	9.3	7.3
	20-24	m	m	m	m	m	m	m	m	m	m	m	m	29.4	58.9	11.7	30.3	59.3	10.4	30.3	56.8	12.9
	25-29	m	m	m	m	m	m	m	m	m	m	m	m	10.3	77.3	12.4	12.5	75.2	12.3	13.0	72.6	14.4
	15-29	m	m	m	m	m	m	m	m	m	m	m	m	39.5	50.3	10.2	41.1	49.4	9.5	41.3	47.1	11.7
Belgium	15-19	85.3	3.9	10.8	89.4	3.7	6.8	89.9	3.6	6.5	89.7	4.1	6.2	89.6	3.6	6.8	89.1	3.8	7.1	92.1	3.1	4.9
	20-24	40.6	42.5	16.9	43.7	38.6	17.7	43.8	40.2	16.0	44.2	42.8	13.0	38.2	44.4	17.4	39.9	43.0	17.1	38.8	44.4	16.9
	25-29	9.3	72.4	18.2	14.4	67.7	17.9	11.8	72.5	15.7	15.0	69.5	15.5	5.8	77.0	17.2	8.9	72.8	18.3	6.0	74.3	19.7
	15-29	43.2	41.3	15.4	47.5	38.2	14.3	46.9	40.2	12.9	48.2	40.0	11.7	43.2	42.8	14.0	44.8	40.8	14.4	44.6	41.4	14.0
Canada	15-19	81.6	9.9	8.5	80.8	10.9	8.3	80.6	11.2	8.2	81.3	11.4	7.3	80.2	11.8	8.0	80.0	11.9	8.1	79.1	12.2	8.7
	20-24	36.8	45.4	17.8	37.1	47.2	15.7	35.8	48.5	15.7	36.4	47.9	15.6	36.5	48.3	15.3	36.7	49.0	14.3	38.1	47.7	14.2
	25-29	10.8	70.1	19.0	10.7	71.2	18.1	10.6	72.2	17.2	11.6	72.1	16.3	12.7	69.8	17.5	12.7	71.2	16.1	11.9	71.9	16.2
	15-29	42.7	42.1	15.2	42.8	43.1	14.1	42.5	43.9	13.7	43.3	43.6	13.1	43.3	43.1	13.6	43.2	43.9	12.9	43.1	43.9	13.0
Chile		m	m	m	m	m	m	m	m	m	m	m	m	m	m	m	m	m	m	m	m	m
Czech Republic	15-19	77.1	15.8	7.2	75.6	14.8	9.7	82.1	10.0	7.9	87.0	6.2	6.8	88.3	5.7	6.0	89.0	5.2	5.8	89.9	4.4	5.7
	20-24	17.1	64.3	18.5	19.6	59.8	20.6	19.7	60.0	20.3	23.1	58.9	18.1	25.7	56.2	18.1	28.7	53.3	18.0	32.3	49.2	18.5
	25-29	1.8	75.1	23.1	2.4	71.7	25.9	2.4	72.1	25.6	3.0	72.1	25.0	2.9	73.3	23.8	3.0	73.0	24.1	3.8	71.6	24.5
	15-29	31.5	52.2	16.3	30.9	50.1	19.0	31.7	49.7	18.5	33.7	48.8	17.4	34.5	48.6	16.9	35.9	47.2	16.9	37.7	45.1	17.2
Denmark	15-19	90.3	7.9	1.8	85.8	10.8	3.4	89.9	7.4	2.7	86.8	9.4	3.8	88.7	8.9	2.4	89.8	7.7	2.5	89.5	8.4	2.1
	20-24	55.0	38.0	7.0	55.8	36.6	7.6	54.8	38.6	6.6	55.3	38.1	6.6	55.3	37.4	7.3	52.1	36.1	11.8	54.0	34.8	11.3
	25-29	34.5	57.8	7.7	35.5	56.7	7.8	36.1	56.4	7.5	32.4	60.0	7.6	35.0	58.3	6.7	23.9	64.6	11.5	28.3	59.8	11.9
	15-29	58.0	36.3	5.7	56.4	37.1	6.5	57.7	36.5	5.8	55.1	38.7	6.2	57.1	37.3	5.6	52.5	38.6	8.9	55.5	35.9	8.6
Estonia	15-19	m	m	m	m	m	m	m	m	m	m	m	m	m	m	m	94.4	2.3	3.3	91.0	1.4	7.6
	20-24	m	m	m	m	m	m	m	m	m	m	m	m	m	m	m	39.7	42.3	18.0	48.6	31.9	19.5
	25-29	m	m	m	m	m	m	m	m	m	m	m	m	m	m	m	14.7	59.8	25.5	14.9	65.3	19.8
	15-29	m	m	m	m	m	m	m	m	m	m	m	m	m	m	m	51.4	33.5	15.1	53.1	31.6	15.3
Finland	15-19	m	m	m	m	m	m	m	m	m	m	m	m	m	m	m	88.1	5.7	6.2	88.9	5.2	5.9
	20-24	m	m	m	m	m	m	m	m	m	m	m	m	m	m	m	52.5	33.1	14.4	53.1	31.5	15.4
	25-29	m	m	m	m	m	m	m	m	m	m	m	m	m	m	m	27.2	58.7	14.1	25.7	58.8	15.5
	15-29	m	m	m	m	m	m	m	m	m	m	m	m	m	m	m	55.6	32.7	11.6	55.2	32.4	12.4
France	15-19	90.0	3.9	6.2	88.7	3.9	7.3	88.2	4.8	7.0	88.1	5.3	6.6	88.3	4.9	6.8	90.3	4.3	5.4	91.3	3.3	5.4
	20-24	38.8	40.7	20.5	37.3	41.5	21.2	39.4	43.0	17.6	39.5	43.4	17.1	39.3	43.1	17.6	40.0	43.3	16.7	39.9	41.3	18.8
	25-29	5.9	70.2	23.9	5.7	71.6	22.8	5.9	73.7	20.4	5.7	74.6	19.7	5.7	74.3	20.0	5.0	74.7	20.3	5.0	75.1	19.9
	15-29	43.9	39.1	17.0	43.1	39.7	17.1	44.1	40.9	15.0	44.0	41.5	14.5	44.6	40.7	14.7	45.1	40.7	14.1	45.9	39.5	14.6
Germany	15-19	m	m	m	89.5	6.0	4.5	87.4	6.8	5.7	88.5	6.4	5.1	90.1	5.2	4.7	91.2	4.1	4.7	93.4	3.0	3.6
	20-24	m	m	m	34.3	49.0	16.7	34.1	49.0	16.9	35.0	48.7	16.4	38.1	46.0	15.9	41.2	43.1	15.6	44.0	38.5	17.5
	25-29	m	m	m	13.6	68.2	18.1	12.7	69.8	17.5	13.5	68.5	18.0	16.3	66.3	17.4	17.9	63.7	18.4	17.6	62.8	19.6
	15-29	m	m	m	44.9	41.9	13.2	44.9	41.8	13.3	46.0	40.9	13.1	48.6	38.8	12.6	50.5	36.7	12.9	52.2	34.3	13.5
Greece	15-19	79.0	9.8	11.2	82.4	8.2	9.4	82.6	8.1	9.3	86.2	6.5	7.3	85.8	6.5	7.8	84.1	6.3	9.6	82.7	6.6	10.8
	20-24	26.7	44.0	29.3	29.5	43.0	27.5	30.7	43.4	25.9	36.2	39.9	23.9	34.8	41.1	24.1	37.5	40.3	22.1	34.7	41.6	23.7
	25-29	4.3	66.1	29.6	5.1	66.4	28.5	5.1	65.8	29.2	6.6	66.1	27.2	5.6	67.1	27.3	6.8	68.0	25.1	5.3	69.0	25.7
	15-29	36.3	40.3	23.4	38.9	39.3	21.8	39.0	39.4	21.5	41.4	38.7	19.9	39.6	40.1	20.3	39.6	40.8	19.6	37.3	42.0	20.7
Hungary	15-19	78.2	10.0	11.8	79.3	9.2	11.6	83.7	7.7	8.6	85.0	6.7	8.3	87.5	4.5	8.0	89.7	3.5	6.8	90.4	3.4	6.2
	20-24	26.5	45.9	27.6	28.6	47.7	23.6	32.3	45.7	22.0	35.0	45.1	20.0	36.9	42.6	20.5	40.5	39.6	19.9	43.8	37.6	18.6
	25-29	7.4	58.9	33.7	8.7	60.1	31.3	9.4	61.4	29.2	9.4	63.4	27.1	8.6	63.1	28.3	12.6	59.9	27.5	12.9	63.2	23.9
	15-29	37.7	38.0	24.2	38.3	39.5	22.2	40.7	39.1	20.2	41.5	39.7	18.9	42.1	38.4	19.5	44.7	36.5	18.8	45.2	37.8	17.1

1.Data for 1997 (Columns 1 to 3) are available on line (see *StatLink* below).

Source: OECD. See Annex 3 for notes *(www.oecd.org/edu/eag2012)*.

Please refer to the Reader's Guide for information concerning the symbols replacing missing data.

StatLink http://dx.doi.org/10.1787/888932667520

C5

Table C5.4a. [2/6] Trends in the percentage of the youth population in education and not in education (1997[1]-2010)

By 5-year age group and work status

	Age group	2005 In education Total	2005 Not in education Employed	2005 Not in education Not employed	2006 In education Total	2006 Not in education Employed	2006 Not in education Not employed	2007 In education Total	2007 Not in education Employed	2007 Not in education Not employed	2008 In education Total	2008 Not in education Employed	2008 Not in education Not employed	2009 In education Total	2009 Not in education Employed	2009 Not in education Not employed	2010 In education Total	2010 Not in education Employed	2010 Not in education Not employed
		(25)	(26)	(27)	(28)	(29)	(30)	(31)	(32)	(33)	(34)	(35)	(36)	(37)	(38)	(39)	(37)	(38)	(39)
Australia	15-19	78.3	14.3	7.4	79.3	13.7	7.1	79.6	13.9	6.5	79.4	14.3	6.3	77.9	13.8	8.3	79.0	12.9	8.1
	20-24	39.4	49.0	11.6	39.0	49.5	11.5	39.1	50.1	10.7	39.3	50.0	10.7	39.9	48.5	11.6	41.5	47.3	11.2
	25-29	16.6	68.0	15.4	16.6	67.7	15.7	17.7	68.0	14.4	15.4	70.5	14.1	15.6	67.5	16.8	18.9	65.2	15.9
	15-29	45.0	43.5	11.4	45.1	43.5	11.4	45.4	44.1	10.5	44.4	45.2	10.4	43.9	43.7	12.3	45.6	42.6	11.8
Austria	15-19	84.4	8.7	6.9	85.0	8.5	6.6	85.6	9.1	5.3	84.3	10.0	5.6	84.3	9.2	6.5	86.6	8.1	5.3
	20-24	30.4	57.2	12.4	32.6	54.8	12.5	32.5	56.5	11.0	32.3	56.3	11.4	33.5	54.6	11.8	34.4	53.0	12.6
	25-29	12.0	74.6	13.4	13.7	71.0	15.3	14.2	70.4	15.4	14.6	71.7	13.7	16.5	68.9	14.6	17.5	67.8	14.7
	15-29	41.3	47.7	11.0	42.9	45.6	11.6	43.1	46.2	10.7	42.6	47.0	10.4	43.6	45.3	11.1	44.8	44.1	11.1
Belgium	15-19	90.1	3.7	6.2	88.9	4.0	7.1	91.9	2.9	5.2	90.5	4.0	5.5	91.1	3.3	5.7	91.8	2.3	5.9
	20-24	38.1	43.6	18.3	35.6	47.6	16.9	39.4	45.2	15.4	41.5	44.4	14.1	44.9	39.0	16.1	43.0	38.9	18.0
	25-29	7.4	74.9	17.7	7.2	75.3	17.5	7.2	75.5	17.2	7.7	75.8	16.5	7.8	75.9	16.3	8.1	73.6	18.3
	15-29	44.4	41.4	14.2	43.2	42.9	13.9	45.5	41.8	12.7	45.9	42.0	12.1	47.2	40.1	12.7	46.8	39.0	14.2
Canada	15-19	80.3	12.7	7.0	81.1	11.5	7.3	80.2	12.5	7.3	80.2	12.5	7.3	80.2	11.6	8.1	81.5	10.2	8.2
	20-24	39.2	46.4	14.5	38.5	48.5	13.0	38.5	47.8	13.7	38.9	48.1	13.0	38.0	46.8	15.2	39.5	45.1	15.3
	25-29	12.5	71.7	15.8	12.3	72.0	15.6	12.2	72.5	15.3	12.4	72.6	14.9	12.0	71.7	16.3	12.9	70.4	16.8
	15-29	44.0	43.5	12.4	44.1	43.9	12.0	43.7	44.2	12.1	43.8	44.5	11.7	43.1	43.7	13.3	43.9	42.5	13.5
Chile		m	m	m	m	m	m	m	m	m	m	m	m	m	m	m	m	m	m
Czech Republic	15-19	90.3	4.4	5.3	91.0	4.5	4.5	92.7	4.4	2.9	92.7	4.5	2.7	92.8	3.7	3.5	93.2	3.0	3.8
	20-24	35.9	47.5	16.6	40.0	45.8	14.1	42.1	46.9	11.0	44.8	44.7	10.6	46.1	40.8	13.1	48.4	38.1	13.6
	25-29	4.4	72.4	23.2	7.7	71.0	21.4	9.0	71.6	19.4	11.1	71.2	17.7	11.2	68.7	20.1	12.0	67.6	20.4
	15-29	39.5	44.6	15.9	42.7	43.2	14.1	44.8	43.5	11.7	46.6	42.5	10.9	47.2	40.0	12.8	48.1	38.7	13.2
Denmark	15-19	88.4	7.3	4.3	88.9	6.7	4.4	84.3	11.6	4.1	86.3	9.7	4.0	86.2	8.7	5.0	87.4	7.0	5.5
	20-24	54.4	37.2	8.3	55.3	38.8	5.9	48.9	43.1	8.0	51.3	40.6	8.2	53.5	36.3	10.1	53.4	34.5	12.1
	25-29	27.0	61.3	11.6	29.4	62.2	8.4	24.8	66.0	9.2	23.7	67.6	8.6	25.2	62.5	12.3	27.6	58.1	14.3
	15-29	55.5	36.3	8.2	58.0	35.8	6.2	52.8	40.1	7.1	54.3	38.8	6.9	55.9	35.1	9.0	57.2	32.3	10.5
Estonia	15-19	92.0	2.9	5.2	90.7	5.6	3.7	86.0	8.2	5.7	88.8	6.3	4.9	89.2	2.8	8.0	92.5	c	6.1
	20-24	50.9	32.7	16.3	47.6	37.0	15.4	45.4	39.3	15.3	46.5	42.8	10.7	46.7	33.5	19.8	50.2	27.3	22.4
	25-29	14.2	61.8	24.0	9.4	75.0	15.6	10.1	71.4	18.4	14.9	66.6	18.5	10.2	61.6	28.2	12.1	61.9	26.1
	15-29	54.0	31.3	14.8	50.7	37.9	11.4	48.0	38.9	13.0	49.9	38.7	11.3	47.4	33.6	19.0	48.7	32.2	19.1
Finland	15-19	90.2	4.5	5.2	91.8	4.6	3.6	92.2	4.3	3.5	90.3	4.6	5.1	90.3	4.5	5.1	91.7	3.2	5.1
	20-24	52.8	34.1	13.0	51.7	35.0	13.3	51.9	34.8	13.3	50.5	37.5	12.0	49.3	35.7	15.1	52.0	32.2	15.8
	25-29	25.7	60.3	14.0	25.6	60.4	13.9	27.2	59.5	13.3	29.2	58.4	12.4	25.4	59.1	15.5	26.3	56.9	16.8
	15-29	55.4	33.7	10.9	55.5	34.1	10.4	56.5	33.4	10.1	56.2	34.0	9.9	54.4	33.6	12.0	56.0	31.3	12.6
France	15-19	90.5	3.2	6.3	89.3	3.7	7.0	90.3	3.4	6.3	90.3	3.9	5.8	90.2	2.9	6.8	88.9	3.2	7.9
	20-24	42.5	39.7	17.8	42.1	38.9	19.0	41.9	40.1	17.9	42.2	41.2	16.6	40.0	40.0	20.0	40.4	39.0	20.6
	25-29	5.1	75.1	19.8	5.5	74.7	19.8	5.5	75.2	19.3	5.2	75.1	19.7	5.0	75.1	19.9	4.3	74.7	21.0
	15-29	46.8	38.7	14.5	46.2	38.7	15.2	46.1	39.4	14.5	45.8	40.2	14.0	44.6	39.7	15.6	43.8	39.5	16.7
Germany	15-19	92.9	2.7	4.4	92.4	3.3	4.2	92.2	3.6	4.2	92.4	3.9	3.7	92.7	3.6	3.8	92.3	4.1	3.7
	20-24	44.2	37.1	18.7	45.5	37.8	16.7	45.7	39.1	15.2	46.7	39.3	14.0	48.5	37.8	13.7	47.5	38.8	13.7
	25-29	18.5	60.3	21.2	18.5	61.5	20.0	18.7	62.8	18.5	19.2	63.8	17.0	18.6	64.5	16.9	18.3	63.9	17.8
	15-29	52.2	33.1	14.7	52.3	34.1	13.6	52.4	35.0	12.6	52.3	36.1	11.6	52.4	36.0	11.6	51.3	36.7	12.0
Greece	15-19	82.2	6.1	11.7	86.3	5.9	7.8	86.7	4.8	8.5	86.8	4.8	8.4	87.9	4.2	7.9	88.8	3.7	7.5
	20-24	40.4	38.0	21.6	44.0	37.7	18.4	47.3	35.0	17.7	48.5	34.4	17.1	47.2	34.6	18.2	46.6	31.8	21.6
	25-29	6.4	69.8	23.7	7.6	70.1	22.2	7.9	70.2	21.9	8.9	70.0	21.1	8.9	69.1	22.0	9.2	67.2	23.6
	15-29	38.6	41.7	19.7	41.4	41.6	16.9	42.8	40.5	16.8	43.7	40.1	16.2	43.4	39.8	16.8	43.9	37.8	18.3
Hungary	15-19	90.6	3.0	6.4	91.3	2.7	6.0	92.3	2.7	5.0	91.8	2.5	5.7	92.7	1.7	5.6	94.0	1.4	4.6
	20-24	46.6	34.5	18.9	47.8	33.7	18.5	49.2	33.9	16.9	48.4	33.2	18.4	49.2	29.9	20.9	48.1	30.4	21.5
	25-29	13.1	63.0	24.0	13.5	62.2	24.3	13.9	63.2	22.9	9.9	67.1	23.1	9.8	65.1	25.1	9.8	61.5	28.6
	15-29	46.3	36.5	17.2	47.3	35.6	17.0	48.6	35.7	15.6	47.2	36.5	16.3	48.1	34.1	17.7	48.3	32.8	18.9

1. Data for 1997 (Columns 1 to 3) are available on line (see *StatLink* below).
Source: OECD. See Annex 3 for notes (*www.oecd.org/edu/eag2012*).
Please refer to the Reader's Guide for information concerning the symbols replacing missing data.
StatLink ᵐˢᴾ http://dx.doi.org/10.1787/888932667520

Table C5.4a. [3/6] Trends in the percentage of the youth population in education and not in education (1997[1]-2010)

By 5-year age group and work status

C5

Country	Age group	1998 In education Total (4)	1998 Not in education Employed (5)	1998 Not in education Not employed (6)	1999 In education Total (7)	1999 Not in education Employed (8)	1999 Not in education Not employed (9)	2000 In education Total (10)	2000 Not in education Employed (11)	2000 Not in education Not employed (12)	2001 In education Total (13)	2001 Not in education Employed (14)	2001 Not in education Not employed (15)	2002 In education Total (16)	2002 Not in education Employed (17)	2002 Not in education Not employed (18)	2003 In education Total (19)	2003 Not in education Employed (20)	2003 Not in education Not employed (21)	2004 In education Total (22)	2004 Not in education Employed (23)	2004 Not in education Not employed (24)
Iceland	15-19	82.2	15.1	c	81.6	17.0	c	83.1	14.8	c	79.5	19.0	c	80.9	14.8	c	88.5	7.6	c	85.4	11.8	c
	20-24	47.8	45.9	6.3	44.8	48.4	6.8	48.0	47.7	c	50.3	45.6	c	53.8	40.1	6.2	57.1	35.1	7.8	56.1	37.5	6.4
	25-29	32.8	57.4	9.8	34.7	58.8	6.5	34.9	59.2	5.9	33.8	61.5	c	36.5	58.8	c	26.8	61.7	11.5	30.2	64.0	5.8
	15-29	55.3	38.6	6.1	54.5	40.7	4.8	56.0	39.9	4.1	54.7	41.8	3.4	57.0	38.0	5.1	59.0	33.5	7.6	57.7	37.3	5.0
Ireland	15-19	m	m	m	79.4	15.4	5.2	80.0	15.6	4.4	80.3	15.5	4.1	81.5	13.6	4.9	81.2	13.5	5.3	83.3	11.8	4.9
	20-24	m	m	m	24.6	64.6	10.8	26.7	63.6	9.7	28.3	62.4	9.3	28.9	60.1	10.9	30.5	58.0	11.5	29.0	59.4	11.6
	25-29	m	m	m	3.1	82.4	14.5	3.3	83.4	13.3	3.3	83.1	13.5	3.6	81.4	15.0	5.0	79.7	15.3	4.8	80.1	15.1
	15-29	m	m	m	37.8	52.3	9.9	37.9	53.2	9.0	37.6	53.5	9.0	37.9	51.8	10.3	37.7	51.0	10.8	37.7	51.6	10.7
Israel	15-19	m	m	m	m	m	m	m	m	m	m	m	m	69.4	6.0	24.6	69.0	5.7	25.2	68.9	5.6	25.6
	20-24	m	m	m	m	m	m	m	m	m	m	m	m	26.8	31.7	41.6	28.1	27.7	44.2	28.6	30.5	40.9
	25-29	m	m	m	m	m	m	m	m	m	m	m	m	19.1	52.2	28.7	19.6	52.7	27.7	20.9	53.9	25.3
	15-29	m	m	m	m	m	m	m	m	m	m	m	m	39.3	29.2	31.5	39.9	27.8	32.3	40.3	29.1	30.5
Italy	15-19	75.4	9.5	15.2	76.9	8.3	14.8	77.1	9.8	13.1	77.6	9.8	12.6	80.8	8.7	10.5	83.8	6.9	9.3	81.2	7.8	11.0
	20-24	35.8	34.1	30.1	35.6	34.5	29.9	36.0	36.5	27.5	37.0	36.9	26.1	38.2	37.5	24.3	44.1	34.2	21.7	37.7	38.7	23.6
	25-29	16.5	54.1	29.4	17.7	53.4	28.9	17.0	56.1	26.9	16.4	58.0	25.6	15.6	59.5	24.8	22.8	54.7	22.5	15.4	59.8	24.8
	15-29	39.5	34.8	25.7	40.1	34.6	25.3	39.9	36.8	23.3	40.1	37.8	22.2	41.0	38.3	20.7	46.6	34.8	18.6	41.2	38.3	20.5
Japan	15-24	60.0	32.4	7.6	60.0	31.0	9.0	62.1	29.2	8.8	62.6	28.9	8.4	58.6	32.0	9.5	58.4	31.7	9.8	59.1	31.7	9.2
Korea	15-19	m	m	m	m	m	m	m	m	m	m	m	m	m	m	m	m	m	m	m	m	m
	20-24	m	m	m	m	m	m	m	m	m	m	m	m	m	m	m	m	m	m	m	m	m
	25-29	m	m	m	m	m	m	m	m	m	m	m	m	m	m	m	m	m	m	m	m	m
	15-29	m	m	m	m	m	m	m	m	m	m	m	m	m	m	m	m	m	m	m	m	m
Luxembourg	15-19	88.6	5.3	6.1	89.2	5.8	5.0	92.2	6.1	c	91.2	7.0	c	91.3	5.7	3.0	92.2	5.7	2.1	91.4	5.5	3.2
	20-24	40.4	50.1	9.5	47.2	43.2	9.6	42.8	48.9	8.2	46.7	44.2	9.0	47.8	45.2	7.0	46.0	45.9	8.1	49.1	40.8	10.1
	25-29	11.9	74.0	14.1	11.3	74.1	14.6	11.6	75.5	12.9	11.6	75.9	12.5	13.9	74.5	11.6	7.6	82.2	10.2	6.1	81.5	12.4
	15-29	42.1	47.5	10.5	44.1	45.5	10.4	45.3	46.6	8.1	46.7	45.1	8.2	48.5	44.0	7.5	46.1	46.9	7.0	46.8	44.4	8.7
Mexico	15-19	46.9	33.8	19.3	49.6	32.7	17.7	47.9	33.8	18.3	50.3	31.9	17.8	53.4	29.0	17.5	54.0	28.2	17.8	54.9	28.0	17.0
	20-24	17.1	55.4	27.4	19.1	54.8	26.1	17.7	55.2	27.1	19.1	53.8	27.1	20.8	52.6	26.6	19.8	52.6	27.6	20.3	52.3	27.4
	25-29	4.2	65.2	30.6	4.9	65.0	30.1	4.0	65.8	30.2	4.1	64.9	31.0	4.6	64.8	30.6	4.2	64.8	31.0	4.4	65.4	30.3
	15-29	24.8	49.9	25.2	26.5	49.4	24.1	25.4	50.0	24.6	26.9	49.5	24.6	28.8	46.9	24.2	28.7	46.6	24.8	29.0	46.7	24.2
Netherlands	15-19	89.7	7.6	2.7	88.2	8.9	3.0	80.6	15.7	3.7	86.5	9.9	3.6	86.7	9.5	3.8	87.0	8.7	4.3	89.2	7.5	3.3
	20-24	50.5	42.0	7.5	50.7	42.5	6.7	36.5	55.2	8.2	44.2	47.8	8.0	45.1	47.7	7.3	44.2	46.5	9.4	46.6	44.2	9.3
	25-29	24.4	64.9	10.7	25.0	65.2	9.8	5.0	83.0	12.1	15.3	73.7	11.0	16.2	71.6	12.2	16.5	71.4	12.1	16.9	71.2	11.9
	15-29	51.5	41.1	7.4	51.8	41.4	6.8	38.1	53.6	8.3	46.8	45.5	7.7	48.1	44.0	7.9	48.6	42.7	8.7	50.6	41.2	8.2
New Zealand	15-19	m	m	m	m	m	m	m	m	m	m	m	m	m	m	m	m	m	m	74.2	16.8	9.0
	20-24	m	m	m	m	m	m	m	m	m	m	m	m	m	m	m	m	m	m	38.5	46.9	14.6
	25-29	m	m	m	m	m	m	m	m	m	m	m	m	m	m	m	m	m	m	17.9	64.4	17.7
	15-29	m	m	m	m	m	m	m	m	m	m	m	m	m	m	m	m	m	m	45.1	41.4	13.5
Norway	15-19	92.1	6.0	1.9	91.9	6.4	c	92.4	5.9	c	85.8	11.1	3.0	85.3	11.5	3.2	86.9	10.4	2.7	87.2	9.9	2.8
	20-24	40.2	51.4	8.4	38.4	53.8	7.8	41.7	50.3	8.0	39.6	51.7	8.7	38.5	51.8	9.7	38.7	50.8	10.4	40.6	49.6	9.8
	25-29	14.4	76.1	9.6	17.2	74.4	8.3	17.5	72.1	10.4	13.9	75.9	10.2	14.2	75.0	10.7	15.4	71.9	12.7	15.4	71.5	13.1
	15-29	46.4	46.8	6.8	46.8	47.1	6.1	48.4	44.6	7.0	44.7	47.8	7.5	44.8	47.2	8.0	46.3	44.9	8.7	47.6	43.8	8.6
Poland	15-19	91.0	4.2	4.8	93.2	2.3	4.6	92.8	2.6	4.5	91.8	2.4	5.8	95.9	1.0	3.1	95.6	1.1	3.3	96.5	0.9	2.6
	20-24	30.8	45.3	23.9	33.1	39.7	27.2	34.9	34.3	30.8	45.2	27.7	27.1	53.8	20.8	25.4	55.7	18.8	25.5	57.5	18.4	24.1
	25-29	5.7	70.5	23.8	5.4	68.0	26.6	8.0	62.9	29.1	11.4	59.9	28.7	14.9	53.3	31.8	17.3	52.3	30.3	15.5	53.7	30.8
	15-29	42.6	39.8	17.6	42.7	37.4	19.9	43.8	34.1	22.1	49.2	30.1	20.7	52.8	26.2	21.0	54.3	25.1	20.5	53.8	25.9	20.3
Portugal	15-19	71.6	20.1	8.3	72.3	19.6	8.1	72.6	19.7	7.7	72.8	19.8	7.4	72.4	20.3	7.3	74.8	16.4	8.8	75.1	15.1	9.8
	20-24	32.4	55.7	12.0	34.9	53.2	11.9	36.5	52.6	11.0	36.3	53.3	10.4	34.7	53.3	12.0	35.2	52.5	12.3	38.7	47.8	13.5
	25-29	9.5	74.8	15.8	11.5	75.1	13.4	11.0	76.6	12.5	11.2	77.3	11.6	10.7	77.1	12.2	11.7	73.7	14.6	11.0	75.0	14.0
	15-29	36.7	51.2	12.1	38.2	50.5	11.3	38.3	51.2	10.5	38.5	51.6	9.9	37.4	51.9	10.7	38.7	49.2	12.1	38.0	49.3	12.7
Slovak Republic	15-19	69.4	12.3	18.3	69.6	10.1	20.4	67.3	6.4	26.3	67.3	6.3	26.4	78.6	5.8	15.6	82.2	5.2	12.6	87.8	4.3	7.9
	20-24	17.4	56.3	26.3	17.4	51.2	31.4	18.1	48.8	33.1	19.4	45.7	34.9	22.1	44.0	33.9	24.0	46.4	29.6	27.5	44.7	27.8
	25-29	1.1	71.6	27.2	1.6	70.2	28.2	1.3	66.9	31.8	2.3	65.0	32.7	2.9	66.6	30.5	2.6	68.3	29.1	4.5	66.6	28.9
	15-29	31.0	45.3	23.8	30.3	43.0	26.7	29.3	40.3	30.4	29.6	39.0	31.4	34.4	38.8	26.8	36.2	39.9	23.9	39.0	39.2	21.8

1.Data for 1997 (Columns 1 to 3) are available on line (see *StatLink* below).
Source: OECD. See Annex 3 for notes *(www.oecd.org/edu/eag2012)*.
Please refer to the Reader's Guide for information concerning the symbols replacing missing data.
StatLink ᔌᔍᔎ http://dx.doi.org/10.1787/888932667520

Table C5.4a. [4/6] Trends in the percentage of the youth population in education and not in education (1997[1]-2010)

By 5-year age group and work status

	Age group	2005 In education Total (25)	2005 Not in education Employed (26)	2005 Not in education Not employed (27)	2006 In education Total (28)	2006 Not in education Employed (29)	2006 Not in education Not employed (30)	2007 In education Total (31)	2007 Not in education Employed (32)	2007 Not in education Not employed (33)	2008 In education Total (34)	2008 Not in education Employed (35)	2008 Not in education Not employed (36)	2009 In education Total (37)	2009 Not in education Employed (38)	2009 Not in education Not employed (39)	2010 In education Total (37)	2010 Not in education Employed (38)	2010 Not in education Not employed (39)
Iceland	15-19	86.4	10.7	c	86.9	9.9	c	83.8	13.3	c	85.5	12.0	c	85.4	10.0	c	85.0	8.2	6.8
	20-24	53.0	37.1	10.0	53.6	41.9	c	55.8	37.8	6.4	56.7	39.8	c	59.1	31.5	9.4	55.3	34.1	10.5
	25-29	30.9	61.5	7.6	33.7	62.3	c	29.0	64.3	6.6	30.6	62.6	6.9	35.5	50.8	13.7	32.9	54.3	12.8
	15-29	57.0	36.2	6.8	58.3	37.8	3.9	56.5	38.2	5.3	57.5	38.2	4.3	57.9	32.5	9.6	55.8	33.9	10.3
Ireland	15-19	82.4	13.1	4.5	81.7	13.3	5.0	82.6	12.3	5.1	81.4	10.1	8.5	83.0	6.0	11.0	85.3	4.2	10.4
	20-24	27.7	60.0	12.3	26.5	61.7	11.8	25.9	62.0	12.1	30.2	55.3	14.6	34.2	45.0	20.8	36.6	36.9	26.4
	25-29	5.3	80.9	13.8	5.6	81.1	13.3	4.9	81.5	13.5	10.1	75.6	14.3	9.7	68.2	22.0	10.9	64.7	24.3
	15-29	36.2	53.4	10.5	34.6	55.0	10.4	33.3	55.9	10.7	36.1	51.1	12.8	37.7	43.7	18.6	40.0	39.0	21.0
Israel	15-19	68.9	6.3	24.7	69.0	6.8	24.3	68.5	5.7	25.7	70.7	7.1	22.2	68.8	6.5	24.7	72.0	5.5	22.5
	20-24	28.3	31.4	40.3	29.3	30.1	40.6	28.5	31.9	39.6	28.9	33.6	37.5	28.5	34.0	37.5	30.9	32.1	36.9
	25-29	21.4	54.3	24.2	24.8	51.8	23.4	24.5	52.0	23.5	24.0	53.1	22.9	26.6	49.2	24.2	27.0	50.1	22.9
	15-29	40.2	30.2	29.6	41.5	29.1	29.4	41.0	29.3	29.7	42.1	30.3	27.5	42.0	29.3	28.7	44.0	28.6	27.4
Italy	15-19	81.8	7.0	11.2	81.6	6.6	11.8	83.5	6.3	10.2	84.5	5.9	9.6	83.8	5.0	11.2	83.6	4.0	12.5
	20-24	38.6	37.3	24.1	40.2	37.0	22.8	41.7	35.7	22.6	42.6	35.4	22.0	42.3	32.9	24.8	40.8	32.1	27.1
	25-29	14.4	59.8	25.8	15.2	60.7	24.1	16.1	58.3	25.6	15.5	60.0	24.5	15.7	57.9	26.4	16.9	54.9	28.2
	15-29	41.5	37.5	21.1	42.7	37.2	20.1	44.5	35.5	20.0	45.3	35.5	19.2	45.3	33.5	21.2	45.3	31.7	23.0
Japan	15-24	59.7	31.5	8.8	56.7	34.2	9.1	58.4	34.0	7.6	58.6	34.0	7.4	58.4	33.1	8.5	61.7	28.4	9.9
Korea	15-19	m	m	m	m	m	m	m	m	m	90.6	2.3	7.0	91.2	1.9	7.0	89.4	2.1	8.5
	20-24	m	m	m	m	m	m	m	m	m	41.1	36.7	22.2	41.2	35.8	23.0	40.9	35.5	23.5
	25-29	m	m	m	m	m	m	m	m	m	9.4	65.1	25.5	9.2	64.2	26.5	9.2	64.9	25.9
	15-29	m	m	m	m	m	m	m	m	m	44.8	36.7	18.5	45.4	35.6	19.0	45.4	35.3	19.2
Luxembourg	15-19	93.4	4.4	2.2	93.1	2.8	4.1	94.3	2.7	2.9	94.0	3.8	2.1	94.5	2.8	2.7	92.1	c	6.3
	20-24	47.4	43.3	9.3	50.3	39.4	10.3	55.1	35.6	9.2	55.9	34.3	9.8	66.0	25.3	8.7	63.1	29.4	7.5
	25-29	8.6	81.2	10.3	9.2	79.6	11.2	7.1	79.1	13.9	11.2	75.8	13.0	7.4	80.7	11.9	15.5	76.9	7.6
	15-29	48.5	44.2	7.3	49.6	41.8	8.6	49.8	41.2	8.9	51.9	39.6	8.5	53.5	38.6	7.9	54.7	38.1	7.1
Mexico	15-19	57.6	24.2	18.2	58.8	23.4	17.8	59.9	22.6	17.5	60.0	22.2	17.8	60.8	20.8	18.4	60.8	20.6	18.6
	20-24	24.3	48.7	27.0	24.3	49.0	26.6	24.5	48.9	26.5	25.1	48.4	26.5	25.7	46.7	27.6	26.1	47.3	26.6
	25-29	5.7	62.8	31.5	6.5	63.4	30.1	6.2	63.2	30.6	6.6	63.9	29.5	6.4	63.2	30.4	6.7	63.5	29.8
	15-29	31.9	43.2	24.9	32.7	43.1	24.2	33.0	42.8	24.2	33.7	42.5	23.9	33.9	41.3	24.8	34.1	41.5	24.4
Netherlands	15-19	89.2	7.0	3.9	91.7	5.2	3.0	88.1	8.3	3.6	90.7	7.2	2.1	89.7	6.8	3.6	89.4	6.8	3.8
	20-24	49.1	41.8	9.1	50.3	42.4	7.3	50.8	42.2	6.9	52.1	42.3	5.6	52.5	39.6	7.9	55.4	36.8	7.8
	25-29	18.2	70.2	11.6	18.1	71.2	10.8	19.8	70.6	9.6	18.7	73.5	7.8	19.1	71.3	9.6	21.1	68.9	10.1
	15-29	52.1	39.7	8.2	53.1	39.8	7.1	53.1	40.2	6.7	54.3	40.6	5.1	54.1	38.9	7.0	55.5	37.3	7.2
New Zealand	15-19	74.9	17.1	8.0	73.2	17.8	9.0	72.6	17.8	9.7	74.7	16.8	8.5	72.7	14.9	12.4	76.5	13.1	10.4
	20-24	38.8	46.7	14.5	37.6	48.8	13.7	38.1	47.7	14.2	38.7	46.1	15.3	38.8	42.9	18.3	38.2	43.4	18.4
	25-29	18.3	65.7	16.1	16.4	67.5	16.2	19.1	64.7	16.2	15.4	68.1	16.5	15.4	66.5	18.1	17.2	62.2	20.5
	15-29	45.7	41.7	12.6	44.1	43.2	12.7	44.9	41.9	13.2	44.6	42.2	13.2	43.7	40.2	16.1	45.1	38.6	16.3
Norway	15-19	87.4	10.1	2.5	82.1	14.5	3.4	80.6	15.8	3.7	78.3	17.7	4.0	80.6	15.2	4.2	81.4	15.1	3.5
	20-24	41.5	48.9	9.6	39.2	51.7	9.1	37.7	53.6	8.8	39.3	53.6	7.0	41.6	49.0	9.4	42.2	48.8	9.0
	25-29	15.7	72.0	12.3	12.2	76.3	11.5	12.2	77.4	10.4	12.6	78.2	9.2	12.7	76.7	10.6	13.5	73.5	13.0
	15-29	48.6	43.4	8.1	45.3	46.8	7.9	44.3	48.2	7.5	44.1	49.2	6.8	45.6	46.5	8.0	46.2	45.3	8.5
Poland	15-19	97.9	0.4	1.7	94.9	1.3	3.8	95.9	1.7	2.5	95.8	1.9	2.4	94.3	2.1	3.6	94.2	2.2	3.6
	20-24	62.7	17.2	20.1	55.1	24.2	20.7	56.4	25.2	18.3	56.8	27.6	15.6	54.4	29.2	16.4	52.8	29.6	17.7
	25-29	16.4	54.3	29.3	12.2	61.2	26.6	12.8	62.9	24.3	11.4	67.1	21.5	12.4	66.8	20.8	12.3	65.7	22.0
	15-29	55.7	26.0	18.4	52.9	29.6	17.4	53.5	31.0	15.5	52.5	33.8	13.7	50.7	35.1	14.2	49.3	35.4	15.2
Portugal	15-19	79.3	12.2	8.4	80.2	12.0	7.8	80.4	11.1	8.6	81.7	11.2	7.1	84.5	8.6	6.9	85.2	7.4	7.4
	20-24	37.4	48.4	14.1	37.7	48.9	13.3	35.5	49.3	15.2	36.5	50.0	13.5	37.9	46.3	15.7	39.6	44.1	16.4
	25-29	11.5	73.6	14.9	12.2	72.9	14.9	12.1	72.4	15.5	11.9	73.0	15.1	14.2	71.0	14.8	13.8	70.5	15.7
	15-29	38.9	48.2	12.9	39.6	48.1	12.4	39.1	47.5	13.4	40.1	47.6	12.2	42.3	44.9	12.8	43.1	43.5	13.5
Slovak Republic	15-19	90.4	3.3	6.3	90.5	2.9	6.7	90.2	4.4	5.4	90.6	3.8	5.7	91.5	4.0	4.5	93.8	1.7	4.6
	20-24	31.0	43.8	25.2	35.4	41.9	22.8	29.4	50.7	19.9	39.3	44.1	16.6	45.3	37.6	17.1	44.8	33.0	22.1
	25-29	6.1	64.9	29.0	5.7	67.9	26.4	6.8	68.0	25.2	6.5	68.7	24.7	7.5	67.6	24.9	7.3	65.1	27.5
	15-29	41.1	38.3	20.5	41.8	39.1	19.1	40.5	42.3	17.2	43.2	40.6	16.2	45.7	38.2	16.1	45.9	35.2	18.8

1. Data for 1997 (Columns 1 to 3) are available on line (see *StatLink* below).
Source: OECD. See Annex 3 for notes (*www.oecd.org/edu/eag2012*).
Please refer to the Reader's Guide for information concerning the symbols replacing missing data.
StatLink http://dx.doi.org/10.1787/888932667520

Table C5.4a. [5/6] Trends in the percentage of the youth population in education and not in education (1997[1]-2010)

By 5-year age group and work status

	Age group	1998 In education Total (4)	1998 Not in education Employed (5)	1998 Not in education Not employed (6)	1999 In education Total (7)	1999 Not in education Employed (8)	1999 Not in education Not employed (9)	2000 In education Total (10)	2000 Not in education Employed (11)	2000 Not in education Not employed (12)	2001 In education Total (13)	2001 Not in education Employed (14)	2001 Not in education Not employed (15)	2002 In education Total (16)	2002 Not in education Employed (17)	2002 Not in education Not employed (18)	2003 In education Total (19)	2003 Not in education Employed (20)	2003 Not in education Not employed (21)	2004 In education Total (22)	2004 Not in education Employed (23)	2004 Not in education Not employed (24)
OECD Slovenia	15-19	m	m	m	m	m	m	m	m	m	m	m	m	m	m	m	92.8	2.4	4.8	92.2	3.5	4.3
	20-24	m	m	m	m	m	m	m	m	m	m	m	m	m	m	m	56.8	30.2	13.0	60.9	27.9	11.2
	25-29	m	m	m	m	m	m	m	m	m	m	m	m	m	m	m	25.3	63.1	11.5	26.6	61.8	11.5
	15-29	m	m	m	m	m	m	m	m	m	m	m	m	m	m	m	57.2	32.8	10.0	58.4	32.4	9.2
Spain	15-19	80.2	9.9	9.8	79.3	11.3	9.4	80.6	11.4	8.0	81.4	11.6	6.9	81.9	11.0	7.2	82.6	10.1	7.3	82.2	10.1	7.6
	20-24	44.3	35.7	20.1	43.6	38.8	17.6	44.6	40.3	15.0	45.0	40.7	14.2	43.4	41.5	15.1	43.5	41.8	14.8	41.3	43.2	15.6
	25-29	15.3	57.3	27.5	15.2	59.6	25.1	16.2	62.4	21.4	17.0	63.1	19.8	16.1	64.2	19.8	15.4	65.0	19.5	15.3	66.2	18.5
	15-29	45.4	35.1	19.4	44.4	37.8	17.8	45.0	39.8	15.3	45.1	40.7	14.2	43.8	41.5	14.6	43.4	42.0	14.6	42.2	43.2	14.6
Sweden	15-19	90.9	4.3	4.7	91.5	4.9	3.7	90.6	5.8	3.6	88.4	7.3	4.3	88.4	7.0	4.6	88.7	7.0	4.2	89.4	5.8	4.8
	20-24	42.6	44.3	13.1	43.8	45.2	11.0	42.1	47.2	10.7	41.2	48.2	10.6	41.7	47.0	11.2	42.3	46.0	11.8	42.8	43.6	13.6
	25-29	24.9	65.0	10.0	22.5	68.1	9.5	21.9	68.9	9.2	22.7	70.0	7.2	22.4	69.5	8.1	22.8	67.9	9.4	21.5	68.0	10.5
	15-29	51.3	39.3	9.4	51.1	40.7	8.1	50.2	41.9	7.9	49.6	43.1	7.3	50.1	42.0	7.9	51.0	40.6	8.4	51.5	39.0	9.5
Switzerland	15-19	85.5	9.6	4.9	84.4	8.0	7.6	84.6	7.5	7.9	85.7	7.5	6.8	86.2	8.0	5.8	83.6	8.6	7.8	84.9	7.9	7.2
	20-24	34.7	54.1	11.3	35.8	55.9	8.3	37.4	56.7	5.9	39.3	52.3	8.4	37.9	52.7	9.4	35.8	51.8	12.4	37.3	51.7	11.0
	25-29	10.1	78.0	11.9	10.3	79.4	10.3	15.1	73.9	11.0	13.5	75.1	11.4	12.6	74.5	12.9	12.2	74.0	13.8	15.7	72.1	12.2
	15-29	41.6	48.9	9.5	42.9	48.4	8.7	45.1	46.6	8.3	46.4	44.7	8.9	44.3	46.2	9.5	42.7	45.8	11.4	45.1	44.7	10.2
Turkey	15-19	40.2	32.1	27.7	42.9	30.2	26.9	39.2	29.6	31.2	41.0	26.7	32.3	42.2	24.8	32.9	45.9	21.3	32.8	43.5	21.2	35.3
	20-24	13.4	44.7	42.0	13.1	45.6	41.4	12.7	43.1	44.2	12.7	43.1	44.2	14.1	40.6	45.3	15.8	36.5	47.8	13.0	39.1	47.8
	25-29	2.9	60.4	36.7	3.4	57.7	38.8	2.9	58.8	38.3	2.6	57.1	40.2	3.0	56.2	40.7	3.7	53.2	43.1	3.1	54.0	42.8
	15-29	19.9	45.0	35.1	21.1	43.7	35.2	18.5	43.7	37.8	18.8	42.4	38.9	19.6	40.8	39.6	21.7	37.2	41.1	19.7	38.4	41.9
United Kingdom	15-19	m	m	m	m	m	m	77.0	15.0	8.0	76.1	15.7	8.2	75.3	16.2	8.6	76.3	14.3	9.4	74.3	16.7	9.0
	20-24	m	m	m	m	m	m	32.4	52.2	15.4	33.5	51.7	14.8	31.0	53.7	15.3	32.6	52.1	15.3	31.1	54.1	14.8
	25-29	m	m	m	m	m	m	13.3	70.3	16.3	13.3	70.6	16.0	13.3	70.7	16.0	15.0	68.7	16.3	14.2	69.0	16.8
	15-29	m	m	m	m	m	m	40.0	46.6	13.3	40.2	46.7	13.1	39.5	47.2	13.3	41.4	44.9	13.6	40.5	46.0	13.5
United States	15-19	82.2	10.5	7.3	81.3	11.3	7.4	81.3	11.7	7.0	81.2	11.4	7.5	82.9	10.2	7.0	m	m	m	83.9	9.2	6.9
	20-24	33.0	52.6	14.4	32.8	52.1	15.1	32.5	53.1	14.4	33.9	50.5	15.6	35.0	48.5	16.5	m	m	m	35.2	47.9	16.9
	25-29	11.9	72.7	15.4	11.1	73.2	15.7	11.4	72.8	15.8	11.8	70.5	17.7	12.3	70.3	17.4	m	m	m	13.0	68.7	18.4
	15-29	43.3	44.5	12.2	43.0	44.4	12.6	43.1	44.6	12.2	44.0	42.7	13.3	45.1	41.5	13.4	m	m	m	44.8	41.3	13.9
OECD average	15-19	79.3	11.6	9.4	80.0	11.4	9.2	80.1	11.4	9.4	80.4	11.3	8.9	81.2	10.4	8.6	83.2	8.7	8.2	83.1	8.8	8.3
	20-24	34.3	47.3	18.5	34.8	47.4	17.8	34.7	48.2	17.7	36.5	46.8	17.2	36.5	45.7	17.7	38.9	43.3	17.8	39.6	42.6	17.7
	25-29	12.4	67.3	20.3	12.7	67.7	19.6	12.2	68.7	19.1	12.7	68.6	19.3	13.0	67.9	19.7	14.0	66.6	19.4	14.0	67.0	19.0
	15-29	41.1	42.8	16.0	41.7	42.9	15.4	41.4	43.6	15.1	42.2	43.1	14.7	42.6	42.2	15.3	44.5	40.3	15.2	44.7	40.2	15.1
EU21 average	15-19	82.6	8.9	8.5	83.1	8.9	7.9	83.2	9.2	7.9	83.8	8.8	7.7	85.1	8.3	6.5	87.0	6.9	6.1	87.4	6.5	6.1
	20-24	35.6	45.6	18.7	36.2	45.6	18.2	35.6	47.0	17.3	37.9	45.6	16.4	38.0	45.6	16.4	40.8	43.1	16.0	42.0	41.4	16.6
	25-29	12.3	66.6	21.0	12.4	67.4	20.2	11.3	69.3	19.4	12.4	68.9	18.8	12.2	69.2	18.6	14.0	67.5	18.5	13.5	67.9	18.6
	15-29	42.2	41.5	16.3	42.5	41.8	15.7	41.9	43.0	15.0	43.1	42.4	14.4	43.5	42.4	14.1	45.9	40.3	13.8	46.1	39.9	14.0
Other G20 Argentina		m	m	m	m	m	m	m	m	m	m	m	m	m	m	m	m	m	m	m	m	m
Brazil	15-19	m	m	m	m	m	m	m	m	m	m	m	m	m	m	m	m	m	m	m	m	m
	20-24	m	m	m	m	m	m	m	m	m	m	m	m	m	m	m	m	m	m	m	m	m
	25-29	m	m	m	m	m	m	m	m	m	m	m	m	m	m	m	m	m	m	m	m	m
	15-29	m	m	m	m	m	m	m	m	m	m	m	m	m	m	m	m	m	m	m	m	m
China		m	m	m	m	m	m	m	m	m	m	m	m	m	m	m	m	m	m	m	m	m
India		m	m	m	m	m	m	m	m	m	m	m	m	m	m	m	m	m	m	m	m	m
Indonesia		m	m	m	m	m	m	m	m	m	m	m	m	m	m	m	m	m	m	m	m	m
Russian Federation		m	m	m	m	m	m	m	m	m	m	m	m	m	m	m	m	m	m	m	m	m
Saudi Arabia		m	m	m	m	m	m	m	m	m	m	m	m	m	m	m	m	m	m	m	m	m
South Africa		m	m	m	m	m	m	m	m	m	m	m	m	m	m	m	m	m	m	m	m	m
G20 average		m	m	m	m	m	m	m	m	m	m	m	m	m	m	m	m	m	m	m	m	m

1.Data for 1997 (Columns 1 to 3) are available on line (see *StatLink* below).
Source: OECD. See Annex 3 for notes (*www.oecd.org/edu/eag2012*).
Please refer to the Reader's Guide for information concerning the symbols replacing missing data.
StatLink ᓂᓕᓄ http://dx.doi.org/10.1787/888932667520

C5

Table C5.4a. [6/6] Trends in the percentage of the youth population in education and not in education (1997[1]-2010)

By 5-year age group and work status

	Age group	2005 In education Total	2005 Not in education Employed	2005 Not in education Not employed	2006 In education Total	2006 Not in education Employed	2006 Not in education Not employed	2007 In education Total	2007 Not in education Employed	2007 Not in education Not employed	2008 In education Total	2008 Not in education Employed	2008 Not in education Not employed	2009 In education Total	2009 Not in education Employed	2009 Not in education Not employed	2010 In education Total	2010 Not in education Employed	2010 Not in education Not employed
		(25)	(26)	(27)	(28)	(29)	(30)	(31)	(32)	(33)	(34)	(35)	(36)	(37)	(38)	(39)	(37)	(38)	(39)
OECD Slovenia	15-19	92.4	2.7	4.9	92.7	3.1	4.2	91.2	4.5	4.3	92.2	3.4	4.4	94.1	3.4	2.5	**95.0**	**1.8**	**3.2**
	20-24	55.7	31.3	13.0	55.8	30.5	13.7	58.7	30.9	10.4	60.6	29.2	10.3	62.9	25.7	11.4	**65.3**	**25.5**	**9.3**
	25-29	24.6	63.9	11.5	26.3	60.3	13.3	26.1	59.5	14.4	26.9	63.2	9.9	27.1	61.3	11.6	**30.4**	**57.2**	**12.4**
	15-29	55.5	34.4	10.1	55.7	33.5	10.8	56.3	33.6	10.1	57.1	34.5	8.5	58.2	32.7	9.0	**60.6**	**30.7**	**8.8**
Spain	15-19	78.2	11.0	10.8	79.5	10.5	10.1	77.8	11.3	10.9	78.9	10.5	10.5	80.4	6.2	13.4	**82.6**	**4.6**	**12.8**
	20-24	35.1	45.5	19.4	34.5	48.6	16.9	34.5	48.2	17.2	34.0	46.5	19.4	34.9	38.9	26.3	**39.3**	**33.3**	**27.4**
	25-29	10.9	69.3	19.8	10.9	70.1	19.1	10.0	72.4	17.6	9.5	71.5	18.9	9.9	63.8	26.3	**11.3**	**60.1**	**28.6**
	15-29	37.1	45.7	17.2	37.1	47.0	15.9	36.3	48.1	15.7	36.3	46.9	16.8	37.4	39.9	22.7	**40.3**	**35.9**	**23.7**
Sweden	15-19	89.6	5.8	4.7	87.7	7.0	5.3	86.9	7.7	5.4	87.4	8.2	4.4	87.9	6.6	5.5	**89.3**	**5.3**	**5.4**
	20-24	42.5	44.1	13.4	43.0	41.8	15.2	39.6	47.3	13.1	39.5	47.5	12.9	39.0	44.5	16.5	**46.3**	**39.4**	**14.3**
	25-29	23.6	66.5	10.0	20.9	67.5	11.6	20.2	69.2	10.6	21.7	68.7	9.5	21.5	67.0	11.5	**24.8**	**63.9**	**11.3**
	15-29	52.9	38.0	9.2	51.5	38.0	10.5	50.3	40.2	9.6	51.3	39.9	8.7	51.0	38.0	11.0	**54.6**	**35.2**	**10.3**
Switzerland	15-19	85.3	7.2	7.5	84.4	8.0	7.6	84.4	7.5	8.2	82.9	7.7	9.4	84.7	7.4	7.9	**88.5**	**6.7**	**4.8**
	20-24	37.9	50.3	11.9	36.9	52.3	10.8	41.0	48.6	10.4	42.7	48.2	9.1	43.4	45.9	10.7	**45.8**	**43.1**	**11.1**
	25-29	12.3	75.9	11.8	14.7	73.8	11.5	12.9	75.2	11.9	14.4	75.5	10.1	14.3	72.9	12.8	**17.2**	**70.0**	**12.8**
	15-29	44.4	45.2	10.4	44.7	45.3	10.0	45.5	44.3	10.2	46.0	44.5	9.6	46.5	43.0	10.5	**49.3**	**41.1**	**9.7**
Turkey	15-19	45.8	18.1	36.1	47.9	17.0	35.0	48.7	16.8	34.5	44.7	18.2	37.1	56.3	15.0	28.7	**59.7**	**14.7**	**25.6**
	20-24	15.4	34.9	49.7	17.3	33.9	48.8	18.6	35.1	46.3	20.0	33.9	46.1	23.9	30.0	46.1	**25.2**	**31.1**	**43.7**
	25-29	4.0	50.2	45.8	5.7	49.4	45.0	4.6	51.5	43.9	4.9	51.6	43.5	7.7	47.4	44.9	**8.1**	**50.1**	**41.8**
	15-29	22.4	34.0	43.6	24.2	33.2	42.6	24.3	34.4	41.3	23.4	34.6	42.0	29.5	30.9	39.6	**31.4**	**32.0**	**36.6**
United Kingdom	15-19	76.0	14.6	9.3	75.7	13.4	10.9	76.2	13.0	10.7	76.5	13.7	9.8	78.3	12.1	9.6	**80.6**	**9.4**	**10.0**
	20-24	32.1	51.0	16.8	30.2	51.6	18.2	29.7	52.3	18.1	28.3	53.4	18.3	31.5	49.3	19.1	**33.7**	**46.9**	**19.3**
	25-29	13.3	70.1	16.6	14.1	69.5	16.4	12.7	71.1	16.2	12.3	71.9	15.8	13.2	68.9	18.0	**14.3**	**67.6**	**18.1**
	15-29	41.2	44.6	14.2	40.6	44.3	15.1	40.1	45.0	14.9	38.2	47.1	14.8	40.4	43.9	15.7	**42.1**	**42.0**	**15.9**
United States	15-19	85.6	8.3	6.1	85.0	8.6	6.3	85.2	8.5	6.3	85.2	7.6	7.2	84.7	6.5	8.8	**85.5**	**6.8**	**7.6**
	20-24	36.1	48.4	15.5	35.0	49.4	15.6	35.7	48.1	16.2	36.9	45.9	17.2	38.7	41.2	20.1	**38.6**	**42.0**	**19.4**
	25-29	11.9	70.0	18.1	11.7	71.5	16.8	12.4	70.7	16.9	13.2	67.3	19.5	13.5	64.7	21.8	**14.6**	**64.2**	**21.2**
	15-29	45.2	41.7	13.1	44.4	42.7	12.8	44.8	42.1	13.1	45.3	40.1	14.6	45.7	37.4	16.9	**46.0**	**37.8**	**16.1**
OECD average	15-19	83.6	8.3	8.2	83.6	8.3	8.2	83.4	8.8	8.0	83.8	8.5	7.9	84.4	7.2	8.4	**85.6**	**6.6**	**8.1**
	20-24	40.3	42.2	17.5	40.4	42.9	17.1	40.6	43.3	16.1	41.7	42.6	16.0	43.1	39.0	17.9	**43.9**	**37.5**	**18.5**
	25-29	14.1	67.1	18.8	14.3	67.8	18.4	14.1	68.1	17.8	14.3	68.3	17.4	14.5	65.9	19.5	**15.7**	**64.3**	**20.0**
	15-29	45.1	39.9	15.0	45.3	40.4	14.3	45.2	40.8	14.0	45.6	40.7	13.7	46.2	38.4	15.4	**47.1**	**37.1**	**15.8**
EU21 average	15-19	87.7	6.1	6.2	87.9	6.1	6.1	87.7	6.6	5.7	88.0	6.4	5.6	88.5	5.1	6.3	**89.4**	**4.4**	**6.5**
	20-24	42.6	41.2	16.1	42.9	41.7	15.4	42.9	42.5	14.5	44.2	41.9	13.9	45.7	37.9	16.4	**46.8**	**35.8**	**17.5**
	25-29	13.7	68.0	18.3	13.7	68.8	17.4	13.7	69.1	17.2	14.3	69.4	16.4	14.1	67.4	18.5	**15.4**	**65.2**	**19.4**
	15-29	46.4	39.8	13.8	46.6	40.1	13.2	46.6	40.7	12.7	47.2	40.6	12.2	47.6	38.3	14.0	**48.6**	**36.6**	**14.8**
Other G20 Argentina		m	m	m	m	m	m	m	m	m	m	m	m	m	m	m	**m**	**m**	**m**
Brazil	15-19	m	m	m	m	m	m	67.0	18.3	14.7	69.1	17.2	13.8	69.9	16.1	14.0	**m**	**m**	**m**
	20-24	m	m	m	m	m	m	24.6	52.0	23.4	23.8	53.7	22.5	23.9	52.8	23.3	**m**	**m**	**m**
	25-29	m	m	m	m	m	m	12.2	66.0	21.8	12.2	67.1	20.7	12.0	66.4	21.6	**m**	**m**	**m**
	15-29	m	m	m	m	m	m	35.1	45.0	19.9	35.4	45.7	19.0	35.6	44.9	19.6	**m**	**m**	**m**
China		m	m	m	m	m	m	m	m	m	m	m	m	m	m	m	**m**	**m**	**m**
India		m	m	m	m	m	m	m	m	m	m	m	m	m	m	m	**m**	**m**	**m**
Indonesia		m	m	m	m	m	m	m	m	m	m	m	m	m	m	m	**m**	**m**	**m**
Russian Federation		m	m	m	m	m	m	m	m	m	m	m	m	m	m	m	**m**	**m**	**m**
Saudi Arabia		m	m	m	m	m	m	m	m	m	m	m	m	m	m	m	**m**	**m**	**m**
South Africa		m	m	m	m	m	m	m	m	m	m	m	m	m	m	m	**m**	**m**	**m**
G20 average		m	m	m	m	m	m	m	m	m	m	m	m	m	m	m	**m**	**m**	**m**

1.Data for 1997 (Columns 1 to 3) are available on line (see *StatLink* below).
Source: OECD. See Annex 3 for notes (*www.oecd.org/edu/eag2012*).
Please refer to the Reader's Guide for information concerning the symbols replacing missing data.
StatLink ⌨ http://dx.doi.org/10.1787/888932667520

HOW MANY ADULTS PARTICIPATE IN EDUCATION AND LEARNING?

- More than 40% of adults participate in formal and/or non-formal education in a given year across OECD countries. The proportion ranges from more than 60% in New Zealand and Sweden to less than 15% in Greece and Hungary.

- In 2007, the annual opportunity costs of employer-sponsored non-formal education represent 0.4% of the GDP in OECD countries for which information is available.

- Across OECD countries, 27% of 55-64 year-olds, but 50% of 25-34 year-olds, participate in formal and/or non-formal education. The lowest overall participation rate of 14% is found among the older cohort with a low level of education, and the highest participation rate (65%) occurs among younger persons with a tertiary education.

Chart C6.1. **Annual labour costs of employer-sponsored non-formal education as a percentage of GDP (2007)**
Employed 25-64 year-olds

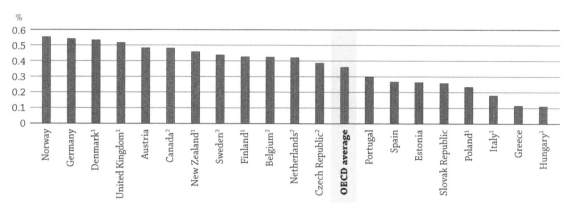

1. Year of reference 2006.
2. Year of reference 2008.
3. Year of reference 2005.
Countries are ranked in descending order of the percentage of GDP spent on the annual labour cost of employer-sponsored non-formal education.
Source: OECD. Table C6.1. See Annex 3 for notes (*www.oecd/edu/eag2012*).
StatLink ᴍꜱ￼ http://dx.doi.org/10.1787/888932663397

■ Context

Investing in education and training after initial education is essential for upgrading the skills of the labour force. Globalisation and the development of new technologies have broadened the international marketplace for goods and services. As a result, competition for skills is fierce, particularly in high-growth, high-technology markets. In order to function effectively in this context, an ever-larger segment of the population must be able to adapt to changing technologies, and to learn and apply a new set of skills tailored to meet the needs of the changing labour market.

Adult learning, as part of lifelong learning, is considered crucial for meeting the challenges of economic competitiveness and demographic change, and for combating unemployment, poverty and social exclusion, which marginalise a significant number of individuals in all countries. Increasing investment in adult learning and reducing inequity in participation are among the policy goals found in many OECD countries (Borkowsky, 2012).

◾ Other findings

- Countries with high participation rates in formal and/or non-formal education invest a relatively high percentage of GDP in employer-sponsored non-formal education and have comparatively high total expenditures on all educational institutions.

- The annual investment in employer-sponsored non-formal education per participant is substantially higher for men than for women, and it increases with the level of educational attainment in all OECD countries.

- Across OECD countries, 17% of 25-34 year-olds and 2% of 55-64 year-olds participate in formal education.

- Younger individuals and people with higher levels of education are more likely to look for information on learning activities. Whereas higher-educated people are more likely to find information when they are looking for it, the information seems to be equally accessible to older and younger individuals.

INDICATOR C6

C6

Analysis

Adult learning for older persons

Adult learning and learning strategies can support the active participation of older people in employment and society. Participation in all types of adult learning – formal, non-formal and informal – tend to decline for older people in many OECD countries (EUROSTAT, 2012; OECD/Statistics Canada, 2011; OECD/Statistics Canada, 2000). This may be due to older individuals placing less value on acquiring new skills, to employers proposing training less frequently to older workers and also to the significantly reduced amount of time (compared to younger people) to recoup the cost of investment in education. Thus, older people are among the social groups that are underrepresented among adult learners.

Participation in formal and non-formal education

Across OECD countries, an average of 8% of adults (25-64 year-olds) participate in formal education. Formal education systems still tend to cater mostly to young people. The youngest adults are much more likely to attend formal studies (17% of 25-34 year-olds) than older individuals: 8% of 35-44 year-olds, 5% of 45-54 year-olds and 2% of 55-64 year-olds are students in formal education. This pattern of lower participation in formal education in successively older cohorts is found in every OECD country. High rates of formal education participation (more than 20% of 25-34 year-olds) are found in Belgium, Denmark, Finland, New Zealand, Norway, Slovenia, Sweden and the United Kingdom. In Belgium, New Zealand, Sweden and the United Kingdom, high participation also extends to the 35-44 year-old cohort, with participation rates in formal education of 14% and higher. In the Czech Republic, Greece, Hungary and Ireland, the participation rate of adults in formal education falls earlier, dropping to 10% or below among the 25-34 year-old cohort (Table C6.5, available on line).

Is there a link between age and participation rates with respect to non-formal education as well? Across the OECD, 38% of 25-34 year-olds and 35-44 year-olds, and 24% of 55-64 year-olds, participate in non-formal education. The pattern is similar for most OECD countries – in other words, the youngest cohort has at least the same access to non-formal education opportunities as older people. Exceptions are Austria, the Czech Republic, Denmark and New Zealand, where the participation rate of the youngest cohort is at least five percentage points lower than that of the second-youngest cohort (Table C6.4b, available on line).

On average, half of the participants in formal education also participate in non-formal education. These individuals take advantage of a variety of learning opportunities.

Across the OECD, 27% of the oldest cohort (55-64 years old), but 50% of the youngest cohort (25-34 years old) participate in formal and/or non-formal education. Age and the level of educational attainment both contribute to the difference in participation in adult learning. The lowest overall participation rate of 14% is found among 55-64 year-olds with a low level of education, while the highest participation rate, 65%, is found among 25-34 year-olds with a tertiary education (Table C6.7, available on line). Among the youngest cohort, people with tertiary education are 2.2 times more likely to participate in formal and/or non-formal education than persons with low levels of education. In the 55-64 year-old cohort, highly-educated people are 3.3 times more likely to participate in formal and/or non-formal education than less-educated people. This increased inequity between individuals with different educational attainment levels in the oldest cohort is found in all OECD countries.

In countries with a low participation rate in formal and/or non-formal education, the inequity in participation between educational groups grows with advancing age (correlation = -0.70). The difference between the youngest and the oldest cohort in the relative advantage of persons with tertiary education is highest (more than five times more likely to participate in formal and/or non-formal education) in Greece, Hungary and Poland and lowest (less than 0.5 times more likely) in New Zealand, the Slovak Republic, Sweden and the United Kingdom (Table C6.7 available on line).

Participation in non-formal education

The pattern and extent of the decline in participation in non-formal education with age varies across countries (Table C6.4a). On average across OECD countries, the youngest age group, which has a participation rate in non-formal education of 37%, is 1.6 times more likely to participate than the oldest age group, with a participation rate of 23%. In Sweden, the participation rate of the older cohort reaches 60%, and it is also higher than 35% in Finland, Norway, Switzerland and the United States. The participation rate is less than 15% in Greece, Hungary, Ireland, Italy, Poland, Portugal and Turkey. The lower the participation rate of older people, the greater the relative advantage of the younger cohort (Chart C6.2).

Chart C6.2.   **Participation in non-formal education, by age group (2007)**

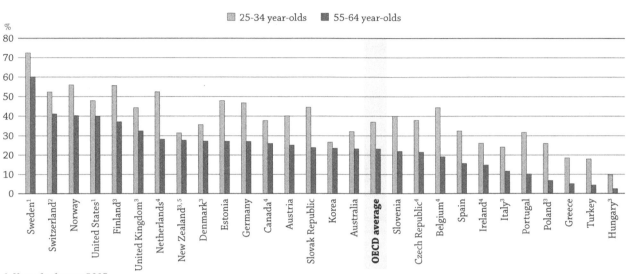

1. Year of reference 2005.
2. Year of reference 2009.
3. Year of reference 2006.
4. Year of reference 2008.
5. Excludes adults who participated only in "short seminars, lectures, workshops or special talks".
Countries are ranked in descending order of the participation rate of 55-64 year-olds (2007).
Source: OECD. Table C6.4a. See Annex 3 for notes (*www.oecd.org/edu/eag2012*).
StatLink http://dx.doi.org/10.1787/888932663416

On average across OECD countries, non-formal education is slightly less workplace-centred for the older cohort than for younger persons: 76% of the 55-64 year-old and 84% of the 25-34 year-old participants in non-formal education receive job-related training or non-formal education for both job-related and for personal reasons. However, the eight percentage-point difference in the OECD averages hides substantial differences between countries. In Austria, Belgium, Ireland, the Netherlands and Turkey, the difference in job-related non-formal education participants between 25-34 year-olds and 55-64 year-olds is 20 percentage points or more, and the non-formal education of the older people is much less workplace focused. In Estonia, Norway, Hungary, the Slovak Republic and the United States, the difference between the age groups is minimal, varying by + or – 3 percentage points or less. There is even slightly more work-centred non-formal education for the older cohort in the Czech Republic and Poland (Table C6.4a).

The time an individual spends in non-formal education activities represents an investment in the individual's skill development for both the employer and the individual. The less work-focused nature of non-formal education for the older cohort is also reflected in the hours of instruction received. Across OECD countries, a participant in non-formal education receives 76 hours of instruction annually. Four out of five of these hours are job-related (Table C6.8, available on line). Among 55-64 year-olds, these averages drop to 65 hours of instruction in all non-formal education, and 40 hours of instruction in job-related non-formal education. For this age group, only two out of three instruction hours are job-related. Participants who are 25-34 years old receive 88 hours of instruction in total, and 70 hours of instruction in job-related non-formal education.

C6

In all OECD countries, the oldest cohort (55-64 year-olds) receives fewer hours of instruction in job-related non-formal education than the population (Chart C6.3). The youngest cohort (25-34 year-olds) receives more such hours of instruction in a majority of 21 countries, but fewer hours in 3 countries (in these countries, the middle age cohorts receive more hours). The difference in instruction hours between the youngest and the oldest cohort amount to more than 30 hours in Belgium, Hungary, Korea and the United Kingdom, and less than 10 hours in Estonia, New Zealand, Poland, Switzerland and the United States (Table C6.8, available on line).

Chart C6.3.   Ratio of mean hours per participant of job-related non-formal education, by age group, to total population (25-64 year-olds) (2007)

■ 25-34 year-olds   ■ 55-64 year-olds

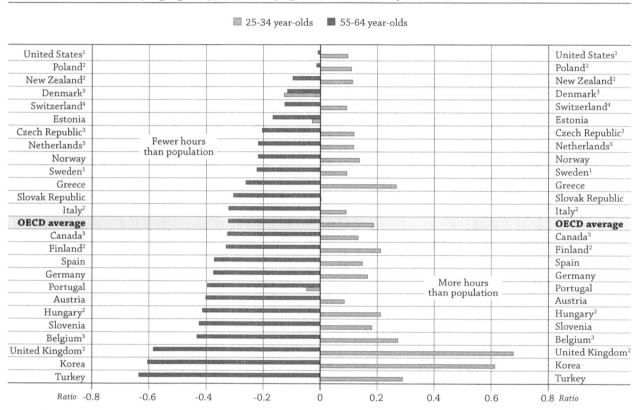

1. Year of reference 2005.
2. Year of reference 2006.
3. Year of reference 2008.
4. Year of reference 2009.

Countries are ranked in descending order of the ratio for 55-64 year-olds.

Source: OECD, Table C6.8, available on line. See Annex 3 for notes (*www.oecd.org/edu/eag2012*).
StatLink ⬛⬛⬛ http://dx.doi.org/10.1787/888932663435

Seeking information and guidance

Effective information and counselling services can help make education and training more accessible to a wider range of people, support learning at all ages, and empower citizens to manage their learning and work. Reaching out to information- and assistance-deprived groups is especially important.

To measure the size of the population outside the education and training system and the information and guidance system, this section looks at the percentage of adults who have not participated in formal and/or non-formal education, and who have not looked for any information concerning learning possibilities within the 12 months prior to being surveyed. Older persons are much more likely to be in this situation than younger persons: 69% among the 55-64 year-olds, compared to 39% of the 25-34 year-olds. In Greece, Hungary, Italy, Poland and Portugal, more than 80% of 55-64 year-olds remain at a distance from adult learning and information and guidance, while less than 50% are in the Netherlands and Sweden (see OECD, 2010, Table C4.2).

Looking for information is an important step towards participating in adult learning. Individuals who have looked for information are twice as likely to participate in formal and/or non-formal education as those who do not. On average, 28% of 25-64 year-olds looked for information on non-formal learning, while 15% of 55-64 year-olds and 38% of 25-34 year-olds did (Table C6.10). On the country level, there is a positive relationship between the rate of participation in adult learning and the rate of individuals looking for information. Independent of the extent to which they are consulted, information systems seem to be mostly successful.

Box C6.1. **Participation in Adult Learning for 65-74 year-olds**

In an ageing society, individuals increasingly need to stay in employment well into their sixties or seventies. Using, updating and acquiring skills remains important into retirement age as a means to promote active citizenship and social participation beyond the workplace.

In 2007, the participation of 65-74 year-olds in formal and/or non-formal learning ranged from more than 20% in the United Kingdom and the United States to 4% in Spain. In all six countries for which data are available, older women participate more often in formal and/or non-formal education than men of the same age (Table C6.11). The steady decline in the participation rate observed for the younger age groups continues for the 55-64 year-olds (Tables C6.7 and C6.11) although not at the same rate for all countries. In the United Kingdom and the United States, the age groups differ least in their participation rates and the participation rate of 55-64 year-olds is relatively high. The drop in participation rates from one age group to the next is largest in countries where the participation rate of the younger elderly is low, as in Spain and Ireland.

In all six countries, older persons with tertiary education participate in formal and/or non-formal education more often than those with low levels of education. In Australia, Germany, Ireland and the United Kingdom, the relative advantage of people with tertiary education is higher for the oldest age group than for the next youngest age group (see chart below). The impact of educational attainment on participation rates is weaker for the young elderly in Spain and the United States.

Percentage of 55-64 year-olds and 65-74 year-olds who have participated in formal and/or non-formal education, by educational attainment (2007)

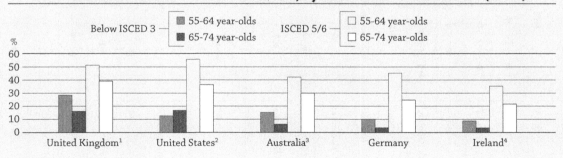

1. Year of reference 2006.
2. Year of reference 2005.
3. The data for 55-64 year-olds and 65-74 year-olds are from different survey sources.
4. Year of reference 2008.
Countries are ranked in descending order of the participation rate of 65-74 year-olds with tertiary education.
Source: OECD. Table C6.11. See Annex 3 for notes (*www.oecd.org/edu/eag2012*).
StatLink ᐧᓵᔥᒍ http://dx.doi.org/10.1787/888932663492

In all countries with comparable data, younger adults seek information more often than older adults. In Greece and Hungary, young people are five times more likely to look for information about educational opportunities than older people, while in Australia, the Netherlands and the Slovak Republic, 25-34 year-olds are no more than two times more likely to do so. However, older people were just as successful in finding information as younger ones (Table C6.10, available on line).

Financial investment in adult learning

Financial investments in adult learning include direct expenditures as well as opportunity costs. At present, there is no OECD-wide information on direct expenditures for adult education. The main opportunity costs consist of the costs of working time devoted to learning instead of productive work, and the foregone earnings of persons who devote time to learning instead of working for pay. The opportunity costs due to the lost productive time of workers attending employer-sponsored non-formal education can be estimated by using a measure of labour cost and taking into account the educational attainment levels, age group and gender of participants. The educational attainment "catches" the effects of the different participation rates and volumes of employees according to industry, occupation and full-time/part-time work – all factors which also affect labour costs.

Chart C6.1 shows the total annual cost of the working time devoted to employer-sponsored non-formal education as a percentage of GDP. On average, 0.4% of GDP is invested in this part of non-formal education. The investment ranges from more than 0.5% in Denmark, Germany, Norway and the United Kingdom to less than 0.2% in Greece, Hungary and Italy. In 2009, OECD countries spent on average 6.2% of GDP on educational institutions (see Indicator B2). The investment in employer-sponsored non-formal education and the total expenditure for educational institutions are positively related (correlation = 0.52). The investment in employer-sponsored non-formal education and the overall participation rate in formal and/or non-formal education by adults are also positively related (correlation = 0.75).

Chart C6.4.   **Annual labour costs of employer-sponsored non-formal education
as a percentage of annual labour costs (2007)**
Employed 25-64 year-olds, by educational attainment

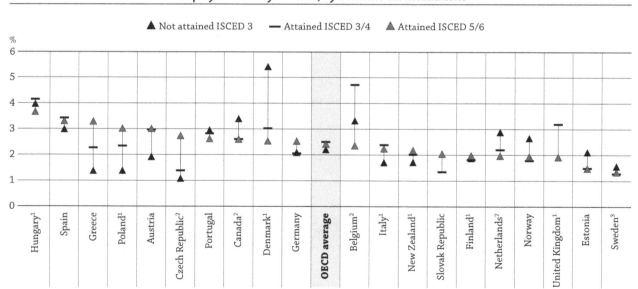

1. Year of reference 2006.
2. Year of reference 2008.
3. Year of reference 2005.
Countries are ranked in descending order of the annual labour costs of persons who have attained ISCED level 5/6.
Source: OECD. Table C6.1. See Annex 3 for notes (*www.oecd.org/edu/eag2012*).
StatLink ⟶ http://dx.doi.org/10.1787/888932663454

In 2007, the annual cost of the working time devoted to employer-sponsored non-formal education per participant amounted to USD 931. This represents 2.4% of the average annual labour cost of a worker. The cost increases from USD 659 for people with a low level of educational attainment, to 866 USD for persons with a middle level of education, to USD 1 235 for workers with high levels of education (Table C6.1). Investment by employers in non-formal education for men is USD 1 087, substantially higher than the figure for women, USD 726 (Table C6.2a, available on line). In the majority of OECD countries, employers invest more in the non-formal education of each participant with a high level of education than in participants with a low level of education. Exceptions are Canada and Denmark, where more investment goes to each participant with a low level of education. The differences in investment according to the educational level of the participants are small in Estonia, Finland, the Netherlands, Norway and Sweden (Chart C6.4).

The expected total cost of working time devoted to employer-sponsored non-formal education over the working life of a person can be estimated using the synthetic cohort method. In the OECD average, the resulting estimate amounts to one year of the annual labour cost of an employed person (Table C6.3). Even though the estimated amount in USD increases with each level of educational attainment, the ratio to the annual labour cost of a worker declines, since the annual labour cost increases more. In each country, the estimated amount invested by employers in men's non-formal education is higher than the amount for women. The annual labour costs are higher for men than for women in each country (see Indicator A10 in OECD, 2010), but the estimated total number of hours in employer-sponsored non-formal education are higher for women than for men in the Czech Republic, Denmark, Finland, Hungary, Portugal and Spain. In the same countries, the ratio of the expected cost of the working time devoted to employer-sponsored non-formal education over the working life to the annual labour cost is higher for women than for men (Chart C6.5).

Chart C6.5. **Ratio of expected cost of working time devoted to employer-sponsored non-formal education to annual labour cost over the working life (2007)**
In equivalent USD converted using PPPs, for employed 25-64 year-olds, by gender

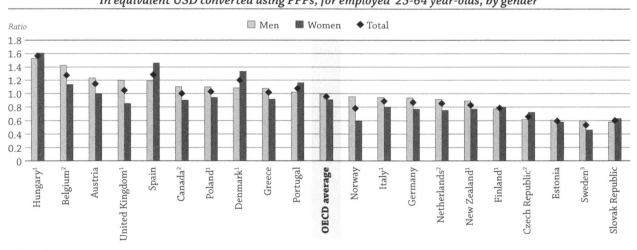

1. Year of reference 2006.
2. Year of reference 2008.
3. Year of reference 2005.
Countries are ranked in descending order of the ratio for men.
Source: OECD. Table C6.3. See Annex 3 for notes (*www.oecd.org/edu/eag2012*).
StatLink ᴍˢᴾ http://dx.doi.org/10.1787/888932663473

Definitions

Formal education is defined as education provided in the system of schools, colleges, universities and other formal educational institutions, and which normally constitutes a continuous "ladder" of full-time education for children and young people.

C6

Non-formal education is defined as an organised and sustained educational activity that does not correspond exactly to the above definition of formal education. Non-formal education may therefore take place both within and outside educational institutions and cater to individuals of all ages. Depending on country contexts, it may cover educational programmes in adult literacy, basic education for out-of-school children, life skills, work skills, and general culture. The EU Adult Education Survey uses an extensive list of possible non-formal education activities, including courses, private lessons and guided on-the-job training to prompt respondents to list all of their learning activities during the previous 12 months. Some of these learning activities might be of short duration.

Low levels of education attained refers to individuals not having attained ISCED level 3.

Middle levels of education attained refers to individuals having attained ISCED levels 3 and/or 4.

High levels of education attained refers to individuals having attained ISCED levels 5 and/or 6.

Methodology

Data for non-European countries were calculated from country-specific household surveys (see Annex 3). Data for countries in the European Statistical System come from the pilot EU Adult Education Survey (AES). The EU AES was conducted by 29 countries in the EU, EFTA and candidate countries between 2005 and 2008. The EU AES is a pilot exercise using a common framework, including a standard questionnaire, tools and quality reporting.

Indicator C6 shows three tables with information on the costs of working time devoted to employer-sponsored non-formal education (NFE) in equivalent USD using the PPP (purchasing power parity) conversion factor for local currencies. A first step in these calculations is the calculation of the hourly cost of working time. Indicator A10 in OECD, 2010 gives the annual labour cost for persons of a given educational attainment level and gender/age group in equivalent USD using the average exchange rate (2007-09) as the conversion factor. The hourly labour cost is calculated using the information on the average hours worked in a country published as part of the OECD labour statistics and also published as part of Indicator C5 in OECD, 2011. The hourly labour cost in equivalent USD using the average exchange rate (2007-09) as the conversion factor is converted into equivalent USD using PPP as the conversion factor. The two conversion factors are published in OECD, 2011, in Tables X2.1 and X2.2.

The formula is:

$$HOUR\_LAB\_COST\_PPP = ANN\_LAB\_COST\_AXR / ANN\_HOURS * AV\_EX\_07\_09/PPP\_09$$

Where:

HOUR_LAB_COST_PPP: Hourly labour cost in equivalent USD using the ppp conversion factor

ANN_LAB_COST_AXR: Annual labour cost using the average exchange rate as conversion factor (see Indicator A10 in *Education at a Glance 2010*: Table A10.1)

ANN_HOURS: average hours worked per country (for full-time employment) (see Indicator C5 in OECD, 2011, Table C5.1a)

AV_EX_07_09: average exchange rate local currency to USD 2007-2009 (OECD, 2011, Table X2.1)

PPP_09: purchasing power parity for local currency to USD (*Education at a Glance 2011:* Table X2.2)

The annual cost of employer-sponsored NFE per participant is calculated as the average number of hours in employer-sponsored NFE multiplied with the hourly cost of the labour.

The estimate of the expected cost of employer-sponsored NFE over a working life is based on the fictive cohort method. The method results in an estimate of the total number of hours devoted to employer-sponsored NFE, which is then multiplied with the hourly labour cost. (A more detailed description of the method can be found in the section *Methodology* for Indicator C5 in OECD, 2011.)

The statistical data for Israel are supplied by and under the responsibility of the relevant Israeli authorities. The use of such data by the OECD is without prejudice to the status of the Golan Heights, East Jerusalem and Israeli settlements in the West Bank under the terms of international law.

References

Borkowsky, A. (2012), *Monitoring Adult Learning Policies: A Theoretical Framework and Indicators*, OECD Publishing.

EUROSTAT (2012), *Database: Custom tables Adult Education Survey*, Retrieved 12-04-2012 *http://appsso. eurostat.ec.europa.eu/nui/submitViewTableAction.do*

OECD (2010), *Education at a Glance 2010: OECD Indicators*, OECD Publishing.

OECD (2011), *Education at a Glance 2011: OECD Indicators*, OECD Publishing.

OECD/Statistics Canada (2000), *Literacy in the Information Age: Final Report of the International Adult Literacy Survey*, OECD Publishing.

OECD/Statistics Canada (2011), *Literacy for Life: Further Results from the Adult Literacy and Life Skills Survey*, OECD Publishing.

The following additional material relevant to this indicator is available on line:

- *Table C6.2a. Annual labour cost of employer-sponsored non-formal education by gender and educational attainment (2007)*
  StatLink ᴹˢ⁴ http://dx.doi.org/10.1787/888932667615

- *Table C6.2b. Annual labour cost of employer-sponsored non-formal education by age group and educational attainment (2007)*
  StatLink ᴹˢ⁴ http://dx.doi.org/10.1787/888932667634

- *Table C6.4b. Participation in non-formal education and purpose of non-formal education, by age group (2007)*
  StatLink ᴹˢ⁴ http://dx.doi.org/10.1787/888932667691

- *Table C6.5. Participation in formal and non-formal education, by age group (2007)*
  StatLink ᴹˢ⁴ http://dx.doi.org/10.1787/888932667710

- *Table C6.6. Participation in formal and/or non-formal education, by gender and age group (2007)*
  StatLink ᴹˢ⁴ http://dx.doi.org/10.1787/888932667729

- *Table C6.7. Participation in formal and/or non-formal education, by educational attainment and age group (2007)*
  StatLink ᴹˢ⁴ http://dx.doi.org/10.1787/888932667748

- *Table C6.8. Mean number of hours per participant and per adult, by purpose of non-formal education, gender and age group (2007)*
  StatLink ᴹˢ⁴ http://dx.doi.org/10.1787/888932667767

- *Table C6.9. Adults who have not participated in formal/non-formal education and have not looked for information, by age group (2007)*
  StatLink ᴹˢ⁴ http://dx.doi.org/10.1787/888932667786

- *Table C6.10. Rate of persons who have looked for and found information about formal/non-formal education, by age group (2007)*
  StatLink ᴹˢ⁴ http://dx.doi.org/10.1787/888932667805

C6

Table C6.1. Total annual labour costs of employer-sponsored non-formal education and annual costs per participant (2007)

In millions equivalent USD converted using PPPs for employed 25-64 year-olds

	Total annual labour cost of employer-sponsored non-formal education	Percentage of GDP	Not attained ISCED 3		Attained ISCED 3/4		Attained ISCED 5/6		Total	
			Annual cost per participant	Percentage of annual labour cost	Annual cost per participant	Percentage of annual labour cost	Annual cost per participant	Percentage of annual labour cost	Annual cost per participant	Percentage of annual labour cost
	(1)	(2)	(3)	(4)	(5)	(6)	(7)	(8)	(9)	(10)
Austria	1 568	0.48	615	1.9	1 363	3.0	1 938	3.0	1 435	2.9
Belgium[1]	1 589	0.42	1 233	3.3	1 963	4.7	1 309	2.4	1 512	3.2
Canada[1]	5 659	0.48	1 103	3.4	1 014	2.6	1 414	2.6	1 227	2.6
Czech Republic[1]	953	0.39	206	1.1	368	1.4	1 482	2.7	519	1.7
Denmark[2]	1 064	0.53	1 718	5.4	1 036	3.0	1 126	2.5	1 149	3.1
Estonia	75	0.26	373	2.1	284	1.5	365	1.5	319	1.5
Finland[2]	779	0.43	672	1.9	661	1.8	960	2.0	794	1.9
Germany	15 793	0.54	868	2.1	924	2.1	1 768	2.5	1 191	2.2
Greece	346	0.11	348	1.4	709	2.3	1 570	3.3	917	2.7
Hungary[2]	204	0.11	539	4.0	762	4.1	1 373	3.7	894	4.0
Italy[2]	3 300	0.18	644	1.7	1 138	2.4	1 688	2.2	1 086	2.3
Netherlands[1]	2 850	0.42	1 168	2.9	1 032	2.2	1 376	2.0	1 158	2.2
New Zealand[2]	525	0.46	471	1.7	679	2.0	869	2.2	715	2.1
Norway	1 045	0.55	1 114	2.7	869	1.8	1 159	1.9	1 029	2.0
Poland[2]	1 474	0.23	131	1.4	348	2.3	796	3.0	461	2.6
Portugal	710	0.30	529	3.0	805	2.8	1 404	2.6	702	2.8
Slovak Republic	324	0.26	c	c	257	1.3	684	2.0	344	1.5
Spain	3 684	0.27	804	3.0	1 082	3.4	1 405	3.3	1 111	3.3
Sweden[3]	1 518	0.44	635	1.6	556	1.3	712	1.3	618	1.3
United Kingdom[2]	10 542	0.52	c	c	1 470	3.2	1 302	1.9	1 448	2.7
OECD average		0.36	659	2.2	866	2.5	1 235	2.4	931	2.4
EU21 average		0.35	617	2.2	868	2.5	1 251	2.5	921	2.5

1. Year of reference 2008.
2. Year of reference 2006.
3. Year of reference 2005.
Source: OECD, LSO Network special data collection, Adult Learning Working Group.
Please refer to the Reader's Guide for information concerning the symbols replacing missing data.
StatLink http://dx.doi.org/10.1787/888932667596

Table C6.3. Expected cost of working time devoted to employer-sponsored non-formal education over the working life and ratio to annual labour cost (2007)

In equivalent USD converted using PPPs for employed 25-64 year-olds

	Not attained ISCED 3		Attained ISCED 3/4		Attained ISCED 5/6		Total		Men		Women	
	Total estimated cost	Ratio to annual labour cost	Total estimated cost	Ratio to annual labour cost	Total estimated cost	Ratio to annual labour cost	Total estimated cost	Ratio to annual labour cost	Total estimated cost	Ratio to annual labour cost	Total estimated cost	Ratio to annual labour cost
	(1)	(2)	(3)	(4)	(5)	(6)	(7)	(8)	(9)	(10)	(11)	(12)
Austria	29 332	0.9	53 028	1.2	76 466	1.2	55 985	1.1	66 220	1.2	39 235	1.0
Belgium[1]	38 334	1.0	82 359	2.0	49 381	0.9	60 619	1.3	72 149	1.4	46 656	1.1
Canada[1]	44 890	1.4	39 759	1.0	54 242	1.0	47 356	1.0	59 111	1.1	33 962	0.9
Czech Republic[1]	7 868	0.4	14 496	0.5	57 656	1.1	20 276	0.7	21 000	0.6	17 837	0.7
Denmark[2]	66 229	2.1	39 103	1.1	44 492	1.0	44 098	1.2	43 374	1.1	42 685	1.3
Estonia	14 067	0.8	11 281	0.6	14 070	0.6	12 443	0.6	15 382	0.6	9 757	0.6
Finland[2]	29 206	0.8	28 406	0.8	38 826	0.8	32 739	0.8	36 294	0.8	29 049	0.8
Germany	34 118	0.8	34 739	0.8	72 633	1.0	46 357	0.9	54 041	0.9	33 948	0.8
Greece	13 852	0.5	24 169	0.8	60 810	1.3	34 510	1.0	40 434	1.1	25 286	0.9
Hungary[2]	30 954	2.3	27 994	1.5	53 487	1.4	35 235	1.6	37 127	1.5	33 343	1.6
Italy[2]	25 700	0.7	44 812	0.9	66 451	0.9	42 708	0.9	50 122	0.9	31 527	0.8
Netherlands[1]	42 421	1.0	41 773	0.9	53 911	0.8	45 824	0.9	51 674	0.9	32 897	0.8
New Zealand[2]	19 147	0.7	28 100	0.8	33 979	0.9	28 545	0.8	33 924	0.9	22 887	0.8
Norway	41 038	1.0	34 809	0.7	45 377	0.8	40 208	0.8	54 740	1.0	25 316	0.6
Poland[2]	5 608	0.6	13 490	0.9	30 968	1.2	17 885	1.0	20 788	1.1	14 500	0.9
Portugal	20 514	1.1	27 681	1.0	53 632	1.0	26 806	1.1	27 932	1.0	25 245	1.2
Slovak Republic	3 760	0.3	9 961	0.5	26 909	0.8	13 391	0.6	14 732	0.6	11 758	0.6
Spain	30 902	1.1	46 045	1.5	54 451	1.3	43 831	1.3	43 105	1.2	44 281	1.5
Sweden[3]	26 605	0.7	22 342	0.5	27 958	0.5	24 673	0.5	29 784	0.6	18 740	0.5
United Kingdom[2]	90 036	2.6	57 252	1.2	50 687	0.7	56 095	1.0	69 723	1.2	38 788	0.9
OECD average	30 729	1.0	34 080	1.0	48 319	1.0	36 479	1.0	42 083	1.0	28 885	0.9
EU21 average	30 586	1.0	34 097	1.0	48 787	1.0	36 316	1.0	41 590	1.0	28 936	0.9

1. Year of reference 2008.
2. Year of reference 2006.
3. Year of reference 2005.
Source: OECD, LSO Network special data collection, Adult Learning Working Group.
Please refer to the Reader's Guide for information concerning the symbols replacing missing data.
StatLink http://dx.doi.org/10.1787/888932667653

C6

Table C6.4a. Participation in non-formal education and purpose of non-formal education, for 25-34 and 55-64 year-olds (2007)

	Participation rate		25-34 year-olds			55-64 year-olds			Ratio of participants in job-related NFE	
	25-34	55-64	Mainly job-related	Both job-related and personal	Mainly for personal reasons	Mainly job-related	Both job-related and personal	Mainly for personal reasons	25-34 [(3)+(4)]/(1)	55-64 [(6)+(7)]/(2)
	(1)	(2)	(3)	(4)	(5)	(6)	(7)	(8)	(9)	(10)
Australia	32	23	26	m	5	14	m	8	0.80	0.62
Austria	40	25	26	6	7	13	c	10	0.80	0.58
Belgium[1]	44	19	35	5	4	11	c	7	0.91	0.63
Canada[1]	38	26	32	m	3	19	m	6	0.84	0.73
Czech Republic[1]	38	22	28	6	4	17	3	1	0.90	0.95
Denmark[2]	36	27	23	10	3	13	10	c	0.90	0.86
Estonia	48	27	41	c	5	23	c	c	0.90	0.90
Finland[2]	56	37	40	8	7	22	5	10	0.86	0.72
Germany	47	27	36	5	5	18	2	6	0.88	0.76
Greece	19	5	15	c	2	4	c	c	0.87	0.75
Hungary[2]	10	2	7	c	2	2	c	c	0.78	0.77
Ireland[1]	26	15	23	m	3	8	m	6	0.89	0.56
Italy[2]	24	12	5	11	4	2	5	2	0.67	0.60
Korea	27	24	8	c	14	7	c	16	0.49	0.33
Netherlands[1]	52	28	39	8	5	16	4	8	0.89	0.70
New Zealand[2, 3]	31	28	24	m	7	19	m	9	0.78	0.68
Norway	56	40	44	7	4	33	c	4	0.92	0.90
Poland[2]	26	7	20	2	4	6	c	1	0.83	0.88
Portugal	32	10	24	2	6	7	c	3	0.81	0.74
Slovak Republic	45	24	36	4	5	21	c	c	0.89	0.92
Slovenia	40	22	24	3	13	10	c	11	0.68	0.50
Spain	33	16	22	2	8	8	c	7	0.74	0.57
Sweden[4]	72	60	44	19	9	39	10	11	0.87	0.81
Switzerland[5]	52	41	39	6	7	26	5	10	0.85	0.74
Turkey	18	4	11	3	4	2	c	2	0.74	0.49
United Kingdom[2]	44	32	22	14	5	14	6	8	0.80	0.61
United States[4]	48	40	23	10	12	19	8	12	0.70	0.68
OECD average	37	23	26	5	6	15	3	7	0.84	0.76
EU21 average	38	22	27	6	5	13	3	5	0.85	0.73

1. Year of reference 2008.
2. Year of reference 2006.
3. Excludes adults who participated only in "short seminars, lectures, workshops or special talks".
4. Year of reference 2005.
5. Year of reference 2009.
Source: OECD, LSO Network special data collection on adult learning activities, Adult Learning Working Group.
Please refer to the Reader's Guide for information concerning the symbols replacing missing data.
StatLink ᵐˢᴸ http://dx.doi.org/10.1787/888932667672

Table C6.11. **Percentage of 55-64 year-olds and 65-74 year-olds who have participated in formal and/or non-formal education (2007)**

Participation rate by educational attainment and gender

	Age group	Not attained ISCED 3	Attained ISCED 3/4	Attained ISCED 5/6	Men	Women	Total
		(1)	(2)	(3)	(4)	(5)	(6)
Australia[1]	65-74	6	9	30	9	14	11
	55-64	15	28	42	25	26	25
	Relative advantage of younger age group	2.5	3.0	1.4	2.9	1.8	2.2
Germany	65-74	4	14	25	13	14	13
	55-64	10	27	45	30	27	28
	Relative advantage of younger age group	2.8	1.9	1.8	2.4	1.9	2.1
Ireland[2]	65-74	4	11	22	6	10	8
	55-64	9	17	35	15	16	16
	Relative advantage of younger age group	2.5	1.6	1.6	2.7	1.7	2.0
Spain	65-74	3	7	9	3	5	4
	55-64	11	26	40	17	17	17
	Relative advantage of younger age group	3.5	3.4	4.2	6.5	3.3	4.3
United Kingdom[3]	65-74	16	16	39	20	24	22
	55-64	28	39	51	33	41	37
	Relative advantage of younger age group	1.8	2.4	1.3	1.7	1.7	1.7
United States[4,5]	65-74	17	20	36	21	29	25
	55-64	13	31	56	33	47	40
	Relative advantage of younger age group	0.8	1.6	1.5	1.6	1.6	1.6

1. The data for 55-64 year-olds and 65-74 year-olds are from different survey sources.
2. Year of reference 2008.
3. Year of reference 2006.
4. Year of reference 2005.
5. Category "Attained ISCED 3/4" excludes persons with attainment at ISCED level 4.
Source: OECD, LSO Network special data collection on adult learning activities, Adult Learning Working Group.
Please refer to the Reader's Guide for information concerning the symbols replacing missing data.
StatLink ⬛ᵐˢ🔗 http://dx.doi.org/10.1787/888932667824

Chapter

The Learning Environment and Organisation of Schools

HOW MUCH TIME DO STUDENTS SPEND IN THE CLASSROOM?

■ Students in OECD countries are expected to receive an average of 6 862 hours of instruction between the ages of 7 and 14, and most of that intended instruction time is compulsory.

■ On average across OECD countries, instruction in reading, writing and literature, mathematics and science represents 55% of the compulsory instruction time for 7-8 year-olds, 47% of the compulsory instruction time for 9-11 year-olds and 41% for 12-14 year-olds.

Chart D1.1. **Total number of intended instruction hours in public institutions between the ages of 7 and 14 (2010)**

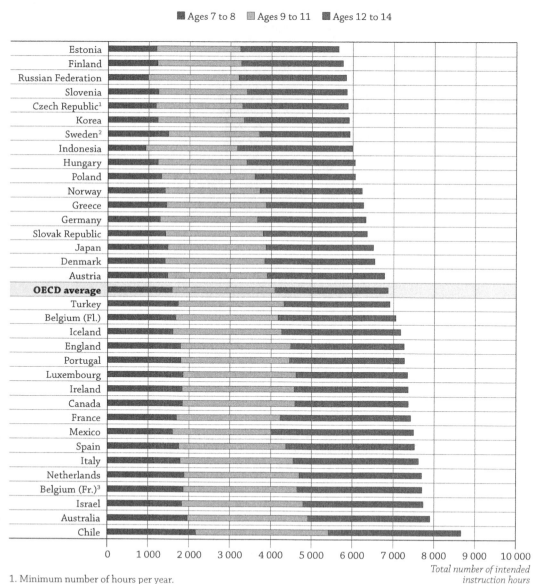

1. Minimum number of hours per year.
2. Estimated because breakdown by age is not available.
3. "Ages 12-14" covers ages 12-13 only.
Countries are ranked in ascending order of the total number of intended instruction hours.
Source: OECD. Table D1.1. See Annex 3 for notes (*www.oecd.org/edu/eag2012*).
StatLink ⓘⓢ⫴ http://dx.doi.org/10.1787/888932663511

Context

Providing instruction in formal classroom settings accounts for a large portion of public investment in student learning and is a central component of schooling. The amount of instruction time and after-school lessons available to students are important indicators of students' opportunities to learn. Matching resources with students' needs and making optimal use of time are central to education policy. Teachers' salaries, institutional maintenance and provision of other educational resources constitute the main costs of education. The length of time during which these resources are made available to students (as partly shown in this indicator) is thus an important factor in determining how funds for education are allocated (see Indicator B7).

INDICATOR D1

Countries make various choices concerning the overall amount of time devoted to instruction and which subjects are compulsory. These choices reflect national and/or regional priorities and preferences concerning what material students should be taught and at what age. Countries usually have statutory or regulatory requirements regarding hours of instruction. These are most often stipulated as the minimum number of hours of instruction a school must offer and are based on the notion that sufficient teaching time is required for good learning outcomes.

Other findings

- In OECD countries, **compulsory instruction time** for 7-8 year-old students averages 774 hours per year and **intended instruction time** averages 790 hours per year. Students aged 9 to 11 receive, on average, about 47 more hours of compulsory education per year than 7-8 year-olds, while students aged 12 to 14 receive about 78 more hours per year than 9-11 year-olds. Students aged 9 to 11 receive just over 48 more hours of intended instruction per year than 7-8 year-olds, and students aged 12 to 14 receive 84 more hours per year than 9-11 year-olds.

- **The proportion of the compulsory curriculum that is devoted to reading, writing and literature varies widely.** For 7-8 year-olds, it ranges from 20% in Iceland to 45% in Denmark, for 9-11 year-olds, it ranges from 13% in England to 32% in the Netherlands, and for 12-14 year-olds it ranges from 11% in Japan and Portugal to 26% in Ireland.

- The **allocation of time for the different subjects** within the compulsory curriculum for 7-8 year-olds and 12-14 year-olds varies less among countries than it does for 9-11 year-olds.

- In OECD countries, the **flexible part of the curriculum** accounts for some 6% of compulsory instruction time for 7-8 year-olds and 9-11 year-olds and 7% for 12-14 year-olds.

- **Decisions about the organisation of instruction are predominantly taken by schools**, while decisions about instruction time are made at the state or central level.

- **Decisions about programmes of study and learning resources are largely decided at the state or central level** or at the school level, but within a centrally established framework.

D1

Analysis

Total intended instruction time

Total intended instruction time is an estimate of the number of hours during which students are taught both compulsory and non-compulsory parts of the curriculum as per public regulations.

On average, students between the ages of 7 and 8 in OECD countries are expected to receive 1 580 hours of instruction, those between the ages of 9 and 11 are expected to receive 2 515 hours, and those between the ages of 12 and 14 are expected to receive 2 767 hours. Most of this instruction time is compulsory (Table D1.1).

While the average intended instruction time for students in OECD countries between the ages of 7 and 14 is 6 862 hours, formal teaching-time requirements range from 5 644 hours in Estonia to 8 664 hours in Chile. During these hours, schools are obliged to offer instruction in compulsory and non-compulsory subjects.

Annual instruction time should be examined together with the length of compulsory education. In some countries with a heavier student workload, compulsory education covers fewer years and students leave the school system earlier; in other countries, a more even distribution of workload and study time over more years ultimately means a larger number of total instruction hours for all. Table D1.1 shows the age range at which over 90% of the population is in education (see Indicator C1). Chart D1.1 shows the total amount of intended instruction time students should receive between the ages of 7 and 14. Intended instruction time does not capture the quality of learning opportunities provided or the level or quality of the human and material resources involved (see Indicator D2, which shows the number of teachers relative to the student population).

In some countries, intended instruction time varies considerably among regions or types of schools. In many countries, although decisions about the organisation of instruction are predominantly taken by school authorities, decisions about instruction time are made by central and state authorities (Table D1.3, available on line). Intended instruction time can also differ from the actual instruction time, as it only captures the time spent by students in formal classroom settings. This is only a part of the total time students spend receiving instruction. Instruction also occurs outside the classroom and/or school. In some countries, secondary school students are encouraged to take after-school classes in subjects already taught in school to help them improve their performance in key subjects. Students can take part in after-school lessons in the form of remedial "catch-up" classes or enrichment courses, with individual tutors or in group lessons provided by school teachers, or other independent courses. These lessons can be financed publically, or can be financed by students and their families (see Box D1.1, *Education at a Glance 2011*). However, time may be lost because of student absences or a lack of qualified substitutes to replace absent teachers.

Compulsory instruction time

Total compulsory instruction time is the estimated number of hours during which students are taught both the compulsory core curriculum and flexible parts of the compulsory curriculum. In OECD countries, students between the ages of 7 and 14 receive an average of 6 710 hours of compulsory instruction (Table D1.1).

Intended instruction time is fully compulsory for all age groups between 7 and 14 years in Australia, Canada, Chile, the Czech Republic, Denmark, England, Estonia, Germany, Greece, Iceland, Indonesia, Ireland, Israel, Italy, Japan, Korea, Luxembourg, Mexico, the Netherlands, Norway, the Russian Federation, Slovenia, Spain and Sweden. Except for Australia, Canada, Chile, England, Iceland, Ireland, Israel, Italy, Luxembourg, Mexico, the Netherlands and Spain, the total length of intended instruction time in these countries is less than the OECD average. Intended instruction time is also fully compulsory at age 15 in these 24 countries, except in Israel, and except in Japan, for which data are missing. In France, although total intended instruction time is fully compulsory for 7-8 year-olds and 9-11 year-olds, it is not so for the older age groups as they can attend one or two non-compulsory subjects. In Finland, total intended instruction time is only fully compulsory for 7-8 year-olds.

OECD countries report an average annual total compulsory instruction time in classroom settings of 774 hours for 7-8 year-olds, 821 hours for 9-11 year-olds and 899 hours for 12-14 year-olds. Most 15-year-olds are enrolled in programmes that provide an average of 920 hours of compulsory instruction.

Instruction time in reading, writing and literature, mathematics and science

In OECD countries, 7-8 year-olds do not necessarily attend separate classes for each subject they study. Students at this age spend an average of 55% of the compulsory curriculum on three basic subjects: reading, writing and literature (30%), mathematics (18%) and science (6%). Together with the arts (12%), physical education (9%) and social studies (6%), these six study areas form the major part of the curriculum for this age group in all OECD and other G20 countries with available data. Religion, modern foreign languages, practical and vocational skills, technology and other subjects make up the remainder (13%) of the compulsory core curriculum for 7-8 year-olds (Table D1.2a and Chart D1.2a).

On average, the largest portion of the curriculum for 7-8 year-olds is devoted to reading and writing, but the differences among countries are large. For example, in Iceland, reading and writing accounts for 20% of compulsory instruction time while in Denmark, Hungary and Turkey, it accounts for 40% or more of compulsory instruction time. The variations between countries in the time spent learning science and arts are even bigger. In Denmark, Estonia, France, Germany, Greece, Ireland, Norway and Turkey, instruction in science accounts for 4% or less of instruction time; in Austria, Canada, Finland, Israel, Luxembourg, the Slovak Republic, Spain and the Russian Federation, it accounts for 8% or more of instruction time; and in Mexico instruction in science accounts for 15% of total instruction time. In Israel and Mexico, instruction in arts accounts for 6% or less of instruction time, while in Finland, it accounts for 21% of total instruction time.

Chart D1.2a. **Instruction time per subject as a percentage of total compulsory instruction time for 7-8 year-olds (2010)**

Percentage of intended instruction time devoted to various subject areas within the total compulsory curriculum

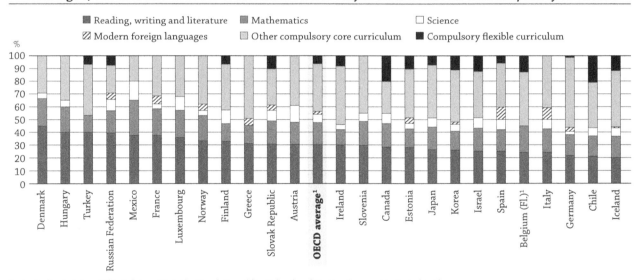

1. Australia, Belgium (Fl.), Belgium (Fr.), the Czech Republic, Poland and Portugal are not included in the average.
Countries are ranked in descending order of the proportion of intended instruction hours devoted to reading, writing and literature.
Source: OECD. Table D1.2a. See Annex 3 for notes (*www.oecd.org/edu/eag2012*).
StatLink http://dx.doi.org/10.1787/888932663530

In OECD countries, 9-11 year-olds do not necessarily attend separate classes for each subject they study. An average of 47% of the compulsory curriculum is composed of three basic subjects: reading, writing and literature (22%), mathematics (16%) and science (8%). On average, an additional 9% of the compulsory curriculum is devoted to social studies and 8% to modern foreign languages. Together with the arts (11%) and physical education (9%), these seven study areas form the major part of the curriculum for this age group in all OECD and other G20 countries with available data. Technology, religion, practical and vocational skills and other subjects make up the remainder (11%) of the compulsory core curriculum for 9-11 year-olds (Table D1.2b and Chart D1.2b).

D1

Chart D1.2b. **Instruction time per subject as a percentage of total compulsory instruction time for 9-11 year-olds (2010)**
Percentage of intended instruction time devoted to various subject areas within the total compulsory curriculum

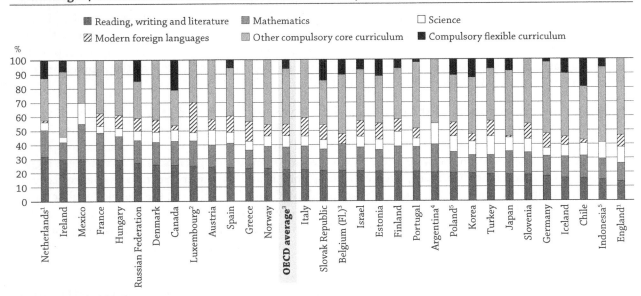

1. Includes 11-year-olds only.
2. German as a language of instruction is included in "Reading, writing and literature" in addition to the mother tongue Luxemburgish.
3. Australia, Belgium (Fl.), Belgium (Fr.) and the Czech Republic are not included in the average.
4. Year of reference 2009.
5. Includes 10-11 year-olds only.
Countries are ranked in descending order of the proportion of intended instruction hours devoted to reading, writing and literature.
Source: OECD. Argentina: UNESCO Institute for Statistics (World Education Indicators programme). Table D1.2b. See Annex 3 for notes (*www.oecd.org/edu/eag2012*).
StatLink ⟨ms⟩ http://dx.doi.org/10.1787/888932663549

There is substantial variation among countries in the allocation of time for the different subjects within the compulsory curriculum for 9-11 year-olds. For example, in England reading and writing accounts for 13% of compulsory instruction time, while in France, Ireland, Mexico and the Netherlands, it accounts for 30% or more of compulsory instruction time. There are also sizeable variations among countries in the time spent learning modern foreign languages. In Argentina, Canada, Chile, Indonesia, Japan, Mexico and the Netherlands, instruction in modern foreign languages accounts for 3% or less of instruction time; in Estonia, Germany, Greece, Israel, Italy, Poland, the Slovak Republic, Slovenia, Spain and Turkey it accounts for 10% or more of instruction time, and in Luxembourg, instruction in modern foreign languages accounts for 21% of total instruction time.

In OECD countries, an average of 41% of the compulsory curriculum for 12-14 year-olds is devoted to three subjects: reading, writing and literature (16%), mathematics (13%) and science (12%). Compared with younger age groups, a relatively larger part of the curriculum for this age group is devoted to modern foreign languages (13%) and social studies (12%), and somewhat less time is devoted to the arts (8%) and physical education (8%). Together, these seven study areas form the major part of the compulsory curriculum for lower secondary students in all OECD and other G20 countries. Technology, religion, practical and vocational skills and other subjects make up the remainder (12%) of the compulsory core curriculum for 12-14 year-olds (Table D1.2c and Chart D1.2c).

The allocation of time for the different subjects within the compulsory curriculum for 12-14 year-olds varies less among countries than it does for 9-11 year-olds. Again, one of the greatest variations is in the time spent teaching reading and writing, which ranges from 11% of compulsory instruction time in Japan and Portugal to 26% in Ireland, where reading and writing includes work in both English and Irish.

Chart D1.2c. Instruction time per subject as a percentage of total compulsory instruction time for 12-14 year-olds (2010)

Percentage of intended instruction time devoted to various subject areas within the total compulsory curriculum

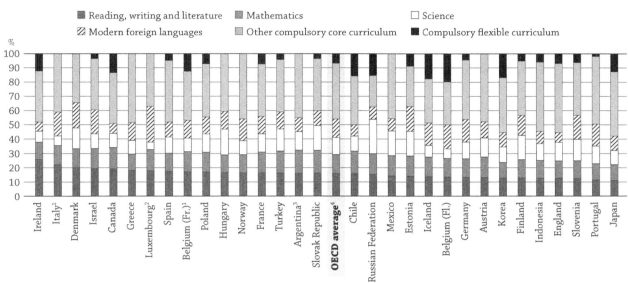

1. Includes 12-13 year-olds only.
2. German as a language of instruction is included in "Reading, writing and literature" in addition to the mother tongue Luxemburgish.
3. Year of reference 2009.
4. Australia and the Czech Republic are not included in the average.
Countries are ranked in descending order of the proportion of intended instruction hours devoted to reading, writing and literature.
Source: OECD. Argentina: UNESCO Institute for Statistics (World Education Indicators programme). Table D1.2c. See Annex 3 for notes (*www.oecd.org/edu/eag2012*).
StatLink ᐧᐧ http://dx.doi.org/10.1787/888932663568

There is also substantial variation in the proportion of compulsory instruction time devoted to particular subjects for 9-11 year-olds compared to 12-14 year-olds. On average among OECD countries, the older age group spends about one-quarter less time studying reading, writing and literature than the younger age group. Conversely, time spent on science, social studies, modern foreign languages, technology and practical and vocational skills increases with students' age. These differences are larger in some countries than in others. For example, the percentage of compulsory instruction time devoted to reading, writing and literature for 12-14 year-olds is around one-half of that for 9-11 year-olds in Austria, France, Mexico and Portugal. Yet in England, the difference is less than 6%. Chile and Italy are the only countries where the proportion of compulsory instruction time devoted to reading, writing and literature is the same for 12-14 year-olds than for 9-11 year-olds. Clearly, countries place different emphases both on subjects and on when they should be taught to students (Tables D1.2b and D1.2c).

Compulsory flexible curriculum

On average among OECD countries, the flexible part of the curriculum accounts for some 6% of compulsory instruction time for 7-8 year-olds and 9-11 year-olds and 7% for 12-14 year-olds. Within the compulsory part of the curriculum, schools, teachers and/or students have varying degrees of freedom to choose the subjects they want to teach or study. The Czech Republic allows complete flexibility (100%) in the compulsory curriculum for 7-14 year-olds and Poland allows this for 7-8 year-olds. They are followed by Australia, which allows 54% flexibility in the compulsory curriculum for 7-8 year-olds, 57% for 9-11 year-olds and 40% for 12-14 year-olds. While Belgium (Flemish Community), Canada, Chile, Iceland and Korea allow 10% or more flexibility in the compulsory curriculum for students in the three age groups, the Russian Federation allows 15% flexibility in the compulsory curriculum for 9-11 year-olds and 12-14 year-olds (Tables D1.2a, D1.2b and D1.2c).

D1

Box D1.1. **How flexible are countries' curricula?**

Canada

In Canada, each province and territory is responsible for education and for the policies and regulations related to curriculum and instruction time. The instructional time figures for Canada largely reflect the mandated minimum instruction hours in each province and territory. In most provinces and territories, the mandated hours of instruction (total intended curriculum) include hours for "compulsory flexible curriculum". The number of hours of flexible curriculum and the way flexible curriculum is administered varies across provinces and territories. In some jurisdictions, schools are free to allocate these hours to any subject they choose, including additional hours for compulsory core curriculum subjects, such as mathematics, literacy, science, etc. In other jurisdictions, compulsory flexible curriculum hours are for certain subjects only. In most provinces and territories, the compulsory flexible curriculum includes one or more elective courses. Students in junior and senior high school choose electives from selected course options (for details, see Annex 3 at *www.oecd.org/edu/eag2012*).

Chile

Schools decide whether to adopt their own curriculum, in which case they must meet a set of minimum requirements to obtain an official authorisation, or adopt the national curriculum designed by the Ministry of Education. Most schools choose to adopt the national curriculum. Within the compulsory part of the national curriculum, there is a flexible portion called "Hours of Free Provision" that must be implemented by schools. Schools can decide autonomously how to use this time in order to reach their educational goals, generally by distributing the objectives among various subjects. Nevertheless, the Ministry of Education establishes some guidelines to help schools make the best use of their flexible time.

The Czech Republic

In the Czech Republic, a binding Framework Educational Programme for Basic Education (FEP) was issued by the Ministry of Education, Youth and Sports for basic school (*základní škola*) (primary and lower secondary education combined), as well as for the lower secondary level/portion of general secondary school (gymnasium). The FEP sets the key competences, the recommended content of education, the different fields of study and cross-curricular topics (including the subjects within them and the number of compulsory hours for each subject), and the outputs of the educational areas. Based on the FEP, schools can set their own curricula for the primary and lower secondary levels of education, i.e. the school can decide how to share/divide the total number of compulsory hours per subject across each particular grade within primary and lower secondary education, as long as the outputs are achieved and the time allocated to individual educational areas/fields is maintained.

England

There is no legal requirement for the length of the school day. The governing body of each school decides when each school day should begin and end, and the length of each lesson. Schools must allow enough lesson time to deliver a broad and balanced curriculum that includes the National Curriculum and other statutory requirements. The National Curriculum prescribes programmes of study for individual subjects and specifies which subjects must be covered at each stage of compulsory education. Schools and teachers decide how to teach this most effectively and design a wider school curriculum that best meets the needs of their pupils. Academies and free schools have the freedom to design their own curriculum, but must teach English, mathematics, science and religious education.

Finland

National regulations issued by the government define the minimum total weekly lessons per year for compulsory/common subjects and voluntary studies in basic education. However, within this framework, local authorities and schools decide on the distribution of lessons in different years/classes.

...

D1

The compulsory curriculum, which is relatively flexible, may include applied and advanced studies in common subjects, modules composed of multiple subjects, optional (or voluntary) foreign languages and subjects related to information technology. In a few schools Latin is offered in upper classes. The content and objectives of optional subjects are decided by local/school authorities, as are the grade levels at which the subjects are offered. A portion of the compulsory curriculum is also flexible.

Iceland

Part of Iceland's total intended curriculum is set aside for elective subjects. A reference timetable, published in the National Curriculum Guides for Compulsory Schools, describes how schools can allocate part of the minimum instruction time stipulated in the Compulsory School Act. Schools are allowed to use part of the flexible time to supplement core subjects or support the schools' own pedagogical objectives or for instruction in areas not included in the National Curriculum Guide. A certain amount of flexible time is set aside for grades 1-4, 5-7 and 8-10. More time is set aside for the flexible curriculum in grades 8, 9 and 10, but schools are free to organise how the total time is distributed among these three grades. The school curriculum should describe how the school intends to use the flexibility allowed, in consultation with local educational authorities and parents, define and explain elective subjects on offer, and present a teaching schedule, learning materials and assessment procedures. Students may be eligible for elective credits from their school if they attend classes in music or language schools or if they participate in sports activities organised within clubs.

Poland

In 2009-10, Poland introduced a new integrated education system for 7-9 year-olds. The traditional system of teaching subjects separately was replaced by education units or activities that are context- and task-oriented and can be planned flexibly as day-long, week-long or even month-long modules. The new core curriculum for compulsory instruction, created by groups of experts appointed by the Ministry of Education, provides the minimum number of instruction hours for each compulsory educational activity (modern foreign languages, music, art, computer science and physical education) for a period of three years. For the remaining instruction hours, teachers can choose between the Polish language, social education, natural science, mathematics and/or technology (on the approval of the school head). Based on this framework, education activities are conducted according to a flexible timetable prepared by the teachers in which the duration of lessons and breaks are adjusted to the pupils' capabilities. One teacher is responsible for the education of the children in his/her class, with the exception of lessons in music, physical education, art, computer science and modern foreign languages, which can be taught by other qualified teachers. For pupils aged 7 to 14, a certain amount of additional flexible time is left to the discretion of the school principal who can allocate this time for compulsory subjects, cross-curricular pathways, remedial classes or to increase educational opportunities of gifted pupils or those with learning difficulties.

Scotland

The Scottish government formulates policy and guidance on the national curriculum; the curriculum is then planned and delivered by schools and education authorities. Flexibility is built into the guidance to allow for local innovation. Education Scotland inspects schools against the standards of the curriculum guidance and advice.

The Slovak Republic

For the first and second grades of primary, lower secondary and upper secondary education, schools create their own individual education programmes based on the framework set in the National Educational Programme. This framework includes a number of compulsory optional lessons that schools can use either as an extension of the compulsory subjects or on other subjects that are chosen and prepared by the schools themselves. Each school can thus design its education programmes to reflect the interest of its pupils.

D1

Non-compulsory instruction time

Among OECD countries, the non-compulsory part of the curriculum accounts for an average of 2% of the total compulsory instruction time for 7-8 year-olds and 9-11 year-olds, and 3% for 12-14 year-olds. Nevertheless, a considerable amount of additional non-compulsory instruction time is sometimes provided. For 7-8 year-olds, all intended instruction time is compulsory in most countries, but additional non-compulsory time accounts for as much as 20% in Turkey, 11% in Belgium (French Community) and Hungary, and 9% in Poland. For 9-11 year-olds and 12-14 year-olds, non-compulsory instruction time is a feature in Austria, Belgium (French Community), Finland, Hungary, Poland, Portugal, the Slovak Republic and Turkey. For 9-11 year-olds, it ranges from 3% or less in Portugal and the Slovak Republic to 20% in Hungary and Turkey, and for 12-14 year-olds, it ranges from 3% in Portugal and the Slovak Republic to 32% in Hungary. In Argentina and France, non-compulsory instruction time is also a feature for 12-14 year-olds (Tables D1.2a, D1.2b and D1.2c).

Level of government at which decisions about the organisation of instruction, programmes of study and learning resources are taken

The extent of authority of state, central, regional, local, and school administrators over the organisation of instruction, programmes of study and learning resources at the lower secondary level varies considerably across countries. While decisions about the organisation of instruction (i.e. assessment of pupils' regular work, assistance to pupils, teaching methods, grouping of pupils, choice of software and textbooks) are taken by schools in at least 70% of countries, decisions about instruction time are more often made at the state or central level (24 out of 37 countries). However, in 11 out of the remaining 13 countries, decisions on instruction time are taken at the local or school level, but within a centrally established framework. Only in England and Indonesia is instruction time decided autonomously by schools (Chart D1.3 and Table D1.3, available on line).

Chart D1.3. **Level of government at which decisions about the organisation of instruction, programmes of study and learning resources in public lower secondary education are taken (2011)**

Percentage of OECD countries reporting decisions taken at each level of government

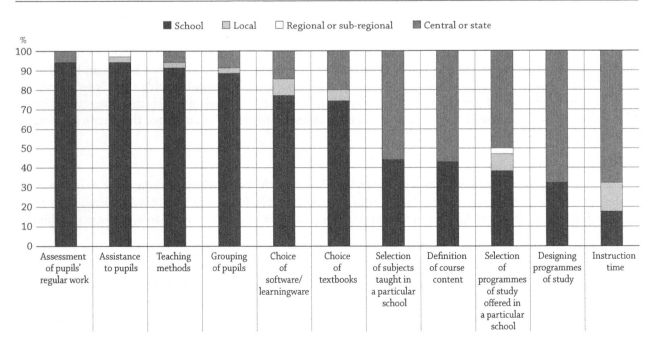

Decisions are ranked in descending order of the percentage of OECD countries reporting these decisions as taken at the school level.
Source: OECD. Table D1.3, available on line. See Annex 3 for notes (*www.oecd.org/edu/eag2012*).
StatLink ⟶ http://dx.doi.org/10.1787/888932663587

How much time do students spend in the classroom? – INDICATOR D1   CHAPTER D

D1

Although decisions about the organisation of instruction are predominantly taken by schools, decisions about programmes of study and learning resources (i.e. the definition of course content, selection of subjects taught in a particular school, selection of programmes of study offered in a particular school, and designing programmes of study) are decided at the state or central level in more than half of the countries. For the remaining countries, although these decisions are in the hands of schools or local authorities, they are subject to an overarching framework set by the central or state government. Only in Indonesia and Scotland are these decisions taken by schools with full autonomy. For the selection of programmes of study offered in a particular school, decisions are taken autonomously by schools in Austria and by local authorities in Sweden, while in France decisions are taken at the school level in consultation with the authorities from the sub-regional level. In Hungary, decisions are also taken at the school level, but in consultation with local authorities. The majority of decisions about the organisation of instruction, planning and structure are taken centrally in Greece and Luxembourg.

Definitions

The **compulsory curriculum** refers to the amount and allocation of instruction time that almost every public school must provide and almost all public-sector students must attend. The measurement of the time devoted to specific study areas (subjects) focuses on the minimum common core rather than on the average time spent, since the data sources (policy documents) do not allow for more precise measurement. The total compulsory curriculum comprises the compulsory core curriculum as well as the compulsory flexible curriculum.

The **compulsory flexible curriculum** refers to the part of the compulsory curriculum where there is flexibility in time spent on a subject and/or a choice can be made between study areas.

Instruction time for 7-15 year-olds refers to the formal number of 60-minute hours per school year organised by the school for class instruction. For countries with no formal policy on instruction time, the number of hours is estimated from survey data. Hours lost when schools are closed for festivities and celebrations, such as national holidays, are excluded. Intended instruction time does not include non-compulsory time outside the school day, homework, individual tutoring, or private study done before or after school.

Instruction time for the least demanding programme for 15-year-olds refers to the programme for students who are least likely to continue studying beyond the mandatory school age or beyond lower secondary education. Such a programme for 15-year-olds may or may not exist, depending on a country's streaming and selection policies. In many countries students are offered the same amount of instruction time in all or most programmes, but there is flexibility in the choice of subjects. Often, such choices have to be made early in the student's school career if programmes are long and differ substantially.

Intended instruction time refers to the number of hours per year during which students receive instruction in the compulsory and non-compulsory parts of the curriculum.

The **non-compulsory part of the curriculum** refers to the average time of instruction to which students are entitled beyond the compulsory hours of instruction. These subjects often vary from school to school or from region to region and may take the form of non-compulsory (elective) subjects.

Typical instruction time for 15-year-olds refers to the programme in which most students at this age are enrolled. The programme may take place in lower or upper secondary education and, in most countries, consists of a general programme. If the system channels students into different programme types at this age, the average instruction time may have been estimated for the most important mainstream programmes and weighted by the proportion of students in the grade in which most 15-year-olds are enrolled. When vocational programmes are also taken into account in typical instruction time, only the school-based part of the programme is included in the calculations.

D1

Methodology

This indicator captures intended instruction time, as established in public regulations, as a measure of exposure to learning in formal classroom settings. It does not show the actual number of hours of instruction received by students and does not cover learning outside of the formal classroom setting. Differences may exist across countries between the regulatory minimum hours of instruction and the actual hours of instruction received by students. A study conducted by Regioplan Beleidsonderzoek in the Netherlands showed that owing to factors such as school timetable decisions, lesson cancellations and teacher absenteeism, schools may not consistently reach the regulatory minimum instruction time (see Box D1.1 of *Education at a Glance 2007*).

The indicator also illustrates how minimum instruction hours are allocated across different curricular areas. It shows the intended net hours of instruction for those grades in which the majority of students are between 7 and 15 years old. Although the data are difficult to compare among countries because of different curricular policies, they nevertheless provide an indication of how much formal instruction time is considered necessary for students to achieve the desired educational goals.

Data on instruction time are from the 2011 OECD-INES Survey on Teachers and the Curriculum and refer to the school year 2009-10.

Data on the level of decision-making about the organisation of instruction, programmes of study and learning resources are from the 2011 OECD-INES survey on decision making in education and refer to the school year 2010-11. More detailed information on definitions and methodology can be found in Indicator D6, "Who makes key decisions in education systems?"

The statistical data for Israel are supplied by and under the responsibility of the relevant Israeli authorities. The use of such data by the OECD is without prejudice to the status of the Golan Heights, East Jerusalem and Israeli settlements in the West Bank under the terms of international law.

References

Notes on definitions and methodologies for each country related to this indicator are provided in Annex 3, available at *www.oecd.org/edu/eag2012*.

The following additional material relevant to this indicator is available on line:

- *Table D1.3. Level of government at which different types of decisions about the organisation of instruction, programmes of study and learning resources are taken in public lower secondary education (2011)*
  StatLink ᵃᵐˢ⌐ http://dx.doi.org/10.1787/888932667938

Table D1.1. **Compulsory and intended instruction time in public institutions (2010)**
Average number of hours per year of total compulsory and non-compulsory instruction time in the curriculum for 7-8, 9-11, 12-14 and 15-year-olds

	Ending age of compulsory education	Age range at which over 90% of the population are enrolled	Average number of hours per year of total compulsory instruction time					Average number of hours per year of total intended instruction time				
			Ages 7-8	Ages 9-11	Ages 12-14	Age 15 (typical programme)	Age 15 (least demanding programme)	Ages 7-8	Ages 9-11	Ages 12-14	Age 15 (typical programme)	Age 15 (least demanding programme)
	(1)	(2)	(3)	(4)	(5)	(6)	(7)	(8)	(9)	(10)	(11)	(12)
OECD												
Australia	17	5 - 16	982	984	997	982	927	982	984	997	982	927
Austria	15	5 - 15	690	766	914	1 005	960	735	811	959	1 050	1 005
Belgium (Fl.)	18	3 - 17	a	a	a	a	a	835	835	960	960	450
Belgium (Fr.)[1]	18	3 - 17	840	840	960	m	m	930	930	1 020	m	m
Canada	16 - 18	6 - 17	917	921	922	919	a	917	921	922	919	a
Chile	18	6 - 15	1 083	1 083	1 083	1 197	1 197	1 083	1 083	1 083	1 197	1 197
Czech Republic[2]	15	5 - 17	588	706	862	794	588	588	706	862	794	588
Denmark	16	3 - 16	701	813	900	930	900	701	813	900	930	900
England	16	4 - 16	893	899	925	950	a	893	899	925	950	a
Estonia	16	4 - 17	595	683	802	840	m	595	683	802	840	m
Finland	16	6 - 18	608	640	777	856	a	608	683	829	913	a
France	16	3 - 16	847	847	971	1 042	a	847	847	1 065	1 147	a
Germany	18	4 - 17	641	793	887	933	m	641	793	887	933	m
Greece	14 - 15	5 - 29	720	812	796	773	a	720	812	796	773	a
Hungary	18	4 - 17	555	601	671	763	763	614	724	885	1 106	1 106
Iceland	16	3 - 16	800	889	969	987	a	800	889	969	987	a
Ireland	16	5 - 18	915	915	929	935	935	915	915	929	935	935
Israel	17	5 - 16	914	990	981	964	m	914	990	981	1 101	m
Italy	16	3 - 16	891	924	1 023	1 089	m	891	924	1 023	1 089	m
Japan	15	4 - 17	735	800	877	m	a	735	800	877	m	a
Korea	14	6 - 17	612	703	859	1 020	a	612	703	859	1 020	a
Luxembourg	15	4 - 15	924	924	908	900	900	924	924	908	900	900
Mexico	15	4 - 14	800	800	1 167	799	a	800	800	1 167	799	a
Netherlands	18	4 - 17	940	940	1 000	1 000	a	940	940	1 000	1 000	a
New Zealand	16	4 - 16	m	m	m	m	m	m	m	m	m	m
Norway	16	3 - 17	701	773	836	858	a	701	773	836	858	a
Poland	16	6 - 18	600	707	765	810	a	656	763	820	865	a
Portugal	15	5 - 17	865	859	908	882	m	900	888	934	934	m
Scotland	16	4 - 16	a	a	a	a	a	a	a	a	a	a
Slovak Republic	16	6 - 16	695	784	822	936	936	709	794	851	936	936
Slovenia	15	6 - 18	621	721	817	908	888	621	721	817	908	888
Spain	16	3 - 16	875	875	1 050	1 050	1 050	875	875	1 050	1 050	1 050
Sweden[3]	16	3 - 18	741	741	741	741	a	741	741	741	741	a
Switzerland	15	5 - 17	m	m	m	m	m	m	m	m	m	m
Turkey	14	6 - 13	720	720	768	810	a	864	864	864	810	a
United States	17	6 - 16	m	m	m	m	a	m	m	m	m	a
OECD average	16	4 - 16	774	821	899	920	913	790	838	922	948	907
EU21 average	16	4 - 16	750	800	877	907	880	767	819	907	941	876
Other G20												
Argentina[4]	17	5 - 15	m	720	744	m	m	m	720	896	m	m
Brazil	17	6 - 16	m	m	m	m	m	m	m	m	m	m
China	m	m	531	613	793	748	m	m	m	m	m	m
India	m	m	m	m	m	m	m	m	m	m	m	m
Indonesia	15	6 - 14	464	747	944	1 020	a	464	747	944	1 020	a
Russian Federation	17	7 - 14	493	737	879	912	m	493	737	879	912	m
Saudi Arabia	11	11 - 17	m	m	m	m	m	m	m	m	m	m
South Africa	15	m	m	m	m	m	m	m	m	m	m	m
G20 average	m	m	733	801	911	935	m	m	m	m	m	m

1. "Ages 12-14" covers ages 12-13 only.
2. Minimum number of hours per year.
3. Estimated minimum numbers of hours per year because breakdown by age is not available.
4. Year of reference 2009.
Source: OECD. Argentina: UNESCO Institute for Statistics (World Education Indicators programme). China: The Ministry of Education, *Notes on the Experimental Curriculum of Compulsory Education*, 19 November 2001. See Annex 3 for notes (*www.oecd.org/edu/eag2012*).
Please refer to the Reader's Guide for information concerning the symbols replacing missing data.
StatLink ᴍˢ🔗 http://dx.doi.org/10.1787/888932667862

D1

Table D1.2a. Instruction time per subject as a percentage of total compulsory instruction time for 7-8 year-olds (2010)

Percentage of intended instruction time devoted to various subject areas within the total compulsory curriculum

	Compulsory core curriculum												Compulsory flexible curriculum	Total compulsory curriculum	Non-compulsory curriculum
	Reading, writing and literature	Mathematics	Science	Social studies	Modern foreign languages	Technology	Arts	Physical education	Religion	Practical and vocational skills	Other	Total compulsory core curriculum			
	(1)	(2)	(3)	(4)	(5)	(6)	(7)	(8)	(9)	(10)	(11)	(12)	(13)	(14)	(15)
OECD															
Australia[1]	m	m	m	m	m	m	m	m	m	m	m	46	54	100	n
Austria	30	17	13	n	x(11)	n	13	13	9	x(11)	4	100	x(11)	100	7
Belgium (Fl.)[1]	24	21	x(11)	x(11)	n	n	10	7	7	n	18	87	13	100	n
Belgium (Fr.)[1]	x(11)	x(11)	x(11)	x(11)	n	n	x(11)	7	7	n	86	100	n	100	11
Canada	28	19	8	7	n	n	7	10	n	n	1	80	20	100	n
Chile	21	16	7	7	n	8	8	8	5	n	n	79	21	100	m
Czech Republic[1]	x(13)	x(13)	x(13)	x(13)	x(13)	x(13)	x(13)	x(13)	n	n	n	x(13)	100	100	m
Denmark	45	21	4	n	n	n	13	6	6	n	4	100	n	100	n
England	m	m	m	m	m	m	m	m	m	m	m	m	m	m	m
Estonia	28	15	4	4	4	n	9	12	n	n	13	90	10	100	n
Finland	33	14	11	n	n	n	21	9	6	n	n	93	7	100	n
France	38	21	4	8	6	2	9	13	n	n	n	100	n	100	n
Germany	22	16	3	3	3	1	14	12	7	n	16	99	1	100	n
Greece	31	15	n	16	5	n	11	7	4	n	11	100	n	100	n
Hungary	40	20	5	n	n	n	13	14	n	5	4	100	n	100	11
Iceland	20	17	7	10	1	3	13	10	x(4)	7	1	88	12	100	n
Ireland	30	12	4	8	x(14)	n	12	4	10	n	12	92	8	100	n
Israel	25	18	8	9	n	1	6	6	12	n	3	88	12	100	n
Italy[2]	24	19	7	11	9	n	15	7	7	n	n	100	x(12)	100	n
Japan	26	18	7	6	n	n	13	10	n	n	12	93	7	100	n
Korea	26	15	6	6	2	n	7	6	n	n	22	89	11	100	n
Luxembourg[3]	36	21	11	n	n	n	11	11	7	n	4	100	n	100	n
Mexico	38	28	15	10	n	n	5	5	n	n	n	100	n	100	n
Netherlands	m	m	m	m	m	m	m	m	m	m	m	m	m	m	m
New Zealand	m	m	m	m	m	m	m	m	m	m	m	m	m	m	m
Norway	33	20	4	5	5	n	15	9	8	n	1	100	n	100	n
Poland[1]	x(13)	x(13)	x(13)	x(13)	x(13)	x(13)	x(13)	x(13)	x(13)	x(13)	x(13)	x(13)	100	100	9
Portugal[1]	32	28	x(4)	20	n	x(11)	x(11)	n	n	x(11)	20	100	m	100	4
Scotland	a	a	a	a	a	a	a	a	a	a	a	a	a	a	a
Slovak Republic	31	18	8	2	4	2	10	8	4	2	n	90	10	100	2
Slovenia	30	19	6	6	n	n	17	13	n	n	9	100	n	100	n
Spain	25	17	8	8	10	n	9	9	x(13)	n	8	94	6	100	n
Sweden	m	m	m	m	m	m	m	m	m	m	m	m	m	m	m
Switzerland	m	m	m	m	m	m	m	m	m	m	m	m	m	m	m
Turkey	40	13	n	17	n	n	13	7	n	n	3	93	7	100	20
United States	m	m	m	m	m	m	m	m	m	m	m	m	m	m	m
OECD average[1]	30	18	6	6	2	1	12	9	4	1	6	94	6	100	2
EU21 average[1]	32	18	6	5	3	n	13	10	5	1	6	97	4	100	1
Other G20															
Argentina	m	m	m	m	m	m	m	m	m	m	m	m	m	m	m
Brazil	m	m	m	m	m	m	m	m	m	m	m	m	m	m	m
China	m	m	m	m	m	m	m	m	m	m	m	m	m	m	m
India	m	m	m	m	m	m	m	m	m	m	m	m	m	m	m
Indonesia	x(12)	x(12)	x(12)	x(12)	n	n	x(12)	x(12)	x(12)	x(12)	x(12)	100	n	100	n
Russian Federation	39	18	9	n	5	4	9	9	n	n	n	93	7	100	n
Saudi Arabia	m	m	m	m	m	m	m	m	m	m	m	m	m	m	m
South Africa	m	m	m	m	m	m	m	m	m	m	m	m	m	m	m
G20 average	m	m	m	m	m	m	m	m	m	m	m	m	m	m	m

1. Australia, Belgium (Fl.), Belgium (Fr.), the Czech Republic, Poland and Portugal are not included in the averages.
2. For 7 and 8-year-olds the curriculum is largely flexible.
3. German as a language of instruction is included in "Reading, writing and literature" in addition to the mother tongue Luxemburgish.
Source: OECD. See Annex 3 for notes (*www.oecd.org/edu/eag2012*).
Please refer to the Reader's Guide for information concerning the symbols replacing missing data.
StatLink ￼ http://dx.doi.org/10.1787/888932667881

Table D1.2b. Instruction time per subject as a percentage of total compulsory instruction time for 9-11 year-olds (2010)

Percentage of intended instruction time devoted to various subject areas within the total compulsory curriculum

	Compulsory core curriculum												Compulsory flexible curriculum	Total compulsory curriculum	Non-compulsory curriculum
	Reading, writing and literature	Mathematics	Science	Social studies	Modern foreign languages	Technology	Arts	Physical education	Religion	Practical and vocational skills	Other	Total compulsory core curriculum			
	(1)	(2)	(3)	(4)	(5)	(6)	(7)	(8)	(9)	(10)	(11)	(12)	(13)	(14)	(15)
OECD															
Australia[1]	m	m	m	m	m	m	m	m	m	m	m	**43**	57	**100**	n
Austria	24	16	10	3	8	n	18	10	8	x(11)	3	**100**	x(11)	**100**	6
Belgium (Fl.)[1]	22	19	x(11)	x(11)	7	n	10	7	7	n	18	**89**	11	**100**	n
Belgium (Fr.)[1]	x(11)	x(11)	x(11)	x(11)	5	x(11)	x(11)	7	7	n	81	**100**	n	**100**	11
Canada	26	17	8	7	3	n	7	10	n	n	1	**79**	21	**100**	n
Chile	16	16	9	9	3	6	10	7	5	n	1	**81**	19	**100**	m
Czech Republic[1]	x(13)	x(13)	x(13)	x(13)	x(13)	x(13)	x(13)	x(13)	n	n	n	**x(13)**	100	**100**	m
Denmark	26	16	7	6	9	n	20	10	4	n	3	**100**	n	**100**	n
England[2]	13	13	12	14	8	13	11	9	3	n	5	**100**	x(12)	**100**	x(14)
Estonia	21	15	7	6	12	4	9	10	n	n	4	**88**	12	**100**	n
Finland	21	18	10	2	9	n	19	9	5	n	n	**94**	6	**100**	7
France	30	19	5	11	9	3	9	14	n	n	n	**100**	n	**100**	n
Germany	17	14	6	6	10	2	15	10	7	n	11	**98**	2	**100**	n
Greece	23	13	6	16	14	n	7	6	6	n	7	**100**	n	**100**	n
Hungary	29	17	6	7	9	n	14	12	n	5	2	**100**	n	**100**	20
Iceland	16	15	8	10	6	3	12	9	x(4)	8	2	**90**	10	**100**	n
Ireland	30	12	4	8	x(14)	n	12	4	10	n	12	**92**	8	**100**	n
Israel	21	17	8	10	11	n	5	6	12	n	3	**93**	7	**100**	n
Italy[3]	22	17	7	11	13	2	14	7	6	n	n	**100**	n	**100**	n
Japan	18	16	10	9	1	n	10	8	n	n	19	**92**	8	**100**	m
Korea	19	13	10	10	5	2	13	10	n	2	3	**87**	13	**100**	m
Luxembourg[4]	25	18	6	2	21	n	11	10	7	n	n	**100**	n	**100**	n
Mexico	30	25	15	20	n	n	5	5	n	n	n	**100**	n	**100**	n
Netherlands[2]	32	19	6	6	1	n	9	7	5	3	n	**88**	13	**100**	m
New Zealand	m	m	m	m	m	m	m	m	m	m	m	**m**	m	**m**	m
Norway	23	16	7	9	8	n	15	11	8	n	3	**100**	n	**100**	n
Poland[5]	20	15	11	5	10	5	5	15	n	n	4	**89**	11	**100**	7
Portugal[6]	21	17	6	11	7	x(7)	12	6	n	n	18	**98**	2	**100**	3
Scotland	a	a	a	a	a	a	a	a	a	a	a	**a**	a	**a**	a
Slovak Republic	22	15	7	10	11	1	8	7	4	1	n	**86**	14	**100**	1
Slovenia	18	16	10	8	11	2	11	11	n	3	10	**100**	n	**100**	n
Spain	24	17	8	8	12	n	8	9	x(13)	n	10	**94**	6	**100**	n
Sweden	m	m	m	m	m	m	m	m	m	m	m	**m**	m	**m**	m
Switzerland	m	m	m	m	m	m	m	m	m	m	m	**m**	m	**m**	m
Turkey	19	13	13	10	11	2	7	6	7	n	6	**93**	7	**100**	20
United States	m	m	m	m	m	m	m	m	m	m	m	**m**	m	**m**	m
OECD average[1]	22	16	8	9	8	2	11	9	4	1	5	**94**	6	**100**	2
EU21 average[1]	23	16	7	8	10	2	12	9	4	1	5	**96**	5	**100**	3
Other G20															
Argentina[7]	20	20	15	15	n	n	10	10	n	n	10	**100**	x(12)	**100**	n
Brazil	m	m	m	m	m	m	m	m	m	m	m	**m**	m	**m**	m
China	20-22	13-15	7-9	3-4	6-8	m	9-11	10-11	m	16-20	7-9	**m**	m	**m**	m
India	m	m	m	m	m	m	m	m	m	m	m	**m**	m	**m**	m
Indonesia[5]	15	15	12	9	n	n	12	12	9	6	6	**94**	6	**100**	n
Russian Federation	27	16	7	6	9	7	7	7	n	n	n	**85**	15	**100**	n
Saudi Arabia	m	m	m	m	m	m	m	m	m	m	m	**m**	m	**m**	m
South Africa	m	m	m	m	m	m	m	m	m	m	m	**m**	m	**m**	m
G20 average	m	m	m	m	m	m	m	m	m	m	m	**m**	m	**m**	m

1. Australia, Belgium (Fl.), Belgium (Fr.) and the Czech Republic are not included in the averages.
2. Includes 11-year-olds only.
3. For 9 and 10-year-olds the curriculum is largely flexible, for 11-year-olds it is about the same as for 12 and 13-year-olds.
4. German as a language of instruction is included in "Reading, writing and literature" in addition to the mother tongue Luxemburgish.
5. Includes 10-11 year-olds only.
6. For 9-year-olds, "Technology", "Arts" and "Practical and vocational skills" are included in "Other".
7. Year of reference 2009.
Source: OECD. Argentina: UNESCO Institute for Statistics (World Education Indicators programme). China: The Ministry of Education, *Notes on the Experimental Curriculum of Compulsory Education*, 19 November 2001. See Annex 3 for notes (*www.oecd.org/edu/eag2012*).
Please refer to the Reader's Guide for information concerning the symbols replacing missing data.
StatLink http://dx.doi.org/10.1787/888932667900

D1

Table D1.2c. Instruction time per subject as a percentage of total compulsory instruction time for 12-14 year-olds (2010)

Percentage of intended instruction time devoted to various subject areas within the total compulsory curriculum

	Reading, writing and literature	Mathematics	Science	Social studies	Modern foreign languages	Technology	Arts	Physical education	Religion	Practical and vocational skills	Other	Total compulsory core curriculum	Compulsory flexible curriculum	Total compulsory curriculum	Non-compulsory curriculum
	Compulsory core curriculum														
	(1)	(2)	(3)	(4)	(5)	(6)	(7)	(8)	(9)	(10)	(11)	(12)	(13)	(14)	(15)
OECD															
Australia[1]	m	m	m	m	m	m	m	m	m	m	m	**60**	40	**100**	n
Austria	13	14	13	12	11	n	16	10	7	2	1	**100**	x(11)	**100**	5
Belgium (Fl.)	14	13	7	9	17	4	4	6	6	1	n	**80**	20	**100**	n
Belgium (Fr.)[2]	17	14	9	13	13	3	3	9	6	n	n	**88**	13	**100**	6
Canada	19	15	10	13	7	3	8	10	n	n	3	**87**	13	**100**	n
Chile	16	16	11	11	8	3	8	5	5	n	3	**84**	16	**100**	m
Czech Republic[1]	x(13)	x(13)	x(13)	x(13)	x(13)	x(13)	x(13)	x(13)	n	n	n	**x(13)**	100	**100**	m
Denmark	20	13	14	9	18	n	11	8	3	n	3	**100**	n	**100**	n
England	13	12	13	13	7	12	9	8	3	n	3	**93**	7	**100**	x(14)
Estonia	14	14	17	9	17	5	7	7	n	n	n	**91**	9	**100**	n
Finland	13	13	17	7	14	n	15	7	5	4	n	**95**	5	**100**	7
France	16	15	13	13	12	6	7	11	n	n	n	**93**	7	**100**	10
Germany	13	13	12	12	16	3	9	9	5	2	1	**96**	4	**100**	n
Greece	18	11	10	12	12	5	6	8	6	3	10	**100**	n	**100**	n
Hungary	17	12	18	12	12	3	10	9	n	3	3	**100**	n	**100**	32
Iceland	14	14	8	8	16	2	6	8	x(4)	5	3	**82**	18	**100**	n
Ireland[3]	26	12	8	15	6	n	4	5	8	x(14)	4	**88**	12	**100**	n
Israel	19	14	10	16	17	4	n	6	9	n	1	**97**	3	**100**	n
Italy[2]	22	13	7	11	17	7	13	7	3	n	n	**100**	n	**100**	n
Japan	11	11	10	9	10	3	7	9	n	n	17	**87**	13	**100**	m
Korea	13	11	11	10	10	4	8	8	n	4	5	**83**	17	**100**	n
Luxembourg[4]	18	15	5	10	25	n	10	8	6	n	3	**100**	n	**100**	n
Mexico	14	14	17	23	9	n	6	6	n	9	3	**100**	n	**100**	n
Netherlands	m	m	m	m	m	m	m	m	m	m	m	**m**	m	**m**	m
New Zealand	m	m	m	m	m	m	m	m	m	m	m	**m**	m	**m**	m
Norway	16	13	10	10	15	n	11	10	7	3	5	**100**	n	**100**	n
Poland	17	14	13	11	12	5	4	14	n	n	4	**93**	7	**100**	7
Portugal[5]	11	11	12	13	15	4	7	9	n	n	15	**98**	2	**100**	3
Scotland	a	a	a	a	a	a	a	a	a	a	a	**a**	a	**a**	a
Slovak Republic	16	16	17	16	10	n	7	7	3	3	n	**97**	3	**100**	3
Slovenia	12	12	15	14	17	2	6	6	n	n	8	**94**	6	**100**	n
Spain	17	13	11	10	10	5	10	7	x(13)	n	11	**95**	5	**100**	n
Sweden	m	m	m	m	m	m	m	m	m	m	m	**m**	m	**m**	m
Switzerland	m	m	m	m	m	m	m	m	m	m	m	**m**	m	**m**	m
Turkey	16	15	15	11	12	4	4	4	5	n	8	**96**	4	**100**	13
United States	m	m	m	m	m	m	m	m	m	m	m	**m**	m	**m**	m
OECD average[1]	16	13	12	12	13	3	8	8	3	1	4	**93**	7	**100**	3
EU21 average[1]	16	13	12	12	14	3	8	8	3	1	4	**95**	6	**100**	4
Other G20															
Argentina[6]	16	16	13	19	10	6	10	10	n	n	n	**100**	x(12)	**100**	20
Brazil	m	m	m	m	m	m	m	m	m	m	m	**m**	m	**m**	m
China	m	m	m	m	m	m	m	m	m	m	m	**m**	m	**m**	m
India	m	m	m	m	m	m	m	m	m	m	m	**m**	m	**m**	m
Indonesia	13	13	12	11	8	4	8	8	7	6	6	**94**	6	**100**	n
Russian Federation	15	14	24	9	9	3	4	6	n	1	n	**85**	15	**100**	n
Saudi Arabia	m	m	m	m	m	m	m	m	m	m	m	**m**	m	**m**	m
South Africa	m	m	m	m	m	m	m	m	m	m	m	**m**	m	**m**	m
G20 average	m	m	m	m	m	m	m	m	m	m	m	**m**	m	**m**	m

1. Australia and the Czech Republic are not included in the averages.
2. Includes 12-13 year-olds only.
3. For 13-14 year-olds, "Arts" is included in "Total compulsory core curriculum".
4. German as a language of instruction is included in "Reading, writing and literature" in addition to the mother tongue Luxemburgish.
5. "Technology" is included in "Arts" for 14-year-olds.
6. Year of reference 2009.
Source: OECD. Argentina: UNESCO Institute for Statistics (World Education Indicators programme). See Annex 3 for notes (*www.oecd.org/edu/eag2012*).
Please refer to the Reader's Guide for information concerning the symbols replacing missing data.
StatLink ᴍˢᴾ http://dx.doi.org/10.1787/888932667919

WHAT IS THE STUDENT-TEACHER RATIO AND HOW BIG ARE CLASSES?

- The average class in primary education in OECD countries has more than 21 students, but classes are usually larger in other G20 countries. Among all countries with available data, the number of students per class varies from more than 29 in Chile and China to nearly half that number in Luxembourg and the Russian Federation.

- In more than two-thirds of the countries with comparable data for 2000 and 2010, classes have tended to become smaller in primary education, most notably in countries that had relatively large classes in 2000, such as Korea and Turkey.

- On average in OECD countries, the number of students per class grows by two or more between primary and lower secondary education. In lower secondary education, the average class in OECD countries has about 23 students.

Chart D2.1. **Average class size in primary education (2000, 2010)**

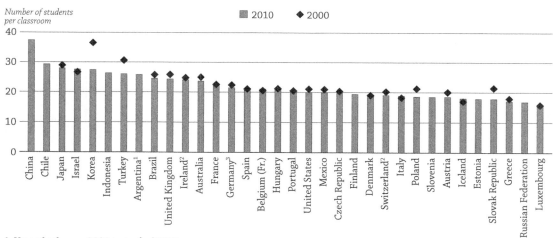

1. Year of reference 2009 instead of 2010.
2. Public institutions only.
3. Years of reference 2001 and 2010.
Countries are ranked in descending order of average class size in primary education in 2010.
Source: OECD. Argentina, China, Indonesia: UNESCO Institute for Statistics (World Education Indicators programme). 2010 data: Table D2.1. 2000 data: Table D2.5 available on line. See Annex 3 for notes (*www.oecd.org/edu/eag2012*).
StatLink 🔗 http://dx.doi.org/10.1787/888932663606

Context

Class size and student-teacher ratios are much-discussed aspects of education and, along with students' total instruction time (see Indicator D1), teachers' average working time (see Indicator D4), and the division of teachers' time between teaching and other duties, are among the determinants of the size of countries' teaching force. Together with teachers' salaries (see Indicator D3) and the age distribution of teachers (see Indicator D5), class size and student-teacher ratios also have a considerable impact on the level of current expenditure on education (see Indicators B6 and B7).

Smaller classes are often perceived as allowing teachers to focus more on the needs of individual students and reducing the amount of class time needed to deal with disruptions. Yet, while there is some evidence that smaller classes may benefit specific groups of students, such as those from disadvantaged backgrounds (Krueger, 2002), overall the evidence of the effects of differences in class size on student performance is weak. There is more evidence to support a positive relationship between smaller class size and aspects of teachers' working conditions and outcomes (e.g. allowing for greater flexibility for innovation in the classroom, improved teacher morale and job satisfaction) (Hattie, 2009; OECD, 2009).

The ratio of students to teaching staff indicates how resources for education are allocated. Smaller student-teacher ratios often have to be weighed against higher salaries for teachers, increased professional development and teacher training, greater investment in teaching technology, or more widespread use of assistant teachers and other paraprofessionals whose salaries are often considerably lower than those of qualified teachers. As larger numbers of children with special needs are integrated into mainstream classes, more use of specialised personnel and support services may limit the resources available for reducing student-teacher ratios.

▥ Other findings

- In 21 of the 26 countries with available data, **the student-teacher ratio decreases between the primary level and the lower secondary level, despite a general increase in class size between these levels** (in all countries with available data except one). This decrease in the student-teacher ratio reflects differences in annual instruction time for students, which tends to increase with the level of education.

- On average in OECD countries, the **availability of teaching resources relative to the number of students in secondary education is slightly more favourable in private than in public institutions**. This is most striking in Mexico where, at the secondary level, there are nearly 17 more students per teacher in public than in private institutions. On average across OECD countries, there is at most one student more per class in public than in private institutions at the primary and lower secondary levels.

- On average among countries with available data, **non-instructional staff represent slightly more than one-quarter of the total education personnel in primary, secondary and post-secondary non-tertiary schools, and more than one-third of the total staff at the tertiary level**. There are more than 10 more education personnel per 1 000 students in tertiary education than at the primary, secondary and post-secondary non-tertiary levels of education.

▥ Trends

From 2000 to 2010, the average class size in countries with available data for both years decreased by one student at both the primary and lower secondary levels, and the range of class size among OECD countries narrowed. At the lower secondary level, for example, class size ranged from 17.4 students (Iceland) to 38.5 (Korea) in 2000 and from 19.4 students (Luxembourg and the United Kingdom) to 34.7 (Korea) in 2010. However, class size has tended to increase in some countries that had relatively small classes in 2000, most notably in Iceland.

D2

Analysis

Average class size in primary and lower secondary education

The average primary class in OECD countries had more than 21 students in 2010. When considering all countries with available data, that number varies widely and ranges from fewer than 17 in Luxembourg and the Russian Federation to more than 29 in Chile and China. There are fewer than 20 students per primary classroom in nearly half of the countries with available data: Austria, the Czech Republic, Denmark, Estonia, Finland, Greece, Iceland, Italy, Luxembourg, Mexico, Poland, the Russian Federation, the Slovak Republic, Slovenia and Switzerland (public institutions). At the lower secondary level, in general programmes, the average class in OECD countries has more than 23 students (in one-quarter of OECD countries, lower secondary schools have between 22 and 25 students per class). Among all countries with available data, that number varies from 20 or fewer in Denmark, Estonia, Finland, Iceland, Luxembourg, the Russian Federation, Slovenia, Switzerland (public institutions) and the United Kingdom to more than 34 students per class in Indonesia and Korea, and to over 50 in China (Table D2.1).

The number of students per class tends to increase between primary and lower secondary education. In Brazil, China, Greece, Indonesia, Japan, Korea, Mexico and Poland, the increase in average class size exceeds four students. Meanwhile, the United Kingdom and, to a lesser extent, Switzerland (public institutions only) show a drop in the number of students per class between these two levels of education (Chart D2.2).

Chart D2.2. **Average class size in educational institutions, by level of education (2010)**

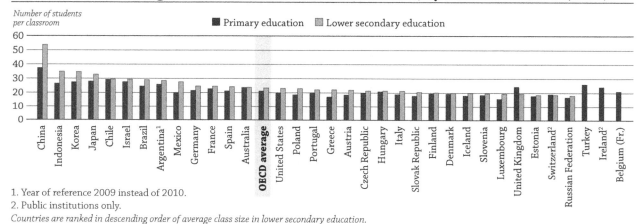

1. Year of reference 2009 instead of 2010.
2. Public institutions only.
Countries are ranked in descending order of average class size in lower secondary education.
Source: OECD. Argentina, China, Indonesia: UNESCO Institute for Statistics (World Education Indicators programme). Table D2.1. See Annex 3 for notes (*www.oecd.org/edu/eag2012*).
StatLink ᵐˢᴾ http://dx.doi.org/10.1787/888932663625

The size of the average primary school class decreased slightly between 2000 and 2010 in countries with available data in both years (21.4 students per class in 2010 as compared to 22.5 in 2000), and this partially results from the fact that some countries implemented reforms on class size during that period (see Indicator B7). However, among countries with comparable data, class size decreased, and most notably (by more than four students) in countries that had larger classes in 2000, such as Korea and Turkey. Class size increased or was unchanged in countries that had the smallest classes in 2000, such as Denmark, Iceland, Italy and Luxembourg (Chart D2.1). In lower secondary school, the gap between the smallest and largest classes narrowed between 2000 and 2010: among countries with comparable data for both years, class size varied from 17.4 students (Iceland) to 38.5 (Korea) in 2000 and from 19.4 students (Luxembourg and the United Kingdom) to 34.7 (Korea) in 2010 (Table D2.1 and Table D2.4, available on line).

The indicator on class size is limited to primary and lower secondary education because class size is difficult to define and compare at higher levels, where students often attend several different classes, depending on the subject area.

Student-teacher ratios

The ratio of students to teaching staff compares the number of students (in full-time equivalent) to the number of teachers (in full-time equivalent) at a given level of education and in similar types of institutions. However, this ratio does not take into account the amount of instruction time for students compared to the length of a teacher's working day, nor how much time teachers spend teaching. Therefore, it cannot be interpreted in terms of class size (Box D2.1).

> ### Box D2.1. **Relationship between class size and student-teacher ratio**
>
> The number of students per class is calculated from a number of different elements: the ratio of students to teaching staff, the number of classes or students for which a teacher is responsible, the amount of instruction time compared to the length of teachers' working days, the proportion of time teachers spend teaching, and how students are grouped within classes and team teaching arrangements.
>
> For example, in a school of 48 full-time students and 8 full-time teachers, the student-teacher ratio is 6 to 1. If teachers' work week is estimated to be 35 hours, including 10 hours teaching, and if instruction time for each student is 40 hours per week, then regardless of how students are grouped in the school, average class size can be estimated as follows:
>
> Estimated class size = 6 students per teacher * (40 hours of instruction time per student/10 hours of teaching per teacher) = 24 students.
>
> Using a different approach, the class size presented in Table D2.1 is defined as the number of students who are following a common course of study, based on the highest number of common courses (usually compulsory studies), excluding teaching in subgroups. Thus, the estimated class size will be close to the average class size of Table D2.1 where teaching in subgroups is less frequent, such as in primary and lower secondary education.
>
> Because of these definitions, similar student-teacher ratios between countries can result in different class sizes. For example, at the primary level, the Czech Republic and Japan have similar ratio of student to teaching staff (18.7 in the Czech Republic and 18.4 in Japan – Table D2.2), but the average class size differs substantially (19.9 in the Czech Republic and 28.0 in Japan – Table D2.1). The explanation may lie in the higher number of instruction time in Japan (Table D1.1) and less teaching time for teachers in Japan (707 hours in Japan compared with 862 in the Czech Republic – Table D4.1).

At the primary level, there are 16 students for every teacher, on average in OECD countries. The student-teacher ratio ranges from more than 23 students per teacher in Brazil, Chile, Mexico and South Africa, to fewer than 11 in Hungary, Luxembourg, Norway, Poland and Portugal (Chart D2.3).

Student-teacher ratios also vary, and to a larger extent, at the secondary school level, ranging from 30 students per full-time equivalent teacher in Mexico to fewer than 11 in Austria, Belgium, Iceland, Luxembourg, Norway, Portugal, Saudi Arabia and Spain. On average among OECD countries, there are about 14 students per teacher at the secondary level (Table D2.2).

As the differences in student-teacher ratios indicate, there are fewer full-time equivalent students per full-time equivalent teachers at the secondary level than at the primary level of education. In most countries, the student-teacher ratio decreases between primary and lower secondary school, despite an increase in class size. This is true in all but five OECD countries: Chile, Italy, Mexico, Poland and the United Kingdom.

Chart D2.3. **Ratio of students to teaching staff in educational institutions, by level of education (2010)**

Number of students per teacher in full-time equivalents

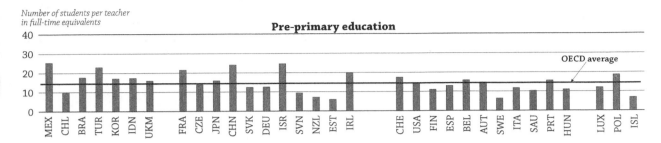

Pre-primary education

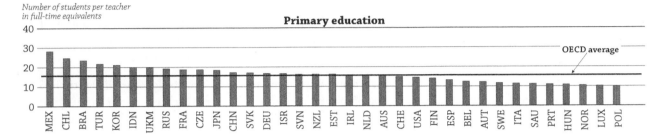

Primary education

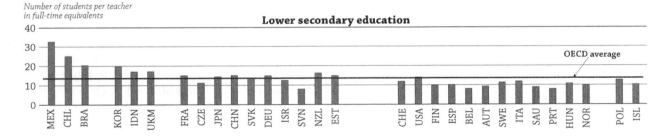

Lower secondary education

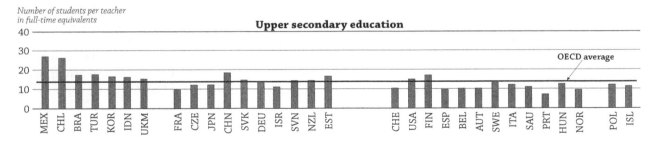

Upper secondary education

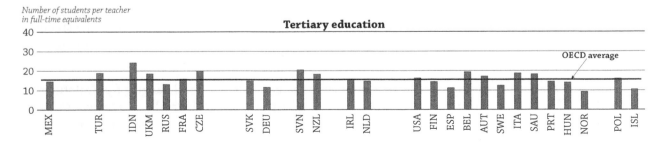

Tertiary education

Countries are ranked in descending order of students to teaching staff ratios in primary education.

Source: OECD. China, Indonesia: UNESCO Institute for Statistics (World Education Indicators programme). Saudi Arabia: UNESCO Institute for Statistics and Observatory on Higher Education. Table D2.2. See Annex 3 for notes (*www.oecd.org/edu/eag2012*).

Please refer to the Reader's Guide for list of country codes for country names used in this chart.

StatLink ⏧ http://dx.doi.org/10.1787/888932663644

This reduction in the student-teacher ratio reflects differences in annual instruction time, which tends to increase with the level of education (see Indicator D1). It may also result from delays in matching the teaching force to demographic changes, or from differences in teaching hours for teachers at different levels of education (the number of teaching hours tends to decrease with the level of education, as teacher specialisation increases). The general trend is consistent among countries, but evidence is mixed as to whether smaller student-teacher ratios are more desirable from an educational perspective at higher levels of education.

For the pre-primary level (see also Indicator C2), Table D2.2 shows the ratio of student to teaching staff and also the ratio of students to contact staff (teachers and teachers' aides). Some countries make extensive use of teachers' aides at the pre-primary level. Fifteen countries reported smaller ratios of students to contact staff (Column 1 of Table D2.2) than of students to teaching staff. However, few countries have large numbers of teachers' aides. As a result, the ratios of students to contact staff are substantially lower than the ratios of students to teaching staff (at least two fewer pupils) in Austria, Brazil, China, France, Germany, Ireland, Israel and the United States. The difference is particularly large in Ireland and Israel, where there are at least 10 fewer pupils per contact staff than per teaching staff.

At the tertiary level, the student-teacher ratio ranges from 20 or more students per teacher in the Czech Republic, Indonesia, Slovenia and South Africa to fewer than 11 in Iceland and Norway (Table D2.2). However, comparisons at this level should be made with caution since it is difficult to calculate full-time equivalent students and teachers on a comparable basis. In 6 of the 12 countries with comparable data at the tertiary level, the ratio of students to teaching staff is lower in more vocationally-oriented programmes (tertiary-type B) than in academic (tertiary-type A) and advanced research programmes. Turkey is the only country with a significantly higher student-teacher ratio in vocational programmes at the tertiary level (Table D2.2).

Teaching resources in public and private institutions

Countries encourage and provide resources to both public and private schools for various reasons. One is to broaden the choices of schooling available to students and their families. Class size is one factor that parents may consider when deciding on a school for their children, and the difference in average class size between public and private schools (and between different type of private institutions) could influence enrolment.

Among countries for which data are available, average class size does not differ between public and private institutions by more than one student per class for both primary and lower secondary education (Chart D2.4 and Table D2.1). However, there are marked differences among countries. For example, at the primary level, in Brazil, the Czech Republic, Iceland, Indonesia, Israel, Poland, the Russian Federation, Turkey and the United Kingdom, average class size in public institutions is larger by four or more students per class. However, with the exception of Brazil and Indonesia, the private sector is relatively small in all of these countries, representing at most 5% of students at the primary level (see Table C1.4). In contrast, average class size in private institutions is larger than that in public institutions by four or more students in China and in Spain, where more than 30% of pupils are enrolled in private institutions.

The comparison of class size between public and private institutions shows a mixed picture at the lower secondary level, where private institutions are more prevalent. The average class size in lower secondary schools is larger in private institutions than in public institutions in 13 OECD countries, although differences tend to be smaller than in primary education.

In countries where private institutions are more prevalent at the primary and lower secondary levels (i.e. countries where more than 10% of students at these levels are enrolled in private institutions), such as Argentina, Australia, Belgium (French Community), Brazil, Chile, Denmark, France, Indonesia, Portugal and Spain, there may be large differences in class size between public and private institutions. However, where these differences are large (a difference of four students or more at both levels in Brazil and Indonesia, and at the primary level only in Argentina, Chile and Spain), private institutions tend to have more students per class than public schools, except in Brazil and Indonesia (see Tables C1.4 and D2.1). This suggests that in countries in which a substantial proportion of students and families choose private schools, class size is not a determining factor in their decision.

Chart D2.4. Average class size in public and private institutions, by level of education (2010)

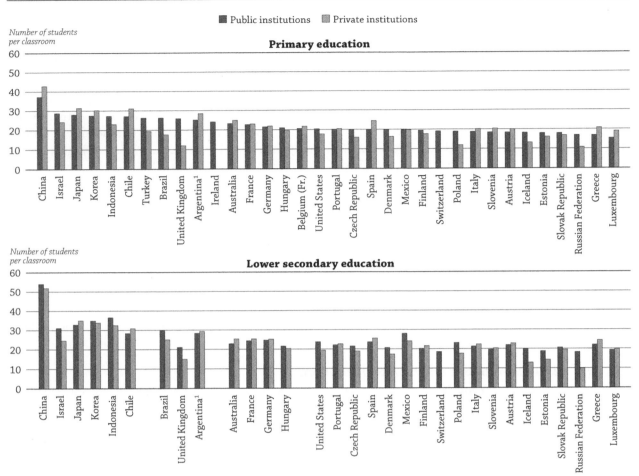

1. Year of reference 2009 instead of 2010.
Countries are ranked in descending order of average class size in public institutions in primary education.
Source: OECD. Argentina, China, Indonesia: UNESCO Institute for Statistics (World Education Indicators programme). Table D2.1. See Annex 3 for notes (*www.oecd.org/edu/eag2012*).
StatLink ᵐˢ᠊ http://dx.doi.org/10.1787/888932663663

Comparing the number of student to teaching staff shows a similar picture. On average among countries for which data are available, ratios of students to teaching staff are slightly lower in private institutions than in public institutions at the lower secondary and combined lower and upper secondary levels, but not at the upper secondary level alone (Table D2.3). The largest differences between public and private institutions are in Brazil and Mexico where, at the lower secondary level, there are at least nine more students per teacher in public institutions than in private institutions. At the upper secondary level in Mexico, the difference between student-teacher ratios in public and private institutions is even larger than at the lower secondary level.

However, in some countries, the student-teacher ratio is lower in public institutions than in private institutions. This is most pronounced at the lower secondary level in Spain, which has some 15 students per teacher in private institutions, but fewer than 9 students per teacher in public institutions.

Teaching staff and non-teaching staff employed in education

The size of the teaching staff has an impact on the training of children and students, and also on expenditure on educational institutions (expenditure on compensation of teachers). However expenditure is also dependent on the size of the non-teaching staff in the education sector. There are significant differences in the distribution of education staff between teaching and other categories among countries with available data, reflecting differences among countries in the organisation and management of schooling. These differences reflect the numbers of staff that countries employ in non-teaching capacities, e.g. principals without teaching responsibilities, guidance counsellors, school nurses, librarians, researchers without teaching responsibilities, bus drivers, janitors and maintenance workers, and administrative and management personnel both inside and outside the school.

At the primary, secondary and post-secondary non-tertiary levels of education, among the 12 OECD countries reporting data for the different categories, the teaching and non-teaching staff employed in primary and secondary schools ranges from about 90 people or fewer per 1 000 students enrolled in Japan and Mexico to 125 or more per 1 000 students in the Czech Republic, Italy and the United States, and exceeds 150 people per 1 000 students in Iceland.

Among these 12 countries for which data are available for the different categories of personnel employed in education, non-instructional staff (staff other than teaching staff, teachers' aides and research assistants) represents on average slightly more than one-quarter of the total education personnel in primary, secondary and post-secondary non-tertiary schools. In five of these countries (the Czech Republic, Iceland, Italy, Mexico and the United States), such staff represents between 30% and 40% of total education personnel; in Chile, this proportion reaches 60% (Table D2.4a). However, in some countries (e.g. Chile, the Czech Republic and Mexico) large shares of non-instructional staff are not necessarily associated with higher-than-average expenditure per student; expenditure per student in these countries is below the OECD average (Table B1.2). This implies that the salary levels for the different categories are low enough to counterbalance the larger proportion of non-teaching staff within the total number of education personnel.

In Hungary, Iceland and Italy, maintenance and operations personnel working in primary, secondary and post-secondary non-tertiary schools represent at least 20 people per 1 000 students enrolled in these schools. Administrative personnel represent 10 people or fewer per 1 000 students enrolled in primary, secondary and post-secondary non-tertiary schools in Chile, France, Hungary, Iceland, Japan, Mexico, Slovenia, the United Kingdom and the United States, and 20 people or more per 1 000 students in Australia and the Czech Republic. In contrast, staff employed in school and higher-level management exceeds 6 people per 1 000 students in Mexico, Norway, the Slovak Republic, Slovenia, the United Kingdom and the United States, and 10 per 1 000 students in Iceland (Table D2.4a). Finally, people employed to provide professional support for students are relatively numerous in Chile, Italy, Slovenia, the United Kingdom and the United States, where there are about 10 per 1 000 students enrolled in these levels.

At the tertiary level of education, there are also significant differences in the distribution of education staff among instructional and other categories of personnel in the nine OECD countries for which data are available. Education staff varies from fewer than 85 people per 1 000 students in France to 160 or more per 1 000 students in Hungary. Compared to the primary, secondary and post-secondary non-tertiary levels of education, there are more than 10 more teaching and non-teaching staff per 1 000 students in tertiary education, on average among the eight countries with available data for the different levels of education.

In tertiary education, non-instructional staff represents an average of nearly 40% of total education personnel, among countries with available data for the different categories. In most of these countries, non-teaching staff represents between 25% and 40% of total staff, but exceeds 50% in Hungary and the United Kingdom (Table D2.4b). In the United Kingdom, this is attributed to the larger proportions of management personnel in comparison to other countries.

Definitions

Instructional personnel (teaching staff) includes two categories:

- **Teachers' aides and teaching/research assistants** include non-professional personnel or students who support teachers in providing instruction to students.

■ **Teaching staff** refers to professional personnel directly involved in teaching students. The classification includes classroom teachers, special-education teachers and other teachers who work with a whole class of students in a classroom, in small groups in a resource room, or in one-to-one teaching situations inside or outside a regular class. Teaching staff also includes department chairpersons whose duties include some teaching, but excludes non-professional personnel who support teachers in providing instruction to students, such as teachers' aides and other paraprofessional personnel.

Non-instructional personnel comprises four categories.

■ **Maintenance and operations personnel** include personnel who support the maintenance and operation of schools, the transportation of students to and from school, school security and catering. This category includes the following types of personnel: masons, carpenters, electricians, maintenance staff, repairers, painters and paperhangers, plasterers, plumbers and vehicle mechanics. It also includes bus drivers and other vehicle operators, construction workers, gardeners and grounds staff, bus monitors and crossing guards, cooks, custodians, food servers and others with similar functions.

■ **Professional support for students** includes professional staff who provide services to students that support their learning. In many cases, these staff originally qualified as teachers but then moved into other professional positions within the education system. This category also includes all personnel employed in education systems who provide health and social support services to students, such as guidance counsellors, librarians, doctors, dentists, nurses, psychiatrists and psychologists, and other staff with similar responsibilities.

■ **School and higher-level administrative personnel** includes all personnel who support the administration and management of schools and of higher levels of the education system. The category includes: receptionists, secretaries, typists and word processing staff, bookkeepers and clerks, analysts, computer programmers, network administrators, and others with similar functions and responsibilities.

■ **School and higher-level management** includes professional personnel who are responsible for school management and administration and personnel whose primary responsibility is the quality control and management of higher levels of the education system. This category covers principals, assistant principals, headmasters, assistant headmasters, superintendents of schools, associate and assistant superintendents, commissioners of education and other management staff with similar responsibilities.

Methodology

Data refer to the academic year 2009-10 and are based on the UOE data collection on education statistics administered by the OECD in 2011 (for details see Annex 3 at *www.oecd.org/edu/eag2012*).

Calculations cover expenditure by public institutions or, where available, by both public and private institutions.

Class size is calculated by dividing the number of students enrolled by the number of classes. In order to ensure comparability among countries, special-needs programmes are excluded. Data include only regular programmes at primary and lower secondary levels of education, and exclude teaching in sub-groups outside the regular classroom setting.

The **ratio of students to teaching staff** is obtained by dividing the number of full-time equivalent students at a given level of education by the number of full-time equivalent teachers at that level and in similar types of institutions.

The statistical data for Israel are supplied by and under the responsibility of the relevant Israeli authorities. The use of such data by the OECD is without prejudice to the status of the Golan Heights, East Jerusalem and Israeli settlements in the West Bank under the terms of international law.

References

Ehrenberg, R., et al. (2001), "Class Size and Student Achievement", *Psychological Science in the Public Interest*, Vol. 2, No. 1, pp. 1-30.

Finn, J. (1998), *Class Size and Students at Risk: What is Known? What is Next?*, US Department of Education, Office of Educational Research and Improvement, National Institute on the Education of At-Risk Students, Washington, DC.

Hattie, J. (2009), *Visible Learning; A synthesis of over 800 Meta-analyses Relating to Achievement*, Routledge, London.

Krueger, A.B. (2002), "Economic Considerations and Class Size", National Bureau of Economic Research Working Paper, No. 8875.

OECD (2009), *Creating Effective Teaching and Learning Environments: First Results from TALIS*, OECD Publishing.

Piketty, T. and M. Valdenaire (2006), *L'Impact de la taille des classes sur la réussite scolaire dans les écoles, collèges et lycées français : Estimations à partir du panel primaire 1997 et du panel secondaire 1995, ministère de l'Éducation nationale, de l'Enseignement supérieur et de la Recherche*, Direction de l'évaluation et de la prospective, Paris.

Notes on definitions and methodologies regarding this indicator for each country are presented in Annex 3 at *www.oecd.org/edu/eag2012*.

The following additional material relevant to this indicator is available on line:

- **Table D2.5. Average class size, by type of institution and level of education (2000)**
  StatLink ⫯⫯ http://dx.doi.org/10.1787/888932668071

D2

Table D2.1. Average class size, by type of institution and level of education (2010)
Calculations based on number of students and number of classes

| | Primary education | | | | | Lower secondary education (general programmes) | | | | |
| | Public institutions | Private institutions | | | Total: Public and private institutions | Public institutions | Private institutions | | | Total: Public and private institutions |
		Total private institutions	Government-dependent private institutions	Independent private institutions			Total private institutions	Government-dependent private institutions	Independent private institutions	
	(1)	(2)	(3)	(4)	(5)	(6)	(7)	(8)	(9)	(10)
Australia	23.2	24.9	24.9	a	**23.7**	22.8	25.3	25.3	a	**23.7**
Austria	18.4	20.0	x(2)	x(2)	**18.4**	21.9	22.8	x(7)	x(7)	**22.0**
Belgium	m	m	m	m	**m**	m	m	m	m	**m**
Belgium (Fr.)	20.6	21.7	21.7	m	**21.0**	m	m	m	m	**m**
Canada	m	m	m	m	**m**	m	m	m	m	**m**
Chile	27.1	31.1	32.5	23.7	**29.3**	28.3	30.7	31.9	24.7	**29.5**
Czech Republic	19.9	15.9	15.9	a	**19.9**	21.5	18.9	18.9	a	**21.4**
Denmark	19.9	16.3	16.3	a	**19.3**	20.7	17.3	17.3	a	**20.0**
Estonia	17.9	16.0	a	16.0	**17.9**	18.7	14.4	a	14.4	**18.5**
Finland	19.4	17.7	17.7	a	**19.4**	20.2	21.7	21.7	a	**20.3**
France	22.6	22.9	x(2)	x(2)	**22.7**	24.3	25.3	25.5	13.4	**24.5**
Germany	21.5	21.9	21.9	x(3)	**21.5**	24.7	25.2	25.2	x(8)	**24.7**
Greece	16.8	20.7	a	20.7	**17.1**	22.0	24.3	a	24.3	**22.1**
Hungary	21.0	19.5	19.5	a	**20.8**	21.5	20.4	20.4	a	**21.4**
Iceland	18.1	13.1	13.1	a	**18.0**	19.9	12.9	12.9	a	**19.8**
Ireland	24.1	m	a	m	**m**	m	m	a	m	**m**
Israel	28.7	24.2	24.2	a	**27.6**	31.0	24.5	24.5	a	**29.4**
Italy	18.8	20.2	a	20.2	**18.8**	21.3	22.4	a	22.4	**21.3**
Japan	27.9	31.4	a	31.4	**28.0**	32.8	34.9	a	34.9	**32.9**
Korea	27.4	30.2	a	30.2	**27.5**	34.9	33.8	33.8	a	**34.7**
Luxembourg	15.3	18.9	19.4	18.9	**15.6**	19.3	19.9	20.0	19.8	**19.4**
Mexico	19.9	19.9	a	19.9	**19.9**	28.0	24.1	a	24.1	**27.6**
Netherlands[1]	22.4	m	m	m	**m**	m	m	m	m	**m**
New Zealand	m	m	m	m	**m**	m	m	m	m	**m**
Norway	a	a	a	a	**a**	a	a	a	a	**a**
Poland	18.9	11.9	11.2	12.1	**18.6**	23.2	17.7	23.7	15.9	**22.9**
Portugal	20.1	20.4	23.5	19.3	**20.1**	22.1	22.6	23.4	21.5	**22.1**
Slovak Republic	17.9	16.8	16.8	n	**17.8**	20.6	19.5	19.5	n	**20.5**
Slovenia	18.4	20.4	20.4	n	**18.4**	19.6	20.3	20.3	n	**19.6**
Spain	19.9	24.5	24.5	24.3	**21.2**	23.7	25.6	25.8	23.9	**24.3**
Sweden	m	m	m	m	**m**	m	m	m	m	**m**
Switzerland	19.1	m	m	m	**m**	18.5	m	m	m	**m**
Turkey	26.3	19.4	a	19.4	**26.1**	a	a	a	a	**a**
United Kingdom	25.8	11.9	19.1	11.7	**24.4**	21.1	14.9	18.9	9.6	**19.4**
United States	20.3	17.7	a	17.7	**20.0**	23.7	19.4	a	19.4	**23.2**
OECD average	21.3	20.3	20.2	20.4	**21.2**	23.3	22.4	22.7	20.6	**23.4**
EU21 average	20.0	18.8	19.0	18.2	**19.8**	21.9	21.2	21.7	18.9	**21.8**
Argentina[2]	25.1	28.4	29.7	24.1	**25.8**	28.3	29.2	30.0	26.7	**28.5**
Brazil	26.2	17.6	a	17.6	**24.6**	29.7	25.0	a	25.0	**29.0**
China	37.1	42.8	x(2)	x(2)	**37.4**	54.0	51.9	x(7)	x(7)	**53.8**
India	m	m	m	m	**m**	m	m	m	m	**m**
Indonesia	27.2	22.9	a	22.9	**26.4**	36.5	32.5	a	32.5	**34.9**
Russian Federation	16.9	10.7	a	10.7	**16.8**	18.2	9.9	a	9.9	**18.2**
Saudi Arabia	m	m	m	m	**m**	m	m	m	m	**m**
South Africa	m	m	m	m	**m**	m	m	m	m	**m**
G20 average	24.4	22.9	~	~	**24.2**	26.7	24.9	~	~	**26.4**

1. Year of reference 2006.
2. Year of reference 2009.
Source: OECD. Argentina, China, Indonesia: UNESCO Institute for Statistics (World Education Indicators programme). See Annex 3 for notes (www.oecd.org/edu/eag2012).
Please refer to the Reader's Guide for information concerning the symbols replacing missing data.
StatLink 🔗 http://dx.doi.org/10.1787/888932667976

Table D2.2. **Ratio of students to teaching staff in educational institutions (2010)**
By level of education, calculations based on full-time equivalents

	Pre-primary education		Primary education	Secondary education			Post-secondary non-tertiary education	Tertiary education		
	Students to contact staff (teachers and teachers' aides)	Students to teaching staff		Lower secondary education	Upper secondary education	All secondary education		Tertiary-type B	Tertiary-type A and advanced research programmes	All tertiary education
	(1)	(2)	(3)	(4)	(5)	(6)	(7)	(8)	(9)	(10)
Australia[1,2]	m	m	15.7	x(6)	x(6)	12.0	m	m	14.9	m
Austria	10.3	14.7	12.2	9.3	10.1	9.6	10.8	x(10)	x(10)	17.1
Belgium[3]	15.9	15.9	12.4	8.1	10.1	9.4	x(5)	x(10)	x(10)	19.3
Canada[2,4]	m	x(4)	x(4)	17.7	15.8	17.1	m	m	18.2	m
Chile	9.4	9.7	24.6	25.1	26.1	25.8	a	m	m	m
Czech Republic	13.6	13.9	18.7	11.2	12.1	11.7	18.6	17.5	20.2	20.0
Denmark	m	m	x(4)	11.5	m	m	m	m	m	m
Estonia	m	6.0	16.2	14.9	16.6	15.9	x(5)	m	m	m
Finland	m	11.0	14.0	9.8	17.1	13.7	x(5)	n	14.4	14.4
France[3]	14.2	21.5	18.7	15.0	9.7	12.3	x(8)	16.4	15.7	15.8
Germany	9.9	12.6	16.7	14.9	13.2	14.4	14.8	14.2	11.1	11.6
Greece	m	m	m	m	m	m	m	m	m	m
Hungary	m	11.0	10.8	10.7	12.5	11.6	15.3	19.5	13.5	13.9
Iceland	6.9	6.9	x(4)	10.3	11.3	10.6	x(5, 10)	x(10)	x(10)	10.5
Ireland[2]	9.0	19.8	15.9	x(6)	x(6)	14.4	x(6)	x(10)	x(10)	15.6
Israel[2]	12.5	24.6	16.6	12.6	11.0	11.7	m	a	m	m
Italy[2]	11.8	11.8	11.3	11.9	12.1	12.0	m	7.3	18.8	18.7
Japan	15.1	15.9	18.4	14.4	12.2	13.2	x(5, 10)	m	m	m
Korea	17.1	17.1	21.1	19.7	16.5	18.0	a	m	m	m
Luxembourg	m	12.0	10.1	x(6)	x(6)	9.1	m	m	m	m
Mexico	25.4	25.4	28.1	32.7	26.9	30.4	a	15.7	14.5	14.5
Netherlands[2]	m	x(3)	15.7	x(6)	x(6)	16.5	x(6)	x(10)	x(10)	14.7
New Zealand	7.1	7.1	16.2	16.3	14.4	15.3	23.0	19.2	18.0	18.2
Norway[2]	m	m	10.5	9.9	9.4	9.7	x(5)	x(10)	x(10)	9.2
Poland	m	18.7	10.0	12.7	12.1	12.3	14.9	10.3	16.0	16.0
Portugal	m	15.7	10.9	7.9	7.2	7.5	x(5, 10)	x(10)	x(10)	14.4
Slovak Republic	12.4	12.5	17.1	13.6	14.6	14.1	14.2	8.5	15.0	14.9
Slovenia	9.4	9.4	16.2	8.0	14.3	11.0	x(5)	x(10)	x(10)	20.5
Spain	m	13.0	13.2	10.1	9.6	9.9	a	9.2	11.7	11.2
Sweden	6.3	6.3	11.7	11.4	13.1	12.3	12.3	x(10)	x(10)	12.5
Switzerland[1,2]	m	17.5	14.9	11.8	10.3	11.4	m	m	m	m
Turkey	m	23.0	21.7	a	17.6	17.6	a	58.7	14.4	18.8
United Kingdom	15.0	15.9	19.8	17.1	15.2	16.0	x(5)	x(10)	x(10)	18.5
United States	11.4	14.6	14.5	14.0	15.0	14.4	18.0	x(10)	x(10)	16.2
OECD average	12.3	14.4	15.8	13.7	13.8	13.8	15.8	16.4	15.5	15.5
EU21 average	11.6	13.4	14.3	11.7	12.5	12.3	14.4	12.9	15.2	15.8
Argentina[4]	m	m	m	m	m	m	a	m	12.6	m
Brazil	13.0	17.7	23.4	20.4	17.3	19.0	a	x(10)	x(10)	m
China	21.6	24.0	17.2	15.0	18.4	16.5	m	m	m	m
India	m	m	m	m	m	m	m	m	m	m
Indonesia	16.1	17.4	19.9	17.0	16.1	16.7	a	x(10)	x(10)	24.1
Russian Federation[2,5]	m	m	19.2	x(6)	x(6)	11.3	x(6)	10.5	13.9	13.1
Saudi Arabia	m	10.3	11.2	8.8	11.0	9.7	a	x(10)	x(10)	18.2
South Africa[4]	m	x(3)	33.6	x(6)	x(6)	24.4	a	x(10)	x(10)	26.6
G20 average	~	17.5	19.4	15.6	15.5	16.2	~	~	~	~

1. Includes only general programmes in upper secondary education.
2. Public institutions only (in Australia, tertiary-type A and advanced research programmes only; in Canada, at the tertiary level only; in Ireland, at the pre-primary and secondary levels only; in Israel, at the pre-primary level only; in Italy, from pre-primary to secondary levels; in the Russian Federation, at the primary level only).
3. Excludes independent private institutions.
4. Year of reference 2009.
5. Excludes part-time personnel in public institutions at lower secondary and general upper secondary levels.
Source: OECD. Argentina, China, Indonesia: UNESCO Institute for Statistics (World Education Indicators programme). Saudi Arabia: UNESCO Institute for Statistics and Observatory on Higher Education. South Africa: UNESCO Institute for Statistics. See Annex 3 for notes (www.oecd.org/edu/eag2012).
Please refer to the Reader's Guide for information concerning the symbols replacing missing data.
StatLink ⬛⬛⬛ http://dx.doi.org/10.1787/888932667995

Table D2.3. Ratio of students to teaching staff, by type of institution (2010)

By level of education, calculations based on full-time equivalents

	Lower secondary education				Upper secondary education				All secondary education			
		Private				Private				Private		
	Public	Total private institutions	Government-dependent private institutions	Independent private institutions	Public	Total private institutions	Government-dependent private institutions	Independent private institutions	Public	Total private institutions	Government-dependent private institutions	Independent private institutions
	(1)	(2)	(3)	(4)	(5)	(6)	(7)	(8)	(9)	(10)	(11)	(12)
OECD												
Australia[1]	x(9)	x(10)	x(11)	a	x(9)	x(10)	x(11)	a	12.3	11.7	11.7	a
Austria	9.2	10.6	x(2)	x(2)	10.3	9.2	x(6)	x(6)	9.6	9.8	x(10)	x(10)
Belgium[2]	7.5	m	8.5	m	10.7	m	9.8	m	9.5	m	9.4	m
Canada[3, 4, 5]	17.8	15.6	x(2)	x(2)	15.9	14.4	x(6)	x(6)	17.1	15.1	x(10)	x(10)
Chile	24.2	26.0	27.8	17.9	26.6	25.7	28.8	14.3	25.7	25.8	28.5	15.3
Czech Republic	11.3	9.6	9.6	a	11.8	14.0	14.0	a	11.5	13.2	13.2	a
Denmark[4]	11.3	12.8	12.8	m	m	m	m	m	m	m	m	m
Estonia	15.0	11.8	a	11.8	16.8	13.2	a	13.2	16.0	12.7	a	12.7
Finland[6]	9.8	9.8	9.8	a	16.4	21.4	21.4	a	13.2	18.7	18.7	a
France	14.7	m	16.3	m	9.6	m	10.0	m	12.1	m	13.1	m
Germany	14.9	14.4	14.4	x(3)	13.4	12.2	12.2	x(7)	14.4	13.7	13.7	x(11)
Greece	m	m	m	m	m	m	m	m	m	m	m	m
Hungary	10.7	10.3	10.3	a	12.6	12.1	12.1	a	11.6	11.5	11.5	a
Iceland[4, 6]	10.3	9.4	9.4	n	11.4	10.8	10.8	n	10.6	10.6	10.6	n
Ireland[2]	x(9)	x(10)	a	x(12)	x(9)	x(10)	a	x(12)	14.4	m	a	m
Israel	12.8	a	m	a	11.0	a	a	a	11.7	a	m	a
Italy	11.9	m	a	m	12.1	m	a	m	12.0	m	a	m
Japan[6]	14.6	12.7	a	12.7	11.5	13.9	a	13.9	13.1	13.6	a	13.6
Korea	19.7	19.9	19.9	a	16.0	17.3	17.3	a	18.0	17.9	17.9	a
Luxembourg	9.4	x(10)	x(11)	x(12)	8.8	x(10)	x(11)	x(12)	9.1	9.2	10.2	8.4
Mexico	35.5	20.3	a	20.3	32.3	15.2	a	15.2	34.4	17.6	a	17.6
Netherlands[2]	x(9)	m	a	m	x(9)	m	a	m	16.5	m	a	m
New Zealand	16.5	13.1	n	13.1	14.4	14.3	19.0	11.8	15.4	14.0	19.0	12.3
Norway	9.9	m	m	m	9.4	m	m	m	9.7	m	m	m
Poland	12.8	10.0	11.9	9.4	11.9	13.6	14.1	13.5	12.3	12.3	13.0	12.2
Portugal	7.7	10.8	10.8	10.9	7.5	6.1	9.5	5.3	7.6	7.4	10.2	6.3
Slovak Republic	13.6	13.1	13.1	n	14.9	12.9	12.9	n	14.2	13.0	13.0	n
Slovenia[2]	8.0	3.8	3.8	n	14.3	13.4	x(6)	x(6)	11.0	12.7	x(10)	x(10)
Spain	8.6	14.9	14.8	15.2	8.6	14.1	13.4	14.9	8.6	14.6	14.6	15.0
Sweden	11.2	12.6	12.6	n	12.8	14.8	14.8	n	12.0	14.0	14.0	n
Switzerland[7]	11.8	m	m	m	10.3	m	m	m	11.4	m	m	m
Turkey	a	a	a	a	18.5	7.2	a	7.2	18.5	7.2	a	7.2
United Kingdom[2]	17.3	16.4	19.8	11.0	12.4	19.8	21.8	11.2	14.5	18.9	21.4	11.1
United States	14.4	10.7	a	10.7	15.6	10.7	a	10.7	14.9	10.7	a	10.7
OECD average	13.5	13.1	12.5	9.5	13.7	13.9	15.1	9.4	13.8	13.6	14.6	9.5
EU21 average	11.4	11.5	12.5	11.7	12.1	13.6	13.8	11.6	12.1	13.0	13.5	10.9
Other G20												
Argentina	m	m	m	m	m	m	m	m	m	m	m	m
Brazil	22.1	12.6	a	12.6	18.9	11.8	a	11.8	20.7	12.2	a	12.2
China	m	m	m	m	m	m	m	m	m	m	m	m
India	m	m	m	m	m	m	m	m	m	m	m	m
Indonesia	21.2	12.6	a	12.6	17.7	14.8	a	14.8	19.8	13.6	a	13.6
Russian Federation	10.1	m	a	m	m	m	a	m	m	m	a	m
Saudi Arabia	10.2	3.4	x(2)	x(2)	10.5	13.8	x(6)	x(6)	10.3	7.0	x(10)	x(10)
South Africa[3]	x(9)	x(10)	x(10)	x(10)	x(9)	x(10)	x(10)	x(10)	25.1	14.3	x(10)	x(10)
G20 average	m	m	m	m	m	m	m	m	m	m	m	m

1. Includes only general programmes in lower and upper secondary education.
2. Upper secondary includes post-secondary non-tertiary education.
3. Year of reference 2009.
4. Lower secondary includes primary education.
5. Lower secondary includes pre-primary education.
6. Upper secondary education includes programmes from post-secondary education.
7. Includes only general programmes in upper secondary education.
Source: OECD. Indonesia: UNESCO Institute for Statistics (World Education Indicators programme). Saudi Arabia, South Africa: UNESCO Institute for Statistics. See Annex 3 for notes (www.oecd.org/edu/eag2012).
Please refer to the Reader's Guide for information concerning the symbols replacing missing data.
StatLink ⟲ http://dx.doi.org/10.1787/888932668014

Table D2.4a. Teaching staff and non-teaching staff employed in primary, secondary and post-secondary non-tertiary education institutions (2010)

Teaching staff and non-teaching staff in primary, secondary and post-secondary non-tertiary educational institutions per 1000 students, calculation based on full time equivalents

	Instructional personnel		Professional support for students	Management/Quality Control/Administration		Maintenance and operations personnel	Total teaching and non-teaching staff
	Classroom teachers, academic staff & other teachers	Teacher aides and teaching/ research assistants		School- and higher-level management	School- and higher-level administrative personnel		
	(1)	(2)	(3)	(4)	(5)	(6)	(7)
OECD Australia	71.9	x(5)	2.6	m	22.4	3.0	**99.8**
Austria	96.0	m	m	m	m	m	**m**
Belgium	95.5	m	m	m	m	m	**m**
Canada[1]	59.0	m	m	m	m	m	**m**
Chile	39.7	4.3	49.5	4.1	3.1	9.1	**109.8**
Czech Republic	73.6	2.0	8.0	4.5	20.5	16.8	**125.4**
Denmark	86.8	m	m	m	m	m	**m**
Estonia	62.5	m	m	m	m	m	**m**
Finland[2]	72.5	9.7	m	2.8	m	m	**m**
France[3]	84.0	7.0	4.8	3.0	3.9	0.9	**103.5**
Germany	61.0	m	m	m	m	m	**m**
Greece	m	m	m	m	m	m	**m**
Hungary[4]	87.1	m	2.7	m	8.8	19.9	**118.4**
Iceland[2, 4]	94.3	8.6	5.9	12.1	4.9	25.3	**151.1**
Ireland	65.7	m	m	m	m	m	**m**
Israel	70.8	a	a	4.6	m	m	**m**
Italy[2, 3, 4]	85.2	3.1	11.8	0.5	12.9	23.1	**136.5**
Japan[2, 4]	65.3	m	5.4	5.6	4.9	5.3	**86.4**
Korea[2]	51.9	m	m	3.0	m	m	**m**
Luxembourg	104.8	m	m	m	m	m	**m**
Mexico[2, 4]	34.4	0.2	1.1	6.3	9.9	4.1	**56.0**
Netherlands[3]	62.1	m	m	m	m	m	**m**
New Zealand	63.0	m	m	m	m	m	**m**
Norway[2, 3]	99.5	10.7	m	9.3	m	m	**119.6**
Poland[2]	88.9	m	6.3	3.3	m	m	**98.5**
Portugal	112.2	m	m	m	m	m	**m**
Slovak Republic[2]	67.6	1.6	m	7.5	m	m	**m**
Slovenia	78.4	9.3	10.2	6.1	1.1	m	**105.2**
Spain	88.6	m	m	m	m	m	**m**
Sweden	83.2	m	m	m	m	m	**m**
Switzerland[3]	76.5	m	m	m	m	m	**m**
Turkey	48.9	m	m	m	m	m	**m**
United Kingdom[2, 4]	57.7	15.5	12.9	6.6	8.2	2.8	**103.7**
United States	68.9	15.5	10.7	6.6	10.0	14.2	**125.9**
OECD average	74.5	7.3	10.2	5.4	9.2	11.3	**110.0**
Average for countries with data on each category	70.0	7.3	10.5	5.5	9.2	11.3	**110.1**
EU21 average	81.8	6.5	7.8	4.0	10.9	12.7	**114.3**
Other G20 Argentina	m	m	m	m	m	m	**m**
Brazil	48.6	m	m	m	m	m	**m**
China	m	m	m	m	m	m	**m**
India	m	m	m	m	m	m	**m**
Indonesia	m	m	m	m	m	m	**m**
Russian Federation	81.6	m	m	m	m	m	**m**
Saudi Arabia	m	m	m	m	m	m	**m**
South Africa	m	m	m	m	m	m	**m**
G20 average	m	m	m	m	m	m	**m**

1. Year of reference 2009.
2. School- and higher-level management excludes higher-level management.
3. Public institutions only.
4. School- and higher-level administrative personnel excludes higher-level administrative personnel.
Source: OECD. See Annex 3 for notes *(www.oecd.org/edu/eag2012)*.
Please refer to the Reader's Guide for information concerning the symbols replacing missing data.
StatLink http://dx.doi.org/10.1787/888932668033

Table D2.4b. Teaching staff and non-teaching staff employed in tertiary education institutions (2010)

Teaching staff and non-teaching staff in tertiary educational institutions per 1000 students, calculation based on full time equivalents

| | Instructional personnel | | Professional support for students | Management/quality control/administration | | Maintenance and operations personnel | Total teaching and non-teaching staff |
	Classroom teachers, academic staff & other teachers	Teacher aides and teaching/research assistants		School- and higher-level management	School- and higher-level administrative personnel		
	(1)	(2)	(3)	(4)	(5)	(6)	(7)
Australia	m	m	m	m	m	m	**m**
Austria[1, 2]	58.5	m	2.6	1.6	32.3	4.2	**99.3**
Belgium	51.7	m	m	m	m	m	**m**
Canada	m	m	m	m	m	m	**m**
Chile	m	m	m	m	m	m	**m**
Czech Republic	50.1	1.8	7.0	1.5	29.3	10.0	**99.6**
Denmark	m	m	m	m	m	m	**m**
Estonia	m	m	m	m	m	m	**m**
Finland	69.6	m	m	m	m	m	**m**
France[3, 4]	64.5	a	1.2	m	8.4	9.4	**83.5**
Germany	86.5	m	m	m	m	m	**m**
Greece	m	m	m	m	m	m	**m**
Hungary[1, 2, 5]	71.7	m	x(5)	x(5)	96.7	x(5)	**168.4**
Iceland[1, 2]	95.5	x(1)	3.2	4.4	35.3	8.4	**146.8**
Ireland	63.9	m	m	m	m	m	**m**
Israel	m	m	m	m	m	m	**m**
Italy[1, 2]	53.5	9.0	3.0	0.4	26.0	2.8	**94.7**
Japan	m	m	m	m	m	m	**m**
Korea	m	m	m	m	m	m	**m**
Luxembourg	m	m	m	m	m	m	**m**
Mexico[1, 2]	68.9	m	6.5	6.3	27.7	10.4	**119.7**
Netherlands	m	m	m	m	m	m	**m**
New Zealand[2]	54.9	m	m	m	m	m	**m**
Norway[4]	108.2	m	m	m	m	m	**m**
Poland[1, 2]	62.7	m	0.1	m	34.3	6.2	**103.3**
Portugal	69.3	m	m	m	m	m	**m**
Slovak Republic[1]	67.3	m	m	0.9	m	m	**m**
Slovenia	48.8	28.9	18.5	2.5	2.7	4.4	**105.8**
Spain	89.6	m	m	m	m	m	**m**
Sweden	80.2	m	m	m	m	m	**m**
Switzerland	m	m	m	m	m	m	**m**
Turkey	53.2	m	m	m	m	m	**m**
United Kingdom[1, 2]	54.2	a	m	43.9	32.2	17.4	**147.7**
United States	61.8	m	m	m	m	m	**m**
OECD average	67.5	13.2	5.3	7.7	32.5	8.1	**116.9**
Average for countries with data on each category	62.1	13.2	5.9	9.1	32.9	8.1	**118.2**
EU21 average	66.2	5.4	2.8	9.7	37.0	8.3	**113.8**
Argentina	m	m	m	m	m	m	**m**
Brazil	38.3	m	m	m	m	m	**m**
China	m	m	m	m	m	m	**m**
India	m	m	m	m	m	m	**m**
Indonesia	m	m	m	m	m	m	**m**
Russian Federation	76.3	m	m	m	m	m	**m**
Saudi Arabia	m	m	m	m	m	m	**m**
South Africa	m	m	m	m	m	m	**m**
G20 average	m	m	m	m	m	m	**m**

1. School- and higher-level management excludes higher-level management.
2. School- and higher-level administrative personnel excludes higher-level administrative personnel.
3. School- and higher-level management excludes school-level management.
4. Public institutions only.
5. Tertiary-type B is partially included with upper secondary education.
Source: OECD. See Annex 3 for notes (*www.oecd.org/edu/eag2012*).
Please refer to the Reader's Guide for information concerning the symbols replacing missing data.
StatLink ᵐˢᵖ http://dx.doi.org/10.1787/888932668052

HOW MUCH ARE TEACHERS PAID?

- The statutory salaries of teachers with at least 15 years of experience average USD 35 630 at the pre-primary level, USD 37 603 at the primary level, USD 39 401 at the lower secondary level and USD 41 182 at the upper secondary level.

- On average in OECD countries, teachers' salaries at the primary-school level amount to 82% of full-time, full-year earnings for 25-64 year-olds with a tertiary education, while teachers' salaries at the lower secondary level amount to 85% of that benchmark, and teachers' salaries at the upper secondary level amount to 90% of it.

- Among the 38 countries with available data, half offer an additional payment to teachers for outstanding performance.

Chart D3.1. Teachers' salaries in lower secondary education (2010)
Annual statutory teachers' salaries after 15 years of experience and minimum training in public institutions in lower secondary education, in equivalent USD converted using PPPs, and the ratio of salary to earnings for full-time, full-year workers with tertiary education aged 25-64

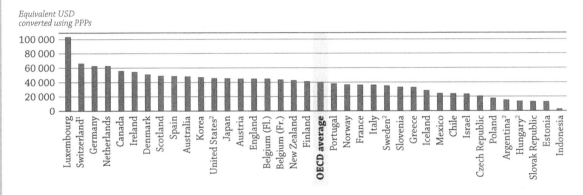

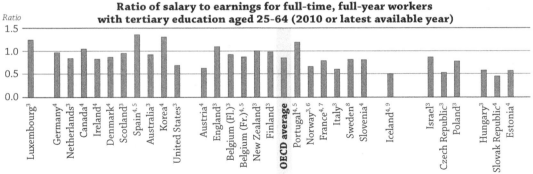

1. Salaries after 11 years of experience.
2. Actual base salaries.
3. Ratio of actual salary, including bonuses and allowances, for teachers aged 25-64 to earnings for full-time, full-year workers with tertiary education aged 25-64.
4. Ratio of statutory salary after 15 years of experience (minimum training) to earnings for full-time, full-year workers with tertiary education aged 25-64.
5. Year of reference 2009.
6. Year of reference 2007.
7. Year of reference 2008.
8. Ratio of actual teachers' salary after 15 years of experience (minimum training), not including bonuses and allowances, to earnings for full-time, full-year workers with tertiary education aged 25-64.
9. Year of reference 2006.
Countries are ranked in descending order of teachers' salaries in lower secondary education after 15 years of experience and minimum training.
Source: OECD. Argentina: UNESCO Institute for Statistics (World Education Indicators programme). Tables D3.1. See Annex 3 for notes (*www.oecd.org/edu/eag2012*).
StatLink ⓘ http://dx.doi.org/10.1787/888932663682

Context

Teachers' salaries represent the largest single cost in school education. Together with alternative employment opportunities, teachers' salaries have an impact on the attractiveness of the teaching profession. They influence decisions to enrol in teacher education, become a teacher after graduation (as graduates' career choices are associated with relative earnings in teaching and non-teaching occupations, and their likely growth over time), return to the teaching profession after a career interruption, and/or remain a teacher (as, in general, the higher the salaries, the fewer the people who choose to leave the profession) (OECD, 2005). Burgeoning national debt, spurred by governments' responses to the financial crisis of late 2008, have put pressure on policy makers to reduce government expenditure – particularly on public payrolls. Since compensation and working conditions are important for attracting, developing and retaining skilled and high-quality teachers, policy makers should carefully consider teachers' salaries as they try to ensure both quality teaching and sustainable education budgets (see Indicators B6 and B7).

INDICATOR D3

Other findings

- In most OECD countries, **teachers' salaries increase with the level of education they teach.** For example, in Belgium, Indonesia and Poland, the salary of an upper secondary school teacher with at least 15 years of experience is at least 25% higher than that of a primary school teacher with the same experience.

- **Salaries at the top of the scale are, on average, 60%, 62% and 63% higher, respectively, than starting salaries in primary, lower secondary and upper secondary education,** and the difference tends to be greatest when it takes many years to progress through the scale. In countries where it takes 30 years or more to reach the top of the salary scale, salaries at at the top of the scale are an average of 77% higher than starting salaries.

- The maximum salary received by teachers with the maximum qualifications and at the top of the salary scale is, on average, USD 46 382 at the pre-primary level, USD 48 436 at the primary level, USD 51 872 at the lower secondary level, and USD 52 962 at the upper secondary level. However, **the salary premium for a higher level of qualification is varied.** Primary teachers holding the maximum qualification in Israel, Mexico, Poland and Slovenia, for example, earn at least 30% more than primary school teachers holding the minimum qualification with similar experience; yet in around 40% of countries, there is no difference.

- The average **statutory salary per teaching hour** after 15 years of experience is USD 49 for primary school teachers, USD 58 for lower secondary teachers, and USD 65 for upper secondary teachers in general education.

Trends

Teachers' salaries rose, in real terms, in most countries with available data between 2000 and 2010. Notable exceptions are France and Japan, where there was a decline in teachers' salaries in real terms during that period.

D3

Analysis

Comparing teachers' salaries

Teachers' salaries are one component of teachers' total compensation. Other benefits such as regional allowances for teaching in remote areas, family allowances, reduced rates on public transport and tax allowances on the purchase of cultural materials may also form part of teachers' total remuneration. There are also large differences in taxation and social-benefits systems in OECD countries. All this should be borne in mind when comparing salaries across countries.

Teachers' salaries vary widely across countries. The salaries of lower secondary school teachers with at least 15 years of experience range from less than USD 15 000 in Argentina, Estonia, Hungary, Indonesia and the Slovak Republic to USD 60 000 or more in Germany, the Netherlands and Switzerland (for teachers with at least 11 years of experience) and exceed USD 100 000 in Luxembourg (Table D3.1 and Chart D3.1).

In most OECD countries, teachers' salaries increase with the level of education taught. In Belgium, the Czech Republic, Denmark and Poland, upper secondary teachers with 15 years of experience earn about 30% more than pre-primary teachers with the same experience. The difference exceeds 50% in Finland, mainly because of the 33% gap between pre-primary and primary teachers' salaries. The differences between salaries at each level of education should be interpreted in light of the requirements to enter the teaching profession (see Indicator D5).

In Australia, Canada, Israel, Korea and Turkey, there is less than a 5% difference between salaries for upper secondary and pre-primary school teachers with 15 years of experience; in England, Greece, Ireland, Portugal, Scotland and Slovenia, teachers receive the same salary irrespective of the level of education taught. In contrast, in Argentina, teachers' salaries decrease with the level of education taught: an upper secondary school teacher earns 17% less than a pre-primary school teacher. In Israel there is a 17% difference between the salaries of an upper secondary teacher and a primary teacher in favour of the latter and this difference is the consequence of the "New Horizon" reform that has been gradually implemented since 2008. The reform has increased salaries for primary and lower secondary teachers. However, another reform, begun in 2012, will also increase salaries for upper secondary teachers. In Luxembourg, primary school teachers with 15 years of experience earned around 50% less than secondary teachers with the same amount of experience prior to a reform in 2009. Now, however, the difference between primary and secondary school teachers' salaries is less than 10%.

Differences in teachers' salaries at different education levels may influence how schools and school systems attract and retain teachers and may also influence the extent to which teachers move among education levels.

Box D3.1. **Actual teachers' salaries**

Statutory salaries as reported by most of the countries in this indicator must be distinguished from actual expenditures on wages by governments and from teachers' average salaries, which are influenced by factors such as the age structure and levels of experience of the teaching force, the prevalence of bonuses and allowances in the compensation system, and the frequency of part-time work.

Table D3.5 (available on line) provides the average actual annual salaries of teachers aged 25-64 including all bonuses, allowances or additional payments for 16 countries with available data. In Chile, Hungary, Israel (pre-primary and secondary levels), Norway (primary and lower secondary levels) and Poland (pre-primary, primary and lower secondary levels), average salaries, including bonuses and allowances, are at least 20% higher than statutory salaries for teachers with 15 years of experience. In contrast, in the Czech Republic, Italy, Luxembourg (pre-primary and primary levels), the Netherlands (lower and upper secondary levels) and Scotland, average salaries of teachers aged 25-64 are at least 5% lower than statutory salaries for teachers with 15 years of experience.

D3

Minimum and maximum teachers' salaries

Education systems face a challenge in recruiting high-quality graduates as teachers. Research evidence indicates that salaries and alternative employment opportunities are important influences on the attractiveness of teaching (Santiago, 2004). The starting salaries of teachers relative to other non-teaching occupations and the likely growth in earnings have a huge influence over a graduate's decision to become a teacher. Countries that are looking to increase the supply of teachers, especially those with an aging teacher workforce and/or an increasing school-age population, might look at implementing attractive starting wages and career prospects. However, to ensure a well-qualified teaching workforce, efforts must be made to not only recruit and select only the most competent and qualified teachers, but to retain effective teachers.

At the lower secondary level, new teachers entering the profession with the minimum qualification earn on average USD 29 801. This minimum salary ranges from below USD 15 000 in Argentina, the Czech Republic, Estonia, Hungary, Indonesia, Poland and the Slovak Republic to above USD 40 000 in Denmark, Germany, Luxembourg, Spain and Switzerland. For teachers at the top of the salary scale and with the maximum qualifications, salaries average USD 51 872. This maximum salary ranges from less than USD 20 000 in Argentina, Estonia, Indonesia and the Slovak Republic to more than USD 75 000 in Luxembourg and Switzerland. Most countries with starting salaries below the OECD average also show lower maximum salaries. The exceptions are France, Japan, Korea and Mexico where starting salaries are at least 5% lower than the OECD average, but maximum salaries are significantly higher. The opposite is true for Australia, Denmark and Norway where starting salaries are at least 10% above the OECD average but maximum statutory salaries are within the OECD average (Chart D3.2 and Table D3.4, available on line).

A number of countries have relatively flat salary scales. For example, the difference between minimum and maximum salaries is less than 30% in Turkey at all levels of education, in Denmark at the pre-primary, primary and lower secondary levels, and in Finland, Norway and Sweden at the pre-primary level. Given the weak financial incentives, these countries may have some difficulties in retaining teachers as teachers approach the peak of their earnings.

Chart D3.2. **Minimum and maximum teachers' salaries in lower secondary education (2010)**
Annual statutory teachers' salaries in public institutions in lower secondary education, in equivalent USD converted using PPPs

1. Salaries at top of scale/minimum training.
2. Actual base salaries.
Countries are ranked in descending order of starting teachers' salaries with minimum training in lower secondary education.
Source: OECD. Argentina: UNESCO Institute for Statistics (World Education Indicators programme). Table D3.4, available on line. See Annex 3 for notes (*www.oecd.org/edu/eag2012*).
StatLink ⬛⬛⬛ http://dx.doi.org/10.1787/888932663701

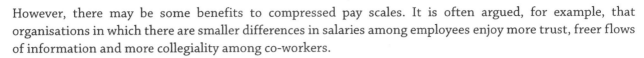

However, there may be some benefits to compressed pay scales. It is often argued, for example, that organisations in which there are smaller differences in salaries among employees enjoy more trust, freer flows of information and more collegiality among co-workers.

In contrast, maximum salaries are at least twice the amount of starting salaries in Austria, Chile, France (lower and upper secondary levels), Hungary (upper secondary level), Israel, Japan (primary and secondary levels), Korea and Poland (pre-primary and primary levels), and they are more than three times the starting salaries in Mexico (pre-primary, primary and lower secondary levels).

The salary premium for a higher level of qualification, at the top of the salary scale, also varies across the countries. At the lower secondary level, while there is no difference between salaries at top of the scale for teachers with minimum and maximum qualifications in 11 of 32 countries with both data, teachers at the top of the scale holding the maximum qualification in France, Hungary, Israel, Norway, Scotland and Slovenia earn at least 20% more than teachers with the same experience, but with minimum training. This salary gap is as wide as 57% in Mexico. A similar picture is seen at the upper secondary level (Table D3.1 and Table D3.4, available on line).

When considering salary structure for teachers, it is important to remember that not all teachers reach the top of the salary scale. For example, in Italy, less than 5% of all teachers were at the top of the salary scale in 2010.

Teaching experience and salary scales

Salary structures define the salaries paid to teachers at different points in their careers. Deferred compensation, which rewards employees for staying in organisations or professions and for meeting established performance criteria, is also used in teachers' salary structures. OECD data on teachers' salaries are limited to information on statutory salaries at four points of the salary scale: starting salaries, salaries after 10 years of service, salaries after 15 years of experience, and salaries at the top of the scale. The salaries discussed here are those of teachers who have the minimum required training. As mentioned above, further qualifications can lead to wage increases in some countries.

In OECD countries, statutory salaries for lower secondary school teachers with 10 and 15 years of experience are, respectively, 25% and 35% higher, on average, than starting salaries. Furthermore, salaries at the top of the scale, which is reached after an average of 24 years of experience, are on average 62% higher than starting salaries. In Hungary, Israel, Italy, Korea and Spain, lower secondary school teachers reach the top of the salary scale after at least 35 years of service. In contrast, lower secondary school teachers in Australia, Denmark, Estonia, New Zealand and Scotland reach the highest step on the salary scale within six to nine years (Table D3.1).

While salary increases are gradual in slightly more than half of the 33 OECD countries with relevant data, in the remaining countries, salary scales include steps of uneven size. For example, in the Czech Republic and Greece, salaries at the top of the scale are around 50% higher than starting salaries, and teachers in both countries must work 32 (the Czech Republic) or 33 years (Greece) to reach the top salary. However, most of the increase in the Czech Republic occurs during the first 10 years of service and salaries rise at a slower rate during the next 22 years; while in Greece, there are gradual salary increases throughout teachers' careers.

Teachers' salaries relative to earnings for workers with a tertiary education

The propensity of young people to undertake teacher training, as well as of graduates from training teachers programmes to enter or stay in the profession will be influenced by the salaries of teachers relative to those of other occupations requiring similar levels of qualifications and likely salary increases. In all OECD countries, a tertiary qualification is required to become a teacher (see Indicator D5), so the likely alternative to teacher education is another tertiary education programme. Thus, to interpret salary levels in different countries and reflect comparative labour-market conditions, teachers' salaries are compared to those of other similarly-educated professionals: 25-64 year-old full-time, full-year workers with a tertiary education (see Indicator A10).

Teachers' salaries at the primary level amount to 82% of full-time, full-year earnings, on average, for 25-64 year-olds with tertiary education, 85% at the lower secondary level, and 90% at the upper secondary level. At this latter level, teachers earn as much or more than workers with tertiary education in 12 countries of the 30 countries with available data (Table D3.1 and Chart D3.1). Relative salaries for teachers are highest in the Flemish Community of Belgium (upper secondary level), Korea, Luxembourg (lower and upper secondary levels) and Spain, where teachers' salaries are at least 20% higher than those of comparably educated workers. The lowest relative teachers' salaries, compared to the salaries of other professionals with comparable education are found in Iceland for primary and lower secondary school teachers, and in the Slovak Republic at all levels of education, where statutory salaries for teachers with 15 years of experience are 50% or less, on average, of what a full-time, full-year worker with a tertiary education earns.

Statutory salaries per hour of net teaching time

The average statutory salary per teaching hour after 15 years of experience is USD 49 for primary school teachers, USD 58 for lower secondary teachers, and USD 65 for upper secondary teachers in general education. Argentina, Chile, the Czech Republic (primary level), Estonia, Hungary, Indonesia, Mexico (primary and lower secondary levels), Poland (primary level) and the Slovak Republic show the lowest salaries per teaching hour – USD 30 or less. In contrast, salaries per hour reach USD 90 or more in Belgium, Denmark, Germany and Japan at the upper secondary level, and in Luxembourg at all education levels (Table D3.1).

As secondary school teachers are required to teach fewer hours than primary school teachers, their salaries per teaching hour are usually higher than those of teachers at lower levels of education, even in countries where statutory salaries are similar (see Indicator D4). On average among OECD countries, upper secondary school teachers' salaries per teaching hour exceed those of primary school teachers by around 31% (Table D3.1). In Scotland there is no difference, while in Denmark, upper secondary school teachers earn double the salary of primary school teachers per teaching hour. In contrast, in Argentina, primary school teachers' salaries per teaching hour exceed those of upper secondary school teachers by 57%.

However, the difference in salaries between primary and secondary teachers may disappear when comparing salaries per hour of working time. In Portugal, for example, there is a 14% difference in salaries per teaching hour between primary and upper secondary school teachers, even though statutory salaries and working time are actually the same at these levels. The difference is explained by the fact that primary school teachers spend more time in teaching activities than upper secondary teachers do (see Table D4.1).

Box D3.2. **Effect of the financial crisis**

The financial crisis that hit the world economy in the last months of 2008 significantly affected the salaries for civil servants and public sector workers in general. The first-order effect of the crisis was a general reduction in GDP growth in the OECD area, and some countries went into recession. The second-order effect was a large increase in national debt that put pressure on government expenditure in many countries. The pressure to trim government spending in order to reduce national debt has resulted, for example, in cuts in teachers' and other civil-service salaries in Estonia, Hungary and Ireland. In Estonia the statutory salaries in 2009-10 fell back to their 2008 levels. In Hungary, the 13th month of salary (a supplemental bonus that was paid to all employees) was suspended in 2009 but a compensatory bonus was paid to all employees in the public sector whose wages where under a determined threshold. In Ireland, teachers' salaries were reduced from 1 January 2010 as part of a public service-wide reduction in pay. In other countries, similar measures were implemented after 2010.

The financial crisis has also had an influence on the supply of teachers. In general, when the general economy is weak, and there is high graduate unemployment and low graduate earnings, teaching might seem to be a more attractive job choice for graduates than other non-teaching occupations (OECD, 2005).

Trends since 2000

Between 2000 and 2010, teachers' salaries increased in real terms in most countries. In Denmark, Estonia, Ireland, Portugal and Scotland, salaries increased at all levels of education by at least 20%. In the Czech Republic (primary and lower secondary levels) and in Turkey, salaries doubled over the past decade. Only in France and Japan did teachers' salaries decrease in real terms by more than 5 % (Table D3.2 and Chart D3.3).

In most countries, salaries increased less since 2005 than between 2000 and 2005. The exceptions to this pattern are Denmark, Estonia, Israel (primary and lower secondary levels) and New Zealand, where most of the increase in teachers' salaries occurred after 2005.

Chart D3.3. **Changes in teachers' salaries after 15 years of experience/minimum training in lower secondary education (2000, 2005, 2010)**
Index of change between 2000 and 2010 (2000 = 100, constant prices)

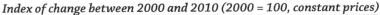

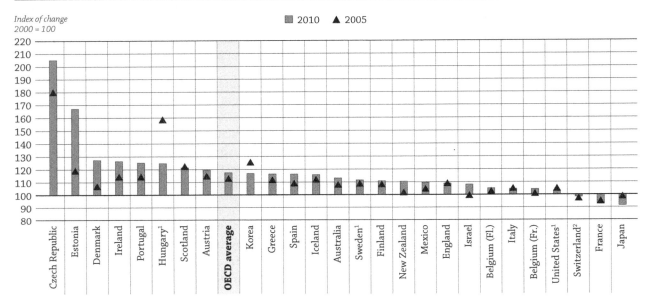

1. Actual base salaries.
2. Salaries after 11 years of experience.
Countries are ranked in descending order of the index of change between 2000 and 2010 in teachers' salaries in lower secondary education after 15 years of experience.
Source: OECD. Table D3.2. See Annex 3 for notes (*www.oecd.org/edu/eag2012*).
StatLink ᴍꜱᴘ http://dx.doi.org/10.1787/888932663720

Additional payments: Incentives and allowances

In addition to basic pay scales, school systems increasingly use schemes that offer additional payments or other rewards for teachers. These may take the form of financial remuneration and/or reduction in the number of teaching hours. Greece and Iceland, for example, offer a reduction in required teaching hours to reward experience or long service. In Portugal, teachers may receive a salary increase and a reduction in teaching time when they carry out special tasks or activities, such as training student teachers or providing guidance counselling. Together with the starting salary, these payments may influence a person's decision to enter or remain in the teaching profession. Additional payments early in a career may include family allowances and bonuses for working in certain locations, and higher initial salaries for higher-than-minimum teaching qualifications.

Data have not been collected on payment amounts but on whether additional payments are available and on the level at which the decision to award such payments is taken (Table D3.3a and Tables D3.3b, D3.3c and D3.3d, available on line, and Annex 3 available at *www.oecd.org/edu/eag2012*).

Additional payments are most often awarded for particular responsibilities or working conditions, such as teaching in more disadvantaged schools, particularly those located in very poor neighbourhoods or those with a large proportion of students whose language is not the language of instruction. These schools often have difficulty attracting teachers and are more likely to have less-experienced teachers (OECD, 2005). These additional payments are provided annually in about half of the countries. Eleven countries also offer additional payments, usually on an annual basis, for teachers who teach in certain fields in which there are teacher shortages.

Additional payments based on teachers' qualifications, training and performance are also common in OECD and other G20 countries. The most common types of payments are for an initial education qualification and/or a level of teacher certification and training that is higher than the minimum requirement. Three-quarters of the countries make these payments available, with about 60% of all countries offering both types of payments. Twenty-two countries offer additional payments for the successful completion of professional development activities. In 16 of these countries, these payments help to determine the base salary, but in Korea they are only offered on an incidental basis.

Two-thirds of the 19 countries that offer an additional payment to reward outstanding teaching do so as incidental payments; 13 countries offer these payments as annual additions to teachers' salaries. In 16 of the 19 countries that offer this performance incentive, the decision to award the additional payments can be made at the school level.

Less than half of all OECD countries offer additional payments based on teachers' demographic characteristics (family status or age), and most of these are annual payments.

Definitions

Actual salaries for teachers aged 25-64 refer to the annual average earnings received by teachers aged 25 to 64, before taxes. It includes work-related payments such as annual bonuses, result-related bonuses, extra pay for holidays and sick-leave pay. Income from other sources, such as government social transfers, investment income, and any other income, which is not directly related to their profession, are not included.

An **adjustment to base salary** is defined as any difference in salary between what a particular teacher actually receives for work performed at a school and the amount that he or she would expect to receive on the basis of experience (i.e. number of years in the teaching profession). Adjustments may be temporary or permanent, and they can effectively move a teacher off the scale and to a different salary scale or to a higher step on the same salary scale.

Earnings for workers with tertiary education are average earnings for full-time, full-year workers aged 25 to 64 and with an education at ISCED 5A/5B/6 level. The relative salary indicator is calculated for the latest year with earnings data available. For countries in which teachers' salary and workers' earnings information are not available for the same year (e.g. Australia, the Flemish Community of Belgium, Canada, Italy and the Netherlands), the indicator is adjusted for inflation using the deflators for private consumption. Reference statistics for earnings for workers with tertiary education are provided in Annexes 2 and 3.

Salaries after 15 years of experience refer to the scheduled annual salary of a full-time classroom teacher with the minimum training necessary to be fully qualified plus 15 years of experience.

Starting salaries refer to the average scheduled gross salary per year for a full-time teacher with the minimum training necessary to be fully qualified at the beginning of the teaching career whereas **maximum salaries** reported refers to the maximum annual salary (top of the salary scale) of a full-time classroom teacher with the maximum qualifications recognised from the point of view of compensation.

Statutory salaries refer to scheduled salaries according to official pay scales. The salaries reported are gross (total sum paid by the employer) less the employer's contribution to social security and pension, according to existing salary scales. Salaries are "before tax", i.e. before deductions for income tax. In Table D3.1, salary per hour of net contact divides a teacher's annual statutory salary by the annual net teaching time in hours (see Table D4.1).

D3

Methodology

Data on statutory teachers' salaries and bonuses are derived from the 2011 OECD-INES Survey on Teachers and the Curriculum. Data refer to the school year 2009-10 and are reported in accordance with formal policies for public institutions.

Measuring the statutory salary of a full-time teacher relative to the number of hours per year that a teacher is required to spend teaching does not adjust salaries for the amount of time that teachers spend in various other teaching-related activities. Since the proportion of teachers' working time spent teaching varies across OECD countries, statutory salaries per hour of net teaching time must be interpreted with caution (see Indicator D4). However, it can provide an estimate of the cost of the actual time teachers spend in the classroom.

Gross teachers' salaries were converted using PPPs for private consumption from the OECD National Accounts database. In the previous editions of *Education at a Glance,* salaries used to be converted using PPPs for GDP. As a consequence, teachers' salaries in USD (Table D3.1) are not directly comparable with the figures published in the previous editions of *Education at a Glance*. Information on trends in teachers' salaries can be found in Table D3.2. As a complement to Table D3.1, which presents teachers' salaries in equivalent USD, converted using PPPs, a table with teachers' salaries in national currency is included in Annex 2. The period of reference for teachers' salaries is from 1 July 2009 to 30 June 2010. The reference date for GDP per capita and PPPs is 2009-10.

For calculation of changes in teachers' salaries (Table D3.2), the deflator for private consumption is used to convert salaries to 2000 prices.

Notes on definitions and methodologies for each country are provided in Annex 3 at *www.oecd.org/edu/eag2012*.

The statistical data for Israel are supplied by and under the responsibility of the relevant Israeli authorities. The use of such data by the OECD is without prejudice to the status of the Golan Heights, East Jerusalem and Israeli settlements in the West Bank under the terms of international law.

References

OECD (2005), *Teachers Matter: Attracting, Developing and Retaining Effective Teachers*, OECD Publishing.

OECD (2008), *Improving School Leadership, Volume 1: Policy and Practices*, OECD Publishing.

Santiago, P. (2004), "The labour market for teachers", in G. Johnes and J. Johnes (eds), *International Handbook on the Economics of Education*, Edward Elgar, Cheltenham.

The following additional material relevant to this indicator is available on line:

- *Table D3.3b. Decisions made by school principal on payments for teachers in public institutions (2010)*
  StatLink 🖳 http://dx.doi.org/10.1787/888932668185

- *Table D3.3c. Decisions made by local or regional authority on payments for teachers in public institutions (2010)*
  StatLink 🖳 http://dx.doi.org/10.1787/888932668204

- *Table D3.3d. Decisions made by the national authority on payments for teachers in public institutions (2010)*
  StatLink 🖳 http://dx.doi.org/10.1787/888932668223

- *Table D3.4. Minimum and maximum teachers' salaries (2010)*
  StatLink 🖳 http://dx.doi.org/10.1787/888932668242

- *Table D3.5. Average actual teachers' salaries (2010)*
  StatLink 🖳 http://dx.doi.org/10.1787/888932668261

- *Table D3.6. Trends in the ratio of salaries to GDP per capita (2000-10)*
  StatLink 🖳 http://dx.doi.org/10.1787/888932668280

Table D3.1. [1/3] Teachers' salaries (2010)

Annual statutory teachers' salaries in public institutions at starting salary, after 10 and 15 years of experience and at the top of the scale, by level of education, in equivalent USD converted using PPPs for private consumption

D3

	Pre-primary education				Primary education			
	Starting salary/ minimum training	Salary after 10 years of experience/ minimum training	Salary after 15 years of experience/ minimum training	Salary at top of scale/ minimum training	Starting salary/ minimum training	Salary after 10 years of experience/ minimum training	Salary after 15 years of experience/ minimum training	Salary at top of scale/ minimum training
	(1)	(2)	(3)	(4)	(5)	(6)	(7)	(8)
OECD								
Australia	34 029	46 318	46 318	46 318	34 193	47 445	47 445	47 445
Austria	30 812	36 361	40 818	60 973	30 812	36 361	40 818	60 973
Belgium (Fl.)	31 193	39 139	44 076	53 949	31 193	39 139	44 076	53 949
Belgium (Fr.)	30 202	m	42 792	52 509	30 202	m	42 792	52 509
Canada	34 437	52 213	54 996	54 996	34 443	52 205	54 978	54 978
Chile	17 820	21 547	23 411	30 866	17 820	21 547	23 411	30 866
Czech Republic	12 578	15 588	16 527	19 089	15 036	18 878	19 949	22 276
Denmark	41 525	44 057	45 257	45 257	43 393	48 540	50 253	50 253
England	30 204	44 145	44 145	44 145	30 204	44 145	44 145	44 145
Estonia	m	m	m	m	11 876	12 576	12 576	17 357
Finland	24 520	28 159	28 159	28 159	29 029	35 335	37 455	39 702
France	24 334	30 572	32 733	48 296	24 334	30 572	32 733	48 296
Germany	m	m	m	m	46 456	m	55 771	61 209
Greece	26 583	30 210	32 387	38 934	26 583	30 210	32 387	38 934
Hungary[1]	10 257	11 554	12 291	16 100	10 701	12 290	13 228	17 644
Iceland	21 477	23 885	23 885	27 328	24 822	27 211	27 930	29 123
Ireland	32 601	47 891	53 677	60 758	32 601	47 891	53 677	60 758
Israel	14 205	18 274	20 076	29 639	17 646	22 415	25 181	36 137
Italy	27 015	29 728	32 658	39 762	27 015	29 728	32 658	39 762
Japan	m	m	m	m	25 454	37 838	44 788	56 543
Korea	26 238	38 551	45 045	74 149	26 776	39 722	46 338	74 149
Luxembourg	65 171	84 194	95 043	114 988	65 171	84 194	95 043	114 988
Mexico	14 302	14 397	18 621	30 602	14 302	14 397	18 621	30 602
Netherlands	m	m	m	m	36 861	44 407	50 621	53 654
New Zealand	m	m	m	m	27 719	41 009	41 009	41 009
Norway	32 041	36 476	36 476	36 476	32 629	35 991	35 991	40 405
Poland	9 526	12 620	15 186	15 824	9 526	12 620	15 186	15 824
Portugal	30 825	34 537	37 542	54 158	30 825	34 537	37 542	54 158
Scotland	30 207	48 188	48 188	48 188	30 207	48 188	48 188	48 188
Slovak Republic	9 033	9 944	10 391	11 546	11 028	12 132	12 688	13 680
Slovenia	26 690	29 608	32 436	33 425	26 690	29 608	32 436	34 074
Spain	37 137	40 480	42 846	51 822	37 137	40 480	42 846	51 822
Sweden[1]	28 777	31 437	32 927	34 162	28 937	32 182	33 374	38 696
Switzerland[2]	40 317	51 301	m	62 811	45 226	57 371	m	70 784
Turkey	22 740	24 455	24 371	26 197	23 130	24 845	24 761	26 587
United States[1]	36 977	m	m	m	36 858	42 889	45 226	52 137
OECD average	27 541	33 649	35 630	43 048	28 523	34 968	37 603	45 100
EU21 average	27 960	34 127	37 004	43 602	28 948	34 477	38 280	44 907
Other G20								
Argentina[1]	14 204	m	17 232	20 907	13 768	m	17 041	20 657
Brazil	m	m	m	m	m	m	m	m
China	m	m	m	m	m	m	m	m
India	m	m	m	m	m	m	m	m
Indonesia	1 638	1 855	2 072	2 361	1 638	1 855	2 072	2 361
Russian Federation	m	m	m	m	m	m	m	m
Saudi Arabia	m	m	m	m	m	m	m	m
South Africa	m	m	m	m	m	m	m	m
G20 average	m	m	m	m	m	m	m	m

Note: Due to a change in the methodology used to convert teachers' salaries into USD, data are not directly comparable with the figures published in previous editions of *Education at a Glance*. Please refer to Table D3.2 for information on trends in teachers' salaries.
1. Actual base salaries.
2. Salaries after 11 years of experience for Columns 2, 6, 10 and 14.
Source: OECD. Argentina: UNESCO Institute for Statistics (World Education Indicators programme). See Annex 3 for notes (*www.oecd.org/edu/eag2012*).
Please refer to the Reader's Guide for information concerning the symbols replacing missing data.
StatLink ᴬᴵˢᴾ http://dx.doi.org/10.1787/888932668109

Table D3.1. [2/3] Teachers' salaries (2010)

Annual statutory teachers' salaries in public institutions at starting salary, after 10 and 15 years of experience and at the top of the scale, by level of education, in equivalent USD converted using PPPs for private consumption

	Lower secondary education				Upper secondary education			
	Starting salary/ minimum training	Salary after 10 years of experience/ minimum training	Salary after 15 years of experience/ minimum training	Salary at top of scale/ minimum training	Starting salary/ minimum training	Salary after 10 years of experience/ minimum training	Salary after 15 years of experience/ minimum training	Salary at top of scale/ minimum training
	(9)	(10)	(11)	(12)	(13)	(14)	(15)	(16)
Australia	34 321	47 445	47 445	47 445	34 321	47 445	47 445	47 445
Austria	32 236	39 275	44 179	63 361	32 680	35 270	45 425	66 487
Belgium (Fl.)	31 193	39 139	44 076	53 949	38 939	49 655	56 638	68 278
Belgium (Fr.)	30 202	m	42 792	52 509	37 736	m	55 157	66 613
Canada	34 443	52 205	54 978	54 978	34 588	52 436	55 191	55 191
Chile	17 820	21 547	23 411	30 866	17 941	22 859	24 820	32 665
Czech Republic	14 916	19 060	20 217	22 522	15 533	20 408	21 449	24 117
Denmark	43 393	48 540	50 253	50 253	44 640	58 256	58 256	58 256
England	30 204	44 145	44 145	44 145	30 204	44 145	44 145	44 145
Estonia	11 876	12 576	12 576	17 357	11 876	12 576	12 576	17 357
Finland	31 351	38 162	40 451	42 879	32 276	41 162	42 809	45 377
France	27 184	33 422	35 583	51 301	27 420	33 658	35 819	51 560
Germany	51 058		61 784	68 552	53 963	m	66 895	76 433
Greece	26 583	30 210	32 387	38 934	26 583	30 210	32 387	38 934
Hungary[1]	10 701	12 290	13 228	17 644	11 755	14 311	15 616	22 963
Iceland	24 822	27 211	27 930	29 123	22 850	26 520	28 103	29 399
Ireland	32 601	47 891	53 677	60 758	32 601	47 891	53 677	60 758
Israel	17 646	20 512	23 047	33 230	13 995	18 770	21 009	31 543
Italy	29 122	32 270	35 583	43 666	29 122	33 056	36 582	45 653
Japan	25 454	37 838	44 788	56 543	25 454	37 838	44 788	58 075
Korea	26 670	39 616	46 232	74 043	26 670	39 616	46 232	74 043
Luxembourg	73 777	92 222	101 775	128 181	73 777	92 222	101 775	128 181
Mexico	18 446	19 018	23 854	39 085	m	m	m	m
Netherlands	38 001	52 425	61 704	66 403	38 001	52 425	61 704	66 403
New Zealand	28 127	42 062	42 062	42 062	28 535	43 116	43 116	43 116
Norway	32 629	35 991	35 991	40 405	35 991	38 817	38 817	42 766
Poland	10 725	14 314	17 300	18 030	12 119	16 348	19 791	20 629
Portugal	30 825	34 537	37 542	54 158	30 825	34 537	37 542	54 158
Scotland	30 207	48 188	48 188	48 188	30 207	48 188	48 188	48 188
Slovak Republic	11 028	12 132	12 688	13 680	11 028	12 132	12 698	13 680
Slovenia	26 690	29 608	32 436	34 074	26 690	29 608	32 436	34 074
Spain	41 518	45 225	47 816	58 065	42 325	46 152	48 818	59 269
Sweden[1]	29 245	33 183	34 481	38 951	30 650	34 918	36 429	41 675
Switzerland[2]	51 240	65 296	m	79 603	59 107	76 207	m	90 374
Turkey	a	a	a	a	23 780	25 495	25 411	27 237
United States[1]	36 772	42 982	45 049	55 259	37 267	44 011	48 446	55 199
OECD average	29 801	36 683	39 401	47 721	30 899	38 190	41 182	49 721
EU21 average	30 202	36 134	40 211	47 287	31 346	37 482	42 470	50 139
Argentina[1]	11 231	m	14 852	18 015	11 231	m	14 852	18 015
Brazil	m	m	m	m	m	m	m	m
China	m	m	m	m	m	m	m	m
India	m	m	m	m	m	m	m	m
Indonesia	1 745	2 053	2 361	2 565	2 021	2 053	2 615	2 849
Russian Federation	m	m	m	m	m	m	m	m
Saudi Arabia	m	m	m	m	m	m	m	m
South Africa	m	m	m	m	m	m	m	m
G20 average	m	m	m	m	m	m	m	m

Note: Due to a change in the methodology used to convert teachers' salaries into USD, data are not directly comparable with the figures published in previous editions of *Education at a Glance*. Please refer to Table D3.2 for information on trends in teachers' salaries.
1. Actual base salaries.
2. Salaries after 11 years of experience for Columns 2, 6, 10 and 14.
Source: OECD. Argentina: UNESCO Institute for Statistics (World Education Indicators programme). See Annex 3 for notes (*www.oecd.org/edu/eag2012*). *Please refer to the Reader's Guide for information concerning the symbols replacing missing data.*
StatLink ᴍˢᴾ http://dx.doi.org/10.1787/888932668109

Table D3.1. [3/3] Teachers' salaries (2010)

Annual statutory teachers' salaries in public institutions at starting salary, after 10 and 15 years of experience and at the top of the scale, by level of education, in equivalent USD converted using PPPs for private consumption

D3

	Ratio of salary to earnings for full-time, full-year workers with tertiary education aged 25-64			Ratio of salary at top of scale to starting salary			Years from starting to top salary (lower secondary education)	Salary per hour of net contact (teaching) time after 15 years of experience			Ratio of salary per teaching hour of upper secondary to primary teachers (after 15 years of experience)
	Primary education	Lower secondary education	Upper secondary education	Primary education	Lower secondary education	Upper secondary education		Primary education	Lower secondary education	Upper secondary education	
	(17)	(18)	(19)	(20)	(21)	(22)	(23)	(24)	(25)	(26)	(27)
Australia[1]	0.92	0.92	0.92	1.39	1.38	1.38	9	55	58	59	1.08
Austria[2]	0.58	0.62	0.64	1.98	1.97	2.03	34	52	73	77	1.47
Belgium (Fl.)[1]	0.93	0.93	1.22	1.73	1.73	1.75	27	58	65	90	1.55
Belgium (Fr.)[2,3]	0.87	0.87	1.12	1.74	1.74	1.77	27	58	64	90	1.55
Canada[2]	1.05	1.05	1.05	1.60	1.60	1.60	11	68	74	74	1.08
Chile	m	m	m	1.73	1.73	1.82	30	22	22	23	1.06
Czech Republic[1]	0.53	0.53	0.57	1.48	1.51	1.55	32	23	31	35	1.50
Denmark[2]	0.87	0.87	1.01	1.16	1.16	1.31	8	77	77	155	2.00
England[1]	0.99	1.09	1.09	1.46	1.46	1.46	12	65	63	63	0.97
Estonia[2]	0.57	0.57	0.57	1.46	1.46	1.46	7	20	20	22	1.09
Finland[1]	0.89	0.98	1.10	1.37	1.37	1.41	20	55	68	77	1.41
France[2,4]	0.73	0.79	0.80	1.98	1.89	1.88	34	36	55	57	1.59
Germany[2]	0.88	0.97	1.05	1.32	1.34	1.42	28	69	82	94	1.35
Greece	m	m	m	1.46	1.46	1.46	33	55	78	78	1.42
Hungary[1,5]	0.58	0.58	0.66	1.65	1.65	1.95	40	22	22	26	1.18
Iceland[2,6]	0.50	0.50	0.61	1.17	1.17	1.29	18	45	45	52	1.15
Ireland[2]	0.82	0.82	0.82	1.86	1.86	1.86	22	59	73	73	1.25
Israel[1]	0.85	0.87	0.92	2.05	1.88	2.25	36	31	39	40	1.31
Italy[1]	0.57	0.60	0.64	1.47	1.50	1.57	35	42	56	58	1.37
Japan	m	m	m	2.22	2.22	2.28	34	63	74	90	1.41
Korea[2]	1.31	1.30	1.30	2.77	2.78	2.78	37	57	74	75	1.31
Luxembourg[1]	1.08	1.24	1.24	1.76	1.74	1.74	30	129	161	161	1.25
Mexico	m	m	m	2.14	2.12	m	14	23	23	m	m
Netherlands[1]	0.70	0.84	0.84	1.46	1.75	1.75	16	54	82	82	1.51
New Zealand[1]	0.98	1.01	1.03	1.48	1.50	1.51	8	44	50	57	1.29
Norway[1,7]	0.66	0.66	0.70	1.24	1.24	1.19	16	49	55	74	1.53
Poland[1]	0.76	0.77	0.75	1.66	1.68	1.70	10	30	35	40	1.32
Portugal[2,3]	1.19	1.19	1.19	1.76	1.76	1.76	34	43	49	49	1.14
Scotland[1]	0.95	0.95	0.95	1.60	1.60	1.60	6	56	56	56	1.00
Slovak Republic[2]	0.45	0.45	0.45	1.24	1.24	1.24	32	15	19	20	1.35
Slovenia[2]	0.81	0.81	0.81	1.28	1.28	1.28	13	47	47	51	1.09
Spain[2,3]	1.21	1.35	1.38	1.40	1.40	1.40	38	49	67	70	1.45
Sweden[5,8]	0.79	0.81	0.86	1.34	1.33	1.36	a	m	m	m	m
Switzerland[9]	m	m	m	1.57	1.55	1.53	27	m	m	m	m
Turkey	m	m	m	1.15	a	1.15	a	40	m	46	1.16
United States[1,5]	0.67	0.69	0.72	1.41	1.50	1.48	m	41	42	46	1.12
OECD average	0.82	0.85	0.90	1.60	1.62	1.63	24	49	58	65	1.31
EU21 average	0.81	0.85	0.90	1.55	1.56	1.60	24	51	61	69	1.35
Argentina[5]	m	m	m	1.50	1.60	1.60	25	25	11	11	0.43
Brazil	m	m	m	m	m	m	m	m	m	m	m
China	m	m	m	m	m	m	m	m	m	m	m
India	m	m	m	m	m	m	m	m	m	m	m
Indonesia	m	m	m	1.44	1.47	1.41	32	2	4	3	1.68
Russian Federation	m	m	m	m	m	m	m	m	m	m	m
Saudi Arabia	m	m	m	m	m	m	m	m	m	m	m
South Africa	m	m	m	m	m	m	m	m	m	m	m
G20 average	m	m	m	m	m	m	m	m	m	m	m

1. Ratio of actual salary, including bonuses and allowances, for teachers aged 25-64 to earnings for full-time, full-year workers with tertiary education aged 25-64 for Columns 17, 18 and 19.

2. Ratio of statutory salary after 15 years of experience (minimum training) to earnings for full-time, full-year workers with tertiary education aged 25-64 for Columns 17, 18 and 19.

3. Year of reference 2009 for Columns 17, 18 and 19.

4. Year of reference 2008 for Columns 17, 18 and 19.

5. Actual base salaries (not including bonuses and allowances) for Columns 20 to 27.

6. Year of reference 2006 for Columns 17, 18 and 19.

7. Year of reference 2007 for Columns 17, 18 and 19.

8. Ratio of actual teachers' salary after 15 years of experience (minimum training), not including bonuses and allowances, to earnings for full-time, full-year workers with tertiary education aged 25-64 for Columns 17, 18 and 19.

9. Salaries after 11 years of experience.

Source: OECD. Argentina: UNESCO Institute for Statistics (World Education Indicators programme). See Annex 3 for notes (*www.oecd.org/edu/eag2012*).
Please refer to the Reader's Guide for information concerning the symbols replacing missing data.

StatLink ᑢᑦ5ᑭ http://dx.doi.org/10.1787/888932668128

D3

Table D3.2. Trends in teachers' salaries between 2000 and 2010 (2000 = 100)

Index of change between 2000 and 2010 (2000 = 100) in statutory teachers' salaries after 15 years of experience/minimum training by level of education, converted to constant price levels using deflators for private consumption

	Primary level							Lower secondary level							Upper secondary level						
	2000	2005	2006	2007	2008	2009	2010	2000	2005	2006	2007	2008	2009	2010	2000	2005	2006	2007	2008	2009	2010
	(1)	(2)	(3)	(4)	(5)	(6)	(7)	(8)	(9)	(10)	(11)	(12)	(13)	(14)	(15)	(16)	(17)	(18)	(19)	(20)	(21)
Australia	100	108	104	105	110	110	113	100	108	105	107	111	110	113	100	108	105	107	111	110	113
Austria	100	111	111	112	112	114	115	100	115	115	116	116	119	119	100	106	107	108	108	111	111
Belgium (Fl.)	100	109	109	108	105	110	111	100	103	103	102	100	105	105	100	103	103	102	100	105	106
Belgium (Fr.)	100	106	107	107	104	112	111	100	101	101	100	98	105	104	100	101	101	100	98	105	105
Canada	m	m	m	m	m	m	m	m	m	m	m	m	m	m	m	m	m	m	m	m	m
Chile	m	m	m	m	m	m	m	m	m	m	m	m	m	m	m	m	m	m	m	m	m
Czech Republic	100	180	181	211	207	212	202	100	180	181	211	212	216	205	100	150	151	185	185	186	179
Denmark	100	107	108	108	110	130	127	100	107	108	108	110	130	127	100	111	114	112	113	126	126
England	100	109	110	110	109	109	109	100	109	110	110	109	109	109	100	109	110	110	109	109	109
Estonia	100	119	131	147	170	184	167	100	119	131	147	170	184	167	100	119	131	147	170	184	167
Finland	100	117	118	121	122	121	120	100	108	109	111	112	112	111	100	109	110	112	113	113	112
France	100	95	94	94	92	91	92	100	95	94	93	91	91	92	100	96	95	94	92	92	93
Germany	w	w	w	w	w	w	w	w	w	w	w	w	w	w	w	w	w	w	w	w	w
Greece	100	112	112	111	113	115	116	100	112	112	111	113	115	116	100	112	112	111	113	115	116
Hungary[1]	100	159	155	149	145	129	125	100	159	155	149	145	129	125	100	158	148	147	139	124	117
Iceland	100	112	118	111	117	125	116	100	112	118	111	117	125	116	100	111	122	120	117	107	99
Ireland	100	116	120	123	122	129	128	100	114	119	122	121	128	126	100	114	119	122	121	128	126
Israel	100	99	102	111	118	127	131	100	100	102	101	107	107	108	100	100	101	100	107	100	100
Italy	100	106	104	103	103	105	105	100	105	104	103	102	104	105	100	105	104	102	102	104	104
Japan	100	99	99	95	92	92	91	100	99	99	95	92	92	91	100	99	99	95	92	92	91
Korea	100	125	127	126	124	120	117	100	126	127	126	124	120	117	100	126	127	126	124	120	117
Luxembourg	m	m	m	m	m	m	m	m	m	m	m	m	m	m	m	m	m	m	m	m	m
Mexico	100	104	106	107	108	108	108	100	105	107	108	109	108	110	m	m	m	m	m	m	m
Netherlands	m	m	m	m	m	m	m	m	m	m	m	m	m	m	m	m	m	m	m	m	m
New Zealand	100	102	102	103	104	105	108	100	102	102	103	104	105	110	100	102	102	103	104	105	113
Norway	m	m	m	m	m	m	m	m	m	m	m	m	m	m	m	m	m	m	m	m	m
Poland	m	m	m	m	m	m	m	m	m	m	m	m	m	m	m	m	m	m	m	m	m
Portugal	100	114	113	112	111	123	125	100	114	113	112	111	123	125	100	114	113	112	111	123	125
Scotland	100	122	122	122	121	121	121	100	122	122	122	121	121	121	100	122	122	122	121	121	121
Slovak Republic	m	m	m	m	m	m	m	m	m	m	m	m	m	m	m	m	m	m	m	m	m
Slovenia	m	m	m	m	m	m	m	m	m	m	m	m	m	m	m	m	m	m	m	m	m
Spain	100	105	106	105	109	113	113	100	109	110	109	110	116	116	100	104	105	103	107	111	110
Sweden[1]	100	106	105	110	107	110	108	100	109	108	112	110	113	112	100	110	109	112	110	112	111
Switzerland[2]	100	102	101	101	100	104	103	100	97	96	96	96	99	98	100	96	95	95	95	98	96
Turkey	100	181	170	178	182	191	202	a	a	a	a	a	a	a	100	199	189	197	202	212	224
United States[1]	100	104	105	105	103	103	103	100	105	106	107	103	103	103	100	98	99	99	103	103	103
OECD average	100	116	116	118	119	123	122	100	113	114	115	116	119	117	100	115	115	117	118	120	119
OECD average for countries with data available for all reference years	100	116	116	118	119	123	122	100	113	114	115	116	119	117	100	115	115	117	118	120	119
EU21 average for countries with data available for all reference years	100	117	118	121	121	125	123	100	117	117	120	121	125	123	100	114	115	118	118	122	120
Argentina	m	m	m	m	m	m	m	m	m	m	m	m	m	m	m	m	m	m	m	m	m
Brazil	m	m	m	m	m	m	m	m	m	m	m	m	m	m	m	m	m	m	m	m	m
China	m	m	m	m	m	m	m	m	m	m	m	m	m	m	m	m	m	m	m	m	m
India	m	m	m	m	m	m	m	m	m	m	m	m	m	m	m	m	m	m	m	m	m
Indonesia	m	m	m	m	m	m	m	m	m	m	m	m	m	m	m	m	m	m	m	m	m
Russian Federation	m	m	m	m	m	m	m	m	m	m	m	m	m	m	m	m	m	m	m	m	m
Saudi Arabia	m	m	m	m	m	m	m	m	m	m	m	m	m	m	m	m	m	m	m	m	m
South Africa	m	m	m	m	m	m	m	m	m	m	m	m	m	m	m	m	m	m	m	m	m
G20 Average	m	m	m	m	m	m	m	m	m	m	m	m	m	m	m	m	m	m	m	m	m

1. Actual base salaries.
2. Salaries after 11 years of experience.
Source: OECD. See Annex 3 for notes (*www.oecd.org/edu/eag2012*).
Please refer to the Reader's Guide for information concerning the symbols replacing missing data.
StatLink ᐧ᠊ᔍᔭ http://dx.doi.org/10.1787/888932668147

Table D3.3a. [1/2] Decisions on payments for teachers in public institutions (2010)

Criteria for base salary and additional payments awarded to teachers in public institutions

	Experience			Criteria based on teaching conditions/responsibilities																			
	Years of experience as a teacher			Management responsibilities in addition to teaching duties			Teaching more classes or hours than required by full-time contract			Special tasks (career guidance or counselling)			Teaching in a disadvantaged, remote or high cost area (location allowance)			Special activities (e.g. sports and drama clubs, homework clubs, summer school, etc.)			Teaching students with special educational needs (in regular schools)			Teaching courses in a particular field		
	(1)	(2)	(3)	(4)	(5)	(6)	(7)	(8)	(9)	(10)	(11)	(12)	(13)	(14)	(15)	(16)	(17)	(18)	(19)	(20)	(21)	(22)	(23)	(24)
OECD Australia	−			−									−	▲						▲				
Austria	−	▲			▲			▲						▲							△			
Belgium (Fl.)	−								△															
Belgium (Fr.)	−											△												
Canada	−	m	m		m	m		m	m		m	m		m	m		m	m		m	m		m	m
Chile	−												−											
Czech Republic	−	▲	△	−	▲	△		▲	△		▲	△		▲	△		▲	△	−	▲	△			
Denmark	−	▲	△	−	▲	△		▲	△		▲	△	−	▲	△		▲	△		▲	△		▲	△
England	−	▲	△	−	▲	△		▲	△					▲	△		▲	△	−	▲	△	−	▲	△
Estonia					▲	△			△			△	−	▲	△		▲	△		▲	△			
Finland		▲		−				▲			▲		−	▲			▲		−	▲	△	−		△
France	−				▲	△		▲			▲						▲		−		△			
Germany	−								△															
Greece	−				▲						▲						▲			▲				
Hungary	−				▲			▲			▲						▲			▲				
Iceland	−	▲	△		▲	△		▲	△				−	▲	△		▲	△		▲	△			
Ireland	−	▲	△		▲									▲										
Israel	−				▲		−	▲		−	▲			▲			▲			▲				
Italy						△			△						△		▲				△			
Japan					▲			▲									▲				△			
Korea					▲				△			△			△					▲			▲	
Luxembourg									△			△												
Mexico	−	▲	△		▲			▲		−	▲		−	▲			▲			▲				
Netherlands	−	▲	△		▲	△		▲			▲			▲	△		▲		−	▲	△		▲	△
New Zealand					▲						▲			▲			▲			▲			▲	
Norway	−				▲				△	−	▲	△		▲			▲			▲	△			
Poland	−		△					▲			▲			▲			▲			▲				
Portugal	−				▲				△		▲								−					
Scotland																	▲							
Slovak Republic	−	▲	△		▲			▲	△		▲			▲	△		▲	△	−	▲	△			
Slovenia	−			−	▲				△			△			△			△						△
Spain	−				▲												▲							
Sweden	−			−					△				−						−				−	
Switzerland	−			−					△			△			△				−		△	−		
Turkey	−							▲			▲						▲							
United States	−				▲								−	▲			▲						▲	
Other G20 Argentina	m	m	m	m	m	m	m	m	m	m	m	m	m	m	m	m	m	m	m	m	m	m	m	m
Brazil	m	m	m	m	m	m	m	m	m	m	m	m	m	m	m	m	m	m	m	m	m	m	m	m
China	m	m	m	m	m	m	m	m	m	m	m	m	m	m	m	m	m	m	m	m	m	m	m	m
India	m	m	m	m	m	m	m	m	m	m	m	m	m	m	m	m	m	m	m	m	m	m	m	m
Indonesia	−	▲		−	▲		−	▲		−	▲			▲		−	▲		−	▲		−		
Russian Federation	−			−			−										▲		−			−	▲	
Saudi Arabia	m	m	m	m	m	m	m	m	m	m	m	m	m	m	m	m	m	m	m	m	m	m	m	m
South Africa	m	m	m	m	m	m	m	m	m	m	m	m	m	m	m	m	m	m	m	m	m	m	m	m

Criteria for:
− : Decisions on position in base salary scale
▲ : Decisions on supplemental payments which are paid every year
△ : Decisions on supplemental incidental payments
Source: OECD. See Annex 3 for notes (*www.oecd.org/edu/eag2012*).
Please refer to the Reader's Guide for information concerning the symbols replacing missing data.
StatLink ⌷⌷ http://dx.doi.org/10.1787/888932668166

Table D3.3a. [2/2] Decisions on payments for teachers in public institutions (2010)

Criteria for base salary and additional payments awarded to teachers in public institutions

	Criteria related to teachers' qualifications, training and performance																		Criteria based on demography						Other		
	Holding an initial educational qualification higher than the minimum qualification required to enter the teaching profession			Holding a higher than minimum level of teacher certification or training obtained during professional life			Outstanding performance in teaching			Successful completion of professional development activities			Reaching high scores in the qualification examination			Holding an educational qualification in multiple subjects			Family status (married, number of children)			Age (independent of years of teaching experience)					
	(1)	(2)	(3)	(4)	(5)	(6)	(7)	(8)	(9)	(10)	(11)	(12)	(13)	(14)	(15)	(16)	(17)	(18)	(19)	(20)	(21)	(22)	(23)	(24)	(25)	(26)	(27)
OECD Australia	–																			▲							
Austria									△											▲						▲	
Belgium (Fl.)	–				▲																					▲	
Belgium (Fr.)	–																									▲	△
Canada		m	m		m	m		m	m		m	m		m	m		m	m		m	m		m	m			
Chile								▲	△							▲											
Czech Republic							–	▲	△															△			
Denmark	–	▲	△	–	▲	△		▲	△	–	▲	△				–	▲	△									
England	–	▲	△				–	▲	△																		
Estonia	–			–				▲	△								▲	△									
Finland	–			–	▲			▲					▲			–											
France																				▲							
Germany																			–			–					
Greece	–				▲																					▲	
Hungary	–								△	–							▲									▲	
Iceland	–	▲	△	–	▲	△					▲	△			△			△					▲				
Ireland	–	▲		–	▲																						
Israel	–												▲							▲			▲				
Italy																				–							
Japan																				▲						▲	
Korea												△											△	▲			
Luxembourg										–										▲							
Mexico	–	▲		–	▲		–	▲		–	▲																
Netherlands	–	▲	△	–	▲	△	–	▲	△	–	▲	△				▲	△										
New Zealand								▲																		▲	
Norway		▲			▲			▲			▲			▲			▲						▲				
Poland	–	▲	△					▲	△	–					△												
Portugal	–			–						–										▲							
Scotland				–																							
Slovak Republic								▲	△		▲												△				
Slovenia		▲			▲				△	–																	△
Spain					▲																						
Sweden	–			–			–						–														
Switzerland																				▲						▲	
Turkey	–				▲				△		▲									▲						▲	
United States	–	▲		–	▲		–		△	–	▲															▲	
Other G20 Argentina	m	m	m	m	m	m	m	m	m	m	m	m	m	m	m	m	m	m	m	m	m	m	m	m	m	m	m
Brazil	m	m	m	m	m	m	m	m	m	m	m	m	m	m	m	m	m	m	m	m	m	m	m	m	m	m	m
China	m	m	m	m	m	m	m	m	m	m	m	m	m	m	m	m	m	m	m	m	m	m	m	m	m	m	m
India	m	m	m	m	m	m	m	m	m	m	m	m	m	m	m	m	m	m	m	m	m	m	m	m	m	m	m
Indonesia	–	▲		–	▲						▲						▲		–	▲		–	▲				
Russian Federation	–			–	▲			▲					–														
Saudi Arabia	m	m	m	m	m	m	m	m	m	m	m	m	m	m	m	m	m	m	m	m	m	m	m	m	m	m	m
South Africa	m	m	m	m	m	m	m	m	m	m	m	m	m	m	m	m	m	m	m	m	m	m	m	m	m	m	m

Criteria for:
– : Decisions on position in base salary scale
▲ : Decisions on supplemental payments which are paid every year
△ : Decisions on supplemental incidental payments

Source: OECD. See Annex 3 for notes (*www.oecd.org/edu/eag2012*).
Please refer to the Reader's Guide for information concerning the symbols replacing missing data.
StatLink ▄▄▄ http://dx.doi.org/10.1787/888932668166

HOW MUCH TIME DO TEACHERS SPEND TEACHING?

- The number of teaching hours per teacher in public schools averages 782 hours per year in primary education, 704 hours in lower secondary education, and 658 hours in upper secondary education.

- The average teaching time remained largely unchanged between 2000 and 2010 at all levels of education.

Chart D4.1. Number of teaching hours per year in lower secondary education in 2000, 2005 and 2010

Net statutory contact time in hours per year in public institutions

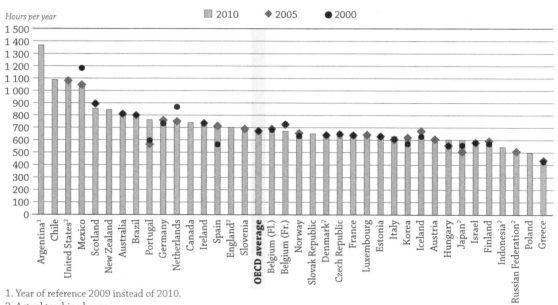

1. Year of reference 2009 instead of 2010.
2. Actual teaching hours.
Countries are ranked in descending order of the number of teaching hours per year in lower secondary education in 2010.
Source: OECD. Argentina: UNESCO Institute for Statistics (World Education Indicators programme). Table D4.2. See Annex 3 for notes (www.oecd.org/edu/eag2012).
StatLink ⬛▨▨ http://dx.doi.org/10.1787/888932663739

🔳 Context

Although statutory working hours and teaching hours only partly determine teachers' actual workload, they do offer valuable insight into the demands placed on teachers in different countries. Teaching hours and the extent of non-teaching duties may also affect the attractiveness of the teaching profession. Together with teachers' salaries (see Indicator D3) and average class size (see Indicator D2), this indicator presents some key measures regarding the working lives of teachers.

The proportion of working time spent teaching provides information on the amount of time available for non-teaching activities such as lesson preparation, correction, in-service training and staff meetings. A large proportion of working time spent teaching may indicate that less time is devoted to tasks such as assessing students and preparing lessons.

In addition to class size and the ratio of students to teaching staff (see Indicator D2), students' hours of instruction (see Indicator D1) and teachers' salaries (see Indicator D3), the amount of time teachers spend teaching also affects the financial resources countries need to allocate to education (see Indicator B7).

Other findings

- **The average number of teaching hours in public primary schools is 782 hours per year**, but ranges from less than 600 hours in Greece and Poland to over 1 000 hours in Chile and the United States.

- **The number of teaching hours in public lower secondary schools averages 704 hours per year**, but ranges from less than 500 hours in Greece and Poland to over 1 000 hours in Argentina, Chile, Mexico and the United States.

- **The average number of teaching hours in public upper secondary general education is 658 hours per year**, but ranges from 377 hours in Denmark to 1 368 hours in Argentina.

- The **composition of teachers' annual teaching time**, in terms of weeks and days of instruction and hours of teaching time, **varies considerably**. As a result, the average number of hours per day that teachers teach also varies widely, ranging at the lower secondary level from three hours or less per day in Greece, Indonesia, Japan, Korea, Poland and the Russian Federation, to more than five hours in Argentina, Chile, Mexico and the United States.

- **Regulations concerning teachers' required working time vary significantly**. In most countries, teachers are formally required to work a specific number of hours per year. In some, teaching time is only specified by the number of lessons per week and assumptions may be made about the amount of non-teaching time required per lesson at school or elsewhere.

- **Decisions about the duties and conditions of service** of lower secondary school teachers in public institutions **are taken at the school or local level** in more than half of countries.

Trends

In most OECD countries with available data, teaching time remained largely unchanged between 2000 and 2010. However, the number of teaching hours changed dramatically in a few countries. It increased by more than 25% in the Czech Republic at the primary level and in Portugal and Spain at the secondary level.

Analysis

Teaching time in primary education

In both primary and secondary education, countries vary in terms of the number of teaching hours per year required of the average public school teacher. Teachers are usually required to teach more hours in primary education than in secondary education.

Annual teaching hours in primary schools range from less than 600 hours in Greece and Poland to 900 hours or more in France, Ireland, the Netherlands and New Zealand, to over 1 000 hours in Chile and the United States (Table D4.1 and Chart D4.2).

There is no set rule on how teaching time is distributed throughout the year. In Spain, for example, primary school teachers must teach 880 hours per year, about 100 hours more than the OECD average. However, those teaching hours are spread over fewer days of instruction than the OECD average because primary school teachers in Spain teach an average of five hours per day compared to the OECD average of 4.2 hours. In contrast, primary school teachers in Korea must complete a very large number of days of instruction – more than five days a week, on average – but their average teaching time per day is only 3.7 hours.

Denmark and Estonia also provide an interesting contrast in policies. They have similar annual teaching time in terms of hours (Chart D4.2), but primary school teachers in Denmark must complete 25 days of instruction more than primary school teachers in Estonia. The difference between the two is explained by the number of hours taught per day of instruction. Primary school teachers in Estonia complete fewer days of instruction than teachers in Denmark, but each of these days includes an average of 3.6 hours of teaching, compared to 3.3 hours in Denmark. Estonia's teachers must provide 20 minutes more teaching time per day of instruction than Denmark's teachers, and this difference is combined with a substantial difference in the number of days of instruction they must complete each year.

In most countries, teaching time in primary schools remained about the same between 2000 and 2010. However, in the Czech Republic, primary school teachers were required to teach 33% more hours, and in Israel and Japan, 12% and 11% more hours, respectively, in 2010 than in 2000. In Belgium (French Community) and Scotland, net teaching time in primary education dropped by 9% and 10%, respectively, between 2000 and 2010 (Table D4.2).

Teaching time in secondary education

Lower secondary school teachers teach an average of 704 hours per year. The teaching time ranges from less than 600 hours in Finland, Greece, Indonesia, Israel, Poland and the Russian Federation to more than 1 000 hours in Argentina, Chile, Mexico and the United States (Table D4.1 and Chart D4.1).

Teaching time in upper secondary general education is usually less than that in lower secondary education. A teacher of general subjects in upper secondary education has an average teaching load of 658 hours per year, ranging from 377 hours in Denmark to 800 hours or more in Australia, Brazil, Mexico and Scotland, and over 1 000 hours in Argentina, Chile and the United States (Table D4.1 and Chart D4.2).

As is the case for primary school teachers, the number of hours of teaching time and the number of days of instruction for secondary school teachers vary. As a result, the average number of hours per day that teachers teach also varies widely, ranging, at the lower secondary level, from three hours or less per day in Greece, Indonesia, Japan, Korea, Poland and the Russian Federation, to more than five hours in Mexico and the United States and more than six hours in Argentina and Chile.

Similarly, at the upper secondary general level, teachers in Denmark, Finland, Greece, Israel, Japan, Korea, Norway, Poland and the Russian Federation teach for three hours or less per day, on average, compared to more than five hours in Argentina, Chile and the United States. Including breaks between classes in teaching time in some countries, but not in others, may explain some of these differences.

Chart D4.2. **Number of teaching hours per year, by level of education (2010)**
Net statutory contact time in hours per year in public institutions

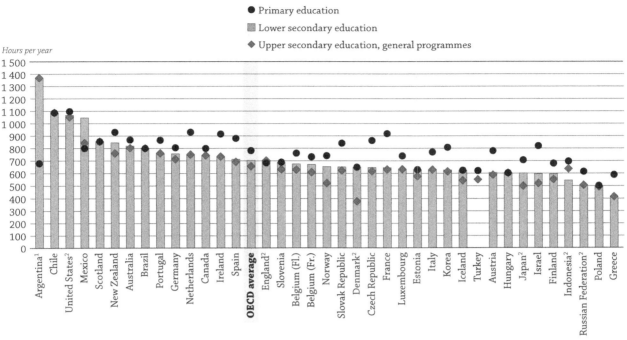

● Primary education

■ Lower secondary education

◆ Upper secondary education, general programmes

D4

1. Year of reference 2009.
2. Actual teaching hours.
Countries are ranked in descending order of the number of teaching hours per year in lower secondary education.
Source: OECD. Argentina: UNESCO Institute for Statistics (World Education Indicators programme). Table D4.1. See Annex 3 for notes (*www.oecd.org/edu/eag2012*).
StatLink ⟨⟩ http://dx.doi.org/10.1787/888932663758

About half of the OECD countries for which data are available saw at least a 5% change, most often an increase, in the amount of teaching time, in either lower or upper secondary schools, between 2000 and 2010. Secondary school teachers were required to teach over 25% more in 2010 than in 2000 in Portugal and Spain (up to 48% more in Portugal at the upper secondary level) (Table D4.2).

Differences in teaching time between levels of education

In most countries, primary school teachers are required to teach more hours per year than secondary school teachers. In the Czech Republic, France, Greece and Israel, primary school teachers have at least 30% more annual teaching time than lower secondary school teachers. In contrast, the difference does not exceed 3% in Poland and the United States, and there is no difference in Brazil, Chile, Denmark, Estonia, Hungary, Iceland, Scotland and Slovenia. Argentina, England and Mexico are the only countries in which the teaching load for primary school teachers is lighter than that for lower secondary school teachers (Table D4.1 and Chart D4.2).

Teaching time at the lower and upper secondary levels is similar across most countries. However, in Japan, Mexico and Norway, the annual required teaching time at the lower secondary level is at least 20% higher than at the upper secondary level and over 70% higher in Denmark.

Teachers' working time

How teachers' hours of work are regulated varies considerably from country to country. While some countries formally regulate contact time with students only, others also set total working hours. In some countries, time is allocated for teaching and non-teaching activities within the formally established working time.

D4

Box D4.1. **Workload and teaching load throughout the career**

Findings from the 2008 Teaching and Learning International Survey (TALIS), conducted in 23 countries, suggest that there are few differences in the workloads of new and more experienced teachers. In most countries, new teachers assumed virtually the same responsibilities as more experienced teachers. On average, new teachers spent slightly more time on lesson planning and slightly less time teaching students and performing administrative duties, but with the exception of a few countries, these differences are small. New teachers in Mexico spent about seven hours less teaching per week than experienced teachers. New teachers in Brazil, Estonia, Italy, Lithuania and Portugal teach 3-5 hours per week less than more experienced teachers.

TALIS 2008 data also show that new teachers report feeling somewhat less effective in their work than more experienced teachers. Moreover, new teachers report spending a smaller proportion of their classroom time teaching. They also report participating in less professional development even though they also report a greater need for professional development in a number of areas than more experienced teachers. On average, nearly one-third of new teachers reported a high level of need for professional development on how to address student discipline and behaviour problems. In addition, 25% of new teachers reported a high level of need for professional development to improve their classroom-management skills, compared to 12% of more experienced teachers.

The similarities in workload between new and more experienced teachers, and fact that new teachers report lower levels of self-efficacy and actual teaching and learning in their classes are important findings for policy makers. If a school or a school system is trying to maximise the effectiveness of its teaching, it would have its more effective teachers spend more time teaching or mentoring new teachers. Instead, TALIS results suggest that there is little job differentiation between new and more experienced teachers. In most countries, teachers were likely to have spent similar amounts of time teaching in the first year of their careers as they were in the last year. Altering related policies so that the more effective teachers, regardless of their seniority, spend the most time teaching or mentoring new teachers could help to improve school performance.

Source: OECD (2012).

In most countries, teachers are formally required to work a specified number of hours per week, including teaching and non-teaching time, to earn their full-time salary. Within this framework, however, countries differ in how they allocate time for each activity (Chart D4.3). The number of hours for teaching is usually specified, except in Sweden; but some countries also regulate the time a teacher has to be present in the school.

Australia, Belgium (Flemish Community, for primary education), Brazil, Canada, Chile, England, Estonia, Finland, Greece, Iceland, Indonesia, Ireland, Israel, Luxembourg, Mexico, New Zealand, Norway, Poland, Portugal, Spain, Sweden, Turkey and the United States all specify the time during which teachers are required to be available at school, for both teaching and non-teaching activities (Table D4.1).

Greece reduces teaching hours according to how many years a teacher has served. At the secondary level, teachers are required to teach 21 class sessions per week. After 6 years, this drops to 19 sessions, and after 12 years to 18 sessions. After 20 years of service, teachers are required to teach 16 class sessions a week – more than 25% less than teachers who have just started their careers. However, the remaining hours of teachers' working time must be spent at school.

In Austria (primary and lower secondary education), the Czech Republic, Germany, Hungary, Japan, Korea, the Netherlands and Scotland, teachers' total annual working time, at school or elsewhere, is specified, but the allocation of time spent at school and time spent elsewhere is not. In some countries, the number of hours to be spent on non-teaching activities is partially specified; but what is not specified is whether teachers have to spend the non-teaching hours at school.

Non-teaching time

In the 22 countries that specify both teaching and total working time, the percentage of teachers' working time spent teaching ranges from less than 40% in Denmark, Hungary, Iceland, Japan, Poland and Turkey at all levels of education, to 100% in Brazil. In 13 countries, the proportion of non-teaching time is higher at the secondary level than at the primary level (Table D4.1 and Chart D4.3).

In the 21 countries that specify both teaching time and the amount of time that teachers are required to be available at school, the percentage of teachers' working time at school spent teaching ranges from less than 40% in Greece (secondary level) and Iceland to 100% in Brazil, Ireland (secondary level) and Mexico (primary level). In 10 countries, the proportion of time spent in non-teaching activities is greater at the secondary level than at the primary level.

D4

Chart D4.3. **Percentage of teachers' working time spent teaching, by level of education (2010)**
Net teaching time as a percentage of total statutory working time and working time required at school

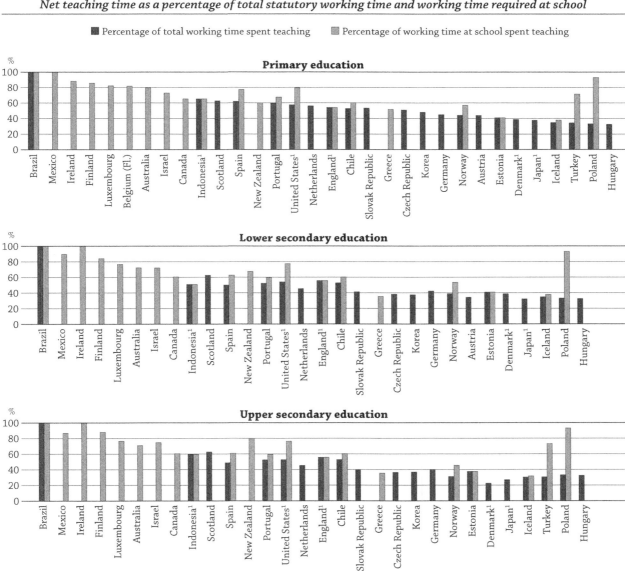

1. Actual teaching time.
Countries are ranked in descending order of the percentage of teachers' working time spent teaching in primary education.
Source: OECD. Table D4.1. See Annex 3 for notes (*www.oecd.org/edu/eag2012*).
StatLink ⓘⓢⓛ http://dx.doi.org/10.1787/888932663777

D4

In Belgium (Flemish Community, for the secondary level), Belgium (French Community), France, Italy, the Russian Federation, there are no formal requirements regarding time spent on non-teaching activities in primary and secondary education. However, this does not mean that teachers are given total freedom to carry out other tasks. In Austria, provisions concerning teaching time are based on the assumption that teachers' duties, including teaching time, preparing lessons and tests, marking and correcting papers, overseeing examinations and handling administrative tasks total 40 hours per week. In Belgium (Flemish Community), the additional non-teaching hours at school are set at the school level. There are no regulations regarding the time devoted to preparing lessons, correcting tests, marking students' papers, etc. The government defines only the minimum and maximum number of teaching periods a week (50 minutes each) at each level of education (Table D4.1).

Box D4.2. **Who makes decisions about the duties and conditions
of service of lower secondary teachers in public institutions?**

		With full autonomy	After consultation with other bodies in the education system	Within a framework set by a higher authority	Other
Teachers' duties	Central	AUT, FRA, IDN, ITA, KOR, LUX, PRT, TUR			GRC
	State	BFR, DEU, MEX, CHE	AUS	ESP	
	Provincial/regional				
	Sub-regional				
	Local			DNK, JPN, SCO,	
	School	ENG, NLD, NOR, SVK	USA	BFL, CAN, CHL, CZE, EST, HUN, ISL, IRL, ISR, POL, SVN, SWE	FIN
Teachers' conditions of service	Central	IRL, ISR, LUX, PRT, TUR			GRC
	State	AUS, BFR, DEU, MEX, CHE			
	Provincial/regional	JPN			
	Sub-regional				IDN
	Local	NOR		CAN, DNK, SCO	FIN, ISL
	School	BFL, ENG, EST, FRA, KOR, NLD, SVK, SWE	USA	AUT, CHL, CZE, HUN, ITA, POL, SVN, ESP	

Source: OECD. Table D6.8, available on line. See Annex 3 for notes (*www.oecd.org/edu/eag2012*).
Please refer to the Reader's Guide for list of country codes for country names used in this chart.

In more than half of countries, decisions on the duties and conditions of service of lower secondary school teachers in public institutions are taken at the school or local level. Decision-making authority may be delegated to the local level to reduce bureaucracy, enhance the quality and effectiveness of teaching, and/ or be more responsive to local needs (Table D6.8, available on line).

In 21 out of 36 countries, decisions on the duties of lower secondary teaching staff in public institutions are taken at the school or local level. In England, the Netherlands, Norway and the Slovak Republic, these decisions are taken with full autonomy by schools. Belgium (Flemish Community), Canada, Chile, the Czech Republic, Estonia, Hungary, Ireland, Israel, Poland, Slovenia and Sweden, however, prefer to counterbalance complete school autonomy with frameworks determined at the central or state level in which individual schools make decisions. In Iceland, these decisions are also taken at the school level, but within a framework established by local authorities. Only in the United States are these decisions taken at the school level in consultation with the local authorities. Although the local authorities

...

in Finland are, as education providers, responsible for deciding what the duties of teaching staff are, they can decide if they wish to delegate decision making to the schools or not, and to what extent. In practice, decisions concerning duties are largely made at school level. In Denmark, Japan and Scotland, these decisions are taken at the local level as opposed to the school level. In contrast, similar decisions are taken at the central and/or state level of government in Australia, Austria, Belgium (French Community), France, Germany, Greece, Indonesia, Italy, Korea, Luxembourg, Mexico, Portugal, Spain, Switzerland and Turkey.

A similar pattern is seen with regard to decisions on the conditions of service of lower secondary teaching staff in public institutions. In 23 out of 36 countries, these decisions are in the hands of schools or local authorities. In Belgium (Flemish Community), England, Estonia, France, Korea, the Netherlands, the Slovak Republic and Sweden, these decisions are taken with full autonomy by schools, whereas in Austria, Chile, the Czech Republic, Hungary, Italy, Poland, Slovenia and Spain, they are taken by individual schools within a framework established by a higher authority. As with decisions on teachers' duties, decisions on conditions of service are taken at the school level, in consultation with the local authorities, in the United States. In Canada, Denmark, Norway and Scotland, decisions on the conditions of service of teaching staff are taken at the local level, while in Iceland, these decisions are outlined in contracts between the association of municipalities and the teachers' union, in compliance with the Compulsory School Act. In Finland, the local authorities as education providers are responsible for determining the conditions of service of lower secondary school teachers. However they can autonomously decide if they wish to delegate decision making to the schools or not, and to what extent. These decisions are taken centrally in Greece, Ireland, Israel, Luxembourg, Portugal and Turkey, and by the state government in Australia, Belgium (French Community), Germany, Mexico and Switzerland. In Japan, similar decisions are taken at the regional level, while in Indonesia, they are taken at the sub-regional level.

Definitions

The **conditions of service of teachers** include the minimum number of hours to be worked per week or per year, the time schedule, the size and level of the groups to teach, the students' abilities, etc. It does not include salaries and bonuses.

The **duties of teachers** refer to the responsibilities and required tasks and activities of teachers.

The **number of teaching days** is the number of teaching weeks multiplied by the number of days per week a teacher teaches, less the number of days on which the school is closed for holidays.

The **number of teaching weeks** refers to the number of weeks of instruction excluding holiday weeks.

Teaching time is defined as the number of hours per year that a full-time teacher teaches a group or class of students as set by policy. It is normally calculated as the number of teaching days per year multiplied by the number of hours a teacher teaches per day (excluding periods of time formally allowed for breaks between lessons or groups of lessons). Some countries provide estimates of teaching time based on survey data. At the primary school level, short breaks between lessons are included if the classroom teacher is responsible for the class during these breaks.

Working time refers to the normal working hours of a full-time teacher. It does not include paid overtime. According to a country's formal policy, working time can refer to:

- the time directly associated with teaching and other curricular activities for students, such as assignments and tests; and

- the time directly associated with teaching and hours devoted to other activities related to teaching, such as preparing lessons, counselling students, correcting assignments and tests, professional development, meetings with parents, staff meetings, and general school tasks.

Working time in school refers to the time teachers are required to spend working in school, including teaching and non-teaching time.

Methodology

Data are from the 2011 OECD-INES Survey on Teachers and the Curriculum and refer to the school year 2009-10.

In interpreting differences in teaching hours among countries, net contact time, as used here, does not necessarily correspond to the teaching load. Although contact time is a substantial component of teachers' workloads, preparing for classes and necessary follow-up, including correcting students' work, also need to be included when making comparisons. Other relevant elements, such as the number of subjects taught, the number of students taught, and the number of years a teacher teaches the same students, should also be taken into account.

Data on the level of decision-making about the duties and conditions of service of lower secondary school teachers are from the 2011 OECD-INES survey on decision making in education and refer to the school year 2010-11. More detailed information on definitions and methodology can be found in Indicator D6, "Who makes key decisions in education systems?"

Notes on definitions and methodologies for each country are provided in Annex 3 at *www.oecd.org/edu/eag2012*.

The statistical data for Israel are supplied by and under the responsibility of the relevant Israeli authorities. The use of such data by the OECD is without prejudice to the status of the Golan Heights, East Jerusalem and Israeli settlements in the West Bank under the terms of international law.

References

For further information about TALIS 2008, see:

OECD (2012), *The Experience of New Teachers*, OECD Publishing.

Visit *www.oecd.org/edu/talis*

Table D4.1. **Organisation of teachers' working time (2010)**

Number of teaching weeks, teaching days, net teaching hours, and teachers' working time over the school year, in public institutions

	Number of weeks of instruction			Number of days of instruction			Net teaching time in hours			Working time required at school in hours			Total statutory working time in hours		
	Primary education	Lower secondary education	Upper secondary education, general programmes	Primary education	Lower secondary education	Upper secondary education, general programmes	Primary education	Lower secondary education	Upper secondary education, general programmes	Primary education	Lower secondary education	Upper secondary education, general programmes	Primary education	Lower secondary education	Upper secondary education, general programmes
	(1)	(2)	(3)	(4)	(5)	(6)	(7)	(8)	(9)	(10)	(11)	(12)	(13)	(14)	(15)
OECD															
Australia[1]	40	40	40	196	196	193	868	819	803	1 093	1 135	1 135	a	a	a
Austria[1]	38	38	38	180	180	180	779	607	589	a	a	a	1 776	1 776	a
Belgium (Fl.)[1]	37	37	37	179	180	180	761	675	630	931	a	a	a	a	a
Belgium (Fr.)[1]	38	38	38	183	183	183	732	671	610	a	a	a	a	a	a
Canada[1]	37	37	37	183	183	183	799	740	744	1 226	1 227	1 232	a	a	a
Chile[1]	38	38	38	179	179	179	1 087	1 087	1 087	1 804	1 804	1 804	2 068	2 068	2 068
Czech Republic[1]	41	41	41	196	196	196	862	647	617	a	a	a	1 696	1 696	1 696
Denmark[2]	42	42	42	200	200	200	650	650	377	m	m	m	1 680	1 680	1 680
England[2]	38	38	38	190	190	190	684	703	703	1 265	1 265	1 265	1 265	1 265	1 265
Estonia[3]	39	39	39	175	175	175	630	630	578	1 540	1 540	1 540	1 540	1 540	1 540
Finland[4]	38	38	38	189	189	189	680	595	553	794	709	629	a	a	a
France[1]	35	35	35	m	m	m	918	646	632	a	a	a	a	a	a
Germany[1]	40	40	40	193	193	193	805	756	713	a	a	a	1 793	1 793	1 793
Greece[1]	36	31	31	177	153	153	589	415	415	1 140	1 176	1 176	a	a	a
Hungary[4]	37	37	37	183	183	183	604	604	604	a	a	a	1 864	1 864	1 864
Iceland[1]	37	37	35	180	180	170	624	624	544	1 650	1 650	1 720	1 800	1 800	1 800
Ireland[1]	37	33	33	183	167	167	915	735	735	1 037	735	735	a	a	a
Israel[1]	38	37	37	183	175	175	820	598	521	1 126	831	700	a	a	a
Italy[4]	39	39	39	175	175	175	770	630	630	a	a	a	a	a	a
Japan[2]	40	40	40	201	201	198	707	602	500	a	a	a	1 876	1 876	1 876
Korea[3]	40	40	40	220	220	220	807	627	616	a	a	a	1 680	1 680	1 680
Luxembourg[1]	36	36	36	176	176	176	739	634	634	900	828	828	a	a	a
Mexico[1]	42	42	36	200	200	172	800	1 047	843	800	1 167	971	a	a	a
Netherlands[3]	40	m	m	195	m	m	930	750	750	a	a	a	1 659	1 659	1 659
New Zealand[1]	39	38	38	194	192	190	930	845	760	1 552	1 251	950	a	a	a
Norway[1]	38	38	38	190	190	190	741	654	523	1 300	1 225	1 150	1 688	1 688	1 688
Poland[1]	38	38	37	186	184	183	502	497	494	540	534	532	1 520	1 504	1 496
Portugal[3]	37	37	37	173	173	173	865	761	761	1 283	1 283	1 283	1 456	1 456	1 456
Scotland[3]	38	38	38	190	190	190	855	855	855	a	a	a	1 365	1 365	1 365
Slovak Republic[1]	38	38	38	189	189	189	841	652	624	m	m	m	1 583	1 583	1 583
Slovenia[1]	40	40	40	190	190	190	690	690	633	m	m	m	m	m	m
Spain[1]	37	37	36	176	176	171	880	713	693	1 140	1 140	1 140	1 425	1 425	1 425
Sweden	a	a	a	a	a	a	a	a	a	1 360	1 360	1 360	1 767	1 767	1 767
Switzerland	m	m	m	m	m	m	m	m	m	m	m	m	m	m	m
Turkey[1]	37	a	37	175	a	175	621	a	551	870	a	756	1 816	a	1 816
United States[2]	36	36	36	180	180	180	1 097	1 068	1 051	1 381	1 381	1 378	1 913	1 977	1 998
OECD average	38	38	38	187	185	183	782	704	658	1 178	1 171	1 114	1 678	1 673	1 676
EU21 average	38	38	38	185	182	182	758	660	629	1 085	1 057	1 049	1 599	1 598	1 584
Other G20															
Argentina[5]	36	36	36	170	171	171	680	1 368	1 368	m	m	m	m	m	m
Brazil[1]	40	40	40	200	200	200	800	800	800	800	800	800	800	800	800
China	35	35	35	175	175	175	m	m	m	m	m	m	m	m	m
India	m	m	m	m	m	m	m	m	m	m	m	m	m	m	m
Indonesia[2]	44	44	44	244	200	200	697	544	638	1 069	1 069	1 069	1 069	1 069	1 069
Russian Federation[2]	34	35	35	164	169	169	615	507	507	a	a	a	a	a	a
Saudi Arabia	m	m	m	m	m	m	m	m	m	m	m	m	m	m	m
South Africa	m	m	m	m	m	m	m	m	m	m	m	m	m	m	m
G20 average	m	m	m	m	m	m	m	m	m	m	m	m	m	m	m

1. Typical teaching time.
2. Actual teaching time.
3. Maximum teaching time.
4. Minimum teaching time.
5. Year of reference 2009.

Source: OECD. Argentina: UNESCO Institute for Statistics (World Education Indicators programme). China: The Ministry of Education, *Notes on the Experimental Curriculum of Compulsory Education*, 19 November 2001. See Annex 3 for notes (*www.oecd.org/edu/eag2012*).
Please refer to the Reader's Guide for information concerning the symbols replacing missing data.

StatLink http://dx.doi.org/10.1787/888932668318

Table D4.2. Number of teaching hours per year (2000, 2005, 2010)

Net statutory contact time in hours per year in public institutions by level of education in 2000, 2005 and 2010

	Primary level			Lower secondary level			Upper secondary level		
	2000	2005	2010	2000	2005	2010	2000	2005	2010
	(1)	(2)	(3)	(4)	(5)	(6)	(7)	(8)	(9)
OECD Australia	882	888	868	811	810	819	803	810	803
Austria	m	774	779	m	607	607	m	589	589
Belgium (Fl.)	767	761	761	682	690	675	638	645	630
Belgium (Fr.)	804	722	732	728	724	671	668	664	610
Canada	m	m	799	m	m	740	m	m	744
Chile	m	m	1 087	m	m	1 087	m	m	1 087
Czech Republic	650	813	862	650	647	647	621	617	617
Denmark[2]	640	640	650	640	640	650	560	560	377
England[1]	m	m	684	m	m	703	m	m	703
Estonia	630	630	630	630	630	630	578	578	578
Finland	656	677	680	570	592	595	527	550	553
France	907	918	918	639	639	646	611	625	632
Germany	783	808	805	732	758	756	690	714	713
Greece	609	604	589	426	434	415	429	430	415
Hungary	583	583	604	555	555	604	555	555	604
Iceland	629	671	624	629	671	624	464	560	544
Ireland	915	915	915	735	735	735	735	735	735
Israel	731	731	820	579	579	598	524	524	521
Italy	744	739	770	608	605	630	608	605	630
Japan[1]	635	578	707	557	505	602	478	429	500
Korea	865	883	807	570	621	627	530	605	616
Luxembourg	m	774	739	m	642	634	m	642	634
Mexico	800	800	800	1 182	1 047	1 047	m	848	843
Netherlands	930	930	930	867	750	750	867	750	750
New Zealand	m	m	930	m	m	845	m	m	760
Norway	713	741	741	633	656	654	505	524	523
Poland	m	m	502	m	m	497	m	m	494
Portugal	815	855	865	595	564	761	515	513	761
Scotland	950	893	855	893	893	855	893	893	855
Slovak Republic	m	m	841	m	m	652	m	m	624
Slovenia	m	690	690	m	690	690	m	633	633
Spain	880	880	880	564	713	713	548	693	693
Sweden	a	a	a	a	a	a	a	a	a
Switzerland	884	m	m	859	m	m	674	m	m
Turkey	639	639	621	a	a	a	504	567	551
United States[1]	m	1 080	1 097	m	1 080	1 068	m	1 080	1 051
OECD average	762	772	782	681	684	704	605	641	658
OECD average for countries with data available for all reference years	757	762	768	673	672	683	602	615	618
EU21 average for countries with data available for all reference years	766	773	778	657	661	671	628	633	635
Other G20 Argentina[3]	m	m	680	m	m	1 368	m	m	1 368
Brazil	800	800	800	800	800	800	800	800	800
China	m	m	m	m	m	m	m	m	m
India	m	m	m	m	m	m	m	m	m
Indonesia[1]	m	m	697	m	m	544	m	m	638
Russian Federation[1]	m	615	615	m	507	507	m	507	507
Saudi Arabia	m	m	m	m	m	m	m	m	m
South Africa	m	m	m	m	m	m	m	m	m
G20 average	m	m	m	m	m	m	m	m	m

1. Actual teaching time.
2. Break in time series following methodological changes in 2006 for Columns 7, 8 and 9.
3. Year of reference 2009 instead of 2010.
Source: OECD. Argentina: UNESCO Institute for Statistics (World Education Indicators programme). See Annex 3 for notes (*www.oecd.org/edu/eag2012*).
Please refer to the Reader's Guide for information concerning the symbols replacing missing data.
StatLink ⬛⬛⬛ http://dx.doi.org/10.1787/888932668337

WHO ARE THE TEACHERS?

- In 19 of 32 OECD and other G20 countries, 60% or more of secondary school teachers were at least 40 years old in 2010. In Austria, the Czech Republic, Estonia, Germany and Italy 70% or more belong to this age group.

- On average in OECD countries, two-thirds of teachers and academic staff are women, but the proportion of female teachers decreases as the level of education increases: from 97% at the pre-primary level, 82% at the primary level, 68% at the lower secondary level, 56% at the upper secondary level, and to 41% at the tertiary level.

- Thirteen OECD countries require that teachers at some or all levels of education participate in continuing training/education to maintain employment.

Chart D5.1. Age distribution of teachers in secondary education (2010)
Distribution of teachers in educational institutions, by age group

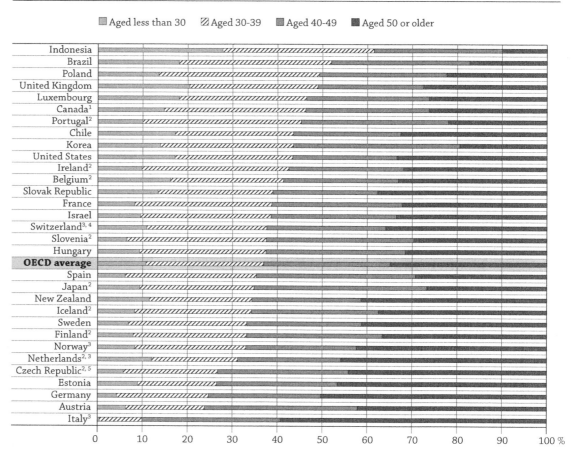

1. Year of reference 2009.
2. Secondary education includes post-secondary non-tertiary education.
3. Public institutions only.
4. Upper secondary education includes general programmes only.
5. Upper secondary education includes tertiary-type B education.
Countries are ranked in ascending order of the percentage of teachers aged 40 or older at the secondary level.
Source: OECD. Indonesia: UNESCO Institute for Statistics (World Education Indicators programme). Table D5.2. See Annex 3 for notes (www.oecd.org/edu/eag2012).
StatLink ⌨ http://dx.doi.org/10.1787/888932663796

Context

The demand for teachers depends on a range of factors such as the age structure of the school-age population, average class size, the teaching load of teachers, required instruction time for students, use of teaching assistants and other "non-classroom" staff in schools, enrolment rates at the different levels of education, in-grade retention rates, and starting and ending age of compulsory education. With large proportions of teachers in several OECD countries set to reach retirement age in the next decade, and/or the projected increase in the size of the school-age population, governments will be under pressure to recruit and train new teachers. Given compelling evidence that the calibre of teachers is the most significant in-school determinant of student achievement, concerted efforts must be made to attract top academic talent to the teaching profession and provide high-quality training (Hiebert and Stigler, 1999; OECD, 2005).

Teacher policy needs to ensure that teachers work in an environment that encourages effective teachers to continue in teaching. In addition, as teaching at the pre-primary, primary and lower secondary levels remains largely dominated by women, this gender imbalance in the teaching profession and its impact on student learning warrant detailed study.

Other findings

- **At the tertiary level, most teachers are men in nearly all countries** except Finland, New Zealand, the Russian Federation and South Africa.

- On average among OECD countries, **58% of primary teachers are at least 40 years old.** However, in seven OECD or other G20 countries – Belgium, Brazil, Ireland, Israel, Korea, Luxembourg and the United Kingdom – more than one-half of the primary teachers are under the age of 40.

- **The duration of teacher training for pre-primary education varies widely** among the 26 OECD countries with data for pre-primary programmes: from two years for basic certification in Japan, Korea and the United States, to five years in France and Portugal.

- For all reporting OECD countries, **the final qualification for teacher-training programmes is a tertiary qualification** (either general tertiary-type A or more vocational tertiary-type B), but the percentage of teachers with such degrees varies among countries.

Trends

Between 1998 and 2010, the proportion of secondary teachers aged 50 or older climbed from 28.8% to 34.2% on average among countries with comparable data. This increase is particularly large in Austria, Germany, Ireland, Japan, Norway, Switzerland and the United Kingdom (an increase of 8 percentage points or more). In contrast, the proportion of teachers under the age of 40 increased slightly from 36.2% to 37.5% on average among countries with available data, but decreased in seven countries, most notably in Austria, Japan and Korea, where these proportions shrank by 14 percentage points or more.

In countries that stand to lose a significant number of teachers through retirement and whose school-age population remains the same or increases, governments will have to boost the appeal of teaching to upper secondary and tertiary students, expand teacher-training programmes, and, if necessary, provide alternate routes to certification for mid-career professionals intent on changing careers. Fiscal constraints – particularly those driven by pension obligations and health-care costs for retirees – are likely to result in greater pressure on governments to reduce academic offerings, increase class size, integrate more self-paced, online learning, or implement some combination of these measures (Abrams, 2011; Christensen, 2008; Peterson, 2010).

D5

Analysis

Demographic profile of teachers

Gender

On average among OECD countries, two-thirds of the teachers and academic staff from all levels of education (i.e. from pre-primary through tertiary education) are women. From pre-primary through upper secondary levels of schooling, the majority of teachers are women in OECD countries, though the proportion of women drops at each successive level of education. However, at the tertiary level, the majority of teachers and academic staff are men in OECD countries. Women represent only 41% of the teaching staff at this level on average among OECD countries. Despite this general pattern, there are large differences between countries at each of the levels of education.

In pre-primary schools, of the 33 OECD and other G20 countries with staffing data, 94% or more of teachers in all but two countries are women. The exceptions are France and South Africa, where 83% and 77% respectively are women. At the primary level, 74% or more of teachers are women in all countries with staffing data, except nine countries: Canada (72%), China (58%), India (46%), Indonesia (60%), Japan (65%), Mexico (67%), Saudi Arabia (50%), South Africa (55%) and Turkey (52%). On average, women occupy 97% of pre-primary and 82% of primary teaching positions in OECD countries (Table D5.3 and Chart D5.2).

Chart D5.2. Gender distribution of teachers (2010)

Percentage of women among teaching staff in public and private institutions, by level of education

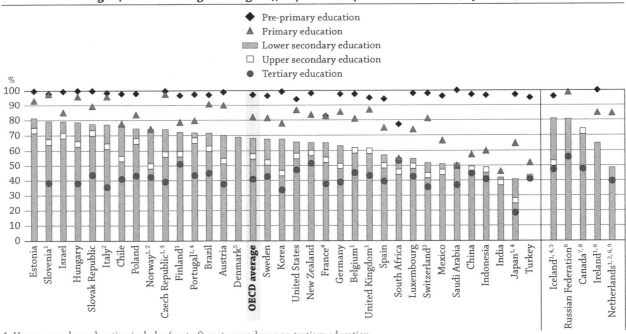

1. Upper secondary education includes (part of) post-secondary non-tertiary education.
2. Public institutions only.
3. Upper secondary education includes tertiary type-B education.
4. Tertiary education includes (part of) post-secondary non-tertiary education.
5. Lower secondary education includes primary education.
6. Lower secondary education includes upper secondary education.
7. Lower secondary education includes pre-primary and primary education.
8. Year of reference 2009.
9. Primary education includes pre-primary education.
Countries are ranked in descending order of the percentage of female teachers at the lower secondary level.
Source: OECD. China, India, Indonesia: UNESCO Institute for Statistics (World Education Indicators programme). Saudi Arabia: UNESCO Institute for Statistics and Observatory on Higher Education. South Africa: UNESCO Institute for Statistics. Table D5.3. See Annex 3 for notes (*www.oecd.org/edu/eag2012*).
StatLink ᕫᕫᓯ http://dx.doi.org/10.1787/888932663815

While a majority of teachers (68%) are women at the lower secondary level in OECD countries, the proportion of male teachers at that level is larger than at the primary level. Among the 28 OECD countries with staffing data, the proportion of female teachers varies considerably, from less than half of the teachers in Japan (41%) to more than 81% in Estonia. At the upper secondary level, the average percentage of female teachers in the 31 OECD countries with staffing data drops to 56% and varies from 26% in Japan to 73% in Estonia. However, among other G20 countries, 80% of upper secondary teachers are women in the Russian Federation.

At the tertiary level, even if most of the teaching staff are men on average in OECD countries, the share of female teachers varies considerably between countries: from about one-third or less of the teaching staff in Japan and Korea (19% and 34%, respectively) to more than half in Finland, New Zealand, the Russian Federation and South Africa (51%, 52%, 56%, and 53% respectively). As at the lower and upper secondary levels, Japan is a significant outlier at the tertiary level of education. However, the smaller proportions of female teachers in Japan, whatever the level of education, may be partly related to weaker involvement of women in the labour market compared with other countries.

Age distribution of teachers

Variations in the size and age distribution of the population, duration of tertiary education, teachers' salaries and working conditions affect the age distribution of teachers. Declining birth rates drive down demand for new teachers. Tertiary education is completed later in some countries than in others. While competitive salaries and good working conditions in some countries attract young people to teaching, they also keep teachers from leaving the profession and thus limit the number of openings.

At the primary level, 58% of teachers are at least 40 years old, on average among OECD countries. The proportion exceeds 70% in the Czech Republic, Germany, Italy and Sweden. In only seven countries – Belgium, Brazil, Ireland, Israel, Korea, Luxembourg and the United Kingdom – are more than half of primary teachers under the age of 40. Only in Belgium, Ireland, Korea, Luxembourg and the United Kingdom does the proportion of teachers under the age of 30 exceed 20% (Table D5.1 and Chart D5.3).

There is a similar age distribution of teachers at the secondary level. On average among OECD countries, 63% of teachers are at least 40 years old. In Austria, the Czech Republic, Estonia, Germany and Italy, 70% or more of secondary teachers are at least 40 years old. Only in Brazil and Indonesia are most secondary teachers (51.9% and 61.5% respectively) below the age of 40. In 11 additional countries, 40% or more of secondary teachers are below the age of 40. The proportion of secondary school teachers aged 50 or older is larger than that of primary school teachers in most countries (in 23 of 30 OECD and other G20 countries). The proportion of teachers aged 50 or older is at least 10 percentage points higher in upper secondary than in primary education in Belgium, the Czech Republic, Estonia, Finland, France, Israel, Italy, the Netherlands, Norway, Poland and the Slovak Republic (Table D5.1 and Chart D5.1).

In addition to prompting recruitment and training efforts to replace retiring teachers, the ageing of the teacher workforce also has budgetary implications. In most school systems, there is a link between teachers' salaries and years of teaching experience. The ageing of teachers increases school costs, which in turn limits the resources available to implement other initiatives at the school level (see Indicator D3).

Despite the larger proportions of teachers aged 50 or over at the secondary level compared to the primary level, young teachers may represent a significant part of the staff (at the primary and secondary levels, 14% and 11% of teachers, respectively, are aged 30 or younger, on average in OECD countries). Only in Austria, the Czech Republic, Estonia, Finland, Germany, Hungary, Italy, Portugal, Slovenia and Sweden, are 10% or fewer of primary and secondary teachers younger than 30. This can be partly explained by the relatively late age at which students complete tertiary education in these countries (see Annex 1).

Change in the age distribution of teachers between 1998 and 2010

Among countries with comparable trend data for both 1998 and 2010, the average proportion of secondary school teachers under the age of 40 increased by 1.3 percentage points between 1998 and 2010, whereas the proportion of those aged 50 or older increased by 5.4 percentage points. In 9 of 16 OECD countries, the proportion of teachers under the age of 40 increased between 1998 and 2010. Yet the range among countries

Chart D5.3.   Age distribution of teachers in primary education (2010)
Distribution of teachers in educational institutions, by age group

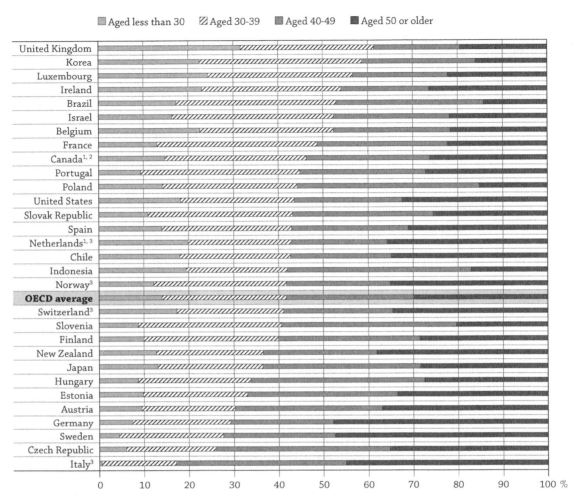

1. Primary education includes pre-primary education.
2. Year of reference 2009.
3. Public institutions only.
Countries are ranked in ascending order of the percentage of teachers aged 40 or older at the primary level.
Source: OECD. Indonesia: UNESCO Institute for Statistics (World Education Indicators programme). Table D5.1. See Annex 3 for notes (*www.oecd.org/edu/eag2012*).
StatLink ᵐˢᵖ http://dx.doi.org/10.1787/888932663834

is wide. In Belgium (Flemish Community), Canada, Germany, Luxembourg and the United Kingdom, the proportion rose by more than 8 percentage points. Conversely, in Austria, Japan and Korea, the proportion dropped by 14 percentage points or more. From 1998 to 2010, the proportion of secondary teachers aged 50 or older increased the most (by at least 8 percentage points) in Austria (from 20% to 42%), Germany (from 40% to 50%), Ireland (from 23% to 32%), Japan (from 18% to 27%), Norway (from 33% to 42%), Switzerland (from 27% to 36%) and the United Kingdom (from 19% to 28%) (Table D5.2).

In all countries, the changes in the number of teachers should be balanced against changes in the school-age population. In countries with a demographic growth and thus an increase in the school-age population over the period, such as Ireland, Israel and Spain (see Indicator C1, Table C1.6), new teachers will need to be recruited to compensate for the significant number of staff hired during the 1960s and 1970s and who will reach retirement age in the next decade. Teacher-training programmes will likely have to grow, and incentives for students to enter the teaching profession may have to increase (see Indicator D3). In contrast, as there can be high individual and social costs when substantial resources are invested in teacher education, countries with a decreasing school-age population, such as Austria, Chile, Germany, Japan, Korea and Poland, need to ensure that the quality of teacher preparation is not undermined by large number of candidates and/or graduates from teacher-training programmes who are not able to find work as teachers (OECD, 2005).

Developing teachers' knowledge and skills

The far-reaching economic and social changes occurring today have made high-quality schooling more important than ever before. Countries are no longer only interested in getting an adequate supply of teachers, but also in raising the quality of learning for all. The latter can only be achieved if all students receive high-quality instruction. Teachers are central to school improvement efforts. Improving the efficiency of schools depends to a large measure on ensuring that competent people want to work as teachers, and that their teaching is of high quality. Countries create these conditions in different ways (Hiebert and Stigler, 1999; OECD, 2005).

Selection into teacher education

Diploma requirements for entry into pre-service teacher-training programmes differ little across OECD and other G20 countries. The minimum requirement is typically an upper secondary diploma. In Brazil, candidates for teacher-training programmes for teaching at the primary level need only a lower secondary diploma. In contrast, candidates for teacher-training programmes for teaching at the lower and upper secondary levels in Italy and Spain need a tertiary diploma, as do candidates for teacher-training programmes for teaching at the upper secondary level in Switzerland (see Annex 3).

In addition, applicants in several countries must pass competitive exams to enter pre-service training programmes. Such exams are required for candidates for pre-primary teacher training in Denmark and Luxembourg; for pre-primary and primary teacher training in Austria; for primary and secondary teacher training in Australia, Germany, Hungary, Indonesia and Mexico; and for all levels of education in Finland, Greece, Ireland, Israel, Korea and Turkey (Table D5.4).

Teachers' educational attainment

The duration of teacher training ranges widely among the 26 OECD countries with data for pre-primary programmes: from two years for basic certification in Japan, Korea and the United States, to five years in France and Portugal. In the countries with data for both pre-primary and primary teacher-training programmes, while the duration of these programmes is similar in 18 countries, it increases from the pre-primary to the primary level by one year in Norway, and by two years in the Czech Republic, Finland and Germany. For lower secondary teachers, the variation in the duration of teacher-training programmes ranges from 3 years in Belgium, to between 5.5 years and 6 years in Austria, Germany and Spain. In the 35 countries with data for both lower secondary and upper secondary teacher-training programmes, while the duration of these programmes is similar in 23 countries, there are some variations in the remaining countries. In Hungary and Switzerland, upper secondary programmes are one year longer than lower secondary programmes, in the Netherlands they are one to two years longer, and in Belgium and Denmark they are two years longer. Teacher training for upper secondary teachers ranges from 3 to 4 years in England and Israel to 6.5 years in Germany (Table D5.4).

The final qualification for teacher-training programmes for all reporting OECD countries is a tertiary qualification (either general tertiary-type A or more vocational tertiary-type B). Yet the percentage of teachers with such degrees varies among countries. At the pre-primary level, data were provided by only 21 countries, of which 7 reported that all of their teachers were qualified according to current standards. At the primary level, 19 countries reported that 92% or more of their teachers were qualified according to current standards, with 7 countries claiming 100% compliance. At the lower secondary level, 20 countries reported that at least 90% of their teachers were qualified according to current standards, with 8 countries claiming 100% compliance. At the upper secondary level, 17 countries reported that at least 92% of their teachers were qualified according to current standards, with 8 countries claiming 100% compliance.

Students in teacher-training programmes in many countries must also participate in a teaching practicum in addition to formal instruction. Among OECD countries, Austria has such a requirement for teacher trainees at the pre-primary or primary level; Denmark has such a requirement for students who want to teach at the pre-primary, primary, or lower secondary level; Mexico has such a requirement for teacher trainees at the primary or lower secondary level; 10 countries have such a requirement for students who want to teach at the primary, lower or upper secondary level; and 20 countries have such a requirement for students who want to teach at any level. While England has no such requirement, Scotland requires a teaching practicum for all students in teacher-training programmes.

Requirements to enter the teaching profession

Twenty-two OECD countries and Brazil require that, in addition to holding a diploma from a tertiary institution, candidates for the teaching profession must also acquire a licence or supplementary credential, pass a competitive examination, and/or participate in an on-the-job teacher practicum as part of an induction process or probationary period. Candidates in Australia, Germany, Israel, Italy (secondary level), Japan, Mexico (upper secondary level) and the United States are required to both pass a competitive examination and acquire a licence or supplementary credential to become a teacher. In Canada, England, Germany, Israel, Japan, Korea, New Zealand (primary and secondary levels), Scotland and the United States, candidates must participate in a teacher practicum to acquire the licence or supplementary credential necessary to become a teacher. Candidates in Greece, Hungary, Ireland, Israel, Luxembourg, New Zealand (primary and secondary levels), Scotland, Spain and Turkey must also participate in an on-the-job teacher practicum as part of an induction process or probationary period. This is only required at the upper secondary level in Austria and Denmark. Moreover, 11 OECD countries and Indonesia require that teachers acquire a licence or supplementary credential at the primary and secondary levels to become fully certified. This is required only at the secondary level in Italy and at the upper secondary level in Denmark (Table D5.5).

Beyond such additional work, 13 OECD countries require teachers at some or all levels of instruction to participate in continuing education. However, this number is likely to increase in the coming years as continuing education for teachers takes on new significance with the rising demand for both differentiated instruction to address a wider range of learning styles and the integration of technology to connect the classroom to the outside world.

Level of government at which decisions about teachers in public lower secondary schools are taken

The division of authority among central, state, regional, local, and school administrators over teacher hiring, dismissal, duties, conditions of service, pay, and professional development in public institutions at the lower secondary level varies considerably across OECD countries (Chart D5.4). While advocates of more autonomy at the local or school level contend that such freedom empowers principals and teachers and fosters greater community involvement, critics counter that such freedom tends to politicise staffing decisions, increase inequality between regions, and atomize standards.

In roughly one-third of OECD countries for which data are available, authority over teacher hiring, dismissal, and duties is highly centralised. In the case of Australia, Austria, Belgium (French Community), France, Luxembourg, Mexico, Spain and Turkey, all such authority rests with state or central administrators, either exclusively or in consultation with school leaders. In contrast, authority in these three domains belongs to local or school leaders alone in Belgium (Flemish Community), Canada, Chile, the Czech Republic, Denmark, England, Estonia, Finland, Hungary, Iceland, Ireland, the Netherlands, Norway, Poland, Scotland, the Slovak Republic, Slovenia, Sweden and the United States (Table D5.6, available on line).

Authority over teachers' pay belongs largely to state or central administrators. Only in the Czech Republic, England, Estonia, Hungary, the Netherlands and Sweden is teachers' pay decided at the school level, either exclusively or within a centrally established framework. Teachers' pay is decided at the local level within a framework established centrally in Chile and within a framework negotiated with teachers' unions in Finland,

Iceland and Norway. In the United States, although individual states often determine a minimum salary schedule for teachers, this may be supplemented by local districts.

The allocation of resources for professional development of teachers is decided at the state or central level in around 40% of the OECD countries while the use of these resources are typically decided at the local or school level. Both allocation and use of such resources are decided by state or central administrators in only seven countries: Belgium (French Community), Chile, Greece, Israel, Luxembourg, Mexico and Portugal. Such joint policy is made at the school level alone in 12 countries: Australia, Denmark, England, Estonia, Hungary, Iceland, Indonesia, the Netherlands, Scotland, the Slovak Republic, Slovenia and Sweden. In three countries – the Czech Republic, Finland and Poland – allocation of resources is decided at the local level while how those resources are used is decided at the school level.

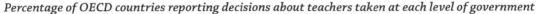

Chart D5.4. Level of government at which decisions about teachers are taken in public lower secondary education (2011)

Percentage of OECD countries reporting decisions about teachers taken at each level of government

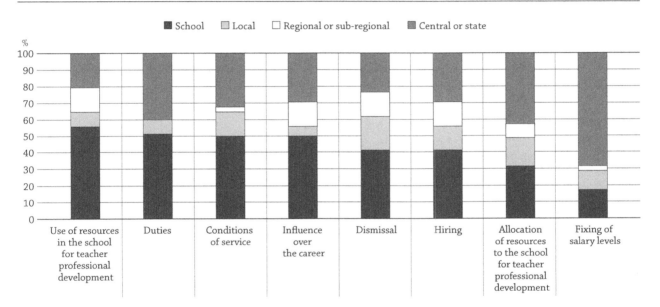

Decisions are ranked in descending order of the percentage of OECD countries reporting these decisions as taken at the school level.
Source: OECD. Table D5.6, available on line. See Annex 3 for notes (*www.oecd.org/edu/eag2012*).
StatLink ᴍᴤᴾ http://dx.doi.org/10.1787/888932663853

Definitions

Credential or licence refers to a certification, licence, or similar document granted by a government agency or institution that attests that a teacher is qualified and meets standards to teach in the public education system. The requirements for a credential exceed the education diploma.

Duration of pre-service training for new teachers refers to the typical number of full-time equivalent years of teacher training required to become a fully qualified teacher according to the formal policy of the country.

ISCED type of final qualification refers to the type of educational qualification (e.g. ISCED 3, 5B, 5A) that a new teacher would be require to have to teach primary, lower secondary, and upper secondary education (general programmes) in the public sector.

A register for teachers refers to an administrative record of teachers that contains a detailed profile of all teachers (e.g. their qualification, experience, career path, etc.).

Teaching practicum provides student teachers and/or inexperienced teachers, as well as experienced teachers, with a guided teaching/learning experience where they can benefit from the instructional expertise of an experienced teacher.

Methodology

Data on teachers by gender and by age refer to the academic year 2009-10 (and 1997-98) and are based on the UOE data collection on education statistics administered by OECD in 2011 (for details, see Annex 3 at *www.oecd.org/edu/eag2012*). Data on teachers by age for 1998 may have been revised in 2011 to ensure consistency with 2010 data.

Data on pre-service teacher-training requirements and requirements to enter the teaching profession are from the 2011 OECD-INES Survey on Teachers and the Curriculum and refer to the school year 2009-10.

Data on the level of decision-making about teachers are from the 2011 OECD-INES survey on decision making in education and refer to the school year 2010-11. More detailed information on definitions and methodology can be found in Indicator D6, "Who makes key decisions in education systems?"

Notes on definitions and methodologies for each country are provided in Annex 3 at *www.oecd.org/edu/eag2012*.

The statistical data for Israel are supplied by and under the responsibility of the relevant Israeli authorities. The use of such data by the OECD is without prejudice to the status of the Golan Heights, East Jerusalem and Israeli settlements in the West Bank under the terms of international law.

References

Abrams, S.E. (2011), "Technology in Moderation", *The Teachers College Record*, available at *www.tcrecord.org/content.asp?contentid=16584*.

Christensen, C.M. (2008), *Disrupting Class: How Disruptive Innovation Will Change the Way the World Learns*, McGraw Hill, New York.

Hiebert, J. and J. Stigler (1999), *The Teaching Gap: Best Ideas from the World's Teachers for Improving Education in the Classroom*, Free Press, New York.

OECD (2005), *Teachers Matter: Attracting, Developing and Retaining Effective Teachers*, OECD Publishing.

Peterson, P. (2010), *Saving Schools: From Horace Mann to Virtual Learning*, Harvard University Press, Cambridge.

The following additional material relevant to this indicator is available on line:

- *Table D5.6. Level of government at which different types of decisions about teachers are taken in public lower secondary education (2011)*
  StatLink 🔢 http://dx.doi.org/10.1787/888932668470

D5

Table D5.1. **Age distribution of teachers (2010)**
Percentage of teachers in public and private institutions, by level of education and age group, based on head counts

	Primary education					Lower secondary education					Upper secondary education				
	< 30 years	30-39 years	40-49 years	50-59 years	>= 60 years	< 30 years	30-39 years	40-49 years	50-59 years	>= 60 years	< 30 years	30-39 years	40-49 years	50-59 years	>= 60 years
	(1)	(2)	(3)	(4)	(5)	(6)	(7)	(8)	(9)	(10)	(11)	(12)	(13)	(14)	(15)
Australia	m	m	m	m	m	m	m	m	m	m	m	m	m	m	m
Austria	9.4	20.8	32.8	34.9	2.1	6.5	15.8	33.1	41.9	2.7	5.8	20.0	35.3	34.6	4.2
Belgium[1]	22.6	29.7	26.0	20.2	1.5	18.1	25.3	24.4	28.8	3.4	15.2	25.2	26.1	29.8	3.8
Canada[2,3]	14.8	31.5	27.5	22.4	3.8	x(1)	x(2)	x(3)	x(4)	x(5)	14.8	31.5	27.5	22.4	3.8
Chile	18.0	24.7	22.5	25.8	9.0	17.5	23.9	22.7	26.5	9.4	17.1	27.5	24.3	23.4	7.7
Czech Republic[1,4]	6.0	19.9	38.7	30.2	5.1	7.3	24.4	31.3	28.4	8.6	4.5	18.3	27.4	34.9	14.9
Denmark	x(6)	x(7)	x(8)	x(9)	x(10)	8.6	30.8	23.5	28.1	9.0	m	m	m	m	m
Estonia	9.8	23.2	33.5	23.8	9.8	9.6	18.1	26.9	28.5	16.9	8.3	17.3	26.7	29.3	18.4
Finland[1]	10.0	29.9	31.5	25.7	2.9	11.2	30.2	28.8	25.7	4.1	5.1	21.0	31.4	30.9	11.7
France	13.0	35.7	29.1	21.4	0.8	10.8	34.0	25.6	26.3	3.4	5.6	27.1	32.4	30.6	4.4
Germany	7.4	21.8	23.0	37.1	10.8	4.8	19.9	23.5	40.5	11.3	3.1	21.7	28.1	36.3	10.8
Greece	m	m	m	m	m	m	m	m	m	m	m	m	m	m	m
Hungary	8.7	25.0	38.8	26.9	0.6	8.0	24.4	34.8	31.2	1.7	10.4	31.4	27.6	25.9	4.7
Iceland[1]	x(6)	x(7)	x(8)	x(9)	x(10)	9.3	29.1	28.4	24.4	8.7	5.6	18.5	27.9	31.8	16.2
Ireland[1]	23.0	31.1	19.6	22.0	4.4	x(11)	x(12)	x(13)	x(14)	x(15)	9.8	32.7	25.5	26.1	5.9
Israel	16.3	36.1	25.7	19.0	2.8	9.9	30.8	30.0	25.0	4.2	9.2	28.1	26.8	25.2	10.7
Italy[5]	0.5	16.6	37.9	39.3	5.7	0.5	11.6	28.1	50.0	9.8	0.4	7.9	32.8	50.0	8.9
Japan[1]	13.1	23.4	35.1	27.8	0.7	10.8	26.8	40.5	21.2	0.8	8.0	24.2	36.7	28.2	2.8
Korea	22.5	36.2	25.3	14.0	2.0	14.8	29.8	38.6	16.0	0.7	13.1	29.5	35.6	20.6	1.1
Luxembourg[6]	24.4	32.3	21.2	21.1	1.1	27.0	31.4	20.9	18.7	2.0	12.7	26.5	31.2	26.2	3.4
Mexico	m	m	m	m	m	m	m	m	m	m	m	m	m	m	m
Netherlands[1,2,5]	19.9	22.9	21.4	29.5	6.3	x(11)	x(12)	x(13)	x(14)	x(15)	12.1	19.1	22.9	35.9	10.0
New Zealand	12.8	23.8	25.2	27.0	11.2	12.0	23.4	24.6	28.1	12.0	11.1	22.1	24.1	29.5	13.3
Norway[5]	12.2	29.6	23.1	24.0	11.1	12.2	29.6	23.1	24.0	11.1	4.9	20.6	25.9	31.1	17.5
Poland	14.1	30.1	40.6	13.8	1.4	14.9	37.6	30.7	15.0	1.7	12.7	34.3	26.7	20.8	5.5
Portugal[1]	9.4	35.4	28.0	25.2	2.0	9.9	34.0	32.8	21.2	2.1	10.1	36.4	32.8	18.6	2.1
Slovak Republic	11.0	32.2	31.3	22.5	3.0	14.6	26.8	21.8	30.7	6.1	12.1	24.1	25.0	31.1	7.7
Slovenia[1]	8.7	32.0	38.9	19.9	0.5	7.5	31.7	31.2	27.0	2.6	5.4	30.3	34.6	25.3	4.4
Spain	14.0	28.9	26.0	26.7	4.4	6.2	29.5	35.3	24.5	4.5	5.9	28.9	35.6	25.3	4.4
Sweden	4.4	23.2	24.9	31.0	16.5	6.8	30.4	26.1	22.7	14.0	6.8	22.9	25.1	27.1	18.1
Switzerland[5,7]	17.3	23.8	24.4	30.0	4.5	12.3	26.7	25.5	29.6	5.9	6.9	26.5	29.6	29.6	7.4
Turkey	m	m	m	m	m	a	a	a	a	a	m	m	m	m	m
United Kingdom	31.7	29.7	19.2	18.0	1.4	22.7	30.3	22.0	21.8	3.2	19.1	27.6	24.4	23.5	5.4
United States	18.1	25.4	24.1	26.3	6.1	18.4	26.7	23.1	25.1	6.7	15.6	25.8	23.1	26.7	8.8
OECD average	14.0	27.7	28.4	25.2	4.7	11.6	27.2	28.0	27.1	6.2	9.4	25.1	28.7	28.6	8.2
EU21 average	13.1	27.4	29.3	25.7	4.2	10.8	27.0	27.8	28.4	5.9	8.7	24.9	29.0	29.6	7.8
Argentina	m	m	m	m	m	m	m	m	m	m	m	m	m	m	m
Brazil	17.2	35.7	32.8	12.2	2.0	18.5	34.0	30.9	14.2	2.5	17.5	33.7	30.7	15.2	2.9
China	m	m	m	m	m	m	m	m	m	m	m	m	m	m	m
India	m	m	m	m	m	m	m	m	m	m	m	m	m	m	m
Indonesia	19.4	22.5	41.0	16.0	1.0	34.0	30.7	26.7	7.7	1.0	19.9	37.5	31.0	10.2	1.4
Russian Federation	m	m	m	m	m	m	m	m	m	m	m	m	m	m	m
Saudi Arabia	m	m	m	m	m	m	m	m	m	m	m	m	m	m	m
South Africa	m	m	m	m	m	m	m	m	m	m	m	m	m	m	m
G20 average	m	m	m	m	m	m	m	m	m	m	m	m	m	m	m

1. Upper secondary education includes post-secondary non-tertiary education (or part of post-secondary non-tertiary for Iceland and Portugal).
2. Primary education includes pre-primary education.
3. Year of reference 2009.
4. Upper secondary education includes tertiary-type B education.
5. Public institutions only.
6. Lower secondary private institutions included with upper secondary institutions.
7. Upper secondary education includes general programmes only.
Source: OECD. Indonesia: UNESCO Institute for Statistics (World Education Indicators programme). See Annex 3 for notes (*www.oecd.org/edu/eag2012*).
Please refer to the Reader's Guide for information concerning the symbols replacing missing data.
StatLink http://dx.doi.org/10.1787/888932668375

Table D5.2. Age distribution of teachers (1998, 2010)

Percentage of teachers in public and private institutions in secondary education, based on head counts

		Secondary education (2010)					Secondary education (1998)					Percentage of teachers under 40 years old		
		< 30 years	30-39 years	40-49 years	50-59 years	>= 60 years	< 30 years	30-39 years	40-49 years	50-59 years	>= 60 years	2010	1998	Dif.
		(1)	(2)	(3)	(4)	(5)	(6)	(7)	(8)	(9)	(10)	(11)	(12)	(13) = (11) - (12)
OECD	Australia	m	m	m	m	m	m	m	m	m	m	m	m	m
	Austria	6.2	17.6	34.1	38.8	3.3	8.1	30.4	41.1	19.5	0.9	23.8	38.5	-14.7
	Belgium[1]	16.2	25.2	25.5	29.5	3.6	m	m	m	m	m	41.4	m	m
	Belgium (Fl.)	18.1	27.4	24.9	27.2	2.4	13.3	24.2	35.3	24.8	1.9	45.5	37.5	8.0
	Canada[2]	14.8	31.5	27.5	22.4	3.8	9.1	24.8	40.9	24.0	1.2	46.3	33.9	12.4
	Chile	17.2	26.3	23.8	24.4	8.2	m	m	m	m	m	43.6	m	m
	Czech Republic[1, 3]	5.7	21.0	29.1	32.0	12.1	m	m	m	m	m	26.8	m	m
	Denmark	m	m	m	m	m	m	m	m	m	m	m	m	m
	Estonia	8.9	17.7	26.8	28.9	17.7	m	m	m	m	m	26.6	m	m
	Finland[1, 3]	7.9	25.3	30.2	28.5	8.2	7.5	25.9	34.8	29.2	2.6	33.2	33.4	-0.2
	France	8.2	30.5	29.0	28.4	3.9	12.6	23.8	33.6	29.1	0.8	38.7	36.4	2.3
	Germany	4.3	20.5	25.0	39.2	11.1	2.6	12.5	44.8	36.6	3.5	24.7	15.1	9.6
	Greece	m	m	m	m	m	m	m	m	m	m	m	m	m
	Hungary	9.3	28.2	31.0	28.3	3.3	m	m	m	m	m	37.4	m	m
	Iceland[1]	8.2	26.0	28.3	26.6	10.9	6.7	24.2	34.2	23.9	11.1	34.2	30.9	3.3
	Ireland[1]	9.8	32.7	25.5	26.1	5.9	14.8	27.8	34.7	19.1	3.7	42.5	42.6	-0.1
	Israel	9.5	29.1	27.9	25.1	8.4	m	m	m	m	m	38.5	m	m
	Italy[4]	0.5	9.5	30.8	50.0	9.3	m	m	m	m	m	9.9	m	m
	Japan[1]	9.3	25.5	38.5	24.8	1.8	13.1	36.8	31.7	16.8	1.6	34.8	49.9	-15.1
	Korea	13.9	29.6	37.0	18.5	0.9	11.9	46.2	25.9	12.6	3.5	43.5	58.0	-14.5
	Luxembourg[4]	18.1	28.3	27.3	23.4	2.9	7.7	26.7	34.5	28.2	2.9	46.4	34.4	12.0
	Mexico	m	m	m	m	m	m	m	m	m	m	m	m	m
	Netherlands[1, 4]	12.1	19.1	22.9	35.9	10.0	m	m	m	m	m	31.2	m	m
	New Zealand	11.5	22.8	24.3	28.7	12.6	10.1	21.7	30.9	28.9	8.4	34.3	31.9	2.5
	Norway[4]	8.3	24.7	24.6	27.8	14.5	12.9	20.5	33.1	27.7	5.8	33.0	33.5	-0.5
	Poland	13.6	35.7	28.3	18.4	4.0	m	m	m	m	m	49.3	m	m
	Portugal[1]	10.0	35.3	32.8	19.8	2.1	m	m	m	m	m	45.3	m	m
	Slovak Republic	13.4	25.5	23.4	30.9	6.9	m	m	m	m	m	38.9	m	m
	Slovenia[1]	6.5	31.0	32.9	26.1	3.5	m	m	m	m	m	37.5	m	m
	Spain	6.1	29.3	35.4	24.8	4.5	m	m	m	m	m	35.3	m	m
	Sweden	6.8	26.4	25.6	25.0	16.2	8.4	17.1	28.6	38.1	7.8	33.2	25.6	7.6
	Switzerland[4, 5]	10.9	26.6	26.5	29.6	6.3	11.3	27.1	34.6	23.9	3.1	37.6	38.3	-0.8
	Turkey	m	m	m	m	m	m	m	m	m	m	m	m	m
	United Kingdom	20.4	28.6	23.6	22.9	4.6	17.3	22.6	40.7	18.5	0.9	48.9	40.0	9.0
	United States	17	26	23	25.8	8	m	m	m	m	m	43	m	m
	OECD average	10.8	26.1	28.2	27.9	7.0	~	~	~	~	~	~	~	~
	OECD average for countries with available data for both reference years	11.0	26.5	28.2	27.4	6.8	10.5	25.8	35.0	25.1	3.7	37.5	36.2	1.3
	EU21 average	10.1	25.7	28.2	29.2	6.8	~	~	~	~	~	~	~	~
Other G20	Argentina	m	m	m	m	m	m	m	m	m	m	m	m	m
	Brazil	18.0	33.9	30.8	14.6	2.6	m	m	m	m	m	51.9	m	m
	China	m	m	m	m	m	m	m	m	m	m	m	m	m
	India	m	m	m	m	m	m	m	m	m	m	m	m	m
	Indonesia	27.8	33.7	28.6	8.8	1.2	m	m	m	m	m	61.5	m	m
	Russian Federation	m	m	m	m	m	m	m	m	m	m	m	m	m
	Saudi Arabia	m	m	m	m	m	m	m	m	m	m	m	m	m
	South Africa	m	m	m	m	m	m	m	m	m	m	m	m	m
	G20 average	m	m	m	m	m	m	m	m	m	m	m	m	m

1. Including post-secondary non-tertiary education (part of post-secondary non-tertiary education for Iceland and Portugal).
2. Year of reference 2009 instead of 2010.
3. Includes tertiary-type B education (for Finland, in 1998 only).
4. Public institutions only (for Luxembourg, in 1998 only).
5. Upper secondary education includes general programmes only.
Source: OECD. Indonesia: UNESCO Institute for Statistics (World Education Indicators programme). See Annex 3 for notes (*www.oecd.org/edu/eag2012*).
Please refer to the Reader's Guide for information concerning the symbols replacing missing data.
StatLink ▀▀ꞙ▬ http://dx.doi.org/10.1787/888932668394

Table D5.3. **Gender distribution of teachers (2010)**

Percentage of women among teaching staff in public and private institutions, by level of education, based on head counts

| | Pre-primary education | Primary education | Lower secondary education | Upper secondary education | | | Post-secondary non-tertiary education | Tertiary education | | | All levels of education |
				General programmes	prevocational/ vocational programmes	All programmes		Type B	Type A and advanced research programmes	Total tertiary education	
	(1)	(2)	(3)	(4)	(5)	(6)	(7)	(8)	(9)	(10)	(11)
Australia	m	m	m	m	m	m	m	m	m	m	**m**
Austria	98.9	90.0	70.1	61.7	49.5	53.1	52.4	x(10)	x(10)	37.7	**64.2**
Belgium	97.6	81.0	61.5	x(6)	x(6)	60.2	x(6)	x(10)	x(10)	45.2	**68.7**
Canada[1]	x(2)	72.4	x(2)	x(6)	x(6)	72.4	m	52.9	39.5	47.7	**m**
Chile	97.8	77.7	76.6	57.2	49.5	54.7	a	41.8	40.8	41.1	**67.6**
Czech Republic	99.7	97.5	73.9	x(6)	x(6)	57.8	x(6)	x(6)	39.2	39.2	**m**
Denmark	m	x(3)	68.8	m	m	m	m	m	m	m	**m**
Estonia	99.6	93.1	81.3	78.7	65.3	73.2	x(5)	m	m	m	**m**
Finland	96.7	78.6	72.0	69.6	52.4	57.9	x(6)	a	51.1	51.1	**70.6**
France	82.6	82.8	65.1	55.0	51.2	53.9	x(8)	41.4	36.8	37.7	**65.8**
Germany	97.5	85.5	63.1	53.2	42.2	49.7	51.6	54.0	35.3	38.9	**64.4**
Greece	m	m	m	m	m	m	m	m	m	m	**m**
Hungary	99.8	95.9	78.5	68.2	53.1	64.5	51.5	49.3	36.9	38.1	**75.6**
Iceland	96.0	x(3)	80.8	x(6)	x(6)	51.6	x(6, 10)	x(10)	x(10)	47.3	**72.0**
Ireland	100.0	84.9	x(6)	65.3	52.2	64.7	x(6)	m	m	m	**m**
Israel	99.4	85.2	79.1	x(6)	x(6)	69.8	m	m	m	m	**m**
Italy[2]	98.4	95.9	77.0	74.7	56.5	63.0	m	32.9	35.6	35.6	**75.9**
Japan	97.1	64.8	40.7	x(6)	x(6)	26.4	x(4, 8, 9)	34.2	17.1	18.5	**46.7**
Korea	99.2	77.9	67.5	46.5	41.0	45.0	a	42.3	31.6	33.8	**55.7**
Luxembourg[3]	98.1	73.9	54.6	54.0	45.4	49.7	m	x(10)	x(10)	42.6	**m**
Mexico	96.2	66.6	51.0	45.2	48.0	45.5	a	m	m	m	**m**
Netherlands[2]	x(2)	84.6	x(6)	48.1	49.8	48.6	x(6)	x(10)	x(10)	39.6	**64.0**
New Zealand	98.1	83.6	65.2	59.4	54.2	58.5	52.4	62.3	47.9	51.5	**69.6**
Norway[2]	m	74.2	74.2	x(6)	x(6)	49.7	x(6)	x(10)	x(10)	42.2	**62.7**
Poland	98.0	83.7	74.4	70.6	62.4	66.3	63.6	67.8	42.5	43.1	**72.7**
Portugal	97.4	79.7	71.7	x(6)	x(6)	66.7	x(6, 8)	x(10)	x(10)	43.5	**70.4**
Slovak Republic	99.8	89.3	77.3	74.6	70.3	71.6	49.8	60.5	43.3	43.7	**75.5**
Slovenia	97.8	97.5	79.1	71.2	62.3	65.8	x(4, 5)	x(10)	x(10)	38.3	**74.1**
Spain	94.2	75.0	57.2	x(6)	x(6)	50.0	a	44.6	38.3	39.5	**64.4**
Sweden	96.4	81.5	67.5	48.1	54.3	52.1	46.6	x(10)	x(10)	42.7	**73.3**
Switzerland[2]	98.0	81.1	51.7	43.4	m	43.4	m	m	35.6	35.6	**59.1**
Turkey	95.2	52.0	a	42.9	40.8	41.9	a	31.3	42.0	40.9	**50.3**
United Kingdom	95.0	87.0	59.9	60.0	59.6	59.8	x(6)	x(10)	x(10)	43.2	**67.0**
United States	94.1	86.7	65.6	x(6)	x(6)	56.5	63.0	x(10)	x(10)	47.1	**69.0**
OECD average	97.1	82.0	68.1	59.4	53.0	56.3	53.9	47.3	38.3	40.9	**66.6**
EU21 average	97.1	86.2	69.5	63.5	55.1	59.4	52.6	50.1	39.9	41.2	**69.8**
Argentina	m	m	m	m	m	m	m	m	48.6	m	**m**
Brazil	97.1	90.7	71.5	63.1	53.3	61.4	a	x(10)	x(10)	44.9	**74.6**
China	97.2	57.6	48.9	46.9	48.5	47.6	m	48.1	25.6	44.7	**55.2**
India	m	46.2	41.9	x(6)	x(6)	38.5	m	m	m	m	**m**
Indonesia	96.7	60.0	48.7	48.2	45.1	47.0	a	x(8)	x(8)	40.8	**57.5**
Russian Federation	m	98.9	x(4)	83.1	64.4	80.5	x(5)	67.7	52.4	55.7	**75.0**
Saudi Arabia	100.0	50.2	49.6	x(6)	x(6)	49.6	a	x(10)	x(10)	36.5	**50.1**
South Africa[1]	77.2	55.1	55.1	45.7	x(3)	45.7	a	x(10)	x(10)	53.3	**62.8**
G20 average	94.5	72.4	53.7	55.4	50.0	52.0	m	45.0	36.4	41.3	**62.1**

1. Year of reference 2009.
2. Public institutions only (for Italy, from pre-primary to secondary levels).
3. Lower secondary private institutions included with upper secondary institutions.
Source: OECD. Argentina, China, India, Indonesia: UNESCO Institute for Statistics (World Education Indicators programme). Saudi Arabia: UNESCO Institute for Statistics and Observatory on Higher Education. South Africa: UNESCO Institute for Statistics. See Annex 3 for notes (*www.oecd.org/edu/eag2012*).
Please refer to the Reader's Guide for information concerning the symbols replacing missing data.
StatLink ᴍᵻᶳᴾ http://dx.doi.org/10.1787/888932668413

D5

Table D5.4. [1/2] Pre-service teacher-training requirements in public institutions (2010)

	Competitive examination required to enter pre-service teacher training				Duration of teacher-training programme in years				Teaching practicum required as part of pre-service training			
	Pre-primary education	Primary education	Lower secondary education	Upper secondary education	Pre-primary education	Primary education	Lower secondary education	Upper secondary education	Pre-primary education	Primary education	Lower secondary education	Upper secondary education
	(1)	(2)	(3)	(4)	(5)	(6)	(7)	(8)	(9)	(10)	(11)	(12)
Australia	m	Yes	Yes	Yes	m	4	4	4	m	Yes	Yes	Yes
Austria[2]	Yes	Yes	a	No	3	3	5.5	5.5	Yes	Yes	a	No
Belgium (Fl.)	No	No	No	No	3	3	3	5	Yes	Yes	Yes	Yes
Belgium (Fr.)	No	No	No	No	3	3	3	5	Yes	Yes	Yes	Yes
Canada	m	No	No	No	m	5	5	5	m	Yes	Yes	Yes
Chile	m	No	No	No	m	m	m	m	m	No	No	No
Czech Republic	No	No	No	No	3	5	5	5	Yes	Yes	Yes	Yes
Denmark	Yes	No	No	No	4	4	4	6	Yes	Yes	Yes	No
England	No	No	No	No	3, 4	3, 4	3, 4	3, 4	No	No	No	No
Estonia	No	No	No	No	4, 5	4, 5	4, 5	4, 5	No	Yes	Yes	Yes
Finland	Yes	Yes	Yes	Yes	3	5	5	5	Yes	Yes	Yes	Yes
France	No	No	No	No	5	5	5	5, 6	Yes	Yes	Yes	Yes
Germany	a	Yes	Yes	Yes	3	5.5	5.5, 6.5	6.5	a	Yes	Yes	Yes
Greece	Yes	Yes	Yes	Yes	4	4	4	4, 5	Yes	Yes	a	a
Hungary	m	Yes	Yes	Yes	m	4	4	5	m	Yes	Yes	Yes
Iceland	m	No	No	No	m	3, 4	3, 4	4	m	Yes	Yes	Yes
Ireland	Yes	Yes	Yes	Yes	3	3, 5.5	4, 5	4, 5	Yes	Yes	Yes	Yes
Israel[3]	Yes	Yes	Yes	Yes	3, 4	3, 4	3, 4	3, 4	Yes	Yes	Yes	Yes
Italy	m	No	No	No	m	4	4-6	4-6	m	Yes	Yes	Yes
Japan[4]	No	No	No	No	2, 4, 6	2, 4, 6	2, 4, 6	4, 6	Yes	Yes	Yes	Yes
Korea	Yes	Yes	Yes	Yes	2, 4, 6.5	4	4, 6.5	4, 6.5	Yes	Yes	Yes	Yes
Luxembourg	Yes	No	No	No	4	3, 4	5	5	Yes	Yes	Yes	Yes
Mexico	m	Yes	Yes	Yes	m	4	4, 6	4, 6	m	Yes	Yes	No
Netherlands[5]	No	No	No	No	4	4	4	5, 6	Yes	Yes	Yes	Yes
New Zealand	No	No	No	No	3, 4	3, 4	3, 4	4	Yes	Yes	Yes	Yes
Norway	No	No	No	No	3	4	4, 6	4, 6	Yes	Yes	Yes	Yes
Poland	No	No	No	No	3, 5	3, 5	3, 5	3, 5	Yes	Yes	Yes	Yes
Portugal	No	No	No	No	5	5	5	5	Yes	Yes	Yes	Yes
Scotland	No	No	No	No	4, 5	4, 5	4, 5	4, 5	Yes	Yes	Yes	Yes
Slovak Republic	m	No	No	No	m	5	5	5	m	Yes	Yes	Yes
Slovenia	m	m	m	m	m	5	5-6	5-6	m	m	m	m
Spain	No	No	No	No	3	3	6	6	Yes	Yes	Yes	Yes
Sweden	No	No	No	No	3.5	3.5	4.5	4.5	Yes	Yes	Yes	Yes
Switzerland	m	No	No	No	m	3	5	6	m	Yes	Yes	Yes
Turkey	Yes	Yes	a	Yes	4-5	4-5	a	4-5	Yes	Yes	a	Yes
United States	No	No	No	No	2-4	4	4	4	Yes	Yes	Yes	Yes
Argentina	m	m	m	m	m	m	m	m	m	m	m	m
Brazil	No	No	No	No	m	m	m	m	No	No	No	No
China	m	m	m	m	m	m	m	m	m	m	m	m
India	m	m	m	m	m	m	m	m	m	m	m	m
Indonesia	m	Yes	Yes	Yes	m	4-5	4-5	4-5	m	Yes	Yes	Yes
Russian Federation	m	m	m	m	m	m	m	m	m	m	m	m
Saudi Arabia	m	m	m	m	m	m	m	m	m	m	m	m
South Africa	m	m	m	m	m	m	m	m	m	m	m	m

1. Tertiary-type A programmes are largely theory-based and are designed to provide qualifications for entry into advanced research programmes and professions with high knowledge and skill requirements. Tertiary-type B programmes are classified at the same level of competence as tertiary-type A programmes but are more occupationally oriented and usually lead directly to the labour market.
2. Refers to pre-primary education provided in primary schools only, for Columns 1, 5, 9, 13 and 17.
3. Year of reference 2012 for Column 7.
4. Year of reference 2007 for Columns 17, 18, 19 and 20.
5. Refers to pre-primary education provided in primary schools for 4-5 year-olds only, for Columns 1, 5, 9, 13 and 17.
6. Refers to full-time teachers only.
Source: OECD. See Annex 3 for notes (*www.oecd.org/edu/eag2012*).
Please refer to the Reader's Guide for information concerning the symbols replacing missing data.
StatLink ⎚⎚⎚ http://dx.doi.org/10.1787/888932668432

Table D5.4. [2/2] Pre-service teacher-training requirements in public institutions (2010)

	ISCED type of final qualification[1]				Percentage of current teacher stock with this type of qualification			
	Pre-primary education	Primary education	Lower secondary education	Upper secondary education	Pre-primary education	Primary education	Lower secondary education	Upper secondary education
	(13)	(14)	(15)	(16)	(17)	(18)	(19)	(20)
OECD								
Australia	m	5A	5A	5A	m	87%	91%	x(19)
Austria[2]	5A	5A	5A	5A	94%	94%	95%	78%
Belgium (Fl.)	5B	5B	5B	5A, 5B	99%	98%	97%	96%
Belgium (Fr.)	5B	5B	5B	5A	100%	100%	m	m
Canada	m	5A	5A	5A	m	m	m	m
Chile	m	5A, 5B	5A, 5B	5A, 5B	m	m	m	m
Czech Republic	5B, 5A	5A	5A	5A	12%	87%	88%	87%
Denmark	5B	5A	5A	5A	100%	100%	100%	100%
England	5A	5A	5A	5A	100%	100%	100%	100%
Estonia	4, 5A, 5B	5A	5A	5A	70%	66%	75%	84%
Finland	5A	5A	5A	5A	m	90%	90%	95%
France	5A	5A	5A	5A	m	m	m	m
Germany	5B	5A	5A	5A	m	m	m	m
Greece	5A	5A	5A	5A	97%	94%	97%	98%
Hungary	m	5A	5A	5A	m	95%	100%	100%
Iceland	m	5A	5A	5A	m	92%	x(18)	82%
Ireland	3, 4, 5A, 5B	5A, 5B	5A, 5B	5A, 5B	m	m	m	m
Israel[3]	5A	5A	5A	5A	74%	83%	92%	87%
Italy	m	5A	5A	5A	m	86%	90%	99%
Japan[4]	5A+5B, 5A, 5A	5A+5B, 5A, 5A	5A+5B, 5A, 5A	5A	74%, 21%, 0.4%	15%, 80%, 3%	5%, 89%, 5%	75%, 24%
Korea	5B, 5A, 5A	5A	5A	5A	100%	100%	100%	100%
Luxembourg	5B	5B	5A	5A	86%	95.6%, 4.5%	100%	100%
Mexico	m	5A	5A, 5B	5A, 5B	m	96%	90%	91%
Netherlands[5]	5A	5A	5A	5A	100%	100%	100%	100%
New Zealand	5B, 5A	5B, 5A	5B, 5A	5A	m	m	m	m
Norway	5A	5A	5A	5A	83%	47%	46.8%, m	20.5%, m
Poland	5B, 5A	5B, 5A	5A	5A	0.9%, 91.5%	0.8%, 98%	99%	98%
Portugal	5A	5A	5A	5A	100%	100%	100%	100%
Scotland	5A	5A	5A	5A	m	m	m	m
Slovak Republic	m	5A	5A	5A	m	93%, 7%	91%, 9%	87%, 13%
Slovenia	m	5A	5A	5A, 5B	m	m	m	m
Spain	5B, 5A	5A	5A	5A	100%	100%	100%	100%
Sweden	5A	5A	5A	5A	54%[6]	82%	x(18)	72%
Switzerland	m	5A	5A	5A	m	m	m	m
Turkey	5A	5A	a	5A	94%	91%	a	98%
United States	5B, 5A	5A	5A	5A	99%	99%	99%	99%
Other G20								
Argentina	m	m	m	m	m	m	m	m
Brazil	3B, 5A	3B	5A	5A	87%	99%	84%	91%
China	m	m	m	m	m	m	m	m
India	m	m	m	m	m	m	m	m
Indonesia	m	5A	5A	5A	m	m	m	m
Russian Federation	m	m	m	m	m	m	m	m
Saudi Arabia	m	m	m	m	m	m	m	m
South Africa	m	m	m	m	m	m	m	m

1. Tertiary-type A programmes are largely theory-based and are designed to provide qualifications for entry into advanced research programmes and professions with high knowledge and skill requirements. Tertiary-type B programmes are classified at the same level of competence as tertiary-type A programmes but are more occupationally oriented and usually lead directly to the labour market.
2. Refers to pre-primary education provided in primary schools only, for Columns 1, 5, 9, 13 and 17.
3. Year of reference 2012 for Column 7.
4. Year of reference 2007 for Columns 17, 18, 19 and 20.
5. Refers to pre-primary education provided in primary schools for 4-5 year-olds only, for Columns 1, 5, 9, 13 and 17.
6. Refers to full-time teachers only.
Source: OECD. See Annex 3 for notes *(www.oecd.org/edu/eag2012)*.
Please refer to the Reader's Guide for information concerning the symbols replacing missing data.
StatLink ⊞⊞⊞ http://dx.doi.org/10.1787/888932668432

Table D5.5. [1/2] Requirements to enter the teaching profession in public institutions (2010)

	Competitive examination required to enter the teaching profession				Credential or licence, in addition to the education diploma, required to start teaching				Credential or licence, in addition to the education diploma, required to become a fully qualified teacher				Teaching practicum required to obtain credential/licence			
	Pre-primary education	Primary education	Lower secondary education	Upper secondary education	Pre-primary education	Primary education	Lower secondary education	Upper secondary education	Pre-primary education	Primary education	Lower secondary education	Upper secondary education	Pre-primary education	Primary education	Lower secondary education	Upper secondary education
	(1)	(2)	(3)	(4)	(5)	(6)	(7)	(8)	(9)	(10)	(11)	(12)	(13)	(14)	(15)	(16)
OECD																
Australia	m	Yes	Yes	Yes	m	Yes	Yes	Yes	m	Yes	Yes	Yes	m	No	No	No
Austria[1]	No	No	a	No	No	No	No	No	No	No	No	No	No	No	No	No
Belgium (Fl.)	No	No	No	No	No	No	No	No	No	No	No	No	No	No	No	No
Belgium (Fr.)	No	No	No	No	No	No	No	No	No	No	No	No	No	No	No	No
Canada	m	No	No	No	m	Yes	Yes	Yes	m	Yes	Yes	Yes	m	Yes	Yes	Yes
Chile	m	No	No	No	m	No	No	No	m	No	No	No	m	No	No	No
Czech Republic	No	No	No	No	No	No	No	No	No	No	No	No	No	No	No	No
Denmark	Yes	No	No	No	No	No	No	No	No	No	No	Yes	No	No	No	No
England	No	No	No	No	Yes	Yes	Yes	Yes	No	No	No	No	Yes	Yes	Yes	Yes
Estonia	No	No	No	No	No	No	No	No	No	No	No	No	No	No	No	No
Finland	No	No	No	No	No	No	No	No	No	No	No	No	No	No	No	No
France	Yes	Yes	Yes	Yes	No	No	No	No	No	No	No	No	No	No	No	No
Germany	a	Yes	Yes	Yes	a	Yes	Yes	Yes	a	Yes	Yes	Yes	a	Yes	Yes	Yes
Greece	Yes	Yes	Yes	Yes	No	No	No	No	No	No	No	No	No	No	No	No
Hungary	m	No	No	No	m	No	No	No	m	No	No	No	m	No	No	No
Iceland	m	No	No	No	m	No	No	No	m	Yes	Yes	Yes	m	No	No	No
Ireland	No	No	No	No	Yes	Yes	Yes	Yes	Yes	Yes	Yes	Yes	m	m	m	m
Israel	Yes	Yes	Yes	Yes	Yes	Yes	Yes	Yes	Yes	Yes	Yes	Yes	Yes	Yes	Yes	Yes
Italy	m	Yes	Yes	Yes	m	No	Yes	Yes	m	No	Yes	Yes	m	No	No	No
Japan	Yes	Yes	Yes	Yes	Yes	Yes	Yes	Yes	Yes	Yes	Yes	Yes	Yes	Yes	Yes	Yes
Korea	Yes	Yes	Yes	Yes	No	No	No	No	Yes	Yes	Yes	Yes	Yes	Yes	Yes	Yes
Luxembourg	Yes	Yes	Yes	Yes	No	No	No	No	No	No	No	No	No	No	No	No
Mexico	m	Yes	Yes	Yes	m	No	No	Yes	m	No	No	No	m	No	No	No
Netherlands[2]	No	No	No	No	No	No	No	No	No	No	No	No	No	No	No	No
New Zealand	No	No	No	No	No	Yes	Yes	No	No	Yes	Yes	Yes	No	Yes	Yes	Yes
Norway	No	No	No	No	No	No	No	No	No	No	No	No	No	No	No	No
Poland	No	No	No	No	No	No	No	No	No	No	No	No	No	No	No	No
Portugal	No	No	No	No	No	No	No	No	No	No	No	No	No	No	No	No
Scotland	No	No	No	No	Yes	Yes	Yes	Yes	Yes	Yes	Yes	Yes	Yes	Yes	Yes	Yes
Slovak Republic	No	No	No	No	m	No	No	No	m	No	No	No	m	No	No	No
Slovenia	m	m	m	m	m	m	m	m	m	m	m	m	m	m	m	m
Spain	Yes	Yes	Yes	Yes	No	No	No	No	No	No	No	No	No	No	No	No
Sweden	No	No	No	No	No	No	No	No	No	No	No	No	No	No	No	No
Switzerland	m	No	No	No	m	Yes	Yes	Yes	m	No	No	No	m	No	No	No
Turkey	Yes	Yes	a	Yes	No	No	a	No	No	No	a	No	No	No	a	No
United States	Yes	Yes	Yes	Yes	Yes	Yes	Yes	Yes	Yes	Yes	Yes	Yes	Yes	Yes	Yes	Yes
Other G20																
Argentina	m	m	m	m	m	m	m	m	m	m	m	m	m	m	m	m
Brazil	Yes	Yes	Yes	Yes	No	No	No	No	No	No	No	No	No	No	No	No
China	m	m	m	m	m	m	m	m	m	m	m	m	m	m	m	m
India	m	m	m	m	m	m	m	m	m	m	m	m	m	m	m	m
Indonesia	m	No	No	No	m	No	No	No	m	Yes	Yes	Yes	m	No	No	No
Russian Federation	m	m	m	m	m	m	m	m	m	m	m	m	m	m	m	m
Saudi Arabia	m	m	m	m	m	m	m	m	m	m	m	m	m	m	m	m
South Africa	m	m	m	m	m	m	m	m	m	m	m	m	m	m	m	m

1. Refers to pre-primary education provided in primary schools only, for Columns 1, 5, 9, 13, 17, 21 and 25.
2. Refers to pre-primary education provided in primary schools for 4-5 year-olds only, for Columns 1, 5, 9, 13, 17, 21 and 25.
Source: OECD. See Annex 3 for notes (*www.oecd.org/edu/eag2012*).
Please refer to the Reader's Guide for information concerning the symbols replacing missing data.
StatLink http://dx.doi.org/10.1787/888932668451

Table D5.5. [2/2] Requirements to enter the teaching profession in public institutions (2010)

	Teaching practicum required after being recruited, as an induction/probation period				Existence of a register for teachers				Compulsory requirement for continuing education to maintain employment in the teaching profession			
	Pre-primary education	Primary education	Lower secondary education	Upper secondary education	Pre-primary education	Primary education	Lower secondary education	Upper secondary education	Pre-primary education	Primary education	Lower secondary education	Upper secondary education
	(17)	(18)	(19)	(20)	(21)	(22)	(23)	(24)	(25)	(26)	(27)	(28)
OECD												
Australia	m	No	No	No	m	Yes	Yes	Yes	m	m	m	m
Austria[1]	No	No	a	Yes	Yes	Yes	Yes	Yes	No	No	No	No
Belgium (Fl.)	No	No	No	No	Yes	Yes	Yes	Yes	No	No	No	No
Belgium (Fr.)	No	No	No	No	Yes	Yes	Yes	Yes	Yes	Yes	Yes	Yes
Canada	m	No	No	No	m	Yes	Yes	Yes	m	No	No	No
Chile	m	No	No	No	m	No	No	No	m	No	No	No
Czech Republic	No	No	No	No	No	No	No	No	No	No	No	No
Denmark	No	No	No	Yes	No	No	No	No	No	No	No	No
England	No	No	No	No	Yes	Yes	Yes	Yes	Yes	Yes	Yes	Yes
Estonia	No	No	No	No	Yes	Yes	Yes	Yes	Yes	Yes	Yes	Yes
Finland	No	No	No	No	No	No	No	No	Yes	Yes	Yes	Yes
France	No	No	No	No	No	No	No	No	Yes	Yes	No	No
Germany	a	No	No	No	a	No	No	No	a	No	No	No
Greece	Yes	Yes	Yes	Yes	Yes	Yes	Yes	Yes	No	No	No	No
Hungary	m	Yes	Yes	Yes	m	No	No	No	m	Yes	Yes	Yes
Iceland	m	No	No	No	m	Yes	Yes	Yes	m	Yes	Yes	No
Ireland	Yes	Yes	Yes	Yes	Yes	Yes	Yes	Yes	No	No	No	No
Israel	Yes	Yes	Yes	Yes	Yes	Yes	Yes	Yes	Yes	Yes	Yes	Yes
Italy	m	No	No	No	m	No	No	No	m	No	No	No
Japan	No	No	No	No	No	No	No	No	Yes	Yes	Yes	Yes
Korea	No	No	No	No	Yes	Yes	Yes	Yes	No	No	No	No
Luxembourg	Yes	Yes	Yes	Yes	Yes	Yes	Yes	Yes	Yes	Yes	Yes	Yes
Mexico	m	No	No	No	m	No	No	No	m	No	No	No
Netherlands[2]	No	No	No	No	Yes	Yes	Yes	Yes	Yes	Yes	Yes	Yes
New Zealand	No	Yes	Yes	Yes	Yes	Yes	Yes	Yes	m	m	m	m
Norway	No	No	No	No	Yes	No	No	No	No	No	No	No
Poland	No	No	No	No	No	No	No	No	No	No	No	No
Portugal	No	No	No	No	Yes	Yes	Yes	Yes	No	No	No	No
Scotland	Yes	Yes	Yes	Yes	Yes	Yes	Yes	Yes	Yes	Yes	Yes	Yes
Slovak Republic	m	No	No	No	m	No	No	No	m	No	No	No
Slovenia	m	m	m	m	m	m	m	m	m	m	m	m
Spain	Yes	Yes	Yes	Yes	No	No	No	No	No	No	No	No
Sweden	No	No	No	No	No	Yes	Yes	Yes	No	No	No	No
Switzerland	m	No	No	No	m	No	No	No	m	No	No	No
Turkey	Yes	Yes	a	Yes	No	No	a	No	No	No	a	No
United States	No	No	No	No	No	No	No	No	Yes	Yes	Yes	Yes
Other G20												
Argentina	m	m	m	m	m	m	m	m	m	m	m	m
Brazil	No	No	No	No	Yes	Yes	Yes	Yes	No	No	No	No
China	m	m	m	m	m	m	m	m	m	m	m	m
India	m	m	m	m	m	m	m	m	m	m	m	m
Indonesia	m	No	No	No	m	Yes	Yes	Yes	m	No	No	No
Russian Federation	m	m	m	m	m	m	m	m	m	m	m	m
Saudi Arabia	m	m	m	m	m	m	m	m	m	m	m	m
South Africa	m	m	m	m	m	m	m	m	m	m	m	m

1. Refers to pre-primary education provided in primary schools only, for Columns 1, 5, 9, 13, 17, 21 and 25.
2. Refers to pre-primary education provided in primary schools for 4-5 year-olds only, for Columns 1, 5, 9, 13, 17, 21 and 25.
Source: OECD. See Annex 3 for notes *(www.oecd.org/edu/eag2012)*.
Please refer to the Reader's Guide for information concerning the symbols replacing missing data.
StatLink ᘻᓱᒲ http://dx.doi.org/10.1787/888932668451

WHO MAKES KEY DECISIONS IN EDUCATION SYSTEMS?

- Decisions about diverse aspects of lower secondary education are most commonly made at the school level in a majority of countries.

- While in most countries decisions on the organisation of instruction are predominantly taken at the school level, decisions related to personnel management, planning and structures, and resources are more likely to be made at higher levels of authority, although countries vary widely in this regard.

- Since 2003, there has been a pattern of fewer decisions taken at the school level in countries with available data.

Chart D6.1. **Percentage of decisions taken at each level of government in public lower secondary education (2011)**

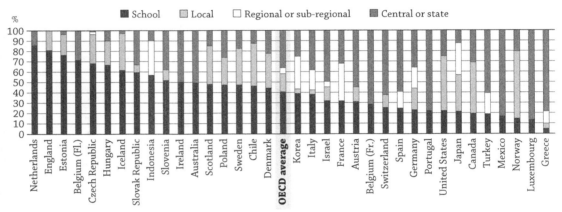

Countries are ranked in descending order of the percentage of decisions taken at the school level.
Source: OECD. Table D6.1. See Annex 3 for notes (*www.oecd.org/edu/eag2012*).
StatLink ᵐˢᵖ http://dx.doi.org/10.1787/888932663872

◼ Context

The division of responsibility among national, regional and local authorities, and schools is a much-debated topic in education policy. Since the early 1980s, a key aim of education reform has been to place more decision-making authority at lower levels of the education system. At the same time, many countries have strengthened the influence of central authorities in setting standards, curricula and assessments. For example, a loosening of "process" and financial regulations has often been accompanied by an increase in the central level control of outputs.

There are many reasons for changes in patterns of decision making and responsibility, and they vary from country to country. The most common reasons to decentralise decision making are increased efficiency and improved financial control; reduced bureaucracy; increased responsiveness to local communities; more creative management of human resources; improved potential for innovation; and the creation of conditions that provide better incentives for improving the quality of schooling.

Although decentralisation initiatives attract considerable attention in policy debates, this indicator finds that decision making at the school level has decreased over the past decade. In most countries, the largest proportion of itemised decisions tracked in this survey are still taken at the school level, but this share is clearly shrinking in 10 of 21 countries, while only 4 countries show an increase in the proportion of decisions taken at the school level. Some of the shift towards more centralised decision making can be explained by the heightened interest in measures of accountability that involve national assessments and national examinations that are

INDICATOR D6

based on centrally established curricula or frameworks. Setting centrally determined frameworks in which individual schools make decisions is a possible counterbalance to full school autonomy.

This indicator shows where key decisions are made in public institutions at the lower secondary level of education. The indicator does not capture the totality of decisions made within a school system. Instead, a representative set of 46 key decisions, organised across four domains, are considered. These decisions are based on earlier rounds of data collection in 2003 and 2007, and were developed with input from representatives from the participating countries. Additional information is available in the *Methodology* section at the end of this indicator and in Annex 3, available at *www.oecd.org/edu/eag2012*.

INDICATOR D6

This indicator presents results from data collected in 2011 on decision making at the lower secondary level of education and updates the previous survey, which took place in 2007. Responses were compiled in each country by a panel of experts representing different levels of the decision-making process at the lower secondary level. Information on the composition of these panels and the methods and process used to complete the survey can be found in the "Notes on methodology" in Annex 3, available at *www.oecd.org/edu/eag2012*. While the questionnaire was largely the same during each round of data collection, the composition of the panel in each country changed, in most cases.

Other findings

- **In 16 of 36 countries, decisions are most often taken at the school level.** Countries that are most decentralised in terms of decision making include the Netherlands, with 86% of decisions taken at the school level, followed by England (81%), Estonia (76%), the Flemish Community of Belgium (71%), and the Czech Republic (68%).

- **In 12 of 36 countries, decisions made at the state or central level were the most prevalent.** Countries with the most centralised decision making include Luxembourg, with 87% of decisions taken at the state or central level, followed by Mexico (83%), Greece (78%), Portugal (78%), and the French Community of Belgium (72%).

- **Decisions on the organisation of instruction are predominantly taken by schools** in all countries included in the survey, except Greece, Luxembourg and Norway. Most decisions on personnel management and the use of resources are taken at the local or school level in around one-half of countries. Decisions on planning and structures are mostly taken at one of the more centralised tiers of government.

- There are substantial differences between countries in the ways in which decisions are taken. On average in OECD countries, **half of the decisions taken at the school level are taken in full autonomy.** Around 40% of decisions taken by schools are taken within a framework set by a higher authority. Decisions taken by schools in consultation with other levels of authority are relatively rare, although in the United States, most decisions taken by schools are taken in consultation with local school district authorities.

- **Schools are least likely to make autonomous decisions related to planning and structures.**

Trends

Between 2003 and 2011, decisions were taken at a more central level in about half of the countries, most notably in Luxembourg and Portugal. The opposite trend was evident in Australia and Iceland. In 10 of these 21 countries, trends show clearly that fewer decisions were being taken at the school level, while only 4 countries showed a clear pattern of greater decision making occurring at the school level (Australia, the Czech Republic, Iceland and the Slovak Republic). In the remaining seven countries, there was no clear pattern or substantial change in the proportion of decisions taken at the school level.

D6

Analysis

Level of decision making in public lower secondary schools

The tables with results indicate six distinct levels of government or education authority at which decisions can be taken (see *Definitions* section at the end of this indicator). The charts, however, group the findings across four different levels of government: the school level, the local level, the regional or sub-regional level, and the state or central level. This grouping allows federal countries and non-federal countries to be compared more readily. For example, the state and national levels are grouped together, since the most central level at which decisions about education are taken in a federal country is typically the state level, and the most central level in a non-federal country is the national level. Similarly, the regional and sub-regional levels refer to the second-most central level in federal and non-federal countries, so it was logical to group these together as well.

The results reveal that the largest share of decisions is taken at the school level. Across the 34 OECD countries with available data, an average of 41% of all decisions itemised in the survey are taken at the school level. On average, 36% of all decisions were made centrally (i.e. the central or state level). Some 17% of the decisions were made at the local level, which is the level just above the school level; and 6% of the decisions were made at the regional or sub-regional level (Table D6.1 and Chart D6.1).

Sixteen of 36 countries reported that the largest proportion of decisions that affect lower secondary education is taken at the school level. The school is by far the most important level of decision making in the Netherlands, with 86% of decisions made at that level, followed by England (81%), Estonia (76%), the Flemish Community of Belgium (71%) and the Czech Republic (68%).

Twelve of 36 countries reported that the largest share of decisions is taken at the state or central level. Luxembourg reports the highest proportion of decisions made at the state or central level (87%), followed by Mexico (83%), Greece (78%), Portugal (78%) and the French Community of Belgium (72%).

The three countries that reported that the largest share of decisions is taken at the local level, meaning by local school districts or local or municipal education authorities, are Norway (65%), the United States (53%) and Canada (49%). In Finland, although the local authorities are, as education providers, responsible for most decisions, in practice many decisions are delegated to schools, particularly those related to staffing. In France, Germany, Italy and Korea, decision making is more evenly distributed among the central, intermediate, and local or school levels (Table D6.1).

Domains of decision making

Decisions about education systems are organised across four general domains of decision making: organisation of instruction, personnel management, planning and structures, and resource management (Tables D6.2a and D6.2b and Chart D6.2). There are large differences in where decisions are made, depending on the domain. Decisions related to the organisation of instruction are predominantly made at the school level (75%), while decisions about planning and structure are most likely to be made at the central or state level (60%).

The left-most bar in Chart D6.2 illustrates the distribution of all decision making across various levels of government or education authority. The next four bars illustrate the breakdown of decision making across four distinct domains. Because a general assessment of the roles played in the decision-making process includes decisions made about different domains, an aggregate measure can mask differences in the degree of centralisation in those areas. For example, a country may centralise almost all decisions about the curriculum, whereas schools may have nearly complete control over decisions about teaching methods. The distribution of decisions taken by each administrative level across the four domains of decision making (see *Definitions* and *Methodology* sections) is an indicator of "functional decentralisation", which takes into account the fact that decision making may be decentralised in certain activities and centralised in others.

Chart D6.2. **Percentage of decisions taken at each level of government in public lower secondary education in OECD countries (2011)**

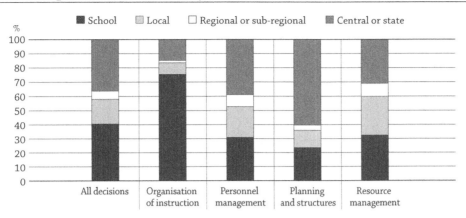

Source: OECD. Tables D6.2a and D6.2b. See Annex 3 for notes (*www.oecd.org/edu/eag2012*).
StatLink ᛗᛁᛊ᛫ http://dx.doi.org/10.1787/888932663891

Organisation of instruction

When decisions are differentiated according to domain, the data show that decisions about the organisation of instruction are predominantly taken by schools in all countries except for Greece, Luxembourg and Norway. Relative to the other domains, decisions on the organisation of instruction are predominantly taken at the school level and this finding is much more consistent across countries (Table D6.2a and Chart D6.3). While the majority of decisions about the organisation of instruction (i.e. pupils' school careers, grouping of pupils, choice of textbooks and software, teaching methods, assessment of pupils' regular work and assistance to pupils) are taken by schools in at least 70% of countries, most decisions about instruction time are made at the state or central level (24 of 37 countries with available data). However, in 11 of the remaining 13 countries, decisions on instruction time are taken at the local or school level, but within a centrally established framework. Only in England and Indonesia is instruction time decided autonomously by schools (Table D6.7, available on line and see Indicator D1).

Planning and structures

For decisions within the domains of personnel management, planning and structures, and resource management, schools generally take fewer decisions and the patterns are more mixed. On average, schools are least likely to have decision-making responsibility in the area of planning and structures, ranging from decisions to open or close a school, through to programme design and accreditation. In 25 of the 36 countries for which data are available, at least 50% of decisions related to planning and structures were taken at the state or central level. In Greece, Luxembourg, Mexico, Portugal and Switzerland all decisions in this domain were made at the state or central level. Even in countries that tend to be more decentralised (i.e. less than 50% of all decisions taken centrally), such as the Netherlands and the Flemish Community of Belgium, the central government has an important role in decision making concerning planning and structures of the education system (Tables D6.1 and D6.2b, and Chart D6.3).

Within the domain of planning and structures, most decisions about programmes of study and learning resources (i.e. the definition of course content, selection of subjects taught in a particular school, selection of programmes of study offered in particular schools, and designing programmes of study) are decided at the state or central level in more than half of the countries (see Indicator D1). In countries where national examinations are administered, decisions about formulating qualifying examinations for a certificate or diploma are taken at the state or central level, except in Indonesia and Israel, and decisions about accreditation (i.e. defining examination content, marking and administration) are also taken at the state or central level, except in Belgium, Estonia, France, Indonesia, Italy and the Slovak Republic (Table D6.9, available on line).

D6

Chart D6.3. Percentage of decisions taken at each level of government in public lower secondary education, by domain (2011)

■ School   ▣ Local   □ Regional or sub-regional   ▦ Central or state

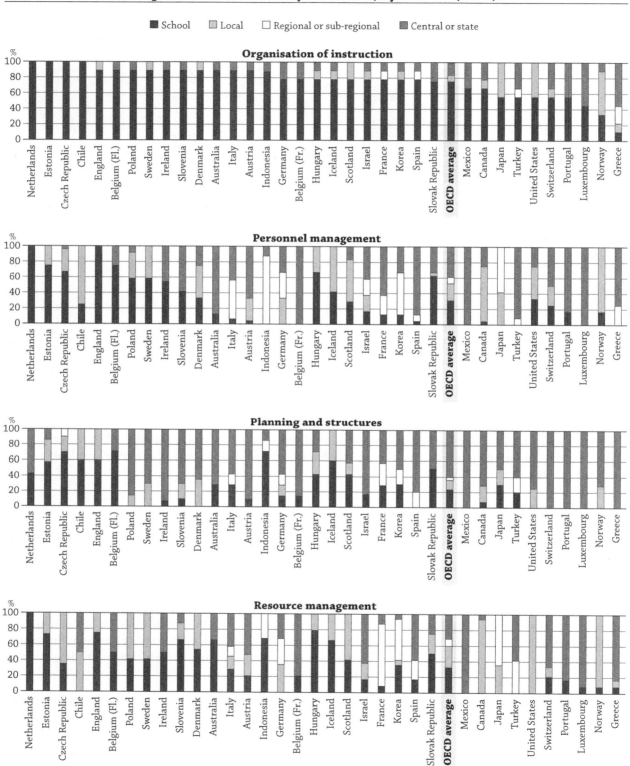

Countries are ranked in descending order of the percentage of decisions about organisation of instruction taken at the school level.
Source: OECD. Table D6.2a and D6.2b. See Annex 3 for notes (*www.oecd.org/edu/eag2012*).
StatLink ⟐⟐ http://dx.doi.org/10.1787/888932663910

In 16 of 36 countries, authority over the creation and closure of schools are in the hands of local authorities. In the Flemish Community of Belgium, these decisions are taken at the school level, but within a framework set by the state government. For the remaining 19 countries, this decision is taken at the state or central level in 14 countries and at the sub-regional or regional level in 5 countries. In contrast, decisions about the creation or abolition of a grade level are mostly taken at the state or central level (21 of 35 countries with available data). In Belgium (Flemish Community), Canada, Chile, the Czech Republic, Denmark, Estonia, Finland, Iceland, Norway and Turkey, these decisions are taken at the school or local level, either exclusively or within a framework established by a higher authority, whereas in Hungary, this decision is taken by local authorities in consultation with school authorities. In England, this decision is taken by local authorities in consultation with central authorities. Only in Germany and Spain is the creation or abolition of grade levels decided at the sub-regional or regional level.

Personnel management

In 18 of 36 countries, more than 50% of decisions about personnel management, including decisions on the hiring and dismissal of staff and on setting salary schedules and conditions of work, are taken at the school or local level. Most decisions in this domain are taken at the school level in Belgium (Flemish Community), the Czech Republic, England, Estonia, Hungary, Ireland, the Netherlands, Poland, the Slovak Republic and Sweden, and at the local level in Canada, Chile, Iceland, Norway and Scotland. In Finland, although the local authorities are, as education providers, responsible for most decisions, in practice many decisions about personnel management are delegated to schools. In Australia, Austria, Belgium (French Community), France, Greece, Luxembourg, Mexico, Portugal, Slovenia, Spain and Turkey, most of these decisions are taken at the state or central level (Table D6.2a and Chart D6.3).

In 21 of 36 countries, authority over hiring and dismissing principals belongs to local or school leaders. In contrast, in Australia, Austria, Belgium (French Community), France, Luxembourg and Mexico, the authority for deciding these matters rests with state or central administrators. In Germany, Greece, Italy, Korea, Spain and Turkey, all such authority rests with sub-regional or regional administrators, but within a framework established by the state or central government. In Japan, the prefectural boards of education have jurisdiction over hiring and dismissing staff (principals and teachers) whose salaries are paid from the prefectural budget, but these decisions are made after receiving recommendations from the municipal boards of education (Table D6.8, available on line).

Authority over setting principals' salaries belongs largely to state or central administrators (23 of 36 countries). Although individual states in the United States often determine a minimum salary schedule for staff (principals, teachers and non-teaching staff), this may be supplemented by local districts. In Denmark, the salary scale is a part of the collective agreement reached between the teachers' union on the one hand and the Danish municipalities and the central government on the other. In contrast, principals' salaries are decided at the local level in full autonomy in Estonia and Sweden and within a framework either established centrally or negotiated with teachers' unions in Chile, the Czech Republic, Finland, Hungary, Iceland, Norway and Poland. In England, although school administrators set salaries, these decisions are made within an overarching framework set by the central government. Only in the Netherlands is the entire salary system the responsibility of both the unions and employer organisations, even if the central level plays a role by setting the financial framework.

In 18 of 36 countries, decisions on the conditions of service of school principals are taken at the school or local level. In contrast, these decisions are taken at the state or central level in 14 countries. Only in Greece, Indonesia, Japan and Korea are these decisions taken at the sub-regional or regional level. Decisions concerning the duties of school principals are made by state or central authorities in 19 of 36 countries, whereas these decisions are taken by local authorities in 12 countries. Only in Belgium (Flemish Community), England, Iceland, Ireland and the Netherlands are decisions concerning the duties of principals decided at the school level, either autonomously or within a centrally established framework.

While authority over non-teaching staff is in the hands of local or school authorities in two-third of countries, decisions regarding their salary are made at the state or central level (19 of 34 countries with available data). In Finland, although the local authorities are, as education providers, responsible for deciding what the duties of non-teaching staff are, they can decide if they wish to delegate decision making to the schools, and to what extent. In practice, decisions concerning duties are largely made at the school level. A similar pattern is evident with regard to authority over teaching staff (see Indicator D5).

D6

Resource management

Decisions about the allocation and use of resources are made slightly less frequently at the central level. In 10 of 36 countries with available data, central authorities made more than half of the decisions related to resource management. In 2011, there were four countries with highly centralised decision making in this domain: Greece, Luxembourg, Mexico and Portugal. In these countries, at least 80% of decisions related to resources were made at state or central level. In the Czech Republic, Denmark, England, Estonia, Finland, Hungary, Iceland, the Netherlands, Norway, Poland, Scotland, Sweden and the United States, all decisions related to resource management were taken at either the school or local level (Tables D6.2b and Chart D6.3). Since 2007, the proportion of decisions taken at the intermediate levels has declined across all countries, except for France, where it increased slightly (Table D6.6d, available on line).

Although state and central authorities in half of the countries decide on how resources are allocated for a school's teaching staff, decisions on how resources are allocated for non-teaching staff are typically taken at the local level. In contrast, in two-thirds of countries, the use of resources for school staff is decided at the school level. Decisions on the allocation and use of resources for a school's capital expenditure are taken by local authorities in at least half of the countries. While the allocation of resources for a school's operating expenditure is largely decided by local authorities, the use of these resources is predominantly decided at the school level (26 of 35 countries). Decisions on the allocation and use of resources for principals' and teachers' professional development are taken at the school or local level in around half of the countries (Table D6.10, available on line).

Influence of non-governmental entities

In addition to recognising the influence of different levels of government on decision making (Tables D6.7, D6.8, D6.9 and D6.10, available on line), many countries have noted that non-governmental entities may also be consulted or may be involved in establishing a framework for decisions taken at lower levels. The most common non-governmental participants are teachers' unions. For example, when teachers' unions negotiate with education authorities to set pay scales, they are helping to establish a framework for decisions related to teachers' salaries for specific teachers. In many countries, teachers' unions are involved in decisions relating to duties and conditions of work, salary scales and instruction time. The participation of teachers' unions in decision making on these issues is notable in Belgium, Denmark, Finland, Iceland, Israel and Sweden (see Annex 3, available at *www.oecd.org/edu/eag2012*).

In the Flemish Community of Belgium, for example, decisions on minimum and maximum instruction times are taken by the state governments, but in consultation with non-governmental entities such as teaching unions and education networks. Teachers' unions, some of which are called trade unions, can sometimes influence decisions on professional development of teaching staff and their careers, as happens in Italy. In Finland and Norway, employers' associations (organisations) are involved in decisions about personnel management, including salaries.

Parents and parents' organisations also have an influence on decision making (see the indicator, "How can parents influence the education of their children?" in OECD, 2010). In Scotland, for example, parent councils often participate in the selection of principals. Schools in Scotland consult with both staff and parents in designing programmes of study, selecting subjects taught in particular schools and defining course content. In Turkey, some decisions, including those on allocation of resources, are taken by the central government with the involvement of parent-teachers' associations. Portugal involves teachers' associations, experts and scientific societies in establishing a framework for instruction time and designing programmes of study.

Decisions taken at the school level and the mode in which these decisions are taken

The mode of decision making refers to whether decisions are made autonomously, after consulting with other bodies, or within a framework set by a higher authority. On average in OECD countries, 41% of all decisions are made at the school level and around half of these decisions are made in full autonomy. Around 44% of decisions taken by schools are taken within a framework set by a higher authority. Decisions taken by schools in consultation with others levels are relatively rare, although in the United States, most decisions taken by schools are taken in consultation with local school district authorities. In addition, 5% of all decisions, on average, are taken at other levels after consultation with schools (Table D6.3 and Chart D6.4).

Chart D6.4. **Decisions taken at the school level in public lower secondary education in OECD countries, by mode of decision making and domain (2011)**

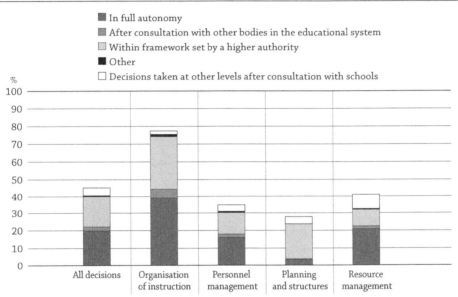

Source: OECD. Tables D6.4a and D6.4b. See Annex 3 for notes (*www.oecd.org/edu/eag2012*).
StatLink http://dx.doi.org/10.1787/888932663929

How to read this chart
The left-most bar on Chart D6.4 represents all decisions that are taken at the school level across the 34 OECD countries. The percentages up to 100% that are not captured by the bars are decisions made at local, intermediate or central level. The remaining four bars depict the four domains of decision making. Each bar is broken into four sections to indicate whether the decisions taken at the school level are made in full autonomy, within a framework set by a higher authority, after consultation with other bodies or other. The white portion of the bar represents the portion of the decisions taken at higher levels that are made after consultation with schools.

Planning and structures is the domain with the lowest proportion of decisions made at the school level. This domain also has the lowest proportion of school-level decisions that are made in full autonomy. Some 32% of all decisions related to resource management are made at the school level. In addition, another 9% of decisions related to resource management are made by higher levels of government, but they are made after consulting with schools. Organisation of instruction is the domain with the highest proportion of decisions made at the school level (Tables D6.4a and D6.4b and Chart D6.4).

There are substantial differences among countries in the mode in which decisions are made (Chart D6.7, available on line). Among the ten OECD and other G20 countries in which most decision making is in the hands of schools, more than 50% of these decisions are taken in full autonomy in Belgium (Flemish Community), England, Iceland, Indonesia, the Netherlands and the Slovak Republic. Such decisions are more often taken within a framework set by a higher authority in the Czech Republic, Estonia, Hungary and Slovenia. For the first six countries, the remainder of decisions is mainly taken within a framework set by a higher authority.

For the latter four countries, they are taken in full autonomy (Table D6.3). In Finland, although the local authorities are responsible for most decisions, they can decide if they wish to delegate decision making to the schools, and to what extent.

Perhaps predictably, decisions taken by schools in countries that tend to have more centralised decision making are more likely to be subject to an overarching framework. This is the case in Austria, Greece and Turkey. However, in the French Community of Belgium, where most decisions are taken centrally and only 28% are taken by schools, schools have full autonomy for most of the decisions they take. In Australia, Denmark, Luxembourg, Portugal, Scotland, Slovenia and the United States, at least 10% of all decisions are taken at other levels, but after consultation with schools.

Changes in decision making over time

Nineteen countries reported data on decision making in 2003, 2007 and 2011; the Slovak Republic and Turkey reported data on decision making in 2003 and 2011 only. On average, changes over time are relatively small, except for the five percentage-point drop in the proportion of decisions made at the school level between 2007 and 2011 (Chart D6.5). Generally, the findings suggest a gradual trend towards centralisation and a decrease in decision making at the lowest level (Table D6.5 and Tables D6.6a, D6.6b, D6.6c and D6.6d, available on line).

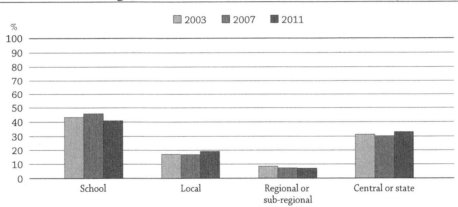

Chart D6.5. **Changes in decision making over time, by level of government (2003, 2007, 2011)**

OECD average for countries with data available for all reference years

Source: OECD. Table D6.5. See Annex 3 for notes (*www.oecd.org/edu/eag2012*).
StatLink ⊛⊠⊒ http://dx.doi.org/10.1787/888932663948

Between 2003 and 2011, decisions were taken at a more central level in about half of the countries, most notably in Luxembourg and Portugal. The opposite trend was evident in Australia and Iceland. Ten of these 21 countries had clear trends showing that fewer decisions were being taken at the school level, while only four countries – Australia, the Czech Republic, Iceland and the Slovak Republic – showed a trend towards more decision making at the school level. In the remaining seven countries, there was no clear pattern or substantial change in the proportion of decisions that was taken at the school level (Chart D6.6).

The Netherlands has one of the most decentralised decision-making patterns; however, the proportion of decisions taken by schools has declined from 96% in 2003 to 86% in 2011. In the countries with relatively more centralised decision making, such as Luxembourg and Mexico, there was a steady decline in the proportion of decisions taken at the school level and an increase in decisions taken at the central level. In the case of Norway, there was a decrease in decision making at both the school and central levels, which was the result of a sharp increase in decision making at the local level over time.

Chart D6.6. **Share of decisions taken at the school level (2003, 2007, 2011)**

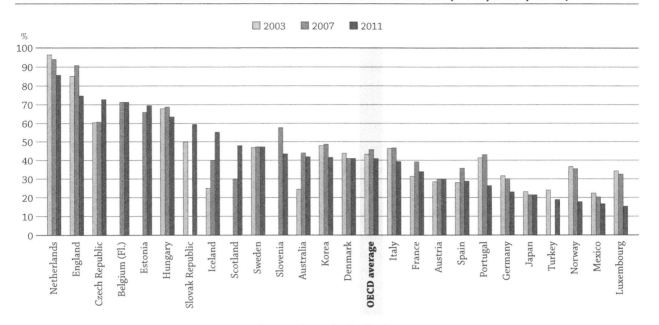

Countries are ranked in descending order of the percentage of decisions taken at the school level in 2011.
Source: OECD. Table D6.5. See Annex 3 for notes (*www.oecd.org/edu/eag2012*).
StatLink http://dx.doi.org/10.1787/888932663967

Definitions

The **central government** consists of all bodies at the national level that make decisions or participate in different aspects of decision making.

The municipality or community is the smallest territorial unit in the nation with a governing authority. The **local authority** may be the education department within a general-purpose **local government** or it may be a special-purpose government whose sole area of authority is education.

The **province** or **region** is the first territorial unit below the national level in countries that do not have a "federal" or similar type of government structure, and the second territorial unit below the nation in countries with "federal" or similar types of governmental structures. Provincial/regional authorities or governments are the decision-making bodies at this level.

School, school board or committee refers to the individual school level only and includes school administrators and teachers or a school board or committee established exclusively for that individual school. The decision-making body – or bodies – for this school may be: an external school board, which includes residents of the larger community; an internal school board, which could include headmasters, teachers, other school staff, parents, and students; and both an external and an internal school board. "School networks", "networks of schools", "didactic circles", and "groups of schools" should be considered as schools.

The state is the first territorial unit below the nation in "federal" countries or countries with similar types of governmental structures. **State governments** are the governmental units that are the decision-making bodies at this level. For countries other than federal or similar, where the extent of the state is identical with that of the country, this level is non-existent.

The **sub-region** is the second territorial unit below the nation in countries that do not have a "federal" or similar type of governmental structure. Sub-regional or **inter-municipal authorities** or governments are the decision-making bodies at this level.

Methodology

Data are from the 2011 OECD-INES Survey on Locus of Decision Making and refer to the school year 2010-11. This indicator shows the percentage of education decisions taken at specific levels in public lower secondary education. Decentralisation is concerned with the division of power between levels of government. This concept has two dimensions: the locus of decision making, that is, the level of decision-making authority; and the mode of decision making, which relates to the degree of autonomous or "shared" decision making.

D6

The questionnaire distinguished between six levels of decision making: central government, state governments, provincial/regional authorities or governments, sub-regional or inter-municipal authorities or governments, local authorities or governments, schools or school boards or committees (see *Definitions* section).

The questionnaire provided information on four domains:

Organisation of instruction: student admissions; student careers; instruction time; choice of textbooks; choice of software/learningware; grouping of students; additional support for students; teaching methods; day-to-day student assessment.

Personnel management: hiring and dismissal of principals, teaching and non-teaching staff; duties and conditions of service of staff; salary scales of staff; influence over the careers of staff.

Planning and structures: opening or closure of schools; creation or abolition of a grade level; design of programmes of study; selection of programmes of study taught in a particular school; choice of subjects taught in a particular school; definition of course content; setting of qualifying examinations for a certificate or diploma; accreditation (examination content, marking and administration).

Resource management: allocation and use of resources for teaching staff, non-teaching staff, capital and operating expenditure, professional development of principals and teachers.

The questionnaire also sought information on how autonomously decisions are taken. The most important factor in determining the mode is "who decides". The following categories are provided: full autonomy; after consultation with bodies located at another level within the education system; independently but within a framework set by a higher authority; other. More detailed information on specific countries (e.g. decentralisation in Denmark; main objectives of Greek education policy; recruitment, selection and allocation of teachers in Norway) is available in the 2004 edition of *Education at a Glance* available at *www.oecd.org/edu/eag2004*.

Some 46 general decisions were included in the survey. These were separated into four domains described above. The number of decisions within each of these domains was not equal, and two of the domains (planning and structures, and resource management) contain fewer than ten items. Adjustments were made to give equal weight to each of the four domains. Because there are different numbers of items (i.e. decisions) in each domain, each item is weighted by the inverse of the number of items in its domain. Some items are split up into sub-items. The sum of weights of sub-items is equal to the weight of an item (in the same domain) without sub-items. Missing and not applicable items receive weight zero, causing other weights to change within a domain.

Notes on definitions and methodologies for each country are provided in Annex 3 at *www.oecd.org/edu/eag2012*.

The statistical data for Israel are supplied by and under the responsibility of the relevant Israeli authorities. The use of such data by the OECD is without prejudice to the status of the Golan Heights, East Jerusalem and Israeli settlements in the West Bank under the terms of international law.

References

OECD (2010), *Education at a Glance 2010: OECD Indicators*, OECD Publishing.

The following additional material relevant to this indicator is available on line:

- *Chart D6.7. Decisions taken at the school level in public lower secondary education, by mode of decision making and domain (2011)*
  StatLink ⟨⟩ http://dx.doi.org/10.1787/888932663986

- *Table D6.6a. Trends in the percentage of decisions about organisation of instruction taken at each level of government in public lower secondary education (2003, 2007, 2011)*
  StatLink ᐧᐧᐧᐧ http://dx.doi.org/10.1787/888932668641

- *Table D6.6b. Trends in the percentage of decisions about personnel management taken at each level of government in public lower secondary education (2003, 2007, 2011)*
  StatLink ᐧᐧᐧᐧ http://dx.doi.org/10.1787/888932668660

- *Table D6.6c. Trends in the percentage of decisions about planning and structures taken at each level of government in public lower secondary education (2003, 2007, 2011)*
  StatLink ᐧᐧᐧᐧ http://dx.doi.org/10.1787/888932668679

- *Table D6.6d. Trends in the percentage of decisions about resource management taken at each level of government in public lower secondary education (2003, 2007, 2011)*
  StatLink ᐧᐧᐧᐧ http://dx.doi.org/10.1787/888932668698

- *Table D6.7. Level of government at which different types of decisions about organisation of instruction are taken in public lower secondary education (2011)*
  StatLink ᐧᐧᐧᐧ http://dx.doi.org/10.1787/888932668717

- *Table D6.8. Level of government at which different types of decisions about personnel management are taken in public lower secondary education (2011)*
  StatLink ᐧᐧᐧᐧ http://dx.doi.org/10.1787/888932668736

- *Table D6.9. Level of government at which different types of decisions about planning and structures are taken in public lower secondary education (2011)*
  StatLink ᐧᐧᐧᐧ http://dx.doi.org/10.1787/888932668755

- *Table D6.10. Level of government at which different types of decisions about resource management are taken in public lower secondary education (2011)*
  StatLink ᐧᐧᐧᐧ http://dx.doi.org/10.1787/888932668774

D6

Table D6.1. Percentage of decisions taken at each level of government in public lower secondary education (2011)

	Central	State	Provincial/ regional	Sub-regional	Local	School	Total
	(1)	(2)	(3)	(4)	(5)	(6)	(7)
OECD Australia	n	51	a	a	a	49	**100**
Austria	33	22	n	a	14	31	**100**
Belgium (Fl.)	n	29	n	a	n	71	**100**
Belgium (Fr.)	n	72	n	a	n	28	**100**
Canada	n	31	a	a	49	19	**100**
Chile	13	n	n	a	41	46	**100**
Czech Republic	1	a	3	n	28	68	**100**
Denmark	22	a	n	a	34	44	**100**
England	n	a	a	a	19	81	**100**
Estonia	4	a	a	n	20	76	**100**
Finland[1]	n	a	n	n	100	x(5)	**100**
France	32	a	16	20	n	32	**100**
Germany	n	36	13	8	21	23	**100**
Greece	78	a	12	a	5	5	**100**
Hungary	10	a	a	n	23	67	**100**
Iceland	3	a	a	a	36	62	**100**
Ireland	50	a	a	a	n	50	**100**
Israel	50	a	5	a	13	32	**100**
Italy	38	a	19	a	4	38	**100**
Japan	13	a	31	a	35	21	**100**
Korea	25	a	32	a	4	39	**100**
Luxembourg	87	a	a	a	a	13	**100**
Mexico	41	43	a	n	a	17	**100**
Netherlands	14	n	n	n	n	86	**100**
New Zealand	m	m	m	m	m	m	**m**
Norway	21	a	a	a	65	15	**100**
Poland	26	a	n	n	26	47	**100**
Portugal	78	a	n	a	n	22	**100**
Scotland	15	a	a	a	37	48	**100**
Slovak Republic	33	a	n	a	7	59	**100**
Slovenia	38	a	n	n	10	52	**100**
Spain	16	43	16	a	n	25	**100**
Sweden	18	a	a	a	35	47	**100**
Switzerland	n	63	a	a	12	25	**100**
Turkey	61	a	20	a	a	19	**100**
United States	n	25	a	a	53	22	**100**
OECD average[1]	24	12	5	1	17	41	**100**
EU21 average[1]	27	9	4	1	13	46	**100**
Other G20 Argentina	m	m	m	m	m	m	**m**
Brazil	m	m	m	m	m	m	**m**
China	m	m	m	m	m	m	**m**
India	m	m	m	m	m	m	**m**
Indonesia	10	a	n	33	a	57	**100**
Russian Federation	m	m	m	m	m	m	**m**
Saudi Arabia	m	m	m	m	m	m	**m**
South Africa	m	m	m	m	m	m	**m**
G20 average	m	m	m	m	m	m	**m**

1. Finland is not included in the averages.
Source: OECD. See Annex 3 for notes (*www.oecd.org/edu/eag2012*).
Please refer to the Reader's Guide for information concerning the symbols replacing missing data.
StatLink ᴍᴤ᷈ http://dx.doi.org/10.1787/888932668508

Table D6.2a. Percentage of decisions taken at each level of government in public lower secondary education, by domain (2011)

	Organisation of instruction							Personnel management						
	Central	State	Provincial/regional	Sub-regional	Local	School	Total	Central	State	Provincial/regional	Sub-regional	Local	School	Total
	(1)	(2)	(3)	(4)	(5)	(6)	(7)	(8)	(9)	(10)	(11)	(12)	(13)	(14)
OECD														
Australia	n	11	a	a	a	89	100	n	88	n	a	n	13	100
Austria	11	n	n	a	n	89	100	25	42	n	a	29	4	100
Belgium (Fl.)	n	11	n	a	n	89	100	n	25	n	a	n	75	100
Belgium (Fr.)	n	22	n	a	n	78	100	n	100	n	a	n	n	100
Canada	n	22	a	a	11	67	100	n	25	a	a	71	4	100
Chile	n	n	n	a	n	100	100	n	n	n	a	75	25	100
Czech Republic	n	a	n	n	n	100	100	4	a	n	n	29	67	100
Denmark	n	a	n	a	11	89	100	25	a	n	a	42	33	100
England	n	a	a	a	11	89	100	n	a	a	a	n	100	100
Estonia	n	a	a	n	n	100	100	n	a	a	a	25	75	100
Finland[1]	n	a	n	n	22	78	100	n	a	n	n	100	x(12)	100
France	11	a	n	11	n	78	100	63	a	25	n	n	13	100
Germany	n	22	n	n	n	78	100	n	33	25	8	33	n	100
Greece	56	a	22	a	11	11	100	75	a	25	a	n	n	100
Hungary	11	a	a	n	11	78	100	n	a	a	n	33	67	100
Iceland	11	a	a	a	11	78	100	n	a	a	a	58	42	100
Ireland	11	a	a	a	n	89	100	46	a	a	a	n	54	100
Israel	11	a	n	a	11	78	100	42	a	21	a	21	17	100
Italy	11	a	n	a	n	89	100	44	a	50	a	n	6	100
Japan	n	a	n	a	44	56	100	n	a	58	a	42	n	100
Korea	11	a	n	a	11	78	100	33	a	54	a	n	13	100
Luxembourg	56	a	a	a	a	44	100	100	a	a	a	a	n	100
Mexico	33	n	a	n	a	67	100	42	58	a	n	a	n	100
Netherlands	n	n	n	n	n	100	100	n	n	n	n	n	100	100
New Zealand	m	m	m	m	m	m	**m**	m	m	m	m	m	m	**m**
Norway	11	a	a	a	56	33	100	n	a	a	a	83	17	100
Poland	11	a	n	n	n	89	100	8	a	n	n	33	58	100
Portugal	44	a	n	a	n	56	100	83	a	n	a	n	17	100
Scotland	n	a	a	a	22	78	100	17	a	a	a	54	29	100
Slovak Republic	25	a	n	a	n	75	100	33	a	n	a	4	63	100
Slovenia	11	a	n	n	n	89	100	58	a	n	n	n	42	100
Spain	n	11	11	a	n	78	100	25	63	8	a	n	4	100
Sweden	n	a	a	a	11	89	100	n	a	a	a	42	58	100
Switzerland	n	33	a	a	11	56	100	n	50	a	a	25	25	100
Turkey	33	a	11	a	a	56	100	92	a	8	a	a	n	100
United States	n	n	a	a	44	56	100	n	25	a	a	42	33	100
OECD average[1]	11	4	1	n	8	75	100	24	15	8	n	22	31	100
EU21 average[1]	12	3	2	1	4	80	100	28	12	6	n	15	39	100
Other G20														
Argentina	m	m	m	m	m	m	**m**	m	m	m	m	m	m	**m**
Brazil	11	n	n	n	n	89	100	m	m	m	m	m	m	**m**
China	m	m	m	m	m	m	**m**	m	m	m	m	m	m	**m**
India	m	m	m	m	m	m	**m**	m	m	m	m	m	m	**m**
Indonesia	13	a	n	n	a	88	100	13	a	n	88	a	n	100
Russian Federation	m	m	m	m	m	m	**m**	m	m	m	m	m	m	**m**
Saudi Arabia	m	m	m	m	m	m	**m**	m	m	m	m	m	m	**m**
South Africa	m	m	m	m	m	m	**m**	m	m	m	m	m	m	**m**
G20 average	m	m	m	m	m	m	**m**	m	m	m	m	m	m	**m**

1. Finland is not included in the averages.
Source: OECD. See Annex 3 for notes *(www.oecd.org/edu/eag2012)*.
Please refer to the Reader's Guide for information concerning the symbols replacing missing data.
StatLink ⬛⬛⬛ http://dx.doi.org/10.1787/888932668527

Table D6.2b. **Percentage of decisions taken at each level of government in public lower secondary education, by domain (2011)**

	Planning and structures							Resource management						
	Central	State	Provincial/ regional	Sub-regional	Local	School	Total	Central	State	Provincial/ regional	Sub-regional	Local	School	Total
	(1)	(2)	(3)	(4)	(5)	(6)	(7)	(8)	(9)	(10)	(11)	(12)	(13)	(14)
OECD														
Australia	n	71	a	a	a	29	**100**	n	33	a	a	a	67	**100**
Austria	70	20	n	a	n	10	**100**	25	27	n	a	27	21	**100**
Belgium (Fl.)	n	29	n	a	n	71	**100**	n	50	n	a	n	50	**100**
Belgium (Fr.)	n	86	n	a	n	14	**100**	n	79	n	a	n	21	**100**
Canada	n	71	a	a	21	7	**100**	n	6	a	a	94	n	**100**
Chile	n	n	n	a	40	60	**100**	50	n	n	a	50	n	**100**
Czech Republic	n	a	10	n	20	70	**100**	n	a	n	n	65	35	**100**
Denmark	64	a	a	n	36	n	**100**	n	a	n	a	46	54	**100**
England	n	a	a	a	40	60	**100**	n	a	a	a	25	75	**100**
Estonia	14	a	a	n	29	57	**100**	n	a	a	n	27	73	**100**
Finland[1]	n	a	n	n	100	x(5)	**100**	n	a	n	n	100	x(12)	**100**
France	43	a	a	29	n	29	**100**	13	a	38	42	n	8	**100**
Germany	n	57	n	14	14	14	**100**	n	31	25	8	35	n	**100**
Greece	100	n	n	a	n	n	**100**	83	a	n	a	8	8	**100**
Hungary	29	a	a	n	29	43	**100**	n	a	a	n	21	79	**100**
Iceland	n	a	a	a	40	60	**100**	n	a	a	a	33	67	**100**
Ireland	93	a	a	a	n	7	**100**	50	a	a	a	n	50	**100**
Israel	83	a	n	a	n	17	**100**	63	a	n	a	21	17	**100**
Italy	57	a	14	a	n	29	**100**	42	a	13	a	17	29	**100**
Japan	50	a	n	a	20	30	**100**	n	a	65	a	35	n	**100**
Korea	50	a	20	a	n	30	**100**	6	a	52	a	6	35	**100**
Luxembourg	100	a	a	a	a	n	**100**	92	a	a	a	a	8	**100**
Mexico	60	40	a	n	a	n	**100**	27	73	a	n	a	n	**100**
Netherlands	57	n	n	n	n	43	**100**	n	n	n	n	n	100	**100**
New Zealand	m	m	m	m	m	m	**m**	m	m	m	m	m	m	**m**
Norway	71	a	a	a	29	n	**100**	n	a	a	a	92	8	**100**
Poland	86	a	n	n	14	n	**100**	n	a	n	n	58	42	**100**
Portugal	100	a	n	a	n	n	**100**	83	a	n	a	n	17	**100**
Scotland	43	a	a	a	14	43	**100**	n	a	a	a	58	42	**100**
Slovak Republic	50	a	n	a	n	50	**100**	25	a	n	a	25	50	**100**
Slovenia	70	a	n	n	20	10	**100**	13	a	n	n	21	67	**100**
Spain	40	40	20	a	n	n	**100**	n	58	25	a	n	17	**100**
Sweden	70	a	a	a	30	n	**100**	n	a	a	a	58	42	**100**
Switzerland	n	100	a	a	n	n	**100**	n	67	a	a	13	21	**100**
Turkey	60	a	20	a	a	20	**100**	58	a	42	a	a	n	**100**
United States	n	75	a	a	25	n	**100**	n	n	a	a	100	n	**100**
OECD average[1]	43	17	2	1	12	24	**100**	19	13	8	1	28	32	**100**
EU21 average[1]	49	11	2	2	11	25	**100**	19	11	5	2	22	40	**100**
Other G20														
Argentina	m	m	m	m	m	m	**m**	m	m	m	m	m	m	**m**
Brazil	m	m	m	m	m	m	**m**	m	m	m	m	m	m	**m**
China	m	m	m	m	m	m	**m**	m	m	m	m	m	m	**m**
India	m	m	m	m	m	m	**m**	m	m	m	m	m	m	**m**
Indonesia	14	a	n	14	a	71	**100**	n	a	n	31	a	69	**100**
Russian Federation	m	m	m	m	m	m	**m**	m	m	m	m	m	m	**m**
Saudi Arabia	m	m	m	m	m	m	**m**	m	m	m	m	m	m	**m**
South Africa	m	m	m	m	m	m	**m**	m	m	m	m	m	m	**m**
G20 average	m	m	m	m	m	m	**m**	m	m	m	m	m	m	**m**

1. Finland is not included in the averages.
Source: OECD. See Annex 3 for notes (*www.oecd.org/edu/eag2012*).
Please refer to the Reader's Guide for information concerning the symbols replacing missing data.
StatLink ⏷ http://dx.doi.org/10.1787/888932668546

Table D6.3. **Percentage of decisions taken at the school level in public lower secondary education, by mode of decision making (2011)**

D6

	In full autonomy	After consultation with other bodies in the educational system	Within framework set by a higher authority	Other	Total, decisions taken at the school level	Decisions taken at other levels after consultation with schools[1]	Total, decisions taken at the school level or after consultation with schools
	(1)	(2)	(3)	(4)	(5)	(6)	(7)
OECD							
Australia	11	n	38	n	**49**	10	**59**
Austria	5	2	20	3	**31**	2	**33**
Belgium (Fl.)	45	n	27	n	**71**	n	**71**
Belgium (Fr.)	25	n	n	3	**28**	6	**34**
Canada	6	n	14	n	**19**	n	**19**
Chile	18	n	28	n	**46**	n	**46**
Czech Republic	19	n	49	n	**68**	n	**68**
Denmark	23	5	16	n	**44**	14	**58**
England	56	4	21	n	**81**	n	**81**
Estonia	31	n	45	n	**76**	n	**76**
Finland	m	m	m	m	**m**	m	**m**
France	18	6	5	3	**32**	6	**37**
Germany	8	3	12	n	**23**	3	**26**
Greece	n	n	5	n	**5**	n	**5**
Hungary	18	5	44	n	**67**	7	**73**
Iceland	36	6	20	n	**62**	n	**62**
Ireland	10	n	40	n	**50**	4	**54**
Israel	12	3	17	n	**32**	4	**36**
Italy	19	n	19	n	**38**	n	**38**
Japan	8	n	13	n	**21**	4	**26**
Korea	29	n	10	n	**39**	n	**39**
Luxembourg	10	n	n	3	**13**	15	**28**
Mexico	11	6	n	n	**17**	n	**17**
Netherlands	57	n	19	9	**86**	n	**86**
New Zealand	m	m	m	m	**m**	m	**m**
Norway	4	6	5	n	**15**	6	**20**
Poland	24	3	20	n	**47**	n	**47**
Portugal	13	n	9	n	**22**	13	**35**
Scotland	25	3	20	n	**48**	26	**74**
Slovak Republic	40	6	14	n	**59**	1	**60**
Slovenia	18	1	33	n	**52**	15	**66**
Spain	15	3	7	n	**25**	n	**25**
Sweden	38	n	9	n	**47**	n	**47**
Switzerland	11	3	11	n	**25**	5	**30**
Turkey	3	3	13	n	**19**	n	**19**
United States	6	12	5	n	**22**	20	**43**
OECD average	20	2	18	1	**41**	5	**45**
EU21 average	24	2	20	1	**46**	5	**51**
Other G20							
Argentina	m	m	m	m	**m**	m	**m**
Brazil	m	m	m	m	**m**	m	**m**
China	m	m	m	m	**m**	m	**m**
India	m	m	m	m	**m**	m	**m**
Indonesia	54	3	n	n	**57**	n	**57**
Russian Federation	m	m	m	m	**m**	m	**m**
Saudi Arabia	m	m	m	m	**m**	m	**m**
South Africa	m	m	m	m	**m**	m	**m**
G20 average	m	m	m	m	**m**	m	**m**

1. The number of decisions taken at other levels but in consultation with schools as a percentage of all decisions.
Source: OECD. See Annex 3 for notes (*www.oecd.org/edu/eag2012*).
Please refer to the Reader's Guide for information concerning the symbols replacing missing data.
StatLink ᴪᴸ http://dx.doi.org/10.1787/888932668565

D6

Table D6.4a. Percentage of decisions taken at the school level in public lower secondary education, by mode of decision making and domain (2011)

	Organisation of instruction							Personnel management						
	In full autonomy	After consultation with other bodies in the educational system	Within framework set by a higher authority	Other	Total, decisions taken at the school level	Decisions taken at other levels after consultation with schools[1]	Total, decisions taken at the school level or after consultation with schools	In full autonomy	After consultation with other bodies in the educational system	Within framework set by a higher authority	Other	Total, decisions taken at the school level	Decisions taken at other levels after consultation with schools[1]	Total, decisions taken at the school level or after consultation with schools
	(1)	(2)	(3)	(4)	(5)	(6)	(7)	(8)	(9)	(10)	(11)	(12)	(13)	(14)
OECD														
Australia	11	n	78	n	**89**	n	**89**	8	n	4	n	**13**	17	**29**
Austria	11	n	78	n	**89**	n	**89**	n	n	4	n	**4**	n	**4**
Belgium (Fl.)	67	n	22	n	**89**	n	**89**	42	n	33	n	**75**	n	**75**
Belgium (Fr.)	67	n	n	11	**78**	n	**78**	n	n	n	n	**n**	8	**8**
Canada	22	n	44	n	**67**	n	**67**	n	n	4	n	**4**	n	**4**
Chile	56	n	44	n	**100**	n	**100**	17	n	8	n	**25**	n	**25**
Czech Republic	22	n	78	n	**100**	n	**100**	33	n	33	n	**67**	n	**67**
Denmark	33	n	56	n	**89**	n	**89**	33	n	n	n	**33**	8	**42**
England	89	n	n	n	**89**	n	**89**	58	17	25	n	**100**	n	**100**
Estonia	33	n	67	n	**100**	n	**100**	25	n	50	n	**75**	n	**75**
Finland[2]	33	n	44	n	**78**	n	**78**	m	m	m	m	**m**	m	**m**
France	56	11	n	11	**78**	n	**78**	8	4	n	n	**13**	n	**13**
Germany	33	11	33	n	**78**	n	**78**	n	n	n	n	**n**	13	**13**
Greece	n	n	11	n	**11**	n	**11**	n	n	n	n	**n**	n	**n**
Hungary	44	11	22	n	**78**	n	**78**	29	n	38	n	**67**	4	**71**
Iceland	44	22	11	n	**78**	n	**78**	33	n	8	n	**42**	n	**42**
Ireland	22	n	67	n	**89**	n	**89**	17	n	38	n	**54**	n	**54**
Israel	22	n	56	n	**78**	11	**89**	n	13	4	n	**17**	4	**21**
Italy	56	n	33	n	**89**	n	**89**	n	n	6	n	**6**	n	**6**
Japan	33	n	22	n	**56**	n	**56**	n	n	n	n	**n**	17	**17**
Korea	78	n	n	n	**78**	n	**78**	13	n	n	n	**13**	n	**13**
Luxembourg	33	n	n	11	**44**	n	**44**	n	n	n	n	**n**	n	**n**
Mexico	44	22	n	n	**67**	n	**67**	n	n	n	n	**n**	n	**n**
Netherlands	78	n	11	11	**100**	n	**100**	58	n	17	25	**100**	n	**100**
New Zealand	m	m	m	m	**m**	m	**m**	m	m	m	m	**m**	m	**m**
Norway	n	22	11	n	**33**	11	**44**	17	n	n	n	**17**	n	**17**
Poland	67	11	11	n	**89**	n	**89**	8	n	50	n	**58**	n	**58**
Portugal	44	n	11	n	**56**	22	**78**	8	n	8	n	**17**	n	**17**
Scotland	33	11	33	n	**78**	n	**78**	n	n	29	n	**29**	17	**46**
Slovak Republic	75	n	n	n	**75**	n	**75**	58	n	4	n	**63**	4	**67**
Slovenia	22	n	67	n	**89**	n	**89**	n	4	38	n	**42**	25	**67**
Spain	44	11	22	n	**78**	n	**78**	n	n	4	n	**4**	n	**4**
Sweden	56	n	33	n	**89**	n	**89**	54	n	4	n	**58**	n	**58**
Switzerland	n	11	44	n	**56**	11	**67**	25	n	n	n	**25**	8	**33**
Turkey	11	11	33	n	**56**	n	**56**	n	n	n	n	**n**	n	**n**
United States	22	22	11	n	**56**	11	**67**	n	25	8	n	**33**	8	**42**
OECD average[2]	39	5	30	1	**75**	2	**77**	16	2	12	1	**31**	4	**35**
EU21 average[2]	45	3	30	2	**80**	1	**81**	20	1	17	1	**39**	4	**43**
Other G20														
Argentina	m	m	m	m	**m**	m	**m**	m	m	m	m	**m**	m	**m**
Brazil	89	n	n	n	**89**	n	**89**	m	m	m	m	**m**	m	**m**
China	m	m	m	m	**m**	m	**m**	m	m	m	m	**m**	m	**m**
India	m	m	m	m	**m**	m	**m**	m	m	m	m	**m**	m	**m**
Indonesia	88	n	n	n	**88**	n	**88**	n	n	n	n	**n**	n	**n**
Russian Federation	m	m	m	m	**m**	m	**m**	m	m	m	m	**m**	m	**m**
Saudi Arabia	m	m	m	m	**m**	m	**m**	m	m	m	m	**m**	m	**m**
South Africa	m	m	m	m	**m**	m	**m**	m	m	m	m	**m**	m	**m**
G20 average	m	m	m	m	**m**	m	**m**	m	m	m	m	**m**	m	**m**

1. The number of decisions taken at other levels but in consultation with schools as a percentage of all decisions.
2. Finland is not included in the averages.
Source: OECD. See Annex 3 for notes (www.oecd.org/edu/eag2012).
Please refer to the Reader's Guide for information concerning the symbols replacing missing data.
StatLink ⟐ http://dx.doi.org/10.1787/888932668584

Table D6.4b. **Percentage of decisions taken at the school level in public lower secondary education, by mode of decision making and domain (2011)**

	Planning and structures							Resource management						
	In full autonomy	After consultation with other bodies in the educational system	Within framework set by a higher authority	Other	Total, decisions taken at the school level	Decisions taken at other levels after consultation with schools[1]	Total, decisions taken at the school level or after consultation with schools	In full autonomy	After consultation with other bodies in the educational system	Within framework set by a higher authority	Other	Total, decisions taken at the school level	Decisions taken at other levels after consultation with schools[1]	Total, decisions taken at the school level or after consultation with schools
	(1)	(2)	(3)	(4)	(5)	(6)	(7)	(8)	(9)	(10)	(11)	(12)	(13)	(14)
OECD Australia	n	n	29	n	**29**	14	**43**	25	n	42	n	**67**	8	**75**
Austria	10	n	n	n	**10**	n	**10**	n	8	n	13	**21**	8	**29**
Belgium (Fl.)	29	n	43	n	**71**	n	**71**	42	n	8	n	**50**	n	**50**
Belgium (Fr.)	14	n	n	n	**14**	14	**29**	21	n	n	n	**21**	n	**21**
Canada	n	n	7	n	**7**	n	**7**	n	n	n	n	**n**	n	**n**
Chile	n	n	60	n	**60**	n	**60**	n	n	n	n	**n**	n	**n**
Czech Republic	n	n	70	n	**70**	n	**70**	19	n	17	n	**35**	n	**35**
Denmark	n	n	n	n	**n**	n	**n**	25	21	8	n	**54**	46	**100**
England	n	n	60	n	**60**	n	**60**	75	n	n	n	**75**	n	**75**
Estonia	n	n	57	n	**57**	n	**57**	67	n	6	n	**73**	n	**73**
Finland	m	m	m	m	**m**	m	**m**	m	m	m	m	**m**	m	**m**
France	n	7	21	n	**29**	14	**43**	8	n	n	n	**8**	8	**17**
Germany	n	n	14	n	**14**	n	**14**	n	n	n	n	**n**	n	**n**
Greece	n	n	n	n	**n**	n	**n**	n	n	8	n	**8**	n	**8**
Hungary	n	7	36	n	**43**	14	**57**	n	n	79	n	**79**	8	**88**
Iceland	n	n	60	n	**60**	n	**60**	67	n	n	n	**67**	n	**67**
Ireland	n	n	7	n	**7**	14	**21**	n	n	50	n	**50**	n	**50**
Israel	17	n	n	n	**17**	n	**17**	8	n	8	n	**17**	n	**17**
Italy	n	n	29	n	**29**	n	**29**	21	n	8	n	**29**	n	**29**
Japan	n	n	30	n	**30**	n	**30**	n	n	n	n	**n**	n	**n**
Korea	n	n	30	n	**30**	n	**30**	27	n	8	n	**35**	n	**35**
Luxembourg	n	n	n	n	**n**	n	**n**	8	n	n	n	**8**	58	**67**
Mexico	n	n	n	n	**n**	n	**n**	n	n	n	n	**n**	n	**n**
Netherlands	n	n	43	n	**43**	n	**43**	94	n	6	n	**100**	n	**100**
New Zealand	m	m	m	m	**m**	m	**m**	m	m	m	m	**m**	m	**m**
Norway	n	n	n	n	**n**	n	**n**	n	n	8	n	**8**	13	**21**
Poland	n	n	n	n	**n**	n	**n**	21	n	21	n	**42**	n	**42**
Portugal	n	n	n	n	**n**	29	**29**	n	n	17	n	**17**	n	**17**
Scotland	43	n	n	n	**43**	43	**86**	25	n	17	n	**42**	46	**88**
Slovak Republic	n	n	50	n	**50**	n	**50**	25	25	n	n	**50**	n	**50**
Slovenia	n	n	10	n	**10**	n	**10**	50	n	17	n	**67**	33	**100**
Spain	n	n	n	n	**n**	n	**n**	17	n	n	n	**17**	n	**17**
Sweden	n	n	n	n	**n**	n	**n**	42	n	n	n	**42**	n	**42**
Switzerland	n	n	n	n	**n**	n	**n**	21	n	n	n	**21**	n	**21**
Turkey	n	n	20	n	**20**	n	**20**	n	n	n	n	**n**	n	**n**
United States	n	n	n	n	**n**	n	**n**	n	n	n	n	**n**	63	**63**
OECD average	3	n	20	n	**24**	4	**28**	21	2	10	n	**32**	9	**41**
EU21 average	4	1	20	n	**25**	6	**31**	25	2	12	1	**40**	9	**50**
Other G20 Argentina	m	m	m	m	**m**	m	**m**	m	m	m	m	**m**	m	**m**
Brazil	m	m	m	m	**m**	m	**m**	m	m	m	m	**m**	m	**m**
China	m	m	m	m	**m**	m	**m**	m	m	m	m	**m**	m	**m**
India	m	m	m	m	**m**	m	**m**	m	m	m	m	**m**	m	**m**
Indonesia	71	n	n	n	**71**	n	**71**	56	13	n	n	**69**	n	**69**
Russian Federation	m	m	m	m	**m**	m	**m**	m	m	m	m	**m**	m	**m**
Saudi Arabia	m	m	m	m	**m**	m	**m**	m	m	m	m	**m**	m	**m**
South Africa	m	m	m	m	**m**	m	**m**	m	m	m	m	**m**	m	**m**
G20 average	m	m	m	m	**m**	m	**m**	m	m	m	m	**m**	m	**m**

1. The number of decisions taken at other levels but in consultation with schools as a percentage of all decisions.
Source: OECD. See Annex 3 for notes (*www.oecd.org/edu/eag2012*).
Please refer to the Reader's Guide for information concerning the symbols replacing missing data.
StatLink http://dx.doi.org/10.1787/888932668603

D6

Table D6.5. Trends in the percentage of decisions taken at each level of government in public lower secondary education (2003, 2007, 2011)[1]

	Central			State			Provincial/regional			Sub-regional			Local			School		
	2003	2007	2011	2003	2007	2011	2003	2007	2011	2003	2007	2011	2003	2007	2011	2003	2007	2011
	(1)	(2)	(3)	(4)	(5)	(6)	(7)	(8)	(9)	(10)	(11)	(12)	(13)	(14)	(15)	(16)	(17)	(18)
Australia	n	n	n	76	56	58	a	a	a	a	a	a	a	a	a	24	44	42
Austria	27	27	27	22	22	22	n	n	n	a	a	a	23	22	22	29	30	30
Belgium (Fl.)	m	n	n	m	29	29	m	n	n	m	a	a	m	n	n	m	71	71
Belgium (Fr.)	m	m	m	m	m	67	m	n	n	m	m	m	m	m	n	m	m	33
Canada	m	m	m	m	m	33	m	m	m	m	m	m	m	m	48	m	m	19
Chile	m	m	n	m	m	n	m	m	n	m	m	n	m	m	53	m	m	47
Czech Republic	7	6	1	a	a	a	1	n	3	n	n	n	32	33	24	60	61	73
Denmark	19	19	22	a	a	a	n	n	n	a	a	a	38	40	37	44	41	41
England	11	4	n	a	a	a	a	a	a	a	a	a	4	5	25	85	91	75
Estonia	m	4	4	m	a	a	m	a	a	m	n	n	m	30	27	m	66	69
Finland[2]	m	m	n	m	m	a	m	m	n	m	m	n	m	m	100	m	m	x(15)
France	24	27	29	a	a	a	10	6	6	35	28	31	n	n	n	31	39	34
Germany	4	4	n	30	31	31	17	17	5	n	n	10	17	18	31	32	30	23
Greece	m	m	74	m	m	a	m	m	12	m	m	a	m	m	7	m	m	7
Hungary	4	4	10	a	a	a	a	a	a	n	n	n	29	27	27	68	69	63
Iceland	25	23	3	a	a	a	a	a	a	a	a	a	50	37	42	25	40	55
Ireland	m	m	50	m	m	a	m	m	a	m	m	a	m	m	n	m	m	50
Israel	m	m	40	m	m	a	m	m	3	m	m	a	m	m	19	m	m	37
Italy	23	31	36	a	a	a	16	16	16	a	a	a	15	6	8	46	47	39
Japan	13	13	13	a	a	a	21	21	21	a	a	a	44	45	45	23	21	21
Korea	9	7	27	a	a	a	34	36	26	a	a	a	8	8	6	48	49	42
Luxembourg	66	68	85	a	a	a	a	a	a	a	a	a	a	a	a	34	32	15
Mexico	30	30	46	45	48	37	2	2	a	n	n	n	a	a	a	22	20	17
Netherlands	4	6	14	n	n	n	n	n	n	n	n	n	n	n	n	96	94	86
New Zealand	25	24	m	n	n	m	n	n	m	n	n	m	n	n	m	75	76	m
Norway	32	25	21	a	a	a	a	a	a	a	a	a	32	40	62	37	35	18
Poland	m	m	26	m	m	a	m	m	n	m	m	n	m	m	29	m	m	45
Portugal	50	57	74	a	a	a	8	n	n	a	a	a	n	n	n	41	43	26
Scotland	m	17	15	m	m	a	m	a	a	m	m	a	m	53	37	m	30	48
Slovak Republic	33	m	40	a	m	a	2	m	n	a	m	a	15	m	1	50	m	59
Slovenia	m	38	41	m	a	a	m	n	n	m	n	n	m	4	15	m	58	43
Spain	n	9	16	57	42	39	15	10	16	a	a	a	n	3	n	28	36	29
Sweden	18	18	18	a	a	a	a	a	a	a	a	a	36	35	35	47	47	47
Switzerland	m	m	n	m	m	67	m	m	a	m	m	a	m	m	7	m	m	26
Turkey	49	m	63	a	m	a	27	m	18	a	m	a	a	m	a	24	m	19
United States	m	m	n	m	m	25	m	m	a	m	m	a	m	m	51	m	m	24
OECD average[2]	21	19	23	10	9	12	7	5	4	2	1	1	15	17	19	44	49	40
OECD average for countries with data available for all reference years	19	20	23	12	10	10	7	6	5	2	1	2	17	17	19	43	46	41
EU21 average for countries with data available for all reference years	20	21	26	8	7	7	5	4	4	3	2	3	15	15	16	49	51	45
Argentina	m	m	m	m	m	m	m	m	m	m	m	m	m	m	m	m	m	m
Brazil	m	m	m	m	m	m	m	m	m	m	m	m	m	m	m	m	m	m
China	m	m	m	m	m	m	m	m	m	m	m	m	m	m	m	m	m	m
India	m	m	m	m	m	m	m	m	m	m	m	m	m	m	m	m	m	m
Indonesia	m	m	10	m	m	a	m	m	n	m	m	35	m	m	a	m	m	55
Russian Federation	m	m	m	m	m	m	m	m	m	m	m	m	m	m	m	m	m	m
Saudi Arabia	m	m	m	m	m	m	m	m	m	m	m	m	m	m	m	m	m	m
South Africa	m	m	m	m	m	m	m	m	m	m	m	m	m	m	m	m	m	m
G20 average	m	m	m	m	m	m	m	m	m	m	m	m	m	m	m	m	m	m

1. In order to compare 2011 data with data from previous years, three new items in the 2011 survey were not included in the calculations.
2. Finland is not included in the averages.
Source: OECD. See Annex 3 for notes (*www.oecd.org/edu/eag2012*).
Please refer to the Reader's Guide for information concerning the symbols replacing missing data.
StatLink ᵐˢᴸ http://dx.doi.org/10.1787/888932668622

WHAT ARE THE PATHWAYS AND GATEWAYS TO GAIN ACCESS TO SECONDARY AND TERTIARY EDUCATION?

- National examinations are most prevalent at the upper secondary level and least prevalent at the primary level. Twenty-three of the 36 countries that reported data had national examinations at the upper secondary level.

- Twenty countries reported that they have alternative routes or flexible pathways that can be used to gain access to tertiary education.

- Countries with standards-based external examinations tend to score higher on the PISA survey.

Chart D7.1. **Examinations and access to secondary and tertiary education (2011)**

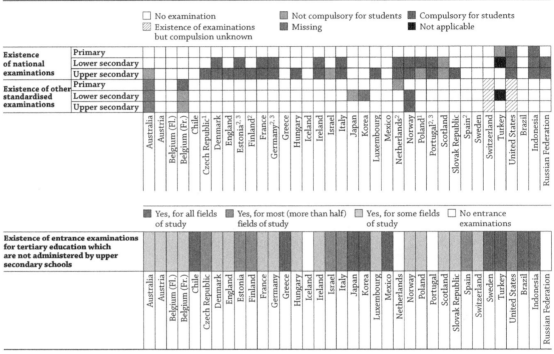

1. Excludes ISCED 3C programmes at the upper secondary level.
2. Includes only general programmes at the upper secondary level.
3. Includes only general programmes at the lower secondary level.
Source: OECD. Tables D7.1a, D7.2a, D7.3a, and D7.1b, D7.1c, D7.2b, D7.2c, available on line. See Annex 3 for notes (*www.oecd.org/edu/eag2012*).
StatLink ⟦⟧ http://dx.doi.org/10.1787/888932664005

■ Context

A number of intrinsic and extrinsic factors motivate students to learn. This indicator identifies some key extrinsic factors that may influence the amount of pressure placed on students to work hard in school, such as the presence and nature of examinations that influence access to secondary and tertiary education. Other factors that can motivate students include requirements for access to tertiary education and the availability and competition for places in tertiary education.

Around the world, there is increasing interest in using standardised tests to measure cognitive knowledge. National assessments and examinations are increasingly used by education authorities to hold schools accountable. Meanwhile, international assessments like PISA are frequently cited by the media and policy makers. Understanding differences among countries' education systems requires having more information about country-specific factors, including the pressure students are under to work hard in school and perform well on examinations. Understanding the requirements associated with the pathways and gateways to secondary and tertiary level education can help explain the differences in country performance on international assessments like PISA.

Other findings

- **National examinations are typically devised at the central level.** Eighteen countries reported that national examinations at the upper secondary level are compulsory for students.

- Most countries report that **results from national examinations at the upper secondary level are shared directly with school administrators, teachers, parents and students,** in addition to education authorities. Eleven countries report general results directly to the news media.

- In addition to national examinations, **seven countries reported using other types of standardised examinations at the upper secondary level.**

- National examinations and other examinations can serve a multitude of purposes. At the upper secondary level, **the most common purpose of national examinations is for student certification, graduation or grade completion** (22 countries). The next most common purpose of national examinations is to determine student entry into tertiary education (20 countries). Other related purposes of the examinations include determining access to selective tertiary institutions (16 countries) and determining access to specific programmes of study at the tertiary level (15 countries).

- **Thirty-two countries reported using entrance examinations for tertiary education** (that are not administered by upper secondary schools). In ten countries, entrance examinations are compulsory for all students who wish to participate in tertiary education. Most countries (21 of 32) reported that the entrance examinations are devised and graded by an individual tertiary institute or a consortium of tertiary institutes. In addition to entrance examinations, other factors, criteria or special circumstances are used by tertiary-level institutions to determine access to tertiary-type A and B programmes. These other factors include Grade Point Average from secondary schools (21 countries), previous work experience (14 countries), applicant letter or written rationale (11 countries) and past service or volunteer work (10 countries). Family background factors, such as ethnicity of the applicant or family income, were used in only 6 and 8 countries, respectively.

- **The ratio of available places to applicants at the tertiary level provides an indicator of the relative competition for places among students.**

Trends

In addition to certifying student performance and signalling student achievement, national examinations are also a prominent means of holding schools and education systems accountable. This method of ensuring accountability has become increasingly important internationally in the past few decades, while the more traditional forms of accountability that focus more on inputs and processes are being used less widely. This shift to greater use of national examinations is also partly attributed to the technological advances that make it easier to test large populations of students regularly.

Analysis

Prevalence of national examinations or other standardised examinations

National examinations are standardised tests that have formal consequences for students, such as whether a student can progress to a higher level of education or obtain an officially recognised degree. Twenty-three of the 36 countries that reported data had national examinations at the upper secondary level (Chart D7.1).

Thirteen of the countries reported data separately for general programmes and pre-vocational/vocational programmes at the upper secondary level. Eight of these 13 countries reported having national examinations for both general and pre-vocational/vocational programmes. Four countries have national examinations for their general programmes but not for pre-vocational/vocational programmes at the upper secondary level. Only Spain reported having national examinations for its vocational programmes but not its general upper secondary programmes (Table D7.1a).

Control of and responsibility for national examinations is usually determined by the level of government or education authority that develops and grades the national examination. In 11 countries, national examinations at the upper secondary level are devised and graded at the national level, and in 4 countries the examinations are devised at the state level, which is typically the most central level at which education decisions are taken in a federal country. Six countries reported that examinations are devised and graded at both the national and school levels, and Poland reported that examinations are devised and graded at both the national and regional levels. In Norway, national examinations for general programmes are devised and graded at the national level, while examinations for the country's pre-vocational/vocational programmes are devised and graded at both the national and regional levels.

A total of 18 countries reported that national examinations at the upper secondary level are nationally standardised; i.e. they are administered and scored under uniform conditions across different schools throughout the country so student scores are directly comparable. Seventeen of the countries reported that national examinations at the upper secondary level are compulsory, five countries reported that the examinations are not compulsory, and Estonia reported that the examinations are only compulsory for general programmes. Nine countries reported that all students take the national examination, and another nine countries reported that between 76% and 99% of students take the examination. In the Czech Republic, between 51% and 75% of students take the national examination at the upper secondary level; this is also true for vocational programmes in the Slovak Republic. In Scotland, most students from general programmes take national examinations, although the few students from pre-vocational/vocational programmes generally do not take them. In Spain, only 10% or less of the country's pre-vocational/vocational students take it.

The manner in which the results from national examinations are shared or communicated is important when considering the nature and purpose of national examinations at the upper secondary level. Twenty-three countries reported that the results from national examinations are shared directly with others in addition to education authorities. This means that designated groups receive the information without having to request it. Twenty-one countries shared the results with school administrators, 18 countries shared the results with classroom teachers, 15 countries shared the results with parents, and 23 countries shared the results with students. Eleven countries reported that they directly shared the results with the news media. The pattern in which countries share the results of national examinations at the primary and lower secondary levels is similar as that reported at the upper secondary level (Table D7.1a, and Tables D7.1b-c, available on line).

Fourteen of 35 countries reported having national examinations at the lower secondary level. These examinations were compulsory for students in 13 of the 14 countries. Estonia, Germany, the Netherlands and Portugal reported the existence of examinations in general programmes and pre-vocational/vocational programmes separately. Only the Netherlands reported having a national examination for both types of programmes, while the other three countries reported having national examinations only for general programmes (Chart D7.1 and Table D7.1c, available on line).

The Netherlands is one of a number of countries that tracks students into either general or pre-vocational programmes after primary education. A new test or assessment will be introduced at the lower and upper secondary level for the general programme. This test is used to provide formative feedback intended to improve instruction; the results have no formal consequences for students. The test administered in pre-vocational programmes at this level does have formal consequences for students and is considered an examination, since the results are used to determine access to specific vocational programmes at the upper secondary level.

Only three countries – Indonesia, Turkey and the United States – reported having national examinations at the primary school level (Chart D7.1 and Table D7.1b, available on line). The United States has a federal system with education largely the responsibility of each state. In 2001, federal legislation mandated that all states administer an annual standardised examination for public schools across grades 3-8, as well as at least one grade at the upper secondary level. States are able to use their examinations for a variety of purposes including, but not limited to, promoting students to the next grade or retaining them, evaluating teachers, and fulfilling graduation requirements. The examinations do not necessarily have consequences for students, but there can be consequences for schools with poor performance (see Annex 3, available at *www.oecd.org/edu/eag2012*).

Countries were also asked about the prevalence of other (non-national) standardised examinations that are administered in multiple schools. Four countries reported having such examinations at the primary level, and five countries reported having such examinations at the lower secondary level. Seven countries reported having such examinations at the upper secondary level: four of these countries reported having examinations for all programmes, and three countries reported having such examinations for pre-vocational/vocational programmes only. Although fewer countries use these types of examinations, they were slightly more prevalent for pre-vocational/vocational programmes compared to general programmes. These examinations are devised at various levels of government and show no clear pattern across the countries that reported using them (Table D7.2a and Tables D7.2b-c, available on line).

Purposes or uses of national and other standardised examinations

National examinations and other examinations can serve a multitude of purposes (Chart D7.2). Responses from countries reveal that the most common use of national examinations at the upper secondary level is for student certification, graduation or grade completion (22 countries). The next most common use was in determining student entry into tertiary education (20 countries). Other related purposes include determining access to selective tertiary institutions (16 countries) and determining access to specific programmes of study at the tertiary level (15 countries) (Tables D.7.1a and D7.2a and Tables D7.1b-c and D7.2b-c, available on line).

Chart D7.2. **Distribution of main purposes of national and other standardised examinations at the upper secondary level in general programmes (2011)**

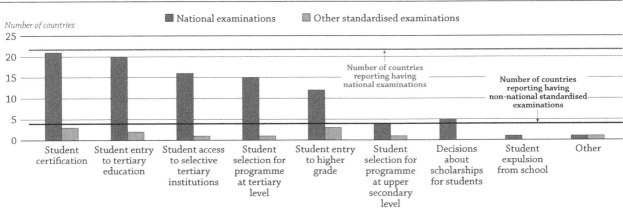

Purposes are ranked in descending order of the number of countries reporting these as one of the national examinations' purposes.
Source: OECD. Tables D7.1a and D7.2a. See Annex 3 for notes (*www.oecd.org/edu/eag2012*).
StatLink ⬛ᵐˢˡ⬛ http://dx.doi.org/10.1787/888932664024

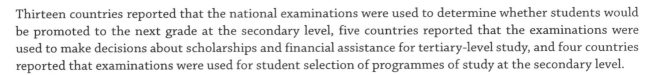

Thirteen countries reported that the national examinations were used to determine whether students would be promoted to the next grade at the secondary level, five countries reported that the examinations were used to make decisions about scholarships and financial assistance for tertiary-level study, and four countries reported that examinations were used for student selection of programmes of study at the secondary level.

The purposes of national examinations at the primary and lower secondary levels are more oriented towards student certification and grade completion. Ten of 14 countries reported that national examinations at the lower secondary level help to determine student entry into upper secondary education, and 9 of 14 countries reported that they are used to determine whether students would be promoted to the next grade (Tables D7.1b-c, available on line).

Use of examinations does not necessarily imply pressure on students to learn. For example, examinations, especially those at lower levels of education, are a formal requirement to progress to the next grade or school level, and the threshold for passing could be relatively low so that most students are not pressured to prepare for these examinations.

Prevalence of entrance examinations to gain access to tertiary education

Entrance examinations are examinations not administered by upper secondary schools that are typically used to determine, or help to determine, access to tertiary-type A and B programmes. Thirty-two countries reported using entrance examinations (Table D7.3a). Of the 32 countries with university entrance examinations, 9 reported that the examination covers all fields of study, 7 countries reported that the examinations cover more than half of the fields of study, and 16 countries reported that the examinations cover only some of the fields of study available at the tertiary level.

Of the 32 countries with entrance examinations, 6 reported that these examinations are devised and graded at the national or state level, 21 reported that they are devised and graded at the school level (i.e. by individual tertiary institutions or a consortium of tertiary institutions), and the United States reported that these examinations are devised and graded by private companies.

Because these examinations are most often devised by individual tertiary institutions, the results are often not comparable with examinations administered by other tertiary-level institutions. Only 12 of the 32 countries with university entrance examinations indicated that these examinations are standardised and comparable.

Ten countries reported that entrance examinations are compulsory for all students wishing to access tertiary education, while 22 countries reported that these examinations are not compulsory for all students. In seven countries, between 76% and 99% of students take the entrance examination, while in four countries, between 51% and 75% of students take the examination. Two countries reported that between 11% and 50% of students take the exam, and nine countries reported that less than 10% of students take the exam.

Twenty-seven countries reported that the results are shared with others in addition to education authorities. These external audiences include students (27 countries), school administrators (12 countries), the news media (5 countries), classroom teachers (5 countries), and parents (4 countries).

In a number of countries, examinations at the upper secondary level are used as an exit requirement as well as for entry into university. For example, in Australia, each state and territory conducts examinations for graduation from upper secondary education that produces a standardised score for entry into university (Australian Tertiary Admission Rank, ATAR). In Greece, the Panhellenic examinations are national examinations devised and administered centrally by the Ministry of Education using the facilities and personnel of upper secondary schools. These examinations are usually taken by students who want to enter tertiary education while they are in upper secondary school, although they can also be taken after students have completed that level of education.

Table D7.3b, available on line, contains descriptive details about each country's entrance examination(s).

Purposes or uses of entrance examinations

The main purposes of entrance examinations overlap with many of the reported purposes of national examinations administered at the upper secondary level. In 22 countries, entrance examinations were reported to be the only available route to some fields of study, while in 5 countries they were reported to be the only available route to tertiary education. Sixteen countries reported that these examinations are used to determine access to selective institutions, and 27 countries reported that these examinations are used to determine access to selective or specific programmes, disciplines, fields of study, or specialisations at the tertiary level. Six countries noted that these examinations are also used to determine whether to award scholarships or financial aid to students (Table D7.3a).

Other factors used to determine access to tertiary education

In addition to entrance examinations, other factors, criteria or special circumstances are used by tertiary-level institutions to determine access to tertiary-type A and B programmes. Chart D7.3 illustrates the relative importance of these other factors.

Chart D7.3. **Influence of factors other than examinations used by tertiary institutions to determine access to the first stage of tertiary education (2011)**

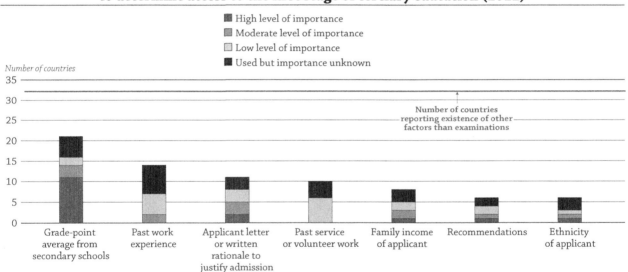

Factors are ranked in descending order of the number of countries reporting these factors as used by tertiary institutions to determine access to the first stage of tertiary education.
Source: OECD. Table D7.4a. See Annex 3 for notes (*www.oecd.org/edu/eag2012*).
StatLink ⌐⌐⌐ http://dx.doi.org/10.1787/888932664043

The most common other factor cited by the 32 countries that use additional criteria or special circumstances to determine entrance into tertiary education is Grade Point Average (GPA) from secondary schools: 21 countries reported using GPA as a criterion, and 11 of these reported that GPA is highly important. Fourteen countries reported that previous work experience is used to help determine access to tertiary institutions, although none of the countries indicated that this criterion was of high importance. Eleven countries indicated that an applicant letter or written rationale to justify admission is considered as a factor, and three countries indicated that this factor is of low importance, but five countries reported that this factor was of moderate or high importance. Ten countries reported that past service or volunteer work is a criterion used to determine access, but this factor was considered to be of relatively low importance (Table D7.4a).

Family background factors, such as ethnicity of the applicant or family income, are used in 6 and 8 countries, respectively. In addition to these generally recognised factors, 24 countries reported that their tertiary-level

D7

institutions used other criteria to determine access to the first stage of tertiary education. These other factors are described in Table D7.4b, available on line. Australia, Brazil, Finland and Korea, for example, reported that some institutions used interviews of applicants, and other countries prioritised some subgroups of students based on gender, past military service, or whether or not the applicant had a disability. Applicants' practical skills are also a factor in a few countries.

Access to tertiary education and existence of alternative routes

The number of available places at the tertiary level, and the degree of competition for these places, are important factors in determining how much pressure students may experience as they go through primary and secondary school. For example, if a tertiary education is guaranteed for all upper secondary graduates, students would probably feel less pressure than if they had to compete with peers or had to meet certain performance standards to be admitted to a tertiary-level institution.

The entry rate into tertiary-type A education, which estimates the proportion of people who will enter tertiary-type A programmes during their lifetime, illustrates the relative accessibility of tertiary education within each country (see Indicator C3). Some 84% of people in Portugal and 83% of people in Poland will ultimately gain access to tertiary-type A institutions. Germany (36%) and Switzerland (33%) have relatively low proportions of students who will eventually gain access to tertiary-type A institutions (Chart D7.4). This may be partly explained by the strong traditions of attending trade schools and apprenticeship programmes in these latter countries. Although Belgium has relatively low entry rates in tertiary-type A education (30%), this is counterbalanced by high entry rates in tertiary-type B education.

Chart D7.4.   **Entry rates into tertiary-type A education (2010)**
Entry rates adjusted from international students

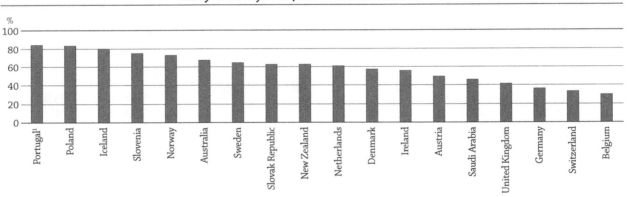

1. Entry rates may be overestimated as they include all students who entered the first year of a programme, not just those students who entered a tertiary-type A or B programme for the first time.
Countries are ranked in descending order of adjusted entry rates for tertiary-type A education.
Source: OECD. Table C3.1. See Annex 3 for notes (*www.oecd.org/edu/eag2012*).
StatLink ⌐᠊ᴵ᠊ᴼ᠊ http://dx.doi.org/10.1787/888932664062

Twenty countries reported that there were alternative routes (instead of or in addition to entrance examinations and the factors listed above) that could be used to gain access to the first stage of tertiary education. These alternative routes are described in Table D7.5, available on line.

The Nordic countries have relatively strong traditions of compensatory adult education and the use of alternative routes to encourage adults to enter tertiary education later in life. In Sweden, higher education institutions can use alternative selection criteria for as many as a third of the places available, though these alternative criteria are mainly used to select from among applicants who have the necessary formal qualifications. In these cases, special tests other than the standard university entrance examination, relevant knowledge, professional or vocational experience, and other circumstances that are relevant to the programme can be considered.

D7

Box D7.1. **How standards-based external examinations are related to student performance**

Findings from the 2009 PISA survey suggest that countries that use standards-based external examinations tend to perform better, even when accounting for national income. Over 10% of the variance in reading performance between countries is accounted for by the existence of standards-based external examinations. In other words, students in school systems that use standards-based external examinations score 16 points higher, on average across OECD countries, than students in school systems that do not use these examinations, based on the bivariate regression model with the existence of standards-based external examination regressed on reading performance. In contrast, the existence of standards-based external examinations tends to be unrelated to equity, i.e. the strength of relationship between students' socio-economic background and reading performance. These findings suggest the need for further research on the relationship between the existence of standards-based examinations and the relative performance of students on assessments such as PISA.

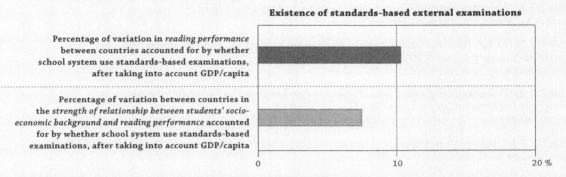

Existence of standards-based external examinations

Note: Relations that are statistically significant at the 10% level (p < 0.10) are marked in a darker tone.
Source: OECD. *PISA 2009 Database*, Table IV.2.1.
StatLink ⟨ms⟩ http://dx.doi.org/10.1787/888932669287

Definitions

"Directly" sharing information or results means sharing information with designated groups without them having to request it. When results are available on line, they are considered to be shared directly.

National examinations are standardised student assessments that have a formal consequence for students, such as an impact upon a student's eligibility to progress to a higher level of education or completion of an officially recognised degree. They assess a major portion of what students are expected to know or be able to do in a given subject.

A **standardised or comparable examination** refers to a test that is administered and scored under uniform conditions across different schools so student scores are directly comparable. In some cases, it also refers to multiple choice or fixed-answer questions as this makes it easy and possible to score the test uniformly. However, with rubrics and calibration of test examiners (persons who manually score open-ended responses), one can also find standardised tests that go beyond multiple choice and fixed answers.

Methodology

Data are from the 2011 OECD-INES Survey on National Examinations and Access to Secondary and Tertiary Education and refer to the school year 2010-11.

Notes on definitions and methodologies for each country are provided in Annex 3 at *www.oecd.org/edu/eag2012*.

The statistical data for Israel are supplied by and under the responsibility of the relevant Israeli authorities. The use of such data by the OECD is without prejudice to the status of the Golan Heights, East Jerusalem and Israeli settlements in the West Bank under the terms of international law.

D7

References

For further information about PISA 2009, see:

OECD (2011), *PISA 2009 Results: What Makes a School Successful? Resources, Policies and Practices*, Volume IV, OECD Publishing.

Visit *www.pisa.oecd.org*

The following additional material relevant to this indicator is available on line:

- *Chart D7.5. Distribution of main purposes or uses of entrance examinations to gain access to the first stage of tertiary education (2011)*
  StatLink ⬛ http://dx.doi.org/10.1787/888932664081

- *Table D7.1b. National examinations at the primary level (2011)*
  StatLink ⬛ http://dx.doi.org/10.1787/888932668831

- *Table D7.1c. National examinations at the lower secondary level (2011)*
  StatLink ⬛ http://dx.doi.org/10.1787/888932668850

- *Table D7.2b. Other (non-national) standardised examinations that are administered in multiple primary schools (2011)*
  StatLink ⬛ http://dx.doi.org/10.1787/888932668888

- *Table D7.2c. Other (non-national) standardised examinations that are administered in multiple lower secondary schools (2011)*
  StatLink ⬛ http://dx.doi.org/10.1787/888932668907

- *Table D7.2d. Other (non-national) examinations that are administered in multiple schools (2011)*
  StatLink ⬛ http://dx.doi.org/10.1787/888932668926

- *Table D7.3b. Tertiary entrance examinations (2011)*
  StatLink ⬛ http://dx.doi.org/10.1787/888932668964

- *Table D7.4b. Other factors, criteria or special circumstances used by tertiary institutions to determine access to the first stage of tertiary education (2011)*
  StatLink ⬛ http://dx.doi.org/10.1787/888932669002

- *Table D7.5. Alternative routes that can be used to gain access to the first stage of tertiary education (2011)*
  StatLink ⬛ http://dx.doi.org/10.1787/888932669021

Table D7.1a. [1/2] National examinations at the upper secondary level (2011)

		Existence	Level of government at which they are devised and graded	Standardised at the national level	Compulsory for students	Percentage of students taking them	Main purposes or uses							
							Student certification/ graduation/grade completion	Student promotion/entry to higher grade	Student entry to tertiary education	Student access to selective tertiary institutions	Student selection for programme/course/tracks at the upper secondary level	Student selection for programme/faculty/ discipline/field/specialisation at tertiary level	Student expulsion from school	Decisions about scholarships/ financial assistance for students	Other
		(1)	(2)	(3)	(4)	(5)	(6)	(7)	(8)	(9)	(10)	(11)	(12)	(13)	(14)
Australia	All programmes	Yes	2	No	No	m	Yes	No	Yes	Yes	No	Yes	No	Yes	No
Austria	All programmes	No	a	a	a	a	a	a	a	a	a	a	a	a	a
Belgium (Fl.)	All programmes	No	a	a	a	a	a	a	a	a	a	a	a	a	a
Belgium (Fr.)	All programmes	No	a	a	a	a	a	a	a	a	a	a	a	a	a
Canada	All programmes	m	m	m	m	m	m	m	m	m	m	m	m	m	m
Chile	All programmes	No	a	a	a	a	a	a	a	a	a	a	a	a	a
Czech Republic	General	Yes	1, 6	Yes	Yes	3	Yes	Yes	Yes	Yes	No	Yes	No	No	No
	Pre-voc. and voc.[1]	Yes	1, 6	Yes	Yes	3	Yes	Yes	Yes	Yes	No	Yes	No	No	No
Denmark	General	Yes	1	Yes	Yes	1	Yes	No	Yes	Yes	No	No	No	No	No
	Pre-voc. and voc.	Yes	1	Yes	Yes	1	Yes	No	No	No	No	No	No	No	No
England	All programmes	Yes	1	Yes	Yes	2	Yes	No	Yes	Yes	Yes	Yes	No	Yes	No
Estonia	General	Yes	1	Yes	Yes	2	Yes	Yes	Yes	Yes	No	Yes	No	No	No
	Pre-voc. and voc.	Yes	1	Yes	No	2	Yes	Yes	Yes	Yes	No	No	No	No	No
Finland	General	Yes	1, 6	Yes	Yes	2	Yes	No	Yes	Yes	No	Yes	No	No	No
	Pre-voc. and voc.	No	a	a	a	a	a	a	a	a	a	a	a	a	a
France	All programmes	Yes	1	Yes	Yes	1	Yes	Yes	Yes	Yes	Yes	Yes	No	Yes	No
Germany	General	Yes	2	No	Yes	1	Yes	Yes	Yes	Yes	No	No	No	No	No
	Pre-voc. and voc.	No	a	a	a	a	a	a	a	a	a	a	a	a	a
Greece	All programmes	No	a	a	a	a	a	a	a	a	a	a	a	a	a
Hungary	General	Yes	1	Yes	Yes	2	Yes	Yes	Yes	Yes	No	Yes	No	No	No
	Pre-voc. and voc.	Yes	1	Yes	Yes	2	Yes	No	No	No	No	No	No	No	No
Iceland	All programmes	No	a	a	a	a	a	a	a	a	a	a	a	a	a
Ireland	All programmes	Yes	1	Yes	Yes	2	Yes	No	Yes	Yes	No	Yes	No	Yes	No
Israel	All programmes	Yes	1, 6	Yes	No	2	Yes	No	Yes	Yes	No	Yes	No	No	No
Italy	All programmes	Yes	1, 6	No	Yes	1	Yes	No	Yes	No	No	No	No	Yes	No
Japan	All programmes	No	a	a	a	a	a	a	a	a	a	a	a	a	a
Korea	All programmes	No	a	a	a	a	a	a	a	a	a	a	a	a	a
Luxembourg	All programmes	Yes	1	Yes	Yes	2	Yes	Yes	Yes	a	No	No	No	No	No
Mexico	All programmes	No	a	a	a	a	a	a	a	a	a	a	a	a	a
Netherlands	General	Yes	1, 6	Yes	Yes	1	Yes	No	Yes	Yes	No	Yes	No	No	No
	Pre-voc. and voc.	No	a	a	a	a	a	a	a	a	a	a	a	a	a
New Zealand	All programmes	m	m	m	m	m	m	m	m	m	m	m	m	m	m
Norway	General	Yes	1	Yes	Yes	1	Yes	Yes	Yes	Yes	Yes	Yes	No	No	No
	Pre-voc. and voc.	Yes	1, 3	Yes	Yes	1	Yes	Yes	Yes	Yes	Yes	Yes	No	No	No
Poland	General	Yes	1, 3	Yes	No	2	No	No	Yes	Yes	No	Yes	No	No	m
	Pre-voc. and voc.[1]	Yes	1, 3	Yes	No	2	Yes	No	Yes	Yes	No	Yes	No	No	Yes
Portugal	General	Yes	1	Yes	Yes	1	Yes	Yes	Yes	Yes	No	Yes	No	No	No
	Pre-voc. and voc.	No	a	a	a	a	a	a	a	a	a	a	a	a	a
Scotland	General	Yes	1	Yes	No	2	Yes	Yes	Yes	No	Yes	Yes	No	No	No
	Pre-voc. and voc.	Yes	1	Yes	No	6	Yes	Yes	Yes	No	Yes	Yes	No	No	No
Slovak Republic	General	Yes	1, 6	Yes	Yes	1	Yes	No	Yes	Yes	No	Yes	Yes	No	No
	Pre-voc. and voc.[1]	Yes	1, 6	Yes	Yes	3	Yes	No	Yes	Yes	No	Yes	Yes	No	No
Slovenia	All programmes	m	m	m	m	m	m	m	m	m	m	m	m	m	m
Spain	General	No	a	a	a	a	a	a	a	a	a	a	a	a	a
	Pre-voc. and voc.	Yes	2	No	No	6	No	Yes	No	No	No	No	No	No	No
Sweden	All programmes	No	a	a	a	a	a	a	a	a	a	a	a	a	a
Switzerland	All programmes	No	a	a	a	a	a	a	a	a	a	a	a	a	a
Turkey	All programmes	No	a	a	a	a	a	a	a	a	a	a	a	a	a
United States	All programmes	Yes	2	No	Yes	2	Yes	m	No	m	m	m	No	No	Yes
Brazil	All programmes	No	a	a	a	a	a	a	a	a	a	a	a	a	a
Indonesia	All programmes	Yes	1	Yes	Yes	1	Yes	Yes	No	No	No	No	No	No	No
Russian Federation	All programmes	Yes	1	Yes	Yes	1	Yes	Yes	Yes	No	No	No	a	No	No
Saudi Arabia	All programmes	m	m	m	m	m	m	m	m	m	m	m	m	m	m

Levels of government
1: Central authority or government
2: State authorities or governments
3: Provincial/regional authorities or governments
4: Sub-regional or inter-municipal authorities or governments
5: Local authorities or governments
6: School, school board or committee

Percentage of students taking national examinations
1: All students
2: Between 76% and 99% of students
3: Between 51% and 75% of students
4: Between 26% and 50% of students
5: Between 11% and 25% of students
6: 10% or less of students

Note: Federal states or countries with highly decentralised school systems may have different regulations in states, provinces or regions. Please refer to Annex 3 for additional information.
1. Excludes ISCED 3C programmes, includes ISCED 3A vocational programmes only.
Source: OECD. See Annex 3 for notes (*www.oecd.org/edu/eag2012*).
Please refer to the Reader's Guide for information concerning the symbols replacing missing data.

StatLink ⫘⫘⫘ http://dx.doi.org/10.1787/888932668812

Table D7.1a. [2/2] National examinations at the upper secondary level (2011)

		How results are shared					
		Shared with external audience in addition to education authorities	Shared directly with school administrators	Shared directly with classroom teachers	Shared directly with parents	Shared directly with students	Shared directly with media
		(15)	(16)	(17)	(18)	(19)	(20)
OECD Australia	All programmes	Yes	Yes	No	No	Yes	No
Austria	All programmes	a	a	a	a	a	a
Belgium (Fl.)	All programmes	a	a	a	a	a	a
Belgium (Fr.)	All programmes	a	a	a	a	a	a
Canada	All programmes	m	m	m	m	m	m
Chile	All programmes	a	a	a	a	a	a
Czech Republic	General	Yes	Yes	Yes	No	Yes	No
	Pre-voc. and voc.[1]	Yes	Yes	Yes	No	Yes	No
Denmark	General	Yes	Yes	Yes	Yes	Yes	Yes
	Pre-voc. and voc.	Yes	Yes	Yes	Yes	Yes	Yes
England	All programmes	Yes	Yes	Yes	Yes	Yes	Yes
Estonia	General	Yes	Yes	Yes	Yes	Yes	Yes
	Pre-voc. and voc.	Yes	Yes	Yes	Yes	Yes	No
Finland	General	Yes	Yes	Yes	No	Yes	No
	Pre-voc. and voc.	a	a	a	a	a	a
France	All programmes	Yes	Yes	Yes	Yes	Yes	Yes
Germany	General	Yes	Yes	Yes	No	Yes	No
	Pre-voc. and voc.	a	a	a	a	a	a
Greece	All programmes	a	a	a	a	a	a
Hungary	General	Yes	Yes	Yes	Yes	Yes	Yes
	Pre-voc. and voc.	Yes	Yes	Yes	Yes	Yes	Yes
Iceland	All programmes	a	a	a	a	a	a
Ireland	All programmes	Yes	Yes	No	Yes	Yes	No
Israel	All programmes	Yes	Yes	No	No	Yes	Yes
Italy	All programmes	Yes	No	Yes	Yes	Yes	No
Japan	All programmes	a	a	a	a	a	a
Korea	All programmes	a	a	a	a	a	a
Luxembourg	All programmes	Yes	Yes	Yes	Yes	Yes	Yes
Mexico	All programmes	a	a	a	a	a	a
Netherlands	General	Yes	Yes	Yes	Yes	Yes	No
	Pre-voc. and voc.	a	a	a	a	a	a
New Zealand	All programmes	m	m	m	m	m	m
Norway	General	Yes	Yes	No	No	Yes	Yes
	Pre-voc. and voc.	Yes	Yes	No	No	Yes	Yes
Poland	General	Yes	Yes	Yes	Yes	Yes	Yes
	Pre-voc. and voc.[1]	Yes	Yes	Yes	Yes	Yes	Yes
Portugal	General	Yes	Yes	Yes	Yes	Yes	Yes
	Pre-voc. and voc.	a	a	a	a	a	a
Scotland	General	Yes	Yes	Yes	Yes	Yes	Yes
	Pre-voc. and voc.	Yes	Yes	Yes	Yes	Yes	Yes
Slovak Republic	General	Yes	No	Yes	No	Yes	No
	Pre-voc. and voc.[1]	Yes	No	Yes	No	Yes	No
Slovenia	All programmes	m	m	m	m	m	m
Spain	General	a	a	a	a	a	a
	Pre-voc. and voc.	Yes	Yes	No	Yes	Yes	No
Sweden	All programmes	a	a	a	a	a	a
Switzerland	All programmes	a	a	a	a	a	a
Turkey	All programmes	a	a	a	a	a	a
United States	All programmes	Yes	Yes	Yes	Yes	Yes	No
Other G20 Brazil	All programmes	a	a	a	a	a	a
Indonesia	All programmes	Yes	Yes	Yes	Yes	Yes	No
Russian Federation	All programmes	Yes	Yes	Yes	No	Yes	No
Saudi Arabia	All programmes	m	m	m	m	m	m

Levels of government
1: Central authority or government
2: State authorities or governments
3: Provincial/regional authorities or governments
4: Sub-regional or inter-municipal authorities or governments
5: Local authorities or governments
6: School, school board or committee

Percentage of students taking national examinations
1: All students
2: Between 76% and 99% of students
3: Between 51% and 75% of students
4: Between 26% and 50% of students
5: Between 11% and 25% of students
6: 10% or less of students

Note: Federal states or countries with highly decentralised school systems may have different regulations in states, provinces or regions. Please refer to Annex 3 for additional information.
1. Excludes ISCED 3C programmes, includes ISCED 3A vocational programmes only.
Source: OECD. See Annex 3 for notes (*www.oecd.org/edu/eag2012*).
Please refer to the Reader's Guide for information concerning the symbols replacing missing data.
StatLink ᵃᵢˢᵖ http://dx.doi.org/10.1787/888932668812

Table D7.2a. [1/2] Other (non-national) standardised examinations that are administered in multiple upper secondary schools (2011)

		Existence	Level of government at which they are devised and graded	Compulsory for students	Percentage of students taking them	Main purposes or uses Student certification/ graduation/grade completion	Student promotion/entry to higher grade	Student entry to tertiary education	Student access to selective tertiary institutions	Student selection for programme/course/tracks at the upper secondary level	Student selection for programme/faculty/ discipline/field/specialisation at tertiary level	Student expulsion from school	Decisions about scholarships/ financial assistance for students	Other
		(1)	(2)	(3)	(4)	(5)	(6)	(7)	(8)	(9)	(10)	(11)	(12)	(13)
OECD Australia	All programmes	m	m	m	m	m	m	m	m	m	m	m	m	m
Austria	All programmes	No	a	a	a	a	a	a	a	a	a	a	a	a
Belgium (Fl.)	All programmes	No	a	a	a	a	a	a	a	a	a	a	a	a
Belgium (Fr.)	All programmes	Yes	2	No	3	Yes	Yes	Yes	No	No	No	No	No	No
Canada	All programmes	m	m	m	m	m	m	m	m	m	m	m	m	m
Chile	All programmes	No	a	a	a	a	a	a	a	a	a	a	a	a
Czech Republic	General	No	a	a	a	a	a	a	a	a	a	a	a	a
	Pre-voc. and voc.[1]	Yes	1, 6	Yes	4	Yes	Yes	No	No	No	No	No	No	No
Denmark	All programmes	No	a	a	a	a	a	a	a	a	a	a	a	a
England	All programmes	No	a	a	a	a	a	a	a	a	a	a	a	a
Estonia	General	No	a	a	a	a	a	a	a	a	a	a	a	a
	Pre-voc. and voc.	Yes	7	No	3	Yes	No	No	No	No	No	No	No	No
Finland	All programmes	No	a	a	a	a	a	a	a	a	a	a	a	a
France	All programmes	No	a	a	a	a	a	a	a	a	a	a	a	a
Germany	General	No	a	a	a	a	a	a	a	a	a	a	a	a
	Pre-voc. and voc.	m	m	m	m	m	m	m	m	m	m	m	m	m
Greece	All programmes	No	a	a	a	a	a	a	a	a	a	a	a	a
Hungary	All programmes	No	a	a	a	a	a	a	a	a	a	a	a	a
Iceland	All programmes	No	a	a	a	a	a	a	a	a	a	a	a	a
Ireland	All programmes	No	a	a	a	a	a	a	a	a	a	a	a	a
Israel	All programmes	No	a	a	a	a	a	a	a	a	a	a	a	a
Italy	All programmes	No	a	a	a	a	a	a	a	a	a	a	a	a
Japan	All programmes	No	a	a	a	a	a	a	a	a	a	a	a	a
Korea	All programmes	No	a	a	a	a	a	a	a	a	a	a	a	a
Luxembourg	All programmes	No	a	a	a	a	a	a	a	a	a	a	a	a
Mexico	All programmes	No	a	a	a	a	a	a	a	a	a	a	a	a
Netherlands	General	No	a	a	a	a	a	a	a	a	a	a	a	a
	Pre-voc. and voc.	Yes	6, 1	Yes	1	Yes	a	Yes	No	No	Yes	No	No	No
New Zealand	All programmes	m	m	m	m	m	m	m	m	m	m	m	m	m
Norway	General	Yes	3	Yes	1	Yes	Yes	Yes	Yes	Yes	Yes	No	No	No
	Pre-voc. and voc.	Yes	3	Yes	1	Yes	Yes	Yes	Yes	Yes	Yes	No	No	No
Poland	General	No	a	a	a	a	a	a	a	a	a	a	a	a
	Pre-voc. and voc.	m	m	m	m	m	m	m	m	m	m	m	m	m
Portugal	All programmes	No	a	a	a	a	a	a	a	a	a	a	a	a
Scotland	All programmes	No	a	a	a	a	a	a	a	a	a	a	a	a
Slovak Republic	All programmes	No	a	a	a	a	a	a	a	a	a	a	a	a
Slovenia	All programmes	m	m	m	m	m	m	m	m	m	m	m	m	m
Spain	All programmes	No	a	a	a	a	a	a	a	a	a	a	a	a
Sweden	All programmes	No	a	a	a	a	a	a	a	a	a	a	a	a
Switzerland	All programmes	Yes	1, 2, 5, 6, 7	m	m	m	m	m	m	m	m	m	m	m
Turkey	All programmes	No	a	a	a	a	a	a	a	a	a	a	a	a
United States	All programmes	Yes	m	m	m	Yes	m	m	m	m	m	No	No	Yes
Other G20 Brazil	All programmes	No	a	a	a	a	a	a	a	a	a	a	a	a
Indonesia	All programmes	No	a	a	a	a	a	a	a	a	a	a	a	a
Russian Federation	All programmes	No	a	a	a	a	a	a	a	a	a	a	a	a
Saudi Arabia	All programmes	m	m	m	m	m	m	m	m	m	m	m	m	m

Levels of government
1: Central authority or government
2: State authorities or governments
3: Provincial/regional authorities or governments
4: Sub-regional or inter-municipal authorities or governments
5: Local authorities or governments
6: School, school board or committee
7: Private company

Percentage of students taking non-national examinations
1: All students
2: Between 76% and 99% of students
3: Between 51% and 75% of students
4: Between 26% and 50% of students
5: Between 11% and 25% of students
6: 10% or less of students

Note: Federal states or countries with highly decentralised school systems may have different regulations in states, provinces or regions. Please refer to Annex 3 for additional information.
1. Includes ISCED 3C programmes only.
Source: OECD. See Annex 3 for notes *(www.oecd.org/edu/eag2012)*.
Please refer to the Reader's Guide for information concerning the symbols replacing missing data.
StatLink ⬛⬛⬛⬛ http://dx.doi.org/10.1787/888932668869

D7

Table D7.2a. [2/2] Other (non-national) standardised examinations that are administered in multiple upper secondary schools (2011)

			How results are shared					
			Shared with external audience in addition to education authorities	Shared directly with school administrators	Shared directly with classroom teachers	Shared directly with parents	Shared directly with students	Shared directly with media
			(14)	(15)	(16)	(17)	(18)	(19)
OECD	Australia	All programmes	m	m	m	m	m	m
	Austria	All programmes	a	a	a	a	a	a
	Belgium (Fl.)	All programmes	a	a	a	a	a	a
	Belgium (Fr.)	All programmes	Yes	Yes	Yes	Yes	Yes	Yes
	Canada	All programmes	m	m	m	m	m	m
	Chile	All programmes	a	a	a	a	a	a
	Czech Republic	General	a	a	a	a	a	a
		Pre-voc. and voc.[1]	Yes	Yes	Yes	Yes	Yes	No
	Denmark	All programmes	a	a	a	a	a	a
	England	All programmes	a	a	a	a	a	a
	Estonia	General	a	a	a	a	a	a
		Pre-voc. and voc.	Yes	Yes	Yes	Yes	Yes	Yes
	Finland	All programmes	a	a	a	a	a	a
	France	All programmes	a	a	a	a	a	a
	Germany	General	a	a	a	a	a	a
		Pre-voc. and voc.	m	m	m	m	m	m
	Greece	All programmes	a	a	a	a	a	a
	Hungary	All programmes	a	a	a	a	a	a
	Iceland	All programmes	a	a	a	a	a	a
	Ireland	All programmes	a	a	a	a	a	a
	Israel	All programmes	a	a	a	a	a	a
	Italy	All programmes	a	a	a	a	a	a
	Japan	All programmes	a	a	a	a	a	a
	Korea	All programmes	a	a	a	a	a	a
	Luxembourg	All programmes	a	a	a	a	a	a
	Mexico	All programmes	a	a	a	a	a	a
	Netherlands	General	a	a	a	a	a	a
		Pre-voc. and voc.	No	a	a	a	a	a
	New Zealand	All programmes	m	m	m	m	m	m
	Norway	General	Yes	Yes	Yes	No	Yes	Yes
		Pre-voc. and voc.	Yes	Yes	Yes	No	Yes	Yes
	Poland	General	a	a	a	a	a	a
		Pre-voc. and voc.	m	m	m	m	m	m
	Portugal	All programmes	a	a	a	a	a	a
	Scotland	All programmes	a	a	a	a	a	a
	Slovak Republic	All programmes	a	a	a	a	a	a
	Slovenia	All programmes	m	m	m	m	m	m
	Spain	All programmes	a	a	a	a	a	a
	Sweden	All programmes	a	a	a	a	a	a
	Switzerland	All programmes	m	m	m	m	m	m
	Turkey	All programmes	a	a	a	a	a	a
	United States	All programmes	No	a	a	a	a	a
Other G20	Brazil	All programmes	a	a	a	a	a	a
	Indonesia	All programmes	a	a	a	a	a	a
	Russian Federation	All programmes	a	a	a	a	a	a
	Saudi Arabia	All programmes	m	m	m	m	m	m

Levels of government
1: Central authority or government
2: State authorities or governments
3: Provincial/regional authorities or governments
4: Sub-regional or inter-municipal authorities or governments
5: Local authorities or governments
6: School, school board or committee
7: Private company

Percentage of students taking non-national examinations
1: All students
2: Between 76% and 99% of students
3: Between 51% and 75% of students
4: Between 26% and 50% of students
5: Between 11% and 25% of students
6: 10% or less of students

Note: Federal states or countries with highly decentralised school systems may have different regulations in states, provinces or regions. Please refer to Annex 3 for additional information.
1. Includes ISCED 3C programmes only.
Source: OECD. See Annex 3 for notes (www.oecd.org/edu/eag2012).
Please refer to the Reader's Guide for information concerning the symbols replacing missing data.
StatLink http://dx.doi.org/10.1787/888932668869

D7

Table D7.3a. **Entrance examinations to enter the first stage of tertiary education (2011)**
Entrance examinations that are not administered by upper secondary schools to access tertiary-type A and B programmes

	Existence of tertiary entrance examinations (not administered by secondary schools)	Level of government at which they are devised and graded	Standardised/comparable	Compulsory for students to gain access to tertiary-type A and B programmes	Percentage of students taking them	Main purposes or uses						How results are shared					
						Only available route into tertiary education	Only available route into some fields of study	Student access to selective tertiary institutions	Student access to programme/faculty/discipline/field/specialisation	Decisions about scholarships/financial assistance for students	Other	Shared with external audience in addition to education authorities	Shared directly with school administrators	Shared directly with classroom teachers	Shared directly with parents	Shared directly with students	Shared directly with media
	(1)	(2)	(3)	(4)	(5)	(6)	(7)	(8)	(9)	(10)	(11)	(12)	(13)	(14)	(15)	(16)	(17)
OECD																	
Australia	3	1	Yes	No	m	No	Yes	No	Yes	No	No	Yes	Yes	No	No	Yes	No
Austria	3	6	No	No	5	No	Yes	Yes	Yes	No	No	No	a	a	a	a	a
Belgium (Fl.)	3	2, 6	Yes	No	m	No	Yes	No	Yes	No	No	Yes	No	No	No	Yes	No
Belgium (Fr.)	3	6	No	No	6	No	Yes	No	Yes	No	No	Yes	No	No	No	Yes	No
Canada	m	m	m	m	m	m	m	m	m	m	m	m	m	m	m	m	m
Chile	1	6	Yes	Yes	2	Yes	Yes	Yes	Yes	Yes	No	Yes	Yes	Yes	Yes	Yes	Yes
Czech Republic	2	6	No	No	m	No	No	No	Yes	No	No	Yes	No	No	No	Yes	No
Denmark	3	6	No	No	6	No	Yes	No	No	No	No	No	a	a	a	a	a
England	3	6	No	No	6	No	No	No	Yes	No	No	Yes	No	No	No	Yes	No
Estonia	2	6	No	No	m	No	No	Yes	Yes	No	No	Yes	m	m	m	Yes	m
Finland	2	6	No	No	2	No	Yes	Yes	Yes	No	No	Yes	Yes	No	No	Yes	No
France	3	6	No	No	6	No	Yes	Yes	Yes	No	No	Yes	No	No	No	Yes	No
Germany	3	6	No	No	m	No	Yes	Yes	Yes	No	No	Yes	No	No	No	Yes	No
Greece	1	1	Yes	Yes	2	No	Yes	No	Yes	No	Yes	Yes	Yes	No	No	Yes	No
Hungary	3	6	No	No	6	No	Yes	No	No	No	No	Yes	No	No	No	Yes	No
Iceland	4	a	a	a	a	a	a	a	a	a	a	a	a	a	a	a	a
Ireland	3	6	Yes	No	6	No	Yes	No	Yes	No	m	Yes	Yes	No	No	Yes	No
Israel	2	6	Yes	Yes[1]	2	No	Yes	Yes	Yes	Yes	No	Yes	No	No	No	Yes	No
Italy	2	1, 6	No	Yes	2	Yes	Yes	No	Yes	No	No	Yes	No	No	No	Yes	No
Japan	1	6	No	No	3	Yes	Yes	Yes	Yes	m	m	Yes	No	No	No	Yes	No
Korea	1	1	Yes	No	m	No	No	Yes	No	No	No	Yes	Yes	Yes	No	Yes	No
Luxembourg	3	6	No	Yes	6	No	Yes	No	Yes	No	No	Yes	Yes	No	No	Yes	No
Mexico	1	6	No	Yes	m	No	No	Yes	Yes	No	No	No	a	a	a	a	a
Netherlands	4	a	a	a	a	a	a	a	a	a	a	a	a	a	a	a	a
New Zealand	m	m	m	m	m	m	m	m	m	m	m	m	m	m	m	m	m
Norway	3	6	No	No	6	No	Yes	No	Yes	No	No	Yes	No	No	No	Yes	No
Poland	3	6	No	No	6	No	Yes	No	Yes	No	No	Yes	No	No	No	Yes	No
Portugal	4	a	a	a	a	a	a	a	a	a	a	a	a	a	a	a	a
Scotland	3	6	No	No	m	No	No	No	Yes	No	No	m	m	m	m	m	m
Slovak Republic	3	6	No	No	m	No	Yes	Yes	Yes	No	No	Yes	No	No	No	Yes	No
Slovenia	m	m	m	m	m	m	m	m	m	m	m	m	m	m	m	m	m
Spain	2	2	Yes	Yes[2]	3	No	Yes	Yes	Yes	No	No	Yes	Yes	Yes	Yes	Yes	Yes
Sweden	1	1	Yes	Yes	m	No	No	No	Yes	No	m	Yes	No	No	No	Yes	No
Switzerland	3	2, 6	No	No	m	m	m	m	m	m	m	m	m	m	m	m	m
Turkey	1	1	Yes	Yes	3	Yes	Yes	Yes	Yes	No	No	Yes	Yes	Yes	Yes	Yes	Yes
United States	2	7	Yes	No	4	No	No	Yes	Yes	Yes	No	Yes	Yes	Yes	Yes	Yes	Yes
Other G20																	
Brazil	1	1, 6	Yes	No	2	No	No	Yes	Yes	Yes	No	Yes	Yes	No	No	Yes	Yes
Indonesia	1	6	No	Yes	3	Yes	Yes	Yes	Yes	Yes	No	Yes	Yes	No	No	Yes	No
Russian Federation	4	a	a	a	a	a	a	a	a	a	a	a	a	a	a	a	a
Saudi Arabia	m	m	m	m	m	m	m	m	m	m	m	m	m	m	m	m	m

Existence of tertiary entrance examinations
1: Yes, for all fields of study
2: Yes, for most (more than half) fields of study
3: Yes, for some fields of study
4: No

Levels of government
1: Central authority or government
2: State authorities or governments
3: Provincial/regional authorities or governments
4: Sub-regional or inter-municipal authorities or governments
5: Local authorities or governments
6: Individual tertiary institute or consortium of tertiary institutes
7: Private company

Percentage of students taking entrance examinations
1: All students
2: Between 76% and 99% of students
3: Between 51% and 75% of students
4: Between 26% and 50% of students
5: Between 11% and 25% of students
6: 10% or less of students

Note: Federal states or countries with highly decentralised school systems may have different regulations in states, provinces or regions. Refer to Annex 3 for additional information.
1. Except to access ISCED 5B tertiary programmes.
2. Except to access ISCED 5B tertiary programmes after completion of general upper secondary education.
Source: OECD. See Annex 3 for notes *(www.oecd.org/edu/eag2012)*.
Please refer to the Reader's Guide for information concerning the symbols replacing missing data.
StatLink ꜱᴛꜱ http://dx.doi.org/10.1787/888932668945

Table D7.4a. Factors, criteria or special circumstances used by tertiary institutions to determine access to the first stage of tertiary education (2011)

Factors, criteria or special circumstances (other than examinations) used by tertiary institutions to determine access to tertiary-type A and B programmes

	Existence of additional criteria or special circumstances for entry into tertiary education	Grade Point Average from secondary schools		Ethnicity of applicant		Family income of applicant		Previous work experience		Past service or volunteer work		Recommendations		Applicant letter or written rationale to justify admission		Other	
		Factor used	Level of importance	Factor used	Level of importance	Factor used	Level of importance	Factor used	Level of importance	Factor used	Level of importance	Factor used	Level of importance	Factor used	Level of importance	Factor used	Level of importance
	(1)	(2)	(3)	(4)	(5)	(6)	(7)	(8)	(9)	(10)	(11)	(12)	(13)	(14)	(15)	(16)	(17)
OECD																	
Australia	Yes	No	a	Yes	m	Yes	m	Yes	m	m	m	m	m	Yes	m	Yes	m
Austria	No	a	a	a	a	a	a	a	a	a	a	a	a	a	a	a	a
Belgium (Fl.)	Yes	No	a	No	a	No	a	No	a	No	a	No	a	No	a	Yes	4
Belgium (Fr.)	Yes	No	a	No	a	No	a	No	a	No	a	a	a	No	a	Yes	4
Canada	m	m	m	m	m	m	m	m	m	m	m	m	m	m	m	m	m
Chile	Yes	Yes	3	No	a	No	a	No	a	No	a	No	a	No	a	Yes	3
Czech Republic	Yes	Yes	m	No	a	No	a	No	a	No	a	No	a	No	a	Yes	m
Denmark	Yes	Yes	4	No	a	No	a	Yes	3	Yes	2	No	a	Yes	3	m	m
England	Yes	a	a	No	a	No	a	Yes	2	Yes	2	Yes	4	Yes	4	Yes	4
Estonia	Yes	m	m	m	m	m	m	m	m	m	m	m	m	m	m	m	m
Finland	Yes	Yes	m	No	a	No	a	Yes	m	Yes	m	No	a	Yes	m	Yes	m
France	Yes	Yes	4	No	a	Yes	3	Yes	3	No	a	No	a	Yes	3	Yes	3
Germany	Yes	Yes	m	Yes	m	No	a	Yes	m	Yes	m	Yes	m	Yes	m	No	a
Greece	Yes	No	a	No	a	No	a	No	a	No	a	No	a	No	a	Yes	2
Hungary	Yes	Yes	4	No	a	Yes	2	No	a	No	a	No	a	No	a	Yes	2
Iceland	Yes	a	a	No	a	No	a	No	a	No	a	No	a	No	a	Yes	4
Ireland	Yes	No	a	No	a	Yes	m	Yes	m	No	a	No	a	No	a	No	a
Israel	Yes	Yes	4	Yes	4	Yes	m	Yes	m	Yes	m	Yes	3	No	a	Yes	m
Italy	Yes	Yes	2	Yes	m	No	a	No	a	No	a	No	a	No	a	No	a
Japan	Yes	Yes	m	No	a	No	a	m	m	m	m	m	m	Yes	4	m	m
Korea	Yes	Yes	4	No	a	Yes	2	Yes	2	Yes	2	Yes	2	Yes	2	Yes	2
Luxembourg	Yes	Yes	3	No	a	No	a	No	a	No	a	No	a	No	a	Yes	4
Mexico	Yes	Yes	4	No	a	Yes	3	No	a	No	a	No	a	No	a	Yes	3
Netherlands	Yes	Yes	2	No	a	No	a	No	a	No	a	No	a	No	a	Yes	2
New Zealand	m	m	m	m	m	m	m	m	m	m	m	m	m	m	m	m	m
Norway	Yes	Yes	4	Yes	2	No	a	Yes	2	Yes	2	No	a	No	a	Yes	3
Poland	Yes	Yes	4	No	a	No	a	No	a	No	a	No	a	No	a	Yes	3
Portugal	Yes	Yes	4	No	a	No	a	No	a	No	a	No	a	No	a	Yes	4
Scotland	Yes	a	a	No	a	No	a	Yes	m	Yes	m	Yes	m	Yes	2	Yes	4
Slovak Republic	Yes	Yes	m	No	a	No	a	Yes	m	m	m	m	m	m	m	m	m
Slovenia	m	m	m	m	m	m	m	m	m	m	m	m	m	m	m	m	m
Spain	Yes	Yes	4	No	a	No	a	No	a	No	a	No	a	No	a	No	a
Sweden	Yes	Yes	4	No	a	No	a	Yes	2	Yes	2	No	a	Yes	2	Yes	m
Switzerland	m	m	m	m	m	m	m	m	m	m	m	m	m	m	m	m	m
Turkey	No	a	a	a	a	a	a	a	a	a	a	a	a	a	a	a	a
United States	Yes	Yes	3	No	a	No	a	Yes	2	Yes	2	Yes	2	Yes	3	Yes	3
Other G20																	
Brazil	Yes	No	a	Yes	3	Yes	4	No	a	No	a	No	a	No	a	Yes	m
Indonesia	No	a	a	a	a	a	a	a	a	a	a	a	a	a	a	a	a
Russian Federation	Yes	No	a	No	a	No	a	No	a	No	a	No	a	No	a	Yes	4
Saudi Arabia	m	m	m	m	m	m	m	m	m	m	m	m	m	m	m	m	m

Levels of importance
1: No importance
2: Low level of importance
3: Moderate level of importance
4: High level of importance

Note: Federal states or countries with highly decentralised school systems may have different regulations in states, provinces or regions. Refer to Annex 3 for additional information.

Source: OECD. See Annex 3 for notes (*www.oecd.org/edu/eag2012*).

Please refer to the Reader's Guide for information concerning the symbols replacing missing data.

StatLink ᠍ᡖ᠍ http://dx.doi.org/10.1787/888932668983

Annex

1

CHARACTERISTICS OF EDUCATIONAL SYSTEMS

Annex 1

Table X1.1a. [1/2] Upper secondary graduation rate: Typical graduation ages and method used to calculate graduation rates (2010)

The typical age refers to the age of the students at the beginning of the school year; students will generally be one year older than the age indicated when they graduate at the end of the school year. The typical age is used for the gross graduation rate calculation.

| | | Typical graduation ages | | | | | |
| | | Programme orientation | | Educational/labour market destination | | | |
	First-time	General programmes	Pre-vocational or vocational programmes	ISCED 3A programmes	ISCED 3B programmes	ISCED 3C short programmes[1]	ISCED 3C long programmes[1]
OECD							
Australia	17	17	17	17	a	a	17
Austria	17-18	17-18	17-19	17-18	17-19	14-15	16-17
Belgium	18	18	18	18	a	18	18
Canada	17-18	17-18	17-18	17-18	a	a	17-18
Chile	17	17	17	17	a	a	a
Czech Republic	18-19	19	18	19	19	a	18
Denmark	18-19	18-19	20-21	18-19	a	27	20-21
Estonia	18	18	18	18	18	18	a
Finland	19	19	19	19	a	a	a
France	17-18	17-18	16-20	17-18	18-20	16-20	17-22
Germany	19-20	19-20	19-20	19-20	19-20	19-20	a
Greece	18	18	18	18	a	18	18
Hungary	18	18	18-19	18	a	18	18-19
Iceland	19	19	17	19	20	17	19
Ireland	18-19	18	19	18	a	19	18
Israel	17	17	17	17	a	a	17
Italy	18	18	18	18	18	17	a
Japan	17	17	17	17	17	15	17
Korea	18	18	18	18	a	a	18
Luxembourg	17-20	17-18	17-20	17-19	18-20	16-18	17-19
Mexico	17-18	17-18	17-18	17-18	a	a	17-18
Netherlands	17-19	17	19	17	a	a	18
New Zealand	17-18	17-18	17-18	17-18	17-18	16	17-18
Norway	18-20	18	19-20	18	a	m	19-20
Poland	19-20	19	20	19	a	a	19
Portugal	17	17	17-19	m	m	m	m
Slovak Republic	18-19	19	19	19	a	17	18
Slovenia	18	18	16-18	18	18	16	17
Spain	17	17	17	17	17	17	17
Sweden	18	18	18	18	18	18	18
Switzerland	18-20	18-20	18-20	18-20	18-20	17-19	18-20
Turkey	17	17	17	17	a	m	a
United Kingdom	16	16	16	18	18	16	16
United States	17	17	m	17	m	m	m
Other G20							
Argentina	m	17	17	17	a	a	a
Brazil	17-18	17-18	18-19	17-18	18-19	a	a
China	17	17	17	17	m	17	17
India	m	m	m	m	m	m	m
Indonesia	17	17	17	17	17	a	a
Russian Federation	17	17	17	17	17	16	17
Saudi Arabia	m	m	m	m	m	m	m
South Africa	m	m	m	m	m	m	m

1. Duration categories for ISCED 3C – short: at least one year shorter than ISCED 3A/3B programmes; long: of similar duration to ISCED 3A or 3B programmes.
Source: OECD. Argentina, China and Indonesia: UNESCO Institute for Statistics (World Education Indicators programme). See Annex 3 for notes (*www.oecd.org/edu/eag2012*).
Please refer to the Reader's Guide for information concerning the symbols replacing missing data.
StatLink ᠁᠍᠍ http://dx.doi.org/10.1787/888932669059

Table X1.1a. [2/2] Upper secondary graduation rate: Typical graduation ages and method used to calculate graduation rates (2010)

	First-time	Graduation rate calculation: gross versus net					
		Programme orientation		Educational/labour market destination			
		General programmes	Pre-vocational or vocational programmes	ISCED 3A programmes	ISCED 3B programmes	ISCED 3C short programmes[1]	ISCED 3C long programmes[1]
OECD							
Australia	m	net	net	net	a	a	net
Austria	m	net	net	net	net	net	net
Belgium	m	net	net	net	a	net	net
Canada	net	net	net	net	a	a	net
Chile	net	net	net	net	a	a	a
Czech Republic	gross	gross	gross	gross	gross	a	gross
Denmark	net	net	net	net	a	net	net
Estonia	m	net	net	net	net	net	a
Finland	net	net	net	net	a	a	a
France	m	net	net	net	net	net	net
Germany	gross	gross	gross	gross	gross	gross	a
Greece	net	net	net	net	a	m	net
Hungary	net	net	net	net	a	m	net
Iceland	net	net	net	net	net	net	net
Ireland	net	net	net	net	a	net	net
Israel	net	net	net	net	a	a	net
Italy	gross	net	gross	net	gross	gross	a
Japan	gross	gross	gross	gross	gross	m	gross
Korea	gross	gross	gross	gross	a	a	gross
Luxembourg	net	net	net	net	net	net	net
Mexico	net	net	net	net	a	a	net
Netherlands	m	net	net	net	a	a	net
New Zealand	m	m	m	m	m	m	m
Norway	net	net	net	net	a	m	net
Poland	net	net	net	net	a	a	net
Portugal	net	net	net	m	m	m	m
Slovak Republic	net	net	net	net	a	net	net
Slovenia	gross	net	gross	net	gross	net	gross
Spain	gross	gross	gross	gross	gross	gross	gross
Sweden	net	net	net	net	n	n	net
Switzerland	m	gross	gross	gross	gross	gross	gross
Turkey	net	net	net	net	a	m	a
United Kingdom	gross	m	m	m	m	gross	gross
United States	net	m	m	m	m	m	m
Other G20							
Argentina	m	net	net	net	a	a	a
Brazil	m	net	net	net	net	a	a
China	gross	gross	gross	gross	m	gross	gross
India	m	m	m	m	m	m	m
Indonesia	m	net	net	net	net	a	a
Russian Federation	m	gross	gross	gross	gross	gross	gross
Saudi Arabia	m	m	m	m	m	m	m
South Africa	m	m	m	m	m	m	m

1. Duration categories for ISCED 3C – short: at least one year shorter than ISCED 3A/3B programmes; long: of similar duration to ISCED 3A or 3B programmes.
Source: OECD. Argentina, China and Indonesia: UNESCO Institute for Statistics (World Education Indicators programme). See Annex 3 for notes (*www.oecd.org/edu/eag2012*).
Please refer to the Reader's Guide for information concerning the symbols replacing missing data.
StatLink ⟨⟨⟩⟩ http://dx.doi.org/10.1787/888932670294

Annex 1

Table X1.1b. Post-secondary non-tertiary graduation rates: Typical graduation ages and method used to calculate graduation rates (2010)

The typical age refers to the age of the students at the beginning of the school year; students will generally be one year older than the age indicated when they graduate at the end of the school year. The typical age is used for the gross graduation rate calculation.

	Typical graduation ages				Graduation rate calculation: Gross versus net			
		Educational/labour market destination				Educational/labour market destination		
	First-time	ISCED 4A programmes	ISCED 4B programmes	ISCED 4C programmes	First-time graduates	ISCED 4A programmes	ISCED 4B programmes	ISCED 4C programmes
OECD								
Australia	18-20	a	a	18-20	net	a	a	net
Austria	18-19	18-19	19-20	23-24	m	net	net	net
Belgium	19-21	19	19-21	19-21	m	net	net	net
Canada	m	m	m	30-34	m	m	m	m
Chile	a	a	a	a	a	a	a	a
Czech Republic	20-22	20-22	a	20-22	gross	gross	a	gross
Denmark	21	21	a	a	net	net	a	a
Estonia	20	a	20	a	m	a	net	a
Finland	35-39	a	a	35-39	net	a	a	net
France	21-24	21-24	a	21-24	m	gross	a	gross
Germany	22	22	22	a	gross	gross	gross	a
Greece	a	a	a	m	m	m	m	m
Hungary	a	a	a	19-20	net	a	a	net
Iceland	27	m	m	27	net	n	n	net
Ireland	23	a	a	23	net	a	a	net
Israel	m	m	m	a	m	m	m	a
Italy	21-22	a	a	21-22	net	a	a	net
Japan	18	18	18	18	m	m	m	m
Korea	a	a	a	a	a	a	a	a
Luxembourg	21-25	a	a	21-25	net	a	a	net
Mexico	a	a	a	a	a	a	a	a
Netherlands	20	a	a	20	m	a	a	net
New Zealand	18	18	18	18	net	net	net	net
Norway	20-22	20-21	a	21-22	net	net	a	net
Poland	21	a	a	21	net	a	a	net
Portugal	20-21	m	m	m	net	m	m	m
Slovak Republic	21	21	a	a	net	net	a	a
Slovenia	19-20	19-20	19-20	a	net	net	net	a
Spain	a	a	a	a	a	a	a	a
Sweden	19-22	m	m	19-22	net	n	n	net
Switzerland	21-23	21-23	21-23	a	m	gross	gross	a
Turkey	a	a	a	a	a	a	a	a
United Kingdom	m	m	m	m	n	n	n	n
United States	m	m	m	m	m	m	m	m
Other G20								
Argentina	a	a	a	a	a	a	a	a
Brazil	a	a	a	a	a	a	a	a
China	m	m	m	m	m	m	m	m
India	m	m	m	m	m	m	m	m
Indonesia	a	a	a	a	a	a	a	a
Russian Federation	18	a	a	18	m	a	a	gross
Saudi Arabia	m	m	m	m	m	m	m	m
South Africa	m	m	m	m	m	m	m	m

Source: OECD. Argentina and Indonesia: UNESCO Institute for Statistics (World Education Indicators programme). See Annex 3 for notes (*www.oecd.org/edu/eag2012*).
Please refer to the Reader's Guide for information concerning the symbols replacing missing data.
StatLink 🔗 http://dx.doi.org/10.1787/888932669078

Table X1.1c. [1/2] Tertiary graduation rate: Typical graduation ages and method used to calculate graduation rates (2010)

The typical age refers to the age of the students at the beginning of the school year; students will generally be one year older than the age indicated when they graduate at the end of the school year. The typical age is used for the gross graduation rate calculation.

	First-time tertiary-type B	Tertiary-type B (first degree)	First-time tertiary-type A	Tertiary-type A (first and second degrees)			Advanced research programmes
				3 to less than 5 years	5 to 6 years	More than 6 years	
OECD Australia	20-21	20-21	21-22	21-22	22-23	24	25-26
Austria	21-23	21-23	23-25	22-24	24-26	a	27-29
Belgium	21-22	21-22	21	m	m	m	27-29
Canada	21-24	21-24	22-24	22	23-24	25	27-29
Chile	22-25	22-25	24-26	23-26	24-26	25-27	30-34
Czech Republic	22-23	22-23	22-24	22-24	25-26	a	30-34
Denmark	23-25	23-25	24	24	26	25-29	30-34
Estonia	21-22	21-22	21-23	21	23	a	30-34
Finland	30-34	30-34	24-26	24	a	a	30-34
France	19-23	19-23	19-24	19-22	21-24	27-29	26-28
Germany	21-23	21-23	24-27	24-26	25-27	a	28-29
Greece	24-25	24-25	23-24	23-24	23-24	a	30-34
Hungary	20	20	22-24	21-23	23-24	a	30-34
Iceland	24	24	23	23	25	n	30-34
Ireland	20-21	20-21	21	21	23	25	27
Israel	m	m	26	26	28-29	a	30-34
Italy	22-23	22-23	23	23	25	a	30-34
Japan	19	19	21-23	21	23	24	26
Korea	20	20	22-24	22-26	24-25	a	30-34
Luxembourg	m	m	m	m	m	m	m
Mexico	20	20	23	23	23-26	m	24-28
Netherlands	m	29	23	23	a	a	28-29
New Zealand	19-21	19-21	21-23	21-23	23	24	27-28
Norway	21-22	21-22	22-27	22-23	24-25	26-27	28-29
Poland	22	22	23-25	23	25	a	25-29
Portugal	25-29	25-29	22	22	22-24	26-28	30-34
Slovak Republic	21-22	21-22	21-22	21-22	23-24	a	26-29
Slovenia	22-25	22-25	24-25	24-25	24-25	n	28
Spain	19-21	19-21	22-23	20-22	22-23	a	30-34
Sweden	21-23	21-23	25	25	25	n	30-34
Switzerland	23-29	23-29	24-26	24-26	25-27	25-27	30-34
Turkey	21	21	22-24	22-23	25-26	30-34	30-34
United Kingdom	19-24	19-24	20-25	20-22	22-24	23-25	25-29
United States	19	19	21	21	23	24	26
Other G20 Argentina	m	20-24	m	20-24	25-29	a	25-29
Brazil	m	m	22-24	22-24	m	m	30-34
China	m	m	m	m	m	m	m
India	m	m	m	m	m	m	m
Indonesia	m	24	m	24	24	24	25-27
Russian Federation	20	20	22	21	22	23	25-26
Saudi Arabia	20-24	20-24	20-24	m	m	m	25-29
South Africa	m	m	m	m	m	m	m

Note: Where tertiary-type A data are available by duration of programme, the graduation rate for all programmes is the sum of the graduation rates by duration of programme.
Source: OECD. Argentina and Indonesia: UNESCO Institute for Statistics (World Education Indicators programme). Saudi Arabia: Observatory on Higher Education. See Annex 3 for notes *(www.oecd.org/edu/eag2012).*
Please refer to the Reader's Guide for information concerning the symbols replacing missing data.
StatLink ᵐˢᴸ http://dx.doi.org/10.1787/888932669097

Table X1.1c. [2/2] Tertiary graduation rate: Typical graduation ages and method used to calculate graduation rates (2010)

	Graduation rate calculation: Gross versus net											
	Tertiary-type B (ISCED 5B)				Tertiary-type A (ISCED 5A)						Advanced research programmes (ISCED 6)	
	First-time		First degree		First-time		First degree		Second degree			
	Graduation rate (all students)	Graduation rate for international/foreign students only	Graduation rate (all students)	Graduation rate for international/foreign students only	Graduation rate (all students)	Graduation rate for international/foreign students only	Graduation rate (all students)	Graduation rate for international/foreign students only	Graduation rate (all students)	Graduation rate for international/foreign students only	Graduation rate (all students)	Graduation rate for international/foreign students only
Australia	net	net	net	net	net	net	net	net	net	net	net	net
Austria	net	net	net	net	net	net	net	net	net	net	net	net
Belgium	m	m	net	net	m	m	net	net	net	net	net	net
Canada	net	net	net	net	net	net	net	net	net	net	net	net
Chile	m	m	net	m	m	m	net	m	net	m	net	m
Czech Republic	net	m	net	net	net	m	net	m	net	m	net	m
Denmark	net	net	net	net	net	net	net	net	net	net	net	net
Estonia	m	m	net	m	m	m	net	m	net	m	net	m
Finland	net	n	net	n	net	net	net	net	net	net	net	net
France	m	m	gross	m	m	m	gross	m	gross	m	gross	m
Germany	gross	m	gross	m	net	net	net	net	net	net	net	net
Greece	m	m	m	m	m	m	m	m	m	m	m	m
Hungary	net	m	net	m	net	m	net	m	net	m	net	m
Iceland	net	net	net	net	net	net	net	net	net	net	net	net
Ireland	net	net	net	net	net	net	net	net	net	net	net	net
Israel	m	m	m	m	net	m	net	m	net	m	net	m
Italy	gross	m	gross	gross	net	m	net	m	m	m	m	m
Japan	gross	gross	gross	gross	gross	gross	gross	gross	gross	gross	gross	gross
Korea	m	m	net	m	m	m	net	m	net	m	net	m
Luxembourg	m	m	m	m	m	m	m	m	m	m	m	m
Mexico	net	m	net	m	net	m	net	m	gross	m	gross	m
Netherlands	net	net	net	m	net	net	net	net	net	net	gross	m
New Zealand	net	net	net	net	net	net	net	net	net	net	net	net
Norway	net	net	net	net	net	net	net	net	net	net	net	net
Poland	net	m	net	m	net	net	net	net	gross	net	gross	gross
Portugal	net	net	net	net	net	net	net	net	net	net	net	net
Slovak Republic	net	m	net	m	net	net	net	net	net	net	net	net
Slovenia	net	net	net	net	net	net	net	net	net	net	net	net
Spain	net	m	net	m	net	m	net	m	net	m	net	m
Sweden	net	net	net	net	net	net	net	net	net	net	net	net
Switzerland	gross	m	gross	m	net	m	net	net	net	net	net	net
Turkey	net	m	net	m	gross	m	net	m	net	m	net	m
United Kingdom	net	m	net	net	net	m	net	net	net	net	net	net
United States	gross	gross	gross	gross	gross	gross	gross	gross	gross	gross	gross	gross
Argentina	m	m	gross	m	m	m	gross	m	gross	m	gross	m
Brazil	m	m	net	m	m	m	net	m	net	m	net	m
China	m	m	gross	m	m	m	gross	m	gross	m	gross	m
India	m	m	m	m	m	m	m	m	m	m	m	m
Indonesia	m	m	net	m	m	m	net	m	net	m	net	m
Russian Federation	m	m	gross	m	m	m	gross	m	gross	m	gross	m
Saudi Arabia	gross	m	gross	m	gross	m	gross	m	gross	m	gross	m
South Africa	m	m	gross	m	m	m	gross	m	gross	m	gross	m

Source: OECD. Argentina, China and Indonesia: UNESCO Institute for Statistics (World Education Indicators programme). Saudi Arabia: Observatory on Higher Education. South Africa: UNESCO Institute for Statistics. See Annex 3 for notes (*www.oecd.org/edu/eag2012*).
Please refer to the Reader's Guide for information concerning the symbols replacing missing data.
StatLink ᴍᴘᴸ http://dx.doi.org/10.1787/888932670313

Table X1.1d. Tertiary entry rate: Typical age of entry and method used to calculate entry rates (2010)

		Typical age of entry		Entry rate calculation: Gross versus net — All students			Entry rate calculation: Gross versus net — International students		
	ISCED 5A	ISCED 5B	ISCED 6	ISCED 5A	ISCED 5B	ISCED 6	ISCED 5A	ISCED 5B	ISCED 6
OECD									
Australia	18	18	22-23	net	m	net	net	m	net
Austria	19-20	20-21	25-26	net	net	net	net	net	net
Belgium	18	18	m	net	net	m	net	net	m
Canada	m	m	m	m	m	m	m	m	m
Chile	18-19	18-19	24-28	net	net	net	m	m	m
Czech Republic	19-20	19-20	24-25	net	net	net	m	m	m
Denmark	20-21	20-22	25-27	net	net	net	net	net	net
Estonia	19	19	24	net	net	net	m	m	m
Finland	19	19	m	net	a	m	m	a	m
France	m	m	m	m	m	m	m	m	m
Germany	19-21	18-21	m	net	net	m	net	m	m
Greece	m	m	m	m	m	m	m	m	m
Hungary	19	19	24	net	net	net	m	m	m
Iceland	20	20	25	net	net	net	net	net	net
Ireland	18	18	m	net	net	m	net	net	m
Israel	22-24	18	27-29	net	net	net	m	m	m
Italy	19	19	24	net	gross	gross	m	m	m
Japan	18	18	24	net	net	net	m	m	m
Korea	18	18	24-29	net	net	net	m	m	m
Luxembourg	m	m	m	net	net	net	m	m	m
Mexico	18	18	24	net	net	net	m	m	m
Netherlands	18-19	17-18	m	net	net	m	net	net	m
New Zealand	18	18	23-24	net	net	net	net	net	net
Norway	19-20	19	26-27	net	net	net	net	net	net
Poland	19-20	19-20	m	net	net	m	net	m	m
Portugal	18	22	24-29	net	net	net	net	net	net
Slovak Republic	19	19	24	net	net	net	net	m	net
Slovenia	19	19-20	24-26	net	net	net	net	net	net
Spain	18	19-20	23-27	net	net	net	m	m	m
Sweden	19	19	24	net	net	net	net	net	net
Switzerland	19-21	21-25	25-27	net	net	net	net	m	net
Turkey	18-19	18-19	25-26	net	net	net	m	m	m
United Kingdom	18	18	23	net	net	net	net	net	net
United States	18	18	24	net	m	m	m	m	m
Other G20									
Argentina	18	18	23	net	net	gross	m	m	m
Brazil	m	m	m	m	m	m	m	m	m
China	15-19	15-19	20-24	gross	gross	gross	m	m	m
India	m	m	m	m	m	m	m	m	m
Indonesia	18	18	25	net	net	net	m	m	m
Russian Federation	18	18	23-24	gross	gross	gross	m	m	m
Saudi Arabia	18	18	m	gross	gross	gross	m	m	m
South Africa	m	m	m	m	m	m	m	m	m

Source: OECD. Argentina, China, Indonesia: UNESCO Institute for Statistics (World Education Indicators programme). Saudi Arabia: Observatory on Higher Education. See Annex 3 for notes (*www.oecd.org/edu/eag2012*).
Please refer to the Reader's Guide for information concerning the symbols replacing missing data.
StatLink ᐃᔕᐃ http://dx.doi.org/10.1787/888932669116

Table X1.2a. **School year and financial year used for the calculation of indicators, OECD countries**

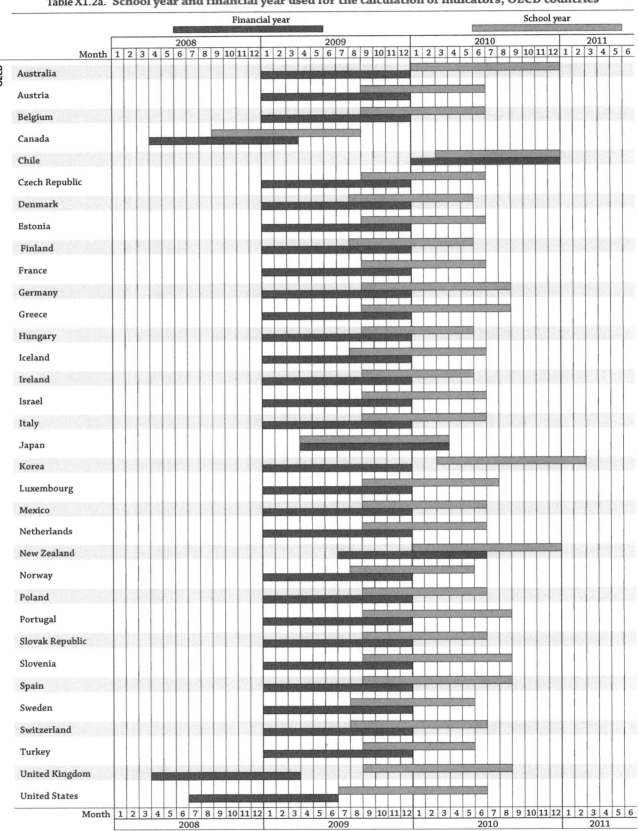

Table X1.2b.   **School year and financial year used for the calculation of indicators, other G20 countries**

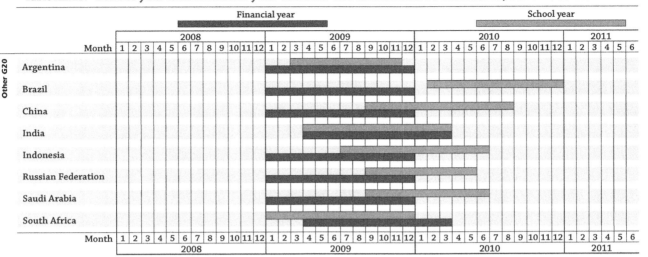

Source: OECD. Argentina, China, India, Indonesia, Saudi Arabia, South Africa: UNESCO Institute for Statistics. See Annex 3 for notes *(www.oecd.org/edu/eag2012)*.
StatLink ᵃⁱˢᵖ http://dx.doi.org/10.1787/888932669154

Annex

2

REFERENCE STATISTICS

Table X2.1. Overview of the economic context using basic variables
(reference period: calendar year 2009, 2009 current prices)

	Total public expenditure as a percentage of GDP	GDP per capita (in equivalent USD converted using PPPs)	GDP deflator (2005 = 100)	GDP deflator (2000 = 100)	Average exchange rates between 2007 and 2009[1]	Purchasing power parity for private consumption (PPP) (USD = 1, 2009)[1]
	(1)	(2)	(3)	(4)	(5)	(6)
Australia	35.1	39 971	115.0	136.9	1.22	1.55
Austria	52.9	38 834	106.9	115.7	0.71	0.87
Belgium	53.8	36 698	108.3	120.2	0.71	0.92
Canada[2]	39.1	38 522	108.2	121.8	1.09	1.31
Chile[3]	20.6	15 107	122.2	161.9	535.26	372.03
Czech Republic	44.9	25 614	107.9	121.3	18.81	14.95
Denmark	58.0	38 299	110.0	123.4	5.30	8.72
Estonia	45.2	19 789	126.6	162.7	0.71	0.62
Finland	55.6	35 848	108.0	112.9	0.71	1.01
France	56.7	33 724	108.0	119.0	0.71	0.92
Germany	48.1	36 048	103.9	109.6	0.71	0.85
Greece	m	29 381	114.3	134.0	0.71	0.78
Hungary	51.3	20 154	119.0	163.2	186.03	145.51
Iceland	51.0	36 718	139.2	169.4	91.88	137.48
Ireland	48.6	39 750	98.3	119.3	0.71	1.02
Israel	42.9	27 454	109.1	116.2	3.88	4.42
Italy	51.7	32 397	109.0	124.4	0.71	0.85
Japan	42.4	32 324	97.0	90.7	104.89	126.04
Korea	33.1	27 171	108.5	124.9	1 102.75	903.08
Luxembourg	43.0	82 972	115.6	133.4	0.71	0.98
Mexico	26.2	14 397	125.1	174.5	11.86	8.83
Netherlands	51.5	41 089	105.4	121.3	0.71	0.88
New Zealand	34.1	29 204	111.6	126.4	1.46	1.61
Norway	46.7	54 708	116.3	137.9	5.93	9.58
Poland	44.4	18 910	112.8	128.0	2.77	2.02
Portugal	49.9	24 580	108.3	126.0	0.71	0.72
Slovak Republic	41.5	22 620	105.8	131.7	0.75	0.59
Slovenia	49.3	27 150	114.0	147.7	0.71	0.68
Spain	46.3	32 146	110.2	135.5	0.71	0.79
Sweden	55.1	37 192	110.0	117.8	7.00	9.24
Switzerland	33.7	44 773	107.3	110.5	1.12	1.69
Turkey	m	14 442	137.0	426.8	1.38	1.12
United Kingdom	51.4	34 483	110.7	123.4	0.56	0.69
United States	42.7	45 087	109.7	123.7	1.00	1.00
Argentina	m	14 677	m	m	m	m
Brazil	34.0	11 155	127.4	201.5	1.9	m
China	m	m	m	m	m	m
India	m	2 976	m	m	m	m
Indonesia	m	4 394	m	m	m	m
Russian Federation	m	18 882	157.7	346.8	27.4	15.42
Saudi Arabia	m	m	m	m	m	m
South Africa	m	2 139	m	m	m	m

1. The average exchange rate and the Purchasing Power Parity for private consumption (PPP) are used in Indicator A11.
2. Year of reference 2008.
3. Year of reference 2010.
Source: OECD. See Annex 3 for notes (*www.oecd.org/edu/eag2012*).
Please refer to the Reader's Guide for information concerning the symbols replacing missing data.
StatLink ⬛ℝ⬛ http://dx.doi.org/10.1787/888932669173

Table X2.2a. Basic reference statistics (reference period: calendar year 2009, 2009 current prices)[1]

	Gross domestic product (in millions of local currency)[2]	Gross domestic product (adjusted to financial year)[3]	Total public expenditure (in millions of local currency)	Total population in thousand (mid-year estimates)	Purchasing power parity for GDP (PPP) (USD = 1)	Purchasing power parity for GDP (PPP) (Euro Zone = 1)	Purchasing power parity for private consumption (PPP) (USD = 1)
	(1)	(2)	(3)	(4)	(5)	(6)	(7)
OECD Australia	1 284 670		450 682	22 163	1.45015	1.8127	1.55
Austria	274 818		145 360	8 363	0.84619	1.0577	0.87
Belgium	340 398		183 229	10 790	0.85966	1.0746	0.91
Canada[4]	1 603 418	1 584 810	619 880	33 720	1.23439	1.5430	1.31
Chile[5]	103 806 380		24 273 284	17 094	401.97839	502.4730	365.72
Czech Republic	3 739 225		1 679 693	10 491	13.91433	17.3929	15.61
Denmark	1 667 839		966 642	5 522	7.88622	9.8578	8.65
Estonia	216 474		97 912	1 340	8.16122	10.2015	0.62
Finland	173 267		96 300	5 339	0.90532	1.1317	1.01
France	1 889 231		1 071 907	64 496	0.86859	1.0857	0.91
Germany	2 374 500		1 142 090	81 875	0.80453	1.0057	0.86
Greece	231 642		m	11 283	0.69877	0.8735	0.77
Hungary	25 622 866		13 148 013	10 023	126.84522	158.5565	143.67
Iceland	1 497 672		763 327	319	127.7634	159.7043	140.60
Ireland	160 596		78 065	4 468	0.90423	1.1303	1.02
Israel	766 273		328 528	7 486	3.7286	4.6608	4.42
Italy	1 526 790		788 951	60 193	0.78294	0.9787	0.85
Japan[6]	470 936 700	472 997 325	200 331 700	127 510	114.25894	142.8237	126.08
Korea	1 065 036 800		352 323 300	48 747	804.1058	1 005.1323	902.83
Luxembourg	37 393		16 095	497	0.90622	1.1328	0.98
Mexico	11 879 676		3 114 065	107 444	7.67963	9.5995	8.73
Netherlands	571 145		294 424	16 526	0.84111	1.0514	0.87
New Zealand	187 802		64 013	4 332	1.48445	1.8556	1.60
Norway	2 356 599		1 101 034	4 827	8.92402	11.1550	9.67
Poland	1 343 366		596 542	38 153	1.86196	2.3275	2.04
Portugal	168 504		84 106	10 632	0.63556	0.7945	0.72
Slovak Republic	62 896		26 079	5 417	0.5133	0.6416	0.60
Slovenia	35 311		17 403	2 042	0.63702	0.7963	0.69
Spain	1 047 831		484 759	45 929	0.70969	0.8871	0.79
Sweden	3 093 843		1 703 862	9 299	8.94568	11.1821	9.31
Switzerland	535 650		180 619	7 801	1.53361	1.9170	1.69
Turkey	952 559		m	71 897	0.91739	1.1467	1.11
United Kingdom	1 393 847		716 432	61 792	0.65415	0.8177	0.70
United States	13 863 600		5 913 918	307 483	1	1.2500	1.00
Euro Zone					0.800		
Other G20 Argentina	1 145 458		m	40 134	1.9481	2.435	m
Brazil	3 185 125		1 082 430	191 796	1.4887	1.8609	m
China	m		m	m	m	m	m
India	61 457 625		m	1 224 614	16.863	21.0788	m
Indonesia[5]	6 422 919 971		m	237 415	6 237.547	7 795.6838	m
Russian Federation	38 786 372		m	141 904	14.47585	18.0948	16.60
Saudi Arabia	m		m	m	m	m	m
South Africa	504 938		m	49 752	4.745	m	m

1. Data on GDP, PPPs and total public expenditure in countries in the Euro zone are provided in Euros.
2. GDP calculated for the fiscal year in Australia and GDP and total public expenditure calculated for the fiscal year in New Zealand.
3. For countries where GDP is not reported for the same reference period as data on educational finance, GDP is estimated as: wt-1 (GDPt - 1) + wt (GDPt), where wt and wt-1 are the weights for the respective portions of the two reference periods for GDP which fall within the educational financial year. Adjustments were made in Chapter B for Canada, Japan, the United Kingdom and the United States.
4. Year of reference 2008.
5. Year of reference 2010.
6. Total public expenditure adjusted to financial year.
Source: OECD. See Annex 3 for notes (*www.oecd.org/edu/eag2012*).
Please refer to the Reader's Guide for information concerning the symbols replacing missing data.
StatLink ᵐˢᴸ http://dx.doi.org/10.1787/888932669192

Table X2.2b. Basic reference statistics
(reference period: calendar year 1995, 2000, 2005 current prices)[1]

	Gross Domestic Product (in millions of local currency)			Total public expenditure (in millions of local currency)			Change in Gross Domestic Product (2005 = 100, constant prices)			
	1995	2000	2005	1995	2000	2005	1995	2000	2005	2009
	(1)	(2)	(3)	(5)	(6)	(7)	(9)	(10)	(11)	(12)
Australia	531 970	708 919	1 001 440	184 270	225 913	309 431	69	84	100	112
Austria	174 794	208 474	245 243	98 361	108 175	122 585	79	92	100	105
Belgium	207 927	252 543	303 357	108 336	123 943	157 976	80	92	100	104
Canada	810 426	1 076 577	1 373 845	392 886	442 560	539 234	72	88	100	103
Chile	28 363 879	40 679 938	77 830 577	6 705 897	10 559 689	15 342 256	66	81	100	112
Czech Republic	1 533 676	2 269 695	3 116 056	798 790	915 413	1 340 123	75	82	100	111
Denmark	1 019 545	1 293 963	1 545 257	604 404	694 479	815 717	82	94	100	98
Estonia	2 766	6 160	11 182	17 866	34 815	3 757	51	71	100	98
Finland	96 064	132 195	157 429	58 947	63 794	78 934	69	88	100	102
France	1 196 181	1 439 603	1 718 047	650 606	744 119	920 351	81	92	100	102
Germany	1 848 500	2 047 500	2 224 400	1 012 330	930 400	1 043 450	89	97	100	103
Greece	88 742	135 043	193 050	40 783	63 627	m	69	82	100	105
Hungary	5 727 829	13 089 047	22 018 283	3 197 916	6 251 647	11 032 047	71	82	100	98
Iceland	454 013	683 747	1 025 740	m	286 259	433 346	64	81	100	105
Ireland	53 692	105 854	163 462	21 841	32 836	55 109	51	79	100	100
Israel	289 038	509 235	601 208	149 518	239 809	273 209	70	90	100	117
Italy	952 158	1 198 292	1 436 379	497 487	550 032	688 367	87	95	100	98
Japan	495 165 500	502 989 900	501 734 400	181 284 700	193 917 400	193 158 000	89	94	100	97
Korea	409 653 600	603 236 000	865 240 900	83 399 300	135 324 800	230 062 600	62	80	100	113
Luxembourg	15 110	22 001	30 283	5 996	8 270	12 573	62	84	100	107
Mexico	2 013 954	6 020 649	9 220 649	384 960	1 139 998	1 979 808	70	91	100	103
Netherlands	305 261	417 960	513 407	172 305	184 612	229 965	77	94	100	106
New Zealand	94 545	117 508	160 573	31 743	m	62 645	72	83	100	105
Norway	943 437	1 481 242	1 958 907	480 575	626 569	818 805	75	90	100	103
Poland	337 222	744 378	983 302	147 561	294 012	427 152	66	86	100	121
Portugal	87 841	127 317	154 269	36 447	52 237	70 363	78	96	100	101
Slovak Republic	19 319	31 177	49 314	9 392	16 255	18 730	67	79	100	121
Slovenia	10 357	18 566	28 722	m	8 636	13 011	68	84	100	108
Spain	447 205	629 907	909 298	198 730	246 542	349 501	70	85	100	105
Sweden	1 809 575	2 265 447	2 769 375	1 175 180	1 248 029	1 491 382	74	88	100	102
Switzerland	373 599	422 063	463 799	157 093	145 394	208 505	85	94	100	108
Turkey	10 435	166 658	648 932	m	m	m	65	80	100	107
United Kingdom	733 266	976 284	1 254 290	322 956	381 199	553 045	71	87	100	100
United States	7 359 300	9 898 800	12 564 300	2 732 629	3 353 547	4 563 353	72	89	100	101
Brazil	646 192	1 179 482	2 147 944	224 283	394 349	670 514	m	m	m	m
Russian Federation	499 375 940	1 389 769 900	2 774 281 100	m	2 016 630	7 380 575	77	79	100	124

1. Data on GDP, and total public expenditure in countries in the Euro zone are provided in euros.
Source: OECD. See Annex 3 for notes *(www.oecd.org/edu/eag2012)*.
Please refer to the Reader's Guide for information concerning the symbols replacing missing data.
StatLink ▰ᵯᵴ▰ http://dx.doi.org/10.1787/888932669211

Table X2.3a. [1/2] Teachers' salaries in national currency (2010)

Annual statutory teachers' salaries in public institutions at starting salary, after 10 and 15 years of experience and at the top of the scale, by level of education, in national currency

Annex 2

	Pre-primary education				Primary education			
	Starting salary/ minimum training	Salary after 10 years of experience/ minimum training	Salary after 15 years of experience/ minimum training	Salary at top of scale/ minimum training	Starting salary/ minimum training	Salary after 10 years of experience/ minimum training	Salary after 15 years of experience/ minimum training	Salary at top of scale/ minimum training
	(1)	(2)	(3)	(4)	(5)	(6)	(7)	(8)
OECD								
Australia	52 865	71 956	71 956	71 956	53 119	73 706	73 706	73 706
Austria	26 817	31 647	35 526	53 067	26 817	31 647	35 526	53 067
Belgium (Fl.)	28 338	35 557	40 042	49 011	28 338	35 557	40 042	49 011
Belgium (Fr.)	27 438	m	38 875	47 703	27 438	m	38 875	47 703
Canada	44 854	68 006	71 632	71 632	44 861	67 996	71 608	71 608
Chile	6 465 240	7 817 297	8 493 461	11 198 117	6 465 240	7 817 297	8 493 461	11 198 117
Czech Republic	195 904	242 785	257 418	297 330	234 194	294 031	310 711	346 961
Denmark	359 285	381 192	391 577	391 577	375 448	419 978	434 802	434 802
England	21 102	30 842	30 842	30 842	21 102	30 842	30 842	30 842
Estonia	m	m	m	m	7 298	7 728	7 728	10 667
Finland	24 725	28 395	28 395	28 395	29 272	35 631	37 769	40 035
France	22 060	27 715	29 674	43 783	22 060	27 715	29 674	43 783
Germany	m	m	m	m	39 688	m	47 647	52 292
Greece	20 521	23 321	25 001	30 055	20 521	23 321	25 001	30 055
Hungary[1]	1 486 200	1 674 024	1 780 884	2 332 740	1 550 400	1 780 752	1 916 568	2 556 456
Iceland	3 066 123	3 409 863	3 409 863	3 901 395	3 543 514	3 884 631	3 987 224	4 157 620
Ireland	32 566	47 840	53 620	60 693	32 566	47 840	53 620	60 693
Israel	63 184	81 282	89 297	131 835	78 491	99 704	112 005	160 740
Italy	22 868	25 164	27 645	33 658	22 868	25 164	27 645	33 658
Japan	m	m	m	m	3 157 000	4 693 000	5 555 000	7 013 000
Korea	23 783 294	34 944 614	40 831 708	67 212 724	24 271 343	36 005 976	42 003 257	67 212 724
Luxembourg	63 895	82 545	93 182	112 736	63 895	82 545	93 182	112 736
Mexico	125 517	126 350	163 419	268 569	125 517	126 350	163 419	268 569
Netherlands	m	m	m	m	32 249	38 851	44 288	46 941
New Zealand	m	m	m	m	44 348	65 609	65 609	65 609
Norway	310 700	353 700	353 700	353 700	316 400	349 000	349 000	391 800
Poland	19 311	25 583	30 785	32 078	19 311	25 583	30 785	32 078
Portugal	22 200	24 874	27 038	39 005	22 200	24 874	27 038	39 005
Scotland[1]	21 104	33 666	33 666	33 666	21 104	33 666	33 666	33 666
Slovak Republic	5 334	5 872	6 136	6 818	6 512	7 164	7 492	8 078
Slovenia	18 459	20 477	22 433	23 117	18 459	20 477	22 433	23 566
Spain	29 374	32 018	33 889	40 989	29 374	32 018	33 889	40 989
Sweden[1]	270 400	295 400	309 400	321 000	271 900	302 400	313 600	363 600
Switzerland[2]	67 633	86 060	m	105 367	75 868	96 241	m	118 743
Turkey	25 847	27 796	27 701	29 776	26 290	28 239	28 144	30 219
United States[1]	36 977	m	m	m	36 858	42 889	45 226	52 137
Other G20								
Argentina	26 345	m	31 983	38 631	24 668	m	30 574	37 114
Brazil	m	m	m	m	m	m	m	m
China	m	m	m	m	m	m	m	m
India	m	m	m	m	m	m	m	m
Indonesia	8 804 400	9 973 200	11 142 000	12 693 600	8 804 400	9 973 200	11 142 000	12 693 600
Russian Federation	m	m	m	m	m	m	m	m
Saudi Arabia	m	m	m	m	m	m	m	m
South Africa	m	m	m	m	m	m	m	m

1. Actual base salaries.
2. Salaries after 11 years of experience for Columns 2, 6, 10 and 14.
Source: OECD. Argentina: UNESCO Institute for Statistics (World Education Indicators programme). See Annex 3 for notes (*www.oecd.org/edu/eag2012*).
Please refer to the Reader's Guide for information concerning the symbols replacing missing data.
StatLink ⟐ http://dx.doi.org/10.1787/888932669230

Table X2.3a. [2/2] Teachers' salaries in national currency (2010)

Annual statutory teachers' salaries in public institutions at starting salary, after 10 and 15 years of experience and at the top of the scale, by level of education, in national currency

	Lower secondary education				Upper secondary education			
	Starting salary/ minimum training	Salary after 10 years of experience/ minimum training	Salary after 15 years of experience/ minimum training	Salary at top of scale/ minimum training	Starting salary/ minimum training	Salary after 10 years of experience/ minimum training	Salary after 15 years of experience/ minimum training	Salary at top of scale/ minimum training
	(9)	(10)	(11)	(12)	(13)	(14)	(15)	(16)
Australia	53 319	73 706	73 706	73 706	53 319	73 706	73 706	73 706
Austria	28 056	34 183	38 451	55 146	28 443	30 697	39 535	57 866
Belgium (Fl.)	28 338	35 557	40 042	49 011	35 375	45 110	51 454	62 028
Belgium (Fr.)	27 438	m	38 875	47 703	34 281	m	50 108	60 515
Canada	44 861	67 996	71 608	71 608	45 051	68 297	71 886	71 886
Chile	6 465 240	7 817 297	8 493 461	11 198 117	6 509 124	8 293 290	9 004 818	11 850 942
Czech Republic	232 328	296 876	314 897	350 793	241 943	317 867	334 084	375 631
Denmark	375 448	419 978	434 802	434 802	386 236	504 046	504 046	504 046
England	21 102	30 842	30 842	30 842	21 102	30 842	30 842	30 842
Estonia	7 298	7 728	7 728	10 667	7 298	7 728	7 728	10 667
Finland	31 614	38 482	40 791	43 238	32 547	41 507	43 168	45 758
France	24 644	30 299	32 258	46 507	24 858	30 513	32 472	46 742
Germany	43 620	m	52 784	58 599	46 102	m	57 150	65 298
Greece	20 521	23 321	25 001	30 055	20 521	23 321	25 001	30 055
Hungary[1]	1 550 400	1 780 752	1 916 568	2 556 456	1 703 208	2 073 468	2 262 636	3 327 156
Iceland	3 543 514	3 884 631	3 987 224	4 157 620	3 262 000	3 786 000	4 012 000	4 197 000
Ireland	32 566	47 840	53 620	60 693	32 566	47 840	53 620	60 693
Israel	78 491	91 239	102 514	147 811	62 249	83 490	93 450	140 307
Italy	24 651	27 316	30 121	36 963	24 651	27 982	30 966	38 645
Japan	3 157 000	4 693 000	5 555 000	7 013 000	3 157 000	4 693 000	5 555 000	7 203 000
Korea	24 175 343	35 909 976	41 907 257	67 116 724	24 175 343	35 909 976	41 907 257	67 116 724
Luxembourg	72 332	90 416	99 782	125 671	72 332	90 416	99 782	125 671
Mexico	161 890	166 906	209 350	343 017	m	m	m	m
Netherlands	33 247	45 866	53 984	58 095	33 247	45 866	53 984	58 095
New Zealand	45 001	67 295	67 295	67 295	45 653	68 980	68 980	68 980
Norway	316 400	349 000	349 000	391 800	349 000	376 400	376 400	414 700
Poland	21 742	29 017	35 071	36 550	24 567	33 141	40 120	41 819
Portugal	22 200	24 874	27 038	39 005	22 200	24 874	27 038	39 005
Scotland[1]	21 104	33 666	33 666	33 666	21 104	33 666	33 666	33 666
Slovak Republic	6 512	7 164	7 492	8 078	6 512	7 164	7 498	8 078
Slovenia	18 459	20 477	22 433	23 566	18 459	20 477	22 433	23 566
Spain	32 839	35 771	37 820	45 927	33 477	36 504	38 613	46 879
Sweden[1]	274 800	311 800	324 000	366 000	288 000	328 100	342 300	391 600
Switzerland[2]	85 956	109 537	m	133 536	99 154	127 839	m	151 605
Turkey	a	a	a	a	27 029	28 978	28 883	30 958
United States[1]	36 772	42 982	45 049	55 259	37 267	44 011	48 446	55 199
Argentina	19 666	m	26 455	32 091	19 666	m	26 455	32 091
Brazil	m	m	m	m	m	m	m	m
China	m	m	m	m	m	m	m	m
India	m	m	m	m	m	m	m	m
Indonesia	9 384 000	11 038 800	12 693 600	13 790 400	10 864 800	11 038 800	14 058 000	15 319 200
Russian Federation	m	m	m	m	m	m	m	m
Saudi Arabia	m	m	m	m	m	m	m	m
South Africa	m	m	m	m	m	m	m	m

1. Actual base salaries.
2. Salaries after 11 years of experience for Columns 2, 6, 10 and 14.
Source: OECD. Argentina: UNESCO Institute for Statistics (World Education Indicators programme). See Annex 3 for notes (*www.oecd.org/edu/eag2012*).
Please refer to the Reader's Guide for information concerning the symbols replacing missing data.
StatLink ᵐˢᵖ http://dx.doi.org/10.1787/888932669230

Table X2.3b. [1/2] Trends in teachers' salaries in national currency, by level of education (2000, 2005-10)[1]

Annual statutory teachers' salaries in public institutions after 15 years of experience / minimum training, by level of education, in national currency

	Primary level							Lower secondary level			
	2000	2005	2006	2007	2008	2009	2010	2000	2005	2006	2007
	(1)	(2)	(3)	(4)	(5)	(6)	(7)	(8)	(9)	(10)	(11)
Australia	50 995	62 240	61 243	63 977	68 586	70 696	73 706	51 016	62 384	62 106	64 984
Austria	25 826	31 050	31 935	32 830	33 717	34 848	35 526	26 916	33 635	34 418	35 467
Belgium (Fl.)	29 579	35 417	36 390	37 236	37 432	39 670	40 042	31 191	35 417	36 390	37 236
Belgium (Fr.)	28 638	33 598	34 825	35 697	35 917	38 872	38 875	30 482	33 973	34 825	35 697
Canada	m	m	m	m	m	m	71 608	m	m	m	m
Chile	m	m	4 430 124	4 636 394	m	8 257 733	8 493 461	m	m	4 430 124	4 636 394
Czech Republic	125 501	250 559	254 921	302 856	309 994	323 789	310 711	125 501	250 559	254 921	302 856
Denmark	285 200	332 015	341 001	346 569	362 222	434 439	434 802	285 200	332 015	341 001	346 569
England	23 193	27 123	28 005	28 707	29 427	30 148	30 842	23 193	27 123	28 005	28 707
Estonia	3 068	4 379	5 039	6 013	7 522	8 439	7 728	3 068	4 379	5 039	6 013
Finland	26 506	33 171	33 868	35 299	36 540	37 417	37 769	31 115	36 109	36 867	38 123
France	27 288	28 395	28 791	29 097	29 271	29 438	29 674	29 456	30 667	31 068	31 274
Germany	37 938	44 370	44 481	45 877	46 295	46 134	47 647	40 597	45 534	45 648	49 861
Greece	15 883	20 572	21 237	21 872	22 989	24 146	25 001	15 883	20 572	21 237	21 872
Hungary[2]	897 168	1 944 576	1 970 676	1 983 240	2 059 668	1 914 504	1 916 568	897 168	1 944 576	1 970 676	1 983 240
Iceland	1 884 000	2 573 556	2 837 950	2 830 814	3 268 766	3 987 224	3 987 224	1 884 000	2 573 556	2 837 950	2 830 814
Ireland	33 370	46 591	49 421	52 177	53 221	55 916	53 620	33 729	46 591	49 421	52 177
Israel	68 421	73 496	77 475	86 089	94 432	105 899	112 005	76 048	82 030	86 256	86 838
Italy	20 849	25 234	25 528	25 799	26 470	27 374	27 645	22 836	27 487	27 797	28 095
Japan	6 645 000	6 236 000	6 235 725	5 958 000	5 753 000	5 720 000	5 555 000	6 645 000	6 236 000	6 235 725	5 958 000
Korea	26 757 000	39 712 000	40 841 220	41 387 505	42 003 300	42 003 300	42 003 257	26 661 000	39 616 000	40 745 220	41 291 505
Luxembourg	m	62 139	63 692	65 284	64 244	67 230	93 182	m	81 258	83 289	85 371
Mexico	86 748	124 082	130 526	137 323	145 917	155 022	163 419	109 779	157 816	166 107	174 854
Netherlands	m	m	m	m	m	m	m	m	m	m	m
New Zealand	49 450	54 979	56 628	58 327	60 660	63 086	65 609	49 450	54 979	56 628	58 327
Norway	m	302 000	305 000	313 000	327 300	337 800	349 000	m	302 000	305 000	313 000
Poland	m	19 022	m	m	26 944	28 902	30 785	m	19 022	m	m
Portugal	17 180	22 775	23 186	23 541	23 987	26 763	27 038	17 180	22 775	23 186	23 541
Scotland[2]	22 743	29 827	30 602	31 241	32 052	32 855	33 666	22 743	29 827	30 602	31 241
Slovak Republic	m	m	m	m	m	7 276	7 492	m	m	m	m
Slovenia	m	17 939	19 025	20 005	20 911	22 361	22 433	m	17 939	19 025	20 005
Spain	22 701	28 122	29 347	29 934	32 193	33 754	33 889	24 528	31 561	32 922	33 580
Sweden[2]	248 300	283 200	283 200	298 800	298 800	313 600	313 600	248 300	290 400	290 400	306 300
Switzerland[3]	85 513	90 483	89 909	91 017	92 617	96 918	96 241	102 409	103 037	102 985	104 157
Turkey	2 638	17 166	17 609	19 822	22 114	25 043	28 144	a	a	a	a
United States[2]	35 323	40 734	42 404	43 633	44 172	44 788	45 226	35 185	41 090	42 775	44 015
Argentina	m	m	m	m	m	m	30 574	m	m	m	m
Brazil	m	m	m	m	m	m	m	m	m	m	m
China	m	m	m	m	m	m	m	m	m	m	m
India	m	m	m	m	m	m	m	m	m	m	m
Indonesia	m	m	m	11 142 000	11 142 000	11 142 000	11 142 000	m	m	m	11 142 000
Russian Federation	m	m	m	m	m	m	m	m	m	m	m
Saudi Arabia	m	m	m	m	m	m	m	m	m	m	m
South Africa	m	m	m	m	m	m	m	m	m	m	m

1. Data on salaries for countries now in the euro zone are shown in euros.
2. Actual base salaries.
3. Salaries after 11 years of experience.
Source: OECD. Argentina: UNESCO Institute for Statistics (World Education Indicators programme). See Annex 3 for notes *(www.oecd.org/edu/eag2012)*.
Please refer to the Reader's Guide for information concerning the symbols replacing missing data.
StatLink ⌨️ http://dx.doi.org/10.1787/888932669249

Table X2.3b. [2/2] **Trends in teachers' salaries in national currency, by level of education (2000, 2005-10)[1]**

Annual statutory teachers' salaries in public institutions after 15 years of experience / minimum training, by level of education, in national currency

	Lower secondary level			Upper secondary level						
	2008	2009	2010	2000	2005	2006	2007	2008	2009	2010
	(12)	(13)	(14)	(15)	(16)	(17)	(18)	(19)	(20)	(21)
Australia	69 794	70 696	73 706	51 016	62 384	62 106	64 984	69 794	70 696	73 706
Austria	36 455	37 664	38 451	29 728	34 265	35 273	36 493	37 508	38 787	39 535
Belgium (Fl.)	37 432	39 670	40 042	39 886	45 301	46 477	47 644	47 976	50 852	51 454
Belgium (Fr.)	35 917	38 872	38 875	39 207	43 704	44 750	45 820	46 039	50 106	50 108
Canada	m	m	71 608	m	m	m	m	m	m	71 886
Chile	m	8 257 733	8 493 461	m	m	4 638 231	4 852 425	m	8 638 812	9 004 818
Czech Republic	316 173	330 923	314 897	152 941	255 125	258 535	323 566	337 024	347 334	334 084
Denmark	362 222	434 439	434 802	335 000	404 229	424 212	423 426	436 926	497 723	504 046
England	29 427	30 148	30 842	23 193	27 123	28 005	28 707	29 427	30 148	30 842
Estonia	7 522	8 439	7 728	3 068	4 379	5 039	6 013	7 522	8 439	7 728
Finland	39 464	40 411	40 791	32 681	38 263	39 066	40 396	41 805	42 808	43 168
France	31 461	31 641	32 258	29 456	30 895	31 296	31 525	31 715	31 896	32 472
Germany	50 544	50 929	52 784	43 920	49 048	49 171	53 640	54 369	55 533	57 150
Greece	22 989	24 146	25 001	15 883	20 572	21 237	21 872	22 989	24 146	25 001
Hungary[2]	2 059 668	1 914 504	1 916 568	1 128 996	2 432 388	2 358 240	2 474 508	2 474 388	2 298 900	2 262 636
Iceland	3 268 766	3 987 224	3 987 224	2 220 000	3 014 000	3 446 964	3 619 000	3 840 000	4 025 000	4 012 000
Ireland	53 221	55 916	53 620	33 729	46 591	49 421	52 177	53 221	55 916	53 620
Israel	95 405	99 247	102 514	75 097	80 052	84 190	85 118	93 786	91 563	93 450
Italy	28 831	29 824	30 121	23 518	28 259	28 574	28 880	29 637	30 661	30 966
Japan	5 753 000	5 720 000	5 555 000	6 649 000	6 237 000	6 235 725	5 958 000	5 753 000	5 720 000	5 555 000
Korea	41 907 300	41 907 300	41 907 257	26 661 000	39 616 000	40 745 220	41 291 505	41 907 300	41 907 300	41 907 257
Luxembourg	93 772	101 058	99 782	m	81 258	83 289	85 371	93 772	101 058	99 782
Mexico	185 616	196 707	209 350	m	m	m	m	m	m	m
Netherlands	48 615	50 955	53 984	44 244	54 712	55 647	47 427	48 615	50 955	53 984
New Zealand	60 660	63 086	67 295	49 450	54 979	56 628	58 327	60 660	63 086	68 980
Norway	327 300	337 800	349 000	m	321 000	324 000	332 500	347 300	362 800	376 400
Poland	30 850	32 920	35 071	m	19 022	m	m	35 459	37 670	40 120
Portugal	23 987	26 763	27 038	17 180	22 775	23 186	23 541	23 987	26 763	27 038
Scotland[2]	32 052	32 855	33 666	22 743	29 827	30 602	31 241	32 052	32 855	33 666
Slovak Republic	m	7 276	7 492	m	m	m	m	m	7 276	7 498
Slovenia	20 911	22 361	22 433	m	17 939	19 025	20 005	20 911	22 361	22 433
Spain	35 200	37 669	37 820	26 366	32 293	33 666	34 339	36 818	38 459	38 613
Sweden[2]	306 300	324 000	324 000	264 700	313 600	313 600	326 900	326 900	342 300	342 300
Switzerland[3]	105 874	110 096	109 537	121 629	120 602	121 187	122 259	124 936	129 158	127 839
Turkey	a	a	a	2 441	17 403	18 074	20 329	22 650	25 625	28 883
United States[2]	44 000	44 614	45 049	37 838	41 044	42 727	43 966	47 317	47 977	48 446
Argentina	m	m	26 455	m	m	m	m	m	m	26 455
Brazil	m	m	m	m	m	m	m	m	m	m
China	m	m	m	m	m	m	m	m	m	m
India	m	m	m	m	m	m	m	m	m	m
Indonesia	12 693 600	12 693 600	12 693 600	m	m	m	11 142 000	14 058 000	14 058 000	14 058 000
Russian Federation	m	m	m	m	m	m	m	m	m	m
Saudi Arabia	m	m	m	m	m	m	m	m	m	m
South Africa	m	m	m	m	m	m	m	m	m	m

1. Data on salaries for countries now in the euro zone are shown in euros.
2. Actual base salaries.
3. Salaries after 11 years of experience.
Source: OECD. Argentina: UNESCO Institute for Statistics (World Education Indicators programme). See Annex 3 for notes (*www.oecd.org/edu/eag2012*). *Please refer to the Reader's Guide for information concerning the symbols replacing missing data.*
StatLink http://dx.doi.org/10.1787/888932669249

Table X2.3c. [1/3] **Reference statistics used in the calculation of teachers' salaries (2000, 2005-10)**

	Purchasing power parity for private consumption (PPP)[1]	Gross domestic product (GDP) (in millions of local currency, calendar year)[1]								
	Jan 2010	1999	2000	2004	2005	2006	2007	2008	2009	2010
	(3)	(4)	(5)	(6)	(7)	(8)	(9)	(10)	(11)	(12)
OECD Australia	1.55	663 810	708 919	926 447	1 001 440	1 091 633	1 185 740	1 255 241	1 284 670	1 386 617
Austria	0.87	199 266	208 474	234 708	245 243	259 034	274 020	282 746	274 818	286 197
Belgium (Fl.)[2]	0.91	238 877	252 543	291 292	303 357	318 697	335 610	346 130	340 398	354 378
Belgium (Fr.)[2]	0.91	238 877	252 543	291 292	303 357	318 697	335 610	346 130	340 398	354 378
Canada	1.30	982 441	1 076 577	1 290 906	1 373 845	1 450 405	1 529 589	1 603 418	1 528 985	1 624 608
Chile	362.80	37 228 111	40 679 938	58 303 211	66 192 596	77 830 577	85 849 774	89 205 487	90 219 527	103 806 380
Czech Republic	15.58	2 149 023	2 269 695	2 929 172	3 116 056	3 352 599	3 662 573	3 848 411	3 739 225	3 775 237
Denmark	8.65	1 213 473	1 293 963	1 466 180	1 545 257	1 631 659	1 695 264	1 753 152	1 667 839	1 754 648
England[3]	0.70	928 871	976 282	1 202 370	1 254 292	1 328 597	1 405 796	1 433 870	1 393 854	1 463 734
Estonia	0.61	5 358	6 160	9 685	11 182	13 391	16 069	16 304	13 840	14 305
Finland	1.01	122 321	132 195	152 266	157 429	165 765	179 830	185 670	172 518	179 721
France	0.91	1 367 005	1 439 603	1 655 572	1 718 047	1 798 116	1 886 792	1 933 195	1 889 231	1 932 802
Germany	0.85	2 000 200	2 047 500	2 195 700	2 224 400	2 313 900	2 428 500	2 473 800	2 374 500	2 476 800
Greece	0.77	125 010	135 043	183 583	193 050	208 893	222 771	232 920	231 642	227 318
Hungary	144.89	11 443 475	13 089 047	20 665 018	22 018 283	23 675 850	24 991 847	26 545 649	25 622 866	26 747 662
Iceland	142.76	632 399	683 747	930 141	1 025 740	1 168 602	1 308 530	1 481 986	1 497 672	1 537 106
Ireland	1.00	91 391	105 854	150 561	163 462	178 297	189 933	179 990	160 596	155 992
Israel	4.45	458 658	509 235	567 292	601 208	648 228	686 512	723 562	766 273	813 021
Italy	0.85	1 133 998	1 198 292	1 397 728	1 436 379	1 493 031	1 554 199	1 575 144	1 519 695	1 553 166
Japan	124.03	497 628 600	502 989 900	498 328 400	501 734 400	507 364 800	515 520 400	504 377 600	470 936 700	479 179 200
Korea	906.46	549 005 000	603 236 000	826 892 700	865 240 900	908 743 800	975 013 000	1 026 451 800	1 065 036 800	1 172 803 400
Luxembourg	0.98	19 887	22 001	27 456	30 283	33 920	37 491	39 437	37 393	40 267
Mexico	8.78	5 037 271	6 020 649	8 561 305	9 220 649	10 344 065	11 290 752	12 153 436	11 879 676	13 043 195
Netherlands	0.87	386 193	417 960	491 184	513 407	540 216	571 773	594 481	571 145	588 414
New Zealand	1.60	111 178	117 508	152 038	160 573	168 663	182 260	185 561	187 802	197 208
Norway[4]	9.70	1 240 426	1 481 242	1 752 812	1 958 907	2 180 801	2 306 445	2 559 914	2 356 599	2 523 226
Poland	2.03	665 688	744 378	924 538	983 302	1 060 031	1 176 737	1 275 432	1 343 366	1 415 362
Portugal	0.72	118 661	127 317	149 313	154 269	160 855	169 319	171 983	168 504	172 670
Scotland[3]	0.70	928 871	976 282	1 202 370	1 254 292	1 328 597	1 405 796	1 433 870	1 393 854	1 463 734
Slovak Republic	0.59	28 109	31 177	45 161	49 314	55 002	61 450	66 842	62 795	65 743
Slovenia	0.69	16 922	18 566	27 165	28 722	31 045	34 562	37 280	35 311	35 416
Spain	0.79	579 942	629 907	841 294	909 298	985 547	1 053 161	1 087 749	1 047 831	1 051 342
Sweden	9.40	2 138 421	2 265 447	2 660 957	2 769 375	2 944 480	3 126 018	3 204 320	3 105 790	3 330 581
Switzerland	1.68	402 907	422 063	451 379	463 799	490 544	521 101	545 028	535 650	550 571
Turkey	1.14	104 596	166 658	559 033	648 932	758 391	843 178	950 534	952 559	1 103 750
United States	1.00	9 301 000	9 898 800	11 797 800	12 564 300	13 314 500	13 961 800	14 219 300	13 863 600	14 447 100
Other G20 Argentina	1.79	m	m	m	m	m	m	1 032 758	1 145 458	1 442 655
Brazil	m	m	m	m	m	m	m	m	m	m
China	m	m	m	m	m	m	m	m	m	m
India	m	m	m	m	m	m	m	m	m	m
Indonesia	5 376.31	1 208 278 251	1 389 769 900	2 295 826 000	2 774 281 100	3 339 216 900	3 950 893 200	4 948 688 400	5 603 871 000	6 422 918 200
Russian Federation	17.01	4 818 191	7 298 009	17 027 191	21 609 766	26 917 201	33 247 513	41 276 849	38 786 372	44 939 153
Saudi Arabia	m	m	m	m	m	m	m	m	m	m
South Africa	m	m	m	m	m	m	m	m	m	m

1. Data on PPPs and GDP for countries now in the euro zone are shown in euros.
2. Data on Gross Domestic Product and total population refer to Belgium.
3. Data on Gross Domestic Product and total population refer to the United Kingdom.
4. The GDP Mainland market value is used for Norway.
Source: OECD. Argentina: UNESCO Institute for Statistics (World Education Indicators programme). See Annex 3 for notes (*www.oecd.org/edu/eag2012*).
Please refer to the Reader's Guide for information concerning the symbols replacing missing data.
StatLink ⬛⬛ http://dx.doi.org/10.1787/888932669268

Table X2.3c. [2/3] Reference statistics used in the calculation of teachers' salaries (2000, 2005-10)

	Total population (in thousands, calendar year)								
	1999	2000	2004	2005	2006	2007	2008	2009	2010
	(13)	(14)	(15)	(16)	(17)	(18)	(19)	(20)	(21)
Australia	19 036	19 270	20 250	20 542	20 871	21 261	21 728	22 163	22 554
Austria	7 992	8 012	8 169	8 225	8 268	8 301	8 337	8 363	8 388
Belgium (Fl.)[2]	10 222	10 246	10 417	10 474	10 543	10 622	10 708	10 790	10 883
Belgium (Fr.)[2]	10 222	10 246	10 417	10 474	10 543	10 622	10 708	10 790	10 883
Canada	30 401	30 686	31 941	32 245	32 576	32 930	33 316	33 720	34 109
Chile	15 197	15 398	16 093	16 267	16 433	16 598	16 763	16 929	17 094
Czech Republic	10 283	10 273	10 207	10 234	10 267	10 323	10 430	10 491	10 517
Denmark	5 321	5 338	5 403	5 419	5 437	5 460	5 492	5 522	5 546
England[3]	58 684	58 886	59 842	60 235	60 584	60 986	61 398	61 792	62 262
Estonia	1 379	1 372	1 351	1 348	1 345	1 342	1 341	1 340	1 340
Finland	5 166	5 176	5 228	5 246	5 266	5 289	5 313	5 339	5 363
France	60 315	60 725	62 491	62 958	63 393	63 781	64 142	64 496	64 848
Germany	82 087	82 188	82 501	82 464	82 366	82 263	82 120	81 875	81 757
Greece	10 883	10 917	11 062	11 104	11 149	11 193	11 237	11 283	11 308
Hungary	10 238	10 211	10 107	10 087	10 071	10 056	10 038	10 023	10 000
Iceland	277	281	293	296	304	311	319	319	318
Ireland	3 755	3 804	4 067	4 160	4 261	4 365	4 443	4 468	4 476
Israel	6 125	6 289	6 809	6 930	7 054	7 180	7 309	7 486	7 624
Italy	56 916	56 942	58 175	58 607	58 942	59 375	59 832	60 193	60 483
Japan	126 667	126 926	127 787	127 768	127 770	127 771	127 692	127 510	127 383
Korea	46 617	47 008	48 039	48 138	48 297	48 456	48 607	48 747	48 875
Luxembourg	431	436	458	465	472	480	488	497	506
Mexico	96 569	98 295	102 888	103 831	104 748	105 677	106 573	107 443	108 292
Netherlands	15 809	15 922	16 276	16 317	16 341	16 378	16 440	16 526	16 612
New Zealand	3 843	3 868	4 101	4 148	4 198	4 241	4 281	4 332	4 384
Norway[4]	4 462	4 491	4 591	4 622	4 661	4 706	4 769	4 827	4 889
Poland	38 270	38 256	38 180	38 161	38 132	38 116	38 116	38 153	38 187
Portugal	10 172	10 226	10 502	10 549	10 584	10 608	10 622	10 632	10 637
Scotland[3]	58 684	58 886	59 842	60 235	60 584	60 986	61 398	61 792	62 262
Slovak Republic	5 396	5 401	5 382	5 387	5 391	5 397	5 406	5 418	5 430
Slovenia	1 984	1 989	1 997	2 001	2 008	2 019	2 022	2 042	2 049
Spain	39 927	40 264	42 692	43 398	44 068	44 874	45 593	45 929	46 073
Sweden	8 858	8 872	8 994	9 030	9 081	9 148	9 220	9 299	9 378
Switzerland	7 167	7 209	7 454	7 501	7 558	7 619	7 711	7 801	7 786
Turkey	63 366	64 259	67 734	68 582	69 421	70 256	71 079	71 897	72 848
United States	279 328	282 418	293 502	296 229	299 052	302 025	304 831	307 483	310 106
Argentina	m	m	m	m	m	m	39 746	40 062	40 412
Brazil	m	m	m	m	m	m	m	m	m
China	m	m	m	m	m	m	m	m	m
India	m	m	m	m	m	m	m	m	m
Indonesia	207 437	205 132	216 826	219 852	222 747	225 642	228 523	231 370	237 641
Russian Federation	147 539	146 890	144 168	143 474	142 754	142 221	142 009	141 904	m
Saudi Arabia	m	m	m	m	m	m	m	m	m
South Africa	m	m	m	m	m	m	m	m	m

1. Data on Purchasing Power Parities (PPPs) and GDP for countries now in the euro zone are shown in euros.
2. Data on GDP and total population refer to Belgium.
3. Data on GDP and total population refer to the United Kingdom.
4. The GDP Mainland market value is used for Norway.
Source: OECD. Argentina: UNESCO Institute for Statistics (World Education Indicators programme). See Annex 3 for notes (*www.oecd.org/edu/eag2012*).
Please refer to the Reader's Guide for information concerning the symbols replacing missing data.
StatLink ⫸ http://dx.doi.org/10.1787/888932669268

Table X2.3c. [3/3] Reference statistics used in the calculation of teachers' salaries (2000, 2005-10)

	Private consumption deflators (2000 = 100)							Reference year for 2010 salary data
	Jan 2000	Jan 2005	Jan 2006	Jan 2007	Jan 2008	Jan 2009	Jan 2010	
	(22)	(23)	(24)	(25)	(26)	(27)	(28)	(29)
OECD								
Australia	100	113	116	119	123	125	128	2010
Austria	100	109	111	114	116	118	120	2009/2010
Belgium (Fl.)[2]	100	110	113	117	120	122	122	1 Jan 2010
Belgium (Fr.)[2]	100	110	113	117	120	122	122	2009/2010
Canada	100	109	111	113	114	115	117	2009/2010
Chile	m	m	m	m	m	m	m	2010
Czech Republic	100	111	112	115	119	122	122	2009/2010
Denmark	100	109	111	113	115	118	120	2009/2010
England[3]	100	107	110	113	116	119	122	2009/2010
Estonia	100	120	125	134	145	150	151	2009/2010
Finland	100	107	108	110	113	116	118	2009/2010
France	100	110	112	114	117	118	119	2009/2010
Germany	100	107	109	110	112	113	114	2009/2010
Greece	100	116	120	124	129	132	135	2009
Hungary	100	137	141	149	158	165	171	2010
Iceland	100	122	128	135	148	169	183	2009/2010
Ireland	100	121	123	127	131	130	126	2009/2010
Israel	100	108	111	113	117	121	125	2009/2010
Italy	100	114	117	120	123	125	126	2009/2010
Japan	100	95	95	94	94	93	92	2009/2010
Korea	100	118	121	123	127	131	135	2010
Luxembourg	100	111	114	117	119	122	123	2009/2010
Mexico	100	137	142	148	155	166	174	2009/2010
Netherlands	100	114	117	119	121	121	122	2009/2010
New Zealand	100	109	112	115	118	121	123	2010
Norway[4]	100	110	111	113	116	119	122	2009/2010
Poland	100	117	119	122	126	130	133	2009/2010
Portugal	100	116	119	123	126	126	126	2009/2010
Scotland[3]	100	107	110	113	116	119	122	2009/2010
Slovak Republic	100	131	136	141	146	149	150	2009/2010
Slovenia	100	131	134	138	145	148	149	2009/2010
Spain	100	118	122	126	130	132	133	2009/2010
Sweden	100	107	109	110	112	115	117	2009
Switzerland	100	103	104	106	108	109	109	2009/2010
Turkey	100	359	392	423	460	496	529	2010
United States	100	111	114	117	121	123	124	2009/2010
Other G20								
Argentina	m	m	m	m	m	m	m	2009
Brazil	100	154	163	171	181	191	202	m
China	m	m	m	m	m	m	m	m
India	m	m	m	m	m	m	m	m
Indonesia	100	155	177	200	229	259	280	2009/2010
Russian Federation	m	m	m	m	m	m	m	m
Saudi Arabia	m	m	m	m	m	m	m	m
South Africa	m	m	m	m	m	m	m	m

1. Data on Purchasing Power Parities (PPPs) and GDP for countries now in the euro zone are shown in euros.
2. Data on Gross Domestic Product and total population refer to Belgium.
3. Data on Gross Domestic Product and total population refer to the United Kingdom.
4. The GDP Mainland market value is used for Norway.
Source: OECD. Argentina: UNESCO Institute for Statistics (World Education Indicators programme). See Annex 3 for notes (*www.oecd.org/edu/eag2012*).
Please refer to the Reader's Guide for information concerning the symbols replacing missing data.
StatLink ᴍᴤᴘ http://dx.doi.org/10.1787/888932669268

Annex 2

General notes

Definitions

Gross domestic product (GDP) refers to the producers' value of the gross outputs of resident producers, including distributive trades and transport, less the value of purchasers' intermediate consumption plus import duties. GDP is expressed in local money (in millions). For countries which provide this information for a reference year that is different from the calendar year (such as Australia and New Zealand), adjustments are made by linearly weighting their GDP between two adjacent national reference years to match the calendar year.

The **GDP deflator** is obtained by dividing the GDP expressed at current prices by the GDP expressed at constant prices. This provides an indication of the relative price level in a country.

GDP per capita is the gross domestic product (in equivalent USD converted using PPPs) divided by the population.

Purchasing power parity exchange rates (PPP) are the currency exchange rates that equalise the purchasing power of different currencies. This means that a given sum of money when converted into different currencies at the PPP rates will buy the same basket of goods and services in all countries. In other words, PPPs are the rates of currency conversion which eliminate the differences in price levels among countries. Thus, when expenditure on GDP for different countries is converted into a common currency by means of PPPs, it is, in effect, expressed at the same set of international prices so that comparisons between countries reflect only differences in the volume of goods and services purchased.

Total public expenditure as used for the calculation of the education indicators, corresponds to the non-repayable current and capital expenditure of all levels of government. Current expenditure includes final consumption expenditure (e.g. compensation of employees, consumption of intermediate goods and services, consumption of fixed capital, and military expenditure), property income paid, subsidies, and other current transfers paid (e.g. social security, social assistance, pensions and other welfare benefits). Capital expenditure is spending to acquire and/or improve fixed capital assets, land, intangible assets, government stocks, and non-military, non-financial assets, and spending to finance net capital transfers.

Sources

The 2012 edition of the *National Accounts of OECD Countries: Detailed Tables, Volume II.*

The theoretical framework underpinning national accounts has been provided for many years by the United Nations' publication *A System of National Accounts,* which was released in 1968. An updated version was released in 1993 (commonly referred to as SNA93).

OECD Analytical Database, February 2012.

Annex

3

SOURCES, METHODS AND TECHNICAL NOTES

Annex 3 on sources and methods is available in electronic form only. It can be found at:
www.oecd.org/edu/eag2012

Contributors to this Publication

Many people have contributed to the development of this publication. The following lists the names of the country representatives, researchers and experts who have actively taken part in the preparatory work leading to the publication of *Education at a Glance 2012: OECD Indicators*. The OECD wishes to thank them all for their valuable efforts.

INES Working Party

Ms. Maria Laura ALONSO (Argentina)

Ms. Marcela JÁUREGUI (Argentina)

Ms. Stephanie BOWLES (Australia)

Mr. Paul CMIEL (Australia)

Mr. Stuart FAUNT (Australia)

Ms. Ashlee HOLLIS (Australia)

Ms. Cheryl HOPKINS (Australia)

Ms. Joanna KORDIS (Australia)

Ms. Shannon MADDEN (Australia)

Mr. Scott MATHESON (Australia)

Ms. Margaret PEARCE (Australia)

Mr. Mark UNWIN (Australia)

Mr. Andreas GRIMM (Austria)

Ms. Sabine MARTINSCHITZ (Austria)

Mr. Mark NEMET (Austria)

Mr. Wolfgang PAULI (Austria)

Mr. Helga POSSET (Austria)

Mr. Philippe DIEU (Belgium)

Mr. Liës FEYEN (Belgium)

Ms. Nathalie JAUNIAUX (Belgium)

Mr. Guy STOFFELEN (Belgium)

Mr. Raymond VAN DE SIJPE (Belgium)

Ms. Ann VAN DRIESSCHE (Belgium)

Mr. Daniel Jaime CAPISTRANO DE OLIVEIRA (Brazil)

Ms. Juliana MARQUES DA SILVA (Brazil)

Ms. Ana Carolina SILVA CIROTTO (Brazil)

Mr. Patric BLOUIN (Canada)

Mr. Patrice DE BROUCKER (Canada)

Ms. Amanda HODGKINSON (Canada)

Mr. Enzo PIZZOFERRATO (Canada)

Mr. Janusz ZIEMINSKI (Canada)

Ms. Ana Maria BAEZA (Chile)

Mr. David INOSTROZA (Chile)

Mr. Francisco LAGOS MARIN (Chile)

Ms. Paola LEIVA (Chile)

Mr. Gabriel Alonso UGARTE VERA (Chile)

Mr. Cristian Pablo YANEZ NAVARRO (Chile)

Ms. Helena CIZKOVA (Czech Republic)

Ms. Michaela KLENHOVA (Czech Republic)

Mr. Lubomir MARTINEC (Czech Republic)

Ms. Michaela SOJDROVA (Czech Republic)

Ms. Stine ALBECK SEITZBERG (Denmark)

Mr. Jens ANDERSEN (Denmark)

Mr. Jorgen BALLING RASMUSSEN (Denmark)

Mr. Henrik BANG (Denmark)

Mr. Erik CHRISTIANSEN (Denmark)

Mr. Leo Elmbirk JENSEN (Denmark)

Ms. Liv Maadele MOGENSEN (Denmark)

Mr. Kristian ORNSHOLT (Denmark)

Mr. Signe PHILIP (Denmark)

Mr. Jens Brunsborg STORM (Denmark)

Ms. Maria SVANEBORG (Denmark)

Mr. Thorbjorn TODSEN (Denmark)

Ms. Tiina ANNUS (Estonia)

Ms. Kristi PLOOM (Estonia)

Ms. Christine COIN (Eurostat, European Commission)

Mr. Richard DEISS (European Commission)

Ms. Margarida GAMEIRO (European Commission)

Ms. Ana Maria MARTINEZ PALOU (Eurostat, European Commission)

Ms. Lene MEJER (Eurostat, European Commission)

Ms. Teresa OLIVEIRA (European Commission)

Mr. Fernando REIS (Eurostat, European Commission)

Mr. Timo ERTOLA (Finland)

Mr. Ville HEINONEN (Finland)

Mr. Matti KYRO (Finland)

Ms. Riikka RAUTANEN (Finland)

Mr. Mika TUONONEN (Finland)

Ms. Pierrette BRIANT (France)

Mr. Luc BRIERE (France)

Ms. Nadine DALSHEIMER-VAN DER TOL (France)

Ms. Florence DEFRESNE (France)

Ms. Saskia KESKPAIK (France)

Ms. Céline LAMBERT (France)

Ms. Florence LEFRESNE (France)

Ms. Valerie LIOGIER (France)

Ms. Claude MALEGUE (France)

Ms. Pascale POULET-COULIBANDO (France)

Ms Marguerite RUDOLF (France)

Ms. Alexia STEFANOU (France)

Mr. Andreas ALBRECHT (Germany)

Mr. Heinz-Werner HETMEIER (Germany)

Ms. Katrin KIRSCHMANN (Germany)

Ms. Christiane KRUGER-HEMMER (Germany)

Mr. Marco MUNDELIUS (Germany)

Mr. Martin SCHULZE (Germany)

Ms. Suzanne VON BELOW (Germany)

Ms. Eveline VON GAESSLER (Germany)

Ms. Dimitra FARMAKIOUTOU (Greece)

Ms. Maria FASSARI (Greece)

Mr. Ioannis GEORGAKOPOULOS (Greece)

Mr. Tünde HAGYMÁSY (Hungary)

Ms. Judit KÁDÁR-FÜLÖP (Hungary)

Mr. Tibor KÖNYVESI (Hungary)

Ms. Judit KOZMA-LUKACS (Hungary)

Mr. László LIMBACHER (Hungary)

Mr. Gunnar ARNASON (Iceland)

Mr. Julius BJORNSSON (Iceland)

Ms. Asta URBANCIC (Iceland)

Ms. Ida KINTAMANI (Indonesia)

Mr. Gilian GOLDEN (Ireland)

Mr. Pat McSITRIC (Ireland)

Ms. Nicola TICKNER (Ireland)

Ms. Sophie ARTSEV (Israel)

Mr. Yoav AZULAY (Israel)

Ms. Nava BRENNER (Israel)

Mr. Yosef GIDANIAN (Israel)

Mr. Yonatan HUBARA (Israel)

Ms. Hava KLEIN (Israel)

Mr. Haim PORTNOY (Israel)

Mr. Giovanni BIONDI (Italy)

Ms. Lucia DE FABRIZIO (Italy)

Ms. Paola DI GIROLAMO (Italy)

Ms. Maria Teresa MORANA (Italy)

Ms. Claudia PIZZELLA (Italy)

Mr. Paolo SESTITO (Italy)

Mr. Paolo TURCHETTI (Italy)

Mr. Jugo IMAIZUMI (Japan)

Ms. Nami JINDA (Japan)

Ms. Erina KAGA (Japan)

Mr. Soichi MURAKAMI (Japan)

Mr. Tatsushi NISHIZAWA (Japan)

Mr. Hiromi SASAI (Japan)

Ms. Yuka UZUKI (Japan)

Mr. Hongseon CHO (Korea)

Ms. Young Hae KANG (Korea)

Ms. Sung Bin MOON (Korea)

Mr. Jérôme LEVY (Luxembourg)

Mr. Javier Antonio FERREIRO BURDICK (Mexico)

Mr. Gerardo FRANCO BARRALES (Mexico)

Mr. Rafael FREYRE MARTINEZ (Mexico)

Mr. Ezequiel GIL HUERTA (Mexico)

Mr. Rene GOMORA CASTILLO (Mexico)

Mr. Hector Virgilio ROBLES VASQUEZ (Mexico)

Mr. Sergio G. ZAVALA MENDOZA (Mexico)

Ms. Danielle ANDARABI (Netherlands)

Ms. Linda SLIKKERVEER (Netherlands)

Mr. Dick TAKKENBERG (Netherlands)

Ms. Pauline THOOLEN (Netherlands)

Ms. Anouschka VAN DER MEULEN (Netherlands)

Mr. Fred WENTINK (Netherlands)

Mr. David SCOTT (New Zealand)

Ms. Marie ARNEBERG (Norway)

Mr. Sadiq Kwesi BOATENG (Norway)

Ms. Siri BOGEN (Norway)

Mr. Kjetil HELGELAND (Norway)

Ms. Anne-Berit KAVLI (Norway)

Mr. Lars NERDRUM (Norway)

Mr. Geir NYGARD (Norway)

Mr. Terje RISBERG (Norway)

Ms. Anne-Marie RUSTAD HOLSETER (Norway)

Ms. Barbara ANTOSIEWICZ (Poland)

Ms. Hanna GOLASZEWSKA (Poland)

Ms. Renata KORZENIOWSKA-PUCULEK (Poland)

Mr. Andrzej KURKIEWCZ (Poland)

Ms. Katarzyna MALEC (Poland)

Ms. Urszula MARTYNOWICZ (Poland)

Mr. Jacek MASLANKOWSKI (Poland)

Mr. Krzysztof MIESZKOWSKI (Poland)

Ms. Anna NOWOZYNSKA (Poland)

Ms. Beatriz GONCALVES (Portugal)

Ms. Joana MENDONCA (Portugal)

Ms. Rute NUNES (Portugal)

Mr. Joao PEREIRA DE MATOS (Portugal)

Mr. Nuno Miguel RODRIGUES (Portugal)

Mr. Joaquim SANTOS (Portugal)

Mr. Mark AGRANOVICH (Russian Federation)

Mr. Evgeny BUTKO (Russian Federation)

Ms. Anna FATEEVA (Russian Federation)

Ms. Irina SELIVERSTOVA (Russian Federation)

Mr. Ahmed F. HAYAJNEH (Saudi Arabia)

Mr. Peter BRODNIANSKY (Slovak Republic)

Ms. Alzbeta FERENCICOVA (Slovak Republic)

Mr. Frantisek ZAJICEK (Slovak Republic)

Ms. Helga KOCEVAR (Slovenia)

Ms. Viljana LUKAS (Slovenia)

Ms. Dusa MARJETIC (Slovenia)

Ms. Marija SKERLJ (Slovenia)

Ms. Tatjana SKRBEC (Slovenia)

Mr. Stojan SORCAN (Slovenia)

Ms. Bheki MPANZA (South Africa)

Ms. Sagrario AVEZUELA SANCHEZ (Spain)

Mr. Eduardo DE LA FUENTE (Spain)

Mr. Jesus IBAÑEZ MILLA (Spain)

Mr. Joaquín MARTIN MUÑOZ (Spain)

Mr. Valentín RAMOS SALVADOR (Spain)

Mr. Ismael SANZ LABRADOR (Spain)

Ms. Carmen UREÑA UREÑA (Spain)

Ms. Anna ERIKSSON (Sweden)

Ms. Maria GÖTHERSTRÖM (Sweden)

Ms. Marie KAHLROTH (Sweden)

Mr. Hans-Ake OSTROM (Sweden)

Mr. Kenny PETERSSON (Sweden)

Ms. Katrin HOLENSTEIN (Switzerland)

Mr Emanuel VON ERLACH (Switzerland)

Mr. Stefan C. WOLTER (Switzerland)

Ms. Hümeyra ALTUNTAS (Turkey)

Ms. Filiz BASOREN ALAN (Turkey)

Ms. Nilgun ÇALISKAN (Turkey)

Mr. Derhan DOGAN (Turkey)

Mr. Unal GUNDOGAN (Turkey)

Mr. Ibrahim Zeki KARABIYIK (Turkey)

Mr. Serdar YILMAZ (Turkey)

Mr. Albert MOTIVANS (UNESCO)

Mr. Markus SCHWABE (UNESCO)

Mr. Said Ould Ahmedou VOFFAL (UNESCO)

Mr. Stephen HEWITT (United Kingdom)

Mr. Stephen LEMAN (United Kingdom)

Ms. Rachel DINKES (United States)

Ms. Jana KEMP (United States)

Ms. Valena PLISKO (United States)

Mr. Thomas SNYDER (United States)

Ms. Kimberly TAHAN (United States)

Network on Labour Market, Economic and Social Outcomes of Learning (LSO)

Lead country: Canada

Network Leader: Mr. Patrice DE BROUCKER

Mr. Paul CMIEL (Australia)

Ms. Shannon MADDEN (Australia)

Mr. Scott MATHESON (Australia)

Ms. Margaret PEARCE (Australia)

Mr. Andreas GRIMM (Austria)

Mr. Mark NEMET (Austria)

Mr. Wolfgang PAULI (Austria)

Ms. Ariane BAYE (Belgium)

Ms. Isabelle ERAUW (Belgium)

Ms. Genevieve HINDRYCKX (Belgium)

Ms. Christine MAINGUET (Belgium)

Mr. Daniel Jaime CAPISTRANO DE OLIVEIRA (Brazil)

Ms. Maria DAS GRACAS COSTA (Brazil)

Ms. Carla Maria MOTTA DO VALLE CASTRO (Brazil)

Mr. Leonardo Kazuo SERIKAWA (Brazil)

Ms. Ana Carolina SILVA CIROTTO (Brazil)

Mr. Patric BLOUIN (Canada)

Ms. Emanuelle CARRIERE (Canada)

Mr. Patrice DE BROUCKER (Canada)

Ms. Dallas MORROW (Canada)

Mr. Patrick TAYLOR (Canada)

Ms. Pascaline DESCY (CEDEFOP)

Mr. Giovanni RUSSO (CEDEFOP)

Mr. Marco SERAFINI (CEDEFOP)

Mr. Alex STIMPSON (CEDEFOP)

Ms. Alena ZUKERSTEINOVA (CEDEFOP)

Mr. Jose ARANGUIZ (Chile)

Ms. Ivonne BUENO (Chile)

Mr. Andres BUSTAMANTE (Chile)

Mr. Mario CAMPOS (Chile)

Mr. Domingo CLAPS (Chile)

Mr. Jaime ESPINA (Chile)

Ms. Paulina HUAIQUIMIL (Chile)

Mr. Osvaldo JARA (Chile)

Ms. Alejandra Garcia MOZO (Chile)

Ms. Julia ORTUZAR (Chile)

Mr. Miski PERALTA (Chile)

Ms. Alexandra RUEDA (Chile)

Mr. Cristian Pablo YANEZ NAVARRO (Chile)

Ms. Sona FORTOVA (Czech Republic)

Ms. Vendula KAŠPAROVA (Czech Republic)

Ms. Michaela KLENHOVA (Czech Republic)

Mr. Jens ANDERSEN (Denmark)

Mr. Andreas GINGER-MORTENSEN (Denmark)

Mr. Leo JENSEN (Denmark)

Ms. Liv Maadele MOGENSEN (Denmark)

Mr. Thorbjorn TODSEN (Denmark)

Ms. Tiina ANNUS (Estonia)

Ms. Kristi PLOOM (Estonia)

Ms. Katrin REIN (Estonia)

Ms. Marta BECK-DOMZALSKA (Eurostat, European Commission)

Mr. Jens FISCHER-KOTTENSTEDE (European Commission)

Mr. Lars JAKOBSEN (Eurostat, European Commission)

Mr. Sylvain JOUHETTE (Eurostat, European Commission)

Ms. Irja BLOMQVIST (Finland)

Ms. Aila REPO (Finland)

Ms. Florence LEFRESNE (France)

Ms. Pascale POULET-COULIBANDO (France)

Mr. Andreas ALBRECHT (Germany)

Mr. Hans-Werner FREITAG (Germany)

Ms. Christiane KRUGER-HEMMER (Germany)

Mr. Marco MUNDELIUS (Germany)

Mr. Christoph SCHNEIDER (Germany)

Mr. Martin A. SCHULZE (Germany)

Ms. Angelika TRAUB (Germany)

Mr. Meike VOLLMAR (Germany)

Ms. Susanne VON BELOW (Germany)

Ms. Eveline VON GAESSLER (Germany)

Mr. Sándor GRAD (Hungary)

Ms. Judit KÁDÁR-FÜLÖP (Hungary)

Ms. Éva TÓT (Hungary)

Ms. Asta M. URBANCIC (Iceland)

Ms. Nicola TICKNER (Ireland)

Mr. Yosef GIDANIAN (Israel)

Mr. Haim PORTNOY (Israel)

Ms. Francesca BRAIT (Italy)

Ms. Angela FERRUZZA (Italy)

Ms. Liana VERZICCO (Italy)

Ms. Nami JINDA (Japan)

Ms. Erina KAGA (Japan)

Ms. Yuka UZUKI (Japan)

Ms. Gloria HUIJUNG CHU (Korea)

Ms. Sung Bin MOON (Korea)

Mr. Cheonsoo PARK (Korea)

Mr. Jerry LENERT (Luxembourg)

Mr. Rafael FREYRE MARTINEZ (Mexico)

Mr. Rene GOMORA CASTILLO (Mexico)

Mr. Juan Manuel HERNANDEZ VAZQUEZ (Mexico)

Mr. Hector ROBLES (Mexico)

Mr. Ted REININGA (Netherlands)

Ms. Tanja TRAAG (Netherlands)

Mr. Bernard VERLAAN (Netherlands)

Mr. David SCOTT (New Zealand)

Ms. Marie ARNEBERG (Norway)

Mr. Sadiq-Kwesi BOATENG (Norway)

Mr. Lars NERDRUM (Norway)

Ms. Ragnhild NERSTEN (Norway)

Mr. Geir NYGARD (Norway)

Mr. Terje RISBERG (Norway)

Mr. Anne-Marie RUSTAD HOLSETER (Norway)

Mr. Jacek MASLANKOWSKI (Poland)

Ms. Anna NOWOZYNSKA (Poland)

Mr. Carlos Alberto MALACA (Portugal)

Mr. Joaquim SANTOS (Portugal)

Mr. Mark AGRANOVICH (Russian Federation)

Ms. Anna FATEEVA (Russian Federation)

Ms. Oega ZAITCEVA (Russian Federation)

Mr. Roman BARANOVIC (Slovak Republic)

Mr. Frantisek BLANAR (Slovak Republic)

Mr. Jaroslav JURIGA (Slovak Republic)

Mr. Gabriel KULIFFAY (Slovak Republic)

Ms. Lubomira SRNANKOVA (Slovak Republic)

Mr. Juraj VANTUCH (Slovak Republic)

Ms. Helga KOCEVAR (Slovenia)

Ms. Tatjana SKRBEC (Slovenia)

Ms. Raquel ALVAREZ-ESTEBAN (Spain)

Ms. Carmen UREÑA UREÑA (Spain)

Mr. Dan ANDERSSON (Sweden)

Mr. Torbjorn LINDQVIST (Sweden)

Mr. Kenny PETERSSON (Sweden)

Ms. Wayra CABALLERO LIARDET (Switzerland)

Mr. Emanuel VON ERLACH (Switzerland)

Mr. Ali PANAL (Turkey)

Mr. Youngsup CHOI (UNESCO)

Mr. Friedrich HUEBLER (UNESCO)

Mr. Hirochimi KATAYAMA (UNESCO)

Ms. Nhung TRUONG (UNESCO)

Mr. Said Ould Ahmedou VOFFAL (UNESCO)

Mr. Anthony CLARKE (United Kingdom)

Mr. Stephen LEMAN (United Kingdom)

Ms. Rachel DINKES (United States)

Ms. Erin ROTH (United States)

Mr. Thomas SNYDER (United States)

Ms. Kimberly TAHAN (United States)

Network for the Collection and Adjudication of System-level Descriptive Information on Educational Structures, Policies and Practices (NESLI)

Lead Country: United Kingdom

Network Leader: Mr. Stephen LEMAN

Mr. Paul CMIEL (Australia)

Ms. Shannon MADDEN (Australia)

Mr. Scott MATHESON (Australia)

Ms. Rachel THOMAS (Australia)

Mr. Christian KRENTHALLER (Austria)

Ms. Kristin SJOHOLM-SCHMID (Austria)

Ms. Helene LENOIR (Belgium)

Mr. M. Francois TRICARICO (Belgium)

Mr. Raymond VAN DE SIJPE (Belgium)

Ms. Ann VAN DRIESSCHE (Belgium)

Mr. Daniel Jaime CAPISTRANO DE OLIVEIRA (Brazil)

Ms. Juliana MARQUES DA SILVA (Brazil)

Ms. Ana Carolina SILVA CIROTTO (Brazil)

Ms. Shannon DELBRIDGE (Canada)

Mr. Angelo ELIAS (Canada)

Mr. Yves SAINT-PIERRE (Canada)

Ms. Louise VAN WART (Canada)

Mr. Cristian Pablo YANEZ NAVARRO (Chile)

Ms. Michaela KLENHOVA (Czech Republic)

Mr. Jorgen Balling RASMUSSEN (Denmark)

Ms. Kristi PLOOM (Estonia)

Mr. Richard DEISS (European Commission)

Ms. Arlette DELHAXHE (Eurydice)

Mr. Stanislav RANGUELOV (Eurydice)

Ms. Petra PACKALEN (Finland)

Ms. Kristiina VOLMARI (Finland)

Ms. Nadine DALSHEIMER-VAN DER TOL (France)

Ms. Pia BRUGGER (Germany)

Ms. Cornelia FRANKE (Germany)

Mr. Marco MUNDELIUS (Germany)

Ms. Dimitra FARMAKIOTOU (Greece)

Ms. Maria FASSARI (Greece)

Mr. Sándor GRAD (Hungary)

Ms. Emese Horváthné BATÁR (Hungary)

Ms. Anna IMRE (Hungary)

Ms. Judit KÁDÁR-FÜLÖP (Hungary)

Mr. Gunnar ARNASON (Iceland)

Ms. Asta URBANCIC (Iceland)

Ms. Ida KINTAMANI (Indonesia)

Mr. Pat McSITRIC (Ireland)

Ms. Nicola TICKNER (Ireland)

Ms. Sophie ARTSEV (Israel)

Mr. Yoav AZULAY (Israel)

Mr. Yosef GIDANIAN (Israel)

Ms. Gianna BARBIERI (Italy)

Ms. Lucia DE FABRIZIO (Italy)

Ms. Ezia PALMERI (Italy)

Ms. Nami JINDA (Japan)

Ms. Erina KAGA (Japan)

Mr. Soichi MURAKAMI (Japan)

Ms. Sung Bin MOON (Korea)

Mr. Gilles HIRT (Luxembourg)

Mr. Rafael FREYRE MARTINEZ (Mexico)

Mr. Sergio G. ZAVALA MENDOZA (Mexico)

Mr. Hans RUESINK (Netherlands)

Mr. Marcel SMITS VAN WAESBERGHE (Netherlands)

Mr. Cyril MAKO (New Zealand)

Mr. Kjetil HELGELAND (Norway)

Ms. Katarzyna MALEC (Poland)

Ms. Anna NOWOZYNSKA (Poland)

Mr. Nuno Miguel RODRIGUES (Portugal)

Ms. Ana VITORINO (Portugal)

Mr. Mark AGRANOVICH (Russian Federation)

Ms. Anna FATEEVA (Russian Federation)

Ms. Alzbeta FERENCICOVA (Slovak Republic)

Mr. Frantisek ZAJICEK (Slovak Republic)

Ms. Helga KOCEVAR (Slovenia)

Mr. Mitja SARDOC (Slovenia)

Mr. Antonio DEL SASTRE (Spain)

Mr. Valentín RAMOS SALVADOR (Spain)

Ms. Camilla THINSZ FJELLSTROM (Sweden)

Ms. Helena WINTGREN (Sweden)

Ms. Rejane DEPPIERRAZ (Switzerland)

Ms. Hümeyra ALTUNTAS (Turkey)

Ms. Filiz BASOREN ALAN (Turkey)

Ms. Dilek GULECYUZ (Turkey)

Mr. Anthony CLARKE (United Kingdom)

Mr. Mal COOKE (United Kingdom)

Mr. Stephen LEMAN (United Kingdom)

Ms. Rebecca McKAY (United Kingdom)

Mr. Thomas SYNDER (United States)

Ms. Kimberly TAHAN (United States)

Other contributors to this publication

Mr. Samuel E. ABRAMS (NESLI consultant)

Ms. Anna BORKOWSKY (LSO consultant)

Mr. Jon LAUGLO (LSO consultant)

Mr. Henry M. LEVIN (NESLI consultant)

Mr. Gary MIRON (NESLI consultant)

Mr. Kenny PETERSSON (LSO consultant)

Mr. Dan SHERMAN (LSO consultant)

Ms. Fung Kwan TAM (Layout)

RELATED OECD PUBLICATIONS

Better Skills, Better Jobs, Better Lives: A Strategic Approach to Skills Policies (2012)
ISBN 978-92-64-17729-1

PISA 2009 Results: Students On Line: Digital Technologies and Performance (Volume VI) (2011)
ISBN 978-92-64-11291-9

PISA 2009 Results: What Students Know and Can Do: Student Performance in Reading, Mathematics and Science (Volume I) (2010)
ISBN 978-92-64-09144-3

PISA 2009 Results: Overcoming Social Background: Equity in Learning Opportunities and Outcomes (Volume II) (2010)
ISBN 978-92-64-09146-7

PISA 2009 Results: Learning to Learn: Student Engagement, Strategies and Practices (Volume III) (2010)
ISBN 978-92-64-09147-4

PISA 2009 Results: What Makes a School Successful?: Resources, Policies and Practices (Volume IV) (2010)
ISBN 978-92-64-09148-1

PISA 2009 Results: Learning Trends: Changes in Student Performance Since 2000 (Volume V) (2010)
ISBN 978-92-64-09149-8

Improving Health and Social Cohesion through Education (2010)
ISBN 978-92-64-08630-2

OECD Employment Outlook 2010 (2010)
ISBN 978-92-64-08468-1

TALIS 2008 Technical Report (2010)
ISBN 978-92-64-07985-4

Taxing Wages 2008-2009 (2010)
ISBN 978-92-64-08299-1

Creating Effective Teaching and Learning Environments: First Results from TALIS (2009)
ISBN 978-92-64-05605-3

Health at a Glance 2009: OECD Indicators (2009)
ISBN 978-92-64-06153-8

OECD Science, Technology and Industry Scoreboard 2009 (2009)
ISBN 978-92-64-06371-6

OECD Reviews of Tertiary Education: Tertiary Education for the Knowledge Society (2008)
ISBN 978-92-64-04652-8

Understanding the Social Outcomes of Learning (2007)
ISBN 978-92-64-03310-8

OECD Revenue Statistics 1965-2005 (2006)
ISBN 978-92-64-02993-4

Teachers Matter: Attracting, Developing and Retaining Effective Teachers (2005)
ISBN 978-92-64-01802-0

Internationalisation and Trade in Higher Education: Opportunities and Challenges (2004)
ISBN 978-92-64-01504-3

....

OECD publications can be browsed or purchased at the OECD iLibrary (www.oecd-ilibrary.org).

ORGANISATION FOR ECONOMIC CO-OPERATION AND DEVELOPMENT

The OECD is a unique forum where governments work together to address the economic, social and environmental challenges of globalisation. The OECD is also at the forefront of efforts to understand and to help governments respond to new developments and concerns, such as corporate governance, the information economy and the challenges of an ageing population. The Organisation provides a setting where governments can compare policy experiences, seek answers to common problems, identify good practice and work to co-ordinate domestic and international policies.

The OECD member countries are: Australia, Austria, Belgium, Canada, Chile, the Czech Republic, Denmark, Estonia, Finland, France, Germany, Greece, Hungary, Iceland, Ireland, Israel, Italy, Japan, Korea, Luxembourg, Mexico, the Netherlands, New Zealand, Norway, Poland, Portugal, the Slovak Republic, Slovenia, Spain, Sweden, Switzerland, Turkey, the United Kingdom and the United States. The European Union takes part in the work of the OECD.

OECD Publishing disseminates widely the results of the Organisation's statistics gathering and research on economic, social and environmental issues, as well as the conventions, guidelines and standards agreed by its members.

OECD PUBLISHING, 2, rue André-Pascal, 75775 PARIS CEDEX 16
(96 2012 03 1P) ISBN 978-92-64-17715-4 – No. 60189 2012

CPSIA information can be obtained at www.ICGtesting.com
Printed in the USA
LVOW021925270213

321976LV00002B/34/P